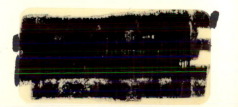

# Historical Dictionary
# of Modern Spain,
# 1700–1988

# Historical Dictionary
# of Modern Spain,
# 1700–1988

ROBERT W. KERN,
*Editor-in-Chief*

MEREDITH D. DODGE,
*Associate Editor*

**Greenwood Press**
New York • Westport, Connecticut • London

**Library of Congress Cataloging-in-Publication Data**

Historical dictionary of modern Spain, 1700–1988 / Robert W. Kern,
  editor-in-chief, Meredith D. Dodge, associate editor.
    p.   cm.
  Bibliography: p.
  Includes index.
  ISBN 0–313–25971–2 (lib. bdg. : alk. paper)
    1. Spain—History—Bourbons, 1700– —Dictionaries.   I. Kern,
  Robert W., 1934–  .   II. Dodge, Meredith D., 1950–  .
  DP192.H57   1990
  946′.003—dc20        89–7471

British Library Cataloguing in Publication Data is available.

Library of Congress Catalog Card Number: 89–7471
ISBN: 0–313–25971–2

First published in 1990

Greenwood Press, Inc.
88 Post Road West, Westport, Connecticut 06881

Printed in the United States of America

The paper used in this book complies with the
Permanent Paper Standard issued by the National
Information Standards Organization (Z39.48–1984).

10 9 8 7 6 5 4 3 2 1

# Contents

# Contributors

*Víctor Alba*, Sitges, Catalonia

*Peter J. Bakewell*, Emory University

*Richard A. Barrett*, University of New Mexico

*Earl R. Beck*, Florida State University

*Susan Benforado*, Museum of New Mexico

*Martin Blinkhorn*, University of Lancaster

*Carolyn P. Boyd*, University of Texas

*Susan L. Brake*, Social Security Administrator, U.S. Government

*William J. Callahan*, University of Toronto

*Ron M. Carden*, South Plains Junior College

*Robert P. Clark*, James Madison University

*James W. Cortada*, IBM Corporation

*Russ T. Davidson*, University of New Mexico

*Meredith D. Dodge*, University of New Mexico

*Nelson Durán*, Consultant, Coral Gables, Fla.

*Victoria L. Enders*, Northern Arizona University

*George Esenwein*, Hoover Institution of Peace and War

*Gilbert G. Fernández*, Tennessee State University

*Pelayo H. Fernández*, University of New Mexico

*Rosa M. Fernández*, University of New Mexico

*Shannon E. Fleming*, Social Security Administrator, U.S. Government

*Douglas W. Foard*, National Endowment of the Humanities

*Patrick Foley*, Tarrant County Junior College

*Willard C. Frank, Jr.*, Old Dominion University

*Shirley F. Fredricks*, Metro State University
*Thomas F. Glick*, Boston University
*Ángel González*, University of New Mexico
*Luis T. González-del-Valle*, University of Colorado
*Helen E. Graham*, University of Southampton
*Linda B. Hall*, University of New Mexico
*Charles R. Halstead*, Washington College
*Carl A. Hanson*, Trinity University
*Glenn T. Harper*, University of Southern Mississippi
*Robert Himmerich y Valencia*, University of New Mexico
*Rick Hendricks*, University of New Mexico
*Richard Herr*, University of California
*Paul Heywood*, University of London
*Oliver W. Holmes*, Connecticut Wesleyan University
*David V. Holtby*, University of New Mexico
*Donald Kagay*, University of Dallas
*Robert W. Kern*, University of New Mexico
*Harry L. Kirby, Jr.*, Louisiana State University
*Steven P. Kramer*, University of New Mexico
*Allen J. Kuethe*, Texas Tech University
*Charles E. McClelland*, University of New Mexico
*Edward E. Malefakis*, Columbia University
*Juan Maura*, University of Vermont
*Regina A. Mezei*, Mercer County Junior College
*Carl J. Mora, Jr.*, Sandia Corporation
*Víctor Morales Lezcano*, Computense University, Madrid
*Stanley G. Payne*, University of Wisconsin
*Paul Preston*, University of London
*Raymond L. Proctor*, University of Idaho
*Rowena Rivera*, University of New Mexico
*Susana Rivera*, University of New Mexico
*Alfred Rodríguez*, University of New Mexico
*Joseph P. Sánchez*, National Park Service
*Nicolás Sánchez-Albornoz*, New York University
*Carlos Seco Serrano*, Universidad Complutense, Madrid
*Adrian Shubert*, York University, Canada
*Donald E. Skabelund*, University of New Mexico
*M. Jane Slaughter*, University of New Mexico

*Leslie Stainton*, Consultant, Ann Arbor, Mich.

*Charlie R. Steen*, University of New Mexico

*Pierre L. Ullman*, University of Wisconsin, Milwaukee

*David J. Viera*, Tennessee Tech University

*Neddy A. Vigil*, University of New Mexico

*Robert H. Whealey*, Ohio University

*Alexandria Wilhelmsen*, University of Dallas

# Preface

The history of Spain continues to attract a wide historical interest in the United States. The civil war (1936–1939) and the Franco era (1939–1975) are only the most recent examples of Spain's long involvement in world affairs. Through the work of Stanley G. Payne, Burnett Bolloten, Edward E. Malefakis, and others, American readers have come to know the agony and frustrations of the Spanish Civil War as well as any period of the twentieth century in Europe. More than two hundred books by American authors have been written about the civil war since 1936. Greenwood Press itself contributed to a synthesis of research on the war by publishing James W. Cortada's *Historical Dictionary of the Spanish Civil War, 1936–1939* (Westport, Conn., 1982).

As a major segment in Western European society, Spain has contributed social and cultural values to Latin America and the American Southwest from the sixteenth to the nineteenth century that still have importance. The work of Hubert Bancroft and Henry Lea established Spain as an early focus of research, and Roger B. Merriman continued this tradition in the 1920s and 1930s, as did scholars on colonial Latin America like James Lockhart, Woodrow Borah, Bailey Diffie, Lewis Hanke, and J. H. Parry. Textbooks by Payne, Richard Herr, Gabriel Jackson, and Harold Livermore have made it possible to teach Spanish history courses as never before.

An equal or larger amount of work has been done by British scholars. The historic rivalry between Spain and Britain has attracted a host of very capable writers, chief among them Sir Raymond Carr, whose *Spain 1808–1939* (1966) remains the classic in the field. Carr's graduate students continue to examine the contours of modern Spanish history and number some distinguished Spanish intellectuals among them, part of the recent revival of historical studies in a very historically minded society.

This work has been done in the face of obstacles. The leyenda negra, the Black Legend of Spanish cruelty and religious bigotry, persuaded early writers

that Spanish culture destroyed much more than it provided. The economic catastrophe of the sixteenth and seventeenth centuries displaced Spain in importance, and added elements of underdevelopment to a culture that once had a
Siglo de Oro, misleading observers about the nature of Spanish ''simplicity.''
Diplomatic problems of the eighteenth century and colonial disintegration in the
nineteenth (concluding with the Spanish-American War in 1898) wiped out a
major Spanish role in world affairs, but the Spanish Civil War and the courtship
of General Franco's regime by U.S. diplomats, culminating in the 1953 Bases
Agreement, proved otherwise.

Spain continues to play an important international role today, despite signals
to the contrary that sometimes mislead scholarly thought. Since 1975, the most
recent reversal has been the appearance of a strong democratic tendency that
dispelled earlier pessimism that Franco's regime was not preparing Spaniards
for political maturity. Perhaps the evolution is more a testimony to Spanish
pragmatism than to the Generalissimo's policies, but it illustrates the difficulty
of interpreting and understanding Spanish history that has always plagued scholars. Today, in fact, observers from eastern Europe now study the transition from
dictatorship to democracy in Spain.

The fact that modern scholarship has acknowledged these problems and transcended many of them makes this an opportune time to do the present volume
on the general history of Spain since 1700. Nearly seventy scholars from the
United States, Britain, Spain, Canada, and Latin America have contributed
entries to this dictionary. The civil war generally has been treated lightly, since
James W. Cortada's *Historical Dictionary of the Spanish Civil War* and Robert
A. Gorman's *Biographical Dictionary of Neo-Marxism* (Westport, Conn.: Greenwood Press, 1985) cover these topics in the 1930s. What makes this volume
distinctive is its wide sweep from the eighteenth century to the late twentieth,
giving the student a unique reference work for the last three centuries of Spanish
history.

Within this time frame, editorial effort has been made to cover seven areas:
political, governmental, diplomatic, institutional, cultural, social, and military
history. The first three no doubt fare better than the others because of a greater
amount of information; but in some cases, the other areas provide the reader
with the only thorough discussion in English available on the topic.

All reference works face space restrictions, so many entries in this volume
are short. The objective of this dictionary is not to provide a definitive, detailed
history for Spain, but to offer a quick reference on a broad range of material
for those interested in basic information. In many cases, however, the material
contains the latest historiographic interpretations or available facts. This is important, particularly since eighteenth-century and late twentieth-century Spanish
history are not well known and works are not readily available. The bibliographic
references accompanying each entry also enhance the usefulness of the
dictionary.

The best way to use this dictionary is to go directly to a particular entry of
interest, all of which are in alphabetical order. Entries are cross-referenced to

suggest other related topics. Asterisks indicate that the item in question is the subject of its own entry. If the reader wishes to see all references to a certain subject, regardless of location in the dictionary, the index is quite complete. In addition, the time line will establish a basic chronology for those uncertain about the main outline of Spanish history, and the bibliography contains the more important works available on the various aspects of the period since 1700.

It should be noted that the spelling of place names corresponds to Carr's usage in *Spain 1808–1939*. When a place name had to be supplied, *Webster's Geographical Dictionary* was used. Finally, it is unfortunate that entries for Camilo José Cela (1916– ) and Ramón del Valle-Inclán (1870–1936) were assigned but never received.

# Acknowledgments

It is not easy to do such a large project as this one in two years without the aid and assistance of a great many people. James W. Cortada, the editor of an earlier volume on the Spanish Civil War, gave a great deal of initial help in getting the present volume started. Stanley G. Payne was kind enough to look at the original list of entries. Alfred Rodríguez of the University of New Mexico did likewise with the literary entries. Many of the contributors themselves added other names to the list. Professor Joan Connelly Ullman also gave me some good advice. One cannot help but be impressed by the talent in this small but vital field of European history.

I owe a great deal to the associate editor of this work, Meredith D. Dodge. She did a superb job of editing the work and came up with many ideas. Edith Jonas, Susan Brake, and Alison Freese performed miracles of proofreading. David Null and the reference staff of Zimmerman Library also gave me many hours of assistance; and other faculty members of the University of New Mexico, well-known for its Hispanic civilization courses, provided entries and assistance for which I am grateful. Thanks are also due to the vice president for research of the University of Mexico, Dr. Paul G. Risser, for additional financial assistance during the course of this project. At Greenwood Press, Cynthia Harris was a sympathetic editor.

Finally, two contributors to this project wish to acknowledge funding agencies that made their research possible. Carl J. Mora, Jr., would like to thank the United States–Spanish Joint Committee for Cultural and Educational Cooperation for travel grants in 1985 and 1987, Juan Antonio Pérez Millán and the personnel of the Filmoteca Española (Madrid), and Jordi Batllé, Ramón Font, and Antonio Kirchner of the Filmoteca, Generalitat de Catalunya (Barcelona), for their kind assistance. Charles McClelland wishes to thank the American Philosophical Society for its support of his research.

# Abbreviations

| | |
|---|---|
| AO | Alianza Obrera |
| BNP | Basque Nationalist party |
| BOC | Bloque Obrero y Campesino |
| CAMPSA | Compañía Arrendataria del Monopolio de Petróleos, S.A. |
| CAPV | Comunidad Autónoma del País Vasco |
| CCOO | Comisiones Obreras |
| CDS | Democratic Center and Social party |
| CEA | Cinematografía Española Americana |
| CEDA | Confederación Española de Derechas Autónomas |
| CERN | European Atomic Energy Commission |
| CGTU | Confederación General del Trabajo Unitario |
| CIFESA | Compañía Industrial Film Español, S.A. |
| CIO | Congress of Industrial Organizations |
| CIU | Convergence and Unity party |
| CNT | Confederación Nacional del Trabajo |
| CNV | Comunión Nacionalista Vasca |
| CONS | Confederación de Obreros Nacional-Sindicalistas |
| CSIC | Consejo Superior de Investigaciones Científicas |
| CTV | Cuerpo de Tropas Voluntarias |
| DRV | Derecha Regional Valenciana |
| EA | Eusko Alkartasuna |
| EAJ | Eusko Alderdi Jeltzalea |
| ECESA | Estudios Cinema Español, S.A. |
| ETA | Basque Homeland and Freedom |

| FAI | Federación Anarquista Ibérica |
| FECSA | Fuerzas Eléctricas de Cataluña, S.A. |
| FET | Falange Española Tradicionalista |
| FJS | Socialist Youth |
| FNAE | Federación Nacional de Agricultores de España |
| FNTT | Federación Nacional de Trabajadores de la Tierra |
| FOUS | Federación Obrera de Unidad Sindical |
| FSA | Federación Socialista Asturiana |
| FUE | Federación Universitaria Española |
| GATT | General Agreement on Tariffs and Trade |
| GEPCI | Federación Catalana de Gremios y Entidades de Pequeños Comerciantes e Industriales |
| ICE | Izquierda Comunista Española |
| JONS | Juntas de Ofensiva Nacional-Sindicalista |
| JSU | Juventudes Socialistas Unificadas |
| KAS | Koordinadora Abertzale Sozialista |
| LOAPA | Pact to Harmonize the Autonomy Process |
| LODE | Law on the Right to Education |
| MDM | Movimiento Democrático de la Mujer |
| MLE | Movimiento Libertario Español |
| MPAIC | Movimiento para la Autodeterminación y Independencia del Archipiélago Canario |
| NATO | North Atlantic Treaty Organization |
| OECD | Organization for Economic Cooperation and Development |
| ORGA | Organización Republicana Gallega Autónoma |
| PCC | Partit del Comunistes de Catalunya |
| PCE | Partido Comunista Español |
| PCI | Italian Communist Party |
| PCV | Partido Comunista de Viscaya |
| PNV | Partido Nacionalista Vasco |
| POUM | Partido Obrero de Unificación Marxista |
| PRI | Partido Revolucionario Institucional |
| PSOE | Partido Socialista Obrero Español |
| PSP | Partido Socialista Popular |
| PSUC | Partit Socialista Unificat de Catalunya |
| PURA | Partido de Unión Repúblicana Autonomista |
| SERA | Extradition Service of the Spanish Republicans |
| SESM | Committee of Sociological Study about the Woman |

| SEU | Sindicato Español Universitario |
| SMA | Sindicato de Obreras Mineros Asturianos |
| UCD | Unión Central Democrática |
| UDPE | Union of the Spanish People |
| UGT | Unión General de Trabajadores |
| UJC | Communist Youth |
| UNESCO | United Nations Educational, Scientific, and Cultural Organization |
| UP | Unión Patriótica |

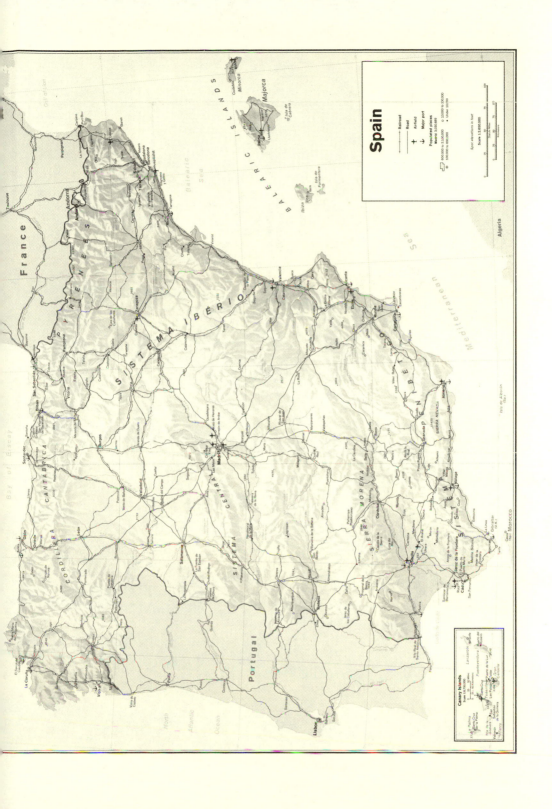

# Spain

# Administrative Divisions

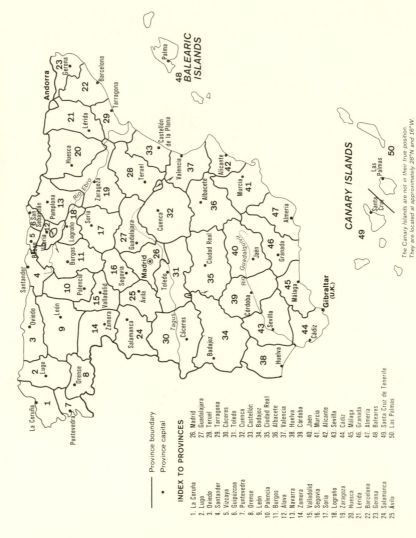

Andorra

23 Gerona

Barcelona

22

21 Lérida

29 Tarragona

20 Huesca

33 Castellón de la Plana

BALEARIC ISLANDS

Palma

48

13 Pamplona
18 Logroño
Río Ebro
Zaragoza 19
17 Soria
27 Guadalajara
28 Teruel

5 San Sebastián
Álava 12
4 Santander
11 Burgos
16
26 Madrid
32 Cuenca
37 Valencia
42 Alicante
41 Murcia

3 Oviedo
10 Palencia
15 Valladolid
25 Ávila
31 Toledo
35 Ciudad Real
36 Albacete
47 Almería

9 León
14 Zamora
24 Salamanca
30 Cáceres
34 Badajoz
40 Jaén
46 Granada
45 Málaga

2 Lugo
8 Orense
1 La Coruña
7 Pontevedra

Segovia
Palencia
Tagus
Río Guadalquivir
39 Córdoba
43 Sevilla
44 Cádiz
38 Huelva

Gibraltar (U.K.)

CANARY ISLANDS

49 Santa Cruz
50 Las Palmas

*The Canary Islands are not in their true position.
They are located at approximately 28°N and 16°W.*

── Province boundary
•  Province capital

## INDEX TO PROVINCES

1. La Coruña
2. Lugo
3. Oviedo
4. Santander
5. Vizcaya
6. Guipúzcoa
7. Pontevedra
8. Orense
9. León
10. Palencia
11. Burgos
12. Álava
13. Navarra
14. Zamora
15. Valladolid
16. Segovia
17. Soria
18. Logroño
19. Zaragoza
20. Huesca
21. Lérida
22. Barcelona
23. Gerona
24. Salamanca
25. Ávila

26. Madrid
27. Guadalajara
28. Teruel
29. Tarragona
30. Cáceres
31. Toledo
32. Cuenca
33. Castellón
34. Badajoz
35. Ciudad Real
36. Albacete
37. Valencia
38. Huelva
39. Córdoba
40. Jaén
41. Murcia
42. Alicante
43. Sevilla
44. Cádiz
45. Málaga
46. Granada
47. Almería
48. Baleares
49. Santa Cruz de Tenerife
50. Las Palmas

# Population

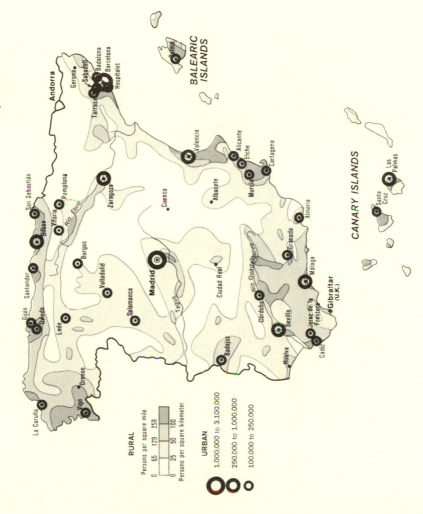

Andorra

Gerona
Sabadell
Tarrasa Barcelona
Badalona
Hospitalet

BALEARIC
ISLANDS

Palma

San Sebastián
Pamplona
Vitoria
Bilbao
Río Ebro
Zaragoza
Valencia
Cuenca
Alicante
Elche
Albacete
Murcia
Cartagena

Santander
Gijón
Oviedo
Burgos
León
Valladolid
Almería
Madrid
Salamanca
Granada
Ciudad Real
Málaga
Tajo
Río Guadalquivir
Córdoba
Gibraltar
(U.K.)
Sevilla
Jerez de la
Frontera
Badajoz
Huelva
Cádiz

La Coruña
Orense
Vigo

Las
Palmas
Santa
Cruz

CANARY ISLANDS

RURAL

Persons per square mile

| 0 | 65 | 129 | 259 |

Persons per square kilometer

| 0 | 25 | 50 | 100 |

URBAN

1,000,000 to 3,100,000

250,000 to 1,000,000

100,000 to 250,000

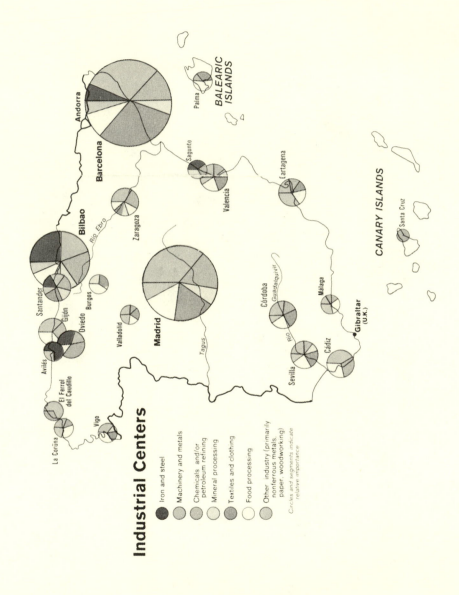

# Industrial Centers

Iron and steel

Machinery and metals

Chemicals and/or
petroleum refining

Mineral processing

Textiles and clothing

Food processing

Other industry (primarily
nonferrous metals,
paper, woodworking)

*Circles and segments indicate
relative importance*

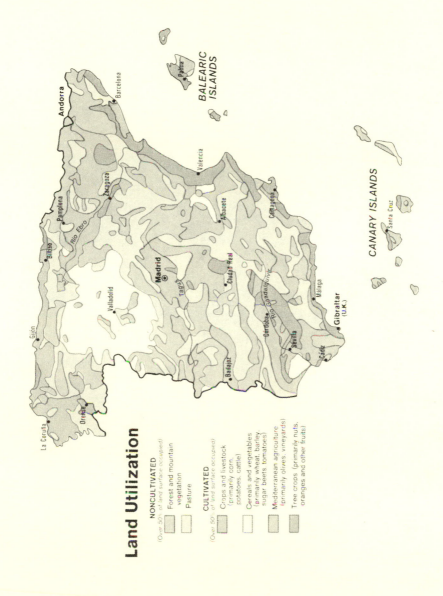

# Land Utilization

**NONCULTIVATED**
(Over 50% of land surface occupied)

Forest and mountain
vegetation

Pasture

**CULTIVATED**
(Over 50% of land surface occupied)

Crops and livestock
(primarily corn,
potatoes, cattle)

Cereals and vegetables
(primarily wheat, barley,
sugar beets, tomatoes)

Mediterranean agriculture
(primarily olives, vineyards)

Tree crops (primarily nuts,
oranges and other fruits)

La Coruña

Gijón

Orense

Bilbao

Pamplona

Andorra

Barcelona

Valladolid

Zaragoza

Rio Ebro

Madrid

Tagus

Valencia

Albacete

Ciudad Real

Cartagena

Rio Guadalquivir

Córdoba

Badajoz

Sevilla

Málaga

Cádiz

Gibraltar
(U.K.)

BALEARIC
ISLANDS

Palma

CANARY ISLANDS

Santa Cruz

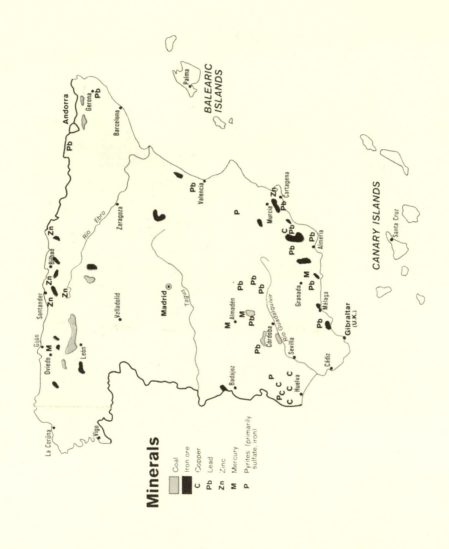

# Minerals

| | Coal |
| :---: | :--- |
| | Iron ore |
| **C** | Copper |
| **Pb** | Lead |
| **Zn** | Zinc |
| **M** | Mercury |
| **P** | Pyrites (primarily sulfate iron) |

BALEARIC ISLANDS

CANARY ISLANDS

Andorra

Gerona **Pb**
Barcelona
**Pb**

Palma

**Pb** Valencia

Zaragoza

Río Ebro

**Zn** Bilbao
**Zn**
Santander
**Zn**
Gijón
Oviedo **M**
León
Valladolid

Madrid

Tagus

**P**

Murcia **Zn**
**Pb Cartagena**
**C** **Pb**
**Pb** Almería
**M**
Granada **Pb**
**Pb** Málaga
Gibraltar
(U.K.)

**M** Almadén
**Pb**
**M**
**Pb** Córdoba
Sevilla
Río Guadalquivir
**Pb**

Badajoz

**P** **P**
**P C C**
**C C C**
Huelva

Cádiz

Santa Cruz

La Coruña

Vigo

# Historical Dictionary of Modern Spain, 1700–1988

# A

ALARCÓN Y ARIZA, PEDRO ANTONIO DE (1833–1891), nineteenth-century writer. Alarcón studied law at the University of Granada and theology at the seminary in nearby Guadix, but in the 1850s, he abandoned these interests to be come a newspaper editor and, eventually, a soldier, politician, novelist, and short-story writer. In his youth, Alarcón was a radical liberal; later, though, he became a staunch conservative and defender of the church in 1855, when his life was spared in a duel. National recognition of Alarcón's work first came with the publication of his war journal, *Diario de un testigo en la guerra de África, 1859–1860* (1862). From then until the late 1880s, he worked as a journalist, held government posts, served in the Cortes, and became a member of the Spanish Royal Academy. He died at the age of fifty-eight after suffering four strokes.

Alarcón's literary fame is largely the result of the popularity of his short novel *El sombrero de tres picos* (1874). This delightful work, inspired by the folk ballad "El molinero de Arcos," relates what happens to a miller when he mistakenly believes that his faithful wife has been seduced by an influential government official. Comical situations develop as the plot unfolds until all is finally resolved happily. Wit, lively dialogue, and rapid action combine with elegant style to make this work a classic of the storyteller's art.

Other publications by Alarcón include the humorous short novel *El capitán Veneno* (1881) and four rather moralistic-didactic full-length novels: *El final de Norma* (1851), *El escándalo* (1875), *El niño de la bola* (1880), and *La pródiga* (1881). Alarcón's outstanding short stories are collected in *Historias nacionales*, *Cuentos amatorios* (both 1881), and *Narraciones inverosímiles* (1882). His complete works also contain a play, travel books, poems, essays, and an autobiography.

Although Alarcón contributed to the development of the nineteenth-century realistic novel, his works have qualities of romanticism as well. He is therefore considered a transitional figure between the two literary movements.

For additional information, see C. de Coster, *Pedro Antonio de Alarcón* (Boston, 1979); and J. F. Montesinos, *Pedro Antonio de Alarcón* (Madrid, 1977).

*H. L. Kirby, Jr.*

**ALAS UREÑA, LEOPOLDO (CLARÍN)** (1852–1901), writer and journalist. Alas was a professor of philosophy of law at the University of Oviedo, a founder of its extension for the education of the working class, novelist, short-story writer, literary critic, and journalistic satirist. Born in Zamora, Alas moved with his family back to Oviedo when he was five and there, in the city of his ancestors, spent most of his life. After preliminary studies at the University of Oviedo, he went to Madrid to complete his formal education. In 1874, he began his journalistic career in the capital on the staff of the newly founded satirical paper *El Solfeo*, whose employees had to adopt musical pseudonyms. Alas kept his for the rest of his life.

Because the government had so little prestige earlier in the century and therefore could not attract talented young men to fill responsible government positions, literary accomplishment had become the way of advancement. As a result, the newspapers, which were controlled by political cliques, issued literary judgments according to the writers' political allegiances, so that literary criticism had become extremely corrupt and unprofessional. Seeing praise bestowed on mediocre writers and talent ridiculed, Clarín undertook the revival of literary criticism. Since he was not only well versed in classical and Spanish literature, but also knowledgeable about the contemporary literary scene in the rest of Europe, he was especially qualified to put mediocrity in its place with his caustic wit and applaud truly meritorious work, though he tempered approbation with mild recommendation for improvement. His commentary earned him more enmity than any other literary figure of his time. As a result, his reputation suffered for years after his death, and his works were seldom reprinted, even though his masterpiece, *La Regenta* (1885), is considered by many critics to be the greatest Spanish novel after *Don Quixote* (1605, 1615). He is also esteemed as Spain's greatest nineteenth-century short-story writer.

Clarín has been called a cerebral writer, and indeed a tendency to exaggerated ratiocination, combined with a fascination with symbolism, occasionally led him astray in the course of his struggle against traditionalism. This attitude was particularly prominent in his relationship with the great novelist Emilia Pardo Bazán,* a faithful Catholic, conservative monarchist, and prominent feminist. Transforming his literary political opposition to her into personal antagonism, Clarín, a committed anticlerical republican, attacked her feminist activity. It has been suggested that, at an abstruse, metaphorical level, Clarín's most famous short story, "¡Adiós, Cordera!," portrays his antifeminist ire. Ironically, during the Spanish Civil War,* one of Clarín's sons was executed by the rightists at about the same time Pardo Bazán's was killed by the leftists.

Clarín was justified in his attacks on the Royal Academy, whose members were political appointees, and in whose writings he did not fail to point out syntactical errors condemned by the grammar of their own institution. He also blamed a serious but avoidable maritime accident on the ineptitude of another sacred institution, the navy.* When challenged to a duel by some officers unless he apologized, Alas announced that he would neither retract his criticism nor fight, the latter a reasonable decision, at least, since he was of almost dwarfish size. It has been suggested that the disparity between his physical and his intellectual stature contributed a certain aggressiveness to his psychological makeup.

For additional information, see D. Torres, *Studies on Clarín: An Annotated Bibliography* (Metuchen, 1987).

*P. L. Ullman*

**ALBÉNIZ, ISAAC** (1860–1909), the first Spanish composer of major international stature to incorporate stylized folk-music elements into his works. Although Albéniz delighted in telling friends that he was a Moor, he was born in Compradón, Gerona, in Catalonia. He gave his first piano recital at the age of four (dressed in a musketeer costume), auditioned for admission to the Paris Conservatory at the age of six (he was granted delayed admission after breaking a large mirror in the conservatory while playing with a ball), and, at the age of nine, ran away from his tax-collector father. He then spent four years wandering through North and South America, often supporting himself by playing the piano, his back to the keyboard, in waterfront saloons and vaudeville houses. His father finally caught up with Albéniz in Cuba and sent him home to Spain.

Upon his return to Europe, Albéniz received a grant from the Spanish government to study piano at the Brussels Conservatory. Despite a disinclination to take his studies very seriously, Albéniz won first prize in piano at the conservatory in 1878. He then traveled with the aging Franz Liszt (1811–1886) in Germany and Italy before touring Europe as a "mature virtuoso" at the age of twenty.

Albéniz began composing at this time. He wrote dozens of salon compositions: waltzes, barcaroles, and fantasies on Italian opera arias. Seeking a new means of expression through composition, Albéniz returned to Spain in 1885 to study with Felipe Pedrell (1841–1920), the self-styled "Wagner of Spain." Pedrell, a composer and music scholar, sought to free Spanish music from a century and a half of stifling Italian domination. He believed, as did Béla Bartok (1881–1945) later in Hungary and Ralph Vaughn Williams (1872–1958) in Britain, that a great and truly national music could be built only on the foundation of native folkloric song. Pedrell's influence turned Albéniz away from salon pieces, but he despaired of teaching Albéniz even the rudiments of composition. As Pedrell said, "he can understand music intuitively and only through the medium of the keyboard."

In 1893, Albéniz settled in Paris and devoted virtually all his time to composition. He met and befriended the French composers Gabriel Fauré (1845–1924) and Paul Dukas (1865–1935), who supplied another major stylistic influence on Albéniz's works, late French romantic or impressionist music.

At this time, Albéniz made an extremely bad business contract with a mediocre British playwright who wanted the composer to write operas, but only from his own libretti. Albéniz produced three operas—*The Magic Opal*, *Henry Clifford*, and *Merlin*, all largely and justly forgotten. Pseudo-Wagnerian treatments of such disparate themes as the War of the Roses and the Arthurian legends are relieved only by the interjection (on the barest of pretexts) of Spanish folk dances.

Albéniz wanted to be remembered as a composer of operas, but it is his work for solo piano, much of which has been transcribed for guitar, that has assured his reputation. Many of his short works have entered the popular repertoire. *The Tango in D* and *Asturias* (known as *Leyenda* in guitar literature) are very accessible to listener and performer alike.

*Ibérica*, written near the end of Albéniz's life, is generally considered his most important work. This is a suite of twelve pieces of uneven quality, each piece representing a region or scene from Spanish life. Written for the piano, the pieces, like much of Albéniz's work, seem to imitate the guitar in an elaborate rhapsodic style. The music at times sounds wild and almost always totally spontaneous, but it is carefully constructed. The dynamics range from fortissimo to pianissimo in the course of a few measures. Only the most technically proficient pianist can even begin to master the pieces, and, indeed, Albéniz almost destroyed the completed manuscript when he realized that it was virtually unplayable. The suite was published in four volumes between 1906 and 1909. Opinion is divided on *Ibérica* and its proper place in the musical repertoire. French and British musicologists tend to be generally more impressed with the suite than the Spanish, who tend to feel that it is too Frenchified.

With the completion of *Ibérica*, Albéniz returned to Spain, where he died at the age of forty-eight.

For additional information, see G. Chase, *The Music of Spain* (New York, 1959); L. E. Powell, *A History of Spanish Piano Music* (Bloomington, 1980); and A. Salazar, *La música contemporánea en España* (Madrid, 1930).

*S. L. Brake*

**ALBERONI, GIULIO** (1664–1752), a cardinal and prime minister during the reign of Felipe V.* Alberoni was born in Italy* where, in 1690, he joined the priesthood. In Parma, he met the French general, the duke of Vendôme (Louis-Joseph de Bourbon, 1654–1712) and accepted employ as his secretary, traveling with Vendôme to Flanders where he met Louis XIV (1638–1715). From France,* Alberoni and his employer journeyed to Spain in 1712. As the envoy of Parma, Alberoni later joined the numerous Italians serving at the Spanish court.

Upon the death of the queen, María Luisa of Savoy, on 14 Feb. 1714, Alberoni emerged as the most influential supporter of Isabel Farnesio (the niece of the late Vendôme), as a suitable wife for king Felipe V. Alberoni also rallied Louis XIV, the princess dos Ursinos (Anne Marie de la Trémouille), cardinal Francisco del Guidice, and the powerful minister Melchor Rafael de Macanaz (1670–1760) to the cause of Farnesio. The wedding was celebrated on 16 Sept. 1714.

In 1717, Alberoni was elevated to cardinal and, with the backing of the new queen, soon became an important figure in the political arena who set about putting Spain's economy—badly disrupted by the War of Spanish Succession*—in order. His reforms centered on trimming government expenditures, ending systemic abuses, restructuring commerce, and promoting the army and navy, all aimed at returning Spain to its earlier prominence. In addition, Alberoni's design for Spain had an international dimension. The cardinal sought an alliance with Britain* and the Netherlands and open confrontation with France, but was frustrated by the formation of the Triple Alliance, which joined France, Britain, and the Netherlands. Alberoni responded by mounting an expedition to occupy Sicily in 1718. The impending invasion led Austria to ally itself with the members of the Triple Alliance to form a Quadruple Alliance. Initially, the war was disastrous for Spain, with the fleet destroyed on 22 Aug. 1718 by the British under the command of John Byng (1704–1757). A series of crushing land engagements saw the French and British land in Spain, while Austria retook Sicily. Alberoni received the blame for Spain's misadventures, and on 4 Dec. 1719 he was removed as prime minister and ordered out of Spain. After a difficult return trip to Italy, Alberoni sought refuge in Genoese territories. Summoned to Rome in 1721, he successfully defended himself and resumed his clerical activities. In 1733, he founded a seminary and in later years served as a papal legate to Ravenna and with the powerful Bologna legation.

For additional information, see R. de Missy, *The History of Cardinal Alberoni . . .* (London, 1719); G. Moore, *Lives of Cardinal Alberoni, the Duke of Ripperda, and Marquis of Pombal, three distinguished political adventurers of the last century* (London, 1814); and S. Harcourt-Smith, *Alberoni or the Spanish Conspiracy* (London, 1943).

*R. Hendricks*

*Related entry*: FELIPE V.


**ALCALÁ ZAMORA Y TORRES, NICETO** (1877–1949), first president of the Second Republic.* Born in Priego, near Cordoba, Alcalá Zamora became a lawyer in the office of Luis Díaz Cobeña (1837–1911), one of the best-known advocates of Madrid. There, he had a brief acquaintance with his later rival and successor as premier, Manuel Azaña.*

A member of the Liberal party and an eloquent orator, he first served in two cabinets of Manuel García Prieto (1859–1938), who had added the word "democratic" to the party's name. In 1917, he became minister of development and in 1922, minister of war. During the dictatorship of Gen. Miguel Primo de Rivera,* Alcalá Zamora joined the opposition and on 17 Aug. 1930, signed the Pact of San Sebastian, which called for establishment of a republic by force to revive civil and religious liberty and grant Catalan autonomy.

When the municipal elections of 1931 gave a marginal victory to republican and socialist parties, Alcalá Zamora, perhaps the most conservative member of the Central Revolutionary Committee formed after the signing of the Pact of

San Sebastian, became premier in the provisional government that wrote the constitution for the Second Republic.

Almost immediately, Alcalá Zamora and his party, the Liberal Republican Right, opposed the efforts of Azaña's Left Republican party to destroy the conservative and antirepublican dominance over Spain's educational system and economic life. Azaña's followers and allied groups, however, dominated the elections for the Constituent Cortes, and Article 26 of the proposed constitution was sufficiently anticlerical to bring Alcalá Zamora's resignation as premier.

Azaña, who replaced Alcalá Zamora as prime minister, was eager to soften his predecessor's opposition, and with the approval of the constitution in Dec. 1931, secured the election of Alcalá Zamora as the first president of the new republic. This uneasy alliance between a relatively conservative president and a liberal-socialist prime minister lasted into 1933, when strikes, rural violence, and the anticipated closing of Catholic schools brought a lessened liberal vote in the municipal elections of Apr. 1933 and blocked Alcalá Zamora's attempt to find a prime minister who might command a majority in the Cortes. He was therefore forced to dissolve it. New elections in Nov. 1933 brought a significant showing of conservative Catholic groups in the Confederación Española de Derechos Autónomas under José María Gil Robles. Alcalá Zamora would not name José María Gil Robles (1898– ) as prime minister because of his antirepublican stance in the elections, however, and Alejandro Lerroux,* leader of the Radical party, was allowed to form a government with CEDA support, but no cabinet ministers.

Lerroux survived for some months in spite of the opposition of workers and Catalan autonomists, but in Oct. 1934 found it necessary to reform his cabinet to include three CEDA members. This cabinet was responsible for harsh military action against striking miners in Asturias and also reversed most of the anticlerical measures passed under Azaña. It lasted until Jan. 1934, when disclosure of corruption among Lerroux's followers and his own rejection of the CEDA and Gil Robles's leadership forced Alcalá Zamora to dissolve the Cortes.

In the elections of 16 Feb. 1936, Azaña and an alliance of parties joined together in the Popular Front and won a victory narrow in terms of popular votes, but impressive in the number of seats gained in the Cortes. Alcalá Zamora immediately named Azaña as premier, but constitutional provisions required a review of his own two dissolutions of the Cortes. In what was perhaps the most serious error of the Spanish republicans, this review condemned Alcalá Zamora for having dissolved the Cortes in 1936, rather than in Oct. 1934. He was impeached as president and replaced by Azaña, which deprived the new president of major political influence. As a result, one of the most sincere leaders of the republic was lost, while the most popular republican politician now existed in isolation.

Alcalá Zamora remained a republican throughout the civil war. In 1941, Gen. Francisco Franco* sentenced him to fifteen years' exile, loss of nationality, and confiscation of his personal estate. He spent most of his remaining life in Buenos

Aires, Argentina, where he played an intellectual role by writing books on themes ranging from Spanish oratory and grammar to the thought of "El Quijote" and international peace. He died in Buenos Aires on 18 Feb. 1949. His will, written in 1942, still praised republican government and implored his fellow Spaniards to affirm and practice "in ideas, religious liberty, and peace, without fanaticism or sectarian persecutions; in sentiment, an intense patriotism . . . ; and in life and conduct, austere simplicity and crystal clarity of action."

For additional information, see R. Herr, *Spain* (Englewood Cliffs, 1971); E. Aguado, *Don Manuel Azaña Díaz* (Barcelona, 1972); R. de la Cierva, *Historia de la Guerra Civil Española*, vol. 1 of *Perspectivas y antecedentes, 1898–1936* (Madrid, 1969); and H. Thomas, *The Spanish Civil War* (New York, 1961).

*E. R. Beck*

*Related entries*: AZAÑA, MANUEL; SECOND REPUBLIC.


**ALEIXANDRE, VICENTE** (1898–1984), one of the most distinguished members of the Generation of 1927.* Aleixandre was born in 1898 in Seville, but spent most of his childhood years in Malaga, his "city of paradise" that figures symbolically in much of his work. In 1909, he moved with his family to Madrid, where eleven years later, he received degrees in law and mercantile management. Illness and the discovery of poetry as his true vocation soon forced him to abandon these careers.

In 1917, Dámaso Alonso (1898– ) lent him an anthology of the great modernist poet Rubén Darío (1867–1916), which caused, in his words, "a revolution in my soul." Shortly thereafter, he began to read other poets, most notably Antonio Machado* and Manuel Machado (1874–1947), and Juan Ramón Jiménez.* He experimented with his own poetry at the age of twenty, but tormented by fear and insecurity, he did not publish until eight years later.

Aleixandre wrote extensively about his own work and his poetic creed. He distinguished between two types of poets. The poets of "minorities" spoke of "exquisitely strict themes, refined partialities, the decanted essences of our meticulous civilization." The others, among whom he counted himself, referred to what is "humanly permanent and sing not what separates in a refined way, but what essentially unites. These are radical poets, and they speak of the primary, elemental forces of human nature." Poetry, for Aleixandre, was fundamentally communication. "Poetry is not a question of ugliness or beauty, but of muteness or communication. . . . In this power of transmission lies perhaps the only secret of poetry." To this end, it must therefore be accessible to a large audience and must also be intimately related to life and to man. "Poetry stems from man and ends in man. Between one pole and the other, it can pass through the entire universe."

Aleixandre's work includes pure poetry, as in *Ámbito* (1928). It was followed by a surrealist period influenced by the reading of Sigmund Freud (1856–1939), which resulted in *La destrucción o el amor* (1935), winner of the National Prize for Literature. *Mundo a solas* (written 1934–1936, published 1950) followed, a transitional work that presents the world in transformation from the previous state of chaos to a world of tranquil serenity that is finally glimpsed in *Sombra de paraíso* (1944). This last work represented a return to authenticity and reality as opposed to the escapism typical of the official poetry of the Franco period. Its free verse broke with the artificial formalism characteristic of earlier movements.

In 1949, Aleixandre was voted a member of the Spanish Academy, and in 1977, coinciding with the fiftieth anniversary of his generation and the first democratic elections held in Spain after the death of Gen. Francisco Franco,* he was awarded the Nobel Prize, because his poetry "with roots in the traditions of Spanish lyric verse and in modern currents, illuminates man's condition in the cosmos and in present-day society."

Aleixandre holds a prominent position in the history of Spanish literature not only for the excellence and originality of his work, but also for his human qualities. He is one of the few writers of his generation who, because of his delicate health, did not go into exile after the defeat of the Second Republic* in 1939, despite his strong anti-Francoist stance. In the difficult and culturally stagnant years of the dictatorship, his legendary home in Madrid on Velintonia Street (now named after him) became a mecca for three generations of poets who looked up to him as a master, mentor, and friend. He is also considered a link between those writers who remained in Spain in interior exile and those who fled the country.

Despite the great variety in his writing, there are undercurrents common to it all, particularly his overwhelming desire for unity, whether with the cosmos or all humanity, and love as the means to reach it. Vicente Aleixandre is an outstanding figure in the history of literature whose influence has been instrumental in the development of contemporary Spanish poetry.

For additional information, see C. Bousoño, *La poesía de Vicente Aleixandre*, 3d ed. (Madrid, 1977); V. Cabrera and H. Boyer, eds., *Critical Views on Vicente Aleixandre's Poetry* (Lincoln, 1979); D. Puccini, *La palabra poética de Vicente Aleixandre* (Barcelona, 1979); and K. Schwartz, *Vicente Aleixandre* (New York, 1970).

*S. Rivera*

*Related entry*: GENERATION OF 1927.


**ALFONSO XII, KING OF SPAIN** (1857–1885), ruled 1875–1885. Alfonso, putatively the son of Isabel II* and her royal consort, Francisco de Asís (1822–1902), was perhaps the most likeable and progressive monarch of Spain during the nineteenth century. His education under royal tutors at court was deficient, but at the age of eleven, he accompanied his mother to Paris after the revolution of Sept. 1868 and attended classes there at the Stanislas college. In 1870, Isabel II abdicated the throne in favor of her son, although there was much subsequent suspicion that she did not regard this act as final. This action came at the time when the revolutionary forces in Spain were debating the choice of an Italian king, Amadeo I,* as a monarch to replace the Bourbon line. Amadeo, however, soon found that conditions did not allow for stable royal government and returned to Italy. Amadeo's reign was followed by the founding of the First Republic,* which proved more chaotic than the monarchy and ended in a brief semidictatorship under one of Isabel's former lovers, Gen. Francisco Serrano (1810–1885), the duque de la Torre.

Meanwhile, after four years' study in Paris, the young prince went to a military academy, the Theresianum, in Vienna. This brought him into contact with the culture of the rest of Europe and marked the beginning of a pronounced Germanophilism. While the prince was in Vienna, his mother briefly entrusted the cause of her son's claim to the Spanish throne to the representation of his uncle, Antonio de Orléans (1824–1890), the duke of Montpensier, who was himself a claimant to the crown. During this short period of cooperation between prince and uncle, Alfonso met and fell in love with his cousin, María de las Mercedes.

Disillusioned with Montpensier's management of her son's claims to the throne, Isabel in 1873 gave the official representation of those claims to Antonio Cánovas del Castillo,* already a well-known political figure, although his most significant political career was to come after Alfonso became king. On 11 Aug. 1874, Cánovas sent the young prince to Sandhurst, the British military school, to provide the future king with a view of government under a constitutional monarchy. Alfonso followed the guidance of Cánovas in the issuance on 1 Dec. 1874 of the so-called Manifesto of Sandhurst, in which he set forth the claim that a Bourbon restoration to the throne in his person would be followed by constitutional government. During this period in Britain, however, Alfonso also took a vacation trip to the continent and visited Germany,* seeing the Krupp factories at Essen, visiting relatives in Munich, and in the process strengthening his Germanophilism.

The chaotic course of Spanish politics had in the meantime been further complicated by civil war, with the Basques* of Biscay, Álava, and Guipúzcoa Provinces joining the neighboring province of Navarre* in a conflict seeking the restoration of their special legal privileges, or fueros, and supporting the cause of the Carlist pretender to the throne, Carlos VII (1848–1909).* By 1874, much of the northern part of Spain was in the hands of the Carlists,* whose troops numbered some sixty thousand men, amply financed and provisioned. The government of the duque de la Torre displayed little energy or initiative in dealing with this real threat to Spanish unity.

The Second Carlist War (1873–1876) emphasized the role of military leaders in Spain, who had already demonstrated their importance in the overthrow of Emilio Castelar (1832–1899), the last president of the First Republic. Although Cánovas was recognized as the spokesman of the Alfonsist cause, significant military leaders were also advocates of the Bourbon restoration and had no intention of leaving that movement entirely in civilian hands. The leading figure involved was Gen. Arsenio Martínez Campos (1831–1900), who had criticized the government of the duque de la Torre and been briefly imprisoned, then placed on reserve status in Madrid. It was, therefore, necessary for him to "borrow" several regiments from a friend in order to make the pronunciamento at Sagunto on 19 Dec. 1874 on behalf of Alfonso, which led to the collapse of the regime of the duque de la Torre and the return of Bourbon rule.

Early in Jan. 1875, Alfonso entered Spain through Catalonia and proceeded to Madrid with a triumphal entry on 14 Jan. Through the first six years of his reign, practically all governmental decisions were made by his prime minister, Cánovas del Castillo, with the king's role restricted to the acceptance and support of those decisions.

Cánovas and his supporters, the Liberal-Conservative party, governed harshly. Press censorship and action against dissident movements were initiated. Francisco Romero Robledo (1838–1906), the minister of the interior, established the pattern of managed elections and caciquismo* that was followed through the remainder of the century. The Second Carlist War was brought to a successful conclusion partially through military action, partially by negotiations with some of its leaders. The young king was allowed to take a brief part in the last battle of the war, even though at that late date the military actions of the Carlists came close to bringing an early end to his reign.

Cánovas was also responsible for the establishment of a new Constitution of 1876. The monarchical principle was proclaimed to be based on "the grace of God." Although the king was designated as a constitutional monarch, the statement of the king's authority set no real limitations. With regard to the Cortes, the monarch had the right to name one-third of the members of the senate, and both houses were placed under the control of the propertied classes. Although the constitution allowed the private exercise of religions other than Catholicism, the interpretation of this provision was extremely restrictive.

Cánovas encouraged the formation of an alternate political party, which at the outset was called the Constitutionalist party and was led by Práxedes Mateo Sagasta,* who had been involved with the government of Amadeo I and that of the duque de la Torre. From the first, Cánovas's conception of two rival political parties debating in the Cortes and sharing power by peaceful change was vitiated by the division within the leading parties and the appearance of third parties that complicated the political spectrum. One personal contribution of the monarch was to convey to political opponents his respect for them personally and his recognition of the possibility of political change.

The king's popularity was increased by aspects of his personal experiences— his marriage to his cousin, María de las Mercedes, whom he chose in spite of family and political objections; her unfortunate death fewer than six months later; and a narrow escape from an assassin's bullet. A second marriage in 1879 was officially arranged with María Cristina de Habsburgo (1858–1929),* but both before and after this marriage, the king's romantic adventures in Madrid had become widely known.

Meanwhile, Cánovas had sent Martínez Campos, the most colorful general of the Carlist War and the author of the pronunciamento of Sagunto, to end the existing revolt in Cuba. Martínez Campos succeeded in this effort by a com-

bination of successful counterguerilla warfare and negotiations with his opponents, and by his demands that Spain undertake a significant reform movement
in Cuba. His proposals stirred opposition in Spain, particularly because they
challenged entrenched economic privileges, especially in Catalonia,* but Cánovas allowed Martínez Campos to form his own cabinet to seek support for these
measures. The cabinet lasted only from 8 Mar. 1879 to 7 Dec. of the same year.
The failure of these reform measures left the problems of Cuba unsolved.

Although the king was reported as carrying out royal duties conscientiously,
his role with respect to domestic politics was minimal. In 1881, however, the
king brought about the first change of ministry since the Restoration, calling for
a temporary alliance of Sagasta's constitutionalists and other party groupings to
head the government. This so-called fusion of parties opposing Cánovas did not
last long, but it did provide a freer atmosphere, allowing the return to their posts
of professors fired for political or religious differences, the reappearance of
opposition newspapers, and the formation of some party groupings combining
the ideals of democracy and monarchy. It was, though, also marked by the
turning out of government officials on a large scale, along with controlled elections and an early splintering of liberal groups over personal differences as well
as budget issues and the reform of the military. Although Sagasta moved early
in 1883 to a purely liberal (the term replacing "constitutionalist") ministry, the
Spanish Left continued to be more divided than the Right, with Cánovas and
his followers now adopting the term "conservative" as the designation of their
party. The liberal interlude had brought the increased activity of the Spanish
socialist movement under Pablo Iglesias (1850–1925) and of southern anarchism.* The Sagasta government acted against both these groups almost as
severely as had Cánovas.

Although Alfonso XII had accepted Sagasta and given encouragement to
leaders even to the left of Sagasta, the liberal government had resulted in considerable disillusionment on the monarch's part. He had found it impossible to
carry through the military reforms he thought were needed and had become
aware of the widespread corruption and inefficiency in the bureaucracy. True
reform, he said on one occasion, would require throwing out the parliamentary
system, purging the bureaucracy, and governing arbitrarily for twenty years,
after which he could go to the country for approval or disapproval of the changes
he had made. Because of the impossibility of this alternative and the fall of a
brief ministry of José Posada Herrera (1815–1885), the result of Cánovas's and
Sagasta's opposition to its proposal for universal manhood suffrage, the monarch
accepted the return of Cánovas early in 1884.

It was, however, during the liberal period that the king's Germanophilism
found expression in strong efforts to establish good relations with Otto von
Bismarck's (1815–1898) Germany. Alfonso XII, despite his marriage to the
Austrian María Cristina, viewed the German leader with a kind of hero worship.
A visit to Germany in 1883 won the respect of Kaiser Wilhelm I (1797–1888)
and his personal interest in the role of the Spanish monarchy, but also earned

Alfonso negative demonstrations in Paris on his return journey to Spain. Advice from the German government always stressed the importance of the king's strengthening of the military and his own control over its leaders.

Many difficulties attended the last period of the monarch's rule. There were several abortive military revolts, severe earthquakes in Granada and Malaga, and a terrible cholera epidemic. The king's own love for Germany was put to some test when Spain lost the ownership of the island of Yap in the Carolines in a controversy with that country. Cánovas governed harshly, becoming involved in a serious controversy with the university students in Madrid. He also exercised greater control over the young monarch, trying to curtail the king's penchant for nightly escapades at the same time that he was showing increasing evidence of the effects of the tuberculosis that cost him his life on 25 Nov. 1885.

Alfonso XII's reign was marked more by hope than accomplishment. His major achievement was the stabilization of the dynasty by his own acceptance of the concept of peaceful parliamentary change. There is no evidence that he gave strong personal support to the reforms for Cuba that Martínez Campos advocated and that might have avoided the Spanish-American War.* His efforts for military reform came to naught because of the opposition of entrenched leaders and those who profited from military expenditures. The system of government encouraged corruption. There was a considerable acquisition of personal popularity. Had the monarch lived longer, more might have been accomplished, but this would have required a stronger hand on the political scene than was possible in this period.

For additional information, see E. R. Beck, *A Time of Triumph and of Sorrow: Spanish Politics during the Reign of Alfonso XII, 1874–1885* (Carbondale, 1979); M. Espadas Burgos, *Alfonso XII y los orígenes de la restauración* (Madrid, 1975); M. Fernández Almagro, *Historia política de la España contemporánea*, 2 vols. (Madrid, 1956–1959).

*E. R. Beck*

*Related entries*: CÁNOVAS DEL CASTILLO, ANTONIO; FIRST REPUBLIC; SAGASTA, PRÁXEDES MATEO.

**ALFONSO XIII, KING OF SPAIN** (1886–1941), ruled 1902–1931. Born 17 May 1886, almost six months after the death of his father, Alfonso XII,* Alfonso XIII was declared king at his birth, but his mother, the Austrian archduchess María Cristina de Habsburgo (1858–1929), acted as regent until he reached the age of majority. Alfonso received an excellent education, but from early childhood bore the weight of already being king. Although María Cristina acted as a faultless constitutional monarch, her regency suffered from the tragic consequences of defeat in the Spanish-American War.* The country Alfonso governed had suffered the loss of its colonies* as well as prestige. He governed through a period when there was a strong ground swell for the "regeneration" of Spain. In the long run, this quest for reform resulted in the loss of his throne.

The system of government that had been created by the Constitution of 1876, under which his father returned to the throne, contemplated a rotation of a "liberal" and a "conservative" party supported by caciques,* which allowed the minister of the interior of each new government to "manage" the election of a majority of the Cortes in support of his party. Each change of ministry carried with it a complete alteration of the government bureaucracy. Alfonso's reign, though, was troubled by personal divisions within each party, and the seeming stability attached to the system during the reign of his father and the regency of his mother was fractured. The growth of left-wing labor movements— socialists and anarchosyndicalists—and of federalist and republican sentiments accentuated these problems.

The monarch's personal actions supported the position of the military, which had been left unreformed after the loss of the war with the United States,* and of the Catholic church, which combatted "liberal" reform movements. In spite of the increasing industrialization of the state, the long-existing poverty of the landless peasants was accompanied by the rapid growth of a depressed class of workers in the cities.

Alfonso married a British princess, Victoria Eugenia of Battenberg (1887– 1969), the granddaughter of Queen Victoria. She brought to her children the disease of hemophilia, which was inherent in the family line. The marriage did not bring close attachment to Britain,* and Spain remained neutral in the spate of alliances preceding World War I.* The major, indeed almost the only, focus of Spanish foreign policy lay in the effort to maintain ownership of a virtually worthless strip of desert in Morocco,* the last remnant of imperial pride.

Both the lack of firm royal leadership and the force of circumstance sabotaged reform efforts in the period before World War I. The first efforts to establish alternatives to church-controlled education came under the conde de Romanones (1863–1951), Álvaro de Figueroa, in 1902. Attempts were also made in that year, during the ministry of Práxedes Mateo Sagasta,* to establish some state supervision over the religious orders in Spain. These moves reflected the growth of criticism of the size and wealth of the Catholic clergy in Spain. In this period, Antonio Maura* formulated his program of "reform from above," but later events were to indicate that neither he nor the monarch intended for reform to interfere with the predominant role of the church. Maura, who had been a liberal, moved to the Conservative party in 1902 and headed his first cabinet from 1903 to 1905. Efforts to control the clergy became moribund during this ministry.

In 1906, the liberals, led by José López Domínguez (1829–1911), moved more strongly against the church, sponsoring civil marriages and sterner state control over religious organizations. Strong public demonstrations in support of the church accompanied Maura's opposition. On 31 May 1906, Alfonso XIII and his bride were the object of an assassination attempt on the return to the palace after the wedding. The bomb used killed thirty-seven and injured more than one hundred spectators and some guards; the monarch and his bride narrowly escaped death. The author of the attempt, one Mateo Morral, was employed in the publishing firm of Francisco Ferrer,* an anarchist who had founded a "Modern School" in Barcelona,* which allowed both sexes to attend and was considered antireligious in its teachings. As a consequence, Ferrer was arrested with Morral and became the symbol of harsh government action. In a strange turn of events, however, the liberal government lasting from 4 Dec. 1906 to 25 Jan. 1907 subsequently established, with the monarch's approval, committees to review the status of education in Spain.

These committees accomplished little, since Maura returned to office with strong Catholic support. In this period, Maura sought to carry out his "reform from above," but with little success. He encountered opposition in his efforts to enlarge the Spanish fleet, and military reforms made no move to reduce either the size of the army* or the hold of the entrenched officer class. The monarch's involvement in deciding military appointments and policies became clear during this period. Maura talked of "uprooting caciquismo," but failed to obtain the necessary legislation. Attempts to liberalize local and regional government were unsuccessful, largely because of opposition from his own party. Only a move to control terrorism gained support and implementation, although its restriction of civil rights was criticized.

During this period, the liberals formed a Left Bloc, which campaigned strongly against Maura's program. The role of the church was a significant point of attack, along with the harsh plight of the Spanish working class, whose condition declined despite a period of some economic recovery. The result was a general strike in Barcelona that joined hostility to the church, protest against unemployment and poverty, and opposition to the beginning of a new military campaign in Morocco and found its new recruits largely among the lowest classes in society. Severely repressive government measures provoked the Tragic Week (26 July–1 Aug. 1909) in which hundreds of strikers were injured or killed. Ferrer was executed in Oct. 1909. These events shocked liberal opinion at home and abroad, and late in the same month, the monarch asked for the resignation of his prime minister at a time when he still held a majority in the Cortes. Whether Alfonso buckled under the domestic and foreign hail of criticism or was more concerned about the Moroccan policy of his minister is uncertain. He did, however, disrupt the normal process of rotation that had existed under his father and mother.

Finding a reliable liberal leader to replace Maura posed some difficulties. Segismundo Moret's (1838–1913) brief cabinet fell when the king denied the right to dissolve the Cortes. It was followed by the cabinet of José Canalejas (1854–1912), who sought to limit the increase of religious orders (but compromised on a moderate law) and used strong measures against a general railroad strike in 1912. His assassination in Nov. 1912 left the monarch without a strong liberal leader. Romanones held office several times, but to no great effect.

Spain's neutrality provided the opportunity for some economic advancement, but the war brought a rise in the cost of living that affected many sections of the population adversely. Economic problems were joined to an increase in the drive for Catalan autonomy. The army was the only source of royal security, but reforms to improve the quality of its leaders and the morale of its troops were met by organized resistance in the form of military "defense committees," which protected the privileges of incompetent officers. The monarch did not seek the reforms needed and maintained friendships with political generals who knew little of campaign tactics.

In 1918, the monarch supported the formation of a "National Government" that was supposed to represent all the parties, but proved ineffective. In the period that followed, cabinets came and went without creating a sense of authority or stability. This allowed the increase of anarchist and syndicalist movements and shattered the king's own confidence in the existing constitutional system. These defects in royal leadership were underscored by events taking place between 21 July and 9 Aug. 1921 at the battle of Anwal* in Morocco. Criminally faulty leadership allowed a few thousand rebellious Riff tribesmen to take the lives of some twenty thousand Spanish soldiers, who found their enemies armed with the rifles and supplied with munitions that had been sent for their own use. The degree of the king's responsibility for this tragedy remains debatable, but parliamentary efforts to investigate the causes led to an army takeover and the military dictatorship of Gen. Miguel Primo de Rivera.*

During Primo's dictatorship, the king had virtually no role; his major American biographer has characterized him as a prisoner of the dictatorship. As a consequence, he could neither take credit for its accomplishments nor be blamed for its failures. The fall of Primo in 1931 brought with it no strong movement to return to the monarchy. Elections in that year brought republican victories in many Spanish cities, although monarchical sentiments still predominated in rural areas. Alfonso would support neither a republic nor a call to arms to protect the throne and left the country without abdicating. From exile, he watched the tragic events of the Second Republic* and the Spanish Civil War* without exercising any significant influence upon them. Gen. Francisco Franco* appeared to prove a hope of restoration for the monarch, but when he assumed power, he indicated that Alfonso could not be considered as a ruler for the new monarchy he intended to create. Shortly before he died in Rome on 12 Feb. 1941, Alfonso abdicated in favor of his son, don Juan (1913– ).

Much of the tragedy of Alfonso XIII's reign must be attributed to circumstances and events beyond his control. No civilian leaders of the stature and determination of Antonio Cánovas del Castillo* or Sagasta were available. The king's strong and determined support might have added to the influence of Antonio Maura, but economic and social changes brought deep divisions among liberal groups. The strength of revolutionary forces made the monarch dependent upon the support of the military and prevented needed reforms. Probably the only real course available to him was a royal dictatorship, but this would have involved breaching the constitution, and Alfonso lacked the courage and determination to take that step. When Primo finally took it for him, he became a spectator on the political scene rather than a participant. This, of course, set the scene for the coming of the republican experiment and the civil war that followed.

For additional information, see C. P. Boyd, *Praetorian Politics in Liberal Spain* (Chapel Hill, 1979); M. Fernández Almagro, *Historia del reinado de Alfonso XIII*, 4th ed. (Barcelona, 1977); V. R. Pilapil, *Alfonso XIII* (New York, 1969); and J. C. Ullman, *The Tragic Week: A Study of Anti-clericalism in Spain, 1875–1912* (Cambridge, 1968).

E. R. Beck

*Related entries*: PRIMO DE RIVERA Y ORBANEJA, MIGUEL; WORLD WAR I.

**ALMIRALL I LLOZER, VALENTÍ** (1841–1904), lawyer and writer, key figure of the late nineteenth-century Catalan political resurgence. A son of a wealthy Barcelona* bourgeois family, Almirall obtained his law degree from the University of Barcelona in 1863, though he practiced little. He participated in the revolutionary activities of 1868 in Barcelona; founded the Federalist Club and its organ *El Federalista*; and transformed it in 1869 into the daily voice of Barcelona's federalists, *El Estado Catalán*. He was responsible for the popular anticlerical weekly *La Campana de Gràcia* and organized the federalist congress that produced the Pact of Tortosa. At the start of the First Republic,* Almirall took his federalist campaign to Madrid* and published *El Estado Catalán* there until June 1873. Then, disillusioned with republican parliamentary strife—his Catalanism intensifying as his republicanism diminished—he returned to Barcelona.

In 1879, Almirall founded *El Diari Català*, the first Catalan language daily, and in 1880, initiated and presided over the first Catalan nationalist congress. In June 1881, he broke with the federalists, headed by Francesc Pi i Margall,* and closed *El Diari Català*, calling for a specifically Catalan political program. In 1882, with the "Renaixença" group, he founded the Catalan center, which under his influence became the first Catalan nationalist political organization. The congress of 1883 adopted his political orientation, and as a result a number of his works, including the "Memorial in Defense of Moral and Material Interests of Catalonia," were published. His "Memorial de Greuges," presented to Alfonso XII* in 1885, became the best-known early statement of Catalan aspirations.

The following year brought Almirall to his apogee: he was named president of the Jocs Florals (floral games, literally poetry contests using the Catalan language), and his major political work, *Lo Catalanisme*, appeared. This systematic exposition of regionalism analyzed the opposing Castilian and Catalan national characters and underscored the determining role of language in Catalan life.

Unfortunately, Almirall's inflexible personality and doctrinal regionalism aggravated discord among other Catalans. Disagreement over the Universal Exposition of 1887 sparked the withdrawal of conservative dissidents from the proposed Catalan Center to form the Lliga de Catalunya. Although Almirall was elected president of the Barcelona Atheneum in 1896, and subsequent attempts were made to draw him back into politics, his recurrent illness and isolation embittered his last years, and he died in 1904.

For additional information, see A. Barcells, ed., *Història dels Països Catalans de 1714 a 1975* (Barcelona, 1980); and J. Vicens i Vives and M. Llorens, *Industrial i Polítics (Segle XIX)*, 3rd ed. (Barcelona, 1980).

*V. L. Enders*

*Related entries*: BARCELONA; CATALONIA.

**AMADEO I DE SABOYA, KING OF SPAIN** (1845–1890), ruled 1871–1873. Amadeo de Saboya (in Italian, Amadeo di Savoia) was born in Turin, Piedmont, on 30 May 1845. The second son of the future Victor Emmanuel II (1820–1878) and Archduchess Marie Adelaide of Hapsburg, he was immediately created duke of Aosta by his grandfather, King Charles Albert (1798–1855), many of whose personal traits—notably his indecision—he inherited.

In Jan. 1869, even before the new constitution establishing a constitutional monarchy had been adopted in Spain, the Spanish government unofficially inquired whether the duke of Aosta would be willing to accept the crown. Much to his father's chagrin, Amadeo flatly refused. In July 1870, however, as the Franco-Prussian War (1870–1871) loomed imminent, Amadeo reluctantly agreed to put forth his candidacy for the sake of European peace. After the outbreak of the war, a vehement appeal to his sense of patriotic and dynastic duty was necessary to keep him from again changing his mind. Finally, on 16 Nov. 1870, the Cortes, by a majority of 191 votes to 153, elected him king.

Gen. Juan Prim y Prats,* who had arranged Amadeo's election, was the leader of the left-center coalition of the Progressive,* Liberal Union, and Democratic parties that had overthrown Isabel II.* Prim had ruled out a republic, favored by many democrats, and had prevailed over the unionists, most of whom would have preferred a Bourbon prince. As Amadeo set sail for Spain on 27 Dec., however, unknown assailants murdered Prim in Madrid. The new king, who had looked to Prim for guidance and support, thus began his reign a political orphan, presiding over a fractious government of less than lukewarm supporters.

The circumstances called for a man of uncommon qualities. Amadeo was a brave prince of good intentions, but rather limited intellect. "A bearded child," one of his ministers called him; "An idiot," was another's less charitable assessment. Tall, thin, dark, with irregular features; high, narrow forehead; dark eyes; a longish nose; a rather prominent mouth, he was not considered "sufficiently royal" by many of his subjects, who mocked his inability to master Spanish.

Francisco Serrano (1810–1885), duque de la Torre, the leading unionist and former regent, formed the king's first cabinet. The difficulty in dividing government offices among the three coalition parties gave Amadeo the first intimation of the intricacies of Spanish politics. Not only had the three parties never been firmly united, but now the progressives, the party of Prim, began to split. The radicals, headed by Manuel Ruiz Zorrilla (1833–1895), proposed sweeping political and economic reforms as the only means for the new constitutional monarchy to strike roots. The constitutionalists, led by Práxedes Mateo Sagasta,* espoused a more conservative policy and regarded the revolutionary chapter as closed.

Despite a comfortable majority in the Cortes, petty bickering prevented Serrano from governing effectively, and he resigned in July 1871. Faced with the definitive breakdown of the revolutionary coalition, Amadeo insisted that there be only two dynastic parties. He pressured the unionists to join the constitutionalists and the democrats to merge with the radicals. Amadeo can, therefore, be regarded as the first Spanish statesman to attempt the turno pacífico, the peaceful alternation of parties. Although Ruiz Zorrilla and Sagasta paid lip service to the idea of a bipartisan system, however, neither was willing to implement it.

After barely three months in office, Ruiz Zorrilla lost a procedural vote to Sagasta and quickly tendered his resignation. A distraught Amadeo was reduced to appealing to the patriotism of José Malcampo y Monje (1828–1880), a rear admiral and political nonentity, to form a colorless government of followers of Sagasta. It proved to be a stopgap measure, as Ruiz Zorrilla paid Sagasta back in kind by handing his protégé a resounding parliamentary defeat.

Unable to evade responsibility any longer, Sagasta at last agreed to form a government on 21 Dec. 1871. His unexpected resignation in May 1872, following a corruption scandal, had nothing to do with Ruiz Zorrilla's fierce opposition. It appears he could not disclose that funds had been used to cover up an indiscretion in the king's private life.

With Ruiz Zorrilla still sulking, the king called upon Serrano to form a government. Serrano believed that the only way to restore order—threatened by a new Carlist insurrection and republican agitation—was to suspend constitutional guarantees. Beset by scruples and advised by his father's ambassador, Amadeo refused Serrano's request.

The fall of the Serrano cabinet and the inevitable return of Ruiz Zorrilla brought about a realignment of political parties. The unionists and many constitutionalists withdrew their support of the dynasty and turned in growing numbers to the idea of a Bourbon restoration. Republicans, on the other hand, were exultant. Since the constitutionalists could not rule, and the radicals could govern only with their permission, they looked forward to the day when they would be rid of the king.

The new Cortes elected in Aug. 1872 was an affront to Amadeo's sense of fair play. It was completely dominated by the radicals and their republican allies; moreover, no conservative figures—neither Serrano nor Sagasta—were returned. By early Feb., when the king provoked an incident with his ministers by refusing to receive them on the occasion of the birth of his third son, it was clear that Amadeo had grown tired of revolving-door cabinets and thought himself the prisoner of a party whose monarchism was very much in doubt. After two years of enduring vitriolic attacks in the press and the theater—"the foreigner," or "Macarronini I," as he was publicly called—the scorn of the upper classes, and the indifference of the masses, he was ready to lay down his burden.

The Hidalgo affair was the excuse the king used to leave "the insane asylum," as he called it, of Spanish politics. Baltasar Hidalgo de Quesada was accused, probably unjustly, by his fellow artillery officers of having joined a Prim-inspired mutiny in 1866 and killed a number of his brother officers. A thankful revolution promoted him and, in 1872, appointed him captain general of the Basque Provinces. Rather than serve under him, all artillery officers went on sick leave. Under pressure from his republican allies who saw in the incident a way of disposing of the king, Ruiz Zorrilla accepted their resignations and ordered the corps reorganized.

Amadeo, himself a military man, sympathized with the officers' position. Ever the constitutional king, however, he was unwilling to ignore the will of the Cortes and the cabinet. As he signed the reorganization decree, he informed an astonished Ruiz Zorrilla of his decision to abdicate. On 11 Feb. 1873, despite all efforts to dissuade him, an uncommonly resolute Amadeo signed his abdication. That same day, the Cortes proclaimed the First Republic.*

Following his abdication, Amadeo returned to Italy and resumed the life of comfortable obscurity he had so reluctantly relinquished. He never again returned to Spain and refused all communication with his former subjects. By his first marriage to Maria Victoria dell Pozzo della Cisterna he had three sons. After her death in 1876, Amadeo married his niece, Laetitia Bonaparte, in 1888 and had another son. On 18 Jan. 1890, he died of pneumonia in Turin.

For additional information, see A. de Figueroa, conde de Romanones, *Amadeo de Saboya, el rey efímero* (Madrid, 1934); and A. de Sagrera, *Amadeo y María Victoria, reyes de España* (Palma de Mallorca, 1959).

*N. Durán*

*Related entry*: FIRST REPUBLIC.


**ANARCHISM.** Anarchism has a long history in particularistic and individualistic Spain, where economic change left peasants isolated, exploited, and vulnerable to peculiar delusions of independence. This southern Mediterranean mood, also common in Sicily and Calabria, was one of primitive rebellion, complete with overtones of messianic expectation, communalism, and universality. Centered in Andalusia,* already unsettled by the War of Independence,* the liberal process of disentailment* and anticlericalism attacked constituted authority and weakened order. Unrest began in the 1840s and 1850s with the burning of notary archives and manor houses; and matured during the First Republic,* when the cantonal movement appeared from peasant sources to interpret the more general regional federalism of Francesc Pi i Margall* as a sanction for the formation of city-states. Idiosyncratic practices ranging from prohibition of alcohol or tobacco to communal property-sharing—unified by an antiauthoritarian philosophy toward national politics, but ironically, quite authoritarian in their own local application—briefly flourished until the army* under Gen. Manuel Pavía y Rodríguez (1827–1895) put an end to this messianic outburst.

The southern roots of Spanish anarchism continued into the twentieth century. The Black Hand (Mano negro) conspiracy of the 1880s, while heavily prosecuted, nevertheless maintained the old grievances until a modern agricultural union, Federación Nacional de Agricultores de España (FNAE), created new militancy from 1917 to 1936 that focused land-reform legislation of the Second Republic* on the region in 1932. The organizational expertise for this mobilization of Andalusian protest came from a second strand of Spanish anarchism that had developed in the north.

Northern anarchism began in 1868, when Giuseppe Fanelli (1827–1877), an Italian disciple of the exiled Russian anarchist Michael Bakunin (1814–1876), arrived in Barcelona* to preach the concept of revolution from below and discuss other Bakuninist ideas recently debated by the First Socialist International (1864–1876). ''Propaganda of the deed,'' Bakunin's euphemism for the use of violence and terror in the revolution from below to bring down the state (symbol of property, power, and social class differences), had a certain appeal to a fledgling and badly organized movement, and as was common throughout Europe during this period, terrorist violence plagued the area for decades. Only a few, such as Anselmo Lorenzo (1841–1914) and Francesc Ferrer,* by advocating popular education and proletarian self-improvement, avoided isolation from the working-class community that limited anarchism's influence.

The larger importance of Fanelli's mission to Barcelona lay in providing a context for an emerging labor movement. Organization of labor syndicates was further along in Catalonia* than elsewhere in Spain, several already having been organized on a basis other than craft. As industrial unions, claiming to represent the working class, they viewed the world more politically than did craft syndicates, asserting their members' power and seeking a philosophy that exaggerated their importance. In time, and with a debt to French industrial unionism of the 1890s and the concept of the general strike propounded (in a different context) by the French philosopher Georges Sorel (1847–1922), Spanish anarchosyndicalism emerged to create the Confederación Nacional del Trabajo (CNT), founded in 1911, after antimilitary and anticlerical riots of Tragic Week in Barcelona (July 1909) were punished by indiscriminate anarchist jailings and the execution of Ferrer.

The CNT rapidly became the largest labor federation in Spain, outstripping the rival socialist Unión General de Trabajadores* (UGT), a group of craft unions. Andalusians in the northeast provided a link between northern and southern anarchism, but the rapid economic expansion during World War I* in any case placed no premium upon craft skills. After failing to gain UGT cooperation in the first large general strike (Aug. 1917), CNT leaders such as Salvador Seguí (?–1923) usually turned to less political forms of labor activity, although this moderation was not enough to prevent the CNT from being banned by the dictatorship of Gen. Miguel Primo de Rivera* in 1923.

In reaction, a more traditional anarchist organization, the Federación Anarquista Ibérica (FAI), was created in 1927. Its main purpose was to organize the movement effectively, a reaction to anarchist failure in the Russian Revolution (1918–1920). By creating affinity groups and regional plenums to coordinate local anarchist groups, the FAI placed greater stress on political action than on labor organization. Anarchosyndicalists, led by Ángel Pestaña (1881–1937) and Juan Peiró (1887–1942), reacted negatively to this approach by forming their own Solidarity group to revive the CNT; a strong union movement was the only solution to the lack of anarchist power. This split persisted throughout the 1930s, and a small syndicalist party stood for election in 1933. The CNT became a battleground among factions.

Some anarchists remained simple quixotic adventurers; Buenaventura Durruti (1896–1936) was typical of this group. The son of a railway worker, he had been drawn to violence by the great strikes before the dictatorship. In exile between 1923 and 1931, Durruti worked on assassination plots in Paris and bank robberies in Latin America. When he returned home with the advent of the Second Republic in 1931, he indiscriminately battled CNT leaders, republicans, and the Right, searching for an opening that might allow the revolution from below to triumph. By 1934, ground down by repeated failures, Durruti was the perfect illustration of anarchist futility in the early Second Republic.

This futility had many causes. Refusal to participate in electorial politics denied the movement a voice in republican cabinets; fear of compulsory labor arbitration by the socialist minister of labor, Francisco Largo Caballero,* led to a series of fruitless strikes; and lingering strife between Solidarity and FAI weakened anarchism almost as soon as it was legalized by the republic. The bizarre tragedy of Casas Viejas (Jan. 1933), involving the deaths of a score of millenarian peasants by republican paramilitary guards, damaged the reputation of Manuel Azaña* so badly that Casas Viejas became an element in the center-right's electoral victory a few months later (Nov. 1933), and led to the banning, once more, of anarchism.

These setbacks sobered anarchists as much as the Primo dictatorship had once enraged them; effectiveness seemed further away than ever, and change was essential. Major alterations came quickly: the CNT-FAI helped form the Popular Front, and anarchists voted for the first time in the Feb. 1936 elections that secured its victory. The Spanish Civil War* forced a CNT-FAI merger that diminished, but did not end, the FAI-Solidarity split. Remarkably, four anarchists (including Federica Montseny,* the only woman in Spain to serve in a ministerial capacity at cabinet level) joined the Popular Front government as ministers of state on 4 Nov. 1936—the first and only case of anarchists joining a government anywhere in the world.

These changes, produced by necessity and grim reality, nevertheless reflected a shift from Bakunin's ''propaganda of the deed'' to the mutualist ideas of Peter Kropotkin (1842–1921). Extensive rural communes (established during 1936 and 1937 in Aragon* and Catalonia), worker management committees (developed in Barcelona at the start of the civil war), and adult education (accelerated by Montseny as minister of welfare and education) were extraordinary changes under the circumstances, but they did not camouflage many serious problems. Violence and lack of discipline made the nationalists and civilians hate the anarchists; difficulties in Catalonia with the regional government; the thesis of the Spanish Communist party* (PCE) that antifascism came before revolutionary goals; and the failure of the anarchist militia (led by Durruti until his death in Madrid on 20 Nov. 1936) to capture Saragossa.

These frustrations finally culminated during the May crisis (1937) in Barcelona, when antagonism between anarchists and communists finally erupted into four days of bitter fighting. Despite efforts by anarchist ministers to find a solution, PCE criticism of the Popular Front cabinet led to its resignation, thus ending official CNT-FAI participation in government; and throughout the remainder of the civil war, the cabinet of Juan Negrín* sided with the PCE. The toll this took was enormous: abolition of the anarchist-dominated Council of Aragon; replacement of rural communes by a return to private farming; the disappearance of worker committees; merger of the militia into the regular (and PCE controlled) republican army; and the exclusion, with Negrín's support, of the Antifascist Militia Committee (controlled by the CNT-FAI) from power in the Catalan regional government. Everything that had been gained was destroyed.

During the final phase of the civil war, anarchists were sometimes persecuted and usually ignored. The CNT did sign a unity pact with the socialist UGT on 18 Mar. 1938, and for a time became more Marxist than anarchist, with Peiró holding a government office. The FAI, which had earlier pushed the CNT to collaborate with the Popular Front government, criticized this step, but the movement had no further alternatives. Exile or imprisonment was the only reality, and before the victory of Gen. Francisco Franco* on 1 Apr. 1939, perhaps 20,000 former CNT-FAI members went into exile; while judicial records indicate that more than 400,000 individuals were accused of anarchist ties in the courts of Franco's new state, although it is difficult to ascertain how many were sentenced on these charges.

At home, insurgence continued sporadically for more than a decade in the northern and southern mountains; while abroad, the CNT relocated in Toulouse and played a role in the exile governments of José Giral (1880–1962) and Rodolfo Llopis (1895– ), gradually forming the Movimiento Libertario Español (MLE) to merge its two organizations. The FAI disappeared almost entirely until 1975; the CNT went through many crises, not the least the efforts of the Falange Española,* itself in decline, to attract former CNT members into the official labor syndicates of the Franco regime. Efforts made in 1961 to stem the collapse of the CNT by cooperating with the UGT in the Alianza Sindical Obrera did result in renewed anti-Franco opposition, but also caused greater suppression within Spain in 1963. The MLE fought back in a series of bombings, protests, and exile actions; but the rise of the Comisiones Obreras movement (CCOO), secretly run by the PCE, further separated the anarchists from Spanish labor, forcing the MLE to cooperate with a series of antiauthoritarian factions: Grupo Primero de Mayo (1966), Acción Sindical (1968), the newspaper *Frente Lib-*

*ertario*, and Movimiento Internacional Libertarias (active in 1968, although older). Even here, however, the traditional anarchist sphere was overshadowed by Maoist and Marxist-Leninist factions of the New Left, such as Basque Homeland and Freedom, Euzkadi ta Askatasuna (ETA) or Fracción del Ejército Rojo. Oddly, the spread of anarchist theories, a general phenomenon after 1968, weakened older, purely anarchist organizations such as MLE, which were not student oriented.

In any case, exile ended with Franco's death, and the anarchosyndicalist CNT has staged a mild comeback, rising to considerable strength in Catalonia and improving its showing in Madrid. The socialist UGT, however, has far outstripped the CNT nationally as a contemporary union.

For additional information, see O. Alberola and A. Gransac, *El anarquismo español y la acción revolucionaria, 1961–1974* (Paris, 1975); E. Comín Colomer, *Historia de la anarquismo español (1830–1948)* (Madrid, 1948); X. Cuadrat, *Socialismo y anarquismo en Cataluña (1899–1911): Los orígenes de la CNT* (Madrid, 1976); J. Gómez Casas, *Anarchist Organization: The History of the F.A.I.* (Montreal, 1986); Eric Hobsbawm, *Primitive Rebels: Studies in Archaic Forms of Social Movement in the 19th and 20th Centuries* (Manchester, 1959); R. W. Kern, *Red Years/Black Years: A Political History of Spanish Anarchism, 1911–1937* (Philadelphia, 1978); C. Lida, *Anarquismo y revolución en la España del siglo xix* (Madrid, 1972); T. Kaplan, *Anarchists of Andalusia, 1868–1903* (Princeton, 1977); J. Mintz, *The Anarchists of Casas Viejas* (Chicago, 1982); and A. Padilla Bolívar, *El movimiento anarquista español* (Barcelona, 1976).

*R. W. Kern*

Related entries: FERRER, FRANCESC; MONTSENY, FEDERICA.

**ANDALUSIA,** Spanish autonomous community including the provinces of Huelva, Cadiz, Seville, Malaga, Cordoba, Jaén, Granada, and Almería. Area: 33,694 sq. mi.; 1986 pop. (est.) 6,735,600. Andalusia is the largest and most populous of all Spanish regions, occupying more than 17 percent of the peninsula and representing about 17 percent of its population. Its resulting high population density and its small contribution to the gross national product, somewhere in the area of 12 percent, mark it as an area of permanent underdevelopment.

The climate and geography vary widely, from the Mediterranean to the alpine. Mountain ranges divide the region along its southwest-northeast axis. The northern rugged Sierra Morena range, which runs through Huelva, Seville, and Cordoba, ends in the south in the Guadalquivir basin. Here are found the large landed estates characteristic of Andalusia's rural economy. To the south, the Baetic Mountains begin in Jaén and terminate in Almería. The slopes of the Baetics gradually descend to the steppe country, a harsh, dry land of malpais and deep gorges. Finally, there is what might be termed Mediterranean Andalusia, the areas southwest from the city of Almería to western Malaga, and center of the region's tourist industry.

This geographical complexity has a counterpart in Andalusia's climatological diversity. Most of the region enjoys mild weather both winter and summer. In the Baetics, however, which have some of the highest peaks south of the Pyrenees, winter temperatures are severe, and snow blocks access to the upper reaches between November and May. With few exceptions, Andalusia is very arid and averages only about seventy-five days of rain annually. Rainfall may vary, though, from a high of forty inches in the Sierra Nevada to a low of four inches in the steppe country. When the rains do come, particularly in the fall, they are torrential.

Andalusia's human geography is as diverse as its physical one. The high population density masks the fact that since 1950, its population has been steadily decreasing, and in some areas, such as Cordoba and Granada, decreasing absolutely since 1960. There are two principal reasons for this population decrease. First is the high incidence of infant mortality. Second is emigration. Since the 1950s, Andalusia has served as a source of immigrants to other areas of Spain, such as Catalonia,* and, increasingly, to Western Europe, particularly France,* Germany,* Switzerland, and Belgium. By 1968, Andalusia was providing 50.1 percent of all legal Spanish immigrants to Western Europe, approximately 42,359 people annually.

Though blessed with many natural resources and potentially very rich, Andalusia has experienced uncertain economic development. Although the nineteenth century saw some French and British exploitation of lead, copper, and iron, production gradually diminished because of exhaustion of the mines, the high cost of extraction, and competition from new international sources. Andalusian underdevelopment is further reflected in its lack of large-scale heavy industry, which accounted for only about 25 percent of the region's labor force and 27 percent of gross Spanish output in the late 1960s. This picture becomes yet more dismal when it is seen that what industrial activity does exist is concentrated almost exclusively in food-processing industries. Primary among the foodstuffs produced are sugar, olives and olive oil, wine, and preserved foods. Fortunately, though, the last two decades have seen a slow but important change in the Andalusian industrial picture. Since the 1950s, the government has taken an active interest in promoting Andalusian development, and chemical factories and steelworks have begun to make their appearance.

If Andalusia's economy has a strong point, it is its agricultural sector. Even here, however, the underpinnings are fragile, and the sources of this weakness must be sought in the region's history.

The question of land and its distribution lies at the heart of Andalusian economic life. Since the eighteenth century, the structure of the rural economy has been characterized by large landholdings, on the one hand, and a vast pool of landless day laborers, on the other. At that time, agriculture held the preeminent place in the region's economy, as it still does today. The three primary landowners were the crown, the church, and the nobility. By and large, the crown held the worst lands, unproductive, uncultivated woodlands and plains. It further possessed tierras baldías, given in usufruct for common use to communities, but sold in times of royal economic need. Unfortunately, since tierras baldías made available for sale were usually purchased by the church, their appearance on the market was of no benefit to potential smallholders.

The church's lands were generally better than the crown's and were also inalienable. They were purchased out of the church's immense revenues and located in the most productive areas, such as the Campiña and El Aljarafe. Land-produced profits were used to further increase holdings of land and real property.

The third group of large landowners were the great noble families, such as the Albas, the Osunas, and the Medinacelis, who held the most productive land in inalienable mayorazgos. Their use of revenues produced by the land differed significantly from the church's in that they were largely spent for conspicuous consumption.

The resulting latifundia system, characterized by lack of productive investment, undercultivation of land, and widespread absenteeism, produced predictable abuses. Outside Andalusia, small landowners constituted as much as 20 percent of the landowning population, while inside the region, they represented only 3 to 7 percent of that population. Further, only 20 percent of those small owners could successfully support themselves year round on the income their land generated. The remaining 80 percent were forced to supplement their earnings by serving as day laborers. They thus joined the estimated four out of five workers in Cordoba and Jaén, and the five out of six in Seville, who also worked as agricultural day laborers.

The pernicious effects of latifundismo extended even to Andalusia's urban areas and also affected the region's economic potential. Seasonal unemployment, poverty, hunger, and famine drove the rural masses into Andalusia's cities. Once there, their only recourse was often begging, which induced the government to undertake periodic campaigns to suppress begging and arrest vagabonds.

With regard to other economic sectors, Andalusia at this time could be characterized as a region of growth without development. Since secular income was drawn to conspicuous consumption, there was a marked lack of investment in productive industry or an improved infrastructure. This, in turn, hastened the deterioration of regional commercial networks. The result, by century's end, was the disappearance of well-being and prosperity from Andalusia.

In the first half of the nineteenth century, a potential solution for some of these problems appeared, as mortmain, mayorazgos, and señoríos were all abolished. The freeing up of land could have benefited the landless, had they possessed the cash to purchase land. They did not, of course, and what had seemed to be an enlightened policy resulted in a retrenchment of latifundismo. The nobility continued to increase its land purchases, but it was now joined by a far more important group—wealthy businessmen. The result was the emergence of a great agricultural bourgeoisie that was often more rapacious than its predecessors.

The masses' lack of land was further exacerbated as municipal councils, often under the control of businessmen, alienated municipal commons. As land previously available for community exploitation passed into private hands, the poor lost access to firewood and pastures. They were further penalized as munici-palities made up lost revenues by taxing staples purchased primarily by the lower-class sector of the population.

In the face of such hardship, Andalusia's landless workers were, with few exceptions, passive. The cause was their lack of organization, their lack of class consciousness, and the failure of urban-based political movements to ally with them. There were, of course, occasional outbreaks of peasant violence, as oc-curred at Loja, Granada, in 1861, but these usually collapsed the moment they encountered opposition. This dismal situation, although not the latifundia system itself, changed soon after the introduction of anarchism* in Spain in 1868.

During the First Republic,* new expectations among the landless resulted in some spontaneous land occupations and social conflict in the countryside, par-ticularly in western Andalusia. Later repression of worker radicalism, however, stunted this protest, but it also left the peasant permanently inclined toward vanguardist radicalism.

With the Restoration came the consolidation of liberal state and society at its most conservative. The key elements of the new order, the 1876 Constitution and the Civil Guard,* produced a stable "official" Spain, but the "real" Spain—the Spain of the countryside—was now defined in terms of problems with the oligarchy and the caciques.* Although some workers' organizations were le-galized in 1881, rural anarchists were severely repressed. Suppression drove the disorganized movement underground, but further encouraged its desperate extremism. Until the early twentieth century, in fact, rural anarchist violence was mostly confined to Cadiz and Seville provinces.

The turn of the century saw a resurgence of anarchism, now influenced by French syndicalism and the general strike, in the Andalusian countryside. The latifundia system had remained largely unchanged, and the result was widespread peasant unrest in Andalusia in 1904 and 1905. Although the socialists had now for the first time undertaken peasant organization in direct competition with the anarchists, this brief, violent period was followed by years of relative peace lasting until around 1917. The principal reason for this was the prosperity en-gendered by Spain's neutrality in World War I,* but the calm was short-lived.

After the war's end, inflationary pressures, the deterioration of the Restoration political system and the emergence of new political groups, and the profound demonstration effect of the Russian Revolution again aroused anarchist hopes in the countryside. The period from 1917 to 1920 witnessed an unprecedented number of mostly nonviolent strikes in rural Andalusia, but the dictatorship of Gen. Miguel Primo de Rivera* in 1923 again forced a halt in rural anarchist activity, but also helped to produce a deeper extremism.

The advent of the Second Republic* and its promise of agrarian reform seemed to offer new hope to Andalusia's dispossessed. While the republic did raise expectations, though, it utterly failed to fulfill them. The government of Manuel Azaña* proved unable to implement in a timely fashion the provisions of the 1932 agrarian-reform law, which included resettlement of the landless and theoretically would have affected about 50 percent of the cultivated land in Andalusia. The resulting frustration in the countryside meant that during this period, rural Andalusia was in a state of constant, though usually nonviolent, turmoil, some of it spontaneous, some of it increasingly led by the socialists. The anarchists, whose earlier role had been so prominent, had begun to devote more attention to urban organization and were now in a period of relative decline; the socialists had, quite naturally, stepped into the breach.

The land question in Andalusia remained unresolved at the outbreak of the Spanish Civil War,* as it did throughout the Franco period. Latifundismo remained in place, Spain continued to be primarily an agricultural country, and the plight of Andalusia's rural poor went largely unchanged. Although some mechanization of agricultural tasks occurred in the late 1950s and early 1960s, far from revolutionizing agriculture, the effect was to cause a massive labor exodus from the Andalusian countryside into the cities.

Even today, large landholdings, absenteeism, widespread unemployment, and poor living conditions characterize Andalusian rural life. It remains to be seen whether, as Spain becomes a postindustrial country at the turn of the twenty-first century, its leaders will have the courage and intelligence to deal with this persistent social failure.

For additional information, see R. P. Clark and M. H. Haltzel, *Spain in the 1980s: The Democratic Transition and a New International Role* (Cambridge, 1987); G. A. Collier, *Socialists of Rural Andalusia: Unacknowledged Revolutionaries of the Second Republic* (Stanford, 1987); J. M. Cuenca Toribio, *Andalucía: Una introducción histórica* (Cordoba, 1980); J. A. Lacomba et al., *Aproximación a la historia de Andalucía* (Barcelona, 1979); and E. E. Malefakis, *Agrarian Reform and Peasant Revolution in Spain: Origins of the Civil War* (New Haven, 1970).

*M. D. Dodge*

*Related entries*: ANARCHISM; SECOND REPUBLIC.


**ANGLO-SPANISH WAR (WAR OF JENKINS'S EAR)** (1739–1748), a war between Spain and Britain* in 1739. This conflict had a number of underlying causes, but principal among them were concessions Spain made to Britain as a result of a series of treaties from the Treaty of Madrid (1667) to the Convention of El Pardo (1739), and particularly the Treaty of Utrecht (1713–1715). The Utrecht agreement granted Britain limited commercial access, which had previously been denied, to Spain's American markets through the asiento de negros (the formal contract for the exclusive right of furnishing black slaves to the colonies*) and the navio de permiso (the right to introduce one five-hundred-ton ship into the market at Portobelo each year). The treaties recognized as legal Britain's de facto possessions in America as of 1670. Differences over the right of possession of Georgia, Gibraltar,* and Minorca also grew out of contrasting interpretations of the treaties' provisions.

According to Spain, Britain abused its trading privileges by engaging in unbridled contraband. Beginning in 1726, Spain began to board all British ships to inspect them for illegal cargo, frequently seizing merchandise from Spanish colonies and imprisoning crews. Spain considered its actions a legal exercise of the right of search and seizure on the high seas, while Britain saw the actions as depredations against legal commerce. Nevertheless, Robert Walpole (1676–1745), Britain's first unofficial prime minister, sought to avoid war at all costs.

A negotiated Convention of El Pardo on 14 Jan. 1739 appeared to have settled the matter. Spain agreed to pay a ninety-five-thousand-pound indemnity to Britain within four months for British losses. Because Britain owed sixty-eight thousand pounds in taxes accumulated by the British South Sea Company, neither side paid as stipulated by the convention. Spain revoked the asiento in May 1739, and the war party in Parliament rallied public opinion to try to bring about Walpole's fall and war with Spain.

The most sensational method employed was the testimony of Robert Jenkins, captain of the brig *Rebecca*. Jenkins, a well-known contrabandist, and his preserved, severed ear made for dramatic testimony of how he was seized by a Spanish privateer off Havana in 1731, hanged by his heels by a Capt. Fandino, and tortured, having his left ear lopped off. The reaction to this outrage was predictable, and Walpole avoided losing office by declaring war with Spain on 19 Oct. 1739. The conflict, one in a series of wars that had begun in 1689, became the latest chapter in the Anglo-Hispanic struggle to dominate world maritime trade.

Fighting began on the high seas and in America, but within a year the conflict merged with the more generalized European struggle caused by the War of the Polish Succession (1733–1735). Spain was drawn into this war because of a series of treaties and the secret First Family Pact with traditional rival France,* now allied with Spain in an effort to recapture Gibraltar in return for the transfer to France of the commercial concessions made to Britain at the Treaty of Utrecht in 1713.

Spain launched privateers from its American ports and did considerable damage to British shipping. The British, in turn, captured Portobelo in 1739. Spaniards in Saint Augustine offered freedom to British slaves and helped to provoke a slave revolt near Charles Town. Gen. James Edward Oglethorpe (1696–1785) attempted to take Saint Augustine in 1740, while other British forces unsuccessfully laid siege to Cartagena de Indias in 1741 and attacked Santiago de Cuba in 1742 to little effect. The same year, Spaniards tried but failed to destroy Oglethorpe's colony in Georgia, while Adm. George Anson (1697–1762) sacked Paita in Peru for the British and captured the galleon en route to Manila from Acapulco in 1743. A treaty signed in Aix-la-Chapelle on 30 Apr. 1748 ended the war.

For additional information, see L. E. Ivers, *British Drums on the Southern Frontier: The Military Colonization of Georgia, 1733–1749* (Chapel Hill, 1974); J. T. Lanning, *The Diplomatic History of Georgia: A Study of the Epoch of Jenkins' Ear* (Chapel Hill, 1936); W. S. Robinson, *The Southern Colonial Frontier, 1607–1763* (Albuquerque,

1979); and O. Shepard and W. Shepard, *Jenkins' Ear: A Narrative Attributed to Horace Walpole, Esq.* (New York, 1951).

R. Hendricks

*Related entry*: NAVY.


**ANWAL** (1921), military disaster in Morocco.* In Jan. 1919, Gen. Dámaso Berenguer* was appointed high commissioner of the Spanish protectorate in Morocco to pacify it by pursuing a program of political bribery and persuasion with military occupation. To assist him, the government reassigned Gen. Manuel Fernández Silvestre (1871–1921) in Feb. 1920 from the military household of King Alfonso XIII* to the command of the Melilla sector. He and Berenguer immediately started to advance troops into the central Rif, occupying the tribal areas of Aith Sa'id, Aith Wurishik, Aith Tuzin, and Tafarsith. The furthest point of Spanish penetration occurred in Jan. 1921, when Fernández Silvestre's forces established positions at Anwal and Tafarsith. This occupation, coupled with poor harvests and difficult economic times, helped stimulate Berber opposition to the Spanish. Resistance was most pronounced in the central Rif among the Aith Waryaghar, where to this point, Spanish political and economic penetration had been slight.

This opposition coalesced around Muhammad ibn Abd al-Krim al-Khatabi (1882–1963) and his brother, Si Mhammad, sons of a lowland Aith Waryaghar notable who, until 1919, had close ties with the Spanish. The brothers evolved into masterful military and political leaders who proposed not only to expel the Christian Spaniards from the central Rif, but to replace tribal anarchy with centralized indigenous authority.

Their first success came on 1 June 1921, when Fernández Silvestre sent a group of Spanish troops and Moroccan regulars to occupy the hill of Dahar Ubarran near the Amquaran River. A force organized by Abd al-Krim al-Khatabi attacked and decimated this position on 2 June, causing 179 casualties and the loss of four mountain cannon, 250 rifles, and an ammunition dump. For the Rifis, this was a major victory, but within a week, the Spaniards again advanced and occupied the hill.

Although Spanish commanders assured the minister of war on 8 July that the Melillan command was adequately protected with some 25,790 troops, most of these forces were scattered throughout the sector in a series of small, fixed positions that were both indefensible and highly vulnerable. Pockets of potential resistance gave the Rifis a perfect opportunity on 16 July to initiate a full-scale attack, and by 21 July, the situation at Ighriben had become so desperate that Fernández Silvestre ordered its evacuation, which resulted in almost three hundred Spanish casualties.

After Ighriben, the Rifis concentrated their attack on the main post at Anwal so ferociously on the morning of 22 July that Fernández Silvestre reluctantly ordered Anwal's four thousand defenders to retreat to Issumar and Bin Tayyib. By this point, however, between four and six thousand Rifis had begun a general attack on the entire length of the Spanish front line, and many other tribes had sent reinforcements. The Spanish retreat turned into a confused and disorganized rout. Fernández Silvestre himself either committed suicide or was killed, and the efforts of his subordinate commanders to contain the retreat proved futile. Frightened and dispirited Spanish units deserted their posts and retreated in waves toward Melilla. By 11 Aug., Melilla was surrounded, and in the process, according to data later provided to the Cortes, the army suffered 13,192 casualties (8,668 dead) and lost 570 prisoners. The Rifis captured twenty thousand rifles, four hundred machine guns, more than a hundred pieces of heavy artillery, and stores of ammunition and other supplies.

Although by mid–1922, the Spanish were able to retake most of the territory, the political repercussions of the disaster were catastrophic for Spain's embattled parliamentary regime and the prestige of the monarchy. The rout toppled the Conservative ministry then in power; and the so-called responsibilities debate that followed was a constant theme in both the press and the Cortes. The acrimonious debate eventually was ended only by the imposition of a dictatorship by Gen. Miguel Primo de Rivera.*

For Abd al-Krim, the fall of Anwal and the subsequent rout heightened his already growing prestige among the Berber tribes, thus enabling him to consolidate his power in the Rif and then to expand his rebellion into the Ghmara and the Jbala. In Feb. 1923, he proclaimed a Rifian republic, which endured until his defeat by coordinated French and Spanish forces in May 1925.

For additional information, see C. R. Pennell, *A Country with a Government and a Flag: The Rif War in Morocco, 1921–1926* (Wisbech, U.K., 1986).

                                                                        *S. E. Fleming*
*Related entries*: ALFONSO XIII; BERENGUER, GEN. DÁMASO; MOROCCO.

**APARISI Y GUIJARRO, ANTONIO** (1815–1872), conservative parliamentarian and Carlist ideologue. Antonio Aparisi launched his political career as an attorney and journalist connected with conservative newspapers in his native Valencia in the period from 1843 to 1857. Notoriety from his articles in *El Pensamiento de Valencia* took him to the Cortes in late 1858, where he remained until 1865. There he opposed the liberal governments of the era as a traditionalist member of the neo-Catholic bloc led by Cándido Nocedal (1821–1885).

Outwardly loyal to Isabel II,* he was a disciple of Juan Donoso Cortés,* warning of the fall of liberal governments and the monarchy itself. He viewed liberalism* as doomed, because it rejected religion and produced a society of greed, competition, and chaos in which demands of the masses would lead to socialism and then to communist dictatorship. His philosophy, which was rooted in Catholic exclusivity, first led him into politics and, after the exile of Isabel II in 1868, to Carlism.* In the Cortes, he opposed disentailment,* freedom of the press and religion, and legislation intended to limit church prerogatives. He rejected parliamentarianism based on parties in favor of the corporate state he thought represented the natural harmony in society. He believed monarchy was the best system for Spain because of the nation's historical tradition and the strength of that form of government and argued that it was easier to check power when it resided in one person than when it rested with the masses.

In 1868, he saw Carlism as the best available vehicle for his political beliefs. He became a member of the privy council of the pretender, Carlos VII (1849–1909), and influenced him ideologically, becoming the first major Carlist ideologue. He wrote Carlos's "Carta-manifiesto" to his brother, Alfonso XII,* a classic writing of Carlism, in addition to the important Carlist documents of 1869–70.

Once a Carlist, he developed the system of ancient foral liberties most prominent among the Basques* into a system of government implemented for a time by Carlos VII in northern Spain during the Second Carlist War (1873–1876). He also gave Carlos's pronouncements the strong social content for which Carlos VII was thereafter known.

Aparisi found a place in history because he became a Carlist. He transformed the nineteenth-century speculative traditionalism of Jaime Balmes (1810–1848) and Donoso Cortés into the platform of an active political movement, thereby joining the philosophic and the concrete. Aparisi's influence lasted long after his death in 1872, because Carlos VII remained the Carlist pretender until 1909. His conservative Carlism continued to be politically significant through the Spanish Civil War.*

For additional information, see A. Aparisi y Guijarro, *Obras de D. Antonio Aparisi y Guijarro* (Madrid, 1873–1877); and R. de Miguel, *Semblanza humana y política de Aparisi y Guijarro* (Valencia, 1980).

*R. A. Mezei*

*Related entry*: CARLISM.


**ARAGON,** region of northern Spain consisting of the three provinces of Huesca, Saragossa, and Teruel. Pop. (1981 est.) 1,213,099; 18,294 sq. mi. Aragon occupies more than 9 percent of Spanish territory and extends from the Pyrenees in the north to the Iberian Mountains in the south. It is bordered on the east by Valencia and Catalonia,* and on the southwest, west, and north by Castile* and Navarre.* Physically, Aragon encompasses three distinct geographical and climatic zones: the Pyrenees and their southern flanks in the north, the arid plain of the Ebro basin in the center, and the mountains and plateaus of the south.

Economically, Aragon is overwhelmingly rural. The entire region has a population density of about 25 people per square kilometer, compared to 160 in Catalonia and 113 in Valencia. It is a region of small, nucleated agricultural settlements and some 820 municipios, of which 650 have fewer than 1,000 inhabitants. The most heavily populated agricultural regions are in the irrigated zones of the Ebro, Cinca, and Esera drainages in the provinces of Saragossa and Huesca. Outside these areas, villages are widely separated and depend upon a relatively poor dry-farm agriculture. Most of these villages have tended to lose population in recent years, as thousands of rural Aragonese have joined the tide of emigration to the cities.

The urban life of Aragon centers around the traditional capital of Saragossa. With a population of approximately six hundred thousand, it is the fifth largest city in Spain and a rapidly growing industrial center, one of the seven "poles" of economic development the government established to create a balance in industrial growth throughout the country. The dominance of Saragossa within Aragon is illustrated by the fact that approximately 45 percent of the Aragonese population is concentrated here. The next largest cities are Huesca, with about forty-five thousand inhabitants, and Teruel, with slightly fewer than thirty thousand.

The history of Aragon is more spectacular before 1700 than after. Roman, Visigothic, and Islamic civilization had washed across the region before Navarre freed Aragon from Islamic control. Ramiro I (1035–1063) then established the Kingdom of Aragon, which, to fight off Castilian claims, federated with Catalonia in the twelfth century and under Jaime the Conqueror (1213–1276) added Valencia and a Mediterranean empire. Up to the time of the death of the childless Martín I (1356–1410), the kingdom had developed a strong noble class and a zealous defender of local liberties in the Justicia. The Compromise of Caspe in 1412 established the Castilian Trastámara dynasty in Aragon, but the rule of Juan II (1458–1479) was marked by the remença riots, and Juan's son, Fernando (1452–1516), married the Castilian Isabel (1451–1504) to create a union that ended the independent history of Aragon.

The relative freedom from taxation, fiercely supported by the Justicia, that Aragon enjoyed during the Hapsburg period (1517–1700) brought it and Catalonia into conflict with Felipe II (1555–1598) and Felipe IV (1625–1665)—in the last case against the conde-duque de Olivares (1587–1645) in the 1640s. Rebellion in the northeast meant the curtailment of the region's fueros, but the Aragonese and Catalans fought back a half-century later by siding with Charles of Austria during the War of Spanish Succession,* which caused Felipe V* to finally revoke traditional liberties altogether by the Nueva Planta decree on 29 June 1707. In the wake of Charles VI's (1685–1740) withdrawal and Castilian reconquest, the audiencia of Aragon created on 3 Apr. 1711 survived as the region's primary administrative body until 1833, when the three modern provinces were created.

The eighteenth century became a time of quiet and recuperation after an age of conflict. Commerce and agriculture improved until Aragon again prospered, largely because of improvements made on the Imperial Canal and other reforms sponsored by the Sociedades Económicas de Amigos del País*. Even in the Enlightenment,* however, a regional writer, José Mor de Fuentes (1762–1848), evoked strong regional feelings. During the War of Independence,* though, the French, who from 1808 to 1812 sought to annex Aragon, laid siege to Saragossa from 21 Dec. 1808 to 21 Feb. 1809 before it capitulated. The French occupation caused a wave of national patriotism, and there was a large Aragonese delegation at the Cortes of Cadiz,* but traditionalism also evoked a strong response to the revival of absolutism after the return of Fernando VII* in 1814, as well as to Carlism* in the 1830s. Aragon, in fact, was a major battleground for Carlism, and Carlists held much of the region at one time or another (including Saragossa in Feb. 1838) from 1834 until their surrender in 1839.

The liberal age brought change. The Progressive party* attracted the region's middle classes, who in 1854–1856 supported Gen. Baldomero Espartero* and demanded new commercial opportunities. The subsequent Liberal Union party rule from 1858 to 1863 brought rapid industrial growth in the 1860s, as railways to the east, west, and south made Aragon a major hub in the new national transportation system. Juan Faustino Bruil (1810–1878) was one of the more successful new industrialists, but as industrial society emerged, republicanism (1868–1873), federalism (1872–1883), Carlism again (1873–1876), and anarchosyndicalism (after the turn of the century) found support in a rather large dissenting sector of Aragonese society.

The most important intellectual voice of Aragon at the end of the nineteenth century belonged to Joaquín Costa,* a native of Huesca. Although he spent most of his life in Madrid, his criticism of the Restoration's corrupt use of caciques* found great popularity at home, and the Cámara Agrícola del Alto Aragon became the type of local institution that Costa believed would lead to local independence, Europeanization, and modernization.

No matter how diligently the Aragonese industrialized, however, they faced greater competition from the Catalans and the Basques* and pressure for free trade from Castile. Intellectual life was likewise diminished by the lure of national centers such as Barcelona* and Madrid. The Catalans were a particular source of discontent in Aragon, especially after their grant of mancomunidad gave them greater control over their own local affairs in 1913. Even though the Liga Regional Aragonesa sought the same treatment in 1913 and the Acción Regionalista de Aragon tried even more forcefully in 1918, national authorities refused to change the region's status, in part because labor unrest in Saragossa seemed worse than in other regions. The Confederación Nacional de Trabajo (CNT), whose strength in Saragossa lay in its appeal to uprooted peasants working on the margin of the skilled industries and to the independent streak in the Aragonese, became so violent that in 1923 it was implicated in the assassination of the local archbishop.

The subsequent dictatorship of Gen. Miguel Primo de Rivera* severely repressed this disorder. Catholic Social Action created a large Catholic union movement in the 1920s. The term *fuero* was reintroduced into jurisprudence and administrative law, although without the same strength as *mancomunidad* in neighboring Catalonia. Aragon, in responding favorably to the dictatorship, avoided the protests that shook Barcelona and Madrid, and when the regime fell and the Second Republic* emerged, it made no impact until the terminology of the republican constitution in Dec. 1931 acknowledged municipal and regional autonomy, which raised perennial Aragonese hopes for some form of regional government. Republicans thus marginally won more votes than did other parties in the elections of 1931, but the hasty land reform passed by the Second Republic in Sept. 1932 alienated Aragonese small farmers, who should not have been included in the legislation at all, and the conservative Catholic Confederación Española de Derechas Autónomas (CEDA) won the elections of 1933 in a back-lash against the ineptness of land reform and failure of the Cortes to produce any sign of regional autonomy for Aragon. The CNT responded to the Right with massive general strikes in Apr. and May 1934, and this dislocation, coming at a time of serious economic depression, stimulated the growth of the right-wing Falange Española* in Huesca, Alcañiz, Teruel, and Saragossa. The scene was set for a series of violent confrontations between Left and Right in the Popular Front elections of Feb. 1936, which prepared the way for the Spanish Civil War* in Aragon.

After the nationalists failed to seize Barcelona on 20 July 1936, Saragossa became the focal point of the civil war in the north. The local garrison, commanded by Gen. Miguel Cabanellas (1872–1938), a republican who initially refused to join the military revolt, was pushed into the nationalist camp by the arrival of Carlist paramilitary Requetés who sealed off the city to the advance units of the Aragon militia organized in Barcelona by the Anti-Fascist Militia Committee and led by anarchist Buenaventura Durruti (1896–1936). The war raged from Huesca in the north to Teruel in the south, but the militia never gained entrance to Saragossa. In the countryside, anarchist communes succeeded in proclaiming a new form of autonomous government and reorganizing agriculture in one of the most revolutionary steps of the civil war, but neither the militia nor the communes had the resources to achieve a lasting result. In the summer of 1938, after an anarchist-communist split caused the cabinet of Francisco Largo Caballero* to fall to Juan Negrín, the communists dismantled the militia and the communes run by the Council of Aragon. Even with communist reinforcements, Saragossa would not fall, and fighting shifted to the Teruel front in Dec. 1937, where a nationalist victory in Feb. 1938 divided the republic in two. The Ebro campaign from July to Nov., the last unsuccessful republican counterattack, left Aragon and the republic in ruins at the end of the war.

In the postwar era, Aragon gained regional status in 1979, when Spain adopted federalism on a nationwide basis. Its economy recovered from the ravages of the civil war, with the region a leading source of coal, electrical appliances, steel, and automobiles for Spain. Agriculture also benefited from further extension of irrigation to the Huesca area.

For additional information, see J. A. Armillas and F. Moreno, *Aproximación a la historia de Aragón* (Saragossa, 1977); and C. Royo Villanova, *El regionalismo aragonés, 1707–1978* (Saragossa, 1979).

*R. A. Barrett and R. W. Kern*

**ARANA Y GOIRI, SABINO DE** (1865–1903), father of nationalism among the Basques* and founder of the Basque Nationalist party* (BNP). Sabino de Arana was born in Bilbao, the last of six children of a well-to-do Carlist family.

His early life was marked by ill health and turbulence caused by his family's exile in France during the First Carlist War (1833–1840). When Arana was seventeen, his father died, and his mother took him and his brother, Luis, to Barcelona,* where exposure to the growing Catalan nationalist movement stimulated in him an intense desire to work for Basque political and cultural independence. At the age of twenty-three, he returned to Bilbao, where he dedicated himself until his death at age thirty-eight to building the Basque nationalist movement.

Arana made numerous seminal contributions to the language and symbolism of Basque nationalism. He worked to revive the Basque language, Euskera, not only for cultural reasons, but also as a medium of political communication. An adult learner of Euskera himself, he published grammars, textbooks, and histories of the language and wrote and published newspapers and magazines in Basque when government policies permitted. He created the word "Euzkadi" to refer to the Basque ethnic nation and coined important political slogans for Basque nationalists, such as "Jaun Goikoa eta Lagi Zarra" ("God and the Fueros") and "Zazpiak Bat" ("Seven are One," a reference to the seven Basque Provinces). He also designed the first Basque flag, the "ikurrina," and founded the first Basque cultural club, the Centro Vasco, in Bilbao. His most important contribution was the establishment of the BNP in 1895. He himself was the first Basque nationalist elected to public office, winning a seat in the Biscayan provincial government in 1898.

Arana was jailed several times, once for an inflammatory telegram he sent to Theodore Roosevelt (1858–1919) congratulating him on the United States* liberation of Cuba from Spanish rule after the Spanish-American War.* During his last jail term, Arana gave a newspaper interview that left the impression he was abandoning the struggle for Basque independence and accepting the need to work with Spain. Upon his release, however, he repudiated that interview and was at work again in the provincial and national elections of 1903 when death ended his career.

For additional information, see M. García Venero, *Historia del nacionalismo vasco*, 3d ed. (Madrid, 1969); J.-C. Larronde, *El nacionalismo vasco: Su origen y su ideología en la obra de Sabino Arana-Goiri* (San Sebastian, 1977); and S. G. Payne, *Basque Nationalism* (Reno, 1975).

R. P. Clark

*Related entries*: BASQUES; BASQUE NATIONALIST PARTY.


**ARANDA, CONDE DE, PEDRO PABLO ABARCA DE BOLEA** (1719–1798), distinguished politician during the reign of Carlos III.* Aranda was descended from a long line of Aragonese nobles, the Jiménez de Urreas, lords of the villa of Epila. In his youth he traveled extensively throughout Europe, studied military tactics in Prussia, and was befriended by leading Encyclopedists in France, among them Voltaire (François Marie Arouet, 1694–1778). Aranda began a military career during the reign of Felipe V,* when he was seriously wounded at the battle of Camposanto and, for his heroic service to the crown, named field marshal. Aranda later served as ambassador to the Polish court and as captain-general in Valencia and Aragon. In 1765, he became grand master of the Spanish Masons and a year later was named president of the Council of Castile and captain-general of New Castile.

Once established at the head of the council, Aranda began to break with tradition. He appeared often in public, had himself driven about Madrid in a regal carriage, and received visitors in his office throughout the day. Together with the marquis of Pombal (Sebastião José de Carvalho e Melo, 1699–1782), the duke of Choisseul (Etienne François, 1719–1785), and the marquis of Tanucci (Bernardo Tanucci, 1698–1783), the prime ministers of Portugal,* France,* and Italy,* respectively, Aranda plotted against the Society of Jesus. Within Spain he was supported by conde de Campomanes,* in France by Voltaire. There is some doubt that he participated in the preparation for the actual expulsion of the Jesuits, and he seems to have maintained good relations with members of the society after their expulsion from Spain in 1767.

Aranda was, in many ways, representative of his time. He was at once an enlightened noble reformer and an autocratic elitist. In the pursuit of his reforms, he was not above abuse of power. He suspended church rights, denied the right to asylum in the church, prohibited freedom of the press, and tortured suspected wrongdoers. Religious ceremony was frequently circumscribed or curtailed. Decisions on these matters were frequently made unilaterally and kept from the king. Beyond his attacks on the church and, not infrequently, the citizenry, Aranda worked diligently for the development of agriculture, industry, and commerce. He directed an impressive construction program for major public buildings in the capital and principal cities of Spain. Some of his most significant legislation concerned the development of hydrological projects and mining.

His methods provoked considerable protest from many quarters, and he was eventually removed from the presidency of the Council of Castile by Carlos III. In recognition of his years of service he was named ambassador to France in 1773. While he was in this post, Spain went to war with Morocco.* Aranda favored the abandonment of all minor Spanish presidios in Africa, particularly Melilla, preserving only Ceuta and Oran. Aranda also favored active participation by Spain in the American Revolutionary War against Spain's enemy, Britain. In this, as in most of his positions, Aranda was at odds with the conde de Floridablanca,* who was fearful of the example set for Spain's own American colonies.

In his capacity as ambassador to France, Aranda met with Benjamin Franklin (1706–1790) and John Jay (1745–1829). In 1779, Jay had been named American minister plenipotentiary and was in Paris seeking Spain's participation in the 1778 Franco-American alliance. The rebel British colonists also sought a $5 million loan and a guarantee of free navigation on the Mississippi. In exchange, the former colonies would see that Florida passed securely to Spain. Despite

Aranda's opinions, Spain frustrated Jay's entreaties. U.S. independence was not recognized, and the Mississippi remained an exclusively Spanish river.

In addition to dealings with the Americans, Aranda maintained a secret correspondence with the future Carlos IV* during his stay in the French capital. Carlos wished to undermine the power of the conde de Floridablanca,* and to this end he cultivated the friendship of his principal rival, Aranda. Their plans for an influential personal minister created an avenue to power later taken by Manuel Godoy. During the negotiations leading up to the signing of the 1783 Treaty of Paris, Aranda represented Spain in its dealings with Britain. In 1792, he was named secretary of state for Carlos IV, but his beliefs were in direct conflict with those of the master he served. As a Freemason he supported the aims of the French revolutionaries; as an elite monarchist he supported his sovereign. When France pursued war against Austria, Aranda was faced with the dilemma of whether to support the royalist or revolutionary army. He put his faith in the inexperienced republicans who promptly were routed. He was replaced in his post by Godoy, who in 1794 exiled him from the court to Jaén. For a year, Aranda was held prisoner in Granada's Alhambra. The following year he was allowed to return to Epila, where he resided until his death.

For additional information, see R. Olaechea and J. Ferrer Benimeli, *El Conde de Aranda*, 2 vols. (Saragossa, 1978); D. Hilt, *The Troubled Trinity: Godoy and the Spanish Monarchs* (Tuscaloosa, 1987); and E. de Tapia Ozcariz, *Carlos III y su época: Biografía del siglo xviii* (Madrid, 1962).

R. Hendricks

*Related entries*: CARLOS III; CARLOS IV; ENLIGHTENMENT, AGE OF; FLORIDABLANCA, CONDE DE.

**ARENAL, CONCEPCIÓN** (1820–1893), nineteenth-century intellectual. Arenal was born in El Ferrol, La Corunna, on 31 Jan. 1820. After dressing like a male to study secretly at the School of Law in Madrid, she married a fellow student, Fernando García Carrasco, with whom she had two sons. His death in 1854 forced her to write for a living.

In 1855, after her first book, *Fábulas y romances*, had appeared, she left Madrid to write in Armano, in the province of Santander, where she produced several sociological studies, including *El visitador del pobre*. Its publication led to her appointment as inspector of women's prisons until 1868. Afterward, she returned to Madrid to edit *La Voz de Claridad* for more than a year and, in 1874, headed the Spanish Red Cross during the Second Carlist War (1873–1876).

The rest of her life was spent representing wealthy Spaniards in the coordination of charitable works, exercising a form of Christian democracy that stressed the importance of social security and Christian good works. She often testified in favor of reform acts in the Cortes and sometimes defended maids and other servants in the courts against wealthy employers who had abused them.

Arenal's death on 14 Feb. 1893 came in Gijón, Oviedo, her home during the last part of her life.

Her major works included *La beneficencia, la filantropía y la caridad* (1861), *Cartas a los delincuentes* (1865), *La mujer del porvenir* (1869), *Cartas a un obrero* (1880), *Cartas a un señor* (1880), *La mujer de su casa* (1883), *El delito colectivo* (1893), *El visitador del preso* (1893), and posthumously, *El pauperismo* (1897) and *La igualdad* (1898).

For additional information, see J. Alarcón y Menéndez, *Una celebridad desconocida* (Madrid, 1914); R. Salillas, G. de Azcárate, and A. Sánchez Miguel, *Doña Concepción Arenal y sus obras* (Madrid, 1894); J. Tobio Fernández, *Las ideas sociales de Concepción Arenal* (Madrid, 1960).

R. W. Kern

**ARIAS NAVARRO, CARLOS** (1908–1989), politician, civil servant, and prime minister. Born on 11 Dec. 1908, Arias Navarro was the product of a lower-middle-class Madrid* family. He studied law at the Central University and, in 1929, secured a civil-service position in the Ministry of Justice. In 1933, he was assigned to the office of the public prosecutor in Malaga. There, when the Spanish Civil War* erupted, he was imprisoned until the arrival of the nationalist army. Joining the insurgent forces, he served as prosecutor for the military judicial corps until his transfer to the air force judicial staff.

In 1944, after serving briefly as public prosecutor in Madrid, Arias was named civil governor of Leon and head of the Falange in that province. He accepted the civil governorship of Santa Cruz de Tenerife in 1949, and after several years in the Canary Islands,* he was made governor of Navarre.* In 1957, he became director general for security. He held the position for eight years and earned a reputation as a champion of order in the regime of Gen. Francisco Franco.*

In 1965, he became mayor of Madrid, a post he held until 1973. His tenure as mayor was marked by massive construction, a dramatic expansion of educational and recreational facilities, and a general modernization of the city. In 1967, he was elected to the Cortes and soon afterward was named to the Council of the Realm.

Arias Navarro entered the cabinet in June 1973 as minister of the interior in the new government headed by Adm. Luis Carrero Blanco (1903–1973). His stay in that post was brief, because the Dec. 1973 assassination of Carrero Blanco brought about a cabinet dissolution, and in Jan. 1974, Franco, ignoring the Council of the Realm, named Arias Navarro premier. The appointment was almost certainly designed to placate moderate elements within the National Movement, while at the same time providing assurances to conservatives.

The overriding task of the new premier was to prepare Spain for the end of the Franco era and to ensure the peaceful transition to power to Juan Carlos I.* His initial ministerial appointments greatly weakened the influence of the Opus Dei* and brought into positions of leadership conservative professionals who, like the premier himself, were loyal followers of the Caudillo relatively uninvolved in the factional politics wracking the movement.

In a televised address to the Cortes on 12 Feb. 1974, the new premier announced a program of limited reform. Mayors and local officials were to be chosen by popular elections; "political associations" within the framework of the National Movement would be permitted; and labor and management would form separate organizations within the official syndicates. At the same time, he affirmed Spanish friendship with the West; called for closer relations with Portugal,* Latin America, and the Arab world; and pledged to work toward membership in the European Economic Community.

The premier's plans for cautious and limited reform were jeopardized by the increasing frailty of the Caudillo—bringing with it fear and intransigence on the part of the so-called Bunker, or archreactionaries—and by the escalating violence of Basque separatists. As a part of his efforts to quell the Basques,* Arias ordered the arrest and then exile of the outspoken bishop of Bilbao. This brought him into conflict with the hierarchy, the Vatican, and—perhaps most significant— with Carmen Franco de Polo (1902–1987), and resulted in a major political setback.

During the waning months of the Franco regime, Arias Navarro attempted to maintain a delicate balance between restless reformists and hard-line conservatives and succeeded in satisfying neither camp. Terrorism continued unabated, and by the summer of 1975, the smoldering controversy over Spanish Sahara had reached a crisis stage. By the time Franco died in Nov. 1975, the government was in a state of near-paralysis. Nevertheless, the transition to monarchy proceeded without immediate disruption, and Arias Navarro retained the premiership, despite increasing evidence that his pace of reform was insufficient to satisfy the popular Juan Carlos or his closest advisors.

The long-anticipated change in government leadership came on 1 July 1976, when, apparently to his surprise, Arias was summoned to the palace and asked to resign. In dismissing the man to whom he had allegedly referred as "an unmitigated disaster," Juan Carlos was in effect severing his last tie to Francoism and placing Spain on the path of rapid and dramatic change.

For additional information, see R. Carr and J. P. Fusi, *Spain: From Dictatorship to Democracy* (London, 1979).

*G. T. Harper*

*Related entries*: FRANCO, GEN. FRANCISCO; JUAN CARLOS I; SUÁREZ, ADOLFO.

**ARMY.** The origin of a continuous, institutionalized, standing army in modern Spain is variously dated from the reign of the Catholic kings or the regency of Cardinal Francisco Jiménez de Cisneros (1463–1517) in the late fifteenth or early sixteenth centuries. For more than one hundred years the finest in Europe, its power and efficiency declined disastrously in the midseventeenth century, pari passu with the general decline of the Spanish monarchy. The country's slow rate of development from that point made it almost inevitable that Spanish military institutions would lack the resources ever to regain their earlier standing.

The modern organizational structure of the army dates more precisely from the Bourbon reforms of the early eighteenth century, when Spanish units were restructured according to the modern French regimental system. During the eighteenth century, Spain's military institutions regained at least a modest degree of their former vigor, as the worldwide empire reached its greatest geographical dimensions.

During the nineteenth and twentieth centuries, however, the Spanish army became much better known for its political than for its military role. It became a leading political actor soon after the advent of modern liberalism,* quickly supplementing weak civilian elites in helping to determine, sustain, or reverse fundamental political changes. In the process, it became the original historical prototype of the modern "praetorian" force. Just as Spain led the way in the attempt to accelerate political modernization in underdeveloped societies, the Spanish army provided the first major example of systematic political intervention in this process.

Much of the organized standing army was destroyed during the War of Independence* against the French invasion between 1808 and 1813. It was often replaced by volunteer partisan bands that practiced guerrilla, or irregular partisan, combat, in perhaps the first significant modern example of guerrilla warfare. During the restoration of absolute monarchy under Fernando VII,* ambitious young officers became increasingly restive with their own diminished peacetime status and the meager, inept administration of the restored system. Individual officers, usually of middle-class background, led a series of abortive revolts beginning in 1815 and finally achieved success five years later with the rebellion headed by Maj. Rafael de Riego (1785–1823) that eventually overthrew the absolutist regime and restored the constitutional monarchy initiated at the Cortes of Cadiz* in 1812. Though this interlude lasted but three years, military commanders also played important roles in championing the expansion of liberalism during the first years of the reign of Isabel II,* starting in 1833.

Several basic aspects must be clearly understood to grasp the character of nineteenth-century praetorianism. First, military leaders normally acted in concert with civilian politicians and in most cases, were eagerly recruited by the latter, who were conscious of the weakness of civilian political groups. During the nineteenth century, there was never any attempt in Spain to establish a military dictatorship in the strict sense, for political activists in the military championed changes in civil institutions within the framework of monarchist and parliamentary government. Whenever a general served as prime minister, he did so as the leader of a primarily civilian political party or as individual officeholder within an organized, civil, nominally constitutional, institutional framework, not as direct dictator or the corporate representative of the armed forces per se. On only two occasions did generals hold the office of chief of state during the nineteenth century—under the regency of Gen. Baldomero Espartero* from 1841 to 1843 and during the brief interlude of Gen. Francisco Serrano (1810–1885) as republican president from 1873 to 1874. Normally, most of the officer corps was not involved in politics; had it been, the military institutions would have dissolved altogether. In most cases, only senior commanders exercised political initiative, most officers simply followed orders. In more radical, but less frequent, circumstances, middle-ranking officers were occasionally active, but junior officers almost never took action on their own, since insubordination for the ranks was severely repressed. The rare example of an attempted sergeants' revolt in 1866 was suppressed with numerous executions.

The actual form of military intervention varied considerably. The classic pronunciamento, a term introduced in connection with the Riego revolt of 1820, was not ipso facto a coup or the beginning of civil war, but a "pronouncement" by one or more generals or sectors of the army that sought to win the support of other sectors or influence a change in general policy or regime. Some pronunciamentos were bloodless, while others led to outright battle. In some cases, a conspiracy was organized to seize power directly, while in others the action was designed simply to influence and change the course of events. In many instances, senior commanders merely lobbied behind the scenes, while on some occasions rebel units would adopt the passive tactic of the cuartelazo, or barracks revolt, to put pressure on the existing government. No military intrigue, coup attempt, or more indirect pronunciamento led to generalized civil war. All the genuine civil wars of the nineteenth century (1821–1823, 1833–1840, and 1869–1876) stemmed from fundamental civic division between liberal and neotraditionalist forces, the latter centered primarily in the northeast.

For the sake of simplicity, the political history of the modern Spanish military may be divided into three periods. From 1815 to 1874, the prevailing tendency of military intervention was liberal, followed by a more centrist phase from 1874 to 1936. The political orientation of the military only developed a strongly rightist-authoritarian identity in 1936. Nonetheless, even during the classic era of liberal pronunciamentos from 1815 to 1874, military intervention also spearheaded almost every attempt to establish more conservative government, and military attitudes began to assume an increasingly rightist tinge from the first years of the twentieth century.

It has nonetheless been argued that the actual political values of the military itself did not change so very much throughout this period. Army officers came primarily from the middle classes and tended to play a role analogous to that of a special, middle-class elite during the heyday of nineteenth-century liberalism, when liberalism was elitist and progressively patriotic. After liberalism was increasingly challenged by democratic and radical forces, the military found itself placed much nearer the center of the political spectrum. In the early twentieth century, when the Spanish system was challenged by revolutionary collectivism and centrifugal regionalism, the reaction of the military placed it on the right.

Moreover, complete political unity within the officer corps itself never existed. For most of this period, army officers reflected many of the divisions existing within Spanish political society in general. From the time of the First Carlist

War (1833–1840) until the early twentieth century, a vague consensus tended to exist on moderate constitutional monarchy, but during most of the years from 1844 to 1868, conservative liberal commanders such as Gen. Ramón Narváez* tended to sustain the highly elitist and restrictive governments of Isabel II. A somewhat more liberal commander such as Gen. Leopoldo O'Donnell* helped to open the way for the progressive biennium of 1854–1856 and the attempt at a broader Liberal Union government of 1858–1863. The most capable and in some ways the most advanced of all the nineteenth-century liberal commanders was Gen. Juan Prim y Prats,* who led the overthrow of Isabel II and inaugurated Spain's first democratic interlude of 1868–1874.

Under the restored Bourbon constitutional monarchy of 1874, the political cycle came full circle. The praetorian hypertrophy of military politics had been the result not so much of the mere ambition of the military itself as of the dysfunctional character of Spanish politics and government and the partial political vacuum that resulted. Once a stable two-party system of moderate liberalism was established under the Restoration, overt intervention largely disappeared for several decades. Even under the Restoration system, however, senior commanders retained a degree of special influence, several serving as temporary prime ministers, and the army enjoyed greater institutional autonomy than in most European countries.

Though most noted for the political role of its leaders, the Spanish army remained an active combat force and was involved in military campaigns for a greater total number of years during the nineteenth century than was the case with most European armies. After the War of Independence, the Spanish army was involved in three lengthy colonial campaigns (1814–1825, 1868–1878, 1895–1898), two of them unsuccessful, as well as continuing garrison duty in the Caribbean and western Pacific and numerous related minor actions. There were three domestic civil wars as well as smaller skirmishes in Catalonia* in 1827 and 1846–1849. In addition, there were two international wars, the Moroccan conflict of 1859 and the Spanish-American War* of 1898, as well as a minor expedition to Portugal* in 1848.

Though most of these were comparatively modest operations, several of them stretched the government's resources to the very limit, and their cumulative cost, a major element in Spain's limited economic growth during the nineteenth century, was very great. The proportionate loss of life in the First Carlist War was greater than in the civil war of 1936–1939, approximately 130,000 Carlist and government troops being killed, while the final Cuban campaign produced 55,000 fatalities, mostly from disease.

The combination of frequent involvement in both active campaigns and political affairs in an underdeveloped country produced an increasingly expensive, but far from proficient, force. The military budget was normally costly, not because of the number of troops under arms or the expenditure on equipment, but because of the unbridled growth of the officer corps, particularly in the senior ranks. During peacetime, the army accounted for approximately 20 percent of the state budget, though that figure declined slightly during the second half of

**Table 1**
**Budget of the Ministry of War as Percentage of Total Spanish Budget, 1850–1900**

| Year | % | Year | % | Year | % |
|------|------|------|------|------|------|
| 1850 | 23.9 | 1870 | 12.7 | 1890 | 17.4 |
| 1855 | 18.1 | 1875 | 43.9 | 1895 | 18.0 |
| 1860 | 18.4 | 1880 | 19.1 | 1900 | 16.9 |
| 1865 | 17.8 | 1885 | 17.2 |      |      |

Source: Daniel R. Headrick, Ejército y política en España (1866-1898) (Madrid, 1981): 273.

the century, as indicated in Table 1. The officer corps first ballooned in size as a result of the War of Independence, and the subsequent civil and colonial wars kept its numbers high throughout the remaining century, rare efforts at reform soon being countermanded by new military expansion, as indicated in Table 2. Withal, the Spanish army remained a weak military institution, lacking funds for the best modern equipment, logistical support and supply facilities, or adequate field training. A disproportionate amount of the budget was required simply to pay officers' salaries.

**Table 2**
**Total Number of Troops and Officers, 1828–1865 (including Civil Guard)**

| Year | Total | Year | Total |
|------|---------|------|---------|
| 1828 | 61,056 | 1850 | 113,440 |
| 1835 | 92,914 | 1855 | 84,668 |
| 1840 | 139,642 | 1860 | 119,067 |
| 1845 | 107,165 | 1865 | 111,177 |

Source: Daniel R. Headrick, Ejército y política en España (1866-1898) (Madrid, 1981): 269-70.

In general, the Spanish army had at least twice the number of officers proportionate to the total number of troops compared with the best European forces of the period, with especial hypertrophy at the rank of general. The 716 generals of 1816 declined after 1823, but numbered 647 once more by 1844 and only fell to 469 twenty years later. During the Restoration period, particularly, there was increasing concern over the need for technical reform of the military, including a reduction in the officer corps. A total of ninety works on military reform were published between 1866 and 1899. The most serious effort, the Cassola reform of 1887, was largely aborted because of political resistance, though the number of generals was reduced to fewer than 300 by 1888.

In the early twentieth century, following the disaster of 1898, the situation of the military slowly changed. For the first time in its history, the Spanish army was seemingly left without a major role to play. The last vestiges of overseas empire had been lost, Spanish leaders showed little appetite to join the competition for what remained to be taken in Africa, and the country was not involved in the international rivalries and military expansion of Europe during the new century. The comparatively impoverished Spanish government showed little interest in serious modern military development that might have provided a new vocational image, while officers resented what they perceived as a general tendency to blame the military itself for the hopeless inadequacy of Spanish arms in 1898.

New domestic social and political changes proved increasingly inimical. Though some middle-class republicans still echoed the "pronunciamento tradition" and looked to liberal sectors of the military to assist in an eventual overthrow of the monarchy, both the new revolutionary worker movements and the increasingly influential Catalan and Basque regionalists spurned the more traditional forms of Spanish patriotism, regarding the military as their foes, and attacked them in their propaganda. The caricatures of fat, middle-aged generals in the Catalan satirical publication *Cu-cut* led to an officers' riot in Barcelona in 1905 and a new campaign of military pressure demanding safeguards for the honor of the armed forces. Thus, in 1906 a liberal government passed a new "Law of Jurisdictions" that transferred legal jurisdiction over cases of potential libel of military institutions to military courts, an action that is usually held to mark, at least to some extent, the return of the military to the political sphere after an absence of three decades.

A new frontier opened for the army in 1909 with the hostilities surrounding Spanish mining enterprises in northern Morocco, followed by the official establishment of the new Spanish Protectorate in 1912. The government took this step reluctantly, feeling dragged in by the irresistible vortex of French imperialism. The northern zone of Morocco was in fact a beehive of autonomous and bellicose Berber Kabyles little disposed to Spanish rule. Initial operations in 1913–1914 showed that a major campaign would be required to subdue and occupy the new protectorate. Though this provided opportunity for one of the first modest uses of military aircraft (after the Italians in Libya in 1911), with the outbreak of World War I,* it was decided to suspend aggressive campaigning for the duration.

Despite official neutrality, World War I had a significant impact on Spain. To the discontent of political progressives, regionalists, and the worker movements was added the mounting resentment of officers in the home garrisons, who denounced political favoritism in promotion, the rapid advancement won by officers who had volunteered for service in Morocco, and the meager pay of junior and middle-ranking officers, which fell farther and farther behind wartime inflation. Such grievances led to the formation of juntas militares in several garrisons during 1916, a form of officers' syndicalism that spread throughout the peninsula the following year. Political progressives who convened the short-lived, independent parliamentary assembly of July 1917 in Barcelona were sufficiently impressed by the junteros' call for patriotic change to hope for military support in a new democratic breakthrough, but the juntas showed that they were mainly concerned about professional grievances and corporate privileges. Though the juntas managed to force two minor changes in national government in 1917–1918, they refused to back any new sector of the civilian opposition, and their own narrow vision and internal contradictions limited their influence in the future, as the government sought to reassert the formal chain of command.

Following the end of War World I, the army undertook to complete occupation of the protectorate. The native Kabyles proved among the most adept guerrilla fighters in the Afro-Asian world of that generation, forcing the Spanish debacle at Anwal* in 1921 in which nine thousand troops were killed and most of the eastern half of the protectorate lost. During the next two years, the political opposition demanded "responsibilities" (full inquiry and prosecution) concerning the role of the crown and army command in this humiliating defeat, while the government feared to attempt an all-out offensive to avenge it. Concurrently, the local army commander in Barcelona, Gen. Severino Martínez Anido (1862–1939), seized control of civil and police command in Barcelona to repress the bloody street conflict between Catalan capitalists and anarchosyndicalist labor. As electoral abstention increased and middle-class progressives demanded fundamental change, several generals considered the possibility of military intervention to solve both the domestic and colonial conflicts. Though a "quadrilateral" of four royalist generals in Madrid plotted temporary dictatorship to save the honor of king and army, it lacked an adequate leader. Instead, Gen. Miguel Primo de Rivera,* captain-general of Barcelona, seized the initiative and carried out the last of the nineteenth-century pronunciamentos on 12–13 Sept. 1923.

The resulting Primo de Rivera dictatorship was unique, the first direct military dictatorship in Spanish history. Though Alfonso XIII* recognized Primo's usurpation, which was invested with powers of government, Primo did not form a regular administration, but a special Military Directory, composed of seven generals and an admiral. With French military assistance, it finally began to solve the Moroccan problem by the end of 1925, but the directory then gave way to a new civilian cabinet, still under Primo's dictatorship. Officers grew increasingly restive with this arbitrary regime, and several abortive conspiracies were organized against it. Primo's overturn of the closed seniority system of the Artillery Corps was bitterly resented, and after it became clear that he planned neither to restore constitutional government nor replace it with a credible new system, a much broader military conspiracy began to form at the beginning of 1930. There was considerable sentiment that the honor of the military had been compromised by arbitrary, increasingly inept, one-man rule, and a small number of officers swung to the side of republican conspirators. Though most of the officer corps remained relatively conservative, respect for the monarchy declined greatly. After the municipal elections of 12 Apr. 1931, only a handful of die-hard monarchist generals attempted without influence to oppose the peaceful inauguration of the Second Republic.*

While the military had done nothing overtly to oppose the coming of the republic, the new regime placed solution of Spain's perpetual civil-military problems high on its agenda. The first republican war minister, Manuel Azaña,* planned both to subordinate the armed forces to the civil government completely and attempt a basic reform of the army's structure. A generous program of retirement at full pay reduced the swollen officer corps from 22,000 to 12,400, and minor structural changes were carried out as well. The basic organization of the army was affected only in secondary ways, for the republic had no interest in subverting the military hierarchy per se and lacked the money to upgrade and drastically reorganize army institutions. An adversary relationship soon developed between republican politicians and much of the officer corps, not because of truly drastic changes, but because of the hostile attitude of the new regime's leaders and their evident determination to put the army in its place. Nonetheless, few officers were monarchists, and an abortive rightist revolt in Aug. 1932 (the "sanjurjada") drew scant support. The military found themselves defenders of the republic when called to suppress the much more extensive revolutionary insurrection in Asturias* and several other regions in Oct. 1934.

As political opinion increasingly polarized between Right and Left, many of the officers came to sympathize with the Right. A semiclandestine officers' organization, the Unión Militar Española, was formed in 1934 and drew the support of a significant minority. After the Popular Front's electoral victory of Feb. 1935, the extreme right placed its hopes for overthrow of the left republican regime almost exclusively with the military. Plotting against the government began soon after the electoral victory, but was divided severely by region, professional subsector, and varying political allegiances. The republican government appointed moderates or liberals to nearly all the top commands, and most officers proved reluctant to commit themselves to serious conspiracy, all the more since the supercharged climate of Spanish affairs guaranteed that the penalty for failure would not be as mild as in previous generations. Gen. Emilio Mola,* former police chief for the monarchy and briefly high commissioner of Spanish Morocco, finally began to take control of the conspiracy after 30 Apr.

1936, but encountered great difficulty in drawing it together. Only after polarization became almost complete following the killing of the rightist politician José Calvo Sotelo* on 13 July did circumstances permit a broadly based revolt.

The rebellion that broke out in widely scattered parts of Spanish territory between 17 and 20 July lacked clear political unity or plan. It was organized above all as a coup by the military to overthrow the existing government, temporarily replace all civilian politicians, and install some sort of more conservative and authoritarian republic. It managed to incorporate only about half the standing army (losing the other half either because units failed to rebel or were intimidated or defeated by the Left), so that all opportunity for a relatively quick coup was lost. The entire country was soon divided between a republican and a rebel, or nationalist, zone, the latter led by a Junta de Defensa Nacional of the senior rebel commanders. It relied especially on the Army of Africa, led by Gen. Francisco Franco,* and drawn from the veteran units in the protectorate, which conquered southwestern Spain and drove on to Madrid. As the struggle for the capital loomed ever nearer, personal supporters of Franco, the most prestigious of all the rebel commanders, arranged his election, with no dissenting votes, as generalissimo and head of the new regime. On 1 Oct. 1936, Franco assumed full powers as nationalist chief of state.

Franco's primary achievement in the civil war was to develop what eventually became the largest mass army in Spanish history. Though it received crucial military assistance from Italy and Germany, it also achieved greater military cohesion than did the opposing republican force, which largely lacked professional leadership and never overcame internal political division. At least 820,000 men served in the nationalist army during the civil war, and altogether a total of more than 1 million were mobilized for all branches of the armed forces and police and auxiliary units. At least 60,000—possibly more—died in combat or from wounds. This mass army was led by large new cadres of alféreces provisionales (temporary second lieutenants), of whom 29,000 were trained, often with German assistance, together with nearly 20,000 new noncommissioned officers (NCOs). This new nationalist army was in large measure Franco's creation and remained loyal to him until his death. It gained the upper hand through the conquest of the northern republican zone during the summer and fall of 1937 and, under conditions of increasing predominance, ground down its foe in the fifteen months that followed.

The army enjoyed a preeminent place in the new regime Franco constructed, forming one of its two main pillars with the new state party, the Falange Española Tradicionalista.* Franco drew heavily on the senior commanders of the military to serve as cabinet ministers and other high officials, particularly during the first twenty years of his regime, yet he was careful not to give the army any autonomous corporate role within the new system. The hundreds of officers who held office in his government administration did so as individual state civil appointees of an organized system under theoretically civilian control, not as corporate representatives of the military.

Though most army commanders favored Spanish entrance into World War II* on the side of Germany* after the fall of France* in 1940, their ardor soon cooled, while they increasingly resented the pretensions and ambitions of the fascistic Falangists. The most severe internal strife in the long history of the Franco regime was that between the Falangists and the military during 1941–1942. Franco cleverly played each group off against the other, though in the long run the military gained more satisfaction than did the Falangists. As the tide of war shifted in Europe, some of the leading figures in the military hierarchy came increasingly to favor the monarchy as the most acceptable formula for solving Spain's political problems. In Sept. 1943, most of the lieutenant generals (the highest regular rank) signed a letter to Franco asking him to restore the monarchy, the only occasion on which most of the high command requested, however momentarily, that their Caudillo resign. Franco finessed the issue skillfully, convincing a number to change their minds and soon promoting more die-hard Franquistas to the highest rank. Virtually the entire army command rallied behind Franco in the face of the leftist insurgency that first flared in the autumn of 1944 and closed ranks firmly before the international ostracism of the Spanish regime between 1945 and 1949, helping to guarantee the security and survival of the system.

In the last eighteen years of the regime, from 1957 to 1975, the role of the military and the importance of the military budget steadily declined as the government placed its main emphasis on rapid economic growth. The army had been expanded once more during the main phase of World War II (though never to more than half its civil-war dimensions) and then declined to 320,000 (including 29,500 officers) in 1950. From that level, it was slowly reduced, reaching 240,000 (including 19,300 officers) in 1970. During World War II, military and police expenditures had at times held about 40 percent of the state budget, but this dropped steadily during the 1950s and 1960s to 14.7 percent for the armed forces alone in 1968 and 13.8 percent in 1975, the last year of the regime. By 1970, the state was spending more on public education than on the military for the first time in Spanish history. The proportion of military figures in Franco's cabinets declined from 46.1 percent in 1941 to 31.6 percent in 1965 and then to 15.8 in 1974, when the only military members were those in charge of the three armed-forces ministries themselves. At the time of Franco's death, the Spanish army remained proportionately one of the weakest and least-modernized forces in Europe and also, compared with the general population, one of the smaller military establishments of the continent. Franco had always been cognizant of his army's technical deficiencies, but showed only limited interest in remedying them, preferring instead to maintain the political and bureaucratic equilibrium of the force that had emerged from the civil war in 1939.

Despite the straitened military budget and the limited combat effectiveness of the army, it was widely believed on the morrow of Franco's death that the military command would intervene—violently, if need be—to prevent any real democratization of government. Sociological investigation in recent years has revealed that nearly 80 percent of the infantry officers were products of self-recruitment within military families, and the attitudes and values of officers were decidedly more conservative, traditionally Catholic, nationalistic, and authoritarian than those of the general population. Yet, though most army and navy officers disapproved of the democratization carried out between 1976 and 1979, there was no overt move to terminate it through armed intervention.

At no time in the history of Spain has the military intervened to overthrow a government that was simultaneously legal and constitutional, maintained order and the established hierarchies, sustained effective leadership and unity, and was supported by a clear and strong majority of the population. All these prerequisites were met by the smooth and peaceful transition, which was carried out by the very laws and mechanism of the Franco regime itself. No plausible opportunity to intervene presented itself in this chain of circumstances, while the government for the most part ably managed the military, with the able leadership of Juan Carlos I* himself.

One abortive coup was attempted on 23 Feb. 1981 after the transition had been completed, at a moment when the prime ministership was changing hands and a regular government momentarily did not exist. The conspiracy behind this move was extensive, but far from being either complete or united, and was forced to rely on a combination of parliamentary coup and pronunciamento technique, hoping that the seizure of parliament would rally other sectors behind it. The king's immediate and effective intervention prevented this, most army commanders proving that in a showdown, they had no stomach for a corporate military revolt against the crown and the general political society. The following year was a time of delicate equilibrium in civil-military relations, but by 1982, supremacy was becoming more firmly established than ever.

The socialist government of Felipe González* that took office in 1982 moved carefully in managing military policy, but soon began to implement the reform program sketched out under the preceding administration of Calvo Sotelo. The two military bills of 1982 and 1984 were designed first of all to provide fundamental increases in the supplies and matériel budget to buy the modern equipment necessary for a professional and apolitical North Atlantic Treaty Organization (NATO) force, and second to reduce considerably the size of the army. The 1984 reform calculated that a smaller group of soldiers could be adequately equipped with modern matériel for the first time in nearly two centuries and would thus also be more likely to concentrate on its professional role. By 1990, the army is to be reduced to no more than 150,000 troops in a recognized unit structure that emphasizes rapid combat deployment and more sophisticated equipment, while the total of officers and NCOs combined will decline from 41,500 to 35,000. In this fashion, the government of democratic Spain in the late twentieth century hopes to put a complete end to the backward, but praetorian, army of earlier generations, replacing it with a smaller but more modern and professionalized force geared to genuine national defense and international security.

For additional information, see M. Ballbé, *Orden público y militarismo en la España constitucional (1812–1983)* (Madrid, 1983); M. A. Baquer, *El modelo español de pronunciamento* (Madrid, 1982); C. P. Boyd, *Praetorian Politics in Liberal Spain* (Chapel Hill, 1979); J. Busquets Bragulat, *Pronunciamentos y golpes de Estado en España* (Barcelona, 1982); G. Cardona, *El poder militar en la España contemporánea hasta la Guerra Civil* (Madrid, 1983); D. R. Headrick, *Ejército y política en España (1866–1898)* (Madrid, 1981); S. G. Payne, *Politics and the Military in Modern Spain* (Stanford, 1967); and C. Seco Serrano, *Militarismo y civilismo en la España contemporánea* (Madrid, 1984).

*S. G. Payne*

*Related entry*: FRANCO, GEN. FRANCISCO.

**ARRIAGA Y RIVERO, FREY JULIÁN DE** (1696?–1776), knight of the Order of San Juan and minister of the Indies and marine (1754–1776). Julián de Arriaga entered the navy as an ensign in 1728. During the course of his service, he attracted the attention of the minister of finance, war, marine, and the Indies, Zenón de Somodevilla, the marqués de la Ensenada.* When the revolt in Leon, Venezuela, erupted against the Caracas Company in 1749, Ensenada named him, with the powers of governor, commander of the pacification expedition sent from Spain. Arriaga suppressed the rebellion with prudence and equanimity, a success that led to his appointment in 1752 as marine intendant for Cadiz and president of the Casa de Contratación. After the fall of his benefactor in 1754, Arriaga succeeded him as minister of the Indies and marine.

Arriaga was a magistrate of unquestioned integrity and a reasonably efficient administrator. Deeply conservative by instinct, he was firmly committed to the principles of aristocracy, privilege, and special arrangement. His years in Cadiz influenced him greatly, and he remained a friend of the Consulado for life. Yet he was very much his own man, largely isolating himself from the political intrigues at court. He commanded the personal respect of political friend and foe alike. Arriaga survived politically the humiliation of Spain at Havana and Manila during the Seven Years' War,* but Carlos III* reduced his powers by establishing the Junta de Ministros to oversee colonial reform. Although most reformist legislation carried Arriaga's signature as minister, much was imposed on him by Leopoldo de Gregorio, the marqués de Esquilache,* and the conde Jerónimo Grimaldi (1720–1786), the other members of the junta. Arriaga understood the need for a reorganization of the colonial military, but he was more moderate on the question of revenue reform than Esquilache was. He opposed the establishment of the intendant system in Cuba and above all the 1765 regulation for free trade in the Caribbean Islands. The reformist visita of José de Gálvez* to New Spain alarmed him deeply.

After the fall of the Esquilache government, Arriaga regained his powers, although he was not consulted about the expulsion of the Jesuits (1767), whom he admired. Old, feeble, and plagued by fading eyesight, he nevertheless enjoyed considerable success in blocking further deregulation of the colonial commercial system and in derailing Gálvez's plan to extend the intendant system to New

Spain. Perhaps his most positive achievement was the remarkable expansion of the fleet that occurred during his tenure as minister of marine. Almost an octogenarian, the venerable Arriaga died on 28 Jan. 1776. He was succeeded by Gálvez as minister of the Indies and González de Castejón for marine.

For additional information, see J. A. Escudero, *Los orígenes del Consejo de Ministros en España*, 2 vols. (Madrid, 1979); and V. Rodríguez Casado, *La política y los políticos en el reinado de Carlos III* (Madrid, 1962).

A. J. Kuethe

*Related entries*: CARLOS III; COLONIES; ENSENADA, MARQUÉS DE LA.


**ASTURIAS,** consisting of the province of Oviedo, bounded by the Cantabrian Sea on the north, Cantabrian Mountains on the south, Santander on the east, and Galicia* on the west. Its capital city is Oviedo, and other major cities include Gijón and Avilés. Pop. (1981) 1,127,007; sq. mi. 4,079.

Agriculturally, Asturias was traditionally one of the regions in which seigneurial jurisdiction was most widespread. Little land was worked directly; almost all was rented to tenants, who made up 85 percent of the population. Independent smallholders comprised only 5 percent, and since most farms were small, there were even fewer agricultural laborers.

The basic unit of rural society was the caserío, an integrated farmstead comprising a house, outbuildings, a garden, orchards, land for cereals, pasture, and rights to use the commons. Agriculture took the form of a subsistence polyculture, giving farmers very little contact with markets. The introduction of corn in the eighteenth century permitted a more intensive agricultural cycle. Increased food production contributed to population growth, which in turn prompted the division of farms, so that by the end of the century, calls for legislation to prevent further divisions were heard.

Asturian agriculture experienced little innovation in the first half of the nineteenth century, until introduction of the potato stimulated extension of cultivation into previously uncultivated lands and supported another spurt of population growth. This led to recurring subsistence crises in the 1850s and 1860s (the second as part of the 1867–1868 national crisis, lasting longer here than elsewhere), prompting the marqués de Composagrado (c. 1809–1870) to write *Manifiesto de hambre* (1854?) to describe the misery of the area. A subsequent trend toward stockraising led to an increase in forage crops and some commercial agriculture, including filberts for the British market, and beans and cattle (raised under a form of sharecropping known as acomunado, whereby the landowner provided the stock to be grown by the tenant, who received a share of the income) for Castile.*

Disentailment,* less important here than in the south, allowed the urban middle classes to buy title to most of the ecclesiastical lands sold under the Juan Álvarez Mendizábal* disentailment of 1837. The conditions of sale made it very difficult for tenant farmers to redeem their leases (foros), until the Madoz law of 1856 eased credit terms. One peculiarity of disentailment in the region was the tiny

**Table 1**
**Coal Production and Miners, 1872–1933**

| Year | Production (metric tons) | Miners |
|------|-------------------------|--------|
| 1872 | 424,499 | 4,292 |
| 1885 | 434,871 | 4,795 |
| 1895 | 1,008,769 | 10,063 |
| 1905 | 1,916,285 | 14,427 |
| 1915 | 2,697,939 | 19,952 |
| 1925 | 3,934,149 | 31,023 |
| 1933 | 3,790,416 | 27,775 |

proportion of the village common lands (about 10 percent) sold; most had little use other than as pasture, and villagers had no incentive to pay for what they already had rights to use. Only some seventeen thousand hectares changed hands, ranking Asturias twenty-sixth among the provinces in this process.

Toward the end of the century, Asturian farmers began to specialize in live-stock. By 1891, the region had 16 percent of the national herd, mostly sold to the colonial market. During the early twentieth century, however, a shift to the production of milk and other dairy products occurred, and by 1922, Asturias produced more than one-fifth of the country's milk, of which two-thirds was consumed within the province.

Industrially, coal mining and iron made Asturias a major center. Large-scale mining began in the 1860s when a number of large companies (Fábrica de Mieres, Duro y Compañía, Hulleras del Turón, and Hullera Española) came to dominate the industry, but since small enterprises remained a persistent characteristic, increased production came not from mechanization, but from an increased number of miners employed, as Table 1 indicates.

Asturian coal suffered from the chronic problem of inability to compete with British imports in its principal market in the Basque* provinces. This was due to the unreliability and high cost of rail transport and to what mine owners said was inadequate tariff protection, even though tariffs on coal increased by 650 percent between 1906 and 1922. World War I* eliminated British imports and gave Spanish coal, of which Asturias produced 75 percent, a monopoly of the national market. Coal prices increased five times between 1913 and 1918; mining companies enjoyed unprecedented profits, but the return to normal conditions at the end of the war created a severe crisis that lasted until the Spanish Civil War.*

**Table 2**
**Iron Production, 1861–1931**

| Year | Production (000 tons) | % National Production |
|------|------------------------|------------------------|
| 1861 | 10 | 28.5 |
| 1871 | 21 | 38.8 |
| 1881 | 38 | 33.3 |
| 1891 | 40 | 25.6 |
| 1901 | 56 | 16.9 |
| 1911 | 73 | 17.8 |
| 1921 | 18 | 7.8 |
| 1931 | 90 | 19.2 |

The most important stimulus for the growth of coal mining was the emergence of an iron industry in Mieres and La Felguera, which began in the 1840s when British investors set up the first foundries. By the 1860s and 1870s, Asturias was the center of Spain's iron industry, as Table 2 shows, but the rapid extension of production in Biscay after 1876 left it far behind.

Demographically, there is little reliable data for the period before the first national census in 1857. The improvement in the food supply from the introduction of corn allowed a rapid population growth, estimated at some 50 percent over the eighteenth century. The Floridablanca* regional census of 1787 put the population at almost 350,000, while estimates for the 1840s range wildly from 372,000 to 685,000. The modern national censuses are shown in Table 3. Asturias experienced its demographic transition earlier than Spain as a whole, although later than Catalonia. Death rates dropped quickly after 1910; and in the 1920s, birth rates fell below the national average for the first time.

Migration had a significant impact on the region's population growth. An old tradition, dating back to the sixteenth century, it grew more important in the eighteenth century when population growth outstripped the ability of the land to sustain it. There were three distinct migratory flows: to Madrid and Andalusia; to the American colonies;* and seasonal migration to adjacent regions. By the end of the eighteenth century, Gaspar Melchor de Jovellanos* wrote of a "migratory mentality" inspired by hopes of becoming wealthy and returning home as an "indiano."

The big jump in emigration came in the second half of the nineteenth century, due to an increase in rural misery; a more favorable political climate in Spain that relaxed restrictions on emigration; and an active search for immigrants by

**Table 3**
**Population, 1857–1970**

| Year | Population | Year | Population |
|------|-----------|------|-----------|
| 1857 | 524,529 | 1920 | 743,726 |
| 1877 | 576,352 | 1930 | 791,855 |
| 1887 | 595,420 | 1940 | 836,692 |
| 1897 | 612,663 | 1950 | 888,149 |
| 1900 | 627,069 | 1960 | 989,344 |
| 1910 | 685,131 | 1970 | 1,045,635 |

the Latin American republics. Asturias was one of the leading sources of emigrants to the Americas, and continued to be in the twentieth century, although by the 1960s, Europe had become the favored target of emigrants. More Asturians now went to France,* Germany,* and Switzerland than to the Americas.

Industrialization caused internal population shifts; geographical distribution shifted from the coast to the interior coalfields. This process also brought urbanization; early in the nineteenth century, Asturias was one of the least urbanized regions in the country, and most people lived in hamlets composed of clusters of farmsteads. Such small centers remained important well into the twentieth century, even in the heart of the coalfields, but large towns and cities came to have an increasing weight. Industrial centers such as Mieres, Sama de Langreo, and La Felguera were among the fastest growing municipalities in the first three decades of the twentieth century.

As there was little immigration to the region before World War I, the mining industry drew its work force from the province, and especially from the areas in and around the coalfields. As a result, the dominant figure among the mine workers was the obrero mixto, the mixed worker, who combined mining with agriculture. Their farming activities gave them an independent mentality that made it difficult for mine owners and managers to impose a satisfactory degree of labor discipline. The mixed worker declined in importance only with the massive immigration during World War I, but he remained prominent throughout the 1920s.

Politically, Asturias produced two of the leading figures of eighteenth-century enlightened despotism: the conde de Campomanes* and Gaspar Melchor de Jovellanos. It also produced the first great hero and martyr of liberalism,* Rafael de Riego (1785–1823), the military officer who initiated the revolution of 1820 and was subsequently immortalized in the unofficial anthem of progressive politics, the "Himno de Riego."

For much of the nineteenth century, however, the most prominent political figures of the region were on the right: Alejandro Mon (1801–1882), the Moderate party minister of finance in 1844 and 1845, who created the fiscal system that remained the basis for government finances for over a century; and Alejandro Pidal y Mon (1846–1913), who led the Catholic Union party that, after flirting with Carlism,* joined the Liberal-Conservative party of Antonio Cánovas del Castillo* in 1883, providing crucial Catholic support for the Restoration system.

Industrialization created new social classes and new political options. Gijón was the home of the Reformist Republican party under Melquíades Álvarez (1864–1936). The strength of the Reformist party, created in 1912, lay in its ability to attract the support of intellectuals such as José Ortega y Gasset* and Manuel Azaña.* For most, including Álvarez himself, republicanism was less important than the realization of a democracy untainted by the corruption of the caciques,* social and agrarian reform, and modern education. The Reformist party was close to the Socialist party, at least until 1923, and during the 1917 general strike, Melquíades Álvarez hid mine labor leaders in his home. During the Second Republic, the Reformist party was renamed the Liberal Democratic party and moved to the right, remaining outside the republican-socialist coalition in the 1931 and 1933 elections, and allying with the Confederación Española de Derechas Autónomas (CEDA) in 1936.

The most important political development in the region was the emergence of labor as a radical force. The anarchists were the first to arrive, briefly organizing metal workers into a branch of the First International in 1871. They returned at the end of the century and built two strongholds in Gijón and La Felguera, but their appeal among miners was always limited.

The socialists, who began to organize only in 1892, ultimately emerged as the dominant force in the working class, especially among the miners. Growth of the party and its affiliated unions was slow and erratic until 1910, when the Sindicato de Obreros Mineros Asturianos (SMA), brilliantly led by Manuel Llaneza (1879–1931), grew into one of the wealthiest and strongest unions. After a prolonged mining crisis began in 1920, however, the SMA's cautious strategy of relying on the government for protection almost destroyed it, although the Second Republic did help the SMA regain its dominant position. A policy of avoiding strikes at all costs soon generated an increasing restiveness among younger members.

The regional branch of the Socialist party, the Federación Socialista Asturiana (FSA), was much smaller than the union and always heavily dependent on it. Founded in 1901, the FSA had over 2,400 members two years later, a figure it would never exceed. During the dictatorship of Gen. Miguel Primo de Rivera,* membership ranged between 400 and 500, but even during the Second Republic, its membership remained static, far smaller than socialist groups in provinces such as Albacete, Tenerife, Lugo, Logroño, and Pontevedra, never known as socialist strongholds.

Labor dominance over the party in Asturias was reflected in the absence of any strictly political figures of prominence in the FSA. Even so, many workers voted socialist without ever joining the party. The first socialist municipal councillor was elected in 1901, the first mayor (in Mieres) in 1918, and by 1920 there were forty-six socialists sitting as local councillors. In the municipal elections of Apr. 1931, which ushered in the Second Republic, eighty-seven socialists were elected. The party followed a similar pattern in national elections: the first socialist deputy was elected in 1918; others were elected in 1919, 1920, and 1923; and during the republic, four socialists were elected in June 1931, as part of the center-left coalition that took twelve of the province's seventeen seats. Running alone in Nov. 1933, the party took four seats once again, although the majority went to the right. As part of the Popular Front in Feb. 1936, the FSA won six seats.

The proclamation of the Second Republic generated great enthusiasm and hope among Asturian workers; but the inability of republican governments to alleviate hardships caused by the collapse of international markets in the coal industry, when combined with fears caused by conservative electoral successes that hinted of fascism, generated a rank-and-file militancy that pushed the region's reformist socialist leaders toward more radical positions. When the Socialist party,* or Partido Socialista Obrero Español (PSOE), national leadership called for an insurrection to block the CEDA's entry into the cabinet in Oct. 1934, only Asturias responded. Workers, led by the miners, took control of the coalfields and laid siege to Oviedo. In areas they controlled, the workers exceeded the limited objectives of the national leadership by creating an incipient socialist society. The "Asturian Commune" was subdued after two weeks only after 26,000 troops had been sent to combat it. A severe repression followed the defeat.

At the outbreak of the Spanish Civil War, Asturias remained loyal to the republic, with the exception of Oviedo, where the military governor was able to retain control despite being besieged. The nationalist rising in Gijón was defeated in Aug. 1936, but in Oct., nationalist troops from Galicia succeeded in breaking the siege of Oviedo and connected the city to nationalist territory by a narrow corridor.

As in other republican areas, the civil war triggered a sweeping social revolution. Only in Feb. 1937 was the interprovincial council of Asturias and León able to replace the Popular Front committee, allow private banks to reopen, and return small businesses that had collectivized to their former owners.

When Santander fell to the nationalists in Aug. 1937, the interprovincial council declared itself sovereign, and in a desperate attempt to stave off defeat, appointed a new military commander and sought to impose stronger discipline on its military forces. On 21 Oct., however, the nationalists entered Gijón and the war in the north came to an end.

The economic policies of the first two decades of the Franco regime favored Asturias's heavy industries. In 1950, broad interventionism led to the creation of a state iron and steel company. By the mid–1950s, Asturias ranked sixth among Spanish provinces in terms of income per capita, but liberal economic policies adopted in 1959 initiated a crisis in the region, causing income per capita to fall. Growth rates fell constantly below the national average from 1960 to 1978, and jobs in heavy industry were lost even at the height of the 1960s "economic miracle." Creation of a state coal company helped slow the decay slightly, but by the time the Socialist party came to power in 1982, determined to reconvert Spain's heavy industrial base to meet the challenge of European Economic Community membership, Asturias had become a classic example of an outdated heavy industrial economy. Socialist reconversion policies generated unrest, including several riots in Gijón.

Despite the Franco regime's prohibition of all independent labor organizations, Asturias became the birthplace of the Comisiones Obreras (CCOO) that challenged the official vertical unions in the 1960s. The CCOO burst onto the scene with a major miners' strike in 1962, and strike activity continued throughout the subsequent period.

Asturias achieved regional autonomy under the Constitution of 1978, which went into effect in the spring of 1981. Since then, the regional government has been controlled by the PSOE.

For additional information, see G. Anes, *Economía y sociedad en la Asturias del Antiguo Régimen* (Barcelona, 1988); J. García Fernández, *Organización del espacio y economía rural en la España Atlántica* (Madrid, 1975); J. M. Moro, *La desamortización en Asturias* (Oviedo, 1981); G. Ojeda, *Asturias en la industrialización española* (Madrid, 1985); D. Ruiz, *El movimiento obrero en Asturias* (Madrid, 1979); and A. Shubert, *The Road to Revolution in Spain: The Coal Miners of Asturias, 1860–1934* (Urbana, 1987).

*A. Shubert*

*Related entries*: JOVELLANOS, GASPAR MELCHOR DE; SECOND REPUBLIC; SPANISH CIVIL WAR.

**ATENEO CIENTÍFICO Y LITERARIO DE MADRID,** a leading intellectual organization. A British observer once compared the Ateneo to the debating societies at Oxford and Cambridge and called it a "Holland of free speech" in Spain. Its library, bar, and auditorium, located a block from the Cortes building and close to the Prado museum, attracted politicians and intellectuals to daily tertulias, formal debates, and occasional concerts.

The organization was founded in 1836 at the very onset of the liberal age. It originally reflected the romantic values liberals had acquired during their French or British exiles. The rediscovery of "Spanishness" promoted a populism tied to foreign ideas of liberalism or radicalism that raised vague expectations of a new Siglo de Oro.

These hopes were dashed by the late 1830s. Liberal divisiveness and authoritarianism during the regimes of Gen. Baldomero Espartero,* Gen. Ramón de Narváez,* and Juan Bravo Murillo* created mistrust and a decline of the Ateneo between 1840 and 1854. Revival came in the late 1850s and 1860s, but this second period of brilliance was more complicated than the earlier one. The moderate historian and Tory-like, liberal-conservative future premier, Antonio Cánovas del Castillo,* presented an early version of his celebrated work, *Historia de la decadencia de España*, at the Ateneo. While he asserted that the conservative character of the Spanish nation, which the Hapsburgs and the church had ignored in the sixteenth and seventeenth centuries, could be relied upon to restore the nation to greatness, other Ateneo members, knowing Cánovas's elitism, disagreed. Francisco Giner de los Ríos,* a leading Krausist, believed that Spaniards needed to be educated before they could accomplish greatness. Liberalism* was in fact a corrupt oligarchical form of government that obstructed education and social improvement. The republican philosopher and historian Nicolás Salmerón* suggested that the Ateneo itself establish model education institutes to educate the nation. A Catalan, Francesc Pi i Margall,* challenged liberals in the Ateneo to abandon centralism for a more democratic federalism that would abolish oligarchy. Soon, of course, these ideas became the substance of the Revolution of 1868 and the First Republic.*

Censorship of ideas began in 1867 at the university level, and Cánovas expanded it at the beginning of the Restoration in 1875. Under the leadership of Francisco Silvela,* the Ateneo lost its openness in the late 1870s, lapsing for a time into neo-Catholic preoccupation, but Krausism and other reform issues refused to disappear. When access to the Ateneo was denied them, reformers such as Gumersindo de Azcárate (1840–1917) and Joaquín Costa* used legal societies and other groups to criticize the Tory politics of Cánovas and his allies. By 1890, the urgency of social and political reform created a third important period in the Ateneo's history.

The catalyst for the Generation of 1898,* for instance, may have been the Ateneo conferences on the "national disaster" in 1900 and on caciquismo and oligarchy in 1903. Azcárate and Costa played major roles in the group and took the Ateneo from debating-society status to an institution that tried to establish a national consensus. Despite efforts of conservative liberals, among them, Álvaro de Figueroa, the conde de Romanones (1853–1950), the Ateneo entered the twentieth century on the side of change. Its discussions and conferences brought together Spanish intellectuals and disseminated the ideas of Miguel de Unamuno,* José María Ortega y Gasset,* and other rising names in arts and letters.

The Ateneo had become so outspoken by 1927 that the dictatorship of Gen. Miguel Primo de Rivera* closed it. Reopened in 1930 and led by Manuel Azaña* just prior to the Second Republic,* its debates were often tumultuous and sometimes bitter. It declined drastically during the era of Gen. Francisco Franco.* Open debate was not part of the Francoist style, and the conferences on national syndicalism were not popular. In any case, a national consensus of Spanish intellectuals was almost impossible to obtain after 1939, since so many of them were in exile.

After the civil war, the Ateneo's building fell into disrepair, and the library was neglected. While it still operates today in refurbished quarters, university campuses have replaced it as a center of intellectual debate.

For additional information, see R. W. Kern, *Liberals, Reformers and Caciques in Restoration Spain* (Albuquerque, 1973); R. M. de Labra, *El Ateneo de Madrid* (Madrid, 1878); and J. B. Trend, *The Origins of Modern Spain* (New York, 1934).

*R. W. Kern*

*Related entries*: GENERATION OF 1898; GENERATION OF 1927; KRAUSE, KARL CHRISTIAN FRIEDRICH.

**AZAÑA Y DÍAZ, MANUEL** (1880–1940), second premier and architect of the Second Republic,* and president of the republic (1936–1939) during the Spanish Civil War.* Azaña, born on 10 Jan. 1880 in Alcalá de Henares to a liberal family, was orphaned in 1890. An intelligent student, he won scholarships to private schools and graduated with honors in law from the University of Saragossa in 1898 and with a doctorate of laws from Madrid in 1900. He practiced in Saragossa and Alcalá for the next five years before becoming a staff member of the justice ministry in Madrid.* In 1911, a scholarship from the Junta para Ampliación de Estudios allowed him to study in Paris.

His subsequent career turned more toward journalism, writing, and scholarship than the law. His first book was published in 1918, and he helped edit the periodical *España* with José Ortega y Gasset.* As a part of the brilliant Generation of 1927,* he published *El jardín de los frailes*, an anticlerical work (1927), a play, and a number of translations, including *The Bible in Spain*, by George Borrow.* His literary career made him eligible for membership in the Ateneo*; and in 1930, he became its president, polishing the oratory he later found useful in politics.

As a politician, Azaña supported the Allies in World War I* by founding a small democratic party. In 1925, during the dictatorship of Gen. Miguel Primo de Rivera,* he created Acción Republicana, a new party that rejected Alejandro Lerroux,* the leading republican who now leaned more toward the right. Azaña became a key figure in the antimonarchical Pact of San Sebastian (Aug. 1930) versus Alfonso XIII.* The municipal elections of 12 Apr. 1931 that created the Second Republic allowed Azaña to emerge from hiding to become minister of war, and on 25 Apr., he retired more than half of the officer corps in a reform designed to remove the military from politics. He also argued to the Constituent Cortes on 13 Oct. that since Spain had ceased being Catholic when the church abandoned the people, it no longer qualified for special privileges in the Constitution of 1931. Coming on the heels of his military reform, the subsequent adoption of Article 26 approving nonreligious control of health, education, and welfare elevated Azaña to premier in place of Niceto Alcalá Zamora (1877–1949) on 9 Dec. 1931.

Azaña remained premier until Sept. 1933. His ambitious efforts to change Spanish society ranged from education to land reform, but he had little to show until the unsuccessful coup d'état of Gen. José Sanjurjo (1872–1936) led to hasty and punitive passage of bills granting Catalan autonomy and land reform. The premier's popularity rose briefly, but revolutionary expectations ran so high in southern rural areas that messianic violence at Casas Viejas (Jan. 1933) led to a score of deaths. Although Azaña was cleared of any responsibility, support for him dropped until Alcalá Zamora, president of the republic, called for new elections held in Nov. 1933.

The second parliamentary elections, won by the Confederación Española de Derechas Antónomas (CEDA), gave Azaña only five seats. He created an Izquierda Republicana party through merger with several other groups, but he was a marked man, and after the Asturian insurrection (Oct. 1934), his arrest and imprisonment for several months by Lerroux (now premier of the CEDA-backed government), despite parliamentary immunity, won him new sympathy. As Lerroux's center-right coalition destroyed the early Second Republic's legislation, Azaña attracted a much larger following that enabled him to play a strong role in the creation of a Popular Front coalition, pitting the factions against one another. When Alcalá Zamora called for new elections, the Popular Front's victory again made Azaña premier on 19 Feb. 1936.

The republican leader quickly amnestied all prisoners, restored Catalan autonomy, outlawed the Falange,* suspended farm rents in Andalusia,* and neutralized popular military figures. Criticism of Alcalá Zamora's delay in calling new elections, however, led to his impeachment and Azaña's presidency on 10 May. This sudden, controversial, and perplexing change, crucial in unhinging republican politics, was a hoped-for pacification of the most radical wing of the Popular Front that depended upon Indalecio Prieto's (1883–1962) succession to the premiership, something that Socialist party politics and Francisco Largo Caballero,* Prieto's rival, would not permit. A weak cabinet that could not control political tempers led to a much more rapid emergence of the Spanish Civil War, although polarization was so great that it may have been inevitable.

Azaña's role in the civil war, limited by the weak powers of the presidency, was a terrible disappointment. Whether his stature might have led to greater European aid and rapport had he remained premier is intriguing but doubtful, since his efforts to bring the war before the League of Nations were unsuccessful, and his other diplomatic initiatives to obtain a negotiated settlement got nowhere. Even his earlier anticommunism was untested at the time, and initially he accepted the procommunist Juan Negrín* as premier in place of Largo Caballero (probably because of old conflicts between Azaña and Largo), although he later became very critical of Negrín and tried to remove him in Aug. 1938.

Azaña retreated from Madrid to Barcelona* in Oct. 1936, where he remained until the May crisis in 1937, when he moved to Valencia,* always growing more isolated and unhappy. He returned to Barcelona in Dec. 1937, by now convinced that the republic had no chance to win the war. The nationalist invasion of Catalonia* forced him to flee to France* on 5 Feb. 1939, and in Paris on 27 Feb., asking Spaniards not to make further useless sacrifices, he resigned. He left Paris for Bordeaux, where he lived in poverty and illness—certainly one of the more tragic stories in Spanish history—until his death on 3 Nov. 1940.

For additional information, see E. Aguado, *Manuel Azaña* (Madrid, 1979); J. Marichal, ed., *Obras completas de Manuel Azaña*, 4 vols. (Mexico City, 1966–1968); and F. Segwick, *The Tragedy of Manuel Azaña* (Columbus, 1963).

*R. W. Kern*

*Related entries*: SECOND REPUBLIC; SPANISH CIVIL WAR.

# B

BALEARIC ISLANDS, archipelago in the western Mediterranean between Spain and Italy* and below southern France* composed of the islands of Majorca, Minorca, Cabrera, Ibiza, and Formentera. It has been a provisional autonomous region of Spain since 1979. Pop. (1982 est.) 669,101. Sq. mi., 1,935.

The Balearic Islands, once an ancient trading center, is now a tourist area, with more than 2 million visitors a year. The economy is dominated by service industries and light manufacturing, particularly of artificial Majorcan pearls at Manacor. Only Formentera specializes in agricultural produce.

After centuries of Greek, Roman, Vandal, Byzantine, and Muslim occupation, the islands came under peninsular control in 1235 through the efforts of an Aragonese king, Santiago I. A further age of somnolent Spanish rule ended when an Anglo-Dutch fleet bombarded Palma, Majorca, in 1706, and Britain* occupied Port Mahon, Minorca, in 1708. The Treaty of Utrecht (1713) ceded Minorca (along with Gibraltar*) to the British from 1713 until 1802. Since the eighteenth-century European powers believed that the archipelago controlled the entire Mediterranean, the British heavily fortified Minorca, and it became the object of Austrian, French, and British ambitions, with Spain struggling to regain Minorca in 1727–1729 and 1779–1783. France and Britain quarreled over the Balearics in 1756, while negotiating the Treaty of Versailles, culminating with the French attack and capture of Minorca between 10 Apr. and 28 June 1756. In 1763, however, the Treaty of Paris gave Minorca back to Britain in exchange for the Antilles and five trading bases in India. The British built a new base, George Town, to protect Port Mahon, but in 1782, a Franco-Spanish force again seized control of the area. Adm. Viscount Horatio Nelson (1758–1805) attacked the fortifications in 1798 during the Egyptian campaign, but in Mar. 1802, Britain abandoned Minorca to Spain, getting Trinidad in exchange.

This long struggle for the Balearics was prolonged by the Barbary pirates of North Africa, whose raids made maritime commerce and life in the port cities risky until the 1820s. The islands had been isolated from Spain for so long that talk of independence was quieted only when the archipelago became a Spanish province in 1833, and even then Madrid* needed a large military garrison to repress signs of support for Carlism* from the region's traditional Catholics. Life did not improve greatly under Spanish sovereignty. George Sand (1804–1876), who lived in Majorca with Frederic Chopin (1810–1849) in 1838–1839, portrayed the conditions of the time rather bleakly in her *Un hiver a Majorque* (1841).

By the midnineteenth century, aided by linguistic ties, the Balearics fell under a strong Catalan influence. During 1868–1874, the Balearics gave support to the federalism of Francesc Pi i Margall.* In the Bourbon Restoration, however, Antonio Cánovas del Castillo* reestablished strong centralized control from Madrid, with fraudulent local elections and heavy-handed oligarchical politics the rule rather than the exception. His successor as leader of the Liberal-Conservative party, Antonio Maura,* a Majorcan who became premier in 1903–1904 and 1907–1909, sought seriously but unsuccessfully to reform local political abuses, inspired by the dismal record in the Balearics. After 1913, however, Maura moved to the right and created an authoritarian movement common in the Mediterranean region during this period.

These ideas probably found a good reception among the many wealthy foreigners now living in the Balearics. The first popularizer of the islands as a vacation resort was the Archduke Louis Salvador of Austria (1772–1806), who wrote the nine-volume *Balearen in Wort und Bilt* to sing its praises. In 1909, the Grand Hotel of Majorca was built, and in 1910, Brazilian proprietors opened the Hotel Formentor—both forerunners of the modern tourism industry. Juan March,* a Majorcan who became the richest man in Spain through his control of the tobacco monopoly, typified island society during the 1920s, when the Balearics became a premier European resort.

The Spanish Civil War* abruptly shattered this gilded isolation. The nationalist generals considered the Balearics and the Moroccan enclaves ideal for the start of their rebellion against the Second Republic.* Gen. Manuel Goded (1882–1936) seized Majorca on 18 July 1936, but was defeated after he flew to Barcelona* to direct the uprising there. This enabled the republicans, already established on Formentera, to take Minorca on 20 July, and successfully invade Ibiza on 9 Aug., under the leadership of Air Force Capt. Alberto Bayo (1894–1961). When Bayo landed on Majorca's east coast on 16 Aug., however, Italian fascists and nationalists were able to defeat his forces by 3 Sept. After a bloody purge of Majorca in Oct. and Nov. 1936, these forces recaptured Ibiza and Formentera at year's end.

Only Minorca remained in loyalist hands, because of a protocol signed by Britain and Italy in Jan. 1937 that barred Italian troops from landing on the island, part of Britain's price for neutrality in the larger war. The republicans used Minorca to stage their successful sinking of the German battleship *Deutschland* on 18 May 1937, although this led to increased Axis submarine attacks on republican shipping and near starvation on Minorca. The agony of this remaining republican stronghold in the Balearics, caught by Georges Bernanos (1888–1948) in his moving *Grands Cimetieres sous la Lune* (1938), became so great that when the nationalists captured Catalonia* on 10 Feb. 1939, Minorcan leaders surrendered the same day on board the British vessel *Devonshire* sent by the British Foreign Office to prevent Italian occupation of the Balearics.

The civil war left the area devastated until the tourist boom regained its prosperous momentum in the 1950s, although the age of mass tourism has had its own destructive impact upon the islands.

For additional information, see J.-L. Colas, *The Balearics* (Chicago, 1967).

R. W. Kern

*Related entries*: MAURA, ANTONIO; SPANISH CIVIL WAR.

**BARCELONA.** Barcelona, located on the Mediterranean coast in northeastern Spain, occupies a plain some three miles wide, bounded by the Besós and Llobregat rivers and the Sierra del Litoral (including Mt. Tibidabo and the Montjuic Mountains). Connected by river valleys to the rest of Catalonia, Barcelona has served as the Catalan capital during two periods of regional autonomy (1931–1939 and 1977 to the present). It was formerly the seat of the condado de Barcelona, which in turn was the nucleus of the medieval kingdoms of Valencia and Majorca, to which were added the kingdoms of Aragon, Naples, and Sicily. It enjoys a temperate climate, with an average humidity of 70 percent, although today its air pollution occasionally approaches alarming levels.

The topography of the city clearly shows the stages of its historical evolution. A knoll in the center of the modern city is ancient Mt. Taber, with Roman walls and ruins from the same era. The barrio Gótico-Catedral, the palace of the Generalitat (the autonomous government), the old palace of the kings of Aragon and the condes de Barcelona, the archbishopric, and El Call (the old Jewish quarter) date from medieval Barcelona, with street names that still preserve the names of professions once followed in them; this section goes as far as the port. At the end of the Middle Ages, the city went beyond its walls and extended past Las Ramblas, now Barcelona's central promenade. In the seventeenth century, the city spread inland and toward the Besós River, but slowly, because it was experiencing a period of economic decline. It was during the period after 1700 that Barcelona acquired its present-day configuration, with a constant expansion along the coast and inland.

The city is divided by an axis from the ocean to the mountains, formed by Las Ramblas, the Paseo de Gracia, and the Plaza Mayor, to the foot of Mt. Tibidabo; and by two transverse axes: the Granvía, from the entrance to the city from the south, by which one comes from Madrid and the rest of central and southern Spain, to the entry from the north, which leads to France and the northeast regions. The other transverse axis is diagonal, further inland than the Granvía, but with similar access. These two transverse axes put Barcelona in contact with what is called the metropolitan area, formed by villages that long ago were separated by the city, but that today constitute an urban unity within it, although preserving their structures and their own municipal authorities. The metropolitan area includes some 3,200 square kilometers (of which some 170 correspond to the city of Barcelona proper), in which about 4 million people live (1.75 million in Barcelona proper).

Barcelona's demography reflects the states of its historical evolution. In 1354, it had 34,024 inhabitants. That fell to 28,940 in 1516, to more than double in 1657 to 64,000, then falling by almost half in 1715 to 37,000. Since then, the increase has been constant, though slow, with an abrupt fall in 1821 because of a yellow-fever epidemic. In 1850, there were 125,000 inhabitants, with 248,000 in 1877 and 509,000 in 1900. The population passed 1 million in 1930, the result of a wave of immigration in the 1920s; 1.5 million in 1960; and in 1980, approached 2 million, then falling somewhat because of population movement to the metropolitan area and the return of many immigrants.

Of Barcelona's inhabitants in the eighteenth century, 90 percent were born in Catalonia. Since that time, the proportion of those born outside Catalonia has been increasing, with the highest percentages occurring in the 1920s and 1960s, when there were great waves of immigration, the first, especially, from Murcia and the second from Andalusia. The existence of large nuclei of immigrants, which in the 1920s were especially concentrated in Barcelona and its metropolitan area and in the 1960s spread throughout all Catalonia, had important social repercussions. The immigration of the 1920s was attracted in large part by anarchosyndicalist organizations, primarily the Confederación Nacional de Trabajo (CNT) and the Federación Anarquista Ibérica (FAI). While the working-class population of the 1960s remained passive in the Franco period, during the years when democracy was reestablished, at least 15 percent was unionized.

Immigration created a linguistic problem that had not existed before: that of part of the population being unable to speak Catalan (in the city of Barcelona, as much as 40 percent) and refusing to learn it. From 1975 on, with the coincidence of a new generation of immigrants' children born in Barcelona or Catalonia and the establishment of democracy and autonomy, Catalan has been gaining ground among immigrants, and today instruction in schools, which under Franco was conducted only in Castilian while Catalan was rigorously prohibited, is bilingual, with a growing predominance of Catalan at the secondary and higher levels. The position of the authorities is that only through education can demography be made to coincide with the language; since Catalan-language education is a problem considered basic in Catalan nationalism and a focal point of much political and administrative activity in Catalonia and Barcelona.

On the other hand, since its founding by Carthaginians and naming (Barcino, by the Romans), Barcelona has provided a home for many groups of foreigners. There have been Greeks, Romans, Germans (Visigoths), Provençals (above all, survivors of the crusade against the Albigensian heretics), Genovese, French (during the French Revolution), and Latin American refugees fleeing the dictatorships that followed the independence of the Spanish colonies* in America.

Later, German and Allied agents during World War I,* German Jews and anti-Nazi elements, and refugees from Spain's center and south during the civil war arrived. The German colony grew greatly during and after World War II.* Today, there are important nuclei of French, British, Germans, Americans, Portuguese, Chileans, Argentineans, and Uruguayans, augmented by illegal immigrants from the southern Sahara and the Maghreb.

Barcelona also has been a source of emigration, first to Latin America and, to a lesser extent, to the United States; to France (especially artists and intellectuals); and, at the end of the civil war, again to France and from there to other places. The city's population declined most dramatically in 1939–1940, the result of the civil war.

All of these complexities make Barcelona a bridge between the lands north and south of the Pyrenees, between Spain and Europe. If in the Middle Ages popular European influences entered the peninsula by the pilgrims' road to Santiago, cultural influences penetrated through Barcelona, combining with Barcelonan and Catalan culture (which also had Valencia and Naples as nuclei). After the fifteenth century, however, Barcelona was restricted to preserving Catalan culture. The Catalan language became a rural language of the people. Barcelona itself, as the seat of societies and academies, or a place of scientific work where the spirit of the Enlightenment* found an echo among Catalan merchants, belonged more to Western Europe than Iberia.

Unlike second-born Castilian sons who went to Castile's American colonies, the Catalans, unable to go to America, without realizing it, created a new bourgeoisie that expanded Barcelona and enriched itself in the slave trade and by the sale of aguardiente produced by the great country estates.

Barcelona also changed physically. Little was built from the fifteenth to the eighteenth century, but following a lull after the War of Spanish Succession* (when Catalonia opposed the Bourbon dynasty), palaces and mansions of the bourgeoisie began to be built. When Carlos III* opened the Indies trade to Catalonia denied them since the discovery of America, a merchant marine developed to sustain a very active trade with Buenos Aires and Havana. A renaissance of the economy, science, and moderate enlightened thought characterized eighteenth-century cultural development not genuinely Catalan or Barcelonan, but an echo of French rationalism. This established the bases for what in the following century was known as the Renaixença (in the literal sense of the term *renaissance*), which led to the transformation of Catalan from a popular spoken language to the language of culture. Barcelona also transmitted French culture to the rest of Catalonia and Spain and became home to historians, poets, novelists, and some scientists at the University of Barcelona.

The most outstanding feature of this period, however, was urbanism. In 1859, engineer Ildefonso Cerdà (1815–1876), author of the *General Treatise of Urbanization* (1867), presented a plan for Barcelona's expansion that presented a bold, innovative idea to establish two large neighborhoods with gardens, schools, theaters, and community and recreation centers in the center of each block of houses. The houses were built, but Cerdà had not taken into account the greed of the owners, who refused to give public access to the centers or allow them to be used for community purposes. The result was a new city, called Eixample, or extension, that was innovative on its face, but very traditional and closed as a community. This betrayal of Cerdà's plan did not stop the new bourgeoisie from converting Eixample into a showcase of modernism. Antoni Gaudí* achieved fame with buildings such as the Pedrera, the Church of the Holy Family, and the Comillas Palace, as well as Güell Park. Among his followers, Lluis Domènec i Muntaner (1850–1923) constructed the famous Palau de la Música Catalana. The Eixample was converted into a museum of modernist facades and interiors, since those architects were also decorators and designers of furniture who joined architecture to sculpture and painting. This was probably Barcelona's period of greatest cultural flowering, and a modernist city with a strong personality arose. The atmosphere influenced the other arts, and artists such as Pablo Picasso,* Joan Miró,* and Salvador Dalí,* and musicians such as Enrique Granados,* Isaac Albéniz,* and Pau (Pablo) Casals,* were formed in Barcelona.

Culturally, Barcelona still lives on in the inheritance of those two generations of creators. Its present-day urbanism is dedicated to saving what was not destroyed by the urbanism of the Franco era—ferociously speculative, typical of a period in which municipal authorities, appointed from above, without election, were distinguished by corruption, indifference to the city's characteristic values, and persecution of Catalan language and culture—a period in which defense of culture and even urbanism was confused with opposition to the Franco regime.

This cultural evolution was linked to the ups and downs of the Catalan economy, always dependent on Barcelona. Like Florence, Venice, and Genoa, Barcelona had been a bourgeois city with a feudal hinterland, tied to the Mediterranean with its Llibre del Consolat de Mar, at one time a truly universal maritime code. The discovery of America, however, moved the center of the Western world from the Mediterranean to the Atlantic, and Barcelona lost its trade and entered a period of decadence that worsened when Catalan participation was barred from America's conquest, colonization, and trade. Fortunately, the emancipation of the serfs in the fifteenth century created the formation of a new bourgeoisie made up of the second sons of peasants freed by the fifteenth-century civil war. In an economically declining Spain of the late sixteenth and early seventeenth centuries, the Catalan second sons transformed urban artisanry into manufacture and created industries that later gave Catalonia a new prosperity, especially when Carlos III authorized trade with the Americas. The merchant marine was reborn and transformed into a transatlantic one, the textile industry prospered, and trade flourished in a Mediterranean that had overcome the sixteenth-century crisis of isolation.

Not until the nineteenth century, however, did Barcelona again become a decisive element in the Spanish economy. For a time, diplomats of the French Revolution thought the bourgeoisie would be attracted to it, and Napoleon Bonaparte (1769–1821) believed he could integrate Catalonia into France. Catholicism's deep roots, however, and a proverbial distrust of France caused Barcelona to send deputies to the Cortes of Cadiz* as liberals. Barcelona and a good part of Catalonia thus sided with political modernization and became a center of liberal tendencies in nineteenth-century Spanish politics. In return, they received from Madrid a systematically protectionist policy that permitted industrialization without fear of foreign competition. New industries like textiles, established along the Llobregat River, outside the city proper, provided the moving force for nineteenth-century prosperity.

Barcelona also became the point of entry into Spain for the industrial revolution, which in many respects remained limited to Catalonia. The first Spanish railroad was built in 1848 from Barcelona to Mataro, center of the knitted-goods industry, and in 1860, it spread further still to the manufacturing cities of Terrassa and Sabadell. The Barcelona stock exchange, established in 1860, followed the formation of a half a dozen local banks. The "gold fever" mood of the 1880s and 1890s witnessed even greater economic growth, such as the creation of the transatlantic and trans-Mediterranean shipping companies, and even more celebration, with the founding of the Teatro del Liceo opera, center of the new bourgeoisie's public life. Loss of profits from overseas colonies in the Spanish-American War* was overcome by the transitory prosperity of World War I* that made Barcelona the refuge of Paris's *belle epoque* spirit.

The end of the war brought a new crisis, but the dictatorship of Gen. Miguel Primo de Rivera* overcame it with the improvement of highways, modernization of the telephone system, a subway, and the international exposition of 1929. The economic depression slowed growth from 1929 to 1936, although it was mitigated by the Generalitat's social policy, which established subsidies for unemployed workers (some six thousand in 1933). Barcelona's economy was radically transformed by the Spanish Civil War* and the collectivization of industrial enterprises, famine and rationing, and inflation accompanying the war.

Once the civil war ended, the old bourgeoisie was replaced by a new one, politically linked to Franquismo, the product of a policy of autarky. It was a bourgeoisie of the *nouveau riche*, based on the black market, real-estate speculation, and municipal corruption, which made great fortunes, but created nothing economically or culturally. With the development policy of ministers of the Opus Dei,* from the 1960s on, a new type of promoter appeared. He was an executive who poorly imitated American techniques to found enterprises that somewhat modernized the economic structure of Barcelona. The city nevertheless continued to suffer municipal corruption, real-estate speculation, and replacement of slums by high-rise public housing. Barcelona found itself surrounded by a belt of bedroom communities and condominiums (the rental apartment has almost disappeared), inhabited by immigrants who did not participate in the life of the city.

This changed after Franco's death in 1975, with elected city councils and new urban policies that removed industries from the city and improved less-favored neighborhoods, for example, through the creation of more green space. The prospect of the Olympics in 1992, which will take place in Barcelona, has accelerated this policy of making the city more presentable, although, despite everything, it continues to be one of the most densely populated cities in the world, surpassed only by Calcutta.

The administration of the city has passed through distinct stages. Medieval Barcelona was ruled by a Consell de Cent (Council of the Hundred) elected by the city's patricians. In the fifteenth century, after bitter struggles, artisans won the right to elect and be elected to the council, which disappeared with the War of Spanish Succession in 1714, at the same time the Generalitat did. Since the thirteenth century, it had been a permanent deputation of the Cortes charged with overseeing the crown's use of tax revenues. From 1714 until after the War of Independence,* the city's government also oversaw the functionaries appointed by the viceroy of Catalonia. With the establishment of nineteenth-century liberalism, the city council was elected by a restricted number of citizens until establishment of universal suffrage, when the parties of the center (autonomists) and the left (republicans) predominated. Primo de Rivera's dictatorship returned to an appointive system from Madrid until the Second Republic* of 1931 returned to elective city councils, which were controlled by the Esquerra Republicana party. During the civil war, this council was replaced by another made up of delegates from different republican and worker parties. During the Franco period, the council was successively administered by military men, mayors, and council members appointed by the Madrid government. In 1979, members of the city council were again elected, creating a majority of socialist council members.

The modern social and political history of Barcelona began with two shocks: the war against Felipe IV (1605–1665) in 1640 and the war against Felipe V* in 1700. The fall of Barcelona in 1714 put an end to all liberties and national institutions. Enlightened policies of the first Bourbons, however, gave the city the opportunity to recuperate, but prosperity and expansion in the nineteenth century led to renewed unrest. Barcelona sided with the liberals in the Carlist Wars (1833–1840), and the militia exercised considerable influence, especially with its "battalions of the tunic" formed by artisans. This did not keep Baldomero Espartero* from the bombing Barcelona in 1843 for refusing to submit to his rule, although liberal skirmishing was nothing compared to the radicalism of the era of industrialism, when workers began organizing, influenced by the doctrines of Mikhail Bakunin (1814–1876) and Karl Marx (1818–1883) imported by artisans returning from Europe or by agents of the First International who visited Barcelona, such as the Bakuninist Giusepe Fanelli (1827–1877) or the Marxist Paul Lafargue (1842–1911). In 1868, thirty-eight workers' societies met to organize a major labor association, and in addition, elections for the city council led to a republican victory.

Owners organized three groups to protect their interests: Casino Mercantil, Fomento de la Producción Nacional (later transformed into the powerful Fomento del Trabajo Nacional de los Industriales), and for landowners the Sociedad Agrícola de San Isidro. Initially, management could count upon the support of labor to cooperate to petition for protectionist policy to favor the development of industry. Catalan industry took advantage of the Franco-Prussian War (1871) to quintuple the number of textile factories.

The First Republic* of 1873 unleashed greater political agitation. Federalist ideas predominated among the working and middle classes, and a Catalan state was briefly proclaimed until the Catalan president in Madrid, Francesc Pi i Margall,* pressed them to remain in the unitary republic. The captain-general of Barcelona, Arsenio Martínez Campos (1831–1900), dissolved the section of the International and the workers' militias and prepared a military coup d'état to end the republic. A group of militiamen led by Joan Martí, the "Xic de les Barraquetes," resisted in the Barcelona suburb of Sarriá, while the bourgeoisie supported Martínez Campos. In reaction, the city was transformed into an anarchosyndicalist focal point over the next fifty years, with many illegal actions (one, a bomb in the Liceo, which caused many deaths) and strikes.

Barcelona thus became socially and politically the most advanced city of Spain. Pablo Iglesias (1850–1925), founder of the Socialist party* (PSOE), chose Barcelona as the place of creation for the Unión General de Trabajadores* (UGT), although it never became firmly rooted in Barcelona. At the same time, catalanismo, the recovery of Catalan nationalism, grew among the middle class and bourgeoisie, whose interests were opposed to those of the large owners and the nobility whom the Madrid government represented.

In 1900, the creation of the Lliga Regionalista party, autonomist and bourgeois, led in 1914 to the establishment of a preliminary form of autonomy, the Mancomunitat of Catalonia, thanks to strong pressure from all parties, from Carlists to republicans, united into the Solidaritat Catalana. The populist republican movement of Alejandro Lerroux* also took root, leading many workers to play a negative role in the Tragic Week in 1909. General strikes, industrial strikes, and terrorism (initiated by gangs in the pay of Germans to prevent sales to the Allies during World War I) became common. The unions had united in the Confederación Nacional del Trabajo (CNT) in 1911 at a congress held in Barcelona that in 1915 adopted an industrial-union organization that, twenty years later, characterized the North American Congress of Industrial Organizations (CIO). Barcelona was also the scene of the Asamblea de Parlamentarios (Assembly of the Parliamentarians) in 1917, which would have discarded the monarchy, if not for the defection of the Lliga, which frightened by the rise of anarchosyndicalism, moderated its catalanismo in exchange for the Madrid government's repression of the worker's movement, done by so-called free unions of gangsters in the pay of owners. Several years of attacks, strikes, bombings, and murder of owners and union leaders followed, until Gen. Miguel Primo de Rivera executed his coup d'état in Barcelona in 1923, which the Catalan bourgeoisie welcomed with relief.

Opposition to the dictatorship was weak, but stronger in Barcelona than in the rest of the country, because there middle- and working-class discontent and Catalan nationalism fused. The dictatorship prohibited Catalan, dissolved the Mancomunitat, and persecuted the CNT unions. The international exposition of 1929 was unsuccessful in extinguishing discontent, and with the fall of the dictatorship in 1930, Barcelona experienced general strikes, student protest, and the formation of new parties like the Esquerra, led by Francesc Macià,* who won the municipal elections of Apr. 1931.

Barcelona now relied on a city council with an Esquerra majority, a restored Generalitat, and a parliament that also had an Esquerra majority. In Oct. 1934, it experienced a tense period when Lluis Companys (1883–1940) proclaimed a Catalan republic and was jailed by the army. The elections of Feb. 1936 reestablished the Generalitat and the parliament. In the months of great agitation that followed, Barcelona was an oasis of tranquility, because the Catalan government followed a less vacillating policy than did Madrid.

The military uprising of July 1936 failed in Barcelona; groups of workers and the assault guard dominated the military. Once the coup had been transformed into civil war, Barcelona became the leading center of revolution: collectivization of industry, formation of militias, and control over foreign trade. There was an uncontrolled repression of the Right, which ended in Sept. 1936 when a government of the Generalitat, composed of all the antifascist parties, was formed. The imposition of the Soviet consul, Antonov Ovseenko (1844–1937), forced Companys to ally with the communist Partit Socialista Unificat de Catalunya* (PSUC) against the CNT and the POUM*; in May 1937, the streets of Barcelona experienced a brief civil war within the civil war. The alliance between the communists and the moderates predominated; Andreu Nin (1892–1937) was kidnapped and assassinated; and the central government was moved from Valencia to Barcelona in 1938, causing the collectivizations to be dissolved and the Generalitat to lose part of its power. Nationalist bombings claimed more than two thousand victims until the city fell in Jan. 1939 to Franco's forces.

During the Franco era, corrupt speculation was worsened by the inordinate growth of summer tourism that destroyed the landscape of the Catalan coast. Bitter over prohibition of Catalan and regional institutions, Barcelona saw three distinct kinds of opposition to the dictatorship (that of workers, of intellectuals and the middle class, and of supporters of catalanismo) manifest themselves in waves of illegal strikes in 1946–1948 and a general strike in 1952. Once again, Barcelona was the center of opposition in Spain and relied on the collaboration of the local Catalan church, more democratic than elsewhere in Spain.

Upon Franco's death in 1975, great demonstrations for autonomy and amnesty forced the Madrid government to accept the return of Josep Tarradellas (1899–

1988), the president of the Generalitat in exile. With the Generalitat's reestablishment, Barcelona elected a socialist municipal council and a Catalan government of the center-right (Jordi Pujol's Convergencia Democrática) which predominated in the Catalan Parliament. The city tried to escape corruption and speculation, recover its traditions, and reestablish its cultural institutions, a difficult task since almost half its population was made up of immigrants who spoke no Catalan.

For additional information, see V. Alba, *Catalonia: A Profile* (New York, 1975); A. Balcells, *Crisis económica y agitación social en Cataluña, 1930–1936* (Barcelona, 1971); F. Candel, *Els altres catalans* (Barcelona, 1964); J. M. Carandell, *Guía secreta de Barcelona* (Madrid, 1984); A. Jutglar, *Història crítica de la burguesa a Catalunya* (Barcelona, 1972); M. Reventós, *Els moviments socials a Barcelona* (Barcelona, 1987); C. Soldevila, *Guía de Barcelona* (Barcelona, 1952); J. Vicens-Vives, *Noticia de Catalunya* (Barcelona, 1960); and P. Vilar, *Cataluña en la España moderna* (Barcelona, 1987).

V. Alba

*Related entry*: CATALONIA.

**BAROJA Y NESSI, PÍO** (1872–1956), novelist, short-story writer, and essayist. This prolific Spanish writer was born in San Sebastian, in the Basque* Provinces. After briefly practicing medicine, he abandoned this career and assumed management of a family bakery in Madrid. He subsequently became a full-time writer and member of the Royal Academy. He is considered by many a member of the Generation of 1898,* in that he shared with its adherents a preoccupation with Spanish history and certain philosophical beliefs popular at the time, especially those of Friedrich Nietzsche (1844–1900) and Arthur Schopenhauer (1788–1860). Baroja viewed German civilization as politically and ideologically superior.

He was a shy man who never married and who tended to complain about his meager monetary resources. He wrote scores of novels; a multivolume autobiography, *Memorias*; a few plays; and collections of essays and short stories.

As was the case with other members of the Generation of 1898, Baroja traveled throughout Spain. His experiences are clearly reflected in many of his early novels and constitute a retelling of his wanderings in artistic terms.

In many of Baroja's works, the plot is of secondary importance. To an extent, some of his novels resemble paintings, portraying a hostile reality and its effect upon man. In them, one detects a sense of disillusionment, pessimism, and, perhaps, melancholy. He is fond of attacking established social patterns.

Baroja's prose is simple and direct. Its remarkable austerity has led to some criticism regarding its quality. As a novelist, he claimed to disdain both sophisticated and popular theories about the genre. In many ways, he was extremely conservative and disliked change. His works were widely read and still attract critical attention today. Notable modern novelists, among them Ernest Hemingway (1899–1961) and Spanish writer Camilo José Cela (1916– ), have commented favorably upon them.

Among Baroja's best works is *Camino de perfección* (1902). In it, the protagonist, Fernando Ossorio, seeks to find meaning in his existence. Since his instincts and ethical beliefs conflict, he is unable to achieve his objective. Throughout, Ossorio moves from one negative environment to another, unable to escape from the world surrounding him. There is no real conclusion to the work, an open-endedness typical of Baroja's fiction. The figure of the objective narrator is very important in *Camino de perfección*; this entity becomes evident throughout the novel as a type of companion for the protagonist. Descriptive passages abound, another common trait of Baroja's narrative.

Among the better-known works Baroja produced are *Vidas sombrías* (1900), *La casa de Aizgorri* (1900), *Paradox rey* (1906), *Zalacaín el aventurero* (1909), *El árbol de la ciencia* (1911), *El mundo es ansí* (1912), and *Juventud, egolatría* (1917).

For additional information, see R. Landeira, *The Modern Spanish Novel, 1898–1936* (Boston, 1985); and B. P. Patt, *Pío Baroja* (New York, 1971).

*L. T. González-del-Valle*

## BASQUE HOMELAND AND FREEDOM, EUZKADI TA ASKATASUNA

**(ETA),** Basque independence organization. Euzkadi ta Askatasuna is an insurgent organization formed in 1959 to secure the independence of the Basque* homeland, Euzkadi, from both Spain and France.* The organization traces its roots to Basque youth groups formed in France in the late 1940s and especially to a small study and action group called Ekin founded in Bilbao by four college students in 1952. For several years, leaders of the more conservative Basque Nationalist party* (BNP) attempted to arrange a merger of Ekin with their own youth wing, Euzko Gaztedi. The failure of these attempts resulted in the founding of ETA in 1959.

Throughout the first half of the 1960s, ETA concerned itself with internal matters such as building its organization, raising funds, and establishing the ideology on which to base its activist strategy. As a result of intense debate within the organization over correct ideological principles, as well as pressure from the Spanish police that led to the imprisonment or exile of a number of its early leaders, ETA gradually became more radical and more inclined toward insurgent violence. In the summer of 1968, a young ETA leader named Txabi Etxebarrieta was stopped at a Civil Guard* roadblock and killed. In retaliation, ETA assassinated a hated Spanish police inspector named Meliton Manazanas (1921–1968). These two deaths initiated a spiral of violence that has continued through the 1970s and 1980s, making ETA the most violent insurgent organization on the European continent. By the end of 1986, ETA had been responsible for approximately five hundred killed and a number of wounded probably half again as large. In the same period, about one hundred etarras (ETA members) had been killed, and many hundreds have been imprisoned or driven into exile in France or the Western Hemisphere.

Almost from its beginning, ETA has been plagued by many internal divisions that have seriously weakened the organization. At times, these splits have been produced by differences of opinion over tactics (for example, the appropriate use of violence) or by conflicts between competing leaders or factions. The principal source of acrimony, however, has been over the correct ideological principles to follow, especially with regard to the identification of the enemy. "Culturalists" within the organization have stressed the ethnic or linguistic basis of the struggle and have defined the enemy as Spain. Marxists, on the contrary, emphasize the class basis of the group and have defined the enemy as capitalism. These two groups have usually lost the debate to the more radical "Third Worlders" who stress both ethnicity and class and define the enemy as all Spaniards and all capitalists, Basque or not. From the mid–1970s, the principal division was between ETA-Militar ("Military" ETA), which tended to emphasize Basque ethnicity and armed struggle in its ideology, and ETA-Político-Militar ("Political-Military" ETA), which focused on Marxism and mass mobilization in its strategy. By the late 1980s, ETA-Militar had emerged as the principal operating wing of ETA, while the "political-military" wing had practically disappeared.

ETA's objectives were publicly announced for the first time in a single set of demands in early 1978, when in a press communiqué the organization presented the five principles of the KAS Alternative. (The acronym KAS stands for Koordinadora Abertzale Sozialista, or Patriotic Socialist Coordinating Council.) The five basic points include amnesty for all Basque political prisoners; legalization of all Basque political parties; withdrawal of all Spanish law-enforcement authorities from the Basque Provinces; measures to improve working and living conditions of the working class; and an autonomy statute that, among other things, recognizes the sovereignty of the Basque nation and its right to self-determination. In later versions, the integration of Navarre* in the Basque Autonomous Community has usually been included in the list. ETA has insisted that any negotiations aimed at ending the violence must accept the KAS Alternative as legitimate demands of the Basque people. This insistence has usually served as one of the reasons given by the Spanish government for refusing to enter into such negotiations, since the KAS Alternative obviously contains demands that no Spanish leader could fulfill.

To accomplish these goals, ETA has waged a campaign of armed struggle against representatives of the Spanish regime, including law-enforcement authorities and elected officials, and especially the hated Civil Guard. Occasionally, the group has also targeted Basques accused of complicity with Madrid or refusing to pay the "revolutionary taxes" ETA levies. ETA's attacks have also caused a number of deaths and injuries among civilian noncombatants. Until the early 1980s, ETA was careful to keep such casualties at a fairly low level, particularly as compared to insurgencies elsewhere, such as Northern Ireland or Lebanon. From the mid–1980s on, however, ETA's armed struggle regularly spread beyond the original target groups, and increasing numbers of uninvolved bystanders began to be caught up in the violence. The worst incident of this sort took place in June 1987, when a car bomb exploded in the parking garage of a Barcelona department store, killing more than twenty people.

The degree to which the Basque people support ETA's insurgency is, not surprisingly, the subject of considerable polemic. Voting data and public-opinion survey responses through the early 1980s suggest that about 5 percent of the Basque people support armed struggle to achieve independence, about 15 percent advocate achieving independence by peaceful means, about 20 percent voted for ETA-surrogate political parties and candidates, between 33 and 50 percent view ETA members as patriots or in some other positive way, and between 50 and 66 percent favor negotiating a settlement between ETA and Madrid. From the early 1980s on, all these percentages tended to rise, some rather dramatically, thus indicating a hardening of popular support for ETA at all levels.

During the first decade after the restoration of democracy in Spain, there were no fewer than six attempts to negotiate a cease-fire with ETA that became public and probably others that never did. Nevertheless, all these attempts failed, partly because of a complete absence of trust between the contending parties, but also because efforts to begin negotiations were sabotaged by strategically placed and timed acts of violence perpetrated by persons on both sides opposed to a cessation of hostilities. During the last half of 1987, there was yet another flurry of excitement in the press as talks between ETA and the Spanish government seemed to offer the prospect that after twenty years, there might really be an end to the insurgency.

For additional information, see R. Clark, *The Basque Insurgents: ETA, 1952–1980* (Madison, 1984); Euzkadi ta Askatasuna, *Documentos* (San Sebastian, 1979–1981); J. M. Garmendia, *Historia de ETA*, 2 vols. (San Sebastian, 1979); G. Jáuregui Bereciartu, *Ideología y estrategia política de ETA; Análisis de su evolución entre 1959 y 1968* (Madrid, 1981); M. Onaindia, *La lucha de clases en Euskadi* (San Sebastian, n.d.); J. M. Portell, *Los hombres de ETA* (Barcelona, 1974); and J. Zulaika, *Itziar: Basque Violence as Metaphor and Sacrament* (Reno, 1989).

*R. P. Clark*

*Related entry*: BASQUES.

**BASQUE NATIONALIST PARTY (BNP),** in Spanish, Partido Nacionalista Vasco (PNV), or in Basque, Eusko Alderdi Jeltzalea (EAJ), the first political party to espouse the principles of Basque* nationalism and the leading party in Basque politics during the 1930s and again after the restoration of democracy.

The PNV traces its origins to 1895, when Sabino de Arana y Goiri* and a handful of followers founded a political "bureau" in Bilbao to contest elections first in the city itself and later throughout Biscay province. After Arana's death in 1903, the bureau was converted into a formal party called Comunión Nacionalista Vasca (CNV), which gradually grew in electoral popularity through the first two decades of the century. From the late teens until 1920, the Basque nationalist movement was divided between the more moderate CNV, which was willing to work for autonomy within the Spanish state, and the more radical Aberri (Homeland) faction, which advocated independence from Spain. In 1921, the Aberri group split away from the CNV to form the original PNV, and for the rest of the decade, Basque nationalism waned as a force in the region.

In 1930, the two factions were reunited under the name Partido Nacionalista Vasco, and the party regained its prominence as the leading party in the Basque country. In the two important Spanish elections of 1933 and 1936, the PNV won 34 percent and 28 percent of the vote, respectively, making it the leading vote-getter, but still far from controlling a majority of the votes, although it came close in its strongholds in Biscay and Guipúzcoa.

When the civil war broke out, the PNV decided to support the republic and was able to hold the provinces of Biscay and Guipúzcoa against the initial uprising of the military insurgents. In Oct. 1936, the Cortes approved the pending Basque autonomy statute, and the PNV gained decisive control of the autonomous government through its dynamic president, José Antonio Aguirre (1904–1960). After the fall of Bilbao in 1937, Aguirre took the government into exile in France,* where it remained until 1940 and the outbreak of World War II.* During the war, the PNV continued to provide most of the leadership of the government-in-exile in Britain,* and in 1945, the government returned to its temporary exile residence in Paris to await the demise of Gen. Francisco Franco.*

Through the Franco years, the PNV retained its infrastructure in Spain under the leadership of Manuel Irujo (1891–1981). After Aguirre's death in 1960, the presidency of the Basque government in Paris passed to the vice-president, Jesús María Leizaola (1896–1989), also of the PNV. While many younger Basques saw the PNV as the party of tired middle-aged men who had lost the stomach for combat, the fact is that this group managed to hold the party together in the anti-Franco underground for forty years under extremely difficult and trying circumstances.

When democracy was restored in Spain after Franco's death, the PNV was in an excellent position to seize the initiative and return to its position as the dominant party in Euskadi. In Mar. 1977, the party held its first free and open assembly in Spain since the civil war. The meeting, in Pamplona, saw the emotional return from exile of leaders such as Irujo. It was also the occasion for approving the party's new platform, which seemed to eschew sovereign independence by pledging to work "for an autonomous Basque state . . . in solidarity with the freedom and rights of the rest of the peoples of the [Spanish] state." At this meeting, the assembly also elected to head the party the charismatic Navarrese leader Carlos Garaikoetxea (1937– ), the choice of Irujo as someone who could link Navarre* to the rest of the party.

For the next seven years, the PNV was the dominant party in Basque politics once again. Its share of the vote rose steadily until the 1982 municipal elections, when it won 39 percent, and the 1984 Basque parliamentary elections, when the ticket headed by the popular Garaikoetxea won an unprecedented 41 percent. Through the early 1980s, however, serious splits developed within the PNV over personal ambitions (Garaikoetxea against Biscayan party leader Xabier Arzalluz (1938– ) and ideological questions (moderation versus intransigence, autonomy versus independence, the provinces versus the Basque government). In late 1984, Garaikoetxea was forced out of the presidency and replaced by PNV leader José

Antonio Ardanza (1941– ). In the 1986 Spanish parliamentary elections, the PNV lost 150,000 votes and dropped to 28 percent of the vote because of this internal strife. Several months later, Garaikoetxea and his supporters split to form a new party called Basque Solidarity (Eusko Alkartasuna, EA), and in the two following elections in 1986 and 1987, the PNV's vote share declined again to 24 and 22 percent, respectively. At the close of 1987, it was clear that the PNV was no longer able to dominate Basque politics as it had in the 1977–84 period.

For additional information, see Partido Nacionalista Vasco, *Planteamientos político, socioeconómico y cultural* (Bilbao, 1977); S. G. Payne, *Basque Nationalism* (Reno, 1975); K. San Sebastián, *Historia del Partido Nacionalista Vasco* (San Sebastian, 1984).

R. P. Clark

*Related entry*: BASQUES.


**BASQUES.** Euskadi, the name Basque nationalists give to their homeland, is located on the littoral of the eastern end of the Bay of Biscay, where the Iberian peninsula curves north to become the southwest coast of France. The region extends inland for some 93 miles, through the juncture of the Pyrenees and Cantabrian Mountain ranges, and thence southward to the Ebro River.

The Basque region covers 12,799 square miles divided into seven provinces (or, as the Basques refer to them, "historical territories"). Labourd (Lapurdi), Basse Navarre (Benafarroa), and Soule (Zuberoa), the three northern provinces, together cover 1,836 square miles (14 percent of the total) and have been governed by France since the sixteenth century. The four provinces on the Spanish side of the border are Álava (Araba), which covers 1,889 square miles (15 percent of the total); Guipúzcoa (Gipuzkoa), 1,238 square miles (10 percent); Navarre* (Nafarroa), 6,461 square miles (50 percent); and Biscay (Bizkaia), 1,374 square miles (11 percent). The 10,963 square miles of Euskadi that lie in Spain are about 3.6 percent of Spain's total land area.

The territory of the Basque region is divided into five distinct zones that are defined by geography, climate, and economics. Traveling from north to south, one encounters first the coastal littoral, perhaps 31 miles wide, where the climate is cool and wet throughout the year. This zone is anchored on the west by the superindustrialized port city of Bilbao and its suburbs, the site of the Basque country's steel and shipbuilding industries, and on the east by the commercial and resort city of San Sebastian, as well as the coastal French Basque region. In between, most of the population lives in small fishing villages and resort towns.

Next are three complex and interlocking mountain zones: the *goierri* region of central Guipúzcoa, located almost wholly in the Cantabrian Mountains; the western Pyrenees, from Guipúzcoa to Roncesvalles, where the mountains range up to sixteen hundred feet; and the central Pyrenees, between Roncesvalles and the Aragon*-Navarre border. In these three subregions, most of the population lives either in midsized towns nestled in the numerous valleys, where many earn their living in small-scale manufacturing enterprises or services, or on the isolated traditional Basque farmsteads known as caseríos (*baserriak*), where sheep are the principal source of livelihood. Finally, the gently rolling plains of Álava and southern Navarre are characterized by a warmer and drier climate and dedicated to livestock and large-scale farming.

According to the 1981 census, the official population of the Basque Autonomous Community (Comunidad Autónoma del País Vasco, or CAPV) was 2,134,967, divided by province as follows: Álava, 260,580; Guipúzcoa, 692,986; and Biscay, 1,181,401. Driven by high rates of both birth and immigration, the population grew rapidly from the mid–1950s to the mid–1970s. Between 1950 and 1970, for example, the population of Biscay nearly doubled, from 570,000 to more than 1 million. From the late 1970s on, however, declining birth rates combined with net out-migration to cause the population to remain constant. In 1981, the CAPV accounted for 5.7 percent of the population of Spain.

There are two reasons that this figure of 2.1 million does not reveal how many Basques there are. First, not all Basques live in the CAPV. Second, the population of the CAPV is not all ethnic Basque. This issue is complicated considerably by the fact that there is no consensus on what the definition of "Basque" is and no agreement on the criteria by which they may be identified or on who may rightfully lay claim to the distinction.

For centuries, the Basque country has been a large-scale source of immigration to other lands, principally those of the Western Hemisphere. Recent estimates by linguists estimate that there are about eighty thousand speakers of Basque living outside Euskadi, which translates into a diaspora population of about one-quarter million. They are distributed roughly as follows: elsewhere in Spain, fifty thousand; elsewhere in Europe, twenty-five thousand; in the United States, fifty thousand; in Latin America, one hundred thousand; in the rest of the world, twenty-five thousand.

More specifically, there are two significant Basque populations living outside the CAPV. The first is in the Spanish province of Navarre, which in 1981 numbered 507,367, and the second is in France, which numbered 236,698 in 1982.

For reasons that are historical, ethnic, linguistic, political, and economic, the relationship of Navarre to the other Basque provinces has been a divisive issue since at least the turn of the century. Although many Basques consider Navarre to be the cradle of their nation (and the important role of the province in Basque political history stretches back to the Kingdom of Navarre in the tenth century), a number of elements prevent the integration of the province into a larger Basque entity. Of crucial importance is the question of collective identity, since most of Navarre's residents consider themselves solely Navarrese or as a mixture of Navarrese and Basque, and only a minority of 7 to 15 percent think of themselves as solely Basque.

The three Basque provinces north of the Pyrenees have been separated politically from the rest of the Basque population since the French-Spanish border treaty of 1512. Despite this lengthy and now seemingly permanent division, many Basque nationalists refuse to relinquish hope that some day the three French Basque provinces will be free to join an independent Basque nation. Since only about one-third of the French Basque population speak Euskera and consider themselves to be Basque rather than French, this reunification seems at best a dream.

If Basque society has sent many of its sons and daughters abroad, the thriving Basque economy has attracted thousands of non-Basque Spaniards who migrated there in search of jobs and a better way of life. Between 1900 and 1980, the number of people immigrating to the Basque region exceeded those who left by nearly 450,000, or an amount equal to nearly one-fourth of the 1981 population. Before World War I,* there was a net outflow of population, and between 1911 and 1951, immigration and emigration were roughly in balance. In the 1950s, however, the region received 130,000 more people than it lost; in the 1960s, this balance soared to nearly 275,000. In the 1970s, the flow began to reverse itself because of political upheaval and economic decline. Since 1976, when Euskadi's economic crisis began, the outflow increased, although it may have peaked in 1979 and 1980. Between 1977 and 1984, net emigration was nearly 51,000.

What these changes have produced is a population that is only marginally ethnic Basque and in many urban industrial areas, distinctly non-Basque in both language and identity. One authoritative study found that only 52 percent of the population was born in Euskadi of parents also born there, 11 percent was born in Euskadi of parents born elsewhere, and 35.5 percent was born outside the region. Census data from 1975 show that 33 percent of the CAPV population moved there from outside the region.

The wealth of the Basque region compared to most of the other regions of Spain is well known. Spurred by the upsurge in iron-ore mining and steel production in the fifty years after 1876, the industrial revolution came to Euskadi decades before it was felt in the rest of Spain, except for Catalonia.* The more industrialized provinces—Guipúzcoa and Biscay—have figured among the richest in Spain since World War I, and since the 1950s, Álava and Navarre have experienced a similar economic boom. In 1983, of Spain's fifty provinces, Álava ranked first in per capita output, Guipúzcoa seventh, Navarre eleventh, and Biscay thirteenth. Similar high rankings were also registered in per capita income: Álava, third; Guipúzcoa, ninth; Navarre, twelfth; and Biscay, fifteenth. As a unit, the CAPV had a per capita income in 1981 about 11 percent higher than Spain's average. In 1986, of Spain's seventeen autonomous communities, Navarre ranked second in standard of living, and the CAPV ranked third (Madrid ranked first). Since the late 1970s, however, Euskadi has experienced a lengthy and severe economic downturn marked by high unemployment rates, numerous business failures, and capital flight. Thus, in 1986, while Spain as a whole registered a growth rate of 3 percent in its gross national product, the CAPV grew only 1.5 percent, with the service sector the only part of the economy showing improvement. Industry stagnated, and agricultural output actually declined by 3.5 percent.

In many ways, the Basque region (as Spain as a whole) has reached the threshold of the postindustrial age, as indicated by such signs as the drop in the role of the primary sector in the economy (only 3.6 percent of the work force in farming and fishing), a declining birth rate (the lowest in Spain), and technology (only slightly fewer telephones per capita than France). While most advanced industrial regions experience a decline in their industrial sector and a consequent increase in services (to perhaps as high as 60 percent of the work force), Euskadi industry has continued to rise to account for 45 to 55 percent of the labor force. Such "overindustrialization" has left the Basque economy impoverished for the important management and coordination services badly needed by advanced industrial societies, as well as excessively vulnerable to harmful trends in the global economy, such as the rise in the cost of energy after 1973.

The Basque region is today, and has been for many decades, the setting for a clash between traditional and modern cultures. Modern cultural values in this context would include speaking Spanish, feeling oneself to be Spanish or perhaps even "European," working in industry or services, pursuing advanced education, and living in a large city. Contrasting traditional values would include speaking the Basque language, Euskera; feeling oneself to be a member of a narrowly defined, local community (one's town, for example); working in fishing or on a small farm; leaving school after the secondary grades; and living in a small village or on a farm. People who try to mix the two cultures are usually comfortably bilingual in Spanish and Euskera and live and work in a Spanish environment while sending their children to a Basque-language school, called *ikastola*. They themselves tend to be Basque as opposed to Spanish or be from a local village, and spend their time in both large cities and small villages.

Those parts of the population who hold traditional cultural values are concentrated in areas where local institutions protect them from intruding modernization. This area could be depicted on a map as an inverted triangle, with the base running along the coast of the Bay of Biscay and the peak lying in the Cantabrian Mountains just south of the juncture of the borders of Álava, Guipúzcoa, and Navarre. Included within the triangle are the two most important sectors of traditional Basque culture: the fishing villages of the coast and the baserriak of the mountains. Despite their isolation, these two important centers of Basque tradition have been in steady decline almost constantly since the introduction of heavy industry to Euskadi in the last quarter of the nineteenth century.

Since language use is such an important determinant of Basque identity and politics, one should note that the use of Euskera has been in steady decline for centuries, an erosion that has accelerated since the 1950s as tens of thousands of non-Basques have migrated to the region. The first official Basque-language census, published by the Basque government in 1984, confirmed what unofficial estimates had already observed: Euskera is a weakened minority language, although not yet a moribund one. Of the CAPV population, 23 percent can understand Euskera, and 21 percent can speak it, but only 13 percent can read and 10 percent write the language. (These data reflect the fact that Euskera has survived principally as an oral language without a significant written tradition and is conserved not by formal teaching in schools, but by informal teaching in the home.) The Basque government has launched a number of important programs to restore the language to a level of parity with Spanish, but only time will tell whether these efforts will succeed.

While most of the details of the early history of the Basques have been lost, the general outline is fairly well known. The Basques are among the oldest peoples of Europe and their language, Euskera, perhaps the oldest surviving language. After having experienced the passage of numerous visiting peoples—Celts, Romans, Goths, Franks, and Muslims, among others—the Basques reached the tenth century of the Christian era still fairly isolated from the flow of European history. In the tenth and eleventh centuries, the rising Kingdom of Navarre absorbed most of the rest of the Basque peoples and created for the first time a more or less unified Basque political entity. With the decline of Navarre, however, the region fell into disorder, and by the sixteenth century, the Basque Provinces had been integrated into the Kingdom of Castile.* From this time until the nineteenth century, relations between the several provinces and the Spanish crown were governed by the foral laws and privileges of medieval Spain. As a result of the centralization of the Spanish state, civil conflict (1822–1823), and the First Carlist War (1833–1840), the Basque fueros were gradually abolished over the course of the nineteenth century. The creation of the Second Republic* in 1931 offered the chance to create a new autonomous Basque regime, but these efforts were cut short by the Spanish Civil War,* begun at least partly because of fears from conservatives that Basque and Catalan autonomy presaged the disintegration of the Spanish state. After the war, the forty-year dictatorship of Gen. Francisco Franco* sought unsuccessfully to suppress all signs of Basque independence, especially the use of their language.

Since the restoration of democracy in Spain in 1977, the Basques have made significant strides toward establishing their own autonomous government. The 1978 Constitution provides for the creation of autonomous communities, and the Basques were the first to seek and obtain such a regime. A major failing in the CAPV is that Navarre is not a member; most Navarrese leaders preferred to have their own separate autonomous community, finally established in 1982. In 1979, however, the Basque Autonomy Statute was approved, and the first Basque Autonomous Parliament was elected in 1980. The statute establishes a parliamentary form of regional government, with an elected parliament choosing a president (*lehendakari*) at least once each four years. The first president was Carlos Garaikoetxea (1937– ), the dynamic and charismatic leader of the Basque Nationalist party* (PNV). Garaikoetxea was elected to a second term in 1984, but he was forced to resign the same year because of a split within the BNP. He was replaced by José Antonio Ardanza, who was reelected in 1986.

The Basque Autonomous Government has made impressive gains in policy areas that are crucial to the survival of Basque culture, especially preservation of the language through Basque-language schools, television in Euskera, and a vigorous publications program. In addition to having received its own independent taxing authority through the concierto económico with Madrid, the government has also established its own autonomous police force, an independent energy agency, and other institutions aimed at securing and preserving Basque self-rule. Much, however, remains to be done to fulfill the promise of the Basque Autonomy Statute.

For additional information, see J. M. de Azaola, *Vasconia y su destino* (Madrid, 1972, 1976); R. P. Clark, *The Basques: The Franco Years and Beyond* (Reno, 1979); R. Collins, *The Basques* (Oxford, 1986); W. Douglass, ed., *Basque Politics: A Case Study in Ethnic Nationalism* (Reno, 1985); W. Douglass and J. Bilbao, *Amerikanuak: Basques in the New World* (Reno, 1975); M. García Venero, *Historia del nacionalismo vasco*, 3d ed. (Madrid, 1969); D. Gómez-Ibáñez, *The Western Pyrenees: Differential Evolution of the French and Spanish Borderland* (Oxford, 1975); J. Intxausti, ed., *Euskal Herria: Historia y sociedad* (San Sebastian, 1985); L. A. Lerena et al., *Pasado, presente y futuro de la economía vasca* (Bilbao, 1984); L. Núñez, *Euskadi sur electoral* (San Sebastian, 1980) and *Clases sociales en Euskadi* (San Sebastian, 1977); and J. I. Ruiz Olabuenaga, *Atlas lingüístico vasco* (Vitoria, 1984).

*R. P. Clark*

**BÉCQUER, GUSTAVO ADOLFO** (1836–1870), Spanish lyric poet. In 1970–1971, the Spanish-speaking world commemorated the hundredth anniversary of Bécquer's death and of the first printing of his works, thus reaffirming his literary stature as one of the greatest Spanish lyric poets of all time. Although rooted in the romantic period, his poems, *Rimas* (1871), established Bécquer as the innovator of a poetic mode, "poesía pura," which reduced poetry to its basic elements, opening the way to a new freedom of poetic expression.

His pure, lyrical style encompassed an enhanced human quality that transcended time and place. Both his prose and his poetry included popular elements, unusual for the literary trends of his time. This popular ingredient was evident in the natural expression of feelings found in his poetry and in the use of popular tales as a source for his *Leyendas* (1860–1864). Bécquer thus paved the way for such famous poets as Juan Ramón Jiménez,* Antonio Machado,* and the Nicaraguan Rubén Darío (1867–1916).

Bécquer, inspired by an unrequited love for Julia Espín, began writing his *Rimas* in his early twenties while living in Madrid. Love, women, the nature of poetry, and death were the major themes of his writing, although his approach to these traditional themes was fresh and set him apart from other romantic poets. After his unhappy marriage to Casta Esteban, a note of irony and melancholy entered his poetry.

Death was an intrinsic part of his life. Born in Seville, Bécquer was one of eight children who suffered the loss of both parents at an early age. The god-mother with whom he lived for a time died when Bécquer was a teenager. His closest brother, Valeriano, died in Sept. 1870. Bécquer himself died only four months later in Madrid after a short illness; he was only thirty-four.

His best-known works are *Rimas, Leyendas, Cartas desde mi celda, Cartas literarias a una mujer,* and *Historia de los templos de España.*

For additional information, see R. Benítez, *Bécquer tradicionalista* (Madrid, 1971); J. P. Díaz, *Gustavo Adolfo Bécquer* (Madrid, 1985); and J. de Entrambasaguas, *La obra poética de Bécquer* (Madrid, 1974).

*R. M. Fernández*

**BERENGUER Y FUESTE, DÁMASO** (1873–1953), Spanish army* general and monarchical politician. Berenguer was born in Remedios, Cuba, on 4 Aug. 1873. The son of an aristocratic Catalan officer serving in the Spanish colonial army in Cuba, he followed in his father's footsteps when he entered the General Military Academy in 1889. He graduated as a cavalry second lieutenant in 1892 and served a brief tour of duty in Spain. In 1894, he was posted to Cuba and took part in the fighting of the mid–1890s as well as the Spanish-American War* against the United States.* His valorous conduct during these campaigns earned him a series of promotions through the rank of major.

In 1898, he returned to Spain and served until 1902 as aide-de-camp to the captain general of Andalusia.* Subsequently, he was transferred to a cavalry regiment, and from 1906 to 1908, he served on the army's Tactics Commission, which revised basic infantry tactics. In 1909, he was promoted to the rank of lieutenant colonel and named aide-de-camp to the minister of war, his first ''political'' assignment.

In Nov. 1909, Berenguer began his long association with Spanish colonial ambitions in Morocco* when he was assigned to command a cavalry squadron in Spain's North African presidio of Melilla. Twenty months later, he organized and assumed command of the first group of indigenous Moroccan forces assigned directly to the Spanish army. He led these troops in the successful Kert campaign of 1911–1912 and was promoted to colonel.

After the establishment of Spain's Moroccan protectorate in Nov. 1912, Ber-enguer and his indigenous troops were transferred to the capital of Tetuan and participated in a series of difficult campaigns to pacify the area around the city. Promoted to brigadier general, he continued to serve in Morocco until Feb. 1916, when he was named military governor of Malaga. In 1918, he was promoted to major general and appointed under secretary of war in the ''National Govern-ment'' of Antonio Maura* from Mar. to Nov. 1918, also serving later as minister of war in the liberal cabinets of Manuel García Prieto (1859–1938) and the conde de Romanones (1863–1950).

On 23 Jan. 1919, Romanones appointed Berenguer high commissioner of Spain's Moroccan protectorate and authorized him to complete the pacification of the zone. For two years, Berenguer's program of slow, well-prepared military advances was mostly successful, but in mid–1921, his subordinate in Melilla, Gen. Manuel Fernández Silvestre (1871–1921), met considerable resistance from the indigenous inhabitants of the central Rif. Led by Muhammad ibn Abd al-Krim al-Khatabi (1882–1963), these Riffian tribesmen precipitated the Spanish retreat at Anwal* that turned into a catastrophic rout and resulted in 13,192 Spanish casualties. Although the territory lost was eventually recaptured, Berenguer bore the chief military responsibility for the debacle and was indicted for negligence and removed from his post in July 1922.

In July 1924, Berenguer was found guilty for the Anwal disaster by the Supreme Military Council, but was immediately pardoned by the Spanish dictator, Gen. Miguel Primo de Rivera,* promoted to lieutenant general, and named as the head of the military household of Alfonso XIII.* Moreover, in 1927, the king conferred the title of conde de Xauen on him for his pre–1921 services in Morocco.

With the fall of Gen. Primo de Rivera from power on 19 Jan. 1930, Alfonso hurriedly entrusted the government to Berenguer on 30 Jan. with instructions to prepare for a return to the pre–1923 constitutional regime. The reestablishment of political liberties under the so-called Berenguer "dictablanda," however, produced an explosion of antimonarchical sentiment and activity. By Aug. 1930, the various republican groups, the Socialist party,* and the Catalan nationalists had agreed upon the Pact of San Sebastian, which elaborated a political platform to usher in, by force if necessary, a republican parliamentary government. Berenguer countered by announcing legislative elections for 1 Mar. 1931, in what turned out to be a futile gesture, since the abortive Jaca insurrection of 12 Dec. 1930, and the lack of solid support for Alfonso, or a return to the ancien régime, even on the part of the old monarchical politicians, signaled the end of Berenguer's ministry on 14 Feb. 1931. Berenguer, however, remained as minister of war in the subsequent government, which was eventually brought down by the proclamation of the Second Republic* in Apr. 1931.

Republican antipathy for the monarchy found a high-profile scapegoat in Berenguer. On 20 Apr. 1931, he was arrested and charged in connection with the courts-martial and executions of the main protagonists of the Jaca rising. After a period of confinement in the Alcázar in Segovia, Berenguer was transferred to a military prison in Sept. 1931. Despite increasingly poor health, he remained incarcerated until Dec. 1932, when the government of Manuel Azaña* "revised" the penalties for the Jaca incident and freed him. Shortly after his release, Berenguer was put on reserve status, effectively ending his military career. Eventually, on 12 May 1935, at the beginning of the last ministry of Alejandro Lerroux,* he was absolved of any criminal responsibility for the suppression of the Jaca insurrection. He survived the civil war and spent his old age in retirement writing memoirs about Morocco and Alfonso. He died in Madrid on 19 May 1953.

For additional information, see D. Berenguer y Fueste, *Campañas en el Rif y Yebvala. Notas y documentos de mi diario de operaciones* (Madrid, 1923) and *De la Dictadura a la República*, 2d ed. (Madrid, 1975); and C. P. Boyd, *Praetorian Politics in Liberal Spain* (Chapel Hill, 1979).

S. E. Fleming

*Related entries*: ANWAL; ARMY; SECOND REPUBLIC.

**BLASCO IBÁÑEZ, VICENTE** (1867–1928), novelist, journalist, and politician. Born in Valencia,* as a high-school student Blasco Ibáñez was already contributing to a small, liberal publication, *El Turia*. He studied law at the University of Valencia and went to Madrid in the early 1880s to seek his fortune. He graduated from law school there in 1888. By then, he was a regular contributor to *El Correo Valenciano* and a liberal activist, which led to his persecution and escape to Paris in 1891.

Between 1892 and 1894, Blasco Ibáñez wrote volumes against the monarchy and the church (for example, *¡Viva la república!* and *Los fanáticos*). He also established a publishing house, La Propaganda Democrática, devoted to his ideas. In 1894, he founded a newspaper, *El Pueblo*, a publication that eventually endorsed granting political autonomy to Cuba.

In 1898, Blasco Ibáñez was elected to the Cortes, a position to which he was reelected six times until he became disillusioned with politics. Subsequently, he traveled extensively and became a supporter of the Allied cause during World War I,* as evidenced by his novel *Los cuatro jinetes del apocalipsis* (1916), eventually made into a film in Hollywood.

Although he was a public figure and essayist, Blasco Ibáñez is remembered primarily as a novelist and short-story writer influenced by nineteenth-century realism and naturalism. In his novels, he is a masterful painter of landscapes. His descriptive passages of his native Valencia and his careful reproduction of Valencian speech are common traits of much of his fiction. His characters are often individuals in conflict with the social environment in which they live.

Among his better-known works are *Arroz y Tartana* (1894), *La barraca* (1898), *Cañas y barro* (1902), *La catedral* (1903), *La horda* (1905), and *Sangre y arena* (1908).

For additional information, see C. Blasco Aguinaga, *Juventud de 98* (Madrid, 1970); A. G. Day and E. C. Knowlton, Jr., *Vicente Blasco Ibáñez* (New York, 1972); and R. Landeira, *The Modern Spanish Novel, 1898–1936* (Boston, 1985).

L. T. González-del-Valle

*Related entry*: VALENCIA.

**BLUE DIVISION** (1941–1943), Spanish volunteer infantry division on the Russian front during World War II.* With the German attack on the Soviet Union (June 1941), the government of Gen. Francisco Franco,* although adamantly maintaining its tenuous position of neutrality, permitted and encouraged the formation of a unit of volunteers to fight against bolshevism. It was hoped that this might in part relieve Axis pressure on Spain to enter World War II as an ally in payment for their assistance to the nationalist side during the late Spanish Civil War.

The Spanish Council of Ministers decided to form a full infantry division, controlled by the Alto Estado Mayor and removed from the politically oriented Falange.* Gen. Agustín Muñoz Grandes (1869–1970) was named division commander. More than 50 percent of the officers and noncommissioned officers had to be professional soldiers of Spain's military forces. In fact, the number far exceeded that percentage. Many professional officers accepted reduction in rank to be accepted. Within hours, thousands of volunteers were arriving from all parts of Spain and from all classes of society.

The original order of battle was four regiments of infantry; one of artillery; an antitank unit; transport service; and battalions of assault engineers, communications, and scouts. There were support units of service and supply, medical services, veterinary and pharmacy, military police, postal service, and 25 chaplains. Anticipating that they would be a motorized division, the proper specialists were included. The grand total was 18,693 officers and troops, including 38 female nurses. Wearing their "blue shirts," from which came their name Blue Division, the first units departed by train on 30 June for Grafenwöhr, Germany.* The last unit arrived on 23 July 1941.

Unlike other foreign volunteers in the German force, they were not made members of the Waffen SS. At Spanish insistence that they were a military force, not a militia of a political party, they were made the 250th Infantry Division of the Wehrmacht and issued army uniforms and equipment. The divisionarios took their military oath in a mass ceremony on 31 July.

To their disappointment and confusion, they were reorganized from a motorized division into a horse-drawn division and equipped with six thousand horses. One infantry regiment was dissolved, with some of its personnel added to other units, while the remainder formed a special battalion known as the 250th Reserve Battalion. The total strength was reduced to seventeen thousand. In addition to the infantry division, a Spanish fighter squadron, the Escuadrilla Azul de Caza, of seventeen pilots and eighty support personnel, was integrated into the Luftwaffe at Tempelhof.

With only a month's training, on 21 Aug. the division started for the Russian front. They moved first by train, but the last six hundred miles were on foot, which took a heavy toll on the horses.

The division was to have been sent to the Moscow center, but bad reports on the quality of the division made the sector commander want no part of them. Thus, they were diverted north to Novgorod, taking up extended positions (10 Oct.) in sleet and snow along the Volkhov River. First losses were recorded two days later. Then, on 18 Oct., they fought their way under heavy fire across the river in what was known as the battle of the Volkhov. The Germans, who had viewed the Latins with scorn, now praised them for their determination and valor. Soon the temperature dropped far below zero, and the Spaniards beat back assault after assault. On 8 Dec., in minus-forty-degree weather, they were ordered back across the Volkhov to defensive positions. At the end of the month, they counted 718 dead, 1,832 wounded, 725 severe cases of frostbite, and 86 missing.

As they repelled assaults on their positions, a special ski company (206 men) was organized and in Jan. crossed the frozen Lake Ilmen to relieve pressure on German forces. The effort was successful but costly, with only 12 combatants surviving. By late Mar. 1942, the division counted 5,125 casualties, with 1,032 killed and 300 frozen. It went on, though, to assist in reducing the Volkhov Pocket. Meanwhile, in Spain, recruitment and training of replacements and rotating personnel were underway.

In Sept. 1942, the re-formed division was ordered into an eighteen-mile front facing Leningrad, where it traded repeated blows with the Red Army. General Emilio Estaban-Infantes replaced Gen. Muñoz Grandes as commander. In minus-forty-degree weather on 16 Jan. 1942, a battalion of five hundred was ordered to relieve pressure on German forces at Maga. The mission was accomplished, but only one officer and eight men remained effective.

The Red Army was determined to destroy the division and on 10 Feb. 1943 launched a massive attack on the narrow Krasny Bor sector held by the 262nd Regiment. Expecting the assault, the Spaniards had reinforced the zone with their limited reserves.

The great mass of the Soviet assault (two divisions and a tank brigade) shattered the companies of the 262nd Regiment, and surviving elements began to fall back. The Assault Engineer Company held its position for twenty-two hours and then fought a two-and-one-half-mile withdrawal to Krasny Bor, where the Soviet assault stalled. The Spaniards lost 2,500 men, including 126 officers. The cost to the Soviets, however, was more than 11,000. The Spaniards continued to hold their front through the spring, summer, and early fall of 1943.

The Allies had largely ignored the existence of the Spaniards in the Soviet Union until the summer of 1943, when they began to make an issue of the Blue Division. Madrid, however, had been considering their withdrawal for some time. The division was ordered to leave its positions at eight in the morning on 9 Oct. 1943 and return to Spain by Christmas. To placate Berlin, some troops were organized into a Spanish legion of three battalions that remained on the front. This legion was caught in the massive Soviet offensive of Jan. 1944. On 21 Feb., Adolf Hitler (1889–1945) ordered the Spaniards returned to Spain. The Blue Air Squadron was also relieved.

In all, some 47,000 Spaniards served on the Russian front. Among the ground forces, they suffered 3,943 dead, 8,466 wounded, 321 captured (of whom 94 died), and 326 missing. The air squadron lost 12 pilots killed, 8 wounded, and 1 captured.

For additional information, see E. Estaban-Infantes, *La División Azul donde Asia empieza* (Barcelona, 1956); R. L. Proctor, *Agony of a Neutral: Spanish-German Wartime Relations and the "Blue Division"* (Moscow, Id., 1974); T. Salvador, *División 250* (Barcelona, 1962); F. Vadillo, *Orillias del Voljov* (Barcelona, 1967), *Arrabales de Leningrado* (Barcelona, 1971), and *Balada final de la División Azul: Los legionarios* (Madrid, 1984).

R. L. Proctor

*Related entry*: WORLD WAR II.

**BORROW, GEORGE** (1803–1881), British Hispanist. As a youth, Borrow read for the law, the best profession, in his view, for those who intended to have none. He worked as a translator and free-lance writer until 1832, when the British and Foreign Bible Society hired him, because of his linguistic abilities, to disseminate vernacular Bibles. His first assignment was to Russia and then, in 1836–1840, to Spain, a mission the society was reluctant to endorse, considering illiteracy, rather than Catholicism,* an insurmountable obstacle to success. The objective was to institute Bible reading in Spanish schools.

Borrow made three separate trips to Spain: Nov. 1835–Sept. 1836, Nov. 1836–Sept. 1838, and Dec. 1838–Apr. 1840. Upon his arrival in Madrid in Jan. 1836, he had a celebrated interview with the prime minister, Juan Álvarez Mendizábal,* who told him that "it is not Bibles we want, but guns and gunpowder" to put down Carlism.* Although Mendizábal's successor, Francisco Javier Istúriz (1790–1871), was more favorable to Borrow's mission, the government ultimately decided for the Catholic position, which was not to permit the dissemination of vernacular Bibles lacking notes. This led to Borrow's arrest (which, characteristically, he welcomed, as a means to gather data for his dictionary of underworld jargon) and to numerous confiscations both of the Castilian version of the dictionary, as well as two translations of St. Luke, Borrow's in caló, the gypsy language, and Dr. Oteiza's in Basque.

In Madrid, Borrow was in contact with a number of intellectuals, including Serafín Estébanez Calderón (1799–1867), who provided him with materials relating to Spanish gypsies. Borrow used both his knowledge of the British gypsy language Romany to learn the Spanish gypsy dialect and the gypsy network as a way of getting around the country on a dangerous mission, avoiding the authorities whenever possible. Upon his return to Britain, Borrow published *The Zincali* (1841), an account of Spanish gypsy customs and language.

In 1843, Borrow published his masterpiece, *The Bible in Spain*, which sold nearly twenty thousand copies in English the first year and established Borrow both as a celebrity and a Hispanist. The book's popularity rested on his forthright and dramatic narrative style that had the effect, according to Borrow's friend Richard Ford (1795–1858), of authenticating the bizarre stories he recounted. In spite of charges by later critics that Borrow fictionalized his experiences, they are for the most part true. Borrow, as did Ford, had a "colonial" attitude, in that he liked Spain while disliking most Spaniards and preferring the company of gypsies to "proper" folk.

Borrow described the book to John Murray, his publisher, as "a queer book . . . containing all my queer adventures in that queer country whilst engaged in distributing the Gospel." His zeal as a missionary has correctly been questioned. Borrow's evangelical spirit was motivated mainly by a fanatical antipapism, and it is quite clear that his true mission was to gather material for an adventure book, not to distribute the Gospel. His religious hypocrisy was concealed by his rhetoric, which seemed ironic to the skeptical, but serious to middle-class British evangelicals.

The Spanish reception of *The Bible in Spain* split along predictable ideological lines. To the conservative critic Marcelino Menéndez y Pelayo,* Borrow was an infidel charlatan, whereas to the future president of the Second Republic,* Manuel Azaña,* he was an unsparing liberal critic of traditional Spanish society. To Azaña, Borrow's most penetrating commentator in any language, the book, like *Don Quixote* (1605, 1615), is superficially the account of his travels from La Mancha to Barcelona and back. According to Azaña, the literary expression of Borrow's love for inns, mule drivers, and the life of the road is filtered through his reading of Cervantes. *The Bible in Spain* shares with *Don Quixote* the tension between realism and chimera. Borrow, like Quixote, was totally convinced of the validity of his mission, impossible by definition, and carried out in a totally different environment.

For additional information, see M. Azaña, "Jorge Borrow y 'La Biblia en España,' " *Obras completas* (Mexico City, 1966–1968); M. Collie, *George Borrow, Eccentric* (Cambridge, 1982); and W. I. Knapp, *Life, Writings and Correspondence of George Borrow* (New York, 1899).

*T. F. Glick*

*Related entries*: BRITAIN; CATHOLICISM

**BRAVO MURILLO, JUAN** (1803–1873), conservative, Catholic politician during the reign of Isabel II.* Bravo was born in the province of Badajoz on 9 June 1803. His father, a professor of Latin, encouraged him to follow a religious vocation, and Bravo studied for more than twelve years before deciding to become a lawyer, although his religious preoccupation remained strong and led him to teach philosophy and theology at Seville for a short time. In 1834, however, he became fiscal of the audiencia of Cáceres and a year later, of Oviedo, although he soon left this post for a legal career in Madrid. In the capital, he defended the court and church against the liberals' confiscation of royal and clerical lands, castigating them for creating an administrative regime rather than a state representing Spanish values. Some of his ideas were incorporated into the Constitution of 1845.

Bravo served briefly as minister of justice in the cabinet of the marqués de Casa Irujo in 1847 and as minister of commerce, industry, and public instruction under Gen. Ramón María Narváez* from 1847 to 1849. While Bravo was minister of the treasury in 1849 and 1850, his efforts to consolidate the national debt won him support from the queen, Isabel II, who nominated him to succeed Narváez on 14 Jan. 1851.

His cabinet, a technocracy made up of enlightened despots, ruled until 14 Dec. 1852. Its major accomplishment was the signing of a concordat with the papacy* on 11 May 1851, which attempted to settle outstanding financial problems caused by liberal confiscation of ecclesiastical properties. New laws facilitating railway finance and construction followed on 3 Dec., and a new code of administrative law was created on 18 June 1852.

These accomplishments led Bravo to draw up a new constitution that would have greatly strengthened executive power, an issue that had been at the heart of parliamentary debate for more than a decade. Opposition arose, because Isabel II welcomed this reform as a defense against growing criticism of the court's wastefulness and inefficiency, and Bravo was finally forced to resign on 14 Dec. 1852. Although he briefly presided over the Cortes in 1858, his authoritarian predilections never again gave him the support necessary to run for national office, and publication of his memoirs, *Opúsculos*, further underscored his dictatorial views. He died in Madrid on 10 Jan. 1873.

For additional information, see J. Bravo Murillo, *Opúsculos*, 6 vols. (Madrid, 1863–1874); A. Bullón de Mendoza, *Bravo Murillo y su significación en la política española* (Madrid, 1950); and J. L. Comellas, *La teoría del régimen liberal* (Madrid, 1962).

*R. W. Kern*

*Related entry*: ISABEL II.


**BRITAIN,** relations with Spain. In many respects, the relationship between Spain and Britain reached its highest intensity a century or more before the start of the eighteenth century with the brief and grim marriage of Felipe II (1527–1598) to Mary Tudor (1516–1558) in 1554. If any child had been born of this union, the later history of Anglo-Spanish relations might have been substantially different, but such was not to be.

By the time of the War of Spanish Succession,* Britain's aim in preventing the Franco-Spanish union, besides the general objective of maintaining a European balance of power, was also the more specific one of gaining freer access to Latin American markets. Combat swirled to and fro across the peninsula from 1704 to 1711. A British general reported in 1710: "We are not masters, in Castile, of more ground than we encamp on." In the end, it was external events that resolved the contest, and Britain by the Treaty of Utrecht gained from Spain Gibraltar* and Minorca, taken in 1704 and 1708, as well as a thirty-year dominance of the asiento de negros, or slave monopoly, together with other general trading rights.

For the next century, Britain's expansion of its commercial access to Spanish America (still the world's main source of bullion) remained a central concern, perhaps the central concern, of Britain in its relations with Spain—until, in fact, independence came to the Spanish colonies, and Spain became irrelevant to their commercial dealings. The slave asiento offered Britain new opportunities for penetrating the colonial market, for two reasons. First, slave ships could be used to carry goods (strictly speaking, contraband) along with the slaves to the major Spanish American ports of entry. Second, the "annual ship" granted to Britain by the Treaty of Utrecht allowed a five-hundred-ton ship loaded with goods to sell goods to the colonies. The terms of this concession had been made still more generous in Bubb's Treaty of 1716, so that throughout the 1720s, British trade with Spanish America prospered at the expense of peninsular merchants. In 1730, for instance, the annual ship was so successful in disposing of its goods at the Portobelo trade fair on the isthmus of Panama that it carried off half the silver sent up from Peru for purchase of European imports, while the Spanish galleons present were unable to sell most of their cargoes.

Events like this kept relations in constant tension in the decades after Utrecht, but other frictions also arose. In 1717, for example, Spain overran Sardinia in an attempt to recover its Italian territories and quickly found itself opposed by an alliance of Austria, France,* Holland, and Britain. One outcome was that half the Spanish Mediterranean fleet was lost in battle with Britain off Sicily in Aug. 1718.

A new round of Anglo-Spanish combat came in 1739 with the Anglo-Spanish War,* which merged into the general European conflict over the Austrian Succession (1740–1748), in which, again, Spain and France were pitted against Britain and Austria. Much of the British war effort was directed against France; Fernando VI (1746–1759), in any case, followed a broadly neutral policy. The treaties concluding the conflict finally extinguished the British asiento, granting cash compensation for the four years it still had to run under the terms of Utrecht, generally giving Britain favorable access to American trade. Spanish-British relations entered a period of ease previously unknown in the eighteenth century.

This respite ended shortly after Spain was drawn into the final stages of the Seven Years' War* by its connection with France. Fernando kept clear, but after his death, Carlos III* took Spain into another Family Compact in 1761, and hence once again into war with Britain. By now British power, especially at sea, was a match for both the Bourbon nations, and the consequences were severe: Spain saw Havana and Manila quickly taken, while France was driven out of North America. At the reckoning in 1763, Britain returned Cuba to Spain, but only in exchange for Florida. France ceded Louisiana to Spain and surrendered all mainland territory east of the Mississippi to Britain. The outcome was that Britain and Spain emerged as the sole two large colonial powers in America, with Britain obviously rising and threatening further expansion. In response, Carlos III set in motion broad reforms in the American empire, designed to strengthen Spain's grip on the colonies and make them more profitable to the home country—aims achieved for a while, but only at the cost of colonial resentment that disposed them to entertain thoughts of independence in the early nineteenth century.

Spain's empire was also weakened by Iberian intervention in the North American War of Independence. France declared war on Britain in 1778, while Spain did so in 1779. This time, stronger at sea than before, the French and Spaniards dominated the Caribbean, and the war at least yielded to Spain the reconquest of Florida, but the new freedom of the United States* became a guiding beacon for emancipation-minded Spanish Americans, and the gain of Florida was a poor exchange for the damage done to Spain's grip on Central and South America.

Revolution came to France, however, before it took root in the colonies. Spain initially and for two years (1793–1795) struck out against the abomination of an atheistic, king-killing neighbor to the north; but then, after invasion and defeats, in 1796 relented, and took up a defensive and offensive alliance with

France against Britain, which enmeshed Spain in the struggles and Napoleonic ambitions of France for almost the next twenty years, first making it Britain's adversary and finally its ally. The immediate effects of the war, declared in 1796, were naval defeat off Cape St. Vincent and the taking of Trinidad. This became a permanent loss in 1802, when Napoleon Bonaparte (1769–1821), in the Peace of Amiens made with Britain, yielded up Spain's title to the island— without so informing the Spanish government. It was an act all too typical of the satellite relationship with France into which Spain had sunk in these turbulent years.

Worse still came in 1803, when, on the resumption of Anglo-French hostilities, Napoleon sold Louisiana (returned to France under duress in 1799) to the United States* to raise money, despite the French obligation by treaty with Spain never to alienate that territory. Late in 1804, Spain was again pulled into the Franco-British power struggle, forced to drain its own and its colonies' resources to finance Napoleon's war effort, and then in Oct. 1805, drawn into crushing naval defeat at Trafalgar.*

Despairing of the French alliance, Spain tried unsuccessfully to change sides. This shift soon took place anyway, on the French invasion of Spain in early 1808 and the imposition of Napoleon of his brother Joseph as José I.* Spain immediately found itself transformed into Britain's ally against France, and Iberia became the main battlefield on which the combat between Europe's two super-powers was fought out between 1808 and 1814. The final success of the Anglo-Spanish-Portuguese alliance against France owed much to the newly revealed guerrilla talents of the Spaniards and to the quality of command provided by British generals such as Sir Arthur Wellesley, later duke of Wellington.*

The Anglo-Spanish alliance held many stresses, chief among them Britain's intentions toward the Spanish-American colonies. As for two centuries past, the British aspiration here was to gain freer access to the market presented by the colonies. As Spain's dominant ally, Britain managed to extract a qualified per-mission to trade with the colonies from the Cadiz government of Spain in 1810. The extent and length of this concession were disputed, however, and it was not enough to stop Britain from contemplating the advantages of an independent Spanish America. To these commercial considerations, political feelings soon gave reinforcement. The restoration of the Bourbon monarchy in Spain in 1814 produced much liberal distaste in Britain, and an inclination to favor freedom in Spanish America. So, for both economic and political reasons, Britain, while not lending official aid to the independence movements, did not discourage private support for them, in the form of loans, supplies of arms, and the partic-ipation of individuals in the armies of liberation.

Once the Spanish-American colonies were independent, British interest in Spain fell off sharply. The markets that Britain had so long coveted were now directly accessible, and the Spanish market itself was of little consequence. Spain ceased to be a significant prize of European conflict, and being neglected by other European powers became its normal condition in the nineteenth century, in marked contrast to the willing or unwilling involvement in alien struggles that had dominated the country's eighteenth-century history.

Despite this disengagement, a few particulars of Anglo-Spanish relations in the nineteenth century are worth noting. Britain, rejecting the notion of intervention, declined to support the French entry into Spain in 1823 that the other participants of the Congress of Verona backed. In 1834, however, Britain retreated from nonintervention in consenting to enter a Quadruple Alliance with Spain, Portugal,* and France. The purpose was in part to suppress the pretenders to the Spanish and Portuguese thrones, don Carlos and don Miguel, respectively, and thus support constitutionality of monarchy and government in both countries. When don Carlos led his reactionary forces from 1834 to 1839 in the first Carlist War (1833–1840), Britain agreed to supply the Spanish government with arms and ammunition to combat this internal threat. In 1835, Britain went on to suspend the Foreign Enlistment Act, so permitting Englishmen to enlist in a foreign legion fighting in Spain for liberalism and constitutionalism against the threat of Carlism.* In general, Britain supported the liberal cause in Spain during the first half of the nineteenth century—for instance, opposing the 1846 plan of a conservative France under Louis Philippe (1773–1850) to tighten the bond between France and Spain through intermarriage of the royal families once again.

The British influence for moderation in Spain appeared clearly again in 1874, when the young Alfonso, son of Isabel II,* reached sixteen, the age of royal majority. He left his cadetship at Sandhurst to return in Jan. 1875 to his country, now exhausted from the chaos of the First Republic* and the rigors of the Second Carlist War (1873–1876). Though Alfonso intervened little in politics during the eleven years of his reign, his admiration of British parliamentary government certainly was in consonance with Spain's inclination to back away from the extremes of republicanism. The outcome was the conciliatory and moderately conservative constitution of 1876, which remained in force until the new collapse of the monarchy in 1931.

The Anglo-Spanish connection, at least at the royal level, was reinstated at the opening of the twentieth century when, in 1906, Alfonso XIII,* son and successor of Alfonso XII,* married Princess Victoria Eugenia (1887–1969). It was not this link, though, so much as conflicting internal inclinations, that kept Spain neutral in World War I*: army,* church, and conservatives generally supported Germany,* which proffered possibilities about Gibraltar*; while liberals, with strong popular support, backed the Allied cause. Twenty years later, Britain itself chose nonintervention in the Spanish Civil War.* Neville Chamberlain (1869–1940) feared that general war might ensue if European nations ranged themselves with the contending factions in Spain. Conservative antipathy to the Red elements of Spanish politics also disinclined them to take any stand against the rigid and militaristic authoritarianism of Gen. Francisco Franco.* Labor leaders in Britain, though naturally sympathetic to the republican cause, equally feared general war if other European countries undertook to give active support to one side or the other in the Spanish conflict. They abandoned non-interventionism only in Oct. 1937. The British government prevailed on Léon Blum (1872–1950), leading a socialist government in France, and strongly supportive of the republic, also to adopt nonintervention, so that the delivery of French arms to Spain, begun in the earliest days of the war, ceased. Individual Britons, to be sure, fought for the republic in the International Brigades,* though of the forty thousand or so foreigners who took part in the war in this way, barely more than two thousand were British citizens.

In World War II,* Spain again kept to neutrality, or at least nonbelligerency, as Franco cautiously observed the ebb and flow of Axis and Allied fortunes. In the immediate aftermath of the war, Franco was seen by the West as the remaining undefeated fascist dictator, and Spain suffered diplomatic ostracism, so that Britain had no ambassador in Madrid from late 1946 until 1951. Relations improved with the admittance of Spain into the United Nations in 1955, but Franco pressed strongly on the issue of Gibraltar after being particularly displeased by a British royal visit to the Rock in 1954. At the same time, however, Anglo-Spanish trade grew, as did also British tourism to Spain.

Indeed, in the decades since World War II, the dominant contact between Britain and Spain has undoubtedly been tourism, as ever-larger droves of Britons have taken to invading Spain by land, sea, and air during the summer months, seeking sun by day, and chicken and chips by night, from Rosas to Malaga. Undoubtedly, these massive, if peaceful, intrusions have been the most direct and influential British action in and on Spain since the War of Independence,* with economic consequences for the country far greater than any brought by the ancient wine trade, or even by British industrial investment in the second half of the nineteenth century. Certainly many tourists have arrived from other European nations, but the British have always been in the forefront. In 1985, for example, Britons accounted for 31.7 percent of nights spent by foreign tourists in Spanish hotels, narrowly outnumbering West Germans at 29.9 percent. British tourism in Spain shows no sign of dwindling, and while it is easy to mock tourism and to deprecate the ugly development that it has stimulated along much of the Spanish coast, nonetheless it is a contact undeniably more beneficent than that which has usually marked the relationship between these two countries over the past several centuries.

For additional information, see W. C. Atkinson, *A History of Spain and Portugal* (Harmondsworth, 1960); R. Carr, *Spain, 1808–1939* (Oxford, 1966); A. D. Francis, *The Wine Trade* (London, 1972); OECD, *Tourist Policy and International Tourism in OECD Member Countries* (Paris, 1987); J. Vicens Vives, *Manual de Historia Economía de España* (Barcelona, 1965); and G. J. Walker, *Spanish Politics and Imperial Trade, 1700–1789* (Bloomington, 1979).

*P. J. Bakewell*

*Related entry*: GIBRALTAR.

# C

CACIQUES, Caribbean term meaning *chief*, synonymously used in the nineteenth century to denote corrupt, powerful local Spanish political leaders. The term, first encountered in contacts with Carib Indians, who called their chiefs caciques, seems to have been adapted by the Spaniards in the period from 1510 to 1516 to describe tax collectors sent out by Fernando of Aragon (1452–1516). Its heaviest use, however, came in the nineteenth century, when liberal dependence upon local powerholders (in contrast to earlier royal centralism) saw the phenomenon of caciquismo grow until the work of Antonio Cánovas del Castillo* and Práxedes Mateo Sagasta* created functional political machines that reached deep into the countryside to control political life, fix elections, and obtain graft from every possible political transaction, especially in Andalusia.*

Unlike urban political machines in the United States* during the same period, which mediated or brokered power between recent arrivals to the United States and more established groups and classes, the liberal political machines of the Restoration (1875–1885) and Regency (1885–1902) periods dictated national policy. Their power came from the distribution of disentailed lands to politicians and their followers as a means of dominion over the political arena. Rural poverty, illiteracy, and powerlessness enabled the Liberal-Conservative and Liberal Fusion parties to ignore regional or radical political inclinations among various constituencies in Spain, as well as neutralize military and church demands, to create a parliamentary regime that lasted from 1876 to 1923. These forty-seven years, although marked with innumerable scandals and turmoil, contrasted vividly to the chaos of the First Republic* and the praetorian pronunciamentos of the period from 1834 to 1875. Eventually, of course, graft permeated many aspects of statecraft and made the system self-destructive.

The disaster of the Spanish-American War* exposed the inroads of caciquismo in Spanish society. Reformers such as Gumersindo Azcárate (1840–1917) and Joaquín Costa* caustically attacked the caciques and their system of caciquismo as the prime obstacle to modernization, and the dictatorship (1923–1930) of Gen. Miguel Primo de Rivera* portrayed the liberal regime as so corrupt and cacique-ridden that his own authoritarianism was initially overlooked. Praetorian modernization could not replace the parties and political bosses who, for better or worse, constituted a national system of politics; while on the other hand, the parties of the Second Republic* were so ideological and factionalized that their competitiveness overwhelmed parliamentary tolerance.

The land-reform bill of 1932 publicized cacique protection of absentee landowners and blockage of agrarian renovation. After the Spanish Civil War,* the term was occasionally used in reference to the return by Gen. Francisco Franco* of the great Andalusian estates to private ownership and the power local landowners held there. Higher taxation of land in the period after 1975 has diminished the problem somewhat of late.

For additional information, see R. W. Kern, *Liberals, Reformers, and Caciques in Restoration Spain, 1875–1909* (Albuquerque, 1973); J. Martínez-Alier, *La estabilidad del Latifundismo* (Paris, 1968) and J. Tussell Gómez, *La crisis del caciquismo andaluz* (Madrid, 1977).

R. W. Kern

*Related entries*: CÁNOVAS DEL CASTILLO, ANTONIO; LIBERALISM; SAGASTA, PRÁXEDES MATEO.


**CALVO SOTELO, JOSÉ** (1893–1936), conservative politician whose assassination triggered the Spanish Civil War.* Calvo Sotelo, born near Pontevedra on 6 May 1893 and raised in Saragossa, studied law in Madrid, where he came under the influence of the reforming ideas of Joaquín Costa.* Calvo did advanced study on legal philosophy with the sociologist and political scientist Gumersindo de Azcárate (1840–1917), and in 1914, joined the youth movement supporting the elitist authoritarianism of Antonio Maura.* Calvo ultimately became Maura's secretary, which broadened his access to power, and in 1919, won a seat in the Cortes.* He was made civil governor of Valencia in 1921.

His greatest prominence came under the dictatorship of Gen. Miguel Primo de Rivera,* when he was appointed director general of local administration (1923) and then minister of economics (1926). He succeeded in significantly reducing the national debt, and his creation of a national petroleum monopoly (Compañia Arrendataria del Monopolio de Petróleos, S.A., CAMPSA) in 1927 appealed to nationalist fervor and formed part of an elaborate economic plan to pursue earlier reformers' demands for economic modernization. With his support, a modern infrastructure, from irrigation projects and highways to government buildings and railway lines, was initiated.

The onset of the depression ruined these plans. Calvo fled to France* at the proclamation of the Second Republic* in 1931 and returned only after the center-right's victory in Nov. 1933 to become parliamentary spokesman for the conservative ideas popular in 1934 and 1935. Although he remained politically authoritarian and corporatist, he never embraced fascism, but his rhetoric after the victory of the Popular Front in the elections of Feb. 1936 made him a marked man. On 13 July 1936, he was kidnapped and executed in retaliation for the murder of a radical military officer the previous day. After the nationalist victory in 1939, Calvo Sotelo's name was used as a patriotic icon and a symbol of martyrdom.

For additional information, see E. Aunós, *Calvo Sotelo y la política de su tiempo* (Madrid, 1941); J. Calvo Sotelo, *Mis servicios al Estado* (Madrid, 1931); and E. Vegas Latapie, *El pensamiento político de Calvo Sotelo* (Madrid, 1941).

*R. W. Kern*

*Related entries*: PRIMO DE RIVERA, GEN. MIGUEL; SECOND REPUBLIC.

**CAMACHO, MARCELINO** (1918– ), trade-union leader. Camacho was born to working-class parents in Osma la Rasa, Soria, on 21 Jan. 1918. He joined the Communist party* (PCE) in 1934 and fought in the republican army through-out the Spanish Civil War.* In 1939, arrested by the junta that seized Madrid* from communist control, he escaped, only to be captured again by the nation-alists, but eluded his jailers on two other occasions before finally being sentenced to six years in prison. In 1941, he was released conditionally to be sent to Tangiers as a member of a disciplinary battalion. Escaping to French Morocco, he found a more secure refuge in Algeria, where he worked as a millwright from 1944 to 1957. During this time, he remained active as a trade unionist and a socialist.

In 1957, an amnesty allowed Camacho's return to Spain. He was employed at Perkins Hispania in Madrid, but between 1964 and 1967, following the com-munist policy of "entrism," he won election to a number of positions within the official labor syndicates and began playing an especially strong role in the new, clandestine Comisiones Obreras (CCOO), an internal movement within many northern syndicates, particularly in Navarre.*

After a tumultuous period of strike action, the Public Order Tribunal ordered his arrest on 1 May 1967 for labor agitation. Released for three months in 1972, he was arrested soon afterward, tried, and sentenced to twenty years' impris-onment. In 1975, after the death of Gen. Francisco Franco,* he was amnestied.

By the early 1970s, Camacho had become the most prominent labor leader in Spain. He was also an active communist, a member of the central committee, and a deputy who represented Madrid from 1977 to 1981. His public confirmation in 1976 of his party membership and role in the party contributed to the realization that the CCOO had evolved from an independent grassroots organization into a communist union federation. Camacho, however, soon had a number of dis-agreements with Communist party leader Santiago Carrillo,* and following the disastrous communist showing in the 1982 elections, he was among those who pressured Carrillo to resign. Camacho himself stepped down as secretary-general of the CCOO in Nov. 1987, but still remains the honorary president of the union.

For additional information, see J. Melia, *Marcelino Camacho* (Madrid, 1977).

*A. Shubert*

*Related entry*: COMMUNIST PARTY.

**CAMBÓ Y BATLLE, FRANCESC** (1876–1947), Catalan regionalist. Cambó, born on 2 Sept. 1876 to a rural family near Gerona, showed exceptional talent in philosophy and law as a student at the University of Barcelona. Through the patronage of the scholar Narcis Verdaguer i Callis (1868–1918), he became a member of the elite Centre Escolar Catalanista and while still in his twenties, contributed to *La Veu de Catalunya*, one of the leading outlets of Catalan opinion.

His political career began in 1900 after several large and violent nationalist demonstrations; few rose so rapidly in peninsular politics. Cambó mastered the use of symbols, the emotional appeal of a regional language, and the unity of a long cultural history to create a bourgeois form of activism. After election to the Barcelona* city council in Nov. 1901, he founded the Lliga Regionalista with Enric Prat de la Riba* as the political arm of the older Unió Catalanista. Despite occasional exiles in France,* Cambó's influence increased with the founding in 1906 of Solidaritat Catalana, a coalition of regionalists, republicans, socialists, Carlists, and the Lliga, to oppose the pro-Castilian, antiregionalist policies of Alejandro Lerroux.* Solidaritat won forty-one of the forty-four Catalan seats in the *diputació*, a provincial government limited to local matters with a council of elected representatives, of which Cambó was one.

The two years that followed saw the genesis of the modern Catalan crisis. As Víctor Alba has noted, the election made a tremendous impression in Spain, since it signified the end of cacique* rule from Madrid* over provincial politics. The Catalans, unfortunately, could not long maintain the class unity that had permitted Solidaritat's victory. Each political party ran its own candidates in the next election, and the bitter street rioting of Barcelona's Tragic Week in late July 1909, in opposition to use of the area's reserves to serve in Morocco,* permitted renewed Castilian control over Catalonia.

The next seven years forced Cambó into intermittent French exile even though Catalonia was granted limited self-rule, or *mancomunitat*, in 1913. Since Cambó blamed the Left for the disaster of 1909, his politics grew more conservative, and at the same time, his status as middleman for foreign companies wishing to do business in northeastern Spain made him wealthy. In many respects, he traded the role of firebrand for oligarch, by actively opposing Catalan separation from Spain in 1917 (working with his archenemy Lerroux in the process), and joining the "National Government" of Antonio Maura* as minister of economic development in 1918. He remained in various other Madrid cabinets until Mar. 1922, perhaps best known for his policy of economic protectionism. The dictatorship of Gen. Miguel Primo de Rivera* in 1923 ended this phase of his career.

As a Catalan nationalist in this period, Cambó moved distinctly to the right. The Lliga never tried a Solidaritat-type coalition again, and while it pressed other regional diputaciones in 1917 to support federalism, its rejection by all but the Basques* ended any further radical initiatives. The appearance of new radical and nationalist groups on their left—the Partit República Català in 1919, Lluis Companys's Unió de Rabassaires in 1921, the Estat Català of Francesc

Macià,* and the Unió Socialista de Catalunya in 1922—caused the Lliga, now led by Cambó after Prat de la Riba's death, to split in two, with the formation of a National Catalan Conference and its new party, Acció Catalana. Cambó's days as a regional nationalist were at an end.

During the next seven years, he successfully concentrated on business by using the Compañía Hispanoamericana de Electricidad to consolidate foreign utility holdings, amassing an even greater fortune. The lure of politics had not ended for him, though. When the dictatorship began to collapse in early 1931, Cambó organized the Partido del Centro Constitucional, a Spanish center party, with great energy but little success, eclipsed in Catalonia by Macià's new left-wing Esquerra Republicana de Catalunya. This failure still left Cambó with the option of rebuilding the Lliga. He renamed it the Lliga Catalana and took advantage of the electorate's conservative mood in Nov. 1933 to win a slight majority over the Equerra in the Catalan chamber. His program of economic conservatism was tempered by the realization that he might be able to win greater autonomy for Catalonia from the dominant Confederación Española de Derechas Autónomas (CEDA) by avoiding anticlericalism, but his plans were upset by Macià's death in Dec. 1933 and the rise of Lluis Companys (1883–1940) as the new Esquerra leader, whose appeasement of the Confederación Nacional de Trabajo (CNT) and support for the rabassaires' land reform caused Cambó and the Lliga to withdraw from the chamber in Jan. 1934. It had been a short moment of triumph for Cambó, but the complexity of ideological Catalan politics in 1934 doomed his oligarchical cultural nationalism as outmoded and obsolete in a period dominated so strongly by the Left and Right.

The Spanish Civil War* in 1936 caused Cambó to go abroad to Italy.* He returned briefly to Barcelona in 1940, but soon left for Buenos Aires, where he died on 30 Apr. 1947.

For additional information, see V. Alba, *Catalonia, A Profile* (New York, 1975); F. Cambó, *Les dictadures* (Barcelona, 1930) and *Per la concòrdia* (Barcelona, 1930); J. Pabón, *Cambó, 1876–1918* (Barcelona, 1952); M. García Venero, *Vida de Cambó* (Barcelona, 1952); and J. M. Nadal, *Seis años con don Francisco Cambó (1930–1936)* (Barcelona, 1957).

R. W. Kern

*Related entries*: BARCELONA; CATALONIA; LERROUX, ALEJANDRO.


**CAMPOMANES, CONDE DE, PEDRO RODRÍGUEZ** (1723–1803), diplomat, statesman, writer, and economist. Rodríguez, born in Santa Eulalia de Serriba in Asturias* on 1 July 1723, was aided in his early education by an uncle who was the canon at the cathedral of Oviedo. He later attended a Dominican school in Santillana, where his scholarly talents were recognized. At ten, he translated verses by Ovid into Spanish; and at eleven, he began studying philosophy, law, and literature. By nineteen, having graduated from Santillana as a lawyer, he continued his studies in the law at Madrid,* eventually publishing *Disertaciones históricas del orden y cavallería de los Templarios* in 1747.

His career as public servant began in 1755 when the marqués de la Ensenada* made him director general of mail services, in which capacity he reorganized the mail system and put it on .an improved fiscal standing. Impressed with Rodríguez's administrative talents, Carlos III* promoted him to the Consejo Real y Supremo de Castilla in 1762. Since the council was the royal executive body in charge of Enlightenment* reforms, Rodríguez was able to propose a series of new laws and regulations in his new role as royal counselor and fiscal of the council. He raised the age of entrance to cloistered life and reduced state aid to monasteries and convents as part of the battle to regain ecclesiastical lands. Eventually, the reclaimed lands were auctioned as taxable properties to increase state revenues, in a process he described in his treatise on regalist land reform, *Tratado de la regalía de amortización* (Madrid, 1765; Venice, 1777; Gerona, 1821), one of the leading works of its kind for the day.

In 1777, the Asturian was named to the presidency of the Consejo Real in hopes that he could rid Spain of its industrial decadence. His writings and actions reflect an ideological trend against cultural or religious practices that interfered with economic progress. When he was named in 1779 to preside over the Mesta, an ancient official corporation of migrant sheep owners, he sought to dismantle its authority to claim land, by right of posesión, used as right-of-way for the semiyearly transhumance. Responding to the outcry that the Mesta claimed land that could be used for farming, Rodríguez began to force the Mesta to recognize the priorities of local landowners over those of sheep owners. His campaign against the right of posesión resulted in the abolition of that privilege in 1786. Two years later, landowners were permitted to enclose their lands and plant crops of their own choosing. Rodríguez emerged as a champion of landowners, who finally saw the interests of the crown coinciding with their desire to put more land under tillage. For this distinguished service to the crown, Carlos III elevated him to become the conde de Campomanes.

His other works were almost as impressive. He was made president of the Academia de la Historia in 1764, a position he held for twenty years. His interest in education resulted in the modification of the university curriculum with renewed emphasis on mathematics, natural sciences, physics, chemistry, and the development of libraries. His study of education, *Discurso sobre la educación popular de los artesanos y su fomento* (1775–1777), combined new ideas concerning the economy and education very strongly, as did his *Discurso sobre el fomento de la industria popular* (1774). Campomanes always sought, as the epitome of the regalist approach to government, a strengthened realm that would benefit and strengthen the monarchy.

Despite his many services to the crown, however, he fell from grace over issues of succession in the period following the death of Carlos III. He was replaced by the conde de Floridablanca* as president of the Consejo Real y Supremo de Castilla, and Campomanes's career as a royal counselor came to an end in 1791, when he was retired to private life by Carlos IV.* He died in Madrid on 3 Feb. 1803.

For additional information, see R. Herr, *The Eighteenth Century Revolution in Spain* (Princeton, 1958); and J. Sarrailh, *La España Ilustrada de la segunda mitad del siglo xviii*, Trans. A. Alatorre (Madrid, 1974).

*J. P. Sánchez*

*Related entries*: ENSENADA, MARQUÉS DE LA; ESQUILACHE, MARQUÉS DE; FLORIDABLANCA, CONDE DE.


**CANARY ISLANDS,** off the west coast of Africa, comprised of the provinces of Las Palmas and Santa Cruz de Tenerife on the islands of Gran Canaria, Fuerteventura, Lanzarote, Tenerife, La Palma, Gomera, and Hierro. It has been an autonomous region since 1979. Pop. (1982 est.) 1,367,646; sq. mi. 2,807.

A subtropical climate and the volcanic soil permit banana growing for sale in Spanish markets, until recently protected by strong tariffs. Over the centuries, some other special crops—orchilla weed for purple dye, winter vegetables, tropical nuts—joined staples like sugar, tobacco, and wine to form a substantial agrarian economy, although today tourism is dominant.

The Canary Islands (a Roman name for the dogs found there) were conquered in 1404–1406 from their original inhabitants, the Guanches (Berber in origin), by a Majorcan Norman clan, the Betencourts. The islands became a Castilian fief and were defended successfully in 1425 against Prince Henry (1395–1460) of Portugal.* In 1479, possession by Spain was acknowledged by the Treaty of Alcaçovas, an important first step in Castile's future transatlantic empire.

As a contraband center for British, French, and Dutch merchants in the seventeenth and eighteenth centuries, the Canaries presented a severe problem for the Consulado in Seville, which in 1611 finally prohibited the islanders from any further trading with the Indies. During the eighteenth century, island pirates became notorious for their diversion of American silver from Spanish convoys to European ports. Strong protectionism under Carlos III* increased illegal trade, although this independence also protected the islands from British capture.

The Canary Islands began their transformation from overseas dependency to peninsular province in 1810 at the Cortes of Cadiz.* In the 1830s, these links were strengthened by the liberals, who welcomed the cosmopolitan economic attitudes of the island merchants. Soon, the islanders were so thoroughly Hispanized that the islands produced the great nineteenth-century novelist Benito Pérez Galdós,* and the premier of the Second Republic* during the Spanish Civil War,* Juan Negrín.*

Much of the Canaries' twentieth-century life, nevertheless, was lived on the margins of Spanish history. On 16 May 1907, fear that Germany* coveted the islands led Britain,* France,* and Spain to sign the Pact of Cartagena as a guarantee of continued Spanish sovereignty. In 1927, Gen. Miguel Primo de Rivera* divided the islands into two provinces for greater representation. In 1936, Gen. Francisco Franco* briefly served as military governor before flying to Morocco* at the start of the Spanish Civil War. By 28 July, his followers had put down scattered republican resistance and secured the islands for the nationalist cause. Throughout the early part of World War II,* the German navy made advantageous use of the Canaries and even tentatively offered to cancel part of Franco's war debt to obtain permanent possession.

In the postwar period, economic life boomed when mass tourism began. The Canaries became an aviation way station between Europe, Africa, and South America. Finally, in the period after Feb. 1976, when the collapse of the Portuguese empire in Africa caused Spain to abandon Western Sahara, a small island independence movement, Movimiento para la Autodeterminación y Independencia del Archipiélago Canario (MPAIAC), unsuccessfully allied briefly with the Algerian Polisario Front. Today, high population density, an unsettled economic life, and proximity to political unrest in Africa are continuing problems.

For additional information, see A. Millares Torres, *Historia general de las Islas Canarias* (Las Palmas, 1975); J. Peraza de Ayala, *El régimen comercial de Canarias con las Indias en los siglos XVI, XVII y XVIII* (Seville, 1977); M. Norena Salto, *Canarias: política y sociedad durante la restauración* (Las Palmas, 1977); and P. Pérez Díaz, *El problema canario* (Las Palmas, 1977).

R. W. Kern

*Related entries*: NEGRÍN, JUAN; PÉREZ GALDÓS, BENITO.

**CÁNOVAS DEL CASTILLO, ANTONIO** (1828–1897), nineteenth-century politician. One of the most prominent figures in the history of nineteenth-century Spain, Cánovas was born in Malaga on 8 Feb. 1828. Son of the master of a secondary school, Cánovas as a youth showed an early interest in writing. After his father died in 1843, his mother obtained the patronage of his uncle, a well-known writer of the day, for a move to Madrid* in 1845. In Madrid, Cánovas took courses in both philosophy and law and received degrees in each, although he never practiced law.

His uncle arranged a sinecure for Cánovas with the company building the first major railroad in Spain; apparently his only obligation was to pick up his paycheck once a month. It was common for literary figures to receive similar favors, and Cánovas had quickly moved into this classification. He had begun some of the historical writing that was to become, after politics, his major interest and accomplishment. He wrote for several newspapers and in 1850, became the director of *La Patria*, founded by Joaquín Francisco Pacheco (1808–1865), the leader of a section of the Moderate party.* A year later, Cánovas was able to bring his family to Madrid, buy a house, and thus provide space for what would become an extensive private library.

Cánovas's entry into politics was facilitated by his friendship with Gen. Leopoldo O'Donnell,* one of the politico-military leaders who dominated so much of the history of Spain during the nineteenth century. Cánovas wrote the Manifesto of Manzanares, which O'Donnell issued as he initiated the Revolution of 1854. It advocated the preservation of the throne, but without the camarilla that dishonored the rule of Isabel II,* and promised both a freer press and governmental reforms. As was to occur twenty years later in the Restoration period, however, Cánovas's promises of reform were more theoretical than concrete.

Although Cánovas was disillusioned by the consequences of the Revolution of 1854 and followed a more conservative course thereafter, he remained O'Donnell's close associate. He served in the Constitutional Cortes of 1855. After filling minor positions in the Ministry of Foreign Affairs, late in 1855, he was appointed the director of the Spanish Agency of Prayers in Rome, a governmental agency established to further the petitions of Spanish Catholics at the papal court. This was a posting that provided both prestige and profit, and Cánovas's private fortune apparently dates from this period. In 1857, Cánovas returned home, serving briefly as civil governor of Catalonia* in 1858 and then as director general of administration and subsecretary of the Ministry of the Interior. In 1864, he became minister of the interior under Alejandro Mon (1801–1882) in 1864 and in 1865, minister of overseas territories under O'Donnell.

Cánovas learned much of practical politics from these varied experiences. His participation in the Revolution of 1854, when O'Donnell was outmaneuvered by his associates and social unrest threatened, left Cánovas with a deep aversion to revolution. His career as an administrator convinced him that there was little political morality in governmental circles. José Posada Herrera's (1815–1885) "management" of the election of 1858 showed Cánovas the potential of controlling the electoral process. His service as minister of the overseas territories introduced him to the central issue of Spain's nineteenth-century dilemma—the contradiction between an anachronistic national pride and the realities of national power. Closer acquaintance with the affairs of the royal family also revealed to him Isabel II's incompetence as a ruler.

As a consequence, the Revolution of 1868 found Cánovas voluntarily sitting on the sidelines. Although he defended Isabel II against charges of wrongfully making use of funds obtained from the sale of the royal jewels, he was among those who exerted pressure on the queen to abdicate in behalf of her son in 1870. He played a relatively minor role in the Constitutional Cortes of 1869, opposing articles granting universal manhood suffrage and the free exercise of religion. Cánovas did not support the choice of Amadeo I* as Spain's first constitutional monarch and accurately predicted that the Italian prince would be unable to rally the support of the nation.

By 1872, Cánovas had become the outstanding spokesman supporting the return of the Bourbons in the person of the future Alfonso XII.* The queen's advisors urged her to give official support to his efforts, but Cánovas's criticism of the queen's past role and her current life-style led her to seek alternatives. Only when Antonio de Orléans (1824–1890), the duke of Montpensier, and Francisco Serrano (1810–1885) had proved their lack of reliability did the queen finally turn to Cánovas. It was probably at his insistence that this was accompanied by a formal ceremony on 4 Aug. 1873 and confirmed by a letter she and the prince signed. As the official spokesman for the future king, Cánovas began the difficult task of creating a broad coalition of support for Alfonso in the midst of deep party division, unbridgeable personal differences, and the queen's continuing machinations.

By this time, Amadeo had returned to Italy, and Spain had begun its chaotic and tragic first trial of republicanism. The brief period from Feb. 1873 to 3 Jan. 1874 saw a kaleidoscope of events as four presidents came and went. The Carlist cause, which had revived after the Revolution of 1868, took on new momentum. A federalist and cantonalist movement added the dissidence of Catalonia and considerable portions of southern Spain to that of the Basque Provinces. There were also in Spain some significant reflections of the social unrest and terrorism connected with anarchism* and the First International. Emilio Castelar (1832–1899), the last of the elected presidents of the First Republic,* sought to establish unity and order; he accomplished much, but only at the price of dictatorial rule. He returned to command a number of conservative generals displaced during the more radical phase of the republic. One of these, Gen. Manuel Pavía (1827–1895), initiated a coup on 3 Jan. 1874 to prevent the return of the extremists on the Left.

Pavía had acted in Castelar's behalf, but the republican leader denounced the military coup. Cánovas and his followers announced their refusal to support any government that did not proclaim its intention to restore the Bourbons under Alfonso. The result was the formation of a "Government of the Executive Power" under Francisco Serrano y Domínguez (1810–1885), duque de la Torre, regent of Spain following the Revolution of 1868 and president of an executive junta, pending the arrival of Alfonso.

Serrano's plans for the future remained uncertain. Some believed he was only awaiting the propitious moment for the restoration of the Bourbons. Others thought he favored giving the crown to the more liberal Orléanist duke of Montpensier. Still others were convinced that Serrano contemplated heading a lifelong grand dukedom. During the latter part of the Serrano government, authority was largely in the hands of the constitutionalists, led by Práxedes Mateo Sagasta.* Later events showed that they had used much the same procedures that Cánovas later employed to secure the electoral support needed to control the Spanish Cortes.

Serrano, however, proved incapable of dealing either with the existing revolution in Cuba or the Carlist revolt at home, and his political base shrank quickly. Cánovas apparently hoped to bring about the restoration of Alfonso XII, but the military pronunciamento at Sagunto on 29 Dec. 1874 by Gen. Arsenio Martínez Campos (1831–1900) cut political maneuvers short. While Alfonso had been at Sandhurst military academy in Britain, he had issued a manifesto written by Cánovas that promised a constitutional monarchy. The military pronouncement at Sagunto, however, was followed by a six-year period during which Cánovas exercised virtually dictatorial power.

Cánovas and his supporters, the liberal-conservatives, took rapid control of the situation. Strict press censorship was imposed. Spain's civil governors and local officials were changed. New elections were held under the management of Francisco Romero Robledo (1838–1906), who had become Cánovas's minister of the interior. Efforts were made to reestablish better relations with the Catholic church. The Second Carlist War (1873–1876) was brought to a successful conclusion, partly through military action and partly by negotiations with some of its leaders.

The Constitution of 1876 was also largely Cánovas's creation. All previous constitutions were declared void, and Spain was returned to an "internal constitution" based upon the role of the king as constitutional monarch "by the grace of God." The king's person was proclaimed "sacred and inviolable," and his authority was said to extend to "everything that conduces to public order at home and the security of the state abroad." The role of the Cortes as the law-making body of the state was confirmed, but the constitution provided that universal manhood suffrage, which had been accepted for the election of the Constitutional Cortes, would not necessarily be extended for later elections. Two years later, the Cortes adopted requirements for the payment of real-estate taxes as a prerequisite for voting. The Senate was to be composed of three groups: those taking office by personal privilege (high church officials, leaders of the army,* counselors and attorneys of the realm, and grandees with an annual income from their estates of seventy thousand pesetas); senators for life named by the king; and elected senators. The consequence of these requirements, of course, was that the conservative and reactionary classes had built-in control of the legislative agencies.

The only portion of the constitution that was vaguely liberal was Article 11, which proclaimed Catholicism the religion of the state and promised state support, but added that "no one shall be molested in Spanish territory for his religious opinions or for the exercise of his own religion except for the respect owed to Christian morality." This liberal phraseology was, however, followed by the words "ceremonies or public demonstrations other than those of the religion of the state, however, will not be permitted." Through the period that followed, the interpretation of this prohibition was to include police action against non-Catholic groups singing hymns with the windows open, a ban on signs marking the places where their church activities were to take place, and government actions against Protestant schools and those who attended them.

Cánovas encouraged the formation of an alternate political party, favoring the Constitutionalist party led by Práxedes Sagasta. From the first, Cánovas's conception of two rival political parties debating in the Cortes and sharing power by peaceful change was vitiated by the existence of divisions within the leading parties and the appearance of third parties that complicated the political spectrum.

After consolidating affairs at home, Cánovas dispatched Martínez Campos, author of the pronunciamento of Sagunto, to end the existing revolt in Cuba. Martínez Campos succeeded in this effort by a policy of successful counter-guerilla warfare and negotiations with his opponents and began to demand that Spain undertake significant reforms in Cuba. His proposals stirred opposition in Spain, particularly because they challenged entrenched economic privileges, especially in Catalonia, and Cánovas allowed Martínez Campos to form his own cabinet to seek support for these measures, although he was personally opposed to the proposed changes. The cabinet of Martínez Campos lasted only from 8 Mar. 1879 to 7 Dec. of the same year. The failure of these reform measures left the problems of Cuba unsolved.

Whether the king himself or Cánovas decided the issue, the king's prerogative was employed in 1881 for the first peaceful alternation of cabinets, the turno pacífico, as he called Sagasta and a temporary alliance of other party groupings to head the government. This so-called Fusion of parties opposing Cánovas did not last long, but did provide a freer atmosphere that allowed the return to their posts of professors who had been fired because of liberal religious views, the reappearance of opposition newspapers, and the formation of some party groupings combining the ideals of democracy and monarchy. It was, however, also marked by the overturn of government officials on a large scale, along with controlled elections and an early splintering of liberal groups over personal differences as well as budget issues and the reform of the military. Although Sagasta moved early in 1883 to a purely liberal (the term replacing *constitutionalist*) ministry, the Spanish Left continued to be more divided than the Right, with Cánovas and his followers now adopting the term "Conservative" as the designation of their party. The liberal interlude brought increased activity by the Spanish socialist movement under Pablo Iglesias (1850–1925) and by anarchists in the south. The Sagasta government acted against both of these groups almost as severely as had Cánovas.

Although Alfonso XII had accepted Sagasta and given encouragement to leaders even to Sagasta's left, the liberal government had disillusioned the monarch. The reforms he sought had not been carried out, and he was aware that corruption was rife. He was also to say that he felt "safer" under the leadership of Cánovas. After the brief ministry of Posada Herrera fell because both Cánovas and Sagasta opposed its proposal for universal manhood suffrage, the monarch accepted the return of Cánovas early in 1884.

Many difficulties attended the last ministry of Cánovas during the rule of Alfonso XII. There were several abortive military revolts, severe earthquakes in Granada and Malaga, and a terrible cholera epidemic. Cánovas governed harshly, becoming involved in a serious controversy with the university students of Madrid. He also exercised greater control over the young monarch, trying to curtail the king's penchant for nightly escapades at the same time that he was showing increasing evidence of the effects of the tuberculosis that cost him his life on 25 Nov. 1885.

On the death of Alfonso XII, Cánovas, or perhaps the queen-regent herself, María Cristina de Habsburgo (1858–1929), exercised the royal prerogative for the second, major turno pacífico, as Sagasta was recalled to power. Sagasta and his followers ruled five years. Some political reforms were made, most notably universal manhood suffrage and the recognition of all political parties not openly antimonarchist. During this period out of power, Cánovas added to his scholarly, primarily historical, pursuits.

On 8 July 1890, Cánovas returned to power, the queen-regent taking this action to avoid the disclosure of a scandal that affected Sagasta's wife, although not the political leader himself. This was, however, the beginning of a period when Cánovas found political difficulties at home and abroad. His first minister of the interior, Francisco Silvela,* failed to manage the elections as well as had Romero Robledo, and Cánovas replaced him with the former partner in government in Nov. 1891. Silvela became a critic, charging poor handling of a case involving corruption in the city government of Madrid. By 1893, Silvela was complaining that Cánovas was old and should retire to allow a more robust conservative party.

On 11 Dec. 1892, Cánovas was again replaced by Sagasta, who began the long Spanish struggle with incipient revolt in Cuba. Neither he nor Cánovas wanted to allow a central, autonomous agency on the island. Cánovas again returned to power on 23 Mar. 1895, by which time full-scale revolt was underway. He was unwilling to discuss reforms until Cuban leaders had indicated their loyalty to Spain. Although Cánovas sent Martínez Campos to Cuba, the general whose reforms might have avoided the loss of Cuba found nothing but military action possible this time. Cánovas responded by more than doubling the Spanish forces on the island, but early in 1896 sent the infamous general, Valeriano Weyler (1838–1930), who took harsh action, including the vicious reconcentración policy. In the Philippines, Gen. Camilo García de Polavieja (1838–1914) also governed repressively, adding to political dissent there. Although Cánovas's policies were not greatly different from those Sagasta had followed, he undoubtedly contributed to the coming of the Spanish-American War* and the loss of Spain's overseas empire. He himself proved a victim of internal dissent and was assassinated by an anarchist at the resort city of Santa Ageda on 8 Aug. 1897.

Cánovas's political career took place during the same period as the Gilded Age in the United States and was marked by the same characteristics of the rapid rise of business with resultant fortunes, a large element of public corruption and political bossism, and a government under the control of a self-satisfied established order. His major goal was to preserve public order and the stability of the monarchy. There was little evidence in Spain that those holding political, social, or religious leadership were concerned with the suffering of the lower classes. In the absence of reform came the origin of revolutionary forces. As a result, Cánovas bears a considerable measure of responsibility for Spain's later problems, a responsibility increased by the fact that his historical research should have shown him that the real reason for the decline of Spain lay in its failure to develop a vital middle class.

For additional information, see J. L. Comellas, *Cánovas* (Barcelona, 1965); M. Fernández Almagro, *Cánovas. Su vida y su política* (Madrid, 1951), and *Historia política de la España contemporánea*, 2 vols. (Madrid, 1956); and R. W. Kern, *Liberals, Reformers and Caciques in Restoration Spain, 1875–1909* (Albuquerque, 1974).

E. R. Beck

*Related entries*: ALFONSO XII; SAGASTA, PRÁXEDES MATEO.

**CARLISM,** Spanish political movement, customarily regarded as on the extreme political Right, officially born in 1833, that still exists in vestigial and fragmented form. The Carlist cause takes its name from don Carlos María Isidro de Borbón, younger brother of King Fernando VII,* and would-be king, Carlos V (1788–1855). On the death of Fernando in 1833, don Carlos contested the right to the throne of his niece, Isabel II,* basing his own claim on the Salic Law, introduced into Spain in 1713 by its first Bourbon king, Felipe V.* The law, barring female succession, was an innovation quite alien to Spanish tradition; Carlos IV* formulated a pragmatic sanction reversing it in 1789, but never unambiguously promulgated it. Don Carlos's claim provided a rallying point for various elements of opposition to early nineteenth-century Spanish liberalism, opposition first manifested during the royalist and malcontent guerrilla activities of the 1820s and crystalized in the First Carlist War (1833–1840). The Carlist program was summed up in the slogan "¡Dios, Patria, Rey!," to which was later added "Fueros" (regional rights and privileges), out of deference to regionalist sentiment.

Once in existence, Carlism proved to possess remarkable powers of endurance and continued to play a significant role in Spanish affairs under a succession of pretenders to the throne: Carlos V himself (pretender 1833–1845); his son Carlos VI, Montemolín (1818–1861, pretender 1845–1860); Carlos VI's brother Juan III (1822–1887, pretender 1860–1868); don Juan's son Carlos VII (1848–1909, pretender 1868–1909); his son Jaime III (1870–1931, pretender 1909–1931); and Carlos VII's brother Alfonso Carlos I (1849–1936, pretender 1931–1936). Following the death of Alfonso Carlos in 1936, the Carlist succession became unclear and disputed.

The Carlist cause was forged from a complex combination of what in the 1820s had been termed apostólico (ultra-Catholic) resistance to liberal secularism and all forms of modernism: an inchoate, popular revolt against various aspects of contemporary socioeconomic change; the growing interference of the central government in regional and local life; and the parallel disruption of local economies by invading capitalist practices. Popular Carlism's main bases lay in a broad arc of northern and eastern Spain incorporating the Basque region, Navarre,* parts of Castile,* Aragon,* Catalonia,* and Valencia,* with small pockets of support elsewhere, for example, in Galicia* and Andalusia.* In Navarre and the Basque country, Carlism won the enduring support of a conservative, deeply Catholic rural and small-town population that, while economically more secure than its counterparts in many other regions, nevertheless felt threatened by liberal erosion of a traditional way of life. Farther east, the movement appears to have offered an outlet for protest to a variety of economically declining and struggling sectors: marginal peasant farmers, especially in upland districts, struggling to survive in an increasingly market-oriented economy; village artisans; urban craftsmen; and small-scale merchants threatened by more modern and more powerful competitors.

Such groups, for half a century at least, were easily mobilized by an elite consisting mainly of clerics; lesser aristocrats; and a broadly middle-class element consisting of Catholic, antiliberal professional men, landowners, and retired army officers. On the whole, the wealthier, more powerful members of Spain's aristocracy and business class preferred the opportunities presented by liberalism to the backward-looking world of Carlism. Considerable support was initially forthcoming from all levels of the Spanish Catholic church, although with the passage of time, this was to prove more enduring among the lower than the higher clergy.

The undeniable fact that, during its nineteenth-century heyday (1833–1876), Carlism provided a channel for early anticapitalist social protest, encouraged Carlist propagandists and historians in the 1970s to argue that true Carlism was an incipiently socialist movement with its roots in the pueblo carlista rather than in a clerical, reactionary elite. It is a doubtful claim that does not necessarily distort the truth of Carlism's complexity any more than those more conventional explanations that have portrayed it as a uniformly, and consciously, conservative or even reactionary cause. What is in any case undeniable is that with the defeat of 1876, Carlism ceased to be a vehicle for genuine social protest. From that point on, the cause fell back upon its more unambiguously conservative strongholds in Navarre and the Basque country and even there assumed increasingly conservative form.

Between 1833 and 1876, Carlism offered an intermittently serious threat to the Spanish liberal system. The most dramatic challenges came in the form of Carlism's three civil wars: the First Carlist War of 1833–1840; the War of the "Early Risers" (matiners, from the Catalan) of 1846–1849; and the Second Carlist War of 1872–1876. All three were fought chiefly in northern and eastern Spain where Carlist support was strongest. The First Carlist War ranged throughout extensive areas of the Basque country, Navarre, Aragon, Catalonia, and Valencia; the war of 1846–1849 was confined mainly to Catalonia; and the Second Carlist War was concentrated in Navarre and the Basque region. Although in the first and third wars the Carlists, especially in Navarre, were able to put full-scale armies into the field, it was the guerrilla struggle, drawing its vigor from a largely sympathetic rural population, that most typified Carlist military activity. The limited nature of this warfare illustrated both the strength and the weakness of Carlism as a military cause. In its home territory, from Biscay east and south to Alicante, Carlism's deep roots made it difficult for the liberal state to defeat. Its relative and increasing weakness elsewhere in Spain, however, rendered it unable to break out of its strongholds and seriously threaten nationwide victory. Although Carlism's struggle threw up first-rate military leaders, notably, in the First Carlist War, Tomás de Zumalacárregui* and Ramón Cabrera (1806–1877), time and resources were wasted in both the 1830s and the 1870s in besieging liberal strongholds within Carlist country, especially Bilbao. In all the Carlist wars, contracting resources, internal divisions over strategy, and the superior power of the Spanish state ultimately produced defeat. Moreover, popular support, while remaining considerable, was never again as great as during the First Carlist War; both the Matiners' conflict and the Second Carlist War were essentially regional conflicts.

From time to time between 1840 and 1872, Carlist leaders flirted with other roads to power: undermining the ruling system through extending influence at court; a possible, but never-achieved, dynastic marriage between Carlos V's son and either Isabel II,* her sister, or her daughter; a military proununcamento, unsuccessfully attempted in 1860 by Carlos VI and a Carlist general; or a peaceful, parliamentary road to power, encouraged by the attraction to the Carlist ranks of neo-Catholic religious conservatives and pursued between Isabel II's fall in 1868 and the renewal of civil war in 1872. Such developments indicated and aggravated a number of complex, sometimes overlapping, differences of emphasis that recurred within Carlism between those upholding the separateness and integrity of Carlism and those prepared to deal with conservative elements within the Spanish establishment; between Carlists of wholly reactionary outlook and others whose populist instincts drew them toward republican and democratic alliances; between supporters of a peaceful road to power and the Carlist war party; and ironically in a dynastic movement, between a generally conservative Carlist elite and pretenders who sometimes showed disturbingly flexible or even liberal tendencies. Both Carlos VI and Juan III eventually abdicated on these grounds.

From the end of the Second Carlist War in 1876 to the fall of Alfonso XIII* in 1931, Carlism labored to survive in the face of a liberal monarchy that was actually conservative enough to undercut Carlism's own conservative appeal. During this period, Carlism experienced increasing difficulty in finding a place in Spanish politics. Its former role as a vehicle for vaguely defined social protest was taken over by the emergent Spanish Left; its regionalist role was successfully challenged by the more modern and single-minded forces of Catalan and Basque nationalism; and conservative lovers of order and religion, no longer scared of liberalism, could contentedly embrace the status quo. Such developments not only lessened Carlism's appeal to the uncommitted, but actually encouraged a leakage of former Carlist support in these directions.

Although the years of the liberal monarchy witnessed Carlism's overall slow decline, they were not wholly unproductive. Two positive achievements, one organizational and the other ideological, deserve mention. After 1876, and more particularly after appointment of the marqués de Cerralbo as Carlos VII's secretary-general in 1888, Carlism underwent a drastic organizational overhaul, for the first time assuming the form of a permanently organized political party instead of a loose cause. Carlism now played a peaceful role in political and social affairs, as indeed it did for most of the period between 1890 and 1923. It nevertheless also remained susceptible to adaptation for conspiratorial and insurrectionary purposes, especially after organization of a paramilitary branch, the Requeté.

On the ideological front, a Galician, Juan Vázquez de Mella,* provided Carlism with a modern, integrated, and sophisticated body of theory and policy between 1880 and World War I.* His traditionalism occupied a place squarely within the European Catholic Right of the late nineteenth and early twentieth centuries. Rejecting liberalism and unrestrained capitalism as well as materialistic socialism, his traditionalism advocated an essentially paternalistic social order, a tempered monarchy with all forms of power decentralized on an essentially corporatist basis. In the early twentieth century, many Carlists involved themselves in social activities, chiefly the development of Catholic rural syndicates and cooperatives and urban trade unions.

These activities allowed Carlism to offer itself as a serious political party and probably slowed its decline. After 1876, nevertheless, it showed few signs of ever again being able to bid for national power. Although Carlos VII was perhaps the most impressive and attractive of all the Carlist pretenders, the liberal monarchy of Alfonso XII* and Alfonso XIII was too well entrenched between 1874 and 1909 to be challenged. Both Carlos and his successor, don Jaime, fell afoul of the chronic Carlist tendency toward schism: in 1888, a Catholic die-hard element, the Integrists, broke away; and in 1919, Vázquez de Mella quarreled with the liberally inclined don Jaime and left to form his own Traditionalist party. During the crisis of the parliamentary system from 1917 to 1923, Carlism was in no shape to take advantage of the situation. The dictatorship of Gen. Miguel Primo de Rivera* created confusion and division in Carlist ranks on what attitude toward the regime was appropriate.

The coming of the Second Republic* in 1931 reversed Carlism's declining fortunes by removing the competition of the liberal monarchy and creating an atmosphere in which an established right-wing movement could offer refuge to conservative Spaniards. During 1931 and 1932, Carlism was renamed the Traditionalist Communion, and emerged as the first serious focus of opposition to the republic. Between 1931 and 1933, years of left-of-center, reforming, and anticlerical government, the schisms of 1868 and 1919 were healed, and Carlism experienced an appreciable revival of popular support, initially in regions of long-standing Carlist tradition (Navarre, the Basque country, Valencia), but later more widely. New members came mainly from elements inflamed by republican anticlericalism and the fear of socialism: the Catholic bourgeoisie; the middling and lesser peasantry; and the artisan sector of the working class. Carlism benefited from the rest of the Right's initial weakness; its own combative image; and its possession of a national organization, however rickety; and of a number of first-class organizers. Although overtaken after 1933 by a larger Catholic party, the Confederación Española de Derechas Autónomas (CEDA), Carlism remained a significant force on the extreme Right, especially in Navarre, Valencia, and western Andalusia.

For three years, the Carlists, under the leadership first of the marqués de Villores and then of the Navarrese conde de Rodezno (Tomás Domínguez Arévalo, 1883–1952), concentrated upon building up the Traditionalist Communion's strength and influence through recruitment, propaganda, electoral and parliamentary politics, and alliances with other rightist organizations. The eventual overthrow of the republic was the aim, but both a clear strategy and a sense of urgency were absent. After Rodezno was replaced in May 1934 by an Andalusian, Manuel Fal Conde (1894–1975), however, emphasis shifted to paramilitary preparation and plans for a Carlist rising.

The official goal of Carlist activity between 1931 and 1936 was the installation of the "Traditional Monarchy" described by Vázquez de Mella and now redrawn by his protégé Víctor Pradera (1873–1936) in *El estado nuevo* (1935). Carlism's traditionalist ideas, however utopian, exercised an important influence during the 1930s upon both the CEDA and the Alfonsist monarchists by giving the entire Catholic right a common ideological basis that ultimately transcended tactical differences. Carlist hopes of installing their monarchy were obstructed, however, by an intractable succession problem. Don Alfonso Carlos, who succeeded don Jaime as pretender in 1931, was a childless octogenarian with no clear heir. Attempts by Rodezno and other Carlist moderates to negotiate a dynastic settlement with Alfonsist monarchists, whereby one of Alfonso's offspring would inherit the Carlist succession, failed between 1931 and 1934; early in 1936, Alfonso Carlos announced that on his death his nephew-by-marriage, prince François-Xavier of Borbón-Parma—don Javier to his Spanish supporters—would act as regent.

Following the Popular Front election victory in Feb. 1936, the Traditionalist Communion began to prepare seriously for rebellion. Since the paramilitary Requeté numbered over thirty thousand and represented the largest and best prepared rightist militia in Spain, Carlism was inevitably drawn into the conspiratorial network that eventually produced the rising of 17–18 July 1936. Although Fal Conde wished to impose strict conditions for Carlism's participation involving a monarchist restoration, he was obliged to yield in the face of pressure from the military leadership and the more flexible Navarrese group led by Rodezno.

Once committed to the rising, Carlism threw in its forces with enthusiasm and played an important role, especially during the early months of the Spanish Civil War.* Between seventy and a hundred thousand enrolled in the Carlist tercios during 1936, although by no means had all been Carlists before the war. The Requeté made a particularly important contribution on the Basque front in autumn 1936; on the Aragon front; in the battles of 1936–1937 at Sierra de Guadarrama north of Madrid; and in several districts of Andalusia. In late 1936, the Requeté, like the militia of the rapidly expanding Falange,* came under increasingly close military control and thereafter lost much of its distinct identity within the nationalist forces. Nevertheless, Carlist claims that without the Requeté the rising might have foundered at the outset have some substance.

For most Carlists, the minimum purpose of the civil war was the destruction of the republic, the Popular Front, and the Spanish Left; and its maximum purpose the restoration, or more properly, the installation of the Carlist monarchy. During the early months of the war, don Javier, Fal Conde, and the national hierarchy strove desperately to keep the maximum goal within view, if only by maintaining and asserting Carlism's autonomy within the nationalist camp. In doing so, they increasingly annoyed the military leadership, especially after the elevation of Gen. Francisco Franco* to the positions of Generalissimo and head of state in late Sept. 1936. An attempt by Fal Conde to create a Royal Carlist Military Academy for the training of Requeté officers was interpreted by Franco as a challenge to his and the army's authority. The ensuing crisis ended with Fal Conde exiled in Portugal,* thus strengthening the hand of Rodezno and the more pliable Navarrese Carlists.

By early 1937, expectation reigned within nationalist Spain that Franco would soon move to create a single party embracing the Falange, the Carlists, and other lesser organizations. For some weeks, negotiations took place between Carlist and Falangist leaders with a view to forestalling forced fusion with a voluntary one. For the Carlists, Fal Conde and don Javier opposed any merger that smacked of fascist totalitarianism rather than Carlist traditionalism. The talks collapsed, and in Apr. 1937, Franco arbitrarily fused the Traditionalist Communion and the Falange into the Falange Española Tradicionalista y de las Juntas de Ofensiva Nacional-Sindicalista (FET), the single party of Spain down to 1975.

Although Fal Conde and other prominent Carlists refused to acknowledge the fusion or to participate in the FET's affairs, Rodezno and numerous collaborationists defied don Javier's orders and accepted state and party office. Rodezno himself became minister of justice in Jan. 1938, the first of four collaborationist Carlists to hold that office under Franco. This effective schism indicated a profound and sincere difference of outlook between the two tendencies headed by Fal Conde and Rodezno. The "Falcondian" view was that the Carlist monarchy could and must be achieved; that a separate and powerful Carlist organization was essential to this end; and that close cooperation with fascists and militarists would mean Carlism's subjection to a modern, oppressive totalitarianism. The rival collaborationist view was that Carlism would never be able to win power alone; that its maximum goals, however desirable, were unattainable; and that Carlism must therefore function as a vital current within a broadly acceptable right-wing regime, in particular by guaranteeing the spiritual, cultural, and educational role of Catholicism and resisting from within the more authoritarian ambitions of others. If the second view proved over the years to be overoptimistic, the first was utterly utopian.

After its revival in the early 1930s, Carlism never recovered from the crisis of 1937. The FET was largely rejected by Carlists, many of whom after the civil war simply retired into private life, clinging to Carlism as a popular and family tradition. They mostly combined loyalty to the memory of the 1936 crusade with disappointment concerning its outcome. Disillusionment increased as time passed, helping to feed a modest Carlist revival during the 1960s.

Those Carlists who remained politically active after 1939 split into several factions and tendencies, a development assisted and exacerbated by the unresolved succession problem. One group remained loyal to the political leadership of Fal Conde and supported the regency of don Javier in its detachment from and criticism of the Franco regime. In 1956, after much hesitation, don Javier yielded to the long-standing wishes of his supporters and claimed the Spanish throne. Of those who embraced the Franco regime, some did it so unreservedly as to cease to be Carlists in anything other than sentimental terms. Others, scarcely if at all less franquista and scornful of the regency, nevertheless continued to seek some kind of eventual monarchist restoration. Most followed Rodezno in pursuing a reconciliation between Carlist collaborationism and the cause of Alfonso XIII's son, don Juan. Reconciliation was eventually achieved, after Rodezno's death, at the so-called Act of Estoril in 1957. Another faction, hostile to the succession of the liberal Alfonsine branch of the Bourbons yet skeptical toward the regency, between 1943 and 1953 upheld the claim of another nephew of Alfonso Carlos, archduke Karl Pius of Hapsburg, who became Carlos VIII.

Following the premature death of Carlos VIII in 1953, don Javier's candidacy in 1956, and the Act of Estoril in 1957, this imbroglio resolved itself into a straight rivalry between Estorilos and Javieristas. Between 1956 and 1969, the former, convinced that the Carlist claim and tradition now rested with don Juan and his son, don Juan Carlos, became, like other collaborationists before them, Carlists in name only. The Javieristas, in contrast, strove during the 1960s to establish a distinctive identity within Franco's Spain. From 1958 onwards, the initiative within the movement was assumed by innovative younger Carlists led by don Javier's son, Carlos Hugo. Until 1965–1966, a populist critique of the regime's content was carefully combined with a respectful attitude toward Franco himself, designed to win official tolerance of Carlist activity and persuade Franco to name Carlos Hugo, rather than Juan Carlos, his successor.

Given the absence, in the increasingly lively political climate of the 1960s, of legal opposition channels, Carlist populism, while alienating some conservative Carlists, brought the movement significant popular support. During the late 1960s, however, Carlist criticism of the regime became so outspoken as to provoke the expulsion of the Borbón-Parma family from Spain in Dec. 1968. This, and the designation of don Juan Carlos as Franco's successor in 1969, threw Carlism once more into crisis. Carlos Hugo and his followers now led a renamed Carlist party into outright opposition, under the banner of a "Carlist socialism" inspired by the supposed revolution manqué of the nineteenth-century pueblo carlista. Many disgruntled conservative Carlists belatedly followed several waves of precursors into the Franco camp, while others assumed a more aggressive rightist stance, either in a reformed Traditionalist Communion or in any of a number of neotraditionalist or neofascist splinter groups.

With the death of Franco and succession of Juan Carlos in 1975, and the subsequent transition to democracy, Carlos Hugo's party lost its raison d'être and the modest support it had briefly possessed. By the mid–1980s, a disillusioned Carlos Hugo had effectively abandoned his affairs. By 1988, while the Carlist party on the Left, and several traditionalist factions on the Right, still exist, it is reasonable to assume that, as a significant political force, Carlism has at last become extinct.

For additional information, see M. Blinkhorn, *Carlism and Crisis in Spain 1931–1939* (Cambridge, 1975); J. del Burgo, *Conspiración y guerra civil* (Madrid, 1970); J. Camps i Giró, *La guerra dels matiners i el catalanism politic (1846–1849)* (Barcelona, 1976); J. C. Clemente, *Historia del carlismo contemporáneo 1935–1972* (Barcelona, 1976), and *Las guerras carlistas* (Barcelona, 1982); J. Extramiana, *Historia de las guerras carlistas*, 2 vols. (San Sebastian, 1979–1980); and R. Oyarzun, *Historia del carlismo* (Madrid, 1969).

*M. Blinkhorn*

*Related entries*: VÁZQUEZ DE MELLA, JUAN; ZUMALACÁRREGUI, TOMÁS DE.


**CARLOS III, KING OF SPAIN** (1716–1788), ruled 1759–1788. Born on 20 Jan. 1716, Carlos was the fifth son of Felipe V* of the House of Bourbon and the first of Isabel Farnesio (1692–1766), Felipe's second wife. Since two of his half-brothers died in childhood, and Luis I (1707–1724) after a brief reign in 1724, Carlos succeeded the childless Fernando VI (1713–1759), who died on 10 Aug. 1759. The king of the Two Sicilies at the time of his Spanish inheritance, Carlos arrived at Barcelona* on 17 Aug.

Carlos is generally ranked the greatest of the Spanish Bourbons. An enlightened and ambitious man, his freedom of mind enabled him to challenge entrenched privileges and search boldly for modern alternatives. His approach to royal government, while rational and liberating, was also highly pragmatic. Its fundamental design was to increase the prosperity and power of the absolutist state and enhance its capacity to wage war.

Influenced by the enlightened teachings of Jerónimo Feijóo,* Carlos demonstrated progressive, efficient rule in Italy* during his brief reign as duke of Parma and Piacenza and after 1734 as king of the Two Sicilies. Carlos's talent was his ability to select capable ministers, support them loyally, and thus minimize the intrigue that inevitably entered the affairs of court. In Naples, he found Bernardo Tanucci (1698–1783), a Tuscan lawyer, who served in his administration and schooled him in the art of good government. Together, they did much to curb the feudal privileges of the nobility; curtail the immunities and temporal power of the church; improve the administration of justice; and promote economic development, fiscal reform, and a revival of science* and the arts. When he abandoned Naples for Spain, Carlos left Tanucci behind to guide his son, who later became Carlos IV,* but corresponded with the Italian until his death in 1783.

Carlos faced his severest trials in Spain early in his reign. Confronted by a world at war, he entered into the Third Family Compact with France* in Aug. 1761, hoping to use his weight to mediate a satisfactory settlement between that power and Britain.* Instead, Spain itself was drawn into the Seven Years' War,* a conflict for which it was ill prepared, as revealed by resounding defeats at Havana and Manila and the loss of Florida in the Treaty of Paris (1763).

Determined to reverse Spain's fortunes, Carlos sustained his commitment to the Family Compact and plunged Spain and its empire into vigorous preparation for war. His instrument was the minister of finance and war, Leopoldo de Gregorio, the marqués de Esquilache,* who had accompanied him from Naples. While Esquilache successfully structured a program to place Havana on a sound military footing, his reforms in Spain generated heated controversy, which contributed to the traumatic Hat and Cloak Riots of Mar. 1766. Forced to exile the Italian, Carlos fled Madrid for Aranjuez under cover of darkness. Frightened and humiliated, he considered transferring the capital to Seville and never again entering Madrid. Carlos nevertheless summoned the courage to return in Dec., after the customary stays of the court at the spring, summer, and fall palaces. Further embarrassments arose when Carlos was forced to yield in the 1770–1771 dispute with Britain over the Falkland (Malvinas) Islands and an invasion of Algiers failed in 1775.

In the face of these reverses, Carlos worked with single-minded determination to reform his domains and reestablish Spain's international standing. As he had in Italy, he found capable magistrates to assist him, including the marqués de Grimaldi (1720–1786); Pedro Abarca y Bolea, the conde de Aranda*; Pedro Rodríguez, the conde de Campomanes*; José Moñino, the conde de Floridablanca*; Miguel de Múzquiz*; and José de Gálvez.* Carlos met daily with his ministers and councils, normally during the morning, and established the Order of Carlos III as recognition for meritorious government service.

To improve governmental efficiency, the administration of justice, and the collection of taxes, Carlos intensified the process of centralization he had inherited from his Bourbon predecessors. He sought to stimulate the economy* through modernized mercantilism and an eclectic combination of deregulation and government enterprise. Legislation of 1765 and 1778 simplified the process of licensing and inspecting ships and opened much of America to most of Spain's principal ports, thus breaking the historic monopoly of the Consulado de Cadiz.

Carlos also weakened the grip of the craft and merchant guilds over their local communities and liberalized standards for membership. To encourage productive enterprise, the political stigma associated with work in the crafts was legally removed. Carlos curtailed the grazing privileges of the Mesta to aid crop production. He attempted land reform, albeit without much success, but the crown lands of the Sierra Morena were productively colonized with foreigners. Through public works, canals were built and roads improved. Although the tendency was to promote freer competition in the marketplace, Carlos also fostered state enterprise by establishing a series of royal factories, making liberal use of foreign technicians. The lucrative royal tobacco monopoly was likewise ambitiously expanded in the colonies.*

A deeply pious man, Carlos nevertheless took a strong regalist position regarding the church, advancing policies to curb its temporal power and privileges, improve the quality of the clergy, and open the door to enlightened thought. Blaming the Hat and Cloak Riots on the ultramontanist Society of Jesus, he expelled the Jesuits in 1767. Reform of the universities followed, including a reorientation of curriculum toward experimental rationalism and greater emphasis on mathematics and science. The grip of the colegios mayores of Salamanca, Valladolid, and Alcalá on appointments to high ecclesiastical and administrative offices and the judicial tribunals of Spain and America was replaced by a system based on merit. With royal support, Sociedades Económicas de Amigos del País* were established throughout Spain to disseminate modern thought, particularly in the applied sciences. A flourishing periodical press added to the flow of information.

His priority was to secure the means to finance an ambitious armament program. While reducing the repressive alcabala, Carlos instituted new taxes on land and rental income. His liberalized commercial policy, although entailing the hope of economic development, was primarily oriented toward enhancing customs revenues. Also bolstered by more efficient collection policies, royal income registered remarkable gains, but much went to the army* and the fleet. In order to free the monarchy from its dependence for emergency finance on privileged corporations such as the Cinco Gremios Mayores de Madrid and the Consulado of Cadiz, Carlos established the Banco de San Carlos in 1782.

Some of his most ambitious reforms concerned the empire. Following the Seven Years' War, Carlos initiated a far-reaching colonial reorganization. Proceeding piecemeal, the crown took the risky step of arming Americans in a disciplined militia system. It assumed responsibility for efficient mail service; radically liberalized commercial policy; introduced intendants to improve provincial administration; and increased royal revenues through raising taxes, expanding royal monopolies, and improving revenue collection. Other innovations included the establishment of the Viceroyalty of Río de la Plata (1776), the Captaincy General of Caracas (1777), and the Commandancy General of the Interior Provinces (1776). Mining reform missions were sent to New Spain, New Granada, and Peru, and botanical expeditions advanced the cause of science in New Granada and Peru.

By the 1780s, Carlos believed with some justification that Spain had become a power of the first order. Royal income stood at unprecedented levels. The army had been expanded, an ambitious ship-building program had made the fleet the second or third largest in the world, and America stood well defended. Military academies had been established for the artillery, cavalry, and infantry. During the War of American Independence (1779–1783), Spain had exacted revenge upon the British with offensive victories in Florida, reacquiring the colony by the Treaty of Paris in (1783), and Carlos ambitiously contemplated the eventual expulsion of the British from Gibraltar, Jamaica, and Belize.

Fundamental problems, however, remained unresolved. Despite administrative centralization, the arming of Americans and the immense military expenditures in the empire amounted to a dangerous transfer of power to colonial hands. Although commercial deregulation provided some stimulus, Spanish industry remained weak, perhaps the victim of heavy taxation and the large investment of American revenues in colonial defense. Capitalist agriculture enabled the aristocracy to gain strength, conserving most of its seignorial privileges, while the mass of the peasantry languished in poverty.

Carlos was an astute and caring monarch. He eschewed personal extravagance except for the hunt, which was his passion. He patronized the decorative arts and brought the painter Francisco de Goya* to court. In Madrid, he championed urban beautification and is especially remembered for founding a botanical garden, an observatory, and a modern hospital. While hunting, he contracted the chill that developed into a fever and brought his life to an end on 14 Dec. 1788.

Carlos married María Amalia de Sajonia (1724–1760) of the House of Saxony, the daughter of King Augustus II (1670–1733) of Poland, in 1738. She bore thirteen children, seven of whom survived childhood. They included two daughters, the malformed María Josefa, and María Luisa, who married Leopold II (1747–1792) of Austria. The five sons were the source of heartbreak and disappointment. The mentally retarded Felipe had to be disinherited. Carlos, the prince of Asturias, and Fernando, king of the Two Sicilies, were mediocrities. The favored Gabriel, who married Mariana Victoria Braganza, died just days before his father. Probably the greatest distinction of Antonio Pascual was his appearance in Goya's portrait of his brother's family. María Amalia died in Sept. 1760, having become ill soon after her arrival in Madrid. Carlos neither remarried nor took a mistress.

For additional information, see J. A. Escudero, *Los orígenes del Consejo de Ministros en España*, 2 vols. (Madrid, 1979); J. Fontana and A. M. Bernal, eds., *El "comercio libre" entre España y América (1765–1824)* (Madrid, 1988); R. Herr, *The Eighteenth-Century Revolution in Spain* (Princeton, 1958); and A. Hull, *Charles III and the Revival of Spain* (Washington, 1981).

                                                                                        A. J. Kuethe

*Related entries*: COLONIES; ENLIGHTENMENT, AGE OF.


**CARLOS IV, KING OF SPAIN** (1748–1819), ruled 1788–1808. Carlos was born 11 Nov. 1748 to Carlos III* and María Amalia de Sajonia and became the prince of Asturias after the death of his mentally defective elder brother Felipe in 1759. Married to María Luisa of Parma in 1765, the couple lived under the approbation of Carlos III for their laziness and moral slackness. Their familial discord was caused by a generational clash between the king, raised to rule by his mother, Isabel Farnesio (1692–1766), and his son, who after his marriage to the sexually promiscuous María Luisa (1751–1819) had to wait more than twenty years for an opportunity to rule, ignored by his father. When his time finally came in 1788, Carlos IV became a monarch without vigor or intelligence.

Much of his early rule was carried on by the condes de Aranda* and Floridablanca,* favorites of his father. Both clearly disapproved of the new king. Court activities, the sizable royal family (six children, although the two youngest were probably not sired by Carlos), uncertainties caused by Carlos's birth in Italy* (which led him to secretly repeal Salic succession laws in 1789), and the outbreak of the French Revolution distracted the king and queen and made them fall prey to a clever guardsman, Manuel Godoy,* who was probably the queen's lover. Carlos, persuaded to pursue the French throne after the execution of Louis XVI (1754–1793), found himself at war with France,* in debt for more than 680 million reales, and pressed to elevate Godoy as the ''Prince of Peace'' for his settlement of the war with France that was a fiasco from start to finish.

For Carlos's eldest son, Fernando (king in 1808 and from 1814–1833), the situation became intolerable as early as 1799, and the court was internally divided until 1808. The international complications of the Napoleonic era (1799–1814) were far beyond the king, and the queen's private life continued to provide the scandal that gravely damaged the prestige of the monarchy. The transfer of Louisiana back to France in 1803 (who promptly sold it to the United States*), and the Treaty of Fontainebleau in 1807 to allow French passage across Spain to overthrow Portugal* were public embarrassments that finally forced Carlos to dismiss Godoy on 29 Oct. 1807 after the Prince of Peace's vain effort to obtain a crown of his own led to intrigues with Emperor Napoleon I (1769–1821), whose designs on Spain and Portugal were apparent. The allies of Godoy soon freed him, however, and created such chaos that Fernando rebelled at Aranjuez in Mar. 1808 and overthrew both Godoy and Carlos to seize the throne himself for a few short days.

Carlos and María Luisa immediately appealed to Napoleon, giving the French emperor the opportunity to intervene openly in Spanish politics by calling all parties to France, where Carlos and Fernando jointly were forced to abdicate. The king and queen lived as pensioners of France at the Chateau de Chambord until after the fall of Napoleon, when they fled to Rome, where Carlos died five years later on 20 Jan. 1819, ostracized for his royal ineptness and the debt of 7.2 billion reales left by his regime.

For additional information, see D. Hilt, *The Troubled Trinity: Godoy and the Spanish Monarchy* (Tuscaloosa, 1987); and G. H. Lovett, *Napoleon and the Birth of Modern Spain*, 2 vols. (New York, 1965).

R. W. Kern

*Related entries*: FERNANDO VI; GODOY, MANUEL; JOVELLANOS, GASPAR MELCHOR DE; INDEPENDENCE, WAR OF.

**CARRILLO, SANTIAGO** (1915– ), Communist party* leader. Carrillo was born in Gijón on 18 Jan. 1915 to a working-class family with socialist sympathies. At thirteen, when he began working, he joined the Juventudes Socialistas, and in 1934, he became its secretary-general at nineteen. Jailed by the Alejandro Lerroux* government for participating in the Asturias uprising of Oct. 1934, he was not freed until the Popular Front elections in Feb. 1936. The months before the Spanish Civil War* were dominated by his first trip to Moscow and the merger of Juventudes Socialistas with the communists to form the Juventudes Socialistas Unificadas (JSU). Carrillo joined the Communist party of Spain (PCE) in Nov. 1936, and during the civil war, he continued working with the JSU, but also became a delegate of the defense junta that ran Madrid* after the republican government moved to Valencia* in Nov. 1936. It was during this period that the junta was accused of executing a number of nationalist prisoners at Parcuellos de Jarama, an issue that has followed Carrillo ever since. At the end of the civil war, he denounced his father, Wenceslao, for participating in the takeover of the junta by Col. Segismundo Casado (1893–1968) that ended communist control of Madrid.

Carrillo fled to France* for a time after the fall of the Second Republic* before moving to Moscow in Sept. 1939, where briefly he became a secretary in the Communist Youth International before traveling through the Americas; he returned to France in 1944. At the end of World War II,* the headquarters of the PCE in exile was moved to Prague, Czechoslovakia, where Carrillo spent some time and rose in the ranks until in 1960 he became the PCE's secretary-general.

Before 1960, the PCE had provided an effective underground opposition to Gen. Francisco Franco,* but its isolation as a clandestine party became apparent when it became badly divided over whether to oppose Spanish admittance to the United Nations and refused to join the Pact of Paris in Apr. 1957 to create a new provisional government to oppose Francoism. While this isolation was partly reversed by PCE participation in the all-factions Munich conference of June 1962 and by PCE penetration in the 1960s of the Comisiones Obreras (CCOO), a fledgling labor organization in northern Spain (led by the communist Marcelino Camacho*), a schism in Oct. 1964 with Fernando Claudín (1912?– ) and Jorge Semprún (1923– ), supporters of an early version of Eurocommunism, rocked the PCE and Carrillo's leadership in Oct. 1964. The CCOO's subsequent militancy became a last-ditch effort to organize a pure workers' party, but while its persecution drew sympathy from Spaniards weary of Franco's regime, leftist attitudes were much more broadly based in the 1970s and the maneuver did not succeed. In any case, the assassination of Francoist Luis Carrero Blanco (1903–1973) in Dec. 1973 led to government persecution of the PCE, despite protests that this group had nothing to do with the assassination.

These prefatory events may explain why Carrillo became such an enthusiastic convert to Eurocommunism in July 1976. He distanced himself from Moscow and party domination over personal tastes and values. Above all, he said, he wanted communists to treasure heretical views rather than continue to evolve in a conservative, Stalinist manner. Subsequently, the Ninth Party Congress in Apr. 1978, following Carrillo's argument in his book *Eurocomunismo y estado*, dropped ''Leninist'' from its title and the goal of creating a dictatorship of the proletariat from its bylaws and endorsed Eurocommunism.

In the meantime, the death of Franco in Nov. 1975 allowed Carrillo to end forty years of exile and return to Spain in Dec. 1976. He was arrested on 22 Dec., but was unexpectedly released on 30 Dec., when he accepted the monarchy and the flag. He took a public role in the early events of the constitutional monarchy as one of the negotiators of the Moncloa Pact (Oct. 1977), an unsuccessful attempt to gain labor peace at a time of high inflation and economic dislocation. In the elections of 1977, the PCE won 9.3 percent of the vote and twenty seats in the Cortes, totals that increased to 10 percent and twenty-three seats in 1979. If these showings were a personal triumph for Carrillo, though, the election of 28 Oct. 1982 that saw the PCE win only four seats was his worst personal defeat. Critics charged that the PCE's Eurocommunism made it indistinguishable from the better-organized, social-democratic Socialist party* (PSOE). A pro-Moscow faction (which included Dolores Ibarruri*) had been dogging Carrillo since he had become a convert to Eurocommunism, and the mood within the PCE soon became rancorous, finally causing him to resign his offices on 11 Nov. 1982.

For additional information, see S. Carrillo, *Demain l'Espagne* (Paris, 1974) and *Eurocommunism and the State* (Westport, 1978); F. Claudín, *Documentos de una divergencia comunista* (Barcelona, 1978); J. Semprún, *Autobiografía de Federico Sánchez* (Barcelona, 1977); and M. E. Yagüe, *Santiago Carrillo* (Madrid, 1977).

*R. W. Kern*

*Related entries*: COMMUNIST PARTY; IBARRURI, DOLORES.

**CASALS, PAU [PABLO]** (1876–1973), cellist. Casals, born near Barcelona* and trained as a cellist in Spain, became an immediate international sensation after his 1899 debut in Paris. He toured extensively for several years, giving as many as 250 concerts a year, and revolutionized cello technique by freeing the arms of the performer at the sides of the instrument. He also was the first cellist to perform all J. S. Bach's (1685–1750) "Six Suites for Unaccompanied Cello" publicly as a whole. He was noted for his interpretation of romantic classical music.

In 1919, he returned to Barcelona and, hoping to create a first-class Spanish orchestra, established the Orquestra Pau Casals. He personally subsidized the Orquestra to keep ticket prices within the reach of even the poorest working men and women.

When the Spanish Civil War* began in 1936, Casals sided openly with the republic. Wartime pressures caused the Orquestra to disband, and in 1938, Casals went into self-imposed exile, first in Paris and later in Prades, a small town in the French Pyrenees. Until 1945, he gave benefit concerts and used the proceeds to organize relief efforts in the refugee camps of southern France, but he then stopped giving public performances to personally protest the Allied decision not to intervene in Spain after World War II.*

The world came to Casals, however, and he resumed performing in 1950 as part of the celebrations honoring the bicentennial of Bach's death. Later, he organized his own personal crusade for peace, touring with a United Nations orchestra and performing his oratorio, *El pessbre* (The Manger). In later years, he never returned to Spain. He died in Puerto Rico in 1973.

For additional information, see P. Casals, *Joys and Sorrows* (New York, 1970); E. Cowling, *The Cello* (New York, 1975); and H. Kirk, *Pablo Casals: A Biography* (New York, 1974).

*S. L. Brake*

**CASTILE,** area of central Spain including the modern provinces of Toledo, Cuidad Real, Cuenca, Guadalajara, Madrid, and Albacete in the Castile–La Mancha region, and Valladolid, Burgos, Leon, Salamanca, Zamora, Palencia, and Segovia in the Leon–Old Castile region. Pop. (1982 est.) 7,409,904; sq. mi. 55,307.

The arid, upland sand- and limestone plateaus of Old and New Castile, the mesetas (in Latin "table," literally table lands) resemble the topography of the U.S. Southwest. Two-fifths of the land is treeless—the Castile of the Mesta, the land of livestock raising. Sheep still dominate the landscape of the Castiles, and more than half Spain's sixteen million sheep are raised in the central regions. The native pasture grasses turn brown early in the summer, and the flocks scatter widely, although the ancient practice of long-distance herding has been motorized. The Cantabrian Mountains of Asturias* and Leon in Old Castile, reaching an elevation of 8,786 feet in the Picos de Europa, water extensive pastures; the Guadarrama range northeast and southwest of Madrid,* with a high point of 8,501 feet, does the same in central Castile.

Rainfall is several inches more than in the western Great Plains of the United States* and six inches greater than in the American Southwest, which permits successful dry-land grain growing as the main cash crop of Castile. The numerous river valleys (including the two largest, the Duero and the Tagus) throughout the mesetas permit more intensive cultivation of fertile pockets of well-watered soils and the production of sugar beets near Valladolid; of esparto grass throughout Old Castile; and of rye, alfalfa, and fruit in the valleys of the whole region.

Population centers in Old Castile were determined by water supply and ease of defense; thus, only Valladolid is centrally located. Burgos commands trade routes from the central mesetas to the northern mountains. Salamanca is an old university town; Avila and Segovia, historic towns that are now tourist centers; while the rest—Leon, Palencia, Zamora, Soria, and Béjar—serve agriculture and local industry.

Madrid marks the division of the two Castiles. It is an urban center now more than 4 million in population, the demographic and governmental center of Spain and also a steadily growing industrial zone. South of Madrid, New Castile (since 1979 renamed Castile–La Mancha) stretches south to the Guadalquivir River valley of Andalusia* and south and west to Estremadura, broken by the smaller mountain ranges of the Sierra de Guadalupe, the Montes de Toledo, the Sierra Morena, and the Serranía de Cuenca. It has a warmer and drier climate than Old Castile and is sparsely populated. Badajoz, Albacete, Cáceres, Toledo, Ciudad Real, and Cuenca lack the size or industry of their counterparts in the north.

Historically, Castile's military tradition began with the Reconquista of the Middle Ages and acquired greatness in the national union and empire of the fifteenth and sixteenth centuries. By the Bourbon era, however, bankruptcy and loss of European empire crippled Castilian power and made the Siglo de Oro but a memory. Taxation remained high, agriculture lay in ruins, and the rural areas of the two Castiles were either abandoned or dangerously underpopulated. The French and Italian advisors of Felipe V,* who did not identify with Castile as had the conde-duque de Olivares (Gaspar de Guzmán, 1587–1645) in the

1630s, sought to improve these conditions by restricting aristocratic status in order to increase tax collections; reforming encomiendas; and, under Fernando VI (1713–1759) in 1749, introducing a single tax (catastro) in Castile. The royal Mesta tax was abolished in 1758 to help promote agriculture.

During the reign of Carlos III,* price ceilings were abolished on grain in 1765 to stimulate the rural economy. The crown granted the right to enclose land in 1788 after centuries of resisting such legislation in the Mesta's behalf. As part of the first real land reform, Pedro Rodríguez, the conde de Campomanes,* and Pedro Abarca de Bolea, the conde de Aranda,* distributed unused Castilian lands to landless peasants and foreign freeholders in 1771. As revenues from wool and grain sales improved, free trade allowed Castilians to import scarce manufactured goods. By the early nineteenth century, Bourbon rule could claim some measure of success in returning Castile to its place of national importance.

The liberals finally abolished two special Castilian privileges, the Council of Castile (1835) and the Mesta (1839). They also continued the slow rehabilitation of Castilian agriculture by seizing ecclesiastical and royal lands, although private owners had difficulty improving the land and private ownership often disrupted local political life. One contemporary problem was the rise of agrarian rents, which increased steeply in some areas and socially destabilized parts of the region. The pattern varied widely; the number of independent small farmers actually increased around Valladolid and Salamanca, while large and small cultivators in the Burgos area offset rising rents or land costs by successfully increasing grain production in classic economic fashion. In contrast to Andalusia, sale on the open market of entailed and mortmain lands confiscated by liberals did not result in the worst types of corruption normally associated with the process.

These changes led to adoption of national free-trade policies in 1869. Castilian crops purchased the new machinery needed to intensify production, but at the expense of manufacturers in Catalonia,* who protested Castilian self-interest and supported protectionism and Catalan regionalism until free trade was abandoned in 1891. Once unleashed, sectional feelings did not disappear after tariff policy had changed. A latent Castilianism equated the good of the nation with the central meseta areas—a counterregionalist attitude that was neo-Catholic, authoritarian, and militaristic. Both Alfonso XIII* and Gen. Francisco Franco* identified with these values, and many Castilians responded enthusiastically to this chauvinism. In any case, Castile benefited the most from the legal and fiscal uniformity imposed by modern government, which had removed the crushing tax burden and military obligations of Olivares's seventeenth-century Castile without weakening the Castilian hold on government employment.

Simultaneously, changes in Madrid unleashed other social forces. The crossroads town of Felipe II's day in the mid–sixteenth century changed into several cities: the nineteenth-century city of great boulevards and the Gran Vía shopping area and the late twentieth-century metropolis of steel-and-glass buildings and superhighways. The Unión General de Trabajadores* (UGT) moved from Barcelona* to Madrid in 1899 and became a major political force. Since Madrid acted as a magnet in drawing unemployed and displaced agricultural workers, politics also changed. The city offset the rural traditionalism of the countryside, although the more Madrid changed, the more the large towns of Old Castile moved right themselves in reaction to the capital's politics. Burgos became the center of Gen. Francisco Franco's nationalist regime during the Spanish Civil War,* while Madrid's loyalty to the Second Republic* during three years of siege demonstrated its radicalism.

The divided political soul of Castile after 1936 and the pan-national problems of the Franco regime up to 1975 may explain the decrease of a militant Castilian spirit in the present era. Castile no longer speaks with one voice, because Madrid's industrialization gave it greater rapport with Barcelona or Saragossa than with Valladolid or Burgos. Many aspects of the past live on, but regionalism, now recognized by the Constitution of 1978, has less impact in Castile than changes introduced by international culture, and Madrid's role in the world economy will bring more changes as Spanish membership in the European Economic Community increases these contacts.

For additional information, see S. Brandes, *Migration, Kinship and Community: Tradition and Transition in a Spanish Village* (New York, 1975); F. Bravo Morata, *Historia de Madrid*, 3 vols. (Madrid, 1966); S. T. Freeman, *Neighbors: The Social Contract in a Castilian Hamlet* (Chicago, 1970); M. Kenney, *A Spanish Tapestry: Town and Country in Castile* (New York, 1966); J. M. Martínez Bande, *La lucha en torno a Madrid* (Madrid, 1968) and *La ofensiva sobre Segovia y la batalla de Brunete* (Madrid, 1972); D. Ridruejo, *Castilla la Vieja* (Barcelona, 1980); D. Ringrose, *Madrid and the Spanish Economy, 1560–1850* (Berkeley, 1983); and R. Way, *A Geography of Spain and Portugal* (London, 1962).

                                                                                          *R. W. Kern*

**CASTRO, ROSALÍA DE** (1837–1885), Spanish-Galician writer. Castro, an illegitimate daughter of a Galician noblewoman and a priest (probably José Martínez Viojo, whose parents raised her until she was thirteen), spent her adolescence with her mother in Santiago de Compostela. She received a good education for the time; began writing early; and was soon a participant in regional literary activities. At nineteen, she moved to Madrid* and married a journalist, with whom she had seven children, including two that died before the age of two.

In her career, Castro published not only in Spanish but also in Galician, a language of northwestern Spain derived from Galician-Portuguese of the twelfth and thirteenth centuries when it was the preferred language for Iberian lyrics. Eventually, she ranked with Gustavo Adolfo Bécquer* as the foremost postromantic poet of the nineteenth century.

Her writings included both poetry and prose, but it was her Galician poetry that brought her fame. Nineteenth-century Galicia* was one of the Spanish regions with strong separatist tendencies and a dream of elevating Galician to a written language in order to restore its culture. Castro's publication of a book of poems entitled *Cantares Gallegas* (1863) in her native language gave her regional popularity and national respect. *Cantares* was inspired by the music and letters of popular Galician songs, a fusion of her creative power with admiration for traditional Galician folk elements and love for the Galician people and countryside. One theme focused on the region's beauty; another described the plight of the poor and their forced departure from the region in search of employment. *Cantares Gallegas* transcended regional boundaries into the realm of universal poetry by the quality of her poetic style and empathy with the people.

The publication of Castro's second and third major poetry collections (of the five she produced) showed a maturity that raised her to a new prominence in Spanish letters. *Follas novas* (1880) and *En las orillas del Sar* (1884) are easy to read because they contain few rhetorical devices or convoluted metaphors. They are direct and sincere, filled with a variety of innovative metrical forms to better express the musicality of her verses. Her themes deal with nature and human emotion; love was particularly important in her work, a driving force that initially brings joy, but ultimately causes sorrow.

Castro's prose has not generated the same acclaim as her poetry. Her early novels and stories drew heavily upon the romantic tradition; her first, *La hija del mar* (1859), was darkly so, but her later novels evolved toward more modern forms until her next-to-last novel, *El caballero de las botas azules* (1866), was a social satire.

Castro's last years were marked by a surge of interest in her own feminism, which biographers have found to be courageous at a time when writing poetry for public consumption was still a male occupation. Her poetry expressed displeasure with all forms of social injustice. In nonfiction, two articles, "Lieders" and "Literatas," became explicit statements of her social ideas.

For additional information, see K. Kulp-Hill, *Rosalía de Castro* (Boston, 1977); M. Mayoral, *La poesía de Rosalía de Castro* (Madrid, 1974); and C. H. Poullain, *Rosalía Castro de Murguia y su obra literaria* (Madrid, 1974).

*N. A. Vigil*

*Related entries*: BÉCQUER, GUSTAVO ADOLFO; GALICIA.

**CATALONIA,** northeastern Spain, with modern provinces of Barcelona, Gerona, Lérida, and Tarragona. Pop. (1983 est.) 5,958,203; sq. mi. 12,327. Descendant of the Frankish marca hispánica, Catalonia from its beginnings seemed marked off from the rest of Spain by its language, culture, and geographical configuration. The castellated aspect of the mountainous region has long served to guarantee the separate existence of this "land of castles" as a political entity. Great Tertiary uplifts dominate most of the zone, from its imposing, northern Pyrenean border to the massive Sierra de Cadi, the district's western boundary; and from the central basin to the steep but regular coastline. The only area not dominated by mountains is the flat, marshy delta land surrounding Tortosa, which shares many of the features of the Valencian huerta. Catalonia's rivers all owe their source to the northern and western mountain ranges. The higher streams, the Fluvia, Ter, Llobregat, and Francoli, empty into the Mediterranean, but offer few navigational possibilities. The Segre, one of Catalonia's medieval borders, flows past Lérida and empties into the Ebro, the region's greatest navigable river and source of much of its irrigation.

The variations of the country's climate and agriculture reflect its serried relief. In the north, winter temperatures can fall well below freezing, and precipitation rates may top forty inches. In the south, average temperature may increase to 90°F in the summer, and rainfall totals may decrease to fifteen inches yearly. Olives, grapes, wheat, and common vegetables are cultivated in the northern and central zones, while almonds, rice, and subtropical fruits are grown in the south. The northernmost districts support most of the country's cattle and sheep industry. In spite of its mountains, the region is relatively poor in usable minerals, the only significant deposits of coal, lead, and potash existing in the upper Llobregat basin.

The Catalan national character was molded in the region's mountainous separateness. Because of these natural barriers, the Catalans have long felt ethnically and culturally distinct from other Spaniards. Reinforcing this perception is the Catalan language, which resembles French as much as it does Spanish. The very nature of the land has forced on Catalans social patterns unshared by the rest of the peninsula. Lacking rich soil, the region's farmers have long been forced to compensate with industriousness; a Catalan saying emphasizes this spirit in the claim that "Catalans get bread out of stones." This ethic of hard work has driven Catalans to take full advantage of every meager opportunity. Inhabiting an area endowed with fine natural harbors, northeastern Spaniards thus became a race of traders and carved out a large economic empire in the Middle Ages.

Bolstered by a reverence for its past, Catalonia has never fit well in a Spanish nation-state dominated by Castile.* This "spoil't child of the Peninsular family" has time and again resisted the central government on the grounds that it has run roughshod over Catalan laws and customs. Because of many centralist attacks on their culture during the last three centuries, Catalans have never lost either their hatred of the Castilian rulers or their firm conviction in the validity of their own culture. This unshakable assurance has served to keep Catalan civilization alive, even during the epochs of darkest repression, then allowed it to come into full flower, finally influencing the course of Spanish policy itself.

The differences between the Catalan periphery and the Castilian center far exceed language. Perhaps no element better explains the dissimilar courses of the two regions than the advance of industry. The medieval Catalan empire was based on the conquest of territories in the central Mediterranean, but also focused on gaining markets for such manufactured goods as textiles, paper, glassware, jewelry, and pottery. These items were produced in Barcelona* and a ring of surrounding towns. Despite the exclusion of Catalonia from American commerce, the trading-manufacturing unity of northeastern Spain retained Mediterranean importance well into the Hapsburg era. Strangely, the political repression directed against Catalonia with the new Bourbon dynasty in 1715 stimulated the region's urban growth and commerce. Catalan shipping was compensated for the loss of Mediterranean markets by the policy of Carlos III* of opening American trade to all Spanish regions after 1765.

The most significant economic feature of the era, however, centered on industrial development. In Barcelona and its environs, manufacture of cotton and calico goods was modernized from the late eighteenth century by the adoption of a factory system and steam-powered weaving equipment. British industrial models were closely followed and improved with the Bergadan loom and perfection of Europe's first thread factory.

The "great and active industry" Arthur Young observed in Barcelona in 1787 had already begun to accentuate Catalonia's difference from the rest of Spain. A small clique of factory owners soon consolidated their hold over Catalan industry and thus began deeply to affect the economy* of the entire peninsula. Characterized by Castilian business leaders as "birds of prey . . . of unbridled voracity," Catalonia's great industrialists further tightened their hold on the economy of the region throughout the nineteenth century by sponsoring railroad construction, modernization of factory equipment, and a thoroughgoing protectionism.

Despite a clear record of success that even Madrid had to respect, Catalan industry underwent a series of structural and external setbacks. With a backward banking system, a fairly narrow band of industrial expertise, and a paucity of natural resources, Catalan manufacturing began to reach its systemic limits at the dawn of the twentieth century. World events also conspired to flatten Catalonia's upward economic curve. The North American victory of 1898 and the end of World War I* robbed Catalonia of lucrative markets. Still, the region's industry remained paramount until after the Spanish Civil War,* when Gen. Francisco Franco* acted to encourage economic growth in other peninsular regions, and the Catalan business community seemed burdened by a sense of malaise. The last two decades of Franco's rule, however, saw a sharp Catalan recovery, with the removal of governmental strictures and a tremendous increase in tourism.

Catalonia's agricultural growth largely paralleled its industrial vicissitudes. With the Decree of Guadalupe in 1486, the Catholic kings virtually ended Catalonia's feudal regime by bestowing on the peasantry control of most of the region's farmland. Because of a constantly growing rural population, however, this boon soon became an onus many peasants escaped by immigrating to nearby industrial towns.

Catalonia's only true agrarian success was attained in viticulture, which is still expanding in such districts as Alt Panadés. The wine industry has been the only real force for drawing people back to the land, and it has done so by guaranteeing them fairly secure, long-term labor conditions with the rabassa morta sharecropping contract. After some major production dips at the turn of the century resulting from phylloxera and blight, the wine trade has reached new heights in the last two decades, with extensive exportation to the North American market. Apart from this achievement, Catalonia's rural districts have remained the region's poorest and still retain strong ties to the conservative, Carlist past.

Catalonia's problems as an industrial society have long made it a seedbed for intellectual movements of all sorts. From the mid–nineteenth century, the zone witnessed the birth of a labor movement. With the establishment around Barcelona of modern factories equipped with ''self-acting machines'' (selfactines), a primitive form of Luddism soon gave way to labor organizations that demanded better wages and conditions. General strikes, such as those of 1855, 1909, 1917–1923, 1931, 1944, and 1951, were called to attain these aims, but often triggered lethal exchanges between industrialists and labor thugs. These eras of unrest often resulted in much broader revolutions that, as in the Tragic Week of July 1909, brought governmental intervention and ended in widespread bloodshed.

Socialism and anarchism* deeply influenced the labor movement. Karl Marx's (1818–1883) view of a gradual, ''scientific'' revolution was disseminated through the Socialist party* (PSOE), the Partit Socialista Unificat de Catalunya* (PSUC), and the Unión General of Trabajadores* (UGT). A far greater number of anarchist workers adhered to Mikhail Bakunin's (1814–1876) philosophy that only violence could change the current society. These ideas, which were passed through the ranks of the Confederación Nacional de Trabajo (CNT) and the Federación Anarquista Ibérica (FAI), led to a great wave of nineteenth-century terrorism, including the bombing of the Liceu opera house in 1893. The split within Catalan labor erupted into open warfare in 1916 and 1937. These divisions, chronicled so movingly in George Orwell's (1903–1950) *Homage to Catalonia* (1938), clearly influenced the defeat of the Second Republic.*

The Catalan bourgeoisie, too, spawned a number of political philosophies intended to advance Catalonia within the Spanish power structure. This elite was deeply frustrated by a backward central government and looked to France* for inspiration in fashion, cuisine, and urban beautification. These commercial leaders wanted to direct the course of their own region and of all Spain. The complex of ideas they formulated came to be known as Catalanisme. Not a unified movement, it attempted to exalt all things Catalan. This romantic idea of the early nineteenth century unleashed a Catalan Renaxença, or renaissance, aimed at perfecting the region's language and investigating its past. The movement so ingrained Catalan culture in the region's populace that years of Francoist repression could not eradicate it. Religious and cultural Catalanisme formed a secret bond among Catalans that again became public in the 1960s, when calls for the right to enjoy their distinct civilization became more urgent. Thus, Madrid rightly construed such innocuous acts as the dancing of the sardana or singing of the regional anthem, ''La Senyera,'' in public as subversive.

In political terms, Catalanisme was a truly nationalistic force that posited a number of solutions to the Catalan problem. The most conservative of these was the call for a form of Spanish federalism similar to the North American system. Three ideologues of the late nineteenth and early twentieth centuries, Francesc Pi i Margall* (Francisco Pi y Margall), Valentí Almirall,* and Enrique Prat de la Riba,* proposed this solution for Spanish nationalities. They insisted that each national area be given its own parliament and that the central government respect its particular laws and customs. Many of these federalist ideas have again surfaced in Catalonia's two twentieth-century experiments with autonomy, from 1913 to 1923 and from 1980 to the present. Despite such centralist attempts at satisfying Catalan regional sentiments, many regionalists have urged separatism. These writers and journalists have systematically rejected a national Spanish allegiance and called for a separate Catalonia. Even with the easing of the government's suppression of Catalan culture in the 1970s and the move toward self-government in the 1980s, a sector of intellectuals and political activists with sympathies for or ties to the terrorist group Free Land (Terra Lliure) still clamor for succession.

The granting of Catalan autonomy in 1980 was characterized by the prime minister, Adolfo Suárez,* as the "only way out of Spain's current problems, but also . . . the principal risk that threatens our fragile democracy." Though Catalan language and culture were freed from centralist restraints by this decree, the turbulent and unhappy past of northeastern Spain has taught its inhabitants— including an entire generation of émigrés headed by such geniuses as Pau (Pablo) Casals* and Pablo Picasso*—that repression of this heritage is only a penstroke away. In addition to this ever-present danger from above, Catalan culture finds itself imperiled by more pressing and mundane threats: the culturally diluting effect of the massive influx of immigration from other Spanish regions and the increased drug use and crime that have followed the era of Francoist order. While Catalonia's rich civilization may change under the relentless pressure of the unitary Spanish state, it seems certain that the Catalans will have the *seny*, or good sense, to remain Catalan and Spanish at the same time.

For additional information, see V. Alba, *Catalonia: A Profile* (New York: 1975); A. Balcells, *El sindicalisme a Barcelona, 1916–1923* (Barcelona, 1966); E. C. Hansen, *Rural Catalonia under the Franco Regime* (London, 1977); G. W. McDonogh, ed., *Conflict in Catalonia: Image of an Urban Society, 1840–1940* (Gainesville, 1986); O. Pi-Sunyer, *Nationalism and Societal Integration: A Focus on Catalonia* (Amherst, 1983); J. Read, *The Catalans* (London, 1978); P. Vila, *Geografía de Catalunya* (Barcelona, 1934), and *La Catalogne dans l'Espagne moderne* (Paris, 1962).

*D. Kagay*

*Related entry*: BARCELONA.


**CATHOLICISM.** Few institutions have occupied a more central or controversial role in the history of Spain than the Catholic church. For 260 of the nearly 300 years that have passed since the first Bourbon king ascended the throne in 1700, Catholicism has been the official religion of the state and the Roman Catholic church its established church. Since the time of the French Revolution, apologists for the church have repeatedly identified it with the historic soul of the nation. Such an interpretation, of course, fails to take into account the broad movements of secularization that have affected Spain as fully as any European country, albeit tardily. When all is said and done, though, religion and the church have been intimately bound up with modern Spain's difficult search for political, social, and economic stability.

The collapse of the traditional absolute monarchy before the triumphant forces of nineteenth-century liberalism* marked a significant divide in the history of Spanish Catholicism. The long conflict between the church and liberalism and, later, pluralistic democracy, began formally in 1810 and did not end until the church accepted the new constitutional and democratic government established in the late 1970s. This prolonged struggle with modern forms of political expression endowed Spanish Catholicism with a particular character that made the church and its place within society a perennial source of intense and sometimes violent controversy.

Until the republican Constitution of 1931 separated church and state for the first time in the nation's history, every Spanish constitution had affirmed, in one way or another, Catholicism's official position. Yet the long confrontation with nineteenth-century liberalism proved a deeply traumatic experience for an institution accustomed to the enormous wealth and privileges it had possessed under absolute monarchy. A centuries-old relationship linking throne and altar gave the church a preeminence unmatched by any other institution in the kingdom save that of the monarchy itself. The church had acquired immense wealth in the form of land and other sources of income, amounting to perhaps as much as one-fourth of the gross national product, while the Inquisition, although less severe during the eighteenth century than in earlier times, had effectively maintained religious orthodoxy.

The eighteenth-century church paid a price for its privileges. The Bourbon kings, Felipe V,* Fernando VI (1713–1759), and Carlos III,* sought to exert ever-greater control over ecclesiastical administration. This movement, known as regalism, progressed erratically at first, but following the Concordat of 1753, which vastly increased the powers of the crown over clerical appointments, the Bourbons succeeded in creating a royal church subject to Rome only in matters of doctrine. Although some bishops, notably Bishop Carvajal y Lancaster (1698–1754) during the 1760s, protested growing state involvement in ecclesiastical affairs, regalism in fact attempted a series of necessary reforms. The expulsion of the Jesuits in 1767 was, to be sure, an example of regalist excess, but in other areas, state intervention proved beneficial. During the second half of the century, the crown appointed bishops with impressive qualifications, while it promoted the foundation of diocesan seminaries and, in general, sought to direct the energies of the clergy toward pastoral responsibilities. Regalist attempts to introduce change into a cumbersome ecclesiastical organization also received the support of a vital minority of reforming clergy, called Jansenists by their detractors and enlightened Catholics by later historiographical admirers. This so-called Jansenism was not a coherent movement, but its advocates, highly educated bishops and priests such as Josep Climent (1706–1781) of Barcelona, saw the necessity of introducing reforms into the church to improve its pastoral effectiveness.

To what extent even limited reform could be imposed on a sprawling organizational structure that had formed in successive stages over the centuries was problematical. The church possessed an unbalanced ecclesiastical superstructure dominated by a privileged clerical elite composed of sixty bishops, twenty-three hundred cathedral canons, and approximately five thousand rich benefice holders who received a disproportionate share of the institution's income. Almost all the kingdom's sixty thousand secular priests lived a precarious economic existence. Considerable wealth was also concentrated in the hands of more than three thousand monasteries, friaries, and convents containing seventy-seven thousand religious, although the riches of the regular clergy were also distributed unevenly.

By modern standards, the eighteenth-century church possessed an abundance of clergy and religious. Yet neither the wealth of the church nor its large body of personnel was primarily directed toward serving pastoral needs. By the end of the century, nearly one-fifth of the country's twenty thousand parishes lacked incumbents because of the aversion of the secular clergy to accepting poorly paid posts in an isolated countryside. Indeed, only one-third of the seculars served in parishes at all. Similarly, the regular clergy, with the exception of the medieval monastic orders, avoided establishing foundations in the countryside, preferring instead to locate in the cities where sources of income were more easily secured.

In spite of these deficiencies, the church retained the allegiance of nearly all the population, although assessing the quality and the extent of that faith poses difficult questions. There is some evidence that evangelizing efforts carried out after the Council of Trent (1545–1547, 1551–1552, 1562–1563) in the north and in Castile* succeeded in conveying a minimal knowledge of doctrine. To what extent this reflected a sincere acceptance of conscience or simple conformity to what has been called a religious ''civilization of habit'' imposed by social custom and the powerful pressure of the civil and ecclesiastical authorities remains a matter of debate. At the level of formal religious observance, at least, the population fulfilled the obligations the church imposed, while also engaging in a variety of sometimes extravagant popular devotions the clergy frequently opposed.

Reforming tendencies within the church began to weaken following the outbreak of the French Revolution as a prophetic and messianic spirit developed that laid the foundations for later clerical intransigence. The church saw the revolution as an impious conspiracy intent upon destroying religion and the established social order throughout Europe. This new militancy had two sides. On the one hand, it allowed the clergy to play a prominent role as propagandists and, sometimes, as combatants in the great national rising against the Bonaparte monarchy in Spain (1808–1813). Napoleon Bonaparte (1769–1821) and his brother Joseph (José I*), whom the emperor had placed on the Spanish throne, were vilified, unjustifiably, as agents of a sinister campaign to destroy Catholicism. On the other hand, the new militancy prepared the way for direct conflict with Spain's first modern parliamentary assembly, the Cortes of Cadiz.*

The struggle between the church and the liberal reformers at Cadiz set a pattern of civil-ecclesiastical relations that endured for more than century. Liberal deputies at Cadiz were neither anticlerical nor anti-Catholic. The Constitution of 1812 proclaimed Catholicism as the official religion of the state and made no concessions toward religious toleration. Abolition of the Inquisition (22 Jan. 1813), however, angered the bishops, although the decision was made primarily for political reasons inherited from eighteenth-century regalism. The Inquisition stood condemned, because it appeared to threaten the sovereign authority of the state.

There were, however, deeper sources of clerical hostility toward liberalism. Although the liberal revolution eschewed popular radicalism as it created a constitutional monarchy, it passed legislation that undermined the traditional hierarchical society in favor of a political philosophy emphasizing the individual and the equality of all subjects before the law. This emphasis on the centrality of the individual in political and social life clashed directly with an eighteenth-century scholastic interpretation of the purposes and organization of society. Many clergy saw society as forming a harmonious unity ordained by natural law and divine providence, but composed of distinct and unequal parts. Liberal individualism thus seemed a shocking and impious rebellion against nature and God.

The church, therefore, welcomed the coup d'état Fernando VII* executed upon his return from exile in France.* The king promptly restored the Inquisition, authorized the reestablishment of the Jesuits, and encouraged the bishops to purge the clergy of liberal sympathizers. There thus began the identification of the church with a repressive regime sympathetic to its interests that made prolonged conflict with liberalism inevitable. It was a struggle the church could not hope to win. After each battle, it faced a more determined adversary intent upon imposing ever-greater state control and forcing ecclesiastical reforms on a recalcitrant clergy.

Thus, the liberal revolution of 1820 sought to rationalize the structure of the regular clergy for the first time by closing approximately one-half of the kingdom's monasteries and friaries. Ecclesiastical reform, though, continued to figure prominently in the liberal program. The government attempted to improve the lot of the parochial clergy by eliminating benefices unconnected to pastoral work, by reducing the number of cathedral canons, and by increasing the income of parish priests. Although liberal concern with ecclesiastical reform never entirely disappeared, it gradually receded before an even stronger determination to break clerical opposition to the new political order.

The church paid a heavy price for its support of a restored absolutism (1823–1833) and the First Carlist War (1833–1840), during which Fernando's brother Carlos, a reactionary prince committed to uphold every particle of clerical privilege, opposed the succession of the king's young daughter Isabel II.* In 1834, the liberals returned to power. They soon imposed a far harsher ecclesiastical settlement than the church might have secured in 1812 or 1820.

Between 1834 and 1843, successive liberal governments carried out a revolution in the ecclesiastical order as thorough as the political revolution directed against the institutions of absolute monarchy. In 1835–1836, the prime minister, Juan Álvarez Mendizábal,* suppressed almost all the male religious orders and ordered the sale of their property for the benefit of the public treasury. Similar legislation in 1841 subjected the property of the secular clergy to the same fate, although the government undertook payment of salaries to diocesan bishops and parish priests. These measures dealt the church a double blow by virtually eliminating the regular clergy and by destroying the economic base that had supported the ecclesiastical establishment for centuries.

The effects of this ecclesiastic revolution and the defeat of Carlism* in 1840 forced the church to abandon its historic identification with absolute monarchy and seek a modus vivendi with a triumphant liberalism. The accession to power in 1843 of the most conservative liberals grouped in the Moderate party,* which saw the church as a useful ally against popular radicalism, opened the road to accommodation. In 1851, the government of Juan Bravo Murillo* concluded a concordat with the papacy* that governed civil-ecclesiastical relations until 1931, save for two brief periods. The concordat affirmed the status of the Catholic church as the established church of the state, confirmed the government's obligation to pay the salaries of the diocesan clergy, and authorized a limited reestablishment of the male religious orders. In return, the papacy accepted the sale of ecclesiastical property carried out until that time and government proposals for a rationalization of diocesan and parish boundaries.

The concordat of 1851 established an uneasy peace between church and state. As a result, the church was able to function normally for the first time in years, but at the cost of supporting the highly conservative moderato political system. In fact, the relationship between moderato governments and the church was never more than a marriage of convenience. Many bishops and priests remained deeply hostile to liberalism in all its political forms, although the church was more than prepared to secure any advantages it could from whatever government was in power. During the authoritarian moderato ministry of Gen. Ramón María Narváez,* the gains were considerable, particularly in education. The Revolution of 1868, however, swept away these new and tenaciously acquired privileges. Although the revolutionary Constitution of 1869 affirmed official ties between church and state, it also established religious liberty for the first time in the nation's history, thereby outraging the clergy and contributing to the outbreak of the Matiners' revolt (1846–1849). The clergy's worst fears appeared close to realization when the First Republic* proposed the outright separation of church and state. The republic's collapse in less than a year under the weight of internal divisions, however, saved the church from disestablishment.

The long conflict over the place of the church within a society governed by nineteenth-century liberal principles consumed clerical energies in the face of immense pastoral problems that emerged, in part, from liberal ecclesiastical reforms. The number of clergy, for example, declined far below eighteenth-century levels. The census of 1860 reported 42,765 secular priests, 1,683 male religious, and 18,817 nuns. This demographic decrease required major administrative changes, particularly in diocesan and parish organization, designed to use existing personnel effectively. In fact, little was done. Madrid, for instance, did not acquire diocesan status until 1885 because of the opposition of the archbishop of Toledo, who resisted losing the most populous city of his see.

To some extent, the church adapted to the new individualistic society liberalism created. The clergy promoted a vast range of new devotions, many imported from abroad, that differed substantially from the collective expression of popular piety characteristic of the eighteenth century. These devotions, simple and affective in emphasis, stimulated the development of a highly individualistic popular religion as cults, such as those to Our Lady of Lourdes, Our Lady of Perpetual Help, and others, spread rapidly. The devotional resurgence exercised a strong emotional appeal, particularly for women.* It was ill suited, though, to retain the allegiance of economically deprived industrial workers in the country's few manufacturing centers. In Barcelona,* for instance, attendance at religious services was clearly slipping by the late 1850s. Further, responses to a massive petition campaign organized in 1869 to protest religious toleration already showed a marked difference between a more religiously inclined north and a relatively indifferent south.

A new phase in the history of the modern church opened with the restoration of the Bourbon monarchy in 1874. The architect of the Restoration (1874–1923), Antonio Cánovas del Castillo,* sought to place the constitutional monarchy on a stable foundation by eliminating military intervention in politics and by creating a credible political opposition destined to take power in due course. Cánovas also believed that the chronic dissension over the role of the church characteristic of liberal politics had to be resolved. He therefore embarked on a delicate balancing policy designed to win clerical support for the regime without alienating the parliamentary opposition that had supported the principle of religious liberty.

To achieve this, Cánovas abrogated the secularizing legislation passed between 1868 and 1873 and allowed the full-scale reestablishment of the male religious orders as long as the state incurred no expense. In the drafting of the Constitution of 1876, the prime minister's abilities were put to the test. The constitution recognized the confessionality of the state, but Article 11 declared that no Spaniard could be prosecuted for private religious beliefs. Although the church campaigned vigorously against this provision, it finally accepted Article 11 grudgingly, as did advocates of full toleration who eventually formed the Liberal party under the leadership of Práxedes Mateo Sagasta.*

Up to a point, Cánovas had won his gamble. His ecclesiastical settlement, however, always remained ambiguous during the Restoration. The hierarchy, to be sure, knew enough not to provoke an open break with a regime that partially served its interests. The clergy, however, always resented the failure of successive governments to heed its theocratic admonitions. The church berated the regime for failing to curb the activities of Protestant churches in spite of their singular lack of proselytizing success, and it complained ceaselessly of the government's refusal to take action against dissent from the norms of Catholic orthodoxy. However flawed the political system of the Restoration may have been, though, it continued to embody, if only to a limited degree, the secularizing and pluralistic principles inherent in nineteenth-century liberalism. Even Cánovas refused to allow the church to dictate public policy.

The relationship between the church and the Restoration was yet another marriage of convenience that suited, for different reasons, the parties involved. Moreover, a significant body of Catholic opinion, notably the Carlists, the integrists of Ramón Nocedal (1821–1885), and the Basque* nationalists of Sabino de Arana y Goiri,* remained implacably opposed to a regime that they believed, for whatever reason, intended to weaken the influence of Catholicism in Spain.

Cánovas's expectation that the issue of the church would be removed as a source of public controversy ultimately proved incorrect. Tension between the church and the regime was chronic, although subdued, until the turn of the century. After 1900, the anticlericalism that never lay far below the surface of Spanish politics surfaced with renewed vigor. It did so for several reasons. After the assassination of Cánovas in 1897, his Liberal-Conservative party moved in a proclerical direction, particularly during the ministry of Antonio Maura,* while the Liberal party, following the death of Sagasta, espoused a policy of moderate anticlericalism in response to the massive growth of the religious orders. By 1900, the number of male religious had increased sixfold over 1860, and the number of nuns had more than doubled. Liberal efforts to limit the growth of the orders led the hierarchy to abandon its always-tenuous political neutrality in favor of support for Maura and the Conservative party. A revival of popular anticlericalism also occurred during the first decade of the century, especially in Catalonia,* where the violent propaganda of the new Radical Republican party fomented deep hostility to the church among the region's large working-class population.

The events of Tragic Week (26 July–1 Aug. 1909) in Barcelona and its environs revealed how weak the protective shell around the church since the beginning of the Restoration had become. Eighty churches, monasteries, convents, and parochial schools were set to the torch in the greatest outburst of popular anticlericalism since 1835. Although the authorities easily quelled the disturbances, the clergy began to lose confidence in the regime's ability to defend the church from anticlerical assaults. These sentiments deepened from 1910 to 1912 during the reforming ministry of José Canalejas (1854–1912). The government's Padlock Law, or Ley del Candado (23 Dec. 1910), affirmed the absolute right of the state to control the growth of the religious orders. Canalejas also made a strong commitment to interpreting Article 11 of the constitution as broadly as possible in support of religious toleration. Opposition to these mild reforms provoked spectacular expressions of Catholic anger in a series of large public demonstrations during 1910 and 1911.

After the assassination of Canalejas in 1912, open conflict between the church and successive governments diminished. It did so in part because the church largely got its way. The Ley del Candado was allowed to lapse, for example. A more significant shift took place, though, as the church increasingly saw the danger of social revolution as the greatest threat to its interests. The destructive effects of World War I* on the Spanish economy* brought severe hardship to the urban working class and to the dispossessed rural proletariat of southern estate lands. Rising militancy among the ever-increasing number of adherents to socialist and anarchist organizations burst forth between 1917 and 1923 in a wave of strikes and agrarian disturbances. For the church and its supporters, these seemed to herald the coming of a revolution that would destroy family, property, and religion. Although successive governments employed brutal force against social dissidents, their inability to put a definitive end to popular unrest further eroded the church's confidence in the liberal regime. This further diminished when it became clear that the Restoration political system would not permit the formation of a great Catholic party, either in the form of a remade Conservative party under the leadership of Maura or of a new Christian Democratic party on the Italian model.

In Sept. 1923, the Restoration collapsed before the military rising led by Gen. Miguel Primo de Rivera.* The church played no role in these events, although the clergy and much of Catholic opinion welcomed the establishment of the dictatorship. The new regime made some concessions to clerical demands by establishing censorship and publicly enforcing Catholic morality, but it did not dramatically expand clerical privileges beyond those enjoyed under the Restoration. The clergy, for example, resented the regime's refusal to increase its salaries to any significant degree. Moreover, the dictatorship's unwillingness to support Catholic labor unions and allow the formation of a Catholic political party irritated activists, such as Ángel Herrera (1886–1979), editor of the influential Catholic daily El Debate. Indeed, as the decade wore on, astute Catholic observers increasingly saw the regime as transitional and stressed the necessity of organizing Catholic forces more effectively for forthcoming political battles. The apparent national tranquility the regime imposed, however, lulled the church and its supporters into a false sense of security.

There is no evidence the church profited from its privileged position under the Restoration and the dictatorship to reverse the obvious progress of secularization among industrial workers and southern agricultural workers that was painfully obvious by the turn of the century. In rural Andalusia,* Estremadura, and La Mancha, clerical observers frequently noted the massive abstention of men from church services. The situation in the industrial towns was no better.

The causes were complex, but the church clearly failed utterly to devise effective strategies to deal with it.

The collapse of the dictatorship in 1930 and the proclamation of the Second Republic* in Apr. 1931 opened a two-year period of far-reaching political reform that demolished the official privileges the church had enjoyed under the Restoration. Article 26 of the Constitution of 1931 ordered the separation of church and state, while the republican government gradually eliminated the state budget for clerical salaries and forbade the religious orders to teach. The authorities also introduced a wide body of secularizing legislation, including laws allowing civil marriage and divorce.

The initial reaction of the church and its supporters to these events was far from uniform. Some bishops, notably the cardinal primate, Pedro Segura (1880–1957), quickly made known their opposition to the new regime. More moderate prelates, though, especially Cardinal Vidal i Barranquer (1868–1943) of Tarragona, attempted to negotiate a modus vivendi with the republic during its first six months. That these negotiations failed, in part because of republican intransigence, was unfortunate. Faced with a secularizing revolution laced with growing social agitation, the church reverted to a historic pattern of resistance similar to its struggle against nineteenth-century liberalism. There was, however, a difference. For the first time in the nation's modern history, the church was able to rely on a mass Catholic party, the Confederación Española de Derechas Autónomas (CEDA), founded in 1933. Defense of religion, indeed, became a useful point of attack on the regime from a variety of right-wing political groups.

The election of a more conservative republican government in 1933 offered the church an uncomfortable breathing space. That the issue of the church and its place within a society undergoing political and social upheaval remained a source of intense controversy became evident in Oct. 1934, when revolutionaries burned churches in the Asturian capital, Oviedo. For the first time since 1835, a significant number of priests were killed during the disturbances.

Between 1931 and 1936, the struggle to defend the interests of the church consumed the energies of both the clergy and their supporters. Little thought was given to devising creative strategies to deal with immense pastoral problems, although there is some evidence that the conservative urban bourgeoisie underwent a religious revival of sorts. The church, indeed, placed its hopes, as it always had when its interests were threatened, on a change of government, rather than on pastoral initiatives of its own making.

The church had no role in the military rising against the republic on 18 July 1936. Leading members of the hierarchy, however, such as Bishop Pla y Deniel (1876–1968) of Salamanca, wasted little time in proclaiming the conflict a life-or-death struggle between Christian civilization and barbarism. Clerical support for the rising was extremely strong, although there were exceptions, notably among the clergy of the Basque Provinces in recognition of the republic's concession of autonomy to the region in 1936.

Open backing of the generals, however, exacted a heavy price. Some 4,184 secular priests, 2,365 clergy from the religious orders, and 283 nuns perished during the great wave of violent anticlericalism that swept republican Spain, particularly during the first three months of the war. The republican authorities, especially in Catalonia, attempted to curtail the activities of extremists engaged in the systematic execution of priests, although with limited success. The scale of reprisals against the clergy, however, served to deepen the commitment of the clergy to the regime of Gen. Francisco Franco.*

Even before the war's conclusion, Franco's nationalist government had begun to dismantle the republic's secularizing legislation. When the conflict ended in 1939, church and state entered into a close relationship unmatched since the alliance of throne and altar during the reign of Fernando VII. Although there were points of conflict between the civil and ecclesiastical authorities over certain issues, such as the censorship of church publications and the extent of state control over Catholic associations, the church profited handsomely from its new position. Indeed, it was able to realize at long last the dreams of generations of clergy through a policy of religious compulsion backed by the full weight of the state. Sociological surveys carried out in the closing years of the regime, however, indicate that the mechanisms of enforced religion the church employed through its dominant role in education and the regulation of public morality proved to be singularly unsuccessful in creating the Catholic Spain that the clergy expected to emerge under the new political order.

The intimate association of church and state in what has come to be known as National Catholicism began to erode during the 1960s. Tension developed, first, as a result of conflict between the regime and Basque and Catalan clergy sympathetic to the realization of political autonomy for their respective regions and, second, because of the support some bishops and priests lent to the demands of both industrial and agricultural workers victimized by accelerating economic development. Further, the declarations of the Second Vatican Council instilled an incipient spirit of pluralism in the Spanish church in spite of the resistance of some members of the hierarchy. By the time of General Franco's death in 1975, much of the lower clergy and many, although not all, bishops had distanced themselves from the regime. Moderate members of the hierarchy, particularly Cardinal Vicente Enrique y Tarancón, supported the peaceful transition to democratic rule between 1975 and 1978.

Under the constitutional monarchy, the church has lost the official privileges it enjoyed under Franco. The Constitution of 1978 separated church and state, although this disestablishment is not without ambiguity. Even the socialist government in power since 1982 has continued to pay the salaries of diocesan clergy. The church has resisted an extensive body of secularizing legislation allowing divorce and limited abortions. Strong tension between church and state also developed over the socialist government's Law on the Right to Education (LODE), which drastically curtailed the administrative powers of the religious orders over the many church schools receiving financial support from the state. Tension is likely to continue, given the historical role of the church in modern Spain and the tendency of the papacy to appoint conservative priests to bishoprics.

Both the civil and ecclesiastical authorities, however, have generally conducted themselves with moderation, seeking to avoid the bitter confrontations of the past. Disestablishment has also encouraged the church to devote its energies and imagination to innovative pastoral initiatives long neglected in its modern history. To what extent these will prove fruitful within an increasingly secularized population is, of course, another question. It appears, however, that at last the Spanish church has learned the lesson that it must rely upon persuasion to realize its religious mission.

For additional information, see J. A. Gallego, *La política religiosa en España, 1889–1913* (Madrid, 1975); E. Appolis, *Les jansénistes espagnoles* (Bordeaux, 1966); W. J. Callahan, *Politics and Society in Spain, 1750–1874* (Cambridge, 1984); V. Cárcel Orti, *Iglesia y revolución en España, 1868–1874* (Pamplona, 1979); G. Hermet, *Les catholiques dans l'Espagne franquiste*, 2 vols. (Paris, 1981); F. Lannon, *Privilege, Persecution and Prophecy: The Catholic Church in Spain, 1875–1975* (Oxford, 1987); M. Revuelta González, *Política religiosa de los liberales del siglo xix: Trienio constitucional* (Madrid, 1973); J. M. Sánchez, *The Spanish Civil War as a Religious Tragedy* (Notre Dame, 1987); J. C. Ullman, *The Tragic Week: A Study of Anticlericalism in Spain, 1875–1912* (Cambridge, 1968).

*W. J. Callahan*

*Related entry*: PAPACY.

**CIERVA Y CORDONIA, JUAN DE LA** (1895–1936), aviation pioneer. Cierva, born in Madrid,* was the son of Rafael, a wealthy professor of mining and a prominent figure in the Liberal-Conservative party and a friend of Antonio Cánovas del Castillo* and Alfonso XIII.* The son's interest in aviation started early with the construction of small gliders, and in 1912, he enrolled at the civil-engineering school in Madrid, since there was no aeronautical engineering available in Spain at the time. Nevertheless, during the six years he studied in Madrid, much of his work was directed to the mathematics and physics of flight. He also constructed his first conventional airplane from a damaged French craft.

When World War I* rapidly advanced aviation technology, the Spanish government responded by creating an official competition. Cierva, supported by thirty-two thousand dollars collected by Spanish aristocrats, built a remarkably sophisticated trimotored biplane bomber in 1918 that became the first airplane built in Spain. Unfortunately, the plane was irreparably damaged by its pilot, and from Cierva's writings, this trauma profoundly affected the future inventor of the autogiro, who decided to focus his talents on the creation of an aircraft that would be stabler, more secure, and more reliable than the conventional airplane.

After many mathematical and physical calculations, Cierva came to believe that an aircraft provided with a rotor, rather than the usual fixed wings, might be the flexible device he sought. He conceived of the rotor as a rotating group of airfoils that would be mounted on a strong shaft above the fuselage of an aircraft propelled by the thrust of a conventional engine. Since the rotor's blades turned by the flow of air past the rotor's blades to provide lift, the rotor theoretically could keep this novel aircraft aloft by itself, even without the use of the motor. Cierva called this "autorotation."

Over the next few years, Cierva experimented with models of all sizes in wind tunnels. Most were put together with the fuselages and motors of obsolete airplanes, on which he installed rotors with from two to five blades. The first few autogiros either did not fly or rose only a few feet off the ground. A technical breakthrough came only when the Spanish inventor realized that rigid rotor blades were of no use, and substituted articulated and flexible rotor blades, hinged at the hub of the rotor to respond differentially to aerodynamic and centrifugal forces involved in rotation. The first successful flight of an autogiro built by Cierva occurred at Getafe airfield near Madrid in Jan. 1923. Flight by autogyration had been proved not only possible but practical.

Having secured the appropriate patents, Cierva decided to market his autogiro. Trials had proved that it had attributes that seemed to give it many advantages over conventional aircraft. It was a relatively safe and useful machine that would not stall or spin and could take off from a very small area and land almost vertically. Moreover, it was capable of cross-country flight at comparatively fast speeds, and its small wings and good maneuverability at low altitudes provided augmented visibility. The autogiros were simple to control and could be flown by a pilot after three or four hours of instruction. They did, however, consume considerable fuel, and their payload was modest.

After demonstrations of the autogiro in Britain,* the Royal Air Force ordered an experimental model to test the craft's military usefulness. This encouraged Cierva to establish a factory in Britain to manufacture and demonstrate the autogiro throughout Western Europe. In addition, he licensed Harold F. Pitcairn and W. Wallace Kellett to build autogiros in the United States* that were wingless and had an enclosed cabin to carry more than the one or two seats of the earlier models. In 1930, Pitcairn, who credited Cierva for the work, won the Collier trophy for the most significant accomplishment in aviation.

Unfortunately, neither Pitcairn nor Cierva sold many autogiros, so the cost of the craft remained high. A few were purchased for mail service or sold to newspapers or wealthy aviators. Lack of economic success, however, did not prevent Cierva from becoming a celebrity in Spain, where Alfonso XIII presented him with the Cross of Alfonso XII. He became a member of the Consejo Superior Aeronática and several other commissions. His autobiography, *Wings of Tomorrow* (1931), sold well in Britain, Spain, and the United States, but economic difficulties kept Cierva in search of capital, and it was on one of these trips that he died in 1935, when the commercial airliner he was on crashed in the fog outside London.

Although Cierva is known as the creator of the helicopter, he did not believe that the serious aeronautical problems that beset this craft could be overcome. Torque appeared to be an insuperable difficulty for the helicopter until its rotor was driven directly by an engine, rather than turned by an induced flow of air like the autogiro. Clearly, however, the invention of the autogiro led to the modern helicopter, since the principle of autorotation and the technology of the rotor blade were first developed by Cierva.

For additional information, see J. Wartela, *Autogiro: Juan de la Cierva y su obra* (Madrid, 1977).

C. R. Halstead

*Related entry*: SCIENCE.

**CINEMA.** Shortly after its beginnings in France, commercial cinema appeared in Spain on 16 May 1896 with the screening of three Lumière films at the Rusia Hotel in Madrid. By June 1896, the first Spanish-made features included such titles as *Llegada de los toreros* and *Maniobras de la artillería de Vicálvaro*. The first Spanish fiction film was *Riña de café* (1897), which Fructuoso Gelabert (1874–1955) made in Barcelona.* The most successful films of the silent era were Florián Rey's (1894–1962) *La aldea maldita* (1929), based on a rural theme, and José Buchs's (1893–1973) *Prim* (1930), a romanticized depiction of the career of the liberal monarchist general Juan Prim y Prats.*

The introduction of sound film coincided with the proclamation of the Second Republic* in 1931. The republican period represents one of the most significant in the history of Spanish cinema. The beginnings of an industrial infrastructure were established with the building of sound stages at Orphea Studios (Barcelona), Ciudad Lineal (Madrid), and Aranjuez (south of Madrid), together with a number of solidly based production companies: Compañía Industrial Film Español, S.A. (CIFESA); Cinematografía Española Americana (CEA); and Estudios Cinema Español, S.A (ECESA), among others.

By 1935, the film industry had experienced impressive growth; for a population of twenty-four million, there were more than three thousand theaters, eleven production studios, eighteen film-processing laboratories, and more than twenty production companies. Since the republican government extended little financial support to the industry, filmmakers developed a ''popular'' cinema that appealed to Spanish moviegoers of the period.

In general, films were based on literary and aesthetic conventions of the silent-film era; popular stage plays, zarzuelas,* and famous novels were adapted for the screen. Cinema imported costumbrismo from literature; and folklore, social satire, romanticism, and humor—all within a Spanish context—characterized most films. The international appeal of Spanish cinema was limited as a result, although some films, such as Florián Rey's famous *Nobleza baturra* (1935), a drama of Aragonese peasant life, were commercial successes in Latin America, as was Benito Perojo's (1894–1974) *La verbena de la paloma* (1935), an adaptation of the popular zarzuela. Luis Buñuel (1900–1983), residing in Paris and already well known for his surrealist films *Un chien andalou* (1928) and *L'âge d'or* (1930), participated in Spanish filmmaking with the controversial *Las Hurdes/Tierra sin pan* (1932) and *Don Quintín el amargao* (1935).

The outbreak of the civil war in July 1936 had an immediate and profound impact on Spanish filmmaking. Most of the studio facilities in Madrid and Barcelona remained under republican control. Nationalist filmmakers used studios in Rome and Berlin to produce some commercial features. Cinematically, the most significant contribution of both republican and nationalist filmmakers was in the area of newsreels and documentaries. Each faction in the republic—socialists, anarchists (in particular through the Generalitat of Catalonia*), and communists—had its own film units with which it recorded and interpreted the conflict.

The nationalists also produced features to mobilize their supporters and justify their cause. Because of their greater political homogeneity, the nationalists' documentary production was less abundant. After the Falangist party had absorbed Carlism,* they were in turn merged into the National Movement of Gen. Francisco Franco.* Documentaries were produced under the auspices of the Falange* and the Juntas de Ofensiva Nacional-Sindicalista (JONS).

The most significant development in cinema after the civil war was the extension of government financial support to the industry. This assistance, however, was accompanied by censorship and encouragement of ideologically acceptable themes. The first and best-made nationalist propaganda film was Luis Sáenz de Heredia's (1907–1974) *Raza* (1941), with a script based on a book written by Franco himself under a pseudonym and loosely based on his own family history. Aside from films of this ''national-crusade'' genre that glorified the nationalist cause, other ''political'' films were historical epics that emphasized national, political, cultural, and linguistic unity under the Castilian monarchies of an earlier age. Juan de Orduña's *Locura de amor* (1948) was the most successful, telling the story of Juana la Loca (1479–1555), mother of Carlos V (1500–1558).

In the 1950s and 1960s, some filmmakers slowly and cautiously attempted to deal with Spanish reality. In 1957, José Antonio Nieves Conde's (1915– ) *Surcos* broke with the historical genre, portraying impoverished peasants trying to adapt to urban life. He was followed by Luis García Berlanga (1921– ), who portrayed certain unpleasant Spanish realities in a series of charming comedies: *Bienvenido Mister Marshall* (1952), *Calabuch* (1956), and *Plácido* and *El verdugo* (both 1951). After collaborating with Berlanga to make *Esa pareja feliz* (1951), Juan Antonio Bardem (1922– ), a member of the clandestine Communist party,* criticized Spanish society in a serious vein with *Calle Mayor* (1954) and *Muerte de un ciclista* (1955). Carlos Saura's (1932– ) *Los golgos* (1959) was a stark, neorealist depiction of life in a Madrid slum whose frankness caused the film to be withheld until 1963 and then released in a highly censored version. Saura's *La caza* (1963) was another landmark film that many saw as a powerful allegory of the civil war.

Berlanga, Bardem, and Saura largely constituted the ''new cinema'' of the 1960s and early 1970s, a cinema the regime permitted to be seen abroad, but whose exhibition was generally curtailed at home. With Franco's death in 1975, Spain set out on uncharted political waters. With the lifting of censorship in 1977, Spanish filmmakers treated a variety of previously prohibited topics, such as the civil war, the political and social repression of the Franco years, and the often-surprising new Spain that democracy was spawning. The cinema of the "transition" (1975–1983) included such landmark films as Víctor Erice's (1940– ) *El espíritu de la colmena* (1973), José Luis Carci's (1944– ) *Asignatura pendiente* (1977) and *Volver a empezar* (1983, winner of the Academy Award for best foreign-language film), Pilar Miró's (1940– ) *El crimen de Cuenca* (1978), and Carlos Saura's *Deprisa, deprisa* (1981).

The 1983 triumph of Felipe González* and the Socialist party* (PSOE) ushered in a full-blown democracy. The socialists initiated an aggressive cultural policy that included strong financial support and international promotion of Spanish cinema, and they appointed Pilar Miró as director-general of cinematography to carry it out. Among the important films produced under the socialist administration are Víctor Erice's *El sur*, Jaime Chavarrí's (1943– ) *Las bicicletas son para el verano*, and Saura's *Carmen* (all 1983); Mario Camus's (1935– ) *Los santos inocentes* (1984); Pedro Almodóvar's (1949– ) black comedy *¿Qué he hecho yo para merecer esto?* (1984) and his daringly erotic *La ley del deseo* (1987); and Pilar Miró's *Werther*, Saura's *Eldorado*, Montxo Armendáriz's *Veintisiete horas*, and Chavarrí's *El año que murió Franco* (all 1987).

Another cinematic development of interest since the death of Franco has been the flowering of the "cinema of the autonomies," principally Catalan and Basque (Euskadi) filmmaking, even though some modest efforts have been attempted by regional governments in Galicia,* Valencia, and Andalusia.* The cinema of Euskadi has been the most ambitious, resulting in excellent and overtly political films such as Imanol Uribe's (1950– ) *La fuga de Segovia* (1981), about a group of Basque Homeland and Freedom* (ETA) guerrillas escaping from prison (1981); *La muerte de Mikel* (1984), depicting a homosexual ETA activist; and Armendáriz's *Tasio* (1984), which documents Basque life in the mountains of Navarre.

Catalan films generally emphasize both "national" and general themes and are sometimes bilingual, as in Lluis-Josep Comerón's *Puzzle* (1986), a suspense film about bank robbers and their hostages, although they are usually dubbed in both Catalan and Castilian versions. Among Catalan films, Antoni Ribas's (1935– ) *La ciutat cremada* (1978) and his trilogy *Victòria (La gran aventura d'un poble)* (1983) are among the most ambitious and important; they are historical epics that trace the development of modern Catalan nationalism from its beginnings in the late nineteenth century. Some more recent Catalan-produced films of significance are Luis García Berlanga's civil-war comedy *La vaquilla* (1985) and Bigas Luna's psychological thriller *Angoiza* (1986).

For additional information, see J. M. Caparrós Lera, *El cine republicano español, 1931–1939* (Barcelona, 1977); J. M. Caparrós Lera and R. de España, *The Spanish Cinema: An Historical Approach* (Barcelona, 1987); V. Higginbotham, *Spanish Film under Franco* (Austin, 1988); and J. Hopewell, *Out of the Past: Spanish Cinema under Franco* (London, 1986).

*C. J. Mora, Jr.*

**CIVIL GUARD (GUARDIA CIVIL),** national paramilitary police force created on 28 Mar. 1844. In the 1840s, following the War of Independence* and the First Carlist War (1833–1840), the Spanish countryside fell into the chaos of banditry. Advisors to the crown recommended creation of a paramilitary national police force to provide order in rural areas and protect property and public security.

The decree of 28 Mar. 1844 created the Civil Guard. The duque de Ahumaja (1802–1884) was named the first director general, with officers and most troops drawn from units of the Spanish army.* It became a highly disciplined force that took its mission seriously. Radical, leftist, and romantic writers denounced the Guardia as excessively brutal, but the middle classes called it the "well deserving." As an agent of the state, it opposed banditry, insurrection, and anarchy, and later, communism, the Basque Homeland and Freedom* movement (ETA), and other groups. Since its founding, many hundreds of Guardia have been killed in the line of duty.

Their uniforms have changed through the decades, but members of the Guardia are still well known by their three-cornered leather hats and great cloaks. Until the 1960s, they commonly patrolled on foot, operating in pairs and often standing opposite each other on remote country roads. They were never stationed in their native regions, thus to discourage close social relations with the local population. This led to popular antagonism in rural areas, even though the Guardia's work was often efficient and professional.

As was the case with the armed forces, with the outbreak of the Spanish Civil War* in 1936, the Guardia's loyalties were divided, although most of its thirty thousand members joined the cause of the nationalists. Some, though, played an important role in holding Madrid* and Barcelona* for the Popular Front. Those who joined the nationalists formed such redoubts as the Alcázar in Toledo and for months withstood the anarchist siege of Santa María de la Cabeza. Some caught in the Popular Front–controlled zone deserted individually and by units when possible.

The director general, under the command of the minister of the interior, was usually a general in the Spanish army. In 1986, however, the director general became a civilian appointee. To many of the officers and men, this was seen as an attempt to politicize the force. It should be recalled, though, that the misguided and abortive attempted coup in 1981 against the Cortes by a small number of the Guardia under Lt. Col. Antonio Tejero Molín, along with some officers of the army, provoked the crisis. Juan Carlos I* brought the situation under control, and the director general and those involved suffered heavy punishments following a celebrated court trial.

The force today numbers about sixty thousand men and officers. Only a few are mounted, and the others are seldom seen on foot. They still operate in pairs. A large part of the force is devoted to traffic control on the highways, and they patrol the back roads and villages of the country. They are equipped with powerful motorcycles and have excellent communications. The "Rural Patrol" usually has cars. As in the past, all are armed with light weapons. Because of their dependability and good training, they are in great demand as guards for foreign embassies and other tasks imposed by Madrid; this has created a shortage of personnel in some areas. Some are highly trained for antiterrorist units and equipped with helicopters and specially trained dogs, as well as special arms. Others are designated as sharpshooters of the most accurate sort. All men undergo extensive training with small arms, however, and are highly effective.

There is a modern center at Valdemoro, south of Madrid, that accepts carefully selected, sixteen-year-old cadets for three years of intensive instruction, which includes demanding physical training, horsemanship, automobile and motorcycle operation, communications, military arts, first aid, and public relations, as well as academic topics such as history and law. Much effort is devoted to techniques of combatting terrorism, a constant threat to the Guardia.

For additional information, see F. Sánchez Aguado, *Historia de la Guardia*, 5 vols. (Madrid, 1984); and Historical Division of the Director General, *Revista de la Guardia* (1968– ).

*R. L. Proctor*

**COLONIES** (1700–1988) of the Spanish Empire. At the start of the eighteenth century, the Spanish Empire had territorial holdings in Europe, Africa, Asia, and America. Although European possessions were lost in the War of Spanish Succession,* the king was still "el rey de las Españas y de las Indias" (king of the Spains and the Indies). The American holdings were the heart of the empire; the Asian and African possessions were of comparatively minor significance.

The first two viceroyalties established in America (New Spain in 1535 and Peru in 1542), together with the more numerous audiencias (appellate tribunals with legislative and administrative authority), were regarded as reinos (kingdoms), equal in status at the Spanish court with the kingdoms of Aragon,* Castile,* Catalonia,* and Valencia.* None was on par with Castile, the premier kingdom, but the Spanish Empire in its totality was identified as "estos reinos y esos reinos" (these [the Iberian] kingdoms and those [the American] kingdoms), each having individual, dynastic loyalties to the monarch.

Carlos I (1517–1556) had separated his domestic and foreign kingdoms in 1524 by establishing the Council of the Indies (Consejo Real y Supremo de las Indias) to administer the American kingdoms in a manner similar to the Council of Castile's administration of the peninsular kingdoms. The council existed until 1834, but its significant functions were taken over by the Ministry of Marine and the Indies in 1714, when Felipe V* consolidated his control over the empire.

In addition to the viceroyalties of New Spain and Peru and their viceregal audiencias of Mexico (1529) and Lima (1542), (where the viceroys served as presidents), there were a number of lesser audiencias. Subordinate to the viceroy of New Spain were the audiencias of Santo Domingo (1511), Panama (1538), Guatemala (initially called Los Confines in 1544), Guadalajara in New Galicia (1549), and Manila in the Philippines (1538). The viceroyalty of Peru's lesser audiencias included those of Santa Fe de Bogotá in New Granada (1549), Charcas (1559), Quito (1564), and Chile (1609).

Within the jurisdiction of each audiencia, gobiernos (provinces) were headed by a governor subordinate to the audiencia in judicial matters and in some administrative actions. The governor was autonomous in civil and military matters, free to forward plans and projects to viceroy or king. Below the provincial level, municipalities (called alcaldías mayores in New Spain and corregimientos in Peru) were administrated by a crown representative, the alcalde mayor or corregidor. Internal municipal government was run by local cabildos (municipal councils). By 1700, most cabildo councilmen (regidores), corregidores and alcaldes, and audiencia judges were American-born members of local elites.

The clergy formed another part of colonial governmental machinery. The king, exercising patronato real (royal patronage over church affairs) nominated, and in effect appointed, the high clergy, while viceroys and governors nominated parish priests, thereby exercising a strong influence over the secular clergy. The clergy, who had their own courts, wielded considerable political and economic power. Three bishops and three archbishops served as viceroys of New Spain before 1700, and four archbishops became viceroys after 1700. The Inquisition also served as a bridge between civil and ecclesiastic government. Hostility between the secular clergy (diocesan priests) and the regular clergy (members of the religious orders), however, caused serious conflicts, as did quarrels between the religious orders. Since the regular clergy were, for the most part, American-born by the 1750s, while bishops and archbishops, as were viceroys and governors, almost exclusively European-born, this split provided a great source of disunity.

By 1700, the Spanish colonies were no longer economically dependent on peninsular Spain. Declining mineral production, disastrous to the crown, was replaced in the colonies by development of other sources of wealth that permitted self-sufficiency in most necessities and some luxury items. Inter-American commerce, contrary to existing laws, became another source of revenue. Well into the eighteenth century, the American kingdoms were appropriating more and more of their own production to pay for their upkeep. This explains why the 20 million Spanish subjects around the world initially took no strenuous moves to sue for independence; Spanish colonials already enjoyed a considerable degree of independence. Thus, by the mid–eighteenth century, as much as 80 percent of local treasury income was spent on local defense, administrative costs, salaries, pensions, grants, and supplies.

It was to end this independence that Carlos III* directed his reforms in the last half of the eighteenth century. Colonial reform became the Enlightenment* effort to create a greater Spain, to regain the power and prestige that had slipped away during the War of Spanish Succession and the Seven Years' War.* At the same time, reevaluation was also needed to adjust the colonial administration to reflect territorial expansion in both North and South America (settlers from Peru who had developed the La Plata basin and the Caribbean coast, or those from New Spain who moved as far north as California), or the new prosperity created by the reworked and new silver-producing regions of Mexico.

A start at reform began in 1714 with the establishment of the Ministry of Marine and the Indies to replace some of the functions of the Council of the Indies. Other attempts included the short-lived elevation of the captaincy general of New Granada to a viceroyalty (1717–1722); its permanent reestablishment in 1739; the 1777 creation of the captaincy general of Venezuela and the nearly simultaneous establishment of the viceroyalty of Río de la Plata (with Buenos Aires as its capital); and the opening of new legal ports in both America and Spain to end the trade monopoly of Seville and Cadiz, legalize intercolonial trade, and allow the crown to collect taxes on formerly contraband trade.

Obsolete governmental, judicial, and ecclesiastic practices were also reformed. The 1749 introduction of the intendancy form of administration in peninsular Spain during the reign of Ferdinand VI (1746–1759) showed the potential of a systematic survey (catastro) to establish a workable tax system. Although the reform was not fully carried out in Castile, intendancy was begun in the Americas in 1764, when it was introduced in Cuba after the British occupation of Havana (1762). The system was later established in Río de la Plata (1782), New Spain (1786), and in most of the other colonies (1790). The intendant system provided a well-paid intendant with an efficient staff in each important colonial city, for the first time allowing a representative of the central government to replace the ill-paid, corrupt, and largely ceremonial corregidor or alcalde mayor. The intendant supervised administration, finance, military, and at times in some places, justice. While corregidores and alcaldes mayores were invariably American-born and served relatively short terms, intendants were, with few exceptions, Spanish-born, and served in one region for years. For the most part, intendancy increased administrative efficiency and eliminated corruption.

The net result produced new types of governmental activities (accurate censuses to use for tax equalization and much greater centralization of general administration, identification of income levels, and surveys of ownership or control of land and resources). The viceroys, elites, and clergy, however, resented these reforms, and reaction in the form of enhanced local particularism (Americanism) grew as the American-born elites were threatened. Resistance to change from reino status to that of colony was varied. Taxation to finance Spain's wars in Europe resulted in riots in Peru (1780) and in New Granada (1781). American industry and production, no longer protected, suffered from Spanish competition. America's function was changed from one of promoting its own self-sufficiency to being a producer of raw materials for the metropolis and a consumer of finished products.

The drift toward independence was also furthered by a combination of diminished loyalty, economic discrimination, government by improvisation, and chance. Carlos IV* came to the throne in 1788, just as reaction to imposed colonialism solidified Americanism into regional nationalistic attitudes. After 1796, the Hispano-French alliance caused a British blockade of Cadiz and the licensing of neutrals to maintain colonial trade. By 1807, Spain's economic monopoly with America was beyond recovery, and a year later, Napoleon Bonaparte (1769–1821) controlled peninsular Spain. In Jan. 1809, a junta, invoking the name of Fernando VII,* decreed that Spanish dominions in America were an integral part of the Spanish monarchy with rights of representation. Three years later, the Cortes of Cadiz* promulgated the Constitution of 1812; Spain and America were viewed as a single nation, but the Americans were denied equal representation and freedom of trade. The independence movements needed no clearer signal to begin. The trajectory of conquest was reversed as the regions last to be developed were the first to rebel. By 1825, the Spanish colonial empire was reduced to Cuba and Puerto Rico in America, and the Philippines and Marianas in the Pacific.

This diminished empire, enhanced in a small way by the occupation of Spanish Guinea [Fernando Poo] (1844), the area around Río Muni (1877), and Spanish West Africa (the Río de Oro region south of Morocco*), declined further after the Spanish-American War,* with the loss of Cuba, Puerto Rico, the Philippines, and the Marianas Islands. Spain's early twentieth-century empire was reduced to Ceuta and Melilla on the Mediterranean coast of Morocco, Spanish Guinea and Spanish West Africa on the Atlantic, and the Spanish zone of Morocco (1912). Even this remnant of an empire fell before anticolonialist sentiments and pressure by the United Nations, with the transfer of control of Spanish Morocco to Morocco (1965) and the attachment of Ceuta to Cadiz and Melilla to Malaga. Spanish Guinea gained its independence as Equatorial Guinea in 1968, and Spanish Sahara was abandoned in 1976.

What follows is a list of Spanish colonial possessions significant enough to warrant the assignment of an administrator with the rank of governor or higher.

## CENTRAL AND SOUTH AMERICA

*Antioquia*—Located in northwestern Colombia immediately south of Panama, Antioquia was subject to the audiencia of Santa Fe de Bogotá (see New Granada). Its last Spanish governor departed in 1811, and the province was incorporated into Gran Colombia and later Colombia.

*Arequipa*—This southern Peruvian province was established as an intendancy under the viceroy of Peru in 1784. One of the last areas controlled by Spain, Arequipa became part of the Republic of Peru in 1825.

*Barinas*—The last separate province created in the captaincy general of Venezuela, Barinas had only two governors from 1786 to 1810. It was incorporated into Gran Colombia in 1819 and later into the Republic of Venezuela.

*Buenos Aires*—During the eighteenth century, Buenos Aires was a province under the audiencia of Charcas. In 1777, the Viceroyalty of Río de la Plata was established and located in Buenos Aires, the capital city. The province was designated an intendancy in 1783 and held that status until independence was achieved in 1816.

*California*—Settlement in peninsular Baja California was initiated by friars just before the eighteenth century began, but serious occupation of mainland Alta California was not undertaken until 1767, to counter the threat of British and Russian encroachment. The two provinces were governed jointly until 1804, at which time each obtained appointed governors. The Californias were under the direct jurisdiction of the viceroy and the viceregal audiencia in Mexico until 1821 (except for the period between 1788 and 1793 and again between 1813 and 1821, when control was exercised by the commandant-general of Provincias Internas Poniente). California became a part of Mexico in 1821.

*Cartagena de Indias*—On the central Caribbean coast of present-day Colombia, Cartagena de Indias was under the jurisdiction of the audiencia of Santa Fe de Bogotá. Transfer from the viceroyalty of Peru came with the creation of the viceroyalty of New Granada. Cartagena became independent in 1811, but fell under Spanish control from 1816 to 1821, at which time it was incorporated into Gran Colombia.

*Charcas*—During the first seventy-five years of the eighteenth century, Charcas included most of the area that later became Bolivia, Paraguay, and Argentina. Its audiencia was subject to the viceroyalty of Peru. Charcas was transferred to the newly created viceroyalty of Río de la Plata in 1777, its area much reduced. Independence forces of the United Provinces of Río de la Plata occupied the area of the audiencia from 1810 to 1816, when Charcas was reoccupied by royalist forces. Spanish authority was extinguished in 1824, and Charcas became the nucleus of the Republic of Bolivia.

*Chiapas*—Also known as Ciudad Real, Chiapas was part of the captaincy general of Guatemala until independence in 1821. It was, however, established as an intendancy in 1786, but little is known about this period. Chiapas, like the rest of the captaincy general of Guatemala, became part of the Mexican Empire in 1821.

*Chile*—Initially named New Estremadura, Chile was controlled from Santiago by a governor and audiencia subject to the viceroyalty of Peru. The governor became captain general as well in 1778. Chile became independent in 1817.

*Coahuila*—This region in what is now northern Mexico became a separate province late in the seventeenth century and, until 1716, included Texas. In 1777, Coahuila came under the jurisdiction of the Provincias Internas, but retained its own local civil administration. Coahuila became a part of Mexico in 1821.

*Cochabamba*—Created an intendancy in 1783 within the viceroyalty of Río de la Plata, Cochabamba included most of the territory of Santa Cruz de la Sierra, in what is now central Bolivia. Effective Spanish control ended in 1810, and this former intendancy was incorporated into the Republic of Bolivia in 1825.

*Córdoba*—The Province of Tucumán was divided into two intendancies in 1783: the southern portion named Córdoba, and the northern, Salta. Both were under the jurisdiction of the viceroyalty of Río de la Plata. Spanish authority ended in 1810, and Córdoba became part of Argentina.

*Costa Rica*—Initially named New Cartago, Costa Rica was a province under the audiencia of Guatemala. It remained a province during the intendancy period and declared its independence in 1821. Costa Rica then became a part of the brief United States of Central America.

*Cuba*—Administered by a governor and captain general, Cuba was subject to the audiencia of Santo Domingo until 1707, when this agency was transferred to Puerto Príncipe, Cuba. After 1764, Cuba became a separate captaincy general with jurisdiction over the provinces of Louisiana and (later) Florida. Cuba was occupied by United States* forces in 1898.

*Cuzco*—This former Inca capital became the seat of an intendancy with an audiencia in 1784. An unsuccessful rebellion against Spanish authority occurred in 1813. By 1824, Cuzco was captured by Peruvian republicans.

*Guanajuato*—This central Mexican region was established as an intendancy under the jurisdiction of New Spain in 1787. After 1821, it became part of Mexico.

*Guatemala*—The captaincy general of Guatemala, with its audiencia, though subordinate to the viceroy and viceregal audiencia in Mexico City, had jurisdiction over the provinces of Honduras, Nicaragua, Costa Rica, and Soconusco. The intendancy of San Salvador was added in 1786. In 1821, when freed of Spanish authority, the provinces of the captaincy general united with the Mexican empire. After the establishment of the Republic of Mexico, the Guatemalan jurisdiction formed the United States of Central America. These provinces and the former intendancy of San Salvador became separate republics after 1840. Chiapas remained a part of Mexico.

*Guayana*—This eastern Venezuelan province included the island of Trinidad. In 1735, Trinidad was established as a separate province, and Guayana was incorporated under the Province of New Andalusia until 1762. Four years later, Guayana was transferred to the captaincy general of Venezuela. Independence forces occupied the province in 1817, and Guayana became first a part of Gran Colombia and then Venezuela.

*Guayaquil*—For more than two centuries a corregimiento under the audiencia of Quito, Guayaquil was designated a province in 1763. Occupied by independence forces in 1820, Guayaquil was first a part of Gran Colombia and then incorporated into the Republic of Ecuador.

*Honduras*—Often called Comayagua after its leading city, Honduras was settled from both New Spain and Panama. From the sixteenth century, the region was under the jurisdiction of the audiencia of Guatemala. Between 1786 and 1812, Honduras was designated as the intendancy of Comayagua and then, until 1821, an alcaldía mayor. Freed of Spanish control in 1821, Honduras first became a part of the Mexican Empire, then a state in the United States of Central America, and finally an independent republic in 1840.

*Huamanga*—Situated in southern Peru, Huamanga was one of the eight intendancies established under the Peruvian viceroyalty in 1784. When Spanish control was terminated in 1824, Huamanga was incorporated into the Republic of Peru.

*Huancavelica*—This region in central Peru, the site of rich mercury deposits, was governed from the sixteenth century by a superintendent of mines appointed by the viceroy. After 1736, this appointment was made by the Council of the Indies. From 1784 to 1824, Huancavelica was an intendancy and thereafter a part of Peru.

*La Paz*—In 1783, the area around Lake Titicaca was organized into the intendancy of La Paz under the jurisdiction of the viceroyalty of Río de la Plata. In spite of rebellion after 1809, Spanish control did not end until 1825, when La Paz was incorporated into the Republic of Bolivia.

*Malvinas (Falkland) Islands*—In the south Atlantic, some four hundred miles east of southern Argentina, the Malvinas were first visited by the French and Spaniards in the sixteenth century. The British had visited them by 1592 and named them the Falkland Islands in 1692. The French abandoned interest in the islands in 1767, and for the next seven years, Spain and Great Britain struggled to control them. By 1774, Spain held undisputed control through the viceroyalty of Río de la Plata until 1810, when the last governor fled. Argentina occupied the islands until 1832, when Britain* reoccupied them.

*Margarita*—A small island off the coast of Venezuela, Margarita was under the audiencia of Santo Domingo until 1739, at which time jurisdiction was transferred to the audiencia of Santa Fe de Bogotá. Jurisdiction again shifted with the 1777 creation of the captaincy general of Venezuela. After 1821, Margarita became a district in New Esparta, a state in the Republic of Venezuela.

*Mérida–La Grita*—By 1700, the provinces of Mérida, La Grita, and Maracaibo had been combined into one administrative unit headquartered at Maracaibo, presided over by a governor and captain general subject to the audiencia of Santo Domingo. In 1740, jurisdiction was transferred to the audiencia of Santa Fe de Bogotá. Eleven years later, the name officially changed to Maracaibo, reflecting the growing significance of the provincial capital. In 1777, Maracaibo was included in the newly created Venezuelan captaincy general. After 1811, it became part of Gran Colombia. Later, Maracaibo was incorporated into the Republic of Venezuela.

*Montevideo*—Founded in 1726, on the north side of the Río de la Plata, in response to the threat posed by Portugal's Nova Colônia do Sacramento, Montevideo was elevated to the rank of province in 1751. It retained this status after the 1780 introduction of the intendancy system. Spain acquired Novo Colônia do Sacramento in 1777, and this territory was added to Montevideo. The viceroy of Río de la Plata moved to Montevideo after his 1810 expulsion from Buenos Aires. Four years later, Spanish authority terminated in Montevideo as well. For the next fifteen years, the area was fought over by the new Argentine government, Portugal, and Britain. In 1830, this part of South America became independent as the República Oriental de Uruguay, with Montevideo its capital.

*Nicaragua*—The governor of Nicaragua, one of the very early Central American provinces (settlement began in 1522), reported to the audiencia of Guatemala. He controlled the western half of the territory, with the British heavily influencing the Moskito Coast until 1782. In 1786, the captaincy general of Guatemala was reorganized under the intendancy system, and the governor of Nicaragua became the governor-intendant of Leon. Rebellion began in 1811, but it took ten years to expel Spanish authority. Initially part of Mexico after the break with Spain, Nicaragua became a member of the United States of Central America before becoming an independent republic in 1839.

*New Andalusia*—This eastern Venezuelan province was often referred to as Cumaná after its main city. New Andalusia was under the jurisdiction of the audiencia in Santo Domingo until 1739, at which time it was transferred to the audiencia of Santa Fe de Bogotá in the newly designated viceroyalty of New Granada. In 1777, jurisdiction was again changed, this time to the captaincy general of Venezuela. New Andalusia was the scene of frequent combat between 1810 and 1821, as nationalists and royalists vied for control. The province was initially included in Gran Colombia, but later joined Venezuela.

*New Spain*—The viceroyalty of New Spain had, by 1700, come to exercise authority over all of the Spanish possessions in North America, Central America, the Caribbean, the Venezuelan coast of South America, and the Philippine Islands through the viceroy and the viceregal audiencia in Mexico City, and the audiencias at Guatemala, Guadalajara (New Galicia), Manila (the Philippines), and Santo Domingo. During the eighteenth century, this span of control was diminished through reorganization. The South American provinces were transferred to the audiencia of Santa Fe de Bogotá, while the crown retained control of the Provincias Internas for a time. Rebellion began in 1810, but was essentially quashed by 1815. Spanish control, however, was so weakened that the viceroy was deposed in 1821, and his replacement left powerless. New Spain then became the independent Mexico.

*New Galicia*—In the early eighteenth century, New Galicia exercised control over the governors of the western and northern frontier regions of Coahuila, New Biscay, New Leon, New Mexico, Sinaloa, Sonora, and Texas through its audiencia. In 1708, the governor-president acquired the added authority and responsibility of a captaincy general. The intendancy of Guadalajara was created in the reforms of 1787, with the governor-president and captain general of New Galicia becoming intendant of Guadalajara. This jurisdiction became part of the Mexican Empire in 1821.

*New Granada*—By 1700, the governor and captain general of New Granada, who was also president of the audiencia of Santa Fe de Bogotá, held jurisdiction over Cartagena de Indias and Santa Marta. From 1717 to 1722, New Granada was elevated to a viceroyalty with authority over New Andalusia, Guayana, Venezuela, Mérida–La Grita, Popayán, and Quito as well as Santa Marta and Cartagena de Indias. In 1739, the viceroyalty was reestablished with these same dependencies in addition to Panama. With the 1777 creation of the captaincy general of Venezuela, the viceroyalty lost control of Guayana, Mérida–La Grita–Maracaibo, New Andalusia, and Venezuela. After 1810, the viceroy's authority was limited to Cartagena, Maracaibo, and Panama, and by 1819, Spanish forces had evacuated the viceroyalty. The creation of Gran Colombia used New Granada as its core. With its 1830 collapse, the republic of New Granada—later Colombia—was established using the 1777 viceroyalty as its territorial base.

*New Biscay*—Eighteenth-century New Biscay maintained control over north-central Mexico under the jurisdiction of the audiencia of Guadalajara. In 1777, it was incorporated into the Provincias Internas, its area adjusted to roughly the boundaries of the present-day Mexican states of Durango and Chihuahua, and in 1787, it was redesignated as the intendancy of Durango. In 1821, this region was divided into the states of Durango and Chihuahua.

*New Leon*—Created from part of eastern New Biscay, New Leon was initially under the jurisdiction of the audiencia of Guadalajara. The province became part of Provincias Internas in 1777, but was detached in 1793 and assigned to the viceregal audiencia in Mexico City. New Leon was not incorporated into the intendancy system. The region became part of Mexico in 1821.

*New Mexico*—In the extreme north of New Spain, New Mexico did not develop beyond a frontier region. Initially under the audiencia of Guadalajara, New Mexico became part of the Provincias Internas in 1777, and with the termination of Spanish control in 1821, became a part of the Mexican Empire and later a state in the Republic of Mexico.

*New Santander*—Efforts to develop this sparsely populated area of northeastern New Spain, south of the Río Bravo del Norte, did not begin until 1746. Initially under the viceregal audiencia in Mexico City, New Santander was incorporated into the Provincias Internas in 1777, and then in 1793, jurisdiction was passed back to the viceroy. When royal control ceased in 1812, New Santander was again put under the jurisdiction of the commandant-general of the Provincias Internas. It became the state of Tamaulipas upon the formation of the Republic of Mexico.

*Oaxaca*—In 1787, the alcaldía mayor of Oaxaca was elevated to an intendancy under the viceroy of New Spain and retained this status until Mexican independence. Oaxaca then became a state in the new Republic of Mexico.

*Panama*—The eighteenth century was one of decline for Panama, as trade routes changed. In 1739, Panama was placed under the jurisdiction of the viceroyalty of New Granada, and by midcentury, its audiencia was abolished. During the wars for independence, Panama hosted the viceroy on two occasions, first from 1812 to 1814, and again from 1819 to 1821, the year the isthmus became a part of Gran Colombia.

*Paraguay*—Eighteenth-century Paraguay, under the audiencia of Charcas, was essentially a social and economic backwater. Its eastern district, Misiones, was under direct control of the Jesuits until after 1767, when the mission clergy were expelled and their holdings divided between Spain and Portugal. Paraguay became an intendancy under the viceroy of Río de la Plata in 1783, subject to the viceregal audiencia in Buenos Aires. Paraguay became independent of both Spanish and republican control from Buenos Aires in 1811.

*Peru*—By 1700, the viceroy of Peru had jurisdiction over all South America except for the Caribbean coast of Venezuela. Control was exercised through the viceregal audiencia in Lima and the audiencias of Charcas, Chile, Santa Fe de Bogotá, Panama, and Quito. Peruvian mineral wealth served as the financial core of the Spanish Empire. Bourbon reforms of the eighteenth century reoriented trade policies and resulted in the formation of the viceroyalties of New Granada and Río de la Plata and the captaincy general of Venezuela. Further decentralization followed the implementation of the intendancy system after 1783, when what was left of the viceroyalty was divided into intendancies (Arequipa, 1784; Cuzco, 1784; Huamanga, 1784; Huancavelica, 1784; Tarma, 1784; Trujillo, 1784; and Puno, 1796 [from Río de la Plata]). Indian uprisings (1780 to 1782, 1809, and again in 1813) did not seriously threaten Spanish authority, but invasion from Chile and then Gran Colombia in 1820 crushed royal resistance. Independence was proclaimed in 1821, and the Republic of Peru established four years later.

*Popayán*—This province, in what is now southwestern Colombia, was within the jurisdiction of the audiencia of Quito in the early years of the eighteenth century. In 1777, Popayán became part of the new viceroyalty of New Granada. By 1820, Popayán was incorporated into Gran Colombia.

*Potosí*—This rich silver-mining area within the viceroyalty of Peru was transferred to the newly created Río de la Plata viceroyalty in 1777. Six years later, it was redesignated an intendancy. The intendant was deposed and executed in 1810, and for the next twelve years, control of the area was disputed between royalist and nationalist forces. Most of the area in the intendancy was incorporated into the Republic of Bolivia.

*Provincias Internas*—The Bourbon response to the growing hostility of northern Mexican indigenous tribes was to establish a march in 1787, under a commandant-general initially independent of the viceroy of New Spain. Later, the viceroy did exercise some control over the commandant-general; the degree, however, depended upon the personalities of the individual officeholders. When first organized, the Provincias Internas included all the northern Mexican provinces except California. From 1788 to 1793, the commandancy-general was divided into an eastern section, with control over Coahuila, Texas, New Leon, and New Santander, and a western section that included Sonora, California, New Biscay, and New Mexico. From 1793 to 1813, the Provincias Internas were again united, but control of California, New Leon, and New Santander reverted to the viceroy in Mexico City. Between 1813 and independence, this jurisdiction was again divided into eastern and western sections, California and New Leon being retained under viceregal control. After 1786, New Biscay was part of the intendancy of Durango.

*Puebla*—An alcaldía mayor since 1555, Puebla was designated an intendancy in 1787. The city and province became part of the Mexican empire in 1821.

*Puerto Rico*—This island in the eastern Caribbean, although discovered and settled early, was politically and economically insignificant. After 1825, Puerto

Rico and Cuba were the only remaining Spanish possessions in the Western Hemisphere. Puerto Rico was ceded to the United States in 1898, as a result of the Spanish-American War.*

*Puno*—This area of southeastern Peru was made an intendancy under the viceroyalty of Río de la Plata in 1783. Because of its distance from Buenos Aires, Puno was transferred to the Peruvian viceroyalty in 1796. Spanish authority was extinguished in 1824, when Puno was incorporated into the Republic of Peru.

*Quito*—Quito was an audiencia under the viceroy of Peru. In 1718, the audiencia was ended, and for four years, Quito was put under the jurisdiction of the newly created viceroyalty of New Granada. When this viceroyalty was terminated in 1722, the Quito audiencia was reestablished under the viceroy in Lima. The viceroyalty of New Granada was restored in 1739, and Quito, its audiencia intact, was reassigned to the new jurisdiction. Spanish authority, intermittent after 1809, was crushed by 1822. From this time until 1830, Quito was part of Gran Colombia, at which time it became the Republic of Ecuador, its area based on the former audiencia, but much reduced in size.

*Río de la Plata*—The viceroyalty of Río de la Plata was established in 1777, with jurisdiction over the provinces of Buenos Aires, Paraguay, Tucumán, Montevideo, the Malvinas Islands, the audiencia of Charcas (from the viceroyalty of Peru), and Cuyo (from Chile). The viceregal audiencia was created in 1783 and located in Buenos Aires. The intendancy system was inaugurated the same year, with the viceroyalty divided into the intendancies of Córdoba, Cochabamba, La Paz, Paraguay, Potosí, Salta, Charcas, and Puno (transferred to Peru in 1796); and the provinces of Mojos, Chiquitos, Misiones, Montevideo, and Malvinas. When British forces occupied Buenos Aires in 1806, the viceroy was replaced by a local citizen after an election, an action the crown accepted. Efforts to reassert crown control led to the removal of the viceregal government to Montevideo in 1810. Buenos Aires declared its independence in 1816. The republics of Argentina, Bolivia, Paraguay, and Uruguay were established within the territory governed by the viceroy of Río de la Plata.

*Salta*—Tucumán Province was divided into two intendancies in 1783. The northern region became the intendancy of Salta; the southern, Córdoba. Both were under the jurisdiction of the viceroyalty of Río de la Plata. Effective Spanish authority ended in 1810. Both were incorporated into the Republic of Argentina.

*San Luis Potosí*—Established as an intendancy under New Spain in 1787, San Luis Potosí eventually became a state in the Republic of Mexico.

*San Salvador*—This region in the captaincy general of Guatemala was designated an intendancy in 1786. Spanish control ended by revolt in 1821. San Salvador became part of the United States of Central America in 1824 and the independent Republic of El Salvador in 1839.

*Santa Marta–Río Hacha*—Located in northern Colombia, this city-province remained under the audiencia of Santo Domingo until 1740, except for the interval between 1719 and 1723, when it was under the short-lived first viceroyalty of

New Granada. After 1740, Santa Marta–Río Hacha was again made a province of the viceroyalty of New Granada and the audiencia of Santa Fe de Bogotá. Santa Marta was one of the galleon entrepôts, and the seat of the viceroyalty from 1810 to 1821, when the rest of New Granada was controlled by independence forces. This province ultimately became part of the Republic of Colombia.

*Santo Domingo*—Diminished in importance as Mexican and Peruvian treasure was exported to Europe, Santo Domingo was also reduced in size by the Treaty of Ryswick that ceded the western third of the island to France* in 1697. Until 1739, the captain general and the audiencia of Santo Domingo exercised authority over Cuba, Puerto Rico, Florida, Mérida–La Grita–Maracaibo, Margarita, New Andalusia, Santa Marta–Río Hacha, Guayana, and Venezuela. With the 1739 establishment of the viceroyalty of New Granada, Santo Domingo was left with Cuba, Puerto Rico, and Florida. Florida was ceded to Great Britain in 1763, as a result of the Seven Years' War. The following year, Cuba was elevated to an independent captaincy general, and in 1797, the audiencia was transferred to Puerto Príncipe, Cuba. Between 1801 and 1809, and again from 1822 to 1844, Santo Domingo was occupied by Haiti. The second Haitian occupation followed a brief period of revolutionary control in 1821. Santo Domingo finally became independent in 1844.

*Sinaloa and Sonora*—This important mining region of northwestern Mexico was initially retained under the control of the viceroy of New Spain, but later transferred to New Biscay. In 1732, Sinaloa and Sonora became a separate province under New Galicia. Between 1777 and 1787, this province became a part of the Provincias Internas, and after that, of the intendancy of Sonora. The region became separate states of Sinaloa and Sonora after Mexican independence.

*Tarma*—Tarma was designated an intendancy under the viceroyalty of Peru in 1784. Spanish control ended in 1823. Two years later, Tarma was incorporated into the Republic of Peru.

*Trinidad*—This island off the coast of Venezuela was a part of the Province of Guayana until 1735, when it was created a separate province under the jurisdiction of the audiencia and captain general of Santo Domingo. Four years later, Trinidad was transferred to New Granada, and then in 1777, to the newly organized captaincy general of Venezuela. In 1797, Trinidad was invaded by Britain and retained by the terms of the 1802 Treaty of Amiens.

*Trujillo*—A northern province of Peru, Trujillo was designated an intendancy in 1784, under the viceroy in Lima. Trujillo was occupied by republican forces under Simón Bolívar in 1824, when this region was incorporated into the Republic of Peru.

*Tucumán*—Tucumán was settled from Peru in the sixteenth century and subordinated to the audiencia of Charcas. In 1776, Tucumán was transferred to the viceroyalty of Río de la Plata. Seven years later, in 1783, this province was divided into the intendancies of Córdoba and Salta, ending its history as an administrative unit.

*Valladolid*—Established in an intendancy in 1767 out of the Michoacán region of west central Mexico, Valladolid became part of the Mexican empire in 1821.

*Venezuela*—A large coastal province, Venezuela was put under the jurisdiction of the audiencia of Santo Domingo until 1777 and then again from 1723 to 1739. From 1717 to 1723, and after 1739, Venezuela was subordinate to the viceroyalty of New Granada and the audiencia of Santa Fe de Bogotá. After 1742, Venezuela came under the audiencia of Santo Domingo, but was still subject to the viceroy of New Granada. Venezuela was elevated to a captaincy general in 1777, and received its own audiencia at Caracas with authority over Maracaibo (Mérida–La Grita–Maracaibo), Barinas, Guayana, Trinidad, and until 1797, Margarita and New Andalusia. The captain general was overthrown in 1810, and control shifted between royalist and republican forces until 1820. Venezuela became part of Gran Colombia in 1820, but the provinces that made up the captaincy general of Venezuela became the Republic of Venezuela in 1830.

*Vera Cruz*—Implementation of the intendancy system elevated Vera Cruz to such status in 1787. The region became a state in independent Mexico after 1821.

*Yucatán*—The captaincy general of Yucatán was under the viceregal audiencia in Mexico City from the sixteenth century. It became the intendancy of Yucatán in 1789 and a part of Mexico after 1821.

*Zacatecas*—Zacatecas was an alcaldía mayor under the viceroy in Mexico City until 1787, when it was elevated to an intendancy in New Spain. The jurisdiction became a Mexican state after 1821.

## NORTH AMERICA

*Louisiana*—Spain acquired Louisiana in 1762, a cession entered into with France to deny the territory to Britain. From 1765 to 1803, Louisiana's governor was subordinate to the governor and captain general of Cuba. Spain retroceded Louisiana to France by the Treaty of San Ildefonso in 1800, with the promise of nonalienation. France reestablished control in 1803 and three weeks later sold Louisiana to the United States.

*Florida*—Colonial Florida was governed from Cuba until it was ceded to Britain in 1764, after the Seven Years' War. Spanish forces reoccupied British West Florida during the American War for Independence. East Florida was ceded back to Spain by the Treaty of Paris in 1793. Spain retained the British division of East and West Florida for ease of administration. The Floridas were sold to the United States in 1819; the transfer was completed in 1821.

*Texas*—The first permanent Spanish settlement in Texas was established in 1682. Texas became a separate province in 1716, divided from Coahuila, but subordinated to the commandant-general of the Provincias Internas in 1777. Texas was incorporated into newly independent Mexico in 1821.

## AFRICA

*Canary Islands*—During the eighteenth century and part of the nineteenth, this group of islands consisting of Gran Canaria, Tenerife, La Palma, Gomera,

Hierro, Lanzarote, and Fuerteventura, were governed by a captain general appointed directly by the crown. In 1821, the Canaries became a metropolitan province of Spain.

*Ceuta and Melilla*—These Spanish plazas on the Mediterranean coast of Morocco had separate governors during the eighteenth and first half of the nineteenth centuries. With the 1847 creation of the captaincy general of North Africa, all the Spanish enclaves in the region were brought under the unitary governance of Ceuta, and its governor became a captain general. In 1913, Ceuta, Melilla, and other small plazas were incorporated into the Spanish zone of Morocco and lost their administrative status. With the 1956 termination of the Spanish zone, Ceuta and Melilla have been governed by mayors—Ceuta attached to Cadiz and Melilla to Malaga.

*Ifni*—On the African coast opposite the Canary Islands, Ifni was occupied in the late fifteenth and early sixteenth centuries as Santa Cruz de la Mar Pequeña and reoccupied as Ifni in 1934. The region became a part of Spanish West Africa in 1952 and after 1958, regained its separate identity. The enclave was transferred to Morocco in 1969.

*Morocco*—Spain established control over northern Morocco (in addition to Ceuta and Melilla) in a 1912 agreement with France. The region was governed by a high commissioner. After 1934, this official also had jurisdiction over Spanish West Africa. In 1956, Spain, along with France, withdrew from Morocco, retaining Ceuta and Melilla.

*Oran*—The city of Oran, just west of the prime meridian on the coast of Africa, was occupied by Spain from 1509 until 1792, except from 1708 to 1732, and after 1792, when it was under the control of the Ottoman Empire.

*Spanish Guinea*—Consisting of the islands of Fernando Poo and Annobon and the coastal enclave of Río Muni, West African Spanish Guinea was ceded to Spain in 1777 by Portugal, in exchange for Novo Colônia do Sacramento in South America, under the terms of the Treaty of San Ildefonso. This holding was not occupied by Spain until 1844, having been leased to Britain in 1827 as a slave-trade interdiction base. Spanish Guinea became an overseas province of Spain in 1959 and four years later, gained some internal autonomy as Equatorial Guinea. Fernando Poo, Annobon, and Río Muni became independent Equatorial Guinea in 1968.

*Spanish Sahara* (Western Sahara)—Spanish Sahara was created in 1958 when Spanish West Africa was divided into the separate provinces of Ifni and Spanish Sahara. Spain relinquished its interest in the area in Feb. 1976.

*Spanish West Africa (Río de Oro)*—Spain secured vague rights to this area of coastal Africa south of Morocco in 1860 and proclaimed a protectorate over it twenty-four years later. Spanish West Africa was transferred to the control of the high commissioner of the Spanish zone of Morocco in 1934. This province was divided into the separate political entities of Ifni and Spanish Sahara in 1958. Ifni was transferred to Morocco that year, while Spanish Sahara remained an overseas province of Spain until 26 Feb. 1976.

## THE PACIFIC

*Guam*—The largest and southernmost of the Mariana Island group, although subordinate to the audiencia of Manila in the Philippines, was isolated enough to permit considerable autonomy. Guam was ceded to the United States in 1898 as a result of the Spanish-American War. The rest of the Marianas were sold to Germany* the following year.

*Philippine Islands*—The governor of the Philippine Islands and the audiencia of Manila were subordinate to the viceroy of New Spain as the eighteenth century began. The British occupied Manila in 1762–1763, withdrawing as a condition of the Treaty of Paris in 1763. The governor received the additional authority and responsibility of captain general (1783), three years before the attempted introduction of the intendancy system. Nationalist sentiment in the nineteenth century ended with the islands being invaded and occupied, when the Philippine Islands were ceded to the United States as a result of the Spanish-American War in 1898.

For additional information, see D. Fieldhouse, *The Colonial Empire: A Comparative Survey from the Eighteenth Century* (London, 1966); D. Henige, *Colonial Governors from the Fifteenth Century to the Present* (Madison, 1970); R. Herr, *An Historical Essay on Modern Spain* (Berkeley and Los Angeles, 1971); R. Labra y Cadrona, *La cuestión colonial* (Madrid, 1861); J. Lockhart and S. Schwartz, *Early Latin America: A History of Colonial Spanish America and Brazil* (New York, 1985); J. Lynch, *The Spanish American Revolutions, 1808–1826*, 2d ed. (New York, 1986); P. Madoz, *Diccionario geográfico-estadístico-histórico de España y sus posesiones de ultramar* (Madrid, 1845); R. Mesa, *El colonialismo en la crisis de xix siglo español* (Madrid, 1967).

*R. Himmerich y Valencia*

## COMMUNIST PARTY OF SPAIN, PARTIDO COMUNISTA ESPAÑOL

**(PCE).** The Russian Revolution of 1917 and the creation of the Communist Third International, or Comintern, attracted parts of the Spanish Left, and Soviet influence in Spain did not have to be subsidized in order to flourish, because many Spaniards took the initiative in spreading Marxist and Leninist propaganda. The party was officially born in Apr. 1920. In 1923, Gen. Miguel Primo de Rivera* proclaimed his dictatorship, bringing to an end the nineteenth-century constitution of liberal oligarchy. In the last free elections under the old rules, the Partido Socialista Obrero Español (PSOE) received 21,400 votes and the Communists 1,400.

Municipal elections in Apr. 1931 repudiated Alfonso XIII* and the military dictatorship he had encouraged since 1923. Economic depression further encouraged disillusionment with the old regime. Alfonso abdicated and the Second Republic* was born. The new government, a coalition of liberal progressives and democratic socialists, immediately prepared a new constitution that tolerated the newly reorganized Communist party.

In 1934, the Soviet Union began urging socialists and liberals in Spain, like those in Britain,* France,* and the United States,* to create a united Popular

Front against the Fascists. Joseph Stalin (1879–1953) for the most part abandoned the exportation of revolution in 1928 after the Chinese fiasco and his repudiation of Leon Trotsky (1879–1940), the prime Soviet proponent of world revolution. The period from 1928 to 1934 saw Stalin stressing a "united front from below," meaning destruction of the independent Left, social-democratic, and Trotskyite groups in favor of a tightly controlled, conspiratorial party available to serve Soviet national interests. From 1934 (after Adolf Hitler's Nonaggression Pact with Poland) to the 1936 outbreak of the Spanish Civil War,* the Soviet dictator was interested mainly in protecting Soviet frontiers from a feared Japanese or German armed invasion; under these circumstances, fomenting social revolution in other countries was no longer helpful to the Soviet Union. Consequently, the Foreign Ministry, under the direction of Maxim Litvinov (1876–1951), assumed a conservative defensive reaction against Hitler's drive to the east. Georgi Dimitroff (1882–1949), secretary of the Third International, encouraged the development of a Popular Front in every country to stand up to Adolf Hitler (1889–1945) and Benito Mussolini (1883–1945) as well.

In the fall of 1934, a violent strike took place in Asturias* in which the Spanish communists played a prominent role. The army* crushed the strike within a month, and the leading communists went into exile or were imprisoned. The republic's conservative government collapsed in Dec. 1935 over a question of taxes and gambling scandals.

The Spanish Communist party tried to attract proletarian voters from other parties between 1935 and 17 July 1936. The old Leninist revolutionary rhetoric was therefore maintained to some extent. At the same time, the communists made new appeals to the conservative petit bourgeoisie and salaried class to stand united in a Popular Front against a possible coup by profascist, reactionary, and nationalistic officers. The Soviet Union worked hard with propaganda and, probably, money, to help the Popular Front governments in both France and Spain win election in the first half of 1936.

On 16 Feb. 1936, a close election in Spain brought to power a coalition of liberals, socialists, communists, Trotskyites, and anarchists, formed into a left-wing alliance of parties known as the Popular Front. The major issue uniting these groups was amnesty for the strikers of 1934. The Spanish Communist party itself received only 3 percent of the vote in the election, which translated into fifteen deputies in the Cortes.

Spain may or may not have been on the verge of social revolution in the months before July 1936. After the Feb. Popular Front electoral victory brought liberals to power in the cabinet, the Left continued agitation for social reform, the president was impeached, peasants took over many large estates, strikes were called, and churches were burned. On the Right, the Falange* and the Carlists expanded their private militias. Francisco Largo Caballero* headed the socialist labor union, the Unión General de Trabajadores* (UGT), and he and the anarchist leaders were advocating more radical revolution. In the spring of 1936, Largo's speeches sounded as Lenin's had from Apr. to Oct. 1917. How Spain in 1936 differed from Russia in Nov. 1917 was in its lack of specific plans from either the Spanish revolutionary socialists or the anarchists to carry out an armed coup. The Spanish Left was too divided among bickering liberals; anarchists; revolutionary socialists; Leninist-Trotskyites, under the banner of the POUM*; and the small, authoritarian Communist party under the sway of Stalinism.

The PCE had forty thousand members as of 17 July 1936, when the Right, soon led by Gen. Francisco Franco,* started the civil war. The major charge advanced after 1937 by liberals, socialists, anarchists, and the so-called Trotskyites was that Stalin sabotaged a potentially revolutionary situation for the diplomatic and domestic interests of his own reactionary power in the Soviet Union.

Although it is unclear exactly how and when the Soviet decision to intervene militarily in Spain was made, it may have occurred at Moscow meetings held as early as 21–26 July. The Comintern may have sent agents to discover what was happening in Spain. World-renowned writer André Malraux (1901–1976), president of the French branch of a communist-front organization called the Committee Against War and Fascism, flew to Madrid* about 21 July to serve as a private volunteer. He later returned to France to recruit pilots and secure some twenty planes, which arrived on 13 Aug. at Barajas, near Madrid, and began operations a few days later. Similarly, the Italian communist Nino Nanetti (?–1937) arrived in Barcelona from Toulouse on 20 July. As early as 1 Aug., the French Communist party began collecting arms for shipment to Spain. On 3 Aug., the Comintern quietly initiated a worldwide call for communists to join the other international volunteers who were flocking to Spain. The Soviet newspapers *Pravda* and *Izvestia* reported on 6 Aug. that Moscow's trade unions had collected 12,145,000 rubles, about $2 million, ostensibly for relief for the Spanish workers' militia.

As the war developed, in early Sept., the Madrid government shifted further to the left. During that month, socialist Francisco Largo Caballero replaced the liberal José Giral (1880–1962) as premier, and two communists were appointed to the Spanish cabinet for the first time. The Soviets thereupon made a second, crucial decision to send their own arms and military advisors to direct the international volunteers. In executing this project, the Soviet Union had the cooperation not only of the French Communist party, but of some French officials as well. As of 12–14 Sept., it became official Soviet policy to send military aid to the republican government of Spain. Shortly thereafter, on 25 Sept., in violation of the spirit of the Nonintervention Agreement, the first of five Soviet ships, the *Neva*, arrived in republican Spain with food, secret arms, and munitions.

In Sept., as the Soviets gradually dispatched weapons, the republicans organized their gold reserves for shipment to the Soviet Union. In mid-Sept., the Bank of Spain prepared to ship to Moscow some 510 tons of gold, which was 72.64 percent of the large Spanish reserves. This was gradually spent on the International Brigades, by the republican war ministries, and by Compañía Arrendataria del Manopolio de Petróleos, S.A.-Gentibus, a new Soviet-Spanish monopoly trading company that centralized republican purchasing activities abroad. Thus, private companies, French cooperation, and the Communist International actually were more important than the government of the Soviet Union in the day-to-day foreign operations that sustained the republican war effort from Sept. 1936 to the end of the war.

It also appears that only $131.3 million of the $178 million in Spanish gold spent in Moscow during 1937 went for weapons, with perhaps an additional $85 million in Soviet-provided credit so spent in 1938. This relatively low figure for direct Soviet participation reflects the indirect operations the Comintern employed in Western Europe. The Soviet Union charged the republic some $518 million in Spanish gold for the services of the International Brigades and for weapons and other goods channeled mostly through France. Russian personnel as such did not play a significant military role on the side of the Second Republic. An estimated total of six to eight hundred Soviet military advisors served in republican Spain at any given time, while throughout the war, the total number of Soviets never exceeded two thousand.

The membership of the International Brigades from Germany, France, Italy, and Poland was more than 60 percent communist. Following a month or more of preparation, the first brigaders charged into battle on 23 Oct.; during the course of the civil war, from 35,000 to as many as 59,400 men served in the International Brigades.

As a result of the new prestige of the Soviet Union, the PCE gained 250,000 members by Mar. 1937. The new recruits came from the peasant, tradesman, and small-manufacturer classes. They allied themselves against the more revolutionary anarchists and some of the socialists. The two communists in the cabinet were of minor significance compared to the fact that the need for arms led to Soviet advisors and agents of the Comintern, particularly the Italian Palmiro Togliatti (1893–1964), influencing the dominant Socialist party members of the government on military tactics.

The standing of the communist and Popular Front alliance was shaken in the eyes of democrats abroad after the riotous days in Barcelona in early May 1937. The upshot was that the central government repressed the independent militias of the anarchists and the POUM and made a united army in which communist advisors held key positions.

In time, however, the Soviets reduced their aid to the republic, while the Axis continued to extend strong support to Franco. The republic's chargé d'affaires in Moscow concluded on 24 Apr. 1939 that "many Russians believe we have lost the war," and he requested recall to Spain before the Soviets made any declaration of withdrawal. After June 1938, the Soviet Union quietly retreated from its Spanish venture, partly because the French imposed heavy restrictions on the transit of Soviet supplies from France to Spain.

By July 1938, the official press organ of the German army had already concluded that the Soviet Union had written Spain off as lost and that it continued to support the republicans only to save face. Mussolini and Hitler, however, remained closer to their Spanish nationalist allies until the end of the war. On 21 Sept. 1938, the republican prime minister officially called for the withdrawal of the International Brigades.

Any hope of international support for the beleaguered Second Republic was further dashed by the Munich Conference in 1938. On 29–30 Sept. 1938, France and Britain coerced Czechoslovakia to cede the Sudetenland to Germany without offering resistance. Stalin, who already suspected the British prime minister, Neville Chamberlain (1869–1940), and the French foreign minister, Georges Bonnet (1889–1973), could have no doubt that the Soviet Union had been isolated from the European concert.

By Feb. 1939, Catalonia had fallen, and the flight of top republican officials showed that many Spanish liberals and socialists had concluded that the Popular Front had lost the civil war. Despite the bitter resistance of Mar., the last month of the war, the communists finally gave up the fight. Party leaders, including Dolores Ibarruri*, fled to Moscow.

Franco's victory brought the suppression of all political parties, but struck particularly harshly at the communists. From 1941 to 1956, the Soviets attempted to encourage guerrilla warfare against the Franco regime. During the economic recovery of Spain in the 1960s, workers organized clandestine unions, Comisiones Obreras (CCOO), in which secret communists took a leading role. The party, whose cadre spoke from Moscow, as early as 1956 began to talk of legal opposition to the Franco regime. After Franco's death, the Spanish Communist party was again legalized in Apr. 1977. Free elections for parliament were held in June of that year, in which the communists received 1.7 million votes, or 9.2 percent of the electorate. The next year, they dropped the term ''Leninist'' and in 1979 increased their vote slightly. Since the communists could scarcely be distinguished from legal parliamentary democratic socialists, however, their vote in the third election of 1982 declined. In June 1986, though, they increased their votes from 3 percent to 4 percent, hardly a trend. In 1986, the Communist party held seven seats in the Cortes.

For additional information, see B. Bolloten, *The Grand Camouflage: The Communist Conspiracy in the Spanish Civil War* (New York, 1961); E. H. Carr, *The Comintern and the Spanish Civil War*, ed. by T. Deutscher (New York, 1984); D. T. Cattell, *Communism and the Spanish Civil War*, vol. 1 (Berkeley, 1956); R. G. Colodny, *The Struggle for Madrid: The Central Epic of the Spanish Conflict* (New York, 1958), and *The Popular Front in Europe*, ed. by H. Graham and P. Preston (New York, 1987); and G. Meaker, *The Revolutionary Left in Spain 1914–1923* (Stanford, 1974).

R. H. Whealey

*Related entries*: CAMACHO, MARCELINO; CARRILLO, SANTIAGO; IBARRURI, DOLORES.

**CORTES OF CADIZ** (1810–1813), first constituent legislature, held during the War of Independence.* The Cortes Generales y Extraordinarias met at Cadiz (Sept. 1810–Sept. 1813) to inaugurate a new regime. While Spain was battling

Napoleon Bonaparte's (1769–1821) armies to retain independence, an internal revolution took place at Cadiz, the seat of Spain's junta-led government and the only city left unoccupied by France.* The Cortes, first called by the regency, ostensibly to vote subsidies for the war effort, wrote a liberal charter that reflected ideas first developed by the French constitutions of 1791, 1793, and 1795. Promulgated in Cadiz on 19 Mar., the Spanish Constitution of 1812 was supplemented by liberal legislation designed to change the socioeconomic structure of Spanish society and reduce the role of the church in Spain.

The Constitution of 1812 was the banner of liberalism* throughout southern Europe and Latin America for decades. Extraordinarily long, 384 articles in all, the charter sanctioned popular sovereignty, division of power, equal representation of all male citizens, creation of social classes to replace legal estates, a unicameral Cortes, and complete centralization of government. Essentially, the Constitution of 1812 provided for a society led by the bourgeoisie and a government directed by the legislative branch. The supplementary enactments included suppression of seignorial jurisdiction, provision for the sale of communal lands, abolition of the guild system, and forced reduction of the number of monasteries and members of religious orders.

The Cortes of Cadiz was able to transform Spain, in theory, because of the exceptional wartime circumstances: the captivity of Carlos IV* and Fernando VII* in France; the national sacrifice against the French; the siege of Cadiz by the French; the liberal atmosphere of the city; and the impossibility of holding regular elections for parliamentary delegates, which allowed the use of substitute delegates, often quite intellectually gifted. Three leaders stood out in taking advantage of those circumstances: Agustín Argüelles (1765–1844), José María Queipo de Llano, conde de Toreno (1776–1844), and Fr. Diego Muñoz Torrero (1761–1829). Before the Cortes met, these three persuaded the Junta to streamline the assembly by transforming the traditional three-estate Cortes into a unicameral legislature. At the inaugural session, their formal declaration of popular sovereignty and division of power caught more traditional delegates by surprise.

The traditionalists at Cadiz, known as apostólicos, were henceforth outmaneuvered badly. Having come to Cadiz to deal with the war effort, they were unprepared for a full-scale liberal attack on Spain's political foundations. A small group, however, managed to emerge as articulate defenders of traditionalism and the fundamental laws: the president of the regency, Pedro Quevedo y Quintano (1736–1818), bishop of Orense; Pedro de Inguanzo (1764–1836), future primate of Spain; Jaime Creus (1760–1825); and Ramón Lázaro de Dou y Bassals (1742–1832).

As finally drawn up, the Constitution of 1812 was primarily a liberal document. Sovereignty rested with the people, whose sacrifices in the war gave them the right to be legislatively represented; the popularly elected Cortes (by males twenty-five years of age or over) would make the laws, which the king would execute through appointment of ministers of state, with both legislature and monarchy guided by a bill of rights. On colonial reform, however, this liberalism grew weak, managing only to extend Spanish citizenship to the colonies,* without granting relief from some of the more obvious problems. On matters of faith, the apostólicos managed to preserve Catholicism* as the state religion.

The second war legislature, the Cortes Ordinarias (Sept. 1813–May 1814), opened at Cadiz and closed at Madrid just as Fernando VII returned from captivity. This legislature, mainly concerned with safeguarding the Constitution of 1812 and forcing the king to ratify it, also began the process of disentailment.* Confiscation of religious property, begun during the Enlightenment,* was now broadened to include noble, crown, common, and unused lands. The bitter debate caused sixty-nine apostólico delegates to write a long critique, the "Manifesto of the Persians" (referring to an apocryphal Middle Eastern custom of allowing anarchy to precede a new reign in order to destroy unpopular laws) that urged renovation of the old order in preference to a continued constitutional regime and its disentailment. Led by Bernardo Mozo de Rosales (1772?—1854?), the future marqués de Mataflorida, the apostólico "Persians" thus influenced Fernando to abolish the constitution and all the innovations of Cadiz in May 1814.

The Cortes of Cadiz and the Constitution of 1812, however, became the icons of nineteenth-century liberalism in Spain. The constitution was revived in 1820, 1837, 1854, and 1869, while the Cortes took on mythic proportions to later generations of liberals.

For additional information, see M. I. Arriazu et al., *Estudios sobre Cortes de Cádiz* (Pamplona, 1967); *Diario de sesiones de las Cortes Generales y Extraordinarias. Dieron principio el 24 de septiembre de 1810, y terminaron el 20 de septiembre de 1813*, 9 vols. (Madrid, 1870); M. Morán Orti, *Poder y gobierno en las Cortes de Cádiz (1810–1813)* (Pamplona, 1986); and F. Suárez, *Las Cortes de Cádiz* (Madrid, 1982).

*A. Wilhelmsen*

*Related entries*: DISENTAILMENT; LIBERALISM; INDEPENDENCE, WAR OF.

**COSTA, JOAQUÍN** (1846–1911), nineteenth-century reformer whose criticism of politics anticipated the Generation of 1898.* Costa was born in Huesca, Aragon,* on 14 Sept. 1846 to a poor family with eleven sons. While studying to be a teacher in Huesca, he wrote his first book, which earned him a scholarship to study law and philosophy in Madrid* in 1869–1873. He worked for the ministry of the treasury from 1873 to 1878, including some time spent in Jaén, and then began practicing law in Madrid and editing publications for the Institución Libre de Enseñanza.*

He soon became an active legal scholar. *Derecho consuetudinario y economía popular de España* (1879) provided a populist defense of customary institutions. Many aspects of traditional life protected cooperative economic practices, which allowed Spaniards to live at peace with one another. Furthermore, as he later argued in *Teoría del hecho jurídico individual y social* (1887), few had the ability to adapt to the unrelenting pressure of the marketplace, and in any case, liberalism* had destroyed the intermediate institutions that protected against great power. Costa became very critical of the centralism and corruption evident in the regimes of Antonio Cánovas del Castillo* and Práxedes Mateo Sagasta.*

Costa was also seriously concerned about the Spanish agricultural crisis. In *Colectivismo agrario en España* (1898), he proposed the creation of model farms and producers' cooperatives to stimulate agricultural productivity. He bitterly attacked the neglect of rural society, which he linked to the machinations of local political elites who depended upon illiteracy and extreme need to maintain control of the countryside. To fight them, he founded the Lliga Nacional de Productores, a hybrid politico-economic party that elected a few members from northern Aragon. It held a series of conferences to investigate and publicize reform possibilities. Publication of *Reconstrucción y europeización de España* and *Caciquismo y oligarchismo como la forma actual de gobierno de España* followed in 1900 and 1903.

Neither study managed to save Costa's party, and he became more strident. He demanded an "iron surgeon" to take control of Spanish modernization and to "Europeanize" Spain. *Crisis política de España* (1900) later became a bible for corporatists such as Gen. Miguel Primo de Rivera* and his son, José Antonio,* each intent upon authoritarian modernization. In *Política hidráulica* (1911), Costa chose irrigation as the focal point of modernization, and many of the projects undertaken in the 1920s had their origin in his work.

Costa's chief importance was as a unique publicist who linked dissenting sectors of rural society with the Madrid intelligentsia. His thought suffered from millenarianism and impatience with the political process, but some of his works on customary social and economic life provided an outstanding history of Spanish local life. The legal historian and activist reformer died on 8 Feb. 1911, bequeathing a legacy of radical populism, defense of traditional society, and corporatism.

For additional information, see M. Gambón Plana, *Biografía y bibliografía de D. Joaquín Costa* (Huesca, 1911); R. W. Kern, *Liberals, Reformers and Caciques in Restoration Spain* (Albuquerque, 1973); C. Martín Retortillo, *Joaquín Costa, propulso de la reconstrucción nacional* (Barcelona, 1981); and E. Tierno Galván, *Costa y el regeneracionalismo* (Barcelona, 1961).

R. W. Kern

*Related entry*: LIBERALISM.

# D

**DALÍ, SALVADOR** (1904–1989), surrealist painter. Dalí, born in Figueras, Catalonia,* on 11 May 1904, was the son of a lawyer. Precociously talented, he was also undisciplined and flamboyant, and although he did well at the National School of Fine Arts in Madrid,* he was expelled in 1924 for revolutionary activity and later served a short jail term in Catalonia for antigovernment activity.

In 1928, Dalí began an extended stay in Paris, where he was soon an important member of the surrealist movement. He and Luis Buñuel (1900–1983) produced two surrealist films, *Un chien Andalou* (1929) and *L'âge d'or* (1931), that gained avant-garde popularity. At the same time, Dalí's paintings, based on the symbolism of dreams, such as the "soft watches" in his famous work *The Persistence of Memory* (1931), assured Dalí a place in the art world. Through his bizarre antics and genius for self-publicity, he became as well known as Pablo Picasso* and Joan Miró,* the other two Spanish painters of note in this period.

The 1930s saw Dalí remain in Paris during the Second Republic* and the Spanish Civil War,* though he professed to be an ardent republican. His *Soft Construction with Boiled Beans—Premonition of Civil War,* was said to epitomize the savagery of the war. In the 1940s, he took up residence in the United States,* where he became as much a media star as an artist. His output of paintings was still impressive, but their subject matter became more religious, although his illustrations based on the New Testament were criticized as being bland and saccharine.

In later life, Dalí returned to Catalonia, but his business affairs were badly handled and many of his prints were sold without his knowledge. In 1982, the death of his wife, Elena Diaranoff, left him alone and vulnerable until his own death on 23 Jan. 1989.

For additional information, see R. Descharnes, *Salvador Dalí: The Work, the Man* (New York, 1984); and M. Secrest, *Salvador Dalí* (New York, 1986).

*R. W. Kern*

*Related entries:* MIRÓ, JOAN; PICASSO, PABLO.

**DATO IRADIER, EDUARDO** (1856–1921), political leader and lawyer. Dato was born in La Corunna to a family of military background native to Murcia. He received his licentiate in law in Madrid in 1875 and quickly acquired well-deserved prestige as a lawyer among Madrid's high society. Elected as a deputy to the last Cortes of the reign of Alfonso XII* in 1884, he represented Leon's Murias de Paredes district for the Conservative party.

After a brief distancing from Antonio Cánovas del Castillo,* Dato was again elected deputy in 1891 and served as the subsecretary of government in the Conservative party government during the turno pacífico. He also arranged for the reentry of Francisco Silvela* and Raimundo Fernández Villaverde (1848–1905) into the party, from which they had been estranged since 1892. When Cánovas's death produced the grave national crisis of 1898, the Conservative Union, which Silvela had established, acceded to power with a program of regeneration from above. Dato received the portfolio for government, developing unusual social legislation that posited resolute state interventionism in Spain's growing labor conflict, along the reformist lines of Leo XIII's (1878–1903) 1891 encyclical *De rerum novarum*. The personal reign of Alfonso XIII* already underway, Dato served as minister of justice in Silvela's second government and continued his reformist work. Upon Silvela's retirement and the assumption of party leadership by Antonio Maura,* Dato loyally supported this political solution, despite the fact that Maura had deserted the Liberal party and that the conservatives considered Dato Silvela's heir.

He presided over the Cortes from 1907 to 1909 during Maura's long cabinet. During the crisis of Oct. 1909, the result of government repression in Barcelona following Tragic Week in July, Dato fully supported Maura, although disagreeing with the methods of Juan de la Cierva (1864–1936), the former minister of government. His alienation from Maura came later, when the latter identified with Cierva, object of the liberal Left's condemnation.

Contrary to the attitude of Maura, who opposed alternating power with the liberals who had broken the Pact of El Pardo, Dato assumed formation of a conservative government in 1913. During his rule from 1913 to 1915, the party remained definitively divided between "competent conservatives" and Maurists. When World War I* began, he maintained Spain's strict neutrality, saving his country from the catastrophe of war, which indirectly stimulated its economic development. Only in 1917 did Dato return to power. This was in response to a serious cycle of disturbances produced in the small colonial enclave of Morocco*; and by the Juntas Militares de Defensa, an expression of military corporatism reacting against the lack of care in granting promotions and compensation for battlefield service. Once in power, Dato reined in the revolutionary outbreak of July and Aug., including political subversion in Barcelona's "assemblies of parliamentarians" and the revolutionary strike called by the Unión General de Trabajadores* (UGT) and the Confederación Nacional de Trabajo (CNT). Although triumphant in the crisis, Dato did not enjoy a parliamentary majority, and the king, under pressure from the Juntas Militares, refused him a decree of dissolution for the Cortes, which was seen as the object of scorn and the president's manipulation. Dato therefore had to leave power, although he returned in 1918 as a member of Maura's National Government to serve as minister of state. He overcame the problems created by submarine warfare that had clouded relations with Germany.*

In the midst of the postwar crisis, he formed his last government in 1920, advocating a program of pacification and social progress, including conciliation with the CNT and the creation of a ministry of labor. With the radicalization of the social crisis in Catalonia, he supported the repressive policy of Severino Martínez Anido (1862–1939) in the civil government of Barcelona against the CNT. The response of the anarchist organization was to assassinate Dato in Madrid* on 8 Mar. 1921.

It has been said that Dato, open to a "modern" understanding of social questions, usually acted so conservatively that whatever "audacity" he had in political matters was negated. He did, however, renovate the programs of the Restoration, just as José Canalejas (1854–1912) had done earlier: both met identical deaths at the hands of revolutionary extremists.

For additional information, see M. García Venero, *Eduardo Dato: Vida y sacrificio de un gobernante conservador* (Vitoria, 1969); and C. Seco Serrano, *Pérfil político y humano de un estadista de la Restauración: Eduardo Dato a través de su archivo* (Madrid, 1978).

C. Seco Serrano

*Related entries:* ALFONSO XIII; SILVELA, FRANCISCO; WORLD WAR I.

**DISENTAILMENT.** The term and its Spanish translation of desamortización refer to the freeing of property from legal restrictions on its sale or transfer. As the term was used in nineteenth-century Spain, it applied to a process whereby the royal government and on occasion municipal councils effected the transfer of entailed property to nonentailed private ownership and appropriated the net sums received from the purchasers for their own use. The most common forms of property (land and buildings) in entail, or vinculación, were of ecclesiastical institutions; of private families that had been set up as mayorazgos, or vínculos; municipal properties; common lands; and waste lands (baldíos, under the control of the crown).

There are earlier examples of the disentail of such lands. In the sixteenth century, Carlos I (1500–1558) and Felipe II (1527–1598) obtained papal approval for the sale of ecclesiastical lands and jurisdictions, and Felipe II sold title to baldío lands to private individuals and to towns, but halted the practice in the

face of strong protests from towns that used baldíos for pastures. Felipe V*
resumed the practice in 1737, but protests again led to its being stopped ten
years later by Fernando VI (1713–1759). In 1768, Carlos III* ordered the sale
at auction of those properties of the recently expelled Jesuits that were not
transferred to other religious or educational bodies. Sales began in 1769 and
continued until 1808.

Precedents thus existed for the modern process of desamortización. This began
with decrees of Carlos IV* of 19 Sept. 1798. One ordered the alienation through
public auction of the real property of charitable institutions such as hospitals,
foundling homes, and the like; of certain kinds of clerical benefices; and of
religious endowments known familiarly as obras pías that were dedicated to the
support of confraternities, memorial masses, and similar activities. Another decree of the same day gave owners of mayorazgos and other lay vínculos permission to sell their real properties, but did not require them to do so. In both
cases, the payments for the properties were to be deposited in a fund for the
amortization of the royal debt, and the former owner was to receive 3 percent
interest on the net amount after liens had been paid off. In 1805 and 1806,
Carlos IV obtained from Pius VII (1792–1878) authorization to disentail the
properties that endowed capellanías colativas, benefices whose holders were
appointed by prelates of the church; and one-seventh of the properties of other
ecclesiastical institutions, including parishes, bishoprics, and monasteries.

About one-sixth of the property of the church was disentailed by 1808. The
appeal to private individuals to dispose of entailed property for the good of
the country was less successful. The immediate motive behind the decrees was
the need to bolster the credit of royal bonds called vales reales, which were
heavily depreciated as a result of the war with Britain.* A second, long-range
motive was agrarian reform. Royal advisors, of whom Gaspar Melchor de Jovellanos* was the best known, argued that transferring property in entail into the
hands of private owners would lead to better agricultural practices as well as
happier and more patriotic subjects. The same motives lay behind later disen-
tailments.

While certain clergymen protested Carlos IV's disentailment, the policy did
not become a political issue until Joseph Bonaparte (1768–1844) became king
of Spain as José I* in July 1808. He continued disentailment and extended it to
all property of the religious and military orders, both of whom he ordered
suppressed (18 Aug. 1809), and that of Spanish grandees who joined the rising
against him. To gain support against José, the Supreme Central Junta that headed
the government loyal to Fernando VII* suspended the disentailment of ecclesiastical properties on 16 Nov. 1808. The partisans of Fernando became divided
over disentailment, however, when the Cortes of Cadiz* approved the sale of
properties of the military orders and of those monasteries and convents that the
war would leave permanently closed (13 Sept. 1813), a measure denounced by
defenders of the church. Ecclesiastical disentail remained a divisive political
issue for decades.

In addition, the Cortes of Cadiz initiated the policy at the national level of disentailing public properties: those of the crown not used as royal residences (22 Mar. 1811) and municipal properties (propios) and baldíos not used for common pastures (4 Jan. 1813), half the baldíos and propios to be sold to apply to the public debt and half to be distributed to soldiers and other persons who contributed to the war effort.

After his restoration, Fernando VII halted disentailment and annulled the sales effected during the war, but many buyers of muncipal lands were able to keep them. The next decades saw rapid alterations in the policy. On 5 Aug. 1818, Fernando VII ordered the sale of baldíos to pay the royal debt. The brief liberal regime established by the Revolution of 1820 revived the legislation of Cadiz and added the sale of the Inquisition's properties (9 Aug. 1820). Upon the overthrow of the regime in 1823, Fernando canceled the sales that it had made, but purchasers succeeded in recovering their acquisitions after his death.

Ecclesiastical desamortización on a large scale was renewed during the First Carlist War (1833–1840). The government of Isabel II* decreed on 8 Mar. 1836 the appropriation for the crown of the properties of all religious orders, male and female, to be sold at auction with the proceeds applied to paying the national debt. (Most male orders were closed at this time and female orders a year later.) Sales began promptly. A law of 29 July 1837 provided for the future disposal of the properties of parishes and bishoprics except for buildings used for religious services, and a subsequent decree of 2 Sept. 1841 began their sale. The author of the laws of 1836 and 1837 was the prime minister, Juan Álvarez Mendizábal,* and credit for initiating the process of ecclesiastical disentail has traditionally but erroneously been awarded to him. His immediate objective was to raise money, but he also saw it as a means for agrarian reform.

By a law of 30 Aug. 1836, the government of Isabel II also abolished the entail of noble and other private estates. A similar law had been enacted on 11 Dec. 1820, but it had been annulled upon the fall of the liberals. Henceforth, all family properties could be divided among the heirs or sold if the owner desired.

Much ecclesiastical property, of both regular and secular owners, was sold in the progressive period (1837–1843). After the Moderate party captured the government, it restricted the sales on 9 Apr. 1845. In 1851, a concordat with the papacy recognized the sales of church properties that had taken place, and authorized the state to sell most of those still in its hands. In return, the state would provide an income for the clergy and maintain the expenses of the church.

The last and most decisive state of disentailment began after the Revolution of 1854. The law of 1 May 1855, named after Pascual Madoz (1806–1870), the progressive deputy who proposed it, again provided for the sale of ecclesiastical properties, in defiance of the concordat. The law was abrogated on 17 Oct. 1856, but an agreement with the pope on 4 Apr. 1860 gave the state title to the remaining ecclesiastical properties in its hands in return for royal bonds for their value at

3 percent interest. In effect, this revived the portion of the Madoz law regulating the disentailment of previous church properties, and it remained in force until 1964.

The Madoz law also provided for the sale of municipal properties, except those that were actually used by villagers in common. The municipalities would receive 3 percent interest on 80 percent of the amount received from the sales. Madoz was guided by a philosophical belief in the need to eliminate legal restrictions on the transfer and use of real property. This section of the law, abrogated along with the rest of the law in 1856, was reinstated on 11 Oct. 1858. Under the Madoz law, disentail of municipal properties continued until the twentieth century. Great amounts of previously common and municipal property went to private hands.

It is not possible at present to say how much property changed hands through disentailment, and it probably never will be, but one can estimate an approximate figure. The property survey of the crown of Castile made under Fernando VI (1713–1759) shows that the church owned land that produced about 20 percent of the total income from farming and pasturage. The ecclesiastical properties were almost all disentailed, and their total sale price was about two-thirds of the total price of all properties disposed of by desamortización in the nineteenth century. Thus, one can estimate that roughly 30 percent of all the land of Castile (measured by the value of its annual product at the time of sale, not its area or economic potential) changed hands as a result of the process of disentailment. At present, one can only guess that a similar proportion of the land in the rest of Spain was also involved. Desamortización applied to buildings, and it affected the course of urban development.

Regional studies indicate that the buyers of disentailed properties can be divided into three types. At the top were buyers who operated on a wide scale, buying properties scattered through various provinces. As a rule, they acquired large properties that they planned to exploit for commercial agriculture or to hold for speculation. Mostly they resided in the larger cities, especially Madrid.* Below them were buyers located in provincial capitals or larger towns, land-owners, merchants, and professional people who bought within the limits of their regional economy, with the intention of exploiting the land commercially or leasing it to tenants. Finally, there were small farmers and other villagers who acquired numerous arable plots, irrigated gardens, enclosed fields, and the like, near enough for them to exploit with their own labor. The share of this last group was not insignificant. This pattern appears to have applied also to houses and other buildings the church owned.

One interpretation of desamortización is that it was part of the bourgeois revolution in Spain, permitting the urban bourgeoisie, long deprived of access to the land, to take it over and introduce its capitalist exploitation. This argument probably misrepresents these developments. The beneficiaries of desamortización were largely people who drew their incomes from the state and church (royal servants, officers of the armed forces, and beneficed clergy) and from land (from those who tilled it for their livelihood up to large landowners and including those involved indirectly in the agricultural economy, such as merchants and local craftsmen). As the nineteenth century progressed, persons involved in developing railroads, urban expansion, and industry appear to have invested in disentailed properties (including those in urban areas). If they were a new social class, they did not replace the old one, but joined it.

There are also differences of opinion on the social and economic effects of desamortización. Critics, notably Álvaro Flórez Estrada (1769–1853) at the time and Joaquín Costa* later, denounced the authors of desamortización for not creating a prosperous peasantry by distributing the land outright or in long-term leases among the lower agricultural class. After 1855, poorer peasants, especially agricultural laborers, probably lost some use of common pastures, but the hardships of the propertyless rural class increased more because of demographic expansion than desamortización.

Another interpretation is that desamortización absorbed capital that would have been more productively invested in industry. A large share of the payments of wealthy buyers were made in depreciated government notes, however, which were of little value for industrialization. Desamortización hastened the commercialization of Spanish agriculture, turning it from pasturage to arable lands. This produced a major change in rural Spain, inevitably accompanied by hardships for some and benefits for others, but in the long run probably contributed to the eventual economic growth and social improvement of Spain.

For further information, see R. Herr, *Rural Change and Royal Finances in Spain at the End of the Old Regime* (Berkeley, 1988); Spain, Ministerio de Agricultura, Pesca y Alimentación and Instituto de Estudios Fiscales, *Desamortización y hacienda pública*, 2 vols. (Madrid, 1986); and F. Tomás y Valiente, *El marco político de la desamortización en España* (Barcelona, 1971).

*R. Herr*

*Related entries:* CACIQUES; ECONOMY; LIBERALISM.


**DONOSO CORTÉS Y FERNÁNDEZ CANEDO, JUAN** (1809–1853), marqués de Valdegamas, Catholic apologist, essayist, legislator, and diplomat. Juan Donoso Cortés was born at Valle de la Serena in May 1809 and died in Paris forty-four years later. His early years gave no hint that he would ultimately emerge as nineteenth-century Spain's most outspoken Catholic apologist. At the age of twelve, he entered the University of Salamanca, Castile's most prestigious educational institution, to study law. There he became the protégé of the noted liberal Manuel José Quintana (1772–1857). Under the influence of this scholar-statesman, Donoso became an advocate of liberalism.* Pursuing interests in literature, philosophy, and history, he soon became a devotee of the French philosophes.

Donoso accepted the new chair of literature at the College of Cáceres as a nineteen-year-old professor in 1828. Four years later, he entered public life when, as a result of his written defense of the right of succession for Fernando VII's daughter, the future Isabel II,* rather than the pretender, don Carlos, the king named Donoso to a position in the ministry of justice. Active in the moderate liberal party of Spanish politics, he became director of the periodicals *El Porvenir* in 1837 and *El Piloto* in 1839 and was elected to the Cortes as a deputy.

Donoso maintained both a strong loyalty to Princess Isabel and María Cristina de Habsburgo (1806–1878), the queen-regent, and a vigorous hatred of the progressive form of liberalism that had emerged in Spanish politics after the mid–1830s. As a result, he followed the royal family into exile in Paris when Gen. Baldomero Espartero,* the progressive regent, came to power in 1840. Donoso spent his three years in France studying the works of and meeting with the nation's leading Catholic thinkers, liberal and conservative: Charles Montalembert (1810–1870), Jean Lacordaire (1802–1861), and even Joseph de Maistre (1753–1821).

With the fall of the progressive Espartero regime in 1843 and the subsequent emergence of more moderate ministries soon thereafter, Donoso and the royal family returned to Spain. Possibly still professing moderate liberalism even after Princess Isabel was proclaimed queen in 1843, he was nonetheless then at least leaning toward conservatism. Among the traumatic events that finally brought him firmly into the conservative camp were his disgust with the anticlerical ethos of Spain's Constitution of 1837, the death of his brother, and the upheaval of European society that the revolutions of 1848 caused. By his death in 1853, Donoso had rejected liberalism in any form and had become a staunch apologist for a society founded upon Roman Catholic precepts.

Among his many published works, Donoso's *Ensayo sobre el catolicismo, el liberalismo y el socialismo* (1851) is his most famous. In that study, he clearly places religion, which to him meant Catholicism, at the center of all human activity.

Donoso was generally ignored during his lifetime. Rejecting the Carlists as obscurantists and supporters of an illegitimate Catholic pretender, he had earned the reputation of being an ultraconservative Catholic clericalist by the time of his death. As has been recently pointed out, to see him in this light would be inaccurate. Donoso is much more meaningful to the contemporary world when viewed instead as a pessimistic prophet of apocalyptic doom for human society, if and when the primacy of religion (Catholicism) and the virtue of order are lost.

For additional information, see J. T. Graham, *Donoso Cortés: Utopian Romanticist and Political Realist* (Columbia, 1974); and J. Donoso Cortés, *Ensayo sobre el catolicismo, el liberalism y el socialismo* (Madrid, 1978).

P. Foley

*Related entries:* CATHOLICISM; LIBERALISM.

# E

## ECONOMY

### EIGHTEENTH CENTURY

The early Bourbon period in Spain, confronted by a rising population and unstable prices common in Europe during the eighteenth century, fell into a steep decline caused by agricultural problems such as the soil exhaustion created by sheep grazing; economic ruin from overtaxation to support foreign wars; and a significant loss of population. Two fundamental social and economic trends, however, countered this slump: a steadily increasing population and an upward trend in prices.

In 1650, population was estimated at 4.5 million; in 1747, 7.4 million; in 1768, when a formal census was taken, 9.3 million; and by the end of the century, almost 11 million. The trend in prices was less steady; the colonial wars that had plagued Spain the previous century persisted into the next, and the wars of Louis XIV (1638–1715) created a sharp rise in prices that did not stabilize until the middle of the second decade of the eighteenth century, when prices began to fall and remained relatively stable until the revival of warfare at mid-century. During the 1750s, prices rose steadily until, by 1790, they were thirty-five times higher than forty years earlier.

A major cause of inflation was an increased colonial production of precious metals after 1750, particularly from Mexican silver mines. Another element was an increased demand for agricultural products to feed a growing population. The censuses of 1768 and 1787 indicate an annual growth rate of 8.3 per thousand, nearly corresponding with the annual 6.8 percent growth rate for continental Europe. The relationship between population growth and rising prices in Spain was the result of Bourbon reforms that linked Spain with the economic development of Western Europe. In contrast with Hapsburg exclusivism, the Bourbons participated in the development of European markets. The inflationary trend of the eighteenth century contrasted sharply with the disastrous fluctuations of prices during the previous century.

Intellectual thought supported these changes. Francisco Cabarrús (1752–1810), financial advisor to Carlos III,* promoted the ideas of Adam Smith (1723–1790), as did, later, Antonio Alcalá Galiano (1789–1865). Mercantilist belief that Spanish economic growth was incompatible with that of other European nations, or that national wealth lay primarily in the soil, were denounced in favor of accumulation of capital by individuals; the rights of property; reduction of tariffs and internal trade barriers; and laissez-faire policies for the development of industry. Others argued that the population growth rate was related to the ability of laborers to earn a living. Class distinctions were a necessary component of socioeconomic development; the lower classes were paid from the wealth of the upper classes, as were the clergy, military, and public servants. Society was divided into two groups: the productive classes which controlled the wealth of the nation, and the unproductive classes which performed the labor. Another commentator, Valentín de Foronda (pseud. for Juan Fabbroni [1752–1822]), an Italian living in Spain, supported the premise that a strong policy on imports should balance the export trade in Europe, because buying and selling strengthened the international economy. He supported free trade and the opening of Spanish ports in the Americas to other European nations, arguing that the old policies were detrimental because they promoted an export trade that worked against a healthy European market.

In eighteenth-century agriculture, although some early changes were made in the general nature of land tenure, the most important reforms came in the 1760s. Five important types of land ownership became a new focus of attention: the royal domain (patrimonio real); church lands (señorío eclesiástico); city, town, and village lands (tierras comunes or tierras concejiles); privately owned lands held in entail (mayorazgos); and privately owned lands not in entail (señoríos legos). The least important were those of the patrimonio real, which often consisted of barren lands or mountains. The most important were the señorío eclesiástico, consisting of city, town, and village properties as well as vacant land throughout Spain and the empire. Church lands were tax exempt, and under royal and canon law, they were held in mortmain (de manos muertas), meaning that they could never be alienated from church ownership. The most extensive landholding pattern was the tierras comunes, consisting of woodlands and wastelands (montes y baldíos) and lands immediately surrounding municipalities, used for pasturage, fuel, and agriculture.

Rivaling the extent of the tierras comunes were the mayorazgos. Under the law of primogeniture, noblemen and even commoners were permitted to create a mayorazgo by bequeathing their property to their eldest sons, thereby disinheriting all other possible heirs in order to perpetuate their family names and protect their lands from being divided into small portions. Under the mayorazgo, future acquisitions of land by marriage or purchase were inalienably joined to it, increasing the economic power of its owner. Critics of mayorazgo argued that this practice put much of the land out of circulation for the majority of Spaniards, and created an idle, overprivileged nobility.

Distinct from the mayorazgos were the señoríos legos, the lands and privileges granted to the aristocracy by the crown. Under such titles, the lord had the right to name judges and local officials to administer his land. In Castile,* Estremadura, western Andalusia,* and Valencia,* more than half the towns owed allegiance to such lords.

By the eighteenth century, monopolistic patterns of land tenure had been established. The few landholders controlled the economy at the expense of a large, poor peasantry that worked the land. In 1760, Carlos III decreed that certain lands in private ownership (tierras de propios) be auctioned regularly. Six years later, another decree provided that taxpayers elect two representatives to each city council to serve as a check on the oligarchical political system. After the riots of 1766, caused by a famine, due to high prices that created shortages, the crown became aware of the need for land reform and the importance of encouraging wheat growing, so that the shortages and high prices could be avoided. In 1767, Carlos opened some lands of the patrimonio real for settlement between Madrid, Seville, and Cadiz, and in the Sierra Morena between Cordoba and Seville. Settlers rented land, houses, tools, and livestock from the crown, in return for a part of their agricultural produce.

In an effort to bring more farm land under control of productive landowners, Carlos III appointed Pedro Rodríguez, conde de Campomanes,* a royal councilor, as president of the Mesta, the royal sheep owners' corporation (first established in 1273). Campomanes used his authority to weaken the institution in 1779 by convincing the Mesta's judges to recognize local interests over those of the sheep owners. The age-old privilege of posesión, by which sheep herds had certain rights of way along the trail known as the transhumancia (stretching from the plateaus of Estremadura to the Pyrenees), was abolished in 1786. Two years later, landowners were given the right to enclose their lands and plant crops of their choosing. Curtailment of privileges held by the Mesta freed land for agricultural use.

Such changes were necessary to meet the demands of the eighteenth-century agricultural crises. The breakup of entailment and monopolistic landholding patterns were at the heart of Bourbon economic policies. To better influence local politics, the crown also established the intendant system in 1718 to direct change. Town council elections for representatives of the underprivileged classes were begun later. The crown, which could not afford to buy back privileges, superimposed a new superstructure over the old to create change. The least affected was the church, an issue that was left to the nineteenth century.

Industrialization became another priority. Colonial commerce and domestic manufacture were linked to the revitalization of industry. In 1730, the crown established the Junta de Comercio y Moneda to make economic policy for mining, manufacturing, and minting. One of the most important changes in commercial policy was the abolition of trade monopolies for Seville, Cadiz, and Castile, to open trade between the Americas and the other Spanish provinces. Creation of American commercial companies, modeled after royal trading companies in Europe, led to the emergence of the Real Compañía Guipuzcoana de Caracas (1728–1784), which established a monopoly for shippers from San Sebastian to Venezuela, whose neglected commerce had fallen into the hands of Dutch smugglers. As a result of the Guipúzcoa monopoly, prices on goods brought to Spain by Dutch merchants fell. The Catalan Company (1765) got trade rights with Puerto Rico, Santo Domingo, Margarita, and Honduras. The Compañía de Filipinas was formed from the defunct board of the Caracas Company. The Reglamento of 1778 eventually worked against monopolistic companies by permitting free trade between Spanish ports and all parts of the Americas except Mexico, Venezuela, and the Philippines. The free-trade policy allowed the Mediterranean ports of Barcelona, Alicante, Cartagena, Malaga, and the northern ports of La Corunna, Gijón, and Santander to trade with the colonies.

Royal policies toward manufacturing had a similar revolution. In 1718, the crown moved to create a number of government-supported factories. Each factory was expected to produce luxury goods that had previously been imported. The first to do so, established at Guadalajara in 1718, competed with Dutch woolens and was successful enough to build branches in Brihuega and Segovia. Other factories sprang up in the next few decades. Madrid became known for its tapestries, San Ildefonso for its mirrors and fine glass, Talavera de la Reina for its silks and ceramics, and Italian artisans produced porcelains at a factory near the Buen Retiro. Royal factories were spread throughout Spain and produced such varied products as guns, swords, paper, stockings, textiles, and glassware. The system succeeded by reducing imports, while attacking the problem of unemployment and stimulating guild membership.

The guilds, in fact, multiplied so rapidly that they covered every trade imaginable. Many trades and industrial activities were monopolized by government-chartered groups and eventually became closed shops ruled by master craftsmen, who exploited their apprentices and unskilled workers. So exclusive had the trades become by the 1780s that the crown broke up the old monopolies by granting new factories in the same fields to compete against them.

Bourbon policies to protect manufacturing from foreign competition with tariffs and restrictions, and to allow it to take advantage of low American raw material prices through free trade, did create an industrial base, but one that had not been tested, when the French Revolution sent shock waves throughout Europe that ultimately allowed the colonies to rebel. Since the format of mercantile companies had been based on a hoped-for revival of colonial trade, the Bourbon plan failed when the French Revolution curtailed transatlantic commerce, although the manufacturing capacity of Spain itself provided the foundation for nineteenth-century expansion.

For additional information, see J. Vicens Vives, *An Economic History of Spain* (Princeton, 1969).

*J. P. Sánchez*

*Related entries:* CARLOS III; COLONIES.

## NINETEENTH AND TWENTIETH CENTURIES

Between 1815 and 1985, the Spanish economy experienced one of the most profound transformations in its history. At the beginning of the nineteenth century, agriculture, the largest sector of the economy, was still rooted in the past. Harvest produce was destined in great part for internal consumption; what remained was usually sold only within the region. Yields depended entirely upon the weather, and the volume sold was dependent upon the fluctuating buying power of Spanish consumers. Manufacturing, too, served largely local markets and fluctuated spasmodically according to erratic demand. In the contemporary era, while agriculture is no longer the largest sector of the economy, both production and consumption of foodstuffs have access to internal and external markets. Industry and services, which constitute the most active sector of an urbanized, capitalist economy, make today's Spain an industrial power, if of the second rank.

This tranformation came against a background of colonial loss. In an economy once controlled by American revenues, the colonial emancipation after the War of Independence* and the loss of Cuba, Puerto Rico, and the Philippines after the Spanish-American War* of 1898 forced the Spanish economy to evolve toward internal self-sufficiency, a readjustment to a national scale. Once this was accomplished, the Spanish national economy slowly matured, and in recent decades became more open and sophisticated, oriented toward and influenced by European economic life, which ultimately made it possible for Spain to join the European Community in 1985.

This transformation, passing through a series of stages, had nowhere to go but up after the Napoleonic Wars, whose destructiveness of men, resources, and the means of production was so great that the postwar period could not bring recovery. Instead, a long, sharp recession saw production, trade, and economic values decline and a capital flight occur. Use of strong protectionism tried to rein in the deterioration of the balance of trade, but the agitated political climate and large public expenditures in the struggle between absolutists and liberals discouraged production and prolonged the depression just as north European countries were accelerating their industrial revolution.

After 1840, the Spanish economy resumed its expansion. The demands of the treasury dictated a vast program of disentailment* of land, a good part of which was in the hands of the church or municipalities. The wealth of the church was sold at auction for the benefit of the state in exchange for its financial support of the church. Towns, in turn, were forced to sell their common lands and invest the profits in public bonds or other debt. In four decades, from approximately 1835 to 1875, a good part of the land changed hands, in greater or lesser proportion according to region.

Agriculture thus absorbed large amounts of capital, which reduced capital available for other types of investments, although protectionist tariffs did make agricultural exploitation highly profitable, even for lands of low productivity,

and a growing population assured sustained demand. Cultivation of lands producing cereal expanded at the expense of many sheep-raising areas. The Mediterranean coast specialized in raising produce for export, such as fruit, wine,
and olives. Old and new owners strengthened their position in the countryside,
while Spain consolidated its agricultural orientation.

Meanwhile, Catalonia* was converted into the country's first textile center.
Its factories spun and wove cotton with steam-powered machines, and its products
successfully displaced from the internal market imported fabrics and artisan
manufacture of hemp, linen, silk, and wool, thus accentuating the rural tone of
the former artisan centers. Catalan fabrics, however, did not conquer foreign
markets rapidly, except in the Spanish colonies of the Caribbean, thanks to
protectionism. The relative prosperity of the textile industry, however, did allow
Catalonia to attract auxiliary industries, such as machinery and chemicals; and
Barcelona's busy port also attracted other industries that depended on the import
of raw materials, such as flour and wool mills.

The Progressive party* government of 1855 took the next step of stimulating
the entry of foreign capital in hopes of accelerating development even further,
principally in railroads, banking, and mining. Powerful French financial groups,
with British capital playing a secondary role, competed to obtain rail concessions,
built the most important lines and, by acquisitions, formed networks. The railroads mobilized Spanish capital, public and private, to facilitate interior communication and trade, contributing to the formation of a national market and
regional specialization; but they did not encourage industry, since rails and rolling
stock were initially imported.

The French also founded great credit societies to support their investments.
Their example awakened in many local capitalists the desire to establish similar
businesses. The country was populated with a web of banks and societies, which
the crisis of 1866 took charge of trimming. The Banco de España emerged from
this test as the principal financial institution, with a monopoly on the issuance
of money.

In mining, the British prevailed. They brought new capital and technologies
to the lead mines, and after 1866, they constructed Río Tinto, the great mining
and chemical complex. Even greater success came later with their development
of the iron mines of Biscay. British steel depended for decades on this high-
quality ore. The minerals and their derivatives constituted at the end of the
nineteenth century the country's second largest export sector, behind agriculture.

Coal imported from Britain and local ore caused the construction of furnaces
around Bilbao. They were the property of Basque entrepreneurs capitalized by
the export of the minerals from their own rural areas. Throughout the area, other
industries soon developed. Iron and steel created the second great industrial
nucleus of northern Spain. In contrast to Catalonia, dizzily producing consumer
goods, Biscay specialized in heavy industry and its derivative industries, such
as shipbuilding and railroads.

The attempt of other regions to industrialize either failed or stagnated, as occurred in Asturias,* despite the fact that it had abundant coal. An industrialization so polarized between two places did nothing but accentuate contrasts. In the face of a Spain eager to modernize itself, the traditional survived, and the agricultural crisis at the end of the nineteenth century made the situation more serious. Populations expelled from rural areas left for Latin America or, on a lesser scale, for North Africa. Thanks to remittances from emigrants, the balance of payments was positive for many years, and the country was able to recapitalize itself.

With the arrival of the twentieth century, the transformation was extended. New sources of energy (hydroelectric power and petroleum) favored the diversification and spread of industry, including food processing, cement, chemicals, paper, machinery, and electric engines. The growth was sustained and reached an exceptional apogee during World War I,* when Spain remained neutral and the belligerents flooded the country with orders for manufactured goods, food, and raw materials. The nation was enriched, although the bonanza did not last.

A very concentrated banking system, with a growing penetration throughout the country, channeled toward industry resources that in great part were stolen from the countryside. Agricultural production and profits began to increase through the introduction of new crops, such as the Valencian orange, for export, or beet sugar for local consumption. The export of minerals, however, began to lose importance. The establishment of strong trade barriers in favor of local products weakened foreign trade. Other signs of the era were the redemption of businesses and property titles in the hands of foreigners, and a progressive state intervention in economic life.

Economic interventionism and nationalism were accentuated in the 1920s, when the state promulgated a wealth of administrative regulations and favored the formation of cartels, and monopolies on oil, tobacco, and the telephone system. The dictatorship of Gen. Miguel Primo de Rivera* tended to organize the economy through the corporativist route and invest great sums in public works: highways and reservoirs for electricity and irrigation. The accumulation and concentration of wealth in a few hands posed the problem of its distribution. Those at the lower income levels, in an age of greater social mobility, naturally held constantly rising expectations. The Second Republic,* which succeeded Primo's dictatorship, showed itself to be more sensitive to their plight. In the few years that the republic lasted, the standard of living among the people improved, and agrarian reform was initiated. The worldwide crisis of 1930, nevertheless, stopped the correction of corporativist tendencies in the Spanish economy.

Social tensions led to the cruel and costly Spanish Civil War,* with broad repercussions worldwide. In the economic order, its salient features were the heavy loss of human life, through death or exile, of a significant part of the population; widespread destruction of buildings, factories, and the communication system; the dissipation of monetary reserves; and debt to acquire financing for the war. A novelty was the implementation in the republican zone of a socialized economy through peasant and industrial cooperatives.

In the rebel zone, corporativist tendencies themselves had full approval of fascist or Nazi allies. Autarky, the tight control of production, trade, money, and prices, and rationing of foodstuffs and goods were not temporary expediencies dictated by the needs of a war economy. They constituted instead part of a plan that remained in force after the war and was completed in the national reconstruction phase with a noticeable widening into the public sector to include railroads and the Instituto Nacional de Industria. Autarky meant a regression (almost a hiatus) for modernization in Spain. Production did not recover its 1929 levels until 1953. Drastically reduced salaries maintained a depressed standard of living. Meanwhile, the black market, product of the peculiar distortions of international isolation, benefited the most inefficient agricultural and industrial sectors at the same time that it encouraged corruption.

Autarky, which failed not only to reestablish the level of economic activity and consumption that Spaniards had previously enjoyed, but simultaneously distanced Spain from an economically recovering Europe, forced the gradual creation of a new economic policy at the end of the 1950s. Through a gradual liberalization of trade and production and an opening to other countries, Spain was able to benefit from the prosperous European 1960s to take full advantage of its idle capacity.

Spaniards emigrated en masse to Europe, and conversely, tourists invaded Spain. Emigrants and tourists provided the strong injection of capital needed by the country, and foreign investments and credits were also common devices. Energy, one of the weak points of the Spanish economy, remained cheap throughout this period. Industry expanded, and its products found easy placement in foreign markets. Industry and services contributed to the greatest growth in the gross national product. In that decade, Spain recorded the highest assessments in Europe. Agriculture, despite mechanization, better use of fertilizers, and intensification, fell behind. Full employment helped incomes to rise, and these helped to increase domestic demand. The Spanish economy had become modern.

The oil crisis of 1973 and the international economic downturn that followed stopped the expansion. The trade balance suffered from the rise in oil prices, but the cabinets of this period of transition from dictatorship to democracy did not dare introduce measures necessary, but unpopular, for adjustment. The European recession had repercussions on Spain as well: the industrial countries stopped demanding manual labor and returned some workers to their country of origin. Unemployment increased in Spain at the same time that salaries were finally free from the artificial restraints of autarky. Inflation and contracting economic activity were consequently higher than in the rest of Europe. From 1982 on, Spain has effected a difficult industrial recovery. Obsolete plants have been closed, and the state has been divesting itself of public enterprises running a deficit. Inflation has remained under control, and exports, more than consumption, have made the economy dynamic. The country again has the fastest-growing tax burden in Europe, reducing the distance that has traditionally existed between Spain and most advanced nations. Exports, strong foreign investment, and the growth of tourism have raised gold and currency reserves very high. This strong accumulation gives great strength to the peseta. Thus, Spain in 1985 entered the European Community and faced, with relative confidence, its imminent full integration.

For additional information, see J. Fontana and J. Nadal, "Spain, 1914–1970," and J. Nadal, "The Failure of the Industrial Revolution in Spain, 1830–1914," in *The Fontana Economic History of Europe*, ed. C. M. Cipolla, vols. 2 and 6 (London, 1973 and 1976); J. Harrison, *An Economic History of Modern Spain* (London, 1978); S. Lieberman, *The Contemporary Spanish Economy: A Historical Perspective* (London, 1982); J. Nadal, A. Carreras, and C. Sudria, eds., *La economía española en el siglo xx: Una perspectiva histórica* (Barcelona, 1987); N. Sánchez-Albornoz, ed., *The Economic Modernization of Spain, 1830–1930* (New York, 1987); and J. Vicens Vives, *An Economic History of Spain* (Princeton, 1969).

*N. Sánchez-Albornoz*

*Related entry:* DISENTAILMENT.

## EDUCATION

### PRIMARY AND SECONDARY

The Enlightenment,* through the work of Gaspar Melchor de Jovellanos,* introduced the idea that educational reform was necessary for general social improvement. In the 1780s, when Jovellanos began to write about education, primary schools were provided by town councils from revenues received from communal lands or by the church and religious orders on a fee basis for the well-to-do and as works of charity for those unable to pay. Jovellanos's extensive writings on education culminated in his plan for public education, presented in Nov. 1809, calling for free public schools run by the state, with science instruction given special emphasis. His influence caused the Cortes of Cadiz* to adopt Article 9 of the Constitution of 1812 to establish free primary instruction by the municipalities.

The commission report implementing these plans was presented in Mar. 1814. Suppressed by Fernando VII,* it was not adopted by the Cortes until June 1821, during the liberal Triennium (1820–1823). Suppressed again by Fernando's return in 1823, the Constitution of 1837 finally accepted it as law, but disentailment* loomed larger as an issue, and political instability kept liberalism* from giving education a high priority until the 1850s, when two new elements again raised it as an important national issue.

One was the Concordat of 1851, according the church a right to establish schools and have all instruction conform to religious teachings. Reaction against this step gave impetus to the ideas of Karl Christian Friedrich Krause,* which sought to free students from religious conventions in their pursuit of knowledge. The Ley Moyano (1857), a far-reaching law that made Spain one of the first states to prescribe compulsory primary education, inadvertently caused education to become a battleground for these differing approaches, although the confusion of the First Republic* and the conservatism of the Bourbon Restoration kept the issue from being fully joined until after the Spanish-American War.*

After 1898, with regard to educational reforms, the church redoubled its resistance to the Krausist notion—now also taken up by the Socialist party,* liberal anticlericals, and anarchists—of secular education, viewing with alarm the concurrent spread of anticlerical attitudes and calls for laic schools, especially as these were perceived in three notable examples of private schools: the Krausist Institución Libre de Enseñanza*; the Escuela Moderna of Francisco Ferrer* and its successors, the Escuelas Racionalistas; and the schools associated with the socialist Casa del Pueblo. Little was done, however, to revamp Catholic educational philosophy to match the demands of an urbanizing and industrializing Spain, although Father Andrés Manjo's (1846–1923) Escuelas del Ave-María, and Father Pedro Poveda (1874–1936), by providing schooling for gypsies in Andalusia,* did experiment with Catholic social action, with education at its center.

This philosophic polarization drastically slowed change. While a ministry of public instruction was established in 1900 to make teachers state employees as a means of increasing their salaries, funding levels for education remained inadequate. Teacher associations tried unsuccessfully to attract public support, arouse enthusiasm in the Cortes, or interest the ministry in their plight; in 1912, a small group even affiliated with a socialist trade union. Throughout the reign of Alfonso XIII,* however, the need for thirty thousand new primary schools and millions of pesetas for pay increases went unmet. Education remained in turmoil, with fifty-two ministers of public instruction holding office between 1900 and 1931.

The Second Republic* sought reform by appointing the socialist Rodolfo Llopis (1895– ) as director general of primary instruction from Apr. 1931 to Apr. 1933. More than any other person, he attempted to institute a laic educational system and improve educational conditions. Obligatory teaching of religion in the public schools ended in May 1931, and the budget request to the Cortes projected higher salaries and the building of twenty-seven thousand new schools in five years. The Cortes, with five teachers as deputies, responded positively only to the latter proposal; misiones pedagógicas sent university students into the countryside to establish new schools.

The chaos created by the pedagogic missions and failure to raise the salaries of teachers played some part in the loss of popularity of the Manuel Azaña* cabinet. By Nov. 1933, in any case, the Catholic opposition had rallied to defend religious instruction in the schools; and a plan to close all religious schools, presented for debate early in 1933, became a main issue in the parliamentary elections that defeated the government.

Educational reform, eclipsed by national politics between 1933 and 1936, revived during the Spanish Civil War.* The republicans viewed education as an instrument of social change; and successive left republican, communist, and anarchist ministers of public instruction supported the creation of Institutos Obreros as secondary schools open without cost to workers aged fifteen to thirty-five. Literacy programs through a cultural militia taught reading and writing to soldiers. Salaries were raised, and curriculum innovations for primary and secondary schools in the republican zone stressed secular, scientific, coeducational programs.

Nationalist views on education, emphatically in favor of returning education to ecclesiastical control, crystalized on 30 Jan. 1938, when Gen. Francisco Franco* appointed Pedro Sainz Rodríguez (1898– ), who had formerly served as a primary-school inspector and monarchist deputy in the Cortes, as minister of education. He issued a series of plans reorganizing education to affirm re-Catholicizing it by basing the new primary-school curriculum on religion, patriotism, and civic and physical education.

This philosophy of "national Catholicism" remained in place until Vatican II (1962–1965), when the church began to distance itself from the Francoist state and accept a diminished presence in the administration of public instruction. Sainz's philosophy, however, stayed in place until 1969, when a survey of educational needs provided the basis for a Ley General de Educación (Aug. 1970), the first comprehensive educational legislation since the Ley Moyano in 1857. In it, the state again became responsible for the administration of public instruction, with church schools subsidized by public revenues. The law sought to foster an educational system to prepare the individual for life and work in a world of rapid change, promote greater participation in political life, and seek a just society.

Socialists, while opposing support of religious education, recognized that only chaos would result if the subsidy was abolished. Religious conservatives, while complaining about secularization, did not have the support necessary to block change in a growing middle-class society that valued education. The law itself met mixed reactions when translated into primary-school curricula, since neither students nor teachers reoriented as rapidly as had been hoped, largely because of inadequate pay, poor teacher education, and failure to provide good textbooks. Up to 30 percent of primary-school children achieved low test scores, and so in 1981, a new curriculum was instituted, more rigorous in promotion policy. Religious education was made optional, and most children took nonsectarian courses in ethics. Acknowledging the emergence of a democratic Spain at the same time, all school children study pluralism, political tolerance, and democracy as the values needed to live together in the modern world.

For additional information, see V. García Hoz, *La educación en la España del siglo xx* (Madrid, 1980); J. M. McNair, *Education for a Changing Spain* (Manchester, 1984); Ministerio de Educación, *Historia de la educación en España* (Madrid, 1979); J. Ruiz Berrio, *Política escola de España en el siglo xix* (Madrid, 1970); and M. Samaniego Bonneu, *La política educativa de la segunda república* (Madrid, 1977).

*D. V. Holtby*

*Related* entries: JOVELLANOS, GASPER MELCHOR DE; KRAUSE.

## HIGHER EDUCATION

The early modern decline of Spain can be measured by the number of universities abandoned by 1700: Palencia, Tudela, Calatayud, Gerona, Lérida, Huesca, and Sigüenza. For those that remained—Salamanca, Valladolid, Barcelona,* Saragossa, Palma de Mallorca, Alcalá de Henares, Santiago de Compostela, and Seville—their provision of civil servants for the church and court broadened under the Bourbons and moved away from the models of Bologna for law and Paris for theology. Bourbon absolutism stressed the need for lawyers of the French variety, narrowly educated in the state's legal code.

Felipe V* initiated curricular renovation in 1717 with the introduction of colegios mayores for advanced students to study royal law. Medical studies were facilitated by additional funding provided during the reigns of Fernando VI (1713–1759) and Carlos III,* when clinical medicine and other practical methods of study were introduced. By the end of the eighteenth century, political theory, economics, and technical studies, already influenced by the Enlightenment, took on new meaning with the advent of the French Revolution.

The result was the emergence in the first half of the nineteenth century of a tentative outline of the modern university. The development of general studies or liberal arts was modest at first, until liberals in 1836 decreased the religious content of university studies. New legislation in 1842 strengthened government control over university studies and centralized educational finance. A new ministry of education increased educational centralization between 1845 and 1857 to further standardize higher education. Creation of the Universidad Central, by moving the university at Alcalá de Henares to Madrid, marked the zenith of higher education reform. The existence of a supposedly model institution in the nation's capital was complemented by expansion of other universities in Valencia,* Granada, and Oviedo. Even the best, unfortunately, remained out-of-date and ill-equipped. Old pedagogical techniques of memorizing the course manual and heavy use of teaching assistants continued, along with lack of laboratories or any practical approach to education.

The second half of the century became a time of trouble for many universities, as students and professors grew increasingly impatient. Student politics mirrored the revolutionary era until Antonio Cánovas del Castillo* curtailed freedom of speech and thought in 1875–1876, preparing the way for the Bourbon Restoration, which allowed corruption and state interference to continue. A challenge came from the Krausist movement, led by Francisco Giner de los Ríos,* who challenged orthodox educational pedagogy by seeking a more flexible, democratic educational format in the Institución Libre de Enseñanza, begun in 1875. While the Free Educational Institute failed as a university, its pedagogical innovations as an elite secondary day school increased pressure upon the state to overhaul higher education. Socialists began adult night-school courses in their Casas del Pueblo, and in Catalonia* the anarchist Francisco Ferrer* created popular schools from the primary level to classes for adult workers.

The state responded with reforms in 1907, creating the Junta para Ampliación de Estudios to build new research facilities; conduct advanced studies; send students abroad for specialized training; and supervise the quality of university studies. An ambitious building program resulted in a new campus for the university in Madrid, using Stanford University in California as a model. The dictatorship of Gen. Miguel Primo de Rivera* invested heavily in higher technical education until the universities turned against his regime in 1928.

Students continued to play an important role in the Second Republic. Misiones pedagógicas sent students into the countryside as teachers, often radicalizing them when they came in contact with rural poverty. The universities themselves were a debating ground for the "Republic of Professors," although ironically, most university professors were too busy with politics to alter conditions on their own campuses.

The Spanish Civil War divided the nation's universities: Barcelona, Madrid,* Murcia, and Valencia remained in the republican zone; while Granada, Oviedo, Salamanca, Santiago, Seville, Valladolid, and Saragossa came under nationalist control. Some suffered physical damage, none worse than in Madrid. Each zone adopted cultural models from their allies, complete with indoctrination and ideological purity. The philosopher Miguel de Unamuno,* rector of Salamanca, objected strenuously to these changes in a famous incident in Oct. 1936 and was soon removed. One noticeable change saw a slight increase in the number of women attending college. Of the nearly thirty thousand college students in 1935, only 9 percent had been female; but by 1940, this had increased to almost 15 percent.

In Apr. 1939, Gen. Francisco Franco placed universities under the joint responsibility of church and state. Religious education resumed its earlier importance, though the church did not have the funds to invest heavily in education. Student syndicates, run by the Falange,* which maintained an active presence on all campuses, exercised strong control over students and professors alike; and a new religious lay organization, the Opus Dei,* created an ambitious and ideologically conservative program for Catholic students at the University of Navarre.

After 1956, a new generation of students became a force in the anti-Franco opposition. Their protests led to cancellation of the school year in 1965, a commonplace event throughout the next decade. Despite efforts by the Opus Dei, beginning in 1962, to combat the spread of disaffection, a new university law had to be promulgated in 1970, offering autonomy from political control. This approach was strengthened after Franco's death in 1975; but as opportunities increased, new pressures developed for easier entrance into higher education, culminating in the student riots of Jan. and Feb. 1987. Years of neglect and isolation also have taken their toll, although with democracy the educational budget has risen drastically. Academic freedom, and with it scholarship, is now approaching West European levels.

For additional information, see C. Ajo y Saínz de Zúñiga, *Historia de las universidades hispánicas: Orígenes y desarrollo desde su aparición a nuestros dias*, 11 vols. (Madrid, 1957–1979); and A. Álvarez de Morales, *La ilustración y la reforma de la universidad en la España del siglo xviii* (Madrid, 1971).

*R. W. Kern*

*Related entries:* KRAUSE; SCIENCE.

**ENLIGHTENMENT, AGE OF.** The Enlightenment was a cluster of newly formulated ideas that became popular in the eighteenth century among educated Europeans and North Americans who were critical of certain aspects of their society, government, and culture. These ideas focused to a great extent on Christian beliefs and institutions and on the nature of the state's authority and social organization. The views of enlightened persons were influenced by the scientific discoveries of recent centuries about the nature of the universe and by a new awareness of non-European societies that European exploration and colonization had discovered. The acceptance that the earth was not the center of the universe and that nature had regular laws that applied everywhere cast doubt on the biblical account of Creation. Descriptions of Chinese Confucian civilization and the reported virtues of Native Americans raised questions about the proper organization of government. The most influential publicists of the new ideas were Frenchmen such as Charles-Louis Montesquieu (1689–1755), François Voltaire (1694–1778), and Jean Jacques Rousseau (1712–1778).

Spaniards had been central to the discovery of the non-European world, but they neither shared in creating the revised view of the universe nor had an eighteenth-century political philosopher to match Montesquieu, Rousseau, or Adam Smith (1723–1790). To appreciate the Spanish Enlightenment, one should not seek features to match those found in France* or elsewhere, but observe Spain's response to common developments in Europe on its own terms.

Many Spaniards were well informed on the progress of ideas. The great precursor of the Spanish Enlightenment was Padre Jerónimo Feijóo,* a Benedictine professor of theology at the University of Oviedo who between 1726 and 1759 published a series of essays that told his countrymen about the state of learning outside Spain: the science and philosophy of Francis Bacon (1561–1626), René Descartes (1596–1650), Isaac Newton (1642–1727), and others. He sought to disabuse his readers of superstitious beliefs, the worship of false miracles, and confidence in worthless medical practices. His books were widely read, and they started many young Spaniards thinking about what might be wrong with their education and their country. The University of Valencia was another center of the early Spanish Enlightenment. The works of José Antonio Piquer (1757–1794), a professor of medicine, and Gregorio Mayáns y Siscar (1699–1781), a professor of law, spread new ideas about medicine, jurisprudence, and ecclesiastical reform beyond their local region.

Under Fernando VI (1713–1759), Spanish translations of French works began to appear, and after the accession of Carlos III* their number multiplied rapidly.

Natural science and political economy were the most common subjects of these works, for these seemed to be the fields that most engaged Spanish minds. In science, most noteworthy were those of the French popularizer Abbé Noël Pluche (1688–1761) and the great French naturalist, the Count of Buffon (1707–1788). By the 1780s, Spanish readers had available in translation the writings of European economists, including Gaetano Filangieri (1752–1788), Antonio Genovesi (1712–1769), and David Hume (1711–1776), and in 1794, Adam Smith's *The Wealth of Nations* (1776).

Spaniards may not have shared in eighteenth-century astronomy, but they were a major element in eighteenth-century botany. Antonio Palau (c. 1750–1805), Ignacio de Asso (1707–1778), and Antonio José Cavanilles (1745–1804) investigated and classified the flora of Spain, while José Celestino Mutis (1732–1808) made that of America known. Fernando VI established the Botanical Garden of Madrid,* which under Carlos III became one of the leading institutions of its kind, serving as a model for others in Barcelona,* Valencia,* and Saragossa.

Spaniards also participated in the progress of economic thought. Under the Hapsburgs, Spain's rulers drew many of their financial resources from the mines of South America. The disastrous seventeenth century showed how unreliable this policy was, and the victories of France under Louis XIV (1638–1715) made many European rulers copy the economic mercantilism of his minister Jean Baptiste Colbert (1619–1683). Under Felipe V,* Jerónimo de Uztáriz (c. 1670–1742?) and José de Campillo y Cossío (1695–1743) published analyses of the Spanish economy that resembled Colbert's thinking. For these writers, a flourishing agriculture, manufacture, and export commerce, supported by a rising population, were the real sinews of a nation. Under Carlos III, a number of Spaniards became respectable political economists in their own right, notably Miguel Antonio de la Gándara (?–?), Bernardo Ward (?–1762 or 1763), and the conde de Campomanes.* The major work, however, one of the great pieces of the European Enlightenment, was the *Informe de ley agraria* (1795) of Gaspar Melchor de Jovellanos.* He had absorbed Smith's arguments in favor of laissez-faire and recommended an end to entail and the right to transfer property freely and enclose land as the best solution of the problems of rural Spain.

Before a book could be published legally, it needed permission from the royal government, and after it appeared, it was subject to the Inquisition's review and condemnation. The Inquisition also stood ready to punish the reading of foreign works it deemed heretical or dangerous. It forbade Montesquieu's *De l'esprit des lois* in 1756, all Voltaire's works in 1762, all Rousseau in 1764, and other major works of the foreign Enlightenment before 1789. As the reception of foreign science and economics show, however, these rules did not make Spain impervious to foreign ideas. Feijóo demonstrated that a circumspect approach could avoid prosecution, and in fact, he received royal support. Writings that cast doubt on the legitimacy of royal government or Catholicism* could not be printed in Spain. Many interested Spaniards, however, learned French, Italian, or English, and obtained surreptitiously imported works, citing their ideas, and occasionally the names of their authors, in the Spanish press.

Spaniards were some years behind the French and British in their familiarity with new ideas, but perhaps not more so than people in other parts of Europe. In the 1780s, Spain experienced a flowering of periodical journals, and of these, the *Correo literario de Europa* (1780–1781, 1786–1787) and the *Espíritu de los mejores diarios que se publican en Europa* (1787–1791) devoted themselves to reviews of foreign books and synopses of articles published abroad. Spaniards who were dissatisfied with conditions in their country had within their reach, if they wished to make the effort, most of the materials that anyone else in Europe had. There was some lag in the entry of new political philosophy because of censorship, but before the death of Carlos III, foreign writing on the subject was known to those who were interested.

A more significant difference was in the number of people involved, far fewer proportionally in Spain than in France or Britian.* In part, this was because Spanish society was less given to reading of any kind. Its educated leisure class was tiny and the number of subscribers to the journals was a smaller part of the population than their British or French equivalents. Enlightened Spaniards were found in Madrid in the royal administration and among the wealthy elite, at the universities, and in major provincial towns. Elsewhere, the well-informed person was often a solitary figure, a curate or notary who kept his interests to himself. Members of all educated classes participated: aristocrats, priests, professors, doctors, lawyers, and merchants. It would be incorrect to label the Spanish Enlightenment a specifically bourgeois movement, as some historians have, for some people in all groups that could afford it were inspired by its critical spirit.

What most distinguished enlightened Spaniards from people like them north of the Pyrenees was the tone of their writings and the themes that inspired them. The social and economic organization of their own society interested them more than epistemology and abstract political philosophy. The seventeenth and eighteenth centuries saw a revival in Europe of the medieval theory of government as a pact between ruler and subjects. After 1770, several Spanish universities, with encouragement from the crown, made the law of nature and of nations the subject of the curriculum for lawyers and clergymen. Its texts accepted the doctrine that governments were based on pacts between people and their rulers that established fundamental laws that the rulers should obey, but did not suggest that subjects had a right to revolt. By the 1780s, the Spanish periodical press was carrying articles on the subject. They used the term "constitution" as well as "pact."

If Spaniards had wished to start a conflagration, they could find the tinder for it in their reading. At least one person was so inclined. The poet León de Arroyal appears to have been the author of the anonymous *Cartas al conde de Lerena* (1787–1789) that argued that the government recognized no rules and could be corrected only by leveling it to the ground and rebuilding it from the start.

Under Carlos III, however, few Spaniards agreed with this statement. Support for the crown was far more common among advanced minds. They were deeply aware of the international decline of their country under the last Hapsburgs and welcomed the revival under the Bourbons. The empire was flourishing, the domestic economy was expanding, and Spain was once again an international power. In their efforts, the Bourbon kings ran into the entrenched position of the aristocracy and the church, and in these disputes, most enlightened persons supported the kings.

Perhaps the most eloquent criticism of conditions in Spain came out in the *Cartas marruecas* of the military officer José de Cadalso (1741–1782), first published posthumously in 1789. His fictional visitor from Morocco made fun of Spanish aristocrats, who owed their privileges to the deeds of ancient ancestors rather than their own services to the realm. Other writers had the same opinion of the aristocracy. Not only were nobles useless, they did harm to the rest of the people. Gaspar Melchor de Jovellanos lamented that their privileges placed the burden of society on the backs of worthier citizens. Moreover, their right to entail (mayorazgo) tied up family properties and thus kept them out of hands that would labor directly on them with more profit for society.

Enlightened Spaniards also found the church at fault. The land it held in entail threatened the welfare of the country, while it permitted a large part of the clergy to enjoy a life of ease and even luxury. The reformers accused the clergy of neglecting the properties in their care and the charitable institutions of the church of preserving the poor in their condition rather than helping them become useful citizens. Jovellanos bitterly summed up their feelings by calling Castile* a skeleton of its former glory now peopled only by churches, convents, and hospitals surviving amid the poverty that they had caused. The reformers urged the king to place limits on the church's right to acquire property.

Criticism of the nobility and clergy could also be heard north of the Pyrenees, but there it might be followed by statements critical of Christian doctrines. This was not the case in Spain. One of the most remarkable features of its Enlightenment was the relationship of progressive Spaniards with Catholicism. A small number of influential clergy, including bishops and members of the royal government, strove to reform and purify the church in Spain. Their movement was known as Jansenism, a name that had originated in France a century before. They objected to extravagant religious ceremonies and processions and the luxurious life of the canons and capellanes. Echoing the Erasmists whom the Inquisition had silenced in the sixteenth century, they wished to preach the moral teaching of Jesus and return to the simple church of ancient times. They supported Carlos III's expulsion of the Jesuits and his reform of the religious orders and universities.

Enlightened Spaniards and Jansenists shared a common opposition to the wealth of the church and the power of Rome and the Jesuits. Jansenists found these destructive of the religious mission of the church, while enlightened social critics believed they hurt the economic welfare of the people. Jansenists objected to the Inquisition, because it banned theological works that expressed their own point of view, and social critics resented its prohibition of works of leading modern thinkers. Many people, as did Jovellanos, could accept both points of view, since they were not inconsistent with each other. This may explain why the Spanish Enlightenment never became anti-Catholic or antireligious, as it did in France. An occasional person, such as the poet Juan Meléndez Valdés (1754–1817), might have deistic tendencies, and the priest José María Blanco would flee to Britain and turn Protestant, but they were rarities. Advanced Spaniards disliked much of what they saw in the church, but for reasons that probably went deep into Spain's past they were not ready to abandon its beliefs. A century later this would no longer be the case.

The welfare of the people dominated enlightened Spanish thought, the need for reforms that would improve the conditions of life. Education, especially university education, should bring curricula up to date. After the expulsion of the Jesuits, Pablo de Olavide (1725–1802) directed the reform of the University of Seville, and those of Valencia, Alcalá de Henares, Saragossa, and Granada followed it. Modern works of mathematics and science, along with the law of nature and of nations, replaced scholastic texts. Eventually Salamanca, the most conservative, fell into line, led, among others, by Meléndez Valdés, who held the chair of humanities.

Enlightened Spaniards also gave active support to the attempts of the kings to introduce economic reforms. Their approval was made manifest by the most typical institution of the Spanish Enlightenment, the Sociedades Económicas de Amigos del País.* Their membership, local citizens that included aristocrats and prelates as well as commoners, sought the improvement of agriculture and manufacture by offering prizes for memoirs dealing with practical questions, establishing "patriotic schools," and publicizing foreign innovations.

Nothing aroused the passion of the reformers more than the improvement of the countryside. Like the attitude toward religion, it was a unique feature of the Spanish Enlightenment. In the spring of 1766, for example, a shortage of bread led to the violent popular revolt in Madrid called the Motín de Esquilache* (the name of the unpopular first minister), which showed that increasing the food supply of the cities was the most urgent domestic problem. Unlike writers on agricultural improvement in Britain and France, who argued for large consolidated farming operations, Spanish reformers, led by Campomanes and Olavide, were convinced that the independent labrador got the most out of the land. Taking up an ideal that went back to antiquity, they wished to make Spain a country of small farms, whose farmers would either own or hold them on permanent tenure. Campomanes and Olavide established agricultural colonies in the Sierra Morena that were organized to produce such a society. The king also ordered the municipalities of Andalusia and Estremadura to distribute uncultivated lands to landless peasants and day laborers, but most municipal governments did not take this action, since it might create an independent lower class.

The European Enlightenment contained at least two profoundly different sets of ideas: a belief in the power of reason and observation to discover the laws of nature in science and politics, and an advocacy of sentiment and the "general will" as man's best guide in political and social relations. The former goes back to seventeenth-century science, and the latter can be associated with Rousseau, its most eloquent spokesman. Spain did not experience this division, because its own version of the sentimental or Rousseauan approach was always powerful. In part this was a matter of timing. The Enlightenment became a major intellectual force under Carlos III, and by then, sentiment was becoming popular in Europe. This characteristic owed more, however, to Spaniards' relation with their past. The Rousseauan position, the belief in the need for conscious commitment to the welfare of the community, was closer to the Golden Rule and to the Catholic doctrine of good works than was the individualism of a thinker such as Adam Smith. Spaniards' preference for it can be associated with the Jansenist desire to purify church practice and emphasize moral behavior.

Arguments could be heard in Spain in favor of self-interest as the stimulus that guides men's activities. The most eloquent defense of this position was voiced by Jovellanos's *Informe de ley agraria*. He and others who recognized the role of self-interest also supported the Rousseauan position, however. Dedication to the welfare of society was their ideal. This was the spirit that lay behind the Sociedades Económicas de Amigos del País. Their choice of name symbolized the new philosophy; they were also called "patriotic societies." Campomanes praised the members of the Economic Society of Madrid for avoiding the dangers of "vanity, jealousy, . . . uncontrolled self-interest," and establishing in their place "good morality, . . . humanity, moderation, the desire to hit the mark, and be useful to one's country."

In the social structure these Spanish reformers envisioned, legal orders that distinguished among members of the community seemed out of place. It had no room for idle aristocrats, and in 1770, Carlos III abolished the rule that kept hidalgos from manual labor. A decade later, he declared various crafts such as tanner, shoemaker, carpenter, and blacksmith, compatible with noble status. Campomanes, who drafted much of the economic legislation of Carlos III, had a vision of prosperous artisans in the villages dedicated to the production of common goods, not finery. Rural artisans would complement that ideal figure of enlightened Spaniards, the independent labrador.

The ideal held by enlightened Spaniards reached out to embrace the king and produce a new concept of monarchy. The ruler became his subject's partner in service to society. A Sevilliano called the king "the First Partner of the Nation," and Francisco de Cabarrús (1752–1810), financial advisor to Carlos III, repeated the image, "the principal partner." Herein lies the crux of eighteenth-century enlightened despotism as experienced in Spain. Instead of a collection of subjects (vasallos) under a prince, it was becoming an association of partners (socios), or, in Jovellanos's words, "consocios" (fellow partners), "conciudadanos" (compatriots). In a community embarked on a common enterprise, sovereignty ceased to mean domination. The enterprise needed a director, and the king was the logical person, so long as he was perceived to be dedicated and competent. Carlos III, with his enlightened counselors, enjoyed this reputation. That is one reason few antimonarchical statements were heard. Unfortunately, Carlos IV* lost this aura.

The typical enlightened Spaniard wanted a society of independent farmers, craftsmen, and curates who taught their flocks the simple morality of Jesus. He believed all these citizens would hold the good of the community, the "nation," above their own welfare and that an enlightened and dedicated king would adopt the policies needed to eliminate the harmful privileges of the aristocracy and the worldly excesses of the clergy. This idea gave the Spanish Enlightenment its unique quality.

For additional information, see M. Menéndez Pelayo, *Historia de los heterodoxos españoles*, 3 vols. (Madrid, 1880–1881); L. Sánchez Agesta, *El pensamiento político del despotismo ilustrado* (Madrid, 1953); J. Sarrailh, *L'Espagne eclairée de la seconde moitié du XVIIIe siècle* (Paris, 1954); R. Herr, *The Eighteenth-Century Revolution in Spain* (Princeton, 1958); A. Elorza, *La ideología liberal en la ilustración española* (Madrid, 1970); and J. Saugnieux, *Les jansénistes et le renouveau de la prédication dans l'Espagne de la seconde moitié due XVIIIe siècle* (Lyon, 1976).

R. Herr

*Related entries:* JOVELLANOS, GASPER MELCHOR DE; CARLOS III; SCIENCE.

## ENSENADA, MARQUÉS DE LA, ZENÓN DE SOMODEVILLA Y BEN-GOECHEA (1702–1781),

eighteenth-century statesman and political figure. Somodevilla (better known by his title of the marqués de la Ensenada) was born on 2 Dec. 1702 in the Castilian town of Alesanco. Surprisingly little is known about Ensenada's early life, and certainly nothing that would suggest he was destined to become chief minister to the Bourbon kings, Felipe V* and Fernando VI (1713–1759). His origins, in fact, were quite humble, and his first post in government service was a simple clerkship in the civil administration of the navy,* to which he was appointed in 1720.

His energy, intelligence, and administrative ability soon became evident, and under the patronage of José Patiño (1666–1763), Felipe V's minister of finance, Ensenada was promoted to commissionary general and chief of ordinance in the Ministry of the Navy. In 1732, having helped organize the expedition to Naples that put Felipe's son, the future Carlos III,* on the Neapolitan throne, he was granted the title of marqués de la Ensenada.

From 1736 to 1742, he continued to oversee various activities within the administration of the navy. In the latter year, by now a trusted member of the crown's inner circle of administrators, Ensenada became secretary of state and war to Felipe, duke of Parma (1720–1765). His career was approaching its zenith, and in 1743, upon the death of Patiño's successor, José de Campillo y Cossío (1695–1743), Ensenada was selected by Felipe V to be minister of finance, war, the navy, and the Indies. He held these four ministries, in effect serving as the crown's chief minister, for eleven years. In 1743, caught up in a palace intrigue involving Spain's relations with France* and Britain,* he was removed from office by Fernando VI ( who had succeeded to the throne in 1746) and sent into confinement in the south of Spain.

On the accession of Carlos III in 1759, Ensenada was allowed to return to Madrid.* Carlos named him to a commission established to reform the system of taxation. In 1766, however, because of his pro-Jesuit stance, he again fell out of favor and for a second time was exiled from Madrid, this time to Medina del Campo. His days in public life were over, and he lived uneventfully in Medina del Campo until his death in 1781.

Ensenada ranks as one of the most imaginative and dynamic of the Spanish Bourbon reformist ministers. Like his patron, José Patiño, he tried to reverse the economic decadence of Spain by introducing a more rational system of taxation and finance and curbing waste and corruption in government, while asserting the central authority of the crown against entrenched local privilege. He also undertook to strengthen the army and the navy; reform the provincial administration (it was under Ensenada that the intendant system was extended to all of Spain); foster commerce and trade; and improve the state of agriculture. He was an advocate of importing foreign technology and advisors and of sending Spaniards abroad for education and training. Ensenada embodied the spirit and policies of eighteenth-century enlightened despotism, and helped prepare the ground for later reform.

For additional information, see R. Herr, *A Historical Essay on Modern Spain* (Berkeley, 1974); and A. Rodríguez Villa, *Don Cenón de Somodevilla, marqués de la Ensenada* (Madrid, 1878).

*R. T. Davidson*

*Related entry:* CARLOS III.

## ESCRIVÁ DE BALAGUER Y ALBÁS, JOSÉMARÍA (1902–1975), founder of Opus Dei. Escrivá was born on 9 Jan. 1902 in Barbastro, Aragon,* the first son in a family of six. The death of his three younger siblings turned the family toward the consolations of religion and no doubt influenced him. After he finished his bachillerato in 1918, he entered the seminary in Logroño to finish his studies for the priesthood at the Pontifical University in Saragossa, where he was ordained on 28 Mar. 1925.

For the next several years, he served parishes in Saragossa and Fombuena, but in Apr. 1927, he was transferred to the diocese of Madrid* to teach canon law at the Academia Cicuéndez. Soon afterward, while on a retreat, the idea came to him to establish an apostolic organization to help laypersons seek holiness within their daily lives. On 2 Oct. 1928, Opus Dei* was founded, an organization Escrivá led until his death.

In 1931, Escrivá opened the Academia Derecho y Arquitectura as the first Opus Dei teaching institute. It was noted for its aggressive defense of the church during the anticlericalism of the Second Republic.* In 1934, he published one of the few new religious works of this period, *Consideraciones espirituales* (later retitled as *Camino* [1939] and in English as *The Way* [1954]), which today has gone through 212 editions in thirty-seven languages. Numerous other publications followed: *La Abadesa* (1944), *Es Cristo que pasa* (1973), and *Amigos de Dios* (1977), among others.

Escrivá hid in Madrid during the Spanish Civil War* before he managed to flee to the nationalist zone, where he was warmly received. The support of Carmen (1902–1987), wife of Gen. Francisco Franco,* allowed Escrivá to expand the Opus at the end of the war into the fastest-growing Catholic organization in Spain. After the bishop of Madrid ordained the Opus's first three priests in 1944, however, controversy arose within the church as to the basic nature of the group. Escrivá was forced to go to Rome in 1947 to petition the Vatican to clarify the status of Opus Dei. A decision remained subject to debate until June 1950, when special lay status distinguished it from mendicant orders. Escrivá's stay in Rome allowed him to broaden his ecclesiastical contacts, and in 1952, after founding the University of Navarre in Pamploma, he began to create educational centers in other countries, which today include two universities in Latin America. Opus Dei chapters quickly spread, but at home its closeness to Francoism became controversial in 1959, when a number of Opus Dei technocrats joined the government to modernize the economy without granting democratic reforms. As the anti-Franco opposition emerged, the Opus was portrayed as a slick version of traditional Catholicism.* Its work was aided by cold-war tensions, and before Escrivá's death in Rome on 26 June 1975, the Opus had chapters in eighty countries.

For additional information, see P. Berglar, *Opus Dei: Vida y obra del fundador Josémaría Escrivá de Balaguer* (Madrid, 1987); S. Bernal, *A Profile of Msgr. Escrivá de Balaguer, Founder of Opus Dei* (Manila, 1977); F. Gondard, *Al paso de Dios: Josémaría de Escrivá de Balaguer, fundador de Opus Dei* (Madrid, 1984); and A. Vázquez de Prada, *El fundador del Opus Dei* (Madrid, 1980).

*P. Foley*

*Related entry:* CATHOLICISM.

**ESPARTERO, BALDOMERO** (1793–1879), victorious Cristero general of the First Carlist War (1833–1840) who later became regent of Spain. Espartero was a Manchego from Granatula de Calatrava. From 1808 to 1814, he fought the Napoleonic invaders and from 1815 to 1826, saw extensive action as part of Spain's futile attempt to crush the South American independence movements.

When Carlist uprisings broke out in Spain in 1833, Espartero immediately came to the defense of Isabel II* and her regent mother, María Cristina. The seven-year civil war that followed occupied Espartero's energies. His finest hours came in Dec. 1836, when his armies ended the two-month Carlist siege of Bilbao and in Sept. 1837, when he prevented a Carlist assault on Madrid.

Espartero's renown increased when he reached an accord with the Carlists at Vergara on 31 Aug. 1839, ending the fighting in the Basque Provinces. Espartero then crushed other Carlist strongholds, and by July 1840, the conflict had ended.

During this time, he also became embroiled in the political struggles of the day. He was instrumental in forcing the regent, María Cristina, to leave Spain, and subsequently the government fell into his hands, causing Espartero to become Spain's first modern caudillo. The militarization of politics became a Spanish reality.

From 1841 to 1843, Espartero served as sole regent for the child-queen, Isabel II. In time, Espartero's policies proved a failure, and he was ousted from office and exiled by a rival caudillo, Gen. Ramón María Narváez.*

In 1848, Espartero returned to Spain. The 1854 revolutionary movement brought him back on the political scene in the Bienio Progresista arrangement. In 1856, Espartero retired to Logroño, where he divorced himself from political life. After the Revolution of 1868, he was nominated as a candidate for the vacant Spanish throne, but refused it. No other military political figure of the century had attained the national acclaim of Espartero. In spite of his common background, he was duque de la Victoria, conde de Luchana y Morella, vizconde de Banderas, and príncipe de Luchana. He was also awarded the Toisón de Oro.

For additional information, see A. Figueroa y Torres, *Espartero, el general de pueblo* (Madrid, 1932); and A. Pirala, *Historia de la guerra civil y de los partidos liberal y carlista. Corregida y aumentada con la Regencia de Espartero* (Madrid, 1873).

G. G. *Fernández*

*Related entries:* ISABEL II; LIBERALISM; PROGRESSIVE PARTY.


**ESPRONCEDA, JOSÉ DE** (1808–1842), Spanish poet of the romantic period. In Spanish literary history, Espronceda is considered the foremost romantic poet and representative figure of that period. Often compared to Lord Byron (1788–1824), Espronceda wrote poems, short fiction, political pamphlets, plays, and a historical novel, all motivated by romantic ideals and the political events that marked his short but extremely active life.

Born in Almendralejo, Badajoz, he spent his youth in Madrid, where at the age of fifteen he was sentenced for conspiring with other students to overthrow the absolutist monarchy of Fernando VII.* During his subsequent exile, he was influenced by French and British literary currents.

Throughout his life, Espronceda, a liberal, immersed himself in politics, often going to prison or into exile, but never ceasing to organize demonstrations, give speeches, and write editorials. With the advent of more liberal governments, he became secretary to Spain's embassy in The Hague and representative from Almería to the Spanish Cortes.

Three women provided inspiration for his work: Teresa, who abandoned her husband and children to follow Espronceda; Carmen, a married socialite with whom he had an affair; and Bernarda, whom he intended to marry the year he died. His experiences with them helped him produce some of the best lyrical efforts of Spanish romanticism.

Espronceda succeeded as poet and activist, moving from neoclassical models to a romantic aesthetic, and from adolescent conspirator to member of the Cortes.

The sentimental and the sociopolitical are always present in Espronceda'a work, although portrayed with an increasing pessimism with the passing of time as he confronted the incongruence between the imaginable and the attainable. In reconciling the idealism of the poet with the realities of the world, Espronceda went beyond the romantics to introduce a realistic spirit in his writings.

For additional information, see G. Carnero, *Espronceda* (Madrid, 1974); J. Casalduero, *Espronceda* (Madrid, 1961); and R. Landeira, *José de Espronceda* (Lincoln, 1985).

*R. M. Fernández*

**ESQUILACHE, MARQUÉS DE, LEOPOLDO DE GREGORIO** (ca. 1700–1785), Italian minister of Carlos III.* Gregorio's birth in Messina, Sicily, and his early military career in Spanish service are obscure, but he had retired from the military when Carlos VII of Naples (later Carlos III of Spain) appointed him to the customs service, probably on the recommendation of Carlos's chief Neapolitan minister (and creator of the regime's strong regalism), Bernardo Tanucci (1698–1783). Gregorio showed so much ability as an administrator that, in 1750, he was made a secretary of state in Naples and became the marqués de Esquilache when Carlos inherited the Spanish throne in 1759. He filled the same position in Madrid,* and in 1763, after Spain suffered setbacks in the Seven Years' War,* replaced Ricardo Wall y Devreus (1695–1777) as minister of war.

Esquilache's regalism made him an active reformer. He overhauled the lottery and used its proceeds to finance an ambitious building program in Madrid, but before it could be remade into a suitable backdrop for Carlos, the Madrileños themselves were prohibited from wearing the hats, cloaks, and swords still popular. The violence unleashed by the "motín de Esquilache" of Mar. 1766 was encouraged by the Jesuits, who were fearful that ecclesiastical lands would be confiscated. Carlos was forced to transfer Esquilache to Naples, but the Jesuits were expelled from Spain a year later.

Esquilache spent much of his later life as ambassador to Venice, where he died on 15 Sept. 1785.

For additional information, see E. Eguía Ruiz, *Los jesuitas y el motín de Esquilache* (Madrid, 1947); and V. Rodríguez Casado, *La política y los políticos en el reinado de Carlos III* (Madrid, 1962).

*R. W. Kern*

*Related entries:* ARANDA, CONDE DE; CARLOS III; ENLIGHTENMENT, AGE OF.

# F

**FALANGE ESPAÑOLA** (or FALANGE ESPAÑOLA TRADICIONALISTA [FET] after Apr. 1937), primary fascist movement of twentieth-century Spain, founded in Madrid in Oct. 1933 by José Antonio Primo de Rivera* and a handful of associates. This small organization, which at first gained few adherents, had been preceded by the even smaller Juntas de Ofensiva Nacional-Sindicalista (JONS), organized in Madrid and Valladolid in 1931 by Ramiro Ledesma Ramos (1905–1936) and Onésimo Redondo (1905–1936). The two groups fused early in 1934 to form the Falange Española de las JONS.

The term "fascist" was at first frequently used by some Falangist leaders, but was soon abandoned officially and in later years spokesmen often denied that the Falange was or ever had been a generically fascist movement. The official Twenty-Seven Points adopted in 1934, however, closely paralleled the doctrines of Italian fascism and other fascist groups. Falangist ideology emphasized the typical fascistic negation (anti-Marxism, antiliberalism, and anticonservatism), the basic fascist goals (a new nationalist authoritarian state; organization of a new regulated, multiclass, integral national syndicalism; the espousal of empire and of a new idealistic, voluntarist, antimaterialist creed), and the typical fascist forms of style and organization (romantic political liturgy, the aim of mass mobilization, the revaluing of violence, exaltation of youth, and a form of the leadership principle). That the Falange was also formally Catholic and spoke of "the eternal values of the individual" did not contradict its basic fascism, for merely formal Catholic identity and similar rhetoric might have been found in Mussolini's movement as well.

Prior to the spring of 1936, the Falange was an insignificant movement with never more than ten thousand members, garnering only seven-tenths of 1 percent of the popular vote in the elections of Feb. 1936. The weakness of fascism in Spain was first of all the result of the general absence of any strong nationalist feeling in the country, where nationalism was weaker than in almost any other continental European state. It was equally attributable to the absence of political space and the absence of secularization in much of Spanish society, where reaction to the Left had taken the form of political Catholicism. A modern and radical secular, nationalist culture did not exist as in Italy, so that both cultural support and unoccupied political space were lacking. Moreover, antifascism accompanied—indeed, almost preceded—the emergence of fascism in Spain. The hostility of the revolutionary Left was intense, leading to attacks on Falangists by the winter of 1934 and a steady spiral of political violence, particularly in Madrid.*

The fear of fascism frequently expressed by the Spanish Left from 1934 to 1936 had little to do specifically with the Falange, but referred primarily to all the combined forces of the Spanish Right and particularly of political Catholicism. In Mar. 1936, following the triumph of the Popular Front, the party was outlawed—allegedly because of its responsibility for political violence—and its chief leaders arrested. Paradoxically, only from that point did the Falange began to gain support rapidly, as disillusioned middle-class and rightist youth turned from the defeated parliamentary parties to join the militant Falangists. Party activists played a major role in the street violence that helped to precipitate the republican regime, finally cooperating with and assisting the military in the insurgency of 18 July 1936.

Once the Spanish Civil War* began, the Falange quickly expanded into a mass movement in the nationalist zone. Yet all political power passed immediately to the military, most of the national Falangist leaders were killed either by republican executions or in battle, and the main function of the wartime Falange was to organize military auxiliaries for the nationalist army.

Once Gen. Francisco Franco* became Caudillo and determined to organize an institutionalized new authoritarian system, a national state party was a prime necessity. Much more than any of the preceding parliamentary or rightist reactionary forces, the Falange was the prime candidate. It propounded extreme nationalism, a new authoritarian state, and a multiclass "national syndicalist revolution" that stood for social reorganization and modernization. The Falangist propaganda system had already expanded rapidly, and on 18 Apr. 1937, Franco announced that the Falange was being merged with the Carlists (the nationalists' other prime political and military auxiliary) to form a new united movement, Falange Española Tradicionalista (FET) de las JONS to serve as a state party for the new regime. Though some Falangists grumbled about being taken over by the military government, there was almost no resistance, though the principal Falangist leader, Manuel Hedilla (1902–1970), failed to cooperate. He was sentenced to several years in solitary confinement, and a number of other recalcitrants served shorter periods in jail.

Franco made it clear that the new movement, in adopting the Falangist doctrine as official state program, was not setting a political limit but marking a beginning, and emphasized the eclecticism of both the membership and philosophy of the new party. All other nationalist political groups were encouraged to join. Even more important, it was the nationalist regime that was taking over the party, not vice versa, creating a state party but not a true party-state.

The functions of the FET were above all threefold: to direct political indoctrination and education for Spaniards, provide reliable personnel for aspects of the government and bureaucracy, and to give content and direction to the regime's social and labor programs. Twelve national services were created, paralleling branches of the state system, to train Falangist personnel and provide political orientation, while the FET itself would be led by its national chief (Franco), a Junta Política (a sort of intraparty politburo) and a national council (a kind of central committee), all members of both bodies personally designated by Franco.

The power structure of the new regime was made clearer when Franco installed his first regular government on 30 Jan. 1938. Of eleven cabinet positions, Falangists received only three (interior, agriculture, and syndical organization). Franco carefully balanced ministries and other top state appointments among the diverse political factions supporting the nationalist movement, and even nominal Falangists would never hold more than a minority of appointments. Nominal FET membership continued to grow, however, eventually reaching an all-time high of more than 900,000 affiliates in 1942, for in the early years of the regime party membership was useful in obtaining state employment and in helping to advance personal and economic interest.

Of all the functions connected with ideology, doctrine, and propaganda, one of the most important was that of state censorship, largely administered by Falangists from 1938 to 1943, when it passed to a newly created ministry of information. The other major function was elaboration of the state syndical system, which only began in earnest after the end of the civil war. An effort to make Falangist-led labor a central part of the Spanish system was soon forced out by military conservatives, who administered the syndicates as a strictly subordinate institution. Much the same might be said of the Falangist youth organization, which at no time actually enrolled more than a comparatively small minority of adolescents and youths, and of the largely abortive Falangist militia, restricted to a very small number and placed directly under military command. Many of the original members (camisas viejas) of the party perished in the civil war, and some of the more idealistic survivors dropped out of the official organization once the conflict ended. In 1940, a small group of veteran Falangists even conspired for months to assassinate Franco before finally abandoning the project as unrealistic.

The ambitions of party activists nonetheless reached their highest level during the era of Axis triumph in Europe from 1940 to 1942. The more radical Falangists looked especially to Germany,* and were certain that its victories would soon lead to the complete fascistization of Spain. Some even went so far as to conspire with Nazi agents for the possible overthrow of Franco and his replacement by a more strongly pro-German government. The main foe of Falangists within the regime during this phase was the military; the resulting tension produced several crises and two reorganizations of Franco's cabinet in 1941–1942. Though Franco gave some satisfaction to the anti-Falangist military, he carefully balanced off the forces involved, for he deemed the FET a necessary fount of indoctrination and personnel for the long-range institutionalization of the regime. His brother-in-law, Ramón Serrano Suñer,* a neo-Falangist of 1937, was considered the main representative of Falangism during the first years of World War II,* but in 1941 Franco found for his purpose an ideal secretary-general of the party in José Luis de Arrese (1905– ), who led the FET until 1945 and steadily deradicalized it, co-opting its cadres into obedient service of the regime.

Though the first five years of the Franco regime were a period of semifascistization, the last thirty-three, stretching from 1942 to 1975, constituted a long period of slowly progressive defascistization. This began in 1942–1943, when it first became clear that the Axis powers might not win the war and that an explicitly nonfascist program and identity might be necessary for the regime to survive. The concept of totalitarianism first began to be rejected officially in 1942, and by 1943 Falangism was being increasingly identified with official Catholicism,* while inspiration from or affinities with central Europe were more and more denied.

The first major wave of defascistization took place in 1945, when the FET became commonly known as the "National Movement" and the fascist salute was officially abolished. The FET-National Movement was not at all eliminated, but generally downgraded and left without a secretary-general, the regime being defined subsequently as a Catholic corporative system of organic democracy. The movement continued to fill some of its accustomed functions, particularly in the regime's social program and syndical system. A new secretary-general was again named in 1948 and upgraded to cabinet rank three years later, and the movement continued to provide a limited degree of political and youth mobilization.

By the mid–1950s, however, the tide was swinging even more heavily against it. Though the only national congress of the movement in the regime's history was held in Oct. 1953, veteran camisas viejas and young Falangists alike murmured their displeasure over the continued de-Falangization of the regime, and by 1956 the movement had begun to lose control of University of Madrid students. Arrese was reappointed secretary-general to bolster the movement, and gained Franco's consent for the preparation of a series of new institutional laws that would restructure the party within the regime and guarantee it a place of major influence in the future, even after the Caudillo's death. These proposals for the institutional re-Falangization of the regime drew protest from every other political and institutional sector, however, and were quashed altogether by Franco early in 1957. The cabinet change that followed further reduced movement influence, introducing new economics ministers connected with the Opus Dei.* In the following year, the new cabinet completed the ideological defascistization of the regime with the publication of official new principles of the movement, which totally repudiated the old Twenty-Seven Points in favor of bland bromides affirming peace, unity, cooperation, and the family, etc., which might have been subscribed to by almost any sort of regime. The new economic ministers then went on to draft the liberalization program that fundamentally altered Spanish economic policy in 1959 and marked a crucial turning point in the history of the regime.

Defeat of the Arrese proposals for re-Falangization was a decisive setback from which the movement never fully recovered, yet its existence was assured so long as Franco survived. He explained candidly in private that he needed some sort of political organization to provide direct political backing for the government, operate the labor program, and provide cheerleading on public occasions. During the 1960s, the main leader of the movement was José Solís Ruis (1913– ), a veteran syndical boss, who thought in terms of "political development" of the system that might offer further cosmetic reforms on the one hand and give the movement the opportunity to function more actively as a liberalized, semirepresentative state party on the other. The examples of Peronist Argentina or the Partido Revolucionario Institucional (PRI), the quasi-official Mexican party, were occasionally invoked. Though the movement still carried 931,802 names on its membership lists in 1963, the great majority represented inactive affiliates that had long since dropped out. Complete loss of support or even control in the universities was acknowledged when the Sindicato Español Universitario (SEU), the Falangist student organization, was dissolved in 1965. A new organic law of the movement and its national council was promulgated two years later, but that merely safeguarded institutional continuity without granting it new functions or influence. The last major legislation of the Franco regime, the Organic Law of the State, approved in 1966, made no mention of the movement at all, though the law did reorganize its national council and grant the latter the right to launch an appeal of contrafuero (unconstitutionality) against any further legislation that might be deemed to infringe the fundamental laws of the state. Such an appeal, however, would be decided by Franco's council of the realm, not by any agency of the movement.

The final phase of the movement revolved largely around the issue of associationism as a new semireform in place of direct political parties. This derived in part from tacit recognition that the old movement as a single state organization was dead, but that the moribund organization might be revived through a new role as "Movement-communion" representing the new interests of Spanish society through partially autonomous political associations formed within the general umbrella of the movement and the regime's fundamental laws. The first attempts to draw up guidelines for political associations in 1969 and 1973 came to naught, however, for Franco feared even an artificial ploy that might too closely resemble competitive multiparty politics. During the last phase of the regime under the quasi-reformist government of Carlos Arias Navarro (1908– ), the Juridical Statute of the Right of Political Association was formally approved by the national council in Dec. 1974, though never fully implemented. It stipulated very demanding requirements for the formation of new political associations in conformity with the principles of the movement and always subject to approval by the national council. This opportunity was generally boycotted by the political opposition, the only new association that fully met the official requirements being the new Union of the Spanish People (UDPE), led by Adolfo Suárez,* planned as a sort of moderate reformist continuation of the movement.

The death of Franco and the accession of Juan Carlos I* sounded doom for the movement, which was officially dissolved in Apr. 1977 as the process of democratic constitution-building began. Most of its nominal members had already ceased to believe in it. Since the mid–1950s, the torch of neo-Falangism had not been carried by the movement but by increasingly numerous small groups and sects of what might be described as crypto-Falangism prior to 1975 and neo-Falangism or neofascism after that date. Their proliferation into a multiplicity of competing sects was as extensive as their overall numbers insignificant. Neo-Falangism never achieved the relative strength of neofascism in Italy, primarily because the original movement had lacked independent strength and had never developed an independent Falangist culture on which to build. The dictatorship had survived so long into the postwar democratic era that Falangism had withered from within. In the new conditions of a transformed and sophisticated industrial society, all the tiny neo-Falangist sects combined could gain no more support than the totally insignificant showing of the original Falange in 1936.

For additional information, see P. Chueca, *El fascismo en los comienzos del régimen de Franco: Un estudio sobre FET-JONS* (Madrid, 1983); S. Ellwood, *Priestas las filas: Historia de Falange Española, 1933–1983* (Barcelona, 1984); J. Jiménez Campos, *El fascismo en la crisis de la Segunda República española* (Madrid, 1979); and S. G. Payne, *Falange: A History of Spanish Fascism* (Stanford, 1961).

S. G. Payne

Related entries: FRANCO, GEN. FRANCISCO; SECOND REPUBLIC; SPANISH CIVIL WAR.

**FALLA, MANUEL DE** (1876–1946), perhaps the best-known Spanish composer of the twentieth century. Falla was born in Cadiz, and although he showed signs of musical talent at an early age, did not become a famous child prodigy as did his contemporaries Isaac Albéniz* and Enrique Granados.* He spent his youth and early manhood in the serious study of musical composition and harmony. He wrote his first major work, *La vida breve*, at the age of twenty-eight for a competition in Madrid. He won, and established enough of a reputation to go to Paris, the mecca for young composers. In Paris, Falla met the most famous composers of the day, Claude Debussy (1862–1918), Maurice Ravel (1875–1937), and Paul Dukas (1865–1935), all of whom deeply influenced him.

During Falla's Paris sojourn from 1907 to Sept. 1914, he sketched his most important works: *El amor brujo*, a ballet; *Noches en el jardín española*, symphonic impressions of an Andalusian garden for piano and orchestra; and *El sombrero de tres picos*, a ballet. After the outbreak of World War I,* Falla returned to Madrid,* where he reworked his compositions for their premieres.

The production of *El sombrero*, which had its premiere in 1919, featured Sergei Diaghalev's (1872–1929) Ballet Russe and stage sets designed by Pablo Picasso.*

In 1922, Falla returned to Granada and left only when career demands forced him to do so. He wrote his *Harpsichord Concerto* for Wanda Landowska (1877–1959) at this time and began work on an opera, *Atlántida*, which remained unfinished at his death. Falla remained in Granada throughout the Spanish Civil War,* but left Spain in 1939. He settled in Buenos Aires, where he remained until his death in 1946.

Falla's harmonies, orchestration, and use of impressions place his music clearly in the French impressionist school. His fame stems from his time in Paris and his international connections, rather than from the creation of revolutionary musical forms or styles. His works have entered the standard repertoire of most modern orchestras and, along with Georges Bizet's (1838–1875) *Carmen* (1875), provide the universal standard of what is thought of as Spanish music.

For additional information, see R. Crichton, *Falla* (London, 1982); S. Demarquez, *Manuel de Falla* (Philadelphia, 1968); and J. B. Trend, *Manuel de Falla and Spanish Music* (New York, 1929).

S. L. Brake

**FEIJÓO Y MONTENEGRO, BENITO JERÓNIMO** (1676–1764), Benedictine friar and intellectual. Feijóo was born in Casdemiro, Orense. He took his vows as a very young man and after studying at Salamanca, gained the chair of theology at the University of Oviedo, where he resided until his death. He is universally recognized as the most significant intellectual voice of the first half of the eighteenth century in Spain. His books of essays, published between 1726 and 1760 in two major collections, gave rise to much stimulating discussion and even nationwide polemics in which his friends, such as Martín Sarmiento (1695–1772), defended his positions before the powerful critic Diego de Torres Villarroel (1693–1770). Although an orthodox believer, Feijóo best represents, because of his religious calling, the triumph of rationalism in the Spain of his day.

Feijóo was properly designated as Spain's first modern essayist. His encyclopedic curiosity found in that literary medium the most appropriate instrument for his goal of bringing news to his contemporaries of the achievements taking place, especially in the natural sciences, beyond his country's borders. He also openly advocated the scientific, experimental method that had produced them; pleaded for basic reform in the educational system and method of his day; and, while carefully and sincerely excluding matters of faith, bravely attacked many of the superstitious, unscientific beliefs of his countrymen.

Feijóo's two major collections of essays, *Teatro crítico universal* (1726–1739) and *Cartas eruditas* (1742–1760), vary little, except in terms of the relative length of the essays contained in each. These, totaling some 260 pieces, have been variously classified by subject matter, and the classifications themselves (medicine, politics, aesthetics, pedagogy, social criticism, literature, natural sciences, astronomy, philosophy, and superstitions) reflect the breadth of the Spanish thinker's interests and studies. The scientific and modern bent of his thought may be properly deduced from the very titles of some of his essays: "The Fallibility of Proverbs," "Parallel between the Spanish and French Languages," "Vox Populi," "Defense of Women," "The Marvels of Nature," "Spanish Glories," and "False Miracles."

The monumental presence of Feijóo and his work in the first half of the eighteenth century reflects a Spain if not nearly abreast of the age's great European centers of knowledge and culture, then not, as often unhappily implied or openly stated, years away from the civilization of which it was a part.

For additional information, see A. R. Fernández González, *Personalidad y estilo en Feijóo* (Oviedo, 1966); I. L. McClelland, *Benito J. Feijóo* (New York, 1969); and G. Marañón, *Las ideas biológicas del Padre Feijóo* (Madrid, 1941).

                                                                                                    *A. Rodríguez*

*Related entry:* ENLIGHTENMENT, AGE OF.


**FELIPE V, KING OF SPAIN** (1683–1746), ruled 1700–1746 as first Bourbon king of Spain. Felipe, born on 19 Dec. 1683, was the second son of the French dauphin and grandson of Louis XIV (1643–1715), whose first wife had been María Teresa (1638–1683), daughter of Felipe IV (1605–1665). He was the duke of Anjou until Carlos II (1661–1700) startled all Europe by naming him as heir to the Spanish throne in his second will. In 1701, Felipe married María Luisa of Savoy (1688–1714), daughter of the duke of Savoy, Victor Amadeus (1666–1732). Two sons, Luis I (1707–1724) and Fernando VI (1713–1759), were produced by this union, but upon Maria's death in 1714, Felipe continued his Italian marriage connection with Isabel Farnesio (1692–1766), who had five children, including the future Carlos III* and don Felipe (1720–1765).

The first years of Felipe's reign were dominated by French interests. A number of advisors, including Anne Marie de la Trémouille, the princess de Ursinos (1641–1722), accompanied the young king to Madrid, and they labored to remodel the Spanish government along the lines of French absolutism. The new regime was headed by a council of state composed of four secretaries with specific responsibilities. In theory, the secretaries would be the heart of a centralized, bureaucratic government, one quite different from the vague, general councils of the Hapsburg period. Louis XIV also interfered directly in Spain's European possessions, particularly in the Italian provinces. His aggressiveness led to a general fear that the French would dominate all aspects of the Spanish regime, a response shared by Spaniards who saw the intrusion of French aristocrats and officials as a direct threat to their place and station. Only the few who had encouraged Carlos II to favor French interests enjoyed prestigious positions. Others took heart from foreign resistance to Felipe and openly sided with the aims of the Grand Alliance, made up of Britain,* Austria, the Dutch republic, Portugal,* Prussia, and Savoy. The members of the alliance proclaimed Archduke Charles (1685–1740) of Austria as king of Spain, and insisted on imposing the terms of a treaty of partition, signed in 1698, which had divided the Spanish inheritance among all the powers. The arrival of Charles in Catalonia* in 1705 precipitated a civil war in which that province and Valencia* proclaimed Charles as king.

Affairs in Spain provided only one theater in a broad struggle that pitted French interests against those of Europe. The war was devastating for France and difficult for Spain, which suffered direct losses in Gibraltar* and the Balearic Islands,* and the intrusion of various foreign armies, including Portugal's, which occupied Madrid* briefly in 1706. Felipe joined a Franco-Hispanic force in Italy* in 1702, while María Luisa served as regent during his absence, but French advisors and the princess de Ursinos dominated matters of state. The princess was a personal representative of Louis XIV, and had the task of supervising both the private and public lives of Felipe and his queen. She proved to be capricious, appointing and dismissing government officials according to whim rather than policy.

Ursinos's presence increased the alienation of Spaniards at a time when Spanish forces were suffering losses, including the sack of Cadiz and defeat in Portugal. The war was a disaster for Spain in the Low Countries and in Italy, but Spanish arms enjoyed some success at home, winning at Almanza in 1707 and Villaviciosa in 1710. In 1709, however, the British seized Minorca and the Austrians won at Almenara and Saragossa. The decisive turn in the fortunes of war came when the German emperor died and the title of Holy Roman Emperor passed to Charles on 27 Sept. 1711. The other members of the Grand Alliance were scarcely enthusiastic about reviving the old empire of Charles V (1500–1558), who had ruled all of the Hapsburg possessions in the sixteenth century, and they opened negotiations with Spain.

In 1713, the British and Dutch settled with Spain in the Treaty of Utrecht. Felipe V guaranteed permanent separation of the French and Spanish crowns, while ceding Gibraltar and Minorca to Britain, and also leasing the transatlantic slave monopoly (asiento) to them. The duke of Savoy received Sicily, and the Dutch expanded their trading rights. In 1714, the Treaty of Rastatt concluded hostilities with the Hapsburgs, who gained all of Spain's provinces in Italy and the southern Netherlands. In the same year, Felipe brought the civil war in the north to a close with the capture of Barcelona,* his only gain from the War of Spanish Succession,* since the price of rebellion in Catalonia and Valencia was the loss of their privileges and the imposition of Castilian control in the Nueva Planta decrees.

A second phase of Felipe's rule followed the war and the death of María Luisa in 1714. The government continued to grow in strength along the lines established during the war; centralization remained a goal, but the administration did not enjoy a greater level of efficiency and control. The direction of policy ceased to be in French hands and passed to those of Felipe's second wife, Isabel Farnesio, sometimes called the "shrew of Parma."

This shift in policy came about as Felipe grew more morose and diffident. Isabel increased her influence, bringing a number of Italians back into Spanish cultural and political life, which caused Felipe to withdraw from most activities. In 1724, he tried to escape responsibility altogether by abdicating in favor of his son Luis, who ruled as Luis I from Feb. to Aug., when he died of influenza. Isabel prevailed on Felipe to resume the throne, but following the birth of her son Carlos, she became obsessed with the idea of gaining provinces for him in Italy, a desire that grew with the birth of each additional child. Her chief advisor, Guilio Alberoni,* convinced her to take advantage of a papal call for a crusade against the Ottoman Turks to gain the money for a military expedition against Sardinia and Sicily in 1717. While the venture proved to be a modest military success, it caused the formation of the Quadruple Alliance among Britain, the Dutch, France,* and the Hapsburgs, all of whom swore to restore the status quo and to prevent similar adventures in the future. A British fleet in Sicily and a French force in Catalonia occasioned a prompt surrender in Madrid.

Isabel was vindicated in her actions by the Treaty of the Hague in 1720, by which don Carlos was to receive Tuscany, Parma, and Piacenza if Spain would renounce all other claims to Italy and dismiss Alberoni. Spain was drawn into the system of alliances through marriages with the French house, but the abrupt cancellation by the French of the betrothal of Louis XV (1710–1774) to Felipe's daughter occasioned a wholesale breach of relations. Isabel had replaced Alberoni as advisor with a Dutch adventurer, Baron Johann Willem Ripperdá (1680–1737), and he used the affront as an excuse to align Spain with the interests of Vienna, a situation that provoked another short war involving all the major states of Europe in 1727. The Treaty of Seville ended the conflict in 1729 by affirming the succession of don Carlos in the Italian duchies, an event that took place in 1731. Later involvements gained additional territory for him, and also for his younger brother, don Felipe.

Felipe V, scarcely involved in these machinations, became slightly less lethargic after 1729, although his classic case of melancholia continued the rest of his life. His administration continued along the lines established early in his reign, advancing the interests of the crown against the privileges and traditions of the provinces and exacting royal taxes whenever possible. More royal institutions, including a Spanish Academy for the improvement of the language, were created, but changes in other areas of West European commerce and education did not take place with the same rapidity in Spain under Felipe, who was increasingly remote from everyone in the last years of his life. He died in Feb. 1746 at Madrid.

For additional information, see W. Hargreaves-Mawdsley, *Spain 1700–1788: A Political, Diplomatic, and Institutional History* (London, 1978).

*C. R. Steen*

*Related entry:* SPANISH SUCCESSION, WAR OF.

**FERNANDO VII, KING OF SPAIN** (1784–1833), ruled 1808–1833. Fernando was born at San Ildefonso on 13 Oct. 1784, third child and firstborn male of Carlos IV* and the infamous María Luisa de Parma (1751–1819). Raised at court, he must have been aware of his mother's liaison with Manuel Godoy,* duque de Alcudia, Príncipe de la Paz, perhaps the most notorious scoundrel in Spanish history. In fact, Fernando first opposed Godoy in 1796 at the age of eleven, when his mother's lover received his second title after negotiating the Treaty of Basle in 1795. The príncipe de Asturias nursed a smoldering resentment of his common-born competitor that made Fernando bitter, isolated, and secretive for much of his life.

The breaking point came after the naval defeat at Trafalgar* on 21 Oct. 1805, when Fernando accused Godoy of misleading the court. Godoy tried to silence the prince by persuading Carlos and María Luisa to arrange a marriage between Fernando and Godoy's sister, a confused episode that almost succeeded. In Oct. 1807, just when Napoleon Bonaparte (1769–1821) had manipulated Godoy and Carlos to participate in the partition of Portugal, Fernando wrote directly to Napoleon, seeking to have the French emperor intervene at the Spanish court against Godoy.

This terrible miscalculation gave Napoleon the opening he sought to add Spain to his empire. Heedless of the new danger, Fernando led the mutiny at Aranjuez, which began late on 16 Mar. 1808 and resulted in Godoy's dismissal two days later, Carlos's abdication on 19 Mar., and Fernando's ascension to the throne. The hollowness of his triumph came when the French general, Joachim Murat (1767–1815), rebuffed his claims and forced the new king to travel to France to meet with Napoleon. Fernando left Madrid on 10 Apr. for what became a six-year sojourn in France, beginning in Bayonne, where he was forced to pardon Godoy. Between 30 Apr. and 10 May, Napoleon tricked him into abdicating.

Fernando spent the next period of his life under house arrest at Valençay while Spain rebelled against the monarchy of Joseph Bonaparte, now José I,* in the War of Independence,* an era of popular sovereignty that witnessed the Cortes of Cadiz's Constitution of 1812. Few of these developments came to Fernando's attention. The collapse of French power allowed his release on 5 Feb. 1814, and his return stirred rival feelings of contempt and adulation. Traditional Spain, reacting to the Cortes of Cadiz's disentailment* and the end of ecclesiastical mortmain, called him the Chosen One and urged him to resume absolutism. The legislators of Cadiz, however, whom Fernando wrongly identified with the French, greeted him unenthusiastically. Not surprisingly, on 4 May 1814, the king revoked the Constitution of 1812 and its laws, while promising reforms within the old order, including freedom of speech and the addition of Latin American representatives to the traditional Cortes.

Fernando ruled six years as absolute monarch. He failed to institute reforms, convene the Cortes, or trust any statesman to lead the government. Haunted by the ghost of Godoy, he could not see the pressing need for good leadership to mobilize Spanish efforts to end the Latin American independence movements. An expedition led by Paulo Morillo (1778–1837) reasserted royal authority in Venezuela, but a similar expedition awaiting passage to the Viceroyalty of Río de la Plata collapsed when its officers rebelled and, under the leadership of Maj. Rafael de Riego (1785–1823), marched on Madrid in 1820 to restore the Constitution of 1812. Absolutism disappeared for almost three years, from 1820 to 1823, in the liberal triennium, and once again, Fernando lived almost as a prisoner, his fate in the hands of urban mobs and shifting political cliques. A new royalist regency was established in Seo de Urgel to defend him, but the July Days revolt in 1822 defeated royalist efforts to come to his defense. A growing republican movement seized power in Feb. 1823 and sent the king to Cadiz in Mar. Finally, in Apr. 1823, Spain's traditionalists, the apostólicos, won with the help of a French army sent by the Holy Alliance and commanded by the duke of Angoulême, Louis XVIII's (1755–1824) nephew.

The king's restoration began the Ominous Decade (1823–1833), Fernando's last, which once again saw the abolition of the Constitution of 1812, but ended with a surprising triumph for the previously discredited liberals. One element in this change of fortune was the king's exhaustion. A difficult life had left him physically unable to provide the leadership to reform the old order into an efficient regime. He turned to moderate liberals with a knowledge of modern finance, an act that outraged traditionalists, who rallied around his younger brother, Carlos María Isidro de Borbón (1788–1855), as the nucleus of the future Carlist movement.

A final, nagging question during this last decade was Fernando's lack of an heir. Of his four marriages, only the last, to his niece, María Cristina (1806–1878), produced two daughters, Isabel II* and Luisa Fernanda, who needed a confusing revision in the succession laws to rule. The change provided the Carlists with the pretext to rebel as Fernando lay dying in Madrid on 29 Sept. 1833. It was a fitting end to a life lived in chaos.

For additional information, see J. L Comellas García-Llera, ed., *Del Antiguo al Neuvo Régimen*, vol. 13 of *Historia general de España y América* (Madrid, 1981), and *El Trienio Constitucional* (Pamplona, 1963); J. M. Cuenca Toribio, *La Iglesia española ante la revolución liberal* (Madrid, 1971); J. Fontana, *Hacienda y estado en la crisis final del Antiguo Régimen español, 1823–27* (Madrid, 1973); D. Hilt, *The Troubled Trinity: Godoy and the Spanish Monarch* (Tuscaloosa, 1987); G. H. Lovett, *Napoleon and the Birth of Modern Spain*, 2 vols. (New York, 1965); M. C. Pintos Vietes, *La política de Fernando VII entre 1814 y 1820* (Pamplona, 1958); F. Suárez, ed., *Documentos del reinado de Fernando VII*, 24 vols. (Pamplona, 1961–19

*R. W. Kern*

*Related entries:* CARLOS IV; CORTES OF CADIZ; INDEPENDENCE, WAR OF.

**FERRER I GUÀRDIA, FRANCESC (FRANCISCO)** (1849–1909), Catalan anarchist. Ferrer was born 10 Jan. 1849 near Barcelona.* His family were practicing Catholics, but his uncle was a freethinker who influenced him strongly, so that Ferrer, when he began to work as a railway conductor, became a Mason and a follower of the republican Manuel Ruiz Zorrilla (1833–1895). The young Catalan often acted as a messenger for the exiled radical leader, and in 1885, had to go into exile himself after a republican coup attempt failed. Ferrer remained in Paris for the next sixteen years, active as a Dreyfusard, a delegate to the Second International, and as an enthusiast for a new form of libertarian education, which was noncoercive, natural, and based on the emotional needs of the child.

Many of these ideas had been worked out at a libertarian primary school in Cempuis, France, and although Ferrer never visited the school, he did correspond with it, so that when the Catalan returned to Barcelona in 1901, the Escuela Moderna he established with money from the inheritance of a friend was very similar. Ferrer believed that education had been dominated by the state as a way to produce obedient workers and by the church to perpetuate superstition. His Escuela Moderna opposed rote learning, lectures, and rigorous discipline. Students were encouraged to improvise and experiment. Libertarian ideas from eighteenth- and nineteenth-century freethinkers made up its educational philosophy.

The school, controversial even at a time when the Spanish-American War* had shaken pedagogical conventionality so deeply that the Institución Libre de Enseñanza* and the Junta para Ampliación de Estudios had begun urging educational renovation to cure Spanish backwardness, lasted only until 1906, when Ferrer was implicated in an assassination attempt on the lives of King Alfonso XIII* and his wife Victoria (1879–1969). The assassin, Mateo Morral, was in fact an employee of the small publishing company Ferrer had started in Barcelona, but when Ferrer came to trial, proof of a conspiracy was lacking, and he was acquitted and released from prison in June 1907.

For the next two years, the anarchist from Barcelona remained active in alternative education circles, founding the International League for the Rational Education of Children in 1908, which attracted the membership of libertarian intellectuals from many countries. Events in Barcelona caught up with him when, on 26 July 1909, the city began a week of rioting to protest the mobilization of Catalan reserves for service in Morocco.* Complex issues of regionalism and radicalism lay beneath the surface, but when order was restored, Ferrer, who seems to have played a very minor role in these events, was arrested on 31 July 1909 and found guilty in a hurried trial that led to his execution on 13 Oct. Ferrer was the best-known radical of the city, and city officials who had never accepted his acquittal in 1907 now made him the scapegoat for Barcelona's Tragic Week. Protest demonstrations in dozens of cities in Western Europe and North America called him a martyr to free thought. In Britain,* George Bernard Shaw (1856–1950), H. G. Wells (1866–1946), and Sir Arthur Conan Doyle (1859–1930) protested side by side with Peter Kropotkin (1842–1921) and other anarchists. As a result, Ferrer became the best known of the Spanish anarchists, despite his short career in Catalonia.

For additional information, see P. Avrich, *The Modern School Movement* (Princeton, 1980); J. Connelly Ullman, *The Tragic Week: A Study of Anticlericalism in Spain, 1875–*

*1912* (Cambridge, 1968); F. Ferrer, *The Origins and Ideals of the Modern School* (New York, 1913); and A. Orts-Ramos and R. Carravaca, *Francisco Ferrer y Guàrdia: Apóstol de la razón* (Barcelona, 1932).

*S. F. Fredricks and R. W. Kern*
*Related entries:* ANARCHISM; BARCELONA; CATALONIA.

**FIRST REPUBLIC** (1873–1874), initial period of republican rule in Spain and a time of considerable revolutionary activity. The First Republic grew out of incessant liberal quarrels between 1834 and 1868 over the form and philosophy of government. Specific discontent focused on the financial ineptitude of the court of Isabel II* and her inability to rule efficiently. In the face of mounting unrest, the queen fled to France in Sept. 1868, and Gens. Francisco Serrano (1810–1885) and Juan Prim y Prats,* leaders of a provisional government, searched for a new dynasty to head a strong constitutional monarchy. In 1869, the search culminated with the selection of an Italian prince, Amadeo I,* after earlier provoking a quarrel between France* and Germany* that eventually caused the Franco-Prussian War (1870–1871). Amadeo's reign lasted only from 2 Jan. 1870 to 11 Feb. 1873 and failed to calm political passions. His abdication led to proclamation of a republic on 14 Feb. 1873.

The First Republic may be divided into four periods. Initially, the small Democratic party, made up of intellectual followers of Karl Christian Friedrich Krause,* sought a unitary republic ruled from Madrid and based on a presidential system. The government of Estanislao Figueras (1819–1882), aided by Nicolás Salmerón,* relaxed the authoritarian norms of previous administrations only to collide with the rising expectations of workers and peasants who believed the millennium had arrived at last. Populism, fanned by vague memories of the War of Independence,* dominated Spain south of Madrid. Failure of the unitary republic led to a second, cantonalist stage. Scores of city-states, or cantons, emerged by July 1873 as entities avowedly independent of Madrid and dedicated to primitive communism—anticlerical in the extreme, sharing land and private property, and often practicing many other libertarian concepts. The inspiration for this radicalism initially came from Francesc Pi i Margall,* a Catalan intellectual who drew vaguely upon the anarchist ideas of Pierre-Joseph Proudhon (1809–1865), Michael Bakunin (1814–1876), and even more distant German idealism to create his concept of federalism. Disgruntled with liberal politics, he thought a weaker central government might permit faster socioeconomic reform, although he never anticipated the intensity of the southern revolt. Pi's presidency did not last out the month of July as the Spanish state melted away, and Salmerón's rule was equally unsuccessful and short-lived.

The third period of the First Republic came with the presidency of Emilio Castelar (1832–1899), a liberal who abandoned the concept of extreme federalism for a reestablished unitary republic. His rule from Sept. 1873 to early Jan. 1874 saw the army* under Gen. Manuel Pavía y Rodríguez (1827–1895) crush the cantonalists, although Cartagena's resistance strained the republic's limited resources just as the revolt centering around Carlism* in the north presented a more dangerous threat. Castelar found himself dependent upon the army and conciliatory toward the church, even though both were hostile to social and economic reform. A period that might have seen the birth of a more tolerant regime was instead spent in furious parliamentary infighting. The apolitical Pavía finally could tolerate no more and staged a military coup d'état on 3 Jan. 1874 in favor of Francisco Serrano, the duque de Torre, the aristocratic general who ruled the republic until 29 Dec. 1874.

This last stage of the First Republic witnessed major efforts to destroy republicanism. Serrano wavered between caudillismo—a monarchy without a king—and cooperation with the Bourbon party of Antonio Cánovas del Castillo,* now operating openly to offset the Carlists' ultramontane aspirations. Serrano himself retained some republican values, such as anticlericalism, but his Napoleonic pose of directing the campaign against the Carlists in the field failed to strengthen his government in Madrid. Cánovas emerged as the more powerful of the two, his monarchist dedication leavened by commitment to an orthodox parliamentary system and free trade, goals that unified the middle class, military, and some of the nobility. Another coup d'état on 27 Dec. 1874 brought him to power, and in his ministerial regency of 1875, the First Republic disappeared when the Carlists were defeated and the monarchy restored in Jan. 1876. The Constitution of 30 June 1876 made it official.

For additional information, see A. Eiras, *El partido demócrata español* (Madrid, 1961); C. Hennessy, *The Federal Republic in Spain* (Oxford, 1962); C. Llorca, *Castelar* (Barcelona, 1968); Marqués de Lema, *De la Revolución a la Restauración* (Madrid, 1927); G. Trujillo, *El federalismo español* (Barcelona, 1967).

*R. W. Kern*

*Related entries:* AMADEO I; PI I MARGALL, FRANCESC.

**FLORIDABLANCA, CONDE DE, JOSÉ MOÑINO** (1728–1808), eighteenth-century royal minister. Moñino, the future conde de Floridablanca, was born in Murcia on 21 Oct. 1728 to a merchant family. His ability as a student led him to legal training at Salamanca and a career in the law, which brought him to the attention of Leopoldo de Gregorio, the marqués de Esquilache,* minister of finance and war and a favorite of Carlos III,* who nominated him as a lawyer for the Council of Castile in 1764. He defended the king against Jesuit attacks after the right to bear arms was prohibited in Madrid following the "Motín de Esquilache" of Mar. 1766 and played a leading role in the subsequent controversy that ended only when the Jesuits were expelled from Spain on 2 Apr. 1767.

Moñino later was able to defend this action to Spanish bishops by arguing that regalism was inescapable because the growth of royal ecclesiastical control, embodied in the Concordat of 1753, made Spanish Catholicism* subject to Rome only in matters of doctrine. The monarchy, not the papacy, was the ideal agency to meet the needs of the Spanish church, a point the Jesuits, fiercely loyal to the papacy, could not accept. The king was so pleased by this defense that he soon made Moñino the conde de Floridablanca and, in 1777, elevated him as chief minister to succeed the marqués de Grimaldi (1720–1786), a position he held until 1792.

As the exemplar of Carlos's enlightened despotism, the new conde accomplished a great deal in the next fifteen years. Creation of the Bank of San Carlos led to royal reform of the currency, credit, and colonial trade. Free trade dramatically altered the imperial economy and encouraged domestic growth. University reform introduced mathematics and science into the curriculum; bureaucratic and judicial changes stressed merit. The conde became a promoter of public works, and the construction of canals and roads aided agriculture and the domestic economy, while his encouragement of the Sociedades Económicas de Amigos del País created a new constituency for change. New taxes on land and rental income also reduced the regressive sales tax.

In foreign affairs, the chief minister aggressively won a rare victory over Britain* in Florida during the War of American Independence and regained the colony by the Treaty of Paris in 1783. This was a high point of his foreign policy that led to rather optimistic offensives in Jamaica, Belize, and Gibraltar* that either failed or were finally checked by the Nootka Sound incident in the Pacific Northwest, when the British expelled Spaniards from Victoria Island in Jan. 1790. War seemed likely until it became clear that Spain's French allies not only had no intention of honoring the Bourbon Family Compact, but in fact constituted a revolutionary threat against the regime.

This disappointment came on the heels of Carlos III's death in 1788. The passing of Floridablanca's royal patron encouraged ambitious rivals to attack the chief minister as corrupt, too powerful, or heretical, but no one, at first, was able to persuade Carlos IV* to replace Floridablanca, and from 1788 to 1790, he continued to reform the judicial system and the royal household. On 18 July 1790, however, a French plot to assassinate him and destabilize Spain seriously wounded the chief minister and allowed his rivals to argue that both his health and the animosity of the French toward him limited his effectiveness. The conde de Aranda* took over many of his functions in Feb. 1792, but fell to Manuel Godoy* in Nov. of the same year, and Godoy dominated the court until 1808, the year of Floridablanca's death on 29 Dec. It can be argued that the conde's active expansion of executive power established a de facto prime ministership in the 1780s that crippled government by council without creating adequate safeguards on the abuse of this power by Godoy in the subsequent period.

For additional information, see A. Domínguez Ortiz, *La sociedad española en el siglo xviii* (Madrid, 1955); R. Herr, *The Eighteenth-Century Revolution in Spain* (Princeton, 1958); and J. Sarrailh, *L'Espagne éclairée de la seconde moitié du xviiie siècle* (Paris, 1954).

*R. W. Kern*

Related entries: CARLOS IV; ENLIGHTENMENT, AGE OF; GODOY, MANUEL; JOVELLANOS, GASPAR MELCHOR DE.

**FOREIGN LEGION** (1920–  ), elite, volunteer professional army constituting a shock force of the Army of Africa. Authorized in Jan. 1920, the first Spanish Tercio de Extranjeros of what was to become, to its officers and men, simply La Legión, was organized by the dedicated and controversial Lt. Col. José Millán Astray (1879–1954), with the young, highly efficient Maj. Francisco Franco* as second in command. The history of the force was shaped by the personalities of these two officers. Its spirit, and the mystique of the legionnaire, reflect that of the colonel, and its cold efficiency and stern discipline that of the major.

Officers were selected from those who had proven themselves in battle, many having commanded units of the fierce Moroccan Regulares. Training and discipline of a force formed from what might be viewed as adventurers and society's castoffs were harsh, and punishments severe.

Patterned on the French Foreign Legion, its first regiment, the Tercio Gran Capitán, was organized at Dar Riffian, near Ceuta. The term "tercio" was borrowed from the famous formations of the Spanish army of the sixteenth and seventeenth centuries. The tactical forces were three banderas, or battalions, of infantry. Each bandera was made up of two rifle companies, one machine-gun company, and platoons of sappers, transport, and supply. Eventually, additional banderas were added.

Although open to foreigners, the legion was primarily made up of Spaniards. Provided with distinctive uniforms and better pay and rations than the regular army,* the legionnaires formed an army within an army. Millán Astray allowed them to leave their former, often questionable, lives behind, permitting them to establish new identities based on the camaraderie of the legion. He insisted they were the elite, who, through self-denial, suffering, and dedication, stood above the others. They had to face the future with stoicism and, in the process, exhibit the military virtues of obedience and bravery with a fierce combative spirit that expressed a contempt for death. In their music, the legionnaires became "El novio de la muerte" ("Death's Bridegroom"). The illogical cry "¡Viva la muerte!" (Long Live Death!) carried them into battle against impossible odds. Millán Astray's own terrible, mutilating wounds stood as evidence of his belief in the creed he established for the legion. The mystique established, the legion acquired throughout its history a reputation not only for cold military professionalism, but also for brutality.

Never a very large force, the banderas of the legion fought 845 engagements between 1920 and 1927. In these conflicts, they counted 8,381 casualties, with some 2,000 dead. The figures include the loss of 45 percent of their officers.

In 1934, banderas led by Lt. Col. Juan de Yagüe Blanco (1891–1952) assisted in suppressing the revolt in Asturias.* The severity of the action added to the legion's reputation for brutality and earned the colonel the sobriquet the Hyena of Asturias.

In 1936, the legion included the First Legion, stationed at Melilla, with three banderas of four companies each; and the Second Legion, of the same strength, in Ceuta. The total force was 3,758 highly trained and well-equipped professionals.

With the uprising, Colonel Yagüe assumed command, and the banderas cast for the nationalists. The Fifth Bandera began flying to Spain on 20 July. In Seville, the banderas formed small battle columns, along with tabores of Moorish Regulares, for the bitter drive on Madrid. Others soon followed. Although vastly outnumbered, the legionnaires shattered the militias being deployed before them, but they suffered in the process. One of the most bitter early engagements was the storming of the walls of Badajoz. Here, one company was decimated charging into fortified machine guns.

The battle columns fought on to Talavera de la Reina, Maqueda, and then into the streets of Toledo to relieve the besieged forces in the Alcázar. They battled to Madrid with their thinned ranks to be stalled by greatly superior forces in the bloody battles for the Casa de Campo, University City, and Carabanchel.

Many banderas of the legion suffered badly and had to be pulled from the line. At the same time, recruitment was undertaken to provide replacements and form new banderas at Talavera de la Reina. Before the end of the civil war, twelve additional banderas of four companies each (seven through eighteen) were committed to the nationalist assault divisions. Here, along with the tabores of Moroccans, they formed the shock forces. Many files in the ranks of replacements and new banderas were made up of captured Popular Front troops. These included anarchists and communists.

During the civil war, the legion had 37,393 casualties. Of these, 7,645 were killed, including 924 officers. Additional losses accrued in the fighting in Sidi Ifni (1957–1958). From its founding through 1958, the total losses of the legion were 9,713 dead, 35,188 wounded, and 1,062 missing. The losses of the Third Legion in the Western Sahara from 1970 to 1976 are not available.

Today, there are banderas manning posts at Melilla and Ceuta. They still constitute a highly trained and disciplined force.

For additional information, see Estado Mayor Central, *La legión española: Cincuenta años de historia*, 2 vols. (Madrid, 1970–1973); F. Franco, *Marruecos, diario de una bandera* (Madrid, 1922); F. Gómez de Travecedo, *La legión española* (Madrid, 1958); and A. Manuel, *Historia militar de la guerra de España*, 3 vols. (Madrid, 1969).

*R. L. Proctor*

*Related entries:* ARMY; MOROCCO.

**FORTUNY Y MARSAL, MARIANO** (1838–1874), realist painter. The son of a carpenter, Fortuny was born in Reus, Tarragona, on 11 June 1838. At fourteen, he began his art studies in Barcelona, receiving his first formal commission two years later in 1854. Winning the Rome Prize in 1857 took him to Italy for the traditional two-year stay. Fortuny's first submission to the Barcelona Salon, in 1859, was executed in Rome.

Commissioned to serve as an official war artist during the Spanish-Moroccan conflict (1859–1860), Fortuny spent two months during 1860 in north Africa recording the exploits of the Catalan corps. After his return to Rome, his work focused on oriental themes, possibly reinforced by a brief visit to Morocco* in 1862. Orientalism made Fortuny's career; the combination of precise painting with exotic subject matter appealed greatly to the buying public.

In 1866, Fortuny went to Paris, where he met Jean Louis Ernest Meissonnier (1815–1891), the reigning artist of Parisian society and salon. Possibly under Meissonnier's influence, he began to paint contemporary themes, although using eighteenth-century settings and costume; these works were part of the rococo revival then in vogue. The rococo pieces, like the orientalist subjects, were immensely popular. Foutuny continued to execute both, along with the occasional commission for religious pictures.

Fortuny married Cecilia de Madrazo, the daughter of the Spanish court painter, Federico de Madrazo,* in 1867. Though living in Rome, the couple traveled to Madrid, Granada, Seville, France,* Morocco, and Britain,* returning to Rome in 1872. Fortuny died of malaria there on 21 Nov. 1874.

Fortuny is best known for his oils and watercolors, works small and intimate, yet filled with detail and suffused with light. He also won renown as an etcher in the tradition of Francisco de Goya,* whose work he had studied in the late 1860s in Spain. Given the brevity of his life, his impact on his contemporaries and successors was substantial.

For additional information, see R. Rosenblum and H. W. Janson, *19th-Century Art*, (New York, 1984).

*S. Benforado*

**FRAGA IRIBARNE, MANUEL** (1922– ), contemporary politician. Manuel Fraga was born in Villalba, Lugo, on 23 Nov. 1922. He studied at Santiago and Madrid,* and subsequently taught politics and law at Valencia* from 1945 to 1948, before joining the faculty of the University of Madrid, while also serving in the diplomatic corps. He headed the Institute of Hispanic Culture from 1951 to 1955 and then served as general secretary of the National Educational Ministry until he was made minister of information and tourism in 1962 at a time when Gen. Francisco Franco* faced new sources of discontent.

The government role of Fraga from 1962 to 1969 was more symbolic than innovative. A member of a new post–civil war generation, not closely associated with the Falange* or army* and hostile to the Opus Dei* after the Matesa scandal in 1969, he lacked the backing to be completely independent; but his efforts to modernize the tourist industry and the media (through the press law of 1966) were spectacular, although eventually Franco came to believe he had gone too far and dismissed him. Nevertheless, he became a leading candidate to take over the reins of power in the twilight years of Francoism.

Fraga's succession, however, never came. After Franco's death in 1975, Fraga joined the cabinet of Carlos Arias Navarro (1908– ) on 13 Dec. 1975 as deputy prime minister for political affairs. His work put him in charge of the ministry of the interior at a delicate moment when the transition from dictatorship to democracy, plagued by problems with Basque Homeland and Freedom* (ETA) and the Left, made his liberalism seem conservative in these changed circumstances, and probably ruined his chances to succeed the unpopular Arias Navarro. Fraga resigned when Adolfo Suárez* was made premier in July 1976, and he created his own Alianza Popular party in 1977. Fraga and Suárez resembled each other politically in hoping to salvage something of Franco's regime, but the new premier had the advantage of a much lower political profile. In the elections of 1977, the Popular Alliance won only sixteen seats, not a good showing compared to Suárez's party or the Socialist party* (PSOE), and although he changed the name of his party to the Democratic Coalition in the parliamentary elections of 1 Mar. 1979, it won only nine seats, which fell to two in the elections of 1982. Fraga has continued to play a political role, but as modern issues have continued to emerge in the 1980s, his opposition to such changes as abortion has clearly marked him as a moderate conservative with uncertain chances in the regime of Juan Carlos I.*

For additional information, see E. R. Arango, *Spain from Repression to Renewal* (Boulder, 1985); Manuel Fraga Iribarne, *Después de la Constitución y hacia los años 80* (Barcelona, 1979), and *El debate naciónal* (Barcelona, 1981); and C. Sentis, *Manuel Fraga Iribarne* (Madrid, 1979).

R. W. Kern

*Related entries:* GONZÁLEZ, FELIPE; JUAN CARLOS I; SUÁREZ, ADOLFO.

**FRANCE,** relations with Spain. France, which extends across Spain's entire northern frontier, has played a major role in the diplomacy of Iberia since the time of Charlemagne. Its importance was never greater than in the eighteenth century, when the Bourbons controlled both countries. Diplomatic realism forced a token separation after the Grand Alliance defeated Louis XIV (1638–1715) and his grandson, Felipe V,* in 1713, but French advisors had accompanied Felipe to Spain, and Anne Marie de la Trémouille (1642–1722), princess of Ursinos, the French wife of a Spanish grandee, tried to make the Spanish court forget the Hapsburg anti-French antagonism of the sixteenth and seventeenth centuries.

Felipe's marriage to Isabel Farnesio (1692–1766) in 1714 initially had the opposite effect; her search to find Italian titles for her sons led to war in Sicily in 1718 between Spain and France. A marriage alliance between the two in 1720 failed four years later, when Felipe's older son, Luis I (1707–1724), died suddenly. Subsequent Spanish-Austrian cooperation in Italy* again created hostilities with France and Britain,* with the French campaigning actively during 1727 in Italy. France was excluded from the settlements of 1729–1731 because it still coveted northern Italy, but diplomatic isolation forced it in 1733 to sign the Treaty of the Escorial, which allied France and Spain to recover Gibraltar* from Britain and settle the Italian question.

This first Bourbon Family Compact, as it was called, had far-reaching consequences. The French briefly aided Spain in the Anglo-Spanish War.* Spain, in turn, was persuaded by the French to join the War of the Austrian Succession (1740–1748), but when Britain sent a fleet against the Spanish-ruled Kingdom of the Two Sicilies, France failed to come to their aid. A new pact, the Treaty of Fontainebleau, had to be signed on 23 Oct. 1743 before Spain received greater cooperation from France in Italy; an Austrian defeat was finally achieved in late 1745. France gained the right to contest Britain for control of Minorca, which did not occur until 1756.

Francophilia grew in Spain during the reign of Carlos III.* Of his advisors, the marqués de Grimaldi and the conde de Aranda* were the most strongly pro-French. On 15 Aug. 1761, Carlos himself took a prominent role in signing the third Bourbon Family Pact which guaranteed military support if either country were attacked by a third party. The Spanish-British campaigns of the Seven Years' War* in 1762 led to the temporary British occupation of Manila and Havana and forced Spain to invoke the treaty first. French support, however, was handicapped by financial difficulties and failed to preserve Canada. The Peace of Paris on 10 Feb. 1763 gave Louisiana to Spain for safekeeping, while Spain gave France Dominica and Fernando Poo in 1778. France, in turn, acquired Spanish assistance in the War of American Independence from 1779 to 1783, which resulted in the Spanish recapture of Florida and Minorca. At the same time, French Enlightenment* thought was having its impact on Spain as well.

The small Spanish profit in its political relations with France soon was lost in the era of the French Revolution. Carlos IV* not only was far weaker than his father, but also faced far greater diplomatic and military changes—opportunities he bungled by claiming the French throne after the execution of Louis XVI (1754–1793) and entrusting royal government to Manuel Godoy,* a guardsman turned lover of the queen, María Luisa de Parma (1751–1819), and would-be prince in his own right. Godoy managed to blunt the attack of French revolutionaries in Catalonia* in 1793–1794, and he obtained the title "Prince of Peace" for his negotiations at the Treaty of Basle in 1795, but his drift toward Napoleon Bonaparte (1769–1821) infuriated patriots like José Moñino, the conde de Floridablanca,* and led to a disastrous involvement with Bonapartism against Britain. In 1807, Godoy and Bonaparte partitioned Portugal* between themselves. When Fernando VII* rose against Godoy in Mar. 1808, France was forced to intervene to protect its Spanish interests. In fewer than two months, Napoleon managed to force both Carlos and Fernando to abdicate, but instead of honoring his commitments to Godoy, Napoleon named his brother Joseph king of Spain (José I*).

This Napoleonic interregnum in Spain lasted from 1808 to late 1813. French-supporters, called afrancesados, drew up Spain's first constitution at Bayonne, but Floridablanca and guerrilla supporters who had defeated the French at the battle of Bailén on 21 July 1808 wrote the Constitution of 1812 at Cadiz, which found much greater support. Napoleon's visit to Spain in Nov. and Dec. 1808 and his eight decrees abolishing the Inquisition and initiating land reforms were not enough to secure the throne for Joseph, who as José I* could never overcome economic difficulties long enough to pursue reform or the war against the guerrillas and the British. Despite able leadership by Mars. Nicolas Jean de Dieu Soult (1769–1851), André Masséna, and Auguste de Marmont, the French retreated across the border to France on 7 Oct. 1813.

The later nineteenth-century history of French-Spanish relations was much more episodic; Spain was mostly a stage set for French involvement based on other considerations. Ironically, another French army, whose units were largely commanded by Napoleon's former generals, intervened in Spain in April 1823, just a decade after the French withdrawal. This time, the army intervened on behalf of a Bourbon, Fernando VII, and with the approbation of most of the elements of Spanish society that had fought against Napoleon.

The government of Louis XVIII (1755–1824) had some natural interest in saving Fernando from the hands of the liberals, thereby guaranteeing France's western frontier and eliminating a political experiment that might inspire French radicals at home. The French government won one diplomatic success: it succeeded in acting independently while assuring that it had the support of the Congress of Vienna powers (only Britain looked askance). The action was a military success as well; it was more a promenade than a war, though the assault on Trocadero resembled a real battle closely enough to lend its name to some Parisian real estate. The only failure of the French commander, the Duke of Angoulême (1775–1844), was in restraining the royalists from wreaking vengeance on the Spanish liberals. This restoration in Spain helped consolidate the restoration in France, at least temporarily, by gaining the support of an army only too happy to see action.

A second, more personal, involvement was the marriage in 1846 of Louis Philippe's son, Antonio of Orléans (1824–1890), the duke of Montpensier, to Luisa Fernanda, the sister of Isabel II.* It came too late to aid the Orléans dynasty in France, and Montpensier, a born adventurer who in 1870 ruined his own slim chance of taking the Spanish throne by killing another candidate in a duel—and who soon afterward was the rumored assassin of Juan Prim y Prats,* one of the generals responsible for the overthrow of Isabel II—obviously did nothing to further relations with France. Only the use by Gen. Leopoldo O'Donnell* of an adventuresome foreign policy to obscure internal corruption during his cabinet from 1858 to 1863 led to French-Spanish cooperation in Mexico (1861–1862) and in the Far East (1861), neither very long-lasting and really little more than adventures.

The most significant event in French-Spanish relations had its most important ramifications in the very balance of forces in Europe. The Hohenzollern candidacy to fill the Spanish throne Isabel II vacated in 1868 posed legitimate security concerns for France. Unwilling to leave well enough alone and graciously accept the withdrawal of the candidacy, the beleaguered French regime gave Otto von Bismarck (1815–1896) the opportunity to have the war he wanted under the best possible circumstances for Prussia. French defeat and the beginning of German dominance on the continent were the result.

There was episodic cultural involvement between France and Spain as well. Spain, seemingly so geographically close, was far removed from France, and not only because of bad roads. It was perceived as different and exotic, qualities that attracted French romantics such as Victor Hugo (1802–1885) and Théophile Gautier (1811–1872). Prosper Merimée's (1803–1870) *Carmen*, set to music by Georges Bizet (1838–1875) in 1875, became the epitome of Spain for many audiences.

Economically, however, French investment in Spain became substantial around midcentury. Railways, Catalan textile mills, and Asturian mines revived links between the two countries that marriage alliances and dynastic policies had failed to restore. Marie Edmé Patrice de MacMahon (1808–1893), marshal of France, and Antonio Cánovas del Castillo* developed a political friendship from their shared conservatism during Cánovas's exile in Paris in the early 1870s. MacMahon's defeat and the rise of radical French republicanism did not seem to alienate Cánovas's conservative regime from continuing its cooperation with France in the Mediterranean for economic gain.

Morocco* was a special case in point. The africanismo interests of Madrid for a new empire converged with the obvious power of Paris in Africa. A partition of Morocco was first discussed in 1902, but the zones of influence were not formally created until 3 Oct. 1904, with Spain controlling the upper one-third of the country. Kaiser William II's (1859–1941) visit to Tangier in Mar. 1905 and the German gunboat *Panther*'s stop at Agadir in July 1911 provided outside pressure that cemented the relationship. The Treaty of Algeciras in Jan. 1906 and the Treaty of Fez in Mar. 1912 worked out the responsibilities of the two powers in the protectorate, the high point of their cooperation.

Spanish neutrality in World War I* irritated the French, who did not cooperate with Spain in Morocco until the Anwal* disaster threatened European prestige after 1920. The dictatorship of Gen. Miguel Primo de Rivera* quarreled with France over anarchist exile raids on the Pyrenees border and over an alleged assassination plot in 1925 to kill king Alfonso XIII* while he was on a state visit to Paris. Even Manuel Azaña* rebuffed French efforts at collective security against Germany* when the French premier, Edouard Herriot (1872–1957), visited Madrid in Nov. 1932, early in the Spanish Second Republic. Spain and France simply were too nationally self-absorbed to be close during this period, and even the emergence in 1936 of Popular Front governments in both countries helped only to a limited extent. After the Spanish Civil War* began in July 1936, the French premier, Léon Blum (1872–1950), made efforts to provide aid to the republic, but was stymied by English opposition as well as by the Radical party's unwillingness within his own governing coalition. The French role in the Non-Intervention Committee delighted the nationalists, but infuriated republicans. Nevertheless, the French did not recognize Gen. Francisco Franco* until very late in the civil war, and weapons crossed the border to the republicans without much difficulty in 1938. The republican cause was valorized by such French intellectuals as André Malraux (1901–1976) in *L'Espror* (1937).

The same ambiguity continued during World War II.* Franco accepted a number of French exiles in flight from the German occupation. The Vichy government, surprisingly, while imprisoning and executing many Spanish exiles, returned very few of the numerous Spanish refugee population in France, and Franco did not press—the jails were crowded enough already. Certainly the most significant diplomatic act Franco took at this time was his recognition on 3 Mar. 1943 of Gen. Charles de Gaulle (1890–1970) and the Free French movement, the first step in his abandonment of the Axis powers.

Immediately after the war, however, French public opinion strongly opposed Franco and his authoritarian state. In Dec. 1945, with Soviet support, France even unsuccessfully proposed a United Nations invasion of Spain. The Pyrenees border was unilaterally closed on 1 Mar. 1946, several weeks after the United Nations had barred Spain from international participation, and it was not reopened until 10 Feb. 1948. Spanish exiles played an important role in French politics during this period, and anti-Franco opposition was noticeable for many years.

Discord produced by Morocco further marred Hispano-French relations in the 1950s. The French grant of independence to Morocco in Mar. 1956 came after six years of growing conflict between the two occupying European powers, with each responsible for encouraging Arab nationalism in the other's zone. Franco was unable to persuade the French premier, Guy Mollet (1905–1975), from restoring Mohammed V Ben Yusef (1909–1961) and as a consequence, had to moderate his own authoritarian attitude toward Morocco. This change of colonial policy became a signal to Spanish society that the Caudillo was no longer so all powerful. Demonstrations by university students and strikes by illegal unions dominated the late 1950s as the regime entered its final stages.

Although relations improved slightly, they were never warm during the Franco period. The French opposed Spanish entry into the Common Market, both out of distaste for the Franco system and concern about competition from Spanish agriculture. The accession of democracy in Spain led to better relations, but not radical change. Valéry Giscard d'Estaing (1926– ) put a hold on the Spanish application for European Economic Community membership because of fears as to how it would affect the Community's agricultural policies. France continued to provide a discreet sanctuary for Basque Homeland and Freedom* (Euzkadi ta Askatasuna, ETA) terrorists, even though they were now attacking a democracy.

The arrival of socialists François Mitterand (1916– ) and Felipe González* in power marked a change. France ended its opposition to Spanish entry into the Common Market and extradited several ETA terrorists to Spain. Spain increased its purchase of arms from France. Was this perhaps a fourth family compact, with socialists substituting for Bourbons?

For additional information, see R. Cameron, *France and the Economic Development of Europe 1800–1914* (Princeton, 1961); and J. Cortada, ed., *Spain in the Twentieth-Century World: Essays on Spanish Diplomacy, 1898–1978* (Westport, 1980).

*R. W. Kern and S. P. Kramer*

**FRANCO BAHAMONDE, FRANCISCO** (1892–1975), Generalissimo of the Spanish armed forces and authoritarian chief of state in Spain from 1936–1939 until his death. The most dominant figure in Spanish history since the sixteenth century, Franco was born on 4 Dec. 1892, the second of four children of a senior naval administrative officer and descended from a long line of naval officers stationed in Andalusia* and in El Ferrol, his birthplace. Unable to gain entrance to the naval academy, Franco graduated from the infantry academy at Toledo in 1910, and soon volunteered for service in Morocco.* There he quickly won a reputation for courage, coolness under fire, leadership ability, and strict professionalism. Through combat duty he gained rapid promotion until being seriously wounded on 29 June 1916, and reached the rank of major before his twenty-fourth birthday. After a tour in command of an infantry unit at Oviedo, Franco returned to Morocco in 1920, to help organize the elite new Spanish Legion, becoming its second commander-in-chief after his predecessor was killed in action. In 1922, he published a book, *Diario de una Bandera*, on military experiences in the Protectorate. Franco also played a major role in the decisive Moroccan campaigns of 1924–1926 that broke the back of the native insurgency and at barely thirty-three was promoted to brigadier, reportedly the youngest general in any European army of that time.

Franco was married in 1923 to Carmen Polo y Martínez Valdés (1902–1987), the twenty-one-year-old daughter of a wealthy Asturian family. This was a love match pursued successfully over several years against the initially strenuous objection of the bride's father and proved a conventionally happy and successful marriage. One daughter, Carmen (or Carmencita), was born in 1927.

After Franco served briefly as head of an infantry brigade in Madrid,* his prestige and achievements won him appointment as the first commandant of the new General Military Academy, opened at Saragossa in 1928. Franco held definite monarchist convictions throughout his life and was strongly identified with the monarchy during the final phase of the reign of Alfonso XIII.* Leaders of the Second Republic* immediately closed the new academy in 1931 and left Franco without assignment for nearly a year. Early in 1932, he was named commander of the garrison at La Corunna and one year later of that of the Balearic Islands.*

Though Franco had not been ostracized by the new regime, he was clearly identified with the political right as a monarchist and nationalist conservative. The political victory of the center-right in Oct. 1933 therefore restored him fully to favor, his brother-in-law Ramón Serrano Suñer* being a leader of the Confederación Española de Derechas Autónomas (CEDA), the largest party in the Cortes. When the revolutionary insurrection of the Worker Alliance broke out in Oct. 1934, Franco was quickly appointed special advisor to the minister of war to help coordinate suppression of the revolt. He was subsequently named commander-in-chief in Morocco and then in May 1935 chief of the general staff when José María Gil Robles (1898– ), the main CEDA leader, became minister of war. During 1935, Franco worked to improve the readiness of the army and to counter liberal and leftist influence in the officer corps. He refused, however, to take any initiative either in Dec. 1935 (when the existing center-right parliament was bypassed in formation of a new cabinet, preparatory to its dissolution) or in Feb. 1936, when the Popular Front won new elections. Though extreme rightists urged military action, Franco insisted that the army was far from united politically and could only act on orders from its constitutional superiors.

When the left republicans returned to power, most senior commands were reassigned, and Franco was soon posted to the Canary Islands,* with the intention of removing him from any place of central influence. Though in contact with military conspirators from Mar. 1936 on, he refused to commit himself categorically to any specific plan for revolt, contending that the situation was too uncertain. He finally arranged to take command of the key Moroccan combat units in connection with the central conspiracy prepared by Gen. Emilio Mola,* but only committed himself to this plan definitively after the assassination of José Calvo Sotelo on 13 July, which largely completed the nation's political polarization.

Franco was flown to Tetuan, capital of the Moroccan Protectorate, on 19 July, to assume command there at the beginning of the Spanish Civil War.* During the next weeks, he labored to transport key combat units to the peninsula and initiate contacts with Rome and Berlin for foreign military assistance. His advance from southwestern Spain toward Madrid began on 3 Aug., but developed somewhat slowly due to limited manpower and resources, so that the final drive on Madrid itself only commenced in October.

The nationalist military movement was led by a Junta de Defensa Nacional formed on 26 July, and nominally headed by the senior rebel general, Miguel Cabanellas (1872–1938). By mid-September, several top rebel commanders became concerned to designate a commander-in-chief to coordinate the climactic battle of Madrid, achievement of a final victory, and the founding of a new government. The initiative was seized especially by Gen. Alfredo Kindelán (1879–1963), head of the air force on the southern front, and several other monarchist generals. The only genuine candidate was Franco, most nationalist commanders tacitly agreeing that he was their most prestigious and effective general. Though Franco himself seems to have made no overt move for self-advancement, his candidacy was promoted by a small group of personal associates and backers, and particularly by monarchists, who sought to have a monarchist made commander-in-chief so as to guarantee restoration of the crown after victory.

Members of the nationalist junta met twice at Salamanca in the second half of Sept. 1936, agreeing upon the principle of the mando único and also upon

the designation of Franco as commander-in-chief and head of the new government. Apparently the only vote not cast for Franco was that of Cabanellas, who
abstained. On 30 Sept., Franco was officially proclaimed chief of state (not
simply interim chief of government or prime minister) of the new regime, and
formally invested with power in a ceremony at Burgos on 1 Oct.

In his inaugural speech, Franco declared that his "hand would not tremble"
until he had achieved victory, rebuilt Spain, and restored it to the status of olden
times. In later years, as Franco's regime stretched on through its fourth decade,
he would be accused of having no real ideology beyond the desire to maintain
his personal power at all costs. However that may have been, Franco always
possessed a fundamental set of political principles which did not change significantly from the 1920s until his death half a century later. He was determined
to create a new authoritarian system on generally corporative principles that
would eliminate political parties and all the forces of liberalism and the left. He
was a staunch nationalist in all major policy areas and for some time hoped to
expand Spanish imperialism as well. In spiritual affairs he was a firm and, in
his own way, devout Catholic, who hoped to preside over the re-Catholicization
of Spain with a broad program of cultural traditionalism. In economic policy,
he was a modernizer, hoping to develop a broad and prosperous national industrial
system, stimulated and guided by nationalist priorities and authoritarian corporatist institutions.

A defender of the Gen. Miguel Primo de Rivera* regime of the 1920s, Franco
was equally concerned to avoid what he termed "el error Primo de Rivera,"
the mistake of having failed to organize a fully structured and institutionalized
new system. During the civil war, he had to devote most of his time to military
affairs, an enterprise in which he was ultimately completely successful, and only
began partially to develop a new political system in 1937. His public statements
made it clear that the new regime drew inspiration from counterparts in Italy,*
Portugal,* and Germany* and would develop a "totalitarian" system. For this
it would need a formal state party, created by the official fusion and incorporation
of the fascist Falange and traditionalist Carlists into the new Falange Española
Tradicionalista (FET)* de las Juntas de Ofensiva Nacional-Sindicalista in Apr.
1937. At the same time, he made it clear that the adoption of the official program
of the Falange marked a beginning, not an end, and would be eclectically
amended or expanded as conditions warranted. Supporters from all other political
groups, either outlawed or dissolved, were urged to join the amorphous new
state party. Franco carefully avoided use of the term "fascist," though it was
commonly employed by some other nationalists. Moreover, he insisted that
totalitarianism was merely part of the Spanish tradition, supposedly having been
invented by the Catholic monarchs in the fifteenth century. He seemed to take
totalitarianism as a kind of code word for authority and unity, never proposing
to take control of all Spanish institutions.

Franco named his first regular council of ministers on 30 Jan. 1938, from
which point his regime began to take clearer shape. Even so, administration

remained geographically dispersed, various ministries being located in different northern provincial capitals. Economic policy was developed ad hoc, though with considerable success, and the new state syndical system was not truly organized until after the end of the war. The entire nationalist zone had lain juridically under martial law from the beginning of the conflict, and this did not change until 1948, but in Feb. 1937, Franco moved to centralize and moderate the military repression, which was less extreme in the last two years of the war.

Franco's diplomacy during the civil war was shrewdly conceived and quite effective. He established close enough ties with Rome and Berlin to guarantee adequate military assistance throughout the war, without submitting to the degree of control exercised by Soviet representatives and advisors over aspects of republican policy. With his adversaries he was implacable, rejecting all suggestions of mediation or compromise, and finally won complete victory on 1 Apr. 1939.

The terms of his triumph made Franco, at least for the next few years, the most absolute and powerful ruler in Spanish history. He was bound by few of the traditional laws, regulations, and customs that had limited the authority of sixteenth-century kings, while having at his disposal the powers and instruments of penetration of a twentieth-century dictatorship. Joseph Stalin (1879–1953), Benito Mussolini (1883–1945), and Adolf Hitler (1889–1945) governed theoretically in association with constitutional structures and parliaments of a sort, but even in theory such things did not at first exist in Spain.

Franco reorganized his cabinet in Aug. 1939, maintaining the semifascist orientation of the civil war, with ministries divided among the various forces that had composed the nationalist movement, but the sudden outbreak of general war in Europe dominated much of his government's activity in the years that followed. The regime remained officially neutral during the first phase, though with some tilt toward Germany. The tilt became complete after the fall of France,* when, at Mussolini's request, Franco followed the Duce's example in declaring a new policy of nonbelligerence that indicated clear preference for the Axis. In the summer of 1940, Franco was in fact eager to enter the war on Hitler's side, but shrewdly perceived that this would not be in Spain's interest unless there existed a clear prior understanding (at a time when Spanish entrance might still have some value in Hitler's eyes) guaranteeing broad expansion of the Spanish empire in northwest Africa as well as extensive economic assistance. In June-July 1940, however, Hitler showed no interest in encouraging Spanish war entry.

This indifference soon changed, however, as Hitler became increasingly concerned to seal off Britain's position in the Mediterranean. From Sept. 1940 through the winter of 1941, the German government placed increasing pressure on Madrid to declare war, but offered little in the way of concrete inducement to do so. Hitler's main consideration was that, after Italy, his principal associate in Western Europe was Vichy France, which he could not afford to alienate through major colonial transfers to Spain. Until Oct. 1940, Franco believed that these complications might soon be worked out, but after his famous meeting that month with Hitler at Hendaye, he came to realize that Germany expected Spain to enter the war virtually without conditions. From that point, the Spanish Caudillo became increasingly reluctant, adopting a stubborn and firmly calculated policy of steady delaying tactics without ever directly rejecting German overtures. As late as 1941, Franco might have been willing to join the conflict had Hitler met his price, but as the war became increasingly costly and complicated, Franco grew steadily more reluctant. Only the invasion of the Soviet Union roused his enthusiasm, but there too he refused to become officially involved, sending only the Blue Division* of volunteers to fight beside the Germans.

Though Franco was not fully convinced that Hitler would lose the war until mid-1944, his policy became increasingly circumspect from the summer of 1942. Before the end of that year, a process of ideological differentiation and even of partial defascistization had begun in Madrid, as the doctrine of totalitarianism was rejected and plans were announced for a new corporative Cortes in place of the old elected parliament. Winston Churchill (1874–1965) and Franklin Delano Roosevelt (1882–1945) both assured Franco that the Allies had no intentions of intervening in Spain so long as Madrid remained formally uninvolved, and in Oct. 1943 Franco resumed a policy of official neutrality. From that time, however, Allied pressure steadily mounted against Madrid. On 1 May 1944, Franco agreed to accept a series of Allied diplomatic and economic demands, and de-emphasized relations with Germany. During the final year of the war, Spain was drawn further into the orbit of Allied activity, though the government and press continued to reveal sympathy for Germany until the end.

After the close of the international conflict, Allied policy became much more hostile. By 1946, all major governments had withdrawn their ambassadors from Madrid, and France officially closed its borders with Spain, while the new United Nations declared the Franco regime an international outcast. Ostracism, which persisted through 1948, was accompanied by the only significant guerrilla insurgency from the Left which Franco ever had to face.

As early as 1943–1944, Franco began to realize that his regime would have to undergo some sort of formalistic metamorphosis to survive German defeat. In 1945, it was redefined as a Catholic corporatist system of "organic democracy." A Fuero de los Españoles (Spanish Bill of Rights) was introduced in July 1945, and in the new cabinet which took office that month Falangists were downgraded in favor of Catholic personnel. A Law of Referendum was passed the following year, and in 1947, the regime was theoretically legitimized as a monarchy through a new law of succession. Overwhelmingly approved by official plebiscite, this made Franco regent for life—a sort of uncrowned king—with the right freely to designate his successor from among members of the royal family.

The development of the cold war put an end to most aspects of ostracism against the regime in Western Europe. Though Franco would never be accepted as legitimate by democratic opinion abroad, the United Nations rescinded its ban in Nov. 1950, and the regime was eventually admitted to the international organization six years later. The partial rehabilitation of Franco was completed in 1953, when the regime signed an official concordat with the Vatican and a ten-year pact with the United States,* providing for military and economic assistance and the construction of American military bases in Spain.

The decade of the 1950s was the most quiet and secure in the history of Franco's regime. The leftist and republican opposition had largely faded away, while the domestic economy had begun to expand rapidly. Franco dominated relations with don Juan (1913– ), legal heir to the throne, and gained his permission to have the latter's own son and heir, young Prince Juan Carlos,* educated within Spain. The final year of the decade saw the opening in 1959 of Franco's grandiose personal mausoleum and monument to the civil war dead, the Valley of the Fallen, on 1 Apr. (the twentieth anniversary of the end of the war), and ended in Dec. with the personal visit of the American Pres., Dwight D. Eisenhower (1890–1969), to Madrid. His only daughter, Carmencita, married the marqués de Villaverde (1934– ), an aristocratic playboy also trained as a professional surgeon, in 1950. They gave Franco seven grandchildren, though he was never pleased with his superficial son-in-law. The family circle always remained comparatively narrow, and the dictator's main diversion, especially during the 1950s, was a numerous series of hunting trips, some quite strenuous, which also became social and political occasions. On one of these, in 1961, Franco suffered his only accident, when a cartridge misfired in his hunting rifle, seriously injuring his left hand. In the early 1960s, Franco developed Parkinson's disease, from which he suffered with increasing severity in his remaining years. During the latter phase, he became much addicted to bullfights and soccer and boxing matches on television, though he continued to hunt and fish and also to make watercolor drawings.

The last major turning point in the regime occurred between 1956 and 1959. After incidents in the universities indicated that the Falange had lost control of university youth, Franco appointed a new secretary-general for the state party. He was allowed to prepare drafts of new laws that would once more give the Falange a major and continuing place in Franco's regime. Opposition from all other groups led him to quash this legislation at the beginning of 1957. He then appointed a new cabinet in which the chief economics ministries were held by members of the Opus Dei.* Since the state was facing a severe financial crisis, the new ministers prepared reforms to liberalize many economic regulations and open Spain to the international market. Franco had grave misgivings, for his nationalism and traditionalism encouraged him to separate Spain as much as possible from the world of Western liberalism and materialism. Only the government's dire financial straits and an appeal to his patriotism led him to approve the Stabilization Plan of July 1959.

The new policy was soon enormously successful, but it changed the direction of the last period of the regime. Thenceforth it became more than ever a "developing dictatorship," undergoing further categorical defascistization and ignoring political indoctrination and mobilization almost altogether. Under this "bureaucratic authoritarianism" without new politicalization, social and economic structures were rapidly transformed, and Spanish people imbibed the common materialism, secularism, and cultural modernism of Western Europe. Thus, by the time that Franco died, the old predominantly rural, conservative, and Catholic society that had carried him to power in the civil war had ceased to exist, and his regime had outlived its own social and cultural basis.

Franco's energy and leadership declined during the 1960s, yet at first his government was not challenged. Indeed, the opposition had long accepted the fact that basic political change would occur only after his death, and the figure of Franco himself had gained a measure of respect and even of legitimacy among a majority of Spaniards, who "waited without haste" for the end of the regime. The government itself emphasized material achievement and growing affluence, hoping that this would divert interest from political change.

By the mid-1960s, Franco's cabinet ministers were beginning to look toward the future, encouraging moderate reforms and the nomination of a royal successor to ensure the stability of Spanish institutions. In 1966, censorship was greatly moderated, and a new organic law attempted to harmonize and update the regime's major legislative statutes. General policy and police restrictions became increasingly moderate, while growing signs of opposition appeared among urban workers, students, leftist groups, regionalists, and even among sectors of the clergy. Franco professed to be unalarmed, and was finally prevailed upon to recognize the thirty-one-year-old Prince Juan Carlos, in July 1969, as his successor and future king of Spain.

During five of the first six years of his regime, Franco had relied especially on his brother-in-law Ramón Serrano Suñer as his chief political advisor. After 1942, he came to depend increasingly on Capt. (later Adm.) Luis Carrero Blanco (1903–1973), the subsecretary of the presidency of government, as his main assistant. Carrero Blanco became the nearest thing to a political alter ego that Franco ever had. In June 1973, after he himself had already turned eighty, Franco named Carrero Blanco president of the government, the first prime minister other than Franco himself in the history of the regime.

The Law of Succession and other fundamental laws were so designed that it would not be easy for Franco's successor to name a new prime minister of his own, and thus Franco was depending on the younger Carrero to ensure continuity of the regime even after his death. The assassination of Carrero Blanco, on 20 Dec. 1973, not merely removed Franco's prime minister, but also the prime guarantor of the future of his system. It was a severe blow to the decrepit, ailing octogenarian, who agonized for days before appointing Carlos Arias Navarro,* outgoing interior minister, as the new president of government.

During the final phase of Franco's life, his government became increasingly isolated. Carlos Arias Navarro's cabinet represented not the historic "families" of the regime—which had largely disappeared—but elements from the hard-core state bureaucracy itself. Though it announced a number of noteworthy reforms, including new multiple "political associations," these largely remained unimplemented, while political opposition and strikes expanded rapidly.

The last drama of Franco's long career began in Sept. 1975, with the execution of five political assassins convicted of the killing of policemen. These executions received an extraordinary volume of international publicity and touched off a series of major demonstrations, sometimes even riots, in major European capitals. Franco once more defied his foes and refused to deviate from his policy, but the strain of these events probably helped to precipitate his final illness in Oct. 1975. Following an initial heart attack, his condition steadily worsened and grew increasingly complicated, as one grave physical malady followed another. He underwent three operations and by the first week in Nov., was being kept alive only by elaborate artificial procedures. After life-support systems were withdrawn, he died just short of his eighty-third birthday on 20 Nov. 1975 (also the thirty-ninth anniversary of the execution of José Antonio Primo de Rivera* by the republicans).

Franco was long considered one of the most successful dictators of the twentieth century simply because of his ability to survive for nearly four decades. Conversely, his long-range plans to create an enduring new authoritarian system and reestablish traditional cultural and spiritual values ended in failure. He was more successful in his other aim of achieving the industrialization and modernization of the Spanish economy, to the extent that some of his foes have feared that he will go down in history as the definitive modernizer of Spain.

Franco displayed undeniable political talent in maintaining the balance and relative unity of the forces supporting his regime and in skillfully adjusting its policy to assure its survival. He also enjoyed good fortune, notably in the fact that during the period in 1940, when he was willing to enter the war on Germany's side, Hitler simply refused to pay his price. Yet even that was not all luck, for unlike Mussolini, Franco placed a definite price on Spanish assistance, and managed thus to retain elements of a rational bargaining position that did not abandon all of Spain's basic interests.

The regime's ultimate success in economic development was eventually its own undoing, for the transformation and modernization of Spain produced a kind of peaceful social cultural revolution that eroded long-term support for the regime itself. Economic modernization could only be completed after the regime abandoned its original model of political economy in 1959, rejecting an extreme form of authoritarian autarky in favor of liberalization and international cooperation. Such success was not due to its original goals and plans so much as to its ability to make creative adjustments to powerful developments which it could not effectively resist.

Franco marked more of an end than of a beginning. His positive historical function was to liquidate some of the problems of the past and close the door on a troubled era of internal conflict, but he could not build the positive institutions of Spain's future.

The ultimate paradox of Franco's career is that although his aim was to prevent the return of multiparty parliamentary democracy to Spain, when he finally died in 1975, he left the country better prepared for democracy than at any point in its history. The democratization of Spain, however, was not the result of Franco's policy itself but of the vast changes that had taken place throughout Spanish society and culture (and to a lesser extent in Western Europe as a whole) since the 1940s, and of the skillful leadership of his successors, combined with the good judgment and discipline of most of the Spanish public.

For additional information, see J.W.D. Trythall, *El Caudillo* (New York, 1970); R. de la Cierva, *Historia del Franquismo*, 2 vols. (Barcelona, 1975–1978), and *Francisco Franco* (Barcelona, 1986); L. Suárez Fernández, *Francisco Franco y su tiempo*, 8 vols. (Madrid, 1984); J. P. Fusi, *Franco: Autoritarismo y poder personal* (Madrid, 1985); and S. G. Payne, *The Franco Regime, 1936–1975* (Madison, 1987).

*S. G. Payne*

*Related entries:* ARMY; SECOND REPUBLIC; SPANISH CIVIL WAR; WORLD WAR II.

# G

GALICIA, northwestern Spain with the modern provinces of Lugo, La Corunna, Pontevedra, and Orense. Pop. (1983 est.) 2,753,836; sq. mi. 11,154. Galicia, a hilly, rocky, occasionally mountainous land flanked by the Atlantic to the west and the Bay of Biscay to the north, has an agrarian economy whose leading products are potatoes, corn, and fish. Since good land is scarce, minifundios are common and have perennially hampered the development of large-scale agriculture. A further problem has been the problem of foros. The church, which once owned much of the land in the region, used the foro to create hereditary leases of its property for a stipulated ground rent, always with the right to sublease, a practice that ultimately led to conflicts within a whole hierarchy of leasers and subleasers. Industry in Galicia has remained even weaker. The large towns of La Corunna, Vigo, and El Ferrol del Caudillo are shipbuilding centers and more recently petroleum refiners, but competition from the nearby Basque Provinces and distance from national markets have limited economic development.

In the past, the early medieval St. James legend made Santiago de Compostela one of Europe's most important cathedral cities, the destination of a pilgrimage route that began in central France. The church's role in the region remained paramount until 1479, when the unification of Castile* and Aragon* incorporated Galicia into Old Castile. Administration in 1495 was put under the Junta del Reino de Galicia, one of the lesser royal subcouncils. The region became a backwater in the sixteenth and seventeenth centuries when the south held the trade monopoly with the Indies. Galicians went to the colonies* as lowly emigrants; "gallego" is still today the colloquial term for a poor immigrant in Argentina and Venezuela. During the reign of Felipe V,* a Galician trading company was created in 1734, but the Atlantic ports of the northwest did not fully benefit from colonial revenues until Carlos III* introduced free trade in 1765, too late to be of significance.

The Bourbon period also witnessed a major Galician land crisis, which has continued to provide its most important historical dynamic in the modern age. Population increases caused commodity prices to rise, making it profitable for the holders of foros (foreros) to sublease to others (subforados), but also encouraging the church to attempt a revocation of foros to regain direct control of its rural properties. By royal decree in 1763, the church lost its case. The foreros won continued possession of their leased lands, but the decree also strengthened subforado rights by creating a noneviction rule and fixing rents. When liberal disentailment* abolished mortmain in 1837, the church's claims were replaced by unprecedented litigiousness between foreros and subforados over the inheritability of their leases and subleases.

By 1863, the middle classes of the Galician towns generally had assumed ownership rights over the former church lands. This was reinforced by the Civil Code of 1889, which determined that no property could be subject to divided control, a stipulation threatening subforados who often had occupied the land for generations. Social conflict continued until the dictatorship of Gen. Miguel Primo de Rivera* decided in 1927 to support the right of the actual occupants to buy out the foro, a ruling that generally supported the subforados. The decision was not, however, accompanied by the provision of any means for poor subforados to make land purchases.

The long years of uncertainty, similar to the Irish troubles, took their toll on Galician society. Famine in 1853–1854 drove tens of thousands to emigrate. Seasonal farm labor in the south provided an even greater outlet. Galicians and other poor northerners, as Raymond Carr notes, became the waiters, water carriers, wet-nurses, and porters of the Spanish cities. Many were attracted to radical causes, while the Galician bourgeoisie tended toward ultraroyalism in the 1820s and supported the Moderate party* until the twentieth century. During the later liberal period from 1875 to 1923, elite political domination of the countryside through caciques* flourished in Galicia, with all its consequent corruption. Eugenio Montero Ríos (1832–1914) became the area's most powerful cacique and used the perfect conditions that Galicia provided to maintain oligarchic control over the region. Scattered republican violence was unsuccessful.

The changes that did occur were the result of cultural nationalism. The scholarly Ramón Menéndez Pidal* rediscovered the thirteenth-century importance of Galician literature, long overshadowed by Castilian. The distinctive Portuguese-influenced dialect of the region stimulated a new awareness of local culture, which Rosalía de Castro* portrayed in her regional novels and Valentín Carvajal (1849–1906) used in his journalism and essays.

As in the Basque Provinces and Catalonia,* cultural renaissance led to consideration of political autonomy. Much of the early debate centered on the heated question of the continued use of Castilian or the adoption of the Galician language. Finally, in 1929, with the founding of the main Galician regionalist party, the Organización Republicana Gallega Autónoma (ORGA), linguistic policy was de-emphasized in favor of a republican political program. Its lesser militancy and late start contrasted sharply with other regionalist groups, but it joined the Pact of San Sebastian in 1930 to overthrow the monarchy and, together with the Partido Galleguista, won sixteen Cortes seats in the first elections for the Second Republic* in 1931.

The land-reform legislation of the republic, which failed to make provision for foro purchases, caused the loss of ten regionalist seats in the elections of 1933, but the antiautonomy position of the center-right coalition between 1933 and 1936 rekindled regional sentiments. This led to both a good showing for the Popular Front in the elections of Feb. 1936 and positive support for autonomy in the plebiscite of 26 June 1936, less than a month before the outbreak of the Spanish Civil War.*

The nationalists, nonetheless, won a quick victory in Galicia by taking advantage of military bases and exploiting the lack of a strong Left. Subsequent executions were heavy for such a basically conservative and Catholic area, however, and may be attributed to efforts to wipe out supporters of regional autonomy. The era of Gen. Francisco Franco* brought a different set of changes. Franco, who had been born in El Ferrol (which had "del Caudillo" added to its name in his honor), attempted to increase state investment in his native region. Cooperatives introduced new crops, better facilities, and some foro purchases to Galician agriculture, and improved transportation links to national markets stimulated increased stock raising. Despite these changes, many Galician farms were too small and inefficient to survive. Some subforados simply abandoned the land for jobs in the towns and cities; emigration to Latin America, Europe, and Madrid climbed, while the Galician foros disappeared in a new age of modern agriculture.

Regionalism revived in the 1960s and 1970s. After Franco's death, autonomy was recognized by the Constitution of 1978 and adopted by Galicia in Apr. 1981, after Catalonia and the Basque country. The achievement of comunidad autónoma was not accompanied by any noticeable increase in radicalism. The regional elections of Oct. 1981, for example, saw the center-right Popular Alliance defeat the mainstream Democratic Center Union party of Adolfo Suárez* in the most important conservative victory of recent times. It showed, perhaps, that Galicia still remains somewhat apart from the rest of the country.

For additional information, see A. Alfonso Bozzo, *Los partidos políticos en Galicia 1931–1936* (Madrid, 1976); F. Carballo, *La iglesia en la Galicia contemporánea* (Madrid, 1978); R. Carr, *Spain 1808–1939* (Oxford, 1966); J. A. Durán, *Historia de caciques, bandos e ideologías en la Galicia no urbana* (Madrid, 1972); A. Eiras Roel, ed., *La historia social de Galicia en sus fuentes de protocolos* (Santiago de Compostela, 1981); M. Murguía, *Política y sociedad en Galicia* (Madrid, 1974); M. Pardo, *La emigración gallega intrapeninsular in el siglo xviii* (Madrid, 1960); X. Vilas Nogueira, *O Estatuto Galego* (La Corunna, 1975); and R. Villar Ponte, *Historia sintética de Galicia* (Santiago de Compostela, 1932).

*R. W. Kern*

## GÁLVEZ GALLARDO, JOSÉ DE, MARQUÉS DE SONORA (1720–1787),

minister of the Indies and governor of the Council of Indies (1776–1787). Gálvez was born of poor nobility in the village of Macharavialla near Malaga and studied theology at the local seminary of San Sebastian, but he later earned a degree in jurisprudence at Salamanca. He practiced law in Madrid where, perhaps because of the influence of his French wife, he became legal counsel for the French embassy. In 1761, he drafted an appeal for the deregulation of colonial commercial policy and administrative and mining reform that apparently attracted the attention of the minister of finance, Leopoldo de Gregorio, the marqués de Esquilache.* In Nov. 1764, he was named alcalde de casa y corte of Madrid, and on 20 Feb. 1765, Esquilache named him visitor-general of New Spain, replacing an appointee who had died en route to that colony. He also became an honorary member of the Council of the Indies with seniority.

As visitor-general of New Spain, Gálvez discharged with ruthless efficiency his instructions to effect fiscal and administrative reform. He also followed royal instructions to expel the Jesuits from the colony, executing eighty-five subjects who protested violently. After the fall of Esquilache, his work came under attack both in the Ministry of the Indies and the council, but Carlos III* personally intervened to save his mission, assigning the question to the sympathetic attorneys of the Council of Castile, Pedro Rodríguez, conde de Campomanes* and José Moñino, the conde de Floridablanca.* While the bulk of his work stood, his plan for intendancies languished.

Upon his return to Spain in 1772, Gálvez assumed his position on the unfriendly Council of the Indies, and in 1774, he also received appointment to the Junta General de Comercio, Moneda y Minas. When Julián de Arriaga y Rivero died in Jan. 1776, Carlos named Gálvez minister of the Indies, but did not attach Marine as was the custom. Instead, Gálvez received the governorship of the council, which enabled him to expedite changes in colonial policy.

Gálvez worked quickly to place the empire on a wartime footing, establishing the viceroyalty of Río de la Plata, the commandancy general of the Interior Provinces, and the captaincy general of Caracas, and he sent regents-visitors to New Granada and Peru and subvisitors to Quito and Chile to effect fiscal and administrative reform. In Oct. 1778, he promulgated the famous free-trade regulation. During both his work in Mexico and as minister, Gálvez was determined to wrest control of the colonial political apparatus from entrenched colonial elites. His harsh policies provoked massive protests in Peru and New Granada, but the victories of his nephew, Bernardo, in Florida, saved his reputation, and in 1785, he received his title of Castile. Gálvez also extended the intendancy system to much of the empire, mainly during the postwar period. During his administration, colonial revenues reached all-time highs, but so did expenditures. He was a controversial figure during his lifetime and remains so today.

For additional information, see H. I. Priestly, *José de Gálvez: Visitor-General of New Spain (1765–1771)* (Berkeley, 1916); and J. A. Escudero, *Los orígenes del Consejo de Ministros en España*, 2 vols. (Madrid, 1979).

A. J. Kuethe

*Related entries*: COLONIES; CARLOS III.

**GANIVET GARCÍA, ÁNGEL** (1865–1898), writer and diplomat. Ángel Ganivet spent his formative years in his native Granada. After receiving a doctorate in philosophy and letters at the University of Madrid in 1890, he joined the diplomatic corps, serving in Belgium, Finland, and Latvia. While in the consular service, he became afflicted by a progressive mental illness that, combined with distress over an unhappy love affair, led to his suicide. He leaped into the Dvina River at Riga four months after Spain's defeat in the Spanish-American War* and eleven days before Spain and the United States* signed the Treaty of Paris.

Ganivet, whose personality was tempered by anguish and Senecan stoicism, wrote only during the last six years of his life while living abroad. The corpus of his work consists of a play, two allegorical-satirical novels (*La conquista del reino de Maya por el úlitimo conquistador español, Pío Cid*, [1897], and *Los trabajos del infatigable creador, Pío Cid*, [1898]), and several collections of essays and letters (among these, *El porvenir de España*, correspondence with Miguel de Unamuno,* published posthumously in 1912).

Ganivet is most remembered, however, for his *Idearium español* (1897), an evocative analysis of Spain's past and present strengths and weaknesses. Although the work is perceptive, it is flawed by contradictions, faulty logic, and some facile generalizations.

In *Idearium*, Ganivet suggested some remedies for his country's difficulties: Spain must cultivate its spirituality, seek expression through action and, rather than Europeanize, strengthen its cultural and intellectual ties with Spanish America.

A particularly noteworthy feature of the *Idearium* is Ganivet's discussion of abulia, or paralysis of the will. Taking the term from medical-psychological literature and examining conditions in his homeland, Ganivet concluded that Spain suffered from abulia on a national scale. The concept would become a common thematic element in the works of the Generation of 1898.* Because of his candor, his aesthetic concerns, and, above all, his preoccupation with Spain's problems, Ganivet is considered a precursor of that literary group.

For additional information, see Á. Ganivet, *Obras completas* (Madrid, 1962); J. Ginsberg, *Ángel Ganivet* (London, 1985); and J. Herrero, *Ángel Ganivet: Un iluminado* (Madrid, 1966).

*H. L. Kirby, Jr.*

*Related entry*: GENERATION OF 1898.

**GARCÍA LORCA, FEDERICO** (1898–1936), Spanish poet and playwright of world renown. García Lorca was born in Fuente Vaqueros, Granada, and his childhood in the Andalusian countryside inspired much of his work. His writing is steeped in the images, folklore, and language of the region.

The oldest of four in a close-knit, affluent family, García Lorca spent his school years in Granada, where as an undisciplined student he struggled through university studies, eventually earning a law degree he never used. He was a gifted pianist before turning to writing in his late teens. His early work, highly autobiographical prose and verse meditations, reveals García Lorca's adolescent despair at life's cruelty, and in particular, his obsessions with love and sexuality, the nature of God, social injustice, and death. These remained central concerns throughout his later writing.

In 1918, García Lorca published *Impresiones y paisajes*, a prose collection in the modernist tradition, culled from a series of university travels through Spain. In 1919, he moved to the Residencia de Estudiantes in Madrid, an offshoot of the Institución Libre de Enseñanza,* where his fellow residents included Luis Buñuel (1900–1975) and Salvador Dalí.* From then on, García Lorca lived a rather carefree existence, drifting between life in the hectic capital city and the pleasant ambience of his family's quiet home in Granada, where he spent most summers and composed many of his major works. Among his close friends in Granada was the composer Manuel de Falla,* with whom García Lorca shared a deep love of popular Spanish music and puppetry.

In Madrid, he was known as a gregarious bard, fond of reciting his poems at café tertulias. He soon caught the eye of writers such as Juan Ramón Jiménez,* who published some of García Lorca's poetry in the early 1920s, but Lorca was more at home among the poets of his own Generation of 1927, such as Jorge Guillén (1893- ) and Rafael Alberti (1902– ). At the Residencia, his contact with Buñuel and passionate friendship with Dalí put García Lorca in touch with the avant-garde trends of his day. Though he flirted with surrealism, García Lorca never abandoned his roots in traditional Spanish culture, and he wrote and delivered several lectures on the subject in the 1920s and 1930s.

By the late 1920s, he had published three collections of poetry, most notably the *Romancero gitano* (1928), which brought him sudden national fame. His early attempts at playwriting were less successful. García Lorca's first play, *El maleficio de la mariposa* (1920), drew a warm response when it premiered in 1927, but he was still thought of primarily as a poet.

As the decade drew to a close, García Lorca suffered a profound emotional crisis, brought on in part by the success of *Romancero gitano*. Many who knew him have attributed this crisis largely to García Lorca's homosexuality, a fact he hid fiercely from most of Spanish society, including his own family, and that seems to have caused him lifelong anguish. In mid–1929, he abruptly left Spain and spent the following year in New York City and Cuba.

His experience abroad gave rise to a radical, new poetry collection, *Poeta en Nueva York* (1929–1930), and fueled García Lorca's desire to write plays. Returning to Spain in 1930, he dedicated the next few years mainly to the theater, creating the works for which he is today best known—*La zapatera prodigiosa* (1930), *Bodas de sangre* (1933), *Yerma* (1934), and *La casa de Bernarda Alba* (1936)—as well as a series of artistically more daring and controversial works he labeled "unproduceable plays." Under the auspices of the Second Republic,* García Lorca directed a traveling student theater company, La Barraca. In 1933–1934, he made a triumphant tour to Buenos Aires to oversee the production of several of his plays. At age thirty-six, he was an internationally recognized playwright who had at last achieved financial independence from his parents.

In July 1936, amid mounting political tensions, García Lorca went home to Granada to be with his family. On 17 July, the Spanish Civil War* broke out, and on 20 July, Granada fell to the nationalists. Though not actively political, García Lorca was known for his left-wing attitudes and his friendships with liberals. Sometime before dawn on 18 or 19 Aug., a nationalist firing squad shot García Lorca, one of thousands executed in Granada in the first months of the war.

During the years of the government of Gen. Francisco Franco,* García Lorca's works were banned in Spain and the truth about his death obscured. At the same time, his reputation grew worldwide as he became the symbolic martyr of the Spanish Civil War. As the years passed and restrictions in Spain gradually eased, Spanish interest in his work intensified, and with Franco's death in 1975, the publication of works by and about García Lorca reached new heights. In 1986, the Spanish government participated in a nationwide tribute marking the fiftieth anniversary of his death.

García Lorca's plays, all in some sense poetic, fall into several categories. In addition to *El maleficio de la mariposa*, and *Mariana Pineda* (1927), his early work consists of the puppet plays *Los títeres de Cachiporra* (1923) and *Retablillo de don Cristóbal* (1931), and the two farces *La zapatera prodigiosa* and *Amor de don Perlimplín con Belisa en su jardín* (1928). While these differ stylistically from one another, all share his lyrical vision and his preoccupation with the destructive powers of love and death, as do the later plays.

These include the three rural tragedies, *Bodas de sangre*, *Yerma*, and *La casa de Bernarda Alba*, along with *Doña Rosita la soltera* (1935), a Chekhovian-style drama set in Granada. The three "unproduceable plays," which he considered to be his "true aim" in the theater, are *El público* (1930), an expressionist drama dealing frankly with homosexuality; *Así que pasen cinco años* (1931); and *[Comedia sin título]* (1935–1936), an unfinished play written in direct response to the political events of its time. None of these three was staged during García Lorca's lifetime.

His first poetry collection, *Libro de poemas* (1921), is a mostly derivative work with strong echoes of the previous poetic generation. The three collections that followed, *Suites* (1921–1923), *Poema del cante jondo* (1921), and *Canciones* (1923–1925), all show a tendency toward briefer poetic forms and are infused with elements of Spanish folklore. *Romancero gitano* is a sophisticated blending of traditional Spanish ballad meter with daring, postsymbolist imagery.

García Lorca's later poetry includes *Poeta en Nueva York*, a quasi-surrealist work in free verse; *Diván del Tamarit* (1931–1934), a more muted and mature collection intended partially in homage to Granada's Arab-Andalusian culture; *Llanto por Ignacio Sánchez Mejías* (1934), García Lorca's moving elegy to a dead bullfighter; and the *Sonetos del amor oscuro* (1935), a series of eleven love poems in the Petrarchan mode.

He also wrote a number of lectures, prose poems, and other incidental poetry; began several additional plays; and sketched some four hundred drawings.

For additional information, see F. García Lorca, *Obras completas*, 3 vols. (Madrid, 1986); and I. Gibson, *Federico García Lorca*, 2 vols. (Barcelona, 1985, 1987).

*L. Stainton*

**GAUDÍ I CORNET, ANTONI** (1852–1926), Catalan architect. Gaudí was born in Reus, Tarragona, on 25 June 1852. He studied at the Escuela Superior de Arquitectura in Barcelona and worked, while still a student, as an assistant on the city's Parc de la Cuitadella, begun in 1872. His first commission, the Vicens house, was undertaken in 1878–1880. In 1884, he was appointed director of works for a new church, the Church of the Holy Family, a neo-Gothic design begun by Francesc de Paula del Villar i Carmona (1826?–1899?), who had employed Gaudí earlier in the restoration of the monastery at Montserrat. By 1893, the exterior of the Holy Family was completed, but the rest of the church, on which Gaudí worked intermittently for the rest of his life—and is still unfinished—reflected a decisive shift in his style from a respectful attempt at accurate historical recreation to an inventive, almost indescribable vision that is as much sculptural as it is architectural. The change shows most clearly in the Holy Family's four towers, a quartet of open-work spires, topped by flowerlike finials and covered with broken-tile ornaments that became one of Gaudí's hallmarks. It is evident, too, in the building's surface, a dense shell of organic carving that gives the church the look of a marine growth.

Religion played a central role in Gaudí's life. He seems to have regarded himself more as a medieval craftsman toiling in the service of his God than as a creator. The aestheticism that is so important to the building—and to art nouveau (c. 1893–1905) in particular—is entirely lacking in Gaudí's creations, although there are undeniable stylistic affinities with art nouveau nonetheless. Gaudí has been hailed as the precursor of some of the world's most advanced architecture, but in fact he was a dead end in terms of architectural development. As had William Morris (1834–1896), he sought to achieve an individual style that was unique.

Domestic buildings of the Gaudí era are characterized by art nouveau exteriors and lush interiors reminiscent of Moorish structures in Spain. Among them are the house of Eusebio Güell (1846?–1918), the Palau Güell, done between 1885 and 1889, and the Casas Battlo and Mila, two luxury apartment buildings, both begun in 1905. The work at Casa Battlo was actually the remodeling of an existing structure. Gaudí used shards of broken glass rather than the more usual tile fragments on the facade, which produced the effect of a large habitable seashell. The earlier Palau Güell (1885), a contemporary of the Holy Family, shared the cathedral's sense of fantasy, particularly in the chimney pots along the roofline, which resemble the cathedral's open-work spires.

Güell was Gaudí's patron. He presided over the architect's most important venture into landscape architecture, the Parc Güell, executed between 1900 and

1914. It was initially to be a garden city, more an exercise in urban planning than in park design. Much of what exists today—grottoes, porticos, benches decorated with broken tile or mosaic ornaments, and a few small buildings—has been built since Gaudí's death and provides only an outline of his plan.

Gaudí, who died in Barcelona on 10 June 1926 in a streetcar accident, endowed all of his creations with a sense of the fantastic and an organic conception that in some cases amount to a sort of deformation. His public reputation, after his death, has remained high in Barcelona and in North America, but less so in the rest of Spain and in Europe. A visionary who was as much a sculptor and designer as an architect, Gaudí's work remains unique.

For additional information, see N. Pevsner, *The Sources of Modern Architecture and Design* (New York, 1968); and S. Tachudi Madsen, *Art Nouveau* (New York, 1956).

*S. Benforado*

*Related entry*: BARCELONA.


**GENERATION OF 1898,** intellectual movement of the late nineteenth and twentieth centuries. The concept of generation, as a principle denoting cohort, finds frequent expression in intellectual history under the general category of literary generations. Through this characterization of literary generation, as cohorts of intellectuals, the Generation of 1898 may be understood.

The designation Generation of Disaster to refer to the Generation of 1898 was first used by the historian and politician Gabriel Maura y Gamazo (1879–1963) in a 1908 issue of the Madrid weekly newspaper *Faro* and popularized by the novelist Azorín (José Martínez Ruiz, 1874–1967), a member of the group, in subsequent newspaper articles in 1910 and 1913. On 23 Feb. 1908, Maura engaged in polemical exchanges with José Ortega y Gasset* and referred to "the generation that arrives today; a generation born intellectually at the root of the disaster." Andrés González Blanco, in *Historia de la novela en España*, also referred to the Generation of the Disaster in 1912. To Azorín, however, goes the credit for publicizing the notion of the Generation of 1898. In a brief note of 1910, "Two Generations," Azorín distinguished his generation from a younger group of uncommitted writers. In a series of articles written in 1913 under the title "The Generation of 1898," Azorín used this designation to define his group of writers. They acquired their name as the events of the Spanish-American War* unfolded, presenting them with the perception of national catastrophe and providing a context for their national and social criticisms.

The war marked Spain's last international conflict as a colonial power, at the close of a period of colonial expansion for some West European countries. The Treaty of Paris (1898), virtually ignored by other European countries, confirmed the Spanish sense of despair and isolation. Defeat in the Spanish-American War, combined with the loss of Cuba, Puerto Rico, Guam, and the Philippines, prompted intellectual responses to the crisis. Spaniards saw the war as a national disaster, and the Generation of 1898 came together to discuss what they considered to be the degeneration of Spain. These intellectuals analyzed the Spanish predicament and voiced their criticisms, reflections, and protests in their creative writings and as literary polemics. Several voiced severe doubts concerning the future development of Spain and Spanish culture, particularly before 1898. Thus, the social and educational reforms planned by Joaquín Costa* and the writings of Damián Isern (1852–1914) about national decadence figured prominently in the writings of the Generation of 1898.

This generation was composed of men such as Ángel Ganivet García,* Azorín, Miguel de Unamuno,* Pío Baroja,* Antonio Machado,* and Ramiro de Maeztu,* writers, scholars, and theorists, in contrast to the preceding generation of scientists, scholars, and researchers. This latter group, in turn, was distinct from the previous generation of Francisco Giner de los Ríos,* which had been one of pedagogues, theologians, and orators. The young men of letters of 1898 spent their early years in an atmosphere of pessimism and soul-searching. The defeat in 1898 intensified this mood until it evolved into a national depression affecting all Spaniards who were concerned about the condition of their country.

The war with the United States* did not cause a breakdown of institutions, but it did focus attention on the fact that Spain was no longer a major European power and that something had to be done to keep Spain from slipping permanently into the category of nations whose grandeur was a memory, rather than a promise of future achievement. Indeed, the publication of Unamuno's *En torno al casticismo* (1895) and Ganivet's *Idearium español* (1897), which formulated "the national question" in spiritual language and provided philosophical answers to the practical problems of Spain, support the position that the group of intellectuals associated with the Generation of 1898 would have existed even had there been no military defeat or loss of colonial possessions. The central theme of Spain's social, political, and intellectual history between 1895 and 1914 was the search for a solution to this crisis.

One of the important repercussions of this state of mind was the appearance of critical social and political literature that is often referred to as the literature of 1898. It influenced subsequent Spanish thinking about the nature of the Spanish problem, the national question and the issue of regeneration, and made efforts to characterize and define the essence of the Spanish soul. These preoccupations distinguished the Generation of 1898 from the contemporaneous literary movement represented by modernism.

The Generation of 1898 began brilliantly in literature with the inspiration of Unamuno and other young writers whose intellectual energies were concentrated on the idea of the regeneration of Spain. Some of the members of the Generation of 1898 displayed an increasing tendency to withdraw from the external world into the internal images of their poetry and novels. Literary genres—the novel, the essay, poetry, and drama—were some of the modes through which they pursued their common goal: the regeneration of Spain. The Generation of 1898 arose to confront this reality. It implied a unity of concern and action that no one doubted at the time, even if literary critics have found the concept difficult to apply. Most called for the regeneration of Spain through action and will, turning to the past as the model for the Spanish future. Indeed, several devoted themselves to the interpretation and reinterpretation of the story of Don Quixote. It is therefore not surprising that some chose the motif of Don Quixote as a framework for their criticism or to find that the theme of the will (la voluntad) was central to some of their novels. After 1905, the tricentennial celebration of the publication of Miguel de Cervantes's (1547–1616) *Don Quixote* (1605, 1615), several of these works appeared: Azorín's *La ruta de Don Quijote* (1912), Unamuno's *La vida de Don Quijote y Sancho* (1912), and Ortega y Gasset's *Meditaciones del Quijote* (1914).

The will must be cultivated on an individual and national basis if Spain were to have any hope of averting the abyss of degeneration. It is from Ganivet that such writers as Azorín, Pío Baroja, and others derived the notion of the will and for whom the question of will was crucial in the development of their literary characters. Between the early 1900s and the 1920s, these intellectuals withdrew from any significant political or institutional activity directly involved with Spain's regeneration and turned their creative energy inward. Their involvement was manifest in mental activity, as the internal ideal of the regeneration of Spain increasingly assumed the form of individualistic expressions in novels and poetry. Instead of seeking to combine the subtle and more intricate balance of thought and action, as was the case with Giner de los Ríos and his followers, this group of intellectuals carried their struggle of defining and revitalizing the Spanish essence away from the concrete problem posed by their social, economic, political, and historical circumstances and projected it onto the characters of their novels and the rhythms of their poetry.

Although certain critics disagree with Azorín's identification of the members of the Generation of 1898 (his membership list included Ramón María del Valle-Inclán (1866–1936), Jacinto Benavente (1866–1954), and Rubén Darío (1867–1916), and excluded Ganivet and Antonio Machado) virtually all agree that a group of intellectuals associated with the designation existed. They were unified through a collective attitude that addressed a common set of problems. Thus, their creative works were directed toward discerning national and spiritual values held in common. After World War I,* however, the creative impulses of the Generation of 1898 began to wane. Despite efforts to regenerate Spanish values, the group association dissolved, leaving the problem of national regeneration for the Generation of 1927* to address.

For additional information, see J. L. Abellán, *Sociología del '98* (Barcelona, 1973); C. Blanco Aguinaga, *Juventud del '98* (Madrid, 1970); R. Pérez de la Dehesa, *El pensamiento de Costa y su influencia en el '98* (Madrid 1966); G. Díaz-Plaja, *Modernismo frente del noventa y ocho* (Madrid, 1951); E. Inman Fox, *La crisis intelectual del '98* (Madrid 1976); L. S. Granjel, *Panorama de la Generación del '98* (Madrid, 1959); H. Jeschke, *La Generación del '98 en España* (Madrid, 1954); and D. L. Shaw, *The Generation of 1989 in Spain* (New York, 1975).

*O. W. Holmes*

*Related entry*: GENERATION OF 1927.

**GENERATION OF 1927,** twentieth-century intellectual movement. The Generation of 1927 originated as a term to characterize a certain similarity of poets and writers in the Spain of the 1920s. The year noted the moment when intellectuals and students began to resist the dictatorship of Gen. Miguel Primo de Rivera* in 1927 as a prelude to the Second Republic.* As with their predecessors, the Generation of 1898,* a national crisis created something of a common mentality, or at least a shared identity, in the years before the Spanish Civil War.*

Some members of the Generation of 1927 actively pursued political careers. Manuel Azaña,* an essayist, and Juan Negrín,* a doctor and sometime writer, became future premiers (and, in Azaña's case, president of the republic), but Azaña and Negrín were not central to the cultural productivity of the Generation of 1927, and to a certain extent, their political careers were exceptional, and it is fair to say that many members of this loose grouping favored drastic change and had a spirit of modernism more radical than the previous generation.

There was close cooperation between the Generations of 1898 and 1927 despite their differences. Many of the younger vanguard poets were first published by *Índice*, founded and directed by Juan Ramón Jiménez,* a nineteenth-century follower of Karl Christian Friedrich Krause,* who had been one of the first to reintroduce modernist themes into Spanish literature. Other members of the Generation of 1927 found expression through the *Revista de Occidente*, the premier Spanish periodical created by José Ortega y Gasset* in 1923. Ortega, whose major works were produced in the 1920s, served as one of the most important links between the two generations by giving editorial assistance to the younger poets and by addressing *The Dehumanization of Art* to their concerns. Along with Américo Castro (1885–1972), Ramón Pérez de Ayala (1880–1962), and Eugenio d'Ors y Rovira (1882–1954), he provided an intellectual leadership that inspired younger Spaniards to develop their own creative endeavors fully.

As the Generation of 1927 matured, four publications became crucial outlets for their art and values. *Litoral* was founded and directed by Emilio Prados (1889–1962) and Manuel Altolaguirre (1906–1939). *Gallo* was begun in 1928 by Federico García Lorca,* and *Lola*, edited by Gerardo Diego (1896– ), appeared the same year. The most important journal, however, was *La Gaceta Literaria*, begun in 1927 and edited by Ernesto Giménez Caballero (1898– ).

The identification of the newer poets with *La Gaceta Literaria* was immediate. In its first issue, it referred to the Generation of 1927 as the "generation of *La Gaceta Literaria*." Literary critic Guillermo de Torre (1900– ), in reflecting on the years from 1927 to 1933 when he served as secretary of *La Gaceta Literaria*, described it as "the true organ of expression of the Generation of 1927." Its first issue of 1 Jan. 1927 contained several photographs of Giménez Caballero filming members of three generations of Spanish intellectuals: Pío Baroja* and Ramón Menéndez Pidal* of the Generation of 1898; Américo Castro and Ortega of the small Generation of 1914; and Rafael Alberti (1902– ), Ramiro Ledesma

Ramos (1905–1936), José Bergamín (1895– ), Antonio Marichalar (1893– ), Ramón Gómez de la Serna (1891–1963), and César Muñoz Arconada (1900–1964) of the Generation of 1927.

A characteristic that linked some of the members of the Generation of 1927 was their willingness to experiment with new techniques and media to produce a much broader and more vivid impact. García Lorca's friendly collaboration with painter Salvador Dalí,* film director Luis Buñuel (1900–1983), and composer Manuel de Falla* showed a new appreciation for combining new techniques to extract the mysterious essence from human experience. Buñuel's *Un chien andalou* (1928) and *L'âge d'or* (1930) became visual demonstrations of the new abstract mysticism and surrealism that emerged in the 1920s.

A second and more important characteristic of the Generation of 1927 was an emphasis on the symbolic form of poetic expression. The new poets focused upon the meaning of an event or a physical detail in a way that contrasted sharply with the Generation of 1898's earlier emphasis upon the landscape of Spain or the national will. In this, they became lineal descendants of the French symbolist poets of the late nineteenth century, and the silent tribute paid to the twenty-fifth anniversary of Stéphane Mallarmé's (1842–1898) death in Madrid's Botanical Garden on 11 Sept. 1923 marked the real beginning of the generation's public life.

A more common characteristic the generation shared was the Andalusian origin of many of its members. García Lorca, Vicente Aleixandre,* Alberti, Luis Cernuda (1902–1963), José Moreno Villa (1887– ), Altolaguirre, Prados, and José María Hinojosa (1904–1936) were southerners who represented a new cultural renaissance in an area that long had been in obscurity and social crisis. Some of the radicalism of the Generation of 1927 may have come from the Andalusians, although this was not exclusive to them, and the values of Salinas, Bergamín, Jorge Guillén (1893–1984), Dámaso Alonso (1898– ), Juan Chabás (1900– ), and Giménez Caballero, while similar, did not originate in Andalusia.

Another general characteristic of the group was a revival of the work of the earlier Spanish poet, Luis de Góngora (1561–1627). Involvement with symbolism led many in the Generation of 1927 into literary innovation that centered on the problem of language. Familiar words acquired novel meanings, and brilliant flights of imagination, provocative metaphors, and images marked their work. Góngora's complicated baroque poetry, which the Generation of 1898 had ignored, provided a model for a new poetic vocabulary in the 1920s. Dámaso Alonso, poet and scholar, discovered in Góngora's complex *Soledades* (1613) abundant metaphors and musical effects that seemed to anticipate in the history of the Spanish language the later symbolist and surrealist styles of modern Europe. The rediscovery of Góngora gave the Generation of 1927 a patriotic enthusiasm and a renewed sense of the past. Many of them participated in the tricentennial homage paid to Góngora during Dec. 1927 in Seville. This program, held at a time of growing political and social discontent, was a key event in the formation of the new generation.

The creative years of the Generation of 1927 were soon eclipsed by the political crisis of Spain. Some, such as García Lorca, had their lives ended violently in their artistic prime, while many others found themselves in exile or silenced after 1939 in the traditionalist confines of the regime of Gen. Francisco Franco.* Their influence on the post–1975 period represents a fragile continuity of the 1920s with the 1970s and 1980s. The fact that Spanish intellectuals have been able to resume an active creative life must be credited in part to the work of the Generation of 1927 sixty years ago.

For additional information, see C. Bassolas, *La ideología de los escritores: Literatura y política en La Gaceta Literaria (1927–1932)* (Barcelona, 1975); M. A. Hernando, *Prosa vanguardista en la generación del '27 (Gecé y La Gaceta Literaria)* (Madrid, 1975), and *La Gaceta Literaria (1927–1932): Biografía y valoración* (Valladolid, 1974); L. Tandy and M. Sferrazza, *Ernesto Giménez Caballero y "La Gaceta Literaria" (o la generación del '27)* (Madrid, 1977).

O. W. Holmes

*Related entry*: GENERATION OF 1898.

**GERMANY,** relations with Spain. In 1870, the unification of Germany was inadvertently stimulated by Spain when Leopold (1835–1905), a Catholic member of the Prussian Hohenzollern-Sigmaringen family, was proposed as a candidate for the recently vacated Spanish throne, much to the consternation of France,* who was goaded by Otto von Bismarck's (1815–1898) famous Ems dispatch into the Franco-Prussian War (1870–1871). The Prussian victory that followed led to the creation of the German Empire.

Early relations between Germany and Spain were marred by the action of a German warship, the *Friedrich Karl*, in seizing a Spanish ship, the *Vigilente*, during the chaos of the Spanish First Republic* in the harbor at Cartagena in 1873, and the Carlist seizure of a German merchant vessel, the *Gustav*, in 1874, which prompted German aid to the central government. Closer ties emerged after the restoration of the Bourbon dynasty in 1875. Alfonso XII* was a Germanophile, having studied at a military academy in Vienna and traveled through Germany in 1872 and 1873. Angered by antimonarchical French republicans in Spain, he proposed a German alliance in 1877 that pledged to put at least two hundred thousand men on Spain's Pyrenean border with France. Bismarck, mindful of Spanish weakness, did not consider this to be a serious offer, although later in 1881, he did upgrade Germany's legation to embassy status and permitted Alfonso and German crown prince Wilhelm (1859–1941) to exchange state visits in 1883. Even so, rival claims over the possession of the Caroline Islands in the Pacific continued to ruffle diplomatic relations, especially when papal arbitration found in Germany's favor in 1884.

The sudden death of Alfonso XII in 1885 did not immediately harm relations. French activity in Morocco* caused Spain to appeal to Germany for aid in 1886, and in an exchange of notes on 4 May 1887, Spain was given protection by the Triple Alliance (Germany, Austria-Hungary, Italy*), an arrangement renewed in 1891. These agreements recognized the status quo in the Mediterranean in return for Spanish assurances that it would not assist France in the event of a war with the Triple Alliance. Over the next several decades, however, this stance was made obsolete by rapprochement with France in Morocco, a course dictated by losses in the Spanish-American War,* which made the African colonies more important and cooperation with France, the leading power there, vital, especially since Britain promised France a free hand in Morocco in 1904, in return for similar freedom in Egypt.

The Spanish quandary was solved by the coronation of Alfonso XIII* in 1903 and his marriage in 1905 to Victoria Eugenia de Battenberg (1887–1969). Almost at once, Spain found itself in the midst of an international power struggle when Kaiser Wilhelm sailed to Tangier to protest French actions in Morocco. Britain, mindful of German expansionism, persuaded Spain at the Algeciras conference of 1906 in Spain to support the position of the Entente Cordiale. Two years later, Alfonso met with Edward VII (1841–1910) at Cartagena to work out an agreement to guarantee the status quo in the Mediterranean and the eastern Atlantic along the African shore. When France later signed the Cartagena Agreement, Spain was, for all practical purposes, an informal member of the Entente.

This new status was not without its problems. In 1911, when Germany sent a gunboat to Fez to again protest French colonialism in the area, France was forced to give Germany territory in the French Congo, and it then demanded of Spain, in Nov. 1912, a restriction of the Spanish zone in Morocco. Alfonso, on a state visit to Paris in May 1913, tried to tie Spanish support of France against Germany to their promise of a free hand for Spain in newly republican Portugal,* then a momentary threat to Madrid's stability. No agreement was reached before World War I* began.

Spain's benevolent neutrality during the war included a series of German contacts by Alfonso to strengthen Spanish diplomatic power. Little came of this except a destabilization of Spanish politics, but at least relations remained cordial after the war. Germany established a German-Spanish Chamber of Commerce and, in 1926, negotiated with the Gen. Miguel Primo de Rivera* dictatorship a commercial treaty that allowed the Germans to build submarines (forbidden by the Treaty of Versailles) at the Echevarrieta shipyards, permitted German mineral exploration in Morocco, and gave the I. G. Farben Company a chemical monopoly in Spain.

The rise of the Second Republic* in Spain coincided with the rise of nazism in Germany. Spanish opponents of the Second Republic found allies in the Reich, particularly in Adm. Wilhelm Canaris (1887–1945), head of German military intelligence, who assured the Spaniards of military assistance to overthrow the republic. In July 1936, Gen. Francisco Franco* sent agents to Berlin requesting aid; Hitler himself approved the request, bypassing the foreign office. The Germans eventually sent 500 million Reichsmarks of aid, including seven thousand airmen of the Condor Legion and thirty antitank companies, ignoring the nonintervention agreement promoted by Britain and France. Although the republic received help from the Soviet Union, German and Italian assistance to Franco was decisive.

In World War II,* once German troops were on the Pyrenees following the invasion of France, Hitler met Franco at Hendaye to try to persuade Franco to join the larger war, but the Caudillo made impossible demands. In Jan. 1941, Franco refused a German request for free transit across Spain to attack Gibraltar,* thus avoiding war against the Western allies, but he did agree to send the Blue Division* to fight in the Soviet Union under German command. Once it was clear in 1943 that Germany could not defeat the Soviets, however, Franco withdrew his support and the Blue Division returned home in 1944. Meanwhile, the Allies won the "wolfram war" by outbiding the Germans for this strategic material. Spain thus gradually shifted its benevolent neutrality from the Axis to the Allies.

A number of Germans took refuge in Spain at the end of the war, and relations with the federal republic of West Germany did not reach a stable basis until 1959, when a new commercial treaty reopened trade on a fairly large scale. A similar treaty with the democratic republic of East Germany was signed in 1973. West Germany benefited more from the continuation of the German-Spanish Chamber of Commerce, but the two Germanies were caught between the superpowers, so that their relations were an extension of those between the United States* and the Soviet Union.

For additional information, see W. L. Beaulac, *Franco: Silent Ally in World War II* (Carbondale, 1986); E. R. Beck, *A Time of Triumph and of Sorrow: Spanish Politics during the Reign of Alfonso XII, 1874–1885* (Carbondale, 1979); G. T. Harper, *German Economic Policy in Spain during the Spanish Civil War* (The Hague, 1967); G. R. Kleinfeld and L. A. Tambs, *Hitler's Spanish Legion: The Blue Division in Russia* (Carbondale, 1979); D. A. Puzzo, *Spain and the Great Powers, 1936–1941* (New York, 1962); and R. Reemtsen, *Spanisch-deutsche Beziehungen zur Zeit des ersten Dreibundvertrages 1882–1887* (New York, 1961).

R. M. Carden

*Related entries*: SPANISH CIVIL WAR; WORLD WAR I; WORLD WAR II.

**GIBRALTAR,** British possession at the southernmost point of the Spanish mainland. Gibraltar is a small peninsula on the eastern shore of the Bay of Algeciras. The name, of Arabic origin, refers more specifically to the mountain that rises over the Straits of Gibraltar just to the south. It has had great strategic value since antiquity, because the straits connect the Mediterranean with the Atlantic.

Gibraltar had already experienced ten sieges when it served as a Spanish naval base between 1541 and 1704. As part of Cadiz's defenses, Gibraltar watched over Spanish imperial naval activity on the south coast. Charles I (1600–1649) of Britain,* Spain's traditional enemy and competitor for colonial trade, commissioned an attack upon Spanish defenses in 1625, which failed to win any territory but continued British pressure until the War of Spanish Succession* in 1704, when Adm. Sir George Rooke (1650–1709) finally captured Gibraltar. In

1713, the Treaty of Utrecht confirmed British possession, which has lasted for more than 280 years.

Spain laid siege to it in 1727 and again in the "great siege" of 1779–1783. Gibraltar survived because it was now heavily fortified, with tunnels through the "Rock" serving as artillery emplacements. Food supplies fell to a dangerously low level in 1781, but the French and Spanish attackers diverted part of their forces to Minorca, and the defenders were able to destroy the French-designed floating batteries.

At the Versailles peace negotiations in 1783, Britain first offered to trade Gibraltar for Puerto Rico, which Pedro Abarca y Bolea, the conde de Aranda,* rejected. When British forces returned to Europe from North America, however, his bargaining positions weakened, and on 3 Sept. 1783, Spain dropped its claim on Gibraltar and accepted Minorca and Florida in its place.

During the period from 1790 to 1813, Britain's acquisition of Malta reduced Gibraltar's strategic importance, although it did play a role in the 1798 British attack on the French in Egypt and off Cape Trafalgar in 1805. Napoleon Bonaparte's (1769–1821) seizure of Spain in 1808 involved the garrison briefly both as a fighting force several times in 1810 and as a supply point for Spanish guerrillas. Mar. Jean de Dieu Soult (1769–1851) occupied neighboring San Roque in Dec. 1811 for a short time without attacking Gibraltar.

After the 1815 peace settlement, Gibraltar continued to lose importance; smuggling goods into Spain was its chief economic role until the opening of the Suez Canal in 1869 increased Mediterranean shipping. The British parliament sometimes debated the return of Gibraltar to Spain as a matter of conscience, and certainly Gibraltar was a thorn in Spain's side, but no serious negotiations took place during the nineteenth century. Britain indirectly aided Spain in its Moroccan campaigns to ease pressure, but German propaganda in neutral Spain during World War I* reawakened Spanish nationalism just as Gibraltar's importance as a submarine base rose.

The chief proposal from 1916 to 1939 favored exchanging Gibraltar for Spain's Moroccan enclave of Ceuta. Both Antonio Maura* and Gen. Miguel Primo de Rivera* supported this approach, but nationalism on both sides blocked serious negotiations. The Spanish Civil War* raised new British fears. During their meeting at Hendaye on 23 Oct. 1940, Adolf Hitler (1889–1945) pressed Gen. Francisco Franco* to attack the British colony, but Franco, carefully neutral, refused to do so.

Gibraltar's importance rose in World War II.* At one point early in the war, British strength fell so low that loss of Gibraltar seemed only a matter of time, but the North African campaign ended this possibility. During the postwar era, new difficulties began in 1950, when Gibraltar demanded and received an elected legislative and executive council, a first step toward self-government under British protection that violated promises made long ago in the Treaty of Utrecht. This disturbed Spanish public opinion, which turned violently anti-British, and the revival of diplomatic relations in 1951 still kept most Spaniards out of the colony. Spain imposed its own border restrictions in 1954 and despite talks in 1963, pressed the United Nations to decolonialize Gibraltar. The United Nations asked both parties to negotiate, but Britain refused. Spain then closed the border in Mar. 1965. A referendum in Gibraltar on 17 Nov. 1966 rejected unification with Spain. In return, the gates between La Linea and Gibraltar were locked and the ferry service to Algeciras suspended.

This last siege of Gibraltar lasted until 10 Apr. 1980, when the present Spanish state agreed to talks. In a rare pro-Spanish move, Britain supported Spain's membership in the European Economic Community, and the border reopened on 8 Jan. 1982. Further discussions continued until 27 Nov. 1984, when the border closed again until 5 Feb. 1985. The historic state visit by Juan Carlos I* to Britain in Apr. 1985 failed to achieve a compromise, and the matter still remains stalemated.

For additional information, see G. Hills, *Rock of Contention: A History of Gibraltar* (London, 1974); R. Serrano Suñer, *Entre Hendaye y Gibraltar* (Madrid, 1947); *Spanish Red Book on Gibraltar* (Madrid, 1965). [Updates are available in later U.N. and British publications.]

*R. W. Kern*

*Related entry*: BRITAIN.

**GINER DE LOS RÍOS, FRANCISCO** (1839–1915), founder of the Institución Libre de Enseñana.* Born in Ronda, Andalusia,* on 10 Oct. 1839, Giner de los Ríos completed primary school in Cadiz and received his secondary education in Alicante. He began his university work in Barcelona,* but completed his study of law in Granada. In 1863, he went to Madrid* and entered the ministry of state in their archives, arranging and copying the correspondence and documents of Felipe II (1556–1598). Over the next two years, Giner de los Ríos frequented the intellectual centers and tertulias of the followers of Karl Christian Friedrich Krause* and quickly became a devoted friend of Julián Sanz del Río (1814–1869). In Oct. 1865, he competed successfully for the chair in the philosophy of law and international law at the University of Madrid. His well-known views as a Krausist troubled the government, however, and he waited a year to assume his chair. He then almost immediately resigned to protest the dismissal of Sanz del Río from the university. The next year, following the Revolution of 1868, both men were reinstated, but their actions presaged another protest of conscience in 1875.

In Feb. 1875, the government of Antonio Cánovas del Castillo* abolished the major educational reform of the Revolution of 1868—the freedom to teach without government censorship. Giner de los Ríos, as the most prominent Krausist at the University of Madrid to refuse to pledge support to Catholicism and the monarchy, received the harshest punishment, imprisonment at Cadiz. While in confinement, he considered an offer from the British to establish a university at Gibraltar* for the professors Cánovas's government had dismissed.

The idea of a university free of state interference became a reality in Aug. 1876, with the founding of the Institución Libre de Enseñanza. Twelve prominent Krausists joined Giner de los Ríos in establishing the new university in Madrid, one dedicated to educating new citizens who would work to improve Spain. Giner de los Ríos realized that any national regeneration had to begin with the youngest children. In 1878, he initiated primary and secondary instruction at the Institución Libre, abandoning its university courses. He freed the institute from state supervision of its curricula and teaching methods. In place of a narrowly scholastic program, the Institución Libre offered a balanced program of physical, intellectual, artistic, and moral education.

Giner remained the intellectual mentor of the institute throughout his life, living in austerity on its premises and always available to the young students, who affectionately called him "Grandfather." His personality and temperament found expression in the pedagogy of the school. He enjoyed hiking in the countryside around Madrid, and his nature walks became the basis of his attention to the physical development of his students. His love of music, especially Mozart's, resulted in linking attendance at concerts with instruction in music appreciation. As a Krausist, Giner de los Ríos was fundamentally a moralist, and the students at the Institución Libre learned how to be future leaders of a reformed Spain. Commitment to self-expression and cooperation were instilled with a sense of social responsibility and personal integrity. The highly esteemed value of toleration was taught by example as well.

Giner de los Ríos consistently kept above the fray by refusing to align himself with any political party or accept frequent offers to enter the ministry of public instruction. Instead, once reappointed in 1881 to his chair in philosophy of law, he remained at the University of Madrid for the rest of his academic career.

Giner de los Ríos radiated a personal warmth and charm that belied the virulent attacks made upon him by the extreme Right. Driven to express his views, he published twenty volumes between 1916 and 1936. To reformers of his and later generations, he stood as an advocate of law and education as the best means to regenerate Spain, specifically through liberal ideals of freedom of speech and press and a constitutional separation of church and state. To his conservative enemies, in both the nineteenth and twentieth centuries, he was a radical seeking to supplant Catholicism with secularism. In fact, he represented the interests of an emerging bourgeois elite.

For additional information, see R. Altamira, *Giner de los Ríos educador* (Valencia, 1915); and I. Turín, *La educación y la escuela en España de 1874 a 1902* (Madrid, 1967).

*D. V. Holtby*

*Related entry*: INSTITUCIÓN LIBRE DE ENSEÑANZA.

**GODOY Y ÁLVAREZ DE FARÍA, MANUEL** (1767–1851), court favorite, chief minister under Carlos IV,* and ally of Napoleon Bonaparte (1769–1821). In 1784, Manuel Godoy, a dashing seventeen-year-old Estremaduran of minor aristocratic stock, joined the Royal Bodyguards assigned to the Spanish royal family. He quickly made a favorable impression on the heir to the Spanish throne, don Carlos, and his wife, María Luisa. Once the prince ascended the throne as Carlos IV in 1788, Godoy's rank and influence rose as well; he was made field marshal, duque de Alcudia, and a grandee of Spain. In 1792, at the age of twenty-five, he was appointed first secretary of state. Together with Carlos IV and María Luisa, Godoy formed a triumvirate that greatly determined the destiny of the Spanish nation until 1808.

The monarchs found in Godoy a loyal and trusted confidant who ran the affairs of state while they pursued their petty personal interests. Whether the favorite was the paramour of María Luisa (sixteen years older than he) has never been conclusively substantiated, but enough circumstantial evidence exists to assume he was.

Godoy's domination of Spain coincided with the French Revolution and the ascendancy of Napoleon—both of which entangled the affairs of Spain with the fate of France.* First was the war in 1793–1795, which ended with the Treaty of Basle (1795) and elevated Godoy to Prince of Peace, even though the war had not gone well for Spain. Afterward, Godoy tied Spain to France in a series of disastrous treaties: the Treaty of San Ildefonso (1796), the second Treaty of San Ildefonso (1800), the Treaty of Paris (1803), and the Treaty of Fontainebleau (1807). In most cases, Godoy sacrificed the interests of the Spanish nation to his personal designs.

Although Godoy's domestic policies essentially continued the enlightened programs of Carlos III,* it was his foreign entanglements with France and his close relationship with the king and queen that unleashed considerable antagonism toward Godoy from many quarters. In time, the strongest opposition centered around the prince of Asturias and heir to the throne, Fernando (Fernando VII*). There ensued a period of considerable intrigue, conspiracy, and recrimination that pitted the members of the immediate royal family against each other, especially Fernando and his parents. In order to strengthen its own particular case, each of the feuding parties placed its respective positions before Napoleon, hoping to obtain his support. As a result, the French emperor was not only exposed to the pathetic state of the Spanish throne, but also gained access to means of arbitrating their squabbles.

On 19 Mar. 1808, Fernando and his partisans carried out a coup d'état at the palace of Aranjuez. The hated Godoy was toppled from power and his life was almost ended by the mob. Carlos IV and María Luisa were forced to abdicate in the name of their son, the new king, Fernando VII. This incident finally led Napoleon to resolve the Spanish quandary once and for all. The French emperor lured all the contending parties to Bayonne, France, where Fernando VII and Carlos IV renounced their rights to the Spanish crown. All the Spanish prisoners were allowed to live comfortably in French territory for the duration of the War of Independence.* The favorite afterward accompanied his masters, Carlos and María Luisa, to exile in Italy,* living with them until their deaths in 1819. Godoy never returned to Spain, dying in Paris on 4 Oct. 1851, just as a new Napoleonic empire was in the process of being revived.

For additional information, see J. Chastenet, *Godoy, Master of Spain 1792–1808* (London, 1953); and D. Hilt, *The Troubled Trinity: Godoy and the Spanish Monarchs* (Tuscaloosa, 1988).

G. G. *Fernández*

*Related entries*: CARLOS IV; FERNANDO VII.

**GONZÁLEZ, ÁNGEL** (1925– ), contemporary poet. Ángel González was born on 6 Sept. 1925 in Oviedo, Asturias.* His father, a professor of education, died when González was two, and he was raised by his mother during the Spanish Civil War,* when one of his brothers was assassinated and another became an exile. His own education was interrupted by the war and by a three-year struggle with tuberculosis from 1944 to 1947. After his recovery, he taught school while he obtained a law degree at the University of Oviedo, working briefly as a music critic before moving to Madrid in 1951 to take a position in the Ministry of Public Works. Three years later, he again briefly returned to journalism in Seville before becoming an editor in Barcelona. He returned to the civil service in Madrid between 1956 and 1972.

His real interest throughout this period was poetry, which he had written since his youth and particularly during his illness, when he read the Generation of 1927* and especially the work of Juan Ramón Jiménez.* Many of his images reflected the northern mountains of Leon, while his technique of "voices" also portrayed the personal and national sense of tragedy felt in the 1940s and 1950s. As a poet of the 1950s, González rejected the strident sociopolitical themes of the postwar period to concentrate upon a richer artistic expression that used a multiplicity of points of view to offer other alternatives to the poet's own words—a conversation with the reader, intermittently interrupted by voices that offer discussion of such themes as the deception of outer reality with a deeper inner veracity, the anticipated yet unexpected changes that time brings, the nostalgia for innocence and idealism in contrast to man's eventual alienation and indifference, or the limited but powerful ability of words to express and explain man's existence and ability to love.

His first book, *Áspero mundo*, published in 1956, won second place in the Premio Adonais awards, and *Grado elemental*, published in 1962, won the Antonio Machado* award. Eight volumes of poetry and other writings followed between 1965 and 1985 and led to the prestigious Príncipe de Asturias award in 1985. He lectured internationally throughout this period, and in 1972, he began his residency at several universities in the United States as well as lecturing in Venezuela, Chile, and Argentina. He teaches today at the University of New Mexico.

For additional information, see L. Alarcón, *Ángel González, poeta* (Oviedo, 1969); and T. Alvarado, *La poesía española contemporánea: Cinco poetas de la generación del Cincuenta* (Bogota, 1980).

*R. Rivera*

**GONZÁLEZ MÁRQUEZ, FELIPE** (1942– ), socialist leader and current premier (1982– ). Felipe González, born in Seville on 5 Mar. 1942, was raised in Andalusia. He studied labor economics and law at the University of Seville and later at the University of Louvain in Belgium, where he came into contact with the social democratic movement. He returned to Seville and became an adjunct professor and labor-law specialist while also playing an active role in the socialist Unión General de Trabajadores* (UGT). Well-known to contemporary socialists, he became a protégé of Willy Brandt (1913– ), leader of the Social Democratic International and premier of the German Federal Republic from 1969 to 1974.

González's political career began in 1965, when he became a member of the Socialist party's provincial council, ultimately becoming its executive secretary from 1970 to 1974. In the latter year, he was elected first secretary of the reconstructed Socialist party* (Partido Socialista Obrero Español, PSOE) at an extraordinary congress of the UGT held in Paris. With the death of Gen. Francisco Franco* in Nov. 1975, the reign of Juan Carlos I* gave the PSOE its first political freedom in nearly forty years. González used this opportunity prudently to build a strong national party. After the elections of 1977 made the PSOE the second largest parliamentary party, González, now a deputy, criticized the program of premier Adolfo Suárez* as nothing more than renovated Francoism. When an international economic slump and the revival of regionalism caused Suárez's resignation on 29 Jan. 1981, an unsuccessful revolt of rightist plotters, military, and Civil Guards* on 26 Feb. strengthened the PSOE position as a less threatening alternative. In the national elections of 28 Oct. 1982, González and the PSOE won 47 percent of the vote, the largest victory in Spanish parliamentary history. They were still in power in 1988.

The policies of González have sought to minimize difficulties for the new democratic regime. Even before the elections, he was one of the creators of the bill to harmonize the autonomy progress (LOAPA), which insisted that all regions, and not just the Basque* country and Catalonia,* develop regional governments. Another key success was his management of previously guarded relations between the Socialist party and the Communist party* (PCE), which subsequently became less sectarian. In the elections of 1982, the Eurocommunist PCE found itself unable to distance itself from the social democracy of the PSOE and was decisively defeated.

As premier, González, who has good European ties, completed the final process of Spanish membership in the European Economic Community; formal membership began in 1986. Military policy and membership in NATO have been more difficult. The well-publicized decision in Nov. 1987 to close the U.S.

air base at Torrejón found González caught between Spanish nationalism/radicalism and a need for pragmatism in international matters. Thus far, at least, he has managed to satisfy both sides (although in Dec. 1988 he faced his first major labor walkouts), illustrating his nonideological practicality.

For additional information, see R. P. Clark and M. H. Haltzel, *Spain in the 1980s* (Cambridge, 1987).

*R. W. Kern*

*Related entries*: JUAN CARLOS I; SUÁREZ, ADOLFO.

**GOYA Y LUCIENTES, FRANCISCO JOSÉ DE** (1746–1828), painter. Goya was born on 30 Mar. 1746 in the village of Fuendetodos, near Saragossa. After early studies with Francisco Bayeau (1734–1795), he repeatedly failed to win admission to the Royal Academy in Madrid, and went in 1770 to Rome, still Europe's artistic center. During his two years in Italy, he won a prize in academy competition at Parma (1771).

Returning to Spain, Goya began to win commissions: paintings for a palace and the cathedral in Saragossa and for the Aula Dei, a nearby Carthusian monastery. In 1773, he married Bayeau's sister, Josefa.

The painter finally established himself in Madrid between 1774 and 1778 with a series of designs for the royal tapestry works of Santa Bárbara. His skill as a portraitist, little exercised before, brought him great success at the court of Carlos III.* In 1785, he was made deputy director of the very Royal Academy from which he had been rejected twenty years earlier. Finally, in 1789, Goya became a court painter for Carlos IV.*

A serious illness in 1792–1793 left Goya deaf; it also profoundly changed his interior vision without, however, slowing his ascent at court. He succeeded Bayeau as director of the Academy in 1795, and became the principal painter to the king in 1799.

In 1800, Goya painted Carlos IV and his family in a work that hangs today at the Prado Museum in Madrid. The royal family looks, a critic has said, "like the corner baker and his wife after winning the lottery." It is one of the paradoxes of Goya's career that he was able to paint such frankly unflattering portraits and not only survive, but triumph, at court. He has been called the first painter to exhibit a modern sensibility. It is likely that his royal but unsophisticated sitters accepted the painter's assessment of their looks, unaware of his capacity for irony and alienation.

Goya fared less well with the *Caprichos*, a set of fantastic prints (1799) that constituted a savage assault on the religious establishment, for which he narrowly avoided prosecution. His anticlerical sentiments, however, did not prevent him from receiving and executing religious commissions; in fact, like many other Spaniards of the Enlightenment,* he remained a practicing Catholic all his life. In 1798, for instance, while working on the *Caprichos*, he painted the celebrated murals for the church of San Antonio de la Florida in Madrid.

Much of Goya's best work, aside from portraiture, was produced privately and never shown beyond the artist's studio, so that it remained unknown to his contemporaries. Such paintings as the clothed and nude Majas, and the so-called Black Paintings, from Goya's country house, did not have a public showing during Goya's lifetime, but became enormously influential later in the nineteenth century. The *Disasters of War*, a set of eighty prints documenting atrocities in the War of Independence* (1808–1810), were not made public until 1862, long after Goya's death, probably because of the artist's fear of prosecution. The posthumous impact of the series, with its eyewitness details combined with a universal outcry against war, has been enormous.

After Carlos IV's abdication, Goya, like other Spanish liberals, welcomed the enlightened attitudes of José I,* while decrying the brutality of the French occupation. The pair of paintings, *3 of May 1808*, done in 1814 to celebrate the Bourbon restoration, are today Goya's most famous works. The paintings show an actual event, an execution by the French in Madrid. Without idealizing his subjects, Goya drew upon a long line of painted Spanish martyrs to create a modern icon: the murderers are faceless, while the victims have the face of every man. As one critic has said, the painting encapsulates the history of the twentieth century.

Fernando VII* pardoned Goya in 1814 for his support of Bonaparte, and Goya continued to work at the Spanish court until 1824, when a new era of reaction sent him into self-imposed exile in Bordeaux, France. Among his late productions are the forays into the new technique of lithography, such as the bullfighting prints published as *Tauromaquia* that later influenced Pablo Picasso.* From Bordeaux, Goya made at least two visits to Madrid before his death on 16 Apr. 1828.

For additional information, see P. Gassier and J. Wilson, *The Life and Complete Works of Francisco Goya* (New York, 1981); and F. C. Licht, *Goya: The Origins of the Modern Temper in Art* (New York, 1979).

S. Benforado

*Related entries*: CARLOS IV; FERNANDO VII; PICASSO, PABLO.


**GRANADOS, ENRIQUE** (1867–1916), with Isaac Albéniz,* one of the first Spanish composers to incorporate the idea of a national Spanish music into his work. Granados, who represents the pinnacle of romantic music in Spain, was born in Lérida, Catalonia.* He displayed his musical talents at an early age and studied with the local bandmaster. As a child, Granados and his family moved to Barcelona,* where he continued his musical studies and performed in many recitals. Already accepted for admission to the Paris Conservatory, he was stricken with typhoid and, by the time he had fully recovered, was too old to begin studies there. He remained in Paris for a short time and upon his return to Barcelona in 1889, began composing and teaching. His simple yet elegant *Twelve Spanish Dances* dates from this early period.

The disaster of the Spanish-American War* and the rebirth of interest in Spanish culture, coupled with the sesquicentennial of the birth of Francisco de Goya,* provided the inspiration for *Goyescas*, a piano suite in six parts. This is a cyclical work that begins with "Flirtations" and ends with "The Specter's Serenade." The music, elegant, restrained, and aristocratic, resembles the style of Frédéric Chopin (1810–1849) or Robert Schumann (1810–1856) and is based on a romantic idea of the manners and style of eighteenth-century Spain. Well-constructed and hauntingly lyrical, the suite was later expanded into an opera.

Throughout his life, Granados was at best a reluctant traveler. It was thus sadly ironic that, after having finally been persuaded to come to New York City for the premier of the opera *Goyescas*, he died on the return trip when his ship was torpedoed by a German submarine on 24 Mar. 1916.

For additional information, see G. Chase, *The Music of Spain* (New York, 1959); A. Livermore, *A Short History of Spanish Music* (London, 1972); and L. E. Powell, *A History of Spanish Piano Music* (Bloomington, 1980).

*S. L. Brake*

**GRIS, JUAN** (1887–1927), artist. José Victoriano González, better known by his chosen name of Juan Gris, was born in Madrid* on 23 Mar. 1887, and died in Boulogne, France,* on 11 May 1927. His relatively short working life as an artist produced a definitive cubist vision and a number of acknowledged masterpieces. Despite association with his more famous compatriot Pablo Picasso* and with Picasso's collaborator, Georges Braque (1882–1963), Gris stands independently as the quintessential cubist, and his works—often gray-toned, as the artist's name suggests—set a new standard for cubism.

Gris had abandoned engineering studies at the Escuela de Artes y Manufacturas in Madrid to begin painting in 1904. Almost entirely self-taught, he moved to Paris in 1906, as did so many other artists, where he lived in the now-historic Bateau-Lavoir, already inhabited by a medley of poets and artists. Gris experimented with the forms of the newly discovered attempt by cubism to show all of a subject from various angles, rather than from the one-point perspective traditional since the Renaissance. His cubist creations progressed from analytic investigations of shattered forms to synthetic, two-dimensional studies made by an accretion of forms. His nonrepresentational productions rarely, if ever, abandoned the subject entirely. Gris did not confine himself to canvas and paints; like his fellow cubists Marc Chagall (1887–1985), Chaim Soutine (1894–1943), Julio González (1876–1942), Amedeo Modigliani (1884–1920), and Jacques Lipchitz (1891–1973), he experimented with collage and sculpture as well.

Gris was something of a painter-philosopher, as Picasso emphatically was not. He wrote a paper entitled "Possibilités de la peinture," which he presented at the Sorbonne in 1924. It serves today as one of the unofficial manifestos of the cubist circle. In contrast to other cubist theoreticians such as Albert Gleizes (1881–1953) and Jean Metzinger (1883–1956), authors of "Du Cubisme," Gris was a far more original artist and thinker.

His sober canvases and collages made him one of the most consistent of the cubists. His death at forty ended a career that was devoted almost wholly to exercises in the new mode of vision established by Gris, Picasso, and Braque.

For additional information, see H. H. Arnason, *A History of Modern Art* (New York, 1968).

*S. Benforado*

*Related entry*: PICASSO, PABLO.

# H

HERNÁNDEZ, RAMÓN (1935– ), novelist, short-story writer, essayist, and poet. Hernández, a professional engineer with the National Institute for the Conservation of Nature and editor of *Vida Silvestre*, an ecological journal, is also a founding member, former executive secretary, and president of the Spanish Writers' Guild, an organization originally concerned with the protection of the rights of authors and the development and promotion of Spanish literature.

During Hernández's childhood, his family experienced repression both in Guadalajara and Madrid* after the Spanish Civil War.* His liberal outlook is reflected in many of the essays he published in the early 1980s in *El Imparcial* (Madrid). As a short-story writer and essayist, he has been a contributor to *Diario 16*, *República de las Letras*, *Ya*, *Anales de la Literatura Española Contemporánea*, and *La Hora de Castilla–La Mancha*. Since 1984, he has been the creative-writing editor for *Siglo XX/20th Century*, a publication of the Twentieth-Century Spanish Association of America. He has taught in the United States on a number of occasions as a visiting professor.

To date, Hernández has written thirteen novels: *Presentimiento de lobos* (1966), *Palabras en el muro* (1969), *La ira de la noche* (1970), *El tirano inmóvil* (1970), *Invitado a morir* (1972), *Eterna memoria* (1974), *Algo está ocurriendo aquí* (1976), *Fábula de la ciudad* (1979), *Pido la muerte al rey* (1979), *Bajo palio* (1983), *Los amantes del sol poniente* (1983), *El ayer perdido* (1986), and *Sola en el paraíso* (1987).

He has received the Águilas and Villa de Madrid prizes for his experimental fiction, best characterized by his use of different points of view, subjective reality, and poetic language. His concern is with mankind in a transcendental sense, and with the conflicts and disorientation resulting from the absurdities of the modern world. The characters in his work, seeking to live full existences, either dream or invent an imagined reality in which they seem to exist, which makes Hernández's works among the best in twentieth-century Spanish fiction.

For additional information, see V. Cabrera and L. T. González-del-Valle, *Novela española contemporánea* (Madrid, 1980); L. T. González-del-Valle and R. Landeira, eds., *Nuevos y novísimos* (Boulder, 1987); and S. Sanz Villanueva, *Historia de la literatura española 6/2* (Barcelona, 1984).

*L. T. González-del-Valle*

**HIERRO, JOSÉ** (1922– ), twentieth-century, post–civil war poet. Hierro was born in Madrid, but his family moved to the northern port city of Santander while he was still a child. When the Spanish Civil War* began, he was too young to be a combatant, but the war touched him and his family in 1937, when the nationalists captured the city and jailed his father. The family was plunged into economic destitution, compounded by Hierro's own arrest in 1939 and imprisonment until 1944.

In prison, he began to write poetry, and after his release, he became active in the literary world, particularly after June 1944, when he became a collaborator in the poetic literary journal *Proel*.

Hierro's philosophy, which *Proel* shared, advocates poetry portraying the immediate, concrete circumstance of the poet. The focus of poetry should be the moment lived, rather than abstractions. He himself has written, in the prologue to his *Obras completas* (1962), that he is a poet of "testimony," living and interpreting a particular historical moment. Shunning both idealization and political commitment, he occupies something of a poetic middle ground.

His poetry expresses the universality of shared experiences and sentiments. His verses play musically upon the senses of the reader. There is a quality of dramatic tension in much of his poetry as he interplays opposing ideas or sentiments.

Hierro's first volume of poetry, *Tierra sin nosotros*, was published in 1947. The same year, he produced another, *Alegría*, which won the Adonais award. In 1950, a new work, *Con las piedras, con el viento*, appeared, followed by *Quinta del 42* in 1953. His *Antología poética*, published later in the year, was awarded the Premio National. *Estatuas yacentes* saw print in 1955. Hierro was further honored in 1957 when *Cuanto sé de mí* won both the Premio de la Crítica and the Premio March. His most recent work is *Libro de las alucinaciones*, which appeared in 1964.

For additional information, see A. de Alborno, *José Hierro* (Madrid, 1981); J. Hierro, *Cuanto sé de mí* (Barcelona, 1964); and E. E. de Torre, *José Hierro: Poeta de testimonio* (Madrid, 1983).

*N. A. Vigil*

# I

**IBARRURI GÓMEZ, DOLORES** (1895–1989), leader of the Spanish Communist party* (Partido Comunista Español, PCE). Born in Gallarta, a mining town in northern Spain, Ibarruri was raised with ten siblings in the precarious economic conditions that miners' families endured in the early decades of this century. Though she was enrolled briefly in normal school, Ibarruri found her course of study interrupted by financial difficulties, and she sought work as a waitress, domestic, and laundress. Her parents were Catholic monarchists, but Julián Ruiz, whom Ibarruri married in 1915, was already an active socialist. With him, she became involved in workers' politics, and it was her publication of an article signed La Pasionaria for *El Minero Vizcaíno* during Easter Week 1918 that gave her the name by which she would thereafter always be known.

The Biscayan socialist section to which she and Julián belonged was one of the first to support Russia's Bolshevik revolution (1917) and affiliate with the Third International, criticizing the existing Socialist party* for weakness and hesitancy as well as evolutionary doctrine. In 1920, she was chosen to be a member of the provincial committee of the Partido Comunista de Viscaya (PCV) and then served as a delegate to the First Congress of the PCE. Throughout the 1920s, Ibarruri, as did so many politically committed women,* struggled to balance the multiple roles of wife, mother, and communist activist. During the dictatorship of Gen. Miguel Primo de Rivera,* which almost destroyed the fledgling PCE, Julián was frequently incarcerated, and Dolores, who was a member of the party's national central committee, also spent time in jail.

She and Julián had six children: two sons; a set of triplet daughters; and another daughter, Eva, born in 1928. From intensely personal experience, Ibarruri learned not only of the political oppression and the struggle to survive that workers' families endured, but also of the often tragic burden of working-class women's pregnancy and motherhood. Only two of her children, Rubén and Amaya, lived beyond infancy.

With the establishment of the Second Republic* in 1931, Ibarruri moved away from regional politics and the traditional roles of wife and mother to become an increasingly important and respected national political leader. Never a great theoretician, she found that her greatest assets were her presence, charisma, and oratorical skills, which made her a heroine to the downtrodden and a patriotic symbol. As a member of the party's central committee, Ibarruri moved to Madrid,* campaigned extensively for the now-legal PCE, and worked on the party paper, *Mundo Obrero*. She was also responsible for organizing women's activities in the party and in 1933 created Las Agrupaciones de Mujeres Anti-fascistas; in 1933, at their first national congress, she was elected president. In this capacity, Ibarruri combined two issues that were central to her political activity: the resistance to fascism and the importance of women to the revolutionary struggle. Preaching the gospel of female emancipation through work, she also criticized her party for failure to deal adequately with women's issues and pushed for women's education, the raising of revolutionary consciousness, and women's involvement in all aspects of public life. In 1933, she was a delegate to the meeting of the Communist International, and in 1935, she attended meetings of the Seventh World Comintern Congress, becoming a member of the executive committee.

During the course of the Spanish Civil War,* La Pasionaria truly gained the stature of mythic heroine and became the symbol of sacrifice and unremitting struggle, perhaps in part because few other PCE leaders in those years could match her charisma. Exhorting Spaniards to resist during the long Battle of Madrid, she coined the famous phrase "No pasarán" ("They shall not pass") and sought to convince Madrileños that it was "better to die on your feet than live on your knees." This is not to imply that her functions were only symbolic or rhetorical. During the war, she was one of sixteen communist deputies in the Cortes and was elected vice-president of that body in 1937. In that position, she traveled throughout Europe, seeking support for the republic and gaining an international reputation. She also served as part of the political bureau of the PCE; headed the Comisión Auxilio Femenino under the defense minister, Francisco Largo Caballero,* that organized one hundred thousand women in anti-fascist activities; and galvanized the women of Madrid into building barricades; digging trenches; and staffing collective dining rooms, laundries, soup kitchens, and first-aid stations. On more formal, institutional levels, Ibarruri pushed for creation of a regular army*; supported use of the International Brigades*; and, as the aid and influence of the Soviet Union in Spain increased, adopted a more conservative international communist line.

Her increased responsibilities and visibility during these years were reflected in changes in her personal life as well. She separated from her husband, and her two surviving children were sent to live in Moscow, a common pattern for the children of communist women activists in this decade. In Mar. 1939, Ibarruri left Spain; intending to stay in France,* she was called to Moscow, which would become her home in exile for almost forty years, although her operational base later became Prague, Czechoslovakia.

In the decades in exile, Ibarruri was unwilling to criticize the Soviet Union and in party disputes over autonomy generally led the staunchly Stalinist group. Her devotion to the Soviet Union is understandable in that it had, after all, given support to her beloved Spain and shelter to her and her loved ones. Amaya, who continued to live there, married a Soviet army officer, and Rubén died in the 1942 fighting at Stalingrad. In the exile PCE organization, Dolores remained a central figure, assuming leadership of the party in 1942, and being formally elected party secretary in 1954. She continued to support guerrilla activity in Spain and maintained a national reputation through speeches on clandestine broadcasts by Radio Moscow and Radio España Independiente. In 1960, she supported Santiago Carrillo* for party secretary and assumed the position of party president created especially for her and through which she presided, but no longer governed. By the late 1960s, she adopted a more autonomous and critical posture for which she then earned opprobrium from her previous supporters.

Her reputation as an international communist leader was also enhanced in these years. She served as vice-president of the Women's International Democratic Federation, traveled extensively (including a visit to Cuba in 1964), and received the Lenin Peace Prize in 1964 and the Order of the October Revolution in 1970.

With the death of Gen. Francisco Franco* in 1975, the PCE was again legalized. La Pasionaria returned to Spain in May 1977, headed the party's ticket in elections that year, and gained a seat in the lower house. In 1983, when Gerardo Iglesias was elected party secretary, Ibarruri again was named party president and remains a powerful symbol in national politics, as the homage paid to her in Dec. 1985 on her ninetieth birthday indicated.

For additional information, see A. Carabantes and E. Cimorra, *Un mito llamado Pasionaria* (Barcelona, 1982); L. Haranburu, *Dolores Ibarruri* (Bilbao, 1977); D. Ibarruri, *They Shall Not Pass* (New York, 1966), *Speeches and Articles* (New York, 1938), and *En la lucha* (Moscow, 1968); T. Pamies, *Una española llamada Dolores Ibarruri* (Barcelona, 1976); and M. Mullaney, *Revolutionary Women: Gender and the Socialist Revolutionary Role* (New York, 1983).

                                                                                            *M. J. Slaughter*

*Related entries*: COMMUNIST PARTY; SPANISH CIVIL WAR.

**INDEPENDENCE, WAR OF** (1808–1814), popular uprising of the Spanish people against Napoleon Bonaparte (1769–1821) and his brother, Joseph Napoleon (José I*), king of Spain, 1808–1814. In 1805, Napoleonic domination of Europe was divided between the French Empire, under Napoleon's direct control; the greater empire, subject to Napoleon; nominal allies, such as Spain (since 1796); and the openly hostile states of Britain,* Portugal,* and Russia. The Peace of Tilsit (7–9 July 1807) altered this balance by temporarily allying the Russian Empire with Napoleon.

If Napoleon ruled continental Europe, however, Britain dominated the seas, and to overcome this obstacle, Napoleon announced a continental blockade (21

Sept. 1806) to prohibit British goods from entering European markets. Portugal, linked to Britain by the 1703 Methuen Treaty, refused to cooperate, whereupon Napoleon ordered an invasion from Spain under the command of Jean Andoche Junot (1771–1813). Accomplished late in 1807, it met little resistance, but the Portuguese court, narrowly avoiding Junot's troops, escaped to Brazil. The French then occupied northern Spain from the Basque* Provinces in the west to Catalonia* in the east to safeguard lines of communication between France and Junot's army in Portugal.

At the same time, Napoleon began to expand his activities from the battlefield to the political arena. His ally who had given the French permission to occupy northern Spain, Manuel Godoy,* the favorite of Carlos IV,* had twice (1805 and 1806) approached Napoleon with plans to divide Portugal so that Godoy would gain his own kingdom. He was discredited by the patriotic reaction to the French occupation, however, and Napoleon began pursuing a tactic to annex Spanish territory north of the Ebro River in exchange for a forced merger of what remained of Portugal and Spain. French troops advanced on Madrid to accomplish this geopolitical sleight of hand, while Godoy and Carlos IV chose to go into hiding in southern Spain.

The reaction to this crisis caused the Motín de Aranjuez (18–19 Mar. 1808), which brought about the fall of Godoy on 23 Mar. Carlos IV abdicated on 19 May in favor of his son, Fernando VII,* although Napoleon refused to recognize the act and, at a meeting in Bayonne, threatened Fernando into returning the crown to his father. Carlos in turn renounced it in favor of Napoleon, and the French emperor astounded Europe by naming his brother, Joseph, as King José I of Spain.

In shocked reaction, the people of Madrid revolted on 2 May 1808. The rebellion was bloodily repressed by Napoleon's lieutenant, Joaquim Murat (1767–1815), but since Spain's best soldiers had been sent to Portugal and the south to fight the British, French troops were able to occupy many of the principal northern cities. As the French army advanced, however, the countryside behind them exploded in guerrilla warfare. Juntas formed in the provinces to mobilize popular support, and by means of a Junta Central, they also sent representatives to Britain to seek aid. Eventually, a meeting of a new Cortes was called, and in late 1810, in the Andalusian city of Cadiz, representatives of the provincial juntas met to begin the work of drafting a constitution. In contrast to the popular forces in rebellion against the French, the representatives at the Cortes of Cadiz* were drawn, in large measure, from an intellectual minority steeped in the liberal ideas of the Enlightenment.* The result of their reformist efforts was the Constitution of 1812.

In reaction, the French utilized the army of Pierre Dupont de l'Etang (1765–1840), already en route to Cadiz to aid remnants of the French fleet who had taken refuge there after the defeat at Trafalgar* (21 Oct. 1805), to seize Vitoria, Valladolid, Segovia, and (passing by Madrid), Toledo. Adrien Jannot de Moncey

(1754–1842), camped between Vitoria and Burgos, moved to Aranda, while Philibert Guillaume Duhesme (1766–1815) occupied Barcelona.

Napoleon then ordered Dupont to Andalusia, Moncey to Valencia, François Joseph Lefebvre (1755–1820) to Saragossa, Joseph Chabran (1763–1843) to Tarragona and Valencia, Duhesme to Gerona, Jean-Baptiste Bessieres (1768–1813) to Burgos, Jean Antoine Verdier (1767–1839) to Logroño, and Antoine Charles Louis Lasalle (1775–1809) to Torquemada, Palencia, Cabezón, and Valladolid. Bessieres defeated Gregorio García de la Cuesta (1740–1812) and Joaquín Blake y Joyes (1739–1827) at Medina del Río Seco on 14 July 1808.

These rapid advances overextended supply lines and delayed the arrival of reinforcements. Soon after Dupont had sacked Cordoba, for example, he encountered a mass uprising and superior forces at the battle of Bailén on 19–21 July 1808, and eighteen thousand French troops were lost. Unable to strengthen the Army of the Center, José Bonaparte was forced to evacuate Madrid and retire to the Ebro.

Other French reverses followed. Moncey failed to take Valencia, Chabran lost in El Bruch, Verdier had to lift the first siege of Saragossa, and Duhesme was unable to take Gerona. A British expeditionary army led by Sir Arthur Wellesley (the future duke of Wellington* [1769–1852]) was landed in Portugal, and in late Aug., Junot was defeated at Vimeiro (21 Aug. 1808) and forced to surrender at the Convention of Cintra (22 Aug.). Napoleon, in the midst of preparations for an east European campaign, nevertheless took personal command, and by using the elite of the Grand Army, won a series of victories that recaptured Madrid in early Dec. and forced the British from La Corunna on 16 Jan. 1809.

The emperor returned to France early in 1809 to deal with a possible outbreak of war with Austria, but his marshals remained: Nicolas Jean de Dieu Soult (1769–1851), Michel Ney (1769–1815), Claude Victor-Perrin (1764–1841), Moncey, and Adolphe Edouard Casimir Joseph Mortier (1768–1835). Soult invaded the north of Portugal and Ney, Galicia. Saragossa and Gerona fell after being besieged a second time, and although Wellington was technically victorious over Cuesta at the battle of Talavera (27–28 July 1809), his losses forced him to retire to Portugal. All over the peninsula, France won victories, but not the war.

In 1810, Napoleon, having dealt with Austria, refocused on Spain. His top marshal, André Masséna (1758–1817), was sent to Spain with reinforcements. French troops penetrated deeply into Portugal, capturing Ciudad Rodrigo before being stopped at Torres Vedras, a triple line of secretly constructed forts north of Lisbon. In the south of Spain, the French entered Andalusia and seized Cordoba, Seville, Granada, and Malaga, before being stopped by the fortifications of Cadiz, which were supported by the guns of British ships in the harbor. Further north, Louis Gabriel Suchet (1770–1826) took Lérida and Tortosa and, in 1811 and 1812, Tarragona and Valencia. Despite these impressive gains, however, the guerrilla war raged more bitterly than ever.

In May 1811, Soult mounted a new offensive in Portugal, but was defeated, near Badajoz, at La Albuera, by William Carr, viscount of Beresford (1764–1854), in what proved to be the turning point of the war. Napoleon, having decided to invade Russia, was seriously neglecting the peninsular front, and a major Anglo-Spanish counteroffensive by Wellington took advantage of French weaknesses to capture Ciudad Rodrigo and Badajoz. While the battle of Arapiles near Salamanca on 20 July 1812 relieved pressure on Madrid for a time, the French were briefly forced out of the capital. Evacuating Andalusia, their forces concentrated in Valencia, and from there, they retook Madrid in Nov. 1812.

Six months later, in May 1813, Wellington once more recaptured Madrid, this time for good. José, defeated at Vitoria (21 June) and San Marcial (31 Aug.), crossed the Pyrenees and abdicated at Fontainebleau on 6 Apr. 1814. Wellington was victorious at Toulouse (10 Apr. 1814) in the last major battle of the war.

The War of Independence, as the first successful rebellion against Napoleon, served as an example for Russia and Germany. The French could never control all of Spain, and the guerrillas made the areas that were under French control precarious. Guerrilla warfare itself was a new phenomenon that anticipated future nationalist-dominated conflicts of "total war." Above all, Spanish geography made it impossible for Napoleon to fight the single, definitive battle that had won him victory after victory in northern Europe.

There was little popular support for José, although some Spaniards did side with France. When José moved his court for the final time, ten thousand Spanish troops accompanied him, and at the end of the war, approximately twelve thousand Spanish families sought refuge in France. In the larger cities, many minor bureaucrats elected to support the French for fear of losing their positions. The "afrancesados," as French supporters were called, included a diversity of individuals from churchmen to writers. Many others sided with France less from ideology than for personal advantage.

Despite such support, French generals often acted arbitrarily by abusing the locals in a variety of ways, most often through outright theft of artistic and ecclesiastical treasures, or by levying irregular taxes, ransom, or quartering requirements. These acts came to contrast negatively with the improvement, over time, of the Spanish resistance. Guerrilla leaders such as Francisco Espoz y Mina (1781–1836) and Juan Martín Díaz (1775–1825) and regulars such as Pablo Morillo (1775–1837) proved themselves adaptable and more than a match for their French counterparts.

For additional information, see Servicio Histórico Militar, *Guerra de la independencia, 1808–1814*, 5 vols. (Madrid, 1972); J. García Prado et al., *Estudios de la guerra de la independencia*, 3 vols. (Saragossa, 1964); R. Carr, *Spain, 1808–1939* (Oxford, 1966); and M. Artola, *La burguesía revolucionaria, 1808–1869* (Madrid, 1973).

*R. Hendricks*

*Related entries*: CARLOS IV; FERNANDO VII.

**INSTITUCIÓN LIBRE DE ENSEÑANZA,** the Free Educational Institute, a private, secular educational association. Organized in 1875, the most famous school in nineteenth-century Spain was a product of the Krausist school of philosophy and of Francisco Giner des los Ríos,* its creator, who like all Krausists placed an almost mystic importance on the value of education. When Manuel Orovio (who had purged the universities in 1867) again became minister of public instruction in the cabinet of Antonio Cánovas del Castillo,* he decreed on 26 Feb. 1875 that all state schools must use textbooks approved by the state. Giner protested the moralistic and Catholic thrust of the order and was briefly arrested.

The Institución Libre began the next year as a university, but when this failed, it was converted into a small, private high school. It combined German educator Friedrich Froebel's (1782–1852) "intuitive" method of instruction—field trips and actual observation—with a British emphasis on tutorials and student papers. In this form, it succeeded as an experimental school. Lectures were replaced by discussions led by a number of professors who in 1876–1881 were barred from state universities. Among them were Manuel Cossío (1858–1935), an art historian; Gumersindo de Azcárate (1840–1917), a sociologist and political scientist; José Castillejo (1877–1945), a historian of ideas, and Fernando de Castro (1814–1884), a political scientist.

The school was always small. By 1884, for example, only about two hundred students attended, although the number grew as the school's excellence became known. Santiago Ramón y Cajal* encouraged the study of science* and modern languages, both missing in traditional curricula, that attracted children of well-to-do and intellectual parents.

After Giner's death in 1899, the Free Educational Institute declined as a school, but its influence remained very much alive in the Generation of 1898.* A residencia was established at the University of Madrid for its graduates, headed by novelist and poet Juan Ramón Jiménez.* In 1907, the school was also instrumental in creating the quasi-public Junta para Ampliación de Estudios to send Spaniards abroad to receive graduate education and make recommendations for the improvement of general education. Azcárate, Marcelino Menéndez y Pelayo,* Ramón Menéndez Pidal,* and other creative Spaniards served on its board and were successful in persuading the state to create a system of consejos superiores de investigaciones in 1910. These institutes promoted study and specialized research in many areas, thus continuing the educational mission of the Free Institute. Intellectuals also adopted the republicanism and anticlericalism of the Institución's founders as an agenda for their generation's political life.

For additional information, see V. Cacho Viu, *La Institución Libre de Enseñanza* (Madrid, 1974); J. Castillejo, *War of Ideas in Spain: Philosophy, Politics and Education* (London, 1937); J. B. Trend, *The Origins of Modern Spain* (New York, 1934); and Y. Turin, *Educación y la escuela y España de 1874 a 1902: Liberalismo y tradición*, trans. J. Hernández Alfonso (Madrid, 1967).

*R. W. Kern*

*Related entries*: ATENEO; EDUCATION; KRAUSE, KARL CHRISTIAN FRIEDRICH.

**INSTITUTO DE REFORMAS SOCIALES,** Institute of Social Reform, state-sponsored agency established in 1903. Salvador de Madariaga (1886–1980) once remarked that the liberal regime in Spain had the saving grace of knowing it was inept. A century of chaos did not blind the liberals to the failings of their own ideology, unlike those whose regimes followed.

The Institute of Social Reform represented one of the liberals' most radical experiments. It was approved in 1903 by Alfonso XIII* after the Senate had initially blocked its creation. José Canalejas (1854–1912), a prominent radical liberal, promoted its acceptance, although the original concept was that of the Krausist intellectual, Gumersindo de Azcárate (1840–1917), a republican reformer since the 1870s. He believed that modern society needed mediating institutions to treat the major socioeconomic problems of modern life. The institute would operate as a social fact-finding body, bringing together representatives of government, industry, and labor to investigate social and industrial conditions in order to prepare social legislation.

Seminal studies prepared under the institute's aegis resulted in many of the reforms accomplished in the early twentieth century, particularly those dealing with child labor and women workers. Unfortunately, Azcárate's death in 1917 deprived the institute of his leadership. The later dictatorship of Gen. Miguel Primo de Rivera* destroyed the institute's operations, although his corporative labor legislation of 1926 copied the use of a collegiate body first proposed by the institute. The Second Republic* later attempted to revive it, but it played only a small role.

For additional information, see S. de Madariaga, *Spain: A Modern History* (New York, 1958).

R. W. Kern

*Related entry*: KRAUSE, KARL CHRISTIAN FRIEDRICH.

**INTERNATIONAL BRIGADES** (1936–1938), volunteers in the Spanish Civil War.* The outbreak of civil war and revolution in Spain immediately fired the political idealism of liberal and left-wing circles in Europe and the Americas. Writers, social activists, and ordinary working-class men and women rallied to the republican cause by enlisting in the International Brigades. This diverse group of foreigners freely offered its services because of the realization that the Spanish conflict was a reflection of the greater ideological struggles that seemed to be intensifying daily in Europe. Although their political motives were mixed, all the volunteers went to fight against fascism. By the time the war had ended in Apr. 1939, some 59,380 participants from fifty-three countries had served in the International Brigades of the republican army.

Since the war, the story of the International Brigades has received considerable public attention. This is hardly surprising, since this remarkable group of men and women exhibited considerable courage and self-sacrifice in the course of a long and bitterly fought contest. Most of the numerous publications on the International Brigades, unfortunately, have been largely shaped by the ideological concerns of the civil-war era. As a result, brigade members tend to be portrayed either as the unsung heroes of the first antifascist crusade or as tools of the Soviet Union, whose real mission in Spain was to help the communists dominate republican military and diplomatic affairs. Both depictions are misleading, since the historical role of the brigades was much more complicated than either of these viewpoints implies.

The republican government was initially opposed to the idea of foreign intervention of any kind, including the participation of individuals acting on their own initiative. Yet in the confusion that reigned during the early weeks of the civil war, it proved to be impossible for the authorities to prevent foreigners (especially those already in Spain) from being caught up in the sweep of events. By Aug. 1936, several hundred antifascists—mainly left-wing French trade unionists and political refugees from Italy*, Germany,* and Central and Eastern Europe—were fighting alongside republican troops. The first non-Spanish units to see action were the French Paris Battalion, which participated in the defense of Irun; the Polish General Dombrowski Battalion; the Italian Guistizia e Liberta Column; and the German Ernst Thälmann Centuria, which had grown to battalion strength by the end of Sept.

These first organized groups of foreign volunteers in the republican camp arose spontaneously and were not part of a coordinated movement to bring antifascists into Spain. This situation, however, did not last for long. As early as 28 July, several prominent members of the Comintern (Third or Communist International), based in Paris, were laying plans to fight for the republican cause. Among these actively promoting this idea were Maurice Thorez (1900- ), head of the French Communist party; Palmiro Togliatti (1893–1964), chief of the Italian Communist party in exile; and Yugoslav communist leader Josip Broz (1892–1980), later known as Tito. Backed by the Soviet Union, which was still temporizing over whether to provide military aid to the republicans, the Comintern launched in Sept. a campaign to recruit an international corps to go to Spain.

While the International Brigades, as this army came to be known, were organized and controlled by the Comintern, not all the volunteers were communist. At least 75 percent were party members, but the rest were men and women of different political persuasions, such as liberals, republicans, and socialists. The fact that such famous figures as Ernest Hemingway (1898–1961), Langston Hughes (1876–1956), Stephen Spender (1909- ), George Orwell (1901–1950), Arthur Koestler (1905–1983), André Malraux (1901–1976), and Simone Weil (1909–1943) became identified with the civil war gave rise to the false impression that most of the foreigners in republican Spain, including the International Brigades, were middle-class poets and writers. Yet the overwhelming majority of brigade volunteers were of working-class origins—seamen, miners, and factory workers.

Prospective candidates, usually screened by local Communist party officials, came from the ranks of men and women who subscribed to the Comintern's nonrevolutionary Popular Front policy. Those who eventually enlisted were quickly funneled through the Comintern's international network. Some were issued false passports (for the Americans, it was illegal to enlist in a foreign army), transported to brigade headquarters in Paris, and then smuggled into Spain either by sea or across the Pyrenees.

The first contingent of volunteers began arriving toward the end of Sept., and by mid-Oct., International Brigade units had established a base of operations in Albacete. In view of the growing presence of foreign troops, the republican government finally overcame its reluctance to use non-Spanish combatants by the end of the month.

Given the diverse nationalities represented in the brigades, it was expedient, whenever possible, to divide the volunteers into linguistic groups. French was the most widely used language, followed by Italian, German, and English. Before June 1937, these lines of demarcation were not always clear cut, and it was not uncommon for an English-speaking unit to be attached to a German or French battalion. Only five brigades (XI-XV) were formed during the war, although it often appeared to foreign observers as though there were many more than this, probably because each brigade was composed of a bewildering array of battalions and smaller army units, some of which—such as the Thälmann, Dombrowsky, and Abraham Lincoln Battalions—were better known than the brigades to which they were attached.

Although the International Brigades were warmly received by almost everyone in the republican zone, they were cautiously greeted by the dissident Marxist POUM* and by Spain's classic revolutionaries, the anarchists* and anarcho-syndicalists of the powerful CNT-FAI organizations. For their part, the libertarians feared that troops under Comintern control could be used to strengthen the official communists at the expense of the revolutionary groups. Their suspicions, which proved correct, prevailed throughout the war. Even so, it is interesting to note that once the foreign volunteers had the opportunity to demonstrate their valor and military skills on the battlefield, some libertarian commanders of the republican army came to admire and respect the contributions of the International Brigades.

In a sense, the formation of the International Brigades reflected the desire of the Communist party and other antirevolutionary elements to reorganize the republican army. The Communist party, for example, promoted the militarization of the militias that had been hastily raised during the early weeks of the war. In their place, the communists wanted to form army units modeled on their own Fifth Regiment, where military authority was concentrated under one command (mando único). Unlike the popular militias, many of which practiced egalitarianism and therefore discouraged formal rituals characteristic of a traditional army, the Fifth Regiment stressed the need for iron discipline and strict adherence to a hierarchical chain of command. Following several disastrous republican defeats in the autumn of 1936, the pressure to refashion the military along these lines was immense. The communists took the first major step in this direction by progressively dissolving its prestigious Fifth Regiment, whose battalions were gradually fused into "mixed brigades" of the "People's Army" that was just beginning to take shape.

The movement to militarize the republican forces paved the way for the introduction of the International Brigades. In fact, the brigades constituted an integral component of the communists' ever-expanding network of power and influence in the republican zone. The foreign troops were directed by some of the Comintern's most seasoned apparatchiks. André Marty (1886–1955), a prominent French communist, headed military operations at Albacete, and he was ably assisted by Italian communists Luigi Longo ("Gallo," 1900– ) and Giuseppe de Vittorio ("Nicoletti," 1892–1948). The International Brigades were also controlled by means of the political-commissariat system of the republican army, the greater part of which was dominated by the communists. Fully integrated into the fabric of brigade operations, the political commissar performed a variety of key roles. The political commissariat of the International Brigades described the commissar as "the soul" of the new army. Besides maintaining the morale of the troops, he was responsible for their political education. This entailed, among other things, regular lectures on the political significance of the war. Dissent, especially if it challenged the official line of the Communist party, was not tolerated, and people suspected of being provocateurs or spies were dealt with harshly. A rigorous discipline was imposed not just to enforce a high military standard, but also to ensure political conformity. This meant that very few members of the International Brigades were ever exposed to other viewpoints. Most volunteers, not surprisingly then, never fully understood either the nature or the implications of the ideological struggles that were increasingly rending apart the various political parties in the republican camp. A case in point is the way in which members of the International Brigades perceived the anti-Stalinist POUM and its allies on the revolutionary Left. Brigade members, uncritically following the official communist line, which went to preposterous lengths to discredit the POUM, supported the far-fetched view that POUMists were Trotskyist saboteurs in the service of fascism.

No hard evidence exists that describes the extent to which the political commissar relied on physical threats and other forms of intimidation to maintain discipline. It is significant, though, that even sources sympathetic to the International Brigades have admitted that sometimes the threat of violence or, on occasion, the actual execution of brigade members, did occur. Estimates of the number of purge victims—either in the form of expulsions or executions—vary considerably. While some veterans of the International Brigade deny that extreme punitive measures were ever taken, others have testified that the overzealous actions of some political commissars resulted in as many as fifty political executions. André Marty, for example, was reputed to be a particularly bloodthirsty commander who was known to his enemies as "the butcher of Albacete."

The military history of the International Brigades began with their arrival at a critical moment. Just as the first recruits were undergoing training in Albacete, nationalist troops were advancing relentlessly on Madrid.* Several thousand troops of the newly formed XI Brigade marched into the capital on the morning of 8 Nov., two days after the republican government had fled to Valencia.* The fate of the city now lay in the hands of the Madrid Defense Council (Junta de Defensa) and the people of Madrid. Republican forces already in the capital were reinforced by the arrival of the first shipments of war matériel from the Soviet Union.

Thanks to the efficient communist-run propaganda machine, the early military feats of the brigades were trumpeted around the world. While these press reports exaggerated the role of brigades in the defense of the city, there can be no doubt that their timely intervention helped to keep the capital from falling to the nationalists. Their presence not only uplifted the morale of the beseiged Madrileños, but also played a particularly important part in the intense and bitter street fighting that occurred at University City and Casa de Campo, the areas of the city that bore the main brunt of nationalist frontal attacks.

The republicans' successful defense of Madrid did not dampen the nationalist resolve to occupy it as soon as possible. As a result, Gen. Francisco Franco* spent the next few months mounting offensives aimed at taking Madrid. The International Brigades saw action in the Jarama Valley and at Guadalajara. The Battle of Jarama was a particularly bloody engagement that involved several brigade units: André Marty Battalion (XIV), Edgar Andrí and Ernst Thälmann Battalions (XI), and the British, French-Belgian, Abraham Lincoln, and Dimitrov Battalions of the recently formed XV International Brigade.

As in the engagement of Jarama, the brigades were used as shock troops in the Battle of Guadalajara. While only three thousand troops saw action, they were involved in the heaviest fighting. This was especially true of the Italian Garibaldi Battalion (XII Brigade), which was attached to the Fourteenth Division of the republican army. It was at Guadalajara that another "civil war" drama was played out: the antifascist Italians of the Garibaldi Battalion came face-to-face with Benito Mussolini's (1883–1945) large expeditionary force that had been sent to help the nationalists. The men of the Garibaldi not only fought valiantly against their countrymen, but also attempted to win them over by widely distributing antifascist propaganda. The Garibaldi Battalion, in the end, helped the republican forces deliver a humiliating defeat to Mussolini's much-vaunted Black Flame and Black Shirt divisions.

With the assistance of the International Brigades, the republicans had scored both a strategic and political victory at Guadalajara. From a military standpoint, the republicans had successfully thwarted the nationalist attempt to mount a flank attack on Madrid from the north. The victory also held enormous propaganda value for the republican cause: it was proclaimed in the prorepublican international press as the antifascists' first significant triumph.

The next three months saw a lull in the fighting, a badly needed respite that allowed the brigades to be reorganized. This was undertaken partly because of the substantial losses they had suffered. By June, nearly 70 percent of the volunteers who had fought during the seige of Madrid were either dead or hospitalized. Another reason for the reorganization was the pressing need to bring about linguistic coherence among the patchwork of nationalities. The XI Brigade grouped together the Germanic and Scandinavian volunteers; the XII Brigade was predominantly Italian; the XIII Brigade was formed by Slavic battalions; the XIV Brigade combined French and Belgian forces; and the XV Brigade consolidated the English-speaking volunteers from the United States,* Britain,* and the Commonwealth countries.

Each of the five permanent brigades established (XI-XV) was usually composed of four battalions of seven hundred men each. Additional military groups, such as machine-gun and transportation units, were assigned to each brigade. All the brigades were eventually incorporated formally into units of the regular republican army, grouped into so-called "International Divisions," such as the 35th, then under the command of Gen. "Gal" (Janos Galicz, ?–1938 or 1939), and the 45th, which was initially commanded by Gen. "Lukács" (Mata Zalka Kemeny, ?–1937).

The International Brigades experienced a steady decline in their overall troop strength, however, from the summer of 1937 until their withdrawal in the autumn of 1938. Fresh recruits from abroad were not forthcoming, and an ever-increasing number of the volunteers already in Spain became casualties of the war. During this period, the brigades were engaged in two major military campaigns: the Battle of Teruel and the Battle of the Ebro.

At Teruel, they were sent into action after the nationalists launched a massive counter-offensive against the republican forces occupying the city. The brigades were thrown into battle at an inauspicious time, not least because it was during the bitterest winter in many years. By the time the nationalists had recaptured Teruel at the end of Feb. 1938, the XI and XV Brigades had incurred catastrophic losses: the Canadian MacKenzie-Papineau Battalion had been decimated, and an entire battalion of the XI Brigade had been virtually annihilated.

The XI, XII, and XV International Brigades—of which only 30 percent were foreigners—participated in the republican army's last major offensive, the Battle of the Ebro. In a desperate effort to prolong their struggle against the nationalists, the republicans launched an attack across the Ebro River in late July 1938. Although the republicans captured 270 square miles in less than a week, they maintained only a tenuous hold on the conquered territory. By mid-Aug., republican troops began a long retreat to their original positions behind the Ebro. Unable to stop the nationalists' inexorable drive, the republicans faced certain defeat.

It was apparent that the International Brigades had lost their raison d'être. Most foreign volunteers had been killed, wounded, or absorbed into Spanish units. The republican premier, Juan Negrín,* thus announced to the League of Nations on 21 Sept. 1938 his intention to withdraw "all non-Spanish combatants engaged in fighting on the government side." At a farewell parade on 15 Nov., approximately six thousand of the remaining foreign volunteers marched through Barcelona to the rousing cheers of thousands of onlookers who had come to pay tribute to the International Brigades. The high point of the procession came in the address of the famous communist leader Dolores Ibarruri* (La Pasionaria), who called the foreign volunteers a "heroic example of democracy's solidarity and universality."

The fate of former brigade members in the immediate post-civil war period was one of severe hardship. Because they were leftists who had been associated with a well-known communist organization, veterans from the Western democracies did not return to a hero's welcome. In the United States, for example, returning volunteers were viewed with suspicion, especially by the government. Even though only some of them were committed communists who adhered religiously to the policies of the Soviet Union, all former brigaders were regarded as potential subversives. The fact that some veterans later loyally served their country during World War II* did little to dispel their negative political reputation. Many suffered persecution as a result of their ties with the International Brigades during the cold-war era of the 1950s and 1960s.

Former brigade members in Europe and the Soviet Union were not treated any better. Volunteers who had been political refugees before the civil war were obliged to find asylum wherever they could. Some joined the republican exiles streaming into France,* only to find themselves a few months later in yet another war. Veterans captured during the German occupation were interred in camps, and those who were spared went underground, playing key roles in the resistance movement. In the Soviet Union, a number of former brigaders from Eastern and Central Europe and the Soviet Union fell victim to the Stalinist purges of the late 1930s. Hungarian General Kléber (M. Z. Stern, 1895–1938), for example, once dubbed as the "saviour of Madrid" by the Stalinist press, was one of those liquidated.

Perhaps the most unfortunate group of surviving International Brigaders, though, were the men captured by the nationalists. Of the estimated 287 prisoners taken, more than half were summarily executed. The rest endured long and hard years of imprisonment in Franco's Spain.

For additional information, see B. Alexander, *British Volunteers for Liberty: Spain, 1936–1939* (London, 1982); A. Castells, *Las brigadas internacionales de la guerra de España* (Barcelona, 1972); J. Delperrie de Bayac, *Les brigades internationales* (Paris, 1968); C. Eby, *Between the Bullet and the Lie* (New York, 1969); V. B. Johnston, *The Legions of Babel: The International Brigades in the Spanish Civil War* (University Park, Pa., 1967); C. Penchienati, *Brigate Internazionali in Spagna: Delitti della "Ceka" comunista* (Milan, 1950); and D. Richardson, *Comintern Army: The International Brigades and the Spanish Civil War* (Lexington, Ky., 1983).

G. Esenwein

*Related entries*: ARMY; COMMUNIST PARTY OF SPAIN; POUM; SPANISH CIVIL WAR.

**ISABEL II, QUEEN OF SPAIN** (1830–1904), ruled 1843–1868. The birth of Isabel, daughter of Fernando VII* and his fourth wife, María Cristina of Naples (1808–1878), caused the promulgation of the 1789 Pragmatic Sanction to permit female succession to the throne for their first child, even though Fernando's younger brother, don Carlos (1788–1855), clearly expected to succeed him. With the king's death in 1833, the three-year-old Isabel was represented by the regency (1833–1843) of her mother, while the First Carlist War (1833–1840) divided Spain between the followers of María Cristina and don Carlos.

The regency saw the birth of liberalism,* party politics among the moderates* and progressives,* and the acceleration of disentailment.* These were difficult, fundamental problems of development that became compounded by the personalities of Isabel and her mother. As regent, María Cristina had no choice but to cultivate liberal support, but her lack of consistency in dealing with ministers of state created chaos, and her marriage three months after Fernando's death to a young guardsman created a scandal by reviving memories of Manuel Godoy.* Once the Carlist War ended, the progressives forced her into exile in 1840, and the hero of the war, Gen. Baldomero Espartero,* became regent-dictator and Isabel's political tutor. María Cristina's attempt to return to Spain failed, but by 1843, Espartero's authoritarianism produced a coalition of moderates who overthrew his ministry, forced him into exile, and put Gen. Ramón Narváez* in his place.

Narváez immediately declared Isabel of age but failed, six months later, to prevent María Cristina from returning to Madrid.* Her continued domination of her daughter forced Narváez to insist on Isabel's marriage as a way of diminishing the former regent's influence on the young queen. The "Spanish marriages" of Isabel and her sister Luisa Fernanda (1832–1897)—Isabel to her cousin (and grandson of Godoy), Francisco de Asís, the duque de Cadiz (1822–1902), and Luisa Fernanda to the duke of Montpensier (1824–1890), a son of Louis Philippe (1773–1850) of France,*—took place on 18 Oct. 1846 and sorely disturbed relations between Britain* and France. Asís's title as king consort had to be changed in 1848 to placate the British. In any case, the addition of two fortune-hunting princes at the court obviously added nothing to its stability.

Isabel herself scandalized Victorian Europe by her love affairs, very much like Queen María Luisa (1751–1819) and her own mother, María Cristina. Although devotedly religious, she was also deeply superstitious and as a result, continuously influenced by priests and lovers alike. She seemed to be without principle, unstable, a liar, and extremely selfish. Despite the exclamation of Gen. Leopoldo O'Donnell* that it was impossible to govern as long as she remained the monarch, the rule of Spain passed for three decades to a series of generals who saw themselves as the only group capable of governing a factious and restive nation.

The governments of her early period were authoritarian to an extreme, but after midcentury, when an improving economy increased railroad construction, land speculation, and foreign capital investment, a middle-class revolt led to the crisis of 1854 and a struggle between Isabel's candidate, Espartero, and Gen. O'Donnell. From 1854 to 1856, the queen packed her mother off to Portugal,* dissolved the Cortes, and allowed reform of the royal household. The national militia was reestablished, a senate was created, and freedom of religion improved;

but when disentailment laws surfaced again, Isabel balked and became increasingly unpopular as an obstacle to economic progress during her last decade of rule. She could only turn to O'Donnell or Narváez each time she was threatened, but O'Donnell's death in 1867 and Narváez's the following year left her without defenders. Under constant attack for her profligate immorality and extravagance, she finally was forced to flee the country on 29 Sept. 1868.

The thirty-six years that remained to her were spent in France and Britain before she returned to Spain in 1878 to attend the wedding of her son Alfonso XII,* who had been made king in 1874. When he died suddenly in 1885, Isabel attempted to usurp the role of regent from his second wife, María Cristina de Hapsburgo (1858–1929), but without success, although her connections in Britain surprisingly allowed her to negotiate the marriage of her grandson, Alfonso XIII,* to one of Queen Victoria's (1819–1901) favorite granddaughters, Victoria Eugenia of Battenberg (1887–1969). Isabel died shortly thereafter in 1904 at the age of seventy-four.

For additional information, see E. Kiernan, *The Revolution of 1854 in Spanish History* (Oxford, 1966); C. Marichal, *Spain, 1834–1844: A New Society* (London, 1977); and J. M. Moreno Echevarría, *Isabel II: Biográfica de una España en crisis* (Barcelona, 1973).

S. F. Fredricks

*Related entries*: FERNANDO VII; LIBERALISM; NARVÁEZ, RAMÓN.


**ITALY,** relations with Spain. For centuries, political, military, economic, and cultural ties have connected the development and destinies of Italy and Spain. Spain's domination of Italian territories began with Aragonese control of Naples and Sicily in the thirteenth century. In the sixteenth century, the Spanish Hapsburgs brought other areas, notably Sardinia and Lombardy, under their sway. For Italy, Spanish hegemony meant the imposition of the aristocratic ideals and structures of Spain, while for Spain, control of Italy was considered essential to establishing a dominant position in the Mediterranean. Individual Spaniards owned land in Italy, and Italians in turn served as Spanish diplomats, while merchants, craftsmen, bureaucrats, and soldiers emigrated to Spain. Commercial connections also developed as, for example, favorable trade status was granted to Florentine wool exported to Spain as a reward for Medici support of Felipe II (1527–1598).

The Peace of Utrecht (1713–1715), which concluded the War of Spanish Succession* and established Bourbon rule in Spain, ended formal colonial status of territory in Italy. Ties between the areas continued, though, through shared dynastic rule and diplomatic interests. In the struggles for a balance of power in the eighteenth century, Italy was often a pawn, particularly as Spain sought to resist Austrian Hapsburg power in Europe, while the Italian states often looked to Spain as a means of evicting the Hapsburgs from the peninsula. When Felipe V* married Isabel Farneso (1692–1766), additional ties were created. They planned for their sons, Carlos and Felipe, to rule autonomous states in Italy, while remaining diplomatically, financially, and militarily dependent on Spain. As a result of the wars and treaties of the eighteenth century, Carlos in 1735 was recognized as ruler of the independent Kingdom of the Two Sicilies, which included Naples and Sicily. When Carlos's third son ascended the Spanish throne as Fernando VI (1713–1759), he inherited that kingdom, and the Spanish Bourbons continued to rule it until Italian unification in 1870. In the meantime, Parma had passed to Austrian control in 1735, but was restored to Spanish Bourbon control under Felipe after the War of the Austrian Succession (1745).

Under the hegemony of Napoleon Bonaparte's (1769–1821) French Empire, Italy and Spain continued to share political administrations and aspirations. Both Joseph Bonaparte and Giocchino Murat (1767–1815), Napoleon's brother-in-law, ruled in the two territories, in fact exchanging positions when, in 1808, Joseph was transferred from the Kingdom of Naples to rule Spain as José I.* Secret societies and patriotic groups resisting French control existed in both Spain and Italy, and Italians hoped to imitate Spain's guerrilla wars against Napoleon.

In the European world restored after Napoleon's defeat, similar liberal and nationalist aims and movements continued to link Italians and Spaniards. The Spanish Revolution of 1820 helped spark a similar revolt in Naples, and the Spanish constitution served as a model for the Neapolitan rebels. With the failure of their rebellion in 1821, many Italians sought exile in Spain, carrying with them the political tradition of the secret Carboneria, which was dedicated to the overthrow of despotic regimes and the establishment of constitutional rule.

The collapse of the Spanish constitutionalist movement in 1823 forced many of the same exiles to seek refuge in London and Brussels, but throughout the nineteenth century, connections between Italian movements for democracy and unification and Spanish desires for political reform continued. Nicola Fabrizi (1792?–?), for example, an activist in the nationalist Young Italy movement, gained experience in wars in Spain and Portugal* from 1832 to 1839 and subsequently developed ideas for victory in the struggle to unify Italy.

After unification was achieved in 1870, the new Italian state shared with Spain both the status of a "lesser power" and a desire to protect its interests in the Mediterranean. The signing of the Mediterranean agreements in 1887 by the two nations, Britain,* Austria-Hungary, and Germany* symbolized the determination to maintain the status quo there and thwart the encroachments of both Russia and France.* Subsequently, little changed in Italo-Spanish relations until the rise of fascism and the appointment of Benito Mussolini (1883–1945) as prime minister in Oct. 1922.

Even then, relations did not change significantly. Mussolini's aggressive plans for expansion in the Mediterranean required a friendly regime in Spain, while Spanish political leaders sought amicable relations with Italy, as evidenced by the warmly received visit of Gen. Miguel Primo de Rivera* to Italy in the 1920s. The establishment of the Second Republic* in 1931 intensified relations between the fascist regime and certain Spanish political groups of the Right as common interests became evident. In 1934, Antonio Goicochea (1876–1953), founder of the conservative, monarchist Renovación Española and its leader in the Cortes, visited Italy and held discussions with Mussolini. Goicochea sought an authoritarian monarchy with Catholicism and traditional institutions as its basis and looked for Italian support to this end. His visit was partially successful in that the Italians gave verbal support to the restoration of the monarchy in Spain, a position consistent with their expansionist aims.

Though the uprising against the republic that began in July 1936 did not have Mussolini's direct connivance, Il Duce immediately sent twelve aircraft to the rebels, and shortly thereafter, Gen. Emilio Mola* sent Goicochea back to Italy to reaffirm Italian support and secure a commitment of concrete aid. Mussolini then reversed the pattern of earlier centuries of Spanish military intervention in Italy by sending four divisions, consisting of aircraft, artillery, tanks, and trucks, to Spain. He also provided foodstuffs and outright loans to the nationalists, which were to be repaid in monthly installments between 1942 and 1967 in accord with an agreement signed in 1940. Mussolini viewed his contributions to the insurgents as a way to enhance Italy's position in the Mediterranean and strengthen his hand in the arena of international power politics.

While Mussolini sent an estimated fifty thousand men to Spain, his antifascist opponents also joined the conflict in support of the republicans. Italians ranging from moderate republicans to members of the Italian Communist party (PCI) who had been forced into exile by 1928 began to build an antifascist coalition with its center in France in the 1930s. With the outbreak of the civil war in Spain, leaders of this movement saw the conflict as an opportunity to actively resist fascism. They immediately contacted leaders of republican Spain and undertook the recruiting of volunteers to fight in Spain. In Aug. 1936, individual Italians joined Spanish militia units, and several Italian units fought in northeastern Spain (among them, the column of 150 men led by Carlo Rosselli, a long-time antifascist activist, who in Nov. 1936 coined the slogan for the Italian volunteers in Spain, "Today Spain, Tomorrow Italy"). Most of the Italian volunteers were members of the Garibaldi Battalion of the Twelfth International Brigade* organized in Oct. 1936. The battalion was expanded to brigade status in the spring of 1937 and counted some 3,354 volunteers.

The Garibaldini first saw action in Nov. 1936 in the initial battle for the defense of Madrid, while fascist troops entered the conflict formally in the fall of Malaga in early 1937, after which they were transferred to the central zone and organized as the Cuerpo de Tropas Voluntarias (CTV). While the Internationals fought at the Jarama River in Feb., the fascist command, on 14 Feb., convinced Gen. Francisco Franco* to allow them to launch an attack in the area of Guadalajara as part of a pincer movement to encircle Madrid, while he simultaneously pursued an offensive at the Jarama.

Ironically, the Battle of Guadalajara (8–23 Mar. 1937) saw Italians fighting Italians in a series of attacks and counterattacks. The International forces were victorious, eventually breaking through CTV lines. The first Italian Division retreated, exposing its flank and forcing the Littorio Division to do the same. In the broadest terms, the victory was a minor one for republican Spain. It had destroyed a threat to Madrid, but made no significant gains. Furthermore, two thousand men had been lost, four thousand wounded, and five hundred taken prisoner, while significant losses of equipment were incurred.

More important, perhaps, were the psychological and political results. The Italian volunteers could use this battle to illustrate the strength of antifascism and thereby encourage resistance to Mussolini in Italy. Mussolini did not publicly acknowledge the results of the conflict until the following summer. Embarrassed by the performance of his crack troops, he was increasingly aware that his goals and those of the nationalist command were not necessarily the same, as Franco had not pushed the expected diversionary offensive on the Jarama. After Guadalajara, the CTV was purged, and Franco made it clear that Italian forces would no longer act independently. In the months that followed, Mussolini became disenchanted with the results of his support for the nationalists, but was bound by his commitments and did not withdraw his troops.

Italian volunteers continued to contribute to the republican effort, fighting at Brunete in July 1937 and Teruel in Jan.-Feb. 1938, though the Twelfth Brigade was increasingly made up of Spanish recruits. The battle on the Ebro that began on Mar. 1938 saw heavy fighting, with Italians once again battling their countrymen. In Sept. 1938, the prime minister, Juan Negrín,* agreed to the withdrawal of the Internationals. In the succeeding months, some seven hundred Italians were formally mustered out, though key Italian leaders such as Palmiro Togliatti remained in Spain until the final moments of the conflict.

Several conclusions may be drawn about the meaning of the Italian-Spanish relationship during the civil war. First, though neither the fascists nor the Garibaldini were instrumental in the overall events of the war, they both made significant contributions. The matériel Franco received from Mussolini was certainly important, while for the republicans, Italian leadership, organization, and example were influential. From Mussolini's point of view, Italian intervention had disappointing results. Italy failed to demonstrate the military prowess of which he dreamed, and he was clearly unable to dominate Franco as he hoped, as events of World War II* later made evident. The antifascists, though on the defeated side, had gained both valuable experience and considerable ideological ammunition in the struggle. It is no coincidence that the Italian leaders and heroes of Spain continued in their opposition and after Mussolini's fall in 1943 became central to the organization and eventual success of the Italian resistance (Sept. 1943–May 1945).

Italy continued to maintain diplomatic relations with Spain, even though Spain's neutrality in World War II increasingly isolated it from other powers. From 1946 to 1950, when members of the United Nations were called on to withdraw their representatives from Madrid, Italy, which had not formally joined the organization, did not. Italy's leftist parties opposed the links with Franco's Spain, but the Italian Foreign Ministry still hoped to recover the money loaned to Spain by Mussolini and to maintain trading links. From 1944 to 1946, Italy adopted a stance that characterized Italian-Spanish relations in subsequent years, staying out of internal politics, with no connections to the Falange,* focused instead on personal and cultural relations. Ties between Catholic-inspired parties were encouraged, though even the Christian Democratic party was far less influential in Spain than in Italy.

Outside the structure of formal government institutions, the parties of the Left in Italy maintained contact with their Spanish counterparts. These ties were particularly important for the PCI and the illegal Spanish Communist party* operating in exile. They intensified in the late 1960s and 1970s as both parties sought to redefine their relations with the Soviet Union and develop theory and practice responsive to shifts in international politics and national conditions. These developments culminated in the 1975 joint statement defining Eurocommunism and the 1977 Declaration of Madrid by the communist parties of Spain, Italy, and France that enunciated their commitments to human rights, universal suffrage, and political pluralism.

In the contemporary setting, both international interests and internal issues continue to link Italy and Spain. Both nations continue to be lesser powers in the arena of international politics. They must weigh affiliation with either the United States* or the Soviet Union and seek to strengthen the European Community. Most recently, socialist-led coalition governments have attempted to move both states in the direction of social democracy and have struggled with common problems of economic development, social unrest, political instability, and the threats posed by terrorist groups.

For additional information, see S. Attanasio, *Gli italiana e la guerra de Spagna* (Milan, 1974); V. Brome, *The International Brigades in Spain, 1936–39* (London, 1965); J. Coverdale, *Italian Intervention in the Spanish Civil War* (Princeton, 1975); C. J. Lowe and F. Marzari, *Italian Foreign Policy, 1870–1940* (London and Boston, 1975); and S. Woolf, *A History of Italy, 1700–1860* (London, 1979).

*M. J. Slaughter*

# J

JIMÉNEZ MANTECÓN, JUAN RAMÓN (1881–1958), poet, Nobel Prize winner. Jiménez was born in Moguer, Huelva. His father, a landowner and winegrower, encouraged the early artistic activity of his son, whom he sent to Seville to study painting. Jiménez quickly abandoned his studies for poetry. In 1900, he traveled to Madrid,* where he published his first two books, *Ninfeas* (1900) and *Almas de violeta* (1900), and met writers who, within the modernist movement, were renovating Spanish literature: Salvador Rueda (1857–1933), Francisco Villaespesa (1877–1936), Ramón Valle-Inclán (1866–1936), and the already famous Nicaraguan poet Rubén Darío (1867–1916). Upon his return to Moguer, Jiménez suffered a serious depression when his father died unexpectedly, and he had to be placed in a psychiatric sanatorium in the south of France.*

In 1901, back in Madrid, he published *Rimas* (1902) and *Arias tristes* (1903). His father's death meant loss of the family fortune, and Jiménez returned to Moguer in 1905. He wrote the lyric prose of *Platero y yo* (1914) and some of his most well-known poetry here, but in 1912, already recognized as the most intense lyric voice of the new Spanish poetry, left for good. For some years, he lived in the famous Residencia de Estudiantes in Madrid, which also sheltered other great figures of Spanish culture of his time, such as Federico García Lorca,* Luis Buñuel (1900–1983), and Salvador Dalí.* In New York in 1916, he married Zenobia Camprubí (1887–1956), who until her death was the poet's constant companion and collaborator. In 1936, a few days after the beginning of the Spanish Civil War,* Jiménez left Spain and took up residence in the United States,* where he dedicated himself to teaching Spanish literature at several universities. Although he maintained his distance from political activity, Jiménez never wished, for fundamentally ethical reasons, to return to the authoritarian and repressive Spain of Gen. Francisco Franco.*

In 1956, he received the Nobel Prize for Literature in recognition, according to the Swedish Academy, of "his lyric purity, which constitutes, in the Spanish language, an example of high spirituality and artistic purity." Three days after award of the prize, Zenobia died, a victim of cancer. Jiménez never recovered from that loss, and he himself died a year and a half later, in the spring of 1958.

Until 1913, date of the publication of *Laberinto*, Jiménez's poetry had remained faithful to the Parnassian-symbolist aesthetic that had dazzled the Spanish poets of his generation. In 1916, however, during a sea journey that carried him to New York to marry, Jiménez composed a kind of lyric diary in which he discovered a new style, direct and apparently simple, lacking the ornamentation, external musicality, and brilliant imagery that had characterized his earlier work. *Diario de un poeta recién casado* (1916), later retitled *Diario del poeta y el mar* (1948), is considered a model of that style, which the author named poesía desnuda.

The first part of the work, five books of poetry that he disdainfully rated "savage rough drafts," owes much to the Spanish and Latin American modernist poets, less in substance to Rubén Darío, contrary to what is customarily said, than to the Andalusian Francisco Villaespesa, an uneven, excessive poet, today forgotten, but very influential in his time. Also important was the influence of French symbolist poets. Nevertheless, the deepest and most personal lyric reverberations in Jiménez came from an eminently Spanish tradition: Gustavo Bécquer*; the *Romances*; and especially, traditional and popular songs, whose rhythmic schema are still seen, masterfully stylized, in almost all the work of Jiménez's second period.

If until *Laberinto* Jiménez's poetry depended on a rich European and Spanish tradition, after *Sonetos espirituales* (1916) and the discovery of poesía desnuda, he created a new Spanish poetic tradition. Jiménez's influence affected all of Spanish-speaking America. His poetry held its preeminent position until, at the beginning of the 1930s, the spread of surrealism and the sociopolitical convulsions culminating in the Spanish Civil War marked the deterioration of the purity that had dominated European lyricism.

As a whole, Jiménez's lyric work was directed to the achievement of natural bliss the poet longs for, perhaps to compensate for the debilitating terror that the idea of death produces in man. The root of that argument may be found in the initial dazzling light that nature awakens in the young poet, who is soon revealed as a man of absorbed contemplation, a solitary and impassioned voyeur of twilight, gardens, and idealized landscapes standing in for absolute beauty. The desire to participate in the wealth he senses in nature gives him a very special sense of the life of the creative act. The poet, conscious that he is an exceptional interpreter of beauty, believes that his work shares the richness and eternity he sees in his contemplated world. The culmination of this process is *Dios deseante y deseado* (1949), in which the poetic personality enthrones itself as a god, immortal at last, in the absolute and eternal kingdom of its own creation. Jiménez, certain he was going to complete that glorious itinerary, had already written in the poem "Espacio": "The gods have no more substance than have I."

Jiménez's work is extensive. From the first period, aside from the titles already mentioned, *Olvidanzas* (1909); the three fascicles of *Elegías* (1908–1910); and *La soledad sonora* and *Poemas mágicos y dolientes*, were published in 1911. *Estío* (1916), *Piedra y cielo* (1919), and *La estación total* (1946), written in Spain before the civil war, anticipated the central cosmic vision of *Dios deseante y deseado*.

After the poet's death, two volumes of unpublished work appeared. Jiménez, always unsatisfied with what he had achieved, spent years attempting to "revive" his immense body of work, giving it some coherence. The effort was too ambitious, and he was never able to complete it. Only the volume entitled *Canción*, published in 1936, collected and put in order all the poems that, dispersed throughout different books, were thematically or formally related with the traditional and popular canciones.

Jiménez was also an outstanding prose writer, although most of his prose pieces, such as *Platero y yo* and the portraits contained in *Españoles de tres mundos, viejo mundo, nuevo mundo, otro mundo (caricatura lírica) (1914–1940)*, have a marked poetic character.

For additional information, see J. Guerrero Ruiz, *Juan Ramón de viva voz* (Madrid, 1961); R. Gullón, *Conversaciones con Juan Ramón Jiménez* (Madrid, 1958), and *Estudios sobre Juan Ramón Jiménez* (Buenos Aires, 1960); G. Palau de Nemes, *Vida y obra de Juan Ramón Jiménez* (Madrid, 1974); A. Sánchez Barbudo, *La segunda época de Juan Ramón Jiménez* (Madrid, 1962); and A. González, *Juan Ramón Jiménez: Estudio* (Madrid, 1973).

*Á. González*

**JOSÉ I, JOSEPH BONAPARTE** (1768–1844), older brother of Napoleon Bonaparte (1769–1821) and king of Spain, 1804–1814. Joseph was born on 7 Jan. 1768 at Corte, Corsica. Poor, not well educated but shrewd, and a republican, he entered political life in the elections of 1789, at the start of the French Revolution, but had to flee to continental France* in 1792, when Britain* seized Corsica. He and his brother were active in ending resistance in the south of France for the National Convention, and at Toulon when it was besieged by the British in 1793. Subsequently, Joseph's career was tied to the military success of his brother, Napoleon. Often, as in Napoleon's early career in Italy,* Joseph served as his representative in Paris, but he was also appointed to administrative positions in Parma and to the post of ambassador to Rome in 1797. The next year, he entered the government of the Directory, joining the Council of Five Hundred and aiding in Napoleon's coup d'état later in 1798.

Thereafter, Joseph held important positions in the government, often managing daily business while Napoleon was away campaigning. In 1806, Napoleon, now emperor, appointed Joseph king of Naples and, in 1808, of Spain. A sensible and sensitive man, he assumed the throne with reluctance, recognizing the unpopularity of the French intervention in Spain and anticipating the meager welcome that awaited him.

His reign was an adventure begun by Napoleon following the failure of Spain to abide by the provisions of the Treaty of Fontainebleau (27 Oct. 1807), by which Carlos IV* was to invade Portugal.* His collapse of will led to a partial French military occupation and the double abdication, at Bayonne, of Carlos and his son Fernando (who had already briefly ruled as Fernando VII*).

Joseph quickly became a symbol of foreign rule and a foil for the emperor's nearly total lack of understanding of Spain. The regime met instant disapproval and became a political and military disaster, costing more in men and money than any of Napoleon's other adventures. Joseph was well intentioned, but lacked the ability for such a task, and he was surrounded by officials appointed in Paris who heeded only those orders that came from the emperor. The new king, moreover, was originally supported at first by an inadequate French force. The result was the spread of resistance and rebellion when Joseph entered Spain, with France controlling only the cities and fortifications where its troops were stationed. Unable to carry out even the rudimentary tasks of government, Joseph was also encumbered by a barrage of advice from Napoleon, who issued orders on every aspect of life and whose relentless interference left Joseph in limbo, especially since his assistants fell into the habit of referring matters of substance to the emperor. Of those who took Joseph's side, the early death of Francisco de Cabarrús (1752–1810) removed the only Spaniard of stature. Mariano Luis de Urquijo (1768–1817), a former associate of Manuel Godoy,* and Gonzalo de O'Farrill (1754–1831), descendant of an Irish adventurer, were of limited value.

The intervention of the British in Portugal and Spain converted an unpleasant situation into disaster. Napoleon's orders called for the mobilization of the Spaniards to resist the duke of Wellington,* but the force necessary for that task placed the French in a position of being at war with the people they were trying to govern, something akin to the situation in the recent wars in Vietnam and Afghanistan. The War of Independence,* which lasted until Wellington crossed the Pyrenees in 1813, was a long and costly series of engagements between British and French armies against a backdrop of irregular but constant Spanish resistance. The French defeat in Portugal in 1808 led to a general uprising in Spain and necessitated the direct intervention of Napoleon at the head of a major army of 150,000 men. He defeated insurgents at Burgos and Espinosa in Nov. 1808, and after his departure, the French enjoyed several other successes, but the engagements caused horror and devastation, with cities such as Saragossa being almost totally destroyed. For Spaniards, it was a time of famine, disease, and utter disorder, without any true political direction from the fragmented Spanish opposition.

Joseph was served by some of France's finest generals, but the troops and resources at their disposal were inadequate to the task of defeating both Wellington's army and the Spanish people. The conflict was fought on several levels, with sieges against insurrectionary towns, maneuvers, and battles against the British army, and brutal assaults on civilian guerrilla opposition that occasionally ended with French atrocities. Joseph could never control the situation; Napoleon directed the military effort even while he campaigned in Eastern Europe, although his orders were utterly nonsensical by the time they arrived in Spain. Joseph, fully conscious of the disastrous events that surrounded him and chagrined by the war, began to offer some resistance to Napoleon's orders, with the result that the two ceased communicating in 1811. At particular issue was the annexation of northern Spain into metropolitan France, which destroyed whatever slight chance Joseph had to develop adequate revenues for his own state.

Following Wellington's victory at Salamanca on 22 July 1812, Joseph began the French withdrawal, and after the battle of Vitoria on 21 June 1813, only a few cities remained in French hands, leaving the way free for reintroduction of the Bourbon regime.

As king, Joseph was an unlikely and unwanted ruler, who exercised minimal power and left no personal mark on Spain. His regime represented a break in Spanish political history and helped accelerate the dissolution of the empire, since the Americans, forced to handle their own affairs during these years, gained a taste for independence. French rule also invigorated Spanish political and cultural life, serving both as a model and an object of scorn and hatred.

For additional information, see G. Lovett, *Napoleon and the Birth of Modern Spain*, 2 vols. (New York, 1965).

*C. R. Steen*

*Related entries*: CARLOS III; FERNANDO VII; GODOY, MANUEL; INDEPENDENCE, WAR OF.

**JOVELLANOS Y RAMÍREZ, GASPER MELCHOR DE** (1744–1811), writer, politician, and intellectual in the era of enlightened despotism. Jovellanos, born to a minor noble family in Gijón on 5 Jan. 1744, abandoned religious studies in 1760 to study law in Avila and Alcalá de Heneres. In 1768, he received a royal appointment as a magistrate judge in Seville, where he remained for a decade, strongly influenced by Pablo de Olavide (1725–1802), a Spaniard born in Peru and educated in France,* who, as one of the most able civil governors under Carlos III,* directed an ambitious project to resettle foreign peasants on church lands in the Sierra Moreno.

The polymath Jovellanos, who never married, led a diverse life in Seville: reforming the criminal laws; patronizing the Salamanca group of poets; studying British and French philosophy; and becoming an early member of the physiocratic Sociedades Económicas de Amigos del País.* Even though Olavide ran afoul of the Inquisition of 1776, Jovellanos was promoted to councilor of state by the conde de Campomanes,* head of the Council of Castile. In Madrid,* Jovellanos made a secular reform of religious colleges; wrote both civic and satiric poetry, epistles, and essays; and became a confidant of the painter Francisco de Goya,* who nominated him for membership in the Spanish Academy for his *Poesías* (1779), and the economist and banker Francisco de Cabarrús (1752–1810), who secured him membership in the Economic Society of Madrid. Cabarrús, like

Olavide, was prosecuted in 1790, and when Campomanes refused to intercede, Jovellanos for a time exiled himself in Asturias.*

This breach created a vacuum of power in Madrid when Carlos IV,* frightened by the French Revolution (1789–1794), turned to the conde de Aranda* in Feb. 1792, and then the following Nov. to the ill-prepared court favorite, Manuel Godoy,* who, until 1808, used the government for his own gain. Jovellanos, who otherwise might have expected high office, found himself unemployed. He remained in Gijón to write his major work, *Informe en expediente de ley agraria* (1795).

The *Informe* began with the premise that the furtherance of individual self-interest should be the chief goal of good government. In agriculture, this could be realized through the abolition of communal lands for private ownership; adoption of enclosure to aid private agriculture; and sale of mortmain and entailed estates to new owners who would live on the land. For the general economy, Jovellanos advocated an end to all restraints on domestic trade; a mercantilist approach to imports and exports; sharply decreased sales taxes; an expanded program of education and public works; and the encouragement of private property. In many respects, the *Informe* was one of the last great Enlightenment manifestos.

The publication of such a powerful work rehabilitated its author's political career. Godoy, urged on by his ally Cabarrús, who had not forgotten Jovellanos's earlier support, appointed the Asturian to the foreign office in July 1797, and in Nov., made him minister of justice. Jovellanos began to plan the confiscation of ecclesiastical property while continuing his earlier educational reforms. The Inquisition, prevented by official order in July 1797 from prohibiting the *Informe*, discredited Jovellanos to the queen, María Luisa (1751–1819). Amid rumors of a plot to poison him, Jovellanos resigned (or was dismissed from office) on 15 Aug. 1798 and returned to Gijón, until Godoy, again reacting to clerical pressure, had him arrested on 13 Mar. 1801.

Jovellanos spent the next seven years as a prisoner in Majorca, incommunicado much of the time. Freed by the Spanish revolt against the French on 2 May 1808, he returned to Madrid in late May and was named to the national junta that led the War of Independence* against France. Cabarrús tried to persuade him to support Joseph Bonaparte (José I*), but Jovellanos refused to leave the junta. Even though the junta was forced to flee to Seville and later Cadiz, Jovellanos kept working on new educational reforms and wrote the manifesto calling for a Spanish Cortes to meet at Cadiz. In 1810, many of the *Informe*'s ideas provided the agenda for the writing of the Constitution of 1812. When the Cortes of Cadiz* replaced the junta in Feb. 1810, Jovellanos, now in ill health, remained in Cadiz long enough to defend his ideas, but in Aug. 1811, when the military situation allowed him to travel, he returned to Gijón. There, caught in a new French advance, he fled to the village of Puerta de Vega, where he died of pneumonia on 27 Nov. 1811.

Jovellanos's influence on nineteenth-century liberalism was profound. His program of physical and economic regeneration through the confiscation of mortmain and entailed lands was realized by Juan Álvarez Mendizábal* in 1836 (who lived in Cadiz during this period) and provided the agenda for a half-century of liberal legislation. Since Jovellanos was no democrat, the limited franchise of moderate party governments would have bothered him less than their neglect of education. Jovellanos's educational ideas, which included *Discurso sobre los medios de promover la felicidad de Asturias* (1781), *Ordenanza para el Real Instituto Asturiano* (1793), *Tratado de educación teórico-práctico* (1802), and *Bases para la formación de un plan general de instrucción pública* (1809), were the necessary intellectual complement of his economic plans and represented a serious effort to educate Spaniards to the levels necessary to maximize their self-interest. Those who profited from the land sales did not wish to broaden general political participation through education, however, and Jovellanos's ideas, banned in 1825, remained little read for more than a century, his reform agenda remaining only partially realized.

For additional information, see J. Agustín Cea Bermúdez, *Memorias para la vida del Excmo. Señor D. Gasper Melchor de Jovellanos, y noticias analíticas de sus obras* (Madrid, 1820); J.H.R. Polt, *Gasper Melchor de Jovellanos* (New York, 1971); J. Prados Arrarte, *Jovellanos, economista* (Madrid, 1967); and L. Sánchez Agesta, *El pensamiento político del despotismo ilustrado* (Madrid, 1953).

R. W. Kern

*Related entries*: CARLOS III; CARLOS IV; ENLIGHTENMENT, AGE OF; DISENTAILMENT; GODOY, MANUEL; LIBERALISM.

**JUAN CARLOS I, KING OF SPAIN** (1938– ), rules 1975– . Grandson of Alfonso XIII,* Juan Carlos was born in 1938 in Rome, home of his parents, Juan de Borbón y Battenberg (1913– ) and María de Borbón-Nápoles. When Alfonso XIII died in 1941, Juan, in accord with the terms of his father's will, became head of the royal house of Spain; Alfonso had previously abdicated the crown in Juan's favor. The royal family established itself in Lausanne in 1942, and Juan Carlos began his first studies in 1946 at the College Ville Saint Jean in Freiburg; his parents later moved to Estoril, Portugal. The Succession Law of 1947 worsened the already tense relations between Juan and Gen. Francisco Franco* by defining the state as a kingdom but leaving the identity of the future king unknown, while setting no date for the restoration. The disparity of criteria between Juan, who wanted to effect a reconciliation between Spaniards alienated by the Spanish Civil War,* and Gen. Franco, who pledged to maintain the irreducible dichotomy between the "two Spains," was only partially overcome in an interview aboard the yacht *Azor*, in which both agreed that prince Juan Carlos would finish his studies in Spain; to do so, Juan Carlos went to Madrid* in 1948. In 1954, a second interview in Estremadura permitted the planning of his advanced studies: a triple military course in the academies of Saragossa, Marín, and Cartagena and two in different colleges at the Central University of Madrid.

In 1961, after Juan Carlos married Princess Sofía (1938–  ) of Greece, daughter of Paul I (1901–1964) and Federica (1917–1964), in Athens, Franco definitively designated the prince to occupy the throne upon his death. A break between father and son was averted by the prince's strong identification with his father and the identification of both with the concept of the monarchy as a guarantee of peace through a constitutionally democratic formula. Don Juan advocated "disruptive" solutions, while the prince harbored the aim of reconciling the two factions of the civil war through a transition "from law to law," facilitated by the Franquista constitution itself.

With the Caudillo's death in 1975, Juan Carlos was proclaimed king in the Cortes, and the difficult transitional period began. Juan Carlos's first official speech affirmed his aim of ruling over all Spaniards and returning their liberties to them, facilitating at the same time a decentralization in accord with Spanish historical tradition and the authentic identity of the peoples of Spain.

The reign faced a first, difficult stage under the government of Carlos Arias Navarro,* whose reform program was so timid that, at the same time that it irritated those determined to maintain the Franquista legacy unchanged, it completely disappointed all those who wanted authentic change, among whom were his ministers Manuel Fraga,* José María Areilza (1909–  ), and Antonio Garrigues (1904–  ). As for the king, he took a series of trips through the interior of his kingdom and beyond its borders in which he repeatedly confirmed his commitment to democratization and national integration. His trip to North America in the spring of 1976 was especially successful, but at home the continuation of the Arias government clashed with these principles, and Arias was dismissed in July 1976. In the resolution of this crisis, Torcuato Fernández Miranda (1915–  ), president of the Cortes and the Consejo del Reino and the king's former teacher, suggested a young former minister, Adolfo Suárez,* as the appropriate person to create the changes necessary for democracy. In a short time, Suárez succeeded in effectively carrying out the transition required by the king. Even the Franquista Cortes accepted his reform program, which implied its own dissolution and the convocation of a new assembly elected through direct universal suffrage. The reform was ratified by referendum in Dec. 1976, and almost immediately the political parties proscribed by Franco were legalized, including the Communist party,* which alarmed the military, but the elections of June 1977 proved to be a great triumph for Suárez and, supported by a newly created centrist party, the Unión Central Democrática (UCD), he began the creation of a new state. The Constitution of 1978, facilitated by the Pacts of the Moncloa among the various political factions, and likewise approved by referendum, successfully culminated in the definitive, "consensual" change in accord with the criterion of the king, who since May 1977 had received leadership of the dynasty from his father's hands. Juan Carlos now transferred sovereignty to the Spanish people, sovereignty he had assumed in 1975 for this sole end.

Before this, the king had facilitated the return of autonomy to Catalonia*; then, the constitution configured the country as a state of autonomous regions, a form similar to a federal system. Since 1976, Juan Carlos had created an increasingly generous amnesty plan capable of liquidating the final results of the civil war. Nevertheless, it was impossible to put an end to the terrorism unleashed since Franco's time by the maximalist Basque organization, Basque Homeland and Freedom* (Euzkadi ta Askatasuna, ETA), launched on the road of violence and a bloody counterpoint to Spain's happy democratic recovery.

With President Suárez's resignation in 1981, Leopoldo Calvo Sotelo (1926- ), also an outstanding member of the UCD, took power, only to face a military conspiracy, encouraged by ultrarightists who had already carried out several frustrated attempts to defeat the regime. On 23 Feb., as Calvo Sotelo was being sworn in by the Cortes, Lt. Col. Antonio Tejero attacked the Cortes. He was the instrument of a coup to reproduce in Spain the process of "political renewal" similar to several unsuccessful "gentle coups" attempted in France during the Fifth Republic under Gaullism. Tejero counted on the captain general of Valencia,* Jaime Milans del Bosch, as his keystone.

The determined attitude of Juan Carlos, in contact with various military authorities, paralyzed the coup from its inception, making the conspirators see that he would never support their claims or surrender to a fait accompli. The attempt was neutralized, reduced to a few Cortes members and some troops in the captaincy general of Valencia. On the morning of 24 Feb., Tejero was forced to surrender, liberating the parliamentarians being held hostage. A short time later, the other plotters were arrested. The definitive triumph of democracy, achieved by the king's energetic action, was endorsed by massive popular demonstrations.

The trial of the coup's leaders took place in 1982. The threat of a coup would arise yet again, though in an unimportant fashion, in the last phase of the UCD government, because Calvo Sotelo could not successfully overcome the party's disintegration in the face of economic crisis and strikes. The alternative of a moderate Left, completely integrated with the regime, produced a victory in the elections of Oct. 1982 by the Socialist party* (PSOE), led by Felipe González.* His accession to power, fully democratic and loyal to the monarchy—even more prestigious since 1981—assured the stability of the regime.

Since then, the king has made many international trips, to the United States again, to the Soviet Union, to Latin America and much of Africa, and to Britain.* Spain joined the North Atlantic Treaty Organization (NATO) in 1982, during the government of Calvo Sotelo, and the European Economic Community in 1985. Facing his own country and the great international forums, Juan Carlos has seen his reputation grow. He received the Premio Carlomagno in 1982 and an honorary doctorate from the Sorbonne in 1985. Felipe, the príncipe de Asturias, swore his oath in the Cortes when he reached his majority in 1986. That same year, Juan Carlos and Sofía celebrated their silver wedding anniversary amid the affection of all Spaniards.

Aside from Felipe, born in 1968, the couple has two other children, the infantas Elena, born in 1963, and Cristina, born in 1965.

For additional information, see R. P. Clark and M. H. Haltzel, eds., *Spain in the 1980s* (Cambridge, 1987).

*C. Seco Serrano*

*Related entries*: FRAGA, MANUEL; GONZÁLEZ, FELIPE; SUÁREZ, ADOLFO.

# K

**KRAUSE, KARL CHRISTIAN FRIEDRICH** (1781–1832), German philosopher. All but forgotten in his native Germany* today, Krause was an heir and revisionist of Kantian idealist philosophy and a contemporary of such better-known figures as Johann Gottlieb Fichte (1762–1814), Friedrich Schleiermacher (1768–1834), and Georg Hegel (1770–1831). His principal historical significance derives from the adoption of his name and some of his ideas by the Spanish Krausism movement. Unlike Hegel's "absolute idealism" and glorification of the state as the ultimate ethical expression, Krause's teachings stressed individual and practical idealism.

Krause studied philosophy with Fichte and Friedrich Schelling (1775–1854) at the University of Jena, where he earned his doctorate and became a private tutor in 1802. He subsequently taught at the Engineering Academy of Dresden (1805) and at the University of Berlin (1814). After joining the Freemasons in 1805 and writing a number of pro-Masonic works, he broke with the movement and thereafter ascribed his frustrated academic career to machinations of this secret society.

Krause failed, as did his philosophical contemporary Arthur Schopenhauer (1788–1860), to obtain a regular professorship. He struggled to maintain his large family on private tutoring fees and income from his many publications. He moved to Göttingen in 1824, but was forced to leave after his students were accused of antigovernment agitation during local disturbances in the wake of the 1830 revolution in France. Relocating to Munich in 1831, he hoped for a regular university position, but his former teacher, Schelling, denounced him as a revolutionary and prevented his appointment. He died in Munich in 1832.

Krause's work was virtually forgotten after his death. In the 1830s, only his students continued to propagate his ideas, often outside the politically reactionary climate of German universities in places such as Belgium. Their activity and publications were responsible for the survival of Krause's thought.

Although a former student initiated a modest revival of interest in Krausist thought at the University of Prague in the 1860s, Krause's works never enjoyed the kind of posthumous revival in his own homeland that Schopenhauer's had. This was largely because of Krause's convoluted prose. Even for German intellectuals schooled in the difficult conceptual language of such romantic idealist philosophers as Fichte and Schelling, Krause's writings posed a challenge. The more charitable historians of German philosophy, when they mention Krause at all, frequently remark on the impenetrability of his prose. It is useful to keep this point in mind when discussing Krausism in Spain: the movement appropriated the spirit, rather than the core, of Krause's ideas.

Why Krause became a Spanish obsession is unclear. As had Fichte and Schelling, he tried to overcome the Kantian dictum that "essence" (or God) lay beyond sense experience and could therefore not be "known" in strict epistemological terms by human "consciousness." Revisionists of Kant's verdict, as were Fichte, Schelling, and Krause, in different ways posited a pantheistic solution: if the idea of God (or essence) was everywhere, then it was in humans as well. A perfect version of the self (ego) would therefore theoretically be able to share to some degree in the perfect essence of the universe, or God. Some hope for human understanding of the essence of the universe could be rescued, but only hypothetically (in the case of an "absolute ego," for example, since all higher essence is by definition absolute).

The Spanish fascination with Krause, rather than the leading philosopher of his day, Hegel, requires further explanation. Hegel's lectures on the philosophy of history posited a progressive march toward unity through historical time between the "world spirit," or essence, and the consciousness of man, always fallible and prone to mistakes, after which reason would finally realize itself on earth. Hegel's teaching, however, could be viewed as a long-term, progressive historical interpretation or as a short-term affirmation of the state as the best current incorporation of historical design of the unknown absolute. The latter reading, which so clearly affirmed the existing order, made Hegel appear to contemporaries as the official philosopher of reactionary Prussia and reactionary causes in general. Hegel's system shared with Karl Marx's (1818–1883) the defect of assuming that the forces of impersonal "realization" would triumph in the end, and that individual effort, disciplined moral behavior, and resistance based on human consciousness were epiphenomena rather than causes of world history. Spanish Krausism contained some residues of this philosophical fatalism, but largely resisted it. It also rejected Hegel's implicit apotheosis of the state, so utterly incompatible with Spanish conditions.

Insofar as Krause's philosophical system was not chosen at random, it appeared to contain some elements more congenial to its Spanish adherents than Hegel's. Krause's philosophy of history ascended through consciousness to an ill-defined fusion with essence, reminiscent of European mystical traditions, followed by a descent into practical work to bring the process of fusion between historical reality and perfect essence that much closer, and more quickly, than by relying on the blind gropings of the "world spirit" that Hegel described. Krause thus posited an active chain between human consciousness and essence that potentially allowed scope for human effort, broke the epistemological "unknowability" line of Kant, and stripped such institutions as state and church of absolutism. While proposing this somewhat confused system, Krause also fell back on traditions of pantheism and German mysticism.

Whatever Krause wrote, he seemed to offer a solution to the dilemmas Kant had left, without doubting the possibilities of human intervention in the process of consciousness-becoming-itself and without painting nineteenth-century institutions such as state and church as the God-willed repositories of the "world spirit."

It is also important to note two further points about Krause in relation to Spain. First, his central philosophical system never seriously penetrated there, although his works on the philosophy of law and ethics did. Second, while Krause's "pantheism" came to be ridiculed in German philosophical circles, movements of that kind were foreign neither to Spanish intellectual traditions nor to the German romantic movement. The latter attracted not only philosophers but literary figures and political thinkers who were drawn to Spain initially because of its exotic and different ways. The bravery of the Spanish people resisting Napoleon Bonaparte (1769–1821) appealed to German nationalists. The attractiveness of Catholicism to the mostly Protestant German romantics in the 1820s, as well as supposed traditions of Spanish mysticism, drew the two cultures closer. Even a conservative romantic from Germany, such as Victor Aimé Huber (1800–1869), took home from his Spanish travels in the 1820s ideas about medieval communitarianism that he tried to turn into housing schemes for the nascent Berlin industrial proletariat thirty years later.

German intellectuals rediscovered Spain in many ways after the end of the Napoleonic Wars, and romanticism was central to that rediscovery and redefinition. Spain, no longer viewed as the homeland of Catholic crusades against German religious heresies, became for the first time in modern history an object of German literary and tourist fascination.

Spain's interest in Germany, on the other hand, was minuscule. The obscurantism of the government of Fernando VII* is legendary, as is the more pragmatic anti-intellectualism of that of Isabel II.* French remained the main language through which new ideas in the rest of Europe could trickle through to Spanish intellectuals. Yet French philosophy, as with many things French after the nationalist uprising against Napoleon, struck even advanced Spanish thinkers as inadequate. In its Enlightenment* guise, it appeared outworn and materialistic; in its new versions, as represented by Victor Cousin (1792–1867) and Auguste Comte (1798–1857), shallow and insufficiently metaphysical. From this Gallophobic stance, coupled with a sense of Spain's isolation from Europe, sprang the seeds of Krausism.

That, and the universal prestige of German philosophy in the early nineteenth century, explain the unusual peregrinations of Julián Sanz del Río (1814–1869), who introduced his version of Krause's thought into Spain. Sanz, of humble social origins, studied law in Granada and Toledo before obtaining his doctorate at Alcalá in 1840. He became acquainted with a major work of Krause's disciple Heinrich Ahrens (1808–1874), *Curso de derecho natural*, published in 1841. Armed with a government grant and the promise of a teaching position in the history of philosophy if he would study its current state across the Pyrenees for two years, Sanz set off for Paris, Brussels (where the political exile Ahrens was teaching), and Heidelberg (1843–1844).

It is unclear how Sanz learned German, but his own testimony indicates that he knew it imperfectly. Undaunted, Sanz nevertheless thought he grasped the essence of Krause's difficult propositions. As usual in intellectual history, the disciple's interpretation of a minor master became more important than correct understanding. Sanz saw in Krause's work a reconciliation of the traditionally separate categories of essence and consciousness through a sort of mystical pantheism. On this rock Sanz built the sect of Spanish Krausism.

The atmosphere Sanz encountered in Heidelberg seems to have been even more important than his fixation with Krause's work. He lived in a professor's home, as was typical for German university students of that day, and had frequent contact with some of the more radical thinkers in the city, thanks to Ahrens's sending him along to friends. The family he lived with counted among its houseguests officially proscribed historians such as George Gervinus (1805–1871), one of the few academic spokesmen for political democracy in mid–nineteenth-century Germany, and, like Krause, a refugee from the persecution of constitutional liberals in Göttingen a few years before.

Thus, Heidelberg represented a new type of academic setting and possibility for Sanz. It must have seemed a model of what could be accomplished against intolerance and authoritarian rule. Whatever hand of censorship repressed its newspapers and free speech, the university community could discuss many matters with relative immunity in its salons. Spanish commentators on Sanz's life typically emphasize his rather cautious letters home about reading and understanding Krause in this period. Perhaps understandably, with an eye to censorship and his future job, Sanz's published letters almost never mentioned the free-wheeling discussions in private homes and restaurants that were typical of the Heidelberg of the time. Sanz used Krause as his entrée, but the immediate experience of Heidelberg's republic of letters clearly molded Sanz's later style in teaching and in building a private circle around him in Madrid.

After returning to Spain and retreating, monklike, for a decade of further reading and study, Sanz finally took up his promised professorship at the Central University in Madrid and quietly propounded his version of Krause's reformist philosophy. His inaugural lecture, later incorporated in his *Ideal de la humanidad para la vida* (1860), adapted the ideas from Krause's *Urbild der Menschheit* (1811) to the conditions of Spain in the 1850s and 1860s. These included the "Commandments of Humanity," ethical precepts reminiscent of Kant's categorical imperative. The phrases seem innocuous today, but aroused increasing suspicion in church and government circles. Murky as they were, they also encouraged independent thought and "self-realization" through "reason."

More important, Sanz continued the practice of Heidelberg in having his best students meet in his modest apartment for wide-ranging discussions that perhaps had little enough to do with Krause. His disciples have attested to his not caring much about examining them on the finer points of Krause's philosophy, but encouraging them to take it as an inspirational departure point. The moral earnestness of Sanz's circle, rather than the admittedly vague interpretations of one of the most elusive German philosophers, appears to have been the key to Sanz's salon. His adepts "understood," as they wrote later, what he "meant," although they later went quite different ways. The common bond was Krause's name and a teacher who believed, through the higher force of reason and personal cultivation of it, in the moral, political, educational, and aesthetic rebirth of Spain.

Sanz del Río and his fellow Krausists stood up for the independence of the Madrid professorate, just as Gervinus, Jakob (1785–1863) and Wilhelm Grimm (1786–1859), and other professors of the "Göttingen Seven" had thirty years before, by refusing an unconditional loyalty oath to their government in 1867. Isabel II's corrupt regime removed them from office, only to suffer the same fate itself a year later. Sanz himself died in 1869. Neither he nor his followers were able to cope with the political turmoil, even when briefly in power, and despite wordy manifestos suffered in turn the persecution, exile, and political frustration under the 1874 Restoration that Krause himself and the Göttingen Seven had experienced in the 1830s in Germany.

Sanz had proposed in his most influential work, *Ideal de la humanidad para la vida*, that Krausist man had a divine image to work toward and realize through reason and education, with the aim of establishing harmony among men and between man and the universe. Blind submission to corrupt or obscurantist institutions, such as the Spanish state and church of his day, would only retard this inevitable human development. Thus, most Krausists could be both religious and in favor of order while still seeming to be opponents of the existing religious and political order. Thus, Isabeline Spain made them martyrs and to some degree heroes, but they were a sect without many followers or concrete political ideas. Gervinus lived long enough in Germany to denounce with his last breath the Bismarckian "power state." He, however, was isolated and shouted down too. Spain had less to cheer about, but the era when Krausism was still vibrant had passed there in the 1870s as well.

It is clear from Sanz's followers' ideas that they wanted to institute a religiously bound, but not church-subservient, educational system, as proposed by Francisco Giner de los Ríos,* and uphold a purer and more abstract ideal of law, such as the German Reichsstaat, the "state of laws," in which a well-educated and impartial bureaucracy would merely apply the legislature's will, without regard to the whim of the monarch. Faint echoes of a liberal Catholicism, as being fought over ferociously in Belgium, Germany, and elsewhere across the Pyrenees in the 1860s and 1870s, could be found in Krausist writings. Krausists were not, however, mobilizers and mass leaders, had little sympathy with modern socioeconomic problems, and missed their chance, if they had one, to become political leaders.

Defeated and persecuted in the Spanish Restoration of 1874; unwilling to follow such newer developments as Comtean philosophy from France, Spencerian sociology from Britain, or even the new faith in pure natural science; and faced with what the Generation of 1898* could only denounce later as one of the worst periods in the history of Spanish universities, Sanz's disciples withdrew into small intellectual groups. Some Krausists, such as Giner and Gumersindo de Azcárate (1840–1917), had an impact on educational, religious, and political and ethical thought in Spain, as well as on such Latin American reform movements as Hipólito Yrigoyen's (1852–1933) Argentine Radicalism.

Spanish Krausists were often identified more by their style of moral earnestness, their belief in the possibilities of harmonic human development through reason and reflection, and their sectlike behavior as a secular priesthood for ethical (rather than material or scientific) progress than for their strict adherence to the murky thought of Krause or Sanz. For this reason, many could subsequently attack or claim for themselves Krausism without the constraints of knowing the philosophical roots of the movement. In that sense, Spanish Krausism loosely sought to copy the German reformist neohumanist movement of the early nineteenth century, with the significant difference that Spain fifty years later lacked the educated middle class, modern educational and scientific institutions, and other preconditions that had caused it to take root in Germany.

For all its bizarre appearances and episodic impact, Spanish Krausism nevertheless contributed to rethinking Spanish church and state traditions. It sought a less frivolous and selfish approach to life, thought, and literature, and welcomed concepts of academic freedom that were obviously desiderata of many reformers in Isabeline Spain. As antitraditionalists who also resisted French or British versions of modernity as too materialistic or shallow, the Krausists also opened and deepened another channel of contact with the rest of the European intellectual world through German idealism. As slight as their impact may have been, for this stance they earned great vilification in their own time and in the twentieth century from radical defenders of Spanish traditionalism.

For additional information, see O. Alvaraz Guerrero, *Política y ética social. Yrigoyen y el Krausismo. Orígenes ideológicos de la UCR* (Fuerte General Roca, 1983); E. Díaz, *La filosofía social del krausismo español* (Madrid, 1973); R. García Mateo, *Das deutsche Denken und das moderne Spanien* (Frankfurt, 1982); J. J. Gil Cremades, *Krausistas y liberales* (Madrid, 1975); J. López-Morillas, *The Krausist Movement and Ideological Change in Spain, 1854–1874* (Cambridge, 1981); F. Martín Buezas, *El krausismo español desde dentro. Sanz del Río. Autobiografía de intimidad* (Madrid, 1978); and A. Posada, *Breve historia del krausismo español* (Oviedo, 1981).

*C. E. McClelland*

# L

LARGO CABALLERO, FRANCISCO (1869–1946), socialist trade-union leader. Largo was born on 15 Oct. 1869 in the Plaza Vieja of the Chamberí district in Madrid.* His working-class parents separated in 1873, with the young Francisco remaining with his mother, who set off to Granada in search of work. It was the beginning of a childhood of extreme hardship. At the age of seven, having returned to Madrid, he was forced to abandon school in order to work. The daily brutality of labor infused him with an acute sense of injustice and an unbreakable hostility toward capitalism. These early experiences would be the wellspring of his activities as a labor leader.

In 1878, he found work as an apprentice plasterer, a skilled trade in which he had some success, working by the time he was sixteen with two assistants of his own. He liked his trade, but since it was seasonal work, he was usually unemployed during the winter and obliged to seek work as a laborer on public road-building projects. It was while he was working on the outskirts of Madrid that he first heard of Pablo Iglesias (1850–1925) and became aware of the May Day call for the workers to form sociedades de resistencia, as primitive trade unions were then called. Inspired by the idea, on 2 May 1890, Largo Caballero joined the bricklayers' union "El Trabajo," which formed part of the Unión General de Trabajadores* (UGT). Shortly afterward, he helped found the union of plasterers and quickly rose to be a member of its executive committee. After he had witnessed so much oppression, the very idea of trade unionism was a revelation to him, and he decided to dedicate his life to it.

The figure of Pablo Iglesias was an inspiration to the young convert. At the same time, Largo's austerity and capacity for hard work, as well as a total dedication to union work, quickly attracted the attention of the founder of the Socialist party* (PSOE). They became friends, but the admiration felt by Largo for Iglesias was such that it can be said that his personality was molded as much by Iglesias's influence as by his harsh early experiences as a young worker. The trade union came to be Largo Caballero's great obsession, and he eventually acquired tremendous authority within the UGT as a result of the care with which he carried out his union duties.

In the autumn of 1890, Largo Caballero took part in the organization of a plasterers' strike, the first carried out in Madrid according to UGT rules. This convinced him of the superiority of socialist methods over the spontaneity of the anarchists.* A certain contempt for the anarchists and an absolute faith in the efficacy of the UGT's organization were to be the two crucial and constant keys to his political life, even at its most dramatic moments, such as his apparent leftward swing or radicalization during the Second Republic* of the 1930s. If he came to take part in politics it was only because he considered it the only way to consolidate the trade-union victories won in the daily struggle against the bosses. In fact, he did not join the PSOE until 14 Mar. 1894, when he entered the Agrupación Socialista Madrileña.

Respected by his comrades, he was elected in 1904 to the council of the Instituto de Reformas Sociales,* where he worked hard for the introduction of such practical reforms as sickness insurance for workers. In Dec. 1905, he was elected a councillor of the Madrid city council, where he dedicated himself to the struggle against corruption. So great was this task that Largo, by this time president of the Agrupación Socialista, had to give up his job as a plasterer in order to dedicate himself full-time to being a councillor.

As a consequence of his role in the affairs both of the UGT and the PSOE as Pablo Iglesias's righthand man, Largo began to find himself ever more involved in the great political and social developments of his time. On 28 July 1909, as a member of the national committee of the UGT, he was arrested when the union called a general strike in protest against the Spanish war effort in Morocco.* He was thereafter arrested on several occasions as a result of his participation in the republican-socialist campaign against the colonial war. The socialist links with the middle-class republicans provoked a leftist rebellion within the ranks of the PSOE that eventually led to the communist schisms of 1919–1921. Largo Caballero stood foursquare with Iglesias in defense of the republican alliance.

In the course of World War I,* shortages and a fierce price inflation so affected the living standards of the working class that there was a certain rapprochement of the UGT and the Confederación Nacional de Trabajo (CNT) in hope of joint strike action. Largo took charge of negotiations with the anarchosyndicalists, an experience that convinced him once more of the CNT's lack of organization and its essential adventurism. Despite his conviction that adequate organization was crucial, however, in Aug. 1917 the UGT was forced by government provocation to declare a revolutionary general strike. A strike committee was formed, composed of Largo, Julián Besteiro (1870–1939), and two others. All four were immediately arrested and condemned to life imprisonment in Cartagena. Having been turned into popular heroes and martyrs, they were successfully presented in absentia as candidates in the 1918 Cortes elections, and Largo Caballero became deputy for Barcelona.*

The brutality of the repression unleashed against the strikers in Asturias* and the Basque* provinces traumatized Largo Caballero, convincing him that the 1917 strike had been a grave mistake. At the XIII Congress of the UGT, from 3 to 10 Oct. 1913, he was elected secretary-general of the union. Having been convinced by the aftermath of the strike never again to risk the well-being of the union in a frontal assault against the apparatus of the state, he soon found himself the target of virulent attacks by the revolutionary wing of the socialist movement. When the PSOE held three important congresses in order to debate entry into the Communist International, the role played by Largo Caballero turned out to be crucial. Negatively influenced by the lack of internal democracy within the Bolshevik party and, more significant, hostile to the idea of subordinating the organizations of the Spanish socialist movement to the discipline and the interest of Moscow, he threw the weight of the Agrupación Socialista Madrileña against entry into the Comintern.

Largo Caballero consistently revealed himself to be a pragmatic trade unionist. It was thus hardly surprising when he opposed any adventurist idea of resisting by revolutionary strike action the military coup of Gen. Miguel Primo de Rivera* on 13 Sept. 1923. Largo's reasoning was that, although the political struggle had been forcibly suspended, the trade-union battle had to go on. When the dictator banned the CNT and the Communist party* but held out the possibility of a trade-union monopoly to the UGT, Largo Caballero was keen on collaboration. Not only was he convinced that the essential task of the UGT was to protect the material interest of its members, but he also saw in the facilities Primo offered to the socialists the chance to eliminate the UGT's anarchosyndicalist rivals. This led to a bitter rivalry with Indalecio Prieto (1833–1962) who believed it to be the moral duty of the socialist movement to defend democratic rights. At first, Largo Caballero collaborated enthusiastically with the new regime, taking part in the Junta de Abastos (Food Supply and Distribution Council) and even in the Consejo de Estado (Council of State). He even made public pronouncements against strike actions. From 1927, however, he began to change his stance when he saw that collaboration was leading to a loss of militants in the UGT, especially among the miners of Asturias.

Largo's rise within the socialist movement continued during this period. At the PSOE's XII Congress, held from 29 June to 4 July 1928, he was elected vice-president. At the UGT's XVI Congress, held from 10 to 15 Oct. 1928, he was once more elected secretary-general. His preeminence, though, was based on his capacity to understand and foster the interests of the socialist rank and file. Reacting to growing working-class militancy against the dictatorship, Largo began to move toward Prieto's position, which had long advocated a broad coalition with republican forces against the dictatorship. Just as the material well-being of the UGT had taken him into collaborationism, now fear of losing members pushed him into the opposition.

By the time the dictator left Spain in Jan. 1930, Largo had already become an enthusiastic advocate of the republican cause. At the Pact of San Sebastian in Aug. 1930, along with Prieto and Fernando de los Ríos (1879–1949), Largo became a minister in the provisional republican government. Contrary to his natural caution, and mistakenly confident of support from republican army officers, he supported the participation of the UGT in a revolutionary strike against the monarchy. More than a radical change in his position, this rashness revealed his almost slavish readiness to follow, or to be seen to follow, the wishes of the rank and file. The strike of 15 Dec. 1930 was a failure, but it was soon forgotten in the triumph of the republican-socialist electoral coalition in the municipal elections of 12 Apr. 1931. When the king fled and the Second Republic was established, Largo accepted the ministry of labor for the same reasons that he first supported and then rejected the dictatorship: his determination to be of service to the working class, and to the UGT in particular, by introducing major social reforms. In fact, he had barely entered the ministry before he was introducing by decree the most important reforms carried out by the Second Republic. The decrees aimed at improving the appalling working conditions suffered by the landless laborers of the latifundio areas of the south included the eight-hour day in rural areas; arbitration committees known as mixed juries; obligatory cultivation to prevent rural lockouts by owners simply refusing to cultivate their land; and the establishment of municipal boundaries to prevent the importation of cheap, outside labor into a given municipality while there was local unemployment.

The cumulative consequence of these decrees, and of Largo's entire period in the ministry of labor, signified a fundamental attack on the repressive social and economic relations that prevailed in rural Spain in the 1930s. The landowners' response took the form of a vicious press campaign denigrating the republic, obstruction in the Cortes of the government's reform program, and a brutal offensive in the countryside against the landless laborers. Given that the purpose of his reforms had been humanitarian rather than revolutionary, Largo was profoundly embittered by the ferocity of the right-wing attack. His adolescent hatred of capitalism was ignited once more.

Under the influence of Luis Araquistáin (1886–1959), who had shared his experience in the Ministry of Labor as undersecretary and then as ambassador in Berlin had witnessed the rise of Nazism, Largo began to doubt the efficacy of democratic reformism in a period in which economic depression rendered capitalism inflexible. By the autumn of 1932, it was possible to discern Largo's growing radicalization in his struggle against the moderate wing of the socialist movement led by Besteiro. At the XIII Congress of the PSOE (6–13 Oct.), Largo Caballero was elected president, while the XVII Congress of the UGT (14–21 Oct.) elected him secretary-general within an executive committee dominated by trade-union bureaucrats loyal to Besteiro. Largo therefore resigned from the UGT, convinced that the mood of the rank and file demanded a more determined, and even more revolutionary, policy.

The employers' offensive of the winter of 1932–1933, as well as the rise of fascism abroad, convinced Largo of the necessity of an exclusively socialist government to carry out a policy of social change. His speeches throughout 1933 showed an ever-greater radicalization in this regard, bringing him into conflict once again with Prieto. He succeeded in stimulating the enthusiasm of the Socialist Youth in Madrid, however, and of many sectors of the working class, especially in the rural south. When the republican-socialist coalition government of Manuel Azaña* fell in Sept. 1933, the socialists decided not to renew their electoral coalition with the republican forces. Ignoring the extent to which it was imprudent to go it alone in an electoral system that favored coalitions, Largo Caballero took the lead in the socialist campaign with great fervor. Along with anarchist abstention, the left-wing division was one of the reasons behind the PSOE's defeat in the elections of Nov. 1933.

Socialist bitterness was no less because the disaster was partly self-inflicted. Throughout 1934, Largo intensified the rhetorically revolutionary tone of his speeches, more than anything else with the twin hopes of frightening the Right out of its vengeful social policies and pushing the president of the Second Republic into calling new elections. On 27 Jan. 1934, when the pro-Besteiro executive of the UGT resigned in protest at the revolutionary tendency, Largo was elected secretary-general. Although he was gaining great popularity among the socialist rank and file, particularly in Madrid and the rural south, with his radicalized rhetoric, he continued to be at heart a reformist trade-union leader obsessed with the material well-being of the UGT. This could be deduced from the contrast between the threatening nature of his speeches and the reality of his day-to-day caution. It was most obvious when he prevented the UGT from mounting solidarity actions with the great harvest strike organized by its rural sections in the summer of 1934. He was convinced that his revolutionary threats would stop the president from inviting the Catholic authoritarian party, the Confederación Española de Derechas Autónomas (CEDA), to take part in the government. When three CEDA ministers were named on 4 Oct. 1934, Largo could not believe it and was reluctant to give the go-ahead for the revolutionary movement that had been half-heartedly planned. After the insurrection of miners in Asturias, he was soon arrested and tried for his responsibility in its preparation.

He passed the greater part of 1935 in prison, where it is alleged that he read for the first time several Marxist classics. At the same time, a fierce internal struggle broke out within the socialist movement. The failure of the Asturian rising had convinced Prieto that the socialists had to rebuild their electoral coalition with the republicans in the hope of regaining power. The young followers of Largo Caballero, many of whom like Santiago Carrillo* and Amaro del Rosal (1904– ) were in jail with him, believed that October had been a disaster because the socialists had been insufficiently revolutionary. At this time, the title of the Spanish Lenin was given currency by the communists, who wished to flatter Largo Caballero. His supporters indulged in virulent polemics against Prieto, who nonetheless maintained a hold on the PSOE's organizational apparatus and even managed to provoke the resignation of Largo from the presidency of the party on 16 Dec. 1935. The Caballeristas desisted only when it became clear there was considerable mass support for Prieto's cooperation with Manuel Azaña in creating the Popular Front. The internal struggle was shelved during the campaign for the Feb. 1936 elections, and Largo carried the greatest propaganda burden.

Once the elections were safely won, Largo devoted his efforts to ensuring that there would be a republican-socialist coalition government. He believed that only an exclusively socialist government could carry through the necessary transformation of Spanish society. Accordingly, he insisted that the republicans go it alone until they had exhausted themselves in carrying out the bourgeois stage of the revolution. His plan was for them to either give way to a socialist cabinet or else be engulfed by a fascist uprising that would itself merely set off a successful revolution. Therefore, in May, when Prieto was invited to form a government, Largo used his power as president of the Agrupación Socialista Madrileña as well as of the PSOE's parliamentary minority to prevent him from doing so. A strong coalition under Prieto would have had a good chance to forestall the military uprising. By keeping a weak republican government under Santiago Casares Quiroga (1894–1950) in power, Largo's action facilitated the work of the military conspirators who were to rise on 18 July 1936.

Perhaps paradoxically, during the civil war itself, there was to be no more faithful defender of the Popular Front line and of the republic than Largo Caballero. Abandoning his immediate revolutionary ambitions, and backed by the Communist party, he put his prestige among the working masses at the service of the threatened regime. On 4 Sept. 1936, he was made prime minister at the head of a wide republican-socialist coalition in which he also held the portfolio of minister of war. Two months later, with the nationalists at the gates of Madrid, he widened his coalition by the inclusion of four anarchosyndicalists. He took the responsibility for the decision to evacuate the government to Valencia.* Under his leadership, although in practice at the hands of the communists, action was taken to counteract the revolutionary advances that had taken place in the power vacuum created by the military uprising. The workers' militias were militarized and state authority reestablished. Nevertheless, Largo found himself rapidly facing an alliance of republicans, moderate socialists, and communists who wished to curtail even further the autonomous institutions of proletarian revolution such as the Council of Aragon. His refusal to agree to the suppression of the press and the POUM* and the CNT earned him the hostility of the communists who had previously been happy to manipulate him.

There can be little doubt that Largo was extremely conservative and inflexible as a wartime leader. By the spring of 1937, he was already the target of criticism from both the communists and the socialist followers of Prieto. In April, having discovered the existence of the communists' private prisons, he provoked the resignation of the communist councillor for public order and began a campaign to limit the power of the communist political commissars. He soon found himself surrounded by enemies within his own cabinet. The final crisis came on 13 May 1937, when he refused to permit the suppression of the POUM. The communists proposed that Prieto replace him as minister of war, which guaranteed his resignation. He was vilified by the communist press as an enemy of the working class. Nevertheless, even after his fall, he continued to enjoy considerable support and prestige among the rank and file.

At the end of the civil war, Largo went into exile in France.* On 30 Nov. 1939, he was arrested by Mar. Henri Phillipe Pétain's (1856–1951) police and imprisoned in various French jails. The government of Gen. Francisco Franco* tried without success to gain his extradition. After having been freed and placed under house arrest in Nyons, however, he was arrested on 19 Feb. 1943 by agents of the Gestapo. Aged seventy-four, he was sent to the concentration camp of Orianenburg. He was liberated at the end of the war by Polish troops and taken to Soviet military headquarters and given medical assistance. In mid-1945, with his health broken, he reached Paris. He died on 23 Mar. 1946 and was buried there as a hero, his coffin accompanied by an immense crowd of French and exiled Spanish mourners. In Apr. 1978, his remains were taken to Madrid and buried in a civil cemetery.

For additional information, see J. Andrés-Gallego, *El socialismo durante la dictadura 1923–1930* (Madrid, 1977); S. Juliá, *La izquierda del PSOE* (Madrid, 1977); F. Largo Caballero, *Discoursos a los trabajadores* (Madrid, 1934), *Escritos de la República* (Madrid, 1985), and *Mis recuerdos: Cartas a un amigo* (Mexico City, 1954); G. Mario de Coca, *Anti-Caballero: Una crítica marxista de la bolchevización del Partido Socialista Obrero Español* (Madrid, 1936); J. Maurín, *Los hombres de la dictadura* (Madrid, 1930); G. Meaker, *The Revolutionary Left in Spain 1914–1923* (Stanford, 1974); A. Pastor Ugena, *La Agrupación Socialista Madrileña durante la Segunda República* (Madrid, 1985); and P. Preston, *The Coming of the Spanish Civil War*, 2d ed. (London and New York, 1983).

*P. Preston*

*Related entries*: SECOND REPUBLIC; SPANISH CIVIL WAR.

**LARRA Y SÁNCHEZ DE CASTRO, MARIANO JOSÉ DE** (1809–1837), writer published under the name Fígaro and other pseudonyms. When Joseph Bonaparte, José I* of Spain, was deposed in 1813, Larra's father, a French sympathizer, was obliged to leave Spain. As a result, Larra received his first formal schooling in France. He later continued his education in Spain, where he studied law and medicine for several years. He eventually abandoned these pursuits to become a writer. His career coincided with the chaotic years of the end of the rule of Fernando VII* and the beginning of the reign of Isabel II.*

Although his literary production includes some poetry, comedies, a novel, and a drama about fifteenth-century Galicia, Larra is mostly remembered for his journalistic work as a theater critic, political commentator, and writer of artículos de costumbres, humorous, satirical essays treating Madrileño life and society and national foibles and customs. "Vuelva usted mañana," one of his most memorable artículos, criticizes indolence as a national Spanish malady. Some of Larra's best work appeared early in his career in two short-lived periodicals, *El Duende Satírico del Día* (1828) and *El Pobrecito Hablador* (1832).

The mordant cast of Larra's writing had roots in his unhappy life. Unloved as a child, he later experienced a tragic love affair in adolescence. He made a mismatched marriage at twenty, and during the remainder of his life was involved in an adulterous love affair that led to his suicide at twenty-eight.

Larra's tragic personal history established him as a central figure of Spain's romantic movement. His biting observations about Spanish society, however, underscored his importance for a later generation of writers. His French education, which had led him to believe in logic and progress, made him optimistic about Spain's future, but in the course of his career, he grew increasingly disillusioned about his country's problems. His critical views of Spain foreshadowed attitudes expressed by the Generation of 1898.*

For additional information, see S. Kirkpatrick, *Larra: El laberinto inextricable de un romántico liberal* (Madrid, 1977); M. J. Larra y Sánchez de Castro, *Obras de D. Mariano José de Larra (Figaro)*, ed. C. Seco Serrano (Madrid, 1960); and P. Ullman, *Mariano de Larra and Spanish Political Rhetoric* (Madison, 1971).

*H. L. Kirby, Jr.*

**LERROUX GARCÍA, ALEJANDRO** (1864–1949), Spanish republican politician and journalist. Lerroux was born on 4 Mar. 1864 in the Cordoban village of La Rambla. The size of his family, which included seven children, and the inadequacy of his father's military pay spelled financial hardship for Lerroux's parents throughout most of their married life and left a lasting impression on him.

Although a quick student, Lerroux had difficulty adjusting to scholarly discipline and preferred the education of the streets to that of the classroom. This predilection and his parents' limited resources sent young Lerroux for a short time to live with his mother's brother, a priest, in Villaveza de Agua, Zamora. His uncle furnished him with a home, a few years of primary education, and ironically, given his later anticlericalism, a firm grounding in church dogma and practice.

With the death of his mother in 1882, the eighteen-year-old Lerroux willingly entered a military preparatory school in Seville for the sons of army officers. For two years, he marked time as an army corporal until he initiated his studies in the Academia Militar de Infantería in Toledo. The lack of necessary financial assistance from his family scotched this ambition, however, and in 1884, he deserted his military post and went to live with his older brother, Arturo, an army officer, in Oviedo. For the next two years, Lerroux worked at odd jobs in Asturias and Galicia. Under his brother's influence, Lerroux started to take an interest in politics. Like Arturo, he was especially attracted to "advanced" anticlerical and conspiratorial republicanism as represented by Manuel Ruiz Zorrilla (1833–1895), leader of the Progressive party.* Consequently, in May

1886, he moved to Madrid and became involved in the Progressive party's various conspiracies against the monarchy.

Blessed with a facile pen, Lerroux began to ghostwrite articles for his brother, who had gained a reputation as a republican activist. In turn, with the help of his brother, he was able to secure a position on the staff of the Zorrillista newspaper, *El País*; he became managing editor of the paper in 1892, and transformed *El País* into one of Madrid's leading dailies, while promoting his own reputation as a republican noteworthy.

With the death of Manuel Ruiz Zorrilla in 1895, the Progressive party split over the question of his successor. After a bitter contest, Dr. José María Esquerdo y Zaragoza (1842–1912) assumed the leadership of the more radical elements of the party. In the process, he convinced Lerroux to leave *El País* and assist him in founding an alternative progressive newspaper, *El Progreso*, in Oct. 1897, where Lerroux assumed a national role in the republican movement. In 1897, he organized a propaganda campaign to spread republicanism in southern Spain; at the same time, he launched a spirited effort in *El Progreso* and on the road to win amnesty for those worker activists who had been incarcerated in Montjuich prison in Barcelona* on charges of having planned and executed a series of indiscriminate bombings in Barcelona in 1896.

Lerroux's "Montjuich campaign" won him wide recognition and popularity among Barcelona's workers. Additionally, it earned him a reputation in government circles as a dangerous subversive. As a result, he was imprisoned during and after the Spanish-American War* for disregarding a press-censorship law concerning the colonial conflict. After his release, Lerroux again threw himself into national republican politics. In Apr. 1899, he stood as an unsuccessful Federalist party candidate for Barcelona in the national election; two years later, he moved permanently to Barcelona and ran in the general election of May 1901 as a candidate of the local Progressive party. It was subsequently rumored, although no proof has ever been presented, that the government of Práxedes Mateo Sagasta* facilitated Lerroux's relocation in order to use him as a counterbalance against Catalan regionalists.

The 1901 election was a watershed in Catalan political history. Not only was it fairly honest, but it also witnessed the emergence of the political arm of the Catalan regionalist movement, the Lliga Regionalista. Furthermore, it foreshadowed the birth in 1903 of the Republican Union, an attempt by the various republican organizations under Nicolás Salmerón,* one of the surviving former presidents of the First Republic,* to present a united front in both national and local elections.

Lerroux added to the special nature of this election by employing campaign methods that were a radical departure from traditional tactics. From the office of the republican daily, *La Publicidad*, he directed an appeal to Barcelona's substantial working-class population for votes and money that both scandalized and fascinated his fellow republicans. Moreover, in various articles, manifestos, and speeches, he elucidated ideas and programs that were a heady mixture of radical republicanism, such as antimonarchism; progressive education and anticlericalism; and a more "modern," if vague, call for state intervention in the country's economic and social sector. While abjuring both anarchism and socialism, the Emperador del Paralelo, as he became known to many of Barcelona's workers, was a spellbinding demagogue who at this point sincerely despised the maldistribution of wealth and the paternalistic attitudes of the upper and middle classes toward the workers. In its place he offered an imprecise vision of social harmony and republican virtue.

Lerroux's tactics and his public warnings during the election that he would not be able to control his working-class supporters if there were an attempt to fix the election proved astute. In the final count, Lerroux and Francesc Pi i Margall* were confirmed as the republican deputies from Barcelona. Lerroux followed his 1901 victory with an even more impressive showing in the general election of Apr. 1903. At this point, he had both the backing of the Republican Union and a substantial working-class base that gave him close to thirty-five thousand votes.

Bolstered by his victory, Lerroux's primary intent was to create a base of support that relied on both sophisticated mass mobilization (a first in Spain) and the creation of a local clientele network not unlike the political machines that were being built in urban America. In addition to these efforts, Lerroux had not, at this point, entirely given up his old progressive predilection for clandestine revolutionary activity, a characteristic that set him apart from the staider and more conventional followers of Salmerón. As such, during the years 1902–1906, he was involved in the revolutionary machinations of the semiclandestine Federación Revolucionaria, led by Vicente Blasco Ibáñez,* a movement that sought to use the army* and armed republicans to overthrow the monarchical political system.

A third electoral victory in Sept. 1905 prompted Lerroux to devote his energies entirely to conventional party politics. As the Salmerón wing of the Republican Union moved in late 1905 to join the Catalan regionalists in a gentlemen's alliance (the Solidaridad Catalana) against an increase in military power, Lerroux founded his own newspaper, *El Progreso*, in June 1906 in order to challenge Salmerón's leadership.

In pursuing this challenge, Lerroux found it difficult to control totally the popular passions he had so effectively aroused. During these years, for instance, some of his younger followers, the so-called Jóvenes Bárbaros, were a perpetually disruptive element in Barcelona politics. Lerroux himself did little to help matters by irresponsibly stirring their passions with such revolutionary and anticlerical demagoguery as his inflammatory "¡Rebeldes! ¡Rebeldes!" article of Sept. 1906. The ardor Lerroux generated, however, eventually backfired. During the electoral campaign of Apr. 1907, an anti-Solidaridad republican attempted to assassinate Salmerón, but instead wounded the Catalan leader, Francesc Cambó.* Public reaction to the episode went markedly against Lerroux, and he lost both a reelection bid in Apr. 1907 and a leadership challenge against Salmerón in June 1907 for control of the Republican Union. Attempting to cut his losses, he severed his ties with the Republican Union and in Jan. 1908 founded the Partido Republicano Radical, a party that at this point embodied all the exaltado element of Lerrouxismo.

Dogged by electoral defeat, Lerroux was further harassed by the Antonio Maura* government. Old charges involving a seditious article he had written some years earlier were brought against him, and without parliamentary immunity, he was forced to flee Spain in Feb. 1908. Lerroux remained in exile in France,* Argentina, and finally Britain* until Oct. 1909, thus fortuitously avoiding the Tragic Week (July 1909) and the direct blame for this event that devolved on other "advanced" political and social figures, such as his old progressive comrade, Francesc Ferrer.* Moreover, he had in the meantime been reelected in absentia to the Cortes (Dec. 1908), and his Radical party won a large majority of seats in the Barcelona city council, thus enhancing his position as the preeminent republican leader in Catalonia.*

The twenty years following his return to Spanish politics in 1909 constituted a second and less dramatic period in Lerroux's career. When he reentered the Cortes in May 1910 as a member of the Republican-Socialist Conjunction, he was a very different man than the one who had fled Spain in 1908. His political priorities had now moved from mass mobilization, clandestine activity, and demagoguery to painstaking party organization, which had as its objective the expansion of the Radical party's base outside the confines of Catalonia. This goal, coupled with the Radical party's often-shady administrative practices in Barcelona's municipal government; Lerroux's own dubious involvement in various lucrative business enterprises; and the emergence of the anarchosyndicalist Solidaridad Obrera in 1907 and the Confederación Nacional del Trabajo (CNT) in 1911 rendered the Radicals increasingly less attractive to Barcelona's workers. In Mar. 1914, for instance, Lerroux was only able to remain in the Cortes by assuming a safe seat from Andalusia.* Later that year, in Sept., he badly misjudged the strength of proneutral sentiment in Catalonia when he declared to the French newspaper Le Journal that Spain ought to assist the Allies against Germany.* On his return to Spain, he was greeted by an angry and threatening mob at the border.

Lerroux did compensate somewhat for the virtual loss of working-class support in Barcelona by expanding the Radical party's base into the rest of Spain (especially Madrid, Aragon,* and Valencia) and by adopting moderate positions on a variety of issues, thus appealing to middle-class opinion. In Oct. 1914, for example, he bluntly noted that the "revolution of the barricades is no longer possible." At the same time, during the summer of 1917, Lerroux endorsed the protest of the military Juntas de Defensa for higher pay and a fairer distribution of decorations and promotions, and he became directly involved in the Assembly Movement, whose goal was the establishment of a politically legitimate alternative to the Restoration political parties.

With the failure of the "Revolution of 1917," however, Lerroux became even more "governmental." During the early 1920s, he and his party were vocal critics of both Catalan separatism and Barcelona's almost endemic class violence. In turn, they tacitly supported a number of government policies, such as Spain's involvement in Morocco.* Such moderation, however, failed to gain much support for Lerroux's "historic" republicanism during the latter years of the parliamentary system, and his prospects for real political power proved even more elusive during the dictatorship of Miguel Primo de Rivera* from 1923 to 1930.

With the waning of the dictatorship in the late 1920s, Lerroux and his radicals moved to take advantage of the growing discontent in Spain with both the regime and, more significant, the monarchy. In Feb. 1926, he helped found the Alianza Republicana, a federation of republican parties and groups whose aim it was to move the nation toward a second republic. With the actual collapse of the dictatorship in Jan. 1930 and the growing enthusiasm during 1930 and 1931 for a republican alternative to the monarchy, Lerroux became a key player on the Spanish political stage. His moderate, responsible brand of republicanism had increasing appeal to Catholics, the bourgeoisie, and the professional and business communities.

Such appeal translated into political power, and Lerroux became one of the leading members of the so-called San Sebastian coalition (Aug. 1930), a political grouping of antimonarchist elements that ushered in the Second Republic.* Following this, he served as foreign affairs minister in the republic's provisional government of Apr. 1931 and in its successor, under Manuel Azaña,* of June-Dec. 1931. Lerroux and his party participated in and remained loyal to Azaña's government until 17 Dec. 1931, when Azaña chose to exclude the radicals and right republicans from his newly formed alliance between the left republicans and the socialists. Azaña's action destroyed both the Alianza Republicana and the San Sebastian coalition, and Lerroux withdrew from the Azaña ministry and moved the Radical party into opposition against the government.

Lerroux's Radical party, one of the most significant factions opposing Azaña, fought enactment of the left republican-socialist coalition's programs including, among others, Azaña's military reforms; an agrarian-reform bill (Sept. 1932) that sanctioned the confiscation of untitled lands in southern Spain; the abolition of capital punishment (Sept. 1932); and, most specifically, the Law of Religious Congregations (May 1933), which excluded monastic orders from engaging in commerce, industry, and teaching. By Sept. 1933, Lerroux was able to rally conservative elements, such as the Agrarian party, the Lliga, and the CEDA, against these proposals and thus topple Azaña from power.

The Bienio Negro of center-right predominance from Sept. 1933 to the end of 1935 witnessed six Lerroux ministries. The first, from 12 Sept. 1933 to 3 Oct. 1933, was short-lived because of a socialist vote of no confidence. After the general elections of 19 Nov. 1933, however, which saw the Radical party, the CEDA (a confederation of regional Catholic parties and interest groups led by José María Gil Robles [1898- ]), and other right and center parties won a majority of seats (372) in the Cortes, Lerroux was able to form a more solid second ministry, with CEDA backing, on 16 Dec. 1933. This government lasted until 2 Mar. 1934 and was replaced by a third Lerroux ministry on 3 Mar. 1934, which lasted until 25 Apr. 1934. During these two ministries and that of Ricardo Samper (1881–1939), which lasted from Apr. to Oct. 1934, the radicals moved to slow the pace of reform, despite the opposition of such a party stalwart as Diego Martínez Barrio (1883–1962), but not to alter drastically the programs of the previous two years. Agrarian reform continued, and the labor tribunals proceeded to render mostly prolabor decisions. The government also continued to expand its educational programs.

In early Oct. 1934, however, the radicals' monopoly of ministerial power ended when the CEDA forced Pres. Niceto Alcalá Zamora* to appoint a coalition ministry under Lerroux with three CEDA members. The establishment of Lerroux's fourth cabinet on 3 Oct. 1934 immediately touched off revolutionary insurrections (4–7 Oct. 1934) in Catalonia and Asturias against the CEDA's accession to power. The fighting was especially fierce in Asturias, where approximately thirteen hundred individuals were killed, three thousand wounded, and numerous atrocities committed on both sides. Despite his statesmanlike approach to the crisis, Lerroux was eventually obliged to call in the battle-hardened Army of Africa to quell the revolt.

Lerroux continued to head a coalition ministry through 2 Apr. 1935, when the CEDA refused to support his decision to commute the death sentences of the leaders of the Asturian insurrection. Forced to flee on 3 Apr. 1935, he had to constitute his fifth cabinet without CEDA participation. This ministry was short-lived, however, and on 3 May 1935, Lerroux was compelled to accept substantive CEDA participation, amounting to five cabinet positions, in his sixth and last government. This cabinet lasted until 22 Sept. 1935 and was characterized by increasingly less pragmatic and more reactionary ministerial policies as it pointedly ignored the Law of Congregations; appointed promanagement members to the labor tribunals; and revised the agrarian-reform law, thus ending the confiscation of large estates.

The collapse of Lerroux's last ministry in Sept. 1935 reflected not only the sharp political differences of various centrist and rightist parties and pressures from a resurgent Left, but also a series of financial scandals (the Straperlo and Nombela affairs) that involved a number of his relatives and close political associates. Although personally exonerated by the Cortes, Lerroux and his party lost their remaining credibility and were rendered impotent in the face of the Popular Front onslaught of early 1936. In fact, the national election of 16 Feb. 1936 was a disaster for the Radical party, which won only eight seats, and for Lerroux personally, as he lost his seat in the Cortes. In every sense, it spelled the end of Lerroux's political career.

The definitive end of Lerroux's role in Spanish politics came on 18 July 1936, the beginning of the Spanish Civil War,* when he hurriedly left Spain for exile in Portugal.* Although he eventually threw his support to the nationalist forces of Gen. Francisco Franco,* his historic association with republicanism and the Second Republic left him persona non grata in certain nationalist circles, particularly among the falangists and Carlists. Consequently, he remained in exile until July 1947, when the Franco government allowed him, then an elderly man, to return permanently to Spain. On 27 June 1949, he died in Madrid of cardiac arrest at the age of eighty-five.

For additional information, see A. Lerroux, *Al servicio de la República* (Madrid, 1930), *Mis memorias* (Madrid, 1963), *La pequeña historia de España, 1930–1936* (Buenos Aires, 1945); J. Pabón, *Cambó*, 3 vols. (Barcelona, 1952–1959); J. Romero Maura, *La rosa de fuego* (Barcelona, 1975); O. Ruiz Manjón, *El Partido Republicano Radical, 1908–1936* (Madrid, 1976); and J. C. Ullman, *La Semana Trágica* (Barcelona, 1972).

*S. E. Fleming*

*Related entries*: SECOND REPUBLIC; SPANISH CIVIL WAR.


**LIBERALISM,** political movement of the nineteenth and early twentieth centuries. Enlightened despotism and self-help organizations such as the Sociedades Económicas de Amigos del País* in late eighteenth-century Spain responded to the growth of a mercantile middle class on the coastal periphery by creating free-trade legislation, financial institutions, and technical schools. The merchants of Barcelona,* Valencia,* Malaga, Cadiz, and La Corunna, economically involved with the French and British, welcomed royal assistance in building roads, introducing new crops, and creating a new, innovative climate for economic growth. José de Moñino, the conde de Floridablanca*; Pedro Abarca y Bolea, the conde de Aranda*; and Pedro de Olavide (1725–1803) facilitated these policies, but the mercantilism of Felipe V* was still new and memories of the great, seventeenth-century economic disaster remained vivid, so economic liberalism proceeded slowly.

Liberalism from nationalist sources, however, emerged more rapidly. From 1790 to 1812, the ineptness of Carlos IV,* ecclesiastical paralysis in the face of the French Revolution's anticlericalism, and the intervention of Napoleon Bonaparte (1769–1821) led to the War of Independence.* The vigor of popular response against the French implanted the idea of national sovereignty in the Constitution of 1812, while the unpopularity of the church led to confiscation of ecclesiastical lands in 1813.

The absolutism of Fernando VII,* restored to the throne in 1814, reversed these changes and led many of this generation into Masonic membership in defiance of the regime. The exaltados' participation in the ill-fated insurrectionist regime of 1820–1823, which held the king captive, might have sealed their fate, had it not been for the financial problems that demanded Spanish participation in the new capital markets of Europe. In 1824, Fernando, his throne again returned to him by the French, acknowledged his gratitude by placing the finance ministry in the hands of Luis López Ballesteros (1782–1853), thereby creating an opportunity for liberals to serve the monarchy.

The strength of this revival became apparent after Fernando's death, when the crown went to his infant daughter Isabel II* rather than his younger brother Carlos. The queen-regent, María Cristina de Habsburgo (1806–1878), appointed Francisco Cea Bermúdez (1772–1850) premier in Sept. 1833 and permitted promulgation of a Royal Statute in 1834. It rejected national sovereignty for an oligarchical concept somewhat similar to French doctrinaire liberalism of the same period. Cea Bermúdez; José Pando Fernández de Pinedo, the marqués de Miraflores (1792–1872); Javier de Burgos (1778–1849); and the other founders of the Moderate party* believed that they were mobilizing a new aristocracy of talent. The moderates ruled until Aug. 1836, when military and social unrest created the conditions necessary for the exaltados to establish the Progressive party.* Leadership devolved upon Juan Álvarez Mendizábal,* who publicly acknowledged national sovereignty as the ultimate legal means for bringing change. The progressives championed nationalism, but personal gain was as much their intent as the moderates', since the underemployed urban middle classes dependent on government posts for a livelihood dominated the party.

The moderate and progressive rivalry lasted until 1923, although the names of the parties changed after 1868. New constitutions alternated power between the two groups in 1837, 1845, and 1854. The ecclesiastical disentailment the progressives began in 1837 benefited the liberals politically, and at the end of the First Carlist War (1833–1840), legal codification provided a modern legal system that further centralized power into their hands. At the same time, the military failure of the Carlists,* who detested both groups, ended any organized resistance to liberalism for nearly a generation.

Despite these triumphs, liberalism suffered severely from factionalism between 1840 and 1869. One problem was caudillismo. Progressive Gen. Baldomero Espartero* and moderate Gen. Ramón María Narváez* tried to personify their beliefs behind pseudo-Napoleonic facades without conspicuous success. In the wake of personalism came a second problem, corruption. The liberals were unwilling either to establish an adequate civil service or to regulate the excesses of industries such as the railroads, then in their formative stages.

Praetorian corruption lasted through a third effort to write yet another constitution in 1854. The progressives, out of power from 1843 to 1854, became increasingly hostile to the monarchy, while moderate Juan Bravo Murillo* defended Isabel II by restricting civil liberties and spending more on public works. The progressives countered by advocating abolition of both sales taxes and conscription. Gen. Leopoldo O'Donnell,* representing a new second generation of Liberal Union progressives, proposed creation of a national militia to dismantle moderate military power.

In fact, popular frustration ran high against both parties in 1854–1856. The threat of democratic radicalism finally led to the separation of the Liberal Union from the progressives in 1858. O'Donnell's Unionist cabinet lasted five years, and his adventuresome foreign engagements in Asia, the Caribbean, and Mexico* distracted public attention from a corrupt domestic administration.

The true crisis of Spanish liberalism came between 1863 and 1874. A stock-market crash and excessive expenditures at court caused political disintegration and a series of insurrections, while the deaths of O'Donnell in 1867 and Narváez in 1868 left only an aged Espartero to defend the throne. Isabel abdicated in

Sept. 1868 and was followed by a generation of new, mostly radical, leaders. Only Práxedes Mateo Sagasta* played any role during this period, although Antonio Cánovas del Castillo* reorganized monarchical conservatives in exile.

Both Cánovas and Sagasta played a major role in the Bourbon Restoration of 1875–1885. Their Liberal-Conservative and Liberal Fusion parties alternated in power whenever one of them encountered political difficulties. They carefully controlled political life with caciques—essentially a boss system of patronage politics that was extremely corrupt at its heart. Until the death of Cánovas in 1897 and Sagasta in 1903, liberalism flourished as never before, quite independent of the army* or the church.

At the same time, however, liberal caudillismo ignored so many modern problems that the successors of Cánovas and Sagasta were confronted with a multitude of new problems. Antonio Maura* failed to obtain local government reform in 1909. José Canalejas (1854–1912) had to fall back on anticlericalism for his program, but after his assassination on 12 Nov. 1912, Maura turned increasingly toward authoritarian dictatorship, clashing with new labor organizations and the Left. In 1923, the dictatorship of Gen. Miguel Primo de Rivera,* who in another age would have made a perfect praetorian liberal himself, banned the liberal parties after reformers had criticized them for years. The movement failed to recover during the Second Republic* or the era of Gen. Francisco Franco.*

For additional information, see M. Fernández Almagro, *Historia política de la España contemporánea* (Madrid, 1982); A. Fernández de los Ríos, *Estudio histórico de las luchas políticas de España del siglo XIX* (Madrid, 1879); C. Hennessy, *The Federal Republic in Spain: Pi y Margall and the Federal Republican Movement 1854–1874* (Oxford, 1962); R. W. Kern, *Liberals, Reformers and Caciques in Restoration Spain* (Albuquerque, 1973); and G. Maura, *Historia crítica del reinado de Alfonso XIII* (Barcelona, 1919).

*R. W. Kern*

*Related entries*: CÁNOVAS DEL CASTILLO, ANTONIO; SAGASTA, PRÁXEDES MATEO.

# M

MACHADO Y RUIZ, ANTONIO (1875–1939), poet and member of the Generation of 1898.* Machado was born in Seville to a family of liberal intellectuals sympathetic to the Institución Libre de Enseñanza.* His father was a well-known folklorist whose books, published under the pseudonym Demófilo, earned him international recognition. His older brother, Manuel (1874–1947), later became an outstanding modernist poet.

During Machado's childhood, the family was economically dependent on his paternal grandfather, a professor of natural science at the Universities of Seville and Madrid.* The family moved to Madrid when Machado was eight, so that he could be educated at the Institución. The deaths of his father in 1893 and his grandfather in 1895 left the family in a precarious economic situation. Machado was unable even to finish his undergraduate studies, but in 1899, he traveled with Manuel to France to work as a translator. Their stay lasted about a year, and permitted him to become acquainted with the new French poetry. In 1902, he published *Soledades*, a first book of poetry that revealed a surprisingly mature poet. In 1907, after finally finishing his undergraduate degree, he became a professor of French at the Institute of Soria at the same time as a new, much-expanded version of his first book appeared under the definitive title *Soledades, galerías y otros poemas*.

Soria, capital of one of the poorest provinces in Castile, brought Machado face-to-face with a landscape and social reality that he had been unaware of. He also met Leonor Izquierdo (1894–1912), daughter of a pension owner, and married her in 1909, when he was thirty-four years old and she barely fifteen. In 1911, during another of Machado's trips to Paris, Leonor was diagnosed as having tuberculosis, which caused him to return. A year later, she died, just a few days after *Campos de Castilla* had appeared, a book in which Machado tempered the intimist attitude characteristic of his earlier work.

Incapable of living in Soria without Leonor's company, Machado sought a transfer to the Institute of Baeza, an Andulusian town where the spectacle of social injustice again had a strong impact upon him. Machado wrote poetry evocative of Leonor and the Sorian countryside. He also studied philosophy and letters, and in 1919 obtained a position at the Institute of Segovia. *Nuevas canciones* was published in 1924 and won him election to the Royal Academy in 1927, although he never gave his inaugural address.

During this period, he met Pilar de Valderrama (1908– ), a married woman of Madrid's high society (alluded to in his verses by the name Guiomar), with whom he had a secret love affair. In 1931, after the proclamation of the Second Republic,* which he greeted enthusiastically, he obtained a position at the Institute of Madrid. He successfully wrote theatrical works in collaboration with Manuel and prose pieces under the names Juan de Mairena and Abel Martín. Many of these works appeared in the Madrid press in 1934.

During the Spanish Civil War,* Machado joined the republican cause, which he defended in many of his writings. The war forced him to move to Valencia* and Barcelona,* where he lived with his mother and his brother José, a draftsman and painter. In late January 1939, the Machados were evacuated to France after the nationalist invasion of Catalonia.* The poet's health deteriorated, and he died on 22 February in the small seaside village of Collioure in southern France. His mother died three days later, and both were buried in Collioure's cemetery.

Machado's poetic work, although relatively limited, has great complexity and richness and is consequently difficult to classify. Each of his major books contains changes of attitude, tone, and preoccupation that temper and even deny their author's earlier positions. *Soledades, galerías y otros poemas* entered the poet's interior universe, the "galleries of the soul," to reveal the blurred reality of his dreams and memories. The poet hopes to discover "a divine truth" to explain the mysterious sense of his existence. Machado showed himself here to be a symbolist, but *Campos de Castilla* revealed a very different poet. He abandoned the nebulous galleries of the soul to confront a concrete exterior world: the symbolist transformed into a singer of Castilian landscapes and peoples who also meditates on the sense of its history. Pessimistic consideration of the present is balanced by a hopeful vision of the future, typical of the Generation of 1898.

In general, the unity of Machado's writing has been ignored. His poetry is not a mixture of diverse elements, but a conjunction whose parts are mutually enriching. His epic, lyric, symbolist, and popular poetry have a profound coherence stemming from two sources: fidelity to the romantic impulse, which explains all the patterns and directions of his work; and his constant dialectical behavior, which motivates and resolves the apparent contradictions that penetrate his changes of attitude.

Machado's late romanticism, faith in the value of ideas within the poem, treatment of public and political themes, and enthusiasm for popular culture collide with his taste for the "purity" that dominated Spanish poetry of the period in which Juan Ramón Jiménez* was the indisputable teacher. After the civil war, however, Machado's humanity, liberalism, and exemplary conduct in defense of ideas (which carried him into exile and, in a certain sense, to his death) earned him the recognition and admiration of young Spanish poets, for whom he became a model and symbol.

For additional information, see J. L. Cano, *Antonio Machado: Biografía ilustrada* (Barcelona, 1975); A González, *Antonio Machado: Estudio* (Madrid, 1986); R. Gullón, *Una poética para Antonio Machado* (Madrid, 1970); R. Gutiérrez Girardot, *Poesía y prosa de Antonio Machado* (Madrid, 1969); A. Sánchez Barbudo, *Estudios sobre Unamuno y Machado* (Madrid, 1970); J. M. Valverde, *Antonio Machado* (Madrid, 1975); and R. de Zubiría, *La poesía de Antonio Machado* (Madrid, 1969).

*Á. González*

**MACIÀ, FRANCESC** (1859–1933), Catalan political leader. Born in Vilanova i la Geltru to a merchant family, Macià completed his basic studies and selected a military career by entering the Academy of Military Engineers in Guadalajara, graduating in 1880. He became a captain in 1882 and later commanded the garrison at Lérida, where he directed military engineering projects for more than twenty years, rising to the rank of colonel.

In 1905, however, Macià became disillusioned with the Spanish army* when soldiers at Barcelona* ransacked the offices of two newspapers, a provocation that caused Catalans to form a popular movement, Solidaritat Catalana. Macià entered politics; was elected deputy of the Borges Branques district; but because of army opposition, was transferred to Santander, an act that led to his resignation from the army. Reelected several times as deputy even after the Solidaritat Catalana party was dissolved by the government in 1909, he resigned in 1914 to protest the national government's policies toward Catalonia.

For a time, Macià was a war correspondent for *La Publicidad*, a Barcelona newspaper tied to the Allied cause, but at the end of World War I,* he returned to Barcelona to participate in the Asemblea de Parlamentaris, an ad hoc effort to create a separatist government. Macià was able to unite the Catalan bourgeoisie with the proletariat in the Federació Democràtica Catalana in 1919, by continuing to criticize the central government, believing that once Catalonia gained its sovereignty, it would form part of a federal union.

Macià also took an active part in the Conferència Nacional Catalana in 1922, proposing the creation of a Catalan state with such passion that he began to attract cadres of young followers who were not interested in the conservative, bourgeois Lliga Regionalista de Catalunya, led by Francesc Cambó.* Out of such recruits, he began forming the Estat Catalá movement, a militantly separatist, paramilitary organization. He posed such a risk to the region's stability that in September 1923, at the start of the dictatorship of Gen. Miguel Primo de Rivera,* Macià was forced into exile.

During his stay in France,* Macià formed the Oficines d'Etat Catalá to unite Catalan separatists living abroad. He began seeking financial support from the Soviet Union, traveling there to meet with Soviet leaders, who refused to assist him. Macià then planned an invasion of Spain through the border town of Prato de Mollo, but this insurrection was foiled when either French or Spanish intelligence or an Italian traitor informed French authorities of the plan. Exiled by the French, Macià entered Belgium, and with the poet Ventura Gassol (1893– ), traveled to Uruguay, Argentina, Chile, Cuba, and New York to solicit financial support, without much success.

After Primo de Rivera's fall, Macià returned to Barcelona and took part in a conference of Catalan leftist parties that formed the Esquerra Republicana de Catalunya. He became the president of the Esquerra's executive council, leading the party to electoral victory in April 1931, just as the abdication of Alfonso XIII* saw the formation of the Second Republic.* Two days later, Macià proclaimed a Catalan republic (and became its provisional president), as a part of a proposed federation of Iberian republics. Heavy pressure from Spanish republicans and socialists soon persuaded him to participate in the Second Republic, but he lobbied the constituent Cortes to include the principle of autonomy in the republican constitution, and then wrote the Estatut d'Autonomia for Catalonia that was passed by the Cortes in September 1932.

Macià remained president of the Generalitat of Catalonia until his death on Christmas Day 1933.

For additional information, see E. Jardi Casany, *Francesc Macià. El cami de la llibertat (1905–1931)* (Barcelona, 1977) and *Francesc Macià, President de Catalunya* (Monserrat, 1981); and M. Cruells, *Francesc Macià* (Barcelona, 1971).

*D. J. Viera*

*Related entries*: BARCELONA; CATALONIA.

**MADRAZO Y KUNTZ, FEDERICO DE** (1815–1894), official painter to the court during the reigns of Isabel II* and Alfonso XII.* Madrazo was born in Rome on 19 February 1815 to Spanish parents. His father, José de Madrazo (1781–1859), a neoclassicist trained in the school of the French master, Jean-Auguste-Dominique Ingres (1780–1867), was director of the Academia de San Fernando in Madrid. Federico studied in Paris with Franz Xavier Winterhalter (1805–1873), court painter to Napoleon III (1808–1873), Eugenie, and the nobles of the Second Empire.

Madrazo's style much resembled that of his teacher. Among his most important works were portraits of Isabel II; the duchess of Medinaceli, and other Spanish grandees; as well as a number of historical subjects, such as *Maria Cristina in the Dress of a Nun by the Bedside of Fernando III*. His highly polished academic paintings, impervious to political and social concerns such as Carlism,* Isabel's exile, and the subsequent Bourbon Restoration, made him the classic court painter of the century.

Madrazo's honors included the Legion d'Honneur (1846); corresponding membership of the French Academy (1853); directorship of the Prado (1856); presidency of the Academy of San Fernando (1859); and foreign membership of the French Academy (1873). He executed major commissions at Versailles and in Madrid,* and produced a quantity of historical and religious paintings and portraits during a long stay in Rome. Late in life, he was associated with such art periodicals as *El artista* and *El semanario pintoresco*, themselves part of a new and growing European interest in the contemporary art world.

Madrazo died in Madrid on 11 June 1894. His son, Raimundo de Madrazo (1841–1920), was also a painter, as was his brother, Luis de Madrazo (1825–1897). His daughter, Cecilia, married the Spanish painter Mariano Fortuny.*

For additional information, see F. Madrazo, *Viaje artístico de tres siglos por las colecciones de cuadros de los reyes de España* (Madrid, 1891).

S. Benforado

*Related entries*: FORTUNY, MARIANO; FRANCE; ISABEL II.


**MADRID,** national capital and Spain's largest city. Pop. (1985 est.) 4,137,000 The city of Madrid, originally Majerit, a tenth-century Muslim alcázar guarding the northern flank of Toledo, became a Christian possession in 1083. As the Reconquest moved south, the Cortes, attracted by Madrid's central location, first met there in 1309. The peripatetic Castilian court located permanently in Madrid when the Escorial was begun nearby in 1560, and later Hapsburg projects included the Plaza Mayor, the Segovia bridge, and the cathedral of San Isidro.

The Bourbons changed the city's face even more substantially. The royal palace (begun in 1734), Biblioteca Nacional, Real Academia de Historia, and Real Academia Española all created a cosmopolitan architectural style for the rapidly growing capital. Carlos III* added the Plaza de la Independencia, the Puerta de Alcalá, and at the heart of the city, the Puerta del Sol. He also planned to build a natural science museum next to the new Retiro park, but it remained incomplete at the time of his death and was converted by Fernando VII* in 1819 to the famous Museo de Prado, one of the world's major art galleries.

As Madrid continued to grow, the nineteenth-century city assumed a bourgeois appearance along the Paseo de los Recoletos and its extension, the Paseo de la Castellana. The stately urban palaces of the wealthy encouraged development to the north of the affluent Alcalá district, one of the first districts in the city to have gas and electrical service. At the same time, the area near the Prado became the home of the Cortes (the national legislature), as well as the Ateneo* (the leading intellectual club), and later the luxurious Palace and Ritz hotels.

In 1910, the barrio of San Bernardo was bisected by the Gran Vía, a modern commercial street that ran south from the Puerta de Alcalá to the Plaza de España, surrounded by the first modern office blocks in the city. A new subway system, the Metro, gradually linked the barrios farther to the west, where a new university began construction in 1920, and the north, one of the fastest-growing areas of residential housing. These public improvements accelerated in the 1920s with the support of Gen. Miguel Primo de Rivera's* dictatorship and the engineering talents of the conde de Guadalhorce (1876–1952) and Manuel Lorenzo Pardo (1881–1963). In the decade before the Spanish Civil War,* enthusiasm for civic improvement by two widely divergent politicians, the conservative José Calvo

Sotelo* and the socialist minister of public works, Indalecio Prieto (1883–1962), added greatly to the construction of highways, railroads, and public facilities such as the Nuevos Ministerios.

The war emphasized the strategic importance of Madrid by recreating its role as a major military objective, as had occurred during the War of Spanish Succession* and the War of Independence.* It also revealed a change in the social composition of the city. While Madrid once had been a society of government office holders, absentee landowners, and the fiscal and social nobility, industrialization began to change its class background during the nineteenth century. Printing, construction, and the service industry attracted poor peasants from as far away as Galicia and Andalusia. In 1899, the major Spanish socialist labor organization, the Unión General de Trabajadores* (UGT), left Barcelona* for Madrid. Its political counterpart, the Socialist party* (Partido Socialista Obrero de España, (POSE), ultimately succeeded in developing a strong constituency. Proletarian militancy, portrayed in *Aurora rojo* (1919) by Pío Baroja,* surfaced during the second decade of the twentieth century. University students added a volatile element to political life by leading the opposition to Gen. Miguel Primo de Rivera's dictatorship. The liveliness of Spanish intellectual life in the early twentieth century also made Madrid special. As the center of the Spanish publishing industry, Madrid was the second home of writers and dramatists. Politics and intellectual life became naturally intertwined. Long before the Cortes debates during the Second Republic,* these two forces permeated the national consciousness by dramatizing and publicizing political issues.

The Spanish Civil War ended Madrid's golden age. As the focal point of Gen. Francisco Franco's first campaign north from Seville, the city, which refused to fall, was seriously damaged after 28 August 1936, when it suffered its first bombing attack, an ordeal that subsequently became an everyday experience. The nationalists reached the southern outskirts of Madrid in early November 1936, causing the republican government to flee to Valencia, a move reminiscent of Joseph Bonaparte's (José I*) several escapes during the War of Independence in the early nineteenth century.

Franco, however, could not capture the city. Madrileños volunteered to join the famous Brigade of Steel formed by the Spanish Communist party (PCE)* and rallied to the passionate cry of ''¡No Pasaran!'' made by Dolores Ibarruri,* La Pasionaria, a communist leader from Asturias. Ibarruri and the PCE, strengthened by the Soviet Union's aid to the republic during the civil war, noticeably dominated life in Madrid during its three years of nationalist siege. A popular spirit of resistance, notably proletarian and Soviet-oriented, seemed dramatically inspirational to foreign observers who flocked to ''democratic'' Madrid, but the underside of life during this period saw thousands take political refuge in foreign embassies and many more arrested for political crimes. As air raids continued and artillery bombardment increased, the city was physically and emotionally scarred, even while the tide of major campaigns moved north by early 1939 to Catalonia* and the French border. During the last months of the war, communist power in Madrid was successfully challenged on the junta of defense by military officers led by Col. Segismundo Casado (1893–1968). Brief fighting in early March 1939 ended with communist defeat and surrender to the nationalists on 28 Mar.

The regime (1939–1975) of Gen. Francisco Franco* initially treated Madrid as an occupied city and ringed it with military bases. Damage from the war took such a long time to repair that the city continued to look worse than some other European cities that had been more seriously damaged in World War II.* Only gradually did new construction fill the empty spaces along the Castellana, after Franco received international diplomatic recognition in the 1950s, and multinational businesses congregated in the capital. A favorable business climate led to all the consequences of modern urban growth such as pollution, urban sprawl, congestion, and destruction, in part, of the older city. For the first time in its history, Madrid became a center of heavy manufacturing, and as such, a magnet for population inflow from the countryside. New, hastily constructed barrios filled in the areas south of the Manzaranes River and to the east of the old city, while suburban development went north and west. Madrid took on the aspect of a major population center, which today has passed 4 million.

When Franco began to encounter problems in the period after 1956, Madrid again (as in the 1920s) became a center of student, worker, and regionalist protest. The climax came on 20 December 1973, with the assassination outside a church in Madrid of Adm. Luis Carrero Blanco (1903–1973), the first premier appointed by Franco. When the Caudillo died in 1975, his passing brought Madrid "out of the bunker," in the words of a Madrid newspaper, soon after. Subsequent democratic changes brought a new era of PSOE power, including a socialist administration for Madrid itself, as well as the cosmopolitan qualities, good and bad, of a modern metropolis.

For additional information, see D. Ringrose, *Madrid and the Spanish Economy, 1650–1850* (Berkeley, 1983); C. Kany, *Life and Manners in Madrid, 1750–1800* (Berkeley, 1932); F. Bravo Morato, *Historia de Madrid*, 4 vols. (Madrid, 1977); E. de Guzmán, V. Marco, G. Sol, and E. Domingo, *Historia de Madrid* (Madrid, 1981); R. Colodny, *The Struggle for Madrid* (New York, 1958); D. Kurzman, *Miracle of November: Madrid's Epic Stand* (New York, 1980); and A. López Fernández, *Defensa de Madrid* (Mexico City, 1945).

R. W. Kern

*Related entry*: CASTILE.


**MAEZTU Y WHITNEY, RAMIRO DE** (1874–1936), member of the Generation of 1898* who became a leading proponent of monarchism. A prolific essayist whose writing career spanned forty years and produced more than thirteen thousand essays, Ramiro de Maeztu usually addressed his countrymen by means of the newspaper columns he produced on an almost daily basis. Beginning in Bilbao in 1895, Maeztu offered his readers commentary on every topic from the

Spanish-American War* to the prospects of the government of Manuel Azaña* of February 1936.

The son of a Basque* merchant and a British diplomat's daughter, Maeztu found his formal education cut short in 1891 by his family's declining fortunes in the Cuban tobacco trade. From 1891 to 1894, he actually joined his father for a prolonged stay on the island as they struggled to salvage the business, but to no avail. The elder Maeztu died in the effort, and young Ramiro returned to find employment in Bilbao on the staff of *El Porvenir Vasco*, where he won some distinction for his columns on the mounting crisis in the Antilles.

The outbreak of war with the United States* in 1898 found Maeztu in Madrid,* where his journalistic endeavors earned him national attention and the friendship of such literary notables as Pío Baroja* and Azorín (José Martínez Ruiz, 1874–1967). The first collection of his essays, *Hacia otra España*, was a classic of the regenerationist literature that flooded the capital in the wake of the disaster of 1898 and established its author's place among that generation of writers.

Maeztu's zeal for reform carried him to Britain* in 1905, where he served for more than a decade as the London correspondent for the Madrid daily *La Correspondencia de España*. His columns from the British capital reveal a steady disenchantment with liberalism* and his growing fascination with collectivist solutions to the problems of industrial society. Initially he embraced Fabian socialism and thrived on the company of H. G. Wells (1866–1946). In time, however, he grew suspicious of that creed's statism and would be counted among the guild socialists who published for Alfred Orage's journal, *The New Age*. By the time World War I* engulfed the continent in 1914, Maeztu was already committed to a syndicalist vision of society that he later described in detail in *La crisis del humanismo*, a collection of essays published in Spain in 1919.

Although he lent his pen to the Allied cause during the war, its outcome profoundly disturbed him. In 1919, Maeztu returned to Spain and began regular contributions to the liberal daily *El Sol*. His columns addressed what he perceived to be the growing menace of communism, which he regarded as the logical result of the West's secular notion of humanism, and increasingly rhapsodized about Spanish tradition, Spanish humanism, and the Spanish Catholic experience. Maeztu was one of the few prominent Spanish writers of his day consistently to support the dictatorship of Gen. Miguel Primo de Rivera,* and he was rewarded for that endorsement by being named Spain's ambassador to Argentina in 1928.

His tenure in Buenos Aires proved to be brief. The fall of the dictator and the advent of the Second Republic* propelled Maeztu once again to Madrid, where he plunged into opposition to the new regime and called for the creation of a "military monarchy." He became the director of a newly organized fortnightly journal, *Acción Española*, which was the publicity arm of a monarchist organization of the same name. So closely were the two linked that when the Sanjurjo conspirators of 1932 were jailed for their efforts to overthrow the republic, the journal was closed and its director imprisoned.

Maeztu's collected essays for *Acción Española* were published in 1935 as *Defensa de hispanidad*. He had concluded by then that "There is no work in universal history comparable to that of Spain" and "The future of the [Hispanic] nations depends on their fidelity to the past." Those lines later earned him an important place in the intellectual panthenon of the Spain of Francisco Franco* and may explain why on 29 October 1936 he fell victim to a republican firing squad.

For additional information, see V. Marrero Suárez, *Maeztu* (Madrid, 1955).

D. W. Foard

*Related entries*: GENERATION OF 1898; SPANISH CIVIL WAR.

**MARCH, JUAN** (1880–1962), financier. March was born in Santa Margarita, Majorca, on 4 December 1880, the son of a laborer and farmer. After attending a Franciscan school near Palma, he began work in the office of a local businessman and soon began to dabble in real estate on the island, while also becoming involved in tobacco smuggling. In 1911, he purchased the monopoly to sell tobacco in all Spanish North Africa, except Ceuta and Melilla.

During World War I,* March dealt with both Britain,* to which he provided information of ship movements in the Mediterranean, and Germany,* with which he traded food and fuel in return for unimpeded passage for his vessels. In 1916, he set up the Transmediterránea shipping company.

In 1921 and 1922, the government tried unsuccessfully to break March's smuggling business. The next year, March was elected to the Cortes for Majorca. Shortly after the coup of Gen. Miguel Primo de Rivera,* March went into exile in France,* but he was soon returned and cooperated closely with the regime. During the later 1920s, he bought two Madrid newspapers and in 1927, obtained the monopoly to sell tobacco in Ceuta and Melilla, which had been left out of the 1911 agreement.

March was involved in discussions with the republican-socialist revolutionary committee in 1930, but he did not commit himself to supporting it. Soon after the creation of the Second Republic,* he lost the tobacco monopoly and was arrested, but not brought to trial. In fact, he was elected to the Cortes in June 1931 and reelected in the next two elections held during the republic in November 1933. and February 1936. Arrested again in June 1932 and sent to prison for having used bribery to get the tobacco monopoly in 1927, he was elected to the Court of Constitutional Guarantees in September 1933, while still in prison, but that election was annulled. Three months later, he escaped from Alcalá de Henares prison and fled to France.

March became involved in a number of conspiracies against the republic in 1935 and 1936 and emerged as the chief financial backer of the generals whose rebellion triggered the Spanish Civil War.* He paid for the plane that took Gen. Francisco Franco* from the Canary Islands* to Morocco* at the beginning of the war and put his own wealth and international connections at the service of the nationalists. Among other assistance he provided, March personally guaranteed a \$4.5 million line of credit for the nationalists from a London bank.

March profited from Spanish neutrality during World War II,* as he had during World War I, and the services he provided for the British subsequently proved to be very valuable. In 1943–1944, he dallied with the anti-Franco opposition, but did not commit himself deeply and did not fall out of favor with Franco as a result.

March needed the assistance of both the British and Spanish governments to carry out his most spectacular financial operation, the seizure of the powerful Barcelona Traction, Light and Power Company. This takeover was complex and controversial and gave rise to the longest case in the history of the International Court of Justice, but its basic lines can be described. In 1948, Barcelona Traction, financially very healthy, was declared bankrupt by a court in Reus because Spanish foreign-exchange regulations had prevented it from paying interest on bonds bought up by March. The company, whose head office was in Toronto, although its ownership was by this time primarily Belgian, fought the bankruptcy through the courts and appeals to the Belgian, Canadian, and British governments. At a crucial moment, the British government inexplicably took a position that greatly favored March, and in January 1952, his firm, Fuerzas Eléctricas de Cataluña (FESCA), took over the company. The former directors tried to use the influence of their lawyer, Ramón Serrano Suñer,* Franco's brother-in-law and former foreign minister, but Franco refused to intervene on their behalf. Belgium took the case to the International Court of Justice in 1958, which ruled, in February 1970, against the Belgian position.

In 1955, March created the March Foundation to support the sciences, social sciences, and the arts. Today it is one of the most important private foundations in Spain. He died in Madrid on 10 March 1962, from injuries sustained in an automobile accident.

For additional information, see B. Díaz Mosty, *La irresistible ascensión de Juan March* (Madrid, 1977); M. Domínguez Benavides, *El último pirata del Mediterráneo* (Barcelona, 1934); and R. Garriga, *Juan March y su tiempo* (Barcelona, 1976).

*A. Shubert*

*Related entries*: BALEARIC ISLANDS; ECONOMY.


**MARTÍNEZ DE LA ROSA, FRANCISCO** (1787–1862), writer and statesman. Martínez, born in Granada, was educated as a lawyer there at the end of the eighteenth century, and spent some of his later life as a professor of literature at the University of Granada. He first rose to political prominence during the Napoleonic invasion as a member of the local defense junta and a patriotic poet and writer. In 1811, British exile allowed him to edit *El Español* and publish his epic *Zaragoza*. Upon his return in 1812, he became a member of the Cortes of Cadiz* during passage of the Constitution of 1812, and also published several plays that used this historic occasion as a backdrop.

In May 1814, the Bourbon Restoration, unimpressed by Martínez's eloquence, sentenced him to a prison term in Peñón de la Gomera, where he read the British and French romantics, composed *El Café*, and began *La niña en casa y la madre en el máscara*, *Los celos infudados*, and *La boda y el duelo* before the 1820 rising of Maj. Rafael Riego (1785–1823) freed him and gave him a seat in the Cortes. Fernando VII* was now a prisoner of the army* and provincial radicalism, and when the Eusebio Bardaxi ministry (appointed in March 1821) could not control the exaltados, as the rebels were called, Martínez, by now a celebrity, took office on 28 February 1822. His own policies, remarkably free of bitterness, sought to support the monarchy with an aristocracy of talent. He wanted a new Siglo de Oro, not another French Revolution.

For a short time, his strategy of a strong executive, a property qualification on manhood suffrage, and creation of a Senate neutralized political extremism, but in the summer of 1822, royal manipulation of the Guards regiments led to the murder of a liberal officer that caused unrest in Madrid.* When the Guards threatened to support a strengthened monarchy, the July Days' riots destroyed Martínez's government and raised the possibility of a republic. The threat was taken seriously by the European powers, who quickly approved intervention at the Congress of Verona, and restored Fernando's absolutism in the summer of 1823.

Martínez de la Rosa spent the next eight years in Paris, writing *Poética*, *Hernani*, *Aben Humeya*, and *La Conjuración de Venecia* during the apogee of French romanticism and the formative stages of liberal doctrinaire thought. In 1831, he returned to Granada as a European man of letters and a very conservative liberal, more than ever an elitist opposed to democratic change. Just when the king's death left María Cristina (1806–1878) queen-regent for her daughter, Isabel II,* Martínez moved back to Madrid in 1833, and quickly revived his leadership at the moment when Fernando's younger brother, Carlos, protested the apparent breach of succession laws so vigorously that ultraconservatives rallied to Carlism.* The queen-regent had only the liberals to defend her interests, and after Fernando's last premier, Francisco Cea Bermúdez (1772–1850) refused either to abandon absolutism or alter the traditional order of church and state, Martínez replaced him in January 1834.

The poet-politician's greatest accomplishment during his second and final premiership was the Royal Statute of 10 April 1834. The statute's descriptive prose conjured up a new Siglo de Oro based upon talent and existing social interests, the doctrinaire approach to liberalism. Without question, the statute of 1834 prepared the way for modern government, with an executive cabinet and legislative politics, but there was nothing faintly democratic about it. As did the doctrinaire François Guizot (1787–1874) of France,* Martínez believed in a nineteenth-century form of enlightened despotism.

As had Guizot, Martínez also faced heavy criticism. The statute's contradictions, soon picked apart by job-seeking lower-middle class deputies, who formed a rival Progressive party* to challenge the Moderate party* in 1834, combined with the exhausting and disheartening First Carlist War (1833–1840), persuaded Martínez to leave office on 7 June 1835. He returned as a deputy to the Cortes in 1836, and briefly as advisor to María Cristina in 1840, but the progressive Gen. Baldomero Espartero* forced him into a three-year French exile. He returned when the moderate Gen. Ramón Narváez* restored moderate rule, and served as ambassador to France and Italy* under Narváez. He was also president of the Cortes during the cabinets of Juan Bravo Murillo* in 1851, Narváez in 1857, and the Liberal Union party's Gen. Leopoldo O'Donnell* in 1860. During this period, he wrote essays, travel books and poetry, much of it about Granada, until his death on 7 February 1862.

For additional information, see L. Díez del Corral, *El liberalismo doctrinarismo* (Madrid, 1956); V. Llorens Castillo, *Liberales y románticos* (Mexico City, 1954); R. Sánchez Mantero, *Liberales en el exilio: La emigración política en la crisis del Antiguo Régimen* (Madrid, 1975); and F. Cánovas Sánchez, *El Partido Moderado* (Madrid, 1982).

*R. W. Kern*

*Related entries*: ESPARTERO, BALDOMERO; LIBERALISM; MODERATE PARTY; NARVÁEZ, RAMÓN.

**MAURA Y MONTANER, ANTONIO** (1853–1925), powerful Liberal-Conservative politician of the early twentieth century, a would-be "regenerator" of his party, four-time premier, and late convert to authoritarian political philosophy. Maura, born in Palma de Majorca on 2 May 1853 to a large and talented Catalan lower-middle class family that had lived in the Balearic Islands* for almost a half-century, began the study of law in 1868 at the Central University in the Madrid* of the First Republic.* His oratory, literary in style but delivered with a strong mallorquín accent, enabled him to obtain a position in the law firm of Germán Gamazo (1838–1901), a Castilian nationalist who was a Cortes deputy and a member of the Liberal Fusionist party. In 1878, Maura married Gamazo's daughter, Constancia, and with his father-in-law's help, was elected to the Cortes from Palma de Majorca in 1881.

The year was significant. Maura entered politics just as the liberal-conservative Antonio Cánovas del Castillo* agreed to share power with the liberal fusionist Práxedes Mateo Sagasta* in the so-called turno pacífico, an effective two-party system that unfortunately buried scandals and malfeasance without debate or investigation and allowed caciquismo to flourish. Maura was one of the first deputies to criticize this system in public. He broke with Sagasta and joined the Liberal-Conservative party to better support the monarchy and the church, both indispensable, he felt, for good government. Soon, however, he quarreled with the interior minister, Francisco Romero Robledo (1838–1906) and later, over naval and imperial reform, with Cánovas himself. The adoption of universal manhood suffrage completed his disillusionment with liberalism, which he characterized hereafter as "mob politics."

By the mid–1890s, Maura's political thought made him the leader of a regeneration movement within the Liberal-Conservative party. A provincial outsider who identified with cosmopolitan Castilian culture, he magnified Castilian nationalism into a metaphysical concept of national honor that saw Spain as the head of a Hispanic empire and, more vaguely, a worldwide civilization in danger of being lost by the petty corrupt policies of Cánovas and Sagasta. His political philosophy held that Spanish liberalism* was an aberrant system in a state that needed the church and throne to overcome regional differences. He sought a nebulous revolution from above that would mobilize institutions and oligarchies into a more effective defense of Spanish culture. In many ways, he typified the first generation of Mediterraneans who began to consider alternatives to liberal parliamentarianism or democracy after Pope Leo XIII's (1810–1903) *Rerum Novarum* (1891) called for change in southern Europe.

Maura fought hard to strengthen the military and introduced conservative reforms for Cuba and the Philippines in an effort to prevent their loss. While none of his measures were successful, his popularity grew among conservatives and nationalists. The assassination of Cánovas in 1897 and Sagasta's failure to avoid the Spanish-American War* (which Maura, as colonial minister, tried desperately to avoid through negotiation) brought the Majorcan closer to national power, and in 1902–1903, Maura served as minister of interior in the cabinet of his friend, Francisco Silvela.* When the two Liberal-Conservatives refused to ''make'' the municipal elections through the use of caciques,* however, the rise of regionalist parties in Catalonia* and republicanism in the big cities so distressed Silvela that he abandoned politics.

As Silvela's successor, Maura formed his first cabinet in 1903. Lasting a year, it sought to introduce a new local-government law designed to destroy caciquismo by use of an indirect, corporative franchise that would create a responsible electorate to curb the Left as well. The newly crowned king, Alfonso XIII,* found Maura's ideas incomprehensible and dismissed him to seek a military government. When this effort failed, Maura returned to power from 1907 to 1909. His second cabinet acted as if it had a regenerationist mandate to lead a revolution from above by reintroducing the local government law; although the Liberal Fusionist party, now excluded from political power, questioned Maura's antidemocratic intent and his efforts to enlist cooperation of conservative Catalan regionalists. A ''¡Maura, No!'' campaign heated political tempers in 1908, and formation of a bloc of regionalists, republicans, and liberals led to a bitter effort to oppose Maura.

In the end, he was defeated by the Barcelona* Tragic Week. The rioting in late July 1909 was a spontaneous revolution from below of anarchists, radicals, and regionalists that clashed with a revolution from above supported by Alfonso XIII's desire for a new empire in Morocco,* praetorian politics, and Maura's own imperialism. Maura resigned in October 1909, under strong liberal fusionist pressure and a split in liberal-conservative ranks led by Eduardo Dato* that all but destroyed the party.

Maura briefly retired from politics, but he remained convinced that his new oligarchy might have saved Spain. In Oct. 1913, he organized a new Maurist movement that has been compared with Charles Maurras's (1868–1952) Action Française, one of the first protofascist parties in Europe. The new organization appealed to conservative Catholic youths (such as José Calvo Sotelo,* an early member), who demonstrated in the streets with banners proclaiming ''¡Maura, Sí!'' or painted the slogan on walls as an early political graffiti. Maura dismissed liberalism as obsolete and demanded a return to traditional religious and social values, an ''essential'' Spain that became the hallmark of Gen. Francisco Franco* after 1939. Maura lacked the vanity, however, to be very convincing as a demagogue; he had been an elitist too long to think in terms of creating a mass movement that might reach beyond the Catholic upper classes.

Maura continued to seek new issues that would permit him to regain political leadership. World War I* gave him a brief anti-British, pro-German platform, but the lukewarm response of those Liberal-Conservatives still loyal to him buried Maura's extremism in the war's larger issues. In 1917, he cooperated with Alejandro Lerroux* and Francesc Cambó* to encourage the military to play a larger political role in Catalan regionalists to break with Madrid, although Maura soon abandoned both when the national mood turned radical. His bitter opposition to the Left allowed him to become premier of a national government in March 1918, a cabinet in which Cambó became Maura's chief assistant in an effort to develop a new industrial program designed to modernize from above. Maura hoped to become the ''iron surgeon'' of national politics—a phrase originally coined by Joaquín Costa*—and more successfully used by Gen. Miguel Primo de Rivera* in 1923. Dato, however, criticized Cambó as a veiled separatist, and the cabinet fell in November 1918. Maura returned as premier one last time in a futile, three-month cabinet to urge the army* to take a more vigorous role in Morocco, a policy that ended disastrously at Anwal.*

Maura lived on until 1925, long enough to hail Gen. Primo de Rivera's dictatorship as liberalism's final defeat. It is a matter of some speculation whether he would have fully cooperated with the later regimes of Primo and Gen. Francisco Franco, but both were influenced by his example.

For additional information, see S. Canals, *Sucesos de 1909* (Madrid, 1952); M. Fernández Almagro and G. Maura, *Porqué cayó Alfonso XIII* (Madrid, 1948); M. García Venero, *Antonio Maura 1907–1919* (Madrid, 1953); J. Ruiz-Castillo, ed., *Antonio Maura: Treinta y cinco años de vida pública* (Madrid, 1953); and D. Sevilla Andrés, *Antonio Maura* (Madrid, 1954).

*R. W. Kern*

*Related entries*: LIBERALISM; SILVELA, FRANCISCO; PRIMO DE RIVERA, GEN. MIGUEL; WORLD WAR I.


**MENDIZÁBAL, JUAN ÁLVAREZ** (1790–1853), politician. Mendizábal was born in Cadiz in 1790 to a family of Jewish descent that ran a clothing business. His political connections, developed during his youth in liberal Cadiz during the War of Independence,* were radical and included membership in the Masonic Grand Orient lodge, which made him privy to Maj. Rafael de Riego's (1785–

1823) rebellion against Fernando VII* in 1820. His early business experience brought him into contact with the British through the export of wine. He gradually moved into land sales, again largely to foreigners who were interested in the great estates of Andalusia.*

Mendizábal's involvement with Riego and the radicals who overthrew the absolute monarchy in 1820 forced him into London exile after their failure in 1823. There he had success as the economic advisor to the Brazilian emperor, Pedro I (1798–1834), for whom he arranged British credit to support the successful candidacy for the Portuguese throne of Maria II (1833–1852), Pedro's daughter. His small banking practice specialized in financing the Latin countries.

After the death of Fernando VII in 1833, the rise of Carlism,* and María Cristina's (1806–1878) acceptance of liberal assistance permitted Mendizábal to return to Spain. In the summer of 1835, his financial expertise was put to the test as minister of finance in the cabinet of the conde de Toreno (1786–1843). The national debt, badly affected by thirty years of political turmoil and American secession (the loss of the mines in Mexico and Peru particularly), demanded a solution, especially since Toreno's abortive effort at debt cancellation on 16 November 1834 had just ruined Spanish credit abroad.

Mendizábal, facing debts of 4.4 billion reales, acted pragmatically by convincing the ministry to embark upon a second effort to abolish entail and mortmain. A debt of this size could be reduced only by placing the remaining lands of the monarchy, aristocracy, and clergy on sale to back state bonds reconsolidating the national debt. A first effort, begun timidly by the Cortes of Cadiz* in 1813, had been revoked with restoration of the absolute monarchy. To accomplish a second effort, Mendizábal was elevated to the premiership (for the only time in his career) from 15 September 1835 to 15 May 1836. Disentailment* legislation, much of which he wrote himself, passed on 29 July 1837 under the Progressive party ministry of José María Calatrava (1781–1847).

The law made national property of the real estate, revenues, rights, and shares of religious communities and orders. Purchasers of these confiscated properties could pay cash or use state script (designed to facilitate middle-income peasants) at 10 percent interest over eight years, with the proceeds supporting Spanish state bonds sold abroad. Regular clergy henceforth were subsidized by the state.

One problem, first experienced by the French in 1792–1793, lay with poor bond performance. Most fell below par, frightening away small purchasers and aiding large purchasers from the upper classes. A greater problem was peasant suspicion of mortgage transactions. Occupation or use made more sense to them than financial encumbrance. As a consequence, peasant unrest dogged the nineteenth-century liberal regimes, from arson of notary archives to eruption of peasant anarchism.* Conservatives also vehemently opposed the law; Carlists called the cash down payment of a fifth of a property's total price Mendizábal's "quinto," a caustic reference to the old royal fifth taken from colonial mining revenues.

Mendizábal's career as a politician was destroyed. Despite considerable financial expertise, he was seldom again consulted on fiscal matters. While the Progressive party's subsequent mismanagement of land sales and bond issues betrayed Mendizábal's intent to establish the peasantry on the land and delayed agricultural modernization, most authorities are clear that the step had to be taken. By the time of Mendizábal's death in 1853, renewal of confidence in the Spanish economy by foreign bankers was already manifest.

For additional information, see J. Vicens Vives, *An Economic History of Spain* (Princeton, 1969); R. Carr, *Spain 1808–1975* (Oxford, 1978); A. García Tejero, *Historia político-administrativa de Mendizábal* (Madrid, 1858); and P. Janke, *Mendizábal y la instauración de la monarquía constitucional en España (1790–1853)* (Madrid, 1974).

*R. W. Kern*

*Related entries*: DISENTAILMENT; LIBERALISM

**MENÉNDEZ PIDAL, RAMÓN** (1869–1967), literary critic, scholar, and historian of Spanish literature. Menéndez Pidal was born in La Corunna and educated at the University of Madrid, where he met his wife, María Goyri, his lifelong collaborator. He studied with and became the disciple of Marcelino Menéndez y Pelayo,* one of the most important nineteenth-century Spanish scholars. His study of the *Poema del Cid* won a special prize from the Spanish Royal Academy in 1893, and his first important book, *La Leyenda de los siete infantes de Lara*, in which he explained the evolution of the Castilian epic, was published in 1896. After beginning his teaching career at the Escuela de Estudios Superiores del Ateneo, he taught philology at the University of Madrid for decades.

In 1902, he was made a member of the academy, and in 1909, his publication of *El Cantar de Mío Cid: Texto, gramática y vocabulario*, the first and clearest study of the phonetic and morphological laws of the Spanish language, made him a world-class linguist and scholar. He visited North and South America to study the diffusion of Spanish romanceros (folk ballads), arguing in his studies of them that in the romancero the work of an individual was polished, altered, and improved by popular collaboration of many authors through the centuries.

The scholar's later work included one of his most important works, *La España del Cid* (1929), in which he argued the significance of the Castilian hero, a spirited defense of the more traditional social images blurred by some of the work of Generation of 1898.* He employed an analytical approach to literary works by studying the relationship between authors and their environment. He also instituted modern scientific study of the Spanish language by introducing new methods of language study and philology. Included in this work was the creation in 1914 of *Revista de Filología Española*, the most prestigious scholarly journal of Spain, which attracted the collaboration of many scholars who became his pupils, including Américo Castro (1885–1972), Rafael Lapesa (1908– ), and Federico de Onís (1885–1965).

For additional information, see E. de Zuleta, *Historia de la crítica española contemporánea* (Madrid, 1966); A. del Río, *Estudios sobre literatura contemporánea española*

(Madrid, 1966); J. Ortega y Gasset, *El espíritu de la letra, III* (Madrid, 1967); and J. A. Maravall, *Menéndez Pidal y la historia del pensamiento* (Madrid, 1960).

*J. Maura*

*Related entry*: MENÉNDEZ Y PELAYO, MARCELINO.

**MENÉNDEZ Y PELAYO, MARCELINO** (1856–1912), Restoration intellectual. "The Spanish Fichte" was the term Luis Araquistáin (1886–1954) used to describe Marcelino Menéndez y Pelayo. Even such an ardent progressive as the republic's ambassador to France* could not deny the enormous erudition of his fellow Santanderino. For much of the last quarter of the nineteenth century, Menéndez y Pelayo was a commanding presence in Spanish letters and his intellectual legacy was evident even during the dictatorship of Gen. Francisco Franco.*

The eldest son of a provincial mathematics professor, he was educated in Santander's best schools and subsequently pursued his undergraduate instruction at the University of Barcelona where he came under the particular influence of the literary historian Manuel Milá y Fontanals (1818–1884). Shortly thereafter, Menéndez completed his doctorate in philosophy and literature at the University of Madrid, earning a prize in 1875 from the faculty of arts and letters. He had gained these distinctions at the age of eighteen and in so doing had bested in oposiciones such formidable contemporaries as Joaquín Costa.*

Thanks to the patronage of the ultramontane leader, the marqués de Pidal (1846–1913), the young montañés intellectual attracted the attention of the author of the Restoration regime, the prime minister Antonio Cánovas del Castillo.* It was he who introduced a bill in the Cortes in 1877 which made it possible for the twenty-year-old Menéndez y Pelayo to contend for the vacant chair of Spanish literature at the University of Madrid. Cánovas, too, had considerable influence in selecting the panel which in the following year awarded the post to Menéndez y Pelayo instead of his rival, the future prime minister José Canalejas (1854–1912).

Spanish conservatism already owed a debt to Menéndez y Pelayo. Even before he faced Canalejas in contending for a professorship at Madrid, he had engaged in a celebrated polemic with the republican intellectual Gumersindo de Azcárate (1840–1917), and some of his colleagues whose works frequented the pages of the journal *Revista de España*. The subject of their disputation had been the reasons, if any, for the historical debility of Spanish science.* Azcárate lamented the vacuousness of the nation's scientific thought in the early modern period, while Menéndez y Pelayo rallied to its defense. Spain, Menéndez contended, had produced a host of noteworthy engineers, cartographers, physicians, and botanists during the sixteenth and seventeenth centuries. Even before Menéndez y Pelayo was able to occupy his chair at Madrid, these ruminations, appearing first as a series of articles in the *Revista Europea*, had been collected and published under the title *La ciencia española* (1876). There would be numerous subsequent editions.

A grant from the city government of Santander made it possible for Menéndez y Pelayo to undertake an archival tour of collections in Portugal* and Italy* that would constitute the basis of his next series of essays. Published collectively in 1880 as the multivolume *Historia de los heterodoxos españoles*, the work is an ardent defense of Spanish orthodoxy which at once seeks to refute the allegation of bigotry that had been increasingly leveled against the nation's religious culture and, at the same time, warn its readers of the dangers posed by the intrusion of alien ideas spawned by the Reformation and the French Revolution. The polemical context which produced *Los heterodoxos* even led Menéndez y Pelayo to praise the work of the Inquisition.

Fewer than two years after the appearance of the first edition of *Los heterodoxos*, its author was elected to the Academia Española. He was only twenty-four at the time. Other distinctions promptly followed. In 1883, the Academy of History selected Menéndez y Pelayo for membership, a tribute to which he responded with an inaugural lecture on the theme. The Academy of Moral and Political Sciences followed in 1890, seconded by the Academia de Bellas Artes de San Fernando in 1892. Before the conclusion of his career, Menéndez y Pelayo had also been accorded the Legion of Honor by the President of the French Republic and was even nominated for the Nobel Prize in Literature by his colleagues at the Academia Española.

Although he thought of *Los heterodoxos* as a general introduction to a much broader study of Spanish literature, his subsequent essays were far less contentious in nature. His collected works began to be published a year before his death and would ultimately encompass some sixty-five volumes, including a thirteen-volume work entitled *Antología de poetas líricos castellanos* (1909). Of equal importance was his 1892 *Antología de poetas hispano-americanos* and his masterpiece of literary criticism, *Historia de las ideas estéticas en España*, which he dedicated to his mentor, Milá y Fontanals.

Once he occupied his chair at the University of Madrid, Menéndez y Pelayo's most demonstrative service to the Restoration regime was to permit his name to be included on the conservatives' lists of candidates at various national elections. Thus, in 1884, he earned a seat in the Cortes as a delegate from Majorca (although he had visited the island only once) and in 1891, Saragossa. Later he represented Oviedo in the Senate and, beginning in 1901, he was listed annually until his death as a member of that body by nomination of the Academia Española.

Menéndez y Pelayo became the director of the National Library and chief of the Archival Corps in 1898. He wasted no time in resigning his chair at the university and taking up this challenging new assignment. His work here, rather than the heated words of *Los heterodoxos*, might best constitute his epitaph. When he died suddenly in 1912, Menéndez y Pelayo was still exercising his office at the National Library, but had arranged in his will to have his entire personal collection of fifty thousand volumes and the facility which housed them turned over to the municipality of Santander.

For additional information, see M. Artigas, *Menéndez y Pelayo* (Santander, 1927); G. de Torre, *Menéndez y Pelayo y las dos Españas* (Buenos Aires, 1943); P. Laín Entralgo,

*Menéndez y Pelayo* (Buenos Aires, 1952); and E. Sánchez Reyes, *Biografía crítica y documental de Marcelino Menéndez y Pelayo* (Santander, 1974).

*D. W. Foard*

**MEXICO,** relations with Spain. Hapsburg rule in Spain ended in 1700 with the death of Carlos II (1661–1700), initiating a century of enormous change that was most strongly felt in the New World colonies. Spain's richest holding, Mexico (New Spain), had developed a considerable degree of autonomy. Royal officials frequently intermarried with colonials, created business enterprises, and developed social networks that connected them closely with the local population and economy.

A further legacy of the Hapsburgs was the view, within New Spain, of itself as one of many nations and communities within the Spanish empire, rather than as a part of Spain proper. This sense of both being unique and at the same time belonging to the Spanish world led, despite occasional strains as colonial interests were subordinated to the needs of the metropolis, to a system that worked satisfactorily until the latter part of the eighteenth century, when more stringent Bourbon political and economic controls made inhabitants of New Spain increasingly more restive. A sense of Mexican nationalism, growing out of separate identity within the empire, had been evolving throughout the first two centuries of Spanish rule, and as the Bourbons moved to unify colonial holdings into a more rigid system, tensions rose as the idea of being a separate nation within an empire was diminished. It is one of the ironies of history that a revived and more competent monarchy under the Bourbons would ultimately drive much of Spanish America, including Mexico, to seek independence.

A stronger focus on the administration of Mexico was not possible during the earliest years of Bourbon rule because of the War of Spanish Succession.* Not until 1759, with the accession of Carlos III,* did Spain acquire a monarch willing to initiate a full-scale program of colonial reform. By this time, Mexico had a thriving economy, with close, though not rigid, ties with Spain. Profound social divisions, however, divided the colony. As John Lynch has noted, Spaniard ruled creole, creole used Indian, and the metropolis (Spain) exploited all three.

The control of New Spain was of great importance to the Spanish crown as a source of colonial revenue. Mexican silver production had been rising throughout the eighteenth century from five million pesos in 1702 to twenty-seven million by 1804. Mexican silver accounted for 67 percent of American precious metals, and one single Mexican area, Guanajuato, produced one-sixth of the American total. Crown revenues reached about fourteen million pesos a year by the end of the eighteenth century, and while more than half was retained for local administration or to support other less profitable colonies, six million remained as profit remitted to Madrid.*

The financial demands of Spain's European wars increased the need for additional revenues by the end of the eighteenth century, and led to a Bourbon policy of replacing creoles with Spaniards in the upper levels of colonial administration and clergy. Even the loyalty of peninsulars in Mexico was alienated in 1804, when charitable funds of the church were sequestered for use in Spain's war with Britain,* part of the Napoleonic confusion of the early nineteenth century. These funds had been widely used for credit in the New World, and proprietors and landowners—creoles and Spaniards alike—were hard pressed to meet their mortgages and loan payments, thus damaging peninsular loyalty, increasing Mexican resentment, and embittering the church. To make matters worse, with the outbreak of the War of Independence* on the peninsula in 1808, the viceroy in Mexico was seized and deposed by Spanish conspirators.

The chaos in Spain permitted a creole independence movement to develop in Mexico after Father Miguel Hidalgo's (1753–1811) rallying cry of "Grito de Dolores" on 16 September 1810 called upon Mexicans to throw off the Spanish yoke. Hidalgo was unable, however, to control his mass army once he had set it in motion, and after the murder of Europeans and looting in San Miguel, Celaya, and Guanajuato, he could not bring himself to unleash such terrible destruction on Mexico City. His retreat prolonged the Mexican struggle for independence a further eleven years by allowing the peninsular and creole elites to submerge their differences and unite against the threat of a real social revolution. Fighting continued sporadically for some time, but by 1819, five years into the reign of the restored Spanish king, Fernando VII,* the new viceroy in Mexico City was able to report that he had the situation entirely under control.

In 1820, however, events in Europe again touched off the Mexican independence movement, this time among the elites themselves. The liberal triennium (1820–1823) in Spain to restore the Constitution of 1812, written by the Cortes of Cadiz,* forced conservatives in Mexico to ally with what was left of the insurgent forces of the earlier period to seek independence. The Plan of Iguala (24 February 1821) promised equality for creoles and peninsulars in a constitutional monarchy (the crown being offered unsuccessfully to Fernando), with Catholicism* as the state religion. Upon the collapse of these arrangements, the failure of Agustín de Iturbide's (1783–1824) short-lived empire (1822–1823) led to full independence, and despite endemic Mexican chaos, Spain was unable to defeat the forces led by Gen. Antonio López de Santa Anna (1794–1876) in the invasion of Tamaulipas in 1829. Spain recognized the independence of its former colony in 1836, but a final effort to reoccupy Mexico came in 1861 with the Convention of London, a pact between Isabel II* of Spain, Victoria I (1819–1901) of Britain, and Napoleon III (1808–1873) of France* to jointly occupy Mexican ports in order to collect claims against the new government. Spain, however, abandoned its efforts the following year in protest of Napoleon III's plan to establish a French-dominated regime in Mexico.

In the late nineteenth century, Spain enjoyed better relations with the conservative Mexican president, Porfirio Díaz (1830–1915), who ruled for most of the period from 1876 to 1911. The centennial of Mexican independence, celebrated in 1910, included participation by the Spanish community, and many symbolic acts of friendship, such as the decoration of Díaz with the medal of

Carlos III and his naming of a major avenue in Mexico City for Isabel the Catholic (1451–1504), marked the occasion. In the subsequent Mexican revolution, however, the antirevolutionary attitude of the Spanish community in Mexico caused Spanish diplomats to work closely with the United States* to persuade the first revolutionary president, Francisco Madero (1873–1913), to resign. When Madero was overthrown in a counterrevolutionary coup d'état by Gen. Victoriano Huerta (1854–1916), Spain was one of the first countries to recognize Huerta's government, and he went into exile in Barcelona when he was overthrown by an associate of Madero, Venustiano Carranza (1859–1920). The partisanship of Spanish nationals caused them to be victimized by Francisco Villa (1877–1923), Carranza's major opponent, and when Carranza regained control of Mexico in late 1915, Spain, more favorable to Carranza than Villa, extended him de facto recognition, the start of nearly two decades of relative placidity in Mexican-Spanish relations.

Even closer relations developed with the Second Republic* when Lázaro Cárdenas (1895–1970) became president of Mexico in 1934. Concerned with the improvement of social conditions in Mexico, he applauded the steps taken by Spain's republican leaders to do the same in Iberia and later sided with the republic in the Spanish Civil War.* Mexico thus joined the Soviet Union as the only other country to recognize the legitimacy of the republican government. Mexican representatives to the League of Nations argued unsuccessfully for League assistance to the republic, forcing the Mexican government to provide the republicans with arms and war matériels itself. Mexico eventually became the haven for approximately thirty thousand Spanish exiles in the period from 1937 to 1945. Refugee children arrived in June 1937 to be raised together in the Escuela España-México in Morelia, Michoacán. They were joined by intellectuals invited by Cárdenas in 1938 to found the Casa de España, an institution financed and sponsored by the Mexican government. The success of the Casa, expanded to include Mexican intellectuals, led to the creation of the Colegio de México in 1940, now one of Mexico's most respected institutions of research and higher education. Although Cárdenas's Spanish policy never enjoyed great support from the Mexican people, there is no question that Spanish refugees made an enormous contribution to Mexican cultural life.

These ties to republican Spain and aversion to the government of Gen. Francisco Franco* proved so strong that Mexico's succeeding presidents continued to refuse to recognize the dictatorship. Only in 1977, two years after Franco's death, did Mexico resume normal diplomatic relations with the new constitutional monarchy, when Mexican president José López Portillo (1920– ) made the first Mexican state visit to Spain, receiving the Order of Isabel the Catholic from King Juan Carlos I.* His visit was considered a great success, and good relations between the two countries have continued to the present.

For additional information, see P. Fagen, *Exiles and Citizens: Spanish Republicans in Mexico* (Austin, 1973); J. Fuentes Mares, *Historia de dos orgullos* (Mexico City, 1984); M. Kenny et al., *Inmigrantes y refugiados españoles en México (Siglo xx)* (Mexico City,

1979); J. Lynch, *The Spanish American Revolutions 1808–1826* (New York, 1973); and C. Illades, ed., *México y españa durante la Revolución Mexicana* (Mexico City, 1985).

*L. B. Hall*

*Related entries*: COLONIES; SECOND REPUBLIC; SPANISH CIVIL WAR.

**MIRÓ, JOAN** (1893–1983), modern Catalan painter. Joan Miró was born at Montroig, near Tarragona, on 20 April 1893 and died at age ninety on 25 December 1983. Best known as a painter, he also achieved a considerable reputation as a sculptor, printmaker, and ceramicist. He is often linked with the surrealists and indeed signed the Surrealist Manifesto in 1924, but his characteristic organic abstractions are not attributable to any one movement or source. His works can appear childlike and abstract, a random assortment of naïve images limned in bright colors. In fact, they employ a consistent, personal system of symbols to convey intense emotions; Miró saw himself as the recorder of those things that cannot be seen. As had his contemporaries and fellow Catalans (either by birth or upbringing), Pablo Picasso* and Salvador Dalí,* Miró absorbed many disparate influences to become an original who, in his turn, had a worldwide influence.

Like so many drawn to Barcelona,* Miró entered the Escuela de Bellas Artes in 1907, where he studied and practiced for more than a decade. In 1919, he made his first trip to Paris, the acknowledged art center of the world and home to the informal assortment of artists known as the École de Paris. There he renewed his acquaintance with Picasso, whom he had known in Barcelona, who by this point had become a major force in the international art scene. Among Miró's other companions were the poet Pierre Reverdy (1889–1960) and the theoretician of dadaism, Tristan Tzara (1896–1963).

Cubism, as practiced by Picasso, rather than by Juan Gris,* another Spanish cubist, influenced Miró during this period, but only in a general fashion. He was not then, or ever, a follower; rather he demonstrated a capacity for original synthesis, much like the Japanese in modern times. Later, Jean Arp (1888–1966) and Paul Klee (1870–1940) similarly served as inspirations for Miró, without, however, directly influencing his work. In later explanations of his evolution, Miró rejected cubism, saying he had always wanted to "smash the cubists' guitar."

Miró's paintings from the 1920s manifest a sort of poetic realism that prefigures his departure into the realm of his own imagination. He came to know André Masson (1896– ), the presiding literary genius behind surrealism; and the tenets of dadaism and surrealism, especially the surrealist fascination with the subconscious, increasingly shaped his art. He flattened the picture plane; reduced representational elements to schematized forms or symbols; and began to create a consistent, personal vocabulary of biomorphic forms (the "things one cannot see"). The ostensible naïveté of his paintings does not conceal their emotional intensity.

In 1931, Miró and Max Ernst (1891–1976) designed sets and costumes for Sergei Diaghilev's (1872–1929) Ballets Russes de Monte Carlo, and two years later, Miró produced his first engravings and collages. Having generally disassociated himself from politics, he did not participate in the Spanish Civil War,* but gradually began to work in what he called his "savage style," which reflected a concern for the Spanish political situation. He did an anti-Franco poster and in 1937, painted an overtly political work, now lost, called *Le Faucheur* for the Spanish pavilion at the Paris Exposition, which hung beside Picasso's *Guérnica*. He also executed sculptures in this period, using rope, nails, and fragments of steel in an effort to convey the same intensity of feeling found in contemporary paintings.

When France* was occupied in 1940, Miró returned to Spain, where he lived quietly until the end of World War II,* when he began dividing his time between Barcelona and Paris, with extensive travel elsewhere. He executed a mural at Harvard University in 1950 and produced ceramic murals for the United Nations Educational, Scientific and Cultural Organization's (UNESCO) Paris headquarters in 1957–1958. His art during this last period was instinctive, rather than intellectual, a constant search for the pictorial equivalents of what he called "the sources of human feeling."

For additional information, see G. H. Hamilton, *Painting and Sculpture in Europe 1880–1940* (Harmondsworth, 1972) and *Joan Miró: A Retrospective* (New Haven, 1987).

S. Benforado

*Related entries*: GRIS, JUAN; PICASSO, PABLO.


**MODERATE PARTY,** liberal political party of the nineteenth century. The moderates were the oligarchs of Spanish liberalism. Their conservative interpretation of liberal doctrines defended property rights against the threat of social revolution, first from lower-middle class merchants and job seekers and then from federalists and democrats. As a party of large landowners and aristocrats, the moderates drew upon the Burkeanism of Gaspar Melchor de Jovellanos* and the French doctrinaire ideas of Francisco Martínez de la Rosa* to support the values of order, liberty, progress, and tradition.

Many of the original moderates came from the liberals of 1834, who served the crown after the death of Fernando VII* at the start of the First Carlist War (1833–1840). Their principles of a strong monarchy, a Cortes without the right to initiate legislation, a Senado composed of aristocrats and clergy, and a high property franchise limiting the electorate, however, met strong opposition in 1836 from other liberals in the Progressive party,* which insisted on national sovereignty rather than sovereignty granted by the crown. The progressives also fought for a more modest property franchise and elective municipal councils.

The moderates gave ground on these points, but they continued to control the Cortes, and had it not been for the rise of Caesarist generals such as Baldomero Espartero,* they might have completely dominated Spanish politics during the late 1830s and early 1840s. The First Carlist War increased the importance of a military elite of praetorian liberals, and until the moderates accepted the leadership of Gen. Ramón Narváez* in 1843, their legislative power was blocked by extraparliamentary executive power. From 1843 to 1850, this impasse was broken by Narváez's long dominance, which saw moderates consolidate their preeminence in the Constitution of 1845, without question the best statement of their principles. They might have ruled longer had they possessed greater party discipline, but local election scandals were so open and outrageous that urban popular opinion turned against them in the 1850s.

In particular, the venality of senatorial oligarchs caused critics to portray them as a threat to general economic development. In the period from 1854 to 1856, when Espartero made a political comeback, the Cortes attempted to revise the Constitution of 1845 to broaden political participation. The effort failed, and moderates in the coalition that supported Liberal Union party rule from 1858 to 1863 under Gen. Leopoldo O'Donnell* were so economically corrupt that they caused a stock market scandal in Paris by manipulating Spanish railway stocks. O'Donnell's fall, despite moderate complicity, brought back Narváez from 1863 until his death in 1868. Moderate party cohesiveness, never good, now lay in ruins, especially after the abdication of Isabel II* in September 1868 led to the more chaotic eras of Amadeo I* and the First Republic.*

The failure of these regimes led to a revival of moderate philosophy under Antonio Cánovas del Castillo* during the Bourbon Restoration (1875–1885) and the subsequent regency of Alfonso XIII* (1885–1902). The more overt types of caciquismo that Cánovas allowed, and, after 1881, that Práxedes Mateo Sagasta* endorsed, tried to recapture the oligarchical nature of earlier moderate rule. Even Antonio Maura,* Cánovas's successor as Liberal-Conservative party leader from 1903 to 1909, implicitly believed in the fitness of oligarchical rule and the prerogatives of this traditional Spain, despite his rhetoric of municipal reform.

Such attitudes contrasted anachronistically with the growth of modern ideological parties in the twentieth century and led to general hostility toward liberalism in the dictatorship of Gen. Miguel Primo de Rivera.* At the end of the Spanish Civil War* in 1939, however, old moderate political values mingled in the wake of the victory of Gen. Francisco Franco* with new corporative concepts as the concept of a traditional Spain was revived.

For additional information, see F. de los Ríos, *Luchas políticas* (Madrid, 1861).

*R. W. Kern*

*Related entries*: ESPARTERO, BALDOMERO; NARVÁEZ, RAMÓN; PROGRESSIVE PARTY.

**MOLA VIDAL, EMILIO** (1887–1937), nationalist general in the Spanish Civil War.* Mola was born on 9 July 1887 in Placetas, Cuba, where his father was stationed as a captain in the Civil Guard.* Descended from a long line of military officers dating back to the War of Independence,* he graduated in 1907 from the Academy of Infantry in Toledo. He quickly volunteered for service in Morocco* when war broke out there in 1909, and he spent the next twenty years in North Africa.

As were other generals of the 1936 insurrection, Mola was molded by the African experience. In its Moroccan territory, Spain had a confused and shifting policy that exasperated the officers there. In the process, they became disenchanted with the governments back home and developed a camaraderie and fierce loyalty to the army that had nurtured them. Mola was a good organizer and trained his native troops well, was wounded twice, and rose to the rank of brigadier general on 2 October 1927.

A second formative experience that prepared Mola for his ultimate role as conspirator was his stint as director general of security in Spain from March 1930 to April 1931. The job of maintaining public order made him unpopular and jeopardized his career, although he became a student of conspiracy and in this capacity put down two military coup attempts and learned about communism and anarchism firsthand.

As security chief, Mola became embroiled in the San Marcos affair of 23–25 March 1931, when Civil Guard troops exchanged fire with leftists blockaded in Madrid's medical faculty. Because the violence spread into the city center, Mola's resignation was demanded, but before action could be taken, he protected the safe exit of Alfonso XIII* from Spain following his abdication. When Mola presented himself to the republican government, he was arrested and imprisoned for crimes committed as security director. After his release on 3 July 1931, he was demoted to the reserves and lost his army pay and pension. During this lean period, he wrote several books defending his action in office and faulting the republic for weakening the armed forces. It took Mola three years to recover his former status, when a rightist coalition under Alejandro Lerroux* gained power, passed an amnesty law in 1934, and named Mola commander of the western military district of Morocco on 4 August 1935, and commander-in-chief of the Spanish army in Morocco in November.

Following its February 1936 electoral victory, the Popular Front dispersed the Spanish high command to remote corners of Spain, but not before Mola met in Madrid with ten other generals and additional representatives of the Unión Militar Española, a secret officers' organization opposed to the republic, to set conditions for rebellion. By this time, Mola, the natural leader of the group, had redefined the army code of loyalty and now believed that insurrection was justifiable to keep the nation from ruin. Mola then joined the Twelfth Infantry Brigade in Pamplona on 15 March 1936.

The coincidence of Mola's presence in the heart of antirepublican Carlist territory made Pamplona the center of the revolt. Mola, soon convinced that anarchy existed throughout Spain, became the principal architect of the uprising as he drew up the command structure and organized garrisons, planned the early strategy of staggered revolts in various centers to be followed by a convergence on Madrid, acquired matériel, and submerged the political differences of the diverse conspirators by keeping politics at bay. After the assassination of José Calvo Sotelo* in Madrid on 13 July, top Carlist leaders agreed to the conspiracy on 14 July, and Gen. Francisco Franco* finally wired his confirmation the following day. Mola himself sought only a strong state with a corporate structure and military governance.

The uprisings occurred more or less at the times planned between 17 and 20 July, but they were put down in key areas. By 20 July, Mola knew that the revolt had failed in Lérida, Valencia, Madrid, and Barcelona,* where his brother Ramón was killed. He also had to deal with the vacillation of some garrisons; the loss of Gen. José Sanjurjo (1872–1936), nominal president of the movement, in a plane crash; a shortage of arms, munitions, and aircraft; and the Basque* resistance which kept the Irun passage open to supplies for the republic. Most serious, however, was the mutiny of the navy in favor of the republic and its blockade of the Moroccan coast, which prevented Franco's twenty-four thousand Moroccan troops from crossing to the peninsula for a time.

The key to Mola's strategy had been a swift attack on Madrid. If the conspirators there could not capture the city, they were supposed to flee north to join Mola's troops. Instead, they were slaughtered in the Montaña barracks before Mola's columns of infantry, Requetés, and Falangists arrived outside Madrid on 21 July, having lost precious time along the way wiping out loyalist resistance. The two Guadarrama passes of Alto de León and Somosierra were not secured until 26 July, and only after huge casualties, after which Mola ordered his troops to dig in. Mola's primary goal had been lost, and although he took Irun on 4 September, San Sebastian on 13 September, and Oviedo on 17 October, by the time he turned south with his main force, Madrid had been fortified with Russian supplies and fresh International Brigades.*

After Franco moved to Burgos, where he was named Generalissimo and head of the nationalist government on 29 September, he put Mola in charge of a November assault upon Madrid. Counting upon the superiority of the African army, Mola planned a diversionary attack by two infantry columns, while three columns of the main force would cut through University City, dividing the capital in half. It was at this hopeful hour that Mola is credited with coining the term "fifth column" to refer to the nationalist sympathizers inside Madrid. On 7 November, however, Gen. Juan Varela's (1891–1951) detailed plan for capturing Madrid fell into loyalist hands, and this information, in addition to Mola's insistence on a suicidal bridge crossing of the Manzanares, pinned down the nationalists at the river and in University City, unable to carry out their strategy despite air support from the Condor Legion. By the end of November 1936, it was apparent that the attack had failed.

In December 1936, Mola abandoned the Madrid front. He was not a part of the further efforts that winter to take the capital. While his ability as an organizer is seldom questioned, his skill as a field commander is more controversial as a consequence of the Madrid failure. In the north, though, he redeemed himself in spring 1937 with the aid of better supplies and German aviation when the brigades of Navarre* began large-scale operations at Vitoria on 25 April. After launching the major northern offensive that would definitively turn the fortunes of war toward a nationalist victory, however, he lost his life on 3 June in a plane crash.

For additional information, see J. M. Iribarren, *Con el general Mola* (Saragosa, 1937); A. de Lizarza Iribarren, *Memorias de la conspiración, 1931–1936* (Pamplona, 1969); B. F. Maíz, *Mola, aquel hombre* (Barcelona, 1976); E. Mola Vidal, *Obras completas* (Valladolid, 1940); J. Vigon, *General Mola (El conspirador)* (Barcelona, 1940); and H. R. Wilson, *The Man Who Created Franco—General Emilio Mola* (Ilfracombe, 1972).

*R. A. Mezei*

*Related entries*: FRANCO, GEN. FRANCISCO; MOROCCO; SPANISH CIVIL WAR.

**MONTSENY Y MANE, FEDERICA** (1905– ), anarchist leader and writer. Montseny, born near Madrid,* was raised on a small farm. Her parents, both teachers, were avowed anarchists who unconventionally educated their only surviving child at home. She developed a strong interest in social theory, literature, and natural science, and soon possessed a strong sense of individualism, self-sufficiency, and a desire for naturalness in her personal relationships.

At eighteen, Montseny edited *La Revista Blanca*, a journal published between 1923 and 1938, for which Montseny wrote at least one essay in each edition. The topics ranged widely, but themes of individualism and social justice, by revolution, if necessary, were common. *La Revista Blanca* kept alive anarchist ideas during the dictatorship of Gen. Miguel de Primo Rivera.*

During this period, she also became an active member of the Federación Anarquista Ibérica (FAI), a militant group founded in 1927 to strengthen anarchist principles among Spanish workers, during a time when the anarchosyndicalist Confederación Nacional de Trabajo (CNT) was banned. Montseny fought for the equality of women in the CNT and FAI and also wrote two novels, dozens of short novels, and many essays on the issue of women's rights and anarchism.* Consistent with her values, she began a lifelong relationship in 1930 with an anarchist comrade. Three children were born to them between 1933 and 1941.

The Second Republic* plunged Montseny into labor politics in Catalonia,* an area of great CNT and FAI strength. Her humanism and support for the ideas of Peter Kropotkin (1842–1921) gradually moved Spanish anarchism toward a more communal philosophy of mutual aid. In 1936, she came out strongly for anarchist participation in the Popular Front elections.

At the start of the Spanish Civil War,* Montseny called for anarchist support of the republic. She helped persuade the anarchist militias to aid embattled Madrid against the nationalists, and she supported the Mujeres Libres organization to set up schools and nurseries for women working in war industries, teaching simple health and sanitation practices, and providing medical care and homes for orphans and unwed mothers. When the anarchists joined the Popular Front government in November 1936, she became minister of public health and public assistance in the Francisco Largo Caballero* government until May 1937—the first woman to hold a portfolio at the national level.

In this capacity, she redoubled her commitment to the social welfare of re-publican Spain, struggling to provide adequate hospital facilities and personnel, sufficient medical and food supplies, and the machinery of a national public-assistance program. Politically, she was instrumental in negotiating a truce to the Barcelona* crisis of May 1937, although communist criticism led to the fall of Largo Caballero's cabinet, Montseny's resignation from the cabinet, and the end of anarchist participation in the republican government.

Although severely criticized by foreign anarchists, Montseny continued to follow a moderate course by supporting a pact of unity between anarchists and socialists in January 1937. Her later involvement in the Spanish Libertarian Movement (MLE), however, was more purely anarchist, but after the nationalist capture of Catalonia, Montseny was forced to flee to France* with her family. She worked briefly for the Extradition Service of the Spanish Republicans (SERA), but her pregnancy made it difficult for her to travel further, and she took refuge in southern France.

The birth of her third child allowed her to avoid extradition back to Spain. The family settled in Toulouse, where she continued to be active in anarchist affairs. The MLE founded a press in Toulouse to publish *Espoir*, *Cenit*, and her own writings: *El problema de los sexos* (1943) and *Pasión y muerte de los españoles en Francia* (1969). She remained active in international anarchist groups, but did not return to Spain until after the death of Gen. Francisco Franco* in 1975.

For additional information, see V. Richards, *Lessons of the Spanish Revolution* (London, 1972); and M. J. Slaughter and R. W. Kern, eds., *European Women on the Left* (Westport, 1981).

*S. F. Fredricks*

*Related entries*: ANARCHISM; BARCELONA; WOMEN.


**MOROCCO,** relations with Spain. Iberian colonialization in North Africa an-tedated the American empire with the Portuguese capture of Ceuta (1415), and the Spanish seizure of Melilla (1497); or developed contemporaneously with the capture of Mazalquivir (1505), Oran (1509); and Bejaia, Tunis, and Tripoli, in Libya (1510). Spain pursued three essential objectives in North Africa: (1) main-tenance of forts along the Mediterranean and Atlantic coasts as an effective frontier against Islam; (2) protection of navigation and trade in waters disputed by European fleets and Berber ships; and (3) development of missionary and mercantile activity. In 1578, the defeat of Sebastian I of Portugal closed off the area only seven years after victory over the Ottoman Turks at the battle of Lepanto (1571) raised expectations that Spain might control the entire area. Only Ceuta, captured in the seventeenth century, subsequently fell into Spanish hands.

Relations did not resume until a treaty of peace and commerce was signed by Carlos III* and Sidi Muhammad ibn Abduh (ruled 1757–1790) on 28 May 1767. Rules regarding commercial exchange in Spanish and Moroccan ports and the right to fish in coastal waters were established, but Madrid failed to obtain an expansion of the presidios (Ceuta, Melilla, Vélez, and Alhucemas) located on the Mediterranean coast of Morocco, as hoped by "retentionists" such as the conde de Floridablanca* (and later, Manuel Godoy* and Juan Donoso Cortés*). An opposing view, held by the conde de Aranda* (and later by Francisco Martínez de la Rosa*), wished to abandon the area as unimportant to the national interest. A step in this direction was taken in 1790, when Spain abandoned Oran, which had played a role as fortress, presidio, urban outpost, and secure harbor against Berber corsairs. Melilla, Vélez, and Alhucemas, now of little value to the defense of the crown's dominions, were soon abandoned as well.

Another treaty, signed by Carlos IV* and Mawlay Sulayman (ruled 1796–1822) at Meknes on 1 March 1799, dealt largely with fishing in waters of the Canary Islands.* Efforts were also made to negotiate Spanish difficulties with tribes of the Rif region, an issue that would remain important in Spanish-Moroccan relations for more than a century. When diplomatic negotiations proved disappointing on this point, Godoy sent Domingo Badía y Leblich (1766–1818), his Catalan agent, to Morocco, in a whimsical attempt to undermine the authority of the sultan and promote Spanish interests in the region. His failure was the last real Hispano-Moroccan contact for more than a half-century, as the War of Independence* and the chaotic reign of Fernando VII* intervened.

In the 1830s, however, conquest of Algiers (a dependency of the Ottoman Turks) by France* raised anxiety in Madrid* that the French were about to conquer what Spain had long coveted. Between 1830 and 1912, the French military and economic empire in the present-day states of Algeria, Morocco, Mauritania, Senegal, and Mali contrasted brilliantly with Spanish impotence, bound as a signatory of the Quadruple Alliance (Britain,* France, and Portugal*) to take no action without Anglo-French agreement.

Barred by this from active participation in the partition of Africa, the Spanish faced a dilemma that produced an Africanism in political and military circles, beginning in 1844, when the French occupation of western Algeria led to a frontier crossing into Morocco during the battle of Isly. Weakness of the sultan of Morocco, Mawlay Abd al-Rahman (ruled 1822–1859), and the protector of Algeria, Abd al-Qadir (1808–1883), was so evident that Spanish Africanists began to argue that a timely Spanish intervention in North Africa could guarantee the security and image of Spain, now converted into a lesser power within the European system. A well-known traveler through North Africa, Manuel Malo de Molina (1843–?), wrote that a French Africa would be, for Spain, a constant ignominy, a blow to national pride.

As a consequence, diplomats during the era of Isabel II* discussed various options with Britain—a trade of Ceuta for Gibraltar*; Spanish military expansion from the presidios inland; or the degree to which Britain would allow Spain to protect Spanish interests in Tetuan, Tangier, and in the waters of the Canary fishing banks. Spanish military power did not impress the British, but the legendary Sir John Drummond Hay, British consul in Tangier from 1845 to 1886, was Francophobic enough to encourage the Spaniards to make the effort.

The first modern Spanish campaign against Morocco began in October 1859 and lasted until March 1860, ostensibly caused by the siege warfare practiced by the Anjera tribe against Ceuta. The peninsular army included Basque tercios, Catalan volunteers, regiments from Granada and Toledo, and other military detachments. Gen. Leopoldo O'Donnell* was put in command, assisted by Gen. Juan Prim y Prats.* Within a short time, Tetuan fell, an event described romantically by Pedro Antonio de Alarcón* in his *Diario de un testigo de la guerra de Africa* (1860), and later more skeptically by Benito Pérez Galdós.* Terms of the armistice signed at Wadras on 25 March 1860, drew a clear border between the presidios and Morocco; allowed Spain to levy customs on commerce; and gave it the right to protect a limited number of Islamic and Jewish subjects of the sultan.

Restoration leaders such as Antonio Cánovas del Castillo,* José Canalejas (1854–1912), Manuel García Prieto (1859–1938), and Álvaro de Figueroa y Torres, the conde de Romanones (1863–1950), approved of continued peaceful penetration of Morocco, but Spain's success interested Britain and Germany,* especially since Sultan Mawlay Hasan (1827–1894) could neither restrain the tribes of the Rif nor protect Morocco adequately from international pressure, although he always managed to avoid total capitulation to European pressures. In 1880, Spain staged the conference of Madrid in an effort to take a lead in protecting European interests in Morocco, but it had little success. For the remainder of the century, Spanish plans for a larger role in the area multiplied to include an enclave on Morocco's Atlantic coast, such as Santa Cruz de la Mar Pequeña (Sidi-Ifni); or a colony further south in the doubtful jurisdiction of Río de Oro (a useful buffer zone for the Canary Islands) or one in the northern areas along the Atlantic. French colonial power, however, was hard to match. The military pressure from southwest Algeria of Mar. Louis Lyautey (1854–1934) and French commercial interests in Casablanca and Agadir far exceeded any Spanish presence in Morocco.

Eventually, of course, the Moroccan issue was subsumed by great power rivalries. France, who feared Anglo-German opposition to its colonial expansion, offered Spain the right to establish a protectorate in northern Morocco, if it would recognize a much larger French protectorate in the south. Spain, fearing British objections, rejected the proposal on 8 Nov. 1902. Within two years, however, growing Anglo-German rivalry led to an Anglo-French Entente of 8 Apr. 1904. Conflicts over Egypt were resolved in favor of Britain, who gave France a free hand to colonize the southern and Atlantic regions of Morocco.

In turn, a Hispano-French treaty on 3 October 1904, publicly affirming Moroccan independence, secretly agreed to a partition. Spain, by acknowledging the Anglo-French Entente, now obtained control over the Mediterranean coast of Morocco. Despite German objections, which were rejected by the Algeciras conference (January to April 1906), partition slowly proceeded in the face of

Moroccan resistance and civil war (1908–1911). The French capture of Fez, a center of anti-European opposition until its fall on 21 May 1911, provoked more German protests; and when the German gunboat *Panther* arrived at Agadir on 1 July, a second Moroccan crisis caused widespread tension until November, when Germany, pressed by Britain, gave France—and indirectly, Spain—a free hand in Morocco. France, by the Treaty of Fez on 20 May 1912, and Spain, in a Hispano-French convention signed several months later, finally achieved the partition sought for such a long time.

The two zones were hardly equal: French territory covered 257,300 square miles, with a population of more than 5 million; while the Rif and Tarafaya totaled 12,400 square miles, with 991,000 inhabitants—a rugged territory, with poor communications, and no outlets to the Mediterranean other than the old possessions of Ceuta and Melilla. Its chief economic asset was the Rif Mining Company, whose activities had triggered tribal protests in 1901—and, in Barcelona,* where the rioting and violence of Tragic Week (July 1909) opposed mobilization of the reserves to serve in Morocco. Almost from the very beginning, public opinion opposed the Moroccan adventure, as Ramón Sender's novel, *Imán* (1930), eloquently describes. More tragic, however, was the schism over Morocco between the army (divided among peninsular officials, respectful bureaucrats, and Africanist officials, all of whom defended promotion for battlefield merit and had a proclivity for coups) and the government, which faced an expenditure (120 million pesetas in 1914; 750 million by 1926–1927) for which the treasury and nation were unprepared and unable to pay.

The first fifteen years of the protectorate's history were dramatic. Political parties, reflecting sharply divided public opinion, polarized on whether or not to remain in Morocco. The high commission of the protectorate and the officer corps also split: some, such as Gen. Dámaso Berenguer,* were willing to yield to reality; while others, such as Gen. José Sanjurjo (1872–1936) and Gen. Francisco Franco,* would not. The disastrous defeat at Anwal* (July 1921) made it even more impossible for either side to compromise, since the complicity of Alfonso XIII* in the Anwal campaign now directly threatened the monarchy.

The dictatorship of Gen. Miguel Primo de Rivera* (1923–1930) hesitated initially on Morocco, but in 1924, he closely followed Mar. Lyautey of France in launching a Franco-Spanish campaign against Muhammad ibn Abd al-Krim al-Khatabi (1882–1963), the brilliant leader of the Rif revolt. Pacification was imposed; military administration of the regions and territories of the Rif was extended for the first time; private Spanish capital went into irrigated agriculture (especially in Arcila and Larache), railway building (Tangier-Fez), as well as mining; while public investment in the zone's cities and towns somewhat offset economic exploitation.

When the democrats of the Second Republic* inherited Morocco in 1931, Manuel Azaña* tried to center policy by replacing military administration with a civil alleviation of Morocco's cost to the national treasury. Progress, impaired by domestic Spanish tensions, meant that little changed in Morocco, especially after 1934, when Franco and other Africanists made common cause with the ruling class of northern Morocco (the old viziers and local notables), who were threatened by democracy. In July 1936, important contingents of Moroccan regulares and tercios of the Foreign Legion* became a bulwark of the insurrection against the republic that resulted in the Spanish Civil War* and the immediate substitution of authoritarian nationalist rule in Morocco.

World War II* spectacularly jolted the Franco-Spanish protectorate by pitting Vichy France (1940–1944), a German puppet state, against Franco's ambitions in the region. At a number of points early in the war, each expected to obtain the other's zone; but in the end, neither Spain nor France profited, and both had to face revived Moroccan nationalism in Fez, Tangier, Casablanca, and Tetuan as the legacy of the war and pan-Arab nationalism. French removal of Muhammad V (1910–1961) in August 1952, for his more pliable cousin, Arafa, who ruled as Hasan II (1929–  ), did nothing to alleviate the crisis, and the Fourth Republic of France (1944–1958) began to evacuate Morocco (and Tunis) in 1954–1955. Franco tried a diplomatic campaign of Hispano-Arab friendship, but on 4 April 1956, the Spanish protectorate was also abandoned to the Moroccan monarchy.

Ceuta, Melilla, and Los Peñones remained as sovereign territory, while Ifni and Río de Oro (Spanish West Africa) became, by sleight of hand, provinces. Decolonialization was accomplished late and badly; Madrid tried to postpone U.N. resolution 1514 (Dec. 1960) on colonies and nonautonomous territories, but without success. The International Court of Justice at the Hague in 1974 found no merit to Spanish claims of sovereignty. Ifni was returned to Morocco in 1969, while Spanish West Africa—despite talk of a referendum—was divided first by Morocco and Mauritania (which surrendered its claim); and then became the object of dispute between Hasan II, who staged a "Green March" to back his annexation, and the Algerian government, which supported the Saharan Polisario Front. The Madrid Agreements of November 1975 tried to make sense out of these developments, but from that moment on, North Africa—the Arab Maghrib—became one of the most conflict-ridden aspects of Spanish foreign policy, as Algeria, Libya, and pan-African organizations such as the Organization of African States in Addis Ababa, Ethiopia, took an active role in the still-continuing struggle between the Polisario Front and Morocco.

In addition, several matters still are pending between Spain and Morocco. One is the status of Ceuta and Melilla, closely linked with Gibraltar, still claimed by Spain. Another is the question of Western Sahara, in which Premier Adolfo Suárez* once claimed Spain still has commitments and obligations resulting from its earlier colonial role. A third concerns fishing and agricultural disputes between Morocco and Spain that, if not resolved quickly, may result in negotiations between Morocco and the European Economic Community (EEC). Even though Spain now is an EEC member, any special ties with its neighbor may be lost unless these disputes are settled quickly. At the same time, the rivalry between Algeria and Morocco in the Maghrib obliges Spain to search out a way of maintaining a policy of equilibrium or status quo between these two young states.

Policies of the current Spanish premier, Felipe González,* seem to be moving in that direction, but his Mediterranean policy, particularly that pertaining to the Maghrib, is still difficult to evaluate.

For additional information, see G. Ayache, *Études d'Histoire Marocaine* (Rabat, 1979); J. M. Cordero Torres, *Organización del Protectorado Español en Marruecos*, 2 vols. (Madrid, 1943); R. Gol Grimau, *Aproximación a una bibliografía española sobre el Norte de Africa: 1850–1980* (Madrid, 1982); C. A. Julien, *Le Maroc face aux imperialismes: 1415–1956* (Paris, 1958); J. L. Miege, *Le Maroc et l'Europe: 1830–1894*, 4 vols. (Paris, 1961); and V. Morales Lezcano, *El colonialismo hispano-francés en Marruecos: 1898–1927* (Madrid, 1976), and *España y el Norte de Africa: El Protectorado en Marruecos, 1912–56*, 2d ed. (Madrid, 1986).

V. *Morales Lezcano*

*Related entries*: ALFONSO XIII; ANWAL; ARMY; BERENGUER, GEN. DÁMASO; COLONIES; FRANCO, GEN. FRANCISCO.

**MÚZQUIZ Y GOYENECHE, MIGUEL DE** (1719–1785), marqués de Villar de Ladrón and conde de Gausa, minister of finance (1766–1785), and minister of war (1780–1785). Múzquiz succeeded Leopoldo de Gregorio, the marqués de Esquilache,* at the ministry of finance following the riots that led to the Italian's exile, and he added the ministry of war after the conde de Ricla's (1720–1785) death. Born in the Valley of Bastán in Navarre, he began his work in the ministry of finance as a young man. He continued to serve under the long succession of ministers, rising to the position of official mayor under Esquilache.

Rational and progressive, the enlightened minister was also prudent and cautious in discharging his responsibilities, an orientation surely influenced by the unfortunate fate of his predecessor. In the court rivalry between the "golillas," led by Jerónimo Grimaldi (1720–1776) and José Moñino, the conde de Floridablanca,* and the Aragonese, led by Pedro Abarca y Bolea, the conde de Aranda,* and Ricla, he maintained a restrained, independent profile. Although his sympathies are generally associated with the latter faction, his most important achievements resulted from collaboration with the former. He is best remembered for his careful, efficient management of the royal treasury and for his work with Floridablanca in establishing the Banco de San Carlos (1782). Although he borrowed heavily from the Cinco Gremios Mayores of Madrid to finance the siege of Gibraltar* early in the War of American Independence (1779–1783), he thereafter handled deficit finance by issuing vales reales, for which the new bank assumed responsibility. In recognition for his wartime services, Carlos III* awarded him the title of conde de Gausa and admitted him to the Orden de Carlos III.

In colonial affairs, Múzquiz was a quiet, cautious force behind commercial deregulation and the destruction of the monopoly held by the Consulado de Cadiz. In 1770, he collaborated with Grimaldi in overcoming opposition to including the Yucatán in the system of "free trade" that Esquilache had devised in 1765, urging a cautious reconsideration of the whole question of colonial trade policy. In 1774, he assumed personal responsibility for liberalizing the

1765 regulation to permit calls at multiple rather than single ports. When José de Gálvez* became minister of the Indies with his support, Múzquiz collaborated closely with him in the several steps that led to the promulgation of the 1778 regulation opening much of America to the major ports of Spain.

Múzquiz was much respected and beloved by Carlos III. His death was a grievous blow to the aging monarch. Pedro López de Lerena (1735–1792) succeeded Múzquiz in both ministries.

For additional information, see J. A. Escudero, *Los orígenes del Consejo de Ministros en España*, 2 vols. (Madrid, 1979); and V. Rodríguez Casado, *La política y los políticos en el reinado de Carlos III* (Madrid, 1962).

*A. J. Kuethe*

*Related entry*: CARLOS III.

# N

**NARVÁEZ, RAMÓN MARÍA** (1800–1868), general, Moderate party* leader, and politician. Narváez, son of a distinguished military family, was born near Granada on 5 Aug. 1800. He joined the royal guards at fifteen; defended Fernando VII* against the army* in the military insurrection of the early 1820s; and rose rapidly as a result of his vigorous leadership of various Army of the North regiments in defense of the central government during the First Carlist War (1833–1840). In 1836, his charisma and energy enabled him to reorganize the national militia. He was appointed captain-general of Castile in 1838, and became a deputy to the Cortes. At a time when the army was the only solid national institution, Narváez stood out as an attractive political general who represented it well.

The Andalusian was not quick enough, however, to prevent Gen. Baldomero Espartero,* an officer very much like himself, from creating an alliance with the Progressive party,* powerful in the Cortes after its sponsorship of the 1837 disentailment.* Narváez retired to Andalusia* until 1843, when he publicly protested the regency of Espartero. He had to exile himself briefly to France,* but the Moderate party—upset by Espartero's free-trade policies and allied momentarily with radicals who protested Espartero's curtailment of civil liberties and the lack of a free press—made Narváez the leader of an insurgency against Espartero. The exiled general landed in Valencia to find Espartero campaigning in Andalusia; Madrid fell quickly, and Espartero soon left from Cadiz for his own exile.

Narváez, made premier in May 1844, badly disappointed provincial radicals who had supported his rebellion. Their democracy was offset by his restrictive Constitution of 1845 that stopped the spread of republicanism by creating a rigid social order, a paramilitary Civil Guard,* and a set of caciques* who monopolized local administration. Even with these restrictions, however, Narváez ruled uneasily; the problems caused by Isabel II* kept him at odds with the queen, and ultraconservatives such as Juan Bravo Murillo* found greater favor from the church. Finally, in Jan. 1851, the general stepped down, although he was never very far from power during the next decade and a half.

Narváez's next cabinet (Oct. 1856) followed another period dominated by the more popular Espartero, who again had been unable to satisfy radical and republican demands. Narváez's regime was predictably authoritarian, almost without politics at all, very much like the administration of Gen. Francisco Franco* in the 1940s and 1950s. Two years later, Isabel II turned to Gen. Leopoldo O'Donnell* to rid herself of her dour critic; but when the Liberal Union cabinet fell, Narváez returned from 1863 to 1865 and again in 1866–1868. He died in office on 10 Apr. 1868; Isabel abdicated on 30 Sept.

The career of Gen. Narváez illustrates many of the problems of nineteenth-century Spain: dominance of the army; fear of a natural political evolution; and uncertainty over fundamental political rights. A Napoleonic image helped elevate men such as Narváez, but restoration values allowed a hopeless monarchy to offset the impact of even limited liberal leadership. The period of the midcentury telescoped the values of the ancien regime, the French revolutionary period, and the restoration into a confused conglomeration that created a hybrid form of government at odds with itself. Narváez could only seek calm by making his ministries devoid of politics; this vacuum, in turn, encouraged ultraconservatives into action that usually provoked democratic, radical, or republican resurgence in a never-ending cycle of reform and reaction that finally purged Spanish liberalism of all but the most cynical kind of machine politics. Narváez's heir became the Restoration politician Antonio Cánovas del Castillo,* who likewise de-emphasized politics for severe, centralized, and corrupt controls.

For additional information, see A. Fernández de los Ríos, *Estudio histórico de las luchas políticas de la España del siglo xix* (Madrid, 1879); M. Fernández Almagro, *Historia política de la España contemporánea* (Madrid, 1956); and C.A.M. Hennessy, *The Federal Republic in Spain* (Oxford, 1962).

*R. W. Kern*

*Related entries*: ESPARTERO, GEN. BALDOMERO; ISABEL II; O'DONNELL, GEN. LEOPOLDO.

**NAVARRE,** a region and province of northern Spain, during the Middle Ages (1160–1512) an independent kingdom, between 1512 and 1839 a kingdom within Spain, and since 1983 an autonomous region. Present-day Navarre occupies an area of 4,055 sq. mi., bounded to the northeast by the Pyrenean frontier with France,* to the east and southeast by the Aragonese provinces of Huesca and Saragossa, to the south and southwest by the river Ebro and the province of Logroño (Rioja), and to the west and northwest by the Basque* sierra and heartland. Navarre's population stands at 486,718 (1975), having risen during this century from 307,669. Both its rate of demographic increase and its population density (46.7 per sq. mi.) are well below the national average, although since 1960 net population decrease has been decisively reversed.

The most striking aspect of Navarre's geography is the contrast between north and south. North of the capital, Pamplona, is the montaña, a region of well-watered hills and mountains, rising in the east to almost 7,000 ft. The montaña is divided by a complex series of narrow valleys, some descending roughly southward toward the rest of the province, but in the northwest sloping westward toward the Atlantic, which dominates their climate. The population of the montaña is scattered mainly in small villages and independent farmsteads (caseríos); land is mostly held in outright ownership and distributed widely and fairly equitably among the population. The chief economic activities are the raising of livestock, cultivation of corn, processing of dairy products, forestry, quarrying and cement manufacturing, and in the far northwest a small amount of iron smelting.

Between the montaña and the Navarrese south lies an intermediate central zone dominated by the capital, Pamplona, nowadays an industrial conurbation with more than 200,000 inhabitants, and also containing smaller, recently industrialized towns such as Viana, Estella, and Sangüesa. Since 1960, central Navarre's small-scale food-processing, textile, paper-making, and leather-goods industries have expanded in size and been joined by large-scale automobile plants and a diverse electronics industry.

South of Pamplona, hills give way to the plains of the ribera, a zone totally different in character, classically Mediterranean in climate, terrain and economic activity. Here, population centers are generally bigger and farther apart than in the north; in nonirrigated areas larger rural properties are common; and the dominant crops are wheat, vines, and, in the fertile valleys of the Ebro and its tributaries, fruit and vegetables, which are largely processed in the ribera's towns.

The contrast between montaña and ribera is heightened by ethnological, linguistic, and cultural elements. Most of northern and western Navarre is culturally Basque, although the Basque language has during the past century become confined to a more limited zone extending from the Araquil Valley in the west to the Salazar Valley in the east. Many northern Navarrese have in consequence been, and remain, emotionally and politically drawn toward the Basque country. The rest of Navarre, while parts of it may have been Basque-speaking at various points in the recent or distant past, has in modern times been wholly Spanish in language, culture, and sentiment, and thus largely unsympathetic toward Basque nationalist aspirations.

A distinctive feature of Navarre's modern and contemporary history, surviving to this day, has been its unique constitutional position within Spain. The formerly independent kingdom of Navarre, founded in 1160 by Sancho the Wise (ruled 1150–1194), was effectively annexed by Fernando II (1452–1516) of Aragon* and donated by him to Castile in 1515. Although by the middle of the sixteenth century Navarre was inescapably part of Spain, it remained officially a separate kingdom. Its partial autonomy was protected by the fuero, a body of customary rights and privileges to which the kings of Navarre had sworn loyalty since 1238, and to which kings of Spain remained subject until 1839. In 1528, the Cortes of Navarre promulgated a revised version of the 1304 Fuero general, the so-called Fuero reducido or recopilado; this in turn was several times revised down to the publication of the *Novíssima Recopilación* of 1738. The distinctive features of the "foral" regime were the Cortes de Navarra, an assembly constructed on a system of estates (ecclesiastical, military/noble, and popular, some members of the last category being elected through open village assemblies); the Diputación del Reino, later known as the Diputación Foral, a council that functioned between meetings of the Cortes and exercised, among other rights devolved by the Cortes, that of sobrecarta, a review of royal decrees and dispositions; and a Consejo Real, or supreme council, presided over by the king or, more often, his viceroy. Navarre also enjoyed privileged fiscal status; until the nineteenth century, the Spanish frontier, for customs and excise purposes, lay not along the Pyrenees but along the Ebro, allowing Navarre the benefits of free trade with, and through, France.

Navarrese autonomy remained essentially intact until early in the nineteenth century, when it began to be seriously challenged both by liberals and by a would-be centralizing crown. Between 1829 and 1936, Navarre lost the right of sobrecarta, saw its Diputación Foral reduced to the status of a mere Diputación Provincial, and suffered the abolition of its Consejo Real. With the conclusion of the First Carlist War (1833–1840), the Madrid Cortes announced, in 1839, that the fueros of both Navarre and the Basque Provinces would be modified. In 1840, the Navarrese Diputación began negotiating a new relationship with Madrid; the outcome was the Ley Paccionada of 1841, the constitutional basis of Navarre's relationship with the rest of Spain ever since. The Ley Paccionada ended Navarre's status as a kingdom, moved Spain's customs barriers from the Ebro to the Pyrenees, and confirmed the dissolution of the Cortes, Diputación Foral, and Consejo Real. In return for these concessions, Navarre retained a degree of autonomy greater than any other part of Spain, including the other Basque Provinces, which, by being prepared to concede less in their negotiations with Madrid, ended by being forced to concede more. The provincial Diputación retained considerable control over Navarre's internal affairs and won the right to raise internally an agreed amount of taxation to be paid to the central government. Although in later years the amount was several times renegotiated, the essential autonomy enshrined in this convenio económico has survived.

Navarre's attachment to its fueros, and in general to a degree of autonomy from central government, helps explain its devotion, during the nineteenth century and part of the twentieth, to the cause of Carlism.* Other reasons are the conservatism of a society, in northern and central Navarre, characterized by a traditionalist resistance to the kinds of change threatened by nineteenth-century liberalism and capitalism and a level of religious devotion unequaled anywhere else in Spain. Although the city of Pamplona, much of the ribera, and, in the north, valleys such as Bidasoa and Roncal emerged as "liberal," and in the 1930s, republican strongholds, most of the rest of Navarre demonstrated its loyalty first to the realista insurgents of the early 1820s and then to the Carlist cause. During the First Carlist War, Navarre, along with the Basque country, parts of Catalonia, and the Maestrazgo district of eastern Spain, was one of Carlism's chief strongholds. It was in the Navarrese town of Estella that the pretender Carlos V established his military capital, and in Navarre that he found his most die-hard support when the tide turned against him in the late 1830s.

From 1839–1840 onward, Carlism became embedded in the political and popular culture of much of northern and central Navarre. For those who embraced it, and who often passed it on as a family tradition to their offspring and grandchildren, it was a matter of self-sustaining sentiment and myth as much as of rational calculation. Carlist rebelliousness, nourished by the increasing impact of capitalism and by the uncomfortable adjustment of the region's new constitutional status, was seldom far beneath the surface of public life. During the Matiners' Revolt (1846–1849), fought mainly in Catalonia, Navarre was the only other region to witness significant disturbances; and when the Carlists under the pretender Carlos VII launched a full-scale civil war between 1872 and 1876, it was Navarre that proved to be the enduring stronghold of a Carlist cause that aroused less response in other regions than had been the case forty years earlier. Even though the defeat of 1876 ushered in a period of prolonged decline for Carlism, in Navarre it remained very much alive—as the events of the 1930s were to demonstrate.

Carlism's durability was assisted by the slow pace of socioeconomic change in nineteenth-century and early twentieth-century Navarre, which did not share in the transformation affecting the coastal Basque Provinces. From 1859 onward, it is true, rail links with Madrid, Saragossa, Guipúzcoa, and Álava were added to a basic road network, radiating from Pamplona and constructed during the late eighteenth and early nineteenth centuries. A projected direct rail link with France, however, never materialized, and communications between Navarre and the Atlantic and Mediterranean coasts remained, as the region's would-be industrial entrepreneurs constantly complained, insufficiently good for significant industrial development to be possible. As late as the 1930s, apart from the Portland cement factory in Olazagutia (in the Araquil Valley west of Pamplona), most Navarrese industry remained small-scale and involved the processing of local produce. Sawmills and paper-making factories exploited the forests of northeast Navarre; iron was smelted in Vera de Bidasoa; and southern agriculture formed the basis of flour milling, sugar refining, fruit canning, and jam making, and the production of wine.

In agriculture, however, important changes did occur, due to the process of religious and civil disentailment* between the 1830s and 1870s, and to the development of a market economy in agricultural produce during the half-century that followed. Disentailment involved the selling off into private hands of church- and municipal-owned land throughout Spain. The effects of disentailment were admittedly less extreme in Navarre than in many other regions. In the case of ecclesiastical disentailment, this was because church lands were simply not extensive in Navarre; in that of civil disentailment, because the Diputación, between the 1850s and 1870s, successfully exploited the Ley Paccionada so as to control, and in effect limit, sales of municipal commons. As a result, although in much of the ribera civil disentailment occurred on a major scale and had the effect of further enriching existing large landowners and urban speculators, in the montaña and most of central Navarre large areas of common land survived. The conservatism of northern and central Navarrese rural society was thereby reinforced, and the gap widened between those districts and a ribera increasingly dominated by rentiers and agricultural entrepreneurs. In the north, Carlist sentiment remained strong, while in the south "liberal" loyalties, mostly involving attachment to the Liberal-Conservative party and sustained by caciques, prevailed until the 1930s among those with an effective political voice.

From the later years of the nineteenth century, southern Navarre began to experience some of the rural unrest that was more typical of other regions. The chief cause was the illegal alienation of surviving commons by wealthier landowners eager to plant wheat, vines, or sugar beets for profit. A particular source of friction was the ploughing of corralizas: tracts of land, sometimes privately owned and sometimes rented from the municipality, on which villagers possessed rights of grazing and wood collection. The effect was to worsen the lot of small farmers and foster the emergence of a rural laboring class whose members then found themselves at the economic mercy of the selfsame corraliceros.

The growth of a market economy in the ribera, and with it of social conflict involving acts of violence and occasional deaths, stimulated not only the emergence, admittedly on a small scale, of socialist and anarchist trade unionism, but also a response from Navarrese Catholics. After 1905, Navarre became one of the chief centers in Spain for the development of Catholic rural syndicates, savings banks, and cooperatives. The sincere intention of Navarrese Catholic priests interested in social action and of their lay collaborators was to protect small farmers and rural laborers against exploitation by the wealthy, as well as against the temptations of socialism. Organizational success was considerable but, as with similar initiatives elsewhere in Spain and abroad, as time passed, they fell largely under the influence, and even the control, of richer landowners; in the 1930s, they were to assist the purposes of the political Right.

By the early twentieth century, Carlism and liberalism had been joined in Navarre by another political force, Basque nationalism. For most Navarrese, the degree of autonomy facilitated by the Ley Paccionada was broadly adequate. On a number of occasions, notably over disentailment in 1861 and in 1891 over the central government's attempt to impose on Navarre the same taxation system as in the rest of Spain (the gamazada), Madrid backed down in the face of resistance from the Diputación and, in the latter case, the population at large. Later, in 1927, the dictator Gen. Miguel Primo de Rivera* was to undergo a similar experience. A few Basque Navarrese, nevertheless, came to see Navarre's future as lying within a fully independent, or at least far more autonomous, Basque country. A number of Navarrese made major contributions to the early development of Basque nationalism. Although attracting some support in northern Navarre, however, Basque nationalism failed even there to achieve the impact it made in Guipúzcoa and Biscay: partly, no doubt, because of the greater autonomy that Navarre already possessed, and partly because the social dislocation of Basque communities by industrialization and Spanish immigration was absent in Basque Navarre.

Throughout the early twentieth century, Navarre stood out as Spain's politically most conservative region, thanks to its relatively stable and prosperous rural society and its high level of religious devotion. This was particularly marked during the Second Republic.* The sudden arrival of an anticlerical, left-leaning republic stimulated a sudden and dramatic revival of Carlism, especially in Navarre, where its roots were deepest and its residual strength greatest. Between 1931 and 1936, Navarre was politically and electorally dominated by this renascent Carlism, strongest in the north and especially the center of the province. Non-Carlist Catholic conservatives, some abandoning "liberal" loyalties, eventually came together to form Unión Navarra, a branch of the Confederación Española de Derechas Autónomas (CEDA). With these forces working closely together under the overall leadership of the cacique of Navarrese Carlism, the conde de Rodezno, Tomás Domínguez Arévalo (1883–1952), Navarre returned large right-wing majorities at the general elections of 1931, 1933, and 1936.

For all of the Right's dominance, however, Navarrese politics during the Second Republic were not entirely monochrome. The authentically liberal tradition of some northern valleys, and of Pamplona, was inherited by republicanism, while the working-class Left, chiefly in the shape of the Socialist party* (PSOE), made a significant impact in the partly industrialized Araquil Valley and throughout much of the ribera, where it espoused the cause of the rural unemployed and advocated the recovery of commons and corralizas. The growth of the Navarrese Left, which came to represent around 20 percent of the overall electorate but a majority in several districts, added a much sharper political focus to the region's social conflicts. Navarre in the 1930s was no Andalusia in this respect, but neither was it the peaceful Arcadia that Navarrese right-wingers like to suggest. It was undoubtedly the emergence of a Navarrese Left that helped drive Carlism in the direction of unambiguous social reaction, and that, after 1934, stimulated the modest growth of Falangism in Pamplona and parts of the ribera.

During 1931 and 1932, Navarrese politics were monopolized by the Basque, or more properly the Basque-Navarrese, autonomy issue. Although it was the Basque Nationalist Party,* far stronger outside Navarre than within, that took the lead in pursuing autonomy, common antagonism to republican leftism and anticlericalism initially persuaded Carlists and other Catholics, in Navarre as well as in the three Basque Provinces proper, to collaborate. The alliance collapsed during 1932, as the Basque nationalists moved toward pragmatic acceptance of the republic as the price for autonomy, while most Navarrese Carlists effectively embraced a militant españolismo and antirepublicanism. The cooling of Navarrese Carlists toward Basque autonomy was actually part of a wider Navarrese ambivalence, sometimes shading into outright hostility, toward involvement in Basque affairs that encompassed left as well as right. Basque nationalism remained very much a minority element in Navarrese politics, appealing to no more than a tenth of the population, mostly north and west of Pamplona.

From 1932 onward, Carlist and general conservative hostility toward the republic increasingly took the form of paramilitarism and preparation for rebellion. By 1934, most Navarrese villages possessed some sort of Carlist organization; many boasted a Requeté, or militia group, some of its members armed with weapons now being regularly smuggled across the French-Navarrese border. During 1936, Pamplona became a leading focus of civilian-military conspiracy, principally involving the new military commandant, Gen. Emilio Mola,* a group of officers attached to the subversive Unión Militar Española, and the provincial Carlists under Rodezno. By mid-July 1936, Carlist-dominated districts were excitedly awaiting orders to mobilize.

From the moment the order arrived, late on 18 July 1936, the Navarrese commitment to the insurgent cause was unequaled in numbers and fervor. Within hours, more than six thousand members of the Requeté had been mobilized; during the next week they continued to pour into Pamplona; by early 1937, perhaps fifty thousand Navarrese had enrolled in the Requeté or the Falangist militia. Entire villages were emptied of their active male population, and it was not unknown for three generations of the same family to be represented in the Carlist tercios. The Navarrese Requeté, under Mola's orders and fanning out from Pamplona, played an important part in the conquest of Guipúzcoa in autumn 1936, the reinforcement of Saragossa, and the advance on Madrid from the north. The role of the Carlist and Falangist militias was not, however, an exclusively military one, for the simple reason that not all prewar Navarre had been rightist territory. During 1936 and into 1937, a ruthless repression was carried out against left-wing activists, mainly in the ribera; the number of deaths remains in dispute, rival claims ranging between 1,000 and nearly 3,500.

Politically, a pattern was set during the first year of the civil war that was to survive throughout the Franco regime. Power in Navarre was allowed to remain in the hands of those collaborationist Carlists and independent Catholics who had helped plan the rising in Navarre. In Franco's Spain, Navarre and its neighbor Álava were the only provinces that were permitted a degree of autonomy in recognition of their exceptional contribution to the nationalist "Crusade." Navarre thus retained most of the administrative and economic freedoms inscribed in the 1841 Ley Paccionada.

On the basis of this autonomy, the province's rulers from the early 1950s, and particularly after 1964, sponsored a policy of industrialization that within twenty years transformed Navarre from a still-overwhelmingly rural-agrarian region to a predominantly urban-industrial one. The change was most marked in and around Pamplona, which, by the mid–1970s, had a population of 219,710—more than 46 percent of the province's total. Economic and social development brought significant political change. Carlism, dominant before and during the civil war, proved with the return of open politics, after 1975, to be a phenomenon of popular culture rather than of modern politics. Now, the region came to be broadly divided between the conservative Unión del Pueblo Navarro and the PSOE, the latter especially strong in the Pamplona region and the ribera. Although Basque nationalism still commanded some loyalty—in particular its radical wing, Herri Batasuna, proved to hold some attraction for disaffected young Navarrese—Navarre's preference for its own autonomy, separate from that of the Basque region, remained evident. In 1982–1983, Navarre, in accordance with the provisions of the 1978 constitution, became an autonomous region, based upon its historic fueros and with its Diputación Foral elevated into a "government." Although a special provision allows for the region's voluntary incorporation into the Basque region (Euskadi), such a development appears unlikely.

For additional information, see J. Andrés-Gallego, *Historia contemporánea de Navarra* (Pamplona, 1982); R. Bard, *Navarra, The Durable Kingdom* (Reno, 1982); M. Cruz Miña Apat, *Fueros y revolución liberal en Navarra* (Madrid, 1981); J. del Burgo, *Historia de Navarra: La lucha por la libertad* (Madrid, 1978); R. Gómez Chaparro, *La desamortización civil en Navarra* (Pamplona, 1967); V. Huici et al., *Historia contemporánea de Navarra* (San Sebastian, 1982); A. Lizarza Iribarren, *Memorias de la conspiración: Como se preparó en Navarra la Cruzada, 1931–1936* (Pamplona, 1953); and R. Rodríguez Garraza, *Navarra de reino a provincia (1828–1841)* (Pamplona, 1968).

M. Blinkhorn

*Related entries*: BASQUES; CARLISM.

**NAVY.** Spanish maritime power, both naval and commercial, has been conditioned by geography and history. The Iberian peninsula is a bastion and a gateway that both links and separates Europe and Africa, as it does the Mediterranean and the Atlantic. This commanding strategic position has situated Spain when strong to exercise influence abroad, and when weak to see its territory and seas coveted by more powerful states seeking advantage at Spain's expense.

By 1700, Spanish maritime power was nearly exhausted. The overseas empire and European dominions were too extensive for a weakened Spain to maintain. The navy, reduced to no more than eight serviceable warships, was burdened by a disunified and inefficient structure, lacked competent seamen and good bases, and was deprived of stores by waste and corruption. Spain remained dependent on the wealth of the Americas, which had to be convoyed through a host of predators in the centuries-long battle of the Atlantic.

In the War of Spanish Succession,* Felipe V,* faced with the allied naval power of Britain* and Holland, sought to restore Spanish maritime power, but had to concentrate on the immediate necessities of a land war. France* tried and failed to defend Spanish maritime interests. Anglo-Dutch forces, in trying to seize strategic bases for a maritime war on France, failed to capture Cadiz in 1702, but easily overpowered the ill-prepared defenses of Gibraltar* in July 1704. A Franco-Spanish naval force reacted quickly, but was defeated in the battle of Malaga in Aug. Britain then so fortified Gibraltar that it has withstood every subsequent Spanish siege. Britain also gained a base at Lisbon by treaty in 1703 and another at Mahon by occupying Minorca in 1708, to gain total control of Spanish waters. Impoverished Spain built only two ships-of-the-line and three frigates during the entire war. Anglo-Dutch forces captured an entire convoy from America in Vigo in 1702 and raided Spanish shipping unmercifully, but failed to control Spain's vital Atlantic routes. Henceforth, Britain would be a Mediterranean as well as an Atlantic naval power and Spain's greatest maritime rival.

By the end of the hostilities in 1714, Felipe V had begun to restore Spanish naval power, combining regional fleets into one united navy and launching a building program. Naval policy, however, was incoherent. Bernardo Tinajero (1649?–1722?), Spain's first designated naval minister, and the fleet's architect, Adm. Antonio Gaztañeta (1656–1728), emphasized Atlantic priorities. New warships were to have the speed, maneuverability, and guns for convoy and patrol operations on Caribbean-Atlantic routes, not the huge and unwieldy battleships necessary to confront the British fleet. An assortment of purchased vessels and the first products of Gaztañeta's building program produced a fleet, by 1718, of twenty ships-of-the-line and thirty-one frigates. The king's chief minister, Cardinal Giulio Alberoni,* hastily employed this raw fleet in pursuit of political ambitions in Italy,* bringing into alliance against Spain both Britain and France. Gaztañeta's squadron was defeated by a British fleet in the battle of Pessaro in 1718, losing twenty vessels. Five others were soon lost in Italian waters, and when Spain then sent another ill-prepared armada to invade Scotland in support of the Jacobites, it was destroyed by storms in 1719. Simultaneously, a French army (now momentarily an enemy rather than an ally) raided the shipyards of northern Spain, destroying warships under construction and burning naval stores. Britain reigned supreme in Spanish waters, capturing Vigo and devastating the northern coast. With too few resources and too many enemies, Felipe V sued for peace in 1720.

José Patiño (1666–1736), chief naval constructor since 1717 and naval minister from 1726 until his death, restored the Tinajero-Gaztañeta Atlantic priorities. He ordered sturdy warships of medium power in the numbers necessary to keep the Atlantic sea lanes open. Between 1719 and 1736, Spain produced fifty-six ships and thirty frigates, sufficient numbers to allow the construction of the first heavy warships designed for fleet action against the British. The main building yards were at Guarnizo (Santander) and Havana (Cuba), the latter because of its access to tropical hardwoods. Patiño in 1726 created naval bases at El Ferrol, Cadiz, and Cartagena, which continue as Spain's primary bases today. He also created a naval academy and a marine corps in 1717 and developed naval regulations (pub. 1748).

Zenón de Somodevilla, marqués de la Ensenada,* naval minister from 1743 to 1754, continued Patiño's programs and reforms. His goal was a secure peace through a navy strong enough to defend sea lanes and coasts and to allow Spain to become the political arbiter between France and Britain. He encouraged the scientific officers Jorge Juan (1713–1773) and Antonio de Ulloa (1716–1795) to incorporate foreign technological advances into the Spanish fleet. He retained a clear distinction between ships designed for transatlantic convoys and those for battle with the British fleet. Ensenada shifted building yards to the protected El Ferrol and Cartagena bases, closing Guarnizo. From 1737 to 1754, forty-seven ships-of-the-line and twenty-two frigates joined the fleet. Despite constant losses from storms, rot, and ship worms, ships-of-the-line in service rose from six in 1719 to thirty-three in 1754, or a third the level of the British navy.

The Spanish campaign to dominate the Caribbean and counter smuggling led to a maritime war with Britain from 1739 to 1748. Each decimated the other's shipping, which the smaller Spanish merchant marine could ill afford. British forces attacked Spanish Pacific ports and sea lanes to the Philippines (1740–1744) and captured the Spanish transshipment port of Portobelo in Panama in 1739. Adm. Blas de Lezo (1688–1741) defeated a British assault on Cartagena de Indias in 1741. Adm. Juan José Navarro (1687–1772), as a result of the battle of Sicily in 1744, temporarily weakened British control of the western Mediterranean, allowing Spanish convoys to support troops in Italy. Adm. Andrés Reggio (1692–1780) successfully defended Cuba in the battle of Havana in 1748.

The Bourbon Family Pact with France in 1761 allowed Spain to shift resources from land defense to naval might. Joining France in war against Britain in 1762, Spain regained the strategic island of Minorca the French had captured in 1756. British sea power concentrated against the Spanish colonies. A British force captured Havana in 1762, overcoming the defenses of Capt. Luis Vicente de Velasco (1711–1762), with Spain losing twelve ships-of-the-line in the harbor and two others under construction. The empire's best shipyard was laid waste. Britain also captured Manila and ravaged Pacific supply lines. With peace in 1763, Spain regained Havana and Manila, but had to cede Minorca and Florida to Britain.

The Havana yard was quickly rebuilt. Despite the shortage of shipwrights and seamen, a depletion of timber, and inflation, the shipyards in the peninsula and in Havana from 1755 to 1782 constructed sixty-four ships-of-the-line and sixty-three frigates. One ship alone consumed three thousand trees and twelve miles of rope. Thirteen very large ships-of-the-line were built, starting in 1769 with the *Santísima Trinidad* (140 guns), all at El Ferrol and Havana. By 1782, active ships-of-the-line stood at sixty-one, nearly double the number in 1754. The cost rose to nearly 30 percent of total government expenditures.

In the War of American Independence, Spain followed France in declaring war on Britain in 1779 in hope of combining to impose a decisive defeat on the common enemy. The allies planned a combined invasion of Britain, but scurvy prevented French ships from operating with the formidable Spanish fleet, which included thirty-nine ships-of-the-line, and the operation was canceled. Spain laid siege to Gibraltar in 1779–1782, both sides making its fate a high priority. Gibraltar operations included the battle of Cape Santa María in 1780, in which Adm. Juan de Lángara (1701–1781) lost six ships-of-the-line, and culminated in a massive attack in 1782, which involved fifty Spanish ships. Britain diverted such heavy naval resources to Gibraltar that French and Spanish fleets could freely operate in American waters. Spain launched amphibious assaults on Pensacola in 1781 and the British naval base in the Bahamas in 1782. French and American ground and naval forces concentrated at the Chesapeake in 1781, the decisive campaign of the American Revolution. In retaining Gibraltar, Britain lost America. The overextended British navy could not prevent the successful Spanish campaign against British shipping in British home waters or the Franco-Spanish reconquest of Minorca in 1781.

Adm. Antonio Valdés (1744–1816), naval minister from 1783 to 1796, built the Spanish navy up to its greatest power at the cost, by 1794, of 39 percent of the state's expenditures. He added 28 ships-of-the-line and 41 frigates to produce a navy that, in 1795, had in service 76 ships-of-the-line, 43 frigates, and 103 other vessels. The Spanish fleet remained roughly equal in numbers to the French navy, which was then disrupted by revolution, while the British fleet was still at least twice as large and much stronger in training. Only in combination with the French could the Spanish navy hope to deter or defeat Britain at sea. Spain continued to keep its sea lanes open, although its merchant fleet was reduced to five hundred vessels, far fewer than the numbers serving other maritime states. In 1785, Carlos III* chose new distinctive red-yellow-red naval and mercantile flags, which in time became the Spanish national colors.

The second half of the eighteenth century was the great age of Spanish naval science. Naval engineers Jorge Juan and Antonio de Ulloa made cartographic expeditions and collaborated in publishing *Observaciones astronómicas y físicas* (1749), which gained European renown, as did Juan's *Examen marítimo* (1771). A naval observatory and scientific center was created in Cadiz in 1753. Mathematician and astronomer Vicente Tofiño (1732–1795) produced accurate coastal and topographic maps. Alejandro Malaspina (1754–1810) circumnavigated the world in a five-year voyage of scientific investigation (1789–1794). Spanish ships explored the west coast of North America, planting settlements as far north as Nootka Sound.

Spanish naval power, having risen to a peak in 1795, began to decline just when it was most needed. Spain was pulled into the wars spawned by the French Revolution, but disruptive conditions reduced Spanish colonial and European trade and severely curtailed warship construction. Between 1795 and 1814, while Spain was locked in deadly struggle, only one ship-of-the-line and nine frigates were added to the navy. In any case, there were two few trained seamen for the ships in service.

Spain joined Britain against the revolutionary French from 1793 to 1795, contributing a squadron to the British siege of Toulon. In 1796, Spain reversed alliances to continue its historic maritime struggle against Britain. The combined Franco-Spanish naval threat caused Britain to evacuate the Mediterranean. Frigate war on commerce was intense on both sides. A Franco-Spanish plan to invade Britain collapsed when Britain defeated Adm. José de Córdoba (?–1809) in the battle of Cape St. Vincent in 1797; Britain then seized Trinidad. The destruction of the French Mediterranean fleet in Egypt allowed Britain to retake Minorca in 1798, dividing French and Spanish Mediterranean bases. In a confused action at Gibraltar in 1801, two very large Spanish ships mistakenly fired on each other; both blew up with a loss of two thousand men. Adm. José de Mazarredo (1745–1812) unsuccessfully pleaded for better fleet training and organization, but the resources and will were not available. The temporary Peace of Amiens, in 1802, returned Minorca to Spain, but Trinidad remained in British hands.

The culmination of Franco-Spanish attempts to contest Britain at sea came in 1805. Napoleon Bonaparte (1769–1821) planned another attempt to invade Britain, but the French and Spanish fleets could not combine to secure transit of the English Channel from the British fleet. Having given up the invasion scheme, Napoleon uselessly ordered to sea the Franco-Spanish fleet at Cadiz (eighteen French and fifteen Spanish ships) to face Adm. Horatio Nelson's (1758–1805) waiting fleet at the battle of Trafalgar.* The allied fleet was ill trained, without experience in combined fleet operations and directed from afar by a French emperor without a seaman's sense. Thus, it sailed without confidence, and despite the courage of Spanish captains and crews, the mortally wounded Spanish commander, Adm. Federico Carlos Gravina (1756–1806), lost ten Spanish ships-of-the-line and a thousand men. It was a total British victory, since surviving allied ships were bottled up in port. Spanish sea power had come to a crushing end. Only in Spanish America at Río de la Plata, where naval forces continued the struggle against Britain, did Spain emerge victorious.

The eclipse of Franco-Spanish sea power led Napoleon to adopt a strategy of economic warfare, in pursuit of which he sent troops into the peninsula in 1808, triggering the Spanish War of Independence.* As the winds of war shifted, Britain now became an ally. Its navy defended Spanish coasts and Minorca from French attack, while by sea Britain sustained the Anglo-Spanish armies that drove the French from Spain. Trafalgar made this decisive British support possible, while the remains of the Spanish navy were left to rot in ports, their crews added to the army. At times, Spanish naval vessels ventured from their besieged base at Cadiz to make assaults on the coast, or to hunt down French commerce raiders, and to transport delegates to the Cortes of Cadiz.* Spanish gunboats helped defeat the French attack on Vigo in 1809, but mostly the War of Independence turned Spaniards away from the sea toward the land. Spanish America, its maritime links with the disordered mother country severed, moved toward independence. Spain was liberated at the expense of her navy and her colonies.

In 1814, there were no more than twenty ships-of-the-line in service, and only five of these were in good condition. Five Russian ships, purchased as a stopgap, were rotten and had to be broken up. By 1833, only three ships-of-the-line and three frigates were left. Decades of war had created a severe shortage of timber, and both pay and maintenance declined. When French troops and naval forces reduced Cadiz in 1823, the decrepit flotilla that defended it could do little.

Without naval power Spain could not control her American colonies. British officers and men volunteered for Latin American service against the privateers that preyed on shipping. A Spanish squadron at Montevideo was destroyed in 1814, and Argentine vessels raided Spanish possessions in the Pacific. In 1815, Spain collected eighteen warships and forty-two transports with 10,000 troops to control rebellious colonies bordering the Caribbean. Cartagena de Indias was taken in 1815 but lost again in 1821. Naval forces of Chile and Peru harassed Spanish sea communications in the Pacific, and a relief expedition was neutralized by mutiny and then isolated in 1818–1819. Chile captured a frigate in 1820; others surrendered by 1822. By 1825, Spanish naval power was swept from the Pacific coast. Colombian corsairs, supported by British and Spanish liberals, attacked shipping off the coasts of Spain and used Gibraltar as a base in 1826. Spain made one last attempt to restore control over Mexico with an amphibious landing that failed at Tampico in 1829. Finally, only Cuba and Puerto Rico were left in the American empire and the Philippines in the Pacific.

Eventually, technology stirred Spanish naval power to rise once again. Although sailing warships were constructed up to 1854, the government in 1834–1835 purchased four British paddle-wheel steamships that operated in the First Carlist War (1833–1840) with other Spanish ships to transport the British Legion, blockade Bilbao, and cooperate with the land forces of Isabel II.* Naval forces recaptured Melilla, which had fallen into the hands of Carlist prisoners in 1838–1839. Thirteen more steamships were acquired by 1846, and another thirteen Spanish-built screw frigates followed by 1865. Spain became a leader in the development of armored screw frigates, six being built in Spain and abroad between 1861 and 1863, including the iron-hulled *Numancia* and *Victoria*. These were some of the most advanced ships of the period, a cause for renewed confidence, and, by 1870, the navy was virtually all steam-powered, including five armored frigates and one armored corvette, ten screw frigates and two screw corvettes, seven paddle-wheel frigates and three paddle-wheel corvettes, and numerous lesser steamships.

Spain sent the new navy to exercise power abroad. It joined a multilateral effort to suppress the Roman Republic in 1848–1849 and effectively supported the army in the first Moroccan War in 1859–1860. A Franco-Spanish naval force intervened in Vietnam in support of Christian missionaries from 1858 to 1863, occupying Saigon and Tourane. When Mexico defaulted on debt payments, Spanish warships joined a multilateral expedition that occupied Veracruz in 1861–1862. The navy also helped secure Santo Domingo in 1861–1865.

Spain then dispatched a squadron to the Pacific coast of South America in 1864. Adm. José Manuel Pareja (1813–1865), who had been born in Peru, commanded five large and two small steamships, to which was added the new *Numancia*. In a dispute with Peru, the fleet, by occupying the Chincha Islands, sparked a popular Peruvian uprising against Spain. When Chile supported Peru, Pareja blockaded Valparaíso. A Chilean vessel captured a Spanish warship in 1865, whereupon Pareja committed suicide. Command of the expedition fell to

Capt. Casto Méndez Núñez (1824–1869). After he had been ordered to take reprisals, he bombarded unfortified Valparaiso, but his ships were damaged while bombarding fortified Callao. He withdrew in 1866, without having achieved any advantage. Most of the squadron returned to the Atlantic, where Méndez Núñez engaged in delicate diplomacy during Uruguay's civil strife. Meanwhile, the *Numancia* crossed the Pacific and became the first ironclad to circumnavigate the world. Contrary to the naval world's fears, this ship demonstrated that steam-powered and iron-hulled warships could absorb extensive hits, survive storms, and operate for months beyond the reach of bases.

The navy was soon involved in civil war at home. In 1868, Adm. Juan Bautista Topete (1821–1885) used warships to begin the overthrow of Isabel II.* When her successor, Amadeo I,* abdicated in 1873, elements in the naval port of Cartagena formed a libertarian canton against the new republican central government. All the warships in port joined, and the naval base became the headquarters of a spreading insurrection. The ships induced coastal towns to join the cantonalist camp. Frightened leaders of the central government, without a navy of their own, declared the ships "pirates" in the hope that foreign navies might reduce the rebel fleet for them. A German warship did capture the steamer *Vigilante*, and the ironclad frigates *Almansa* and *Victoria* were surprised in the act of intimidating Almería and Malaga. Until a centralist blockade squadron was built up, however, cantonalist warships continued to go to sea to gain support and supplies from coastal towns, although one expedition to Valencia and Barcelona was terminated when the *Numancia* collided with and sank the paddle-wheel frigate *Fernando el Católico*. Eventually the centralist squadron was able to blockade Cartagena, destroy the frigate *Tetuán*, and blow up the town's ammunition supply. As centralist troops closed in to occupy Cartagena, cantonalist leaders escaped in the *Numancia* through the blockade to Oran in Jan. 1874.

War in northern Spain against Carlist rebels continued from 1872 to 1876. Foreign navies, protecting blockade-runners bearing their flags who tried to break through the central government's blockade of rebel ports, strained international relations. Government warships continued to bombard Carlist positions even after a Carlist shot killed the government's naval commander, Adm. Victoriano Sánchez Barcáiztegui (1826–1875).

During and after this period, Spain acquired 186 steam gunboats for colonial service from 1860 to 1881. To counter the Cuban insurrection (1868–1878), Spain had thirty built in the United States* from 1870 to 1872 to blockade the Cuban coast and cooperate with ground forces. To expand Spanish control over the Philippine archipelago and reduce piracy in its southern waters, seventy-two gunboats were employed from 1860 on, forty-nine being built at Cavite and other Pacific yards for this service. Warships stationed in the Philippines were in constant action between 1861 and 1877, but hard service and typhoons quickly wore them out.

Warship construction in this era lacked a clear strategy. Three screw frigates entered service from 1879 to 1881 and ten small cruisers for overseas use in the early 1880s. The European powers were then engaged in large building programs, stimulating a major debate within the Spanish navy over strategic priorities. The ongoing development of ship technology, a rapid rise in costs, and the constant political restructuring of naval administration prevented solutions to the dilemma of too many tasks and too few means. Yet Spain kept its lead in the development of armored steam warships and remained competitive in the race for naval power. Admirals debated whether to push for an expensive fleet of heavily armored battleships to counter other European battle fleets, or for a more modest fleet for colonial use and commerce raiding that would be within Spanish financial means. A compromise in 1887 settled on a fleet of large cruisers and small torpedo boats.

The result was a fleet that by 1898 included one short-range battleship, eleven larger and ten smaller cruisers for extended service and, for coast and harbor defense, fourteen torpedo gunboats and thirteen small torpedo boats. As a compromise between distinct strategies, the new cruisers were too large for the needs of colonial service or commerce raiding, but too small to battle a major navy. Nevertheless, on paper, the new navy was the world's seventh largest, ranking in 1898 just behind the rising navy of the United States.

The navy did technologically improve. Naval engineers experimented with submarines as early as 1859, and Isaac Peral (1851–1895) produced the world's first practical submarine in 1888. Under the influence of Fernando Villamil (1845–1898), Spain in 1886 produced the first torpedo boat destroyer, *Destructor*. The merchant marine also rose from a total of 90,919 tons of steamships in 1873 to 273,819 tons by 1890, maintaining its position as the world's fifth largest steam-powered merchant fleet. Successful shipping firms operating more than two hundred steamships plied the Mediterranean, Atlantic and Pacific trade routes.

This advance was dramatically reversed by the Spanish-American War* in 1898. When the U.S. battleship *Maine* blew up in Havana harbor, evidence pointed to an internal explosion, but the U.S. declared war nevertheless in April. The Spanish fleet was hampered by a lack of training, munitions, and supplies. Confidence was low, but honor and politics compelled the navy to fight for Cuba and the Philippines. In Manila Bay, an assortment of nine old and worn-out ships commanded by Adm. Patricio Montojo (1839–1917), anchored as a floating battery, was quickly destroyed by an American squadron in May. In the Atlantic, a squadron of four cruisers and three destroyers commanded by Adm. Pascual Cervera (1839–1909) sailed too soon for Cuba. A few weeks more and another cruiser and three more destroyers would have been ready, along with the recently purchased *Cristóbal Colón*, potentially Spain's most powerful vessel, which had not yet received its main guns. The haste to reach American waters left the squadron short of munitions and fuel to destroy Key West or blockade the U.S. coast. As a result, Cervera was himself blockaded and destroyed at Santiago de Cuba in July.

Meanwhile, a collection of smaller warships defending Puerto Rico had to be scuttled. In the Caribbean as in the Philippines, defeat at sea led to the surrender of Spanish land forces. In Spain, a reserve squadron under Adm. Manuel de la Cámara (1836–1920) prepared to raid the U.S. Atlantic coast, but public pressure diverted it to relieve the Philippines instead. This fleet of one battleship, one armored cruiser, and three destroyers, along with armed merchant ships, supply ships, and transports carrying four thousand troops, had only reached the Red Sea when the defeat at Santiago prompted its recall. In all, Spain had lost fourteen cruisers and a host of other vessels in the war, a major reason for its capitulation.

The shock of the Disaster of 1898 produced soul-searching, but naval reconstruction did not occur until the intense European rivalries of World War I* caused Spanish leaders to worry that foreign states might again grab strategic Spanish territory such as the Balearic or Canary Islands. Despite poor finances, Spain launched a series of building programs to hold the balance between foreign navies and to defend Spanish possessions and sea lanes. Starting in 1908, under the leadership of Adm. José Ferrándiz (1847–1918), Spain built three dreadnought battleships and twenty-two coastal torpedo boats. Adm. Augusto Miranda (1855–1920) and his successors, aided by British engineers and investments, expanded the program after 1915, incorporating lessons of the war and adding to the navy through 1936 a mobile force that included eight cruisers, fifteen destroyers, twelve submarines, one seaplane carrier, numerous lesser vessels, and 108 naval aircraft. Despite the shipwreck of a battleship and a cruiser, and the sinking of sixty-eight ships by the Germans during World War I,* the new fleet by 1936 stood as the eighth largest in the world, while the merchant marine went from 479 steamships grossing 1,180,000 tons in 1914 to 600 merchant and 270 fishing vessels in 1936.

In the Rif War (1913–1927) in Morocco,* the new navy performed well, particularly in the decisive amphibious landing at Alhucemas in 1925 that involved seventy-three ships and twenty-six landing craft. The Second Republic,* however, by renouncing war as an instrument of statecraft, used the navy only under League of Nations' control to enforce sanctions against Italy in 1935 after the Ethiopian campaign. Increasing political and social polarization split the service; radicalized sailors gravitated toward social revolution, while shipyard strikes slowed construction programs and weakened maritime commerce. Naval officers feared the intervention of other powers in Spain and yearned for order.

At the onset of the Spanish Civil War,* the naval bases of El Ferrol and Cadiz fell to the nationalist rebels, Cartagena and Minorca to the republic. Most of the 1,248 officers favored the nationalists, while most of the 4,600 petty officers and 12,000 seamen favored the republicans. Those caught in the wrong zone either served or were executed. The republic retained a battleship, three cruisers, fourteen destroyers (and two under construction), and all twelve submarines. The nationalists gained control of a battleship, one cruiser (and two under construction and one being rebuilt), and a destroyer. During the course of the war, both sides added many lesser ships and auxiliaries, while Italy ceded the nationalists two submarines and four destroyers. The nationalist naval staff was led by chief of staff Adm. Juan Cervera (1870–1952) and fleet commander Adm. Francisco Moreno (1883–1945); while the republican fleet command alternated between Lt. Comm. Miguel Buiza (1898–1963) and Luis González de Ubieta (1899–1961).

The land war depended on a continuous flow of war supplies by sea, and the civilian population in the republican zone was dependent on seaborne food and fuel, so the naval war focused on control of vital sea lanes. In the first phase (July–Sept. 1936), the republic commanded the seas and blockaded the Strait of Gibraltar to isolate nationalist forces in Spanish Morocco. Only in the north were nationalist warships able to support land operations. The battle of Cape Spartel in Sept. shifted the naval initiative to the nationalists. In the second phase (Sept. 1936–Oct. 1937), republican caution and strategic errors allowed weaker nationalist forces to control the straits, transport nationalist forces from Morocco to the peninsula, raid the republican Mediterranean coast and supply lines and blockade the north. Italian and German naval forces aided the nationalist effort with clandestine naval warfare and intelligence collection. The republican navy concentrated on protecting its own supply lines, mostly with the Soviet Union, but attacks on this traffic led to reduced Soviet material support. Nationalist supply lines were left unhindered, encouraging Italy and Germany* to maintain their support of the nationalist cause. With the collapse of the republican northern front, the third and last phase (Oct. 1937–Mar. 1939) concentrated on the nationalist blockade and raids against republican Mediterranean ports, while the republican navy could barely maintain coastal communications among these ports. By 1938, the nationalist naval campaign had won the battle of supply, ensuring an eventual nationalist land victory. Republican naval losses included a battleship, three destroyers, and eleven submarines; nationalist losses included a battleship and a cruiser. The Spanish merchant fleet lost nearly a hundred vessels.

Spain remained a nonbelligerent in World War II,* its experienced navy, despite its losses in the civil war, being the most powerful neutral navy of the era. A naval building program began again in 1942, but a lack of resources forced delays. The navy could not prevent Spain from losing eighteen merchant ships to Allied and twelve to Axis attacks.

Since 1945, the navy has remained an instrument of Spanish policy of defense against Soviet expansion, since 1963 as an ally of the United States, and since 1982 as a member of the North Atlantic Treaty Organization (NATO). The navy's mission has been to control the Strait of Gibraltar and the Cadiz-Canaries-Azores triangle, with strategic emphasis upon antisubmarine warfare and a limited amphibious capability. Naval construction since 1945 includes the aircraft carriers *Dédalo* and *Príncipe de Asturias*, the cruiser *Canarias*, nineteen destroyers, and eight submarines, making the navy the fifth most powerful in the world. Naval personnel has risen from 22,300 in 1946 to 64,700 (including 12,000 marines) in 1987. The merchant marine has grown from 1,064 vessels, grossing 1,068,900 tons in 1946 to 2,767 vessels, including 107 tankers, grossing 8,112,200 tons, in 1987.

For additional information, see E. Manera et al., *El buque en la armada española* (Madrid, 1981); C. Fernández Duro, *Armada española: Desde la Unión de los reinos de Castilla y de Aragón*, 9 vols. (Madrid, 1895–1903); J. P. Merino Navarro, *La armada española en el siglo XVIII* (Madrid, 1981); J. Cervera Pery, *Marina y política en la España del siglo XIX* (Madrid, 1979); A. R. Rodríguez González, *Política naval de la restauración (1875–1898)* (Madrid, 1988); R. Cerezo, *Armada española, siglo, XX*, 4 vols. (Madrid, 1983); and F. de Bordejé, *España, poder marítimo y estrategia naval* (Madrid, 1982).

*W. C. Frank, Jr.*

**NEGRÍN LÓPEZ, JUAN** (1892–1956), prime minister of the Second Republic* from 1937 to 1939. Juan Negrín López, born in 1892 to wealthy parents from the Canary Islands,* was educated primarily in medicine at several German universities, particularly Leipzig, which he attended during World War I,* exposing him to the ferment of European politics from 1914 to 1917. Negrín came to Madrid as a professor of physiology at the University of Madrid, part of a new scientific effort begun by Santiago Ramón y Cajal,* the neurologist famous for his revival of Spanish science* and a man of letters politically close to the Generation of 1898.*

Negrin remained at the university until 1931 and also headed the physiology laboratory for the Junta para Ampliación de Estudios, an autonomous committee of prominent scholars established in 1907 by Krausists to promote higher education in Spain. Negrín soon emulated his predecessors by writing for the newspaper *El Sol* (Madrid) and the periodical *Revista de Occidente* (Madrid) and in general by informally becoming a part of the Generation of 1927* that rose to prominence in the years before the Second Republic.

With the advent of the republic, Negrín began a new political career as a member of the moderate socialist faction led by Indalecio Prieto (1883–1962), for whom he won election as a deputy from Madrid in 1931, 1933, and 1936. His interests lay in improving public health, educational reform, and other, mainly practical, efforts at modernization that Prieto's group sought. Much of Negrín's private life revolved around acts of philanthropy from his own funds; he often provided books and medical or scientific instruments to others.

Not until 1934, when the center-right government began arresting peasant protesters, did Negrín show his political temper by bitterly attacking this policy. During the chaotic months in spring 1936 after the Popular Front elections, however, Negrín regained his composure by working with Prieto to protect the republic's social program from destruction. This attitude continued during the early months of the civil war. What had been gained must be built upon, he said, and it became his political credo when, in Sept. 1936, he was made minister of finance in the Francisco Largo Caballero* cabinet. His reform of the Carabineros (customs officials and guards) created an effective republican force presumably for this purpose, although his critics later argued that the Carabineros more closely resembled a private army.

Clearly Negrín was a compassionate man, often intervening early in the war to prevent political reprisals. Gabriel Jackson portrays him as a bourgeois intellectual, fluent in German, passable in French and English, and even able to speak a little Russian. He was a man reassuring to foreign journalists as the model of a Western premier or president and certainly more attractive to outsiders than the anarchists or Largo Caballero himself.

A darker image of Negrín also began to emerge, however, with the transfer of Spanish gold reserves to Soviet custody in Sept. and Oct. 1936. As Soviet influence grew in the republican government, Negrín turned away from Largo Caballero and became a bitter enemy of the POUM* and the Confederación Nacional del Trabajo (CNT). Later speeches made it clear that he disagreed with the possibility of maintaining both revolutionary and antifascist policies, but his Carabineros, who triggered the May crisis in Barcelona* by seizing border posts from the other groups, provoked bitter sectarian feuding and led the way to communist dominance of the republic.

When Largo Caballero resigned the premiership in protest, the president of the republic, Manuel Azaña,* asked Negrín to form a cabinet on 18 May 1937. POUM members were arrested and sometimes executed; the CNT soon lost its power in Catalonia* and Aragon*; and communists surfaced more prominently in the cabinet and army.* By abolishing the revolutionary regime, Negrín believed that the Western powers might finally intervene against the nationalists. Only in this way could the achievements of the republic be salvaged.

Negrín, of course, misread the strength of Western appeasement, but he also miscalculated badly in relying so heavily upon the communists, since fear of Soviet penetration, already strong, replaced criticism of revolutionary excesses. Finally, on 1 May 1938, Negrín issued a thirteen-point program that promised to end foreign interference, but the outcome of the war now so clearly favored the nationalists that Negrín's promises made no impact abroad. He was left dependent upon Joseph Stalin (1879–1953), who soon concluded that the civil war offered no further opportunities for the Soviet Union.

One of the major casualties of this reliance in Mar. 1938 was the friendship of Negrín and Prieto. Prieto had acted as minister of defense under his former protégé since May 1937, but the loss of Teruel in Feb. 1938 made him favor a negotiated peace. Negrín added Prieto's portfolio to his own in early Apr. and thereafter managed the declining republican war effort himself. The failure of the Ebro campaign (July–Nov. 1938) left Negrín without further recourse, and after the nationalist conquest of Catalonia, the premier, on the verge of flight, promoted two of his communist aides, Antonio Cordón and Juan Modesto, to replace him. Almost immediately, Negrín's opponents, led by Col. Segismundo Casado (1893– ), created a National Council of Defense that governed republican Spain in the month that was left to it. Negrín returned from abroad, but it was too late to salvage any honor from the defeat.

Negrín took refuge first in France* and then Britain* during World War II.* He returned to Paris in 1945, still active in exile politics, and died there on 12 Nov. 1956.

For additional information, see M. Ansó, *Yo fui ministro de Negrín* (Barcelona, 1976); B. Bollotin, *The Spanish Revolution: The Left and the Struggle for Power during the Civil War* (Chapel Hill, 1979); and G. Jackson, *The Spanish Republic and the Civil War 1931–1939* (Princeton, 1956).

R. W. Kern

*Related entries*: GENERATION OF 1927; SCIENCE; SPANISH CIVIL WAR.

**NEWSPAPERS.** Royal licenses to publish were created by a decree in 1502 to ensure that nothing contrary or offensive to Catholicism,* good manners, or the prerogatives of the king appeared in print. The first daily newspaper in Madrid appeared in Feb. 1758, and Carlos III* relaxed controls at the start of his reign to spur literacy and popular education. Increasing political polarization, however, caused him to issue the Reglamento de Imprentas in Oct. 1788 as the first formal legislation to control and censor newspapers. His successor, Carlos IV,* so feared the role of journalism in the French Revolution that he had all but two official papers suppressed in 1791.

In 1810, the pendulum swung the other way. Freedom of press was given legal recognition in the Ley de Libertad de Imprenta issued by the Cortes of Cadiz,* ratified by Article 371 of the Constitution of 1812. As a result, some fifty newspapers were founded in Spain between 1808 and 1814. The restoration of Fernando VII,* however, closed all but two official papers until the liberal triennium (1820–1823), when an estimated seven hundred were founded. Suppression returned with Fernando from 1823 to 1833 in defense of absolutism, and it was not until the Constitution of 1837 that the Cadiz law was reinstated.

In the liberal era from 1837 to 1923, control and censorship continued to compete with freedom of expression, but politicians increasingly doubled as journalists to find an outlet for their partisan views. So common did the role of politician-journalist become that in the 1840s, thirteen former journalists held ministerial office, while in the provisional government of 1868–1869, four of the cabinet ministers were journalists. In June 1883, a new Ley de Imprenta, by introducing fines and suspension against editors and directors rather than against the papers themselves, allowed legislators to parlay their parliamentary immunity into new jobs with newspapers. Only a military career was more valuable to nineteenth-century politicians.

The largest newspapers between 1875 and 1900 were *La Correspondencia de España* and *El Imparcial*, with the latter going from 20,000 circulation to 150,000 in 1900. Altogether, 520 general newspapers were published nationally. Ideology ranged from *La Atracción* (1847), the first labor paper; *El Socialista* (1886), published by the Socialist party* (PSOE); *La Gaceta del Norte*, a Catholic paper founded in Bilbao to counter anticlericalism; *El Debate* (1910), the Catholic newspaper of Madrid, with a circulation of 150,000 by 1920; *ABC*, a monarchist daily, published in Madrid, one of the most fashionable newspapers; to *Solidaridad Obrera* (1907), the anarchist paper published in Barcelona.

*El Sol*, one of the most significant dailies, appeared in 1917. In an era of increasing national difficulty, *El Sol* provided an outlet for the modernizing ideas of the Generations of 1898* and 1927.* Initially supportive of the dictatorship of Gen. Miguel Primo de Rivera* in 1923, *El Sol* broke with the dictatorship when one of its regular columnists, Miguel de Unamuno,* was exiled in Feb. 1924. Primo gave heavy-handed treatment to dissent; newspapers from 1923 to 1930 were subjected to government control and censorship on a scale not seen since the days of Fernando VII. *El Sol* became so antigovernment that on 15 Nov. 1930, its editor, José Ortega y Gasset,* proclaimed the monarchy and dictatorship dead, and urged Spaniards to rebuild the nation. Five months later, the municipal elections were so emphatically republican that Alfonso XIII* fled the country.

Relations between the press and the Second Republic* were mercurial. The attack on *ABC*'s offices in May 1931 by an antimonarchical mob, the paper's suppression, and its editor's arrest became harbingers of the ill will between opposition newspapers and the republic over the next five years. The long-standing tension between a free press and one controlled by the party in power was quickly decided in Oct. 1931, when premier Manuel Azaña,* a former journalist and editor, secured enactment of the Ley de Defensa de la República to permit closure of papers deemed a threat to public order. The constitution approved in Dec. 1931 guaranteed a free press and no censorship, but the chilling effect of the law persisted in Article 25 and vitiated its promises.

Newspaper closures increased in frequency and duration as threats to public order became occasions for journalists to call high government officials to account. The two worst moments were the Casas Viejas incident in Jan. 1933, when the deaths of a score of peasant protestors made Azaña vulnerable to criticism; and the Asturias* uprising in Oct. 1934, when Alejandro Lerroux* faced insurrection in the north. As ideological lines increased, press freedom decreased dramatically and then disappeared altogether in the Spanish Civil War.*

*ABC* provides the most extreme case. The paper, owned by a nationalist conspirator, was seized by the republican government and controlled by left republicans from July 1936 to Feb. 1939. Other newspapers took their cue from the *ABC* example and aligned with the most powerful faction in their area. Journalism became a difficult business; shortages of paper, difficulties in repairing presses, damage to buildings, and deaths of journalists (some as political reprisals) were common.

The regime of Gen. Francisco Franco* began to plan for its postwar control of the press with a new Ley de Prensa in Apr. 1938, which remained in effect for twenty-eight years. The press was subject to total control, including pre-publication censorship and government appointment of all newspaper editors and senior staff journalists. Franco purged journalists sympathetic to the republic and replaced them with pronationalist writers. *Arriba*, the official paper of the government and the most prominent of the twenty-eight papers published by the

Movimiento, began in Madrid on 29 Mar. 1939, although there had been earlier papers in Burgos. A subsidized network of communications (including radio and television) grew until Movimiento papers numbered forty-one by 1965, usually with low circulations. While *Arriba* had a circulation of less than ten thousand, the still private *ABC* was over a hundred thousand, while the sports paper, *Marca*, had a circulation of over two hundred thousand.

This dullness came from institutionalized bureaucratic control of the press through establishment of state-approved journalism schools and then, in 1951, the creation of the Ministry of Information. Under the heavy-handed control of its ultraconservative minister, Gabriel Arias Salgado (1904– ), the new ministry made even the official papers of the church protest its unbridled censorship. Franco replaced Arias Salgado in 1962 with Manuel Fraga Iribarne* who, in Apr. 1966, issued a new press law, the Ley de Prensa e Imprenta, which ushered in a more sophisticated approach to press control. In place of an official censor, the threat of sanctions against editors made self-censorship the new mechanism of control.

By the early 1970s, journalists were regularly testing the limits of governmental control, and one group of investors in 1972 sought to found a truly independent newspaper. Their petition was not granted until after Franco's death in 1975, but when the new paper *El País* appeared on 4 May 1976, it marked a new era for the Spanish press. Finally, in Apr. 1977, two months before the first democratic elections, the government rescinded limits on press freedom altogether. The Constitution of 1978 guaranteed freedom of the press and outlawed prior censorship.

In the decade since 1978, the government has moved cautiously but firmly to dismantle the Movimiento's newspapers, beginning with *Arriba* and seven others between 1978 and 1980. In 1977, the total circulation of all state-owned papers was 450,000 and declining; all but five of the papers lost money, and the socialist government has continued slowly to close them. *El País*, on the other hand, became the largest daily in Spain, with a circulation of 348,000, while *ABC* has 240,000. In short, the Spanish press is now a responsible and free institution.

For additional information, see J. M. Desvois, *La prensa en España (1900–1931)* (Madrid, 1977); R. Graham, *Spain: A Nation Comes of Age* (New York, 1984); H. F. Schulte, *The Spanish Press, 1470–1966: Print, Power, and Politics* (Urbana, 1968); and M. Tuñón de Lara et al., *Prensa y sociedad en España (1820–1936)* (Madrid, 1975).

*D. V. Holtby*

# O

O'DONNELL Y JORIS, LEOPOLDO, DUQUE DE TETUÁN (1809–1867), general and statesman. O'Donnell was born in Tenerife, Canary Islands,* on 12 Jan. 1809. Of Jacobite stock, the family had sided with Fernando VII* and against the liberals. In 1833, O'Donnell broke with family tradition by joining the liberal side in the First Carlist War (1833–1840). He ended the war a lieutenant general with a reputation for bravery and courage that earned him the titles of conde de Lucena and vizconde de Aliaga.

Although an avid reader, he never quite mastered spelling and syntax; his lack of oratory skills was the butt of many jokes. During the Carlist War, O'Donnell married Manuela Bargés, a widow several years his senior who exerted great influence over all aspects of his life. He lived modestly, without ostentation. He was neither a gambler, as was Gen. Juan Prim y Prats,* nor a notorious womanizer, as was Gen. Ramón María Narváez.* Physically and morally, he was rara avis among Spanish soldiers and politicians.

At the end of the war, O'Donnell sided with the moderates and against Gen. Baldomero Espartero* and the ruling Progressive party.* Forced to escape to France after the abortive coup of Oct. 1841, his role in the eventual ouster of Espartero was rewarded in 1843 with the government of Cuba. His five-year administration, harsh and high-handed, fanned Cuban animosities toward Spanish rule.

For two years after his return to Spain, as director general of infantry, he reasserted his influence over the army,* especially his associates of 1841–1843. O'Donnell's open disagreements with the reactionary policies of Juan Bravo Murillo* and Luis José Sartorius (1820?–1871) led to the Vicalvarada (28 June 1854), a conservative military pronunciamento he had hoped would bring his more liberal group to power. As the revolt petered out, however, O'Donnell sought wider support and issued the Manzanares Manifesto on 7 July, promising sweeping liberal reforms. Overnight, the moderate revolt became a progressive revolution and events left O'Donnell behind. A frightened Isabel II* turned to Espartero.

From its inception, the 1854–1856 progressive bienio was in a situation of unstable equilibrium. It could expect no sympathy from the moderates or the crown and only half-hearted cooperation from O'Donnell, who bided his time at the Ministry of War. When social revolution threatened in the summer of 1856, he was quick to act forcefully with the support of the queen, whose religious scruples had been offended by the 1855 disentailment bill.

At last head of the government (14 July), O'Donnell adopted a broad policy of conciliation and liberal union. His Acta Adicional was a generous constitutional amendment intended to win over the defeated progressives. By then, though, Isabel was bent on a reactionary course and eager to be rid of the last vestiges of the "impious" bienio. By Oct., Narváez and the moderates were back in the saddle.

O'Donnell's fall was a blessing in disguise. It allowed his followers to make the Liberal Union into an effective political force capable of picking up the reins of power after the political bankruptcy of the moderates became evident. On 28 June 1858, O'Donnell began his long cabinet, the most stable government of Isabel's reign. His Liberal Union was an innovative solution to the problem of a stalemated liberal system. It gathered together progressive moderates and moderate progressives. Availing itself of the political moratorium thus created, it sought to broaden the basis of support for liberalism* by activating and modernizing Spanish society, incorporating its middle strata, heretofore excluded from political life.

Disentailment* (the sale of church and other mortmain property) was reenacted, this time with the pope's blessings. Its proceeds underwrote the 1859 Extraordinary Budget of 2 billion reales, an eight-year plan for the development of the country's infrastructure and the refurbishing of its armed forces. This massive injection of public funds into the economy* coincided with the boom in foreign investment in railroad construction and the banking and credit industries and contributed to the aura of prosperity that surrounded O'Donnell and his government.

O'Donnell paid special attention to the modernization of the army (ultimately his power basis) and the navy.* He endeavored to create an efficient modern army out of what was barely a praetorian guard and sought in military glories abroad a means of integrating the nation, a patriotic dogmatism that would make Spaniards more receptive to political action. O'Donnell's modest, homemade imperialism, Benito Pérez Galdós* claimed, refreshed the atmosphere and purged the blood corrupted by partisan bickering. Most of O'Donnell's foreign adventures—Annam, Mexico, the reannexation of Santo Domingo, the War of the Pacific with Chile and Peru—should be seen in this light, despite their ultimate sterility.

The Moroccan War of 1859–1860, on the other hand, pleased the country at large and allowed the army to regain its self-confidence in the first major foreign war since Napoleonic days. O'Donnell himself led the troops in this difficult campaign. The fall of Tetuan, which earned him a dukedom, generated a paroxysm of patriotic frenzy. His pampering of the generals made them one of the Liberal Union's most solid bulwarks.

As the giddiness of the victory began to dissipate, however, political realities again came to the fore. O'Donnell and his party were expected to reconstruct the system using, and limited by, its existing elements. The reshuffling had to be from the top down, beginning with the throne. O'Donnell would not attempt it: his conservative instincts and personal devotion to the queen forbade it. As it became increasingly apparent that Unionism thus shackled was powerless, his supporters began to defect. Compromise rather than dogmatism was the key feature of the Liberal Union. Not an abstract thinker, O'Donnell believed that by bringing men together he was accomplishing political union; all his efforts were aimed at welcoming and accommodating defectors from both parties. Promises and commitments became indispensable for the sake of lasting conciliation and a stable government; naturally, they limited O'Donnell's freedom of action without guaranteeing the converts' loyalty. Many grew tired of merely temporizing with one another and demanded action in accordance with their respective ideas. The jealousies and rivalries among Unionist chieftains were a major cause of the dissidence that plagued the Liberal Union and helped bring about its fall in Feb. 1863.

Shortly before his resignation, O'Donnell approached Prim, a leading progressive, with the proposal that they alternate in power. The queen, ever distrustful of the party of progress, had other ideas. Her refusal to summon the progressives to power pushed them into retraimiento and, eventually, revolution. The series of colorless moderate cabinets of 1863–1865 proved too weak to cope with the end of Unionist prosperity and the progressive threat. As a last resort, Isabel turned once again to O'Donnell on 21 June 1865. Seeking to conciliate the progressives, he recognized the Kingdom of Italy* over the queen's objections, granted a generous amnesty, and passed a new electoral law that almost trebled the number of electors. It was to no avail. Railing against the "traditional obstacles," the progressives persisted in retraimiento. On 3 Jan. 1866, Prim staged an abortive pronunciamento. Giving up his attempt at conciliation, O'Donnell battened down the hatches against the approaching storm; it was, he said, a matter of "either revolution or dictatorship." On 22 June, an artillery sergeants' revolt in Madrid's San Gil barracks was put down with great loss of life. O'Donnell's harsh repression only underscored his political failure.

Isabel dismissed him on 10 July, turned to Narváez, and embraced reaction. A wounded O'Donnell promised never to serve the queen again and went into self-imposed exile in France.* Despite pressures from his own followers in the army, O'Donnell refused to join Prim's revolutionary efforts. He would lend his name to a movement against the regime only if a satisfactory replacement could be found for the "traditional obstacles" the revolution had determined to sweep away. He believed that Isabel's abdication in favor of the future Alfonso XII* would be the only solution. Leaving aside the thorny question of the regency the new king would require, though, there remained the impossibility of persuading the queen to abdicate.

O'Donnell's Liberal Union was the only political force that could have saved the throne. While he lived and remained loyal to the queen and her dynasty, the Unionist generals dared not move against Isabel. On 5 Nov. 1867, however, typhus and death overtook him in Biarritz. His death removed the last barrier to understanding between the Liberal Union and the progressives, which guaranteed the success of the September Revolution of 1868.

For additional information, see N. Durán, *La Unión Liberal y la modernización de España isabelina* (Madrid, 1979); M. Ibo Alfaro, *Apuntes para la historia de D. Leopoldo O'Donnell* (Madrid, 1868); F. Melgar, conde de Melgar, *O'Donnell* (Madrid, 1946); and C. Navarro y Rodrigo, *O'Donnell y su tiempo* (Madrid, 1869).

N. Durán

*Related entry*: LIBERALISM.

**OPUS DEI,** conservative religious order officially known as the Prelature of the Holy Cross and Opus Dei. Opus Dei was founded on 2 Oct. 1928, by a young priest, Fr. Josémaría Escrivá de Balaguer y Albás,* who three years after his ordination, while on a religious retreat, was inspired to create a new Catholic lay organization to defend the church. He later argued that the objective of Opus Dei was to help ordinary people lead a Christian life in the secular world without drastic modification of their professional or social obligations.

From 1928 to 1936, Opus Dei broadened its ranks to include women as well as men, and developed a worldwide network of corporate activities and institutions designed to educate, train, and provide Catholic spiritual formation. In the ideological climate of the 1930s, however, revival of Catholic influence was controversial. The movement was portrayed either as a neoconservative and reactionary Catholic religio-political movement on the right or as a form of traditional Catholicism blended with an American "success" formula. Even older religious orders reacted negatively when the movement continued to grow at their expense. Eventually, it found favor with Gen. Francisco Franco* and his wife, Carmen (1902–1987), in the nationalist zone during the Spanish Civil War.*

In the postwar period, not surprisingly, some of Franco's cabinet ministers were drawn from the Opus Dei membership. Laureano López Rodó (1920– ) best typified this new generation of devout, technocratic civil servants, but the Matesa scandal of 1969 illustrated the difficulties of combining the work of church and state. Matesa, a textile company, had been a creditor of the Industrial Credit Bank, a government agency. Three Opus Dei economics ministers became implicated in a scheme to illegally and privately invest abroad funds diverted from the loan; two were subsequently convicted in July 1970. Opus was attacked by members of Franco's cabinet such as Manuel Fraga Iribarne,* who accused it of corruption. The publicity made the organization appear to be a far right-wing group of manipulators, and there is no question that the incident badly damaged the Opus Dei's political status in Spain.

By 1988, nevertheless, the Opus Dei's corporate activities have mushroomed to include many new centers, academies, colleges, and a university that educates and trains students in agricultural, vocational, technical, and academic areas, with a strong religious emphasis. All the centers focus on Catholic doctrine and celebrate religious retreats, days of recollection, and other spiritual activities. There are three categories of Opus institutions: adult technical training centers or trade schools, conference centers, and collegiate-level colleges and universities, each with a different approach. The most prestigious Opus institution of higher learning is the University of Navarre that Escrivá founded in Pamplona in 1952. As a major university, it has earned a reputation in church history, theology, philosophy, international law, and journalism. There are other Opus universities at Piura, Peru, and La Sabana, Colombia.

Despite this success, the legal status of Opus Dei within the church remained confused for some time. The 1917 Code of Canon Law made no allowance for a secular organization of such deep religious obligations. Escrivá insisted that Opus Dei always remained obedient to local bishops and the pope, although there was little acceptance of this until the bishop of Madrid on 19 Mar. 1941 made Opus Dei into a "pious union," or special lay association, permitted by canon law. The Vatican, on 8 Dec. 1943, gave approval to the formation of the Priestly Society of the Holy Cross for the ordination of Opus Dei clergy, but no priests could be taken from diocesan or regular clergy already ordained. In 1944, the first three members of the Priestly Society of the Holy Cross were ordained, and today there are more than a thousand priests affiliated with the organization.

Final resolution of the Opus's ecclesiastical position in the church evolved between 1946 and 1983. The movement needed a juridical clarification of its status to obtain ecclesiastical authority beyond the boundaries of the Madrid diocese; one that would not place limitations upon the movement like those of secular institutes whose members take vows of poverty, chastity, and obedience. The Opus Dei has no such permanent vows, since they might hamper secular activities. To seek a final resolution, Fr. Álvaro del Portillo (1914– ) was sent to Rome in 1946, and Escrivá joined him a year later. On 16 June 1950, the Vatican finally permitted the Opus to operate internationally. This decision was ratified by the Second Vatican Council and incorporated in a new code of canon law signed by Pope John Paul II (1920– ) on 25 Jan. 1983, which made the Opus Dei into a personal prelature of the pope. The Prelature of the Holy Cross and Opus Dei formally inaugurated its new headquarters at the Basilica of Santo Eugenio in Rome on 19 Mar. 1983.

The movement thus continued to grow and establish itself. Escrivá died on 26 June 1975 and was succeeded by Álvaro, one of the three original priests ordained by the Priestly Society of the Holy Cross in 1944. The Opus Dei today has a membership of 75,000 in eighty countries, but since the death of Franco, its influence in Spanish affairs has declined.

For additional information, see P. Berglar, *Opus Dei: Vida y obra del fundador Josémaría Escrivá de Balaguer* (Madrid, 1987); Dominique Le Tourneau, *What Is Opus Dei?* (New York, 1975); J. J. Thierry, *Opus Dei: A Close Up* (New York, 1975); and A. Saez Alba, *La otra 'Cosa Nostra,' La Asociación Católica de Propagandistas* (Madrid, 1974).

*P. Foley*

*Related entries*: CATHOLICISM; ESCRIVÁ DE BALAGUER, JOSÉMARÍA; PAPACY.

**O'REILLY, ALEJANDRO DE, CONDE DE O'REILLY** (1723–1794), lieutenant general of the army.* Born of Irish nobility, O'Reilly immigrated to Spain while a child. He began his military career as a cadet in the Regiment of Hibernia, seeing action in Italy* from 1734 to 1736 and 1740 to 1748. Wounds received at the battle of Camposanto left him with a permanent limp. Later attached to the Austrian and French armies to study tactics, he was promoted to colonel upon the personal recommendation of Louis XV (1710–1774). Distinguished service in the Portuguese theater during the Seven Years' War* led to his promotions to brigadier and to field marshal.

In 1763, O'Reilly accompanied an expedition to Cuba to assist in reclaiming Havana from the British, restore the colonial army, and raise a disciplined militia. The model he established for militia organization was eventually extended to much of the empire. He also drafted a report on political and economic conditions that contributed to the 1765 royal decision to open the Caribbean island trade to most of the major ports of Spain. His work in Cuba completed, O'Reilly was ordered to Puerto Rico to reorganize the military and study political and economic conditions. After a return to Spain, where he drafted the army ordinances of 1768, he was sent to Louisiana to crush the insurrection that had ousted Spanish rule. Firmly establishing control through military force, he went on to issue comprehensive regulations for the future governance of the colony.

Upon O'Reilly's return to Spain, his career reached its zenith. Promoted to lieutenant general, he was named inspector general of the army of America in 1770 to coordinate the military preparations in connection with the Falkland (Malvinas) Islands crisis (1770–1771). From this position, he extended the military reform to Santo Domingo and New Granada. A favorite of Carlos III* and Jerónimo Grimaldi (1720–1776), he acquired his title of nobility, became governor of Madrid, and founded the Military Academy of Avila for the infantry.

O'Reilly's star waned when he failed as commander of the 1775 expedition to punish the Dey of Algiers. The public outcry forced Carlos to remove him to Cadiz, naming him captain general, a post he held until 1786. During the War of American Independence (1779–1783), this appointment enabled him to continue the work he had begun in America as he directed the dispatch to Havana of the Army of Operations, which helped reconquer Florida. He made peace with his old enemy Pedro Abarca y Bolea, the conde de Aranda,* to overthrow José Moñino, the conde de Floridablanca,* in 1792 but gained little. He died on 23 Mar. 1794.

For additional information, see A. J. Kuethe, *Cuba, 1753–1815: Crown, Military, and Society* (Knoxville, 1986); and B. Torres Ramírez, *Alejandro O'Reilly en las Indias* (Seville, 1969).

                                                                    *A. J. Kuethe*

**ORTEGA Y GASSET, JOSÉ** (1883–1955), essayist, philosopher, critic, and a prominent member of the Generation of 1898.* Ortega, born on 9 May 1883, was the second of four children of José Ortega Munilla, a popular novelist with strong ties to the followers of Karl Christian Friedrich Krause* and editor of the *Los Lunes*, the literary supplement of *El Imparcial*. Despite the Krausist connections, José and his brother were sent to a Jesuit boarding school near Malaga, an experience that Ortega remembered as one of indoctrination rather than education and that became an element in his exaggerated Dewey-like ideas on the subject. He then enrolled at the Jesuit University of Deuesto, where he remained one year. After brilliantly passing an examination at the University of Salamanca before a panel that included Miguel de Unamuno,* he enrolled at the University of Madrid in 1898, receiving his doctorate in philosophy in 1904. A year later, he left for Berlin, then went on to the University of Marburg. Before returning to Spain in 1908, steeped in neo-Kantianism, Ortega had seriously studied Greek, Latin, and German culture. That same year, he obtained his first teaching position, followed two years later, at age twenty-seven, by his appointment to the chair of metaphysics at the University of Madrid.

Ortega now set upon his lifelong task of raising the intellectual level of Spain by publishing serious journals; the weekly *El Faro* in 1908, a mouthpiece for the Generation of 1898; and *Europa* in 1910, revealing by its title his strong Europeanizing tendencies and thus his break with Unamuno. Each journal lasted only a year, but Ortega went on to organize the League for Political Education, which also lasted a year, though its principles were carried on in a new journal, *España*, that he started in 1915 and directed during its first eight years. *El Espectador*, an annual written totally by him, developed a large readership and lasted from 1916 to 1934. He also wrote extensively for *El Imparcial* until 1917, when his support for Catalan officers who had formed committees of defense in the army* made him join the more liberal and influential *El Sol*, edited by Nicolás María Urgoiti (1869–1951). When the latter became one of the owners of the newly formed and prestigious Espasa-Calpe publishing house, Ortega was put in charge of its "Biblioteca de Ideas del Siglo XX." In 1923, he also started the famous *Revista de Occidente*, which survives today after an interruption caused by the Spanish Civil War.*

Politically, Ortega initially sympathized with socialism, since he believed that it would bring the rise of a true aristocracy of talent, as defined in *The Revolt of the Masses* (1930), something that could not occur under capitalism. He never joined a socialist party, however, choosing instead to enroll in the Republican party in 1912. Indeed, he saw Marxism, with its basis in class struggle, as irrelevant in a land like Spain where all classes were relatively poor. In any case, he later included the concept of revolution within a theory of cultural cycles obviously influenced by Oswald Spengler (1880–1936). Ultimately, he lost his enthusiasm for socialism, which he felt used culture for its own purposes and thus threatened to falsify it. For Ortega, as for Ernest Renan (1823–1892), whom he admired, culture is the very manifestation of human progress from the lower levels of being and thus cannot be subsidiary to an economic system.

Ortega cultivated a European viewpoint long before he began to acquire an international reputation, thanks to the *Nouvelle Revue Française*, which in 1923 published an article of his. In 1911, his criticism of Italy* for its conquest of Libya became a cause célèbre. During World War I,* he remained neutral, wishing other intellectuals would do the same, but in "The Genius of War" (1916) and "La interpretación bélica de la historia," (1919) he made it clear that he was not a pacifist. In *Invertebrate Spain* (1921) and *The Modern Theme* (1923) he used a European viewpoint to discuss Spain, since his political outlook was doubtlessly affected by World War I and the founding of the League of Nations, as well as the military rebellion and general strike of 1917. In these works, he voices some of the same complaints previously uttered by the Generation of 1898 with words like casticismo and abulia, but he does so in his own terms, partly influenced by Spengler.

Although Ortega, unlike other intellectuals such as Unamuno, appears to have flourished under the Gen. Miguel Primo de Rivera* dictatorship, he circumscribed his political criticism and activity until 1928, when an article evincing his new championship of partial regional autonomy was censored. In 1924, *La deshumanización del arte* appeared, and *El Sol* began to print the several parts of *Ideas sobre la novela*. In 1928, he was invited to Buenos Aires for a series of lectures; he returned to Madrid the next year in time to join several of his colleagues in resigning their chairs when the dictatorship closed the universities. Ortega then arranged to offer the rest of his course in several theaters. The lectures were well attended, by students as well as by other protesters and intellectuals, which made him even more of a celebrity. On 1 Feb. 1930, the government of Gen. Dámaso Berenguer* restored the professors to their posts, but by then Ortega had become a convinced republican. His use of the phrase "Delenda est monarchia" at the end of some political articles brought enough pressure on *El Sol* to persuade him to leave it for *Crisol*, likewise financed by Nicolás María Urgoiti of the Espasa-Calpe publishing house, which followed the principles of the Group at the Service of the Republic, led by Antonio Machado.* The manifesto of this group was written by Gregorio Marañón (1887–1960), Ortega, and Ramón Pérez de Ayala.* Of the fourteen seats it obtained in the elections for a constituent assembly after the fall of the monarchy, Ortega won two, one of which he then resigned. For a time, he was very active in politics, especially in support of Catalan regional autonomy, but disappointment with the course of affairs eventually set in and he dissolved the Group at the Service of the Republic.

With the coming of the Spanish Civil War, Ortega emigrated to France* with his family. Because of illness, he declined an invitation to Harvard University, but later went on a lecture tour of Dutch universities at the invitation of historian Johan Huizinga (1872–1945). He lived in Paris, Vichy, Lisbon, and Argentina, returning to Spain in 1945. Though officially restored to his university chair in 1946, he did not resume his teaching. Instead, in 1948 he and Julián Marías (1914– ) founded the Instituto de Humanidades, where Ortega occasionally lectured, until it was closed by Gen. Francisco Franco* in 1950. A series of lectures in Germany in 1949, especially one at the Free University of Berlin on the cultural integrity of Europe, won him enthusiastic audiences, but a second tour, four years later, is generally considered to have been a failure.

For Ortega, the university was not merely a vehicle for his ideas. He viewed it as the center of intellectual activity and the nucleus for intellectual regeneration. In his *Idea of the University*, he sought a central liberal curriculum, free of the technical specialization that could be imparted by other institutions. He thus proposed a core of five disciplines: physics, biology, history, sociology, and philosophy.

It may be surprising at first that the author of *Ideas of the Novel*, *The Dehumanization of Art*, "Sobre el punto de vista en las artes," "Meditición del marco," *Papeles sobre Velázquez y Goya*, *Velázquez*, *Idea del teatro*, "Azorín: primores de lo vulgar," "Apatía artística," " ¿Qué pasa en el mundo?," and many other works on literature, the plastic arts, and even music, would fail to assign to the arts their own place in this curriculum. Nevertheless, literary theory at the time had not yet succeeded in making a good case for the centrality of the arts in its own formulations. Though Ortega, qua critic, admired works of art as microcosms, he was, qua philosopher, wary of subjectivity. In *The Dehumanization of Art*, his approach is historiographic and sociological, and in *Ideas on the Novel*, historiographic and psychological. As he was drawn to classicism, his aesthetics contained a great deal of the neoclassic (he saw *Don Quixote* [1605;1615] in terms of tragedy and comedy) and exhibited a wariness of nineteenth-century realism, such as his ongoing annoyance with the art of Pío Baroja.* He was likewise made uneasy by what he perceived as the influence of decadence and even symbolism in Spanish poetry.

*The Revolt of the Masses* is doubtlessly Ortega's best-known work. Because of its brilliant use of similes and splendidly justified etymology, it has attained the literary stature that all great essays fully deserve. Not surprisingly, historiographers find it highly rhetorical and thus approach it with caution. Western civilization is threatened by hyperdemocracy, which caters to the tastes of the mass man who is not bothered by the fact that he thinks like everyone else, the opposite of the intellectual whose questioning nature may encourage him to become a true aristocrat if he makes himself into a leader. The influence of Spengler is considerable here and elsewhere, perhaps even on Ortega's interest in Gottfried Leibnitz (1646–1716), for it was Spengler who attempted to classify historical epochs according to the progress of mathematics, and Ortega perceived the unavoidable connection between Leibnitz the mathematician and Leibnitz the philosopher.

Indeed, it is in the philosophical essay that Ortega is most felicitous, for the course of his philosophical development is of more enduring interest than his immediate reaction to historical events. Once his studies in Germany had allowed him to shake off the early influence of Friedrich Nietzsche (1844–1900), the neo-Kantian idealism learned in Marburg began to assert itself. It was not long, though, before he introduced his countrymen to Edmund Husserl's (1859–1938) phenomenology, from which he would soon distance himself. In *Meditations on "Quixote"* (the book that earned him renown in Spain), we sense a trend toward biologism and vitalism necessary for the expression of his perspectivist ideas. Ortega's belief that Spaniards needed to acquire the kind of conceptual ability found in the German mind in order to supplement Mediterranean sensuality led him to formulate his own philosophy of ratiovitalism. At first, he dwelt on biologism and vitalism in order to reject idealism. He perceived the difficulty of approaching consciousness simultaneously through the subject and the object, because of the threefold relation—presence, absence, and reference—between them. By emphasizing perspectivism, he insisted on the relativism of reality. Ratiovitalism finds a middle ground between the two extremes of rationalism and relativism by positing reason as a sixth sense, a necessity of human life differentiating mankind from animals. Accordingly, human life manifests a tension between the purely biological and the spiritual. Moreover, the hierarchic classification of reality, informed by our own estimative faculties and those of our fellow humans, emanates from the spiritual aspect of our nature.

A look back at Ortega's career shows that his influence spread far beyond his country and his times. Always committed to the intellectual renovation of a backward Spain, Ortega is the model of a true humanist. In tackling any topic, he used to the fullest a thorough knowledge of philosophy, especially the role of language in the concept of the self in relation to society. It often allowed him to begin the discussion of a topic with an etymological and semantic focus on the accepted terms in which it had been traditionally presented. Thus, when he asked how something that lasted eight hundred years could be called a reconquest, Ortega showed his willingness to reexamine the very foundation of Spanish historiography. Because of his partial repudiation of Unamuno, however, he avoided the exploration of intrahistoria, minimizing also the importance of Semitic elements of Hispanic culture, for he held that the type of German people who settled in Spain (the Goths rather than the Franks) were more important in determining the Spanish character than the Moorish invasion. Had Ortega faced this problem squarely, as did Américo Castro (1885–1972), he would have been more cogent in his attempt to recreate a historiography with elements he picked and modified out of Spengler. It is true that Ortega, like Castro, was also influenced by Wilhelm Dilthey (1833–1911). Unlike Unamuno, though, Ortega was a europeísta, eager to see Spain modernized politically and economically so that it could eventually join the rest of Europe. Accordingly, he attempted to instill in his compatriots an intellectual discipline that would emulate the search of German philosophy for methodical ratiocination. At the same time, by demonstrating the dynamic and creative relation existing among beliefs, doubts, and ideas, Ortega sought to overcome the somewhat romantic encouragement of the deleterious doubting attitude that permeated the writings of Unamuno and other members of the previous generation. This was the origin of his desire to replace with a strong sense of discipline the struggle with faith and accepted values so typical of the latter.

For additional information, see J. W. Díaz, *The Major Themes of Existentialism in the Work of José Ortega y Gasset* (Chapel Hill, 1970); J. Ferrater Mora, *José Ortega y Gasset: An Outline of His Philosophy*, 2d. ed. (New Haven, 1963); J. F. Lalcona, *El idealismo político de Ortega y Gasset* (Madrid, 1974); R. McClintock, *Man and His Circumstances: Ortega as Educator* (New York, 1971); C. Morón Arroyo, *El sistema de Ortega y Gasset* (Madrid, 1968); V. Ouimette, *José Ortega y Gasset* (Boston, 1982); and P. W. Silver, *Ortega as Phenomenologist: The Genesis of "Meditations on Quixote"* (New York, 1978).

*P. L. Ullman*

*Related entries*: GENERATION OF 1898; GENERATION OF 1927; UNAMUNO, MIGUEL DE.

# P

**PAPACY,** relations with Spain. For most of its modern history, Spain has been an officially Catholic state maintaining formal diplomatic links with the papacy. Relations between Madrid and Rome have been close, but rarely straightforward and comfortable. More often than not, the relationship has been complex and difficult. On occasion, it has been hostile. This situation developed, in part, from the ambiguous position of the papacy itself with respect to the Spanish government and church. Until 1870, the pope functioned as a temporal ruler over a central Italian state frequently involved in European diplomatic struggles. His role as a secular Italian ruler inevitably produced conflicts with Spanish governments moved by their own strong perceptions of their national interest. At the same time, the pope served as the spiritual and ecclesiastical head of the Spanish church, a position that involved more than providing moral leadership. How far papal control extended over clerical appointments and church revenues was a perennial source of contention between Madrid and Rome, particularly during the eighteenth century.

In the long history of Spanish relations with the papacy, there is no question that the period of Bourbon absolutism between 1700 and 1808 was among the most conflictive. The points at issue were many and varied. Some were directly political, such as the total break in diplomatic relations (1709) initiated by Felipe V* in reprisal for Pope Clement XI's (1649–1721) recognition of the Hapsburg pretender to the throne during the War of Spanish Succession.* In the course of prolonged diplomatic jousting, the king ordered the expulsion of the nuncio and the appropriation of certain ecclesiastical revenues falling under papal jurisdiction.

Such direct political conflicts, however, were secondary to a larger struggle involving the temporal administration of the Spanish church. At one level, this was a simple battle over who would control an immense apparatus of clerical patronage and the revenues that accompanied it. It has been estimated that fifty thousand benefices existed within the eighteenth-century Spanish church. Appointment to thirty thousand of these, and they tended to be the least lucrative, were given to lay patrons. The right to name incumbents to the remaining benefices rested historically with the papacy, which maintained a special agency, the Dataria, to process the claims of Spaniards wishing to hold such positions. This service, naturally, did not come cheaply, as Rome derived a handsome income from these appointment prerogatives.

Given the importance of patronage in any form for the functioning of the early modern European state and the financial resources involved, Catholic monarchs everywhere sought to strip the papacy of its traditional appointment rights. What is surprising is that Spanish kings were less successful than their counterparts in France* and Portugal* in achieving this objective. Fernando and Isabel had secured the right (universal patronage) to appoint to virtually all benefices, save those falling under lay patronage, in the kingdom of Granada and in the Spanish overseas dominions. The Hapsburgs also had obtained the right of "presentation," that is, the privilege of nominating candidates for bishoprics to the pope, who retained, however, the ultimate power of confirmation. During the reign of Felipe IV (1621–1665), a serious but unsuccessful effort was undertaken to persuade the pope to concede the right of universal patronage over those benefices in the rest of Spain traditionally granted by Rome.

The eighteenth-century Bourbons inherited the historic preoccupation of the Spanish crown with extending its control over ecclesiastical patronage. They approached the task with grim, persistent determination. In the Concordats of 1717 and 1737, the papacy fended off royal pressure for expanded patronage rights. Thanks to the diplomatic skills of Manuel Ventura de Figueroa, legal counselor of the Spanish embassy in Rome, timely bribes delivered to officials of the papal curia, and the temporizing nature of Pope Benedict XIV (1740–1758), the crown finally wrested the concession of universal patronage from the papacy in the Concordat of 1753. Opinion at the royal court correctly welcomed it as a major triumph for the monarchy over the papacy. Some royal officials were so carried away by the euphoria of the moment that they compared the concordat's historical importance to that of the Reconquista, the great medieval crusade that had driven the Moors from Spain.

At another level, however, the long campaign to secure the unfettered right to appoint to the vast majority of benefices not falling under lay patronage was more than just a struggle over money and jobs. It represented a sustained attempt by successive monarchs aided and abetted by regalist bureaucrats to assert total control over the administration of the Spanish church save in matters of doctrine. And on occasion, the crown was not averse to becoming involved in doctrinal controversies with Rome. Whether the eighteenth-century Bourbons intended creating a Spanish national church, a Catholic version of what Henry VIII (1491–1547) had established in Britain during the Reformation, is dubious. Neither monarchs nor their ministers ever denied the primacy of the pope, although some royal officials wished to circumscribe papal authority in ways completely unacceptable to Rome. The Bourbons, however, did attempt to create a royal church that, in practical terms, meant control over its personnel, finances, and internal discipline.

The aggressive regalist policies of the Bourbons and their bureaucracy clearly implied a reduction in papal authority over the Spanish church. This led inevitably to periodic conflicts with the papacy, although the struggle waxed and waned according to circumstances. An early controversy developed over a document, the *Memorial de los 53 Puntos* (1713), written by the attorney general of the Council of Castile, Melchor de Macanaz (1670–1760), who vigorously attacked the abuses suffered by the Spanish church at the hands of Rome and stoutly defended royal demands for greater powers over ecclesiastical appointments. Although initially disposed to defend his minister before a vigorous counterattack launched by the Inquisition, the king decided against a direct confrontation, but at the price of sacrificing his audaciously regalist minister.

Later monarchs were more determined, especially during the reign of Carlos III* (1759–1788), who had received a thoroughly regalist education as king of Naples before assuming the Spanish throne. A series of controversies involving the complex issue of Jansenism brought relations between Rome and Madrid to a low ebb early in the new reign. Although the dispute had doctrinal overtones, it was primarily a clash over the extent of papal authority over the Spanish church. Pope Clement XIII's (1693–1796) condemnation (1761) of a work, the *Catechism* of Mésenguy, which had attacked the Jesuits and questioned certain aspects of papal authority, received a violent reception in the Bourbon courts of Italy and Spain.

The king riposted with a Pragmatic Sanction (18 Jan. 1762) imposing the *exequatur*, a formal prohibition against the publication in Spain of any papal brief or bull until it had received royal authorization, a measure defended on the grounds that it was "an inalienable regalian right" of the crown. Although the king subsequently removed the exequatur, it revealed how far the crown was prepared to go in asserting its supremacy over ecclesiastical affairs.

By the early 1770s, the Spanish monarchy had secured its position vis-à-vis Rome to the point that, in 1773, it was able to pressure a reluctant Pope Clement XIV (1705–1774) to suppress the Jesuits, already expelled from Spain in 1767 because of their perceived opposition to the enlightened absolutism of Carlos III. Through the 1780s and early 1790s, periodic skirmishes took place between Rome and Madrid, although the outbreak of the French Revolution and the later French invasion of Italy imposed a truce of sorts. Toward the end of the revolutionary decade, the reform-minded ministry of Mariano Luis Urquijo (1768–1817), lasting from 1798 to 1800, embarked on another regalist offensive to take advantage of the humiliating captivity of Pope Pius VI carried out by the French Directory and of the vacuum created in Rome by the pope's death in 1799. The government ordered that matrimonial dispensations previously the prerogative of Rome would now be granted by the Spanish bishops and that the king should provide official confirmation of new bishops on a temporary basis, thus denying the papacy one of its traditional rights. Although the fall of Urquijo in 1800 led to the decree's abrogation, the monarchy of Carlos IV* under the direction of Manuel Godoy* was prepared to take whatever advantage it could of the papacy's abasement at the hands of the French to enlarge its control over the Spanish church.

These later conflicts were carried on as if nothing had changed in Europe. The upheaval caused by the French Revolution, however, and later by Napoleon was transforming the rules of the game. For both the Spanish monarchy and the papacy, jurisdictional conflicts and the struggle over money and patronage began to recede before a simple struggle for survival. As Europe emerged from the long years of the revolutionary and Napoleonic wars and the dramatic social and political changes that accompanied them, Rome and Madrid entered another phase in their relations in which new, although equally difficult, questions had to be resolved.

None of these was more fundamental than the situation of the Spanish church under liberalism.* Although it inherited its ideas on ecclesiastical reform from the regalists of the eighteenth century, liberalism approached the issue of the church from a newer point of view that emphasized a sharper distinction between the civil and ecclesiastical powers than had been characteristic of absolute monarchy. Suppression of the Inquisition (1813) by the liberal Cortes of Cadiz* revealed a strong commitment to the supremacy of civil authority in its relations with the church.

An ambitious program of ecclesiastical reform advanced during the liberal triennium (1820–1823) produced serious conflicts with Pope Pius VII in the period from 1800 to 1823. Although he defended his powers in the confirmation of bishops and resisted an attempt to alter Spain's ecclesiastical organization, the pope approached the task in a different way than his eighteenth-century predecessors. He was less concerned with protecting papal jurisdiction for its own sake than with defending the Spanish church before the uncertainties created by the liberal revolution. Wishing to secure for the Spanish church the best terms possible in a time of dramatic political change, he followed a policy of moderation even at the cost of accepting unpalatable reforms, including the closure of one-half of the kingdom's monasteries and convents. Relations between Madrid and Rome were anything but comfortable during this period, particularly during the more radical phase of the liberal revolution, when a total diplomatic break initiated by Madrid occurred in 1823.

The pope's commitment to defending the Spanish church as best he could before liberal reforms feared by many of the clergy marked a turning point in the relationship between the papacy and the Spanish government. Eighteenth-century regalism had enjoyed considerable support among bishops and priests, whose anti-Romanism was often as strong as that of royal bureaucrats. Although some priests, such as Joaquín Lorenzo Villanueva (1757–1837) and Cardinal de Borbón (1777–1823) of Toledo, remained committed to the regalist tradition, most of the bishops and priests now looked to the papacy to defend clerical interests. By assuming the role of protector of the Spanish clergy, Rome acquired a valuable ally in its dealings with Madrid. In these circumstances, the old Bourbon idea of a royal or national church, still espoused by some liberals, could never be realized.

None of this was particularly evident when liberalism secured its final triumph over the old absolutist order beginning in 1834. On the contrary, government ecclesiastical legislation between 1834 and 1843 dealt a shattering blow to the traditional organizational and financial base of the church through the suppression of most of the male religious orders; the sale of their property as well as that of the secular clergy; the abolition of the tithe; and, from 1840 to 1843 during the regency of Gen. Baldomero Espartero,* a concerted attempt to reduce papal authority in Spain to the purely ceremonial. Before this ecclesiastical revolution imposed by liberalism, the Spanish church was thrown into disarray. It looked increasingly to the papacy of Pope Gregory XVI in the period from 1831 to 1846 for defense against the liberal onslaught. Although in practical terms there was little the pope could do, his vigorous attacks (1836, 1841) on liberal religious policy and the moral support he provided the Spanish church in its time of trial reinforced the loyalty of the clergy toward Rome. Relations between successive liberal governments and the papacy became increasingly hostile, in part because under Austrian pressure the pope refused to recognize Isabel II* as the kingdom's legitimate sovereign over the claims of Carlos, brother of Fernando VII.* By 1843, relations between Madrid and Rome could not have been worse.

That an accommodation was finally reached in 1851 with the concordat that would govern church-state relations until 1931 was the result of several circumstances. Political changes in Spain saw the most conservative liberals gathered in the Moderate party* come to power in 1843, thus opening the road to conciliation. The Moderates, who had an oligarchic view of politics and feared a popular revolution, saw the church as a possible ally in their efforts to build a socially and politically conservative regime. The election of Pope Pius IX (1846–1878), who early in his reign viewed liberalism with less hostility than his predecessor, also facilitated an accommodation. Papal recognition of Isabel II as queen of Spain in 1848 removed an important roadblock in the way of an agreement. Moreover, the massive resistance of the clergy to the Espartero regency's scheme for a national church made clear that a unilateral ecclesiastical settlement imposed by the liberal state had become impossible.

Long and difficult negotiations for a new concordat began in 1844. Although successive moderate ministries desired an agreement, they had no intention of abandoning the traditional regalian rights enjoyed by Spanish governments over the church, because they feared being accused of selling out to Rome by the opposition progressives. The pope, in turn, was determined to secure an adequate financial settlement for the Spanish clergy, whose economic situation had deteriorated badly following the sale of ecclesiastical lands.

The Concordat of 1851 amounted to a pragmatic deal between the moderates and the papacy rather than a sincere reconciliation between the civil and ecclesiastical powers. The government secured recognition of the monarchy's historic regalian rights in episcopal appointments and obtained papal acceptance of the sale of church property carried out until this time. It also won Rome's support for a limited reform of Spain's archaic diocesan and parish organization. In return, it formally acknowledged the church as the established church of the state and committed itself to paying the salaries of the bishops and the parochial clergy through the national budget.

The government gave little away in the concordat save, perhaps, a commitment to avoid further anticlerical legislation that the moderates were not about to undertake in any event. By recognizing the official status of the church and agreeing to pay clerical salaries, Madrid simply confirmed what every liberal government since 1834 had pledged, although not always fulfilled. The concordat, however, remained an ambiguous document. Rome and the Spanish clergy interpreted it as a specific commitment by the government to make Spain a thoroughly Catholic state through subsequent legislation and administrative action in the areas of censorship, education, and the regulation of public morality. The Moderates, however, saw the concordat in much narrower terms as an essentially political arrangement designed to win clerical support for the conservative regime they were constructing. They were unwilling, for example, to authorize a massive reintroduction of the male religious orders, even though an ambiguous clause in the concordat might have allowed them to justify such a concession to the church.

What the papacy gained from the concordat was explicit recognition that the liberal state, at least when dominated by the more conservative elements, would not undertake to resolve ecclesiastical questions unilaterally as it had more or less done since 1834. Henceforth, ecclesiastical disputes arising from the terms of the concordat had to be settled through formal negotiations between Madrid and Rome. In practical terms, this meant that the papacy now formally represented the collective interests of the Spanish church and its clergy before the government.

As a result of the Concordat of 1851, relations between Madrid and Rome were generally amicable until the Revolution of 1868, although there were periodic bouts of tension. The semiauthoritarian government of Gen. Ramón Narváez,* lasting from 1866 to 1868, for instance, refused to authorize publication of Pius IX's celebrated indictment of liberalism, the *Syllabus of Errors*. It was also unwilling to make more than token gestures to defend the papacy's temporal power in spite of the clamors of Catholic opinion for active intervention against the Kingdom of Italy, which was in the final stages of its campaign against the Papal States.

The climate of accommodation created by the Concordat of 1851 disappeared during the revolutionary periods from 1854 to 1856 and 1868 to 1873, when relations between Spanish governments and the papacy deteriorated. The decision of the progressive government in 1854 to resume selling whatever church lands remained unsold produced strong tensions, as did the establishment of full religious liberty for the first time in the nation's history in the Constitution of 1869.

Upon the end of the revolutionary period and the reestablishment of the constitutional monarchy that would endure until 1923, relations between the Vatican and Madrid became stable and relatively accommodating. Antonio Cánovas del Castillo,* architect of the Restoration settlement, early announced government support for the 1851 concordat, which had lapsed, to all intents and purposes, during the revolutionary period. The Constitution of 1876 explicitly recognized the official status of the church, although Pius IX objected strenuously to Article 11, in which the state pledged that no one would be prosecuted for his or her private religious beliefs. In the end, the papacy grudgingly accepted the article, although its interpretation would remain a matter of debate.

Relations between Restoration ministries and the papacy were not always smooth, although they generally remained civil. After 1900, however, they became more difficult. The Liberal party, with its tradition of mild anticlericalsim and a stronger commitment to upholding the state's regalian rights in ecclesiastical affairs, wished to impose limits on the growth of the religious orders, which had proliferated by the turn of the century, and to implement the administrative reorganization of the church called for in the 1851 concordat. The liberal government of Práxedes Mateo Sagasta,* lasting from 1901 to 1902, attempted to renegotiate the concordat's terms. A draft revision produced by the marqués de Terverga in 1902 for the cabinet became the basis for fruitless negotiations with Pope Pius X (1835–1914). Although the papacy was willing to make some concessions in the direction of administrative changes, it refused significant compromise on the question of the religious orders. The Vatican, indeed, saw itself called to defend the regular clergy under its interpretation of the 1851 concordat. In 1904, the conservative government of Antonio Maura* managed to reach a limited agreement with the papacy on the religious orders. This convenio, although imposing some restrictions by suppressing communities having fewer than twelve members and by requiring government approval for the establishment of new orders, aroused the fierce opposition of the liberals and never received parliamentary approval.

Controversy over the Convenio of 1904 reflected a broader conflict over the place of an established church within an increasingly secular and pluralistic society. Powerful figures within the Liberal party saw the terms of the Concordat of 1851 as anachronistic and demanded that the church's official privileges be curtailed, while republicans strongly reaffirmed their historic commitment to the outright separation of church and state. The efforts of José Canalejas y Méndez (1854–1912), prime minister from 1910 to 1912, to restrain the growth of the regular clergy and interpret Article 11 of the constitution as generously as possible in the direction of religious toleration created renewed tension with Rome. No significant changes in the concordat were ever introduced, though, either during the later Restoration or the dictatorship of Gen. Miguel Primo de Rivera* from 1923 to 1930.

The papacy successfully defended the church and the clergy from any diminution of their legal and financial rights as defined in the 1851 concordat. Whether this uncompromising policy was wise is another matter. The revival of anti-clericalism on several fronts after the turn of the century and its potentially dislocating effects on the country's political stability were recognized by the Liberal party in its desire to negotiate a modification of the church's privileged situation. Enormous social and economic changes in early twentieth-century Spain contained dangerous implications for the church, but neither the clergy nor the papacy was willing to adjust to these new realities through a revised concordat carried out within the regalist framework that long had governed relations between the Vatican and Madrid.

Establishment of the Second Republic* in 1931 ended the possibility of a negotiated settlement. Initially, Pope Pius XI (1922–1939) was disposed to make concessions to the new regime that the papacy would not have dreamed of granting to a Restoration government. For a brief time, an agreement seemed possible, but the commitment of leading republican politicians to a separation of church and state without compromise ended negotiations. Between 1931 and 1933, the Second Republic proceeded unilaterally to abrogate the Concordat of 1851. The Constitution of 1931 separated church and state for the first time in the nation's history; the government gradually eliminated its subsidy for clerical salaries, suppressed the Jesuits, and curtailed the teaching activities of the other religious orders. By 1933, relations between Madrid and the Vatican had become tense. In the encyclical *Dilectissima nobis* (3 June 1933), Pius XI attacked the ecclesiastical legislation of the republic, particularly censuring a new law severely limiting the role of the religious orders. With characteristic prudence, however, Pius XI, advised by his secretary of state, Cardinal Eugenio Pacelli (1876–1956, Pope Pius XII 1939–1956), and the nuncio in Madrid, Archbishop Tedeschini, continued to maintain formal diplomataic relations with the republic. Yet a residue of the historic regalism of the Spanish state remained even in the republic, which insisted on retaining the right in certain circumstances to veto episcopal appointments made by the pope.

Upon the outbreak of the civil war, the papacy followed a cautious policy. It continued to maintain relations with the republic and refused accreditation to the ambassador dispatched by the nationalist government. Although large-scale executions of the Spanish clergy during the first six months of the conflict provided the Vatican with a powerful motive for supporting the regime of Gen. Francisco Franco,* there were serious difficulties to overcome. The execution of Basque* priests by the military government, apprehensions about the possibly fascist and totalitarian character of the new regime, as well as uncertainty about the kind of ecclesiastical settlement the nationalists envisaged for the church kept the Vatican from extending full diplomatic recognition until 1938.

From the papacy's point of view, these concerns had some justification. In one respect at least, Gen. Francisco Franco showed himself to be a worthy heir of the Bourbons and nineteenth-century liberals by insisting upon retaining the regalist rights of the state in episcopal appointments as embodied in the Concordat of 1851. The papacy, which had only grudgingly accepted this concession in the first place, disliked it even more by the 1930s. In any event, it argued that the 1851 agreement had lapsed and that the nationalist government possessed no automatic right to what the Vatican saw as extinguished privileges. The Franco regime, however, felt its regalist oats and refused to move from its determination to win for itself the powers enjoyed by the old monarchy. After difficult and sometimes tense negotiations, a convenio was reached in 1941 in which Pope Pius XII reluctantly conceded a modified version of royal patronage to Gen. Franco. The terms of this agreement were subsequently incorporated into a new concordat in 1953.

The concordat was anachronistic from the day of its signing. The new direction Pope John XXIII (1958–1963) and the Second Vatican Council gave to the Catholic world, calling for the church to renounce outmoded privileges, as well as the growing disenchantment of many Spanish bishops and priests with the regime, created widespread sentiment for a fundamental revision in relations between the Vatican and Madrid. The Franco government itself, believing that the Spanish church was biting the hand that fed it, also favored renegotiation, although for different reasons. Discussions began during the last years of Franco's life, but were carried on without success.

After the death of Franco in 1975, the elaboration of a new agreement between the Vatican and Spain's new democracy became possible. Two sets of agreements, or acuerdos, in 1976 and 1979 laid the foundation for fundamental changes in church-state relations. The Vatican accepted the separation of the civil and ecclesiastical powers and the introduction of full religious toleration, while Madrid renounced its regalian rights, particularly over patronage, contained in the 1953 concordat.

The acuerdos, however, were far from being free of the old ghosts of regalist-papal controversies. As in 1851, the papacy succeeded in winning a negotiated rather than a unilateral settlement for the Spanish church, and in the dramatically changed circumstances of Spain in the 1970s, it did not do badly. The state agreed to continue to pay clerical salaries for an extended period; it recognized the right of Spaniards to receive a religious education, if they so desired; it allowed the church to establish universities if it wished and carry out the reorganization of diocesan and parish boundaries on its own initiative; and it imposed no controls over the religious orders. The Bourbon and liberal regalists of the past would not have been pleased. What democratic Spain received from these arrangements were less specific concessions than the general and sincere acceptance on the part of the papacy and the Spanish church of the new political order and the pluralistic character of society. There have been points of conflict between the Vatican and Madrid since, particularly with the socialist government that came to power in 1982, but they have been resolved through negotiation. The great regalist battles of old seem unlikely to be repeated.

For additional information, see J. Becker, *Relaciones diplomáticas entre España y la Santa Sede durante el siglo xix* (Madrid, 1908); C. Corral et al., *Los acuerdos entre la*

*Iglesia y España* (Madrid, 1980); J. Andrés Gallego, *La política religiosa en España, 1889–1913* (Madrid, 1975); A. Marquina Barrio, *La diplomacia Vaticana y la España de Franco, 1936–1945* (Madrid, 1983); R. Olaechea, *Las relaciones hispano-romanas en la segunda mitad del siglo xviii*, 2 vols. (Saragossa, 1965); J. Pérez Alhama, *La Iglesia y el Estado español: Estudio histórico-jurídico a través del Concordato de 1851* (Madrid, 1967); J. M. Sánchez, *Reform and Reaction: The Politico-Religious Background of the Spanish Civil War* (Chapel Hill, 1964); L. Sierra Nava, *La reacción del episcopado español ante los decretos de matrimonios del ministro Urquijo de 1799 a 1813* (Bilbao, 1964).

W. J. Callahan

*Related entry:* CATHOLICISM.


**PARDO BAZÁN DE QUIROGA, EMILIA** (1851–1921), countess, poet, essayist, novelist, professor, and literary critic. Emilia Pardo Bazán was born on 16 Sept. 1851 to a wealthy gentry family in Corunna. In 1869, her father, the explorer and writer José Figueroa y Mosquera (1839–1872), became a progressive deputy to the Cortes in Madrid,* and in 1871, he received the pontifical title of conde de Pardo Bazán (which in 1908 was recognized by Alfonso XIII* to honor her accomplishments).

Despite social advantage, her education of three years at a French school in Madrid was meager, although she and her family traveled throughout Europe in her adolescence, and her later friendship with Francisco Giner de los Ríos,* an educator influenced by the ideas of Karl Christian Friedrich Krause,* gave her access to the world of ideas. Even so, her career was remarkable, given the limited role played by women in the late nineteenth century and the fact that she was only sixteen when she married in 1871. Her son Jaime was born in 1876, a doubly important date since it also marked the publication of her first book of poetry, named for her son and written during her pregnancy. The same year, her *Estudio crítico de padre Feijóo* won a national prize for biography. Her first novel, *Pascual López: Autobiografía de un estudiante de medicina*, was serially published in 1879. Later novels included *La tribuna* (1882), her acclaimed *Los pazos de Ulloa* (1886), and its sequel, *La madre naturaleza* (1887). The last two were naturalistic in approach and dealt with themes of personal decadence, incest, and psychological conflict.

By 1877, Pardo Bazán began another career as journalist with *La Ciencia Cristiana, La Época*, and other papers of the late nineteenth century. A series she wrote on Émile Zola (1840–1902) and French naturalism (collected in 1891 as *La cuestión palpitante*) antagonized many Spaniards who considered Zola to be pornographic for his blunt observations of human behavior or atheistic for his rejection of the Catholic concept of free will in favor of the influence of environment. The real issue, however, soon became Pardo Bazán's role as a woman writing about these subjects. A wall of intolerance existed in Spain to the intellectual development of women, and even her husband left her after she refused to give up her career.

As a consequence, she became an active feminist who extolled the need for women to assume a more important place in society. She unsuccessfully sought membership in the all-male Spanish Academy, but in 1916 she became literary chair of the Ateneo* and the first woman to be appointed professor at the Central University of Madrid. Her long relationship with the novelist Benito Pérez Galdós,* a kindred spirit, further marked her unconventionality.

Pardo Bazán ultimately became one of the most prolific writers of nineteenth-century Spain. The caliber of her work and dedication are impressive. She wrote of her native Galicia* in a sensitive and realistic way that preserved northwestern Spain for future generations of readers. She developed the short story, the novel, and poetry to such an extent that she is remembered as one of the best writers of the time and one of the most important early realist writers of Spain.

For additional information, see F. Carlos and S. de Robles, *Emilia Pardo Bazán: Obras completas*, 2 vols. (Madrid, 1947); and W. T. Patterson, *Emilia Pardo Bazán* (New York, 1971).

*N. A. Vigil*

*Related entries:* CASTRO, ROSALIA DE; PÉREZ GALDÓS, BENITO; WOMEN.

## PARTIT SOCIALISTA UNIFICAT DE CATALUNYA (PSUC),

Catalan political party in the Spanish Civil War.* The PSUC came into being on 23 July 1936, rising to prominence during the civil war to play a crucial role in determining the course of Catalan politics. During the thirty-six-year dictatorship of Gen. Francisco Franco,* the PSUC survived in exile and as an underground organization within Spain itself. After the death of Franco in Nov. 1975, the party reestablished itself as an important regional political force.

In the months leading up to the civil war and revolution (1936–1939), negotiations to bring about the fusion of several small left-wing Catalan parties had ended inconclusively. The crucible of the civil war, however, provided the impetus needed for the creation of a new party. Formed only a week after the military rebellion began, the PSUC was an aggregate of four Catalan-based organizations: Unió Socialista de Catalunya, Partit Comunista de Catalunya, Federació Catalana del Partido Socialista Obrero Español, and the Partit Català Proletari. With an initial membership of between three to six thousand, the PSUC hardly appeared as a threat to its principal political rivals, the anarchosyndicalists of the Confederación Nacional de Trabajo (CNT), the anarchists of the Federación Anarquista Ibérica (FAI), or the anti-Stalinist Marxists of the Partido Obrero de Unificación Marxista (POUM*). During the next few months, however, the growth of PSUC and its affiliates was spectacular. By Sept. 1936, the party claimed fifty thousand adherents, and by the end of the war it had grown to ninety thousand. Perhaps a better index of the party's popular support in Catalonia* was the ever-expanding membership of the PSUC-controlled socialist trade union, the Unión General de Trabajadores* (UGT). Within six months, the Catalan section of the UGT mushroomed from sixty thousand to more than half a million members.

In the civil war, among the numerous political parties in republican Spain, formation of the PSUC held greatest significance for the Spanish Communist party* (PCE), which had repeatedly failed to recruit a mass following in Catalonia, home of Spain's largest work force. The PCE never abandoned its efforts to secure a foothold in the region, and with the PSUC's creation, the PCE and Comintern managed to dictate its policies, even though PSUC was a regional party, composed largely of moderate elements, many of whom were independent catalanistas.

This dominance came about through the leadership of Joan Comorera (1895–1960), the secretary-general of the PSUC, Rafael Vidiella (1891- ), and other leading members of the party, who came from the PCE. In addition, the Comintern assigned an agent to act as a political advisor, the Hungarian communist Erno Gero ("Pedro," ?–1939?), who soon became the de facto director of the PSUC. Gero, a former secretary to the famous Hungarian communist Bela Kun (1885–1937), was an experienced apparatchik who closely supervised every aspect of the party's activities, from monitoring the political content of the PSUC's chief organ, *Treball*, to arbitrating intraparty disputes. Fluent in Catalan and conversant with local customs, Gero proved to be particularly adroit at harnessing the catalanista elements within the party hierarchy that might have objected to the PSUC's subservience to the PCE.

These intimate ties with the official communists obliged the PSUC to follow uncritically the prevailing Comintern interpretation that republican Spain was passing through a bourgeois democratic phase of historical development rather than experiencing a profound social and economic revolution. The PSUC enthusiastically embraced the communists' antirevolutionary programs that sought to conduct the war along conventional lines and restore national rule in the antifascist zone. As a loyal member of the Comintern, the PSUC, following the PCE's lead, sought to advance the Soviet Union's foreign policy objectives by forestalling the workers' revolution in Spain in order to induce the Western democracies to intervene on behalf of the republican government, something not possible as long as the republic was perceived as a revolutionary workers' state.

In Catalonia, the PSUC initially faced overwhelming opposition to its program as the tide of revolution swept through the northeast in the summer of 1936. Only the middle-class left republican party, the Catalan Esquerra, could be regarded as a potential ally. Both groups sought to curtail the extensive power and influence of the radical left in the region by rolling back the revolutionary movement that had been triggered by the military insurrection of July 1936. The alliance between PSUC and the Esquerra, however, was at best a temporary marriage of convenience, not least because the overall aims of PSUC and the Esquerra were incompatible. While the Esquerra strove to establish an independent Catalan state, the PSUC subordinated its regionalist aspirations to the broader goals of communism and the Comintern. In the course of the war, for example, the PSUC did its utmost to integrate Catalan economic and political affairs into the framework of the central republican government.

The PSUC itself attracted tradesmen, artisans, small manufacturers, and other lower-middle-class businessmen who felt most threatened by the revolution. Unlike the Esquerra, however, the PSUC forcefully challenged the revolutionary agenda of the anarchosyndicalists, left socialists, and especially the POUM by brazenly defending the interests of the Catalan middle classes through organization of the Federación Catalana de Gremios y Entidades de Pequeños Comerciantes e Industriales (GEPCI), a consortium of small businessmen and manufacturers.

Because the CNT and FAI were by far the most powerful revolutionary forces in Catalonia, the PSUC at first avoided direct confrontation with these groups. This was not the case with the small but vociferous POUM, which early in the war became the PSUC's archrival. To the PSUC and communists, the POUM was more than just a renegade Marxist party; it was above all an outspoken critic of the Stalinist Popular Front program. The PSUC, by falsely branding the POUM as a "Trotskyite" group of spies and saboteurs, went to extraordinary lengths to equate the POUM's anti–Popular Front views with a profascist position.

After the POUM was ejected from its only seat in the Generalitat government of Catalonia in Dec. 1936, the PSUC became increasingly bolder in its campaign to subdue the region's revolutionary movement. By the spring of 1937, PSUC had grown confident enough to force a showdown with both the anarchosyndicalists and the POUM. Tension between the prorevolutionary groups on the one hand and the PSUC and Esquerra on the other climaxed during the May events in 1937. On 3 May, the PSUC police commissioner forcefully challenged anarchosyndicalist control over the central telephone exchange in Barcelona* (the Telefónica), an incident that touched off a general strike and led to open warfare between the opposing sides. Barcelona was paralyzed by a "civil war within a civil war" during the next four days. By the time the combatants withdrew from the barricades on 7 May, it was apparent that the antirevolutionary forces had emerged victorious.

The May events also provoked a serious crisis in the central government of Valencia, forcing the resignation of the left socialist premier, Francisco Largo Caballero.* For the remainder of the war, Juan Negrín,* a moderate socialist ally of the communists, headed the republican government. Negrín had considerable antipathy toward the revolutionary wing of republican society, and both PSUC and the PCE prospered under his administration. In Catalonia, this was illustrated by the freedom PSUC received to persecute the POUM and its allies, mirroring the Stalinist show trials concurrently taking place in the Soviet Union. The PSUC's efforts to present the POUM as a party "in the service of international fascism" were given tacit support by the Esquerra and other antirevolutionary organizations. This witch-hunt, by the autumn of 1937, destroyed the power and influence of the POUM in republican affairs. Only in recent years have prominent PSUC members publicly confessed that the campaign against the POUM represented a dark period in the party's history.

The PSUC's rise to political power in Catalonia greatly facilitated communist attempts to consolidate authority in republican territory. After the Negrín government transferred from Valencia to Barcelona in Nov. 1937, its insistence upon national control met stiff resistance from regionalist parties. By effectively promoting an agenda that called for economic and military centralization, however, the PSUC managed to overcome this kind of opposition, so that the national government eventually was able to assert its complete authority over the Generalitat.

The nationalist victory in 1939 ushered in a long and harsh period of repression for the Spanish left. The PSUC itself, with its members either imprisoned, forced underground, or exiled, came dangerously close to extinction. Not the least of the party's problems was its bitter resentment by socialists, anarchosyndicalists, and other left-wing parties that had experienced its heavy-handed tactics during the civil war.

Power struggles within the exiled communist movement also exacted a heavy toll. One source of friction was the issue of the PSUC's relationship with the PCE and Comintern. Comorera belatedly refused to surrender PSUC autonomy to the PCE and was forced to step down as secretary-general in 1949, replaced by José Moix (1899– ), a PCE candidate. Until Franco's death in 1975, both parties shared the same principles and general style of political organization. Their interdependence was illustrated by the automatic induction into the PSUC of PCE members living in Catalonia.

A dramatic change, however, began in the late 1950s and early 1960s, when PSUC secured for itself a substantial working-class following through its active participation in the Comisiones Obreras (CCOO), illlegal trade-union groups that sprang up to oppose Franco's state-run Organización Sindical. Today the CCOO is one of the largest of the Spanish labor federations, and despite strong competition from other leftist groups, the PSUC by the 1970s had become the predominant force within the Catalan Comisiones.

The PSUC also began to broaden its political appeal by enthusiastically endorsing Catalan rights and presenting itself as a regional party. It has played a central role, as a result, in several regional coalitions, including the Asemblea de Catalunya (1971) and the Consell de Forces Politiques (1975). Ties with noncommunist social groups, such as neighborhood and legal associations, and with the academic community aided this process, as did its particularly successful, popularly oriented publishing ventures. Since the 1960s, for instance, the party has extended its reading audience by producing journals like *Nous Horitzons*.

Following the demise of the Franquista system, the PSUC emerged as one of the most potentially powerful political forces in Catalonia during the democratic transition. In the 1977 general elections—the first free elections in Spain since 1936—the PSUC received over 18 percent of the votes cast (550,000) in the region, and sent eight deputies to the Cortes. Since then, however, its popularity at the polls has declined. Several factors have contributed to this, not the least being numerous splits that have periodically occurred within the Spanish communist movement. In the immediate post-Franco period, for example, serious ideological conflict arose between the Madrid-based PCE and the Catalan-based PSUC. The PCE's commitment to Eurocommunism—a doctrine that rejected Marxist-Leninist politics in favor of a peaceful and democratic approach to change—generated heated debates throughout the communist movement, but particularly within the PSUC itself. Its members were evenly divided into two camps. A Leninist group (the históricos) adamantly opposed Eurocommunism not only because it was anti-Soviet, but also because it challenged the long-standing Marxist tradition of the party. Opposing the prosoviéticos were two moderate factions. The left-Eurocommunists were in favor of democratic reforms, but they did not want to lose the left-wing ideological identity of the PSUC. To the right of this group were the banderas blancas, "white flags," who interpreted Eurocommunism as a movement that embraced a variety of democratic perspectives not necessarily Marxist. Factional tensions eventually surfaced at the Fifth PSUC Congress held in early 1981, and after much debate, it was decided to drop the phrase "Eurocommunism" from the PSUC program.

Rather than uniting the party, this decision served to deepen party divisions. In 1982, a Leninist faction broke away from the PSUC to form the Partit del Communistes de Catalunya (PCC). Since then, the PSUC has been under the moderate leadership of such figures as Antonio Gutiérrez Díaz (1909?– ), Gregorio López Raimundo (1914– ), and Rafael Ribó (1919?– ). Despite some occasional lapses, the PSUC today has evolved into a party substantially different in character from the civil war era. Now in the vanguard of the national trend to defend regional rights against centralized control, the PSUC is understandably optimistic about its future in the Catalan political arena.

For additional information, see V. Alba, *The Communist Party in Spain* (New Brunswick, 1983); J. Almendros, *Situaciones españoles, 1936–1939: El PSUC en la guerra civil* (Barcelona, 1976); B. Bolloten, *The Spanish Revolution* (Chapel Hill, 1979); M. Caminal, *Joan Comorera* (Barcelona, 1984), vols. 1–3; J. L. Martín i Ramos, *El origens del partit socialista unificat de Catalunya, 1935–1939* (Barcelona, 1977); E. Mujal-León, *Communism and Political Change in Spain* (Bloomington, 1983); and L. Ponamariova, *La formación del partit socialista unificat de Catalunya* (Barcelona, 1977).

G. Esenwein

*Related entries:* BARCELONA; CATALONIA; COMMUNIST PARTY; SPANISH CIVIL WAR.

**PÉREZ DE AYALA, RAMÓN** (1880–1962), poet and novelist. A major literary figure of twentieth-century Spain, Pérez de Ayala was known as a poet, essayist, and novelist. He demonstrated great cultural breadth, having mastered Greek, Latin, and six modern languages. He received a solid, humanistic education from the Jesuits and in 1902 earned a law degree from the University of

Oviedo, then called the Athens of Spain because of its outstanding faculty. After studying aesthetics in Italy and Germany, he traveled in France, Britain, and the United States.

In 1914, Pérez de Ayala served as a war correspondent for *La Prensa* (Buenos Aires) and thereafter as a contributor. With José Ortega y Gasset* and Gregorio Marañón (1887–1960), he founded in 1931 the Group for the Defense of the Republic. He served as republican ambassador to Britain between 1931 and 1936, but went into French exile to protest left-wing influence on the republic during the civil war. He lectured in South America in 1940 and took up residence in Buenos Aires until his return to Spain in 1954.

Pérez de Ayala was elected to the Spanish Academy in 1928 and in 1926 received the National Prize for Literature. In 1936, he was granted an honorary doctorate by the University of London and received a medal from the Spanish Society of New York in 1949. He was awarded the Juan March Prize for Creative Writing in 1960.

His poetry portrays land, sea, river, and fire as man's pathway through life. His hundreds of essays reveal a richness of style and vast knowledge. Interspersed with humor and irony, his fiction is notably intellectual and speculative about the nature of knowledge, art, and language. Perspective reaches harmony, while the catharsis of tragedy becomes tolerance.

Pérez de Ayala's autobiographical novels (1907–1913) analyze Spain's crisis of conscience; the three *Poematic Novels of Spanish Life* (1916) are little masterpieces. His major novels turn to universal themes portraying symbolic characters of great moral strength and psychological depth. *Belarmino y Apolonio* (1921) pits a philosophical vision of the world against a dramatic one. *Luna de miel, luna de hiel* (1923) and its sequel, *Los trabajos de Urbano y Simona* (1923), trace love's course from Edenic innocence to marital happiness. Love and honor are interwoven in *Tigre Juan* (1926) and its sequel, *El curandero de su honra* (1926).

For additional information, see A. Amorós, *La novela intelectual de Ramón Pérez de Ayala* (Madrid, 1973); M. C. Rand, *Ramón Pérez de Ayala* (New York, 1971); and F. W. Weber, *The Literary Perspectivism of Ramón Pérez de Ayala* (Chapel Hill, 1966).

P. H. Fernández

**PÉREZ GALDÓS, BENITO** (1843–1920), novelist of realism and naturalism. Galdós was the most important literary figure of nineteenth-century Spain and is widely considered Spain's most outstanding novelist since Miguel de Cervantes (1547–1616). A long life, assiduously and exclusively dedicated to writing (he never married, for example), produced an extraordinarily voluminous body of work: forty-six volumes of *Episodios nacionales*, a fictionalized history of Spain from 1805 to 1880; forty-two volumes containing thirty-four separate novels; twenty-four plays; and fifteen volumes of stories, essays, and other writings.

Galdós is considered the renovator of the Spanish novel in the 1870s and 1880s. He absorbed the norms and purposes of European realism and naturalism, albeit always characteristically Hispanized, and remained attuned to the powerful, Cervantine presence in his creativity. In the 1890s and early 1900s, he developed his innovative narrative techniques in such novels as *Realidad* (1889), *Misercordia* (1897), and *El caballero encantado* (1905). Although Galdós was generally rejected by the highly individualistic Generation of 1898* that followed, his influence is easily seen in its major narrators: Miguel de Unamuno,* Pío Baraja,* and Ramón María del Valle-Inclán (1866–1936).

From the moment of his appearance upon the Spanish literary scene in 1868, Galdós came to personify the modern and Europeanizing outlook that represented Spain's drive toward assimilating and concretizing the major aesthetic, social, and political tendencies that characterized Western Europe. In his early years, Galdós actually entered the religious and political frays of his day through his narrative work, offering a polemically critical perception of the traditionalist elements of his society in such novels as *Doña Perfecta* (1876), *Gloria* (1876–1877), and *La familia de León Roch* (1878). Even in the period from 1881 to 1897, when he removed his art from the partisan politics of the day and produced his best and most lasting work, his informed portrayal of his country and countrymen, especially the urban middle class, leaves little doubt about his liberal views. Novels such as *La desheredada* (1881), *Tormento* (1884), *Lo prohibido* (1885), and his masterpiece, *Fortuna y Jacinta* (1886–1887), offer a microscopically critical, if never negatively revolutionary, reproduction of the salient shortcomings of Spain's then-dominant social class.

Later, perhaps beginning with *Torquemada en la hoguera* (1889), his masterful short novel, Galdós's views became somewhat radicalized by the neo-Christian teachings of Leo Tolstoy (1828–1910). Novels such as *Ángel Guerra* (1890–1891), *Nazarín* (1985), and *Misercordia* are in many ways extraordinary literary examples of the fictionalization of the Russian thinker's hopes for mankind.

Still later, there appears to be a further radicalization of Galdós's political and social thought, with perhaps more revolutionary attitudes expressed literarily, especially in his theater. Plays such as *Electra* (1901), which actually became a rallying cry for a younger generation of Spaniards, and *Casandra* (1905) reflect a profound skepticism regarding the ability of Spain's political institutions to solve the country's mounting social problems. This attitude was apparent in Galdós's offer to lend his prestige and services to the Republican party (then a revolutionary political force) and in his 1906 election as a republican member of the Spanish Cortes.

Like other Spanish artists and thinkers of the nineteenth century, Galdós suffered from the neglect of things Spanish that characterized European attitudes, particularly those of the British and French, until the twentieth century. Only in

recent times, and primarily because of American Hispanists, has he been recognized for his extraordinary artistic merit.

For additional information, see S. Gilman, *Galdós and the Art of the European Novel,
1867–1887* (Princeton, 1981); J. F. Montesinos, *Galdós*, 3 vols. (Madrid, 1968, 1973);
and C. P. Snow, *The Realists* (London, 1978).

*A. Rodríguez*

**PICASSO, PABLO RUIZ Y** (1881–1973), artist. Picasso, born on 25 Oct.
1881, in Malaga, grew up in Andalusia* and after 1885, when his father was
appointed professor at the Academy of Fine Arts (La Lonja), in Barcelona.*
Picasso excelled at the academy and also studied briefly at the Royal Academy
of San Fernando in Madrid.* His early works were signed ''Ruiz'' until he
adopted his mother's surname, evidently because it was unusual and more memorable.

During his student years (c. 1896–1900), Picasso refined his astonishing gifts
as a draughtsman and painter. He gained an understanding of European trends
from associating with avant-garde artists and writers at the Barcelona cafe, Els
Quatre Gats. His work at this time recalls the postimpressionists in style and
subject. Other artistic influences included Catalan Gothic sculpture, paintings
by El Greco (1541–1614), and the work of two great figures from Spain's Siglo
de Oro, Francisco de Zurbarán (1598–1664) and Diego de Velázquez (1599–
1660). In 1900, Picasso headed for Paris, a mecca for artists. Although he
returned to Spain frequently, sometimes for lengthy stays, until his self-imposed
exile began in 1936, France* was his adopted home for the rest of his life.

Picasso's long and varied career exhibits remarkable consistency in subject
matter and formal considerations. Conflicts recur in his work throughout the
decades, as do such thematic preoccupations as the artist and his model, the
portrayal of women in his life, the commedia dell'arte, the minotaur, and the
bullfight. The latter two commingle in a series of remarkable antiwar images
inspired by the Spanish Civil War,* the most famous of them *Guérnica*, done
in 1937. Picasso produced considerable bodies of work in painting, sculpture,
prints, drawings, ceramics, book illustration, and set design.

Picasso's career is too long to discuss in detail, except in relation to Spain
itself. Between 1901 and 1904, he was in Paris, Barcelona, and Madrid, executing city scenes, interiors, and figure studies which tended to be blue in color.
Many theories have been advanced about the sources of this blue period, none
of them definitive, but the uncertainties of Picasso's life may have affected both
his spirits and his palette. The paintings of itinerant circus folk (c. 1905) belong
to his rose period, so named for the paintings' predominant color. The classic
nudes of late 1905 and 1906 derive, in part, from Picasso's knowledge of pre-
Roman Iberian sculpture. Cubism, his most revolutionary and influential phase
(c. 1908–1912), though primarily French, began with a summer spent at Horta
del Ebro in Spain. Later developments, such as his post–World War I* involvement with dada; the neoclassicism of the 1920s; and the surrealist-linked imagery

of the 1930s, relate more to international art movements than to Picasso's Spanish roots.

Picasso's antifascist sympathies were strengthened by the outbreak of the Spanish Civil War. The republican government appointed him director of the Prado Museum in Madrid, a responsibility he seems to have taken seriously and to have maintained, from Paris, at least until the republic's fall in 1939. He donated proceeds from sales of his *Dream and Life of Franco*, a 1937 poem and etching that catalogued images of war, to the republic. The same year, he was invited to do a painting for the Spanish pavilion at the 1937 World's Fair in Paris; this became *Guérnica*, inspired by the Condor Legion's bombing on 26 Apr. 1937 of a small Basque* town. The painting toured the United States* in 1938 to raise more funds for the republic. Later, it became a celebrated attraction at the Museum of Modern Art in New York City. As stipulated in Picasso's will, the painting returned to Spain with the revival of democracy.

Picasso stayed in Paris throughout World War II,* joining the Communist party in 1944. Strong antinazi and antiwar sentiments inspired such postwar works as *The Charnel House*; the well-known image of the dove in flight which served as a logo for a world peace conference; and his peace chapel in Vallauris, France. Picasso refused to return to Spain until Franco was gone. The Caudillo died two years after the artist's own death, at age ninety-one, on 8 Apr. 1973, at Mougins (Alpes-Maritimes), France.

For additional information, see A. Barr, *Picasso: Fifty Years of His Art* (New York, 1946); and W. Rubin, ed., *Pablo Picasso: A Retrospective* (New York, 1980).

*S. Benforado*


**PI I MARGALL, FRANCESC (FRANCISCO)** (1824–1901), journalist, politician, second president of the First Republic,* and theoretician of federalism. Pi, born in Barcelona on 19 Apr. 1824, was the son of a textile worker who had been in the liberal uprising of 1820. Pi studied Greek and Latin classics at the Seminario Conciliar, and his exposure to Catalan romanticism at the Sociedad Filomática developed a strong literary inclination soon demonstrated in his contribution on art and architecture to *España Pintoresca* in 1842. Moving to Madrid* in 1847, he pursued a career as journalist and critic, collaborating on *El Renacimiento* and *El Correo*. An article in *El Correo* opened a ministerial crisis and closed the paper. His subsequent employment in the Madrid office of a Barcelona bank terminated with the 1847 financial crisis. Turning again to writing, Pi covered Andalusia* and Catalonia* for *Recuerdos y Bellezas de España* (1848); the impressions of Spain's problems gathered from travel and research consolidated his political philosophy. In 1849, he joined the Democratic party on the advice of his friend Estanislao Figueras (1819–1882), remaining henceforth a confirmed republican. His political radicalism reflected a fundamental heterodoxy: he saw Christianity as merely an intermediate stage in human evolution and the church and monarchy as obstacles to freedom. Ecclesiastical authorities banned this freethinking rationalism when it appeared in his *Historia de la Pintura*.

Pi emerged as a leading political activist and thinker in the revolutionary developments of 1854. As a member of the central committee of the Democratic party, and thus associated with the "vicalvarada" and the manifesto of Antonio Cánovas del Castillo*, Pi narrowly escaped arrest in Jan. He collaborated with the Madrid revolutionary junta, his radicalism exceeding even theirs. His antiabsolutist, anti-Catholic tract *El Eco de la Revolución*, which called for radical structural change, universal suffrage, and freedom of religion and expression, provided economic and social content to the revolution, and earned him a jail sentence. His contacts with workers increased; he taught at the Madrid Fomento, defended workers' associations before the Cortes, and was consulted by Catalan workers on their organizational efforts. This publicity increased his prestige, and he was only narrowly defeated by Gen. Juan Prim y Prats* for the Cortes in 1854.

Pi's theoretical formulations complemented his political activism, and his articles and books were dedicated to the reformation of Spain. His chief work, *La reacción y la revolución* (1854), proclaimed the absolute incompatibility of monarchy and democracy, and affirmed democracy as the goal of human development. In 1856, he helped found the antimonarchical journal *La Razón*, soon suppressed by the Liberal Union. In 1857, after a brief retreat in the Basque* country where he met his future wife, Petra Arsuaga, he was called by the democratic leader Nicolás Rivero (1814–1878) to edit the party paper *La Discusión*. His effectiveness hampered by the censors who often condemned his work on name recognition alone, Pi turned to the practice of law. In 1859, Figueras helped him establish a legal practice and a more secure living.

Pi i Margall is most often linked with the revolutionary interlude of 1868–1874 and the political failure of the First Republic. In June 1866, Pi had been an active participant in the abortive San Gil revolt and sought political refuge in Paris with his family until the events of Sept. 1868 brought him back to Madrid. Elected to the Constituent Cortes from Barcelona, Pi spoke for the minority democrats of the Federal Republican party, defending a federalist program and soon emerging as head of the party. With the fall of Amadeo I,* the assembly elected Pi as a minister in Figueras's government. In this position, he forestalled a coup by the majority radicals by suppressing the permanent commission of the Cortes and thus guaranteed free elections on the form of government. Pi i Margall followed Figueras as the second president in Apr. 1873. On 7 June, the Cortes voted in the Federal Republic, and Pi, caught between a federalist cantonalist insurrection and the opposition of antifederalist democrats, and insisting on a legalist solution to the constitutional problem, resigned on 18 July. He defended his role from his seat in the Cortes until the Restoration when, seeking temporary exile in Andalusia, he used his retirement to write, republish, and reflect on his political failure.

*Las nacionalidades* (1879) was Pi's most representative work. In it, the French positivism and the influence of Pierre Joseph Proudhon (1809–1865) acquired during his Parisian exile (Pi had translated *Du Principe fédératif* while in Paris) mitigated the Hegelianism of his early years. His central theory of "pactism," with indigenous roots in Catalan tradition, preceded his contact with Proudhon's thought. Pi insisted on the necessity of a federalism of mutual association, not one imposed from above, that would limit the power of the state in favor of municipalities and regions and would reflect Spanish reality.

In 1880, the Federal party split, Figueras rejecting Pi's doctrine of pactism and probably the discipline he imposed as party leader. Other secessions followed, including that of Valentí Almirall,* who founded the Catalan Center party. In 1883, the federalist assembly at Saragossa adopted the federalist constitution, the keystone of Pi's legalist approach, as the party program, and Pi consistently refused to compromise his position for political advantage. His intransigence separated him from his own followers. His journal, *El Nuevo Régimen*, founded in 1890, increasingly became his mouthpiece. He protested the war against Cuba and defended Catalanisme against accusations of separatism, which did not win the catalanists to his federalism. In Spanish historiography, Pi is associated with political failure. His characteristics of doctrinal purity and intransigence; his honesty in politics, business, and personal matters; and his independence of thought isolated him in his later years. These same qualities were the stuff of which myths are made and enabled his admirers to convert his name into a symbol, a banner of republican propaganda.

For additional information, see A. Barcells, M. Ardit, and N. Sales, *Historia dels Països Catalans de 1714 a 1975* (Barcelona, 1980); A. Jutglar, *Història crítica de la burgesia a Catalunya* (Barcelona, 1972) and *Pi y Margall y el federalismo español*, vols 1 & 2 (Madrid, 1975); and J. Vicens Vives and M. Llorens, *Industrials i polítics del segle xix*, 3d ed. (Barcelona, 1980).

*V. L. Enders*

*Related entry:* CATALONIA.

**PORTUGAL,** relations with Spain. After 1700, relations between Spain and Portugal gradually moved toward mutual accommodation. Although the two periodically found themselves on opposite sides in major European conflicts, the climate that arose in the eighteenth century reflected Spanish acceptance of the fact that Portugal was a sovereign state, not a wayward province to be brought under Castilian aegis by marriage or military force. Recognition of this fact stemmed in part from Spanish weakness and growing Portuguese economic strength, much of which could be attributed to income derived from the sugar, tobacco, hides, and gold of colonial Brazil. Adroit alliance building by the Portuguese, particularly their reinforcing ties with an increasingly powerful and expansive Britain during the latter half of the seventeenth century, also made Portugal a more formidable neighbor. With the end of the War of Restoration (1640–1668)—Portugal's lengthy struggle to shake off sixty years of Spanish rule (1580–1640)—a Spain debilitated by economic and military setbacks reluctantly recognized Portuguese sovereignty. Spanish weakness was further revealed in the Treaty of Colônia do Sacramento of 1681, by which Spain ceded control over territory in the Río de la Plata estuary to Portugal after key outposts were captured by Brazilian colonials.

During the War of Spanish Succession,* Spain and Portugal became antagonists again, this time in a struggle over whether the Bourbon or Hapsburg dynasty would succeed to the Spanish throne left vacant with the death of the childless Hapsburg monarch, Carlos II (1661–1700). Conflict between the two Iberian powers was precipitated in 1704, when Portugal dropped its support for the Bourbon claimant to the throne, Philip, Duke of Anjou (Felipe V*), who was preferred by the Spanish, and backed the Hapsburg pretender, the archduke Charles (1685–1740), who was championed by Britain* and Holland. The peninsular struggle moved back and forth, with the Portuguese occupying Madrid* in 1706 and Spanish forces winning a major victory at Caia in 1709. On 6 Feb. 1715, France,* Spain, and Portugal formally ended their involvement in the conflict by signing the Treaty of Utrecht. Portugal recovered Colônia do Sacramento, which had been abandoned in 1705 to Spain.

After 1715, the two Iberian nations again moved toward a modus vivendi. Many Spaniards still clung to the hope of reconstituting an Iberian union led by Madrid, an idea the Portuguese viewed with suspicion. Nonetheless, Portuguese diplomats such as Luís de Cunha (1662–1749) sought to arrange marriage alliances between the two countries. The Portuguese, who had returned to a policy of neutrality held during the early years of the War of Spanish Succession, later acted as mediators, helping to defuse conflict between Britain and Spain. This effort culminated with the Peace of Aix-la-Chapelle (1748), by which Spain recovered Parma, Piastella, and Guastella in Italy.*

On 13 Jan. 1750, Spain and Portugal signed the Treaty of Madrid, which dealt largely with colonial occupation that ran counter to previous agreements, particularly the 1494 Treaty of Tordesillas. The Treaty of Madrid recognized Spanish sovereignty over the Philippines, which technically lay within the Portuguese colonial sphere defined by Tordesillas. By the same token, Spain accepted Portuguese control over western Brazil (Maranhão, Mato Grosso, and Amazonas). Colônia do Sacramento, well within the Spanish sphere, was ceded to Madrid by Lisbon.

Although substantially altered by the 1761 Treaty of Pardo because of difficulties of implementation in the Platine region, the Treaty of Madrid did much to establish the principle of uti possidetis in Luso-Spanish relations. Though not really observed, another innovation in the treaty stipulated that should the two countries become antagonists in Europe, their colonial possessions would remain at peace with each other. This clause arose in part from the realization that colonial strife played into the hands of European powers seeking to gain control of the Americas.

During the Seven Years' War,* Spain and Portugal again found themselves pitted against each other as members of opposing camps. Portugal, in its ancient alliance with Britain, and Bourbon Spain, then closely tied to France, were drawn into a global struggle not of their own making. In 1762, the Bourbon camp directed an ultimatum at Portugal, ordering it to declare war on Britain. Portugal refused and a Franco-Spanish force occupied the cities of Miranda, Bragança, Castelo Rodrigo, and Almeida. An armistice soon followed, though, as Britain emerged victorious from the war. Spain withdrew its forces from Portugal, but the Portuguese received no compensation in the Treaty of Fontaine-bleau (3 Nov. 1762). Indeed, Portugal's role as junior partner to Britain was such that it was not even admitted as a signatory at Fountainebleau. On the losing side, Spain did not suffer such ignominy, but was again reminded that relations with Lisbon ultimately ran through London.

During the 1770s, the question of Colônia do Sacramento, then a century old, was resolved, largely in Spain's favor. Spanish colonials had taken additional territory in the Platine region, including the island of Santa Catarina. Portugal, less well financed as the prosperity derived from Brazilian products waned after 1750, had little leverage in the long-running struggle. Moreover, Britain was too preoccupied with the revolt of its colonies in North America to be of much help, even if it had wanted to support the Portuguese in South America. Spain was thus able to gain Portuguese assent to the Treaties of San Ildefonso (1 Oct. 1777) and Pardo (11 Mar. 1778), by which Portugal ceded Colônia do Sacramento. Lisbon also gave up the West African islands of Ano Bom and Fernando Poo.

The French Revolution shattered the old alliance system in which Spain and Portugal were enmeshed. In the years preceding the revolution, Portugal had sought to stay on a neutral path between its powerful, if not necessarily reliable, ally Britain and the Franco-Spanish bloc. Spain, on the other hand, hewed more closely to the interests of its senior partner, France, and was usually more partisan in the competition between London and Versailles. With the establishment of a militant republic in France, however, Britain sought and gained Spanish support for the opening of a second front, the Pyrenees, against revolutionary France.

The Anglo-Spanish rapprochement did not appear to require the involvement of Portugal, which initially sought to hold to its policy of neutrality. Portuguese sentiment against the threatening behavior of republican France, though, led to alliance with Spain (15 July 1793) and a further treaty with Britain (26 Sept. 1793). Portugal sent an expeditionary force to aid Spain against the French in Rousillon and Catalonia (1793–1795). On 22 July 1795, however, the chief Spanish minister, Manuel Godoy,* negotiated a separate peace with France. This left Portuguese expeditionary forces in Spain isolated in hostile environs, from which they retreated with great difficulty.

Godoy's separate peace recast the old opposition between Spain and Portugal that, again, was more a function of great power antagonism than a fundamental rift between the two Iberian nations. Nevertheless, Godoy, who admired Napoleon Bonaparte (1769–1821) and dreamed of a kingdom of his own, prepared to invade Portugal at the instigation of his French allies, who reminded the Spanish minister that Portugal's alliance with Britain placed it in the enemy camp. Thus, in 1801, after making unacceptable territorial demands on Portugal, Spain invaded its neighbor. With his victory in the so-called War of the Oranges, which lasted only from 20 May to 6 June 1801, Godoy forced Portugal to sign the Treaties of Badajoz, one with Spain and one with France. Portugal agreed to close its ports to the British, open them to France and its allies, and pay an indemnity. Brazilian boundary adjustments favorable to Spain were also imposed, and the Portuguese frontier town of Olivença and its environs were taken by Madrid.

During the next several years, Spanish foreign policy vacillated between the Napoleonic and British camps. Under the influence of Godoy, Spain championed the French emperor, plotted against France with the Russians, or tried a policy of neutrality. Franco-Spanish interests came together in the secret Pact of Fountainebleau, signed on 27 Oct. 1807, which divided Portugal into three Spanish-controlled kingdoms, the southernmost becoming a hereditary state led by Godoy. Portugal's colonies were to be seized and divided between France and Spain. In late 1807, a Franco-Spanish force led by Andoche Junot (1771–1813) invaded Portugal, capturing Lisbon on 30 Nov. The Portuguese royal family fled to Brazil, establishing a court in exile in the vast American colony. Godoy's duplicity was soon repaid by Napoleon, who occupied Spain in 1808 and demanded cession of the Spanish provinces north of the Ebro River. Napoleon subsequently imposed his brother Joseph on Spain as José I,* replacing Carlos IV.* Portugal remained a French military colony until the British in 1809 established themselves in Portugal.

Following the Congress of Vienna in 1815, Luso-Spanish relations were less vulnerable to competing big-power alliances. Both nations were economically dependent on Britain, which served to stabilize relations in Europe and helped spare Spain and Portugal from conflict. Thus, during much of the nineteenth century, Luso-Spanish relations remained harmonious. In 1816, two marriage agreements were successfully concluded by the Iberian crowns. When liberal revolutions took power in both countries in 1820, relations were not seriously disturbed. During the decade, a number of liberal politicians in both countries revived the old idea of an Iberian union. Thereafter, when Spain and Portugal were respectively beset by the Carlist and Miguelist uprisings, improving relations were shaken. For example, in the case of the uprising in Portugal on behalf of Miguel (1802–1866), Spain briefly invaded on behalf of the other claimant, Pedro (1798–1834). This invasion was soon blunted by the ongoing constant in Luso-Spanish relations, the threat of British intervention in support of Portuguese sovereignty.

For the most part, relations thereafter focused on prosaic matters such as treaties of commerce and navigation, pacts for extradition of criminals and deserters, postal and telegraphic conventions, and copyright agreements. After 1860, when Spain and Portugal also signed numerous multilateral agreements, these agreements were themselves occasionally involved in conflict. In 1840, for example, upset by Portugal's lack of support for Spanish actions against Algeria, Madrid used the 1835 treaty for free navigation of the Duero River as a pretext for mobilizing troops against the Portuguese. British diplomacy defused the contretemps.

Iberistas continued to call for an Iberian union. During the 1854 revolution in Spain, for example, the idea of replacing unpopular Queen Isabel II* with Pedro V (ruled 1837–1861) of Portugal gained much support. The queen, however, managed to hold her throne until 1868 after the British let it be known that they were not enthusiastic about the prospect of an Iberian union.

After the Franco-Prussian War (1870–1871), as Britain and France moved closer together, their accommodation found reflection in Luso-Spanish relations, and during the 1920s, the rule of Gen. Miguel Primo de Rivera* pursued a policy of signing bilateral treaties of arbitration and cooperation. One such pact, the 1928 treaty calling for arbitration of disputes over use of the Duero River, was heralded by Madrid as an important contribution to international law. Other agreements included treaties on passports (1922, 1926),'delimitation of the Luso-Spanish frontier (1926), fishing on the Minho River (1927), and use of hydroelectric power on the Duero River (1927).

With the establishment of the Second Republic* in 1931, Madrid sought to cultivate closer ties with the Portuguese, then under the authoritarian control of Dr. Antonio de Oliveira Salazar (1889–1970). The right-wing Salazar regime soon showed itself wary of the lingering hopes for unification of Spanish iberistas and also evinced little sympathy for the republicanism of its neighbor, but when Gen. Francisco Franco* and his nationalist forces invaded Spain, Salazar moved quickly to help the Spanish rebels. At one point, Salazar proposed sending Portuguese troops to support Franco's forces in the Spanish Civil War.* Eventually, upward of twenty thousand Portuguese, most of them volunteers, fought for the nationalists. Perhaps more important, Portugal acted as a conduit for aid sent to Franco by Nazi Germany.* Franco's brother Nicolás (1891–  ) was allowed to use Lisbon as a headquarters for the purchase of arms and petroleum. Portugal's role as a refuge for nationalists and as a source of war matériel during the early stages of the civil war played a crucial role in Franco's ultimate victory.

In 1938, Salazar formally recognized the nationalist regime, then based in Burgos. This recognition foreshadowed the Iberian Pact of 17 Mar. 1939. Conceived as a treaty of nonaggression and friendship, the pact obliged the two countries to come to the defense of each other's territory and refrain from entering any agreements involving aggression against the other. On 29 July 1940, the pact was amended with a protocol, inspired by Salazar, which aimed at assuring Spanish neutrality in World War II.* Salazar feared that if Spain sided with the Axis powers, Britain would be more prone to invoke its ancient alliance, thereby placing Portugal in renewed conflict with its Iberian neighbor. The protocol in effect agreed to keep Germany out of Spain and Britain out of Portugal. Although the British called on Portugal for use of its Atlantic islands in 1943, the protocol helped Iberia exist as a zone of peace throughout the war. In 1949, both the treaty and the protocol were renewed.

Calls for an Iberian union were still heard from a wide range of opinion on both sides of the border, but the trend was toward great bilateral cooperation in the postwar era. In 1969, for example, the Spanish foreign minister, Gregorio López Bravo (1923– ), declared that Spain would pursue closer relations with Portugal. The Portuguese revolution of 1974 and the death of Franco in 1975 came conveniently close together and facilitated amicable relations as the two countries turned toward democracy. The demise of the Iberian dictatorships also allowed for greater integration of the two nations into the European community. Both joined the European Economic Community together on 1 Jan. 1986.

For additional information, see J. Becker, *La historia de la relaciones exteriores de España en el siglo xix*, 3 vols. (Madrid, 1924–1927); J. W. Cortada, ed., *Spain in the Twentieth-Century World: Essays on Spanish Diplomacy, 1898–1978* (Westport, 1980); W. N. Hargreaves-Mawdsley, *Eighteenth-Century Spain 1700–1788* (Totowa, 1979); J. López Oliván, *Repertorio diplomático español* (Madrid, 1944); J. del Nido Y Segalerva, *La unión ibérica* (Madrid, 1914); and P. Soares Martínez, *História diplomática de Portugal* (Lisbon, 1986).

*C. A. Hanson*

**POUM (PARTIDO OBRERO DE UNIFICACIÓN MARXISTA),** independent Marxist organization in the Spanish Civil War.* The POUM, founded in Sept. 1935, was actually an amalgamation of two revolutionary Marxist-Leninist parties centered in Catalonia,* the Bloque Obrero y Campesino (BOC, or Workers' and Peasants' Bloc) and the Izquierda Comunista Española (ICE). While POUM never attracted a mass following, it was endowed with some of Spain's most sophisticated political thinkers. The party managed, throughout its brief existence, to exert an influence disproportionate to its size.

The POUM made its debut at a time when the development of the Spanish Left as a whole was profoundly influenced by the rise of fascism in Europe and particularly in Spain itself, where the extreme Right appeared to be making advances at an alarming rate. The idea of forming a united workers' front as a way of stemming the tide of fascism was considered by many European left-wing groups, but it was first put into practice in Spain as the Alianza Obrera (AO). The tactic's originator, the Marxist theoretician and BOC leader Joaquín Maurín (1893–1973), envisaged the AO as an alliance among worker and peasant organizations transcending the ideological barriers that had long divided the Spanish Left. In this way, Maurín thought it was possible to unite workers without destroying existing organizations. As it happened, the AO was put to the test only once: during the abortive Asturias* uprising of Oct. 1934. Thanks largely to a compact between socialist, Trotskyist, anarchosyndicalist, and communist unions, workers managed to run a commune for nearly two weeks before being overwhelmed by government troops.

The months following the Asturias rebellion saw the Left in disarray: nearly thirty thousand workers were imprisoned and many left-wing unions were forced underground. In this climate of repression, Maurín and the BOC struggled to keep the AO movement alive among parties still deeply committed to a revolutionary agenda. Their efforts particularly appealed to the ICE, which had recently broken with Leon Trotsky (1877–1940) and disassociated itself from his Fourth International movement. In late Sept. 1935, the two parties met clandestinely in Barcelona* and agreed to unite as the POUM. *La Batalla*, formerly the daily organ of the BOC and now the principal mouthpiece of the new party, announced the significance of the fusion as the first step in the creation of a revolutionary socialist workers' party.

With approximately 6,500 adherents, the BOC was by far the larger of the two parties. Although considerably smaller in size, with between four and five hundred members scattered throughout Spain, the ICE nonetheless made its presence felt through the important cadre of intellectuals it contributed to the party: Andreu Nin (1892–1937), Juan Andrade (1903-?), and Ignacio Iglesias (1899-?). From the moment it was founded, the POUM defined itself as a revolutionary Marxist-Leninist organization, opposed not only to the reformism of the Socialist party* (PSOE), its labor union, the Unión General de Trabajadores (UGT) and the Moscow-oriented policies of the official Communist party* (PCE), but also the revolutionary adventurism of sections of the anarchosyndicalist Confederación Nacional de Trabajo (CNT), dominated by the Federación Anarquista Ibérica (FAI). The major points of its platform can be summarized as follows. (1) The party sought to bring about a democratic-socialist revolution in Spain, in which the Spanish proletariat would accomplish a bourgeois revolution before a socialist one. (2) The AO would serve as an organ for exercising political power during the transitional period between the two revolutionary phases. (3) After the socialist revolution, Spain would be reorganized along federalist lines to form a federation of socialist republics (Unión Ibérica de Repúblicas Socialistas). (4) The POUM would ally itself with the nonaligned London Bureau composed of factions of the French and Italian Socialist parties, the British Independent Labour party, and dissident sections of the German Communist party.

Because so much of the literature on the Spanish Civil War has inaccurately characterized the POUM as a Trotskyist or quasi-Trotskyist party, it is important to explain briefly the relationship between the POUM and Trotskyism. Given its Trotskyist background, the ICE was initially viewed with suspicion by many bloquistas, who feared that Trotskyist elements would attempt to use the POUM as a vehicle for their own purposes. Most ICE members loyal to Trotskyist politics, in fact, refused to join the POUM. Some chose to enroll in the PSOE and practice the policy known as the "French turn" of entering socialist organizations in order to radicalize them from within. Others decided to form a Spanish section of the Trotskyist Fourth International movement.

While ICE members entering POUM had formally severed their ties with Trotsky, it is true that some still held Trotskyist viewpoints. For example, two of POUM's chief theoreticians, Nin and Andrade, subscribed to the notion of the "permanent revolution" and argued that a Spanish revolution would not pass through distinct stages, as orthodox Marxists categorically asserted, but rather would be a continuous process in which the democratic (bourgeois) and socialist (proletarian) stages would be combined. In addition, many POUMists concurred with Trotsky's critique of Stalinism, thus placing themselves in diametric opposition to the PCE.

No matter how sympathetic some POUMists were to Trotsky, however, the fact is that the party never followed what can be called a Trotskyist program because, unlike Trotsky himself, POUM theoreticians rejected the view that conditions in Spain were analogous to those in the Soviet Union. Trotsky believed that the POUM lacked the political leadership necessary to give it a true revolutionary orientation. For this reason, he frequently inveighed against members of the POUM executive, both before and during the civil war. Finally, while individual POUMists such as Andrade maintained fraternal relations with the tiny Trotskyist (or bolshevik-Leninist) groups operating in Spain during the civil war, the POUM itself repeatedly rejected their respective bids to enter the party as a faction.

By the end of 1935, a majority of the Spanish Left had abandoned the Alianza Obrera in favor of a Popular Front strategy. In contrast to the AO, which comprised only worker and peasant groups, the Popular Front policy called for the collective resistance to the threat of fascism by means of an alliance between workers' organizations and middle-class parties. Even though the POUM itself was in principle opposed to class collaboration, the pressures to join the Popular Front in late 1935 were immense. Not only was it widely believed that Spain was at the point of falling victim to the clerical-fascist parties, but a Left victory seemed the only hope for the prompt release of the many workers imprisoned after the Asturian revolt. For purely tactical reasons, the POUM agreed to participate in the electoral bloc that brought the Left to power in the Feb. 1936 general elections.

Although the POUM won a seat in the Cortes, it continued to denounce parliamentary democracy on the grounds that it bolstered capitalism and thereby strengthened reactionary forces. The POUM attached significance to its parliamentary role only insofar as it fostered what was perceived as the historical development of a democratic-socialist revolution. Failing this, the POUM believed that a working-class dictatorship would have to be achieved by means of armed insurrection.

The military rising of July 1936 not only triggered a civil war but also unleashed a popular revolution in parts of the republic. It was quickly apparent that, although the mosaic of republican groups were united in their opposition to the nationalists, they were deeply divided over the nature of the conflict. The revolutionary Left (CNT-FAI, left socialists, and POUM) saw the war as an integral part of a general revolution unfoldinig in Spanish society. For its part, the POUM believed that the situation demanded the creation of Marxist-dominated worker militias, and the complete reorganization of the economy along socialist lines: in short, the establishment of working-class hegemony at every level of social life.

Opposing the revolutionary interpretation of events were the moderate socialists, middle-class republican parties, and the official communists. The war, according to them, was simply a struggle between democratic and fascist forces. In contrast to the revolutionaries, who strove to do away completely with the state and its institutions, they aimed to restore parliamentary democracy in Spain by means of conventional warfare. It was the tension between the pro- and antirevolutionary elements that generated the climate of hostility and bitter recriminations in the republican zone throughout the war, and ultimately determined the fate of the POUM itself.

From the outset of the war, it was apparent that POUM faced enormous obstacles in its struggle for political power. During the crucial first moments of the military rebellion, the party lost its secretary general, Maurín, who was captured by nationalist troops and held prisoner for the remainder of the war. Since Maurín was a highly effective leader who enjoyed the support of POUM members, his absence undoubtedly created problems for the party. Maurín's friend, Nin, chosen as the POUM's new leader, lacked the same degree of support as his predecessor. The POUM was further handicapped by the fact that it was a relatively small party (ten thousand members by July 1936); lacked firm allies on the left; and had relinquished control of its trade-union arm, the Federación Obrera de Unidad Sindical (FOUS), with a membership of approximately sixty thousand members, early in the civil war so that FOUS members might play a vanguard role in the reformist Catalan UGT only to see this branch of the UGT eventually fall under the control of the POUM's archrival, the communist-dominated Partit Socialista Unificat de Catalunya* (PSUC).

The POUM looked to the anarchosyndicalists as a potential ally, notwithstanding their profound differences over ideological and practical matters. They hoped above all to influence the CNT-FAI representatives to adopt POUM positions on key issues. As a preliminary step toward consolidating the revolutionary gains of workers, for example, the POUM urged the CNT-FAI to help them conquer political power. POUM members also appealed to the anarchosyndicalists to join them in presenting a united front against the antirevolutionary parties in the republican bloc. The POUM's hopes of forging such a partnership were soon disappointed. The anarchosyndicalists, who constituted the predominant revolutionary force in Catalonia, did not feel compelled to follow the directives of a Marxist party that, irrespective of its anti-Stalinism, embraced the Bolshevik Revolution. With the exception of the UGT's left wing, in fact, the anarchosyndicalists distanced themselves from Marxist organizations.

Nevertheless, the POUM refused, despite its isolation and minority position, to compromise its revolutionary program, especially if it meant making concessions to the bourgeoisie. It amply demonstrated this by its political posture in the Antifascist Militia Committee and the Generalitat. When Nin, for example, served as councillor of justice (Oct.–Dec. 1936), he strove to abolish judicial procedures and practices inherited from the pre–civil war period in order to establish a proletarian form of justice.

Ignored by the anarchosyndicalists and shunned by the republican parties, the POUM fell prey to its principal foe, the PSUC. Nominally a socialist party, PSUC, affiliated with the Communist International (Comintern), was effectively controlled by communists. Established shortly after the outbreak of civil war, it had rapidly risen to prominence as a formidable opponent of revolutionary groups such as POUM, and helped oust Nin from the Generalitat cabinet in Dec. 1936, thus depriving the POUM of its only portfolio.

By the spring of 1937, it was apparent that the struggle between the pro- and antirevolutionary forces was coming to a head. Alarmed that the revolution was increasingly being subordinated to the war effort, Andrade and other POUMists began calling for an alliance, a Frente Obrero Revolucionario, among ultraleft groups. This drive climaxed during the May crisis of 1937, when the radical Left centered in Catalonia was embroiled in open warfare with the PSUC and the middle-class republican parties of the Generalitat.

The events of May, as a turning point in the civil war, determined the fate of the revolutionary movement that had begun in July 1936. Fighting erupted on 3 May after the PSUC police commissioner, Eusebio Rodríguez Salas (1891–1953?), ordered assault guards to occupy the central telephone exchange in the center of Barcelona, controlled by a committee dominated by anarchosyndicalists, who considered the exchange strategically valuable. News of the occupation spread rapidly throughout the city, and by nightfall Barcelona had become an armed camp. Sporadic but intense street fighting continued until the morning of 7 May, when the revolutionaries withdrew from the barricades. Seizing the opportunity to settle long-standing political scores, the communists launched a campaign of persecution against the POUM. To convince other republican groups of the need to eliminate the POUM altogether, the communists denounced their adversaries in the harshest terms. The PCE newspaper *Frente Rojo*, for example, branded the party as a band of spies and traitors, likening POUMists to Trotskyists and saboteurs in the Soviet Union. The anti-POUM campaign was not confined to Spanish borders, since the communists enlisted an impressive array of public figures and international celebrities, including the surrealist poet Louis Aragon (1895-1987), the French writer André Malraux (1901–1976), and the British author Ralph Bates (1899–1978?). Even documents were falsified by the communists in a desperate attempt to link the POUM to Francoist agents working in the republican army.

At the same time, an international campaign was launched in support of the POUM. Foreigners willing to speak out for the release of POUM leaders included the British author George Orwell (1903–1950), who had served in the POUM militia; Fenner Brockway (1888–1987?), leader of the Independent Labour party in Britain; the French novelist André Gide (1869–1951); and American left-wing intellectuals such as Sidney Hook (1902–1989), Bertram Wolfe (1896–1977), and Victor F. Calverton (1900–1940). Despite their efforts, however, the calumnies about the POUM prevailed until long after the civil war had ended.

Although less overtly hostile toward the POUM than the communists, most Catalan and central government officials did not oppose the idea of persecuting the POUM, because they identified the POUM and other revolutionary elements as "uncontrollables" who posed a threat to public order. The power of the revolutionaries had to be sharply curbed in order for the government to conduct its affairs without hindrance.

In fact, the events of May provoked a cabinet crisis in the central government at Valencia and forced the resignation of the premier, Francisco Largo Caballero,* who refused to bow to communist pressures to indict the POUM as a treasonous party. Largo's departure from the cabinet tipped the balance in the cabinet in favor of the antirevolutionary elements. The POUM was vigorously persecuted under the administration of Juan Negrín,* premier from May 1937 until the end of the war.

The POUM's political isolation made it a relatively easy target. This was true even with regard to the anarchosyndicalist movement, for the tactical alliance between POUM and revolutionary elements in the CNT during May had dissolved as quickly as it had arisen. In June 1937, following the arrest of POUM leaders, many of the party's rank and file and foreign supporters were rounded up by the police. The most celebrated victim of this repression was Nin, who was taken to a prison outside Madrid,* where he was apparently tortured and then murdered by the communists.

The repression of the POUM effectively destroyed the party. With the leadership in jail and the POUM militia dissolved, the party existed only as an underground movement and in the unions where it had formerly exercised influence. *La Batalla* was produced clandestinely and only irregularly.

At the POUM trials of Oct. 1938, prosecutors failed to establish that the party was part of a rearguard conspiracy or "Fifth Column" movement. Despite relentless communist efforts to convince them otherwise, the tribunal refused to convict any POUMist as a traitor, although each defendant received a harsh prison sentence for participating in the May crisis.

Because the charges leveled against the POUM were never substantiated, the POUM repression later proved to be an embarrassment for those involved in the case. Writing some years after the war, the French communist Georges Soria (1922?- ), the Spanish communist leader Santiago Carrillo,* and others reluctantly conceded that the POUM had been unfairly maligned and that this incident represents a dark page in the history of the communist movement.

Just before troops led by Gen. Francisco Franco* occupied Catalonia in Jan. 1939, many POUMists managed to escape from prison, eventually making their way across the Pyrenees to join the growing numbers of republican refugees in France. POUM groups appeared after the war in France and Mexico, and for many years the French branch was active in publishing materials about the party.

Their numbers gradually died out, however, and after Franco's death in 1975, the POUM, unlike the CNT, PCE, or PSOE-UGT, was not revived.

For additional information, see J. Andrade, *La revolución española día a día* (Barcelona, 1979); V. Alba and S. Schwartz, *Spanish Marxism versus Soviet Communism* (Brunswick, 1988); F. Bonamusa, *Andreu Nin y el movimiento comunista en España (1930–1937)* (Barcelona, 1977); J. Gorkin, *Canibales políticos* (Mexico City, 1941); Joaquín Maurín Juliá papers, Hoover Institution, Stanford; J. Maurín, *Revolución y contrarevolución en España* (Paris, 1966); A. Nin, *Por la unificación Marxista* (Madrid, 1978); P. Pagès, *Historia del Partido Comunista de España* (Barcelona, 1978); R. Tosstorf, *Die POUM im spanischen Bürgerkrieg* (Frankfurt am Main, 1987).

G. Esenwein

*Related entries:* BARCELONA; CATALONIA; SPANISH CIVIL WAR.

**PRAT DE LA RIBA I SARRÁ, ENRIC** (1870–1917), Catalan nationalist, first president of the Mancomunitat (1914–1917). Born in rural Catalonia* to a prosperous, conservative Catholic family, Prat early imbibed the romantic Catalanisme of La Renaixença. His legal studies in the tradition of Friedrich Savigny (1779–1861), combined with the positivism of Auguste Comte (1798–1857) and the traditionalism of Hippolyte Taine (1823–1893), molded the mind of the future conservative theorist of the Catalan bourgeoisie.

At eighteen, he began law studies in Barcelona* and joined the Centro Escolar Catalanista, becoming its president in 1890. Shortly thereafter, he was made secretary of the newly founded Catalanist Union, and in that capacity he supported the 1892 Catalan regional constitution. He finished his licentiate in Barcelona and his doctorate in law at the University of Madrid during the next two years, and then in 1895 he became one of the founders of the *Revista Jurídica de Cataluña*, writing economic, sociological, and historical articles.

Catalan nationalism early emerged as his central focus. In 1896, under the presidency of Valentí Almirall,* he was elected secretary of the Barcelona Ateneo. Introducing a lecture series there two years later, Prat explored "the Fact of Catalan Nationality" that formed the basis of his classic *La Nacionalitat Catalana*, published in 1906. He collaborated on *La Renaixença* and the *Revista de Catalunya*, among other publications. The Spanish defeat of 1898 intensified Prat's aspirations toward Catalan autonomy and he published two manifestos, "To the Catalans" and "To the Catalan People," in which he developed the theme of the economically powerful Catalan bourgeoisie hampered politically by a decadent centralist state.

In 1898, Prat, Josep Puig i Cadafalch (1869–1956), and other Catalans transformed *La Veu de Catalunya* into a daily and politically interventionist Catalan newspaper, with Prat becoming editor in 1899. He negotiated the merger of the Catalan National Center and the Regionalist Union in 1901 into the Lliga Regionalista, the party of Catalonia's bourgeoisie, which sought to achieve autonomy for the region within a Spanish state. Prat became secretary of the party and *La Veu* became the voice of the Lliga. These activities, in addition to the stress of an arrest for nationalist activities in 1897, and imprisonment in 1902 for an article in *La Veu*, made him gravely ill, and he spent 1902–1904 in a French sanatorium.

Prat's return to Barcelona marked his active emergence into government participation. He was elected provincial deputy from Barcelona in 1905, and at the general assembly of Spanish Deputations meeting in Barcelona in 1906, Prat presented a project for a local law based on municipal and regional autonomy. On 14 Apr. 1907, Prat was elected president of the Barcelona provincial deputation and won reelection every two years until his death. His ideas on regional autonomy were accepted by the national government of José Canalejas (1854–1912), and the Mancomunitat was constituted in Apr. 1914. Prat was elected president, a post he occupied until his death in 1917.

Prat's object as a nationalist was to strengthen a Catalan culture neglected by the central state. While president of the provincial diputació, he was able to create a special commission for cultural renovation. The Institute for Catalan Studies was created in 1907 to provide a center for advanced studies related to Catalonia's culture and directed by leading specialists. In 1913, the Institute published the work of the philologist Pompeu Fabra (1868–1948), which established the orthographic norms of Catalan. The diputació also began the restoration of the Palace of the Generalitat and reorganized the Industrial University of Barcelona. While president of the Mancomunitat, he established the Library of Catalonia, a number of local libraries, schools for librarians and the dramatic arts, and schools for local administrators and nurses. An office of juridical studies, a service to preserve monuments, and a meteorological station were among his other achievements. He was also instrumental in creating the Catalan economic junta on 6 Aug. 1914. His written works included *Corts catalanes* (1906), *Les Mancomunitats* (1912), *Per Catalunya i l'Espanya gran* (1916), *Message en defensa dels drets de la llengua catalana* (1916), and *Història de la nació catalana* (1917).

Quiet and reserved, Prat de la Riba nevertheless came to champion Catalonia; his effectiveness is seen in the enormous demonstration of popular grief at his death on 1 Aug. 1917 and in the regular reprintings of his classic *La Nacionalitat Catalana*.

For additional information, see J. Bofill, *Prat de la Riba i la cultura catalana*, ed. J. Casassas (Barcelona, 1979); and J. M. Figueres, *Prat de la Riba* (Barcelona, 1983).

*V. L. Enders*

*Related entries:* BARCELONA; CATALONIA.

**PRIM Y PRATS, JUAN,** conde de Reus, vizconde del Bruch, marqués de Wad-Ras (1814–1870), general, politician, and leader of the Revolution of 1868. Prim was born on 6 Dec. 1814 in the Catalan town of Reus. He saw extensive military service during the First Carlist War (1833–1840) and by the latter year held the rank of colonel. In 1841, he was elected deputy from Tarragona and in 1843 was named by Gen. Francisco Serrano (1810–1885) governor of Madrid* and subsequently of Barcelona.* His harsh suppression of a series of uprisings won him the favor of the government and the titles conde de Reus and vizconde del Bruch. Prim's fortunes waned, however, when he came into open conflict with the Moderate party,* and his participation in a conspiracy against Gen. Ramón Narváez* resulted in a death sentence that, though commuted, led to a brief, self-imposed exile. Returned to favor in 1847, he was named governor of Puerto Rico.

In 1856 Prim became captain general of Granada and from there in 1859 led a successful expedition to Melilla and into Morocco.* He emerged from the Moroccan War (1859–1860) as marqués de Castillejos, marqués de Wad-Ras, and one of the most popular men in Spain; he was certainly the hero of the Catalans. In 1861, he commanded the combined Anglo-French-Spanish expedition to Veracruz, Mexico, and secured reparations from the Benito Juárez (1806–1872) government. His refusal to support French ambitions in Mexico* earned him the enmity of Napoleon III (1808–1873) and the suspicions of his own government.

Upon his return to Spain, Prim moved ever closer to revolutionary elements and at least by the mid–1860s had become the acknowledged military chief of the antidynastic Progressive party.* His involvement in a series of feeble revolts led to exile and forced him to the reluctant conclusion that only through cooperation with disaffected Liberal Union party members and even republicans could he hope to topple the government of Isabel II.* From headquarters in London, he masterminded a conspiracy that led eventually to the Sept. 1868 revolution and the overthrow of the Bourbon throne. Early in 1869, Prim became head of the government under a Serrano regency and undertook to find for Spain a suitable monarch. The failure of the Hohenzollern candidacy in the summer of 1870 resulted in an invitation to Amadeo I,* second son of Victor Emmanuel (1820–1878), to accept the crown. The new king reached Spain on 30 Dec. 1870, only to learn that Prim had died of wounds inflicted by unknown assassins who were almost certainly members of an extremist republican faction. Prim's death severely undermined the Savoy dynasty and contributed heavily to its early failure.

For additional information, see V. Álvarez Villamil and R. Llopsis, eds., *Cartas de conspiradores: La Revolución de Septiembre, de la emigración al poder* (Madrid, 1919); R. Muñiz, *Apuntes históricos sobre la Revolución de 1868* (Madrid, 1884); and R. Olivar Bertrand, *El caballero Prim* (Barcelona, 1952).

G. T. Harper

*Related entry:* FIRST REPUBLIC.


**PRIMO DE RIVERA, JOSÉ ANTONIO** (1903–1936), son of the dictator and founder of the Falange Española.* José Antonio was the eldest son of the second marqués de Estella and was born in Madrid where his father, Gen. Miguel Primo de Rivera,* had been posted as a lieutenant colonel in the Spanish army. José Antonio's mother died only five years later, following the birth of the family's sixth child, and he was reared by a pair of maiden aunts who saw to it that he attended some of the capital's finest schools. Although one of José Antonio's biographers insists that he was "a normal student, not excessively brilliant," he was admitted to the University of Madrid in 1917 to prepare for a career in law. In Jan. 1923, he was licensed to practice law, and six months later he was awarded a doctorate; but rather than enter the profession, he decided to meet his military obligation and so enlisted for duty in the army.

The young Primo promptly was attached to a cavalry unit in Barcelona,* where his father had gained national attention as the region's captain-general. José Antonio had little time to become acquainted with the Catalan capital. On 12 Sept. 1923, Gen. Primo de Rivera staged the pronunciamento that would overthrow the Restoration regime and establish his dictatorship. His eldest son followed him to Madrid where, after completing his military duties, he spent the next several years pursuing his career in the law.

Initially, both Primos thrived in their new stations, but as the general's fortunes declined José Antonio became "obsessed" (to use one biographer's phrase) with rescuing his father's reputation. He was bitter when the monarchists abandoned his father and sent him into exile in Jan. 1930, but José Antonio was especially dismayed by the vehemence of Spanish intellectual opposition to his father's regime. As a student, he had joined his peers in revering such luminaries as Miguel de Unamuno* and José Ortega y Gasset.* Now, as his friends and mentors celebrated the twilight of the reign of Alfonso XIII,* José Antonio could find few who shared his esteem for his father. He was, in fact, even stripped of his military connection as a consequence of his heated attack upon Gen. Gonzálo Queipo de Llano (1875–1951), an outspoken opponent of the dictatorship.

Within a month of Miguel Primo de Rivero's death in Paris in Mar. 1930, most of his former ministers and what remained of his following coalesced to form a national political organization to replace Primo's ill-fated Unión Patriótica (UP). They styled it the Unión Monárquica Nacional, and soon had convinced José Antonio to accept the office of vice-secretary. He was also encouraged to make good use of *La Nación*, the newspaper created by the general to serve the UP. Between 1930 and 1932, José Antonio contributed no less than forty articles to its columns. He could be heard as well on radio.

The Second Republic* was constituted despite his opposition, and in Oct. 1931, José Antonio sought to gain a seat in the Cortes as a representative from Madrid to defend his father's record and continue his work. Madrid voters failed to share his enthusiasm for such a mission and elected a scholar in his place.

At this juncture, José Antonio again took up his law practice, shunned politics, and even thought of emigrating to America. In Dec. 1931, however, he was briefly detained by security forces on suspicion of plotting the overthrow of the government, and in Aug. 1932, he and his brother Miguel spent several months in Madrid's Model Prison in the wake of the failed military plot of Gen. José Sanjurjo (1872–1936). Both were released in Oct., when the allegations against them were dropped.

While José Antonio may not have participated actively in the Sanjurjo revolt, he made no effort to disguise his enmity to the republican regime. He spoke frequently across the nation against the philosophical foundations of democratic government, defended one of his father's ministers from parliamentary investigators, and in Mar. 1933, lent his name to an article that appeared in the first edition of a newspaper that bore the title *El Fascio*.

There is some disagreement about the nature of this publication, since it has been maintained that its publisher may simply have been capitalizing on reader interest in Nazi Germany rather than seeking to provide a forum for a Spanish rendition of fascism. José Antonio's contribution, however, represents far more than a mere apology for monarchism. His essay indicted the entire liberal interpretation of the law and maintained that it produced "the gravest inequity" by "making the worker the slave of the capitalist." He called for the creation of a new state in which class struggle would become incompatible with the "transcendent unity" of the nation. While he would later deny that the word "fascism" really described his vision for Spain's future, the term was probably applicable.

Although this first edition of *El Fascio* was promptly confiscated by the government, it did not escape the attention of the monarchist newspaper *ABC*, which chided its contributors for having produced a mere imitation of fascism. José Antonio did more than pen a response; he promptly set about creating a mechanism to propound these notions. Within two months, he had received enough financial backing to announce the formation of what his propaganda leaflets called the Movimiento Sindicalista Español. Operating from his law office in Madrid, the movement became sufficiently visible to gain him a place at a meeting of several opposition groups convened by Bilbao financiers at San Sebastian, in Aug. 1933, to find a common approach to the impending elections for the Cortes scheduled for November. While no formal structure emerged, a determination was made to announce its creation in some kind of public forum.

That forum was a meeting on 29 Oct. 1933, attended by nearly two thousand people at Madrid's Teatro Comedia and transmitted nationally by radio. The hall had been donated by a friend of Primo, and those who crowded into its seats were treated to orations that assailed capitalism for having degraded the workers, socialism for proclaiming eternal class conflict, and all existing parties for dividing the nation. "The 'Patria' is a transcendent synthesis," Primo intoned, and "no other dialectic is admissible save the dialectic of fists and pistols when justice or the 'Patria' is offended."

Some take these words to have been prophetic, even momentous. Until this speech, no responsible person from Spain's conservative class had advocated violence, a campaign of official terror, or the type of street gangsterism that José Antonio Primo de Rivera now embraced. At the time of his address, the movement that José Antonio so boldly proclaimed had yet to agree upon its tactics, its program, or even its name.

Even without these prerequisites, the meeting at the Teatro Comedia was a clear success. Inquiries about membership in the "poetic movement" (as José Antonio had described it in his speech) came in from across the nation and even beyond. José Calvo Sotelo,* the exiled former minister of finance and preeminent monarchist, wrote from Paris to ask to be included in the new organization. His application was eventually denied as José Antonio's movement struggled to distinguish itself from the traditionalist and conservative parties that already dotted the landscape of the political Right.

Self-definition was a preoccupation of the emerging movement in the weeks immediately following the meeting, even though José Antonio also busied himself with campaigning in Cadiz in another attempt to gain a parliamentary seat. On 2 Nov., after an entire day of meeting behind closed doors in Madrid, it was decided that the organization should be named Falange Española, a term suggesting national solidarity that several would later claim to have coined. Even this much clarification of the group's purposes was costly since several leading members promptly withdrew from any further association with the group. The bad news of these defections was mitigated by José Antonio's electoral victory. Thanks to a boycott of the voting staged by the region's anarchists and the timely support of an old-fashioned cacique,* the citizens of Cadiz sent a leading Falangist to represent them in the Cortes, according him a parliamentary immunity from arrest.

Further definition of the Falange emerged on 7 Dec. 1933, when the first edition of the movement's newspaper, *F. E.*, rolled off the presses. It contained a lengthy statement clarifying some of the ambiguities remaining about the organization while still retaining Primo's distinct notion of Spain as "a unity of destiny" now threatened by regional separatism, by the clash of political parties, and by class conflict. The remedies proposed by the Falange were vague, but explicit enough to demonstrate hostility to the existing republican regime. Abolition of political parties and the Cortes would lead to a new state that recognized the integrity of the family as the basis for social unity, the autonomy of the municipality as the basis for territorial unity, and the guild or corporation as the basis of a new economy.

The republic's first response to these verbal forays was to seize this edition of *F. E.* and delay its distribution for a week. Once the publication was finally delivered to newsstands, the Falange discovered that dealers were reluctant to put the newspaper on display for fear of offending substantial numbers of their customers. The organization of the Sindicato Español Universitario (SEU) as a rival to the socialist-dominated, national student syndicate, the Federación Universitaria Española (FUE), provided an immediate source of street vendors for the Falange's newspapers and ultimately proved to be a fountainhead of the organization's membership prior to the civil war.

In 1933, writers both in *El Sol* (a Madrid daily that supported the republic) and *Il Populo d'Italia* (Benito Mussolini's own daily) had ridiculed the Falange for all of its theorizing and posturing on the question of violence. In early 1934, the issue ceased being theoretical. Youths selling *F. E.* on street corners in Madrid and elsewhere became targets for antifascist violence. Rather than remaining content with staging massive funerals for the victims, José Antonio authorized his associates to begin a Falangist policy of reprisal for every assault. Thus began the "street gangsterism" noted earlier. One of José Antonio's senior lieutenants would recall that the Falangist leader later confessed that he had authorized this action only after a prolonged personal struggle.

In these circumstances, it is not surprising that the Falange would be more interested than ever in locating allies. For more than a year, José Antonio had been meeting with representatives of another diminutive fascist group that could trace its origins back to 1931 and boasted a youthful following of about three hundred members. Styling itself the Juntas de Ofensiva Nacional Sindicalista (JONS), its membership was concentrated primarily in Valladolid and Madrid, and its most prominent leader was Ramiro Ledesma Ramos (1905–1936). On 11 Feb. 1934, Ledesma's fascists voted to merge their organization with the Falange, officially creating the Falange Española de las Juntas de Ofensiva Nacional-Sindicalista. In addition to relatively insignificant numbers, the JONS lent to the new organization all the symbols, élan, and ideology of national syndicalism, a doctrine that sought to win the support of the industrial working class for a revolutionary restructuring of society within the framework of the nation.

To accommodate the new members, the movement was reorganized. While retaining its national council and its executive committee (the Junta Política), the Falange now acquired a dual leadership consisting of José Antonio and Ledesma Ramos. It was then decided to celebrate the creation of the "FE y de la JONS" by staging a combined national meeting at Valladolid in March. The gathering would be an imposing event, attracting nearly three thousand to the ancient Castilian city's Teatro Calderón. It also attracted the Falange's mortal enemies, and before the day had ended, there had been still another battle in the streets and another fatality in the movement's ranks.

How revolutionary the new organization was is still debated by historians, but clearly the revolutionary nature of José Antonio's movement was sufficient to cost the Falange the financial backing of the nation's monied elite. Funds dried up, membership stabilized, and ambitious plans for the future (such as the publication of a Falangist daily newspaper) were shelved. By late 1934, the embattled fascists could no longer even pay their electric bill at party headquarters.

Ledesma sought deliverance from this dreary plight by enlisting the aid of the Spanish proletariat. In Aug. 1934, he convinced the Falange's Junta Política to permit him to organize local chapters of a nationwide Confederación de Obreros Nacional-Sindicalistas (CONS). The workers organized in their shops and factories by the CONS, he hoped, would reject both the Marxist labor unions and the Catholic syndicates in favor of the Falange's vision of a national-syndicalist Spain. It would be their numbers and their resources that would rescue the Falange from oblivion.

Hard pressed by the conservative cabinet of Ricardo Samper (1881–1938) that had banned any further issues of *F. E.* and even brought charges of impeachment against him the Cortes, José Antonio spent much of the summer of 1934 seeking a quiet accommodation with representatives of the monarchist organization, Renovación Española. Ultimately, he enjoyed no more success in that endeavor than Ledesma did in creating juntas of CONS. By the end of the summer, José Antonio determined that the Falange could not continue pursuing two policy directions at once, and he informed the Junta Política that the movement's leadership arrangement was absurd. When the Falange's national council convened in Madrid on 4 Oct., it abolished the organization's executive triumvirate and created a single executive officer (jefe único) in its place. Sensing the drift of the meeting, Ledesma Ramos then moved that the office be conferred upon José Antonio. His resolution was adopted unanimously.

Even as the Falange debated its future, Spain's prospects were being decided in the streets. A general strike called by the socialists on 4 Oct. became a call for armed rebellion against the government. While five Falangists were killed in Asturias* in the suppression of the rebellion, the most dramatic act taken by the organization's national council during the crisis was to stage a noisy demonstration in Madrid against Catalan secession. Even the horrendous events that had actually produced armed workers seizing industrial property were not enough either to augment significantly the sagging ranks of the Falange or to revitalize its treasury.

Ledesma apparently despaired of the predicament and began making overtures to his former associates in the JONS about abandoning the Falange and starting anew without the ubiquitous José Antonio. The Falange's jefe único learned of these machinations and summoned a meeting of the organization's Junta Política, which, on 16 Jan. 1935, voted to expel Ledesma Ramos. The chimera of a fascist breakthrough to the Left did not, however, vanish with Ledesma's expulsion from the Falange. Throughout 1935, José Antonio continued to negotiate with a splinter faction of the anarchist movement, headed by Ángel Pestaña (1881–1937), to establish a mass base for Spanish national syndicalism, and as late as the winter of 1936, he continued to hope that Indalecio Prieto (1883–1902) could be convinced to abandon the Socialist party* (PSOE) for some kind of coalition with the Falange. While his only really radical point was a proposal to nationalize credit, José Antonio's rhetoric was sufficiently progressive to be described as "bolshevik" by a rightist deputy who sought to refute his speech, on 23 July 1935 in the Cortes, on agrarian reform.

A few weeks earlier, José Antonio had convened a meeting of the Junta Política at Gredos to consider privately what would appear to have been a desperate ploy. The Falange, he argued, could rally its membership at Toledo and march upon Madrid, where, with the help of the officers of the Unión Militar Española, it might execute a dramatic seizure of power. Lack of support quickly dissuaded him.

Far more promising was the possibility of enhancing the Falange's stature by electoral victory that beckoned to it suddenly when the Cortes was dissolved and new parliamentary elections were called for Feb. 1936. As early as Nov. 1935, the Falange's national council had considered this eventuality and debated whether to enter into a coalition with the nation's conservative parties to contest the elections. The council was deeply divided on the issue and authorized José Antonio to enter into such negotiations only as an equal partner within the prospective coalition. In the end, José María Gil Robles and his associates in the National Front proved unresponsive to the notion. The Falange generally faced the elections in isolation from the two contending coalitions vying for Spain's future. The immediate results for the Falange were disastrous, since it lost every seat it contested. Even José Antonio was defeated in his endeavor to retain his constituency in Cadiz, and with it went his parliamentary immunity.

The consequences of this debacle were not long forthcoming. In response to an attempt by Falangist gunmen to assassinate a socialist law professor at the University of Madrid, the newly elected government of Manuel Azaña* banned the Falange on 14 Mar. 1936 and arrested its Junta Política, including José Antonio. Despite these reverses, the Falange's fortunes had dramatically changed with the defeat of Gil Robles's National Front. Since electoral opposition to the Popular Front had conspicuously failed, it now became clear that only the Falange and the Carlists had paramilitary means to forestall the Azaña regime. Early in May 1936, the Right entered the name of José Antonio as a candidate for election to the Cortes for Cuenca (primarily as a chance for renewed parliamentary immunity), and before the end of the month, the imprisoned Falangist leader had been approached by Gen. Emilio Mola* about the Falange's participation in a military uprising against the republic.

While he eventually sanctioned Falangist participation in the military uprising, José Antonio continued to fear that his comrades would be used as shock troops in a conservative cause. When the uprising finally did occur in July, he and other members of the Junta were dispersed to provincial prisons where they were supposed to be safe from attempts at rescue. In José Antonio's case, these precautions proved effective. After several abortive efforts to negotiate his release as a part of an exchange of prisoners and a total of five trials for various offenses against the republic, he was executed by firing squad on 20 Nov. 1936.

Franco's Spain reserved its highest honors for him by enshrining his remains near the tomb of Gen. Franco at the Valley of the Fallen in a spot inscribed simply "José Antonio." It has been claimed that the adoration after his death was a phenomenon artificially stimulated and organized for reasons of state, a verdict that can be tested only by the decades.

For additional information, see F. Bravo Martínez, *José Antonio: El hombre, el Jefé, el Camarada* (Madrid, 1940); S. Dávila, *José Antonio, Salamanca y otras cosas* (Madrid, 1967); I. Gibson, *En busca de José Antonio* (Barcelona, 1980); A. Muñoz Medina, *Un pensador para un pueblo* (Madrid, 1969); S. G. Payne, *Falange: A History of Spanish Fascism* (Stanford, 1961); C. Rojas Vila, *Prieto y José Antonio: Socialismo y Falange ante la tragedia civil* (Barcelona, 1977); A. Río Cisneros, ed., *Obras de José Antonio Primo de Rivera* (Madrid, 1966); H. G. Southworth, *Antifalange* (Paris, 1967); and F. Ximénez de Sandoval, *José Antonio: Biografía apasionada* (Barcelona, 1941).

*D. W. Foard*

*Related entries:* FRANCO, GEN. FRANCISCO; SECOND REPUBLIC; SPANISH CIVIL WAR.

**PRIMO DE RIVERA Y ORBANEJA, MIGUEL,** second marqués de Estella (1870–1930), general and dictator of Spain, 1923–1930. Primo de Rivera was born in Jerez de la Frontera on 8 Jan. 1870, the sixth of twelve children of Miguel Primo de Rivera y Sobremonte, a retired staff colonel from a prominent liberal military family, and his wife, Inés de Orbaneja y Pérez de Grandallana, daughter of a wealthy noble landholder from Jerez. In 1882, he was sent to study in Madrid, where he soon decided on a military career, entering the newly created Academia General Militar in Toledo in 1884. This decision won him the attention of his uncle, Lt. Gen. Fernando Primo de Rivera y Sobremonte, the marqués de Estella, a leading Restoration general closely allied with Gen. Arsenio Martínez Campos (1831–1900), the Conservative party, and the court. His uncle's position and patronage aided Primo's rapid advance through the military ranks after his commission as an infantry second lieutenant in 1889.

Nevertheless, Primo did not owe his success entirely to his political connections. Temperamentally impetuous and decisive, he won quick promotion through courageous leadership in battle. His bravery under fire at Cabrerizas Altas near Melilla in 1893 was rewarded with the Cross of San Fernando, promotion to captain, and appointment as an aide to his uncle. In 1895, as a result of his involvement in the assault by junior officers on the offices of two progressive dailies in Madrid, he was sent to Cuba as an aide to Gen. Martínez Campos. There he volunteered for action, earning another merit promotion and two decorations for valor. In Mar. 1897, he joined his uncle in the Philippines, where he was promoted to lieutenant colonel for his skillful negotiation of the Pact of Biac-na-bató, by which Emilio Aguinaldo (1869–1964) agreed to abandon the rebellion in return for a comfortable exile in Hong Kong.

Returning to Madrid to a post in the war ministry, in 1902 Primo married Casilda Sáenz de Heredia y Suárez de Argudín, the daughter of a wealthy former colonial administrator and his Cuban wife. Six children, including the eldest, José Antonio Primo de Rivera,* the future founder of the Falange Española,* were born to the marriage before her death in childbirth in 1908. Promoted to colonel by seniority in Nov. 1908, Primo volunteered for action in North Africa in 1909, and again in 1911, when he was wounded in the foot and promoted to brigadier general at age forty-one, the first graduate of the Academia General Militar to achieve that rank. His merit promotion to division general was the result of his battlefield action in Tetuan in 1913, for which he also was awarded a second Cross of Military Merit.

Perhaps because of his sympathy for the Allies, Primo was without assignment after his promotion until 1915, when he was appointed military governor of Cadiz. In Mar. 1917, on the occasion of his induction into the Real Academia Hispano-Americana de Ciencias y Artes de Cadiz, he urged the exchange of Ceuta for Gibraltar,* a suggestion that earned him immediate dismissal. Unimpressed with the impoverished strip of North Africa allocated to Spain despite his extensive service there, Primo would reiterate this proposal in the Senate (where he represented Cadiz from 1918 on) in Nov. 1921, after the disaster at Anwal.* As in 1917, his outspokenness would be rewarded with abrupt termination of his duties.

After 1917, as the deepening social and political crisis of the Restoration system magnified the power of the army, Primo became increasingly active in civil-military politics. Although he was initially unsympathetic to the Juntas de Defensa (which in turn viewed his career as a blatant example of the favoritism that often governed military promotions and appointments), he eventually overcame his reputation as an undeserving beneficiary of political patronage and became a spokesman for the antioligarchical, but also socially conservative, majority in the military bureaucracy, a role for which his expansive, unpretentious personality and simplistic political ideas well suited him. His influence with the juntas made him indispensable to politicians seeking to balance the military factionalism that pitted junteros against africanistas and palaciegos. From 1918 on, he held several influential posts, including, after his elevation to lieutenant general in July 1919, appointment as captain-general in Valencia (July 1920–July 1921), Madrid (Oct.-Nov. 1921), and Barcelona (Mar. 1922–Sept. 1923). The death of his uncle in 1921 brought him the title of marqués de Estella and a tax-free grandeza de España.

Primo's mounting frustration with the parliamentary regime and the dynastic parties grew out of their inability to deal decisively with the political and social problems of the postwar era or to respond positively to the popular opinion mobilized by the postwar crisis, particularly after the disaster at Anwal. Political immobilism and electoral manipulation, violent social conflict, the military collapse in eastern Morocco* in 1921, the reluctance of the dynastic parties to address forthrightly the question of political responsibilities for the disaster, and, most important, their inability to end the unpopular war in Morocco, led Primo to conclude that only a dictatorship could break the impasse at which the regime had apparently arrived. His pessimism was shared by many other Spaniards, including the king, Alfonso XIII.*

Standing in the way of a dictatorship were the lack of a suitable leader and the serious divisions in the army, whose effective power had increased as the moral authority and political will of the civilian politicians had declined. During the summer of 1923, Primo promoted his own candidacy among the Catalan bourgeoisie and the junteros in the Barcelona garrison. Meanwhile, the belated and timid efforts of the liberal coalition government of 1923 to reassert the principle of civil supremacy both in the peninsula and in Morocco temporarily united the officer corps in defense of its corporate interests. In late Aug., the government's indecision in the face of a renewed Rif offensive convinced the "Quadrilateral"—a group of africanista conspirators in Madrid—to throw their support to the general, who had twice publicly advocated abandoning the protectorate. In the early hours of 13 Sept., Primo ordered his troops to seize the communications offices in Barcelona and issued a manifesto "to the country and the army" indicating his intention to assume the role of dictator. The halfhearted resistance of Manuel García Prieto's (1859–1938) cabinet was overcome by the king's decision to support the pronunciamento and by the disinclination of the officer corps and the country to defend the discredited parliamentary regime. On 15 Sept., a royal decree created a military directory composed of eight brigadier generals and headed by Primo de Rivera.

In Sept. 1923, Primo described his dictatorship as a "brief parenthesis" in the constitutional life of the nation, during which the strict application of the military virtues—honor, patriotism, obedience, and discipline—would root out political corruption and social disorder and create the climate necessary for national regeneration. He estimated that ninety days would be sufficient to cleanse the political landscape; lay the "responsibilities" issue to rest; and find a "rapid, dignified and sensible" solution to the Moroccan war; whereupon he and the army would withdraw to make way for the "new men" who would spontaneously emerge to rebuild the nation once the grip of the caciques* had been broken.

In its initial phase, the military directory was little more than a front for the purely personal dictatorship of Primo de Rivera. Relying on military personnel to maintain order and authority, he dismantled the old regime, the Cortes and constitutional guarantees were suspended, and martial law and prior censorship were imposed. Military officers replaced civil governors throughout Spain, mayors and town councils were disbanded and reorganized under the supervision of military "governmental delegates," the judicial system was investigated, and the revolutionary syndicalist movement was virtually destroyed. Responding to the prevailing military hostility to "separatism," the dictator also repressed all manifestations of regionalism or nationalism in Catalonia.*

As it became clear that national regeneration would require more than ninety days, however, Primo tentatively embarked on an extended and, ultimately, unsuccessful effort to institutionalize and legitimize his regime. The military directory was reorganized in Dec. 1923, giving it greater administrative structure and responsibility. A new municipal statute, drawn up in early Mar. 1924 by a former Maurist, José Calvo Sotelo,* was intended to decentralize and reorganize the state from the bottom up by restoring independence and vitality to local authorities through corporatively based elections. To mobilize a new political class to assume local leadership roles, Primo's supporters, led by the rightist Asociación Católica Nacional de Propagandistas, organized the Unión Patriótica (UP), which became the official government party in Apr. 1924. Tightly centralized under the civil governors, however, the Unión Patriótica lacked sufficient autonomy or popular support to assume the democratic and renovationist role that the dictator had originally envisioned.

Despite these early efforts to institutionalize his power, Primo continued to promise a prompt conclusion to his dictatorship. The chief obstacle was the Moroccan War, which continued to defy easy resolution. By late May 1924, however, he had decided upon a retreat to the coastal strongholds, a policy to which he adhered in the face of serious opposition from the African army and mounting aggression from the forces of the Rif leader, Muhammad ibn Abd al-Krim al Khatabi (1882–1963). To meet these threats, he assumed personal command of the withdrawal operations from Xauen to the "Primo de Rivera line" near Tetuan in Nov. 1924, a difficult retreat that cost nearly two thousand Spanish lives but that probably forestalled a more serious defeat. It is unclear whether Primo ultimately intended to abandon the protectorate or to force a situation that would bring the French into the war against Abd al-Krim, but Franco-Spanish collaboration became a reality when the Rif leader invaded the French zone. In Sept. 1925, a successful amphibious landing was made at Alhucemas Bay in the central Rif; six months later, Abd al-Krim surrendered, leaving only minor operations to bring a conclusion to the war in July 1927.

Encouraged by the popular acclaim that greeted the victory at Alhucemas, Primo reneged on his commitment to return power to civilian hands and openly endeavored to perpetuate his rule by restructuring Spanish political institutions along authoritarian lines. On 4 Dec. 1925, he announced the formation of a civilian directory composed of technocrats and politicians from the UP, which had attracted sufficient recruits to permit the reduction of the military presence in the state administration. The UP leadership also supplied a nationalist, Catholic, authoritarian, and corporativist ideology that was intended to legitimize the regime by winning the allegiance of the conservative classes, if not the liberal democratic intellectuals and politicians who rejected the ideological and political monopoly claimed by the new party. On the third anniversary of the coup, the UP organized a plebiscite to demonstrate popular support for a corporatively elected assembly to the king, who was reluctant to break so definitively with the Constitution of 1876. Finally, in Sept. 1927, Alfonso XIII agreed to the convocation of a national assembly that, although lacking legislative powers, would prepare a new constitution.

Because the electoral methods and procedural rules of the assembly lacked democratic guarantees, it was boycotted by the dynastic politicians, the liberal intelligentsia, and the organized working class, thus failing to acquire the popular legitimacy that Primo desired. The draft constitution, unveiled in 1929, was a rightist document that provided for the supremacy of the state, a strong executive authority vested in the king, corporate representation in a limited legislature, and restricted individual rights. The proposal was strenuously criticized not only by the growing republican opposition, but also by many liberal monarchists as well.

The economic policies of the dictatorship reflected the nationalist and regenerationist sentiments of Primo de Rivera as well as the corporativist ideology of his finance minister, José Calvo Sotelo. The regime actively stimulated economic growth and development through an extensive program of state intervention. Tariffs, subsidies, public works, state monopolies, and official encouragement of industrial concentration provided profits for Spanish capitalism and a significant expansion and modernization of the economy as a whole. A series of government agencies, culminating in a new ministry of national economy in 1928, represented and protected the corporate interests of Catalan and Basque* industrialists and, to a lesser degree, large landholding interests. Small entrepreneurs, farmers, and commercial interests fared less well, however, and would later register their discontent by supporting the republican movement.

Economic expansion required social peace and working-class cooperation, as did Primo's claim that his regime represented the interest of all Spaniards. Acknowledging the social and economic grievances of the revolutionary Left, and inspired by the example of fascist Italy,* his minister of labor, Eduardo Aunós (1894–1953), implemented an ambitious corporativist program of social welfare and labor legislation that was designed to encourage the collaboration of the moderates in the Socialist party* (PSOE) and its trade-union affiliate, the Unión General de Trabajadores* (UGT). The centerpiece of the program was the corporative comités paritarios, or labor arbitration boards, which were dominated by the UGT. Francisco Largo Caballero,* head of the UGT, was also a member of the advisory council of state. A stable, or even improved, standard of living for urban workers and acceptable levels of unemployment purchased the social peace the dictatorship required, but the collaboration of the socialists was opportunistic, disappearing once the political tide began to turn against the dictatorship. At the same time, the regime's conciliatory social policies and the prolabor bias of the arbitration boards were resented by employers and landowners.

To pay for its economic and social programs, the dictatorship attempted to increase revenues by curbing tax evasion and by imposing new and heavier direct and indirect taxes on the propertied classes. Although state income rose, the hostility of the middle classes to progressive taxation forced the regime to rely extensively on public loans to meet expenditures, a tactic that succeeded only so long as it enjoyed public confidence. Mounting deficits, inflation, and the decline in the peseta, after 1928, further eroded the dictator's support among Spanish business interests.

It was the diminishing support of the officer corps that decisively weakened the dictatorship. From the beginning dependent upon the military, Primo nevertheless felt confident enough after the creation of the civil directory in 1925 to inaugurate a reform program designed to professionalize and modernize the armed forces. Though not ill conceived, his reforms damaged corporate interests without achieving technical efficiency and were too often arbitrarily administered. Conflicts between economically distressed and underemployed peninsular officers and the africanistas, whose careers flourished as a result of the merit promotions lavishly distributed during the concluding phases of the Moroccan War, were an endemic source of discontent. The extension of merit promotions to the hitherto-exempt artillery corps provoked rebellions in 1926 and 1929, and drove the corps as a whole into the republican opposition. The resurrection of the Academia General Militar in Saragossa, in 1927, failed to achieve its mission of diminishing interbranch rivalries. The evident political vulnerability of the dictatorship encouraged dissident officers to join the civilian opposition, to the dismay of those—among them the king—who were worried about the growing politicization of the officer corps. When a direct appeal to the captains general for support in Jan. 1930 did not elicit an enthusiastic response, Primo was forced to resign. He died of diabetic complications in Paris on 16 Mar. and was buried without official ceremony in Madrid a few days later. After the Spanish Civil War,* Gen. Francisco Franco* promoted him posthumously to captain general, and his tomb was transferred to the city of his birth.

An authoritarian military regime similar to those that arose elsewhere in Europe between the wars, the dictatorship of Gen. Primo de Rivera had a lasting impact on Spain. In a negative way, it had made possible the democratization of political life during the Second Republic* by destroying the Restoration political system and damaging the prestige of the king and the army, making it impossible to return to the old order after his departure from office. The economic development promoted by the regime also hastened the pace of urbanization and social modernization and thus fostered the political mobilization that led to the republican triumph in 1931. Equally important, the ideology and institutions of the dictatorship provided inspiration and leadership for the authoritarian Right that emerged in opposition to the republic in the 1930s. In many ways, it was a precursor of and model for the military dictatorship of Gen. Franco that governed Spain for forty years after the civil war.

For additional information, see S. Ben-Ami, *Fascism from Above: The Dictatorship of Primo de Rivera in Spain, 1923–1930* (New York, 1983); M. T. González Calbet, *La dictadura de Primo de Rivera: El directorio militar* (Madrid, 1988); G. Maura Gamazo, *Bosquejo histórico de la dictadura* (Madrid, 1930); P. Pérez, *La dictadura a través de sus notas oficiosas* (Madrid, 1930); J. Rial, *Revolution from Above: The Primo de Rivera Dictatorship in Spain, 1923–1930* (Fairfax, 1986); A. de Sagrera, *Miguel Primo de Rivera: El hombre, el soldado, el político* (Jerez de la Frontera, 1973); J. Tussell Gómez, *Radiografía de un golpe de estado: El ascenso al poder del General Primo de Rivera* (Madrid, 1987); and J. Velarde Fuertes, *Política económica de la dictadura* (Madrid, 1973).

*C. P. Boyd*

*Related entries:* ALFONSO XIII; ANWAL; MOROCCO.


**PROGRESSIVE PARTY.** The Progressive party originated in 1834, when the regency of María Cristina, faced by the First Carlist War (1833–1840), permitted the Moderate party* to organize the defense of the central government. Progresista creator, Salustiano Olózaga (1805–1873), pressed for a return to the anticlericalism, disentailment,* and rigorously controlled constitutional monarchy of the Cortes of Cadiz*; when this did not occur, he drew upon the exaltados tradition of the early 1820s, a mixture of liberalism and romanticism characterized by the martyred Maj. Rafael de Riego (1785–1823), who exerted a posthumous influence akin to that of Augustino César Sandino (1893–1934) in contemporary Nicaragua.

The troubled times of the Carlist War allowed the progressives to take advantage of provincial unrest to install their first cabinet in 1835. The premiership of Juan Álvarez Mendizábal* saw the near completion of disentailment as the final secularization of mortmain and entailed lands begun at Cadiz. This gesture toward popular sovereignty, more beneficial to urban speculators and the politicians themselves, backfired when confusion and resentment enabled Gen. Baldomero Espartero* to ignore the party and take over the regency of María Cristina (1806–1878) from 1840 to 1843; his rule devastated civil liberties and revealed the dark side of the Progressive party. Since no political organization in nineteenth-century Spain could resist the strong national power of the army,* however, Espartero's expediency and authoritarianism damaged civil control of government.

In 1843, Espartero's fall to the Moderate party's Gen. Ramón María Narváez* caused a decade-long progressive hiatus. During this period, they developed all the characteristics of an embittered opposition party—hypercriticism, demagoguery, jealousy of prerogatives, desperation for power—ending any connection with Cadiz or Riego; jobs and political profits were more important. Economic dislocation finally opened the way for the bienio progresista (1854–1856), but the return to power was so rancorous that no agreement on constitutional revisions could be reached, and the creation of a national militia was the Revolution of 1854's only accomplishment. Efforts to go further only encouraged radical and republican unrest.

After this failure, the Progressive and Moderate parties began a slow collapse. Economic growth allowed the coalition Liberal Union cabinet of Gen. Leopoldo O'Donnell* (1858–1863) to adapt laissez-faire to the now stagnant liberalism from above that both parties practiced. The progressives quarreled more with Isabel II,* but they were not free to challenge her regime as long as the moderates remained close to the throne. When she abdicated in 1868, rising regional and radical ideologies made the party obsolete, although Antonio Cánovas del Castillo* did adapt their sense of order, limited participation in government, and severely restricted franchise for use in the Bourbon restoration by his Liberal-Conservative party, bulwark of liberal politics until the dictatorship of Gen. Miguel Primo de Rivera* abolished the nineteenth-century political system in 1923.

For additional information, see A. Jutglar, *Ideologías y clases en la España contemporánea* (Barcelona, 1969); and L. Sánchez Agesta, *Historia del constitucionalismo español* (Madrid, 1955).

*R. W. Kern*

*Related entries:* CÁNOVAS DEL CASTILLO, ANTONIO; ISABEL II; LIBERALISM; NARVÁEZ, GEN. RAMÓN MARÍA.

# R

RAMÓN Y CAJAL, SANTIAGO (1852–1934), histologist, neurologist, Nobel laureate. Ramón y Cajal was born in Navarre* on 1 May 1852, the son of a country surgeon. He studied medicine at the University of Saragossa; received the undergraduate degree in 1873, which licensed him to practice medicine; and spent two years as a military doctor in Cuba. After two more years of private and personal study in Saragossa, he obtained the doctorate as an external student at Madrid* in 1877. While still preparing for this examination, he returned to an assistantship in the medical faculty at Saragossa and there began a lifelong love affair with microscopy. He was appointed professor of anatomy at Valencia* (1884) and of histology at Barcelona* (1887) and Madrid (1892–1922), all the while becoming absorbed in the morphology of the nervous system.

At the time, staining technique was too primitive to follow nerve fibers through a mass of tissues. The key exploratory tool, developed by Camilio Golgi (1843–1926) at Pavia, had escaped general notice. Nerve tissue resisted organic dyes, but Golgi had discovered that silver chromate was absorbed by nerve fibers, setting them in black relief against the surrounding neuroglia (the supporting nerve tissue). Ramón y Cajal viewed sections of brain tissue prepared by a colleague at Valencia using Golgi's method, apparently in 1885, and found his vocation.

His own work reached a peak at Barcelona in 1888, which he called "my greatest year." The gross form of the nerve cell was already known: a cell body with a single, generally long, extension to one side and one or more generally shorter extensions to the other side, known as the axon and dendrites, respectively. By improving on Golgi's method, Ramón y Cajal saw many details missed before, clearly discerning the brushes at the tips of these extensions. He drew two morphological conclusions: that the brushes terminate in the neuroglia and are not fused in a network, such as Golgi thought (as part of established reticular theory), and further that while the brushes of one cell come very close to those of another, there is no mechanical connection. From these, he extracted two physiological consequences: the cell bodies and their extensions must form an integral chain that conducts nerve impulses; these impulses, moreover, must bridge the gaps as electricity through contacts between conductors. Wilhelm His (1831–1904) had already suggested that the nerve cell—body, dendrites, and axon—was the fundamental unit of the nervous system; Ramón y Cajal's work established this concept. His work completed the cell theory of biology, for previously the nerve fibers were thought to be a partial exception. Wilhelm von Waldeyer-Hartz (1836–1921) applied the term "neuron" in 1891. The term "synapse" for a gap was added by Sir Charles Sherrington (1857–1952) in 1897.

Like all Ramón y Cajal's major discoveries, this one was a triumph of technique and persistence. The fabric of gray matter is so dense that there would have been no hope of seeing all this had it not been for a brilliant idea in which His shared about the same time: each looked to the developing embryo, before a thicket of nerve tissue was formed.

Ramón y Cajal took his preparations to the 1889 meeting in Berlin of the German Anatomical Society, and there gained the approval of His, Waldeyer, and Rudolf von Kölliker (1817–1905). The years 1890–1891 saw the diffusion of his neuronal theory—"my Palm Sunday," he called this period—even as he studied how the neuron develops from a globular embryonic nerve cell.

By 1891, he was also at work, along with researchers in Belgium, on the physiology (functioning) of neurons. Their morphological approach established that the direction of an impulse is from the dendrites toward the axon, then from the axonic brushes across the synapses into the dendrites of a contiguous neuron (the law of polarity). In 1895, he enunciated his principle of the neural avalanche: every impression received by the dendrites is propagated in the manner of a cascade, involving more and more neurons. It was for this that, in 1906, he shared the Nobel Prize in medicine with Golgi.

There are suitable entries on Ramón y Cajal in the dictionaries and encyclopedias of science history, but he has been unaccountably passed over in most histories of science or biology. His work, however, has been treated with new consideration in the recent chronicles of computer design, for electrical circuits mimicking neural assemblies show promise in machines that learn inductively from their experience.

Ramón y Cajal was a polymath: he undertook scientific investigations of the paranormal, invented an improvement on Thomas Edison's (1847–1931) phonograph, and published a book on the theory and practice of color photography. After his retirement, the government created a biological foundation, the Instituto Cajal, of which he served as director. In 1907, he was appointed to head the Junta para Ampliación de Estudios, a government commission that sought to create research facilities to improve Spanish education. Much of the system's later improvement came from the Junta's influence.

In his later years, Ramón y Cajal was stalked by illness: malaria from Cuba, tuberculosis after 1878, and heart disease after 1899. He fell into depression at

Spain's hardships and Europe's catastrophe in World War I.* Spain lost its greatest scientist at Madrid on 17 Oct. 1934.

For additional information, see D. Cannon, *Explorer of the Human Brain* (New York, 1949), and *Vida de Santiago Ramón y Cajal* (Mexico City, 1952); P. Laín Entralgo and A. Albarracín Teulon, *Nuestro Cajal* (Madrid, 1967); G. Marañón, *Cajal: Su tiempo y el nuestro* (Madrid, 1951); V. Pratt, *Thinking Machines* (Oxford, 1987); and S. Ramón y Cajal, *Recollections of My Life* (Philadelphia, 1937).

D. E. Skabelund

*Related entry:* SCIENCE.


**RIDRUEJO, DIONISIO** (1912–1975), poet and essayist whose political odyssey led him from the ranks of the Falange* to prominence in the democratic opposition to the regime of Gen. Francisco Franco.* Dionisio Ridruejo affixed his name to the roster of the Spanish fascist movement at Segovia in May 1933. Another two years would transpire before he met José Antonio Primo de Rivera,* but Ridruejo's devotion to that movement would propel him to important posts in its leadership.

In spite of his father's untimely death when Dionisio was only three years old, his family indulged the whims that drove him first to study industrial engineering, then law, and ultimately journalism. He was, in fact, vacationing in Segovia from a term at Ángel Herrera's school for journalists when the civil war erupted in July 1936.

Although Ridruejo yearned to join the fighting in the Guadarrama passes, the young Falangist was obliged to content himself with propagandizing for the cause. Before the end of 1936, he had been appointed jefe provincial of the Valladolid region and had addressed the nation in radio broadcasts from nationalist transmitters.

Ridruejo's prominence in the Falange might have been perilous for him when in Apr. 1937 Gen. Franco brought some Carlists into the organization and formed a unified Falange Española Tradicionalista y de los JONS (FET). He confronted the general personally with his protest over this action, but actually emerged from the crisis with greater responsibility. A vital element in his survival was the working relationship he developed in these crucial months with Ramón Serrano Suñer.* The two collaborated in drafting the statutes of the new organization unification had created. Before the year had ended, Serrano had been appointed minister of the interior, while Ridruejo had been named to the unified movement's National Council and its executive committee, the twelve-member Junta Política. Next in his list of promotions, he was named jefe del servicio nacional de propaganda, an office in the Interior Ministry that gave him oversight of certain aspects of the nation's communications, including films, the publication of books, and scripts for radio broadcasts.

He plunged into this work with great intensity, but soon discovered the limits of even his high offices. His Falangist schemes for a syndicalist structure for the Spanish economy* were scuttled, as were other totalitarian prescriptions for the nation's educational system. Even more vexing was the collapse of his program for winning over the population of Barcelona* after nationalist troops occupied the city in Jan. 1939. Ridruejo had intended to shower Barcelona with propaganda in Catalan, but his designs were vetoed by the local military command. While Franco's forces celebrated their triumph in the spring of that year, Dionisio Ridruejo was hospitalized for exhaustion.

His three-month convalescence at Montseny did yield an impressive result— Ridruejo's first major book of verse, his *Primer libro de amor*. He had earlier published volumes of his classical style of poetry, but this one would enjoy several editions and attract a national readership. Returning to the service of the Franco regime, Ridruejo was promoted in Aug. 1939 to the post of director general de propaganda, a niche from which he orchestrated the ceremony of moving the remains of José Antonio Primo de Rivera from Alicante to the Escorial. He also accompanied Serrano to Berlin in Sept. 1940, as Germany* brought pressure on the Franco regime to take an active part in the Axis war against Britain,* and attended the meeting at Hendaye the following month when Hitler pleaded his case personally with Franco.

The poet was eager for Spain to enlist in the Axis cause and reacted to Gen. Franco's cautious nonbelligerence with growing frustration. In Feb. 1941, he quit his governmental post and in June added his name to the list of volunteers for the Blue Division* that would fight alongside the Germans in their invasion of the Soviet Union. For Dionisio Ridruejo, the subsequent ten months of duty on the eastern front proved to be decisive. Within three months of his return to Spain in Apr. 1942, he had resigned from all his offices in the FET and in Oct. was detained by the regime and exiled to Ronda.

It is the second edition of his *Poesía en armas* that recalls his bitter ordeal at the Novgorod sector in the Soviet Union. The verses only hint at the author's mounting disaffection with the cause he had so loyally served. Certainly, one important element leading to his detention was the political demise of his colleague Serrano, who had been dismissed from his governmental offices in Sept. Furthermore, Ridruejo was suspected of complicity with the young Falangists who just before Serrano's fall had clashed violently with Carlists at Begona.

In this first collision with the Franco regime, Ridruejo's penalties were mild. His house arrest in Ronda lasted only eight months, after which he was allowed to reside in Catalonia. By 1943, the ban on his publications had been lifted, and he was permitted to resume his career in journalism. Gen. Franco himself approved Ridruejo's 1948 certification as correspondent in Rome for Spain's news agency, and the regime did not interfere when, in 1950, his *En once años* captured that year's Premio Nacional de Literatura.

In the 1950s, Ridruejo's name figured as prominently and as often in the opposition to the Franco government as it did in the literary world. By 1956, the poet's newly found passion for democratic reform in Spain led to his second arrest and a confinement in Madrid's Carabanchel prison, which introduced him to such veterans of the opposition as Enrique Tierno Galván.* Following their release in 1957, the two attempted to form the Partido Social de Acción Democrática, an anticommunist opposition to the dictatorship. There would be other such efforts (among them, the creation of the Unión Social Demócrata Española in 1974, in which Ridruejo had a role), more exile (from 1962 to 1964, for having participated in the Congreso del Movimiento Europeo at Munich), and three more terms in prison (1964, 1966, and 1974).

When Dionisio Ridruejo died on 26 June 1975, before the end of Franco's dictatorship, the turbulent postwar years had already witnessed the publication of his most memorable works. Among them are *Dentro del tiempo* (1960), *Hasta la fecha* (1961), *Escrito en España* (1962), and *Castilla la Vieja* (1973).

For additional information, see J. Aguirre, ed., *Dionisio Ridruejo* (Madrid, 1976); D. W. Foard, "Poet on Ice," in *Germany and Europe in the Era of the Two World Wars*, ed. F. Homer and L. Wilcox (Charlottesville, 1986); D. Ridruejo, *Casi unas memorias* (Barcelona, 1976); R. Serrano Suñer, *Anteayer y hoy* (Barcelona, 1982).

D. W. Foard

*Related entries*: FALANGE; FRANCO, GEN. FRANCISCO.

**RODRIGO, JOAQUÍN** (1901- ), composer. Rodrigo was born in Sagunto, Valencia,* and has been blind since the age of three. He studied music in Valencia, but also spent several years in Paris in the 1920s where he studied with Paul Dukas (1865–1935). He returned to Spain at the outbreak of the Spanish Civil War* and has lived in Madrid* ever since. As the most important Spanish composer of the late twentieth century, his works, especially his concerti for guitar and orchestra, are extremely well known. Rodrigo is, like Ralph Vaughn-Williams (1872–1958) and Samuel Barber (1910–1981), a musical conservative. He does not employ any rigid or radical theories about serialism, atonalism, or the necessity of creating new and alien musical sounds. He has returned to the music of Spain in the seventeenth century and combined it with musical technique of the twentieth century to produce a uniquely lyrical and Spanish style.

His most popular work, *Concierto de Aranjuez*, written in 1939, is a concerto in three movements for orchestra and solo guitar. The second movement, perhaps the best example of Rodrigo's craft, is a well-balanced, sonorous interplay between the guitar and orchestra that progresses logically to its climax.

*Fantasía para un gentilhombre*, written in 1954 for Andrés Segovia,* is another example of Rodrigo's musical conservatism. The piece, which is divided into five parts, is based on music written by Gaspar Sanz, a court composer for Felipe IV (1605–1665). Once again, baroque lyricism and balance between the orchestra and soloist are the hallmarks and provide a stark contrast to Igor Stravinsky's (1882–1971) *Pulcinella*, also a twentieth-century reworking of music of the baroque era.

Other important works by Rodrigo include his *Concierto andaluz* for four guitars and his harp concerto. He has also written numerous pieces for solo guitar and piano.

For additional information, see V. Vayá Pla, *Joaquín Rodrigo* (Madrid, 1977); A. Livermore, *A Short History of Spanish Music* (London, 1972); and A. Fernández-Cid, *La música y los músicos españoles en el siglo xx* (Madrid, 1963).

S. L. Brake

# S

SAGASTA PRÁXEDES MATEO (1825–1903), liberal leader of the Bourbon Restoration (1875–1885) and the regency of Alfonso XIII.* Sagasta was born in Torrecilla, Navarre,* in 1825. He became an engineer and participated in the construction of Spain's first railways before being appointed chief of public works in Zamora, affiliated with the Progressive party.* His anticlericalism forced him to spend 1856 in French exile, but during the Liberal-Union era (1858–1863), he was elected to the Cortes and developed a reputation as an orator.

The revival of the Moderate party* in 1863 made him so hostile to the monarchy that he conspired with Gen. Juan Prim y Prats* in the uprising of San Gil (1866), for which he was condemned to death and had to flee to France* again. Revolution in 1868 dislodged Isabel II* and brought Sagasta to power as minister of interior and later as foreign secretary, but Prim's assassination in Dec. 1870 ended Sagasta's radicalism and made him oppose Manuel Ruiz Zorrilla (1833–1895), the Progressive party leader. As premier from 21 Dec. 1871 to 26 May 1872, Sagasta did his best to support Amadeo I* as king, but when radical sentiments grew he was pushed to the right and out of power.

After Gen. Manuel Pavía (1827–1895) destroyed the First Republic* late in 1873, Sagasta obtained several important ministerial positions, and then on 3 Sept. 1874, he became premier again, only to be supplanted by Antonio Cánovas del Castillo* on 3 Dec. As architect of the Bourban Restoration, however, Cánovas recognized Sagasta as a trustworthy leader, now unsympathetic to radicalism and a politician whose technical background would be valuable in the public sector. Sagasta publicly supported the Restoration program on 7 Nov. 1875, helped Cánovas write the Constitution of 1876, and in turn was permitted to form the Liberal party (later the Liberal Fusion party) as the loyal opposition to Cánovas's liberal-conservative organization. No other groups were permitted to stand for election.

Sagasta and Cánovas continued to cooperate until the latter's assassination in 1897. In Feb. 1881, they became notorious for agreeing to alternate in power whenever a cabinet faced difficulties and avoid investigating the circumstances leading to the previous cabinet's fall. Thus Sagasta was premier from 1881 until 13 Oct. 1883 and then twice again (27 Nov. 1885 to 5 July 1890 and 11 Dec. 1892 to 21 Mar. 1895) until Cánovas's death. His sixth and seventh ministries (3 Oct. 1897 to 4 Mar. 1899 and 6 Mar. to 6 Dec. 1901) remained faithful to the old Restoration values, but alienated Alfonso XIII, who blamed the liberal politicians for national disaster. He died a very unpopular man on 5 Jan. 1903.

Sagasta was a pragmatic politician. What idealism he had was destroyed by Amadeo's ill-fated monarchy and the First Republic.* His brand of liberalism, like Cánovas's, was founded upon the principle of stability at any cost. Problems were hidden, elections were rigged, and financial bribery or administrative graft held together the corrupt and often-challenged Restoration system. During his long ministry from 1885 to 1890, prosperity and social peace gave Sagasta a chance to cleanse gubernatorial practices, but instead he permitted cronies to loot the state. The "disaster" Spanish reformers and the Generation of 1898* attack referred to the use of caciques* by Sagasta and Cánovas.

For additional information, see C. de Romanones, *Sagasta o el político* (Madrid, 1930); and M. Fernández Almagro, *Historia política de la España contemporánea* (Madrid, 1969).

*R. W. Kern*

*Related entries*: AMADEO I; CÁNOVAS DEL CASTILLO, ANTONIO; LIBERALISM.

**SALMERÓN, NICOLÁS** (1838–1908), president of the First Republic.* Nicolás Salmerón, born in Almería on 10 Apr. 1838, studied philosophy at Granada and in Madrid,* and became a philosophy professor at the Central University of Madrid. In the 1860s, he took an active role in the work of the Ateneo Científico y Literario,* the leading Spanish intellectual club that at the time included Francesc Pi i Margall* and Emilio Castelar (1832–1899), who, like Salmerón, were interested in the ideas of Karl Christian Friedrich Krause* and general political reform.

In 1867, Salmerón took part in a revolutionary rising against the monarchy by the small Democratic party. Its failure forced him to serve a short jail term, which he used to good advantage by writing his influential book, *La forma del gobierno* (1868), advocating the creation of a federal state to modernize more effectively the economy and administration through regional planning—a conviction he shared with Pi i Margall. Federalism became the starting point of modern Spanish regionalism, one of the great national controversies until it was put into effect by the adoption of regional autonomy in 1979.

After an unsuccessful campaign in 1869, Salmerón was elected to a Cortes seat in 1871. He played an important legislative role in 1872 and 1873, first by drafting a model federalist constitution and then as minister of justice in Estanislao Figueras's (1819–1882) weak republican government in Feb. 1873. As local cantonal revolutions spread, Salmerón broke with Pi i Margall. Federalism meant economic development to Salmerón and revolutionary freedom to Pi. Thus, after Salmerón was elected Cortes president in July 1873, he refused to support Pi's radical federal cabinet and was instrumental in ending its short life.

Salmerón became Pi's successor on 18 July 1873. He believed that federalism had no future if it was to be simply a regime of southern anarchist rebels. He appealed for support from the north and permitted the army, led by Gen. Manuel Pavía y Rodríguez (1827–1895), to attack to the south. On 7 Aug., Valencia* fell, a crucial victory in the campaign of reconquest, but as the military victories continued, a more conservative national mood grew, and federalism became unpopular. Despite Salmerón's moderation, he fell on 7 Sept. 1873 to Emilio Castelar's national unity cabinet. Salmerón resigned from the Cortes on 2 Jan. 1874, when the military deposed Castelar. A year later, he failed to regain his parliamentary seat in the elections held by the ministerial regency of Antonio Cánovas del Castillo.*

The conservatism behind the Bourbon Restoration forced Salmerón to spend the next decade in France,* where a fellow exile, Manuel Ruiz Zorrilla (1833–1895), persuaded him to join the ranks of Spanish republicanism. Although Salmerón and Ruiz Zorrilla later quarreled, when Salmerón returned to Madrid after an amnesty to resume a teaching career in 1884, he joined the small Republican Central party. Nevertheless, he won a Cortes seat from Barcelona in 1893 as a regionalist, but when Pi died in 1901, Salmerón founded a Republican Union party in 1903. Its confusion of republicanism and regionalism caused it to fail, and Salmerón abandoned republicanism in 1906 to join a Catalan nationalist movement, Solidaritat Catalana, thus leaving a confused political heritage for early twentieth-century radicals.

For additional information, see C. Hennessey, *The Federal Republic in Spain: Pi y Margall and the Federal Republican Movement, 1868–1874* (Oxford, 1962); and M. Fernández Almagro, *Historia política de la España contemporánea (Madrid, 1963)*.

                                                                    *R. W. Kern*
*Related entries*: CÁNOVAS DEL CASTILLO, ANTONIO; FIRST REPUBLIC; PI I MARGALL, FRANCESC.


**SCIENCE.** In the last quarter of the seventeenth century, the scientific revolution made itself dimly felt in Spain through the works of novatores, or "innovators" (a derogatory term applied to them by scholastic opponents). The most characteristic way of broaching the new Newtonian cosmology, tainted in the eyes of conservatives by Copernican heliocentrism, or the circulation of the blood, which ran contrary to the canons of Galenic physiology, was by introducing such topics in the form of notes to, or commentaries upon, official science. Prominent among the novatores were Juan de Cabriada (1665–1714) and Juan Bautista Juanini (1633–1691) in medicine; and in the physical sciences, Vicente Mut (1614–1681), Juan Caramuel (1606–1682), and José de Zaragoza (1627–1679).

In the early eighteenth century, advocacy of the new medicine broke into the open in anti-Galenic polemics waged by skeptics such as Miguel Boix i Moliner (1636–1722) or Martín Martínez (1684–1734), the latter a follower of the new clinical medicine of Thomas Sydenham (1624–1689) and William Cullen (1710–1790). Martínez was vigorously defended by Benito Feijóo,* who popularized themes introduced by novatores and was an often-caustic critic of scholastic science. The "skeptical-medicine" controversy of the 1720s was on the leading edge of the early Enlightenment critique of scholasticism and involved, besides Feijóo, a number of other progressive clerics such as Martín Sarmiento (1695–1772) and Francisco José de Isla (1703–1781). In the course of the eighteenth century, the medical revolt against orthodoxy was embodied in a series of important new institutions, from the Academy of Medicine in Seville (1697) to the Royal College of San Carlos (surgery) in Madrid (1787).

In 1736, the Spanish crown joined with the French in support of an expedition to Peru and Ecuador to measure a degree of terrestrial meridian. This enterprise was perceived in scientific circles as providing a test of Newtonian cosmology. The participation of naval officers Jorge Juan (1713–1773) and Antonio de Ulloa (1716–1795) in the La Condamine expedition converted them into public figures and, through their subsequent service to the state as technical experts, changed the perception of science, at least by official Spain, whereby it became an activity worthy of government support. Ulloa, for his efforts, was elected as a fellow of the British Royal Society, one of a number of Spaniards to enjoy that distinction in the eighteenth century.

Because of the notoriety of the La Condamine venture, the Spanish government realized that the endless debate with Portugal* over the boundaries of their New World possessions might be more appropriately resolved by astronomers than by historians. Accordingly, the boundary commission was staffed with naval officers trained in astronomical observation and surveying, notably Dionisio Alcalá Galiano (1762–1805), José Varela (1748–1794), and Diego de Alvear (1749–1830). As early as the 1750s, the Bourbon government was spending about .5 percent of its annual budget on science-related projects in the military academies alone. This figure doubtless grew in subsequent years, in order to finance scientific expeditions and the scientific projects of the navy,* the principal incubator of science in the last third of the century.

Under Carlos IV,* a particularly gifted generation of astronomers—the most talented and productive group of Spanish scientists to appear until the twentieth century—was organized into a hydrographical survey (the future Depósito Hidrográfico) under the direction of Vicente Tofino (1732–1795), to carry out coastal surveys throughout the empire and gather observations related to the problem of longitude, meteorology, and navigation. Among the members of this group were José de Mazarredo (1745–1812), José Espinosa y Tello (1763–1795), José Vargas Ponce (1760–1821), and later, José de Mendoza y Ríos (1762–1816), and Felipe Bauzá (1764–1834)—the latter two, like Ulloa, fellows of the Royal Society. Spanish officers attached to the expedition of Alejandro Malaspina

(1754–1810) carried out important astronomical observations: those of the transit of Mercury in 1789 were subsequently used to establish the anomalous action of that planet's perihelion that was later to play such a prominent role in the general theory of relativity.

Mazarredo, Alejandro Malaspina, and others likewise participated in the longitude debate by testing rival chronometers made by British and French instrument makers. As a result of French distrust over the way these instruments were maintained by the navy, Mazarredo was able to send a number of young Spaniards to Paris to master the art of instrumentation. Virtually all these trainees died in an epidemic, although some modest advances in instrumentation were made by survivors, such as Cayetano Sánchez (1769–1800). Tables of nautical astronomy prepared by Mendoza y Ríos in 1801 were widely used by all the European naval powers in the first third of the nineteenth century.

Enlightenment Spain also enjoyed the presence of another group of naturalists of great talent: the Linnean botanists associated with the Royal Botanical Garden in Madrid (but originally founded at Migas Calientes in 1755 by the anti-Linnean José Quer [1695–1764]). Under the long administration of the autocratic director, Casimiro Gómez Ortega (1740–1818), three major and a number of minor botanical expeditions were sent to explore the economic potential of New World flora: the expedition to New Granada directed by José Celestino Mutis (1732–1808); to Peru, led by Hipólito Ruiz (1752–1816), and José Pavón (1757–1819); and that to New Spain, under the direction of Martín de Sessé (1751–1808) and José Mociño (1757–1819). The New Granada expedition evolved under Mutis's creative entrepreneurship into a powerful, multifaceted scientific institution that produced a brilliant generation of criollo naturalists, including the botanist Francisco Antonio de Zea (1766–1822) and the astronomer and naturalist Francisco de Caldas (1768–1816). Mutis, though generally remembered as a botanist, was an articulate follower of Isaac Newton (1642–1727), who translated the *Principia* (1686) into Spanish for use in his classes at the Colegio del Rosario in Bogotá. In the Río de la Plata, Félix de Azara (1746–1821), working alone but in close contact with naturalists he had met while in the employ of the boundary commission, carried out important studies of South American fauna, and his book on the birds of Paraguay has been long recognized as a classic of descriptive zoology.

Meanwhile, in Mexico, another outstanding institution, the Real Seminario de Minería, coalesced around the figures of Fausto de Elhuyar (1755–1833) and Andrés Manuel del Río (1765–1849), both discoverers of elements (tungsten and vanadium). The advance in chemistry was related to the Royal Chemistry Laboratory and to the government's successful importation of the new chemistry of Antoine Lavoisier (1743–1794), the French chemist, in the persons of Louis Joseph de Proust (1754–1826) and François Chavaneau (1754–1842). Both were contracted as professors of the Real Seminario Patriótico at Vergara. Proust subsequently moved to the Artillery Academy at Segovia, Chavaneau to Madrid* to direct the Royal Laboratory.

The Napoleonic invasion and War of Independence,* together with the Latin American independence movements, put an end to Spanish science of the Enlightenment, destroying its infrastructure (and in the case of New Granada, its personnel, as most of the disciples of Mutis were executed). Under the regressive rule of Fernando VII,* scientists were identified as liberals, and medical leaders such as Mateo Seoane (1791–1870) spent his entire career as a toxicologist in Paris. Under the Revolution of 1868, the banner of science was carried by an "intermediate generation" of modest practitioners who played the important role of training the generation of researchers who attempted to reconstruct the bases of science in the wake of the revolution. Virtually all these men of 1868 held chairs of natural history or medicine, and it was in the biological sciences that the impulses of 1868 were translated into effective research programs.

Inasmuch as the revolution coincided with the European reception of Darwinism, an entire generation of Spanish biologists built their careers on evolution and were stigmatized by the traditional elite because of it. The university crisis of 1876, whereby the conservative government sought to assert its control over higher education, was motivated by "fear of monkeys" (in Julio Caro Baroja's [1914– ] characterization); and the Darwinian leadership, including marine biologist Augusto González de Linares (1845–1904) and geologists Salvador (1853–1911) and Laureano Calderón (1847–1894), lost their university chairs. These three were prominent in the foundation of the Institución Libre de Enseñanza,* a secondary school that promoted British-style science and the ideas of Karl Christian Friedrich Krause.* Future leaders of Spanish medical research, among them neurohistologists Luis Simarro (1851–1921) and Santiago Ramón y Cajal,* were socialized as evolutionary biologists during this period. The aftermath of the revolution also stimulated the foundation of extra university research institutions such as Pedro González de Velasco's (1815–1882) Free Practical School of Medicine and Surgery in Madrid.

Another indirect fruit of the revolution was the "Polemic of Spanish Science," initiated by the publication of *La ciencia española* (1876) by Marcelino Menéndez y Pelayo* and the controversy stimulated by the Spanish edition in the same year of John William Draper's (1811–1882) *Historia de los conflictos entre la religión y la ciencia*, translated by Augusto T. Arcimis (1844–1910), meteorologist and professor at the Institución Libre. Menéndez y Pelayo attempted to retrieve a scientific heritage for traditional Spain in the face of liberal criticism to the effect that the church and the Inquisition had stifled scientific inquiry. This polemic soon devolved into a set piece of the broader ideological debate, producing a host of defensive self-justifications and special pleadings on behalf of Spanish culture, reaching a reductio ad absurdum in the infamous dictum of Miquel de Unamuno,* "¡Que inventen ellos!" ("Let others invent."). If the polemic served any useful purpose at all, it was to locate the issue of science in Spanish political consciousness, pending the arrival of a generation that had more to offer than invective.

Santiago Ramón y Cajal, the outstanding figure of fin de siècle Spanish science, was not an isolated genius as he is often presented, but the product of a solid, if modest, histological tradition, of which the leading figure was his own teacher, Aureliano Maestre de San Juan (1828–1890). Ramón y Cajal's discovery of the neuron led to his sharing of the Nobel Prize with Camillo Golgi (1843–1926) in 1906. Ramón y Cajal and Simarro trained a talented group of neurologists. Simarro's students, Nicolás de Achucarro (1880–1918) and Pío del Río Hortega (1882–1945), produced work (on neuroglia and microglia, respectively) of near-Nobel category. Ramón y Cajal was able to convert his prestige into official interest in the sponsorship of science. He became the first president of the Junta para Ampliación de Estudios, established in 1907. Under the leadership of the Junta's dynamic secretary, José de Castillejo (1873–1945), a large number of researchers in the physical and biological sciences were sent abroad (mainly to West European laboratories) to master the techniques of modern experimental research. The returnees were the nucleus of the scientific generation of the 1920s that, in a number of fields, produced world-class scientists.

Histology was not the only biomedical field in which Spain excelled. Another was physiology, a discipline that under the coordinated leadership of Juan Negrín* in Madrid, and Ramón Turró (1854–1926) and August Pi i Sunyer (1879–1965) in Barcelona,* blossomed in the second decade of the century. Negrín's laboratory was housed in the Residencia de Estudiantes, a Junta facility in Madrid, while Turró's, the Municipal Laboratory of Barcelona, attracted a nucleus of young bacteriologists and physiologists all imbued with an explicitly Pasteurian view of disease. The problems that attracted Spanish physiologists of this generation were related to the "correlation," or interaction, of human systems, notably the endocrinological with the neurological (the physiology of adrenaline was the characteristic research area). Turró was responsible for the American scientist Walter Cannon's (1871–1945) lifelong interest in Spain, and the crucial experiments in the latter's "adrenaline theory" were carried out in 1921–1922. Negrín, who, like Cannon, conducted adrenaline research under explicitly Darwinian presuppositions, was the teacher of Salvador Ochoa (1905– ), who can perhaps be reckoned as Spanish physiology's Nobel winner, although by the time he won it in 1959, he was an American citizen. A related field, endocrinology, was founded by a solitary researcher, Gregorio Marañón (1887–1960), who forged a working disciplinary group of his own students and colleagues. Marañón introduced a doctrine of internal secretions, on the basis of which he fashioned a theory of psychosexual development, intertwined with Freudian concepts.

Freudian ideas were initially received by neurologists of the school of Ramón y Cajal (José María Villaverde [1888–1936], Gonzalo R. Lafora [1886–1971], and José María Sacristán [1887–1957]), and later, a number of psychiatrists who used Freud to initiate dynamic, psychologically informed, clinical psychiatry (José Sanchis Banus [1893–1932], César Juarros [1879–1942], and Emilio Mira y López [1890–1964]). Sanchis Banus and Juarros, both elected deputies to the

Constituent Cortes of the Second Republic,* were vociferous leaders of the sexual-reform movement, the former's speech in the Cortes in favor of the divorce statute constituting a historic benchmark of Freudian discourse in prewar Spain. Mira y López gave the first university-level course on psychoanalysis, introduced the Rorschach test, and was the founder of child psychiatry in Spain.

Progress in the exact and physical sciences was more difficult. Spanish mathematics of the late nineteenth century struggled to keep abreast of European mathematics of the previous generations, although toward the end of the century Eduardo Torroja (1847–1916) and Zoel García de Galdeano (1846–1924) made great strides in the effort to catch up. In 1915, under the Junta's aegis, Julio Rey Pastor (1888–1962) founded the Mathematical Laboratory, whose members were able to effect a giant leap toward parity with Europe, best symbolized by their leadership in the reception of relativity in Spain during the 1920s. When Albert Einstein (1879–1955) visited Madrid and Barcelona in 1923, the maturity and perspicacity of mathematicians such as Estaban Terradas (1883–1950) and Josep María Plans (1878–1934) were evident to him.

Twentieth-century physics had a parallel history, coming from nowhere to significant participation in European physics by the mid–1920s, thanks again to the Junta's stimulus. Blas Cabrera's (1878–1946) Junta-sponsored Laboratorio de Física was the kernel that, with the help of a grant in 1925 from the International Education Board of the Rockefeller Foundation, became the National Institute of Physics and Chemistry. Cabrera's laboratory-institute totally dominated research in physics and chemistry between 1910 and 1937. Part of its success came from its complete autonomy from the stagnant university structure. Its leading members were Cabrera himself in magnetism; Miguel Ángel Catalán (1897–1957) in spectroscopy; and Enrique Moles (1883–1953) in physical chemistry. Spanish physicists, like their mathematician colleagues, were virtually unanimous in their support of relativity, in part because there had been no classical electrodynamic tradition (James Clerk Maxwell [1831–1875]) to oppose it.

Around the turn of the century, in the wake of the Spanish-American War,* conservative and liberal education ministers made a concerted effort to remove higher education from the ideological arena and encourage public discussion in matters of science and technology, in the interests of modernization. This ambience of civil discourse informed and stimulated the real advances in science that were registered before the Spanish Civil War.* Examples of its action were the self-conscious autonomy and impartiality of the Junta para Ampliación de Estudios, which backed research and researchers on merit only, without subjecting each proposal to ideological scrutiny; and the fact that relativity was embraced by a broad sector of the conservative Right, although a few Catholic intransigents viewed it—as they viewed all new ideas—as a threat to traditional values. Engineers, in general a politically conservative group, were conspicuous in their acclamation of Einstein and the new physics.

Faculties of natural and physical sciences were chronically underfunded and did not even begin to function effectively until they were restructured in 1900. As a result, mathematical instruction was better taught in the engineering schools, such as the Escuela de Caminos (Civil Engineering School), the Jesuit Instituto Católico de Artes e Industrias in Madrid, and the Escola d'Enginyeria Industrial in Barcelona.

In industrializing countries during the first third of this century (Brazil presents a comparable example), aviation was viewed as a royal road to modernization. Thus, in Spain, pioneer aviator Emilio Herrera (1879–1967), who, along with Alfredo Kindelán (1879–1962) had seen Wilbur Wright (1867–1912) fly at Le Mans in 1908, inaugurated modern aerodynamics at a wind tunnel of his own design at Cuatro Vientos in Madrid. In 1928, he founded the Escuela Superior de Areotécnica, which was, in the period ending in 1936, the best engineering school in the country. Juan de la Cierva* was world renowned for the invention of the autogiro, which combined aspects of the airplane and helicopter. Leonardo Torres Quevado (1852–1936) built a series of dirigibles (the "Astra" series). Torres was a multifaceted inventor, a pioneer cybernetician who built an automatic chess player and a master of instrumentation who constructed custom-made scientific instruments for the Madrid science community at his automation laboratory.

Although the dictator Gen. Miguel Primo de Rivera* attempted to curry favor with scientists by supporting the Rockefeller grant and encouraging the institutionalization of oceanography (under Odón de Buen [1863–1945], whom the Right had decried as a notorious Darwinian several decades earlier), scientists were prominent in the political opposition to the dictatorship as well as in the emergence of the Second Republic. The political generation of the republic was the first of Spanish politicians to receive its tonality from science. Interestingly, virtually all the protagonists in the polemic over the reform of the Madrid Faculty of Medicine—Negrín, José Sánchez Covisa (1881–1941), Gustavo Pittaluga (1876–1955), and Marañón—were elected deputies to the Constitutent Cortes, about 10 percent of whose members held medical degrees. In addition, a number of physical scientists such as Manuel Martínez Risco (1888–1954, physicist and relativist), José Giral (1879–1962, chemist), and Honorato de Castro (1884–1945, astronomer) were also elected, as well as the geologist José Royo Gómez (1895–1961). Negrín and Giral both became prime ministers in the 1930s.

In exile, the republican scientists virtually remade their respective disciplines in Latin American host countries: in Mexico, Isaac Costero (pathological anatomy), Rafael Méndez (pharmacological cardiology); Dionisio Nieto (neurology); and José Puche Castillo (1919– , physiology); and elsewhere: Pi i Sunyer and Ramón Carrasco Formiguera (physiology, in Venezuela); Ismael Escobar (physics, in Bolivia); Royo Gómez (geology, in Colombia and Venezuela); Pittaluga (parasitology, in Cuba); Mira y López (psychodiagnostics, in Brazil); Ángel Garma (psychoanalysis, in Argentina); and surprisingly many more.

Under Gen. Francisco Franco,* the country had to face, once again, the destruction of its scientific infrastructure. The Junta was replaced by the Consejo Superior de Investigaciones Científicas (CSIC), whose charter called explicitly for a return to the "unity of Catholic science" that had prevailed before the Enlightenment. Most disciplines lost their best practitioners or saw them incapacitated; some lost all their personnel (Dionisio Ridruejo* referred to the early CSIC as a "cage without birds"). In Spanish physics, with the theoretical revolutions of relativity and quantum physics regarded as tainted by Franco's German allies, the major research area of the 1940s was optics, the seventeenth-century field par excellence. To cite an analogous case: inasmuch as Freud was banished from psychology and psychiatry, the mandarins of post–civil war psychiatry, such as Juan José López Ibor (1908– ), turned the clock back; banished Freudians from positions of influence; and served up a thin gruel of third-rate German psychiatry leavened with Catholic homilies instead. Certain institutions, such as the Madrid Museum of Natural History, once a Darwinian stronghold, were literally pillaged by their ostensible caretakers. Under the direction of an official ideology that rejected modern science, and lacking significant numbers of researchers working at European levels in most disciplines, license was given for any kind of pseudoscience, no matter how ludicrous. Examples are the spate of antirelativist tracts that appeared in the 1950s and 1960s, of which Julio Palacios (1891– ) was the most significant author, and a number of parapsychoanalytic doctrines from which the sexual content was carefully pruned.

In the mid–1960s, when Spanish investment in research lagged behind that of most West European countries (0.17 percent of the gross national product in 1966), the Franco system, under the leadership of education and science minister Manuel Lora Tamayo (1904– ), began to take an interest in science policy per se. Lora worked closely with the Organization for Economic Cooperation and Development (OECD), whose 1968 report on Science and Development in Spain was linked, in turn, to the ministry's white paper on science, issued in 1969 by Lora's successor, J. L. Villar Pallasi (1922– ). These studies revealed both the low priority given to scientific research by the economists directing the country's development and the relatively high level of achievement in science considering the government's lack of support.

Both biology and physics did eventually make spectacular recoveries. In biology, the neo-Darwinian synthesis was reintroduced in the late 1950s under the protective cloak of Catholic paleontologists such as Miguel Crusafont Pairo (1910–1983), who diffused Pierre Teilhard de Chardin's (1881–1955) evolutionary philosophy, while at the same time pursuing an evolutionary-research program. Theoretical biology made inroads even in the kinds of applied institutes favored by the regime, such as the emergence of Ramón Margalef (1919– ) in theoretical ecology at the Instituto de Investigaciones Pesqueras in Barcelona. In physics, there has been notable success in a number of mainly theoretical fields, such as high-energy physics, and the participation of Spanish researchers in prestigious international centers such as the European Atomic Energy Commission (CERN).

For additional information, see J. M. López Pinero, ed., *Diccionario histórico de la ciencia moderna en España*, 2 vols. (Barcelona, 1982). On the eighteenth century, see M. E. Burke, *The Royal College of San Carlos* (Durham, 1977); A. R. Steele, *Flowers for the King* (Durham, 1964); and I. Engstrand, *Spanish Scientists in the New World: The Eighteenth-Century Expeditions* (Seattle, 1981). On Darwinism, see T. F. Glick, "Spain," in *The Comparative Reception of Darwinism*, ed. T. F. Glick, 2d ed. (Chicago, 1988). On twentieth-century science, see T. F. Glick, *Einstein in Spain: Relativity and the Recovery of Science* (Princeton, 1988), and "Emilio Herrera and Spanish Technology," in *Flying: The Memoirs of a Spanish Aeronaut*, by E. Herrera (Albuquerque, 1984).

*T. F. Glick*

*Related entries*: CIERVA, RAMÓN DE LA; EDUCATION; KRAUSE, KARL CHRISTIAN FRIEDRICH; RAMÓN Y CAJAL, SANTIAGO.


**SECOND REPUBLIC** (14 Apr. 1931–1 Apr. 1939). Along with the First Republic in France* and the Weimar Republic in Germany,* the Second Republic in Spain is one of the critically important republican regimes in European history. Like them, it had international as well as national significance. Like them also, its short life was packed with high drama, in which idealism alternated with tragedy. That this should prove so is somewhat surprising, since the Second Republic had an apparently healthy birth amid peaceful conditions that contrasted sharply with the fierce conflicts and powerful foreign and domestic pressures under which its French and German counterparts saw light. Yet its end was a terrible one. Indeed, it is difficult to decide when to date the Second Republic's end. Should it be 18 July 1936, when a civil war started that drastically altered its nature and made impossible the achievement of its most cherished goals? Or should it be 1 Apr. 1939, after three years of bloodshed, when the republic was denied control of even the tiniest vestige of Spanish soil by the victory of Gen. Francisco Franco*?

This entry has opted for the more restrictive definition. It will discuss the peacetime republic rather than its wartime continuation, partly because the first phase more fully embodied the hopes of its founders, partly because the second phase will be covered in the article on the Spanish Civil War.*

During the peacetime republic, five subperiods are worth noting: (1) Apr.-Dec. 1931, when a center-left coalition tried to establish a moderate regime acceptable to all; (2) Jan. 1932–Sept. 1933, when a leftist coalition was ascendant; (3) Oct. 1933–Oct. 1934, when a center-right coalition cut back the leftist reforms, but without entirely abandoning the initial republican heritage; (4) Oct. 1934–Feb. 1936, when rightist forces sought, though still by constitutional means, to undo this heritage more fully; (5) Feb.-July 1936, when a Popular Front government tried desperately to prevent the fierce political polarization that now characterized Spain from leading to either rightist or leftist dictatorship, or from erupting into civil war. Its failure was sealed by the military insurrection of 18 July 1936.

## THE FOUNDING OF THE REPUBLIC (APR.–DEC. 1931)

To understand the character assumed by the republic, one must first understand the bifurcated soul of modern Spain. For longer than anywhere else, "two Spains," a liberal-progressive and a conservative-reactionary one, had struggled for mastery of the nation. The first rejected the Spanish past as harmful and sought to restructure politics and society in new ways. The second treasured this past and was unwilling to change it profoundly. The conflict first became intense in 1812, at the Cortes of Cadiz.* It continued for the next 120 years, with major crises in 1820–1823, 1833–1843, 1854–1856, 1868–1874, 1909–1910, 1917–1923, and 1930–1931. In contrast to the general European experience, no clear victor emerged in this long struggle, but neither was it a meaningless, merely repetitive process, as is sometimes asserted. Unlike their German counterparts, the conservatives proved uniquely incapable of dealing with the problems of modernization that confronted Spain and gradually discredited themselves, especially among intellectuals. The liberals slowly increased in strength, and their influence became more diffuse and firmly rooted. The issues that initially divided the two forces clustered around the problem of creating a constitutional, parliamentary government, with the need to reduce the political role played by the church and by the army* assuming greater importance than elsewhere. By the early twentieth century, other issues even less typical of Western Europe were added: agrarian reform, the regionalist aspirations of Catalonia* and the Basque* country, and a large and unusually millenarian working-class movement. Because long delayed (as well as because of nineteenth-century conservative ineptitude), the democratic revolution in Spain faced a much greater accumulation of unresolved problems when it finally gained power in 1931. And, unlike in Britain,* France, or Italy,* it was not brought into being solely by middle-class forces, but included a very active working-class component. A much more burdensome social and political agenda, and a much greater diversity of political forces, thus constituted the special characteristics of the Second Republic.

The republic was nevertheless established with surprising ease. In Aug. 1930, amid the intense political agitation that followed the collapse of the dictatorship of Gen. Miguel Primo de Rivera,* several middle-class parties and the socialists formed a coalition at San Sebastian to overthrow the monarchy. Its first attempt, in Dec., failed, but defeat quickly turned into victory, as the courts refused to convict the conspirators, and then as republican candidates won massive victories in the municipal elections of 12 Apr. 1931. Lacking the will and support necessary to void the electoral results, Alfonso XIII* fled Spain, and a republic was proclaimed on 14 Apr. Bloodshed had been avoided, and jubilation reigned. A "niña bonita," a "beautiful lass" of a regime, had been born that would finally resolve Spain's many ills.

This optimism initially seemed justified. The San Sebastian coalition converted itself into a provisional government headed by a moderate, Niceto Alcalá Za-

mora.* For the next few months, the government displayed great vigor, effectiveness, and unity. The basis for a permanent restructuring of Spain was laid
in an unprecedented outpouring of position papers and decrees that covered every
field. Especially notable were the provisional measures taken in agrarian reform,
Catalan autonomy, and the army reforms that brought it more fully under civilian
control. Yet by the summer of 1931, strains had begun to appear, both within
the coalition and in the country at large. These had many sources. The San
Sebastian coalition was unusually broad: it ranged from relatively conservative
groups that had accepted republicanism mainly because of their despair over the
ineptitude of the monarchy, to the socialists, who, though generally moderate,
included radical members and in any case advocated a program of profound
social reform. There were also other internal cleavages: over regionalism, with
the Esquerra party often preoccupied with Catalan autonomy at the expense of
national issues; over the question of styles of governance, with idealistic, intellectual leaders such as Manuel Azaña* deeply distrustful of the Radical party
because of its tendencies toward corruption and opportunism.

Profound divisions appeared in the country at large as the initial enthusiasm
waned. The deep-seated anticlericalism of Spanish republicanism led to policy
errors, above all the failure to check a wave of church burnings in May and
often excessive antichurch rhetoric and legislation. This weakened the provisional
government by making it difficult for Catholic moderates to continue their collaboration. It also increased opposition among the many millions of Spaniards
who were still believers and gave the antirepublican Right a popular rallying
point to replace the largely discredited monarchical ideal. Opposition grew on
the Left as well. The powerful anarchosyndicalist union, the Confederación
Nacional de Trabajo (CNT), moved toward a second, social revolution that would
supersede the democratic revolution that had just occurred. Even among the
socialists, strong pressures appeared for radical social action.

These tensions led to an uncomfortable summer and autumn of 1931. The
violence of the church burnings in May was followed by considerable working-
class and peasant violence in Andalusia* in June and July. After the Constituent
Cortes was convened on 14 July (a date selected to symbolize the republic's
affinity for the French Revolution), serious differences among the parties began
to appear, especially in regard to the clerical provisions of the constitution and
to the definitive versions of the agrarian-reform law and the Statute for Catalan
Autonomy. In Oct., the first split occurred in the San Sebastian coalition as the
Catholic moderates, led by Alcalá Zamora, left the government over religious
and social issues. Manuel Azaña, the left republican leader, took over as prime
minister until the constitution was passed in Dec. At that point, two major
decisions were made. New elections, which probably would have revealed a
significant centrist and rightist shift in public opinion, were not held, and the
Constituent Cortes continued as the republic's first regular parliament. More
important still, when pressed by the radicals, the largest of the middle-class
republican parties, to end collaboration with the socialists and pursue more

limited goals, Azaña and the left republicans, who held the balance of power, opted for the socialists. The radicals thereupon also abandoned the coalition, which was reduced to its left republican and socialist components. Nevertheless, there was no sharp change in policy. The Azaña forces still held a considerable parliamentary majority, and not all ties with the moderate Catholics and the radicals had been broken. Indeed, Alcalá Zamora was made president of the republic, and though Alejandro Lerroux,* leader of the radicals, announced a policy of obstruction in the Cortes, this did not mean total opposition. The ambitious program defined by the provisional government would not be cut back significantly. The republic would try to achieve simultaneously political, social, and fiscal reform, while also carrying out economic modernization, expansion of the educational system, and liberalization of fundamental civil rights.

### THE AZAÑA COALITION (JAN. 1932–SEPT. 1933)

The left republican-socialist coalition led by Azaña proved to be the most durable governing coalition the republic would know. It was nevertheless always potentially fragile. This was partly because of the fragmentation of left republican forces. Azaña, despite the charisma that now surrounds him, was politically handicapped because his was only one, and only the third largest, of several left republican parties. Differences between the left republicans and the socialists were still more important. In spite of their initial eagerness to collaborate with the republic, the socialists were a Marxist, working-class party whose fundamental orientation differed profoundly from that of the bourgeois parties. The reverse was also true: the left republicans, for all their early respect for the moderation and high moral tone of the socialists, were primarily concerned with middle-class, not social, issues. The common idealism of the two forces and their mutual goodwill caused them to join together in government, but did not guarantee that their collaboration would be either intense or effective. This was shown by the parliamentary paralysis of the first nine months of 1932, especially in relation to the agrarian-reform and Catalan bills, which were given legislative priority. Regarding agrarian reform, the Azaña parties needed five months to sort out their differences as to the scale and nature of the reform and agree on a bill to present to the Cortes. Once debate began in May, the left republican commitment to this fundamental social legislation proved so weak that the parliamentary opposition, though vastly outnumbered in votes, could sabotage its progress by presenting innumerable amendments and technical objections to it. Consequently, by early Aug., three months after debate had begun, only four of the bill's articles had been approved. As to the Catalan bill, the tale is similar, but the roles partially reversed; neither the socialists nor many of the non-Catalan left republicans believed enough in regional autonomy to make special efforts on its behalf.

While parliament debated, the condition of the country in many ways deteriorated. In the political field, this stemmed mainly from the growth of rightist opposition, especially among Catholics. It is frequently argued, and with some justice, that the Azaña republic paid a high political price for its anticlericalism and should have compromised with the church. Such a compromise, however, would have required abandoning such goals as the right to divorce and the secularization of the educational system, which the Azaña forces, still supremely confident, would not do. In the social field, the troubles stemmed partly from the effects of the worldwide economic depression, which finally began to reach Spain. The resulting unemployment was augmented by the attempt of landowners and industrial employers to cut back on hiring so as to escape the increase in labor costs that republican legislation and the great unionization drive of the previous year had produced. Higher pay alone did not satisfy workers who were employed; the republic had awakened much greater expectations, which they set out to fulfill through strikes and, in the countryside, through sporadic efforts to seize land. Special intensity was added to the resulting turmoil both by ancient animosities that still gripped so socially polarized a society—the hatred between the Civil Guard* and the peasants was particularly notorious—and by the fuller radicalization of those huge sectors of the working classes loyal to the anarcho-syndicalist CNT.

A new start was made possible by a fortuitous event. In Aug. 1932, army units headed by Gen. José Sanjurjo (1872–1936) attempted to overthrow the government. The coup failed miserably, but its menace revived enthusiasm for the republic. The changed atmosphere transformed the Cortes debates, as both the agrarian-reform and the Catalan autonomy bills sped toward passage in Sept. It was reflected also in the executive, when in late Oct., Azaña temporarily granted land to approximately forty thousand peasants in Estremadura and Andalusia* in anticipation of their permanent settlement under the agrarian-reform law.

The new vigor and unity ended almost as abruptly as it had begun, amid the furor that followed the police massacre of some twenty peasants in the hamlet of Casas Viejas during an attempted CNT revolution in Jan. 1933. The moral legitimacy of the governing coalition was severely damaged, and the socialists had special difficulty in explaining the event to their followers. A further blow to the confidence of the Azaña forces was struck in Apr., when municipal by-elections in several provinces gave majorities to noncoalition parties, especially the radicals and some rightist groups. This time the response to crisis was not a rallying of forces, but one of mutual recriminations. The process began among sectors of the largest left republican party, the radical socialists, who asserted that a wrong turn had been taken in Dec. 1931, when Azaña chose to govern with the socialists rather than the radicals. The republic had thereby been given too social a cast; the socialist alliance should be abandoned in favor of a purely middle-class coalition that would not try to do everything at once, but would follow a less ambitious program in all fields. The socialists were quick to respond in kind. The reason for past failures was not that too much had been attempted, but that the left republican parties had not seized the initiative. They had been too legalistic on agrarian reform, first allowing it to bog down in parliament and then delaying its application until myriad technicalities had been fulfilled. They were also too cautious fiscally and did not do enough to help the unemployed or to protect the unions against retaliation from the employers. Perhaps the socialists had been wrong to place faith in an alliance even with the purportedly progressive elements of the middle classes; perhaps the workers had to take power by themselves.

Neither left republican nor socialist dissidents could yet gain ascendancy in their parties, but the wounds they inflicted sufficed to paralyze the coalition much more completely than in the previous year. It had shown little vitality during the Cortes debates of the spring of 1933, even though a strongly emotional issue for Spanish republicanism—legislation regulating the church's role in society— dominated the agenda. During the summer, when supplementary agrarian legislation was being discussed, the coalition's effectiveness disappeared almost entirely. Azaña did not rise to the occasion; he sought to smooth over the divisions that had appeared, but never provided the dynamic leadership that might have revivified the coalition. Meanwhile, the situation in the country at large deteriorated. New rightist parties critical of the Second Republic, such as the massive Catholic Confederación Española de Derechas Autónomas (CEDA), were formed; unemployment continued to rise, and strikes more than doubled in number throughout 1932 (becoming five times as numerous as in 1931). The level of violence also rose as deaths occurred in more and more outbreaks of social conflict. The final blow came in early Sept., when elections held among some thirty-five thousand municipal officials to select judges for the newly established Supreme Court gave a two-to-one majority to candidates not affiliated with the coalition. At this point, the president, Alcalá Zamora, concluded that the government no longer represented the nation and asked Lerroux, the radical leader, to form an alternative ministry. Since this could not win a vote of confidence in the existing Cortes, national elections were proclaimed for Nov. The idealistic phase that had characterized the republic since Apr. 1931 came to an end, and the reconciliation of a full-scale democratic revolution with profound social reform that the Azaña coalition represented had proven, at least temporarily, a failure.

### THE PERIOD OF LIMITED REACTION (OCT. 1933–OCT. 1934)

The Nov. legislative elections produced a drastically different Cortes from the one elected in June 1931. The aura of enthusiasm surrounding the early republic had largely evaporated. The Azaña forces further damaged their cause, both by having idealistically granted the vote to women (still strongly influenced by Catholicism*) and especially by falling even more subject to the animosities that had arisen during the summer of 1933 once they lost office. The electoral law favored large coalitions; the socialists and left republicans were now too divided to form them. Consequently, with about 40 percent of the vote, the leftist forces won only some 20 percent of the Cortes seats. Centrist and rightist parties gained power, but while these agreed that the direction of government should be altered, they were not united enough to form even as coherent a majority as the Azaña forces had been in 1932 and early 1933. The radicals, though increasingly conservative, still retained some leftist impulses. On the right, the CEDA emerged as the largest party in the Cortes, but it was not closely linked to the smaller secular rightist parties that the elections also strengthened. A complex situation arose in which the radicals ran the government, but depended on CEDA votes to pass legislation in the Cortes. The key political figures now became Lerroux, of the radicals, and José María Gil Robles (1898– ), of the CEDA.

So poorly articulated a governing coalition could not carry out a full-scale reaction. Nevertheless, several Azaña measures were reversed, especially the law excluding the church from the field of secular education and some of the more controversial agrarian legislation. Land reform was carried out at a slower pace, and labor unions were no longer protected, so that wages fell and many union leaders lost their jobs. There were attempts to narrow the scope of Catalan autonomy, and the conspirators involved in the Sanjurjo coup were pardoned. All these were relatively limited measures, but they had drastic consequences for two reasons. Having given birth to the republic and dominated its first phase, the leftist parties felt they had acquired a revolutionary legitimacy that was being violated by the new government. In the politically polarized climate that had appeared in Europe since 1931, as the nazis took power in Germany and other radical rightist forces threatened in other countries, the new directions being mapped might—the Left thought—lead to a full-scale fascist reaction if unchecked.

These frustrations and fears were particularly strong among the socialists, whose radicalization in the second half of 1933 advanced rapidly under the leadership of Francisco Largo Caballero.* Largo Caballero's line was contested by many older leaders clustered around Julián Besteiro (1870–1940), but was enthusiastically backed by the younger militants and won equivocal support from Indalecio Prieto (1883–1962), the third major socialist figure. How, though, was the new radical line to be made effective? Largo Caballero's attempts in the spring of 1934 to form a massive "Workers' Alliance" failed, because the anarchists—in any case exhausted and disorganized by the defeat of their second attempt at a nationwide insurrection in Dec. 1933—refused, except in a few localities, to forgive the socialists their recent participation in the Azaña government. A nationwide harvest strike in June against cutbacks in the agrarian legislation led only to the crushing of the socialist rural unions. All that was left was a vague plan to launch a revolution if the CEDA, which had thus far not been given ministerial posts, entered the government. This would be taken as a sign that fascism was imminent and would be resisted.

Yet the CEDA was the largest party in parliament and considered its exclusion from power illegitimate. Moderates, such as Alcalá Zamora, who initially suspected the CEDA were forced by its pressure to change their opinion, and on 5 Oct. 1934, three CEDA ministers were included in a new cabinet headed by Lerroux. Unable to back down from the challenge, the socialists proclaimed their revolution. This was so poorly prepared, however, and so many of the local union leaders were unwilling to take risks for it, that it resulted only in brief bouts of street fighting by a few militants in most of Spain. It acquired greater resonance in Catalonia, where the autonomous government, under Luis Companys (1883–1940), precipitously declared its support for the revolution, but collapsed without resistance when the local Spanish army units moved against it. Only Asturias* kept the revolution from being a total fiasco. There, all three Spanish worker movements—the socialists, anarchosyndicalists, and communists—had been able to form a common movement around the slogan, "Unión, Hermanos Proletarios," which from the mining and industrial centers took control of the entire province and resisted the armies sent against it from the surrounding provinces and from Spanish Morocco.* Two weeks of savage fighting were needed to crush the Asturias rising, and barbaric acts were committed by both sides. Each was widely publicized, and both sides had many martyrs. Although it could not yet be expressed openly, the psychological polarization of Spanish society moved forward rapidly.

## THE PERIOD OF RIGHTIST ASCENDANCY (OCT. 1934–JAN. 1936)

The socialists clearly had been mistaken in equating CEDA entry into the government with fascism. Despite the shattering crisis of Asturias, nobody seriously tried to overthrow the republic. The failed leftist revolution meant, however, a sharp turn to the right, as labor unions for all practical purposes ceased functioning, the Catalan government was suspended, and many of the socialist and left republican deputies who had escaped jail stopped attending Cortes sessions. The Left became institutionally voiceless, which in turn meant that the center's independence from the Right was weakened. A period of conservative ascendancy began, but it was neither turned in anticonstitutional directions nor used with generosity or intelligence. No attempt was made at national reconciliation. Thousands of militant workers were kept in prison, and a scandalous effort was made to implicate Azaña and other left republican leaders in the Oct. revolution. Above all, no positive legislative program was proclaimed. Rather, the CEDA, the small secular rightist parties, and—with some misgivings—the radicals, set out to reverse almost the entire progressive legislation of the Azaña period.

This movement began relatively slowly but gained momentum, as the few enlightened leaders in each party were defeated by their more reactionary colleagues. The chief victim was the CEDA minister of agriculture, Manuel Jiménez Fernández, appointed in Oct. Guided by principles of social Catholicism, he tried to substitute for the Azaña coalition's agrarian reform a law that, if much weaker in its benefits for landless workers, would at least have benefited most poor tenant farmers and peasant proprietors. He was hounded from office, however, by opposition from his own party in Mar. 1935. With him disappeared the last vestige of idealism in government. The new agrarian law passed in July was so mean spirited that it victimized more peasants than it helped, especially by making possible the expulsion of tenant farmers. Several more tens of thousands of peasants lost their land when those settled by Azaña in late 1932 were also evicted. In addition, union protection of all kinds was eroded. As to nonsocial issues, no attempt was made to restructure Catalan autonomy on a basis that, while penalizing the region for its support of the Oct. revolution, would have allowed some rights to be exercised. The cutting back of army power was stopped, and the more conservative generals again gained favor. The school-building program was reduced in size. A policy of negativism reigned, as Gil Robles himself sometimes complained.

To this moral bankruptcy was added political inefficiency, as the centrist and rightist parties could not unite except on an ad hoc basis. One new cabinet followed another, leading to much government bumbling, especially in resolving the budget crisis. The confusion became intolerable in the autumn of 1935, when a financial scandal wrecked the Radical party, rendering it unable to provide even the nominal leadership it had given in the past. With Lerroux discredited, Gil Robles thought the time had come for him to take over as prime minister. Alcalá Zamora, though, refused to sanction the full assumption of office by the CEDA, partly because of lingering doubts as to whether it was genuinely re-publican, partly because the Left would be further alienated, partly because it was unclear that the CEDA could govern any more effectively than the radicals had, given the incoherence of the existing parliament. Consequently, the pres-ident proclaimed new elections for Feb. 1936. These mirrored in reverse the 1933 elections. The Right and center were too divided to form electoral alliances, and the CEDA, as had the socialists earlier, fell into the error of believing it could win a majority running alone. The Left, meanwhile, had been sufficiently chastised to coalesce—with difficulty—into a Popular Front. The main reason for the electoral results was the negativism of the previous two years. The multitudes injured by governmental policies flocked to the polls, but since nothing had been done to benefit any large groups of people, there was little similar fervor among supporters of the center and Right. In the elections of 16 Feb. 1936, the center parties practically disappeared, and the rightist parties, whose followers were more loyal, gained no ground. The Popular Front won a slight majority in the vote, which because of the electoral laws was translated into a sweeping majority in the Cortes.

## THE PEACETIME POPULAR FRONT GOVERNMENT (FEB.–JULY 1936)

The new leftist government, though again headed by Azaña, found itself in an entirely different position from that of 1932–1933. The chief difference was not that the Communist party* now formed part of the coalition, as it was still too tiny to have much influence. Rather, the mood of the working classes as a whole had altered drastically. The political victory they and the middle classes had won on 14 Apr. 1931 had been celebrated with jubilation. Their success in the elections of 16 Feb. 1936 was a social victory from which they expected immediate and drastic social improvements, as well as vengeance for the tribulations they had suffered since 1934.

The Largo Caballero wing of the Socialist party,* not the CNT, took the lead in radicalism. The landless peasants should not wait for the government to institute agrarian reform, but should themselves seize land and challenge the government to evict them. Strikes should no longer be used to gain modest wage concessions, but should aim at more drastic transformations of social relationships. The Caballeristas resumed talk of forming "worker alliances" against the bourgeoisie with the CNT and the communists; their rhetoric was replete with threats of revolution should the government not cooperate. The Caballeristas did not entirely control the socialist movement, to be sure. In this new atmosphere, however, their strength grew rapidly, especially in the unions. They quickly overshadowed the more moderate socialist wing now led by Prieto, who thought that the Oct. 1934 failure had proved the impossibility of successful social revolution in Spain. For all its defects, the only realistic policy would be a return to close collaboration with the left republicans, as in 1931–1933. A deep schism thus developed, and since most socialists now passed over to radicalism of an intensity previously manifested only by the CNT, a volatile situation without precedent confronted the new Azaña regime.

Given the socialist refusal to enter it, the government was composed solely of left republicans. It tried to grant enough concessions to calm working-class passions, without giving in completely to their demands. The legalistic orientation of the first Azaña period was abandoned; decisive actions were taken. The agrarian reform in particular began to be applied rapidly. The peasants evicted in 1935 were restored to the farms, and much more land was transferred in the five months between Mar. and July than in the five previous years. This policy of conciliation was not enough to bring about labor peace. If farm invasions began to diminish in Apr., with the passing of the planting season, the number of strikes increased rapidly, far surpassing both in number and scale those of 1932 and 1933. There is no reason to suppose, however, that working-class agitation had become unstoppable or that it would cause the government to collapse. Much more virulent social movements had occurred in Germany and Italy from 1919 to 1921 without resulting in a worker triumph. There is also no evidence that the Caballeristas, the CNT, or the communists were actually planning revolution, even to the extent that the socialists had planned it in 1934. Given time, carefully balanced policies, and a continuation of the self-confidence Azaña displayed from Feb. to May, the exalted mood of the workers might have passed and the stability of the republic restored, with the Prieto wing of the socialists rejoining the government.

If it is uncertain that Azaña was mistaken in his overall social policy, greater mistakes were made in other areas in May. For reasons that remain unclear, the government decided to remove Alcalá Zamora from the presidency on technical grounds that violated the spirit if not the letter of the constitution. Its legitimacy was consequently weakened, as was its efficiency, because Azaña, the strongman of the peacetime republic, now assumed the presidency and left control of day-to-day events to Santiago Casares Quiroga (1894–1950), an undistinguished crony. The new prime minister was not up to the level of the crisis. By the summer of 1936, despite many islands of tranquility, Spain was suffused with unresolved tension.

It was not only worker pressure that was at fault. The radicalization of the Left had been matched by a radicalization of the Right since Feb. The Falange,* a small fascist party previously marginal to the political process, had grown rapidly and tried to destabilize the republic by assassinations and by street fighting in the major cities. Much more important, army officers coordinated by Gen. Emilio Mola* had begun to plot a coup d'état. Conscious of the strength and militancy of the worker organizations, the conspiracy was organized with unprecedented precision. Rumors of what was happening reached the government, but lulled by memories of the failure of Sanjurjo's coup in 1932 and distracted by the agitation coming from the Left, Quiroga did nothing to stop it. Neither a new reshuffling of army commands nor an imaginative proposal that might open up new directions of peaceful political development was forthcoming from the government. The coup was scheduled for the latter part of July. Since some of the potential participants were still vacillating, it might or might not have succeeded had it occurred as planned. On the 13th, however, the legitimacy of the republic was further eroded by the most important single act of leftist violence in its history. In retaliation for the killing by Falangists of a republican police official, a handful of leftist extremists assassinated José Calvo Sotelo,* who since Feb. had become the moral leader of the Right in parliament. The shock galvanized the energies of the opposition, and the coup was moved up to the 18th to take advantage of it. Even with this impetus, however, it was only partially successful. Instead of seizing control of Spain at a single stroke, as they had expected, the conspirators plunged the country into a brutal civil war that cost hundreds of thousands of lives before it was settled three years later. Instead of forestalling social revolution, they made this revolution possible because in the portions of Spain that remained republican, the government depended so completely on worker support to defeat the rebels that it could no longer try to control their most radical demands. To a large extent because it had attempted to do too much, and ultimately could not reconcile a full-scale democratic revolution with profound social reform, the peacetime republic had failed, a victim of the heavy burden of unresolved issues it had inherited from Spain's past, as well as to its own perhaps inescapable divisions.

For additional information, see G. Jackson, *The Spanish Republic and the Civil War, 1931–1939* (Princeton, 1965); E. Malefakis, *Agrarian Reform and Peasant Revolution in Spain* (New Haven, 1970); P. Preston, *The Coming of the Spanish Civil War: Reform, Reaction and Revolution in the Second Republic* (London, 1978); and R. Robinson, *The*

*Origins of Franco's Spain: The Right, the Republic and Revolution 1931–1936* (Newton Abbott, 1970).

*E. E. Malefakis*

**SEGOVIA, ANDRÉS** (1893–1987), guitarist. Born in Linares, Segovia was largely self-taught and developed new techniques for playing the guitar. He was responsible for the reintroduction of the guitar as a concert instrument, transcribed works by J. S. Bach (1685–1750) and early vihuelists and lutenists, and commissioned major concert works for the guitar by several leading composers, including Manuel Ponce (1882–1948) and Joaquín Rodrigo.* His students, among them John Williams (1941– ), have continued his tradition.

For additional information, see A. Segovia, *An Autobiography of the Early Years* (New York, 1976).

*S. L. Brake*

**SENDER, RAMÓN JOSÉ** (1901–1981), novelist of exile after the Spanish Civil War.* Sender, born 3 February 1901, in Chalamera de Cinca, Huesca, grew up in nearby Alcolea (the setting for *El lugar del hombre* [1939]), where he worked on his grandfather's farm. Unable to get along with his father, he was sent to school in Huesca and then to preparatory school in Saragossa, where he first demonstrated his literary skill by winning first prize in a short-story contest.

After college work in Teruel and a brief stay in law school, he worked as a journalist in Huesca before returning to law school. Again unsuccessful, he was drafted by the army in 1923 to serve in Morocco,* the background for his first novel, *Imán* (1930).

In 1924, Sender joined the staff of the prestigious Madrid newspaper, *El Sol.* In 1927, he was arrested in a demonstration against the dictatorship of Gen. Miguel Primo de Rivera,* and was held in prison without trial for three months (described in *Orden público* [1931]), before being freed at the insistence of the Press Association. He left the employ of *El Sol* in 1930 and over the next six years wrote seven novels (including one of his most important works, *Siete domingos rojos* [1932]), five books of journalism, and a travel narrative, *Madrid-Moscú*, based on a 1934 trip to the Soviet Union. He also married Amparo Barayón, a native of Zamora. Two children, Ramón and Andrea, were born in 1935 and 1936.

With the outbreak of the Spanish Civil War, Sender sent his wife and children to Zamora. Although he had often criticized the Second Republic,* he nevertheless joined the republican army as a private. In *Contraataque* (1939), he later wrote of this time as one of political murder and sectarian crimes. Promoted to the rank of major, he won the Military Cross of Merit for valor on the southern front, but his wife Amparo was arrested by nationalist sympathizers in Zamora and executed without trial on 11 Oct. 1936, not long after his brother Manuel had been killed in Huesca. He retrieved his children, put them in the care of the International Red Cross in France,* and returned to Spain. In his novels *Los cinco libros de Ariadne* (1957), a highly autobiographical work, and *El rey y la reina* (1949), his view of the war, unlike the romantic works by non-Spanish writers, was powerfully realistic.

In late 1938, when it appeared that the republic was doomed, Sender left for France to reclaim his children and arrived penniless in New York City (Mar. 1939). Leaving his children with Jay Allen (1900– ), an American journalist Sender had met during the war, he departed for Mexico City to join its growing colony of Spanish exiles. The two children were later adopted by Julia West, a Children's Aid Society worker.

In Mexico,* Sender was actively involved in founding the publishing firm Ediciones Quétzal, which published several of his works. In 1942, a Guggenheim Fellowship allowed him to return to the United States.* He lived in Santa Fe, New Mexico, where he married and taught Spanish literature at the University of New Mexico. During this period, he wrote *Requiem por un campesino español* (published in Mexico as *Mosén Millán* [1953] and New York [1960]), his most mature work. In 1962, he returned to France to renew old friendships. The prohibition on his works having been lifted in Spain, he returned there after the first volume of *Crónica del Alba* (1966) won Sender the Premio de la Literatura. In 1965, *Valle-Inclán y la dificultad de la tragedia* was published in Madrid, and *Mr. Witt en el cantón*, (the 1935 winner of the Premio Nacional de la Literatura) was reprinted in 1968. His new best-selling novel, *En la vida de Ignacio Morel*, won the Premio Planeta, Spain's most lucrative literary award. He returned to the United States to teach at the University of Southern California until his death on 16 Jan. 1982.

For additional information, see R. Sender Barayón, *A Murder in Zamora* (Albuquerque, 1989); M. C. Penuelas, *Conversaciones con Ramón J. Sender* (Madrid, 1970); and J. Rivas, *El escritor y su senda (Estudio crítico-literario sobre Ramón J. Sender* (Mexico City, 1967).

*R. Rivera*

**SERRANO SUÑER, RAMÓN** (1901– ), foreign minister under Gen. Francisco Franco* and head of the Falange.* Serrano was born in Cartagena, one of seven children of a civil engineer and his wife. A bright student, he received his legal education in Madrid* and graduated with honors, which enabled him to do postgraduate work in Italy* early in the dictatorship of Benito Mussolini (1883–1945). Impressed with fascism, he returned to Spain and became a government lawyer in Saragossa, where in 1931 he met and wed Zita Polo, sister of Carmen Polo (1902–1987), the wife of Gen. Franco, director of the Saragossa military academy. The two brothers-in-law formed a close social and political friendship that in five years propelled Serrano into a meteoric political career.

Politics had fascinated Serrano since his youth, and in the era of the Second Republic,* he gravitated to the right. This was not surprising, because Serrano was bourgeois, Catholic, and conscious of traditional Spanish values. In Nov. 1933, he was elected to the Cortes as a Confederación Española de Derechas Autónomas (CEDA) representative from Saragossa. Handsome, intelligent, cultured, and relatively vocal, Serrano prospered as a deputy and led the CEDA youth movement, but on the eve of the Spanish Civil War,* believing the republic to be a disaster, he broke with CEDA leader José María Gil Robles (1898– ), who was unwilling to take violent action against the state. Serrano, arrested by republican officials, went through a harrowing experience that turned his hair gray, but with the collusion of at least one foreign government whose diplomatic representatives were sympathetic to the insurgents, he became a member of a prisoner exchange and was thus able to make his way to Salamanca, where his brother-in-law, now generalissimo of the nationalist army and head of state of the rebel government, assigned Serrano a series of important positions.

His first task became the reorganization of the small fascist party, the Falange, as the sole political party of nationalist Spain. Taking a mélange of amorphous conservative factions clustered around the military leader, he welded them into a more cohesive entity, but with the Falange stripped of its radical social program. From Franco's point of view, the metamorphosis was invaluable, since it generated a group with greater appeal to Spaniards moving toward the nationalist camp. In addition, the Falange, now resembling a more standard fascist party, was soon regarded favorably by fascist Germany* and Italy. It quickly became the only legal party of nationalist Spain, with Serrano as its secretary-general, now dressed in flamboyant party uniforms rather than business suits. Many thought he symbolized the youth, vigor, and determination of the Falange—and perhaps its fanaticism as well, since his behavior, after two of his brothers had been executed by the republicans, was extreme.

When the civil war drew to a close, Franco recognized the need for a cabinet government in his evolving administration. At this juncture, the Generalissimo designated his brother-in-law as minister of the interior with control over the police and censorship. He supervised the creation of a vast and oppressive prison system to incarcerate republican prisoners, and his subordinates destroyed what was left of free expression and intellectual vitality, which stunted Spain for more than a generation. To what extent Serrano was personally responsible for these policies is not fully clear, but he obviously condoned them. Perhaps it was the atmosphere of the time, but in any case, he strengthened the Falange along the lines of a totalitarian party.

By mid–1939, Franco sought Serrano's advice about a wide range of domestic and foreign issues. Many personnel appointments were made on his brother-in-law's recommendations, but Franco also began grooming Serrano as a diplomat. The latter's first assignment was to Italy, where Serrano conferred with Benito Mussolini (1883–1945) and his foreign minister, Count Galeazzo Ciano (1903–1944). Back in Spain, he made a series of speeches on foreign-policy matters, often revealing the regime's official position. As World War II* approached, he was described as "the second most powerful man in Spain," and in the early phases of the war, this was certainly true.

Franco sent Serrano to Rome and Berlin in Sept. and Nov. 1940 with plenipotentiary powers to gather information and postpone, if possible, a declaration of belligerency, since the reconstruction of Spain took precedence over anything else. Serrano performed brilliantly in his role. He grasped the full measure of Adolf Hitler's (1889–1945) interest in Spain, but detected that the Germans had no appreciation of Spanish aspirations to exploit the French and British weaknesses in North Africa. Indeed, the German foreign minister, Joachim von Ribbentrop (1893–1946), was gauche enough to request a piece of Spain's metropolitan territory in return for the satisfaction of Franco's imperial schemes. Serrano rejected this request firmly, which made Ribbentrop crudely threaten a German invasion of Spain if greater cooperation were not forthcoming. At the same time, however, Serrano avoided a complete break in order to assure Franco a place at the peace conference that both parties felt would soon follow the catastrophic defeats of the Allies in Europe. The real importance of his intransigence came in forcing Hitler to meet with Franco at Hendaye, on the French border, to broach a joint attack on Gibraltar.* Serrano, who prepared the protocol that summarized the meeting, left the document so vague and legalistic that Ribbentrop called him "a Jesuit." Hitler would later refer to Serrano as "the worst kind of business politician."

Franco was so pleased with the work of his brother-in-law that he made him foreign minister. The main focus of Serrano's diplomatic policy tilted toward Italy in hopes that Mussolini could intercede with the Germans. In Feb. 1941, when he accompanied Franco in his meeting with the Italian leader, he saw his policy succeed when Mussolini agreed to defend the Spaniards against German criticism. Success in Italy, however, meant new hostility from Britain* and the United States,* both involved in an economic blockade of Spain. Serrano's earlier enthusiasm for fascism proved to be an impossible handicap, as did Franco's occupation of Tangier in Nov. 1940, which the foreign minister stoutly defended despite British displeasure. His support of the Blue Division* to fight as a German ally on the Russian front, perhaps designed to ease tensions with the most powerful of the Axis powers, certainly made Serrano a main target of British and American hostility, and when it became clear in the early fall of 1942 that both intended to retake Axis territory in North Africa, Serrano was summarily dismissed from office.

The main incident leading to his fall involved a violent clash between Falangists and Carlists.* Behind it lay a desperate effort to maintain the fervor of Spanish fascism in those disappointing times. In any case, Serrano had a host of enemies who regarded him as an intrusive upstart. Monarchists and Catholic traditionalists viewed him as an irresponsible adventurer who had needlessly exacerbated relations with Britain, a country much of Spain's elite admired, while Falangists felt that he had emasculated the Falange since 1937. His descent into oblivion was striking and illustrated how fragile the Spanish diplomatic situation was during World War II.

Serrano returned to Madrid after the war and established a lucrative law practice. The coolness between him and his brother-in-law increased when, in the immediate postwar era, Serrano attempted to publish his diplomatic memoirs to prove to the United Nations that Spanish diplomacy had not been pro-German during the war, as public opinion assumed. Franco, however, felt that knowledge of the Hendaye Protocol might destroy new contacts with the United States, and so the book's publication was delayed.

This controversy made Serrano more hostile to the Franco regime. In the 1950s, he fought official censorship, defended literary figures, and sought to speed the return of distinguished intellectuals who were refugees abroad. He also became a part of the movement inside and outside Spain to prepare for the restoration of the monarchy. In his twilight years, he has assumed the role of a mellow statesman and a historical resource.

For additional information, see R. Serrano Suñer, *Entre Hendaye y Gibraltar* (Madrid, 1948).

*C. R. Halstead*

*Related entries*: FRANCO, GEN. FRANCISCO; WORLD WAR II.


**SEVEN YEARS' WAR** (1756–1763), eighteenth-century Spanish war. The Seven Years' War took place in Europe between Prussia and its ally Britain* against Austria and its allies Saxony, France,* Russia, and Sweden. The war began when Frederick the Great (1712–1786) of Prussia sought to consolidate his geographical gains, particularly in the formerly Austrian territory of Silesia. He was also aware of a plot by Austria, Russia, and Saxony to partition Prussia. At the same time, Britain was seeking any excuse to remove France as a colonial power in North America. The Treaty of Aix-la-Chapelle in 1748 concluding the Anglo-Spanish War* (War of Jenkins's Ear) had failed to settle differences between France and Britain over trade and possession of territory in North America. A line of French forts from Montreal to New Orleans seemed to threaten Britain's Atlantic-seaboard colonies.

Frederick feared that the colonial dispute between the two larger powers might be fought out in Europe and at a time when his traditional ally France had allied instead with Archduchess Maria Theresa (1717–1780) of Austria. To prevent further losses, he concluded the Convention of Neutrality with Britain, whose entrance into the general European conflict led the French to attack the British-occupied Minorca and caused Britain to declare war on 18 May 1756.

Spain found itself drawn into this conflict by its alliance with France in the Family Compact of 15 Aug. 1761. The terms of this agreement made the enemies of the two Bourbon nations mutual foes and pledged a common defense for their territorial possessions throughout the world. A secret convention obliged Spain to declare war on Britain on 1 May 1762 if it had not concluded peace with France. In exchange, France would return Minorca to Spain and delay peace with Britain until all pending disputes between Spain and Britain could be resolved.

Spain had a number of claims against Britain concerning violation of Spanish territorial waters, refusal to allow Spanish fishermen on the Grand Banks off Newfoundland, and its exploitation of Honduras. When all but the second point were being discussed by diplomats, Britain demanded an explanation of Spain's compact with France. After learning of the accord's secret provision, Britain declared war on Spain on 4 Jan. 1762. Spain followed with its own declaration twelve days later and with France tried to force Portugal* to declare war against its longtime ally Britain. When the Portuguese refused, Spain invaded Portugal and captured Almeida. In response, Britain sent eight thousand troops to Lisbon, who effectively stopped the Spanish campaign.

After the failure of the Portuguese expedition, Spain's participation in the Seven Years' War centered on the West Indian colonies. In Mar. 1762, Adm. Sir George Pocock (1706–1792) led an expedition against Havana that, after a three-month struggle, forced Spain to cede the city and surrounding area to the British crown. Another British fleet operated in the Caribbean and seized the French colony of Martinique. A further Spanish loss was suffered in the Pacific Ocean, when a small British fleet captured Manila, the largest city of the Philippines. Franco-Hispanic military action, which included a raid on Newfoundland and the capture of the Portuguese colony of Colônia do Sacramento in Brazil, did not match the British successes.

War weariness at home, however, soon forced John Stuart, earl of Bute (1715–1792), who in 1762 had replaced William Pitt (the Elder, 1708–1778) as the head of the British government, to begin negotiations late the same year with France and Spain. The Peace of Paris was formulated on 10 Feb. 1763, with its terms generally unfavorable to France, since the Mississippi became the boundary between Britain and France, ceding everything east of the river, except New Orleans, to Britain. French losses included territorial rights to Canada, where they gave up everything except fishing rights to the St. Lawrence and Newfoundland banks and two small island enclaves for the fishermen. In the West Indies, Martinique, Guadeloupe, Marie Galante, and St. Lucia were returned by the British, who kept only Grenada and the Grenadines. In Africa, Gorée returned to French possession, while Senegal was kept by Britain, and in India, where France kept its trading establishments, it was not allowed to construct fortifications or have soldiers in Bengal. Spain, in turn, abandoned its claims to fishing rights off Newfoundland, allowed the British to continue cutting wood in Honduras, and restored Colônia do Sacramento and Almeida to Portugal. Britain returned Havana and Manila to Spanish control and got Florida in exchange. Minorca returned to British control for Belle Ile. Finally, to compensate Spain for its larger losses, France put Louisiana under Spanish control.

Britain's withdrawal from the war left Prussia and Austria without allies, since Russia and Sweden had disengaged earlier. The two Central European powers agreed to a peace treaty on 5 Feb. 1783 that essentially restored their relations to antebellum status.

The major results of the war saw the emergence of Prussia as a counterbalance to Austrian supremacy, the rise of Russia to major diplomatic status, and the elimination of France as a colonial power in North America.

For additional information, see A. Guerra y Sánchez, ed., *A History of the Cuban Nation*, vol. 2; *Colonial Wars, Conflicts and Progress: From 1697–1790* (Havana, 1958); F. W. Longman, *Frederick the Great and the Seven Years' War* (New York, 1908); and M. Peters, *Pitt and Popularity: The Patriot Minister and London Opinion during the Seven Years' War* (Oxford, 1980).

R. Hendricks

*Related entries*: BRITAIN; FRANCE; PORTUGAL.


**SILVELA Y DE LE VIELLEUZE, FRANCISCO** (1845–1905), nineteenth-century liberal politician. Francisco Silvela, born in Madrid on 15 Dec. 1845, was intellectually so gifted that after his law studies, he gained a quick reputation by 1869 as a writer and orator. Much of his time was devoted to café society, but in 1869 he was elected as a conservative deputy representing Avila in the Constituent Cortes and to the Cortes in 1871, where he again won a reputation for oratory. In 1875, he served as minister of the interior in the regency for a brief time, and in 1883, he became minister of justice in the cabinet of Antonio Cánovas del Castillo,* the liberal-conservative leader. Throughout this period, he defended the party effectively in the Cortes and filled a number of offices.

In 1892, however, he broke with the liberal conservatives in a controversy over electoral corruption. In the next few years, Silvela's dissidence led him further away from party orthodoxy and into criticism of municipal administration and Cuban policy. Cánovas's assassination, on 8 Aug. 1897, elevated Silvela to liberal-conservative leadership and to the premiership on 4 Mar. 1899.

As leader, Silvela stepped into an impossible situation of national despair and political confusion in the wake of the Spanish-American War.* His cabinet made some progress in decreasing the national debt, but regionalist dissent, radical political change, and a desperate need for social and economic modernization prevented municipal administrative reform and dictated the continued use of electoral fraud. Silvela fell on 23 Oct. 1900, to the Liberal Fusion party. He returned as premier one last time between 6 Dec. 1902 and 20 July 1903, but national chaos continued, and now the new king, Alfonso XIII,* actively opposed the patriarchs of the old liberal order. Silvela lost party support to Raimundo Fernández Villaverde (1848–1905) and finally retired from politics, dying in Madrid on 29 May 1905, one of the last, but least successful, of the nineteenth-century liberals.

For additional information, see F. Silvela, *Discursos políticos, 1885–1890* (Madrid, 1892).

R. W. Kern

*Related entries*: CÁNOVAS DEL CASTILLO, ANTONIO; LIBERALISM.

## SOCIALIST PARTY, PARTIDO SOCIALISTA OBRERO ESPAÑOL

**(PSOE).** From its foundation in Madrid on 2 May 1879, the PSOE struggled to establish a significant presence in Spanish political life. The party's slow growth during its first thirty years of existence was regionally concentrated. Only in Madrid,* where socialism attracted support from print workers, and Asturias* and the Basque* country, where it appealed to dockers and metalworkers, did the party have any early success in penetrating the labor movement. Elsewhere, especially among the textile workers of Catalonia* and the landless laborers of Andalusia,* it was forced to cede dominance to revolutionary anarchism* notable for its readiness to challenge state power.

Under the leadership of Pablo Iglesias (1850–1925), a dour ascetic whose commitment to socialism was unshakable and who dominated the party until his death in 1925, the PSOE was hampered by both organizational inflexibility and theoretical poverty. Although the party leaders saw themselves as orthodox Marxists, their understanding of Marxism was derivative, highly deterministic, and inappropriate to the historic moment through which they were passing. Crucially, through not questioning faith in historical progress, they failed to elaborate an agrarian policy. While the PSOE espoused a revolutionary rhetoric, it remained committed to legalistic, reformist practice. Indeed, the party concentrated on building up its own organizational strength at the expense of analyzing the aspirations of the Spanish labor force.

This emphasis on organization was reflected in a determination to guard against what was seen as the corrupting influence of all other antidynastic movements. Thus, the PSOE remained isolated from political initiatives sponsored by anarchists and republicans against the Restoration monarchy. By 1909, the damaging costs of this policy of isolation were apparent, and the PSOE entered an electoral alliance with the republic movement. Immediately, Iglesias was elected to the Cortes in 1910; more significant, however, legalist reformism was confirmed as the dominant mode of action in the socialist movement.

Nonetheless, between 1910 and 1923, the PSOE's fortunes fluctuated. A period of consolidation and growth during World War I* led to the party's hesitant involvement in the crisis of 1917. The result of a concatenation of diverse protests against the status quo, involving discontented junior army officers, the Catalan bourgeoisie, and the PSOE, the crisis culminated in a ramshackle and abortive revolutionary uprising in the major cities. Easily defeated, it led to the state's severe repression of the socialist movement. The consequent trauma exacerbated and hardened divisions within the PSOE that had been incipient since the electoral alliance with republican forces. As a result, the party was rent during the trienio bolchevique (1918–1921) by a bitter struggle between supporters of the legalist, reformist line and sympathizers with the Bolshevik revolution. Eventually, the revolutionaries seceded from the PSOE to form the first Spanish Communist party* (PCE).

Although the 1917 rising was defeated, social and political unrest throughout much of Spain in the following years led to the collapse of the regime in 1923.

Gen. Miguel Primo de Rivera,* whose dictatorship survived until 1930, assumed power in order to shore up the threatened interests of the ruling classes. A central element of the dictator's strategy involved the repression of independent political-party and trade-union activity. While the PSOE's freedom of action was circumscribed, however, the socialist union movement, the Unión General de Trabajadores* (UGT), led by PSOE executive members Julián Besteiro (1870–1939) and Francisco Largo Caballero,* was invited to collaborate in the dictatorship's plans to reorganize labor relations. Despite the opposition of two leading PSOE members, Indalecio Prieto (1883–1962) and Fernando de los Ríos (1879–1949), the UGT agreed to work with the dictator's comités paritarios.

The Primo dictatorship, perhaps the most undistinguished period in the PSOE's history, saw the socialists benefit in both organizational and numerical terms by escaping the repression visited upon its anarchist and communist rivals. When support for the dictatorship began to fade after 1927, the socialist movement was able to capitalize upon its privileged treatment under Primo. As the republican movement regrouped under the leadership of Manuel Azaña,* the PSOE took its place at the head of a broad antimonarchical coalition, formalized by the Pact of San Sebastian in late 1930. With the declaration of the Second Republic* on 14 Apr. 1931, the PSOE stood at the center of the political stage for the first time in its history.

The relationship between the PSOE and the republic, however, was always marked by ambivalence and confusion. Although the party accepted three ministerial posts, the republic was supported only insofar as it was seen as the necessary precursor to socialist revolution; ultimately, it was an obstacle to overcome. In fact, the arrival of the Second Republic deepened divisions that had first developed during the Primo dictatorship.

Participation in government was opposed by those PSOE leaders, such as Besteiro, who believed that the party should not interfere in the teleological march of history, but instead await its proper historical moment. Others, like Largo Caballero, the republic's first minister of labor, felt the PSOE should help consolidate what was seen as the long-overdue bourgeois democratic revolution.

The division between those two groups had alternatively been identified as one between ''worker corporativists'' and ''political reformists.'' Whereas the former sought improvements in the conditions of the work force as their primary aim, no matter what the form of political regime, the latter sought the establishment of liberal democracy as an essential precursor to socialist revolution. Ultimately, both groups were frustrated as the attempted reforms of the republic's first government were undermined by the land-based reactionary conservative opposition. The failure of reform, especially in agrarian legislation, contributed to the collapse of the republican-socialist alliance. In the general elections of Nov. 1933, the PSOE stood on its own and suffered a demoralizing defeat as the right-wing Radical-CEDA coalition swept to victory.

Electoral defeat was a key element in the PSOE's post–1933 ''radicalization,'' marked by the adoption of an ostensibly revolutionary position and seen by many as being directly responsible for the collapse of the Second Republic. In spite of prolonged scholarly debate, the precise causes and impact of the PSOE's radicalization remain unresolved. It is, however, generally agreed that the failure of agrarian reform efforts between 1931 and 1933 led to profound disillusionment among some leading socialists, particularly Largo Caballero, with the republic. Other reasons put forward include the impact of grass-roots militant pressure on the party leadership, especially that from southern landworkers and the Madrid UGT; the fear that the Confederación Española de Derechas Autónomas (CEDA) represented a Spanish equivalent to German and Italian fascism; and the constrictive influence of the PSOE's simplistic understanding of Marxism that posited reform or revolution as the only available alternatives.

The radicalization of the PSOE was opposed by leading party members such as Besteiro, Ríos, and Prieto. The main impetus behind the adoption of more extremist positions derived from the party's Madrid section; its youth group; and members of the Federación Nacional de Trabajadores de la Tierra (FNTT), the affiliated landworkers' association founded in 1930. The most vocal sponsor of the PSOE's more radical posture during 1934 was Largo Caballero. His insistence on the need to combat the CEDA threat led ultimately to the revolutionary rising of Oct. 1934 in direct response to the ministerial appointments of three CEDA members.

The Oct. rising was easily defeated. Poorly coordinated, the planned revolution collapsed quickly in both Madrid and Barcelona.* Only in Asturias, where it received the support of the anarchists, did the rising survive for a fortnight. The repression unleashed by the government in its aftermath, however, was fierce. Several PSOE leaders, including Largo Caballero and Besteiro, were jailed for life, party premises were closed, and the socialist newspaper was banned. The failure of the Oct. rising confirmed the divisions that had developed in the party during the course of the republic. The radical wing, known as the Caballeristas, now called for the bolshevization of the PSOE and began to establish contact with the PCE and other Marxist groups. Others, such as Prieto, who had escaped to France,* were convinced that the PSOE must rebuild its alliance with the republicans and return to reformist legalism.

Throughout 1935, the two wings of the PSOE bitterly contested control of the party's direction. The revolutionary rhetoric of the Caballeristas contributed to the polarization of Spanish politics, which was further destabilized by a series of corruption scandals involving the Radical-CEDA government. It was Prieto, however, in alliance with the republic leader, Manuel Azaña, who gained the political initiative within the PSOE. Their combined efforts to reconstruct the 1931 republican-socialist electoral coalition led to the creation in early 1936 of the Popular Front, a wide-ranging alliance of leftist forces. In spite of communist claims to authorship of the concept, the Popular Front represented a triumph for the Prietistas over Largo Caballero. Essentially moderate, it won the closely fought and highly disputed general elections of 16 Feb. 1936, thereby ensuring the release of the jailed PSOE leaders. By prior arrangement, no socialists took office in the new government.

Nonetheless, the activities of the FNTT, which encouraged members to exact revenge for the right-wing dominance of the previous two years, together with the continued rhetorical extremism of the Caballeristas, lent credence to rightist scare-mongering about a red threat. For all the Popular Front's moderation, violence escalated. An attempt to introduce a calming influence by installing Prieto as prime minister foundered on his fear of Largo Caballero's opposition. When the Spanish Civil War* eventually broke out in July, the divided PSOE was in poor condition to respond effectively. Moreover, the party had by this stage begun to be infiltrated by the PCE, a key element in the remarkable usurpation of the republican war effort by the PCE in the following months. The first move in this direction had come with the unification of socialist and communist youth movements in June.

In Sept. 1936, in response to the steady military gains of Gen. Francisco Franco,* Largo Caballero was made premier of a government that included six socialists. The presence of three communist ministers, however, signaled the start of the PCE's rise to political dominance. In accordance with Soviet instructions, the PCE moved to crush any revolutionary aspirations on the republican side. The infamous May Events of 1937, in which anarchists and the quasi-Trotskyist POUM* were purged, marked the end of Largo Caballero's influence. The UGT leader was ousted in the summer, leaving Prieto, as defense minister, as the only obstacle to communist domination. He did not survive long: by Apr. 1938, the enigmatic Juan Negrín,* a fellow socialist who supported communist policies, had replaced both Prieto and Largo Caballero. Thereafter, as the Second Republic slid to defeat, the PSOE fell into rapid decline.

The end of the civil war found the PSOE a broken and defeated party. While leadership attempted to regroup in exile, the party within Spain was forced underground. The PSOE's structure made it unsuitable for clandestine political activity; six entire interior executive committees were captured by the Franco authorities between 1946 and 1953. The exile leadership, under Rodolfo Llopis (1895– ) in Toulouse, became caught up in a sterile debate over the party's role during the civil war and repeatedly called for European intervention against Franco. Although unjustifiable, the subsequent communist slur that the PSOE was "de vacaciones" (on vacation) during the Franco regime underlined the seeming invisibility of socialist opposition.

The 1960s saw a gradual revival of the PSOE. Spain's industrialization and changing social structure spawned the development of both an industrial working class and an entrepreneurial middle class that reacted against the political restrictions of Francoism. PSOE militants within Spain realized the need to adapt the party's strategies to the new sociopolitical situation. The so-called Seville-Bilbao-Asturias triangle arose to challenge the Toulouse leadership; in the early 1970s, control of the party was wrested from Llopis by the youthful Felipe González* and Alfonso Guerra (1940– ).

After the death of Franco in 1975, the PSOE played a key role in the transition to democracy. To this end, the new leaders set about rebuilding the PSOE in the image of other European social-democratic parties. The party's legalization in 1977 was followed by the controversial abandonment of Marxism by González in 1979. This move, which ironically made explicit what had been implicit through much of the party's history, confirmed the dominance of the González-Guerra leadership. In spite of opposition from leftist critics, the message of moderate modernization helped confirm the PSOE's growing ascendancy over the PCE and set it on the road to its triumphant electoral victory of 1982. With absolute majorities in the Cortes, the PSOE for the first time took sole power in Spain, a feat it repeated in the elections of 1986.

For additional information, see S. Juliá, ed., *El socialismo en España* (Madrid, 1986), and *Socialismo y guerra civil* (Madrid, 1987); P. Preston, *The Coming of the Spanish Civil War* (London, 1978); R. A. H. Robinson, *The Origins of Franco's Spain* (Newton Abbot, 1970); and E. Díaz, *Socialismo en España: El partido y el estado* (Madrid, 1982).

*P. Heywood*

*Related entries*: GONZÁLEZ, FELIPE; LARGO CABALLERO, FRANCISCO; SPANISH CIVIL WAR.

**SOCIEDADES ECONÓMICAS DE AMIGOS DEL PAÍS,** cultural centers in the last quarter of the eighteenth century dedicated to the spread of the ideas of the Enlightenment.* In 1764, the establishment of the Sociedad Económica Vasca, modeled on the academies that abounded in French cities, began to hold discussions for its membership, with competitions to test mastery of the topics. The guiding principle of the society was to encourage the exchange of information and introduce the latest intellectual ideas. Influenced by the French Encyclopedists, the Spanish cultural societies focused on the study of the sciences and took a scientific, investigative approach to other disciplines.

The most important of these societies was the Sociedad Económica de Madrid, dominated by the conde de Campomanes.* At his urging, the social elite of the Spanish capital joined the society, thus giving it considerable influence among both intellectuals and government officials. Campomanes felt that, in order to solve Spain's economic problems, the causes of the current situation had to be carefully examined. The economy had a force of its own and could not be corrected merely through legislation. The methods of production, machinery, and techniques needed to be studied and modernized. Campomanes also cautioned that Madrid could not solve the local problems of each province. These tasks were beyond the pale of government officials who could not possibly keep abreast of the latest advances in industry. The important job of modernization would be carried out not through legislation, but by example promoted by the cultural societies. The members of such societies should work for the common good, not for their own benefit.

Following Madrid's example, the principal cities and towns of Spain soon founded similar societies, which rapidly became centers for instruction and investigation. The work of the societies went beyond education; they supported the arts, maritime industries, local law enforcement, the unemployed, and the homeless. Ideally, each society began its work by taking a census to record all workers and other inhabitants, particularly emigrants, the unemployed, and mendicants, as well as statistically to chronicle the agricultural, riparian, maritime, and urban industries; natural resources; and transportation. Within the society, members specialized in specific fields.

Despite their popularity, the societies met with considerable resistance from the church, which sought to protect its traditional economic prerogatives challenged by the would-be reformers, and the guild organizations, which resisted infringement of their role in technical training and industrial innovation.

Unfortunately, outside major population centers, the societies found little support. Many of the societies nevertheless managed to function well into the nineteenth century, but their role in education was eventually subsumed by the country's universities.

For additional information, see R. Krebs Wilckens, *El pensamiento histórico, político y económico del Conde de Campomanes* (Santiago, 1960); P. Demerson, J. Demerson, and F. Aguilar Piñal, *Las Sociedades Económicas de Amigos del País en el siglo xviii: Guía del investigador* (San Sebastian, 1974).

*R. Hendricks*

*Related entries*: CAMPOMANES, CONDE DE; ENLIGHTENMENT, AGE OF.

**SPANISH-AMERICAN WAR** (1898), last imperial war of Spain in the Americas. Relations between Spain and its Cuban colony were originally disturbed by eighteenth-century uprisings against Spanish mercantilism over cheap royal purchases of tobacco sold at much higher prices in Europe or the inability of sugar producers to trade their surpluses with other nations. Liberalism* removed these economic obstacles in time to prevent Cuba from joining the other American colonies* that freed themselves in the early nineteenth century, but the emergence of a plantation society based on black slavery also made the Cuban planter elite back away from independence in fear of its social and political consequences.

Cuban similarity to southern regions of the United States* caused Thomas Jefferson (1743–1826) to consider annexing the island. Presidents James Polk (1795–1849), Franklin Pierce (1804–1869), and James Buchanan (1791–1868) attempted vainly to purchase Cuba from Spain in the 1840s and 1850s. The Ostend Manifesto (1854) openly discussed seizure of the island, and filibustering expeditions to Cuba showed an inclination to take it by force if necessary, but this phase of U.S.-Cuban involvement ended with the victory of antislavery forces in the American Civil War (1861–1865).

British abolitionism, actively focused on Cuban slavery after 1835, was indirectly responsible for formation of a Cuban reform party in 1865 to support gradual abolition of slavery, equal rights of Cubans, and greater political freedom. Peninsulars (Spanish residents in Cuba) resisted, but advisors of Isabel II,* panicked by Santo Domingo's sudden independence in 1865, called for local elections to create a reform commission. Dominated by Cubans, it accepted a gradual end of slavery and pressed for other reforms, but proslavery peninsular protests made Gen. Ramón Narváez* disband the commission early in 1867.

Rebellion broke out in Cuba in Oct. 1868 and lasted a decade. Although it was a limited war, Cuban exhaustion finally led to the Peace of Zanjón that ended the Ten Years' War on 11 Feb. 1878. Slavery was replaced by patronato, a form of tutelage that led to full emancipation on 7 Oct. 1885. Creole demands for administrative autonomy within the empire, however, went unanswered, and Spanish premiers such as Antonio Cánovas del Castillo* or Práxedes Mateo Sagasta,* facing unrest at home, relied upon caciques* and authoritarian military governors rather than reform in Cuba.

An additional complication was the growing U.S. stake in the Cuban economy. Development of beet sugar in Europe made North America the only major market for Cuban cane sugar, and U.S. capital financed the expansion of productive facilities to the virtual exclusion of Spain. This close association revived the earlier fixation that Cuba properly belonged within the U.S. orbit.

Not all Cubans accepted the U.S. as a replacement for Spanish colonial rule. The major Cuban intellectual and nationalist figure in the years just before the Spanish-American War, José Martí (1853–1895), was one who did not. Educated at the University of Saragossa (1874), he was a poet, journalist, and essayist who returned to Cuba (1878) to become a leader of Cuban autonomy forces. Threatened with arrest (1881), Martí fled to New York City and called for a national rising against Spanish occupation of the island and creation of a Cuban republic independent of the United States (1887). Because Cuba had become the focal point of two major colonial powers, Martí's patriotic anti-imperialism anticipated contemporary Third World thought on the problem of dependence. In other ways, his mixture of romanticism, the ideas of Karl Christian Friedrich Krause*, and economic independence was similar to that of the Filipino nationalist leader, José Rizal (1861–1896).

Both Martí and Rizal separately founded new independence parties in 1892, Martí the Partido Revolucionario Cubano and Rizal the Liga Filipina. In the case of Cuba, however, as long as the Spanish government kept the 1891 reciprocal trade agreement in place, trouble was avoided, but when the U.S. adopted new restrictive tariffs in 1894, Spain again surrounded Cuba with protectionism. Sugar exports plummeted, and some Cubans privately appealed to U.S. officials to intercede with Spain, but Martí took the decisive step of planning a revolt. On 24 Feb. 1895, a new separatist war broke out in Oriente and Matanzas, and soon afterward, the reformist Gen. Arsenio Martínez Campos (1831–1900) was appointed governor general. After the death of Martí in a minor battle in May, however, the Cubans fought with such determination that Martínez Campos was militarily defeated and finally replaced by Gen. Valeriano Weyler (1838–1930) in Dec. 1895.

In an attempt to isolate the rebels, Weyler used trochas (cleared lines of defense) and forced relocation of rural populations so cruelly that Cuban resistance actually intensified. Cánovas's unpopular cabinet, lacking the military means to end the revolt, rejected several offers in 1896 from the U.S. president, Grover Cleveland (1837–1908), to mediate a settlement based on Spanish reforms. Spain's last chance to avoid the disaster of 1898 was blocked by the persistent authoritarianism of the old Restoration administrative system and the advanced age and exhaustion of its leaders. Cánovas was assassinated on 8 Aug. 1897, only to be replaced once again, in Oct., by Sagasta.

In the United States, pressure to follow manifest destiny by intervening in Cuba stemmed from persistent economic difficulties in the early 1890s that had already destroyed the reciprocal-trade agreement in 1894. Outward expansion by means of imperialism was cheered by William Randolph Hearst (1863–1951), newspaper proprietor of yellow journalism fame, and Theodore Roosevelt (1858–1919), seeking a "bully pulpit" from which to proclaim U.S. virtues. The new president, William McKinley (1843–1901), while more circumspect, nonetheless increased pressure on Sagasta to resolve the Cuban crisis. By the end of 1897, some progress had been made. Weyler was replaced, a political amnesty released political prisoners, a draft constitution was published, and a new autonomous government took over in Havana on 1 Jan. 1898. Cuban public opinion, however, interpreted the reforms as a sign of weakness surely leading to independence, and peninsulars convinced that social revolution would follow independence believed that it was imperative for the United States to intervene. Their role in the unsolved sinking of the U.S.S. *Maine* in the harbor at Havana on 15 Feb. 1898 has always been suspected, but as far as U.S. public opinion was concerned, Spain itself was the culprit.

The press's clamor for war undermined McKinley's negotiations to acquire Cuba from Spain by diplomatic means. The U.S. Congress voted additional military funds on 19 Mar., threatening to issue a war proclamation of its own, forcing McKinley to capitulate on 11 Apr. by announcing a declaration of war. Congress, disclaiming any intent to annex Cuba, declared war on 20 Apr., thus beginning the Spanish-American War, an event much greater in its preliminaries than in actuality.

Spanish indignation at the United States for rejecting its concessions temporarily overcame the unpopularity of the Cuban cause. The navy* was hastily sent to Cuba with reinforcements, but before fighting began on the island, an American squadron commanded by Adm. George Dewey (1837–1917) destroyed the weak Pacific fleet of the Spanish navy at Manila on 1 May. Emilio Aguinaldo (1869–1964), leader of the Filipino independence movement since Rizal's execution on 30 Dec. 1896, returned from exile to Manila on 24 May. Spain, so distracted by these faraway events that it sent additional ships eastward, had to recall them when Aguinaldo proclaimed independence on 13 May. All Luzon except Manila was freed by 31 May, and Manila fell on 13 Aug., the day after war in the Caribbean ended.

War in Cuba began in June with the linkage of U.S. and rebel forces in the eastern provinces, but despite victories at El Caney and San Juan Hill in early

July, the mythology that grew up around these battles ignored the miserable conditions, military inexperience, and racial prejudice toward the Cubans. The major engagement was another naval disaster, the blockade of the Spanish fleet in the harbor of Santiago and its destruction on 3 July. Once the lifeline to Iberia was cut, resistance in Cuba collapsed and the U.S. invasion of Puerto Rico on 25 July caused only minor skirmishes. An informal truce was followed by the signing of a peace protocol on 12 Aug. Manila fell the next day after U.S. troops were positioned to protect the Spanish garrison from the Filipinos. Spanish and U.S. diplomats, meeting through the autumn, signed the Treaty of Paris on 10 Dec. 1898. Spain withdrew from Cuba and ceded Puerto Rico, Guam, and the Philippine Islands to the United States.

Spain was paid $20 million for the Philippines, but no amount of money could salvage the disaster of the Spanish-American War for the losers. Any pretense of great-power status had been destroyed, and the promise of change that liberalism had held out from the War of Independence* to the end of the nineteenth century now vanished. Even regeneration and modernization, sought by the Generation of 1898* to remedy problems revealed by the war, would cause difficulties during the Second Republic,* more than thirty years later.

For the victors, Cuba began greater U.S. involvement overseas and its own difficulties with empire. The national celebration over the victory in Cuba altered attitudes about foreign policy, interventionism, and war at the start of the twentieth century, just as the United States became a superpower.

For additional information, see E. May, *Imperial Democracy: The Emergence of America as a Great Power* (New York, 1961); L. A. Pérez, *Cuba between Empires 1878–1902* (Pittsburgh, 1983); J. Suchlicki, *Cuba from Columbus to Castro* (Washington, 1986); and H. Thomas, *Cuba: The Pursuit of Freedom* (New York, 1971).

*R. W. Kern*

*Related entries*: ARMY; CÁNOVAS DEL CASTILLO, ANTONIO; COLONIES; GENERATION OF 1898; NAVY; SAGASTA, PRÁXEDES MATEO.


**SPANISH CIVIL WAR** (1936–1939). Spain has known several civil wars, especially the Carlist Wars of 1833–1840 and of 1872–1876, but these were relatively limited struggles, both in their intensity and in the areas they ravaged. They differed from the Spanish Civil War as traditional European wars differed from the two World Wars of the twentieth century. The war was a total conflict, one in which each side attempted fully to mobilize its resources, in which the enemy was demonized and his complete destruction sought, in which all aspects of life in every region were deeply affected. The totality of the struggle stemmed partly from its being simultaneously a social, political, regional, and religious conflict, without being restricted to one or another of these aspects, as has been the case with most civil wars in world history. Also important was the high degree of ideological polarization, some of it indigenous and resulting from the hopes, fears, and frustrations generated by the experience of the Second Republic,* some reflecting the intense ideological polarization that gripped Europe as a whole during the 1930s. One other frequently forgotten factor contributed to the war's totality: for all its backwardness relative to Britain,* France,* or Germany,* Spain was a modern nation, with modern means of transportation and communication which made possible rapid, decisive actions of all types. Never before or since has a civil war occurred in so advanced a nation; although newer and more destructive weapons were used in subsequent civil wars, of course, none of the Asian, African, or Latin American societies in which they were fought possessed as modernized a social or physical infrastructure as did Spain between 1936 and 1939.

Unique in the above ways, the Spanish conflict was also unique in others. One was the manner in which it began. The army officers who in the spring of 1936 began to conspire together had no intention of launching a civil war. Harking back to Spain's century-long tradition of military intervention in politics, they sought rather to stage a coup that would oust the Popular Front government elected in Feb. and replace it with a conservative body that would stop "dangerous" political and social experimentation and "restore order." They knew that the Popular Front enjoyed wide support, and expected strong opposition from the large and very active working-class organizations that had arisen under the republic. But given the careful preparations made for the coup, above all by Gen. Emilio Mola,* its chief coordinator, they expected to be able to crush this opposition relatively quickly by decisive military action.

## INCOMPLETE MILITARY INSURRECTION AND SOCIAL REVOLUTION, JULY 1936

To some extent their hopes proved accurate. The insurrection started on the afternoon of 17 July in Spanish Morocco. The triumph of the army* there was immediate and complete as no other force existed in the colony capable of resistance. On the mainland during the next three days, the rebels also easily won control of the huge regions of Old Castile and Leon, as well as of the province of Navarre.* This too was no surprise as these areas had long been marked by political conservatism: they were strongly Catholic rural regions without significant urban or rural proletariats because there were no large cities and most peasants held some property. The local populations did not resist the military coup; rather, they tended to join it, especially as volunteers in the Carlist and Falangist militia units that were immediately formed.

Several of the truly indispensable rebel victories cannot be explained by structural factors, however. Seville and Saragossa, after Barcelona* the two greatest urban strongholds of the most militant workers' group in Spain, the anarchosyndicalist Confederación Nacional de Trabajo (CNT),* fell to the rebels largely because of the decisiveness and brilliant psychological ploys used by the local commanders, especially by Gen. Gonzalo Quiepo de Llano (1875–1951) in Seville. The same was true in Oviedo, one of the chief bastions of the socialist Unión General de Trabajadores* (UGT), and to a lesser extent in such radical centers as Cadiz, Córdoba, Huelva, and Granada. The confusion and disorganization of the working classes that permitted these defeats was all the more important because as the cities went, so too went the regions. The republic's loss of Saragossa was immediately followed by the loss of the entire western half of Aragon.* And in Andalusia,* the revolutionary peasant organizations of the CNT that had for so long agitated the region proved no match for the army once the provincial capitals were lost.

If events defied sociology in several regions, they nevertheless conformed to it in others. In the major cities of Madrid,* where the UGT predominated, and Valencia,* where working-class loyalties were mixed, it was the rebel leaders who were confused and disorganized and so allowed to pass the decisive moment that might, against all odds, have given them victory. In Barcelona, the rebels struck fairly quickly, but the CNT was too numerous and militant to be defeated once the local police units joined them in resisting the coup. No rising occurred, or it was quickly defeated, in most industrial and port cities along the Cantabric coast—San Sebastian, Bilbao, Santander, Gijón—as well as in most provincial capitals of New Castile, northern and eastern Andalusia, and along the Mediterranean coast.

Within three days, by 21 July, the coup was decided almost everywhere. Had it either succeeded or failed, no civil war would have occurred, because two sides capable of carrying it out would not have arisen. Because the coup partly succeeded and partly failed, however, civil war suddenly became a reality.

Superficially, the republic seemed in the more advantageous position. Except for Seville and Saragossa, the largest cities and the chief industrial centers all remained in its hands. It controlled major agricultural areas, particularly the rich irrigated plains along the Mediterranean coast from which many of Spain's exports originated. The republic was also the legitimate government and controlled the state apparatus, along with the huge gold reserves Spain had accumulated during World War I* and the assets of the major banks. The air force had been relatively untouched by the conspiracy and remained loyal to the republic. The attempted revolts by naval officers had usually been put down in blood by shipboard mutinies of the seamen, so most of Spain's fleet was also at its disposal. Of the militarized police units, the Assault Guards, the Carabineros, and even significant segments of the Civil Guard* had stayed on its side. Nor had the army proved unanimous in its rebellion; indeed, numerically almost half of the officers had *not* risen against the republic, and several top generals were executed by the rebels for resisting the coup.

Other circumstances rendered these advantages illusory, however. Most important was the collapse of authority on the republican side. The coup justified itself as necessary to stop imminent social revolution; in fact, it set off precisely such revolution in the places where it was defeated. Like the coup itself, however, the social revolution was incomplete. The working-class organizations—especially the CNT with its libertarian ideology, but also the UGT—seized farms, factories, and shops to collectivize them, and created their own armed militias. They disregarded government directives when it suited them and, in effect, set up states within the state. They would not go on to try to seize full state power, though. As in the early stages of the Russian Revolution, a situation of divided authority existed within the republican zone. This was made still more extreme, because, in addition to its power disputes with the worker organizations, the national government's authority was often contested by the regional governments in Catalonia and the Basque* region, as well by the ad hoc governmental entities that sprang up in Asturias,* Santander, and eastern Aragon. To make matters worse, local union groups often defied national union leadership, and the committees that took over local government were as prone to disregard orders from the regional governments as they were from the national.

Against such obstacles, the Madrid government could make little headway: it was a feeble government that had lost control of its forces of coercion and was headed by a stopgap cabinet under José Giral (1880–1962), composed solely of middle-class progressives, without working-class representation. The cabinet had been hastily put together on the night of 19 July, after two previous cabinets had fallen that same day. None of the leading figures of the peacetime republic were included in it, nor did it receive strong guidance from the president, Manuel Azaña,* who had been the charismatic leader of the peacetime republic, but who now began his rapid slide toward political irrelevance and isolation. Taking all the above elements together, it seems safe to assert that authority in a large, modern state has probably never before or since been so weak and fragmented as it was in republican Spain during the first three months of the civil war.

Republican disunity might not have mattered so much had not precisely the opposite condition prevailed on the other side: the degree of unity among the rebels was nearly as exceptional historically, in a situation of civil war, as was the degree of disunity among the loyalists; divisions of the kind that handicapped the Whites in the Russian Civil War, or especially the Islamic groups in today's civil war in Lebanon, did not exist. It should be emphasized that this unity had a de facto and almost fortuitous nature. The army leaders shared only their antirepublicanism, and differed significantly as to what the future government should be. The civilian groups supporting the coup also ran the full gamut of rightest opinion—from Falangist to Carlist to monarchist to conservative republican to social Catholic. None of these factions was strong enough to establish its ascendancy over the others, however, let alone question the predominance of the army. This might have changed had the two most charismatic prewar leaders of the Right—the monarchist, José Calvo Sotelo* and the Falangist, José Antonio Primo de Rivera*—still been active. The first had been assassinated on 13 July, however, and the second arrested and then executed by the republican authorities. Among the army generals, Gen. Francisco Franco* had major advantages in establishing his ascendancy: he was the most prestigious officer of the prewar period and on 19 July assumed command of the units in Morocco,* the Spanish army's most powerful striking force. His path would have been more difficult, however, had not Gen. José Sanjurjo (1872–1936), the intended coup leader, died in a plane crash while returning from exile in Portugal,* and if other possible rivals had not been removed from the competition in a variety of ways.

## THE EARLY MONTHS OF THE WAR (AUG. 1936–MAR. 1937)

At the very start, the unity of command among the rebels was not as effective as it would later become: suspicions and rivalries sometimes prevented their armies from coordinating their activities, perhaps most important in late Aug. when—rather than trying to do it alone via a southern route—the Army of Africa might have joined with the northern forces to attack Madrid from the heights the rebels controlled in the Guadarrama Mountains. The contrast with the other side was nevertheless striking. For several weeks, the republican army's chain of command broke down almost completely. This was not only because of the circumstances mentioned earlier: the weakness of the Giral government, the fragmentation of political authority, and the appearance of autonomous CNT and UGT militia units that disregarded orders. The professional army units that had remained on the loyalist side were also incapacitated partly by the revolutionary fervor, partly because their commanders were often suspected of being crypto-rebels, who had been caught in republican territory by accident and were slyly awaiting the moment when they could safely betray the loyalist cause. The result was that, striking from the positions they had won during the coup of 18–21 July, the rebels went from victory to victory during the next two months; meanwhile, the best the loyalists could do was to carry out misconceived and quickly frustrated offensives in a few places while engaged in mostly ineffective holding actions on other fronts.

The failed republican offensives are quickly summarized: a massive but confused attempt by CNT militia units from Barcelona to dislodge the rebels from Saragossa and Huesca and thus regain western Aragon; an army-navy* expedition to retake the Balearic Islands,* also launched from Catalonia; an army campaign from Castile* to recover Cordoba and northern Andalusia; and several assaults on Oviedo from the surrounding regions of Asturias. The rebels' operations were centered on a northern theater, directed by Mola, and a southern one, headed by Franco. Mola was the less successful: the professional forces under his command were small and poorly armed; moreover, he had to keep many of them on the Aragon and Guadarrama fronts to guard against republican attacks, however inept. Nevertheless, by early Sept., he had taken the cities of Irun and San Sebastian, thus closing the French frontier to republican forces in the north, a particularly grave defeat since these forces were already cut off from the main republican zone in the south, center, and east by the military uprising's success in Old Castile, Navarre, and eastern Aragon.

Franco's victories were more spectacular, commanding as he did the Army of Africa, Spain's best, and being too distant from Barcelona and Madrid to fear attack from the loyalist militias, who were prone to remain close to home. German airplanes enabled him to bypass the republican naval blockade and by early Aug., had transported enough troops from Morocco to Seville to permit the formation of small striking forces. One of these devoted itself to mopping up operations in the Andalusian countryside and to linking the isolated rebel garrison in Granada to the rest of the rebel zone. The other, more significant, pushed north into Estremadura, taking Lérida and Badajoz by 14 Aug., then turning west along the Tajo River valley to take Talavera by 3 Sept., the last important stronghold on the road to Madrid. At this juncture, an often-criticized decision was made to turn south to rescue the rebels holed up since July in a military fortress within the city of Toledo. The valor of the "defenders of the Alcázar," who for two months held a single building against repeated republican attacks, had become a moral symbol of the rebel cause, and their rescue on 28 Sept. occasioned great jubilation. The drive on Madrid, however, had been postponed for three weeks, a perhaps fatal delay given that the republic transformed itself into a much more credible opponent during Sept.

On 4 Sept., faced with defeats in Talavera, Irun, and the Balearic Islands, the Giral government stepped aside; a new government headed by the most charismatic working-class leader, Francisco Largo Caballero,* in which worker rather than middle-class ministers predominated, assumed power. Caballero immediately reorganized the army command structure on all levels, raising its efficiency, centralizing its operations, and weakening—though not ending—the role played by union militias. This was a major step toward lessening the ambiguities and multiple power centers that had incapacitated the republic; since the defeats inflicted by the nationalists (as the rebels now began to call themselves) had been so disastrous, the changes were accepted on all sides, even by most of the CNT, the chief proponent of decentralization and spontaneous action. In late Sept., the republican war effort was further strengthened as the first systematic arms shipments began to arrive from abroad.

Foreign intervention has long been a controversial aspect of the civil war; indeed, in some earlier accounts the Spaniards were reduced almost to irrelevance in their own struggle, with the decisive actions being attributed to foreign influences. A balance has now been restored, and a consensus formed around the following points. The war was primarily Spanish, both in its origins and in its course; intervention of the scale of the United States* in the Vietnam War (and probably even of the French in the American War of Independence) never took place. Nevertheless, foreign intervention was decisive at a number of critical junctures. The first was the German air transport of Army of Africa units to Spain in Aug. and Sept. This would be strengthened at the turn of 1937 when the German Condor Legion became the chief air force on the nationalist side, and by the arrival of Italian army divisions to supplement the nationalist land forces. For the rest of the war, the nationalists would continue to receive supplies from both Germany and Italy.* Without these, they would not have been able to conduct an effective war effort and might eventually have been forced to accept a negotiated peace with the republicans.

As to the loyalists, the Popular Front government in France had briefly helped them at the outbreak of hostilities, but had stopped doing so because of domestic pressures and fears that the Spanish war might escalate into a general European conflict. These fears were inspired largely by Britain and led to the creation of the Non-Intervention Committee, in which the European powers agreed not to supply either side. In fact, though, the fascist governments of Italy and Germany never honored their commitment, thus providing justification for the Soviet Union also to begin sending arms on a small scale in late Sept. This scale increased in Oct. and stayed large for most of the rest of the war. Similar support from France always remained a hope of the republicans; on some brief occasions the Popular Front government did indeed send supplies or otherwise lend its support, because its heart, though weak and vacillating, was basically with the republican cause. The position of the conservatives in power in Britain was firmer: though they continued to pay lip service to the legitimacy of the republic because of domestic political considerations and feared the influence Germany and Italy were gaining on the nationalist side, they never seriously considered helping the loyalists. In their view, the democratic republic of the past had de facto ceased to exist because of the social revolution in its territories, a revolution that injured British economic interests in Spain and might someday enable communism to be established there. Nonconfrontation was also at the core of the policy of appeasement which increasingly dominated British diplomacy.

When Franco resumed his offensive in the direction of Madrid in Oct., he found the going against the revitalized republican forces much tougher. Nevertheless, his advance continued and by 5 Nov. had become so threatening that Largo Caballero's government decided to abandon the capital and continue the war from Valencia. A great drama now unfolded. Madrid did not fall: Franco's troops launched what was to have been their final assault on the 7th and had gained some footholds in the western part of the city by the 15th, but they were never able to move further. The reorganized loyalist army fought fiercely; it held air and tank superiority because of the Russian supplies; it was strongly backed by the International Brigades* recruited mostly among antifascists throughout Europe, who now saw their first military action. The seemingly unremitting nationalist advance had been stopped; morale soared; José Miaja (1878–1958), the commanding general, became hero of the day; and the republic had gained its first victory, albeit a defensive one. Franco's failure at Madrid meant that what appeared destined to be a short war would become a long one, between much more evenly matched contestants than had seemed possible in Aug. or Sept.

Madrid would remain the center of military operations for the next four months as Franco, having failed in a frontal assault, tried to take it by a series of flanking operations. The first were in the north and west of the city, in Dec. and Jan., and proved inconclusive. In Feb., a stronger offensive was launched to the southeast of Madrid, in the Jarama Valley, to cut communications with Valencia. Fiercely contested, the struggle continued for three weeks and left many casualties (including in the American Abraham Lincoln Brigade, which saw its first action at the Jarama) before being broken off. In Mar., the third major attack was launched, this time from the northeast, with a recently arrived Italian division in the vanguard. Poor weather conditions hampered the offensive, which was shorter and less bloody than Jarama had been despite the greater number of troops committed. Nevertheless, the psychological effects of the victory at Guadalajara were probably exceeded only by the defense of Madrid in Nov. On four successive occasions republican armies had held firm. Foreign troops had openly fought against them and been defeated. So high was morale that people tended to forget the serious loss the republic had just suffered in Andalusia, when the major port city of Malaga had collapsed in early Feb. before a joint Italian-nationalist attack.

## THE TIDE TURNS IN FAVOR OF THE NATIONALISTS (APR.– NOV. 1937)

Now the war settled down into a truly protracted struggle. Having failed to take Madrid either by frontal or flanking attacks, Franco gave up all hope of a quick victory and set as his goal the piecemeal destruction of the republic. To carry it out, he further consolidated his already formidable power. In Apr., the Falangists and Carlists, the main civilian supporters of the rebels, were deprived of their frequently disputatious autonomy and forced to unite into a single movement, the Falange Española Tradicionalista (FET),* which was rendered innocuous by the leaders Franco appointed. His brother-in-law, Ramón Serrano Suñer,* began to convert the Junta Tecnica, a provisional body created the previous year to run nonmilitary affairs, into a real government. Church support for the nationalist cause was enhanced by several measures, culminating in the Spanish episcopate's collective letter of July 1937, which officially condemned the republic and lauded the nationalists for having protected religion. German and Italian support of Franco and his policies was strengthened in various ways. The possibility of a rival arising among the nationalist generals disappeared completely as Mola remained content with his position as field commander in the north, and Quiepo de Llano, whose brilliance in seizing Seville during the July uprising had been so vital to the rebel cause, was isolated as commander on the increasingly inactive Andalusian front.

The main theater of war now became the northern republican zone, against which Mola began what was destined to become a seven-month offensive on 31 Mar. 1937. The disadvantages of the loyalists in this region were legion. It was cut off from the main republican zone by hundreds of miles of nationalist-held territory. Its land routes to France had been severed the previous Sept. Sea connections with the outside world were also increasingly disrupted as the nationalist navy, based in Galicia,* gained control of the Bay of Biscay, and as the British accepted the naval blockade in Bilbao in Apr. The republican air force had trouble operating in the northern zone because of weather and geographical conditions. In addition, political authority there was still seriously fragmented, despite Largo Caballero's reforms. Four governmental entities operated: the national government; the Basque regional government legally constituted in Oct. 1936; and two quasi-legal provincial governments, one in Santander and another in Asturias. The purposes and nature of these governments were quite different, with the extremes represented by the middle class, religiously oriented Basque government, whose main quarrel with the nationalists was that they would not recognize Basque autonomy, and the worker-dominated, revolutionary oriented government in Asturias.

The only advantage enjoyed by the republicans was the highly accidented, mountainous terrain of most of the northern zone; the taking of a peak did not lead to a breakthrough, but meant merely that another would have to be taken, and then still another. With defensive positions being so frequent and so formidable, Mola's advance was a slow, agonizing one, especially after the attempt to break republican morale by the first saturation bombardment of a civilian target in world history, the infamous attack by the Condor Legion on Guérnica on 26 Apr., proved counterproductive. Mola's death in a plane crash further disoriented the offensive. By 19 June, however, a major objective had been achieved, the taking of Bilbao. In July and Aug., operations slowed down as the nationalists had to divert forces to beat back major republican offensives first on the Madrid front, at Brunete, then on the Asturias front, at Belchite. Nevertheless, on 26 Aug., another major northern city, Santander, fell. The fighting became even more desperate as the nationalist forces closed in on the fiery revolutionary bastion of Asturias. It took until 19 Oct. to conquer Gijón, but by the end of the month, the nationalist victory had become complete.

The loss of the northern zone meant a significant shift in the relative strength of the two combatants. The north was the center of Spanish mining and heavy industry; although these resources had not been used effectively by the republicans, because of the revolutionary fervor and divisions among them, they now were again rendered efficient with surprising speed. The almost constant nationalist superiority in arms during the rest of the war stemmed not only from the more constant supplies received from Italy and Germany, but also from increased steel and iron production in Bilbao; the improved economic position of the nationalists depended in part on the coal exports they organized from Asturias. Another fundamental change was that the nationalists no longer had to fight on two fronts, but could now move their troops at will against the single, though massive, loyalist zone that remained. A third structural transformation was that the nationalist navy, previously concentrated in the Bay of Biscay, could now be transferred to the Mediterranean, where it gained ascendancy over the republican fleet, and made it much more difficult for Russian arms to reach the loyalists. This, rather than any change in Joseph Stalin's (1879–1953) attitude toward the republic, would seem to be the main reason for the sporadic nature and occasional paucity of Soviet supplies in the future. The demographic base of the republic had shrunk—and that of the nationalists had expanded—by at least two million people. Finally, with the liberal Catholicism* of the Basques silenced, the church could rally behind Franco even more unanimously than before. No comparable change in the fundamental structure of the war had occurred previously. The republic was from now on permanently at a disadvantage.

## NEGRÍN'S RESTRUCTURING OF THE REPUBLIC (MAY 1937–FEB. 1938)

Nevertheless, the republic did not collapse: the war continued for another eighteen months and would see some of the republicans' most heroic moments. A major reason lies in the political transformation that had occurred in the spring of 1937, at about the time Franco was strengthening his own political position. Since the republicans had been more divided than the nationalists, however, the internal struggle was fiercer and more complex. Largo Caballero's reforms of the previous autumn had centralized authority and strengthened the republican army considerably, but had by no means been complete. They were least effective as the distance from the central government increased: in Malaga, in the northern zone, and in Catalonia. Malaga fell in Feb., the north was besieged after Mar., so it was in Catalonia, which in any case exceeded the other two in demographic and economic importance, that the need for further change was greatest.

Catalonia was also the focal point of centralization for political reasons: its government was very autonomously inclined; it was also the chief stronghold of the anarchosyndicalist CNT and of a new, left-communist organization called the Partido Obrero de Unificación Marxista (POUM*). None of these forces were consistently cooperative with the national government, but the most extreme opposition came from the POUM, which despite its small size thought it could repeat the feat of the bolsheviks and energize the republic into victory through a second revolution that would enable it to implement the POUM's harsh policies. The Catalan autonomists and the CNT were more ambiguous: older and less fanatical forces, both recognized that the war had at least partially vitiated many of their dreams. An autonomous Catalonia had been born, only to find itself torn apart by conflicts between the middle-class autonomists and the workers organized by the CNT and the POUM. The CNT suffered even greater trauma: its libertarian ideal of free individuals in small, consensual communities had proved ineffective in organizing a war effort. Yet neither could change course completely and accept the total centralization required by the war. This was particularly true in the CNT, whose national leaders gradually began to bow to the new realities after the disastrous defeats of Aug. and Sept. 1936, but whose local organizations and massive rank and file had more difficulty in adjusting.

These conflicts were complicated by others. Largo Caballero's decision to move the government out of Madrid in Nov. 1936 had damaged his prestige; he gained the reputation of being a bumbling administrator, unable to deal with crisis or formulate military strategy properly. He was seen also as a person too soft to carry to their conclusion the centralizing reforms he had inaugurated previously. His most intense opponents came to be the communists, who from a weak faction during peacetime had been transformed by the war into a major force, partly because their Fifth Regiment proved far the best of the militia units formed in July 1936, partly because the Soviet Union was the republic's chief arms supplier, partly because many thousand middle-class individuals and peasant proprietors had flocked to the party as protection against pressures to join the more purely worker-oriented CNT or UGT. The communists had become perhaps the main pillar of the republic; without their support it would collapse.

The crisis, whose remote origins stretched back to Jan., began to reach a head in late Mar. and throughout Apr., as Mola mounted his campaign in the north; the disputes between Largo Caballero and the communists became more open; and as local conflicts among CNT, POUM, communist, and autonomist followers escalated in Catalonia. It exploded into violence on 3 May, when the Catalan government tried to regain control of the central telephone exchange in Barcelona, held by the CNT since July 1936. The "May events" are extremely complicated and cannot be described here. Suffice it to say that George Orwell's (1903–1950) classic account in *Homage to Catalonia* (1938), though sincere, is politically innocent: the local CNT organizations and especially the POUM were not simply hapless victims of stronger forces. The effect of the events was shattering: for five days, in Barcelona and in other parts of Catalonia, republicans had fought against republicans, not against Franco. Though order was restored on 8 May, the consequences continued to be felt long after. The Catalan government was effectively displaced by the central government, lessening the enthusiasm of the autonomists for the war. The morale of the CNT was also weakened, especially in its local organizations and among its rank and file. The POUM was outlawed. Finally, the May events triggered the fall of Largo Caballero. Objecting to his "softness" in handling the conflict and its aftermath, the communist ministers resigned from his government. Had they been alone in their dissatisfaction, he might have been able to hang on as premier. Many left republicans, however, and, more important, the Indalecio Prieto (1883–1962) wing of the deeply divided Socialist party* also wanted to oust him. On 15 May, Caballero was forced to resign; on 17 May, another socialist, Juan Negrín,* replaced him as prime minister.

Negrín differed radically from Caballero. A noted scientist and university professor, one of the distinguished intellectuals recruited to Spanish socialism in the 1920s, he had played a minor political role prior to the war. From now onward, he would dominate the scene completely; what Azaña had been to the peacetime republic, Negrín became to the republic at war. Moreover, unlike Azaña, he was not given to doubts and depression; his boundless energies were brought entirely to bear on restructuring the republic to release its fullest war-making capacity. This meant above all reversing more completely than Largo Caballero had done the social revolution triggered by the army coup of July 1936.

As Negrín saw it, the social revolution handicapped the republic's war effort. This had been especially true at the beginning, when militia autonomy went unchallenged, and when the lack of governmental authority had permitted small groups and individuals to engage in a hysteria of violence in which tens of thousands of persons, especially priests, were assassinated. The collapse of military discipline had permitted the rebels to consolidate their uprising, and the spontaneous terror had cost the republic dearly both in world opinion and in the fear felt by many middle-class individuals within Spain who did not support Franco. Largo Caballero's reforms, however, had brought both these sources of weakness under control, and the May events (together with the loss of the north) had lessened the significance of rival governmental authorities. What remained to be done, along with completing the above processes, was to render the republic into an effective military machine.

Dismantling the social revolution was the key to this in several ways. Perhaps the most important was that it was economically inefficient in a society that desperately needed greater production. Collectivization, or "worker control," of factories might occasionally bring heroic efforts and record output, but normally it resulted in confusion, disputes, and reduced production. Bilbao and Asturias had given ample proof of this; the industrial centers of Catalonia were perhaps less chaotic, but far from increasing output to meet wartime necessities, their productivity also had dropped sharply from peacetime levels. Agriculture was less seriously affected, since it was less complicated technically, and a smaller proportion of the land had been collectivized. In that sector too, though, productivity had fallen, despite CNT claims to the contrary. This was especially significant given that the large urban population on the loyalist side faced ever-greater food shortages, and the agricultural export crops on which the republic's foreign currency earnings primarily depended were not being shipped. There were also the continued effects on morale of the social revolution, even after the early terrorism had ceased. Spain was not composed simply of propertyless workers and peasants; there were many million small property holders or white-collar employees who feared that their status might be diminished and who were intimidated by the latent violence with which the social revolution operated. Finally, there were the international consequences. Negrín hoped to swing the tide established in 1936 and induce especially the French, but perhaps also even the British and the Americans, to support the republic. These were all capitalist countries for whom social revolution was abhorrent.

The obstacles Negrín faced were formidable. With Mola well into Biscay when he took office, the structure of the war had already become unfavorable to the republic. Neville Chamberlain (1869–1940), for whom the policy of appeasement attained nearly religious sanctity, had just come into office in Britain, and Léon Blum (1872–1950), the republic's greatest sympathizer in France, would fall shortly thereafter. Equally important, if dismantling the social revolution would raise the morale of some, it would lessen the commitment to the republic by those large sectors of the population committed to it, especially as harsh measures would be required to carry it out.

Finally, Negrín himself suffered from the stigma of being associated with the communists. This stigma proved severe, one that still unjustly haunts his reputation, because the communists were rapidly converting themselves into the most widely hated force in the republic. This was partly because of their brutality, which can best be illustrated by what happened after the May events in Catalonia. International communism was entering its worst Stalinist phase and regarded the POUM as Trotskyists who must be eradicated. So the POUM was not merely outlawed after May, but subjected to fierce persecution that culminated in the murder of its main leader, Andreu Nin (1892–1937), in one of the secret prisons the communists maintained throughout Spain to deal with their enemies. Some of the hatred, however, resulted from the single point in which the communists did truly coincide with Negrín—their desire to pursue the war in Spain ruthlessly, putting aside for its duration all revolutionary considerations. This, along with their brutality, had earned them the hatred first of the CNT and then of the Largo Caballero wing of the socialists. As their preponderance was accentuated, and as the war continued to be lost despite all efforts, it would be followed by the hatred both of Prieto's wing of the socialist movement and of the very people to whom Negrín and the communists tried to appeal by their socially conservative policies, the left republicans and most other middle-class groups.

It would be impossible to reconstruct here the details of Negrín's restructuring of the republic, as it was achieved by a series of partial measures too numerous to mention. Suffice it to say that it had proceeded quite far by early Aug. 1937, when the last of the semilegal governmental entities that had sprung up in 1936, the CNT-dominated Council of Aragon, was forcibly disbanded, along with most of the many hundred collective farms the council had sponsored. At that time too, a gesture was made toward reconciling Catholic opinion, by again legalizing religious services so long as they were celebrated privately. As an example of how much remained undone, though, and of how Negrín, despite his imperiousness, was not quite as dictatorial as his coalition partners began to portray him, it was not until fifteen months after he assumed office, on 17 Aug. 1938, that his government dared take over all the munitions factories in Catalonia.

Military reorganization got underway more quickly and began to show its fruits in July 1937, with the drive from Madrid toward Estremadura, and in Aug., when the campaign on the Aragon front was launched. Both were stopped, the first at Brunete, the second at Belchite, but they had forced Franco to divert troops from the northern front and had proven that the republican armies were capable of going on the offensive rather than waiting for the enemy to attack. The army displayed its new strength more dramatically on 15 Dec., when it launched a surprise attack against Teruel. This was the first time the loyalists had conquered a provincial capital, a political triumph that frightened Franco and caused him to call off a planned offensive against Madrid so as to counterattack. Freezing weather and republican determination to hang on converted Teruel into one of the war's longest and cruelest battles. It was not until two months later, in late Feb. 1938, that the nationalists were able to defeat the defenders.

## THE LAST PHASE OF THE WAR (MAR. 1938–MAR. 1939)

The strain of so dogged an effort on the loyalists was immense. On 9 Mar., when Franco's forces pushed eastward from Teruel into Aragon, the republican front gave way completely, for the first time since Sept. 1936. Panic seized many units as they fled before the onslaught. By 3 Apr., the nationalists had entered southern Catalonia and taken the city of Lérida. On the 7th, the source of most of Barcelona's hydroelectric power fell to them. On the 15th, Franco's troops reached the Mediterranean near the mouth of the Ebro River, again dividing the republic in two zones.

Franco was faced with a major decision. Many of his generals advocated striking northward into Catalonia, the most important industrial region of the republic and its capital since Oct. 1937, when the Negrín government had moved to Barcelona from Valencia. The republican rout had been so great that Catalonia could easily be taken, they argued, and the war brought to an end. Franco decided to move south instead, perhaps because his 1936 experience against Madrid made him reluctant to attack so densely populated an area, perhaps because he feared that too rapid an advance might provoke France— where Léon Blum had again returned to office in Mar.—into intervening.

The nationalist drive lost momentum as it turned south. The terrain was more difficult, and republican resistance had stiffened, partly because important new supplies had been received during the brief period Blum held power. Castellón, only a few miles from where the nationalist armies had reached the Mediterranean on Apr. 15, was not taken until 13 June. By mid-July, on the second anniversary of the military uprising, they had only barely reached the outermost defensive perimeter of the city of Valencia. Franco was severely criticized for his caution; signs of dissidence against him reappeared for the first time since early 1937.

On the republican side, meanwhile, the collapse of the Aragon front in Mar. had provoked a crisis. Indalecio Prieto, minister of defense and the leading symbol of the Socialist party once Largo Caballero had fallen (Negrín himself tended to be regarded as an upstart and outsider), concluded that a republican victory had now become impossible and urged that the government begin peace negotiations. The communists reacted sharply, and demanded that Negrín dismiss Prieto and assume the war ministry himself. This took place on 5 Apr., alienating yet another major political faction. During the next three months, while Franco was bogged down on the Levante front, Negrín and the communists carried out their greatest organizational miracle, as they funneled the republic's depleted resources into a surprise attack from Catalonia across the Ebro River into Aragon on 25 July. Franco again decided to accept the challenge rather than outflanking it, and the longest, bloodiest battle of the entire civil war ensued. For four months, until 16 Nov., a few square miles of the loyalist-held salient was fiercely fought over. In some ways, because of the rough terrain, the battle of the Ebro was a concentrated version of the northern campaign of 1937. In others, because of the intense artillery bombardments employed, it more nearly resembled the western front during World War I. In the end, the superior forces of every type that the nationalist side had now accumulated prevailed. And even more than at Teruel, the republic found itself exhausted by the great effort it had made.

The finale was now near. On 23 Dec., the largest nationalist armies ever assembled crossed the Ebro into Catalonia. At first there was some resistance, but by mid-Jan., the republican retreat turned into a rout. There was no attempt to repeat the Madrid miracle of Nov. 1936 by making a stand at Spain's other great city, Barcelona. Morale had been too depleted by the continuous military losses, by the disillusionment that prevailed among the anarchosyndicalists and the Catalan autonomists, by the confusion and despair the many thousand refugees who had crowded into the city during the past year had brought with them, by the lack of heat and light since winter had fallen, and—not least—by the physical depletion of the population, which had long suffered from food shortages and was now on the verge of starvation. The city was abandoned on 25 Jan., and Franco's troops occupied it without fighting on the 26th. With Barcelona gone, a mass exodus of hundreds of thousands of civilians and soldiers streamed toward France and crossed its borders during the first nine days of Feb. The government of the republic was but one small particle carried along with them: Azaña, his dreams of a progressive democratic Spain long since shattered by the horrors the war had brought, was the first to cross the border, on the 4th; Negrín and his ministers followed, on the 7th. Amid unprecedented human suffering, the defeat in Catalonia had been total.

Yet there was one final chapter to be written. The southern republican zone, a huge territory of perhaps 150,000 square kilometers and eight million people, was still unconquered. A stand might still be made there, Negrín and the communists reasoned. At best, resistance might last long enough to merge the Spanish war with the general European war that was now imminent; in this case, the republic might still emerge victorious as France and Britain realized the folly of their nonintervention policies and came to its rescue. At worst, a determined stand could exact more favorable peace terms from Franco who, especially with the Law of Political Responsibilities he proclaimed on the very day the last republicans were crossing into France, showed every sign of planning vengeance on all who had opposed him. So Negrín returned to Spain on 10 Feb. to try to rally resistance.

His task was hopeless. On the 27th, Azaña resigned as president and the head of parliament, and Diego Martínez Barrio (1883–1962), who should have succeeded him under the constitution, refused the post. The republic was legally a shambles. More important, Negrín had lost all political credibility, because of his military failures, his intransigence, and his reputed philocommunism. The population did not want to continue fighting, especially perhaps in Madrid, which had experienced even worse food shortages than Barcelona. Nor were the army commanders more sanguine; indeed, one of them, Colonel Segismundo Casado (1893–1968), had entered into secret contacts with Franco, hoping to extract, as one military man to another, a conciliatory peace from him.

The denouement occurred in Mar., as Casado gathered other officers and several political leaders into his conspiracy; people as respected as Gen. José Miaja (1878–1958) for the army, Julián Besteiro (1870–1940) for the socialists, and Cipriano Mera (1879–1975) for the CNT were included. On 5 Mar., the National Defense Council, a rival government to Negrín's, was created. Negrín and most of the top communist leadership recognized their impotence and immediately fled Spain. Only the local communist forces in Madrid resisted and were put down only after fierce fighting, which probably claimed more victims than had the May events of 1937 in Barcelona. Once again, a small-scale civil war among republicans had broken out within the greater civil war. When it was over, the futility of Casado's hopes for a conciliatory peace became manifest. Franco refused all negotiations and insisted on unconditional surrender. Since there was no soul left in the republic, it collapsed without struggle as the nationalist armies began to move again in late Mar. Madrid surrendered on the 28th, most of the provincial capitals on the 29th and 30th, and the naval base of Cartagena on the 31st. On Apr. 1, Franco could issue his final war bulletin stating simply that "the war has ended."

## FINAL CONSIDERATIONS

The war really had not ended, but only ceased to be fought openly. It continued in the hearts of much of Spain's population, in great part because the Francoist forces imposed so harsh a peace, one with tens of thousands of executions and millions of acts of lesser vengeance against the defeated "Reds," that it could not soon be forgotten. The church had suffered greatly from republican persecution during the war, but it now displayed its own lack of charity by lending moral sanction to the regime's rule of violence. All moderate opinion was silenced. A price would be paid in that, with the ostracism of half its population, Spain entered into the dreariest years of its long history—economically, culturally, and politically—in the 1940s. The Franco regime would also have cause to regret its excesses after the end of the World War II,* when hostile world opinion sometimes threatened to topple it. This was little comfort to the victims who now suffered its ravages.

Why was the Franco government so vindictive? It is not enough to say that vindictiveness usually prevails after fratricidal conflicts, because Franco far exceeded customary levels, whether those of civil wars in other countries or those that characterized previous Spanish internal conflicts. Yet no explanation other than an orgy of vindictiveness seems logical. Everything that happened in Europe from 1939 to 1942, the years of the worst repression, reinforced rather than threatened the position of the victors. The republicans themselves certainly constituted no menace: those who remained behind were utterly voiceless and without organization; the hundreds of thousands who had gone into exile fell into a frenzy of mutual recrimination that rendered them impotent. Would the republic have imposed as savage a peace had it prevailed? Probably not, because after the loss of the north, it could have won the war only if the French or British had decided to assist it. Had this occurred, the main source of brutality still operative within the republic, the Communist party, would have become isolated, as all its many enemies turned against it while most of those, like Negrín, who had collaborated with it for reasons of wartime necessity, would have abandoned it to its fate now that its help was no longer needed.

Was Prieto right in wanting to try to negotiate an end to the war in Mar. 1938, or did Negrín's intransigence serve some useful purpose? In retrospect, it is easy to condemn Negrín, but we must remember that at the time France had just reopened its borders to supplies, Europe had just been provoked by the Nazi occupation of Austria, and that the Munich pact, the full surrender to aggression, would not occur until late Sept. The bloodshed at the Ebro and elsewhere might have proved worthwhile had the diplomacy of the Western democracies been less dominated by the illusions that haunted it during the 1930s and been motivated instead by the power-politics concerns that traditionally determine the foreign policies of most states.

A more meaningful question is whether Franco could have ended the war earlier. Here the answer may well be yes. He probably could have done so militarily, had he been a more imaginative strategist, one not so obsessed by frontal attacks, one who more often dared to employ flanking movements, particularly in response to the republican crossing of the Ebro in July 1938, but also when his armies first approached Madrid, in late Aug. and early Sept. of 1936 as well as at the battle of Teruel, in the winter of 1937–1938. Even more probably, the war could have ended sooner had not Franco been so determined to impose unconditional surrender. The population on the republican side was war weary by the spring of 1938; conciliatory overtures on Franco's part may well have started a process of erosion that would have caused troops on the Levante front to fight with less determination from May to July of 1938 and made it impossible for the republic either to launch or to maintain for so long its resistance on the Ebro.

Would the republic have been stronger had not the social revolution occurred? That is a complicated question. On the one hand, without the social revolution the wartime republic may well never have come into being. Without the outpouring of the urban masses in the streets of Barcelona, Madrid, and Valencia, it is hard to imagine that the army and militarized police units that were not part of the conspiracy would by themselves have had the stamina to defeat the military uprising in those cities, nor is it clear that the demoralized, confused middle-class governments that succeeded one another on 19 July would have been able to generate in their own hearts the will to resist. On the other hand, for the myriad reasons earlier elucidated, the social revolution so damaged the republican war effort that by the time it was brought effectively under control (it was never fully ended), structural conditions, both domestically and internationally, had become so unfavorable to the republic that it was doomed to defeat. This is the ultimate paradox of the Spanish Civil War: without the social revolution, the republic might have collapsed within days or weeks of the military uprising. Because of it, the republic had no real chance of winning the war that the social revolution had made possible.

However important to clarifying our understanding, speculations of this kind are ultimately unanswerable. What is clear is that the coup a portion of the Spanish army planned quickly converted itself into the most decisive and traumatic event in modern Spanish history except for the War of Independence* against Napoleon Bonaparte (1769–1821) at the start of the nineteenth century. By processes too complex and subtle to go into here, the trauma was transcended and the outcome of the war was reversed over the past half-century much more completely than anyone could have imagined in 1939. The wound, however, was a very deep one.

For additional information, see M. Aznar, *Historia militar de la guerra de España (1936–1939)*, 2 vols. (Madrid, 1940); B. Bolloten, *The Spanish Revolution* (Chapel Hill, 1978); P. Broué and E. Témime, *The Revolution and the Civil War in Spain* (Cambridge, 1972); R. de la Cierva, *Historia ilustrada de la guerra civil española*, 2 vols. (Barcelona, 1970); R. Colodny, *The Struggle for Madrid* (New York, 1958); G. Jackson, *The Spanish Republic and the Civil War* (Princeton, 1965); S. Payne, *Politics and the Military in Modern Spain* (Stanford, 1967); R. Salas Larrazabal, *Historia del ejército popular de la república*, 4 vols. (Madrid, 1974); and H. Thomas, *The Spanish Civil War* (New York, 1977).

*E. E. Malefakis*

*Related entries*: ANARCHISM; ANDALUSIA; ARAGON; ARMY; BARCELONA; BASQUES; CATALONIA; CASTILE; CATHOLICISM; COMMUNIST PARTY; FALANGE; FRANCO, GEN. FRANCISCO; GALICIA; LARGO CABALLERO, FRANCISCO; MADRID; NAVARRE; NAVY; NEGRÍN, JUAN; SECOND REPUBLIC; SERRANO SUÑER, RAMÓN; SOCIALIST PARTY; VALENCIA; WORLD WAR II.


**SPANISH SUCCESSION, WAR OF** (1701–1714). The inheritance of the Spanish throne, endlessly discussed by European diplomats during the reign of the childless Carlos II (1661–1700), who had remained chronically ill throughout his life, twice had been the subject of European conferences (Oct. 1698 and Mar. 1700), with Austria claiming the throne each time. French influence at the Spanish court, however, stressing the greater ability of France to maintain the empire intact, persuaded Carlos to name Philip, duke of Anjou, second son of the French dauphin, and grandson of Louis XIV (1638–1715), king of France, as successor, thus raising fears concerning the European balance of power.

While Britain* (England until the Act of Union on 1 May 1707, Britain thereafter) and Holland (the United Provinces in this era) initially accepted Felipe V* as the new king of Spain, the emperor of Austria, Leopold I (1640–1705), continued to press the claim of his son, the Archduke Charles (later Charles VI of Austria) (1685–1740); and when Louis XIV declared that Felipe V would not renounce his rights to succession to the French crown, Britain and Holland, who were primarily interested in protecting their access to trade with Spain's American colonies,* joined with Austria in the Grand Alliance of 1701. Portugal* and Savoy became members of the alliance in 1703.

The purpose of the Grand Alliance was to dismember the Spanish empire. Britain would receive Minorca, Gibraltar,* Ceuta, and one-third of the Indies; Holland, another third of the Indies and part of Flanders; while Austria would get Milan; Portugal would annex Galicia and Estramadura; and the Archduke Charles would become Carlos III of Spain.

Hostilities broke out in northern Italy* in 1701, when prince Eugene of Savoy, the general of the Austrian empire, crossed the Alps and fell on the Duchy of Milan. Easy victories came quickly, but the following year Felipe V arrived from Spain and the war became more difficult, particularly in the battle of Luzzara (15 Aug. 1702), where both sides fought valiantly before settling down in their trenches to pass the winter. Louis XIV's offensive in 1703, an invasion of Germany,* scored a victory at Höchstädt, but failed to take Vienna. In Galicia, a combined British-Dutch fleet destroyed the Spanish fleet returning from the Indies at the battle of Vigo (23 Sept. 1702), opening the Atlantic coast of the Iberian peninsula to Portugal.

After Archduke Charles was proclaimed King Carlos III* of Spain in 1703, the French were repeatedly devastated by the combined forces of the duke of Marlborough (John Churchill, 1650–1722) and the duke of Savoy in 1704. France reinforced Spain under the command of the duke of Berwick (Jacques Fitz-James, 1660–1734) and by Feb. entered Madrid. In Mar. 1704, Archduke Charles arrived in Lisbon with British and Dutch troops. Felipe, forced to return to Spain to meet the threat that faced him in Portugal, could not prevent the British from taking Gibraltar after the largest naval engagement of the war, the battle of Malaga (24 Aug. 1704) saw the French fleet under the command of the count of Toulouse (Louis-Alexandre de Bourbon, 1678–1737) meet an allied fleet of British and Dutch ships under the command of Sir Clousdsley Shovel (c. 1650–1707) and Sir George Rooke (1650–1709). The battle, which lasted most of the day, was the final major sea battle of the war.

Throughout 1705 the war expanded into Spain. Catalonia,* Aragon,* and Valencia,* long known for their separatist inclinations, declared their support for the Archduke Charles, and after he arrived in Barcelona* in Oct., Spain had, in effect, two kings. In 1706, Felipe abandoned Madrid and withdrew the court to Burgos; Archduke Charles arrived in Madrid and declared himself Carlos III, although a less than enthusiastic welcome soon forced him on to southeastern Spain. The British capture of Alicante, Majorca, and Ibiza; Spanish loss of Flanders at the battle of Ramilles (23 May 1706); and loss of the duchy of Milan at the battle of Turin (7 Sept. 1706) made 1706 a disastrous year for Felipe, but the next twelve months saw a remarkable turnaround. The battle of Almansa in Apr. 1707 preceded the fall of Valencia and the destruction of the town of Jativa; Valencian traditional rights were revoked in June. Finally, in Nov., Philippe, duke of Orléans (1679–1723), recaptured Lérida.

The next year produced only minor activity in Spain, but led to a series of disappointing foreign developments for Felipe. Oran fell to the Moors, the island of Sardinia was occupied by the British, and Mahon was surrendered without resistance. In Flanders, Eugene and Marlborough, acting in concert, scored a major victory at Oudenarde (11 July 1708) and captured Lille, thus threatening France* from the north, a struggle that continued in Flanders during 1709 with the surrender of Tournay, the battle of Malplaquet (11 Sept. 1709) and the siege and fall of Mons (20 Oct. 1709). Pressured by the Austrians, Pope Clement XI (1700–1721) recognized the Archduke Charles as king of Spain, an action that produced a rupture between Spain and the Vatican. Victories by the forces of the Archduke Charles at Almenara (27 July 1710) and Saragossa (20 Aug. 1710) allowed him to return triumphant to Madrid, which Felipe V had left for Valladolid. Again he was received coldly and departed quickly. Felipe V, in the meantime, was victorious on the western front at Brihuega (9 Dec. 1710) and Villaviciosa (10 Dec. 1710); in the east, the supporters of Archduke Charles lost everything but Barcelona. Only in the United Provinces did the war continue to go against Spain, as victory after victory went to the allied army, and France's frontiers were dangerously exposed.

In the end, however, the opposing sides were brought to the peace table not by the military situation, but by the deaths of the dauphin of France (the father of Felipe V) and the Austrian emperor, Joseph I (1678–1711), brother of the Archduke Charles, which fundamentally altered the situation by mid–1711. Had Archduke Charles triumphed in Spain, he would have recreated the empire of Carlos I (1500–1558), a situation the allied nations did not want. Frustrated, Charles left Spain for Austria to take the imperial crown as Charles VI.

Peace negotiations began at Utrecht in 1712, but the process of settling the war among so many parties was long and complex and resulted in a number of treaties. On 11 Apr. 1713, the main Treaty of Utrecht allowed Spain to keep its American possessions. In exchange, Felipe renounced his right to succession in France. The agreement granted Britain limited commercial access to Spain's American markets through the asiento de negros (the formal contract for the exclusive right of furnishing black slaves to the colonies) and the navío de permiso (the right to introduce one five-hundred-ton ship into the market at Portobelo each year). The treaties recognized Britain's de facto possessions in America as legal, back to 1670, and gave Britain formal possession of Minorca and Gibraltar. The Low Countries (Spanish Netherlands) were transferred to the Hapsburg empire and Sicily to Savoy. Peace was reached with the United Provinces in June 1714. A further obstacle to concluding the war was removed when Catalonia and Majorca, which had continued to resist, capitulated in Sept. 1714. The final combatant, Portugal, agreed to peace with Spain in 1715.

For additional information, see H. Kamen, *The War of Succession in Spain, 1700–15* (Bloomington, 1969); and J. P. Le Flem, J. Pérez, J. M. Pelorson, J. M. López Piñero, and J. Fayard, *La frustración de un imperio, 1476–1714*, Vol. 5 in Manuel Tuñón de Lara, *Historia de España* (Barcelona, 1986).

                                                                    *R. Hendricks*

*Related entry*: FELIPE V.

**SUÁREZ GONZÁLEZ, ADOLFO** (1932– ), contemporary political leader. Adolfo Suárez was born on 25 Sept. 1932 in Cebreros, Avila. A bright student, he received a doctorate in law at the University of Madrid and almost immediately began a governmental career during the period of change that marked the second half of the Franco era. Far less traditional or ideological than earlier Francoists, he became associated with the conversion of national syndicalism to social democracy, and some of his early work was in social policy.

His bureaucratic career led to a number of posts: procurator of the Cortes, vice general secretary of the National Movement (1961–1964) and director general of government radio and television (1965–1968 and 1969–1973), where he relaxed censorship and improved programming of state-owned media. He left government service in 1975 to create the Union of the Spanish People, a conservative, middle-class party of former supporters of Gen. Francisco Franco,* who saw the need for change.

After Franco's death in Nov. 1975, the premier, Carlos Arias Navarro,* appointed Suárez as director of the National Movement. His success in preventing this long-divided but still potent force from obstructing the transition from dictatorship to democracy may have been his most important contribution to the post-Franco era, and on 26 Mar. 1976, Suárez replaced the unpopular Arias Navarro as premier. Although it was not readily apparent, the Franco era was definitively over.

The appointment of Suárez was not without repercussions. Manuel Fraga Iribarne* and José María Areilza y Martínez de Rodas (1909– ) resigned from the government to protest the selection of a moderate over liberals, a sign of disappointment with the king's choice. Suárez's moderation, however, protected the new regime against a backlash from Franco supporters, and in the summer of 1976, he was able to form the Democratic Center Union (UCD) as a mainstream party to pursue democratic change. The Law of Political Reform of 18 Nov. created popular sovereignty, universal suffrage, and supported political pluralism. The Cortes was remade into a congress of 350 deputies elected by proportional representation and a senate of 207 elected by a simple majority. The king could submit bills, dissolve the Cortes, and call new elections. Suárez consulted widely before drafting the law.

By 15 June 1977, the impact of these early reforms turned the parliamentary elections into a triumph for Suárez and the UCD, which picked up 165 seats, while the Socialist party* (PSOE) picked up 116. With his cabinet intact, he remained a strong influence during the Cortes's constitutional debates, completed on 28 Sept. 1978 and ratified by 87 percent in the national referendum of 6 Dec. Throughout this process, Suárez worked closely with Juan Carlos I.*

The next two years proved to be much more difficult. Although the UCD added three seats to its total in the elections of 1 Mar. 1979, economic and regional difficulties caused Suárez's popularity to decline. Unemployment and the Basque Homeland and Freedom* (ETA) almost succeeded in destabilizing Spain to a far greater extent than the Falange and Right had in 1976. A nadir was reached on 9 Jan. 1979, when Supreme Court justice Miguel Cruz Cuenca was assassinated by the ETA, and again in 1980 when regional demands became chaotic. In early Jan. 1980, even the UCD criticized Suárez for a lack of debate within the party and for secretive and authoritarian leadership, and on 29 Jan., a frustrated Suárez resigned the premiership. Only three weeks later, a coup d'état tried to topple the constitutional monarchy.

Suárez sought to regain office in 1981 and early 1982, but without UCD support, he failed to overturn Leopoldo Calvo-Sotelo Bustelo (1926– ), the new UCD premier. Suárez resigned from the UCD on 28 July 1982 to found the small Democratic Center and Social Party (CDS), but the PSOE's overwhelming victory of 28 Oct. 1982 gave the CDS only two seats. Suárez had gone from acclaim to obscurity in six short years, but his contribution to the establishment of Spanish democracy was nonetheless extraordinary.

For additional information, see E. R. Arango, *The Spanish Political System: Franco's Legacy* (Boulder, 1978); and R. P. Clark and M. H. Haltzel, *Spain in the 1980s* (Cambridge, 1987).

*R. W. Kern*

*Related entries*: GONZÁLEZ, FELIPE; JUAN CARLOS I.

# T

TIERNO GALVÁN, ENRIQUE (1918–1986), Spanish intellectual and politician. Born in Madrid, although of Sorian descent, Tierno entered law school in 1934. When the Spanish Civil War* began, he joined the republican army, remaining in a concentration camp for nine months at the end of the war. He was able to complete his licentiate in philosophy and letters in 1944, a doctorate in law in 1945, and assumed the chair of constitutional law at the University of Murcia in 1948. Moving to the University of Salamanca in 1953, he began a notable intellectual and political career by founding the *Boletín Informativa del Seminario de Derecho Político*, which permitted him to develop cautiously his Marxist humanism, and the Asociación para la Universidad Funcional de Europa (1959) to prepare the way for Western-style democracy in Spain. His intellectual interests included the essay, sociology, and the history of ideas. Between 1961 and 1962, he lived in the United States* and taught at Princeton University as a visiting professor.

At that time, he had already begun open political activity, initiating contact with the various groups opposed to the government of Francisco Franco,* ranging from the supporters of Juan de Borbón y Battenberg (1913– ) to the intellectual group surrounding Dionisio Ridruejo.* In 1965, he lost his chair in constitutional law for having joined and led growing student protest. He lived for a time in exile in the United States and assumed professorships at Princeton and Bryn Mawr, as well as at the University of Puerto Rico.

At the end of this decade of agitation, he returned to Spain and practiced law, clandestinely undertaking the task of renovating the socialist movement despite the opposition of its aging leader in exile, Rodolfo Llopis (1895– ). In Salamanca, he founded the Partido Socialista del Interior, transforming it in 1973 into the Partido Socialista Popular (PSP). The Franco government watched him closely, and in 1970, Tierno and a number of others were fined for having signed a written appeal to William Rogers (1913– ), the U.S. secretary of state, and for meeting in Madrid with Walter Scheel (1919–1985), the future president of the Federal Republic of Germany, then visiting Spain. Both cases underscored the government's inadequacy in preparing for Spain's integration with the rest of Western Europe.

In the meantime, Tierno continued to publish, mainly sociological and historical essays, but when Franco died in 1975, the PSP found itself linked to the Junta Democrática, which had been organized in Paris in 1974. Two years later, the PSP joined the Plataforma de Convergencia Democrática in a united, disruptive effort popularly known as the Platajunta. Spain's political parties were legalized in 1977 following the acceptance by referendum of political reform proposed by the president, Adolfo Suárez.* The 1977 elections—the first under the new democracy to elect the Constituent Cortes—spelled defeat for the PSP, but Tierno himself won election as a deputy and in 1978 joined the Socialist party* (PSOE). Although the PSOE treated Tierno deferentially, he maintained his doctrinal distance, opposing both the separation from Marxism advocated by Felipe González* in the 1978 party congress and, later, remaining in the North Atlantic Treaty Organization (NATO).

After the 1979 municipal elections, Tierno, with the support of the Communist party* (PCE), was elected mayor of Madrid as the PSOE candidate. In this position, he proposed transforming the spirit of the city. His comprehensive "opening" to youth gave him great popularity, as did his bold encouragement of the Movida Madrileña, an expression of popular culture with a postmodernist keynote. His proclamations were masterpieces, both for their literary execution and their winsome style, charged with irony. Aside from this, he always knew how to join unwavering loyalty to his ideas with scrupulous respect for his adversaries.

Operated upon for incurable cancer in 1985, Tierno presented before an end he knew to be soon and inevitable an elevated example of stoicism and serenity in his few remaining months of life. At his death on 19 Jan. 1986, the people of Madrid rendered him an exceptional homage and attended his funeral in large numbers.

For additional information, see E. Tierno Galván, *Cabos sueltos* (Barcelona, 1981).

*C. Seco Serrano*

*Related entries*: GONZÁLEZ, FELIPE; JUAN CARLOS I; MADRID.


**TRAFALGAR, BATTLE OF** (1805). The battle of Trafalgar took place between noon and 4:30 P.M. on 21 Oct. 1805, in coastal waters off Cape Trafalgar, a promontory on the southern coast of Spain midway between Cadiz and Gibraltar.* In contention in this action were a French fleet, commanded by Vice-Adm. Pierre Charles Villeneuve (1763–1806), reinforced by a Spanish squadron under Adm. Federico Gravina (1756–1806), and a British fleet led by Vice-Adm. Horatio Lord Nelson (1758–1805). The outcome of the action was a resounding British victory.

Trafalgar was a crucial battle in the series of contests between Napoleonic France* and Britain* for control of Europe, that occupied the early years of the nineteenth century. Into this dispute, Spain was drawn, unwillingly, in 1804, on the French side. The battle took place amid British fears of a French invasion of the British Isles. Broadly, Napoleon Bonaparte's (1769–1821) plan was to unite his various fleets in the English channel and its approaches so as to secure his army of invasion from the British navy, whose task was to prevent this assembly of French ships.

The story of Trafalgar begins at the Mediterranean French port of Toulon, the base of a large fleet, which Nelson had the task of blockading. This he did successfully in 1803 and 1804; but in March 1805, the French force under Villeneuve managed to evade Nelson's watch; and, following Napoleon's newest project, left the Mediterranean for the West Indies. Six Spanish ships from Gibraltar, under Gravina, joined the French as they passed. Once in the Antilles, Villeneuve was to take various islands for France before returning to European waters and uniting with other French naval units to participate in the invasion. The expectation was that much of the British navy would be fruitlessly seeking the French vessels in the western Atlantic while the attack on Britain took place.

Nelson did indeed pursue Villeneuve to the Antilles, barely missing him there, and then almost caught up with him off northwestern Spain on the return sailing in July and Aug. 1805. Villeneuve then made a poor decision that prejudiced Napoleon's invasion plans and led directly to Trafalgar: finding the British naturally prepared to stop him from joining other French naval forces in the Channel, he went south, following a fallback scheme of Napoleon's, to seize Gibraltar and incorporate into his fleet a Spanish squadron from Cartagena. En route, he and Gravina entered Cadiz, which the British promptly blockaded. Nelson, after a brief leave in Britain to recuperate from his long watch over Toulon and rapid double crossing of the Atlantic, arrived off Cadiz on 28 Sept. 1805 to take command of the blockading fleet. He tempted Villeneuve to leave port by standing well out to sea. His ruse brought success on 19 Oct., the French commander also being stirred to action by news that a replacement for him was about to arrive. The combined French and Spanish fleet now consisted of thirty-three ships of the line, the Spanish contingent of fifteen including four vast vessels carrying a hundred guns or more (the average on both sides being about eighty). Against these, Nelson could put up twenty-seven.

Villeneuve set a southerly course for the Strait of Gibraltar, shadowed by the British on 20 Oct. At dawn the next day, Nelson was nine miles west of the Franco-Spanish fleet, upwind in a light northwesterly breeze. During the morning the distance closed. Villeneuve turned north again to allow a dash for Cadiz if necessary. His ships proceeded in line-ahead, with the Spanish vessels intermingled with the French. Nelson, abandoning the conventional battle form of broadsides between parallel lines of ships, split his force into essentially two divisions, with the intent that these should sail obliquely at the opposing line and separate it into three segments. His plan was to engage the rear and central segments with his entire fleet, leaving the leading segment unopposed, but isolated from the battle for long enough to enable the British fleet to overcome the majority of their opponents. This tactic succeeded brilliantly, the Franco-Spanish vanguard, under Rear-Adm. Pierre Dumanoir (1770–1829), playing little part in the fighting.

The first shots in the battle came shortly after noon on 21 Oct. 1805, directed by the French *Fouqueux* at the leader of Nelson's rear division, Vice-Adm. Cuthbert Collingwood (1748–1810) in the *Royal Sovereign*. Collingwood's first major engagement, however, was with the 112-gun Spanish *Santa Ana*, flagship of Vice-Adm. Ignancio María Alava y Navarrete (1752?–1817). *Santa Ana* was obliged to strike her colors at 2:15 P.M. Nelson, meanwhile, in his flagship *Victory*, had been in close combat with the greatest of the Spanish battleships, the *Santísima Trinidad* (140 guns), and with Villeneuve's flagship, *Bucentaure*, four hundred of whose crew were killed or wounded by *Victory's* first broadside as she passed under her enemy's stern.

Much of the battle was in fact fought by ships at such close quarters that their spars and rigging intertwined. The effects of broadsides at this point-black range were naturally devastating, and the resulting carnage great. The allied fleet suffered casualties of 5,860 men killed or wounded, and the British, 1,690. Among the British losses was Nelson himself, mortally wounded by a musket ball fired from the French *Redoubtable*. He died as the fighting drew to a close. Gravina, also, was mortally struck, dying in Cadiz a few days later. Villeneuve survived the battle, but committed suicide at Rennes on his way to Paris to face an inquiry.

The loss of vessels on the Franco-Spanish side was also great. Nelson's notion of victory was always to annihilate his enemy, though on this occasion he aimed for the destruction or capture of only twenty Spanish and French ships. Seventeen were taken as prizes by the British, and one, the French *Achille*, blew up in combat. The British lost no ships, though several, including *Victory* and *Royal Sovereign*, were partly or wholly dismasted. The British were subsequently less fortunate with their prizes. Largely as a result of the storm that blew up after the battle, and Collingwood's failure to anchor the fleet for safety, all but four of the captured vessels sank, or were scuttled or wrecked.

British success at Trafalgar is generally ascribed to the superiority of Nelson's battle tactics, which enabled him in effect to equalize the numbers of ships in combat; to the higher rate of fire achieved by the British ships; to inattention or confusion in the allied command, which resulted in Dumanoir's ships failing to turn back in time to reinforce the embattled Franco-Spanish center and rear; and to a distinct lack of enthusiasm for the contest on the Spanish part. The broad outcome of the battle was to establish the British Royal Navy as the dominant force at sea during the balance of the Napoleonic Wars, and beyond. The French remained strong in numbers of ships, but Napoleon barely tried to employ them, preferring to pursue his campaigns thereafter with the land forces whose use he understood so profoundly. For Spain, however, Trafalgar came to have a deeper and more enduring meaning. The defeat was all the more bitter because it was the outcome of an unwanted alliance, an alliance into which the country had been bludgeoned as a subordinate partner. It seemed to mark the end of an age. Just as naval victory at Lepanto in 1571 had marked the noontide of Spanish fortune and power, so Trafalgar in 1805 seemed to signal an eventide. It was truly a national disaster, to which were to be added over the immediately following years still greater afflictions: Napoleon's invasion and occupation of Spain, and, yet more grievous, the loss of the American empire.

For additional information, see G. Bennett, *Nelson the Commander* (New York, 1972); and J. Cerva Pery, *Marina y política en la España del siglo xix* (Madrid, 1979).

*P. J. Bakewell*

*Related entries*: GIBRALTAR; INDEPENDENCE, WAR OF; NAVY.

# U

---

**UNAMUNO Y JUGO, MIGUEL DE** (1869–1936), philosopher and one of Spain's leading intellectuals. Born in Bilbao of Basque* parentage on 29 Sept. 1869, Unamuno witnessed the Carlist siege of the city, an experience that inspired his first novel. Raised in a deeply pious Catholic family, Unamuno suffered his first spiritual crisis at puberty when, propelled by a need to rationalize his faith, he read with religious fervor all of the books in his father's library. His higher education led him from Bilbao to Madrid,* where he received his doctorate in philosophy in 1884. Much of his time was spent at the Ateneo,* where he followed the latest intellectual currents of Karl Christian Friedrich Krause,* regeneration, and positivism. It was during this period that he lost his religious faith.

From 1884 to 1891, Unamuno worked as a private tutor in Bilbao while preparing for the competitive teaching examination, which won him the chair of Greek language at the University of Salamanca, where he lived the rest of his life. Between 1894 and 1897, professing to be a socialist, he contributed more than two hundred articles to *La Lucha de Classes*, published in Bilbao. In 1897, however, he suffered a spiritual crisis that influenced his thought. Before a fixation on death appeared, Unamuno's work had been dominated by empirical positivism, but after 1897, his orientation was motivated by a thirst for personal immortality and the need for self-confession. He described his experiences in essays, fiction, and letters to friends, while keeping a diary that recorded his self-censure. In 1900, he became rector of Salamanca and professor of the history of the Spanish language, while at the same time accepting the role of critic of Spanish-American literature for the newspapers *La Lectura* in Madrid (until 1906) and *La Nación* and *Caras y Caretas* in Buenos Aires (until 1935). These outside commitments led to his dismissal from the rectorship in 1914, and he traveled to Italy* to cover World War I* as an Allied sympathizer. In the postwar era, he became an outspoken critic of Alfonso XIII* and the dictatorship of Gen.

Miguel Primo de Rivera* and was exiled to the Canary Islands* in 1923. When the editor of the French newspaper *Le Quotidien* arranged his escape, Unamuno spent the period until 1930 in Paris writing for the European and South American press, tormented that his work would disappear.

Returning to Spain in 1930, Unamuno resumed his rectorship and teaching duties at Salamanca. The Second Republic* honored his work by creating a chair at the university in his name. In addition, he was elected deputy to the new Cortes from 1931 to 1933, although he soon became disappointed in the new republic and criticized its politics. When the Spanish Civil War* broke out, Unamuno originally supported Gen. Francisco Franco,* but in a debate with a nationalist general in Oct. 1936, he made his famous defense of freedom and denunciation of the rebellion that resulted in his house arrest just when he was to receive an honorary doctorate from Oxford University. He died on 31 Dec. 1936.

The essays of Unamuno raised this genre to new heights in Spain. In 1895, *En torno al casticismo* set forth two of his main concerns, Spain's historical destiny and the meaning of history, which provided a superb analysis of Spanish cultural problems. Unamuno called for renovation through assimilation of new ideas and the search for Spain's "eternal tradition"—the spiritual heart of its history—Europeanization without de-Hispanization.

The theories put forth in Unamuno's essays outline his philosophy. Reality is an eternal flux; time resides within reality and in the eternal present as well. This eternal tradition is the patrimony of humankind. History must distinguish between events (sucesos) and fundamental realities (hechos). The latter constitute intrahistory, the permanent substance of history. In Spain, authentic tradition (true casticismo), as outlined in his 1905 essay, *Vida de Don Quijote y Sancho*, must study intrahistory in its present stage and take pride in Spanish aims common to all humankind. Don Quixote symbolized the quest for personality as opposed to the emphasis on fact; his purposeful deeds sought to do good and strive for immortality. Ironically, Unamuno's nationalistic messianism made a religion out of Quixotism. The book was called "the bible of Spain," and Quixote became "the Christ" of the nation, but Unamuno rejected hero worship for Don Quixote, since each individual must fulfill his own needs first.

In philosophy, the Basque writer's main work, *Del sentimiento trágico de la vida en los hombres y en los pueblos*, postulates a radical humanism by making "the man of flesh and blood" the object of all philosophy. Man is an end, not a means, and civilization's direction must have man as its goal. In other words, all systems of ideas must foster life, since man's essence is his longing never to die and to be himself without ceasing to be real, "to be others as well, to encompass the totality of all things visible and invisible, to extend myself to the limitless in space and prolong myself to the endlessness in time." Suffering, however, is the substance of life, the root of personality, and the most immediate revelation of consciousness. In this sense, eternal anguish is the source of the tragic sense of life, "something far deeper, more intimate, and more spiritual than suffering.'' Anguish causes consciousness to turn back to itself to create the passionate longing never to die that leads to active, creative doubt and a fuller life. Man agonizes in an unceasing conquest of his own being, fighting against death and nothingness without hope or desire for victory, since this struggle is the spur man needs for constant self-affirmation. In fact, faith is a matter of will not composed of reason so much as the creation of what we do not see. Unamuno's man of flesh and blood creates his own personal God and bases his belief on the creative force that sustains this God: the will to be (al querer ser). Finally, in *La agonía del cristianismo*, the philosopher further develops the idea of struggle, with Christianity conceived of as the conflict (*agon*) between mind and heart or letter and spirit.

The novels and dramas of Unamuno were often anticipated in his sixty or more short stories. Except for a first long narration, his fiction broke with traditional realistic style to devise a new genre he called the nivola. Autobiographical, personal, confessional, existential, and philosophical, it emphasized contemporary man's sense of alienation and immortalized the self through a novelistic creation. The nivola has been called a naked novel, containing no description of scenery, setting, or physical appearance, and a plot meager in events, where characters agonize in a narrow dimension. Unamuno's reality was the ''poetic or creative reality of man,'' with the division between fiction and reality meaningless—''Don Quixote is as real as Cervantes; Hamlet or Macbeth as real as Shakespeare'' and Unamuno himself a mere pretext to make available his story and that of his fictional characters whose agony is made out of their desire to be or not to be.

The nivola aspired to explore epistemological reality in order to understand man's personality. The exclusion of the external world gives extra depth and power to these stories. The plot is created as the work evolves, characters are formed ex nihilo by events, dialogues are ''monodialogues'' that allow the character introspective indulgence, and words assume utmost importance, since the characters exist only by virtue of what they say.

*Paz en la guerra*, published in 1897, combines the historic realism of the Matiners' Revolt with autobiography and the search for inner peace that could be achieved by harmony with universal laws, so that history and intrahistory complement each other. *Amor y pedagogía*, published in 1902, contains a virulent indictment of science and scientific method as unable to fill the void in man's ontological complexity. *Niebla*, published in 1914 and Unamuno's most translated and provocative novel, reflects the concept of the tragic in the modern world by juxtaposing acting and insincerity with authenticity and intimate truth. The reality of a literary character is fictitious when seen from a human point of view, as is man's when seen by God. The protagonist, in a pilgrimage toward his existential awareness, experiences tedium in his life and believes himself to be fate's toy until chance events accumulate in the character's stream of consciousness and outline his true being. *Abel Sánchez*, published in 1917, takes the Cain and Abel story to epic proportions with intense exploration into the psyche of the protagonist, who witnesses the horrifying alienation of his selfhood until he becomes the victim of his own overwhelming hatred. *La tía Tula* (1921), a product of Unamuno's disillusionment after World War I, proposes a society based not on the concept of patria (the universal brotherhood of man), but on matria (a society based on maternal love), a work that supports feminism, if somewhat abstractly. Other works in this genre include *Cómo se hace una novela* (1927) and *San Manuel Bueno, mártir* (1931), perhaps his best novel, again with a confessional tone and symbolic setting and characers. A rural priest, who represents Unamuno's creative doubt, loses his faith and seeks to save his personality through good works, a mission that leads to his martyrdom because he makes life tolerable and pleasant for his people by carrying for them the burden of truth.

Unamuno's first collection of poetry came late, at age forty-three, although he wished above all to be considered a tragic poet. His metaphysical poems of human affirmation humanized the external world and everything human or divine, personalizing and providing consciousness for the whole universe. Three titles stand out. *Poesías* (1907) contains his best poems. His poetric creed here was a refutation of modernism. *El Cristo de Velázquez* (1920) became one of the most important Spanish religious poems since the sixteenth and seventeenth centuries. Here he wanted to formulate "the faith of my people [and] its realistic Christology." Finally, the posthumous *Cancionero* (1953) contains short poems of popular language translated back into traditional versification.

The theater of Unamuno was another of his lifelong interests to create metaphysical theater intended as the personal stage of the individual's conscience— man as author, actor, and observer of himself. The formula of essential dramatism he used was set on a bare stage, which put him in the vanguard among dramatists of this century, but these internal dramas lacked theatricality and were too static and abstract to be commercially successful. His best-known play is *El otro*, which he wrote in 1926. The Cain and Abel theme is treated as a split personality embodied in twins whose antagonism leads to fratricide. The protagonist, whose personality remains an unsolved mystery, becomes both the assassin and the victim, with his remorse driving him to madness and suicide.

Unamuno played the game of paradox in all his works. Deeply religious, philosophically an impassioned personalist, he wrestled constantly with the problem of faith and the mystery of his personality, yet he found solace in the beauty of nature and the serene ambience of daily life. He rejected the process of formal logic and reasoning and derived his conclusions through a method of passion (paradoxes were truths beyond reason and logic) that made art into the transmission of feeling. "I feel, therefore I am," allowed him to live words, since words are the idea in action. He wrote as he spoke, naturally and alive, though at times harshly, disdaining artifice. He was one of the greatest confessionalists in literature, weaving his gigantic personality into all of his work.

For additional information, see R. E. Batchelor, *Unamuno: A European Perspective* (Oxford, 1972); C. Blanco Aguinaga, *El Unamuno contemplativo* (Mexico City, 1959);

P. H. Fernández, *Miguel de Unamuno y William James: Un paralelo pragmático* (Salamanca, 1961); J. Ferater Mora, *Unamuno: A Philosophy of Tragedy* (Berkeley, 1962); M. García Blanco, *Don Miguel de Unamuno y sus poesías* (Salamanca, 1954); P. Ilie, *Unamuno: An Existential View of Self and Society* (Madison, 1967); M. Nozick, *Miguel de Unamuno* (New York, 1971); V. Ouimette, *Reason Aflame; Unamuno and the Heroic Will* (New Haven, 1974); D. G. Turner, *Unamuno's Webs of Fatality* (London, 1974); and M. J. Valdés, *Death in the Literature of Unamuno* (Urbana, 1966).

*P. H. Fernández*

*Related entries:* GENERATION OF 1898; GENERATION OF 1927.

**UNIÓN GENERAL DE TRABAJADORES (UGT).** Although intimately associated throughout its history with the Socialist party,* or Partido Socialista Obrero Español (PSOE), the Unión General de Trabajadores (UGT) was not initially linked to the PSOE in any formal sense. In a bid to widen the union's appeal, early leaders of the UGT—none more so than the dominant socialist, Pablo Iglesias (1850–1925)—insisted that the organization was independent and did not belong to any political party. This position of formal autonomy was maintained until the UGT's XIV Congress in 1918, thirty years after its founding in Barcelona.* The UGT, nonetheless, was to all intents and purposes a socialist body from its inception; indeed, its creation was wholly sponsored by PSOE leaders.

The UGT officially came into being in Aug. 1888, nine years after the PSOE. Its creation represented a logical development of previous syndical initiatives, associated principally with the Federación Regional Española, the Spanish branch of the International Working Men's Association (founded in Barcelona in 1869), the Asociación General del Arte de Imprimir, a typographers' association instrumental in the birth of the PSOE; and the Barcelona-based Federación Tipográfica y de las Industrias Similares. Like the PSOE, the UGT's early years were marked by painfully slow growth. With fewer than four thousand members during its first year, the union struggled to attract twenty-five thousand affiliates by the turn of the century and failed to top two hundred thousand until 1919. That same year, union membership in France,* Britain,* and the United States* stood at over two million. Not until establishment of the Second Republic* in 1931 did the UGT really achieve national status, reaching a peak of just under two million members in 1938. This expansion, however, was curtailed by the victory of Gen. Francisco Franco,* who banned the union. The UGT's history until the Spanish Civil War* was marked by a number of features common also to the PSOE. Principal among these were ideological ambiguity, organizational centralism and rigidity, and political moderation in labor struggles. While the lack of rigid ideological definition was a deliberate strategy, it also reflected a genuine confusion among socialists over the aims and methods of their struggle. Early PSOE leaders espoused a Marxism marked by simplistic reductionism inappropriate to the historic moment in which they were operating. Whereas late nineteenth-century Spain was predominantly an agrarian society with vestiges of feudal power remaining identifiable, socialists analyzed their country using imported and distorted notions derived from French Marxist popularizers. Rather than concentrate on agrarian relations of production and the prevailing state structure, socialist theory described the political struggle as a straightforward one between the bourgeoisie and proletariat, notwithstanding that both these classes were numerically and politically weak.

This theoretical confusion was reflected in the organization of the UGT, which concentrated on urban sectors of the Spanish work force. Early members of the union were drawn predominantly from industrial workers, especially the Madrid building trades and the printing industry. By 1900, the UGT also managed to attract significant membership from Asturian miners and Biscayan metalworkers. The union made little headway among textile workers in Catalonia,* even though the UGT's headquarters was in Barcelona, because of a failure to grant organizational autonomy to the Catalans. In 1899, the union's administrative center moved to Madrid.* The extent of its failure to make a major presence in Barcelona can be gauged from the fact that in 1893, 20 percent of the UGT's paltry membership of just over 8,500 was based in Barcelona; by 1910, when overall affiliation to the UGT had risen to 41,000, there were only 635 members (1.5 percent) in Barcelona.

Perhaps even more important, UGT leaders made virtually no effort to expand into the countryside until the 1930s. Failure to achieve significant penetration among the massive rural work force, especially the landless braceros of Andalusia,* was a major contribution to the union's slow growth. The dominance of urban workers in the UGT had a major impact upon the union's organization. The UGT, like the PSOE, was effectively run from Madrid, where building workers exercised influence. It has been suggested that the history of the UGT was made by bricklayers of Madrid, miners of Asturias, and metalworkers of Bilbao. Madrid was the fulcrum of the UGT, and within Madrid, the Federación Local de Obreros de la Edificación accounted for a quarter of the membership, which in turn represented over half the UGT's total membership. In 1905, in a total membership of 36,500, Madrid (18,809), Alicante (6,709), Biscay (4,464), and Asturias* (3,155) were the four largest.

The importance of the building trades gave a special character to the UGT. Since they were prone to dispersal in small units of production and threatened constantly by a labor reserve ready to take their jobs, the union acted as a defensive body that protected its members through strong union leadership; although caution, legalistic tactics, and nonconfrontation were common. Strict rules existed to regulate strikes; the UGT's III Congress in 1892 ruled that strike calls were invalid if less than twenty employees were involved or the strike was judged by the national committee to have no realistic possibility of success. An 1896 amendment transferred decision making to local federations; but in 1902, a further regulation forbade strikes if strike funds did not exist, or if a majority of workers had not been UGT members for at least a year.

This legalistic moderation in the UGT was a logical response to the reality of state power. Socialist leaders had seen their anarchist rivals subjected to almost unremitting repression since the founding of the Federación Regional Española, the Bakuninist branch of the International Working Men's Association, established in 1869. Although much larger (especially in Andalusia and Catalonia), the anarchists were subject to massive fluctuations of fortune; brief periods of success were usually followed by intensified state repression, especially after the formation of the anarchosyndicalist Confederación Nacional de Trabajo (CNT) in 1911. At another level, however, UGT legalism reflected its confused theoretical legacy. Despite opposition to the Restoration monarchy, UGT leaders still saw the state as the ultimate guarantor of any progress achieved by the union: the state was the only entity that might exert authority over owners and employers once agreements had been reached. The UGT's ambivalence derived from the division between revolutionary rhetoric, based on a poor understanding of Marxist theory, and reformist practice, based on a pragmatic political approach, which lay at the heart of the socialist movement. The two major leaders of the UGT before the Spanish Civil War, Iglesias and Francisco Largo Caballero,* were both dour, ascetic individuals who held leadership of the PSOE and UGT concurrently; and both exhibited a tendency to compromise that belied the radical content of their political pronouncements.

Official UGT policy, however, did not go entirely unchallenged. Between 1910 and 1914, bitter divisions over the issue of trade union tactics developed within the socialist movement, leaving it badly weakened on the eve of World War I.* In some areas, UGT strike actions became increasingly independent of the socialist central apparatus. In the Basque* country, for instance, powerful mine labor leaders contested the centralism and caution exhibited by socialist leaders. A series of clashes culminated in a bitter conflict over the 1913 Río Tinto miners' strike, which the Basques* wanted to convert into a general strike, with the ultimate aim of radicalizing the socialist movement. Iglesias, in collaboration with Asturian mine leaders, opposed the move and engineered the expulsion of two Basque leaders from the UGT and PSOE.

Although the leadership generally managed to defeat other local initiatives, divisions over tactics remained an endemic feature of the UGT until 1936. It occasionally flirted with revolution, as evidenced by the 1916 Pact of Saragossa with the anarchists and its involvement in the confused general strike of 1917; but in general the UGT line was marked by respect for legality, and reflected a reformist approach to socialism that stressed evolution rather than revolution. This was never more clearly demonstrated than during the dictatorship of Gen. Miguel Primo de Rivera,* when the UGT agreed to collaborate with his plan to reorganize labor relations along corporativist lines.

This decision intensified divisions among the socialists. Primo's offer of UGT participation in the Consejo de Trabajo was based on his positive assessment of the union's sense of responsibility. Two lines emerged within the movement in response to the offer: UGT leaders who were also on the PSOE executive, such as Largo Caballero or Julián Besteiro (1870–1939), argued that the union should take advantage of the offer to reinforce the socialist organization. Gains made at such cost over the years should not be squandered by resistance to a dictator who would only bring about the UGT's repression; the dictatorship, moreover, did not alter the validity of the evolutionist approach to a socialist future.

The second line, taken by PSOE leaders who were not members of the UGT, particularly Indalecio Prieto (1883–1962), argued that collaboration would undermine UGT prestige by opening it up to charges of opportunism. They contended that socialists should oppose Primo's regime as a matter of political principle.

The two positions have been described as worker corporativism and political reformism. Early in the dictatorship, the corporativists held sway. The structure of the UGT, based on small-scale urban concerns federated to particular associations, indeed lent itself well to participation in the corporative framework established by the dictatorship. Largo Caballero and Besteiro became staunch defenders of the regime's comités paritarios, joint committees of workers and employers.

By 1927, however, as Primo's support began to fall away, the UGT distanced itself from his regime. Prompted by Prieto, the socialists established close contact with the renascent republican movement, headed by Manuel Azaña.* Largo Caballero, ironically, became one of Primo's most committed opponents; his entire career was marked by an expedient ability to bend to political circumstance. Collaboration with the republican forces, in any case, left the socialists in prime position to take political advantage when the dictatorship finally collapsed.

The declaration of the republic catapulted the organized socialist movement into a position of unprecedented importance. Collaboration had allowed socialists to reap a tarnished reward of being the most coherently structured political force in Spain at the outset of the new democratic regime. The collapse of the monarchy coincided with a massive increase of UGT membership; it rose from 225,000 in 1930 to nearly 960,000 the following year. Both the PSOE and UGT, consequently had central roles in the Second Republic, and Largo Caballero became minister of labor in the 1931 republican-socialist administration.

The republic, widely welcomed by laboring classes as an opportunity to rectify past injustices, was obliged to reform the Spanish agrarian structure. Agrarian laborers joined the UGT-affiliated Federación Nacional de Trabajadores de la Tierra (FNTT, founded in 1930); it grew from 153 sections with 29,084 members that year to 2,541 sections with 392,953 members two years later. The FNTT played an immensely significant role as a source of radical pressure on the socialist leadership, but in the end, the UGT disappointed its rural supporters.

Soon after taking office, Largo Caballero introduced a series of measures aimed at improving the harsh working conditions in the southern countryside: the eight-hour day; establishment of arbitration committees known as jurados mixtos; a law of obligatory cultivation to prevent rural lockouts by landowners; and the decree of municipal boundaries to prevent the importation of cheap labor in the midst of local unemployment. These measures proved ineffective because the new government underestimated the tenacity of the Right in resisting reform, and this intransigence was assisted by the lack of state machinery to enforce reform. The various landed interests, far from being a feudal remnant, as the socialists thought, organized quickly and effectively as a reactionary conservative bloc, and simply ignored the new laws, knowing that there were few available sanctions against them.

For all the reforming zeal of the republican-socialist coalition, its working-class supporters were soon disillusioned. The promised changes proved illusory, and pressure for more positive measures intensified after the republic's birth in the wake of twin economic disadvantages: the economic mismanagement already suffered under Primo, and the world depression unleashed in 1929. Although UGT leadership was in the hands of gradualist moderates like Largo Caballero and Besteiro, its position was made difficult by demands for action from an unceasingly militant rank and file. Should the UGT fail to deliver, there existed an anarchist option, a point not lost on socialist leaders.

These divisions deepened between reformists and revolutionaries as rightist resistance to reform continued to frustrate the government; and as a result, the PSOE broke its coalition with the republicans before the general elections of Nov. 1933. The right-wing Confederacíon Española de Derechas Autónomas (CEDA) swept to victory and immediately set about undoing the legislation of the previous two years. This led to the radicalization of the socialist movement (or at least a part of it), and the veteran UGT stalwart, Largo Caballero, became a self-appointed standard-bearer of revolution. Largo's main concern was to stem the alarming decline in membership that had hit the UGT in 1933: from its high point of just under a million members in 1931, affiliation declined to 800,000 in 1932, and to 400,000 in 1933.

Largo's disillusionment with a reforming republic had developed from a number of factors: resistance of the Right to his labor legislation; the obvious weakness of the jurados mixtos; decline in UGT membership; the hostility of the CNT; growing combativeness of landowners and employers; and fear that the CEDA represented a Spanish version of fascism. While reformist sectors of the UGT-PSOE counseled caution and worked to reestablish contacts with the republicans, the more militant UGT elements increasingly demanded a revolutionary seizure of power. By early 1934, Largo Caballero, as the dominant figure in the UGT-PSOE, adopted a dual policy of maintaining normal activity through the legal channels of the republic, while making semiclandestine preparations for a revolutionary strike against what was seen as a growing fascist menace.

These preparations, involving collaboration with other Marxist workers' organizations in the Alianza Obrera (created in 1933), culminated in the Oct. 1934 Asturias rising. Largo, who had denied official backing to an FNTT rural general strike in June (which collapsed and was followed by severe repression, leading to intense criticism of the UGT-PSOE), responded to this pressure by opposing the naming of three CEDA ministers in Oct. The insurrection that followed met the same fate as the June general strike; and again, poor coordination among the socialists aided the government. The rising was swiftly crushed everywhere except in Asturias, and a draconian repression ended by jailing Largo Caballero and Besteiro.

The defeat of the October rising created two radically different socialist conclusions: Largo believed that, since its failure rose from insufficient revolutionary commitment, the movement should be "bolshevized"; while Prieto was convinced that revival of the alliance with the republicans would win back power through the ballot box. This acrimonious debate dominated socialist politics in 1935, until it was resolved in Prieto's favor by the formation of the Popular Front coalition (authored by Azaña and Prieto). The now-revolutionary Largo Caballero, by sanctioning UGT unification with the communist Confederación General del Trabajo Unitario (CGTU) in late 1935, opened the way to communist participation in the Popular Front.

The Popular Front's victory (Feb. 1936) pushed Spanish politics leftward; but the government, exclusively republican in accordance with an earlier agreement, was unable to respond effectively to the challenge of antirepublican conspiracies or the Left's eagerness to exact revenge for hardships suffered during the Bienio Negro. The FNTT encouraged its members to take the law into their own hands, especially if they had been evicted by landowners. As a prelude to the Spanish Civil War, in Salamanca and Toledo, estates were invaded; while in Badajoz, mass land seizures led to a bloody incident at Yeste: seventeen peasants were killed, as many wounded, and fifty FNTT members were arrested.

The civil war fundamentally altered the nature and significance of UGT activities. Obligatory republican union membership increased UGT affiliation at just under two million in 1938; but although Largo Caballero became premier in Sept. 1936, UGT influence declined as the Soviet-backed Communist party* (PCE) took charge of the republican war effort by exploiting the split between the ever more revolutionary Largo Caballero and the reformist Prieto, whose alliance-seeking, antifascist moderation won communist sympathy over the social revolutionary aspirations of left socialist, anarchists, and dissident Marxists.

During the war, the UGT took charge of some early collectivization experiments, and also became involved in the operation of nationalized industries. Its autonomy as a socialist trade union, however, was severely circumscribed by the civil war. Divisions within the republican camp further undermined its capacity for independent action. By the end of the war in Apr. 1939, the UGT and PSOE were broken organizations, devastated by defeat and dissension. Declared illegal by the new state of Gen. Francisco Franco,* the union was forced underground and into exile. In contrast to the PCE, the socialists were poorly prepared for an underground struggle, and what remained of the movement within Spain suffered severe persecution under Franco. The exile UGT, meanwhile, suffered various factional splits: while a significant part joined forces with the communist opposition, another section reconstituted the UGT on a territorial basis rather than according to member's profession, with a national assembly replacing the national committee.

Although the UGT formally remained in existence throughout the Franco regime, its capacity for effective opposition to the dictator was limited. The official vertical syndicates were challenged principally by PCE-infiltrated Comisiones Obreras (CCOO), formed originally as independent clandestine unions in the early 1960s. The CCOO won semilegal status and after the death of Franco in 1975 emerged as the most important union organization in Spain until the early 1980s. The UGT, which had to reconstitute itself during the restoration of democracy, did not surpass the communist-led CCOO until the victory of the PSOE in the 1982 elections, when the UGT finally obtained the largest number of affiliations in the labor movement. Relations between the UGT and PSOE, however, have not been close in recent years, as the PSOE leader and premier, Felipe González,* has been forced to follow an industrial modernization program stressing labor efficiency.

For additional information, see P. Biglino, *El socialismo español y la cuestión agraria, 1890–1936* (Madrid, 1986); P. Heywood, *Marxism and the Failure of Organised Socialism in Spain, 1879–1936* (Cambridge, 1989); S. Juliá, ed., *El socialismo en España* (Madrid, 1986), and *Socialismo y guerra civil* (Madrid, 1987); M. Pérez Ledesma, *El obrero consciente* (Madrid, 1987); P. Preston, *The Coming of the Spanish Civil War* (London, 1978); and A. del Rosal, *Historia de la UGT de España, 1901–1939*, 2 vols. (Barcelona, 1977).

*P. Heywood*

*Related entries*: LARGO CABALLERO, FRANCISCO; SOCIALIST PARTY.


**UNITED SOCIALIST YOUTH (JUVENTUDES SOCIALISTAS UNIFICADAS, JSU),** 1936–1939. The JSU was founded in Apr. 1936 when the Socialist Youth (FJS) joined its communist counterpart, the UJC. The youth leaders envisaged unification as paving the way for the fusion of the adult parties, as well as a means of consolidating the forces of the Spanish Left. At this time, unity was at a premium, as the very existence of the Second Republic* as a vehicle of social and economic reform was threatened by violent conservative reaction in the form of the military conspiracy that eventually unleased the civil war (17–18 July 1936). For the Spanish Communist party* (PCE), socialist-communist unity was a key objective, especially in light of the Comintern's new international antifascist alliance strategy of the Popular Front.

At its creation, although nominally independent of both parent parties, the JSU was predominantly socialist. Young communists were outnumbered more than ten to one by their socialist counterparts, out of a total membership of approximately fifty thousand. Yet by Jan. 1937, six months after the start of the civil war, the JSU had been radically transformed. A massive, post–18 July influx turned the JSU into a youth movement of some two hundred thousand members that was firmly under the leadership of the PCE. This control, evident in the JSU's spearheading of popular frontism, was sustained through imposition of a democratic-centralist structure. The PCE's hold on the JSU had been facilitated when a significant sector of the Socialist Youth's national leadership, and most notably Santiago Carrillo,* had transferred their allegiance to the PCE in early Nov. 1936 during the nationalist siege of Madrid. Another element facilitating PCE control was the massive influx of new members that effectively swamped the "old guard" young socialists.

Thus, between Apr. 1936 and Jan. 1937, the Socialist party* (PSOE), which before 1936 had been the party of the Spanish working class par excellence, effectively lost its own youth movement, and with it, the single greatest guarantee of its own political future. The youth unification was a symptom of the PSOE's internal crisis, which itself accelerated the process of erosion within the Spanish socialist movement. By the end of the civil war in Apr. 1939, the PCE had eclipsed the PSOE as the major force of democratic opposition to Gen. Francisco Franco,* a state of affairs that lasted until the 1970s. The loss of the Socialist Youth was a key element in this eclipse. Moreover, the experience of socialist-communist unity in the JSU during the civil war had an enduring impact on the attitudes and responses of the Spanish socialist movement in exile. As will be seen, developments in the JSU during World War II* are thus crucial to an understanding of the exiled PSOE's enduring anticommunism, a position that impeded the unity of the anti-Francoist opposition until the 1970s.

At the practical level, the JSU played a vital role in the republican war effort. Its cadres shored up the strength of the Popular Army with 70 percent of its membership (250,000) mobilized by the spring of 1937. The most salient political feature of the JSU's brief existence, however, was the virulent organizational rivalry between socialists and communists therein. Socialists were rapidly excluded from leadership posts. By spring 1937, FJS discontent was being expressed in ideological terms. The youth dissidents criticized the way the policy of massification had depoliticized the JSU. The deliberate dilution of the socialist principles that had traditionally underpinned the FJS, undertaken in order to make the JSU attractive to as wide a range of young Spaniards as possible, constituted for the young socialist dissidents the unacceptable face of Popular Front policy. In response, the JSU leadership leveled against the dissidents the same accusations of infantile leftism and treason as the PCE brought against the anti-Stalinist POUM.* This sectarianism was eventually responsible for the violent breakup of the JSU in the final months of the civil war, when FJS dissidents reestablished an independent Socialist Youth, electing a short-lived national executive in Madrid in Mar. 1939. After the republican defeat, the socialist youth secretariat established in exile was recognized in Aug. 1939 by the Socialist (Youth) International as the sole legitimate representative of Spanish socialist youth.

The tensions inside the JSU during the war reflected in microcosm the severe organizational rivalry increasingly apparent between the PSOE and the PCE. Forming as they did the bedrock of the Spanish Popular Front, the two adult parties were locked into a dual struggle. They were both competing for rank-

and-file members and domination of the republican state and its war effort. It is worth stressing that this was predominantly an organizational, rather than an ideological, conflict. For the PSOE, the PCE's appropriation of the JSU had been the first stage in its bid to absorb the socialist constituency en masse. Following close on developments in the youth organization, July 1936 saw the unification of socialists and communists in Catalonia* in the Partit Socialista Unifcat de Catalunya* (PSUC), which, subject to democratic-centralist discipline and affiliated with the Comintern, effectively became the Communist party of Catalonia. The PCE also made inroads into the hierarchy of the socialist-controlled labor federation, the Unión General de Trabajadores* (UGT), even securing two co-opted posts on the UGT's national executive committee by Oct. 1937. In order to avoid the distortions of post hoc cold-war analyses, however, it is important to set the growth of the PCE in the context of the time. It was partly the result of the PSOE's long-standing internal crisis. Most crucial, though, it was nonintervention in the civil war, fostered by Britain* and France,* and the effective embargo on arms sales to the republic that this imposed, that laid the foundations for the PCE's expansion. Much of its political influence during the civil war stemmed from the fact that it was the channel by which vital Soviet aid reached a beleaguered republic abandoned by the Western democracies.

For additional information, see R. Casterás, *Las JSUC: Ante la guerra y la revolución (1936–1939)* (Barcelona, 1977); and R. Viñas, *La formación de las Juventudes Socialistas Unificadas (1934–1936)* (Madrid, 1978).

*H. E. Graham*

*Related entry:* SPANISH CIVIL WAR.

**UNITED STATES OF AMERICA,** relations with. The history of relations between Spain and the United States began when Spain supported the thirteen British colonies in their rebellion against Britain* during the 1770s and early 1780s in an attempt to blunt British capability either to expand control over Spanish colonies in the New World or to apply sufficient resources to protect Gibraltar,* which Madrid* wanted to seize. Following the war, however, the new American nation simply assumed the role of the British, forced both Britain and Spain from North America (except in Canada), and locked the Spaniards out of Georgia, Florida, and the lower Mississippi region. By 1820, the United States had more than doubled the size of its territory, mostly at Spain's expense.

By the treaty of La Granja, signed on 1 Oct. 1800, Spain turned over Louisiana to France* in exchange for territories in Europe, thinking that the French would provide a buffer between the United States and Latin America. Napoleon Bonaparte (1769–1821) sold Louisiana and all territories west of it to the United States in 1803, again putting the young nation next to Spanish territory. Rivalry in North America continued with military clashes, particularly in 1806–1807. Little could be done by Madrid, though, to stop the massive flow of North Americans into the south and southwestern part of the continent. In 1817 and 1818, American troops invaded Spain's colony in Florida and displaced the

Spaniards. Clearly, the balance of power in the New World was turning against Spain.

These events were paralleled by rebellions throughout all Central and South America that had been brewing since the late 1700s and that ultimately led to the loss of all Spanish colonies except for Cuba and Puerto Rico by the early 1820s. Discontent over Spanish rule in Hispanic America, the example of the United States successfully rebelling against Britain, and Napoleon's invasion and occupation of Spain made it propitious for Latin Americans to rebel against the homeland. Unable to assert authority capably in the New World at that moment, Spain's influence there receded, while that of the United States grew.

The loss of Latin America was so devastating to Spain that its significance can hardly be exaggerated. First, it cut off a major source of tax revenue and trade profits to such an extent that in the three decades following (1830–1860), Spanish taxation policies and strategies had to be totally revamped. Second, it reduced Spain to the status of a minor power both in Europe and around the world. Third, it fueled the growth in world-power status of the United States. The loss of the colonies did not in itself make the United States a world power, a process that would take another 150 years; it did, however, create a political vacuum in the New World that attracted the energies of the United States.

The Washington government initially showed interest in Latin America because of the possibilities of trade, which under Spanish control was severely restricted to give advantage to Spanish traders. The North Americans encouraged the rebels publicly and privately provided them with arms and other forms of support, which in themselves hardly caused the loss of the colonies. Officially the United States remained neutral. Spain sought to retain the colonies and gain European support for preserving legitimate authority, while holding back a perceived rising tide of republican governments in a period when Europe had had enough of French revolutions and wars. Spain effectively blocked potential British and French intervention in Latin America by encouraging rivalry between the two European powers with the United States. It was during this period that the United States introduced the Monroe Doctrine (1823), which held that no American territory could be allowed to be subjected to European domination.

With the loss of the colonies by the mid–1820s, relations between Spain and the United States settled down to a pattern of hostility over Cuba. The North Americans wanted to increase trade with the island, but Spain constantly blocked such expansion. During the years of the American Civil War (1861–1865), the possible loss of Cuba was a serious concern to Madrid. Spain briefly occupied Santo Domingo and soon after became involved in a war with Chile and Peru. Hostility and mistrust doggedly influenced Spanish efforts to keep the Americans out of Cuba. During the Cuban rebellion of the late 1860s, friction with the United States flared when it was proved that private U.S. citizens, with the sympathy of the American government, had supported the rebels.

The Spanish-American War* of 1898 was the dramatic signal that the United States was achieving world-power status and represented the death knell for the

Spanish empire that Christopher Columbus had established some four hundred years earlier. The symbolism was not lost on either nation. The crux of the problem was increasing trade between Cuba and the United States in the second half of the nineteenth century at the expense of Spain; Madrid's inability to provide efficient, colonial administration of the island; and a rising tide of Cuban nationalism that the Spaniards could not suppress. The Ten Years War (1868–1878) between Cuba and Spain hinted at 1898. The public in the United States sympathized with the Cuban nationalists: Spain managed to retain control, but was absolutely convinced that the American government wanted to see Madrid lose the colony. By then, its loss of Cuba would have represented a major crisis in domestic Spanish politics, and no government thought it could weather such a storm. Cuba became a symbol of earlier Spanish glories and thus could not be allowed to slip from Madrid's hands.

In early 1895, a major Cuban revolution erupted that could not be contained militarily. The Spanish colonial forces suggested compromising with the Cubans, which Madrid would not agree to for domestic political reasons. Europe and the United States sought to mediate the problem between 1895 and early 1898 to protect their interests. Meanwhile, pressure grew in the United States to intervene, especially as trade relations became increasingly disrupted and newspaper reports recounted alleged Spanish atrocities against Cuban civilians. In Feb. 1898, a letter written by the Spanish ambassador to the United States, Enrique Dupey de Lóme (1851–1904), critical of Pres. William McKinley (1843–1901), was published in the American press, and one week later, the USS *Maine*, then at dock in Havana harbor, exploded, killing more than 250 of its crew. Spain was blamed for the explosion, and tensions mounted, which led to U.S. military intervention in Cuba. The excuse was the *Maine*, but the reasons behind it had grown out of a half-century of rivalry.

The summer war quickly ended with Spain out of the colony. By the Treaty of Paris (1899), Spain lost Cuba, Puerto Rico, some minor islands in the Caribbean, and the Philippines. It led to a self-examination of Spanish society and culture and to a growing repudiation of Spain's cultural heritage in Hispanic America. With the loss of its Caribbean holdings, Spain had to establish new diplomatic goals and priorities. In the early decades of the twentieth century, it refocused attention on European and North African affairs. Since Spain was no longer a military threat to the New World, its diplomatic relations with Latin American countries improved, which led to increased trade relations. Thus, Spain's contacts with its former colonies stabilized and relations with the United States became less threatening, giving Spain a more traditional agenda by becoming active in North Africa. In Europe, anxiety over U.S.-Spanish relations abated, creating fewer tensions between Madrid and other European capitals over the matter of the New World.

The quiet interlude of growing trade relations, expanded tourism, and cultural contacts in Spain's relations with the United States after 1898 was shattered by the Spanish Civil War.* Trade relations had deteriorated during the early 1930s, as the Second Republic* had sought to implement new economic policies within the context of growing, worldwide protectionist trade practices, all set within an expanding world economic depression.

With the outbreak of war in July 1936, Spain's relations with the United States changed profoundly. The republican government attempted to curry support and assistance for its cause, and the nationalists did the same. Both sides used diplomatic representatives to obtain political, economic, and military support for their cause. As a result, most governments and their citizens early associated the events in Spain with those developing on a much vaster scale within European politics. The United States viewed the Second Republic as a legitimate, liberal government, while a minority faction, primarily outside government, sought support for the nationalists to restore more traditional ways in a nation that had recently experienced republicanism. The government of the United States sought to remain neutral in the conflict, helping neither side. The emotions of the American public, however, ran high. Volunteers in the Abraham Lincoln Brigade fought for the republic, while the American Catholic church suggested quietly that perhaps the nationalists were merely Spaniards not dedicated to fascism.

Over the next three years, the Second Republic failed to gain active support from the U.S. government in the form of arms sales or outright denunciation of the nationalists. For that matter, Gen. Francisco Franco* experienced the same failure. Trade relations between the two countries came to a virtual halt except for some minor sales of oil to Spain and periodic, illegal (by U.S. law) shipments of arms to both sides. U.S. influence in Latin America grew at a more rapid rate, especially now that Spain had, at the moment, little to offer its Hispanic kin. As time wore on, Americans throughout the New World saw that the Second Republic was doomed. They also believed Franco's forces would develop a dictatorship with fascist overtones.

The lack of American diplomatic support for either side was primarily the result of Washington's policy of avoiding as much as possible involvement in European military problems that might lead to another war. Both sides in the civil war would have claimed an enormous political victory had the United States actively supported one side or the other. American backing might have caused the French and the British, for example, to provide the military aid the Second Republic so desperately wanted. The fact remained, though, that the continuing difficult relations between Spain and the United States did not improve throughout the 1930s.

With the end of World War II,* Benito Mussolini (1883–1945) and Adolf Hitler (1889–1945) were gone, but Franco survived, to the irritation of the American public. The Allies ostracized Spain diplomatically, not even allowing it to join the United Nations until the mid–1950s. Franco even managed to become attractive as the cold war heated up, because his government was vehemently anticommunist. As the North Atlantic Treaty Organization (NATO) defense structure came into being in the late 1940s and early 1950s, the need for Allied military facilities in southern Europe made it possible for Franco to bring his nation into the mainstream of West European affairs. In Sept. 1950, the United States made a loan to Spain, trade relations improved, and, on 26 Sept. 1953, a formal agreement, the Pact of Madrid, was signed.

This set of three agreements has governed U.S.-Spanish relations down to the present. The first dealt with defense, the second with aid for mutual defense, and the third with economic assistance to Spain. The package allowed for the establishment of American military bases in Spain and military and economic aid. Spain was linked to NATO, repeating, in effect, Otto von Bismarck's (1815–1898) effort to involve Madrid in Europe's system of alliances in the 1880s. For Spain, this meant solid help for decades and closer integration into European affairs. It also signaled that pressure to destroy the Franco regime would subside. The Pact of Madrid gave Spain's government a stamp of approval from the strongest nation in the world.

The rest of the 1950s was spent implementing the treaty, improving the Spanish economy, and constructing a series of bases managed jointly by Spanish and American forces. Between 1951 and the end of 1959, total military assistance to Spain amounted to $849.3 million. Economic aid provided an additional $370.9 million. Combined military and economic funding from the United States during the 1960s totaled an additional $1.37 billion.

Similar amounts of money poured into Spain during the 1970s and into the 1980s. During the 1960s, Spain's economy grew faster than any other in Western Europe, while trade relations with the United States expanded. Trade between the two averaged several hundred million dollars in the early 1960s, but was more than $2.5 billion by the early 1970s. Tourism also played a significant role. In 1962, 8.6 million tourists came to Spain from all nations, and by 1970, the number equaled Spain's population. In the late 1960s, it was not uncommon for 600,000 to 700,000 Americans to visit Spain. In 1971, the figure exceeded 1.3 million.

Yet the centerpiece of relations continued to be the bases. Friction over these has been a constant feature of Spain's relationship with the United States. The benefits to both were so great, however, that each time the pacts had to be renewed, intense negotiations took place (and the rent increased), but they were signed throughout the 1960s into the 1980s. The last negotiation in 1987 forced the United States to give up Torrejón air base near Madrid.

An important event in the history of U.S.-Spanish relations occurred with the death of Franco in Nov. 1975 and the rapid restoration of a parliamentary democracy in that country in the late 1970s. The Spanish economy survived the change, although not without the difficulties of inflation and high unemployment. Western Europe sought closer ties to Spain, allowing it to join the European Economic Community in the 1980s, thus drawing it even further into the mainstream of European affairs. Spain became less dependent on the United States, and Madrid was thus able to demand a higher price for use of the bases. In the meanwhile, voices critical of the pact could increasingly be heard. For its part, the United States wanted to retain the bases and Spain's tight linkage to NATO in support of the Western alliance in southern Europe. American policy was successful if for no other reason than that the bases agreements were renewed in 1953 and in 1970, and periodically over the next decade and a half. The Spanish economy, more fully integrated into Europe's by the late 1970s, also augured for a stabler economic order, as Spain became a society with many of the same political features evident throughout Western Europe. During the 1980s, there were moments of challenge. On 3 Dec. 1982, Spain's first socialist government since the 1930s came to power with Felipe González* as its young prime minister after open and free elections. Despite his early criticism of the bases agreement, González directed his government to renew the Pact of Madrid in 1983. He took the position that these were Spanish bases "loaned to the United States." In short, what had been happening in the late 1970s and early 1980s was a growing relationship between Madrid and Europe, on the one hand, and on the other, a concurrent decline in its dependence on the United States. Because of these changes, relations between the two countries became less important to either than they had been in the previous sixty or seventy years.

For additional information, see J. Becker y González, *Historia de las relaciones exteriores de España durante el siglo xix*, 3 vols. (Madrid, 1924–27); J. W. Cortada, *Spain and the American Civil War: Relations at Mid-Century, 1855–1868* (Philadelphia, 1980), and *Two Nations over Time: Spain and the United States, 1776–1977* (Westport, 1978); E. R. May, *Imperial Diplomacy: The Emergence of America as a Great Power* (New York, 1961); R. Rubottom and J. C. Murphy, *Spain and the United States since World War II* (New York, 1984); B. P. Thompson, *La ayuda española en la guerra de la independencia norteamericana* (Madrid, 1967); and R. P. Traina, *American Diplomacy and the Spanish Civil War* (Bloomington, 1968).

                                                                                        *J. W. Cortada*

*Related entries*: COLONIES; CUBA; GONZÁLEZ, FELIPE; JUAN CARLOS I.

# V

VALENCIA (also called the Levante), region of east-central Spain consisting of the modern provinces of Castellón, Valencia, and Alicante. Area 4,150 sq. mi.; pop. (1981) 3,646,765. The capital and major city of the region is also called Valencia.

The interior boundary of the Valencian region is formed by the Iberian and Baetic mountain ranges that, though not huge, provide an effective barrier between Valencia and Aragon* or Castile,* its neighbors to the west and northwest. Catalonia* and Andalusia* further delimit Valencia to the north and the far south, while the Mediterranean forms a continuous coastal zone of more than 350 miles on the east.

The central region of Valencia, around the traditional capital, long has been one of the most fertile and productive agricultural areas in Iberia, even though the annual rainfall is less than twenty inches a year. The huerta, as this area of rich farmland is called, has an elaborate irrigation system developed by the Muslims, who controlled Valencia c. A.D. 725–1235. With irrigation and a mild Mediterranean climate, it is possible to produce two to four crops each year. Valencia is one of the prime European citrus-producing centers, home of the Valencia orange, but rice, vegetables, wine, olive oil, and flowers are also grown commercially, much of which is exported.

The western mountains drop to rolling hills in the southernmost province of Alicante, and the climate becomes drier, hotter, and less Mediterranean, less temperate. Agriculture is important, but less intensively practiced, with more grain grown and less diversity in the range of products, although the palm-date industry is unique. Tourism has recently played an important role in some areas.

The industrial activity of the region is surprisingly busy. From its original Muslim artisan base, Valencia has developed iron and steel, furniture, automobiles, shoes, textiles (especially rugs), and recently electronics as its main industrial base in such towns as Alcoy, Elche, Elda, Sagunto, and the city of

Valencia itself, which in recent years has engaged in a successful program of industrial recruiting. In addition, fishing and marine activity have traditionally provided a large number of jobs along the coast, although the importance of this sector has declined in recent decades.

Historically, the period from 1700 is less important than the earlier centuries, when Valencia had gone from Muslim rule to autonomous independence under the Crown of Aragon in 1245. This autonomy, which permitted a separate legislature and legal code, was guaranteed in the Act of Union in 1319 and reconfirmed in 1418, but the centralization begun by Fernando and Isabel from 1479 to 1516 challenged the hegemony of the Catalan middle class in Valencia. After the Germanía uprising in 1519 against Carlos I (Charles V), the integration of Valencia into the Castilian orbit began during the later years of Hapsburg rule (1517–1700). The Inquisition was quite active in the region during the second half of the sixteenth century, and the expulsion of New Christian Muslims (Moriscos) in 1609 removed a quarter of Valencia's population—perhaps as many as 150,000, the greatest part of Moriscos expelled. The disappearance of skilled artisans and agriculturalists began an economic crisis that lasted until the end of the century. As the lands vacated by the Moriscos were resettled by Christian peasants from other regions, the terms imposed by noble or ecclesiastical landowners caused outbreaks of protest that culminated in 1693 with unsuccessful demands for cessation of Aragonese taxes and a limitation of feudal dues.

When the Bourbons established their rule in Spain at the beginning of the eighteenth century, Felipe V* severed Valencia's connection with Aragon in the Nueva Planta decree of 1707, which suspended the autonomy of Valencia and imposed Castilian laws. A royally appointed audiencia and captain general were created to rule the region and Catalan was prohibited from administrative use; the Council of Castile, rather than of Aragon, routinely handled Valencian matters at the national level. Corregidors administered judicial affairs and local government until alcades mayores were given responsibility for local judicial matters under Carlos III,* which left royal executive power in the hands of the corregidors. At the municipal level, Hapsburg sale of the office of regidores had led to abuse, and Felipe V confiscated the titles and appointed royal nominees in their place. In 1766, Carlos III also opened up municipal government to popularly elected síndicos to better represent the common people. The Cortes of Valencia, however, which had met fourteen times during the sixteenth and seventeenth centuries, ceased meeting altogether under centralized Bourbon rule and was absorbed into the Castilian Cortes, which met only six times in the eighteenth century. Not surprisingly, anti-French attitudes in Valencia, strong in the seventeenth century, focused on the new Bourbon regime in the eighteenth and forced the government to centralize Valencia even more than originally might have been intended.

Yet the new economic revival of Spain generally benefited Valencia. Its traditional trade with the eastern Mediterranean, which had dropped precipitously after an outbreak of plague in 1630, regained its strength by 1755. Population decline ended, and the city of Valencia, fourth largest in Spain with a population of eighty thousand, maintained its standing as population rose in the later centuries. Rural depopulation gradually stopped, and by the end of the first century of Bourbon rule, growth had gone beyond pre-expulsion levels and the huerta came to have the greatest rural density in Europe. Carlos III prevented landowners from dispossessing tenants arbitrarily, which increased agricultural productivity as a degree of peace calmed the countryside. Rural poverty still marked the mountain areas, but a revival of the wool industry aided these areas somewhat. The water tribunals kept popular control of irrigation until capital-intensive agriculture created new problems after 1850. The silk industry also met difficulty in the early nineteenth century as new French techniques lowered costs and increased productivity, almost ruining the industry by the end of the century. Cotton textile production was lost to the Catalans and Britain.

The old anti-French attitudes in Valencia made it a center of opposition to Manuel Godoy* and the Napoleonic regime of 1808–1814, and although the French had large garrisons in the region, Valencia contributed one of the largest contingents to the national junta's army. José I* (Joseph Bonaparte) nevertheless thought that the city of Valencia was secure enough to take refuge there on several occasions, since its long distance from the Peninsular Army in Portugal kept the most intense aspects of the war away from the region. Likewise, the liberal struggles of 1814–1833 flared up only occasionally, as in 1817, although the merchant class had liberal sympathies, but in 1835, the progress of liberalism reached its peak when tax protestors and fugitives from the Carlist civil war in the north stormed the prisons and challenged the royal government. By 1840, Valencia was a bastion for the Progressive party* and supported Gen. Baldomero Espartero* against regent María Cristina (1806–1878). The subsequent Moderate party* period (1843–1854 and partially thereafter until 1868) was unpopular enough to stimulate the popularity of federal republicanism. From 1869 to 1939, the movement for regional autonomy periodically animated the area's political life, especially in the so-called Renaxença of the late nineteenth and early twentieth centuries, a revival of Catalan poetry and intense romanticism that greatly influenced the novelist Vicente Blasco Ibáñez,* whose Blasquismo was an amalgam of federalism, bombast, and anti-clericalism. At the same time, the Left also became more important with the rise of Anselmo Lorenzo (1841–1914) and the Comarca Valencania in the 1880s (which in 1911 joined the anarchosyndicalist Confederación Nacional de Trabajo [CNT]), and the socialist Federación de las Agrupaciones Valencianas. Other mainstream nationalist organizations included the Asemblea Regionalista Valenciana and the Unió Valenciana.

The advent of modern ideological parties led to unrest in 1917 and 1918. Of the thirteen major strikes in the region during these two years, the most serious occurred when railway workers walked out on 23 July 1917 and then merged their dispute into the first national general strike of 10 Aug. Labor violence remained lower than in Madrid and Barcelona, but regionalist unrest increased and led to demands by Unió Valenciana, Blasquismo, and other federal and republican groups for mancomunidad that reached a high point by Jan. 1919. Sectarian infighting among the anarchosyndicalists, socialists, and more bourgeois nationalists finally enabled the government to regain control, and while the dictatorship of Gen. Miguel Primo de Rivera* initially had little difficulty in the region, it did not win over a substantial portion of regional opinion because his regime, though more hostile to Catalonia, was so thoroughly antiregional. In any case, a backlash began in 1927 when the Federación Anarquista Ibérica (FAI) was founded at a beach resort near Valencia, and a major effort to overthrow the dictatorship by José Sánchez Guerra (1879–1954) was mounted in 1929 from the region. Voters supported republican candidates in the 1931 municipal elections, which overthrew the regime and created the Second Republic.*

The period from 1931 to 1936 saw the region commit itself to labor as the CNT grew to 54,000 members and the socialist Unión General de Trabajadores* (UGT) reached 56,000 members, while the Spanish Socialist party* (PSOE) grew to 5,220 members and the FAI reached 2,500. In the center, the Partido de Unión Republicana Autonomista (PURA) cooperated with the republican alliance formed by Manuel Azaña,* while on the center-right the Derecha Regional Valenciana (DRV) ultimately developed a loose coalition in the CEDA. Along with the older Blasquismo movement, regional autonomy was a constant topic among these parties, but national politics outpaced the regional debate, and the elections of Nov. 1933, won by the Confederación Española de Derechas Autónomas (CEDA), blocked further legislative action and moved many of the debators further toward the left.

The three years of the Spanish Civil War* saw the region spared from military campaigning until the nationalist army broke through in the northern part of the region from Teruel to Vinaroz by 20 Apr. 1938. The initial struggle saw Gen. Manuel Goded (1882–1936) defeated at Barcelona before he could lead a nationalist rising in Valencia. Local fighting lasted until 24 July, but then local political leaders found themselves caught between the anarchist-dominated Anti-Fascist Militia Committee of Catalonia and Aragon, and the socialist-dominated central government of Madrid. An enforced political neutrality settled over the region, while the harbor at Valencia funneled aid sent by the Soviet Union to the republic. The Spanish Communist party* (PCE) subsequently made some inroads into local politics, and the arrival of the Popular Front cabinet from besieged Madrid in early Nov. 1936 brought more, but so many political leaders from other regions inhibited local politics and generally rendered Valencia relatively neutral from the kind of sectarian politics that erupted in Barcelona. This included curbs put on the much larger anarchist groups of the region, a disappointment to their comrades in Catalonia and Aragon.

During the civil war, the city of Valencia was often bombed; the waters offshore became the scene of extensive naval warfare; and after the breakthrough that divided republican territory, the nationalist advance south toward the temporary capital placed Valencia in jeopardy after 5 July 1938, although a new line of defense at the small town of Viver and the Ebro campaign soon afterward stopped the nationalist advance until 30 Mar. 1939, at the very end of the civil war, when Alicante and Valencia were simultaneously occupied.

The early postwar period was difficult, because Valencia was so thoroughly identified with the republican cause. Military occupation was the norm until 1945, and all Valencian parties were banned and prosecuted, the public use of Catalan was forbidden, and the Falange* worked hard in the region. Agriculture suffered from the failure to establish suitable credit programs for small farmers, and with the average size of farms in the huerta around two acres, only the few large properties in this area of great productivity were able to modernize their operations. Spain's poor European reputation kept many (but not all) products of Valencia out of the European Economic Community (EEC), with Britain, as the best customer until it too entered the EEC. The agriculture of the Levante was fundamentally sound, though, and so Valencia remained reasonably prosperous. The development plans of the 1960s made Valencia one of the "poles"of new industrial growth, and with the arrival in the early 1970s of the largest Ford Motor Company plant in Europe, this strategy succeeded. Regionalist legislation in 1979 did not give Valencia regional status until 1982, which removed an old issue, and in any case, with the growth of an industrial working class, the PSOE rather than regionalist political groups has emerged as the majority party in the area.

For additional information, see M. Ardit, *Revolución liberal y revuelta campesina: Un ensayo sobre la desintegración del régimen feudal en el País Valenciana 1793–1848* (Barcelona, 1977); A. Cucó, *El valencianismo político 1874–1939* (Barcelona, 1977); V. Gascón Pelegrí, *La revolución del 68 en Valencia y su reino* (Castellón de la Planta, 1975); and J. A. Lacomba, *Crisi i revolució al País Valencia (1917)* (Valencia, 1968).

R. W. Kern

*Related entries:* BLASCO IBÁÑEZ, VICENTE; FIRST REPUBLIC; SECOND RE-PUBLIC.


**VÁSQUEZ DE MELLA Y FANJUL, JUAN** (1861–1928), philosopher of Carlism.* Born in Cangas de Onís, Asturias,* of an Asturian mother and Galician father, Mella became a Carlist at the University of Santiago de Compostela. Even before graduation, he had acquired a reputation as an orator and journalist in defense of traditionalist causes.

As a journalist, he moved from *El Pensamiento Galaico* to write articles for *Restauración* of Madrid,* sit on the editorial board of *El Correo Español* (the official Carlist organ), and to found his own *El Pensamiento Español* when he split with the Carlist pretender don Jaime Borbón y Parma (1852–1931) in 1918. Mella attracted greater national attention, however, as a deputy to the Cortes, serving from 1893 to 1919 (with a six-year hiatus between 1900 and 1905) mostly representing Navarre. A reluctant participant in a system he did not support—he favored instead a corporate system—he nonetheless participated in Cortes debates; speaking in a rough, deep voice; presenting cohesive, ideological speeches in defense of the church, monarchy, and local autonomy that impressed even his opponents. He gave his greatest and most numerous speeches outside the Cortes before groups less hostile to his ideas.

Mella's stature in the Cortes encouraged nontraditionalist parties to try to recruit him. He rejected an offer from Antonio Cánovas del Castillo* to serve in an 1895 cabinet and turned down two seats offered to Carlists in the conservative ministry of Antonio Maura* in 1913. Mella was not driven by personal political ambition, refusing even to become the official leader of Spanish Carlism when asked to do so by Carlos VII (1848–1909). Nevertheless, he became a respected advisor to both Carlos VII and don Jaime, although he broke with the latter in 1918 when Jaime's manifesto banned pro-German activities among the Carlists. Since 1915, Mella had favored the Central Powers in World War I,* a product of his animosity toward Britain,* the captor of Gibraltar* and Spain's historic maritime rival. In Jan. 1919, he founded his own Partido Católico Tradicional, which appealed to many prominent Carlists, but weakened official Carlism at a time when its pretender was in exile and the movement not yet fully recovered from the Integrist schism of Ramón Nocedal (1821–1885).

Mella's political ideas during this period represented the mainstream of traditionalist thought up to the Spanish Civil War.* He adapted the neo-Scholastic principles set down by Juan Donoso Cortés,* Jaime Balmes, (1810–1848), and Antonio Aparisi y Guijarro* to the social changes of his era, while expanding the concept of social sovereignty, an assertion of society's supremacy over the state at a time when he feared the state was becoming too powerful. This concept followed from the Aristotelian idea that the state is formed of lesser societies that precede it historically and that it is eventually called upon to coordinate. Society, Mella argued, enjoys an inner dynamic, based on the social nature of man, which gives it a life that is not only independent of the state, but that shapes the state in its own image and limits it. Since no level has the right to assume the functions of lesser ones, social sovereignty was the most effective check against the possibility of authoritarian government. Mella believed that it is in the context of political and social sovereignty that limits on power should be discussed. The highest organs of social sovereignty were the regional and national Cortes that mirrored society and represented not only territorial entities, but the significant economic and professional groupings.

With the advent of the Basque* nationalist movement and serious civil strife in regionalist Catalonia,* the issues of separatism and regionalism became more critical in Mella's time than in the early days of Carlism. Since he viewed the region as the last step of social sovereignty before the state, he regarded regionalism as a legitimate political program while condemning separatism as unnatural. He defined regions as "incipient nations" with different linguistic, physical, and cultural characteristics, but that were not strong enough to make a distinct nation. At some historical point, the regions, unable to fulfill their needs, form nations in a federated mode. Mella defended Spain as a nation, the product of common historical endeavors to which all of its regions had contributed. Therefore, the various active regionalist movements were justified in seeking to recover historic rights and liberties.

Unlike earlier traditionalist thinkers, Mella accepted the legitimacy of circumstantial political parties that represented interest groups on particular issues. In conformity with traditional corporativism, he found general political parties divisive and counter to the natural harmony in society, faulting them for trying to make their program that of the state and for vitiating their principles to capitalize on the issues of the day. Circumstantial parties, on the other hand, were acceptable because they sought neither to monopolize power nor destroy variety in a corporately organized civil society. They arose to deal with a specific problem, but once it was solved, they had no reason for being and disappeared—making the point that men should not be represented by permanent parties.

Modernization and industrialization, other areas not covered by earlier Carlist philosophers, were discussed by Mella in Carlos VII's 1897 *Acta de Loredán*. Critical of the unchecked individualism of liberalism and capitalism, he upheld the right of workers to form trade unions based upon an individual's right of association to perfect himself. Owners, managers, and workers, however, should belong to the same union. At the top would be the integral syndicate, a union of all syndicates, which worked for the common good. In a properly organized society, though, the strike should not occur, although the strike or lockout in pursuit of social justice was legitimate and moral, as long as public and social services necessary to the common good were not curtailed. Pained by the constant strikes that disrupted Spanish society, he believed that the state could solve the problems that led to strikes by enacting social laws and creating *tribunales integrales* to arbitrate labor conflicts. Some of his ideas appeared in the labor-arbitration schemes adopted in the 1920s.

Mella actively led his faction until 1925, when serious illness restricted his activities. Even after his death three years later, his followers were not not finally reincorporated into Carlism until Oct. 1931.

For additional information, see O. Lira, *Nostalgia de Vázquez de Mella* (Santiago de Chile, 1979); M. Rodríguez Carrajo, *El pensamiento socio-político de Mella* (Madrid, 1974), and *Vázquez de Milla: Sobre su vida y obra* (Madrid, 1973); and J. Vázquez de Mella y Fanjul, *Obras completas de Vázquez de Mella*, 30 vols. (Madrid, 1931–1947).

*R. A. Mezei*

*Related entries*: CARLISM; CATALONIA; NAVARRE.

# W

**WELLINGTON, ARTHUR WELLESLEY, FIRST DUKE OF** (1769–1852), leading general during the War of Independence* and the outstanding British commander of land forces of his age. Wellington was born in Ireland, the fourth son of Garrett Wellesley (1735–1781), first earl of Mornington and the descendant of an old Anglo-Irish family. Outshone as a child by his brothers, Wellington was entered on a military career by his family as a last resort. It proved, however, to be exactly the stimulus that his considerable intellectual powers were awaiting, and Wellington in his twenties began to devote himself to study of both the organizational and theoretical aspects of army affairs.

Wellington's military career against the French in Holland and Belgium in 1794–1795, and in India as a colonel and then major general (for his victory at Assaye [23 Sept. 1803]), served as a prelude for his service in Iberia. Early in 1808, the British foreign secretary, George Canning (1770–1827), gave him the task of collaborating with Gen. Francisco de Miranda (1754–1816), the Venezuelan revolutionary leader, in planning a revolt in that Spanish colony. The intent was to weaken Spain, then allied with Napoleon Bonaparte's (1769–1821) France.* A British force of nine thousand men was assembled at Cork. Wellington, now a lieutenant-general, took command in June 1808 just as a Spanish delegation arrived in Britain* to seek help against the recent French invasion of northern Spain and the imposition as king of Napoleon's brother, Joseph (José I*). With Spain now an ally rather than an enemy, Wellington's army was diverted to the Iberian peninsula, and became the nucleus of the British force that fought the French in Portugal* and Spain until 1813.

On 8 Aug. 1808, Wellington landed his army in Portugal, which had been invaded by France in 1807. His strategy throughout his peninsular campaigns was to use Portugal as a base from which to attack the French in Spain, and to which to retire during the winter. The first task, however, was to eject the French from Portugal. This seemed easily done, at first, as two quick victories at Rolica and Vimeiro, some forty miles north of Lisbon, on 17 and 21 Aug. led to an armistice and French evacuation of the country. This success was soon reversed by French victories over the Spanish in Nov. 1808; the explusion of Sir John Moore (1761–1809) from La Corunna in Jan. 1809; and a French return to northern Portugal in Mar.

Wellington, after several months in Britain, returned to Lisbon in Apr. 1809 as supreme commander of British and Portuguese forces in Portugal. His first business was to remodel army structure; he created autonomous divisions for the first time in the British army. Another notable innovation, already tried in 1808, was to strengthen the skirmishing force of the allied army by adding riflemen to each brigade. Here Wellington imitated the French use of sharp-shooters (*tirailleurs*), sent with deadly effect ahead of the main body of the army.

The first allied success of 1809 was the explusion of the French, under Mar. Jean Soult (1769–1851), from Oporto on 12 May, and soon after from Portugal as a whole. French losses at Oporto were some four thousand, against allied casualties of five to six hundred. Wellington then entered Spain on 4 July; now, for the first time, he had to collaborate with Spanish generals and their forces. This relationship was never easy; Wellington considered the Spanish courageous, especially admiring the guerrilla fighters against the French; but he found the generals and their armies disorganized and unprofessional. Despite these diffi-culties, the allies overcame the French in July 1809 at Talavera, seventy miles southwest of Madrid. Here on 27–28 July, what Wellington called "a murderous battle," was fought, in which twenty thousand allied troops suffered five thou-sand casualties, and forty thousand French troops lost seven thousand. It was as an outcome of this victory that Wellington received his familiar title in the British peerage, being named Viscount Wellington of Talavera.

After Talavera, the British and Portuguese forces retired to Portugal, in large part for lack of provisions. Spain's alleged failure to provide supplies became a constant source of friction among the allies. French sacking of the countryside certainly did not help. In Portugal, Wellington now set about creating above Lisbon the solid defenses that became known as the Torres Vedras lines, which in reality consisted of 152 fortified positions, or redoubts, arranged in five ranks, and controlling all entry to the capital.

In 1810, the number of French troops in Spain rose to 350,000, commanded by Mars. Michel Ney (1769–1815) and André Masséna (1758–1817). The latter's advance into Portugal in Sept. 1810 led to the notable battle of Bussaco (27 Sept.), just north of Coimbra, where the French lost 4,600 men to the allies' 1,252. Wellington then fell back on the Torres Vedras defenses, the strength of which was unknown to the French. When Masséna reached the outermost line, however, he quickly realized the solidity of the obstacle, and after a brief skirmish at Monte Agraco retreated north, in Nov. 1810, to Santarém. Harried by Wel-lington in the early spring of 1811, Masséna abandoned Portugal in Apr., being brought to battle just over the border, at Fuentes de Oñoro, on 5 May. French losses again exceeded the allies', and Masséna retreated to Ciudad Rodrigo, nearby to the east. Meanwhile, in May 1811, Gen. William Carr, the viscount of Beresford (1768–1854) won a costly victory over Mar. Soult at Albuera, near Badajoz.

It was the next year, however, that saw the French grip on Spain finally pried loose. A successful assault on Ciudad Rodrigo in 1812 w as followed in May by another on Badajoz, both of them French strongholds in the west. With these successes, Wellington found himself raised to earl in Britain, and to duque de Ciudad Rodrigo and grandee of Spain. The major allied victory of the second half of the year came at Salamanca (22 July), where the French lost fourteen thousand to the allies' five thousand. Thence Wellington occupied Madrid (12 Aug.), to immense popular adulation, expelling King José I. In Sept., the Spanish Cortes named him generalissimo of the allied forces, an appointment that had long been the aim of British diplomacy, while in Britain, he found himself raised from earl to marquess.

By the winter of 1812–1813, all of Spain south of the Tagus was free of the French. That winter also brought the disaster, for France, of the loss of Napoleon's Grand Army in retreat from Moscow. The tide had finally turned against France. On the peninsula, Wellington, after wintering again in Portugal (where he reportedly spent much time foxhunting) reentered Spain in May 1813, leading an allied army of about a hundred thousand men. Two-thirds of these he sent up into the northern mountains to outflank the French on their right, while he himself undertook to drive them eastward toward their own border. Matters came to a head at Vitoria on 21 June 1813. There, the French force, directed by José himself, was routed by the allies, though Wellington failed, because of rain, difficult terrain, and his own army's disposition to looting, to achieve his aim of capturing the enemy force. José was able to lead 55,000 men back into France.

The fall of 1813 saw further hard fighting in the Pyrenees between the allies and Soult's troops. Eventually the French were forced back over the frontier to Bayonne; and in Feb. 1814, Wellington renewed his northward advance, defeating Soult at Orthez (27 Feb.), and finally, after a hard-fought contest, entered Toulouse (12 Apr.). On the previous day, though Wellington did not know it, Napoleon had abdicated. The long struggle that Britain had led against him was done.

On his return to London, Arthur Wellesley was created duke of Wellington in recognition of his extraordinary labors and successes in the War of Independence. His importance was not merely that he had played a large part in freeing Spain and Portugal of French occupation, but rather that he had for some years been the British commander in the only land arena available to Britain in her contest with Napoleonic France. Because France came to control most of northwestern Europe, the main British effort on land against Napoleon was necessarily concentrated in Iberia. Wellington, therefore, was acting on a continental stage when he engaged the French at Bussaco, or at Salamanca, or at Vitoria. In observance of this last success, indeed, a Te Deum was sung at the cathedral of St. Petersburg. Never before had the victory of a foreign army received that accolade.

For additional information, see M. Glover, *Wellington's Army in the Peninsula, 1808–1814* (Newton Abbot, U.K., 1977); E. Longford, *Wellington: The Years of the Sword* (New York, 1969); and J. K. Severn, *A Wellesley Affair: Richard Marquess Wellesley and the Conduct of Anglo-Spanish Diplomacy, 1809–1812* (Tallahassee, 1981).

P. J. Bakewell

*Related entries*: INDEPENDENCE, WAR OF; JOSÉ I.

**WOMEN.** The history of Spanish women from the Middle Ages to the early eighteenth century was defined by both family interests and class status. Lower-class women engaged in familial agricultural labor and simple survival, while aristocratic women were the crucial figures in marital alliances and often the vehicles for inheritance of property. Among the most powerful of medieval Spanish women were the heads of monastic institutions. The abbess of Las Huelgas in Burgos, for instance, controlled sixty villages and twelve subordinate convents. The legal tradition, while defining women as *sexus imbecilitas*, gave those of noble birth a separate identity with rights of inheritance, the ability to maintain separate property and familial control over dowries. Women of common birth received virtually no protection or legal definition other than of a subordinate person.

The informal power noblewomen could exercise was eroded by growth of more centralized political institutions from which they were excluded. The church limited the autonomy of women's religious orders by decreeing that all nuns be cloistered; while on a theological level, the cult of the Virgin, translated into the Marianismo that accompanied male machismo, was put in place and created separate spheres of life for each gender. Elevation of maternal virtues was accompanied by doctrines of innate female weakness and intellectual inferiority as well as the symbol of Eve as a potentially disruptive figure, capable of evil.

Throughout the Hapsburg period (1517–1700), women kept daily life going during a time of protracted warfare when the absence of men was common. The Council of Trent's (1546–1563) ideal of sacramental marriage, however, placed family authority firmly with husbands, and civil law itself described the male as head of the "marital community" with the sole power over the family, even over a wife's separate property. These developments had less effect on the lower classes where medieval family patterns continued and women participated in agricultural labor and in some cases, in home industries—thus removing working-class women from upper-class ideals of female chastity and virtue, or isolation in the home.

Certainly the most prevalent discriminatory attitude toward Spanish women could be found in the common argument that women were basically inferior and uneducable, or that women were totally dependent on men and happy to remain at home. While the humanist scholar Juan Luis Vives (1492–1540) had written numerous works advocating the education of young women and a more equal participation in marriage by educated wives and husbands, and a few educated women like María de Zayas Sotomayor (?–1725) gained a degree of public acclaim, such scattered episodes of emancipation did little to alter women's second-class status. Under Bourbon rule in the later eighteenth century, the "age of the salon" brought the sexes together socially, particularly in Madrid. This was also the age of Don Juanismo, though, and models of sexual license did little to empower women and instead reinforced older stereotypes of female immorality and the fear of female promiscuity.

On a practical level, the reforming zeal of Carlos III* did result in the establishment of 32 schools for girls, but their primary goal was to prepare young women for marriage. As late as 1797, there were only 1,575 women teachers in Spain in a general population of 10.5 million. This pattern continued into the nineteenth century. A royal order in 1816 asked only that girls be taught to read and write, while educational plans in 1825 spoke simply of the domestic arts. A new law of public instruction in 1857 did call for the creation of separate schools for boys and girls, and the Escuela Normal Femenina received new support. By 1860, there were 4,690 schools educating 260,000 girls, while 13,189 schools for boys had 634,735 students. Nevertheless, more than 65 percent of the male population and 85 percent of the women remained illiterate.

The opportunity for educational reform came from the Spanish popularity of the ideas of Karl Christian Friedrich Krause.* A conference held on 21 Feb. 1869 stressed the obligation of all Spaniards to educate themselves fully. Concepción Arenal* inspired other women of the late nineteenth century, but it was the writer Emilia Pardo Bazán* who became most celebrated as the first woman to apply for a membership in the Spanish Academy and to teach very briefly at the university level. As late as the 1880s, however, only a few women attended university courses in Madrid.

In the nineteenth-century economy, most Spanish women were engaged in agriculture (nearly 60 percent) and domestic service, with smaller numbers working in textile and tobacco factories. By 1900, only 15 percent of the female population worked formally, constituting 18.9 percent of all workers. Women generally earned one-half to two-thirds of the male wage for equal work, while women in domestic service often worked ten hours a day for three pesetas a week. Without pressure, the state was slow to develop regulatory powers. When three women workers died in an 1884 explosion at the state arms factory in Toledo, for example, their relatives received no insurance settlement, but the relatives of the male workers who died with them did receive settlement. Working hours and conditions for women were not covered by any legislation until the law of 8 Jan. 1907 prohibited a workday of more than eleven hours. A royal order in 1908 prohibited women and children from working in dangerous jobs, and the Cortes in 1912 passed the "ley de silla"—the chair law—to provide female factory workers with some comfort while on the job. During the same period, women obtained between four and six weeks' maternity leave and one hour per day for mothers to nurse their children. The problems of domestic workers were not addressed until 1926, and then only minimally.

Change, when it did occur in the early twentieth century, included a decline in the birthrate that, following general European patterns, dropped from 33.8 per 1,000 inhabitants in 1900 to 28.3 per 1,000 in 1930. Health care remained inadequate, and high rates of infant and maternal mortality persisted. Women's presence in the workplace actually declined during these decades. By 1930, only 9 percent of women were listed as wage earners, constituting 12.6 percent of the work force. Single women made up 66 percent of the female work force in 1930, while only 19 percent were married and 14 percent were widows. Only 23.6 percent of working women in 1930 found employment in agriculture, while 31.6 percent were in industry and 30.7 percent in domestic service.

Educational opportunities continued to broaden. By 1930, 52 percent of young girls were in school, only 2 percentage points below boys, and illiteracy rates had diminished to 45 percent of the female and 37 percent of the male population. Legal changes opened the universities to women in 1910, so that 2 percent of the university students in 1919 and nearly 6 percent in 1930 were women. Other reforms between 1910 and 1918 guaranteed wider employment opportunities and opened access to professions such as law, medicine, and architecture.

Many of these changes were the result of increased worker organization and militancy. The Left gradually recognized the importance of the woman question, and the Spanish Socialist party* (PSOE) acknowledged the equality of the sexes in its constitution, but most male socialists saw this as a secondary issue until the Agrupación Femenina Socialista pressed the issue. Among the anarcho-syndicalists in the Confederación Nacional de Trabajo (CNT), Federica Montseny* edited *La Revista Blanca* and was the CNT's most able theorist. The CNT, however, was not profeminist, even though one of the early anarchists, Anselmo Lorenzo (1841–1914), had sympathized with the plight of women in industrial society. Teresa Claramunt (1888?–1937?), one of Lorenzo's associates, became an active labor organizer among female textile workers in Barcelona.

Other organizations devoted specifically to women's rights also emerged in these decades. Building on existing city or regional feminist groups, the Asociación Nacional de Mujeres Españolas was organized in 1919 and began publishing *El Pensamiento Femenino*. In 1926, a like-minded group, the Lyceum Club, was founded by María de Maeztu (1882–1947) with lawyer Victoria Kent (1899–1981?) as vice-president to pursue women's suffrage and modernization of legal rights. By the end of the 1920s, however, it was still the PSOE that discussed the broadest range of women's issues. Among a number of other socialist women, Margarita Nelken (1897–1968) helped to create an influential bloc within the party, supported by several influential socialist intellectuals such as Luis Araquistáin (1888–1959) and Luis Jiménez de Asúa (1889–1970). Together they stressed female suffrage, sexual education, legalized prostitution, birth control, and increased opportunities for women. Others outside the PSOE, such as Kent, Dolores Ibarruri,* and Clara Campoamor (1888–1948), joined them to press for a complete revision of legislation affecting women at the start of the Second Republic* in 1931.

In political and legal terms, the years of the republic and the Spanish Civil War* witnessed significant female organization, activism, and efforts to implement reform. The elections to form the constituent assembly used universal manhood suffrage, and many deputies feared granting women the vote would bring the ''politics of the confessional'' into national life. The large Radical party opposed any change in the voting profile, and other deputies favored only a conditional grant that could be revoked if women proved too reactionary. The PSOE's support for a universal franchise proved too strong, however, and subsequent elections added Kent, Campoamor, and Nelken to the Cortes in 1931 and 1932. Women voted for the first time in the elections of Nov. 1933, and although the center-right won, subsequent analysis shows that women tended to vote about equally for the two extremes rather than exclusively for the Center-Right. Five women were elected to Cortes seats in 1933.

The Constitution of 1931 clearly improved the legal status of Spanish women. Article 40 prohibited discrimination of any type; Article 43 made marriage and family an obligation of both sexes and permitted divorce proceedings to be initiated by either party (in contrast to nineteenth-century law that allowed males alone to sue for divorce in case of adultery). The age of civil adulthood for women was dropped from twenty-six (imposed by the Code of 1889) to twenty-three, as compared to twenty-one for men. Article 25 rejected privileges of family status or gender and allowed women to make and sign contracts and administer estates, an important legal equalization.

Much still remained to be done. Socialist deputy Margarita Nelken campaigned for restriction of free labor in religious communities, social reform for prostitutes, and the development of health and retirement plans to cover single women. Above all, she hoped to spread some of the benefits of improved legal and social conditions to rural women whose lives had remained largely unchanged.

The 1933 victory by the Center-Right effectively halted change and even threatened to dismantle what already had been accomplished. In the civil war, politics also overshadowed feminist goals and pushed women into other avenues of political and military activity. Between 1936 and 1939, thousands of women were mobilized to provide support for military units, perform civil services, and even to fight as they did in the Aragonese militias and as members of guerrilla groups in the south. Women also assumed positions of leadership. Federica Montseny became the first female Spanish cabinet minister as minister of health and education in the Popular Front government from Nov. 1936 to May 1937. Dolores Ibarruri, La Pasionaria, gained international attention as one of the leaders of the Communist party* and the best-known republican propagandist of the era.

On both sides of the conflict, the number and size of membership in women's organizations increased significantly. Among supporters of the republic, in addition to the women's organizations already mentioned, new groups appeared such as the Comité Nacional de Mujeres contra la Guerra y el Fascismo (popularly known as Mujeres Antifascistas), which was founded in 1933 by Ibarruri as an affiliate of the international committee of the same name to publish the magazine *Mujeres*. Anarchist women published *Mujeres Libres* in Apr. 1936 and eventually created a widespread organization with some 20,000 members. Among the nationalists, the Falange* had created a Sección Femenina in 1933 as an elite organization, but by 1939 it had a membership of 580,000 women. Acción Católica also continued to be an important mechanism for organizing women, though its activities were less political and focused upon charitable parish work and religious spiritual life. Both of these groups agreed in their emphasis on morality, austerity, maternity, and the family.

Franco's victory destroyed radical feminism and erased many rights and responsibilities women had gained under the republic. The franchise and legal equality given to women by the Second Republic disappeared; the legal code of 1889 was reestablished in Mar. 1938, and divorce was prohibited in Aug. 1938. Women could not work without permission from Servicio Social, whose social philosophy came from the Fuero del Trabajo of Mar. 1938 that sought to protect women from the rigors of work in order to protect the integrity of the family. Divorce, abortion, and contraception were prohibited on 24 Jan. 1941. The new regime reinforced the idea of the family as the origin and prototype of the ideal society and the cradle of Christian values, with the woman-wife-mother at its center. "Rechristianization" of the home and a cult of morality were directed specifically at women.

At the same time, the women's section of the Falange set out to create the "national syndicalist woman." The leader of the women's section of the Falange during the 1940s was Pilar Primo de Rivera (1913– ), sister of its founder, José Antonio Primo de Rivera.* She urged women to give up public life altogether for the peace of home and family. Youth groups trained girls in the domestic arts and prepared them for a mandatory three-month term of state service (expanded in 1946 to educational work).

The experiences of women under Franco were as contradictory as the policies of the regime that hoped to make Spain a "modern" state economically while maintaining traditional social structures and values. In 1950, 50 percent of the Spanish population was still engaged in agriculture, while only 11.8 percent of women were working, constituting 16 percent of the work force, with half in the service sector. In contrast to the rest of Europe, these figures were quite low and did not begin to increase appreciably until the next decade. The birthrate, however, continued to fall to 21.7 per 1,000 inhabitants by 1960, and education for women continued its gradual expansion so that in the 1950s females made up 38 percent of high-school students and more than 14 percent of university students, while the illiteracy rate for women in 1950 was down to 18.3 percent (compared to 9.9 percent for men).

Improving literacy made it more difficult to counter feminist criticism of Spain from abroad, and in the 1950s and 1960s, when Spain ended its international isolation, feminism revived once again. In 1948, the condesa of Campo Alange's (1922– ) book, *La mujer en España: Cien años de su historia*, while conservative, had showed more gender consciousness than any previous work during the Franco years, and her Committee of Sociological Study about the Woman (SESM) promoted feminist studies at the university level. Women participated in the student strikes of the 1950s and 1960s, and others were drawn into political activity by the Asturian strikes of the early 1960s and the reborn union movement that followed.

In broad terms, the death of Franco in 1975 and the advent of the new constitutional monarchy had significant impact on women's activism and place in society. The number of women working increased from 23 percent of the work force in 1968 to 29.2 percent in 1980. Of those employed in 1980, however, 65 percent were between the ages of fourteen and twenty-four and only 10 percent of married women worked. Legal reform in 1961 guaranteed equal pay for equal work, and the Constitution of 1978 included an equal-rights provision, prohibiting discrimination in access to employment, training, advancement, and working conditions. Nevertheless jobs are still gender-defined, and women's jobs are lower paid, with 60 percent of women working in the service sector in 1980.

Other legal reforms have eliminated the most oppressive portions of the Family Law Code. Women are no longer treated as minors and have equal rights to marital property; adultery is no longer a criminal offense, and divorce is legal; and responsibility for children is held jointly by both parents. Women now are also granted fourteen weeks of maternity leave and have job security. Sale of contraceptives and provision of family-planning information are legal, although abortion is not and remains a controversial issue.

Educational opportunities have continued to expand, and by 1980, girls made up 47 percent of students in primary schools, 50 percent of those on the secondary level, and 40 percent of university enrollments. Women are still concentrated in traditional fields such as teaching, and few enter engineering or architecture. Illiteracy rates have diminished, but more women (12 percent) than men (5 percent) remain unable to read or write. Equity in education and professional advancement has been a target of various women's organizations, and clearly the emergence of a visible and varied feminist movement has been a major development in Spain during the last two decades.

In 1965, women of the Communist party and independents formed the Movimiento Democrático de la Mujer (MDM) as a mass movement for working-class women, and this was followed by a rebirth of women's organizations in other political parties such as the PSOE. In 1973, professional women founded the Asociación para la Promoción y Evolución Cultural to seek feminist opportunities in business, education, and science, but after 1975 they broadened their agenda to target discrimination in work and family life and to challenge gender stereotypes. Since then, many other groups have formed both on local and national levels to support such issues as divorce, birth control, and homosexual rights. As elsewhere in Europe, there are divisions between the autonomous groups and those affiliated with political parties, and difficulties on both sides in reaching less privileged social groups. Women are playing more important political roles in neighborhood groups and workers' councils, but only 1.1 percent of mayors and fewer than 5 percent of elected deputies are female, and women are still excluded from the most important decision-making positions of the state. This is not peculiar to Spain, although women's legislative participation is on the low end when compared to the other nations of Western Europe. Today Spanish women more closely resemble their counterparts in the region than in previous decades, both in the problems they face and in their vision of emancipation.

For additional information, see C. Alcalde, *La mujer en la Guerra Civil Española* (Madrid, 1981); R. M. Capel Martínez, ed., *Mujer y sociedad en España, 1700–1975* (Madrid, 1982); M. Angeles Durán, *El trabajo de la muier en España* (Madrid, 1982); P. Fernández-Quintanilla, *La mujer ilustrada en la España del siglo 18* (Madrid, 1981); E. García Méndez, *La actuación de la mujer en las Cortes de la II República* (Madrid, 1978); A. González, A. López, A. Mendoza, and I. Ureña, *Los orígenes del feminismo en España* (Madrid, 1980); L. Gould Levine and G. Feiman Waldman, *Feminismo ante el Franquismo: Entrevistas con feministas de España* (Miami, 1980); M. Nash, *Mujer, familia y trabajo en España 1875–1936* (Barcelona, 1983); C. Ottolenghi, *Women in Spain*, supplement no. 8 to *Women of Europe* (Brussels, 1981); A. M. Pescatello, *Power and Pawn: The Female in Iberian Families, Societies, and Culture* (Westport, 1976); G. M. Scanlon, *La polémica feminista en la España contemporánea (1968–1974)* (Madrid, 1976); and M. J. and P. Voltes, *Las mujeres en la historia de España* (Madrid, 1986).

*M. J. Slaughter and R. W. Kern*

*Related entries*: IBARRURI, DOLORES; SECOND REPUBLIC; SPANISH CIVIL WAR.

**WORLD WAR I** (1914–1918). The impact of World War I on Spain remains of lesser importance than World War II.* Nothing like the civil war elevated Spain to international notice in 1914–1918 the way it did in 1939–1945, the political system remained unchanged (but grew less stable) and, perhaps most important, the war remained more distant from the Mediterranean. Yet, World War I nevertheless strongly influenced Spanish society. Moderate liberalism as the dominant philosophy of government, already under challenge, failed to cope with new social and economic problems. The army that would rebel in 1936 substantially increased in size and changed its tactics. Above all, the war shattered nineteenth-century conventions and introduced a spirit of change that also influenced the later civil war generation.

Precisely because Spain had no overriding reasons to enter the war, the question of whether to enter and on which side remained significant the whole time. The king played an important but tergiversating role in the debate; this kind of incompetent activism helped weaken the monarchy's stature and in some ways was the most important consequence of the war in Spain. Initially, the cabinet of Eduardo Dato,* which remained in office until the spring of 1915, had no difficulty keeping Spain neutral, but as fighting increased in late 1914, partisans of the Allies, the aliadofilios, and of Germany, the germanofilios, emerged noisily to lobby for the two sides. Nowhere was this split more noticeable than in the royal household, where the Austrian mother, María Cristina de Habsburgo (1858–1929), of Alfonso XIII* favored the Central Powers, while his wife, the British Victoria Eugenia de Battenberg (1887–1969), favored the Allies. Alfonso himself leaned slightly toward France,* Spain's cooperative partner in Morocco.* The problems faced by the French were the lack of an influential figure to press Alfonso to make a firm decision and the further handicap of their close relations with Britain,* whose possession of Gibraltar* ensured Anglophobia throughout Spain. Both France and Britain relied heavily upon their investments in Spain and the nearly 30 percent of overseas sales they provided for Spanish exports to keep Spain favorable to the Entente.

Germany* was a lesser market and a recent diplomatic threat in the Balearic Islands* and Morocco, yet its conservatism and the Catholicism of Austria appealed to the Spanish church, army, and aristocracy. Moreover, the Germans quickly established an active propaganda network set up by German businessmen August Hofer, Wilhelm Rautzenberg, and Karl Koppel, who also subsidized regular newspapers, a tactic not followed by the Allies until 1917. The German Foreign Office made an informal offer in Oct. 1914 to ally with Spain by offering aid in the recapture of Gibraltar if Spain would harass the British fleet in the Mediterranean. Dato refused, but Alfonso seized this opportunity to imitate the Italians by revealing the offer and inviting a counteroffer that guaranteed benevolent neutrality to the Allies in exchange for Gibraltar. Unlike the Italian case, where Austrian rather than Allied territory was involved, this proposal was rejected by London and Paris, as was a second offer made by Alfonso in May 1915, when Italy* joined the Entente. The king then discussed a new policy of benevolent Spanish neutrality with the German military attaché in Madrid, Arnold Kalle, over German use of Spanish naval facilities, although this initiative was later withdrawn.

Dato was replaced by a "national government" (Dec. 1915–Apr. 1917) composed of liberals and conservatives led by Álvaro de Figueroa, the conde de Romanones (1853–1950), a well-known aliadofilio who personally believed that Spain should join the Entente. Even the stormy Antonio Maura,* a former premier and Conservative party leader halfheartedly pursuing an authoritarian policy of "Maurismo," leaned in this direction. The only concession to Alfonso's erratic diplomacy was the appointment of the pro-German Miguel Villanueva Gómez (1852–1931) as foreign minister, an indication that despite an intention to concentrate upon domestic concerns, the national government continued to face thorny diplomatic distractions.

These problems became evident in 1916 when Alfonso sought to obtain German ships interned in Spanish ports at the start of the war to compensate Spanish losses suffered in Germany's submarine war. His real intent, however, was to secure a major role in possible peace negotiations, thus stabilizing his much damaged prestige. Kaiser Wilhelm II (1859–1941), however, was advised that Romanones would make the interned ships available to the Entente or that the idea had originated with the British and French in the first place. The Germans countered with vague economic incentives for Spain and went so far as to commission Alfred Helbig, of the Krupp von Bohlen firm, to study new German-financed mining and harbor projects in exchange for food imports, a project that finally created the Hesperides Company in 1917 to purchase foodstuffs for Germany, although his efforts were soon eclipsed by the *Sussex* incident in Mar. 1916.

The *Sussex* was a channel steamer sunk by a German submarine. Among the passengers lost were a number of Spaniards, including the famous composer Enrique Granados* and his wife. The aftermath of this tragedy saw Alfonso reverse himself by informally threatening to break relations with Germany, which forced Wilhelm to send a special message to the Spanish king by submarine in June 1916 that released ten interned German and two Austrian ships to Spain. Pro-German newspapers made a great deal out of this maneuver, and Alfonso, ever optimistic, believed a new high point had occurred in Hispano-German relations, although in fact the British threatened to occupy Spanish harbors if Madrid did not formally protest the *Sussex* incident. The king was forced to do so on 15 July 1916, and the Cortes subsequently tightened harbor controls to make British blacklisting effective. The fickle Alfonso then reversed himself again in Aug. after Portugal* and Rumania joined the Allies by remarking publicly that the Entente would ultimately triumph, which of course encouraged Romanones and other aliadofilios to tilt again toward France and Britain.

The drumbeat of diplomacy continued through 1916 and early 1917 as the German Admiralty, pressed by the Foreign Office, offered to end submarine attacks on Spanish shipping to Britain if a like number of ships were permitted to trade with German ports. When Britain vetoed this, submarine attacks were stepped up, and for once Wilhelm's effort to restore personal diplomacy with Alfonso failed in Dec. 1916. Unrestricted naval warfare further antagonized Spanish opinion in the following months, particularly after three German submarines put in for repairs in Spanish ports and then slipped out again in the summer and fall of 1917 to avoid being interned.

The war's economic and social consequences now took on new significance. Much of 1915 had been filled with domestic economic and political concerns. Growth of socialist and anarchosyndicalist labor confederations flourished in a period of increasing employment and prosperity, mixed with a rapidly rising cost of living that stirred labor unrest and continuing regionalist agitation in Catalonia.* All sectors of Spanish society with a grievance reacted to rising costs, government control of the railroads, shortages of goods, and political inattentiveness with an eruption of violence. Catalonia, which had achieved a degree of administrative independence in 1913, was shaken by separatist demands in July 1917, and a month later, the first general strike of any consequence in

Spanish labor history occurred. Its impact was more serious in Andalusia,*
especially Cordoba province, where rural strikes continued into 1919. Most
alarming to the king, however, was the juntero movement in the army,* which
threatened to topple the monarchy by removing its main prop as noncommissioned officers demanded increased pay and other military reforms.

Domestic turmoil, which to some degree had the Entente's aid and certainly
its sympathy, curbed Alfonso's erratic diplomacy. The national Spanish newspaper, *El Sol*, subsidized by the British, exposed alleged spying and plotting by
personnel of the German embassy in the spring of 1918 and demanded their
expulsion. Economic pressure led to the signing of a special commercial treaty,
the Cortina Agreement, with Britain in Dec. 1917, a forerunner of similar agreements with France and the United States* in 1918, making Spain, for all practical
purposes, an Entente-dominated state without any special claims on the Western
powers.

This failure to profit from neutrality already had led to political changes. The
national government, which fell on 19 Apr. 1917, was followed by several
ineffectual cabinets before Antonio Maura became premier on 22 Mar. 1918.
His domestic authoritarianism masked Spain's embarrassing diplomatic slide
toward international impotence. Maura demanded that Germany pay damages
for shipping losses and in fact obtained seven ships in Sept. 1918, which forestalled a break in relations at the end of the war.

Looking back, Alfonso clearly lost most by his erratic behavior. His unpopularity and reputation as a poor policymaker dogged him until his abdication in
1931. Liberal politicians, harassed by diplomatic confusion into domestic inattentiveness, also gave up an opportunity to reclaim their prestige. The years
immediately following the war saw social chaos multiply, and this was the real
heritage of World War I.

For additional information, see R. M. Carden, *German Policy toward Neutral Spain
in World War I* (New York, 1987); R. Carr, *Modern Spain 1898–1975* (Oxford, 1977);
L. Gelos Ferreira de Vaz, *Die Neutralitätspolitik Spaniens während des ersten Weltkrieges*
(Hamburg, 1966); and G. H. Meaker, *The Revolutionary Left in Spain 1914–1923* (Stanford, 1974).

R. M. Carden

*Related entries*: ALFONSO XIII; MAURA, ANTONIO.

**WORLD WAR II** (1939–1945). The years of World War II were fraught with
the greatest danger to the national security of Spain. Adolf Hitler's (1889–1945)
armies overran many parts of Western Europe, while the Allies were prepared
to retaliate by invading any portion of the European continent to drive the Nazis
from power. Spain was geographically located next to the fighting, with German
forces, for example, on its northern border in France* and Allied naval facilities
housed on Gibraltar* to the south. With Spain also the largest European land
mass next to the western Mediterranean and so close to the battlefields of North
Africa, its geopolitical position hardly ensured isolation from active involvement.
In short, Spain stood the real possibility of being invaded and occupied by at
least one foreign power.

Not since the days of the Napoleonic Wars had Spain faced such a threat, and never had that problem come at a worse time. Spain had just concluded fighting a bloody and economically expensive civil war that, for all practical purposes, had ended in early Apr., barely five months before the start of World War II. Complicating Spain's predicament was the fact that Spain and both the Allies and Axis understood the Iberian nation's vulnerability all too well and wanted to use it for their own ends.

The damage the civil war caused was so extensive that Spain was scarcely in any military or diplomatic position to stave off invasion, let alone take some active role in the war. Out of a population of some 24.5 million Spaniards, approximately 500,000 had died of all causes. Another 300,000 had left Spain to go into exile, bringing the total loss to about 3.3 percent of the 1936 population. These statistics did not include the loss in productivity caused by those too seriously wounded to serve their nation further, either as soldiers or as active members of the economy. Most Spanish cities had suffered bombardment and the two largest—Barcelona and Madrid—were extensively damaged. More than half the bridges, highways, and railroad lines were either severely damaged or unusable. The nation also faced potential starvation. The national treasury was bereft of gold or hard currency. While there are few reliable statistics on trade or production for the early 1940s, it appears that economic activity had dropped to almost half (if not more) of what it had been in 1936. Finally, the nationalist army was exhausted and, with its arms either antiquated or too few to challenge the armies of either the Axis or Allies, could not be counted on to protect the nation. Add to all these problems the political necessity Gen. Francisco Franco* felt to consolidate his power, and one has a prescription for diplomatic neutrality or at least an urgent need to avoid being an active participant in the war.

Franco's government, therefore, crafted a strategy to keep Spain out of World War II. To do that, the government had to walk a delicate tightrope between either side, sufficiently appeasing each so that neither would invade Spain or force it into the war. At the same time, Franco had to reconstruct the economy and needed help from the belligerents to do it. To accomplish these very difficult tasks required day-to-day tactical moves that favored one side or the other, depending on conditions on Europe's battlefields and the Spanish government's assessment of who might win the war. Thus, before Adolf Hitler occupied southern France, Madrid could drag out discussions with Berlin concerning Spain's possible entry into the war, but after German troops were stationed on the Franco-Spanish border, the Caudillo had to associate himself (at least publicly) more with Berlin than before. When the military balance of power shifted to the Allies in the second half of 1942, Spain gradually distanced itself from the Germans and moved closer to the British and Americans.

The history of Spanish foreign policy during World War II was thus in large part the story of how Madrid protected Spain from occupation while reconstructing the economy. It was a foreign policy the government implemented successfully. Neither side convinced Spain to join the war, and no foreign armies occupied Spain. It also meant that at the end of World War II, after Hitler and Benito Mussolini (1883–1945) were both dead and their regimes gone, Franco's dictatorship remained. In terms of economic reconstruction, Spain managed a slow recovery during the war, an effort that extended into the late 1950s.

From the earliest days of World War II, the Germans wanted Spain involved actively in the war for several reasons. First, the Iberian peninsula was the closest source of wolfram ore, which was used to harden steel for weapons. Second and more important, Spain lay next to Gibraltar, home of a large British naval base that controlled access to the western Mediterranean. Third, Spain could become a convenient conduit for supplies to outfit German forces in North Africa. The Allies, less concerned with wolfram since they had access to the ore in South America or from the Soviet Union, were eager to protect the naval base at Gibraltar, while preventing Hitler from supporting his forces in North Africa. The United States* usually shared the same concerns and priorities as the British throughout the war. As for Portugal,* Lisbon worked with Madrid to remain out of the war. The other political facet was Mussolini's Italy,* which was part of the Axis alliance. In terms of diplomacy, Madrid tried to wedge Italy between Spain and Germany* at different times, but clearly Rome was a minor element when compared to the influences of Berlin, Washington, and London.

During the summer of 1939, before World War II started, Spain kept its distance from the Allies. Madrid played the Germans off the Italians in discussions about joining the Axis alliance, but at least negotiated with Berlin over the nature of future relations and Spain's list of requirements for participation: food, fuel, and arms, and later, territory from French colonial holdings in North Africa. At the same time, Franco purged the foreign ministry of republicans and appointed an army colonel, Juan Beigbeder (1888–1957), as foreign minister in Aug. 1939. Franco selected this Arabic-speaking officer with an eye to someday enhancing Spain's role in North Africa—the traditional focus of Spanish empire building outside the New World and the locale of much activity during the first third of the twentieth century.

With the start of the war, however, Spain's North African aspirations, while never gone, had to play a secondary role as the realities of political and economic conditions prevailed. Spain relied on the United States for almost all its supplies of petroleum, which came from South America. The British were in a strong position to influence the amount of such supplies shipped to Spain, and both Allies profoundly influenced the flow of wheat into Spain that Franco so desperately needed. The Germans talked about providing these necessities to Spain, but as time passed could scarcely provision themselves adequately. Spain's initial reaction, therefore, to the start of World War II was to declare its neutrality in Sept. 1939.

Until June 1940, when France yielded to the Germans, the Spanish government could steer a course between the two sides with relative ease. The situation then became more dangerous for Spanish policymakers. By June, Italy had entered the war on the Axis side, German troops were garrisoned in southern France, and the Allies did not appear to have good prospects for winning the war. Hence the Spanish approached the Germans with an extensive list of demands in exchange for Spain entering the war. The list, designed to stave off Spain's participation in the fighting, included all French Morocco, the Oran sector of Algeria, Gibraltar, and other tracts of land in North Africa. If the Germans won the war and Spain had to participate in it, Spain wanted to be a victor with a previously agreed upon list of spoils.

Franco shifted slightly closer to the Axis in July, when he declared Spain had adopted the position of "nonbelligerency," the tactic taken by Mussolini just before entering the war. By early fall, Franco had concluded (correctly as it happened) that the Germans wanted Gibraltar for themselves and did not want to turn it over to Spain. Madrid resisted German pressures to join the war through various diplomatic tactics. Meanwhile, Spain remained economically dependent on the British and had to carry favor at that court.

Hitler made the next move by requesting Franco to meet him at Hendaye, France, on the border with Spain. Several days before the meeting in Oct. 1940, Franco named Ramón Serrano Suñer,* a prominent leader within the Falange,* as foreign minister. At Hendaye, Hitler pressured Franco to enter the war. The Caudillo calmly argued that he really wanted to, but was prevented at the moment by the lack of food, weapons, and other economic necessities, suggesting that the Germans supply these. He believed the Germans could not because of their needs elsewhere.

Hitler was frustrated at Hendaye at his inability to force Franco into the war despite the Spaniard's almost teasing hint that he wanted to participate. Franco played a good game, and in fact, his representatives had already worked out some joint diplomatic stratagems with Vichy France, which simply encouraged Madrid's tactics at Hendaye. Germany reacted to the Hendaye meeting by increasing pressures on Madrid to enter the war that fall. There were even suggestions that if Spain did not, the Germans might invade Iberia.

When Hitler decided in July 1940 to invade the Soviet Union the following spring, he had to defer any attempt to take Gibraltar. Although Franco did not know of this decision, it ultimately worked in Spain's favor as the invasion date approached. By the spring of 1941, the great threat of Spain having to succumb to German pressure had decreased enormously, and this became increasingly obvious after the invasion of the Soviet Union. Franco's ability to stave off Hitler from the fall of 1939 to the spring of 1941 thus represented his greatest diplomatic victory during the war and perhaps of his entire career as chief of state, because it was during that period from the start of the war until mid–1941 that Spain had been most vulnerable to invasion. Since Hitler had not hesitated to invade so many other European countries, for Spain to avoid the same fate was quite remarkable. While crises and pressures would continue to characterize the triad of relations among the Allies, Axis, and Spain until the end of World

War II, the threat to Spain diminished over time and was never again as it had been before mid–1941.

While dealing with severe pressures from the Germans, the Spaniards had also to treat with the Allies, who used as well whatever resources they had to keep Franco out of the Axis camp. The Allies slowed exports of food and petroleum to Spain. The result was near famine in certain provinces during the winter of 1940–1941. The Spanish withstood the storm and negotiated with the Allies, constantly reminding London and Washington of Madrid's intention to stay out of the war.

Most Allied policymakers concerned with Spain were still suspicious. Revelations from diplomatic archives during the 1960s and 1970s confirmed this distrust. For example, when the Germans invaded the Soviet Union in June 1941, taking Hitler's attention off the West, it gave Franco the opportunity to obtain retribution for civil-war punishment inflicted on the nationalists by Moscow, which was now an Ally. He mustered the Blue Division,* an army unit sent to fight with Germany in the Soviet Union, as a token of his support of Berlin and to establish a bargaining position should Germany win the war there. Other gestures during 1941 and 1942 included moving some Spanish workers to Germany and providing access to Spanish naval bases for German submarines needing refueling. True to Spain's interest in cutting its own course through the diplomatic tangles of the period, the government of Madrid quietly helped Jews fleeing Nazi persecution by allowing them to enter Spain and, in many cases, by providing aid to move to Allied-occupied territories throughout the war.

None of these activities lessened the need for food. In 1940, Spain and Argentina signed the first of many accords providing for the sale of grain to the Spaniards. Once it became evident to the British that Spain intended to stay out of the war—and as a means of further encouraging its neutrality—London permitted renewed trade with Franco, even encouraging the less willing United States to increase the shipment of food and fuel to Spain. In 1942, Franco removed the pro-Axis Serrano Suñer from the foreign ministry and replaced him with the more pro-British Francisco Gómez-Jordana y Sousa (1876–1944). It should be noted that Serrano Suñer was ousted from office less for diplomatic considerations than because of domestic political concerns. The changing of the guard did, however, allow the regime to install a foreign minister more appealing to the Allies at minimal cost to Spanish strategies of soothing the Germans. Count Jordana had already been foreign minister just before World War II and proved to be a consummate diplomat in executing Spanish plans. The strategy worked; the Allies saw his appointment as a Spanish signal that Madrid was shifting away from the Axis and slowly toward the Allies.

By the fall of 1942, it was apparent to Spain that Britain* and the United States had the necessary resources to mount an offensive to push Germany back. Such a maneuver would probably include North Africa, home of long-standing Spanish interests. Spain attempted to discourage an Allied invasion of North Africa, even threatening to defend Spanish-held territories, but to no avail. When the invasion came, Spain's hopes for leadership in North Africa died. Yet it was also evident that the Germans might never be able to invade Spain, because if ever there had been a time to do so, it would have been during the summer to resupply Axis armies under Allied attack. The Allies might have done the same, but instead went to great lengths to assure Spain that they would not, so as to encourage the Spaniards to prevent German access into the Iberian peninsula.

From Madrid's point of view, there was still the danger of an Allied attack on Western Europe via Spain from Gibraltar. Madrid and Lisbon, already bound together by various commercial and diplomatic treaties, worked together to declare an "Iberian Bloc" as part of their effort to blunt this possibility. In reality, the Allies had not planned to invade Iberia and so found it easy to use that fact in dealing with both capitals. Such an invasion would have broadened the theater of war too much. The thought of resisting millions of Iberians in essentially mountainous terrain was not all that welcome either. Until late summer 1943, though, Franco still believed that the Germans could win the war and thus continued to walk a fine line between both factions. With Germans to the north and Allies to the south, the military risk to Spain was still perceived as great. Furthermore, economic reconstruction had barely begun, and Franco was still consolidating his power over Spanish affairs. By the end of 1943, however, Franco decided to alter Spanish strategy and shifted to the Allies. First, the Blue Division was quietly repatriated over a period of months. Second, Spain retreated from its position of nonbelligerency to neutrality, but this time intent on coop-eration with the Allies. Thus, the Spanish press's hostility toward the Allies was curbed gradually; refugees of interest to the Allies were helped; and downed Allied pilots were allowed to pass quietly through Spain to Gibraltar. The Ger-mans were told that these gestures were necessary because the Allies held Spain in an economic stranglehold. Once again, Hitler was given the opportunity to supply these commodities to Spain, but the German leader could not.

The shift in Spain's position was deliberately slow in order not to offend too seriously one side or the other. Clearly, during all of 1943 a shift was discernible, and in 1944, obvious. Jordana executed this policy in 1943–1944 as Franco turned his attention increasingly to domestic issues. Historians as a whole have concluded, as did Allied diplomats of the time, that Jordana did his job well, and when he died of long-standing illness in Aug. 1944, contemporary diplomats and later historians considered the event significant. At the time, Allied diplomats in Spain realized that Jordana had designed the shift and worried about whether his replacement could be as effective and friendly.

In fact, Jordana's successor, José Lequerica (1891–1963), once an ambassador and vocal in previous years in his admiration of the Axis, continued his pred-ecessor's policies. Cultural ties to Hispanic America were emphasized, while interest in becoming closer to Western Europe received added emphasis. It was already evident that Spain's aspirations in North Africa would not be satisfied, because the Allies had committed themselves to restoring France's holdings in the area. It was also obvious that Gibraltar would remain British. During 1944,

Allied diplomats noticed that even Franco was changing his image; pictures of Hitler and Mussolini in the Caudillo's office were removed, replaced with one of the pope.

Diplomacy, often a personal odyssey, is portrayed by historians using the names of nations or capital cities as protagonists as if diplomatic actions were impersonal events executed with monolithic support by government agencies. In a dictatorship such as Franco had established in Spain, that might have been the case, because diplomacy was always an individual event. Despite Spain's foreign ministers and their staffs, ultimately and in practice policy emanated from Franco. He had sympathized with the Axis powers during World War II, yet they were not going to win. He had been forced by the politics of war to downplay his own Falange and decrease the influence of his pro-Axis advisors. In the process, both the Soviet Union—his hated enemy from the civil war and the bastion of anti-Catholic and antimonarchist, heretical communism—was in the ascendancy with the British and Americans as well. All three Allies had become incredibly powerful nations, and they were all antifascist.

As difficult as these circumstances must have been personally for Franco, he made possible the change in Spain's attitude toward the Allies discernible as the months went by, but he tied these strictly to the Allies' success on the battlefield. By the time the Allies invaded mainland Europe in June 1944, any vision of the Axis winning had nearly evaporated in Madrid. The foreign office and various commercial agencies within the Spanish government had just ended months of heated economic rivalry in Spain between the Allies and the Axis, who acquired wolfram through preemptive buying strategies. By then, the Spanish government publicly dropped its support of the Axis.

In retrospect, Franco's policies had been successful. Spain stayed out of the fighting (with the exception of the Blue Division), and the mainland had not been invaded. Petroleum and food had been obtained from the Allies. Most important to Franco, the government he had established had been preserved and even strengthened. He had failed, however, to take advantage of the war to enhance Spain's position in North Africa, although he had tried. His role in South America was superfluous. Gibraltar also remained in British hands. Yet on balance, Spanish foreign policy was prudent and realistic, and Spain's diplomacy was executed with considerable skill.

The impact of World War II extended beyond 1945. From the point of view of the victors, Franco had been too close to the Axis since 1936. He now entered a period in which Hitler and Mussolini were dead, Joseph Stalin (1879–1953) still ran a powerful nation, and Western Europe was hostile to dictators and fascism in general. Spain faced a postwar period of animosity and anger directed toward both Franco and his government.

It was this legacy of criticism that provided an important consequence of World War II for Spain. Between 1945 and Nov. 1975 when Franco died, the Caudillo's history of friendship with Germany and Italy made Spain's full integration into European affairs difficult. Although time eased many feelings,

Spain always remained apart, but never more so than in the first eight years following World War II.

The fundamental Spanish question before the Allies was whether they should allow the Franco regime to survive. Clearly the French were critical of the protofascist regime. Exiled Spanish republicans wanted the restoration of the Second Republic,* while both Britain and the United States identified Franco with the fallen Hitler and Mussolini. The Soviet Union, which had supplied the republicans during the civil war and was a mortal enemy of Franco, also supported the notion of a new government in Madrid. Franco reacted by posting troops on the French border and by telling the victorious powers that changes in the composition of his regime would be undertaken. The Soviets raised the issue of a new government for Spain at the Potsdam Conference. The Mexican government led the charge to keep Franco's Spain out of the newly formed United Nations. Franco countered by claiming he was the victim of a communist plot, but this proved a weak defense against world public opinion that he ran a fascist dictatorship. Clearly, Spain was on the diplomatic defensive in the late 1940s.

To make his regime more palatable, in July 1945 Franco promulgated a declaration of civil rights for all Spaniards. He brought more monarchists into the cabinet and appointed Alberto Martín (1905– ), once director of Catholic Action in Spain, as foreign minister. He reduced the role and visibility of the Falange and let the world know of his intention to restore the Spanish monarchy at some unspecified future date.

Yet these steps did not prevent Spain from being isolated diplomatically. At the United Nations in 1946, the Spanish regime was criticized by Poland, Mexico,* Czechoslovakia, Denmark, Norway, and even Panama and Venezuela. The Soviet Union was loud in its complaints, and Guatemala joined in blocking Spain's membership in technical agencies. In short, Spain was not allowed to join the United Nations. Franco's saving grace was the fact that the Allies— Britain, the United States, the Soviet Union, and to a lesser extent the new French government—were not united completely on what to do about Spain. The United Nations as a whole voted not to exchange ambassadors with Spain, but Argentina defied the ban. To build support, Spain launched an aggressive and successful effort in the late 1940s to establish closer bonds with nations of the Middle East, links that remained close over the next forty years.

As the 1940s progressed, international circumstances again worked to favor Spain. In 1948, the Berlin crisis made very obvious the extent of the cold war. Franco had an impeccable record of being hostile to the Soviets and to communism in general. Spain's location in southern Europe made it a logical candidate to extend the emerging North Atlantic Treaty Organization (NATO) alliance, providing a solid phalanx against Soviet intrusion westward from northern Europe down to Gibraltar. The first significant steps taken to draw Spain into the Western alliance came from the United States in 1948–1949. The Korean War simply increased Franco's attractiveness to the West as memories of World War II faded in a Europe rapidly recovering from the war. In 1950, the United

Nations rescinded its 1946 measure isolating Spain. Within a year, Spain had normal diplomatic relations with most governments; the major exceptions were the Soviet Union and Mexico.

The end of the anti-Franco era became clear in 1953. After two years of negotiations with Washington, the two governments signed the Pact of Madrid. This set of three agreements brought millions of dollars in economic and military aid to Spain in exchange for a U.S. military presence on bases built during the 1950s. For all intents and purposes, Franco's Spain had become a part of NATO. That same year, Franco normalized relations with the Vatican. Finally, in 1955, Franco's Spain was admitted to the United Nations with the strong support of Arab and Latin American governments.

Diplomatically, the war was now behind Franco. Yet full integration into Europe awaited his death in the 1970s. This was not so much because of his role in favoring the Axis, but because Franco preserved his authoritarian rule for so many decades during a period when the nations of Western Europe nourished their own parliamentary democracies. Yet the period of World War II should not be discounted. Not since Napoleon Bonaparte (1769–1821) had set upon a path to conquer Europe had Spain been so threatened by invasion. Spain had lived from hand to mouth, experiencing severe shortages of food, fuel, medicine, transportation, and jobs. In fact, that description applied to Spain throughout the 1940s and to a lessening degree into the 1950s. Such hardships simply heightened the importance of Spain's having normalized relations with the United States and the value of the Pact of Madrid. The aid was worth more to a poor country than simply the pride of international acceptance. It also made possible the continuance of Franco's rule.

Set in a historical context, however, World War II did remind all the major powers of Spain's geopolitical position in the western Mediterranean, while causing Madrid to reassert its historical agenda of active diplomacy in North Africa and with the Middle East. While the deprivations caused by the civil war and then world war were felt longer in Spain than elsewhere in Europe, ultimately Spain's importance as a component of the West made World War II seem like the distant past. Through the precarious years from 1939 to 1945, Spanish foreign policy had been practical and its execution often bordering on the brilliant.

For additional information, see W. L. Beaulac, *Franco: Silent Ally in World War II* (Carbondale, 1986); J. M. Doussinague, *España tenía razón (1939–1945)* (Madrid, 1950); K. -J. Ruhl, *Franco, Falange y 'Tercer Reich': España en la segunda guerra mundial* (Madrid, 1986); R. Serrano Suñer, *Entre el silencio y propaganda: La historia como fue. Memorias* (Barcelona, 1977); and X. Tusell and G. G. Queipo de Llano, *Franco y Mussolini. La política española durante la segunda guerra mundial* (Barcelona, 1985).

*J. W. Cortada*

*Related entries:* FRANCO, GEN. FRANCISCO; SERRANO SUÑER, RAMÓN.

# Z

**ZARZUELA** is a term used to describe a variety of works for the Spanish musical theater. The word has its origin in the seventeenth century when musical plays were staged in a country estate of Felipe IV (1605–1665), which was surrounded by blackberry bushes, or zarzas. The early zarzuelas were written and produced for the royal court and had subject matter closely akin to the Italian operas of the time, namely, mythological stories, fantasies, or heroic escapades.

In the early eighteenth century, the subject matter of the zarzuela became increasingly political and satiric. No longer were the stories centered around nymphs and Greek heroes, but around ordinary citizens of Spain. As the stories became more political, zarzuela went underground, performed only in private homes for small audiences. By 1780, zarzuela had virtually vanished from the scene, eclipsed by the increasing preponderance of Italian opera.

Zarzuela burst back upon the Spanish musical and theatrical scene in the 1830s. One of the first successful zarzuelas was *El Novio y el Concierto* by Tomás Breton (1850–1913?), a satire of Italian opera. Hundreds of zarzuelas of varying length and quality followed. Virtually every Spanish city had its zarzuela theater, and touring companies took zarzuelas throughout Spain and to Latin America.

Some of the most important nineteenth-century zarzuelas are Francisco Asenjo Barbieri's (1823–1894) *Pan y Toros* and *El Barberillo de Lavapies*, Breton's *La Verbena de la Paloma* and Pascual Arrieta's (1820–1891) *Marina*, which is sometimes referred to as the first Spanish opera.

Zarzuelas can be one, two, or three acts. They consist of songs, spoken dialogue, and dances. The subject of the modern zarzuela is usually romantic love, and most have happy endings. The dances are not ballets, but are generally folk dances. Nonsinging character parts abound. Musically, zarzuela ranges from simple popular song to elaborate coloratura arias.

In the 1920s and 1930s, zarzuela experienced yet another rebirth. Such composers as Federico Torroba (1891–1982) and Pablo Sorozabal (1897–   ) wrote zarzuelas with more serious qualities. Yet however close they may have come to the grand opera, they have never lost the provincial Spanish flavor that characterizes zarzuela.

For additional information, see G. Chase, *The Music of Spain* (New York, 1959); A. Fernández-Cid, *La música y los músicos españoles en el siglo xx* (Madrid, 1963); and A. Salazar, *La música contemporánea en España* (Madrid, 1930).

*S. L. Brake*

**ZUMALACÁRREGUI, TOMÁS DE** (1788–1835), Carlist general. Zumalacárregui was a Basque* from Guipúzcoa who volunteered to fight the French invaders from 1808 to 1814. When a liberal regime was established between 1820 and 1823, Zumalacárregui fought to overthrow it. In 1833, he joined the Carlist cause and soon became commander-in-chief of all Carlist forces in the Basque-Navarre* region.

As the ablest, most colorful, and respected Carlist military leader in the First Carlist War (1833–1840), Zumalacárregui had at his disposal a small, raw fighting force. He immediately set out to build an army by increasing its numbers, training his soldiers in the art of warfare, insisting on exemplary bravery, and demanding unflinching loyalty. In addition, he made maximum use of all physical and human resources available to him. Fighting in a mountainous, rugged terrain, he began by carrying out a guerrilla campaign of surprise, striking and eluding the so-called Cristinos (troops of the Madrid government led by María Cristina [1806–1878], regent for Isabel II,* the daughter of Fernando VII*) in order to bewilder and exhaust the government's army.

By mid–1835, Zumalacárregui had assembled a reputable fighting force that brought him the respect and fear of the enemy as well as of his men. Even though four well-known and seasoned Cristino generals were pitted against him, his strategy successfully confined the Cristinos to a series of fortified cities, while the Carlists moved through the region with surprising ease.

Eager to achieve a major victory, the Carlists attacked the Cristino-held city of Bilbao in June 1835. On the 15th, Zumalacárregui was wounded by an enemy bullet in the right leg and, after failing to receive appropriate medical treatment, died of an acute infection on 24 June 1835. His death was a severe blow to the Carlist war effort, since no leader emerged who approximated Zumalacárregui's tactical and organizational ability and who possessed his leadership qualities.

For additional information, see J. Coverdale, *The Basque Phase of Spain's First Carlist War* (Princeton, 1984); and B. Jarnes, *Zumalacárregui, el caudillo romántico* (Madrid, 1931).

*G. G. Fernández*

*Related entry*: CARLISM.

# Chronology of Spanish History, 1700–1988

## THE WAR OF SPANISH SUCCESSION, 1700–1714

### Dynasty

| 1683 | Dec. 19 | Philip of Anjou (1683–1746), grandson of Louis XIV (1638–1715), is born at Versailles. |
|------|---------|-------------|
| 1700 | Nov. 3 | The will of Carlos II (1662–1700) names Philip of Anjou as heir. |
|      | Nov. 16 | Following the death of Carlos II, Philip assumes the Spanish throne as Felipe V. |
| 1701 | Feb. | Felipe enters Madrid. |
|      | May 8 | Felipe V swears to observe the ancient laws of Spain. |
|      | Nov. 27 | Felipe m. María Luisa of Savoy (1687–1714). *Children*: Luis I (1707–1724), k. of Spain 1724; Fernando VI (1713–1759), k. of Spain 1746–1759. |
| 1702 | May 4 | Archduke Charles (later Charles VI, 1685–1740) of Austria is made k. of Spain by the Grand Alliance. |
| 1705 | Oct. 14 | Charles invades Catalonia and captures Barcelona. His claim is supported by Aragon. He takes the title of Carlos III. |
| 1711 | Sept. 27 | Charles drops his Spanish claims when the death of Emperor Joseph makes Charles the Hapsburg emperor as Charles VI (1711–1740). |
| 1712 | Feb. 3 | The agreement at Fontainebleau accepts Felipe's renunciation of all claims on the French throne. |

Some dates vary considerably from source to source. Every effort has been made to achieve accuracy, but occasionally only the year can be given for an event. Dates that are in doubt are marked by a question mark.

| 1713 | May | The introduction of Salic law excludes female succession to the Spanish throne as a further bar to the unification of the French and Spanish thrones. |
| | June 13 | Felipe V is recognized as k. of Spain by the Grand Alliance. Austria rejects the treaty and insists that Spain is still a Hapsburg possession. |
| 1714 | Feb. 14 | María Luisa dies. |

## Favorites/Chief Ministers

| 1701– 1714 | | Anne Marie de la Trémouille, princess of Ursinos (1641–1722), is the French widow of the duque de Bracciano, a Spanish grandee, who acts as liaison between the court of Felipe and Louis XIV and is Felipe's chief advisor. |

## Political Life

| 1705 | May | Administrative reform creates a 24-province nation. An economic council also begins. |
| 1707 | Feb. | The Councils of Castile and Aragon are merged. |
| | June 29 | Catalan and Valencian liberties are abolished. Royal courts curtail traditional liberties. The Catalans briefly go to war in 1714 to regain them. |

## War and Diplomacy

| 1698 | Oct. 11 | In the First Treaty of Partition, Charles of Bavaria claims Spain, the Indies, and the Spanish Netherlands for the Hapsburgs, while Louis XIV of France claims Spanish possessions in Italy. |
| 1700 | Mar. 13 | In the Second Treaty of Partition, Charles again claims Spain and the Indies, while Naples, Sicily, and Lorraine are given to the French dauphin, and Milan is claimed by the duke of Lorraine. |
| | Nov. 3 | Carlos II names Philip of Anjou, grandson of Louis XIV, heir to the Spanish throne. |
| | Nov. 16 | Carlos II dies. Philip assumes his inheritance. |
| 1702 | Sept. 7 | Austria, Prussia, Britain, Savoy, and Portugal (in 1703) ally in the Grand Alliance vs. France and Spain in support of conflicting Austrian and French claims to the Spanish crown. The Grand Alliance supports Charles of Bavaria. |

| 1704 | Apr. 13 | Felipe declares war on the Grand Alliance. |
| | May | Charles sends British and Dutch troops to Portugal to attack western Castile. |
| | July 20–27 | A British admiral, Sir George Rooke, sacks Cadiz and Vigo. |
| | Aug. 4 | Britain seizes Gibraltar from Spain. |
| 1705 | Aug. 22 | Charles lands in Barcelona. The duke of Peterborough invades the rest of Catalonia for Charles. |
| 1706 | June 26 | Charles's forces invade Castile from Portugal and briefly occupy Madrid. Felipe flees to Burgos. |
| | Oct. | Felipe defeats Charles's army and retakes Madrid. |
| 1707 | Apr. 25 | Felipe's victory of Almansa (Albacete) recaptures Valencia and Aragon. |
| 1708 | Sept. | Britain captures Minorca. |
| 1710 | July 17 | Charles's Austrian army wins the battle of Almenara. |
| | Aug. 20 | The Austrians again defeat the Spaniards at Saragossa. |
| | Sept. 28 | Charles pushes his campaign south and briefly captures Madrid again. |
| | Dec. 3 | The Spanish victory at Villaviciosa frees Madrid from the Austrians. |
| 1711 | Sept. 27 | Charles ends his efforts to capture Spain and returns to Vienna to become k. of Austria and the Holy Roman Emporer. |
| 1712 | Nov. 5 | Felipe renounces his claim on the French throne, opening up peace negotiations. |
| 1713 | Mar. 14 | The T. of Utrecht recognizes Felipe V as k. of Spain upon his promise not to unite the thrones of Spain and France. Spain gives Sicily to Austria, and Gibraltar, Minorca, and the Atlantic slave-trade monopoly to Britain. The conference ends on 13 June. |
| | July 13 | The Catalans declare war on Felipe in defense of their autonomy. |
| 1714 | Mar. 6 | By the T. of Rastatt, Spain gives the Netherlands, Naples, Sardinia, and Milan to Austria. Austria, however, still refuses to recognize Felipe. |
| | Sept. 7 | By the T. of Baden, Spain relinquishes its claims on the Low Countries. |
| | Sept. 12 | Barcelona falls to Felipe. |
| 1715 | Feb. 6 | By the Peace of Madrid, Spain and Portugal settle border and colonial disputes. |

## THE BOURBON ASCENDANCY, 1714–1759

### *FELIPE V (1683–1746)*

#### Dynasty

| | | |
|---|---|---|
| 1714 | Sept. 16 | Felipe m. Isabel Farnesio (Elizabeth Farnese) (1692–1766). *Children*: Carlos III (1716–1788), duque de Parma 1731–1735, k. of Sicily 1735–1759 and k. of Spain 1759–1788; Felipe (1720–1765), duque de Parma 1748–1765; Luis Antonio (1727–1785), conde de Chinchón. |
| 1721 | Feb. | Construction begins on La Granja palace. |
| 1724 | Jan. 10 | Felipe briefly abdicates after the death of a fourth son, Fernando. |
| | Aug. 31 | Luis dies. |
| | Sept. 17 | Felipe resumes his rule. |
| 1746 | July 9 | Felipe dies. |

#### Favorites/Chief Ministers

Cardinal Giulio Alberoni (1664–1752) is an Italian favored by Isabel to find Italian crowns for her sons. He is active from 1714 to 1719.

Baron Johann Willem Ripperdá (1680–1752) is a Dutch Catholic who also seeks to recapture Italy for Isabel, but without success.

José Patiño, the marqués de Castelar (1660–1733), is an Asturian who becomes the first Spaniard to reach high rank in Felipe's court. A new era of reform emerges.

Zenón de Somodevilla y Bengoechea, the marqués de la Ensenada (1702–1781), is a Castilian of humble birth who continues the reform program and is particularly effective in strengthening the Spanish navy between 1742 and 1763.

#### Political Life

| | | |
|---|---|---|
| 1714 | June | A Committee of State is created to centralize the bureaucracy. |
| 1715 | | The Spanish Academy is created by royal order. |
| 1716 | Mar. 3 | The final stages of the *Nueva Planta* decree by Alberoni ends the traditional rights of Catalonia and Valencia. It also attempts to codify Spanish law. |
| 1717 | Jan. | The House of Trade (Casa de Contratación) is transferred from Seville to Cadiz. |

| 1719 | Feb. 5 | Alberoni leaves office. |
|------|--------|-------------------------|
| 1724 | Oct. 20 | Ripperdá becomes chief minister. |
| 1726 | May 26 | Ripperdá flees after diplomatic setbacks. José Patiño gradually assumes his role. |
| 1742 | Sept. | The marqués de la Ensenada emerges as the most important of Felipe's ministers. |

## War and Diplomacy

| 1716 | May | Alberoni negotiates a treaty with Britain that ends Spanish recognition of the Stuarts for support against French influence in Spain. |
|------|-----|----|
| 1717 | Aug. 2 | The Spanish seizure of Sardinia is the first step taken in Italian politics to secure positions for Farnesio's sons. |
| 1718 | July | Spain captures Sicily. |
| | Aug. 2 | The Quadruple Alliance unites Britain, France, Holland, and Austria in campaigns in Sicily and Catalonia against Spain. |
| | Aug. 11 | Admiral Byng defeats the Spanish off Cape Passaro. |
| 1719 | Mar. | Spain loses Sicily and Sardinia to Savoy. |
| | Apr. 13 | The Spanish invasion of Scotland begins and lasts until 10 June, the chief offensive against the Quadruple Alliance, but also the last Spanish effort to invade Britain. |
| 1720 | June 20 | In the T. of the Hague, Felipe abandons his Italian claims for future succession rights of Farnesio's sons in northern Italy. |
| | June 21 | A marriage alliance with France is signed to ally the two Bourbon nations. Prince Luis of Asturias is betrothed to Louise Elizabeth of Orleans. Louis XV is betrothed to the infant daughter of Felipe and Isabel. |
| 1724 | Aug. 31 | The death of Luis nullifies the marriage pact with France. |
| 1725 | Apr. 28 | In the T. of Vienna, Ripperdá negotiates Austrian recognition of Felipe in return for his abandonment of any claim on the French throne and recognition of the Italian duchies as Austrian fiefs. In return, Prince Carlos gains the right of succession in Parma, and Spain wins the opportunity to garrison the duchies. |
| | Sept. 3 | In the T. of Hanover, Britain, France, Prussia, and Holland ally vs. Spain and Austria. Raids on Spanish shipping in the Caribbean become common. |
| 1726 | Oct. | Ripperdá threatens to invade Britain unless Gibraltar and Minorca are returned. This plan is so unpopular that he is overthrown and forced to flee to Holland. |
| 1727 | Feb. | Campaigns begin vs. Britain at Gibraltar and vs. France in Italy. The siege of Gibraltar lasts four months. |

| 1728 | Mar. 6 | By the Convention of Prado, Spain negotiates an end to the war vs. Britain. Gibraltar is lost. |
|------|--------|---|
| 1729 | Nov. 9 | By the T. of Seville, Spain wins the right of succession in the Italian duchies by giving France and Britain some commercial rights in Latin America. |
| 1731 | Jan. 10 | By the T. of Vienna, Isabel's son Carlos is made duque de Parma after negotiations with Britain, Holland, and Austria. France is now diplomatically isolated. |
|      | July 22 | By the Pragmatic Sanction, Britain and Holland join Spain in guaranteeing female succession rights in Austria. Spain receives Parma and Piacenza. Austria is now diplomatically isolated. |
| 1733 | Nov. 7 | By the T. of the Escorial (sometimes called the First Family Pact, or First Bourbon Pact), the first lasting pact between the Bourbons in France and Spain, the T. of Utrecht is ignored to create diplomatic and military cooperation. France promises to support Spain vs. Britain in the recapture of Gibraltar and to recognize Carlos as the duque de Parma. Spain agrees to aid France vs. Austria. |
|      | Dec. 15 | The War of Polish Succession begins with Spain vs. Austria at French insistence. France aids the Spanish navy in the conquest of Sicily and Naples. |
| 1734 | Apr. | Carlos is crowned k. of the Two Sicilies. The duchies revert to Austrian control. |
| 1736 | May 18 | Spain and France defeat Austria in Italy. |
| 1738 | Nov. 18 | By the T. of Vienna, Austria recognizes Carlos as k. of Naples and Sicily so long as he remains independent of Spain. In return, France accepts Austria's Pragmatic Sanction. |
| 1739 | Oct. 19 | The Anglo-Spanish War (or War of Jenkins's Ear) begins between Spain and Britain over Georgia and Florida and the question of free commerce for Britain in the Spanish empire. |
|      | Nov. 22 | Britain sacks Portobelo but fails to blockade El Ferrol to keep the Spanish fleet from reinforcing Cuba. |
| 1740 | Oct. | The War of Austrian Succession continues the Anglo-Spanish War in a larger context, but Austrian weakness after the death of Emperor Charles VI allows Isabel Farnesio to press for a new confirmation of her sons' Italian claims. |
| 1741 | May 28 | Spain joins France and Prussia vs. Austria and sends three armies to Italy, where Savoy defeats the Spaniards and Carlos is forced to declare neutrality of the Two Sicilies after the British fleet intervenes. France fails to come to Spain's assistance. |
| 1742 | July | In the T. of Breslau, Prussia and Poland leave the war, while Spain is defeated by Austria and driven back to Naples. |
| 1743 | Oct. 25 | In the Pact of Fontainebleau, the Bourbons agree, in their Second Family Pact, to give French support to Spain in Italy, but the combined force fails to defeat the Austrians until |

Nov. 1745, when Charles Emmanuel III (1701–1773) of Savoy is defeated and Piacenza and Pavia are captured.

|      | Dec. 8 | Spanish and French troops enter Milan. |
| 1746 | Mar. 14 | Savoy reconquers Piacenza with Austrian aid. |

## Colonies

| 1714 | Mercantile efforts intensify as laws developing chartered companies for colonial trade are written. The companies include Honduras (1714), Caracas (1728–1778), Galicia (1734), and Havana (1740–1765). |
| 1720 | Spanish control of Texas is recognized by France. |
| 1721 | The Comuneros revolt in Paraguay, lasting until 1735, becomes a serious challenge to Spanish colonial rule. |
| 1739 | The viceroyalty of New Granada is created in the northern Andean region of Peru. |
|  | Spanish control of Florida is challenged by Britain until 1741. |
| 1743 | José de Campillo y Cossío (1695–1743), one of Felipe's ministers, advocates abandonment of the Cadiz trade monopoly and other reforms to revitalize the American economy. |

## Economics

| 1703 |  | Restrictions on aristocratic status are made to end tax avoidance and improve the economy. Further restrictions are introduced in 1758, 1785, and 1800. |
| 1714 | Nov. 19 | Inland customs posts are abolished between Castile and Aragon after earlier cancellation of local autonomy statutes in Aragon and Valencia. |
| 1717 | Aug. 31 | All internal customs offices are abolished. Spain becomes a customs-free union. |
|  | Oct. 25 | Sale of Asian silks and other fabrics is prohibited to encourage domestic production. |
| 1718 |  | A royal textile factory is established in Santander (and later in El Escorial) to improve the quality of textile weaving. |
|  | Nov. 23 | Labor grants (encomiendas) are made crown property, and new tax laws are applied to holders of such grants. As a result, this colonial labor system quickly disappears. |
| 1742 |  | Jerónimo de Uztáriz (1702?–1742?) advocates a postmercantilist policy in his *Teoría y práctica de comercio y marina*. |

## FERNANDO VI (1746–1759)

### Dynasty

Fernando m. Barbara de Braganza (1711–1758) of Portugal. They have no surviving children.

### Favorites/Chief Ministers

The marqués de la Ensenada continues in office until the loss of the South American colony of Sacramento to Portugal makes him unpopular in 1754.

José de Carvajal y Lancaster (1696–1754) pursues more aggressive colonial and economic policies until his sudden death.

Ricardo Wall y Devreus (1695–1777), a Spaniard of Irish extraction, becomes foreign minister from 1754 to 1763.

### Political Life

1749        The intendant system is intensified between 1749 and 1768.

1751        Tariff protection for Catalan textiles is achieved through reciprocity agreements with Britain and France.

### War and Diplomacy

1748    Apr. 30    The T. of Aix-la-Chapelle sees Austria acknowledge Farnesio's sons as rulers of Parma, Piacenza, and Guastalia, while Spain recognizes the Pragmatic Sanction.

1750        The T. of Madrid resolves boundary issues concerning Paraguay (Colônia do Sacramento) with Portugal.

1752    June 14    In the T. of Aranjuez, Spain and Austria sign a mutual guarantee of the Italian truce.

1753    Jan. 11    A concordat with the Vatican gives greater royal control over ecclesiastical administration in exchange for greater flexibility of the church in colonial society.

1756    June 24    France defeats Britain in Minorca and occupies the island.

### Colonies

1756        The Royal Company of Barcelona is created for colonial trade.

1758        The Assembly of Merchants is formed in Madrid to enter the colonial trade.

## Economics

1748            In the T. of Aachen, Britain negotiates a special tariff reduction
                for goods imported into Spain by selling the slave monopoly
                back to the Spaniards.

1749   Oct. 10  The marqués de la Ensenada creates a single tax (catastro)
                levied on income from rural and urban property. It is not put
                totally in place until 1770 and does not apply to all classes.

1750            Despite the Caravajal-Keene agreement, Spain is unable to
                obtain from Britain or France commercial reciprocity or revision
                of the navigation laws, which prohibit exporting goods to these
                countries in Spanish ships.

1752   Dec. 4   The Company of Five Guilds is created for colonial trade and
                quickly becomes one of the largest.

1753   Nov.     Construction of the Castilian canal begins as a project to
                improve agricultural conditions.

1758            The royal Mesta tax is abolished to encourage agricultural
                stability.

## Culture

Ignacio de Luzán (1792–1754), a student of the Italian
philosopher Vico, becomes Spain's leading Baroque writer.

# AGE OF THE ENLIGHTENMENT, 1759–1788

## CARLOS III (1759–1788)

### Dynasty

María Anna of Saxony (1724–1760) d. a year after becoming q.
of Spain. Carlos does not remarry. *Children:* Carlos IV (1748–
1819), k. of Spain 1788–1808; Fernando (1751–1825), k. of
Naples 1759–1808, k. of the Two Sicilies 1816–1825.

1785            Carlos III considers dividing the Spanish empire to create a
                monarch for the Americas. The plan is not carried out before his
                death.

### Favorites/Chief Ministers

The marqués de Esquilache (1700–1785) and the marqués de
Grimaldi (1720–1786), advisors to Carlos in Naples, continue
their work in Spain, but loss of Florida in 1763, inflation, and
bad harvests make them unpopular. The riot of 10 Mar. 1766,
when prohibition of traditional capes and hats (to make
identification of criminals easier) causes the "Motón de
Esquilache," leads to their disfavor.

Pedro Pablo Abarca de Bolea, the conde de Aranda (1719–1798), is the Francophile leader of the Council of Castile who expels the Jesuits and promotes agricultural reform. His opposition to participation in the War of American Independence for fear of its impact on the Spanish colonies lessens his stature.

José Moñino, the conde de Floridablanca (1728–1808), is a lawyer from Murcia who follows a regalist program of reform designed to strengthen the crown. His philosophy, however, goes beyond the liberal aristocratic policies of Aranda.

## Political Life

| 1761 | May | Urban reconstruction of Madrid is ordered. |
|---|---|---|
| 1763 | Apr.? | Carlos III orders the first restriction of ecclesiastical mortmain. |
| 1766 | Mar. 10 | Riots in Madrid discredit the Jesuits for leading the unrest. Local government reform creates appointive municipal councils, a modern provincial structure, and a professional bureaucracy. |
| 1767 | Apr. 2 | The Jesuits are expelled as enemies of the crown. |
| 1769 | | University reform permits a greater degree of academic freedom. |
| 1770 | | Major tax reforms weaken noble and ecclesiastical exemptions. |
| 1778 | | The Inquisition tries Pablo de Olavide (1725–1802), an associate of Campomanes in the reform of agrarian and educational affairs. The verdict is inconclusive. |
| 1783 | Mar. 18 | All stigmas attached to work are abolished by Carlos III. The traditional idea of the Caballero is destroyed. |

## War and Diplomacy

| 1761 | Aug. 15 | In the Third Family Pact, Spain and France agree to defend the Bourbon states of Italy and of one another if attacked by a third party. |
|---|---|---|
| 1762 | Jan. 2 | Britain declares war on Spain and Naples. Spain invades Portugal in a minor campaign and succeeds in taking Colônia do Sacramento in southern Brazil. Havana and Manila are captured by Britain. |
| | Feb. 4 | Spain and France amend their earlier pact by allying vs. Britain in the Seven Years' War. |
| 1763 | Feb. 10 | The Peace of Paris ends the war by returning Havana and Manila to Spain. France gives Louisiana to Spain as compensation for its loss of Florida. The French empire in America is lost. |
| 1767 | May 20 | Peace treaty with Morocco is signed. |

| 1771 | Jan. | Spain cedes the Malvinas (Falkland) Islands to Britain after expulsion of settlers threatens war. French unwillingness to aid Spain damages the Bourbon alliance. |
| 1774 | Dec. | The siege of Melilla by the sultan of Morocco and Algiers leads to a North African war. Its end is inconclusive. |
| 1776 | June 27 | Aid to the rebels in North America vs. Britain is ordered. |
| 1778 | Mar. 11. | France takes Dominica and Fernando Poo as payment for Louisiana in the T. of Pardo. |
| 1779 | June 23 | In the War of American Independence, Spain joins France in supporting the United States vs. Britain. Gibraltar withstands the siege. |
| 1782 | Feb. 5 | Spain regains Minorca from Britain after a successful campaign that began in Dec. 1781. |
| 1783 | Sept. 3 | By the T. of Versailles at the end of the American war, Spain's recapture of Florida and Minorca is recognized. |

## Colonies

| 1761 | Aug. 15 | The Seven Years' War begins. Many of its campaigns are in the colonies. |
| 1763 | Mar. 4 | The mission of José de Gálvez studies the empire to increase revenues and end smuggling. His work continues until 1771. |
| | | The General Trading Company of the Five Greater Guilds of Madrid is chartered to enter colonial trade. |
| 1765 | Oct. 15 | A general colonial trade reform abolishes the convoy system (flota) and allows nine Spanish ports to trade freely with the colonies. The Castilian monopoly of trade is broken. |
| 1772 | July 5 | Free trade in colonial cotton is permitted for all Spanish ports. |
| 1778 | Feb. 2 | Royal control over shipping to the viceroyalties of Peru, Chile, and Buenos Aires is abolished. |
| | May 11 | Portugal abandons its claim on Fernando Poo to Spain. |
| | Oct. 12 | Colonial free trade is formally promulgated. |
| 1780 | Nov. | The Tupac Amaru revolt in Peru opposes Spanish labor policies and administration. |
| 1781 | May 9 | Bernardo de Gálvez recaptures Pensacola from the British in the Florida colony. |
| | June | The Spanish Philippines Company is created. |

## Economics

| 1760 | May 15 | Carlos III abolishes protectionism for textiles. Catalan production is harmed. |
| 1765 | July 11 | Abolition of price ceilings on grain is announced. |

| 1766 | May 2 | Municipal common lands are made available for private purchase to stimulate agricultural production. |
| 1771 | Apr. 9? | Pedro Campomanes and the conde de Aranda write the first land reform act for unworked ecclesiastical lands or former Jesuit properties. The plan includes resettlement of landless peasants and recruitment of skilled foreign farmers. |
| | Sept. 14 | Importation of all cotton textiles is prohibited. |
| 1775 | | Founding of the Royal Economic Society of Madrid gives royal support to economic change. |
| 1776 | | The Superintendency of Mails and Posts is created. Postal service becomes a regular function of the government. |
| 1780 | Sept. 20 | Royal promissory notes introduce paper currency. |
| 1782 | | Founding of the Bank of San Carlos produces the first national bank of Spain. |
| 1788 | June 15 | The right to enclose land is granted by the crown after centuries of resisting such legislation in order that the Mesta's flocks might pass freely between northern and southern pastures. |

## Culture

Benito Jerónimo Feijóo y Montenegro (1676–1764) writes *Teatro crítico universal* and *Cartas eruditas*, which adopt Jansenism as the main philosophic current of the Spanish Enlightenment. He stresses the limitation of the papacy's authority, better clerical education, and the reduction of ecclesiastical wealth.

The painter Francisco José de Goya y Lucientes (1746–1828) begins his long career as the court's portrait artist.

The conde de Peñaflorida organizes a physiocratic organization called the Economic Friends of the Nation to sponsor model farms, scientific projects, and educational experiments in support of enlightened goals.

Pedro Rodríguez de Campomanes, the conde de Campomanes (1723–1802), proposes in his *Tratado de la regalía de amortización* the redistribution of religious property to improve agriculture and the national economy. His *Discurso sobre el fomento de la industria popular* advocates the program of the Economic Friends of the Nation.

# AGE OF THE FRENCH REVOLUTION, 1788–1808

## *CARLOS IV (1788–1808)*

### Dynasty

| | | |
|---|---|---|
| 1765 | Dec. 9 | Carlos m. María Luisa of Savoy (1751–1819). *Children*: Carlota (1775–1830), q. of Portugal; Luisa (1782–1824), q. of Etruria (Parma); Fernando VII (1784–1833), k. of Spain 1808 and 1814–1833; Carlos María Isidro (1788–1855), founder of the Carlist line who styled himself as Carlos V 1833–1855; María Isabel (1789–1848), allegedly Manuel Godoy's daughter; Francisco de Paula (1794–1865), allegedly Godoy's son and the father of Francisco de Asís (1822–1902), husband of Isabel II. |
| 1789 | Sept. 30 | The Pragmatic Sanction abrogates the Salic laws of succession because Carlos IV had been born in Italy, making it technically illegal for him to succeed his father. The abrogation is done in a secret session of the Cortes, but the legislation is never published. Abrogated in 1830 but reaffirmed two years later, the Sanction allowed Fernando VII to name his infant daughter Isabel as his successor, a shock to the followers of his brother, Carlos. |
| 1801 | Jan. | Carlos informally surrenders his rule to favorite Manuel Godoy after a decade of misrule at home and a vain effort abroad to succeed Louis XVI in France. |
| 1807 | Oct. 30 | Carlos IV arrests Fernando for having created his own cabinet and for planning to take complete control of the monarchy. He is freed on 5 Nov. |
| 1808 | Mar. 16 | The Tumult of Aranjuez sees Crown Prince Fernando lead a violent effort to displace Godoy. |
| | Mar. 19 | Godoy is imprisoned. Carlos IV abdicates to Fernando VII. |
| | Mar. 23 | Gen. Joachim Murat occupies Madrid with the French army to protect the royal family. |
| | Mar. 31 | Carlos IV protests to Napoleon Bonaparte that his abdication has no validity. |
| | Apr. 1 | Napoleon orders Murat to arrest Carlos and Fernando. |
| | Apr. 9 | Carlos and María Luisa take refuge in the Escorial. |
| | Apr. 10 | Fernando leaves Madrid for France to seek support from Napoleon for his succession. |
| | Apr. 30 | Carlos and María Luisa arrive at Bayonne to meet with Napoleon. |
| | May 5 | Carlos surrenders all claims to the throne. |

> May 6        Fernando abdicates as king after pressure by Napoleon.

## Favorites/Chief Ministers

> The conde de Floridablanca continues as chief minister of
> Carlos (1788–1792) and follows the same policies of regalism
> and reform he used in the reign of Carlos III. Increasingly,
> however, he runs into complications caused by the French
> Revolution.
>
> Manuel Godoy (1767–1851) is a guardsman who becomes
> María Luisa's favorite and is made a colonel in the Royal
> Bodyguards. On 27 Nov. 1789, he becomes a Knight of the
> Order of Santiago despite being a commoner. On 21 Apr. 1792,
> he is made duque de Alcudia and later becomes a grandee and a
> councilor of state. His rise is completed on 17 Nov. 1792, when
> he becomes chief minister. He remains the most powerful
> politician in Spain thereafter until 1808, but his greed makes
> him constantly seek new honors and riches.

## Political Events

| | | |
|---|---|---|
| 1790 | June 18 | Hispano-French relations worsen after an unsuccessful French attempt to assassinate Floridablanca. |
| 1792 | Feb. 28 | The conde de Aranda replaces Floridablanca as chief minister after waging a long campaign for the office. Floridablanca's Francophilia and a tax revolt by Galicians contribute to his downfall. |
| | Nov. 17 | Manuel Godoy replaces Aranda as chief minister. The ostensible reason is the need for military leadership after the French victory over Austria makes Spain vulnerable to the French Revolution. |
| 1793 | Mar. | France declares war vs. Spain. |
| 1794 | Feb. 3 | Juan Bautista Picornell leads an unsuccessful republican uprising against the monarchy. |
| 1795 | Sept. 4 | Godoy is made the "Prince of Peace" for his negotiations with the French at the T. of Basle. |
| 1797 | Dec. 15 | The reformer Gaspar Melchor de Jovellanos (1744–1811) is made minister of justice to counter growing criticism of Godoy's corrupt use of power. Jovellanos represents the enlightened tradition of Carlos III. |
| 1798 | Mar. 28 | Francisco Saavedra replaces Godoy as chief minister after war with Britain creates a near-bankruptcy. |
| | Aug. 7 | Illness forces Saavedra to resign. |

| | Aug. 15 | Jovellanos also resigns due to illness. Rumors circulate widely that Jovellanos and Saavedra have been poisoned. |
| --- | --- | --- |
| | Aug. 20 | Mariano Luis Urquijo (1768–1817) becomes chief minister. A lawyer from Bilbao, he is close to Godoy and continues his influence in the government. |
| 1800 | Dec. 6 | Lucien Bonaparte (1775–1840) visits the Spanish court and becomes Godoy's confederate. They propose a marriage alliance between Napoleon Bonaparte and the infante María Isabel. The treaty is rejected by Paris, but the fortunes of Spain and France are closely linked thereafter. |
| 1801 | Jan. | Pedro Ceballos (1764–1840) replaces Urquijo as chief minister after Pius IX's complaints about Urquijo's anticlericalism. Ceballos is a cousin by marriage of Godoy and a compliant facade for him. Urquijo is jailed for a year and Jovellanos for seven. |
| | Mar. 31 | Godoy is made commander of the Spanish military. He remains the power behind the throne until Apr. 1808, a period almost exclusively devoted to international affairs. |
| 1808 | Apr. 21 | Godoy, jailed by the Tumult of Aranjuez, is freed by the French. He flees to southern France on 27 Apr. to meet Napoleon Bonaparte, who rejects his plea for a crown within the French empire. |
| | May 2 | Public disorder in Madrid creates a major crisis when the last members of the court leave for France. The violent French military reaction is portrayed in Goya's *The Disasters of War*. |

## War and Diplomacy

| 1789 | Apr. | The Nootka Sound incident begins when Spain and Britain make rival claims for Vancouver Island. War seems imminent until it becomes clear that France is in no position to aid Spain. An indemnity is paid to protect continued Spanish activity in the area on 28 Oct. 1790. |
| --- | --- | --- |
| 1793 | Mar. 7 | France declares war vs. Spain when Carlos IV claims the French throne through his Bourbon ancestry. |
| | Mar. 23 | The Spanish join Britain vs. France in the First Coalition. |
| | Nov. 7 | Spanish armies invade France and threaten Perpignan. |
| 1794 | Feb. 8 | The capture of Figueras begins a successful French campaign in Catalonia and the Basque Provinces. |
| 1795 | July 22 | In the T. of Basle, Spain ends its war with France by making border concessions and surrendering Dominica to France. |
| 1796 | Aug. 18 | In the T. of San Ildefonso, Spain allies with France vs. Britain. The heir-apparent Fernando is antagonized by Godoy's title of "Prince of Peace" earned by his negotiations. |

| 1797 | Feb. 14 | The French and Spanish fleets are defeated at Cape St. Vincent by the British. |
| 1798 | Nov. | Britain recaptures Minorca from Spain. |
| 1800 | Oct. 1 | By the Second T. of San Ildefonso, Spain receives the kingdom of Etruria (formerly Parma) for Luisa and her husband Luis, and in return cedes Louisiana to France. The treaty is protested by Luisa's brother, who had been deposed by Napoleon. |
| 1801 | Mar. 31 | In the War of Oranges, Spain declares war on Portugal to satisfy Godoy's ambition for his own throne and Napoleon's anger at Portugal's refusal to close its ports to British shipping. |
| | June 6 | By the T. of Badajoz, Portugal's defeat in the War of Oranges forces it to pay an indemnity and cede Olivenza and surrounding territory to Spain. France receives a part of Guyana and the promise that Portugal will close its ports to Britain. |
| 1802 | Mar. 27 | By the T. of Amiens, Spain receives Minorca from Britain in exchange for Trinidad. |
| | Sept. | Napoleon annexes Parma and Piacenza to France. |
| 1803 | Oct. 9 | By the T. of Neutrality, Napoleon demands a subsidy from Spain for its military protection. |
| 1804 | Dec. 12 | In the War of the Third Coalition, Spain declares war on Britain. |
| 1805 | Oct. 21 | In the Battle of Trafalgar, the Spanish fleet is badly defeated. |
| 1806 | Nov. 21 | Spain joins the continental blockade. |
| 1807 | Oct. 27 | By the T. of Fontainebleau, Portugal is partitioned between Godoy and Napoleon. Prince Fernando fails to overthrow Godoy's influence at the court and is imprisoned in Oct. and Nov. |

## Colonies

| 1789 | | Free trade raises greater demands for foreign trade and leads to growing conflict between peninsulars and creoles. |
| 1797 | Dec. 18 | Spanish colonies are allowed to trade with neutral non-Spanish ports for the duration of the war. |
| 1803 | Aug. 9 | The Venezuelan Simón Bolívar (1783–1830) travels to Europe seeking support for Latin American independence. |
| 1804 | Jan. 1 | Haiti frees itself from France in the first successful Latin American colonial revolt. |
| 1806 | Feb. | The Miranda expedition begins when Francisco Miranda (1754–1816) sails from New York City to Venezuela with 200 men to free the colony. He is unsuccessful. |

|      | Apr.    | Sir Home Popham attacks Buenos Aires, but he is defeated by a creole army. |
|------|---------|---------------------------------------------------------------------------|
| 1807 | June    | Bolívar returns to Caracas where he conspires to overthrow Spanish rule. |
| 1808 |         | Viceroy José de Iturrigaray (1742–1815) unsuccessfully seeks the crown of Mexico. |

## Economy

| 1795 | | Gaspar Melchor de Jovellanos writes the *Informe sobre la ley agraria* as the most radical assertion of freeing the land from entailment. |
|------|--|------|

## Culture

| 1799 | Feb. | The *Caprichos*, Goya's satirical engravings of the royal family, are shown for the first time. |
|------|------|------|

# WAR OF INDEPENDENCE, 1808–1814

## *JOSÉ I (JOSEPH BONAPARTE, 1808–1814)*

### Dynasty

### FRANCE

| 1808 | June 6  | Napoleon names his brother Joseph (1768–1844) as k. of Spain. Joseph becomes José I. José m. Julia Clary (1771–1845). *Children*: Zenaida (1801–1854); Carlota (1802–1839). |
|------|---------|------|
|      | June 15 | The Assembly of Bayonne meets under French auspices. It writes Spain's first constitution. |
|      | July 7  | José swears to uphold the new constitution. |
|      | July 20 | José enters Madrid. |
|      | July 25 | José is proclaimed the king of Spain in Madrid. |
|      | July 31 | José flees Madrid for Vitoria after the defeat at Bailén. |
|      | Nov. 4  | Napoleon Bonaparte arrives at the Spanish border. |
|      | Dec. 3  | Napoleon recaptures Madrid. |
|      | Dec. 4  | Napoleon proclaims the destruction of the feudal regime and abolishes the Inquisition and monasteries. |
| 1809 | Jan. 19 | Napoleon Bonaparte returns to France. |
|      | Jan. 22 | José reoccupies Madrid. |

1810    Feb. 1    José travels to Seville and later to Malaga and Granada in an effort to consolidate his regime.

1812    Aug. 31   José flees Madrid for Valencia as the peninsular army approaches, but he reconquers the capital on 4 Nov.

1813    Mar. 17   The king abandons Madrid for Valladolid.

        May 25    José tries to rally his forces, but the defeat at Vitoria forces him to return to France on 29 June.

## SPAIN

Carlos IV lives in freedom at the Château de Chambord in France, while Fernando is put under house arrest at Valençay for the duration of French occupation of Spain.

## Favorites/Chief Ministers

## FRANCE

Count Francisco de Cabarrús (1752–1810), a Spanish nobleman (though born in France) and founder of the Bank of San Carlos, acts as minister of finance for José.

Mariano Luis de Urquijo (1768–1817), former minister under Carlos IV and ally of Godoy (who barred him from joining the National Junta), acts as secretary of state until 1813.

Gonzalo de O'Farrill (1754–1831), descendant of an Irish adventurer and a captain general during the reign of Carlos IV, acts as the minister of war in the new government.

Other officials include the ministers Miguel José de Azaña, the duque de Santa Fe, and the Neapolitan André-François Miot de Melito.

## SPAIN

The former councilor of state Gaspar Melchor de Jovellanos (1744–1811) becomes the leader of a national junta and later of the Cortes of Cadiz. He uses the French occupation to seek popular sovereignty and economic reform.

The Aragonese grandee José Palafox (1780–1847) is the defending general at the siege of Saragossa and represents a conservative patriotic spirit, often critical of republicanism.

The man of letters Agustín Argüelles (1776–1844) takes over the writing of the Constitution of 1812 at the Cortes of Cadiz after Jovellanos's death.

The Asturian conde de Toreno (1786–1843), a historian and classical liberal, supports the constitution to obtain a free market for Spain.

## Political Life

### FRANCE

| | | |
|---|---|---|
| 1808 | July 14 | The Bayonne constitution is written by 150 Francophile delegates (afrancesados) as Spain's first constitutional document. It provides an advisory Cortes elected by universal manhood suffrage, protection of individual rights, and reform of justice and taxation. Many of its provisions are never promulgated. |
| | Aug. 26 | José wins confirmation of his title at an extraordinary convocation of the General Council of Biscay in Bilbao. |
| | Dec. 12 | Napoleon Bonaparte issues eight decrees in Burgos that abolish the Inquisition, limit landholdings, and do away with the vestiges of feudalism. |
| 1809 | Feb. 6 | José introduces a modern cabinet system with seven ministries (foreign relations, church, finance, war, navy, Indies, and interior) and a council of state. |
| | Apr. 2 | José begins secret negotiations with the General Junta for a truce, but he fails. |
| | May 22 | The parliament of the Supreme Council begins its supervision of the ministries and the formulation of state policy. |
| | June 3 | The parliamentary council consolidates the public debt by issuing bonds and liquidating part of the crown properties. Some of the church's properties are added to these assets on 9 June, with an office to handle land sales. The bonds often circulate as paper currency and are printed in excess of the property that backs them, and as a consequence, inflation soon becomes a serious problem. |
| | Aug. 19 | The title of grandee is abolished, and the aristocracy is converted into a service nobility. |
| 1810 | Feb. 8 | Catalonia, Aragon, Navarre, and the Basque provinces are removed from José's control by Napoleon Bonaparte. Burgos and Vallodolid are added in May. José rules only New Castile, the southern half of Old Castile, and Andalusia. José threatens to abdicate. |

| | | |
|---|---|---|
| | Apr. 17 | Prefects are established to supervise local governmental matters of finance, the police, and the militia. A prefectural council coordinates their efforts at the national level, but it is unable to control corruption. |
| | Oct. 10 | The king announces an administrative reform for Andalusia, but it is not carried out. |
| 1811 | May 15 | José confers with his brother in Paris and demands the restoration of his territory and monarchical powers. No compromise is reached, and José returns to Madrid on 15 July. |
| 1812 | Mar. 13 | José's powers are restored by his brother as Napoleon prepares to leave for the Russian front. |
| | Mar. 16 | The bad harvests of the previous summer begin to create famine conditions in Madrid. |

## SPAIN

| | | |
|---|---|---|
| 1808 | May 11 | The Council of the Regency, set up to continue royal government, finds itself unable to rule effectively. |
| | May 24 | Asturias rises against the French. Provincial juntas organize opposition, and popular revolt spreads throughout much of Spain during the next few months, particularly in the south. |
| | Sept. 26 | A National Junta is formed in Aranjuez to replace the Council of the Regency. It has twenty-four members representing a variety of national groups. |
| | Oct. 26 | The Junta declares war on France. |
| 1809 | May 22 | The Junta creates a Cortes to write a new Spanish constitution. |
| 1810 | Sept. 24 | The Constituent Cortes begins its sessions in Cadiz. |
| 1812 | Mar. 19 | The Constitution of Cadiz includes a grant of popular sovereignty and fundamental liberties to the Spanish people, separation of church and state, and confiscation of church property. Colonial reforms are postponed. |
| 1813 | Feb. 22 | The Inquisition is abolished. |
| | Sept. 14 | The Constituent Cortes ends its sessions. On 14 Jan. 1814, the regular Cortes meets for the first time in Cadiz and quickly moves to Madrid. It is abolished by Fernando VII on 4 May 1814. |

## War and Diplomacy

| | | |
|---|---|---|
| 1808 | July 19–21 | Spanish irregulars defeat Gen. Pierre Dupont at the battle of Bailén. |
| | Aug. 21 | Sir Arthur Wellesley (later the duke of Wellington) leads a British expeditionary army in freeing Portugal at the start of the War of Independence. |

|      | Nov. 5 | Napoleon Bonaparte arrives in Vitoria and relieves José as commander of the Grande Armée. He recaptures Madrid on 4 Dec. after the battle of Somo Sierra (30 Nov.) but leaves on 19 Dec. for the front at Valladolid and returns to France on 19 Jan. 1809. |
| 1809 | Jan. 19 | The British under Sir John Moore are defeated at La Corunna by Mar. Nicolás Soult and the French. |
|      | Feb. 20 | Spanish defenders surrender Saragossa to the French. |
|      | Apr. 22 | The duke of Wellington returns to Portugal with a new British army to take command of the anti-Napoleonic opposition. |
|      | July 27 | The battle of Talavera between Britain and France protects Portugal but is unable to prevent the French from advancing into Estremadura and Andalusia. The battle continues through 29 July. |
|      | Nov. 19 | The French defeat the Spanish irregulars in the battle of Ocaña, threatening Andalusia. |
| 1810 | Jan. | José captures all of Andalusia except Cadiz. |
|      | July 10 | Mars. André Masséna and Nicolás Soult defeat Wellington at Ciudad Rodrigo and drive the Peninsular Army back to Portugal. |
| 1811 | Mar. | The siege of Almeida and Badajoz prepares the way for a new counterattack by Wellington in Spain. His campaign continues in Apr. |
|      | May 5 | Wellington defeats Masséna at the battle of Fuentes de Oñoro. |
|      | May 16 | The battle of Albuera sees Gen. William Carr, viscount of Beresford defeat Soult as French power weakens. |
| 1812 | Jan. 14 | Mar. Louis Gabriel captures Valencia. |
|      | Jan. 19 | The British capture Ciudad Rodrigo. |
|      | Mar. 16 | José is restored as French military commander in Spain. |
|      | Apr. 6 | Badajoz falls to Wellington. |
|      | July 20 | José and the Army of the Center leave Madrid to join Mar. Auguste de Marmont and the French Army of Portugal at Salamanca. |
|      | July 22 | Wellington wins the battle of Salamanca. |
|      | Aug. 3 | José returns to Madrid, only to evacuate it on 9 Aug., making his headquarters in Valencia. |
|      | Aug. 12 | Wellington enters Madrid but marches north on 1 Sept. |
|      | Nov. 2 | José regains Madrid. |
| 1813 | May 17 | José leaves Madrid for the last time. |
|      | June 21 | The French are routed at the battle of Vitoria. |
|      | July 12 | Mar. Soult replaces José as commander of the French forces in Spain. |

Oct. 7        Wellington crosses the Bidassoa River into France as the
              Peninsular War ends.

## Economy

1809    June          The Bourbon debt is paid by José through new bonds based on
                      national properties. They soon fall to a quarter of their face
                      value.

1812    June 17       The assets of ecclesiastical communities are seized by order of
                      the Cortes of Cadiz.

1813    Jan. 4        The Cortes orders the abolition and sale of communal lands.

        July 8        The order to enclose farm property stresses the development of
                      private property.

## Colonies

1808    Sept. 15      José de Iturrigaray is deposed as viceroy of New Spain.

1809    Sept. 16      Miguel Hidalgo y Costilla (1753–1811) leads Mexico in revolt
                      vs. Spanish rule. He is captured on 21 Mar. 1811 and executed
                      on 26 July.

1810    Apr. 19       A revolt in Caracas begins the War of Independence in South
                      America. Simón Bolívar, one of its leaders, is sent to Britain to
                      obtain aid. Francisco de Miranda returns from Britain to take
                      command of the revolutionary forces.

        Apr. 20       A United States of Venezuela is created.

        June 25       A colonial revolt begins in Río de la Plata, led by Manuel
                      Belgraño (1770–1820), but he is overthrown by a junta loyal to
                      Fernando on 25 May 1810. Fighting continues, however.

        July 10       Spanish colonies in South America refuse to acknowledge
                      Joseph Napoleon as José I.

        Oct. 10       Colombia breaks relations with Spain.

1811    May 4         Paraguay announces its independence from Spain.

1812    July 5        The T. of San Mateo in Venezuela ends Miranda's attempt to
                      win independence. He dies in prison at Cadiz on 22 Dec.
                      1815.

1813    Aug. 4        Bolívar briefly captures Caracas.

        Nov.          José María Morelos y Pavón (1765–1815) captures Oaxaca and
                      holds it until Dec.

1814    Jan.          Bolívar leads an army from Colombia to capture Caracas where
                      he gains the title of "liberator."

        Sept. 14      A congress at Chilpancingo declares Mexican independence
                      from Spain. It fails when Morelos dies in 1815.

# THE RESTORATION, 1814–1833

## *FERNANDO VII (1814–1833)*

### Dynasty

| | | |
|---|---|---|
| 1814 | Feb. 5 | Fernando is freed by Napoleon. |
| | Mar. 24 | Fernando VII returns to Spain after six years of captivity in France. |
| 1820 | Mar. 9 | The king is forced to accept a constitutional monarchy. |
| 1823 | Oct. 1 | Fernando VII is restored to the throne for a second time. |
| 1829 | Dec. 9 | After childless marriages to María Antonia of Naples (1784–1808), Isabel of Braganza (1797–1818), and María Josefa Amalia of Saxony (1806–1829), Fernando m. María Cristina de Borbón in 1829 (1806–1878). *Children*: María Isabel Luisa (1830–1904), q. of Spain as Isabel II 1843–1868; Luisa Fernanda (1832–1897), duchess of Montpensier (by marriage to a son of Louis Philippe). |
| 1830 | Mar. 29 | While ill, Fernando signs a decree permitting a return to Salic law, abolished by Carlos IV in 1789. Female succession is not permitted, thus making Fernando's younger brother Carlos heir to the throne. |
| | Oct. 10 | María Isabel Luisa (Isabel II) is born. |
| 1832 | Oct. 1 | Liberals are strengthened in the court at the expense of the Carlists. |
| | Dec. 31 | Fernando once again abolishes Salic law to allow his infant daughter to succeed him. |
| 1833 | Apr. 29 | Carlos declares himself the legitimate successor to Fernando. |
| | May 6 | Fernando condemns Carlos to exile. |
| | Sept. 18 | Fernando VII dies. María Cristina is made regent for her daughter, Isabel II. |
| | Oct. 27 | The Carlist revolt begins in northern Spain. Of crucial importance is a defense of conservative Catholicism vs. liberal ecclesiastical disestablishment. Hapsburg financial support of the Carlists is constant until 1885. |

### Favorites/Chief Ministers

| | | |
|---|---|---|
| 1820 | Jan. 1 | Maj. Rafael de Riego (1785–1823) is a Masonic military officer who revolts vs. orders to embark for Latin America and pronounces in favor of the Constitution of 1812. Although initially defeated, the army rallies to him by 7 Mar., and he enters Madrid on 12 Aug. |

|       | Aug. 5  | Gen. Evaristo San Miguel (1785–1862) is a radical general who attempts to create a dictatorship to support the military radicals. |
| 1821  | Mar. 1  | The liberal former secretary of the Cortes, Eusebio Bardaxi (1776–1842) is sufficiently moderate to be the only politician acceptable to the king. He provokes provincial radicals to further violence. |
| 1822  | Feb. 28 | Francisco Martínez de la Rosa (1787–1862) creates a conservative liberal ministry that proposes constitutional reforms unacceptable to the military radicals. He is overthrown on 7 July. Soon after, the European powers decide to intervene in Spain and eventually order the French to aid Fernando in 1823. |
| 1823  | Dec. 6  | The economic liberal Luis López Ballesteros (1782–1853), the finance minister in the first regular cabinet of the second restoration, wins the king's respect for his financial expertise in handling the growing economic crisis. Ballesteros is thus able to slowly popularize liberal thought. |
| 1832  | Oct. 1  | Francisco Cea Bermúdez (1781–1834) is a moderate politician who organizes the first liberal cabinet during Fernando's reign. |

## Political Life

| 1814  | Apr. 22 | Traditionalists demand revocation of the Constitution of 1812. |
|       | May 4   | Fernando VII revokes the Constitution of 1812 to restore absolutism by a royal revolution. |
|       | May 10  | Liberal leaders are arrested to prevent a defense of constitutionalism. |
|       | Sept.   | The first revolt against absolutism fails in La Corunna. Fernando uses more than thirty royal secretaries from 1814 to 1820. |
| 1819  | July    | New unrest with absolutism spreads. |
| 1820  | Jan. 1  | Maj. Rafael de Riego begins his revolts vs. royal plans to crush Latin American independence. The army gathered for this enterprise ultimately marches on Madrid and captures the capital on 7 Mar. |
|       | Mar. 24 | A provisional council for the re-creation of a constitutional monarchy is named. |
|       | July 9  | A new radical Cortes assembles in Madrid. |
|       | Nov.    | A royalist regency is created in Seo de Urgel. |
| 1822  | June 30 | Fighting between army and civilians begins in Madrid. |
|       | July 8  | The July Days revolt sees the royalists fail to free Fernando. |
| 1823  | Feb. 19 | The Regency Riots bring the threat of a republic. |
|       | Mar. 8  | Fernando is forced to swear loyalty to the Constitution of 1812. |

| Mar. 10 | The king is taken captive and imprisoned in Cadiz for planning to overthrow the revolution. |
| May | French troops sent by the Congress of Verona enter Spain. |
| Aug. 31 | The French victory at the battle of Trocadero restores absolutism. |
| Oct. 1 | Fernando returns to the throne. All legislation passed between 1820 and 1823 is annulled. |
| Nov. 7 | Maj. Riego is executed. Military tribunals continue to purge liberals and radicals. |

| 1827 | Sept. 10? | The Revolt of the Aggrieved in Catalonia is the first Carlist revolt against Fernando. Economic difficulties frustrate the punishment of moderate liberals. |
| 1830 | July 18 | The July Revolution in France begins to create unrest in Spain. |

## War and Diplomacy

| 1814 | May 30 | By the T. of Paris, Britain and France agree to persuade Spain to end slavery in Cuba. |
| | July 5 | The restoration of Fernando is formally approved by the European powers. He promises to crush the Latin American rebellions and consider means to abolish Cuban slavery. |
| 1815 | Feb. 8 | By the Declaration of Vienna, slavery is abolished in principle, but Cuban slavery remains an unresolved problem. |
| | June 8 | At the Congress of Vienna, Spain is urged to take action vs. the Latin American revolts. |
| 1817 | Sept. 17 | The Anglo-Spanish T. opens West Indian trade to Britain. |
| 1818 | Oct. 24 | Spain cedes Florida to the United States. |
| 1822 | Nov. 22 | The Congress of Verona discusses Spanish problems. |
| 1823 | Apr. 7 | On orders of the Congress of Verona, the duke of Angoulême leads a French invasion of Spain to restore Fernando VII. |

## Colonies

| 1814 | Apr. | Uruguay declares its independence. |
| | June | Bolívar is forced to abandon Caracas and return to Colombia. |
| | | Spain reconquers Chile. |
| 1815 | May 11 | Gen. Pablo Morillo (1775–1837) reconquers Venezuela. |
| 1816 | Mar. | The Mexican revolt is temporarily stalled. |
| | July 9 | Río de la Plata declares its independence and creates the nation of Argentina. |
| | Nov. 20 | The Assembly of Angostura, convened by Bolívar, renews the struggle for independence. |

| 1817 | Feb. 15 | José de San Martín (1778–1850) declares the independence of Chile. |
| | May | Xavier Miña, a Spanish liberal, attempts to free Mexico. |
| 1818 | Apr. 5 | Bernardo O'Higgins wins final independence of Chile at the battle of Maipú. |
| 1819 | Aug. 7 | Simón Bolívar's capture of Bogota liberates New Granada from Spanish rule. |
| | Dec. 17 | The constitution of Gran Colombia is proclaimed. |
| 1821 | Feb. 24 | The Plan of Iguala in Mexico marks a conservative reaction to the Revolution of 1820 in Spain. |
| | Aug. 24 | The T. of Cordoba grants Mexico independence. |
| 1822 | June 24 | The battle of Carabobo frees Venezuela and Colombia from Spain. |
| | July 28 | José de San Martín announces the independence of Peru. |
| 1823 | June 24 | The United Provinces of Central America are created. |
| | July 21 | Agustín de Iturbide becomes emperor of Mexico. |
| | Dec. 2 | The Monroe Doctrine hinders Spain's reconquest of the Americas. |
| 1824 | Dec. 12 | The battle of Ayachucho is the last major Spanish effort to regain the colonies. |
| 1829 | Mar. | Spaniards are expelled from Mexico. A military effort fails to recapture the former colony on 28 Sept. |

## Economy

| 1815 | Mar. 3 | Fernando decrees the sale of uncultivated and unused lands of the crown. |
| 1819 | July 22 | The king orders the sale of these lands to peasant cultivators. |
| 1820 | Oct. 1 | The revolutionary Cortes reconfirms the 1812 seizure of ecclesiastical property. |
| | Oct. 26 | The property of monastic orders with fewer than twenty-five members is confiscated. |
| 1822 | June 29 | Half the uncultivated lands and royal property are offered for sale to ease the national debt. |
| 1826 | Mar. 8 | A new tariff law creates the concept of a protected market. The London bond market is used to raise new capital. |
| 1829 | June 9 | The Bank of San Carlos is reorganized as the Bank of San Fernando. |
| 1831 | Sept. 10 | The Madrid stock exchange is created by royal decree. |
| 1832 | Feb. 20 | The mechanization of the Catalan textile industry begins. The Güell and Muntadas families control the market and greatly increase productivity. |

## THE LIBERAL AGE, 1833–1868

### ISABEL II (1833–1868)

#### Dynasty

| | | |
|---|---|---|
| 1833 | Sept. 18 | María Cristina is made regent for her daughter Isabel. |
| 1834 | July 11 | Carlos (now styling himself Carlos V) returns to Spain and appoints Tomás Zumalacárregui commander of the Carlist forces. |
| 1840 | Oct. 7 | Queen regent María Cristina abdicates in the wake of Moderate party opposition. Gen. Baldomero Espartero becomes regent on 9 May 1841. |
| 1843 | Nov. 10 | Isabel II comes of age and is crowned. |
| 1844 | Mar. 23 | María Cristina returns to Spain with the support of the moderates and France. |
| 1846 | Oct. 18 | The Spanish marriages occur when Isabel II m. her cousin, Francisco de Asís, the duque de Cadiz (1822–1902), who was the son of Francisco de Paula (himself allegedly the son of Manuel Godoy and Queen María Luisa). The infanta Luisa Fernanda m. the duque de Montpensier (1824–1890), son of Louis Philippe of France. *Children*: Isabel (1851–1931), the countess of Girgenti; Alfonso (1857–1885), k. of Spain 1875–1885; Pilar (1861–1879); María de la Paz (1862–1940) m. Louis Ferdinand of Bavaria; Eulalia (1864–1958) m. Antoine of Orleans. |
| 1854 | Aug. 28 | Isabel is forced to flee the country briefly to escape the Revolution of 1854. |
| 1855 | Apr. 28 | The queen threatens abdication to block further confiscation of church lands. |
| | July 7 | Don Carlos V d. in exile. Carlist leadership goes to his son, the conde de Montemolín (1818–1861), who returns on 2 Apr. 1860, in an abortive bid for the throne as Carlos VI. Gen. Jaime Ortega (1816–1860), captain general of the Balearic Islands and a secret Carlist, is defeated and executed; Montemolín renounces his claims. |
| 1866 | June 30 | The duque de Montpensier and his wife Luisa are exiled for plotting with Gen. Juan Prim to seize the throne. |
| 1868 | Aug. | A political campaign vs. Isabel blames her for misrule and military favoritism. |
| | Sept. 18 | Adm. Juan Bautista Topete y Carballo (1821–1885) rebels in Cadiz to replace Isabel with her sister Luisa. The Gens. Prim and Serrano join the rebellion to end Bourbon rule altogether. |
| | Sept. 30 | Isabel II flees Spain for French exile. |

## Favorites/Chief Ministers

| | | |
|---|---|---|
| 1834 | Jan. 15 | Francisco Martínez de la Rosa returns to form a conservative liberal cabinet aligned with the regency to deal with the Carlist threat. |
| 1836 | Sept. 15 | Juan Álvarez Mendizábal (1790–1853) is able to obtain British loans to finance government efforts in the Carlist war. |
| 1840 | Sept. 9 | Gen. Baldomero Espartero (1793–1879) forms a regency that deposes María Cristina. His Progressive party becomes the chief political faction of the period. |
| 1843 | June 27 | Gen. Ramón Narváez (1800–1868) establishes a moderate provisional government in Valencia. He becomes premier on 4 Sept. 1844, after the progressives are weakened by democratic and republican factions. He heads six other cabinets between 1846 and 1868. |
| 1851 | Jan. 14 | Juan Bravo Murillo (1803–1873) forms an authoritarian moderate cabinet to negotiate a new concordat to stop the confiscation of church property. He goes into exile on 14 Dec. 1852. |
| 1854 | June 28 | Gen. Leopoldo O'Donnell (1809–1867) enters politics in the Revolution of 1854 and replaces Espartero on 13 July 1856, for three months. His liberal union cabinet, however, rules from 1858 to 1863. |

## Political Life

| | | |
|---|---|---|
| 1834 | Apr. 10 | The Royal Statute creates limited constitutional rule. |
| | Aug. | Radical unrest in the south calls for reforms. |
| | Dec. 25 | An amnesty is granted to liberals. |
| 1836 | May 15 | The Moderate party cabinet of Francisco Javier Istúriz unsuccessfully defends the Statute of 1834. |
| | Aug. 12 | The Sergeants' Revolt in La Granja occurs when María Cristina gives in to radical pressure and restores the Constitution of 1812. A progressive cabinet supported by Mendizábel and the radical militia takes office on 15 Aug. |
| 1837 | June 28 | The Constitution of 1837 seizes all monastic property. The single chamber created in 1812 is replaced by a Senate and a House of Deputies. |
| 1838 | Nov. | An unsuccessful conservative revolt by Gen. Narváez is put down in Seville. |

| | | |
|---|---|---|
| 1840 | June 4 | A new municipal statute provokes further moderate and progressive enmity over the franchise and degree of popular political participation. |
| 1842 | May | The moderates begin to oppose Gen. Espartero and the progressives. |
| | Nov. 15 | An uprising in Barcelona vs. Espartero fails. |
| 1843 | May 27 | An unsuccessful rising vs. Espartero in Reus worsens the political situation. |
| | June 11 | Moderates and anti-Espartero progressives in Alicante, Valencia, and Cartagena are led by Narváez vs. Espartero. |
| | July 15 | Narváez captures Madrid. |
| | Aug. 14 | Espartero flees to Britain. |
| | Nov. 20 | A coalition cabinet formed by Salustiano Olózaga (1805–1873) unsuccessfully mediates the difficulties between the moderates and progressives. |
| | Dec. | Radical and Democratic party unrest is crushed by Narváez. |
| 1844 | Mar. 28 | The Civil Guard is created as a national constabulary. |
| 1845 | May 24 | The moderate constitution of 1845 is based upon the limited Constitutionalism of the 1834 Royal Statute. |
| 1848 | Mar. 1 | Fear of revolution provokes a grant of emergency powers to Narváez. |
| | Mar. 26 | Unrest in Madrid is caused by the Revolution of 1848 elsewhere in Europe. |
| | June 23 | Carlist unrest in Catalonia ends in Nov. |
| 1852 | May | Bravo Murillo's proposed constitutional reforms are opposed as too authoritarian. |
| 1853 | Mar. | A railway scandal threatens to destabilize politics when the court's involvement is revealed. Controversy lasts until Dec. |
| 1854 | Jan. 13 | Five progressive gens. are exiled to prevent political problems. |
| | June 28 | Gen. O'Donnell leads a progressive seizure of power. The Revolution of 1854 fails to achieve lasting reform, but it does call for the writing of a new constitution. |
| | July 17 | Madrid rises in insurrection to return Espartero to power. |
| | Sept. 17 | Progressives and democrats form a new Liberal Union party to create a new reform program. |
| | Nov. 8 | The Constituent Cortes begins its sessions. Its major accomplishment is an economic modernization of Spain. |
| 1856 | Jan. 13 | The Constitution of 1856 embodies popular sovereignty and liberty of belief (but not of worship), but this constitution is never promulgated. |
| | July 17 | Espartero returns to power when debate over a more democratic constitution leads to an insurrection in Madrid. |

|        | Oct. 12  | Narváez's return marks the end of the Revolution of 1854, but he is unable to reestablish the hegemony of the moderates. |
| 1858   | June 30  | O'Donnell and the Liberal Union return after months of reactionary rule. They stay in office for almost five years with a policy of new colonial expansion, economic growth, and electoral manipulation. |
| 1863   | Mar. 3   | A railway scandal topples O'Donnell and brings back a moderate cabinet led by the marqués de Miraflores. |
| 1865   | June 21  | O'Donnell forms his final cabinet. He dies on 5 Nov. 1867. |
| 1866   | June 22  | The mutiny of San Gil supports a more democratic general., Juan Prim, the conde de Reus. It fails, but the revolutionary movement continues to grow. |
|        | July 10  | Narváez creates an authoritarian cabinet in response to national unrest. He dies on 23 Apr. 1868. |
|        | Aug. 16  | A secret meeting of progressives and democrats in Belgium creates a new revolutionary coalition. |
| 1868   | Apr. 23  | Luis González Bravo's moderate cabinet antagonizes public opinion by defending Isabel II, more unpopular than ever before in a period of economic decline and rising court expenses. |
|        | July 7   | A new liberal union and progressive pact excludes democrats and republicans from the planned overthrow of the monarchy. |

## War and Diplomacy

| 1834 | Apr. 22  | The Quadruple Alliance of Britain, France, and Portugal supports Spanish constitutional changes. |
| 1835 | June 24  | The Carlist military leader, Tómas Zumalacárregui, d. in the battle of Bilbao. |
|      | July 16  | The government defeats the Carlists in the battle of Mendigorria. |
|      | Sept. 12 | The "royal expedition" of don Carlos reaches Madrid before it is defeated—the last Carlist offensive. |
| 1838 | Jan.     | The First Carlist War disintegrates into isolated guerrilla campaigns. |
| 1839 | Feb. 17  | Final Carlist military efforts collapse. |
|      | Apr.     | Negotiations with the Carlists begin. |
|      | Aug. 31  | The T. of Vergara ends the First Carlist War. |
|      | Oct. 26  | Local privileges are abolished in the Basque Provinces. |
| 1840 | May 28   | Espartero ends Carlist guerrilla activity in the north. |
| 1846 | Feb.     | The war of Matinero ("early risers" or the religiously devote) begins. Sometimes called the Second Carlist War, it lasts until 1849. |

|      | Oct. 18  | The Spanish marriages cause a breakdown of relations between France and Britain over British fears of French and Spanish cooperation. |
| 1851 | Mar. 16  | The Concordat of 1851 is signed with Rome. Church expenses are paid from bonds raised by sale of confiscated church lands. |
| 1859 | Nov. 28  | The Moroccan War begins when O'Donnell seizes Ceuta and Melilla as part of a new imperial policy. |
| 1861 | Sept. 1  | Santo Domingo is annexed by Spain. |
|      | Dec. 8   | Spain cooperates with France in the seizure of Mexico. |
| 1862 | Apr. 9   | Spanish intervention in Mexico ends. |
| 1865 | May 5    | Spain bows to U.S. pressure and relinquishes Santo Domingo. |
|      | Sept. 29 | The War of the Pacific with Chile begins. |
| 1866 | Mar. 31  | The Spanish navy bombards Valparaiso. |
|      | May 2    | Chile defeats Spain in the battle of Callao. |
|      | June 15  | The War of the Pacific ends without diplomatic settlement. |

## Economy

|      |          |  |
| 1834 | Mar. 6   | Titles are confirmed for all disentailed properties sold in 1813 and 1822. |
| 1837 | July 29  | All ecclesiastical property is confiscated by the state. |
|      | Aug. 1   | Titles to confiscated property are reconfirmed. |
|      | Nov. 1   | A new naval law prohibits purchase of ships abroad to benefit domestic ship construction. |
| 1839 | Oct. 25  | New laws promote the mining industry. |
| 1841 | July 9   | A new tariff protects more than 1,500 items. |
| 1843 |          | The business cycle drops steeply; a recession begins. |
| 1844 | Dec. 31  | A royal order begins the distribution of railway franchises. |
| 1845 | Apr. 9   | Sale of confiscated ecclesiastical properties is restricted by the moderates as a step toward the Concordat of 1851. |
| 1848 | Oct. 28  | The first rail line opens in Barcelona. Almost five thousand km. of track is built by 1865. |
| 1849 | Oct. 5   | Another tariff reform reduces the number of excluded items. |
| 1851 | Mar. 16  | The papacy accepts the property confiscations in Spain. Property held by the state but not yet distributed is returned, and the state pays an annual sum in support of the clergy. |
| 1855 | May 1    | The progressives again order communal lands to be sold in order to lower the public debt, despite the Concordat's prohibition of further sales. |
|      | Nov.     | The Bank of Bilbao is founded. |
| 1856 | Jan. 28  | The Bank of Spain is created as a branch of the Treasury. |

| | | |
|---|---|---|
| | Sept. | Spain complies with the Concordat by ending land sales. |
| 1859 | | The first blast furnace is constructed at La Felguera. |
| 1860 | Apr. 4 | New talks with the papacy over land seized in 1855–1856 end with the promise of a future financial settlement with the church. |
| 1865 | | Development of the Bessemer process creates a boom in the Asturian iron and steel industry. |

### Culture

Ángel de Saavedra, the duque de Rivas (1791–1865), develops the genre of romantic poetry and drama.

José de Espronceda (1808–1842) is another romantic writer of note.

José Zorrilla (1817–1893) becomes the most widely read romantic poet of the era.

Gustavo Adolfo Bécquer (1836–1870) writes both poetry and prose of a psychologically romantic nature.

Rosalía de Castro (1837–1885) is the first woman writer of the modern period.

| | | |
|---|---|---|
| 1859 | Aug. | The Floral Games are started in Catalonia as poetry contests to encourage the linguistic development of the Catalan language. |
| 1867 | Sept. | Krausist professors at the University of Madrid are fired by a neo-Catholic minister of education. |

## CONSTITUTIONAL MONARCHY, 1868–1873

### AMADEO I (1871–1873)

### Dynasty

| | | |
|---|---|---|
| 1868 | Oct. 3 | Don Juan (1822–1887), the second son of Carlos V, abdicates as the Carlist pretender. Don Carlos VII (1848–1909), don Juan's son, becomes the new Carlist pretender on 19 Oct., but his claim to the throne is rejected by Prim and Serrano. |
| 1870 | Jan. | The crown of Spain is rejected by Gen. Espartero, Luís I (k. of Portugal), Ferdinand of Saxe-Coburg (widower of Maria II, q. of Portugal 1834–1853), and Prince Leopold of Hohenzollern-Sigmaringen, whose candidacy indirectly causes the Franco-Prussian War. By Nov., only one foreign prince, the duke of Aosta, Amadeo of Savoy, is left in the running. |
| | Mar. 12 | The duque de Montpensier kills Enrique (son of Francisco de Paula) in a duel. Montpensier's candidacy for the kingship is ruined. |
| | June 25 | Isabel abdicates in favor of her son, Alfonso. |

| | Nov. 16 | The duke of Aosta, Amadeo of Savoy (1845–1890), the second son of King Victor Emmanuel II (1820–1878) of Italy is selected as k. of Spain. |
| | Dec. 30 | Amadeo arrives in Cartagena. His chief supporter, Gen. Prim, is dead, assassinated in Madrid, a victim of a plot rumored to have been led by the duque de Montpensier (brother-in-law of Isabel II) or the progressives. |
| 1871 | Jan. 3 | Amadeo is crowned. |
| 1872 | May 2 | Don Carlos VII returns to Spain, but is initially unsuccessful in starting another war for Carlist succession. He briefly returns to his exile. |
| 1873 | Feb. 11 | Amadeo abdicates due to his own unpopularity and the political paralysis of the constitutional monarchy. |

## Favorites/Chief Ministers

| 1869 | June 18 | Gen. Juan Prim, the conde de Reus and the marqués de Castillejos (1814–1870), becomes premier of a coalition cabinet that forms the constitutional monarchy. He is assassinated on 30 Dec. 1870, before Amadeo can take the throne. |
| | | Gen. Francisco Serrano (1810–1885) acts as the president of the constitutional monarchy, works closely with Prim before the latter's death, and continues as the bulwark of Amadeo's regime in its first year. |
| 1871 | June 24 | Manuel Ruiz Zorrilla (1833–1895) is the leading radical republican whose cabinet seeks major social change. He is handicapped by national turmoil and his own hostility to Amadeo. |
| | Dec. 21 | Práxedes Mateo Sagasta (1827–1903) becomes the new head of a revitalized Progressive party. He dissolves the Cortes because it is dominated by radicals and republicans, but the elections return thirty-six Carlists, forcing him to resign on 10 May 1872. Political unrest continues to grow until Amadeo abdicates. |

## Political Life

| 1869 | Feb. 14 | The Constituent Cortes meets to write a new constitution. |
| | May 9 | A rally at Tortosa leads to a pact between provincial representatives vs. the central government. |
| | May 21 | The Cortes defends monarchy as the only form of government for the Constitution of 1869. |
| | June 6 | The Constitution of 1869 creates a constitutional monarchy with a weak Senate and a strong House of Deputies. It is modeled on the Constitution of 1812. |

|        |          |                                                                                                                                                                                                                                                                        |
|--------|----------|------------------------------------------------------------------------------------------------------------------------------------------------------------------------------------------------------------------------------------------------------------------------|
|        | June 28  | The Cortes is dissolved, and new elections are scheduled. When it reassembles on 15 Sept., it is dominated by radicals and republicans.                                                                                                                                  |
| 1872   | Apr. 20  | Growing rural unrest in the north and south threatens the political balance. New parliamentary elections on 24 Apr. return thirty-five Carlist deputies who protest the military budget and threaten a new Carlist war.                                                   |
|        | Nov.     | Andalusian towns break away from the central government to form cantons, or city-states. In the north, the Second Carlist War, which lasts until 1876, begins.                                                                                                           |
| 1873   | Feb. 11  | The first republic is proclaimed after Amadeo's abdication.                                                                                                                                                                                                             |

## Colonies

|        |          |                                                                                                                                                                                                                                                               |
|--------|----------|---------------------------------------------------------------------------------------------------------------------------------------------------------------------------------------------------------------------------------------------------------------|
| 1868   | Sept. 23 | The "Grito de Lares" movement begins to seek Puerto Rican independence. Rebels seize Lares, but are defeated on 5 Oct.                                                                                                                                        |
|        | Oct. 5   | The Ten Years' War begins as Cuba's first rebellion to achieve independence. Formation of a Republican party by Carlos de Céspedes intensifies debate over slavery and the usefulness of autonomy vs. independence.                                           |
| 1869   | Apr. 2   | The Convention of Guamairo by Cubans asks for U.S. annexation.                                                                                                                                                                                               |
| 1870   | Mar.     | Gen. Prim's tax increase and use of conscription to strengthen the army antagonizes many Cubans. The rebellion intensifies, and Spain eventually sends more soldiers than in the earlier War of Independence throughout Latin America.                        |
| 1872   | Jan.     | The Cavite revolt of Filipino soldiers is punished by death sentences vs. Filipino priests and the arrest and deportation of critics who demand that the Philippines become a province of Spain and its administration be opened to Filipinos.                 |
|        | Dec. 23  | The intention to abolish slavery in Cuba and Puerto Rico is announced. The Cortes approves the measure on 23 Mar. 1873, but the law is put aside by the regime's instability and not promulgated until 1880.                                                   |

## Economics

|        |          |                                                                                         |
|--------|----------|-----------------------------------------------------------------------------------------|
| 1868   | Oct. 19  | The real is replaced by the peseta as the basic unit of currency.                       |
|        | Nov. 22  | Foreign ships are allowed to carry Spanish cargos.                                       |
| 1869   | Mar. 14  | A change in mining law abolishes royal ownership and allows privatization.               |

## Culture

Julián Sanz del Rio (1814–1869) emerges as a leading educator after a visit to Germany in 1843, which brings him in contact with Karl Christian Friedrich Krause. Sanz's Krausism stresses democracy, self-improvement, and the autonomous university.

# THE FIRST REPUBLIC, 1873–1874

## Dynasty

1873    July        Don Carlos returns to Spain and establishes his capital at Estella. The Carlists control most of the area north of the Ebro River.

## Favorites/Chief Ministers

Francesc Pi i Margall (1824–1901) rules only a short time in 1873, but his federalist ideas are very influential.

## Political Life

1873    Feb. 12     The president of the Cortes, Estanislao Figueras (1819–1882), is unable to successfully follow a policy of republicanism from above and goes into exile.

        June 9      Pi's federalist cabinet lasts only until 18 July.

        July 19     Pi's successor, Nicolás Salmerón (1838–1908), faces a Cortes divided by Carlism and cantonalism. He begins the campaign vs. cantonalism, but Carlism is a more difficult problem.

        July 27     A new federalist constitution includes provisions that separate church and state, create religious freedom, abolish the nobility, and provide democratic representation with an elected president and a responsible ministry.

        Aug. 20     Emilio Castelar (1832–1899), a liberal, creates a cabinet that lasts until 2 Jan. 1874. He diminishes radicalism and secures the power to defeat the cantons.

1874    Jan. 2      The army leader and conqueror of the south, Gen. Manuel Pavía y Rodríguez (1827–1895), overthrows Castelar. Praetorianism replaces civilian politics.

        Jan. 5      Gen. Francisco Serrano returns to power in a military cabinet during the worst months of the Second Carlist War.

        Sept. 4     Sagasta forms a new cabinet that is secretly committed to a Bourbon restoration.

Dec. 3     The historian and old Liberal Union politician Antonio Cánovas del Castillo (1828–1897) forms a cabinet that is a prelude to his ministerial regency.

Dec. 29    Gen. Arsenio Martínez Campos (1831–1900) announces his support for a Bourbon restoration. Cánovas converts his cabinet into a ministerial regency to restore Alfonso XII.

## War and Diplomacy

| | | |
|---|---|---|
| 1873 | July 26 | Gen. Manuel Pavía destroys the canton of Valencia. |
| | July 31 | Cantonalism in Seville is defeated. Cadiz also falls on 4 Aug. |
| | Aug. 21 | The Carlists win their first victory in the Second Carlist War at the battle of Arrichulegui. |
| | Sept. 19 | The Carlists lose the battle of Tolosa. |
| | Sept. 28 | A radical naval attack on Alicante is repulsed by the central government. |
| | Oct. 6 | The Carlists win the battle of Maneru in Navarre. |
| | | The battle of Escombrera Bay keeps the cantonalists from breaking the blockade of Cartagena. |
| | Oct. 8 | The central government wins the battle of La Junquern in Catalonia vs. the Carlists. |
| 1874 | Jan. 12 | Cartagena is captured by the central government to end the cantonal revolt. |
| | Feb. 28 | The Carlists besiege Bilbao. President Serrano takes command in the field. |
| | May 2 | Gen Manuel de la Concha (1819?–1874) outflanks the Carlists to end the siege of Bilbao. |
| | June 6 | The Carlists lose Gondesa. |
| | June 27 | The government's military commander, Gen. Concha, is killed in battle. |
| | July 13 | The Carlists capture Cuenca. |
| | July 17 | The Carlists massacre their prisoners. |
| | Aug. 14 | Gen. Serrano's government is recognized by the major European powers. |
| | Sept. 9 | The Carlists are defeated at Mora. |
| | Nov. 4 | The Carlists bombard Irun. |
| | Nov. 10 | The government defeats the Carlists in the battle for Irun. |
| | Dec. 10 | Carlist ranks break, and they take refuge in Pamplona. |

## Colonies

1874   Dec. 4   The cabinet and ministerial regency of Antonio Cánovas del Castillo creates a conservative consensus to end the Cuban war without reforms.

## Economy

1874   Mar. 19   The Bank of Spain expands its role in the economy by taking a thirty-year monopoly on the issuance of bank notes.

# THE RESTORATION, 1875–1885

## Dynasty

1875   Jan. 1   Gen. Serrano departs for exile in France.

Jan. 10   Alfonso (1857–1885) arrives in Barcelona and on 14 Jan. in Madrid.

Feb. 6   Alfonso leads the army in capturing Pamplona. Estella remains in Carlist hands.

1876   Feb. 19   Estella falls. Don Carlos leaves Spain on 28 Feb. for exile.

June 1   Alfonso is crowned as Alfonso XII.

1878   Jan. 23   Alfonso m. Mercedes, the daughter of the duque and duquesa de Montpensier, his first cousin. She d. on 23 June of the same year from a gastric fever.

1879   Nov. 25   Alfonso m. María Cristina de Hapsburg (1858–1929). *Children*: María de las Mercedes (1880–1904), duchess of Bourbon; María Teresa (1882–1912); Alfonso (1886–1941), k. of Spain 1902–1931.

1885   Nov. 26   Alfonso XII d. suddenly. His son is born posthumously.

## Favorites/Chief Ministers

Antonio Cánovas del Castillo (1828–1897) is premier in 1876–1879 and again in 1880–1881 and 1884–1885. His power is absolute and his belief that politics must be contained within a small elite puts stress upon strong political controls.

Práxedes Mateo Sagasta (1827–1903) is Cánovas's partner. After creating what later becomes the Liberal Fusion party, he agrees to peacefully avoid controversy and so becomes premier in 1881–1882.

## Political Events

| 1875 | Feb.      | The ministerial regency ends academic freedom and begins censorship. |
| 1876 | Sept. 12  | An interim cabinet allows Cánovas to campaign for a conservative Cortes. |
|      | Oct. 4    | Elections for the Constituent Cortes are won by the monarchists. |
| 1876 | Feb. 14   | The Cortes assembles to write a new constitution. |
|      | June 30   | The Constitution of 1876 gives official political parties more freedom while banning parties of the Left and Right. Cánovas draws upon British parliamentary practice for inspiration. |
| 1879 | Mar. 3    | Cánovas's first cabinet ends with the elevation of Gen. Martínez Campos as premier in recognition of his Cuban victory. |
|      | Dec. 9    | Cánovas forms a new cabinet. |
| 1880 | May 23    | The Liberal Fusion party is created by Sagasta. |
| 1881 | Feb. 10   | Sagasta's first cabinet comes to office. He and Cánovas will share power to avoid responsibility and conceal scandals. |
| 1882 | May 1     | The Spanish Socialist party (PSOE) begins to organize. It sponsors the General Workers' Union (UGT). |
| 1883 |           | The "Black Hand" movement of agrarian anarchists conducts a wave of terrorism in southern Spain. Trials and severe punishments follow in 1884. |
| 1885 | Oct. 1    | The Catalan *Memoria a Alfonso XII* is the first open sign of growing regionalist sentiment since the First Republic. |

## War and Diplomacy

| 1875 | July 6   | All Carlists are expelled from Castile. |
|      | Aug. 26  | Seo de Urgel is surrendered by the Carlists. |
| 1876 | Feb. 28  | The fall of Estella ends the Second Carlist War. |

## Colonies

| 1876 | Feb.     | Gen. Arsenio Martínez Campos is appointed commander of Spanish forces in Cuba. |
| 1878 | Feb. 11  | The Truce of Zanjón issues a general pardon to most rebels in Cuba and demands that others go into exile. |
| 1879 | Nov.     | Martínez Campos makes the 1872 law abolishing slavery effective in Cuba as of 1888. This order is later modified. |

## Economy

| 1875 | July     | The olive oil crop fails 1875–1877. |
| 1876 | July 21  | The Basque region is integrated into a final customs union with the rest of the country. |

| 1881 | The Transatlantic Co. is founded in Barcelona. It quickly becomes the largest Spanish shipping corporation. |
| 1890–1892 | Phylloxera destroys grapevines of the wine industry. |

## THE REGENCY, 1885–1902

### Dynasty

| 1885 | Dec. 2 | María Cristina is appointed regent. |
| 1886 | May 17 | Alfonso is born six months after his father's death. |
| 1902 | May 17 | Alfonso XIII comes of age. |

### Favorites/Chief Ministers

| 1885 | Nov. 26 | Sagasta creates his second cabinet, which lasts until 1890 because the king's death raises fear that Cánovas's authoritarianism may provoke difficulties. Sagasta also leads cabinets in 1892–1895, 1897–1899, and 1901–1902. |
| 1890 | July 5 | Cánovas returns to office when universal manhood suffrage makes government stability important, but when instability fails to materialize, Sagasta returns in 1892. Cánovas's last cabinet comes in 1895–1897. He is assassinated on 8 Aug. 1897. |

### Political Life

| 1887 | Feb. 27 | The Senate adopts trial by jury. It goes into effect on 29 May 1889. |
| 1890 | May 5 | Universal manhood suffrage is passed by the Cortes. |
| | July 5 | Cánovas replaces Sagasta as premier. The next period sees political corruption reach new heights. |
| 1892 | Mar. 7 | The *Bases de Manresa* is written by Catalan regionalists to demand greater autonomy. |
| 1893 | June 3 | The colonial question of Cuba and the Philippines produces a deadlock in the Cortes. |
| | Nov. 7 | An anarchist bombs the Liceo theater in Barcelona. |
| 1894 | | The Basque Nationalist party (BNP) is created under the leadership of Sabino de Araña. |
| 1895 | Mar. 21 | The last Cánovas cabinet is installed. He is assassinated on 8 Aug. 1897. |
| 1900 | Feb. 19 | The Regionalist Union is formed by Narciso Verdaguer and Francesc de Asís Cambó in Catalonia. |

| 1901 | Mar. 9 | The last Sagasta cabinet comes to office. |
| | May 19 | Catalan regionalists win seven parliamentary seats. The House of Deputies includes 224 liberals, 157 monarchists, and 16 republicans. |

## War and Diplomacy

| 1898 | Feb. 15 | The USS *Maine* explodes in Havana harbor. |
| | Mar. | "Yellow journalism" in the American press urges intervention in Cuba. |
| | Apr. 24 | The United States declares war on Spain. |
| | May 1 | The Spanish fleet is defeated in Manila harbor by Adm. George Dewey (1837–1917). |
| | June 6 | American troops begin landing in Cuba. |
| | Aug. 12 | A peace protocol is signed to end the Spanish-American War. |
| | Dec. 10 | The T. of Paris forces Spain to cede Guam, Puerto Rico, and the Philippines to the United States, while Cuba becomes independent. The U.S. Senate confirms the treaty 6 Feb. 1899. |

## Colonies

| 1886 | Sept. | Cuban slavery is abolished two years earlier than stipulated. |
| 1887 | Mar. 10 | The formation of an autonomy party in Puerto Rico calls for colonial reform. |
| | | A Filipino leader, José Rizal (1861–1896), publishes *Noli Me Tangere*, which bitterly attacks Spanish rule in the Philippines. |
| 1891 | | Rizal publishes *El filibusterismo*, which criticizes the slowness of Spanish reform in the Philippines. |
| 1892 | Jan. | The Cuban writer and patriot José Marti (1853–1895) creates the Cuban Revolutionary party to seek Cuban independence. |
| | Feb. 28 | The Club Boriquén is founded as a nationalist group in New York City to help Cuba win its freedom. |
| | July 2 | The Philippine League is created by José Rizal as a Filipino independence movement. |
| | July 6 | Rizal is arrested by Spanish officials and later executed in prison on 30 Dec. 1896. |
| | | A secret society, the Katipunan (Sons of the People), led by Andrés Bonifacio, organizes to force the Spaniards out of the Philippines. |
| 1893 | June 3 | Cuban colonial reforms are proposed in the Cortes. Guerrilla movements begin in Cuba and the Philippines. |

| 1894 | Feb. 13 | The Maura Law is introduced in the Philippines to curb growth of large estates by requiring deeds to be obtained within a year. Filipinos, however, benefit little from the law, and the independence movement grows. |
| 1895 | Feb. 24 | José Martí returns to Cuba to lead the Cuban revolt. He is killed on 19 May. |
|  | Dec. 22 | A Puerto Rican section is added to the Cuban Revolutionary party. |
| 1896 | Feb. 10 | Gen. Valeriano Weyler (1838–1930), captain general of Cuba, declares a state of emergency. |
| 1897 | Mar. | The Pact of Biacnabato is signed by Emilio Aguinaldo and Spanish officials. The Filipino independence movement is forced to abandon its rebellion, and its leaders are exiled to Hong Kong. |
|  | Oct. 4 | Sagasta grants Cuba autonomy without withdrawing Spanish forces. |
| 1898 | Jan. 11 | Gen. Andrés González Muñoz (1840–1898), governor of Puerto Rico, is assassinated. |
|  | Feb. 9 | An autonomous Puerto Rican government is organized; its legislature meets on 17 July, only to be temporarily suspended by the U.S. Gen. John R. Brooks on 9 Dec. |
|  | May 1 | Adm. George Dewey destroys the Spanish fleet in the harbor at Manila. |
|  | May 12 | San Juan is shelled. |
|  | June 10 | The U.S. navy attacks Guantánamo. |
|  | June 17 | Santiago is shelled. |
|  | June 23 | The United States begins landing troops in Cuba. |
|  | July 3 | The Spanish fleet is destroyed off Santiago. The city surrenders on 16 July. |
|  | July 25 | The United States invades Puerto Rico. |
|  | Aug. 12 | Spain asks for a truce to consider peace terms. Manila surrenders the next day. |

## Economy

| 1888 |  | Naval construction undergoes a major period of growth in the Basque Provinces. |
| 1902 | Feb. 17 | The first Spanish general strike takes place in Barcelona. |

## Culture

Juan Valera (1827–1905) creates an Andalusian school of literature.

Francisco Giner de los Ríos (1839–1899), a student of Sanz del Río, becomes the presiding force behind the Institute of Free Education and is the leading Krausist.

Gumersindo de Azcárate (1840–1905), a Krausist and director of the Institute, is the leading essayist and reformer of the period.

Benito Pérez Galdós (1843–1920), a prolific writer, vividly examines national history in the multivolume *Episodios nacionales*.

Joaquín Costa (1846–1911), an Aragonese lawyer and political essayist, provides early leadership for reform.

Ángel Ganivet (1865–1898) inspires the Generation of 1898 by his *Idearium español*, a bitter castigation of the politics that caused the colonial crisis.

Azorín (José Martínez y Ruiz, 1874–1967), a Castilian journalist with strong nationalist tendencies, encourages debate about the Spanish-American War.

## SPAIN AFTER THE DISASTER, 1902–1923

### Dynasty

| | | |
|---|---|---|
| 1902 | May 17 | Alfonso XIII comes of age and is crowned. |
| 1905 | June 1 | An unsuccessful anarchist attack is made on Alfonso while he is on state tour in Paris. |
| 1906 | May 18 | Alfonso m. Victoria Eugenia of Battenberg (1887–1969), Queen Victoria's granddaughter. Their carriage is bombed after the ceremony. *Children*: Alfonso (1907–1938), resigned rights to the throne in 1933; Jaime (1908– ), resigned rights to the throne in 1933; Beatriz (1909– ); María Cristina (1911– ); don Juan (1913– ), given succession rights in 1941 but never rules; Gonzalo (1915–1934). |
| | May 31 | An attempted royal assassination is made in Asturias. |
| 1921 | May | The kind denounces parliamentary government. |
| | July 21 | Rumors of royal involvement in the Anwal disaster in Morocco circulate. |
| 1923 | July 11 | The Cortes reviews the Anwal disaster. |
| | Sept. 19 | Alfonso agrees to take action vs. the liberal parliamentary government. |

### Favorites/Chief Ministers

| | | |
|---|---|---|
| 1902 | Dec. 12 | Francisco Silvela (1845–1905) succeeds Cánovas as liberal conservative premier but is unable to achieve any major reforms. |

| 1903 | Dec. 6 | Antonio Maura (1853–1925) follows Sagasta as Liberal Fusion leader and premier. He seeks a reform of local government in his cabinets of 1904 and 1907–1909, but fails to obtain it. |

## Political Life

| 1902 | Dec. 12 | The Silvela cabinet creates the Institute of Social Reform. |
| 1903 | Dec. 6 | The Maura cabinet is unable to reform local government laws before it quarrels with the king over military appointments and civilian control of the military. |
| 1906 | Jan. 14 | Alfonso decrees a new law of military jurisdictions during a period of social unrest. Military justice is used to punish political acts. |
| | Feb. 11 | Catalan Solidarity is created as a Catalan regionalist party. |
| 1907 | Jan. 25 | Maura's long cabinet attempts to diffuse regionalism by ending local government corruption. |
| | Apr. 21 | Catalan Solidarity wins 41 of 44 seats in regional elections. Alejandro Lerroux (1864–1949) leads an anticlerical and antiregional Radical Republican party (with subsidies from Madrid). |
| 1909 | July 26 | The Tragic Week in Barcelona reacts to the mobilization of Catalan reserves to serve in Morocco by anticlerical and antigovernment rioting. Constitutional guarantees are suspended. The rioting ends on 31 July. |
| | Oct. 20 | The trial of Barcelona rioters culminates with the execution of the anarchist Francesc Ferrer. |
| | Oct. 21 | Maura's cabinet resigns in the Wake of Tragic Week. |
| 1910 | Feb. 9 | José Canalejas (1854–1912) forms a liberal cabinet. |
| 1911 | Sept. 8 | The anarchosyndicalist National Confederation of Labor (CNT) is founded. It is soon the largest labor organization in Spain. |
| 1912 | Nov. 12 | The liberal premier José Canalejas is assassinated by an anarchist in Madrid. |
| 1913 | Oct. 27 | The cabinet of Eduardo Dato (1856–1921) takes office after Maura makes it clear that he favors a personal dictatorship. |
| 1914 | Apr. 6 | Catalonia receives limited self-government. |
| 1917 | May 26 | Unions are formed in the army to obtain pay increases and take political action. The court and conservative politicians fear that the army has become radicalized and order courts-martial of the leaders. |
| | June 10 | The king dismisses the court-martial order, but junior officers begin to discuss replacing the monarchy with a new regime that can "regenerate" the nation. |

| | | |
|---|---|---|
| | June 11 | The second Dato cabinet faces opposition from Catalans, socialists, and republicans. The military unionists are prosecuted. |
| | July 5 | Catalan deputies in the Cortes demand a constituent assembly to consider autonomy for Catalonia. |
| | July 19 | An illegal Catalan assembly is prevented from meeting. |
| | Aug. 13 | A massive general strike, prohibited by the government, is continued by the CNT after it breaks with the UGT over tactics. The Russian Revolution exerts a strong influence. |
| | Nov. 3 | The cabinet of Manuel García Prieto (1859–1938) bans all political activity. |
| 1918 | Mar. 22 | Maura's cabinet styles itself a "national" government and attempts to develop a dictatorship. It falls on 9 Nov. |
| | Oct. 27 | A congress of agricultural workers demands rural reform. Unrest in Córdoba province reaches a new high when dozens of villages hold general strikes. |
| 1919 | Jan. 24 | The Catalans draft an autonomy program after the government's suggestions are criticized as too weak. |
| | Feb. 5 | A labor dispute at an electrical company in Barcelona leads to a general strike and a lockout. Strong measures to pacify the city fail until late in the year. |
| | Mar. 8 | A strike at the British-owned Río Tinto mine near Huelva creates hostility toward foreign-owned industries. |
| | May | A third agricultural strike in Córdoba forces a military occupation of the province. |
| 1920 | Apr. 15 | The Spanish Communist Party (PCE) is founded. |
| | Aug. 2 | Ángel Pestaña and Andreu Nin travel to Moscow for the second congress of the Comintern. They later reject ties between the CNT, PCE, and the Comintern. In 1930, Nin creates the Trotskyist POUM. |
| | Aug. 14 | The last Maura cabinet supports Gen. Dámaso Berenguer's efforts to obtain a Moroccan victory. Military operations are greatly increased but lead to the Anwal disaster in July 1921. |
| 1921 | Mar. 8 | Premier Eduardo Dato is assassinated. |
| | July 21 | The military disaster at Anwal creates a lasting political crisis. |
| | Oct. 20 | The Cortes debate on Anwal attacks the military. |
| 1922 | May | Francesc Macià forms the Catalan Seperatist party in Barcelona. |
| | June | Investigation of the Anwal disaster finds more than thirty officers and the Supreme Council of the Army and Navy guilty of serious errors. |
| | Dec. 7 | The cabinet of Manuel García Prieto dislodges Liberal–Conservative party rule as political opinion turns against the conservatives and the king. |

| 1923 | July 11 | The Cortes creates a commission to recommend the action to be taken on the fact-finding Picasso report analyzing the Anwal disaster. |
| | Sept. 23 | Gen. Miguel Primo de Rivera (1870–1930) dismisses the Cortes and establishes a military dictatorship. The CNT and liberal parties are banned. |

## War and Diplomacy

| 1904 | Aug. 7 | France and Spain agree to continued Spanish control of the northern Mediterranean coast of Morocco. |
| 1906 | Jan. 16 | The Algeciras conference confirms the French and Spanish protectorates in Morocco while leaving Morocco sovereign. The conference ends on 17 Apr. |
| 1909 | Apr. | A new military campaign begins in Morocco. The mobilization of military reserves leads to the Tragic Week in Barcelona. |
| | July 9 | Attacks by Rif tribesmen on Melilla come in reaction to the Spanish expansion of its territory. Fighting continues until Oct. |
| 1912 | Nov. 27 | A new Franco-Spanish agreement on Morocco allows Spain a free hand in northern Morocco. |
| 1914 | Aug. 7 | Spain declares its neutrality in World War I. |
| 1919 | Jan. 28 | The Spanish Foreign Legion is created. |
| 1920 | | The Rif War intensifies as Spain expands its Moroccan territory. The mountain tribesmen find a talented military leader in Abd al-Krim al-Khatabi who finds it easy to arm his followers from the glut of weapons left over from World War I. |
| 1921 | July 21 | The disaster at Anwal occurs when Gen. Manuel Fernández Silvestre and 20,000 Spaniards are defeated by Rif tribesmen under Abd al-Krim al-Khatabi. More than 12,000 are killed or captured, and Silvestre commits suicide. |

## Economics

| 1912 | Dec. 8 | A CNT congress demands full bargaining rights for labor. |
| 1916 | May 16 | The pact of Saragossa links the CNT and UGT in a protest campaign to fight inflation and low wages. |
| 1917 | Oct. | A farm labor strike begins in the south which will last spasmodically until 1923. |
| 1919 | Feb. 21 | A wave of strikes in Barcelona leads to a state-of-siege declaration by Gen. Joaquín Milans del Bosch. Greater social violence follows. |

1920    May 8      A ministry of labor is created to seek new legislation for strike
                    arbitration and problems of the work place.

        Nov. 8     A lockout of workers by Gen. Severiano Martínez Anido in
                    Barcelona disrupts electrical service and causes many other
                    production cuts.

## Culture

José Echegaray y Eizaguirre (1832–1906) wins the 1904 Nobel
Prize for literature. He is a dramatist.

Santiago Ramón y Cajal (1852–1934) revives scientific studies.
He receives the 1906 Nobel Prize for medicine and physiology.

The Castilian scholar Marcelino Menéndez y Pelayo (1856–1912)
investigates the history of Spanish literature and religious life.

The Basque writer and academic Miguel de Unamuno (1869–
1936) is one of the most famous members of the Generation of
1898. He uses Don Quixote as a paradigm for his examination
of the Spanish soul. In existential philosophy, he writes *Del
sentimiento trágico de la vida* (1913).

Vicente Blasco Ibáñez (1867–1928) develops a highly stylized
neoromantic genre dealing with life in Valencia and the
Levante.

Ramón Menéndez Pidal (1869–1967) revives interest in Spanish
medieval studies.

Antonio Machado (1875–1939) becomes one of the most
popular poets of the modern period.

The Basque novelist Pío Baroja (1872–1956) produces modern
realistic works like *Aurora rojo*.

José Ortega y Gasset (1883–1955) represents the mainstream of
the Generation of 1898, particularly in *España invertrabrata*.
His *Revolt of the Masses* in 1930 gives him a worldwide
reputation. He also founds the *Revista de Occidente* and helps
create *El Sol* as the foremost newspaper in Spain between 1918
and 1936.

Jacinto Benavente (1866–1954) wins the 1922 Nobel Prize for
literature.

## THE FIRST ERA OF DICTATORSHIP, 1923–1931

### Dynasty

1928               The monarchy experiences new unpopularity as the dictatorship
                    is faced by increasing difficulties.

1931    Apr. 14    Alfonso and the royal family leave Spain after a republican victory in the municipal elections.

## Favorites/Chief Ministers

1923    Sept. 12    The florid and colorful Gen. Miguel Primo de Rivera (1870–1930) seizes control of the government to protect the king and becomes the "iron surgeon" of Spanish regeneration. Primo, vaguely influenced by Pope Leo XIII's *Rerum novarum* (1891), is anticacique and antiliberal, while his economics are mildly corporativist and nationalist.

1925    Dec. 3    The socialist UGT leader Francisco Largo Caballero (1869–1946) takes advantage of Primo's anti-CNT prejudice to become a councillor of state. Partly through his efforts labor arbitration procedures are formulated.

The corporatist José Calvo Sotelo (1893–1936) becomes the cabinet minister most responsible for economic modernization and public works. He is also the force behind the reorganization of the state's economic planning and helps create a new ministry of economics.

1929    July    The conservative journalist José Sánchez Guerra (1897–1964) protests Primo's restriction of open politics and conspires vs. him. His rebellion in Valencia is a signal that politicians have lost patience with the dictatorship.

## Political Life

1924    Mar. 8    Municipal reform introduces elective local government offices, but the law is not promulgated until 1931.

        Apr. 14    Primo forms the Patriotic Union as the basis of a single-party system.

        Nov. 7    A border raid on Vera del Bidosa is made by anarchist exiles from France.

1925    Dec. 3    Primo's military cabinet is converted into a civilian one with the addition of Calvo Sotelo, Largo Caballero, and others.

1927    July 26    The Iberian Anarchist Federation (FAI) is formed as a militant anarchist organization. It is closely related to the CNT, but the relationship is often tense.

1928    Apr. 8    Student opposition to the dictatorship leads to strikes and demonstrations.

1929    Jan. 29    An unsuccessful coup vs. the regime is made in Valencia by Sánchez Guerra.

        Mar. 17    The universities are closed for opposing the regime.

1930    Jan. 28     Primo resigns his office as opposition mounts and the depression causes further difficulties.

        Jan. 30     Gen. Berenguer continues the military dictatorship after Primo's departure.

        Aug. 17     The Pact of San Sebastian is made by opposition parties to pursue a common strategy and avoid conflict in future elections. Only the CNT refuses to join.

        Sept.       The end of censorship leads to growing criticism of the regime.

        Dec. 12     A military revolt by elements of the army at Jaca reveals the loss of unity in the military.

1931    Jan. 31     Elections are announced for Apr. Gen. Berenguer resigns on 13 Feb.

        Apr. 12     The republicans win the local elections.

## War and Diplomacy

1924    Jan. 5?     Abd al-Krim al-Khatabi's announcement of a new Rif state creates a new unity between Spain and France.

        Feb. 7      The Tangier convention promises military cooperation between France and Spain in the Rif War.

1925    Sept.       The battle of Alhucemas destroys the Rif rebels.

1926    May         Abd al-Krim al-Khatabi makes peace.

## Economics

1926    Nov. 27     A new corporative labor code creates "mixed juries" to minimize unions in new labor councils dominated by employers and the government.

1927    June 27     Calvo Sotelo nationalizes foreign oil companies to form CAMPSA as the government oil monopoly.

## Culture

The journalist and professor Manuel Azaña (1880–1940) uses republican views and numerous intellectual friendships to become one of the leading politicians of the Generation of 1927.

The doctor and historian Gregorio Marañón (1887–1960) rejects the leadership of Alfonso XIII.

The Andalusian poet and dramatist Federico García Lorca (1898–1936) develops an abstract modern style. He is murdered at the beginning of the civil war.

The writer Ramón Sender (1901–1981) follows the perspective of a moderate leftist.

# THE SECOND REPUBLIC, 1931–1936

## Dynasty

| 1933 | June 11 | The Prince of Asturias, Alfonso, m. a Cuban woman and cedes his rights to the throne. |
| | June 21 | The deaf mute Jaime cedes his rights to the throne. |
| 1934 | | Gonzalo d. in an automobile accident in Austria. |
| 1935 | May | In exile Alfonso XIII criticizes right-wing efforts to restore the monarchy at the expense of national stability. |
| | Oct. | Alfonso's son and heir to the throne, Juan (1913– ), m. María de Mercedes (1910– ) of Borbón-Sicily-Orleans. *Children*: Pilar (1936– ); Juan Carlos (1938– ), k. of Spain 1975– . |
| 1936 | May 10 | Alfonso XIII urges his followers not to use violence in their struggle with the Left. |

## Favorites/Chief Ministers

| 1931 | Apr. 14 | The moderate Catholic republican Niceto Alcalá Zamora (1877–1949) becomes the premier during the early months of the republic, but he resigns in Oct. 1931 over the religious provisions of the new constitution. He is then made president of the republic. After five years he is impeached in May 1936. |
| | Oct. 14 | The leader of the Left Republican party, Manuel Azaña, is made premier and holds office until the spring of 1933. Azaña's persecution by the Right restores his popularity, and he returns as premier after the Popular Front's victory in Feb. 1936. Three months later, after Alcalá's impeachment, he is made president of the republic until the end of the civil war. |
| 1933 | Dec. 12 | The Radical party leader, Alejandro Lerroux (1864–1949), is made premier after a Catholic electoral victory in Nov. 1933 raises fear of clerical fascism. |
| | | The leading Catholic politician, José María Gil Robles (1898–1980), is the power behind Lerroux's premiership. Although he is feared for his ultraright position, Gil Robles is motivated more by a desire to protect Catholicism. |

## Political Life

| 1931 | Apr. 18 | A Catalan regional government is formed. |
|------|---------|------------------------------------------|

      May 3     Lluis Companys creates the left nationalist Esquerra party in Barcelona.

      June 28    Elections for the Constituent Cortes gives a majority to the left republicans and the PSOE (socialists).

      July 14    Debate begins on the constitution.

      Oct. 13    The religious provisions of the constitution force the resignation of the premier, Alcalá Zamora, with Azaña succeeding him.

      Dec. 9     The constitution is adopted. A regular government led by Azaña is installed.

1932   Jan. 19    The CNT revolts in Llobregat, Catalonia.

      Mar. 14    The debate on agrarian reform begins in the Cortes.

      Apr. 9     The Catalan autonomy bill is introduced.

      Aug. 10    An unsuccessful revolt led by Gen. José Sanjurjo (1872–1936) causes a radical backlash that leads to military cutbacks, passage of Catalan autonomy, and a radical new land-reform bill on 9 Sept.

1933   Jan. 11    A score of peasant demonstrators are killed at Casas Viejas in Andalusia. The Azaña cabinet suffers a political embarrassment.

      Feb. 28    A group of small Catholic and conservative parties creates the Spanish Confederation of the Autonomous Right (CEDA) to challenge the Left for control of the Second Republic.

      June 8     Azaña resigns as premier but submits a new cabinet four days later.

      Aug. 6     The Basque autonomy statute is debated but not passed before Azaña loses his majority.

      Oct. 29    The Falange is created by José Antonio Primo de Rivera as a quasi-fascist party.

      Nov. 19    The Right wins electiorial control of the Cortes. The CEDA and Lerroux's radicals are the biggest winners.

      Dec. 16    Alejandro Lerroux is made premier.

1934   Jan. 14    Lluis Companys is elected president of Catalonia.

      Feb. 13    The Falange and other groups unite in a Spanish fascist movement led by José Antonio Primo de Rivera.

      Apr.       A resurgent Catalan nationalism merges with radicalism in defense of earlier republican legislation annulled by Lerroux.

      Sept. 5    Peasant protest in Catalonia further complicates its political life.

      Oct. 4     Fear of a Gil Robles cabinet worsens the political crisis.

| Oct. 5 | The Asturian revolt of the Workers' Alliance is crushed by the Foreign Legion, commanded by Gen. Francisco Franco. Fighting ends on 12 Oct., but repression lasts for months. |
|---|---|

| 1935 | Aug. | A Popular Front coalition is formed by the Center-Left to coordinate their efforts in the next election. |
|---|---|---|

| 1936 | Jan. 6 | The Cortes is dissolved after a gambling scandal, and new elections are called. |
|---|---|---|
| | Feb. 16 | The Popular Front wins a narrow victory in the national elections over the Right. Azaña forms a new Center-Left cabinet on 19 Feb. |
| | Mar. 15 | The Falange is declared an illegal party by the government. José Antonio Primo de Rivera is arrested and on 5 June transferred to prison in Alicante. |
| | May 10 | Azaña is elected president of the second republic. Santiago Cásares replaces him as premier. Extreme political instability leads to a near civil war as political factions take their ideologies into the streets. The Spanish Military Union begins to plan a rising against the republic. |
| | July 12 | Lt. José Castillo, a left-wing officer, is assassinated by the Falange in Madrid. The next night Calvo Sotelo is murdered in retaliation. |
| | July 18 | The Spanish Army of Morocco rebels vs. the republic. Francisco Franco flies to Morocco from the Canary Islands to lead a nationalist revolt on 19 July. |

## THE SPANISH CIVIL WAR, 1936–1939

### Favorites/Chief Ministers

REPUBLICANS

| 1936 | July 19 | José Giral (1880–1962) is the first republican premier in the civil war. He is neither political nor popular. |
|---|---|---|
| | Sept. 4 | Francisco Largo Caballero (1869–1946) infuses great spirit into the premier's office and presides over a cabinet of socialists and communists (and later anarchists). In May 1937, however, he breaks with the communists. |
| 1937 | May 15 | Juan Negrín (1889–1956) is a socialist university professor who replaces Largo Caballero. Either he sees no way to resist Franco without Soviet aid, or he assumes that no revolution of the type Largo Caballero and the anarchists favored could succeed. |

NATIONALISTS

| 1936 | Oct. 1 | Gen. Francisco Franco (1892–1975) is made head of state and generalissimo of the nationalist forces. The character of the state |
|---|---|---|

he leads is unclear until Mar. 1938, when a corporative basis is provided for his authoritarian regime.

## Political Life

### REPUBLICANS

| | | |
|---|---|---|
| 1936 | July 18 | The Giral cabinet distributes arms to the people as fighting spreads. |
| | July 20 | The Antifascist Militia Committee is created by the anarchosyndicalist and anarchist CNT-FAI, United Catalan Communist Party (PSUC), and radical Catalan nationalists in Barcelona. It organizes a militia army of Aragon to march on Saragossa. |
| | | Madrid, Bilbao, and Valencia also remain a part of the republic. |
| | July 31 | Lluis Companys is confirmed as the president of Catalonia. José Antonio de Aguirre (1904–1960) is made the president of the Basque Provinces. |
| | Aug. 12 | All religious institutions are closed. |
| | Sept. 4 | Largo Caballero forms a Popular Front cabinet. |
| | Oct. 8 | Home rule is given to the Basques. |
| | Nov. 5 | The republican government moves from Madrid to Valencia. The CNT-FAI joins the cabinet and fills four ministerial positions. |
| | Nov. 20 | The anarchist leader Buenaventura Durruti d. on the Madrid front. |
| 1937 | May 4 | The May crisis occurs when anarchists and communists clash in Barcelona as the Popular Front divides into sectarian factions. The crisis is ended by a truce on 8 May. |
| | May 15 | Largo Caballero breaks with the communists but is forced to resign. Juan Negrín becomes the new premier of a cabinet largely dominated by communists and socialists. His cabinet is confirmed on 18 May. |
| | June 11 | The Trotskyist POUM is outlawed and its members arrested. Andreu Nin is killed by the NKVD on 20 June. |
| | July 30 | The People's Militia is abolished in Aragon, and the Council of Aragon, previously affiliated with the Antifascist Militia Committee, is integrated into Negrín's government on 10 Aug. |
| | Oct. 1 | Largo Caballero is removed as head of the Socialist party. |
| | Oct. 29 | Republican Pres. Azaña moves his headquarters from Valencia to Barcelona. |

|         | Nov. 18  | Indalecio Prieto (1883–1962) is made minister of foreign affairs in an attempt to maintain a PSOE (Socialist party) role in the republic. He is dismissed on 5 Apr. 1938. |
|---------|----------|---|
| 1938    | Aug. 17  | Negrín nationalizes the Catalan munitions industry. |
|         | Aug. 18  | The republic seeks a compromise peace. |
|         | Nov. 15  | The International Brigades and other foreign volunteers are withdrawn in hopes that the German and Italian troops on the nationalist side will do likewise. |
| 1939    | Jan. 23  | Martial law is declared as the Second Republic struggles to maintain order in the face of defeat. |
|         | Feb. 1   | The last meeting of the republican Cortes is held in Spain. |
|         | Feb. 4   | Azaña resigns as president of the republic. |
|         | Mar. 5   | Col. Segismundo Casado (1893–1960) creates the National Defense Council to replace the republican government in peace negotiations with Franco. |
|         | Mar. 8   | Casado puts down a communist revolt in Madrid. |
|         | Mar. 31  | The Second Republic surrenders. |

## NATIONALISTS

| 1936    | July 21  | Gen. Emilio Mola (1887–1937) holds Burgos, Saragossa, and the north after Gen. José Sanjurjo (1872–1936) is killed in a plane crash. |
|---------|----------|---|
|         |          | Catalonia, part of Aragon, and the Basque Provinces remain republican. Gen. Gonzalo Queipo de Llano (1875–1951) holds Seville for the nationalists. |
|         | July 23  | The nationalists form a Junta of National Defense as their ruling body. |
|         | Aug. 6   | Franco arrives in Seville. |
|         | Sept. 13 | The Carlists capture San Sebastian. |
|         | Sept. 21 | Military leaders make Franco the head of the National Defense Council, and he begins to create a state. |
|         | Oct. 1   | Franco proclaims a new nationalist government in Burgos. An all-military cabinet is named on 3 Oct. |
|         | Nov. 20  | José Antonio Primo de Rivera is executed in Alicante. |
|         | Dec. 5   | All government employees must join the National Movement. |
| 1937    | Feb. 7   | The Falange and the Carlists fail to unify in the National Movement. Franco orders them to do so on 19 Apr. |
|         | Apr. 19  | Franco proclaims himself "jefe nacional." |
|         | June 1   | Gen. Mola d. in an airplane accident. |
| 1938    | Jan. 3   | Civilians are added to the nationalist government in Burgos. Chief among them is Ramón Serrano Suñer, Franco's brother-in-law. |

| Mar. 9 | Franco issues the *Fueros de los españoles* as the corporative basis of nationalist Spain. As a labor charter, it introduces the concept of a national-syndicalist state. |
| Apr. 5 | The nationalists abrogate Catalan autonomy. |
| Apr. 22 | A strict press law imposes censorship. |
| May 3 | The Jesuits are welcomed back to Spain. |
| July 18 | Franco assumes the title captain general of the army and navy usually reserved for monarchs. |

1939 Feb. 9     The Law of Political Responsibilities establishes punishment for all opponents of the nationalists.

Apr. 1          Franco announces the end of the civil war.


## War and Diplomacy

## REPUBLICANS

1936 July 26    The Comintern, in Prague, issues a call for volunteers to defend the republic.

Aug. 2          France protests Italian aid to the nationalists.

Aug. 6          The first proposal for the creation of a nonintervention committee is made by France.

Aug. 15         Britain bans sale of war material to Spain.

Aug. 23         The Soviet Union accepts nonintervention, but begins purchasing arms for the republic on 29 Aug.

Sept. 9         The Nonintervention Committee begins meeting in London with Britain and France as its major leaders. Portugal joins on 14 Sept., but the USSR says on 6 Oct. that it will obey an embargo on aid only if Italy and Germany do.

Oct. 6          Largo Caballero begins negotiations for military aid with the Soviet Union. Spanish gold reserves are used for collateral, and the first shipment of arms is received on 26 Oct.

Nov. 7          The siege of Madrid begins. The first volunteers of the International Brigades see action on 8 Nov. Madrid is saved by 20 Nov.

Dec. 10         The Nonintervention Committee refuses to mediate the civil war.

1937 Jan. 8     Britain and Italy conclude a gentleman's agreement on the status quo in the Mediterranean.

Feb. 7          The battle of Jarama again saves Madrid from nationalist capture.

Feb. 20         The Nonintervention Committee bans all foreign volunteers from Spain without success.

Mar. 18    The International Brigades defeat Italian troops at Guadalajara. In London, Britain refuses a republican offer of its Moroccan colonies in exchange for more favorable treatment.

Apr. 19    The Nonintervention Committee begins to monitor Spanish waters to intercept war-related shipping.

Apr. 26    The bombing of Guernica wins the republic worldwide sympathy.

May 1    The United States passes the Neutrality Act, which bars all aid to Spain.

July 25    The republican campaign of Brunete stalls, as does the later Belchite campaign.

Sept. 10    The Nyon conference discusses submarine attacks on shipping.

Dec. 15    The republican campaign to capture Teruel begins.

1938    Feb. 22    The nationalists recapture Teruel.

Mar. 9    The republic is cut in two when the nationalists reach the Mediterranean coast between Valencia and Barcelona.

Mar. 13    France begins to give aid to the republic.

May 1    Negrín promises democracy in exchange for aid. The offer is ignored.

May 13    The republic makes a final request for the assistance of the League of Nations, but it is rejected.

June 27    The Soviet Union agrees with the Nonintervention Committee that volunteers should be removed from the civil war. The International Brigades leave Spain on 15 Nov.

July 25    The Ebro campaign is the republic's last offensive. It fails by 16 Nov., and the nationalists invade Catalonia on 23 Dec.

1939    Jan. 25    Barcelona surrenders to the nationalists.

Mar. 8    Fighting breaks out in Madrid between political factions.

Mar. 26    The republican air force surrenders.

Mar. 31    Cartagena's surrender marks the end of republican military efforts.

## NATIONALISTS

1936    July 20    The first Italian aid is received by the nationalists.

July 22    Gen. Mola captures Galicia.

July 26    Adolf Hitler agrees to aid Franco. The first elements of the Condor Legion leave Germany on 31 July.

July 28    Italian bombers reach Morocco. Italy diplomatically recognizes the nationalist regime.

Aug. 11    Mérida falls to the nationalists. Badajoz surrenders on 14 Aug. A massacre in the bullring there shocks world opinion.

|           | Aug. 28  | Madrid is bombed for the first time. |
|-----------|----------|--------------------------------------|
|           | Sept. 13 | The Carlists capture San Sebastian. |
|           | Sept. 25 | Toledo falls to the nationalists. The siege of the Alcázar has won great sympathy for its defenders. |
|           | Nov. 2   | Nationalist troops reach the southern edge of Madrid. |
|           | Nov. 20  | Franco fails to capture Madrid, greatly extending the war's duration. |
|           |          | José Antonio Primo de Rivera is executed. |
| 1937      | Feb. 7   | Malaga is captured. |
|           | Apr. 20  | The campaign to recapture the Basque Provinces begins. Guernica is bombed on 26 Apr. Bilbao falls on 16 June. |
|           | July 1   | The Spanish bishops publicly support Franco. |
|           | Oct. 19  | Gijón falls to the nationalists. All of Asturias is captured by 21 Oct. |
|           | Oct. 22  | Franco establishes diplomatic relations with Britain. |
|           | Dec. 1   | Japan diplomatically recognizes Franco. |
|           | Dec. 8   | Barcelona is bombed for the first time. |
| 1938      | Feb. 22  | Teruel is recaptured. |
|           | Mar. 6   | The nationalist cruiser *Baleares* is sunk. |
|           | Mar. 9   | The republic is cut in two when the nationalists reach the Mediterranean coast between Valencia and Barcelona. |
|           | May 11   | Portugal recognizes nationalist Spain. |
|           | Nov. 16  | The nationalist territory lost in the Ebro campaign is recaptured. |
|           | Dec. 23  | Nationalist troops enter Catalonia. |
| 1939      | Jan. 25  | Barcelona is captured. The nationalists close the French border of Catalonia on 10 Feb. |
|           | Mar. 8   | Nationalist troops finally enter Madrid. |
|           | Mar. 31  | The surrender of Cartagena ends the civil war. |

## Economy

### REPUBLICANS

| 1936 | Aug. 5  | A War Industries Commission is created in Barcelona by the Antifascist Militia Committee. Agriculture in Catalonia and Aragon is reorganized into communes. |
|------|---------|--------------------------------------------------------------------|
|      | Oct. 7  | The republican government collectivizes all nationalists' property. |
|      | Oct. 24 | All Catalan industries are nationalized as a result of the merger between the Catalan state and the Antifascist Militia Committee. |

|      | Oct. 26 | Spanish gold reserves are pledged to the Soviet Union in return for military aid to the republic. |
|------|---------|---|
| 1937 | June 7  | Negrín returns Catalan property to private ownership. |
| 1938 | Aug. 17 | The republic renationalizes the Catalan munitions industry. |

### NATIONALISTS

| 1938 | Nov. 19 | Franco gives Germany mining concessions as a settlement for military aid he has received. |
|------|---------|---|

## Culture

### REPUBLICANS

| 1936 | Aug. 19 | Federico García Lorca is murdered. |
|------|---------|---|
|      | Oct. 12 | Miguel de Unamuno castigates nationalist Gen. José Millán Astray for the inhumanity of the war. He is dismissed as rector of the University of Salamanca on 30 Oct. and d. under house arrest on 31 Dec. |

### NATIONALISTS

| 1936 | Oct. 29 | Ramiro de Maeztu (1874–1936) dies. He was the most conservative member of the Generation of 1898. |
|------|---------|---|

## THE CONSOLIDATION OF FRANCO'S POWER, 1939–1945

### Dynasty

| 1941 | Feb. 1  | Alfonso XIII abdicates in favor of his youngest son, Juan. Alfonso d. on 28 Feb. |
|------|---------|---|
| 1942 | Nov. 11 | Juan makes his first appeal to Spaniards that he is the legitimate heir to the throne. |
| 1943 | June    | A petition of leading Spanish monarchists asks Franco to restore the monarchy. Many of them are subsequently punished. |
| 1944 | Dec.    | Juan organizes his private council of state as a prelude to an Allied-sponsored restoration that never comes. |
| 1945 | Mar. 19 | In the Lausanne manifesto, don Juan calls upon the Spanish people to oust Franco. |

### Favorites/Chief Ministers

| 1938 | Jan. 30 | Gen. Francisco Franco (1892–1975) uses the title of Caudillo to head the state, the government, the Falange, and the military. |
|------|---------|---|
| 1939 | Aug. 9  | Gen. Agustín Muñoz Grandes (1896–1970) is made the secretary-general of the Falange, now called the National Movement. |

| 1940 | Oct. 16 | Ramón Serrano Suñer (1901– ), Franco's brother-in-law, becomes foreign minister. He is sympathetic to the Axis powers and remains influential in diplomatic life until he is dismissed on 3 Sept. 1942. |
| 1942 | Sept. 3 | Gen. Francisco Gómez Jordana y Souza, the count of Jordana (1876–1944), succeeds Serrano Suñer as foreign minister in 1942, and steers a cautious middle road between the Axis and Allies until his death on 3 Aug. 1944. |

## Political Life

| 1938 | Mar. 9 | The concept of a national-syndicalist state is introduced. All production is in the service of the state, and there is no right to strike. The church and state are united. |
| 1939 | Aug. 9 | Franco's first peacetime cabinet includes the Gens. Muñoz Grandes and Gamero del Castillo and the Falangists Serrano Suñer, Manuel Valdés, José María Alfaro, and Dionisio Ridruejo. |
| 1940 | Oct. 17 | Cabinet changes include Serrano Suñer as foreign minister and Demetrio Carceller as minister of commerce and industry. |
| 1941 | Aug. | The first exile party, the National Union of Spaniards (dominated by socialists), is created in Mexico. |
| 1942 | Aug. 19 | Tension within the ruling circles of Franco's elite surfaces when Carlists attack Falangists. |
| | Sept. 3 | A new cabinet replaces Serrano Suñer with Gen. Jordana. One reason for Serrano's fall is his encouragement of the Falange to act like a fascist party, the cause of the Aug. riots. |
| 1943 | Mar. 17 | A Cortes of Franco appointees is formed. |
| 1944 | June | The Spanish Committee of Liberation is created as an exile group to promote the armed liberation of Spain. |
| | Aug. 19 | A new cabinet adds several moderates, but the profascist José Félix de Lequerica is made foreign minister after Jordana's death. |
| | Oct. | The National Alliance of Democratic Forces is created in Mexico City as the official Spanish exile government. |
| | Dec. 23 | A more liberal penal code is issued. |
| 1945 | July 17 | A new and more moderate framework for the state is published in the *Fuero de los Españoles*, as the end of World War II makes the regime vulnerable. |
| | July 21 | A new cabinet replaces fascists like Lequerica and José Luis de Arrese (secretary-general of the Falange) with more moderate politicians like José Antonio Girón, Raimundo Fernández Cuesta, Martín Artajo, and José Ibáñez Martín (a member of the Opus Dei). |

| Aug. 21 | A government-in-exile led by José Giral is created by exile groups in Mexico City. |

## War and Diplomacy

| 1939 | Mar. 17 | A treaty of friendship is signed by Spain and Portugal. |
| | Mar. 27 | Spain joins the Axis Anticomintern Pact. |
| | Mar. 31 | Spain signs Friendship Pact with Germany. |
| | May | German and Italian troops begin to leave Spain. |
| | Sept. 4 | Spain announces its neutrality in World War II. |
| 1940 | June 14 | Spanish troops seize Tangier. |
| | Oct. 1 | Serrano Suñer meets with Mussolini in Rome. |
| | Oct. 16 | Serrano Suñer is appointed foreign minister. |
| | Nov. 18 | Serrano Suñer meets Hitler at Berchtesgarden. |
| | Dec. 5 | Adm. Wilhelm Canaris brings Hilter's ultimatum to Franco in Madrid. Spain must join the Axis alliance, but Franco refuses. |
| 1941 | Feb. 12 | Franco and Mussolini meet in Italy. Franco tells the Italian dictator that Spain does not have the resources to join the Axis. |
| | Oct. 22 | Franco meets Hitler at Hendaye. |
| 1942 | Feb. 12 | Franco and António Salazar of Portugal confer on the war. |
| | June 27 | Spain sends the Blue Division to the eastern front as a German ally vs. the Soviet Union. |
| | Sept. 3 | Serrano Suñer is dismissed as foreign minister. |
| 1943 | Mar. 3 | Spain recognizes the Free French movement and begins to moderate its diplomatic position. |
| | Apr. 16 | Franco asks the Allies to accept a negotiated peace in Europe. His memorandum is ignored. |
| | Oct. 1 | Spain shifts its diplomatic status back to neutrality. |
| 1944 | Feb. 20 | Hitler releases the Blue Division from the eastern front. |
| | May 3 | The United States sells oil to Spain in return for a Spanish embargo on mineral shipments to Germany. |
| | May 24 | Winston Churchill hints at the possibility of normal diplomatic relations with Spain after the war. |
| 1945 | May 8 | Spain breaks relations with Germany. |
| | June 19 | Mexico successfully proposes that Spain be excluded from membership in the United Nations organization. |
| | Aug. 2 | The Potsdam conference adopts a motion that no nation associated with the Axis should become a member of the United Nations. It also demands that Spain evacuate Tangier. |
| | Dec. 19 | France breaks diplomatic relations with Spain. |

## Economy

| 1939 | Apr. 3 | Rationing is continued through the entire period. |
| | May 1 | The official labor syndicates begin functioning. |
| 1941 | Feb. 1 | The Spanish rail system is nationalized into the Spanish National Railways (RENFE). |

# SPAIN FROM OUTCAST TO ALLY, 1946–1956

## Dynasty

| 1947 | Mar. 31 | The Law of Succession names Franco as Caudillo for life and creates a regents' council and a council of the realm to prepare for monarchical restoration. Spain is defined as a Catholic state and a kingdom temporarily led by the caudillo. |
| | July 6 | The national referendum on the succession law overwhelmingly passes. |
| 1948 | Aug. 27 | Don Juan and Franco meet to discuss the education of Juan Carlos and Alfonso in Spain. Don Juan now lives in Portugal. |
| 1954 | Dec. | The second meeting of don Juan and Franco is marked by the pretender's demand for liberty of the press, independence of the judiciary, social justice, labor freedom, and "authentic" political representation. Franco rejects his demands. |

## Favorites/Chief Ministers

José Ibáñez Martín (1896–1969) is a leading member of the Opus Dei, a Jesuit lay organization. As cabinet member, he is given responsibility for education, involving him in the development of a Catholic university infrastructure. The cabinet of 1945 is, in general, the most stable of the Franco years and lasts until 1957.

## Political Life

| 1947 | Jan. 9 | Members of the National Alliance are put on trial. |
| | | Rodolfo Llopis replaces José Giral as head of the exile government. |
| | Mar. 2 | Anarchist guerrillas in the Sierras are defeated, and their leaders, Amador Franco and Antonio López, killed. |

| | | |
|---|---|---|
| | Apr. 9 | Members of the Spanish University Federation (SEU) are put on trial to prevent student unrest. |
| | July 11 | The referendum on the succession law isolates the government-in-exile. Basque and Catalan nationalist groups abandon it, and a period of political lethargy begins. |

## War and Diplomacy

| | | |
|---|---|---|
| 1946 | Feb. 9 | The General Assembly of the United Nations declares that Franco is not a democratic leader and thus bars Spain from international participation. |
| | Mar. 1 | France closes its border with Spain. |
| | Mar. 8 | The Soviet Union asks the Security Council of the United Nations to discuss the Spanish situation. Debate begins on 17 Apr., but the final report is not issued until 13 Dec. Joint action will be taken if a responsible government is not established "within a reasonable time." Diplomatic relations are discouraged in the meantime. |
| | Apr. 4 | The American, British, and French Declaration on Spain condemns the lack of freedom in Spain. It calls for Franco's resignation and asks for a provisional government to consult the Spanish people on the form of their government. The positive vote received by Franco's succession law, however, dissuades any further action. |
| | Nov. 8 | The United States supports Spain for the first time in the United Nations. |
| | Dec. 13 | The U.S., reversing course, continues to boycott Spain. |
| 1948 | Feb. 10 | France reopens its border with Spain. |
| | Mar. 30 | The U.S. House of Representatives votes to include Spain in the Marshall Plan. Upon reconsideration, the vote is rejected 1 Apr. |
| 1950 | Jan. 18 | The United States asks the United Nations to end its ban on diplomatic relations with Spain. U.S. labor groups protest this change of relations on 5–14 Feb. |
| | Aug. 1 | Spain offers troops to serve on the U.N. side in the Korean War. |
| | Sept. 25 | The U.S. Congress adds Spain as a Marshall Plan recipient. |
| | Nov. 4 | The United Nations ends its boycott of Spain. |
| | Dec. 10 | Spain renews its claims on Gibraltar. |
| | Dec. 12 | Gen. Charles de Gaulle supports the full diplomatic rehabilitation of Spain. |
| 1951 | May 16 | Spain is admitted into the World Health Organization. |
| 1952 | Mar. 12 | Discussion begins with the United States over the creation of American military bases in Spain. |

| | Nov. 19 | Spain joins UNESCO. |
| 1953 | Aug. 27 | A new concordat is signed with the Vatican. |
| | Sept. 26 | Spain accepts the U.S. bases agreement. The U.S. Congress ratifies it on 30 Nov. |
| 1954 | Jan. 28 | Anglo-Hispanic talks on Gibraltar end inconclusively. |
| | Feb. 15 | The first U.S. military and economic aid reaches Spain. |
| | Dec. 29 | Talks between monarchists and the regime end without resolution of outstanding conflicts. |
| 1955 | Jan. 10 | U.S. food relief begins. |
| | Dec. 14 | Spain is admitted into the United Nations. |

## Economic Life

| 1945 | May 8 | The Argentine dictator Juan Perón makes a loan to Spain. A second loan is negotiated on 3 Apr. 1948. |
| | Oct. 30 | Britain and France extend loans to Spain in exchange for agricultural produce. |
| 1949 | Feb. | Chase National Bank makes a private loan to Spain. |
| 1950 | Sept. 26 | A Marshall Plan loan is approved by the U.S. Congress. |
| 1951 | Mar. 16 | The United States makes a wheat loan to Spain. |

# SPAIN IN TRANSITION, 1956–1975

## Dynasty

| 1957 | July 15 | Franco affirms that monarchy will be the form of government in the future. |
| 1960 | Mar. 29 | Another meeting between don Juan and Franco agrees that don Juan Carlos will be educated in Spain without prejudice to don Juan's succession rights. Those rights, however, still remain unclear. |
| | Apr. 25 | Don Juan Carlos returns to Spain. |
| 1962 | June 14 | Don Juan Carlos (1938– ) m. Princess Sophia (1938– ) of Greece. *Children*: Elena (1963– ); Cristina (1965– ); Felipe (1968– ). |
| 1963 | Dec. 27 | The birth of a first child to Sophia and Juan Carlos allows don Juan to visit Spain. |
| 1968 | Nov. 22 | The Organic Law proposes monarchy as the form of government in the future without specifying the order of succession. |

|       | Dec. 21 | A number of leading Carlists are expelled from Spain as Franco prepares to recognize don Juan Carlos as his successor. |
| 1969  | Jan. 7  | Don Juan Carlos agrees to be Franco's successor "in due time." Formal confirmation is made on 22 July. |

## Favorites/Chief Ministers

|       | Feb. 25 | The Opus Dei provides Franco with a ready-made elite that is loyal to conservative principles. It reaches a high point of success with the formation of technocratic cabinets in 1957 and 1965. |
| 1957  |         | |
|       |         | Manuel Fraga Iribarne (1922– ) becomes minister of information and tourism. He is committed to creating an "opening" for greater liberalization within the regime. Some see him as the first modern politician of the Franco years. |

## Political Life

| 1956  | Feb. 1  | A major student revolt demands a free national congress of students. The Falange loses law school elections on 4 Feb., and the universities are closed 10–13 Feb. Intellectuals like Gregorio Marañón, Dionisio Ridruejo, and Pedro Laín Entralgo are accused of fomenting trouble, and the film director Juan Bardem is arrested. |
|       | Feb. 23 | The student trial causes a national furor. A nephew of Calvo Sotelo is among the defendants, and José María Gil Robles acts as their lawyer. A number of more radical student groups form. |
|       | Mar.    | Price increases lead to questions about the success of modernization. Strikes challenging economic policies begin on 13 Apr. The government orders wage increases on 28 Apr. |
|       | Nov. 15 | Juan Negrín d. in exile. The threat of communism is no longer as strong. |
| 1957  | Feb. 25 | The first Opus Dei cabinet sees five members of the organization join six generals. Laureano López Rodó becomes the technical secretary of Franco's inner cabinet. |
|       | Mar. 22 | A new law permits the collective punishment of opposition groups if no defendants can be found in cases of antiregime opposition. |
|       | Apr. 21 | The Paris Agreement unites all opposition parties except the PCE, POUM, and part of the CNT. It asserts the need for the creation of a new provisional government. |
| 1958  | Mar. 4  | A strike in Asturias affects 15,000 workers. It spreads to five major industries in Barcelona and to the steel mills of Bilbao. Underground unions begin to challenge the official syndicates. The strike ends on 17 Mar. |

| Mar. 14 | Asturias is placed under martial law. |
| Mar. 18 | New principles of the National Movement are drawn up. Spain is a "traditional, Catholic, social and representative monarchy," and the National Movement is a "communion of Spaniards in the ideals that gave life to the Crusade." |
| Mar. 29 | Student protest in the medical schools causes their closure for the rest of the term. |
| Apr. 17 | A new legal codification permits limited bargaining rights for workers and gives women full property rights. |
| May 5 | A "day of national reconciliation" is sponsored by the PCE, with little success. |

| 1959 | Jan. 19 | The Spanish Union is organized by Gil Robles and other conservatives as a semiofficial monarchist opposition party. |
| | May 14 | A Christian Democratic Left party is organized. |
| | June 3? | The law of public order places new restrictions upon the right of association and public assembly. |
| | June 18 | A peaceful national general strike is met with force. |
| | July 22 | The Opus Dei ministers introduce the first economic plan as a program of stabilization. |
| | Sept. 7 | The Valley of the Fallen is completed as a memorial to the civil war. |

| 1960 | Jan. 4 | Francisco Sabater Llopart (El Quico), one of the most active political bandits of the postwar era, attacks a police post near Gerona and is killed. |
| | Feb. 18 | Bombings in Madrid are the responsibility of the Iberian Revolutionary Liberation Council, an exile group in Mexico City, rumored to have ties with Fidel Castro's Cuba. One person is executed on 8 Mar. for his part in the bombings. |
| | Mar. 22 | The death of the old Basque leader José Antonio de Aguirre (1904–1960) causes demonstrations in the north. The formation of the Euzkadi ta Azkatasuna (ETA) as a revolutionary branch of the Basque Nationalist party comes soon after. |
| | June 13 | Basque priests protest police violence. |
| | June 26 | Railway bombings by the "social brigade" at a number of stations kill one and injure many more in a two-day spree. |

| 1961 | July 18 | The ETA performs its first act of violence. |
| | Oct. 8 | The arrest of El Campesino, an old republican gen., marks a new hard line amnesty. |

| 1962 | Feb.? | The Omnium Cultura is formed in Barcelona as a Catalan nationalist organization. |
| | Apr. 17 | The Asturias strike movement surfaces again when illegal Workers' Commissions (CCOO) make large gains at the expense of the official syndicates. |

| | | |
|---|---|---|
| | June 5–6 | The Munich congress sees all opposition groups meet together for the first time. Even formerly conservative politicians attend. |
| | July 11 | A new cabinet is installed with a new office of vice president for Gen. Muñoz Grandes. Manuel Fraga Iribarne is made minister of information and tourism, and Laureano López Rodó gets new economic powers. |
| 1963 | Apr. 20 | Another amnesty problem occurs when republican returnee Julián Grimau is executed for crimes committed during the civil war. |
| 1964 | Mar. 4? | Asturian strikes again cause a national crisis. The CCOO organizes nationally as a permanent labor organization. |
| | Oct. | A schism within the PCE develops between Fernando Claudín and Jorge Semprún, who are critical of PCE Leninism, and Santiago Carrillo, the party leader. |
| | Oct. 30 | Intellectuals protest against repression in Asturian mining strikes. |
| 1965 | Feb. 23–25 | Huge student demonstrations begin in Madrid and elsewhere. The universities are closed, and Enrique Tierno Galván is dismissed from the University of Salamanca. |
| | Mar. 13 | Workers in Asturias demonstrate in solidarity with the students. |
| | July 8 | A new cabinet is created with López Rodó elevated to ministerial rank. The cabinet seeks technocracy rather than democracy. |
| | Sept. 2 | Student rights are limited. |
| 1966 | Mar. 18 | Fraga introduces a new press law that allows some relaxation of censorship. His new concept of an "opening" also introduces fines for violations of Movement principles. |
| | Apr. 27 | Students demand a free student association outside government control. Universities are closed in Madrid and Barcelona. |
| | Nov. 22 | The introduction of a new Organic Law reiterates monarchy as the future form of the state without clarifying succession. |
| | Dec. 14 | The national referendum on the Organic Law is overwhelmingly accepted. |
| | Dec. 27 | The ETA's fifth congress (continued in Mar. 1967) abandons cultural nationalism for national liberation theory, influenced by Federico Krutwig Sagredo's book, *Vasconia* (1963). |
| 1967 | Feb. 24 | The cabinet liberalizes religious laws. |
| | Mar. 4 | The ecclesiastical hierarchy takes stronger control over the Catholic social action movement. |
| | July 28 | Vice-President Muñoz Grandes's hostility toward the Opus Dei leads to his resignation from the government. Adm. Luis Carrero Blanco replaces him on 21 Sept. |

|        |          |                                                                                                   |
|--------|----------|---------------------------------------------------------------------------------------------------|
|        | Oct. 27  | Antigovernment riots occur in several cities. They continue on 30 Nov. and 12 Dec.                 |
| 1968   | Mar. 18  | Fraga Iribarne introduces a new press law.                                                        |
|        | May 22   | An educational reform relaxes control over student organizations. Other reforms of education and student life are made on 23 Sept. |
|        | June     | The ETA carries out its first assassination of a policeman. In Aug., Melitón Manzanas, a high-ranking police official in the Basque Provinces, is assassinated. |
|        | Nov. 22  | Organic Law of State is completed.                                                                |
| 1969   | Jan. 24  | A resumption of workers' protests causes a state of emergency which lasts until 25 Mar.            |
|        | Aug. 14  | The Matesa scandal begins when loans from the Industrial Credit Bank to Matesa are illegally invested abroad. Three Opus Dei ministers are implicated. Fraga allows full press coverage of the scandal since he dislikes the Opus. Another critic, José Solís, minister of the National Movement, is dismissed in Oct. |
|        | Oct. 29  | A new cabinet is formed in the aftermath of the Matesa scandal. Fraga is dismissed and the "opening" closes. López Rodó is made foreign secretary. |
| 1970   | Jan. 25  | Newspapers are banned for continuing to cover the Matesa scandal. Discontent with the regime reaches a new high, and expectations about the future rise. |
|        | May 7    | The Matesa trial begins. Two former ministers who belong to the Opus Dei are convicted on 17 July. |
|        | July 26  | The Opus Dei publicly denies any involvement in the Matesa scandal.                                |
|        | Dec. 3–28| The ETA is put on trial in Burgos for the Manzanas assassination. Six are sentenced to death, and nine others are sentenced to terms averaging thirty-five years. |
| 1971   | Feb. 8   | A new antidissent bill is introduced with heavy penalties for criticism of the regime.            |
|        | Mar. 15  | Forty ETA members are arrested on charges of terrorism as protests of the Burgos decision spread.  |
|        | Apr. 1   | Fraga attacks the role of the Opus Dei in the cabinet.                                             |
|        | July 1   | The church criticizes the treatment of political prisoners.                                       |
|        | Oct. 19  | CCOO leaders arrested.                                                                             |
| 1972   | Jan. 6   | New unrest affects the universities as students ally with the CCOO.                                |
|        | Jan. 20  | The Spanish bishops ask for separation of church and state.                                        |
|        | May 29   | A revised law of public order restricts freedom of thought and association.                        |

| Sept. 12 | University officials quit in Madrid and Salamanca in reaction to new government rules concerning the conduct of higher education and student life. |
| Oct. 10 | Members of the university staff in Valencia quit in protest of the new rules. |

1973

| June 8 | Adm. Luis Carrero Blanco is appointed prime minister as Franco's health worsens. |
| June 14 | ETA activity increases as a result of the repression of the Pamplona general strike, which lasts until 25 June. |
| Dec. 20 | Prime minister Carrero Blanco is assassinated by an ETA terrorist group, outside a church in Madrid. The same day, leaders of the CCOO receive prison terms as their trial ends. |
| Dec. 29 | Carlos Arias Navarro, former mayor of Madrid with only six months' experience in the national government, is made prime minister. |

1974

| Jan. 3 | A new cabinet contains no Opus Dei members and few military men. Pío Cabanillas, Fraga's ally, is more liberal than most. |
| Feb. 12 | A new "opening" comes when Arias announces reforms to end press censorship, allow political associations to operate, reform the Cortes, make local government more democratic, and revise labor laws. |
| Feb. 29 | Arias criticizes the Basque church for supporting the ETA and puts the bishop of Bilbao under house arrest. |
| Mar. 2 | A Catalan anarchist is executed for political crimes. |
| Apr. | Jordi Pujol (1930– ) founds the Democratic Convergence as a regional party in Catalonia. |
| June 16 | Gen. Manuel Díez-Alegría is dismissed as chief of the army. The right fears that he will become the Gen. Spínola of Spain— an indication of how much the Portuguese revolution is feared in Spain. |
| July 9 | Franco is incapacitated by illness. His powers are shifted to don Juan Carlos and Arias in July and Aug. Franco returns on 2 Sept. |
| July 29 | The opposition forms a democratic junta. |
| Sept. 13 | A bombing attributed to the ETA kills twelve in Madrid. |
| Oct. 29 | Franco reacts to this violence by dismissing Pío Cabanillas and reinstituting press censorship. |
| Dec. 23 | The new law of political association is less liberal than expected. Its rules are complicated, and the final approval of new political associations is closely controlled by the state. |

1975

| Feb. 5 | A new strike movement lasts until Mar. and demands further liberalization of the regime. Spaniards increasingly criticize the "bunker" mentality of Franco's government. |

| Apr. | State of emergency in the Basque Provinces. |
|---|---|
| June 3 | Moderates form a coalition called the Platform of Democratic Convergence. |
| July 16 | Sixteen political associations demand Franco's resignation. |
| Aug. 8 | A new antiterrorist law is issued. |
| Sept. 21 | Five convicted of terrorism are executed. |
| Oct. 30 | At the age of eighty-two, Franco suffers a heart attack. The first of a series of operations is performed on 4 Nov. He dies on 20 Nov., lies in state 21 Nov., and is buried on 23 Nov. |

## War and Diplomacy

| 1956 | Apr. 4 | Franco meets Mohammed V (1910–1961) of Morocco in Madrid. The Moroccan king's restoration by France on 4 Nov. 1955 is recognized by Franco, but no decisions are reached on the Spanish enclaves in Morocco. |
|---|---|---|
| | May 7 | King Feisal II (1935–1958) of Iraq visits Madrid to discuss the Algerian revolution of 1 Oct. 1954. |
| 1962 | Feb. 9 | Spain begins negotiations for membership in the European Economic Community (EEC). |
| 1963 | Mar. | Spain joins the General Agreement on Tariffs and Trade (GATT) as a preliminary step to EEC membership. |
| | Sept. 26 | The U.S.-Spanish economic agreement gives Spain $100 million for military modernization. |
| 1965 | Sept. 9 | General De Gaulle gives French support for Spain's EEC entry. |
| 1966 | Jan. 17 | An atomic bomb is accidentally dropped on southern Spain by the United States. There are no casualties, but new opposition to the bases agreement grows. |
| | June 16 | The United States sponsors Spain's application for NATO membership. |
| | Nov. 17 | Entry points to Gibraltar are closed as Spain increases pressure on Britain to abandon the colony. |
| 1969 | Mar. 26 | The bases agreement with the United States is extended. |
| 1970 | Oct. 1 | U.S. Pres. Richard Nixon (1913– ) visits Madrid. |

## Colonies

| 1956 | Apr. 4 | Spain gives up its Moroccan protectorate, but it keeps the enclaves of Ceuta and Melilla. |
|---|---|---|
| 1964 | Oct. 19 | Spanish Guinea (including Fernando Poo) is granted self-government. |

| 1966 | Nov. 18 | The colonialism committee of the United Nations urges Spain to free Spanish Guinea. |
| 1968 | Oct. 12 | Spanish Guinea is given its independence and with Río Muni becomes Equitorial Guinea. |
|      | Dec. 18 | The United Nations asks Spain to free the Spanish Sahara. |
| 1969 | Mar. 5 | Unrest in Guinea forces Spaniards to flee their former colony. |
| 1975 | Jan. 30 | Morocco claims sovereignty over Ceuta and Melilla. |
|      | June 27 | Spain closes Ceuta's borders. |
|      | June 30 | All non-Spaniards are expelled from the enclaves. |

## Economics

| 1957 | Mar. 6 | Spain accepts the EEC's principles. |
|      | Apr. | Steps are taken to stabilize the peseta. |
| 1958 | Apr. 17 | Labor is given limited bargaining rights. |
|      | May | A workers' commission is established at La Camocha mine in Asturias. It will lead to the creation of the CCOO as a national labor organization in 1964. |
| 1959 | July 22 | A stabilization plan, sponsored by Opus Dei ministers, includes devaluation of the peseta and puts the rate of exchange under new controls. Exports are increased. |
| 1963 | July 19 | The largest strike to date begins in Asturias. It lasts until 2 Sept. |
|      | Dec. 28 | López Rodó creates a five-year plan to place more stress on the private sector and de-emphasize corporatism. |
| 1964 | Mar. 4 | New Asturian strikes are forcibly repressed. Many arrests follow, and workers are fired as lockouts and labor purges begin. The strikes continue through May, and councils of workers and employers are formed in July. The CCOO becomes a permanent union organization under the leadership of a communist, Marcelino Camacho. |
| 1967 | Feb. 9 | A strike at Standard Electric brings labor unrest to Madrid. The strike lasts until 13 Feb. |
|      | Mar. 1 | Marcelino Camacho is arrested in a crackdown on the CCOO. |
|      | Apr. 22 | A general strike in Bilbao protests the state's treatment of CCOO leaders. |
| 1971 | Apr. 29 | Limited freedom of association is decreed for nonpolitical workers' meetings. |
|      | Oct. 19 | CCOO leaders are again arrested. |
|      | Nov. 19 | Another five-year plan of economic development is created. |

**Culture**

José María Ortega y Gasset returns to Madrid in 1946, but his writings are not published in Spain until his death in 1955.

Pablo Picasso (1881–1973) spends his life after 1936 in French exile. The Catalan's *Guérnica* is the most memorable artwork of the Spanish Civil War. It is returned to Spain by terms of Picasso's will.

Joan Miró (1893–1983) is a Catalan abstractionist whose work becomes fashionable in the postwar period.

Claudio Sánchez-Albornoz (1893–1986) is a leading historian and exile leader.

Alfonso Sastre (1926– ) is a contemporary dramatist.

Juan Ramón Jiménez (1881–1958) wins the 1956 Nobel Prize for literature.

Pedro Laín Entralgo (1908– ) is an expert on intellectual history. He is the rector of the University of Madrid from 1951 to 1956, but he later criticizes the regime's cultural policies.

Dionisio Ridruejo (1912–1975) is a poet who becomes a Falange leader and a cabinet minister in 1939. He grows disenchanted with Franco, however, and sides with the students in their protest vs. the regime on 1 Feb. 1956. He is arrested for organizing a writers' conference to protest censorship on 9 Nov. 1961, and often lives in exile until his death.

Severo Ochea (1905– ), born in Spain but a naturalized United States citizen, wins the 1959 Nobel Prize for medicine and physiology.

| | | |
|---|---|---|
| 1964 | Sept. 30 | "Twenty-five Years of Peace" begins a celebration of Franco's rule. Intellectuals like José Bergamín, Laín Entralgo, and Alfredo Sastre lead protests. |
| 1975 | Jan. 20 | The editor of *Cambio 16* is indicted for violating terms of the press law. The publication is suspended for months. |

## CONTEMPORARY SPAIN, 1975–1988

**Dynasty**

| | | |
|---|---|---|
| 1975 | Nov. 22 | Don Juan Carlos is crowned as Juan Carlos I. |
| | Nov. 24 | The king indicates an intent to pursue political democracy and membership in the EEC. |
| 1976 | June 2 | Juan Carlos supports Adolfo Suárez over Fraga and López Rodó for the premiership. |
| | June 14 | Don Juan formally accepts the monarchy of Juan Carlos. |

| 1981 | Feb. 23 | The king plays a key role in frustrating the insurrection of Lt. Col. Antonio Tejero Molín and Gen. Jaime Milans Bosch by openly rejecting their demands for the creation of a military regime and by calming national political passions. |
| | Nov. 7 | Juan Carlos visits the United States and on 10 May 1984, the Soviet Union. |
| 1986 | Jan. 30 | Prince Felipe is sworn in as heir apparent. |

## Favorites/Chief Ministers

| 1976 | July 3 | Adolfo Suárez (1932– ) creates the Democratic Center Union (UCD) as the government party from 1977 to 1981. Suárez's background as a successful bureaucrat and head of the National Movement (although for less than a year) causes the king to choose him to create a democratic government. He uses a center party backed by right-wing voters to pursue left-of-center policies. |
| 1982 | Dec. 2 | Felipe González Márquez (1942– ) is the first socialist since Juan Negrín to lead a Spanish government. González develops the socialist PSOE into a broad coalition that uses the theme of social justice without extreme sectarianism. |

## Political Life

| 1975 | Dec. 4 | Juan Carlos keeps Arias Navarro as premier of a broad coalition cabinet that includes Fraga, José María de Areiza, and Adolfo Suárez. |
| 1976 | Mar. 3 | Five workers are killed in a political demonstration in Vitoria as labor protests the slow pace of change and the cabinet's moderation. |
| | Mar. 26 | The anti-Franco opposition creates the Democratic Coordination as a coalition party. Fraga has its leaders arrested on 3 Apr. Juan Carlos believes that this violates his democratic program, and he begins to support Suárez over Fraga or Arias. |
| | Mar. 28 | The church supports freedom for labor unions. |
| | July 1 | Arias Navarro resigns. He is too closely tied to the Franco years. |
| | July 3 | The cabinet of Adolfo Suárez is composed mainly of young, right-wing Christian Democrats. |
| | July 13 | Suárez renews Spain's EEC application. |
| | July 14 | New liberal penal reforms are proposed. |
| | Aug. 4 | A sweeping political amnesty is made. Jailed communist party members are freed on 30 Aug. |

| | | |
|---|---|---|
| | Oct. 9 | The Right forms the Popular Alliance as a coalition party. |
| | Nov. 19 | The political-reform law is the first constitutional reform made by the new monarchy. It accepts popular sovereignty, universal suffrage, and political pluralism. The Cortes is composed of a Congress of 350 deputies elected by proportional representation and a Senate of 207 elected by a simple majority. The king can submit bills, dissolve the Cortes, and call new elections. |
| | Dec. 15 | The national referendum on the political-reform law is 90 percent affirmative. |
| 1977 | Jan. 23 | Rightists bomb the Atocha station in Madrid. Ten die as unrest and uncertainty sweep the city. There is fear of both the Left and the Right. |
| | Feb. 8 | The political-reform law is amended by the Cortes to bar the military from politics. |
| | Feb. 11 | Adolfo Suárez and Santiago Carrillo secretly meet. The PCE leader promises that his party is interested only in peaceful change. Suárez legalizes the PCE on 7 Apr. |
| | Feb. 12 | The government makes a sweeping arrest of rightists. |
| | Mar. 2 | Eurocommunist parties hold their annual meeting in Madrid. |
| | Apr. 7 | The National Movement disbands. No successor party is created. |
| | May 14 | Basque riots cause the death of six persons. |
| | June 15 | Free national elections, the first since 1936, give the UCD 165 seats, the PSOE 118, the PCE 20, Fraga's Popular Alliance 11, and the BNP 8 in the House. The UCD also wins a majority in the Senate. Suárez wins 80 percent of the vote. |
| | July 4 | Suárez reforms his cabinet, but there are few surprises. |
| | July 22 | The new Cortes opens and begins to draft a new constitution. It is not approved until 29 Sept. 1978. |
| | Sept. 29 | The Cortes restores the Catalan state (Generalitat). Josep Tarradellas, its president in 1939, ends his exile and returns. No local elections are held until 1981. |
| | Oct. 5 | The Moncloa Pact is an agreement between Suárez and the Left that promises to index wage increases with inflation, raise welfare benefits, and introduce the progressive income tax. In Feb. 1978, Suárez says the pact is "virtually dead." |
| | Dec. 31 | The Basque Provinces are granted autonomy. |
| 1978 | Feb. 2 | Sexual equality is passed by the Cortes. |
| | Feb. 12 | The CCOO wins a series of affiliation victories without government opposition. |
| | Feb. 24 | The first crisis of the democratic era begins when the Left challenges Suárez's cabinet over its weak economic efforts. |

| | | |
|---|---|---|
| | Apr. 19 | The PCE holds its first legal congress since 1938. Eurocommunism becomes its official philosophy. "Leninist" is dropped from the party title, and Santiago Carrillo is reappointed as its president. |
| | Apr. 26 | Contraception is legalized by the Cortes. A debate over abortion is quickly stalemated. |
| | Sept. 28 | The Constitution of 1978 is approved by the Cortes. It incorporates recognition of constitutional monarchy as the basic form of government, autonomy of the nationalities (balanced by the indissoluble unity of the nation), and disestablishment of the church (while acknowledging its historical role). |
| | Oct. 5 | The ETA begins a campaign of terrorism that lasts through Dec. Two high-ranking police officials are killed on 21 July, many ETA members are arrested, and the ETA responds with great violence. |
| | Dec. 6 | The constitution is approved by 87 percent in a national referendum. |
| 1979 | Jan. 9 | Supreme Court judge Miguel Cruz Cuenca is assassinated by the ETA. |
| | Jan. 23 | A government wage ceiling provokes new labor unrest. |
| | Jan. 30 | France arrests thirty Basque terrorists. |
| | Feb. 1 | New antiterrorist legislation is drafted by the Cortes. |
| | Mar. 1 | National elections see the UCD win 165 seats, a gain of 3. The PSOE takes 121 seats, adding 3. Fraga's new party, the Democratic Coalition, wins only 9 seats, a loss of 7 over his old party, the Popular Alliance. A new Andalusian socialist party wins 6 seats. Jordi Pujol's Catalan Democratic Convergence Party merges with the Catalan Democratic Union to create the Convergence and Unity Party (CIV). |
| | May 30 | National economic difficulties lead to an unsuccessful censure motion vs. Suárez. |
| | July 17 | A Basque autonomy statute is passed by the Cortes. It is approved by referendum on 7 Oct. Carlos Garaicochea (1939– ) becomes the pres. of the new Basque autonomous government. |
| | Sept. 30 | The PSOE drops "Marxist" from its official party title. |
| | Nov. 11 | A pro-Franco rally is held in Madrid. |
| | Dec. 11 | Controversy over an abortion trial raises heated debate. A campaign begins in support of abortion. |
| 1980 | Jan. 10 | A Basque police chief is assassinated by the ETA. |
| | Jan. 11 | The Catalans and Basques start home rule. |
| | Mar. 12 | The Aragonese protest construction of atomic energy plants. |

| | Mar. 21 | Elections for the Catalan parliament are won by the CIV with 28 percent of the vote. Jordi Pujol becomes Catalan pres. when Tarradellas steps down. |
| | Apr. 1 | The Basque parliament is opened. |
| | May 30 | Suárez still faces criticism over economic conditions. |
| | Aug. 19 | Hunger marches occur in Andalusia. |
| | Oct. 23 | A home-rule bill for Andalusia is passed by the national Cortes. |
| | Dec. 21 | A similar home-rule bill is passed for Galicia. |
| 1981 | Jan. 29 | Suárez resigns the premiership after the UCD criticizes him for a lack of internal debate within the party and for secretive and authoritarian leadership in general. He seeks to return to office without the UCD. |
| | Feb. 16 | A general strike in the Basque Provinces raises national tensions. |
| | Feb. 23 | The Civil Guard revolts when Lt. Col. Antonio Tejero Molín seizes the Cortes at gunpoint. Gen. Jaime Milans Bosch, commander of the Valencia military region, issues a state-of-emergency decree and presses the king to create a military regime. Juan Carlos refuses and the revolt fails. The king's popularity reaches a new high. |
| | Feb. 26 | A new cabinet led by Leopoldo Calvo Sotelo (1926– ) is formed. The premier and many of the ministers are UCD members. |
| | Apr. 3? | A referendum in Galicia approves home rule. The UCD and PSOE hold talks on improving the autonomy process. |
| | June 22 | In a radical reaction to the Jan. revolt, the national Cortes moves to the left and passes a divorce bill. In July and Aug., cuts are made in the military budget. At the same time, autonomy is approved for Galicia and a slower process created for Andalusia. |
| | July 28 | In a more conservative mood, the Cortes passes the Organic Law on the Harmonization of the Autonomy Process Bill (LOAPA), an act designed to sort out and organize the autonomy process. |
| | Oct. 20 | The Popular Alliance defeats the UCD in the Galician elections, a victory for the Right. |
| 1982 | Mar. 25 | The defendants in the abortion trial are found guilty. |
| | May 23 | The PSOE defeats the UCD in the Andalusian elections. In other elections, Murcia votes for home rule, as do Valencia in June and Castile, the Canary Islands, and Navarre in July. |
| | June 3 | The plotters of the 1981 revolt are found guilty. |
| | July 28 | Suárez resigns from the UCD to form the Democratic Center and Social party (CDS). |

| | | |
|---|---|---|
| | Aug. 27 | The national Cortes is dissolved and new elections are called. |
| | Oct. 2 | Military officers are arrested for planning another revolt the day before the elections on 27 Oct. |
| | Oct. 28 | In the national elections, the PSOE wins an overwhelming victory by gaining 202 seats. Suárez's new CDS wins only 2 seats, the PCE only 4 (down from 23), and the UCD 12. The PSOE's 47 percent of the vote is the greatest electoral triumph in Spanish parliamentary history. |
| | Nov. 11 | Santiago Carrillo resigns as leader of the PCE in the aftermath of the party's poor showing in the elections. |
| | Dec. 2 | Felipe González is sworn in as the premier of the new socialist-dominated cabinet. |
| 1983 | Feb. 2 | Rumesa, a large manufacturing company with eighteen banks and four hundred companies established through government aid during the Franco era, is found to be fraudulently insolvent. The state takes over its operations on 23 Feb. A bank holiday is declared. |
| | Mar. 2? | Felipe González announces a new restructuring of Spanish industry, a sweeping modernization of productive facilities. |
| | May? | The PSOE wins regional elections. |
| | July? | The national Cortes passes González's industrial restructuring bill. |
| | Aug. 10 | The Supreme Court rules that regional governments should control many aspects of local life, a major decision in the 150-year-long quarrel over democratic local government. |
| 1984 | Jan. 24 | A major government offensive is started vs. the ETA. |
| | Feb. 26 | The PNV defeats the ETA in elections for the Basque parliament. |
| | Mar. 19 | The national Cortes approves entry into the EEC. |
| | July 3 | José María Ruiz Mateos, owner of Rumesa, seeks political asylum in West Germany. |
| | Aug. 14 | The ETA rejects government talks. |
| | Sept. 24 | France begins to cooperate with Spain vs. ETA. |
| | Nov. 1 | The state imposes new controls on church-run schools. |
| | Dec. 22 | José Antonio Ardanza becomes premier of the Basque Provinces. |
| 1985 | Aug. 2 | Rumesa is sold to private investors. |
| | Sept. 11 | Spain joins the EEC. |
| 1986 | Jan. 1 | Spain's membership in the EEC formally begins. |
| | Mar. 12 | The national referendum to stay in NATO passes by 89 percent. |
| | Apr. 20 | Santiago Carrillo is expelled from the PCE. |
| | Apr. 22 | The national Cortes is dissolved and new elections are called. |

|          | Apr. 25  | An ETA bombing in Madrid kills five. |
|----------|----------|--------------------------------------|
|          | June 22  | The PSOE wins 184 of the 350 Cortes seats in the national elections, a drop from 202. González continues as premier. |
|          | July 21  | The ETA kills nine Civil Guards in Madrid. González rejects any further negotiations with the ETA. |
|          | Oct. 31  | The first civilian head of the Civil Guard is appointed. |
|          | Nov. 30  | Elections for the Basque parliament sees the PNV split four ways. The PSOE increases its seats. |
|          | Dec. 2   | Manuel Fraga resigns as head of the Popular Alliance. |
| 1987     | Jan. 23  | Students demonstrate for university reform and open admissions. It is the largest protest in recent years. |
|          | Feb. 23  | The PNV and PSOE form a coalition government in the Basque Provinces. |
|          | Feb. 24  | The national cabinet eases antiterrorist laws. |
|          | June 10  | The PSOE loses control of twenty-one of twenty-seven large cities in local elections. Increased student and labor hostility is a consequence. |
|          | June 19  | An ETA car bomb outside a Barcelona supermarket kills fifteen. |
|          | Oct. 4   | The police seal the border to prevent the ETA from using French territory for attacks. More than five hundred have been killed in the ETA's campaigns. On 29 Nov., an even larger police action attacks the ETA. |
|          | Dec. 15  | An ETA bomb kills eleven in Saragossa. |
| 1988     | Feb. 22  | PCE elects Julio Anguita as the new secretary-general of the party. |
|          | July 18  | In a cabinet reshuffle, the writer and former communist Jorge Semprún is made minister of culture. |
|          | Nov. 17  | Some of the participants in the military coup of 1981 are paroled. |
|          | Nov. 26  | Fraga returns to political life by becoming the leader of the Popular Alliance party. |
|          | Dec. 14  | The UGT strikes and leads a protest vs. González over the high level of unemployment and the need for wage increases. Serious strains appear in the PSOE leadership. |

## War and Diplomacy

| 1975 | Dec. 1  | Spain attempts to administer the Spanish Sahara jointly with Morocco and Mauritania. When this arrangement fails, Spain leaves the Sahara. Moroccan and Algerian guerrillas struggle to control the area. |
|------|---------|----------------------------------------------------------------------------------------------------------------------------------------------------------------------|
| 1977 | Feb. 9  | Spain and the U.S.S.R. resume diplomatic relations. |

|       | July 28   | Diplomatic ties are restored with Mexico for the first time since the civil war. |
|-------|-----------|----------------------------------------------------------------------------------|
| 1978  | Sept. 6   | Adolfo Suárez begins a state visit to Latin America. |
| 1979  | Jan. 3    | The Concordat of 1953 lapses with the Vatican without a new agreement. |
| 1980  | Apr. 10   | Tension between Britain and Spain over Gibraltar eases with the signing of new accords. |
|       | June 26   | U.S. Pres. Jimmy Carter (1920– ) visits Spain. |
|       | Sept. 8   | The national Cortes votes in favor of Spain's membership in NATO. |
| 1981  | Nov. 13   | Spain gets a seat on the U.N. Security Council. |
|       | Nov. 27   | Britain supports Spanish membership in the EEC. |
| 1982  | Jan. 8    | The Spanish border with Gibraltar is opened. |
|       | May 8     | Spain's entry into NATO is approved. |
|       | Nov. 7    | Juan Carlos makes a state visit to the United States to reassure Pres. Ronald Reagan (1911– ) that González's election is no threat to democracy. |
|       | Dec. 15   | U.S. Sec. of State George Shultz (1920– ) meets Felipe González in Madrid. |
| 1983  | May 3     | González begins a diplomatic tour of Latin America. |
| 1984  | Mar. 19   | Prolonged diplomacy precedes the national Cortes's approval of EEC membership. |
|       | Nov. 27   | The Gibraltar pact between Britain and Spain receives preliminary approval before it stalls over the ultimate disposition of the colony. The border is closed again until 5 Feb. 1985. |
| 1985  | May 6     | Pres. Ronald Reagan visits Juan Carlos and Felipe González in Madrid. |
| 1986  | Jan. 14   | The Gibraltar conference remains stalemated. |
|       | Apr. 22   | Juan Carlos makes a state visit to Britain to press Spanish claims for Gibraltar. |
| 1987  | Nov. 13   | The United States and Spain fail to agree on provisions concerning Torrejón air base. Spain bars F–16 jet fighters from U.S. base at Torrejón, outside Madrid. |
| 1988  | Jan. 20   | The United States agrees to abandon its base at Torrejón within three years. |

## Economics

| 1976  | Nov. 19   | Labor unions are legalized. |
|-------|-----------|-----------------------------|
| 1977  | Oct. 5    | The Moncloa Pact indexes wages to inflation. It represents an effort to negotiate responsibly with labor. |

| 1979 | Jan. 23 | New government wage ceiling leads to new strikes. |
| 1980 | Mar. 5 | Unemployment reaches its highest level in the democratic era. |
| 1983 | Jan. 30 | Wage controls are extended. |
| | Feb. 25 | The Rumesa scandal leads to a banking crisis. The Rumesa properties are subsequently sold to private investors. |
| 1985 | June 20 | PCE-led one-day strike vs. the austerity measures of González becomes the first major national strike since 1977. |
| 1986 | Oct. 17 | Barcelona wins international competition to stage the 1992 Olympic Games. |
| 1988 | Dec. 14 | The UGT protests the economic policies of Felipe González with a one-day national general strike. Divisions appear between the PSOE and the UGT, both branches of the socialist movement. |

## Culture

| 1976 | May 4 | Juan Luis Cebrián edits a new national newspaper, *El País*. *Diario 16* resumes publishing. |
| 1977 | Jan. 4 | The political-reform act abolishes censorship. |
| | Mar. 12 | The poet Vicente Aleixandre (1898– ) wins the Nobel Prize for literature. |

# Selected Bibliography

The following bibliography is designed for the general reader or the beginning student of modern Spanish history who requires an introduction to the basic monographic literature of the field. Its scope and content are therefore limited in several ways, above all, by the language, place, type, and format of publication. As a general rule, only books written in Spanish or English have been included, the major exception being for studies dealing with the eighteenth century, on which French scholarship—not surprisingly—has left its distinctive signature. Furthermore, wherever they exist, both English-language translations as well as revised or later editions have been cited. The bibliography is also weighted in favor of contemporary treatments, although older works and classic studies are interspersed throughout. An effort has also been made, broadly speaking, to concentrate on monographs. Government reports, documentary collections, and other such published primary material have generally been excluded, as have articles in magazines and scholarly journals. It is assumed that the reader in search of these resources will either already have sufficient knowledge of where to find them or will consult the bibliographies appended to the books. A small number of memoirs and journalistic accounts—primarily for the section on the Spanish Civil War—have also been listed.

The bibliography has been further limited by the sheer volume of work produced over the last twenty-five years. The tendency among both Spanish and non-Spanish historians studying the modern era to gravitate toward the eighteenth century and the Napoleonic intervention was strongly reinforced under the Francoist regime, with its apotheosis of the values of Catholic, imperial Spain and its singular distaste for the more pluralist, secular-minded traditions spawned in the nineteenth century. The death of Franco in 1975, however, fueled a great surge of interest, which had been gathering force for a decade, in studying Spain's more recent past. By the late 1970s, historical interest in examining the problems of nineteenth-century Spain and the Spanish Civil War and pre–civil war periods, not to speak of the Francoist era itself, had become, to borrow Sir Raymond Carr's phrase, "a growth industry." Hundreds of books by Spaniards and non-Spaniards alike began appearing on library shelves. To more than skim the surface of this production, in a listing of this length and scope, would obviously be impossible.

The bibliography has been arranged into eight topical-chronological sections, which parallel the usual divisions of modern Spanish history. These are followed by a section covering bibliographies and guides and a final section listing journals. The latter are further subdivided into those published within and outside of Spain. With regard to the Spanish periodicals, it should be noted that the many local historical journals sponsored by the Consejo Superior de Investigaciones Científicas (CSIC) have not been included. The general section, as its name implies, contains works that either cover the entire range of modern Spanish history or overlap several periods. Within all sections, titles have been listed alphabetically by main entry. In conclusion, I should like to acknowledge my debt to two leading historians of modern Spain, Richard Herr and Sir Raymond Carr. The bibliographic essays appended to their books have served as the basis for many of my selections.

R. T. Davidson

## GENERAL WORKS

Alba, Víctor. *The Communist Party in Spain*. Translated by Vincent G. Smith. New Brunswick: Transaction, 1983.

―――. *Twentieth-Century Spain: Republic, Dictatorship, and Monarchy*. Translated by Barbara Lotito. New Brunswick: Transaction, 1978.

Ardit Lucas, Manuel. *Revolución liberal y revuelta campesina. Un ensayo sobre la desintegración del régimen feudal en el país valenciano (1793–1840)*. Barcelona: Ediciones Ariel, 1977.

Artola, Miguel. *Antiguo Régimen y revolución liberal*. Barcelona: Ediciones Ariel, 1978.

―――. *La burguesía revolucionaria (1808–1869)*. Madrid: Alianza Editorial, 1973.

―――. *El latifundio: propiedad y explotación: SS. xviii–xx*. (Estudios). Madrid: Servicio de Publicaciones Agrarias, 1978.

―――. *Partidos y programas políticos, 1808–1936*. 2 vols. (Biblioteca Cultura e Historia). Madrid: Aguilar, 1974–1975.

*El Banco de España, una historia económica*. Madrid: Servicio de Estudios del Banco de España, 1970.

*El Banco de Vizcaya y su aportación a la economía española*. Bilbao: Banco de Vizcaya, 1955.

Beltrán Flórez, L. *La industria algodonera española*. Barcelona: 1943.

Bernal, A. *La propiedad de la tierra y las luchas agrarias andaluzas*. Barcelona: Ediciones Ariel, 1974.

Brenan, Gerald. *The Spanish Labyrinth: An Account of the Social and Political Background of the Civil War*. 2d ed. Cambridge: University Press, 1950.

Bruguera, F. G. *Histoire contemporaine d'Espagne, 1789–1950*. Paris: Ed. Ophrys, 1953.

Busquets, Julio. *El militar de carrera en España: Estudio de sociología militar*. Barcelona: Ediciones Ariel, 1967.

Callahan, William J. *Church, Politics, and Society in Spain, 1750–1874*. Cambridge, Mass.: Harvard University Press, 1984.

Carmona García, Juan Ignacio. *Una aportación a la demografía de Sevilla en los siglos xviii y xix: Las series parroquiales de San Martín (1750–1860)*. Seville: Diputación Provincial, 1976.

Caro Baroja, Julio. *Los pueblos de España*. 2d ed. 2 vols. (Colección Fundamentos, 54–55). Madrid: Ediciones ISTMO, 1976.

Carr, Raymond. *Modern Spain, 1875–1980*. Oxford: Oxford University Press, 1980.

———. *Spain, 1800–1975*. 2d ed. (Oxford History of Modern Europe). Oxford: Clarendon Press, 1982.

Carrera Pujal, Jaime. *Historia de la economía española*. Prologue by Román Perpina Grail. 2 vols. Barcelona: Bosch, 1943–1944.

———. *Historia política de Cataluña en el siglo xix*. 7 vols. Barcelona: Bosch, 1951–1958.

Carrión, Pascual. *Estudios sobre la agricultura española, 1919–1971*. Madrid: Edic. de la Revista de Trabajo, 1974.

———. *Los latifundios en España: Su importancia, origen, consecuencias y solución*. Prologue by Fernando de los Ríos. (Horas de España). Barcelona: Ediciones Ariel, 1972.

Casares Alonso, Aníbal. *Estudio histórico económico de las construcciones ferroviarias españolas en el siglo xix*. (Estudios del Instituto Iberoamericano de Desarrollo Económico). Madrid: Publicaciones de la Escuela Nacional de Administración Pública, 1973.

Castells Arteche, José Manuel. *Las asociaciones religiosas en la España contemporánea, 1767–1965: Un estudio jurídico-administrativo*. Prologue by M. Artola. (Biblioteca Política Taurus, 21). Madrid: Taurus, 1973.

Castro, Américo. *The Structure of Spanish History*. Translated by Edmund King. Princeton: Princeton University Press, 1954.

Checkland, S. G. *The Mines of Tharsis: Roman, French and British Enterprise in Spain*. London: George Allen and Unwin, 1967.

Cierva, Ricardo de la. *Historia básica de la España actual: (1800–1974)*. 12th ed. (Espejo de España, vol. 8: Serie La Historia Viva). Barcelona: Planeta, 1981.

Comín Colomer, Eduardo. *Historia del anarquismo español: 1836–1948*. Madrid: Editorial R.A.D.A.R., [1948].

Cortada, James W. *Two Nations over Time: Spain and the United States, 1776–1977*. Westport, Conn.: Greenwood Press, 1978.

———, ed. *Spain in the Twentieth-Century World: Essays on Spanish Diplomacy, 1898–1978*. (Contributions in Political Science, 30). Westport, Conn.: Greenwood Press, 1980.

Cuenca Toribio, José Manuel. *Estudios sobre la iglesia española del xix*. (Libros de Bolsillo Rialp, 63). Madrid: Ediciones Rialp, 1973.

———. *La iglesia española ante la revolutión liberal*. (Libros de Bolsillo Rialp, 58). Madrid: Ediciones Rialp, 1971.

Delgado, Jaime. *España y Mexico en el siglio xix*. 3 vols. Madrid: CSIC, 1950.

Díaz del Moral, J. *Historia de las agitaciones campesinas andaluzas–Córdoba*. Rev. ed. Madrid: Alianza Editorial, 1973.

Elorza, Antonio, and María del Carmen Iglesias. *Burguesía y proletarios: Clase obrera y reforma social en la restauración, 1884–1889*. (Papel, 451). Barcelona: Editorial Laia, 1973.

Fernández de Pinedo, Emiliano. *Crecimiento económico y transformaciones sociales del país vasco (1100–1850)*. Madrid: Siglo Veintiuno, 1974.

Fernández Albaladejo, Pablo. *La crisis del antiguo régimen en Guipúzcoa, 1766–1833: Cambio económico e historia*. Madrid: Akal, 1975.

Fontana i Lázaro, Josep. *Cambio económico y actitudes políticas en la España del siglo xix*. 3d ed. (Ariel Quincenal, 88). Barcelona: Ediciones Ariel, 1980.

———. *La hacienda en la historia de España, 1700–1931*. Madrid: Instituto de Estudios Fiscales, 1980.

Frías, Lesmes. *La provincia de Castilla de la Compañía de Jesús desde 1863 hasta 1914*. Bilbao-Deusto: El Mensajero del Corazón de Jesús, 1915.

———. *La provincia de España de la Compañía de Jesús 1815–1863: Reseña histórica ilustrada*. Madrid: Sucesores de Rivadeneyra, 1914.

Fusi Aizpurúa, Juan Pablo. *Política obrera en el país vasco (1880–1923)*. Madrid: Ediciones Turner, 1975.

García Delgado, José Luis. *Orígenes y desarrollo del capitalismo en España: Notas críticas*. (Divulgación Universitarias, 76: Cuestiones Españoles). Madrid: Editorial Cuadernos para El Diálogo, 1975.

García Escudero, José María. *Historia política de las dos Españas*. 2d ed. Madrid: Editora Nacional, 1976.

García Venero, Maximiano. *Historia de los movimientos sindicalistas españoles (1840–1933)*. Madrid: Ediciones del Movimiento, 1961.

———. *Historia del nacionalismo catalán (1793–1936)*. Rev. ed. 2 vols. (Colección "Tierra, Historia y Política": Serie Historia). Madrid: Editora Nacional, 1967.

———. *Historia del nacionalismo vasco (1793–1936)*. Madrid: Editora Nacional, 1945.

García-Villaslada, R., ed. *Historia de la iglesia en España*. 5 vols. Madrid: Autores Cristianos, 1979.

Gil Delgado, Francisco. *Conflicto iglesia-estado*. Madrid: Sedmay Ediciones, 1975.

Gil Munilla, Octavio. *Historia de la evolución social española durante los siglos xix y xx*. Madrid: Publicaciones Españolas, 1961.

Harrison, Joseph. *An Economic History of Modern Spain*. Manchester: Manchester University Press, 1978.

Hennessy, C.A.M. *Modern Spain*. (Historical Association Pamphlet, No. 59). London: Historical Association, 1965.

Herr, Richard. *An Historical Essay on Modern Spain*. Berkeley: University of California Press, 1974.

Iturralde, Juan de. *El catolicismo y la cruzada de Franco*. 2d ed. 2 vols. San Sebastian: Gráficas Izarra, 1978.

Jover Zamora, José María. *Conciencia burguesa y conciencia obrera en la España contemporánea*. 2d ed. (Colección "O Crece o Muere," vol. 6). Madrid: Ateneo, 1956.

———. *Política, diplomacia y humanismo popular: Estudios sobre la vida española en el siglo xix*. (Ediciones Turner, 24). Madrid: Turner, 1976.

Kenny, M. *A Spanish Tapestry: Town and Country in Castile*. Bloomington: Indiana University Press, 1962.

Lacomba Avellán, Juan Antonio. *Introducción a la historia económica de la España contemporánea*. 2d ed. (Colección Biblioteca Universitaria de Economía: Manuales). Madrid: Guadiana de Publicaciones, 1972.

López Ontiveros, Antonio. *Emigración, propiedad y paisaje agrario en la campiña del Córdoba*. (Colección Elcano, 3). Barcelona: Ediciones Ariel, 1974.

Lorenzo, César M. *Los anarquistas españoles y el poder (1868–1969)*. (España Contemporánea). Paris: Ruedo Ibérico, 1972.

Madariaga, Salvador de. *Spain*. New York: Frederick Praeger, 1958.

Martínez Albiach, Alfredo. *Religiosidad hispana y sociedad borbónica*. (Publicaciones de la Facultad Teológica del Norte de España, Ser. A, no. 6). Burgos: 1969.

Martínez Cuadrado, Miguel. *La burguesía conservadora, 1874–1931*. (Historia de España Alfaguara, vol. 6). Madrid: Alianza Editorial Alfaguara, 1973.

———. *Elecciones y partidos políticos de España, 1868–1931*. 2 vols. (Biblioteca Política Taurus, 13/1–13/2). Madrid: Taurus, 1969.

Moxó, Salvador de. *La disolución del régimen señorial en España*. Madrid: CSIC, 1969.

Nadal Oller, Jorge. *El fracaso de la revolución industrial en España, 1814–1913*. 5th ed. (Ariel Historia, vol. 5). Barcelona: Ediciones Ariel, 1982.

———. *La población española: Siglos xvi al xx*. Rev. ed. (Colección Ariel, vol. 12). Barcelona: Ediciones Ariel, 1984.

Nieto, Alejandro. *La retribución de los funcionarios en España (Historia y Actualidad)*. Madrid: Revista de Occidente, 1967.

Olábarri Gorbazar, Ignacio. *Relaciones laborales en Vizcaya (1890–1936)*. Durango: Leopoldo Zugaza, Editor, 1978.

Padilla Bolívar, Antonio. *El movimiento socialista español*. (Colección Textos, 32). Barcelona: Planeta, 1977.

Payne, Stanley. *A History of Spain and Portugal*. 2 vols. Madison: University of Wisconsin Press, 1973.

———. *Spanish Catholicism: An Historical Overview*. Madison: University of Wisconsin Press, 1984.

Peers, E. Allison. *Catalonia Infelix*. London: Methuen, 1937.

———. *Spain, the Church, and the Orders*. London: Burns, Oates, and Washbourne, 1945.

Pérez Garzón, Juan Sisinio. *Milicia nacional y revolución burguesa: El prototipo madrileño, 1808–1874*. Prologue by Manuel Espadas Burgos. (Evolución Socio-Económica de la España Moderna y Contemporánea). Madrid: CSIC, 1978.

Peset Reig, Mariano, and José Luis Peset. *La universidad española (siglos xviii y xix): Despotismo ilustrado y revolución liberal*. (Biblioteca Política Taurus, 23). Madrid: Taurus, 1974.

Pitt Rivers, Julian. *The People of the Sierra*. Chicago: University of Chicago Press, 1961.

Posada, Adolfo. *Evolución legislativa del régimen local en España, 1812–1909*. Madrid: Instituto de Administración Local, 1982.

Preston, Paul. *Las derechas españolas en el siglo xx: Autoritarismo, fascismo y golpismo*. Madrid: Editorial Sistema, 1986.

Pugés, Manuel. *Cómo triunfó el proteccionismo en España: La formación de la política arancelaria española*. Prologue by Pedro Gual Villabí. Barcelona: Editorial Juventud, 1931.

Rama, Carlos. *La crisis española del siglo xx*. 3d ed. Mexico City: Fondo de Cultura Económica, 1976.

Ramos Oliveira, Antonio. *Politics, Economics and Men of Modern Spain, 1808–1946*. Translated by Teener Hall. London: Victor Gollancz, 1946.

Ringrose, David R. *Madrid and the Spanish Economy, 1560–1850*. Berkeley: University of California Press, 1983.

———. *Transportation and Economic Stagnation in Spain, 1750–1850*. Durham: Duke University Press, 1970.

Roldán, Santiago, et al. *La consolidación del capitalismo en España 1914–1920*. 2 vols.

(Libros de Bolsillo, 7). Madrid: Confederación Española de Cajas de Ahorro, 1974.

Romero de Solís, Pedro. *La población española en los siglos xviii y xix: Estudio de sociodemografía histórica.* Madrid: Siglo Veintiuno, 1973.

Saez Marín, Juan. *Datos sobre la Iglesia española contemporánea, 1768–1868.* (España en 3 Tiempos). Madrid: Editora Nacional, 1975.

Sánchez Agesta, Luis. *Historia del constitucionalismo español: La revolución liberal.* Madrid: Instituto de Estudios Políticos, 1955.

Sánchez-Albornoz, Nicolás. *Las crisis de subsistencias de España en el siglo xix.* (Universidad Nacional del Litoral, Instituto de Investigaciones Históricas, Serie C: Colección de Estudios y Monografías, no. 1). Rosario, Arg.: Instituto de Investigaciones Históricas, 1964.

———. *España hace un siglo: Una economía dual.* Barcelona: Ediciones Península, 1968.

———. *Jalones en la modernización de España.* (Ariel Quincenal, 114). Barcelona: Ediciones Ariel, 1975.

———. *Modernización económica en España, 1830–1930.* (Colección Alianza Universidad, 419). Madrid: Alianza Editorial, 1985.

Sardá Dexeus, Juan. *La política monetaria y las fluctuaciones de la economía española en el siglo xix.* (Colección Demos). Barcelona: Ediciones Ariel, 1948.

Saurín de la Iglesia, María Rosa. *Apuntes y documentos para una historia de Galicia en el siglo xix.* La Coruna: Diputación Provincial, 1977.

———. *Sociedad, literatura y política en la España del siglo xix.* (Biblioteca Universitaria Guadiana). Madrid: Guadiana de Publicaciones, 1973.

Schwartz Girón, Pedro, ed. *Ensayos sobre la economía española a mediados del siglo xix.* Madrid: Servicios de Estudios del Banco de España, 1970.

Shubert, Adrian. *Hacia la revolucion: Orígenes sociales del movimiento obrero en Asturias, 1860–1934.* Barcelona: Editorial Crítica, 1984.

Simón Segura, Francisco. *La desamortización española del siglo xix.* Madrid: Ministerio de Hacienda, Instituto de Estudios Fiscales, 1972.

Soldevila Zubiburu, Fernando. *Historia de Catalunya.* 3 vols. Barcelona: 1934–1935.

———. *Historia de España.* Barcelona: Ediciones Ariel, 1957–1959.

Tallada Pauli, José María. *Historia de las finanzas españolas en el siglo xix.* Madrid: Espasa-Calpe, 1946.

Témime, Emile, et al. *Historia de la España contemporánea, desde 1808 hasta nuestros días.* Translated by Albert Carreras. (Ariel Historia, vol. 31). Barcelona: Ediciones Ariel, 1982.

Torres Balbás, Leopoldo, et al. *Resumen histórico del urbanismo en España.* Madrid: Instituto de Estudios de Administración Local, 1954.

Tortella Casares, Gabriel. *Los orígenes del capitalismo en España: Banca, industria y ferrocarriles en el siglo xix.* 2d ed. (Serie de Historia). Madrid: Tecnos, 1973.

Tuñón de Lara, Manuel. *La España del siglo xix (1808–1914).* Barcelona: Editorial Laia, 1973.

———. *Estudios sobre el siglo xix español.* 8th ed. Madrid: Siglo Veintiuno, 1984.

———. *El movimiento obrero en la historia de España.* 3 vols. (Ediciones de Bolsillo, 502: Historia). Barcelona: Editorial Laia, 1977.

Tusell Gómez, Xavier. *La España del siglo xx: Desde Alfonso XIII a la muerte de Carrero Blanco.* (Colección Imágenes Históricas de Hoy, 7). Barcelona: DOPESA, 1975.

Ubieto, A., et al. *Introducción a la historia de España*. 7th ed. Barcelona: Editorial Teide, 1970.

Vicens Vives, Jaime. *An Economic History of Spain*. Translated by Frances López-Tropillas. Princeton: Princeton University Press, 1969.

———. *Approaches to the History of Spain*. Translated and edited by Joan Connelly Ullman. 2d rev. ed. Berkeley: University of California Press, 1972.

———. *Cataluña en el siglo xix*. Translated by E. Borrás Cubells. Prologue by Emilio Giralt y Raventós. Madrid: Ediciones Rialp, 1961.

———, ed. *Historia social y económica de España y America*, vol. 5: *Burguesía, industrialización, obrerismo*. Barcelona: Editorial Teide, 1959.

Vilar, Pierre. *Spain: A Brief History*. Translated by Brian Tate. Oxford: Pergamon Press, 1967.

Villacosta Baños, Francisco. *Burguesía y cultura: Los intelectuales españoles en la sociedad liberal, 1808–1931*. (Estudios de Historia Contemporánea). Madrid: Siglo Veintiuno, 1980.

Viñas Mey, Carmelo. *La reforma agraria en España en el siglo xix*. Santiago de Compostela: Tip. de "El Eco Franciscano," 1933.

Wais San Martín, Francisco. *Historia general de los ferrocarriles españoles*. 2d ed. (España en 3 Tiempos). Madrid: Editora Nacional, 1974.

## THE EIGHTEENTH CENTURY AND THE WAR OF INDEPENDENCE, 1700–1814

Artola, Miguel. *Los afrancesados*. Prologue by Gregorio Marañón. Madrid: Sociedad de Estudio y Publicaciones, 1953.

———. *Los orígenes de la España contemporánea*. 2d ed. 2 vols. (Colección Historia Política). Madrid: Instituto de Estudios Políticos, 1975–1976.

Anes Alvarez, Gonzalo. *El antiguo régimen: Los Borbones*. 6th ed. (Historia de España Alfaguara, vol. 4). Madrid: Alianza Editorial, 1983.

———. *Las crisis agrarias en la España moderna*. (Biblioteca Política Taurus, 16). Madrid: Taurus, 1970.

———. *Economía e "Ilustración" en la España del siglo xviii*. 3d ed. (Ariel Quincenal, vol. 19). Barcelona: Ediciones Ariel, 1981.

Corona Baratech, Carlos. *La doctrina del poder absoluto en España: En la crisis del xviii al xix*. (Cuadernos de la Cátedra Feijóo, no. 13). Oviedo: Universidad de Oviedo, 1962.

———. *Revolución y reacción en el reinado de Carlos IV*. (Biblioteca del Pensamiento Actual, 68). Madrid: Ediciones Rialp, 1957.

DeFourneaux, Marcelin. *L'Inquisition espagnol et les livres français an XVIIIe siècle*. Paris: Presses Universitaires de France, 1963.

———. *Pablo de Olavides ou l'Afrancesado (1725–1803)*. Paris: Presses Universitaries de France, 1959.

Delpy, Gaspard. *Feijóo et l'esprit Européen: Essai sur les idées-maîtresses dans le "Théâtre Critique" et les "Lettres érudites" (1725–1760). . . .* Paris: Librairie Hachette, 1936.

Demerson, Georges. *Don Juan Meléndez Valdés y su tiempo, 1754–1817*. Translated by Angel Guillén. 2 vols. Madrid: Taurus, 1971.

Desdevizes de Dézert, Georges Nicolas. *L'Espagne de l'ancien régime*. 3 vols. Paris: Société Française d'imprimerie et de Librairie, 1897–1904.

Domínguez Ortiz, Antonio. *La sociedad española en el siglo xviii*. 2 vols. (Monografías Histórico-Sociales, vols. 7–8). Madrid: CSIC, 1955.

Elorza, Antonio. *La ideología liberal en la ilustración española*. Madrid: Tecnos, 1970.

García-Baquero González, Antonio. *Comercio colonial y guerras revolucionarias: La decadencia económica de Cádiz a raíz de la emancipación americana*. Seville: Escuela de Estudios Hispano-Americanos, 1972.

Glover, Michael. *The Peninsular War, 1807–1814: A Concise Military History*. London: David and Charles, 1974.

Gómez de Arteche y Moro, José. *Guerra de la Independencia: historia militar de España de 1808 a 1814*. 14 vols. Madrid: Imp. y Lit. del Depósito de la Guerra, 1868–1903.

Hamilton, Earl. *War and Prices in Spain, 1651–1800*. (Harvard Economic Studies, 81). Cambridge, Mass.: Harvard University Press, 1947.

Helman, Edith. *Trasmundo de Goya*. Madrid: Revista de Occidente, 1963.

Herr, Richard. *The Eighteenth Century Revolution in Spain*. Princeton: Princeton University Press, 1958.

Herrera García, Antonio. *El Aljarafe sevillano durante el antiguo régimen: Un estudio de su evolución socioeconómica en los siglos xvi, xvii y xviii*. Cadiz: Publicaciones de la Excma. Diputación Provincial de Sevilla, 1980.

Herrero, Javier. *Los orígenes del pensamiento reaccionario español*. 2d ed. (Colección I.T.S.). Madrid: Editorial Cuadernos para el Diálogo, 1973.

Juretschke, Hans. *Vida, obra y pensamiento de Alberto Lista*. Madrid: CSIC, 1951.

Kamen, Henry. *The War of Succession in Spain, 1700–1715*. Bloomington: Indiana University Press, 1969.

Kany, Charles E. *Life and Manners in Madrid, 1750–1800*. Berkeley: University of California Press, 1932.

Klein, Julius. *The Mesta: A Study in Spanish Economic History, 1273–1836*. (Harvard Economic Studies, 21). Cambridge, Mass.: Harvard University Press, 1920.

Lasarte, Javier. *Economía y hacienda al final del antiguo régimen*. Madrid: Instituto de Estudios Fiscales, 1976.

Lovett, G. H. *Napoleon and the Birth of Modern Spain*. 2 vols. New York: New York University Press, 1965.

Marías, Julián. *La España posible en tiempo de Carlos III*. 2d ed. Barcelona: Planeta, 1988.

Martínez Robles, Miguel. *Los oficiales de las secretarías de la corte bajo los Austrias y los Borbones: 1517–1812: Una aproximación a esta temática*. Madrid: Instituto Nacional de Administración Pública, 1987.

Mercader Riba, Juan. *Barcelona durante la ocupación francesa (1808–1814)*. Madrid: CSIC, 1949.

———. *José Bonaparte, rey de España: 1808–1813*. 2 vols. Madrid: CSIC, 1971–1983.

———. *La ordenación de Cataluña por Felipe V: La Nueva Planta*. Barcelona: 1951.

Merino Navarro, José P. *La armada española en el siglo xviii*. Madrid: Fundación Universitaria Española, 1981.

Mickun, Nina. *La Mesta au xviii siècle*. Budapest: Akadémiai Kiadó, 1983.

Morales Moya, Antonio. *Reflexiones sobre el estado español del siglo xviii*. Madrid: Instituto Nacional de Administración Pública, 1987.

Pike, Ruth. *Penal Servitude in Early Modern Spain*. Madison: University of Wisconsin Press, 1983.

Priego López, Juan. *Guerra de la independencia, 1808–1814*. 4 vols. Madrid: Librería Edit. San Martín, 1966–1976.

Rodríguez Díaz, Laura. *Reforma e ilustración en la España del siglo xviii: Pedro Rodríguez Campomanes*. (Publicaciones de la Fundación Universitaria Española; Monografías, 15). Madrid: Fundación Universitaria Española, 1975.

Sánchez Agesta, Luis. *Moratín y la sociedad española de su tiempo*. Madrid: Universidad de Madrid, 1960.

———. *El pensamiento político del despotismo ilustrado*. Madrid: Instituto de Estudios Políticos, 1953.

Sarrailh, Jean. *L'Espagne éclairée de la seconde moitié du xviii$^e$ siècle*. Paris: Klincksieck, 1954.

Solís, Ramón. *El Cádiz de las Cortes: La vida en la ciudad en los años de 1810 a 1813*. Prologue by Gregorio Marañón. Madrid: Instituto de Estudios Políticos, 1958.

Spell, Jefferson Rea. *Rousseau in the Spanish World before 1833*. Austin: University of Texas Press, 1938.

Vilar, Pierre. *La Catalogne dans L'Espagne moderne: Recherches sur les fondements économiques des structures nationales*. 3 vols. Paris: S.E.V.P.E.N., 1962.

Walker, Geoffrey J. *Spanish Politics and Imperial Trade, 1700–1789*. Bloomington: Indiana University Press, 1979.

Zegrelle, Arsène. *La diplomatie Française et al succession d'Espagne*. 2d ed. 6 vols. Braine-le-Comte: Zech, 1895–1899.

# FERDINAND VII, 1814–1833

Alvarez Pantoja, José María. *Aspectos económicos de la Sevilla fernandina (1800–1833)*. 2 vols. Seville: Diputación de Sevilla, Facultad de Filosofía y Letras, 1970.

Anna, Timothy E. *Spain and the Loss of America*. Lincoln: University of Nebraska Press, 1983.

Artola, Miguel. *La España de Fernando VII*. Introduction by Carlos Seco Serrano. 3d ed. Madrid: Espasa-Calpe, 1983.

Arzadún y Zabala, Juan. *Fernando VII y su tiempo*. Madrid: Editorial Summa, 1942.

Comellas, José Luis. *Los primeros pronunciamientos en España, 1814–1820*. Madrid: CSIC, 1958.

———. *Los realistas en el Trienio Constitucional, 1820–1823*. Introduction by Federico Suárez Verdeguer. (Colección Histórica del Estudio General de Navarra. Serie Siglo XIX, no. 1). Pamplona: n.p., 1958.

Costeloe, Michael P. *Response to Revolution: Imperial Spain and the American Revolutions, 1810–1840*. Cambridge: Cambridge University Press, 1986.

Fontana i Lázaro, Josep. *Hacienda y estado en la crisis final del antiguo régimen español: 1823–1833*. Madrid: Instituto de Estudios Fiscales, 1973.

———. *La quiebra de la monarquía absoluta: 1814–1820*. 3d rev. ed. (Ariel Quincenal, 108). Barcelona: Ediciones Ariel, 1978.

Gil Novales, Alberto. *Las Sociedades Patrióticas*. 2 vols. Madrid: Tecnos, 1975.

González, Muñíz, Miguel Angel. *El clero liberal asturiano (De Martínez Marina a Díez Alegría)*. Salinas: Ayalga Ediciones, 1976.

González Palencia, Angel. *Estudio histórico sobre la censura gubernativa en España (1800–1833)*. Madrid: Tipografía de Archivos, 1934–1935, 1941.

Moral Ruiz, Joaquín del. *Hacienda y sociedad en el Trienio Constitucional (1820–1823)*. Madrid: Instituto de Estudios Fiscales, 1975.

Pintos Vieites, María del Carmen. *La política de Fernando VII entre 1814 y 1820*. (Colección Histórica del Estudio General de Navarra. Serie Siglo XIX, no. 2). Pamplona: Studium-Generale, 1958.

Revuelta González, Manuel. *Política religiosa de los liberales en el siglo xix: Trienio Constitucional*. (Historia de España en el Mundo Moderno, 4). Madrid: CSIC, 1973.

Rivas Santiago, Natalio. *Luis López Ballesteros, gran ministro de Fernando VII*. Epilogue de Gregorio Marañón. (Páginas Inéditas de la Historia Contemporánea de España). Madrid: Editorial Mediterráneo, 1945.

Robertson, William Spence. *Rise of the Latin American Republics as Told in the Lives of Their Liberators*. New York: D. Appleton-Century, 1918.

Sarrailh, Jean. *Martínez de la Rosa*. (Clásicos Castellanos, 107). Madrid: Espasa-Calpe, 1972.

Suárez, Federico. *Las crisis política del antiguo régimen en España (1800–1840)*. (Biblioteca del Pensamiento Actual). Madrid: Ediciones Rialp, 1950.

———. *"Los Sucesos de La Granja."* Madrid: CSIC, 1953.

Torras Elías, Jaime. *Liberalismo y rebeldía campesina, 1820–1823*. Barcelona: Ediciones Ariel, 1976.

Van Aken, Mark J. *Pan-Hispanism: Its Origins and Development to 1866*. Berkeley: University of California Press, 1959.

## EARLY LIBERALISM TO THE BOURBON RESTORATION, 1833–1874

Alonso, José R. *Historia política del ejército español*. Madrid: Editora Nacional, 1974.

Alonso Baquer, Miguel. *Ejército en la sociedad española*. Madrid: Ediciones del Movimiento, 1971.

Areilza, José María de. *Historia de una conspiración romántica*. Madrid: S. Aguirre, 1950.

Barreiro Fernández, José Ramón. *El carlismo gallego*. Santiago de Compostela: Picosacro, 1976.

Brandt, Joseph. *Toward the New Spain*. Chicago: University of Chicago Press, 1933.

Burgos, Francisco Javier. *Anales del reinado de Isabel II*. 6 vols. [Reprint of the 1850–1851 ed.] Ann Arbor: University Microfilms International, 1978.

Cacho Viu, Vicente del. *La Institución Libre de Enseñanza*. Prologue by Florentine Pérez-Embid. (Colección Rialp, de Cuestiones Fundamentales, vol. 7). Madrid: Ediciones Rialp, 1962- .

Carrasco Canals, Carlos. *La burocracia en la España del siglo xix*. (Estudios de Administración General). Madrid: Instituto de Estudios de Administración Local, 1975.

Christiansen, E. *The Origin of Military Power in Spain 1800–1854*. London: Oxford University Press, 1967.

Comellas, José Luis. *Los moderados en el poder, 1844–1854*. (Historia de España en el Mundo Moderno, vol. 3). Madrid: CSIC, 1970.

Coverdale, John F. *The Basque Phase of Spain's First Carlist War*. Princeton: Princeton University Press, 1984.

Cuenca Toribio, José Manuel. *La iglesia española ante la revolución liberal*. (Libros de Bolsillo Rialp, 58). Madrid: Ediciones Rialp, 1971.

Eiras Roel, Antonio. *El partido demócrata español, 1849–1868*. (Publicaciones de la Facultad de Filosofía y Letras de la Universidad Católica de Navarra. Colección Histórica, Serie Siglo XIX, 4). Madrid: Ediciones Rialp, 1961.

Fernández Almagro, Melchor. *Historia política de la España contemporánea*. Madrid: Pegaso, 1959.

Fernández García, Antonio. *El abastecimiento de Madrid en el reinado de Isabel II*. (Biblioteca de Estudios Madrileños, 14). Madrid: CSIC, Instituto de Estudios Madrileños, 1971.

Fontana i Lázaro, Josep. *La revolución liberal: Política y hacienda en 1833–1845*. (Publicaciones; Instituto de Estudios Fiscales, 38). Madrid: Instituto de Estudios Fiscales, 1977.

García Tejero, A. *Historia político-administrativa de Mendizábal*. Madrid: Establecimiento Tip. de J. A. Ortigosa, 1858.

Gómez Chaix, Pedro. *Ruiz Zorrilla, el ciudadano ejemplar*. (Vidas Españoles e Hispanoamericanas del Siglo XIX, no. 41). Madrid: Espasa-Calpe, 1934.

Hennessy, C.A.M. *The Federal Republic in Spain: Pi y Margall and the Federal Republican Movement, 1868–1874*. Oxford: Clarendon Press, 1962.

Holt, Edgar. *The Carlist Wars in Spain*. Chester Springs, Penn.: Dufour Editions, 1967.

Houghton, Arthur. *Les Origines de la restauration des Bourbons en Espagne*. Paris: E. Plon, Nourrit et Cie., 1890.

Janke, Peter. *Mendizábal y la instauración de la monarquía constitucional en España (1790–1830)*. (Historia). Madrid: Siglo Veintiuno, 1974.

Jobit, Pierre. *Les Éducateurs de l'Espagne contemporaines*. 2 vols. (Bibliothèque de l'École des Hautes Études Hispaniques, Fasc. 19–20). Paris: E. de Boccard, 1936.

Kiernan, V. G. *The Revolution of 1854 in Spanish History*. Oxford: Clarendon Press, 1966.

Lida, Clara, and Iris Zaval, eds. *La revolución de 1868: Historia, pensamiento, literatura*. New York: Americas Publishing, 1970.

López Morillas, Juan. *The Krausist Movement and Ideological Change in Spain, 1854–1874*. Translated by Frances M. López-Morillas. 2d ed. Cambridge: Cambridge University Press, 1981.

Lloréns Castillo, Vicente. *Liberales y románticos: Una emigración española en Inglaterra (1823–1834)*. Mexico City: El Colegio de México, 1954.

Múgica, José. *Carlistas, moderados y progresistas*. (Claudio Antón de Luzuriaga). San Sebastian: 1950.

Olivar Bertrand, Rafael. *Prim*. 2 vols. (Colección Políticos y Financieros). Madrid: Tebas, 1975.

Oyarzún, Román. *La historia del carlismo*. (El Libro de Bolsillo, 180. Sección Humanidades). Madrid: Alianza Editorial, 1969.

Pabón, Jesús. *La subversión contemporánea y otros estudios.* (Bitacora, 13). Madrid: Narcea, 1971.

Peset Reig, José Luis, and Maríano Peset. *Muerte en España: Política y sociedad entre la peste y el colera.* (''Hora H,'' 24). Madrid: Seminarios y Ediciones, 1972.

Pirala y Criada, Antonio. *Historia contemporánea: Anales desde 1843 hasta la conclusión de la actual guerra civil.* 6 vols. Madrid: Manuel Tello, 1867–1879.

———. *Historia de la guerra civil: Y de los partidos liberal y carlista corregida y aumentada con la historia de la regencia de Espartero.* 3 vols. Madrid: F. G. Rojas, 1889–1891.

Revuelta González, Manuel. *La exclaustración, 1833–1840.* (Biblioteca de Autores Cristianos, 383). Madrid: La Editora Católica, 1976.

Schramm, Edmund. *Donoso Cortés, su vida y su pensamiento.* (Vidas Españoles e Hispanoamericanas del Siglo XIX, 54). Madrid: Espasa-Calpe, 1936.

Simón Palmer, María del Carmen. *La enseñanza privada seglar en Madrid, 1820–1868.* Prologue by Vicente Palacio Atard. (Biblioteca de Estudios Madrileños, vol. 15). Madrid: Instituto de Estudios Madrileños, 1972.

Simón Segura, Francisco. *La desamortización española del siglo xix.* (Publicaciones, vol. 22). Madrid: Instituto de Estudios Fiscales, 1973.

Termes Ardévol, Josep. *Anarquismo y sindicalismo en España: La Primera Internacional, 1864–1881.* (Horas de España). Barcelona: Ediciones Ariel, 1972.

Tortella Casares, Gabriel, et al. *La banca española en la restauración.* 2 vols. Madrid: Servicio de Estudios del Banco de España, 1974.

Trend, J. B. *The Origins of Modern Spain.* New York: Russell and Russell, 1965.

Villaroya, Joaquín Tomás. *El sistema político del Estatuto Real (1834–1836).* (Colección Histórica-Política). Madrid: Instituto de Estudios Políticos, 1968.

## THE LATE NINETEENTH CENTURY TO THE DICTATORSHIP OF PRIMO DE RIVERA, 1874–1923

Abad de Santillán, Diego. *Contribución a la historia del movimiento obrero español: Desde sus orígenes hasta 1905.* Puebla, Mex.: Editorial Cajica, 1962.

Aguiló Lúcia, L. *Sociología electoral valenciana, 1903–1923: Las elecciones en Valencia durante el reinado de Alfonso XIII.* Valencia: Facultad de Derecho, D. L., 1976.

Alvarez Junco, José. *La ideología del anarquismo español (1869–1910).* (Historia). Madrid: Siglo Veintiuno, 1976.

Alzaga, Oscar. *La primera democracia cristiana en España.* (Colección Horas de España). Barcelona: Ediciones Ariel, 1973.

Andrés Gallego, José. *La política religiosa en España, 1889–1913.* (España en 3 Tiempos). Madrid: Editora Nacional, 1975.

Azaola, José Miguel de. *Vasconia y su destino.* Madrid: Ediciones de la Revista de Occidente, 1972.

Balcells, Albert. *Cataluña contemporánea,* vol. 2: *1900–1936.* (Estudios de Historia Contemporánea). Madrid: Siglo Veintiuno, 1974.

———. *El sindicalismo en Barcelona, 1916–1923.* Barcelona: Editorial Nova Terra, 1965.

———. *Trabajo industrial y organización obrera en la Cataluña contemporánea, 1900–1936.* (Ediciones de Bolsillo, 386). Barcelona: Editorial Laia, 1974.

Beck, Earl R. *A Time of Triumph and of Sorrow: Spanish Politics during the Reign of Alfonso XII, 1874–1885*. Carbondale: Southern Illinois University Press, 1979.

Benet, Josep. *Margall y la Semana Trágica*. Translated by J. Palacios. (Colección Ibérica, 7). Madrid: Ediciones Península, 1966.

Bernis y Carrasco, Francisco. *Consecuencias económicas de la guerra. . . .* Madrid: Impr. de E. Maestre, 1923.

Boyd, Carolyn. *Praetorian Politics in Liberal Spain*. Chapel Hill: University of North Carolina Press, 1979.

Buenacasa, Manuel. *El movimiento obrero español (1888–1926): Historia y crítica*. Barcelona: Impresos Costa, 1928.

Burgos y Mazo, Manuel de. *El verano de 1919 en gobernación*. 2 vols. in 1. Cuenca: Imp. de E. Pinos, 1921.

Cardona, Gabriel. *El poder militar en la España contemporánea hasta la guerra civil*. (Historia). Madrid: Siglo Veintiuno, 1984.

Castillo, Juan José. *Propietarios muy pobres: Sobre la subordinación política del pequeño campesino en España*. Madrid: Servicio de Publicaciones Agrarias, 1979.

Cierva, Ricardo de la. *Historia de la guerra civil española*. 4th ed. 2 vols. Barcelona: Editorial Danae, 1971.

Durán, José A. *Agrarismo y movilización campesina en el país gallego*. (Historia de los Movimientos Sociales). Madrid: Siglo Veintiuno, 1976.

———. *Historia de caciques, bandos e ideologías en la Galicia no urbana: Rianxo 1910–1914*. 2d ed. (Historia). Madrid: Siglo Veintiuno, 1972.

Elorza, Antonio. *Socialismo utópico español*. (El Libro de Bolsillo, 268. Sección Clásicos). Madrid: Alianza Editorial, 1970.

Fernández Almagro, Melchor. *Cánovas: Su vida y su política*. 2d ed. (Colección Políticos y Financieros). Madrid: Tebas, 1972.

———. *Historia del reinado de Alfonso XIII*. 2d ed. Barcelona: Montañer y Simón, 1933.

Fernández Almagro, Melchor, and Gabriel Maura y Gamazo. *Porqué cayó Alfonso XIII*. 2d ed. Madrid: Ediciones Ambos Mundos, 1948.

García Escudero, José María. *De Cánovas a la república*. 2d ed. Madrid: Ediciones Rialp, 1953.

García Nieto, J. A. *El sindicalismo cristiano en España: Notas sobre su orígen y evolución hasta 1936*. Bilbao: Instituto de Estudios Económico-Sociales, Universidad de Deusto, 1960.

García Venero, Maximiano. *Antonio Maura: 1907–1909*. Madrid: Ediciones del Movimiento, 1953.

———. *Historia de las Internacionales en España*. 3 vols. Madrid: Ediciones del Movimiento, 1956–1958.

———. *Melquíades Alvarez: Historia de un liberal*. Prologue by Azorín (José Martínez y Ruiz). Madrid: Editorial Alhambra, 1954.

———. *Santiago Alba, monárquico de razón*. (Evocaciones y memorias). Madrid: Aguilar, 1963.

———. *Vida de Cambó*. (Biblioteca Biográfica). Prologue by Gregorio Marañón. Barcelona: Editorial Aedos, 1952.

Gómez Molleda, María Dolores. *Los reformadores de la España contemporánea*. Prologue by Vicente Palacio Atard. (Historia de España en el Mundo Moderno, vol. 2). Madrid: CSIC, 1966.

Headrick, Daniel R. *Ejército y política en España. (1866–1898).* (Historia). Madrid: Editorial Tecnos, 1981.

Kern, Robert W. *Liberals, Reformers and Caciques in Restoration Spain 1875–1909.* Albuquerque: University of New Mexico Press, 1974.

Lacomba Avellán, Juan Antonio. *La crisis española de 1917.* (Colección "Los Contemporáneos," 19). Madrid: Editorial Ciencia Nueva, 1970.

Laín Entralgo, Pedro. *España como problema.* 3d ed. (Ensayistas Hispánicos). Madrid: Aguilar, 1962.

———. *La generación del noventa y ocho.* 9th ed. (Colección Austral, no. 784). Madrid: Espasa-Calpe, 1979.

Lalcona, Javier F. *El idealismo político de Ortega y Gasset. Un análisis sintético de la evolución de su filosofía política.* (Libros de Bolsillo para el Diálogo. Serie Cuestiones Españolas, 64). Madrid: Editorial Cuestiones para el Diálogo, 1974.

Lida, Clara E. *Anarquismo y revoluciones en la España del xix.* (Historia). Madrid: Siglo Veintiuno, 1972.

Martí, Casimiro. *Orígenes del anarquismo en Barcelona.* Prologue by Jaime Vicens Vives. (Centro de Estudios Históricos Internacionales, Serie Monografías, no. 1). Barcelona: Editorial Teide, 1959.

Maura y Gamazo, Gabriel. *Historia crítica del reinado de Alfonso XIII.* 2 vols. Barcelona: Montañer y Simón, 1919–1925.

———. *Así cayó Alfonso XIII.* Mexico City: Imprenta Mañez, 1962.

Maurice, Jacques, and Carlos Serrano. *J. Costa: Crisis de la restauración y populismo, 1875–1911.* (Estudios de Historia Contemporánea). Madrid: Siglo Veintiuno, 1977.

Maurín, Joaquín. *La revolución española: De la monarquía absoluta a la revolución socialista.* (Colección "Crítica Social"). Madrid: Editorial Cenit, 1932.

———. *Revolución y contrarevolución en España.* Paris: Ruedo Ibérico, 1966.

Meaker, G. H. *The Revolutionary Left in Spain 1914–1923.* Stanford: Stanford University Press, 1974.

Pabón, Jesús. *Cambó, 1876–1918.* 3 vols. Barcelona: Editorial Alpha, 1952–1969.

Payne, Stanley. *Basque Nationalism.* (The Basque Series). Reno: University of Nevada Press, 1975.

———. *Politics and the Military in Modern Spain.* Stanford: Stanford University Press, 1967.

Pike, Frederick B. *Hispanismo, 1898–1936: Spanish Conservatives and Liberals and Their Relations with Spanish America.* Notre Dame: University of Notre Dame Press, 1971.

Ramsden, Herbert. *The 1898 Movement in Spain: Towards a Reinterpretation. . . .* Manchester: Manchester University Press, 1974.

Reventós Carner, Juan. *El movimiento cooperativo en España.* Barcelona: Ediciones Ariel, 1960.

Romero Maura, Joaquín. *La rosa de fuego: Republicanos y anarquistas; la política de los obreros barceloneses entre el desastre colonial y la Semana Trágica.* Barcelona: Ediciones Grijalbo, 1974.

Ruiz Manjón, Octavio. *El partido republicano radical, 1908–1936.* (Colección Historia Política). Madrid: Tebas, 1976.

Ruiz González, David. *El movimiento obrero en Asturias: De la industrialización a la*

*II república.* (Crónica General de España, vol. 26). Madrid: Ediciones Jucar, 1979.

Seco Serrano, Carlos. *Alfonso XIII y la crisis de la restauración.* 2d ed. (Libros de Historia, vol. 1). Madrid: Ediciones Rialp, 1979.

———. *Perfil político y humano de un estadista de la restauración: Eduardo Dato.* Madrid: Real Academia de la Historia, 1978.

Serrano Sánz, José María. *El viraje proteccionista en la restauración: La política comercial española, 1875–1895.* Prologue by José Luis García Delgado. Madrid: Siglo Veintiuno, 1987.

Sevilla Andrés, Diego. *Antonio Maura: La revolución desde arriba.* Prologue by Melchor Fernández Almagro. (Biblioteca Biográfica, 5). Barcelona: Editorial Aedos, 1953.

Solé-Tura, Jordi. *Catalanismo y revolución burguesa.* (Libros de Bolsillo, Cuadernos para el Diálogo, 24). Madrid: Edicura, 1970.

Solozábal Echevarría, Juan José. *El primer nacionalismo vasco: Industrialización y conciencia nacional.* (Temas de Ciencias Sociales, 8). Madrid: Tucar, 1975.

Termes Ardévol, José. *El movimiento obrero en España: La Primera Internacional (1864–1881).* Barcelona: Publicaciones de la Cátedra de Historia General de España, 1965.

Tuñón de Lara, Manuel. *Medio siglo de cultura española, 1885–1936.* (Bruguera Libro Blanco, V. 1511/30). Barcelona: Bruguera, 1981.

Turin, Yvonne. *L'Éducation et l'école en Espagne de 1874 à 1902: Liberalisme et tradition.* Paris: Presses Universitaire de France, 1959.

Tusell Gómez, Xavier. *Historia de la democracia cristiana en España.* 2 vols. (Colección I.T.S.). Madrid: Editorial Cuadernos para el Diálogo, 1974.

———. *Oligarquía y caciquismo en Andalucía (1890–1923).* (Ensayos Planeta de Historia y Humanidades, 18). Barcelona: Editorial Planeta, 1976.

———. *La reforma de la administración local en la España del primer tercio del siglo xx.* Alcalá de Henares: Escuela Nacional de Administración Pública, 1973.

———. *Sociología electoral de Madrid (1903–1931).* (Libros de Bolsillo, Cuadernos para el Diálogo, Cuestiones Españoles, 17). Madrid: Cuadernos para el Diálogo, 1969.

Ullman, Joan Connelly. *The Tragic Week: A Study of Anticlericalism in Spain, 1875–1912.* Cambridge, Mass.: Harvard University Press, 1968.

Varela Ortega, José. *Los amigos políticos: Partidos, elecciones y caciquismo en la restauración, 1875–1900.* (Alianza Universidad, 199). Madrid: Alianza Editorial, 1977.

Winston, Colin M. *Workers and the Right in Spain, 1900–1936.* Princeton: Princeton University Press, 1984.

Zuyazagoitia, Julián. *Pablo Iglesias: Vida y trabajos de un obrero socialista.* Madrid: Ediciones Españolas, 1938.

## THE DICTATORSHIP AND THE SECOND REPUBLIC, 1923–1936

Aguirre y Lecube, José Antonio de. *Entre la libertad y la revolución, 1930–1935: La verdad de un lustro en el país vasco.* 2d ed. Bilbao: Editorial Geu, 1976.

Alcalá-Galiano, Alvaro. *Caída de un trono (1931)*. Madrid: Compañía Iberoamericana de Publicaciones, 1933.

Andrés Gallego, José. *El socialismo durante la dictadura, 1923–1930*. (Colección Historia Política). Madrid: Tebas, 1977.

Arrarás, Joaquín. *Historia de la segunda república española*. 5th ed. 4 vols. Madrid: Editora Nacional, 1968–1970.

Aunós, Eduardo. *La política social de la dictadura*. Madrid: n.p., 1944.

Balcells, Albert. *Crisis económica y agitación social en Cataluña, de 1930 a 1936*. (Horas de España). Barcelona: Instituto Católico de Estudios Sociales de Barcelona y Ediciones Ariel, 1971.

Ben-Ami, Shlomo. *Fascism from Above: The Dictatorship of Primo de Rivera in Spain, 1923–1930*. Oxford: Oxford University Press, 1983.

———. *The Origin of the Second Republic in Spain*. Oxford: Oxford University Press, 1978.

Bertrán Güell, Felipe. *Preparación y desarrollo del alzamiento nacional*. Valledolid: Librería Santarén, 1939.

Blinkhorn, M. *Carlism and Crisis in Spain: 1931–39*. Cambridge: Cambridge University Press, 1975.

Brademas, John. *Anarco-sindicalismo y revolución en España, (1930–1937)*. (Horas de España). Barcelona: Ediciones Ariel, 1974.

Buenacasa, Manuel. *La CNT, los "Treinta" y la F.A.I*. Barcelona: Talleres Gráficos "Alpha," 1933.

Burgo, Jaime del. *Conspiración y guerra civil*. Madrid: Alfaguara, 1970.

Chapaprieta Torregrosa, Joaquín. *La paz fué posible: Memorias de un político*. Prologue by J. Chapaprieta Otsein. (Horas de España). Barcelona: Ediciones Ariel, 1971.

Cordero, Manuel. *Los socialistas y la revolución*. (Temas de Actualidad). Madrid: Impr. Torrent, 1932.

Galindo Herrero, Santiago. *Los partidos monárquicos bajo la segunda república*. 2d ed. (Biblioteca del Pensamiento Actual, 61). Madrid: Ediciones Rialp, 1956.

Gil Robles, José María. *No fué posible la paz*. (Horas de España). Barcelona: Ediciones Ariel, 1968.

Grossi Mier, Manuel. *La insurrección de Asturias*. (Crónica General de España, vol. 19). Madrid: Ediciones Jucar, 1978.

Jackson, Gabriel. *The Spanish Republic and the Civil War, 1931–39*. Princeton: Princeton University Press, 1965.

Juliá Díaz, Santos. *Madrid 1931–1934: De la fiesta popular a la lucha de clases*. (Historia). Mexico City: Siglo Veintiuno, 1984.

———. *Orígenes del Frente Popular en España (1934–1936)*. (Estudios de Historia Contemporánea). Madrid: Siglo Veintiuno, 1979.

Kern, Robert W. *Red Years, Black Years: A Political History of Spanish Anarchism, 1911–1936*. Philadelphia: Institute for the Study of Human Issues, 1978.

López de Ochoa y Portuando, Eduardo. *De la dictadura a la república*. Prologue by Eduardo Ortega Gasset. Madrid: Editorial Zeus, 1930.

Maíz B., Félix. *Alzamiento en España, de un diario de la conspiración*. Pamplona: Editorial Gómez, 1952.

Malefakis, Edward. *Agrarian Reform and Peasant Revolution in Spain: Origins of the Civil War*. New Haven: Yale University Press, 1970.

Manuel, Frank E. *The Politics of Modern Spain*. New York: McGraw-Hill, 1938.

Martínez Barrio, Diego. *Orígenes del frente popular español*. (Cuadernos de Cultura Española, 14). Buenos Aires: Publicaciones del Patronato Hispano-Argentino de Cultura, 1943.

Maura y Gamazo, Gabriel. *Bosquejo histórico de la dictadura*. Madrid: Tipografía de Archivos, 1930.

Pabón, Jesús. *Días de ayer, historiadores contemporáneas*. Barcelona: Editorial Alpha, 1963.

Paniagua, Xavier. *La sociedad literaria: Agrarismo e industrialización en el anarquismo español (1930–1939)*. (Temas Hispánicos). Barcelona: Crítica, 1982..

Payne, Stanley. *Falange: A History of Spanish Fascism*. Stanford: Stanford University Press, 1961.

———. *The Spanish Revolution*. (Revolutions in the Modern World). New York: W. W. Norton, 1970.

Peirats, José de. *La C.N.T. en la revolución española*. 3 vols. Buenos Aires: Ediciones C.N.T., 1952–1955.

Pérez Yruela, Manuel. *La conflictividad campesina en la provincia de Córdoba (1931–1936)*. (Serie Estudios). Madrid: Servicio de Publicaciones Agrarias, 1979.

Preston, Paul, ed. *Revolution and War in Spain, 1931–1939*. London: Methuen, 1984.

Primo de Rivera y Orbaneja, Miguel. *El pensamiento de Primo de Rivera, sus notas, artículos y discursos*. Prologue by José María Pemán. Madrid: Imprenta Artística Sáez Hermanos, 1929.

Ramos Oliveira, Antonio. *La revolución española de octubre: Ensayo político*. Madrid: Editorial España, 1935.

Robinson, Richard Alan Hodgson. *The Origins of Franco's Spain; The Right, the Republic and Revolution, 1931–1936*. (Library of Politics and Society). Newton Abbot, Devon: David and Charles, 1970.

Sánchez, José G. *Reform and Reaction: The Politico-Religious Background of the Spanish Civil War*. Chapel Hill: University of North Carolina Press, 1964.

Sánchez García-Saúco, Juan Antonio. *La revolución de 1934 en Asturias*. (España en 3 Tiempos). Madrid: Editora Nacional, 1974.

Tuñón de Lara, Manuel, et al. *La crisis del estado: Dictadura, república, guerra (1923–1939)*. Barcelona: 1981.

———. *La España del siglo xx, 1914–1939*. 2d ed. (Club del Libro Español). Paris: Librería Española, 1973.

Tusell Gómez, Xavier. *Las elecciones del frente popular en España*. 2 vols. (Libros de Bolsillo. Cuadernos para el Diálogo, Divulgación Universitaria, 31–32. Cuestiones Españolas). Madrid: Cuadernos para el Diálogo, 1971.

Varela Díaz, Santiago. *Partidos y parlamento en la II república española*. (Colección Monografías: Sección 6, Derecho, Economía, Ciencias Sociales y Comunicación Social). Madrid: Fundación Juan March, 1978.

Velarde Fuertes, Juan. *Política económica de la dictadura*. 2d ed. (Biblioteca Universitaria Guadiana). Madrid: Guadiana de Publicaciones, 1973.

## THE CIVIL WAR

Abella, Rafael. *La vida cotidiana durante la guerra civil*. (Colección Panorama, 11). Barcelona: Planeta, 1978.

Alba, Víctor. *Historia del P.O.U.M.* 2 vols. (Colección Nartex, no. 4). Barcelona: Editorial Pórtic, 1974.

———. *El marxismo en España, 1919–1939: Historia del B.O.C. y del P.O.U.M.* 2 vols. Mexico City: B. Costa-Amic, 1974.

Alvarez del Vayo, Julio. *Freedom's Battle.* Translated by Eileen E. Brooke. London: W. Heineman, 1940.

Aznar, Manuel. *Historia militar de la guerra de España.* 4th ed. 3 vols. (Libros de Historia). Madrid: Editora Nacional, 1969.

Bernecker, Walther L. *Colectividades y revolución social: El anarquismo en la guerra civil española, 1936–1939.* (Serie General, Temas Hispánicos, 101). Barcelona: Crítica, 1982.

Bolloton, Burnett. *The Grand Camouflage: The Communist Conspiracy in the Spanish Civil War.* London: Hollis and Carter, 1961.

———. *The Spanish Revolution: The Left and the Struggle for Power during the Civil War.* Chapel Hill: University of North Carolina Press, 1979.

Borkenau, Franz. *The Spanish Cockpit: An Eye-Witness Account of the Political and Social Conflicts of the Spanish Civil War.* London: Faber and Faber, 1937.

Bosch, Aurora. *Ugetistas y libertarios: Guerra civil y revolución en el país valenciano (1936–1939).* (Estudios Universitarios, vol. 9). Valencia: Institución Alfonso El Magnánimo, Diputación Provincial de Valencia, 1983.

Broué, Pierre, and Emile Témime. *The Revolution and the Civil War in Spain.* Translated by Tony White. London: Faber and Faber, 1972.

Burdick, Charles W. *Germany's Military Strategy and Spain in World War II.* Syracuse: Syracuse University Press, 1968.

Burgo, Jaime del. *Conspiración y guerra civil.* Madrid: Alfaguara, 1970.

Carr, Raymond. *The Republic and the Civil War in Spain.* (Problems in Focus Series). London: Macmillan, 1971.

Casado, Segismundo. *The Last Days of Madrid. . . .* Translated and introduced by Rupert Croft-Cooke. London: P. Davies, 1939.

Casanova, Julián. *Anarquismo y revolución en la sociedad rural aragonesa, 1936–1938.* (Historia de los Movimientos Sociales). Madrid: Siglo Veintiuno, 1985.

———. *Caspe, 1936–1938: Conflictos políticos y transformaciones sociales durante la guerra civil.* Saragossa: 1984.

Castells Peig, Andreu. *Las brigadas internacionales de la guerra de España.* (Horas de España). Barcelona: Ediciones Ariel, 1974.

Cattell, D. T. *Communism and the Spanish Civil War.* Berkeley: University of California Press, 1955.

———. *Soviet Diplomacy and the Spanish Civil War.* Berkeley: University of California Press, 1957.

Cierva, Ricardo de la. *Historia ilustrada de la guerra civil española.* Barcelona: Ediciones Danae, 1970.

Coverdale, J. F. *Italian Intervention in the Spanish Civil War.* Princeton: Princeton University Press, 1975.

Cruells, Manuel. *Mayo sangriento: Barcelona, 1937.* Translated by Joaquín Garay Escoda. Barcelona: Editorial Juventud, 1970.

Edwards, Jill. *The British Government and the Spanish Civil War, 1936–1939.* Prologue by Hugh Thomas. London: Macmillan, 1979.

Fagen, Patricia Weiss. *Exiles and Citizens: Spanish Republicans in Mexico.* (Latin American Monographs, no. 29). Austin: Institute of Latin American Studies, University of Texas Press, 1973.

Fraser, Ronald. *Blood of Spain: The Experience of Civil War, 1936–1939.* Harmondsworth: Penguin Books, 1981.

García Venero, Maximiano. *La falange en la guerra de España, la unificación y Hedilla.* Paris: Ruedo Ibérico, 1967.

Garitaonandia, Carmelo, and José Luis de la Granja, eds. *La guerra civil en el país vasco, 50 años después.* Bilbao: Servicio Editorial, Universidad del País Vasco, 1987.

Garrido González, Luis. *Colectividades agrarias en Andalucía: Jaén (1931–1939).* (Estudios de Historia Contemporánea). Madrid: Siglo Veintiuno, 1979.

Gibson, Ian. *The Death of Lorca.* London: W. H. Allen, 1973.

Gómez Casas, Juan. *Los anarquistas en el gobierno (1936–1939).* (Serie La Guerra Civil; Mosaico de la Historia, vol. 5). Barcelona: Editorial Bruguera, 1977.

Kleine-Ahlbrandt, William L. *The Policy of Simmering: A Study of British Policy during the Spanish Civil War, 1936–1939.* The Hague: 1962.

Martínez Bande, José Manuel. *Los cien últimos días de la república.* (La Vida Vivida). Barcelona: L. Caralt, 1973.

Mintz, Frank P. *La autogestión en la España revolucionaria.* Madrid: La Piqueta, 1977.

Orwell, George. *Homage to Catalonia.* London: Secker and Warburg, 1938.

Paul, Elliot. *The Life and Death of a Spanish Town.* New York: Modern Library, 1937.

Peers, E. Allison. *The Spanish Tragedy, 1930–1937: Dictatorship, Republic, Chaos, Rebellion, War.* Rev. ed. London: Methuen, 1937.

Pike, David Wingate. *Conjecture and Deceit and the Spanish Civil War.* Stanford: Stanford University Press, 1970.

———. *Vae Victis! Los republicanos españoles refugiados en Francia, 1939–1944.* Paris: Ruedo Ibérico, 1969.

Preston, Paul, ed. *Revolution and War in Spain, 1931–1939.* London: Methuen, 1984.

Ramos, Vicente. *La guerra civil (1936–1939) en la provincia de Alicante.* 3d ed. 3 vols. (Ediciones Biblioteca Alicantina: I, Historia y Geografía). Alicante: Biblioteca Alicantina, 1972– .

Salas Larrazábal, Ramón. *Historia del ejército popular de la república.* 4 vols. Madrid: Editora Nacional, 1973.

Serrano Suñer, Ramón. *Entre el silencio y la propaganda, la historia como fué.* 2d ed. (Espejo de España, vol. 35). Barcelona: Editorial Planeta, 1978.

Sevilla Andrés, Diego. *Historia política de la zona rosa.* 2d ed. (Libros de Periodismo Rialp: Serie Grandes Reportajes, 5). Madrid: Rialp, 1963.

Steer, George Lowther. *The Tree of Gernika: A Field Study of Modern War.* London: Hodder and Stoughton, 1938.

Thomas, Gordon, and Max Morgan-Witts. *The Day Guernica Died.* London: Hodder and Stoughton, 1975.

Thomas, Hugh. *The Spanish Civil War.* 3d ed. London: Hamish Hamilton, 1977.

Traina, Richard P. *American Diplomacy and the Spanish Civil War.* Bloomington: Indiana University Press, 1968.

Tuñón de Lara, Manuel. *La guerra civil española: 50 años después.* Madrid: Labor, 1986.

Viñas, Angel. *La Alemania nazi y el 18 de julio.* 2d ed. (Alianza Universidad, 81). Madrid: Alianza Editorial, 1977.

————. *El oro de Moscú: Alfa y omega de un mito franquista.* (Colección Dimensiones Hispánicas, 23). Barcelona: Ediciones Grijalbo, 1979.


## FRANCO AND FRANCOISM, 1939–1975

Abella, Rafael. *Por el imperio hacía Dios: Crónica de una posguerra (1939–1955).* (Espejo de España, vol. 45). Barcelona: Planeta, 1978.

Agirre, Julen. *Operation Ogro: The Execution of Admiral Luis Carrero Blanco.* Translated and introduced by Barbara Probst Solomon. New York: Quadrangle/New York Times, 1975.

Amodia, José. *Franco's Political Legacy: From Dictatorship to Facade Democracy.* London: Allen Lane, 1977.

Amsden, J. *Collective Bargaining and Class Conflict in Spain.* London: Weidenfeld and Nicholson, 1972.

Anderson, Charles W. *The Political Economy of Modern Spain: Policy Making in an Authoritarian System.* Madison: University of Wisconsin Press, 1970.

Artigües, Daniel. *El opus dei en España, 1828–1962: Su evolución ideológica y política de los orígenes al intento de dominio.* 2d ed. (España Contemporánea). Paris: Ruedo Ibérico, 1971.

Ben-Ami, Shlomo. *La revolución desde arriba: España, 1936–1979.* (Colección Aula Hispánica). Barcelona: Riopiedras, 1980.

Biescas, José Antonio, and Manuel Tuñón de Lara. *España bajo la dictadura franquista, 1939–1975.* 2d ed. (Historia de España, vol. 10). Barcelona: Labor, 1983.

Blaye, Edouard de. *Franco and the Politics of Spain.* Translated by Brian Pearce. Harmondsworth: Penguin, 1976.

Blinkhorn, R. M., ed. *Spain in Conflict.* London: Sage, 1986.

Brenan, Gerald. *The Face of Spain.* London: Turnstile Press, 1950.

Carr, Raymond, and Juan Pablo Fusi Aizpurúa. *Spain: Dictatorship to Democracy.* 2d ed. London: George Allen and Unwin, 1981.

Cierva, Ricardo de la. *Historia del franquismo.* 4th ed. 2 vols. (Espejo de España, vol. 19). Barcelona: Planeta, 1976–1978.

Clavera, Joan, et al. *Capitalismo español: De la autarquía a la estabilización (1939–1959).* 2d ed. (Cuadernos para el Diálogo: Divulgación Universitaria, 52–53; Serie Cuestiones Españoles). Madrid: Editorial Cuadernos para el Diálogo, 1978.

Crozier, Brian. *Franco.* Boston: Little, Brown, 1968.

Ellwood, Sheelagh M. *Spanish Fascism in the Franco Era: Falange español de los Jons, 1936–76.* London: Macmillan Press, 1987.

Fontana, J., ed. *España bajo el franquismo.* Barcelona: Crítica, 1986.

Fraga Iribarne, Manuel, et al. *La España de los años 70.* 3 vols. Madrid: Moneda y Crédito, 1972– .

Fraser, Ronald. *The Pueblo: A Mountain Village on the Costa de Sol.* London: Allen Lane, 1973.

Fusi Aizpurúa, Juan Pablo. *Franco.* Translated by Felipe Fernández-Armento. Preface by Raymond Carr. New York: Harper and Row, 1987.

Gallego Méndez, María Teresa. *Mujer, Falange y franquismo.* (Biblioteca Política Taurus, vol. 48). Madrid: Taurus, 1983.

Gallo, Max. *Spain under Franco: A History*. Translated by Jean Stewart. London: Allen and Unwin, 1973.

Gironella, José María, and Rafael Borrás Betriu. *100 españoles y Franco*. (Espejo de España, vol. 50). Barcelona: Planeta, 1979.

González, Manuel Jesús. *La economía política del franquismo (1940–70): Dirigismo, mercado y planificación*. (Serie de Historia). Madrid: Tecnos, 1979.

Gunther, Richard P. *Public Policy in a No-Party State: Spanish Planning and Budgeting in the Twilight of the Franquist Era*. Berkeley: University of California Press, 1980.

Hermet, Guy. *The Communists in Spain: Study of an Underground Political Movement*. Translated by S. Seago and H. Fox. (Saxon House Studies). Farnborough, Hants: Saxon House, 1974.

Hills, George. *Franco: the Man and His Nation*. London: Hale, 1967.

Jackson, Gabriel. *Historian's Quest*. New York: Alfred A. Knopf, 1969.

Jerez Mir, M. *Elites políticas y centros de extracción en España, 1938–1957*. Madrid: Centro de Investigaciones Sociológicas, 1982.

López Pina, Antonio, and Eduardo L. Aranguren. *La cultura política de la España de Franco*. (Biblioteca Política Taurus, 31). Madrid: Taurus, 1976.

Maravall, José. *Dictatorship and Political Dissent: Workers and Students in Franco's Spain*. New York: St. Martin's Press, 1978.

Martínez-Alier, Juan. *La estabilidad del latifundismo....* (España Contemporánea). Paris: Ediciones Ruedo Ibérico, 1968.

Medhurst, Kenneth. *Government in Spain: The Executive at Work*. (The Commonwealth and International Library; Governments of Western Europe). Oxford: Pergamon Press, 1973.

Miguel, Amando de. *Manual de estructura social de España*. (Biblioteca Universitaria). Madrid: Editorial Tecnos, 1974.

Ortzi. *Historia de Euzkadi: El nacionalismo vasco y ETA*. (España Contemporánea, vol. 18). Barcelona: Ruedo Ibérico, 1977.

Payne, Stanley G. *Franco's Spain*. (Europe Since 1500). New York: Thomas Y. Crowell, 1967.

Peers, E. Allison. *Spain in Eclipse, 1937–1943*. London: Methuen, 1943.

Pérez Díaz, Victor. *Pueblos y clases sociales en el campo español*. (Sociología y Política). Madrid: Siglo Veintiuno, 1974.

Preston, P., ed. *Spain in Crisis: The Evolution and Decline of the Franco Regime*. Hassocks, Eng.: Harvester Press, 1976.

Ramírez Jiménez, Manuel. *España, 1939–1975: Régimen político e ideología*. (Punto Omega, vol. 249. Sección Historia Social y Política). Madrid: Guadarrama, 1978.

de la Souchère, Éléna. *An Explanation of Spain*. Translated by E. R. Levieux. New York: Random House, 1964.

Stein, Louis. *Beyond Death and Exile: The Spanish Republicans in France, 1939–1955*. Cambridge, Mass.: Harvard University Press, 1979.

Tamames, Ramón. *La república: La era de Franco*. 10th ed. (Alianza Universitaria, vol. 7). Madrid: Alianza Editorial, 1983.

Tusell Gómez, Xavier. *La oposición democrática al franquismo, 1939–1962*. (Espejo de España, vol. 31). Barcelona: Planeta, 1977.

Whitaker, Arthur P. *Spain and the Defense of the West*. New York: Harper and Brothers, 1961.


## BIBLIOGRAPHIES AND GUIDES

Alberich, José. *Bibliografía anglo-hispánica 1801–1850. Ensayo bibliográfico de libros y folletos relativos a España e Hispanoamérica impresos en Inglaterra en la primera mitad del siglo diecinueve*. Oxford: Dolphin, 1978.

*Los archivos para la historia del siglo xx*. Madrid: Ministerio de Cultura, 1979.

Broué, Pierre, Pierre Vilar, and Ronald Fraser. *Metodología histórica de la guerra y revolución española*. 2d ed. (Colección Libro Historia, vol. 2). Barcelona: Fontamara, 1982.

Burgo, Jaime del. *Bibliografía del siglo xix: Guerras carlistas, luchas políticas*. Prologue by Federico Suárez Verdeguer. 2d ed. Pamplona: Diputación Foral de Navarra, 1978.

Cierva, Ricardo de la, et al. *Bibliografía sobre la guerra de España (1936–39) y sus antecedentes históricas*. Madrid: Ministerio de Información y Turismo-Ariel, 1968.

Conard-Malerbe, Pierre. *Guía para el estudio de la historia contemporánea de España*. (Estudios de Historia Contemporánea, Siglo XXI). Madrid: Siglo Veintiuno, 1975.

Cortada, James W. *A Bibliographic Guide to Spanish Diplomatic History, 1460–1977*. Westport, Conn.: Greenwood Press, 1977.

———. *Historical Dictionary of the Spanish Civil War, 1936–1939*. Westport, Conn.: Greenwood Press, 1982.

*Diccionario bibliográfico de la guerra de la independencia española (1808–1814)*. 3 vols. Madrid: Servicio Geográfico del Ejército, 1944–1952.

Feliu Monfort, Gaspar. *Bibliografía de historia económica de Cataluña (1950–1970)*. Barcelona: Caja de Ahorros de la Diputación, 1971.

García Ballesteros, Luis. *Bibliografía histórica sobre la ciencia y la técnica en España*. Granada: Universidad de Granada, 1974.

García Durán, Juan. *La guerra civil española: Fuentes (archivos, bibliografía y filmografía)*. Prologue by Gabriel Jackson. Barcelona: Crítica, 1985.

Giralt i Raventós, Eusebio, et al. *Bibliografía dels movimento socials a Catalunya, Pais valenciailes Illes*. Barcelona: Lavinia, 1972.

*Indice histórico-español*. Barcelona: Centro de Estudios Históricos Internacionales, Universidad de Barcelona, 1953.

Lamberet, R. *Monnements ouvriers et socialistes (chronologic et bibliographie): L'Espagne 1750–1936*. Paris: Les Editions Ouvrieres, 1953.

Palacio Atard, Vicente. *Cuadernos bibliográficos de la guerra de España (1936–1939)*. [8 fasicles]. Madrid: Facultad de Letras, Universidad de Madrid, 1966.

Rees, Margaret. *French Authors on Spain, 1800–1850*. (Research Bibliographies, 10). London: Grant and Cutler, 1977.

Sánchez Alonso, Benito. *Fuentes de la historia española e hispano-americana*. 3d ed. 3 vols. Madrid: CSIC, 1952.

Tuñón de Lara, Manuel, et al. *Historiografía española contemporánea: X coloquio del Centro de Investigaciones Hispánicas de la Universidad de Pau. Balance y resumen*. Madrid: Siglo Veintiuno, 1980.

———. *Metodología de la historia social.* 4th ed. Mexico City: Siglo Veintiuno, 1979.
Ullman, Joan Connelly. "Sir Raymond Carr: The Origins of Modern Spanish Historiography." In *Society for Spanish and Portuguese Historical Studies. Bulletin* 12 (Oct. 1987): 8–12.

## JOURNALS

### Journals Published in Spain

*Anales* (Barcelona), 1947- , irreg.
*Anales de economía: Revista Trimestral* (Madrid), 1941- .
*Anuario de estudios americanos* (Seville), 1944- .
*Anuario de estudios atlánticos* (Madrid), 1955- .
*Anuario de estudios sociales y jurídicos* (Granada), 1972- .
*Anuario de historia económica y social* (Madrid), 1968- .
*Anuario de historia moderna y contemporánea* (Granada), 1974- .
*Anuario de historia del derecho español* (Madrid), 1924- .
*Anuario de la aristocracia y alta sociedad española* (Madrid), 1971- .
*Anuario de las relaciones laborales en España* (Madrid), 1975- .
*Anuario hispanoamericano* (Madrid), 1954- .
*Arbor; Revista general de investigación y cultura* (Madrid), 1944- .
*Archivo documental español* (Madrid), 1950- .
*Archivo hispalense: Revista histórica, literaria y artística* (Seville), 1886?- .
*Archivo ibero-americano* (Madrid), 1914- .
*Boletín de la real academia de historia* (Madrid), 1877- .
*Boletín de la real academia española* (Madrid), 1914- (pub. suspended 1936–1944).
*Boletín de investigaciones y estudios locales* (Madrid), 1960- .
*Boletín, americanista* (Barcelona), 1959- .
*Boletín del centro de estudios del siglo xviii* (Oviedo), 1973- .
*Cuadernos de la cátedra Miguel de Unamuno* (Salamanca), 1948- .
*Cuadernos bibliográficos de la guerra de España* (Madrid), 1966- .
*Cuadernos de historia* (Madrid), 1967- .
*Cuadernos de historia diplomática* (Saragossa), 1954- , irreg.
*Cuadernos de investigación histórica* (Madrid), 1977- .
*Cuadernos hispanoamericanos* (Madrid), 1948- .
*Economía y sociología agraria* (Madrid), 1971- .
*Estudios de historia moderna* (Barcelona), 1950- , irreg.
*Estudios de historia social* (Madrid), 1977?- .
*Estudios eclesiásticos* (Madrid), 1922- .
*Estudios geográficos* (Madrid), 1940- .
*Estudios* (Saragossa), 1977- .
*Estudios y documentos* (Valladolid), 1979- .
*Hidalguía, la revista de la geneaología, nobleza y armas* (Madrid), 1953- .
*Hispania, revista española de historia* (Madrid), 1940- , irreg.
*Hispania sacra: Revista de historia eclesiástica* (Madrid), 1948- .
*Historia 16* (Madrid), 1976?- .

*Missionalia hispánica* (Madrid), 1944- .
*Moneda y crédito* (Madrid), 1942- .
*Revista de archivos, bibliotecas y museos* (Madrid), 1871-  (pub. suspended 1932–1946).
*Revista de estudios políticos* (Madrid), 1940- .
*Revista de geografía* (Barcelona), 1967- .
*Revista de historia militar* (Madrid), 1957- .
*Revista de Indias* (Madrid), 1940- .
*Revista general de legislación y jurisprudencia* (Madrid), 1852- .
*Revista de política social* (Madrid), 1947- .
*Revista de Occidente* (Madrid), 1923- .
*Revista de trabajo* (Madrid), 1938- .
*Revista internacional de sociología* (Madrid), 1941- .
*Testimonio* (Barcelona), 1976?- .


## Journals Published Outside of Spain

*American Historical Review* (Washington, D.C..), 1895- .
*Annales: Économie-société-civilisation* (Paris), 1929- .
*Bulletin hispanique* (Bordeaux), 1899- .
*Cahiers du monde hispanique et luso-bresilien* (Toulouse), 1963- .
*Cuadernos americanos* (Mexico City), 1941- .
*Cuadernos de historia de España* (Buenos Aires), 1941- .
*European History Quarterly* (Lancaster), 1971-  (Formerly *European Studies Review*).
*The Historical Journal* (Cambridge), 1923- .
*History of European Ideas* (Oxford), 1980- .
*France-Iberie recherche. Thèse et documents* (Toulouse), 1970- .
*Historia* (Lisbon), 1978- .
*Iberian Studies* (Nottingham), 1972- .
*Ibérica: Cahiers ibériques et ibero-américains de l'université de Paris-Sorbonne* (Paris),
    1977- .
*Journal of Contemporary History* (London), 1966- .
*Journal of Economic History* (Wilmington, Del.), 1941- .
*Journal of European Studies* (Buckinghamshire), 1971- .
*Mélanges de la casa de Velásquez* (Paris), 1965- .
*Journal of Modern History* (Chicago), 1929- .
*Revue historique* (Paris), 1876- .
*Society for Spanish and Portuguese Historical Studies. Bulletin.* (La Jolla, Calif.),
    1969?- .

# Index

## About the Editors

ROBERT W. KERN is Professor of Iberian History at the University of New Mexico, Albuquerque. He coedited *European Women on the Left* (Greenwood Press, 1981) and wrote *Liberals, Reformers and Caciques in Restoration Spain* and *Red Years/Black Years: A Political History of Spanish Anarchism* as well as several works on labor history.

MEREDITH D. DODGE received her doctorate in Ibero-American Studies from the University of New Mexico in 1984. She is assistant editor at the Vargas Project (UNM), which recently published *Remote Beyond Compare: Letters of Don Diego de Vargas to His Family from New Spain and New Mexico, 1675–1706*. Her most recent edited work, in collaboration with Peter J. Bakewell and John J. Johnson, is the two-volume *Readings in Latin American History*.